C for Engineers and Scientists

An Interpretive Approach

Harry H. Cheng
University of California-Davis

Boston Burr Ridge, IL Dubuque, IA New York San Francisco St. Louis
Bangkok Bogotá Caracas Kuala Lumpur Lisbon London Madrid Mexico City
Milan Montreal New Delhi Santiago Seoul Singapore Sydney Taipei Toronto

The McGraw·Hill Companies

C FOR ENGINEERS AND SCIENTISTS: AN INTERPRETIVE APPROACH

Published by McGraw-Hill, a business unit of The McGraw-Hill Companies, Inc., 1221 Avenue of the Americas, New York, NY 10020.

This book is printed on acid-free paper.

1 2 3 4 5 6 7 8 9 0 DOC/DOC 0 9

ISBN 978–0–07–337605–9
MHID 0–07–337605–1

Global Publisher: *Raghothaman Srinivasan*
Director of Development: *Kristine Tibbetts*
Developmental Editor: *Lorraine K. Buczek*
Senior Marketing Manager: *Curt Reynolds*
Project Manager: *Melissa M. Leick*
Lead Production Supervisor: *Sandy Ludovissy*
Associate Design Coordinator: *Brenda A. Rolwes*
Cover Designer: *Studio Montage, St. Louis, Missouri*
Compositor: *Macmillan Publishing Solutions*
Typeface: *10/12 Times Roman*
Printer: *R. R. Donnelley Crawfordsville, IN*

Library of Congress Cataloging-in-Publication Data

Cheng, Harry H.
C for engineers and scientists : an interpretive approach / Harry H. Cheng. – 1st ed.
p. cm.
Includes index.
ISBN 978–0–07–337605–9 — ISBN 0–07–337605–1 (hard copy : alk. paper) 1. C (Computer program language) I. Title.
QA76.73.C15C465 2010
005.13’3–dc22

2008052747

www.mhhe.com

About the Author

Harry H. Cheng is a professor in the Department of Mechanical and Aeronautical Engineering, Graduate Group in Computer Science, and Graduate Group in Electrical and Computer Engineering at the University of California, Davis. He is also the Director of the Integration Engineering Laboratory at the University of California, Davis. Before joining the faculty at the University of California, Davis, he worked as a senior engineer on robotic automation systems in the Research and Development Division at United Parcel Service from 1989 to 1992. He is the founder of SoftIntegration, Inc. which provides infrastructure software and services for rapid development and deployment of application software. He received an M.S. degree in Mathematics in 1986 and a Ph.D. degree in Mechanical Engineering in 1989 from the University of Illinois at Chicago.

Dr. Cheng has been teaching computer programming in C for engineering applications, engineering software design, robotics, and computer-aided design at the University of California, Davis since 1992. His research is focused on computer-aided engineering, mobile agent-based computing, intelligent mechatronic and embedded systems, and innovative teaching. He has published over 130 papers in refereed journals and conference proceedings and holds one U.S. patent. He received a Research Initiation Award from the National Science Foundation, the Best Paper Award at the IEEE/ASME International Conference on Mechatronic and Embedded Systems and Applications, the Procter and Gamble Best Paper Award, as well as the Waldron Award at the Applied Mechanisms and Robotics Conferences. He received an Outstanding Contribution Award from United Parcel Service Inc.

Dr. Cheng is the original designer and implementer of an embeddable C/C++ interpreter Ch for cross-platform scripting, shell programming, two- and three-dimensional plotting, numerical computing, and embedded scripting. His C/C++ interpreter has been widely used in both academia and industry. He participated in revision of the latest C standard, called C99, through ANSI X3J11 and ISO S22/WG14 C Standard Committees and made contributions to new C99 numerical features of complex numbers, variable length arrays, and IEEE floating-point arithmetic, which had been implemented in his C/C++ interpreter.

Dr. Cheng is a Fellow of the American Society of Mechanical Engineers (ASME) and a Senior Member of the Institute of Electrical and Electronics Engineers (IEEE). He has presented tutorials on real-time Linux for the control of mechatronic systems at the ASME IDETC. He is the Chair of the Technical Committee on Mechatronic and Embedded Systems in ITS of the IEEE Intelligent Transportation Systems Society. He is the General Chair of the 2009 ASME/IEEE International Conference on Mechatronic and Embedded Systems and Applications. He was the Chair of the Technical Area of Embedded and Ubiquitous Computing and Chair of Technical Area of Computers in Electromechanical Systems in the ASME Division of Computers and Information in Engineering. He served as the Conference Chair and Program Chair of the IEEE/ASME International Conference on Mechatronic and Embedded Systems and Applications. With all of his excellent accomplishments in this field, Dr. Cheng is excited to offer this manual to share his knowledge with students.

Contents

CHAPTER 15

‡Dynamic Data Structures and Cross-Platform Software Development 614

CHAPTER 16

‡Scientific Computing in the Entire Real Domain in C99 674

CHAPTER 17

‡Programming with Complex Numbers in C99 and C++ 699

PART II

Object-Based Programming in C++ 724

CHAPTER 18

CHAPTER 19

CHAPTER 20

PART III

Numerical Computing in Ch 794

CHAPTER 21

Preface

C is one of the most popular programming languages used in engineering and science. It is the language of choice for many engineers and scientists. This book is designed to teach students how to solve engineering and science problems using the C programming language. The book teaches beginners with no previous programming experience the underlying working principles of scientific computing and a disciplined approach for software development. All the major features of C89 and C99 are presented with numerous engineering application examples derived from production code. The book reveals the coding techniques used by the best C programmers and shows how experts solve problems in C. It can also serve as a reference book for seasoned programmers.

Prerequisites

The mathematical prerequisite for the book is trigonometry, except for Chapters 22 and 23 (section 23.11), which require a calculus background. No prior computer or programming experience is required. However, if students have experience in other programming languages, the material in the first few chapters can be covered quickly. For upper-division students, discussions on number systems and the introduction on vectors and matrices can be skipped.

Special Features

This book grew out of my sixteen years of teaching introductory computer programming in C for engineering applications and engineering software design at the University of California, Davis since 1992. It also reflects my unique experience in the design and implementation of a cross-platform C/C++ interpreter Ch as well as my extensive industrial and research work on solving engineering problems in C and C++. The book is written with the following distinct features.

- *Complete C coverage.* This book completely covers the C language in Part I, which is organized cumulatively so that each chapter builds on information presented in the earlier chapters. A single topic is presented in a section first and then reinforced and cross-referenced in other sections and chapters. The text is logically organized and heavily cross-referenced and indexed to serve as a reference for serious programmers.
- *Extensive coverage of major C99 features.* C99 features four variable length arrays (VLA), type generic functions, IEEE 754 floating-point arithmetic, complex numbers, and new data types bool and long long, which are used for numerical computing. They overcome the shortcomings of C89 for solving problems in engineering and science.
- *Plotting for visualization.* A picture is worth a thousand words. A plotting C++ library is used for visualization for solving many problems in engineering and science in both the text and exercises. All plots including those in exercises in this book were generated using simple functions or member functions in this plotting library.

- *Cross-platform software development.* All code examples in Parts I and II have been tested in Windows, Linux, Mac OS X, Solaris, HP-UX, FreeBSD, and QNX in C/C++ compilers and cross-platform C/C++ interpreter Ch. The implementation and platform-specific issues are presented with examples throughout the book in sections titled **"Making It Work"** at the end of each chapter in Parts I and II. Building and distributing static and dynamic libraries using make files on these platforms is also demonstrated.
- *64-bit programming.* Whenever the code produces different results for 32-bit and 64-bit machines, it is pointed out in the text. All results have been tested in multiple platforms using C/C++ interpreter and compilers.
- *Extensive coverage and unique presentation of difficult concepts.* Difficult topics such as arrays, pointers and many related subjects, binary and text mode for accessing files, byte order (endianness), structure alignment, dynamic data structures, static and dynamic libraries, internal representation of floating-point numbers, and hardware interfaces are thoroughly covered using multiple forms of presentation with many sample application programs.
- *LAPACK (Linear Algebra PACKage) written in Fortran and its C version, CLAPACK, are introduced.* Mixed-language programming with both row-wise and column-wise arrays is addressed.
- *Commonly used Unix commands are used for cross-platform software development.* In addition, the input/output redirection is introduced at the beginning for using data files in programs.

In addition, the companion CD contains Ch, a cross-platform C/C++ interpreter, with a complete reference manual in a PDF file for all functions in the C standard libraries. I originally designed and implemented Ch to make my job of teaching and research easier. As the user base increased, Ch evolved from a special-application program to a general-purpose computing environment with wide applicability. Ch was never meant to be a new language. Conforming to the C standard is its prevailing design goal. As a complete C interpreter, Ch conforms to the C89 standard and supports major features in C99. C expressions, statements, functions, and programs can be executed in Ch interactively without compiling and linking the code. It can be used for quick testing and trying difficult C features such as pointers and arrays, especially for classroom presentation and discussion sessions. ChIDE, a user-friendly Integrated Development Environment (IDE), can be used to execute functions and programs with detailed line-by-line traces. The Ch environment for Windows contains nearly 250 commonly used Unix commands, such as **vi**, **ls**, **rm**, **awk**, **sed**, **gzip**, and **tar**. It can also be used by students to learn Unix in a familiar Windows environment for a smooth transition from Windows to Unix. Ch has been well received by both instructors and students. In this book, many succinct C code and statements are executed in Ch interactively with output to illustrate numerous programming features and concepts.

Furthermore, many illustrations are used to clarify difficult concepts for beginners. Flowcharts, pseudocode, and procedures are used to describe complicated algorithms. The disciplined approach, various features of C, programming style, modular programming, code reuse, and algorithm development for solving problems in engineering and science are illustrated by over 350 well-documented complete sample programs consisting of more than 14,000 lines of code. Many of these programs are derived from the real-world production code. Earlier example programs are gradually rewritten to make them more concise, efficient, powerful, useful, or user-friendly. This way, students do not struggle with trying to understand new features and new programs at the same time. The top-down and bottom-up software design and refinement are presented with large-scale application examples.

Finally, over 500 carefully designed exercises for solving many problems in engineering and science reinforce concepts presented in the text. Abundant exercises are designed for teaching multiple sessions without repeating problems.

Organization of the Book

The text is divided into four parts. Part I is about structured programming in C, which is the major focus of the book.

Part II moves from structured programming to object-based programming in C++. It presents a C++ class for graphical plotting.

Part III introduces computational arrays as first-class objects and advanced numerical functions in Ch. They can be used conveniently to solve linear systems, nonlinear equations, ordinary differential equations, etc., for problems in engineering and science. The concepts presented in Part III are applicable to other numerically oriented programming languages such as Fortran and MATLAB.

Part IV introduces array-based numerical computing in MATLAB as a second programming language compared to C. It may serve as a quick reference for programming in MATLAB for C programmers.

The chapter on an introduction to Fortran as a second programming language in comparison with C can be downloaded in a PDF file from the website for the book. The comparison study presented in this chapter will also be very useful for those who have the prior programming experience in Fortran to learn C.

Appendix A lists keywords in C and Ch. Appendix B lists C99 features supported in Ch. Appendix C lists C++ features supported in Ch. Appendix D lists ASCII codes.

Sections and chapters marked with the double dagger symbol '‡' in the title can be skipped without hindering learning about the later chapters. The materials marked with the symbol '‡', however, are very useful for those who plan on serious software development in C, need to read existing C code written by experienced programmers, or intend to take other advanced courses.

Part I is organized cumulatively except for Chapter 16, "Scientific Computing in the Entire Real Domain in C99," and Chapter 17, "Programming with Complex Numbers in C99 and C++." These two chapters can be read after Chapter 11, "Pointers," is finished. Other parts are self-contained. After covering sections not marked with the symbol '‡' in Part I, one can move to Part II. Likewise, after finishing Chapter 10, "Arrays," in Part I, one can continue to Part III or Part IV.

Using this Book as a Textbook

This is a comprehensive book on software development for solving problems in engineering and science with complete coverage of the C language and other programming languages. The materials are more than enough for a one-semester course. Early drafts of this book have been used as a textbook for a number of courses. Following are some possible ways to use the book as a textbook.

- **Computer Programming for Engineering Applications** or **Engineering Problem Solving**. In this freshman introductory course, it is assumed that students have no prior computer and programming experience. All sections and chapters not marked with the symbol '‡' are covered in one quarter. It takes eight weeks to cover Chapters 1 to 14 in Part I, one week on computational arrays in Chapter 21 (in Part III) and plotting in Chapter 20 (in Part II), and one week on Chapter 23 (Part IV) for comparison study with MATLAB. If it is a semester course, additional topics marked with the symbol '‡' may be covered. Experience indicates that students who have C can pick up MATLAB quickly.
- **Introduction to Programming in C.** The book can be used as a gentle, slow-paced introduction to computer programming using the C language. It is assumed that students do not have any prior computer or programming experience. Example programs can be presented using ChIDE with detailed line-by-line traces. In this case, only sections in Chapters 1 to 10 not marked with the symbol '‡' and the first two sections in Chapter 14 will be covered.

- **Introduction to C Programming.** For this upper-division undergraduate course, it is assumed that students have prior programming experience in other programming languages or software packages. The materials in early chapters are presented much faster. The most time is spent on Chapters 1 to 14 in Part I. It takes one-and-a-half weeks to cover numerical computing in Ch in Part III and plotting in Chapter 20 (in Part II).
- **Using this book as a supplementary textbook.** The text can also be used as a supplement for some upper-division or graduate courses in engineering and science, such as numerical analysis, control, mechatronics, embedded systems, mechanism design, and engineering software design, in which C programming is needed.

C89 and C99 Standards

There are two versions of the international standards for C. The first version was ratified in 1989 by the American National Standards Institute (ANSI) C standard committee. It is often referred as ANSI C or C89. The second C standard was completed in 1999. This standard is commonly referred to as C99. C99 is a milestone in C's evolution into a viable programming language for numerical and scientific computing. It can significantly simplify programming tasks for solving problems in engineering and science. An increasing number of C compilers support C99 features. Major numerical features in C99 are presented in this book for applications in engineering and science. However, Microsoft Visual C++ still does not support major features in C99 for numerical computing. All programs using C99 features have been tested with both the GNU gcc compiler in Linux and the cross-platform C/C++ interpreter Ch. If a C99 feature is used, it will be pointed out explicitly in both the text and title of the section or chapter. Programs using C99 features have a comment with the compilation option `-std=c99` at the beginning to distinguish from those using C89 features only. For example, the program `funcname.c` in Program 6.16 in Chapter 6 contains the comment

```
Compile in gcc, use command 'gcc -std=c99 funcname.c'
```

Websites for the Book and Teaching Resources

The McGraw-Hill website for the book is

http://www.mhhe.com/cheng

Many teaching resources are available at no cost from this website to instructors who adopt this book as a textbook for their classes. They include 1,400 PowerPoint slides complementary to this book with many different example programs ready for classroom presentations, over 200 companion PowerPoint slides for discussion sessions, *Instructor's Guide* (containing sample general information, syllabus, homework assignments, quizes, and midterm and final examinations), and *Solutions Manual* and the source code for solutions for exercises in each chapter. The site also contains useful resources for students, including a chapter on Fortran as a second language in comparison study with C in a PDF file.

The author's website for the book is

http://iel.ucdavis.edu/cfores

This website contains the source code for all example programs presented in the book, frequently asked questions, supplementary materials, errata, and numerous other resources. The first line of each example program contains its file name so that it can be found easily in the downloaded source code. The website also has a link to a discussion forum for students to exchange ideas and share learning experiences.

Contacting the Author

I sincerely appreciate any criticisms, comments, identification of errors in the text or programs, and suggestions for improvement in future editions from both instructors and students. I can be reached over the Internet at

cfores@ucdavis.edu

I will post corrections and clarifications on the author's website for the book.

Electronic Textbook Options

This text is offered through CourseSmart to both instructors and students. CourseSmart is an online resource where students can purchase access to this and other McGraw-Hill textbooks in a digital format. Through their browsers, students can access the complete text online for one year at almost half the cost of a traditional text. Purchasing the eTextbook also allows students to take advantage of CourseSmart's Web tools for learning, which include full text search, notes and highlighting, and e-mail tools for sharing notes between classmates. To learn more about CourseSmart options, contact your sales representative or visit *www.CourseSmart.com.*

Acknowledgments

First and foremost, I would like to thank the numerous undergraduate and graduate students who used drafts of this book to learn computer programming for solving engineering problems and software design. Their feedback and suggestions greatly improved the text. I also would like to acknowledge my former and current graduate students, especially Bo Chen and Stephen Nestinger, for their numerous thoughtful comments and suggestions.

The insightful criticisms and suggestions of many reviewers have greatly improved the accuracy and presentation of this book. I would like to acknowledge their efforts. They include David Auslander (University of California-Berkeley), Rebecca Bates (Minnesota State University-Mankato), Thomas Daniels (Iowa State University), Paul Furth (New Mexico State University), Tom MacDonald (Eivia, Inc.), Gary Nutt (University of Colorado–Boulder). I am especially grateful to Tom MacDonald, David Auslander, and Paul Furth for scrutinizing the text and programs with countless suggestions. However, I take the full responsibility for any errors. I also would like to thank Paul Furth for providing several exercise problems in Chapter 10.

The outstanding team at McGraw-Hill has been delightful to work with on this project. It includes Raghu Srinivasan, Lorraine Buczek, and Melissa Leick, Curt Reynolds, Laura Lawrie, and Susan McClung. I appreciate their extraordinary efforts in publishing this book.

Finally, I would like to thank my wife, Dawn Cheng, and daughter, Deanna Cheng, for their support and understanding over the many years during which this book has been developed and written.

Harry H. Cheng
November 20, 2008

PART I

Structured Programming in C

CHAPTER 1

Introduction

The computer is one of the most important inventions of the 20th century. Computers have a profound impact on our lives and play an important role in our society. For example, computers control our transportation systems, electric power systems, telephone systems, student records in schools, bank accounts, and other such systems. But, what is a computer and how does it work?

A *computer* is a machine that manipulates data based on a list of instructions called a *program*. A computer can process information and perform mathematical calculations much faster than human beings. A program, installed on a computer, tells the computer when to obtain information, how to process information and perform calculations, and what output to produce. Instructions of a program are executed by a *central processing unit* (CPU), which is also commonly referred to as a *microprocessor*. Personal computers (PCs), such as desktop computers, laptop computers, or tablet computers, are general-purpose computers, which can execute different programs for different tasks. For example, a computer game is a program which can be executed on a PC. A game program processes user input and takes actions based on its instructions. The Internet Explorer Web browser is another program which can be executed on a PC. If the user types a Web address in the browser, the browser program processes the user input, communicates with another program running at that Web address to obtain information over the Internet, and finally displays the result in the Web browser accordingly.

Unlike a PC, an embedded system is a special-purpose computer designed to perform one or a few dedicated functions. In fact, of the 9 billion microprocessors manufactured in 2005, less than 2 percent became the brains of new personal computers and more powerful workstations. The other 8.8 billion went into embedded systems used in industrial machines, medical equipment, traffic light controllers, automobiles, vending machines, household appliances, cellular phones, personal digital assistants (PDAs), toys, etc. For example, a robot typically contains an on-board embedded computer. According to a robot program, executed on a computer in the robot, the robot can make intelligent decisions and take actions based on external sensory information from position, force, vision, and other sensors. A computer or robot serves only the commands programmed into it. When a computer or robot does something smart, it is because a smart person has written a smart program to control it.

C is the language of choice for writing programs for billions of embedded systems that interact with hardware. C and its variant, C++, are also the languages of choice for writing games, Web browsers, word processors, and most programs that run on your PC. This book teaches you how to write your own programs so that a computer or robot will do what you want it to do.

This chapter introduces general computer hardware architecture, various computer software, and different computer languages. The history of C and its evolution reflect its important roles in the information age.

1.1 Computer Hardware

Computer hardware is the physical part of a computer. Tiny computers, single board computers (SBCs), PCs, workstations, and supercomputers are examples of computer hardware. An SBC and a finger-size tiny computer are shown in Figure 1.1. They are complete computers built on a single circuit board. They are smaller than PCs and commonly embedded in instruments, industrial equipment, medical instruments, etc. Tiny computers use microprocessors, such as an ARM 32-bit reduced instruction set computing (RISC) processor manufactured by ARM, Inc., that consume less power than those used in SBCs and PCs. SBCs and PCs typically use x86-compatible microprocessors such as the Pentium processor made by Intel, Inc. or the Athlon processor by Advanced Micro Devices, Inc. Workstations are more powerful desktop computers typically installed with a Unix operating system, which will be described in the next section. Nowadays, the line between PCs and workstations is a blur. Supercomputers were computers that were considered, at the time of their introduction, to be the fastest in terms of calculation speed. However, today's supercomputers tend to become tomorrow's ordinary computers. The computational speed of a microprocessor on a PC is now faster than that of a 10-year old supercomputer. Computer hardware in embedded systems, such as those in robots, automobiles, traffic light controllers, however, may not be seen by normal users. Almost all digital computers are built on the *stored program architecture* or *von Neumann architecture*, named after one of its originators, John von Neumann. The overall structure of a von Newmann computer is shown in Figure 1.2. In this prevalent computer architecture, *both programs and data* are stored in the same memory. The main components of a computer consist of the CPU, main memory, external memory, and input and output devices. Details about these components are described in the paragraphs below.

Figure 1.1: A single board computer and a tiny computer.

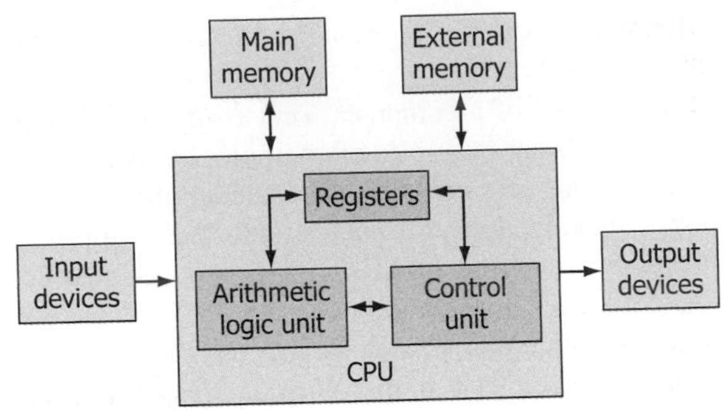

Figure 1.2: A typical computer hardware configuration using the von Neumann architecture.

1.1.1 CPU

The control unit (CU), arithmetic and logic unit (ALU), and registers are collectively known as the *central processing unit* (CPU). Nowadays, these components are typically constructed on a single integrated circuit called a *microprocessor* or *processor*.

The *arithmetic and logic unit* can perform arithmetic operations such as addition and substration. It can also perform logic operations in comparing numbers on whether one is equal to, greater than, or less than the other. More complicated mathematical operations and expressions are broken down by programs into simple steps that the ALU can perform.

The CPU contains a special set of internal memory called *registers* that can be read and written to much faster than main memory. Registers are used for most frequently needed data, such as intermediate results during a calculation, to reduce main memory access.

The *control unit* directs various components of a computer. It reads instructions of a program in main memory one by one. The CU decodes each instruction and turns it into a series of control signals that operate the other parts of the computer. The CU also fetches data values from main memory or input devices and places them into registers. After the ALU performs operations on the data, the CU moves the result, stored in registers, to main memory or output devices.

Microprocessors are becoming increasingly more powerful. Gordon E. Moore, a co-founder of Intel, observed in 1965 that the number of transistors that can be inexpensively placed on an integrated circuit increases exponentially, doubling approximately every two years. This theory is called Moore's law. Based on Moore's law, the processing capacity of computers doubles every two years, which is likely to continue into the near future.

1.1.2 Main Memory and External Memory

A computer's *main memory* or *primary memory* is used to install both programs and data. It comes in two principal varieties: *random access memory,* or RAM, and *read-only memory,* or ROM. RAM can be read and written to at any time. ROM is pre-loaded with programs and data that never change and is typically used to store computer's initial start-up instructions. In embedded systems that may not have external memory such as a disk drive, all of the programs required to perform the tasks may be stored in ROM. Computer programs stored in ROM are typically called *firmware*. Unlike ROM, the contents of RAM is erased when the power to the computer is turned off. Some computers use RAM *cache memories,* which are slower than registers but faster than main memory.

A computer's *external memory*, also called *secondary memory* or *external storage*, is used to store programs and data permanently even when the computer is turned off. Typical external memory devices are hard disks, CDs, universal serial bus (USB) flash drives, tape drives, and floppy disks. External memory is cheaper than main memory and can store more information.

1.1.3 Input and Output Devices

Input/output (I/O) is the means for a computer to communicate with the outside world. A computer receives information from input devices and sends results back to output devices. The keyboard, mouse, and microphone are typical input devices. Common output devices include monitor displays, printers, and speakers for audio output. External memory, such as hard disks, CDs, USB flash drives, tape drives, and floppy disks, serves as both input and output devices. Another form of input and output devices is data acquisition boards, which are popularly used on a computer to receive and send analog or digital signals for applications in engineering and science. For example, a robot may receive sensory input signals through a data acquisition interface circuit board.

1.2 Computer Software

What distinguishes a computer from other machines is its programmability. *Computer software* is a general term used to describe a collection of computer programs that can be loaded into main memory and executed in the CPU of a computer. Therefore, software is also an essential part of a computer. There are different ways to categorize software systems on a computer. The simplest way is to divide software into two categories: *operating system* and *application software*. Figure 1.3 shows the interaction of computer users with computer

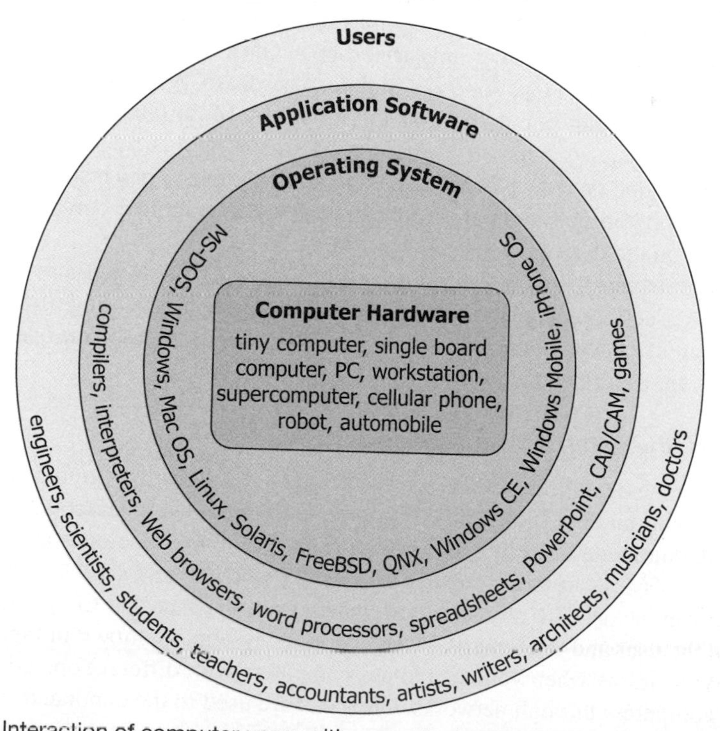

Figure 1.3: Interaction of computer users with computer hardware through computer software.

hardware through application software and operating systems. An alternative classification is to divide software systems into *system software* and *application software*. The system software includes the operating systems and programming software such as compilers and interpreters. Programs presented in this book and exercise programs that you are going to write belong to application software. However, to write your application software, you need an operating system and programming software. In this section, functions of these different software are described.

1.2.1 Operating Systems

An *operating system* (OS) is a software program that is responsible for the management and coordination of activities and the sharing of the resources of a computer. It acts as a host for application programs running on the computer. It relieves the burden of application programs from dealing with the low-level details so that they can be written more easily. Almost all computers have an operating system.

When a computer is powered on, the initial code executing on the computer at startup (boot) is typically loaded from firmware stored in ROM. The firmware loads and executes the code for the operating system located in external memory. When an application program is executed, the operating system creates a *process* by setting aside some main memory, loading the program code from external memory into main memory, and running it. The operating system stores various information for each running process, including the size of memory used by the process and a unique identifier called the *process identifier* (PID). The operating system ensures that each process gets a share of CPU time to execute its code.

Commonly used operating systems are listed in Figure 1.3. Microsoft Windows is the most popularly used operating system on PCs. The operating systems Linux, Solaris, HP-UX, AIX, and FreeBSD are commonly referred to as *Unix* because they are derived from the Unix operating system developed in the 1970s. The Mac OS X from Apple, Inc. is also based on Unix. A *real-time operating system* is intended for time-deterministic real-time applications such as the control of industrial robots. QNX and Windows CE are examples of real-time operating systems running on PCs. Windows Mobile, a subset of Windows CE, is used as an operating system in some PDAs and cellular phones such as those built by Motorola, Inc. The iPhone OS is used in Apple's iPhone.

However, some embedded systems use dedicated operating systems. For a resource-limited small device, the functionalities of an operating system and application program might be combined as a single special-purpose program to run on the device.

An operating system typically contains many *utility programs*, such as those listed in Table 2.1 in Chapter 2. They can be used to manage the system by creating, copying, deleting files, etc. One of the most important utility programs is a *command shell*, which provides a user interface to the operating system. Details about command shells are described below.

GUI and Command Shells for User Interface

Users may interact with the operating system (such as Windows on PCs) by a graphical user interface (GUI, pronounced "gooey") with buttons and menus. However, users may also interact with the operating system through an interactive command shell by typing commands. Command-line interfaces are more commonly used in Unix. When a user logs in to a computer, an interactive command shell will be executed and ready for the user to type commands. The term *shell* originates from the fact that the program is an outer layer of interface between the user and the innards of the operating system, as shown in Figure 1.3. A command-line interface is more desirable when you need to use computers with different operating systems and when remotely accessing computers through networks. Once you are used to the command-line interface, you can interact with a computer more quickly. For example, multiple folders can be created by typing only a single command in a command shell. Examples of using a command shell are presented in section 2.2.2 in Chapter 2.

Table 1.1 Command shells for operating systems.

Shell	Application areas	Inventor
Bourne shell	Command shell and system administration	Stephen Bourne
Korn shell	Command shell and system administration	David Korn
BASH shell	Command shell and system administration	Brian J. Fox
C shell	Command shell and system administration	Bill Joys
Tcsh shell	Command shell and system administration	Ken Greer
Ch (C/C++) shell	Command shell and system administration	Harry H. Cheng
MS-DOS Shell	Command shell in Windows only	Tim Paterson

The commonly used command shells and their inventors are listed in Table 1.1. The Bourne shell (a program named **sh**), developed by Stephen Bourne, was the original command shell distributed with Unix. The Korn shell (**ksh**) and BASH (**bash**) extend the Bourne shell with user-friendly features. Programs can also be written in a command shell. The C shell (**csh**) was originally developed by Bill Joys with its syntax modeled after the C language. The Tcsh shell (**tcsh**) extends the C shell with user-friendly features. The design of the Ch shell (**ch**) is similar to the C shell. The Ch shell supports all features of the C language. Although these shells originated under Unix, all these command shells can run under most operating systems. By default, Windows only comes with the MS-DOS shell (**cmd**).

1.2.2 Application Software

Application software refers to programs developed to assist computer users in completing specific tasks. For example, Web browsers such as Internet Explorer can be used to access websites on the Internet, word processors such as Microsoft Word for writing documents, spreadsheets such as Microsoft Excel for processing data, Microsoft PowerPoint for presentation, CAD/CAM (computer-aided design and computer-aided manufacturing) software for design and manufacturing, and games for entertainment. Compilers and interpreters allow users to develop their application programs.

1.3 Computer Programming Languages

Computer programming languages can be classified into high-level and low-level languages. High-level languages are easier to use and more portable than low-level languages. Most software is written in high-level languages. The working principles of different computer languages are described in this section.

1.3.1 Machine Code and Assembly Languages

Machine code, also called machine language, is the lowest-level computer language. It contains instructions and data directly executed by a CPU. Each instruction consists of a sequence of 0s and 1s. For example, for a Rabbit 3000 8-bit microprocessor, the machine code below

```
00011001
```

stands for an operation of adding integer values in registers `"hl"` and `"de"` in the CPU with the sum in register `"hl"`. A machine code instruction set may have all instructions of the same length, or may have variable-length instructions. Every CPU has its own machine code or instruction set. Therefore, machine code is machine dependent.

Machine code consists of highly inscrutable sequences of 0s and 1s. The assembly language uses more meaningful symbols, such as "add", to represent machine instructions in a one-to-one symbolic mnemonic form. The assembly language is at a higher level than that of machine code. The symbolic mnemonic representation for an assembly language is usually defined by the microprocessor manufacturer. A utility program called an *assembler* is used to transfer assembly language statements into machine code. On the other hand, a utility program called a *disassembler* can be used to transform machine code into assembly code. For example, for a Rabbit 3000 8-bit microprocessor, the assembly statement below

```
add    hl,de
```

is the symbolic mnemonic representation of the previous machine code. It can be translated into the previous machine instruction by an assembler. Like the machine code, an assembly language program offers precise control over the way the CPU carries out the instructions. Nowadays, the assembly language is used primarily for programming resource-constrained embedded systems and mission critical real-time systems. Although an assembly language program can be very compact and efficient, it is machine-dependent, tedious, hard to read, and difficult to change.

1.3.2 High-Level Compiled Languages

To make the computer accessible to users other than computer specialists, high-level programming languages have been developed. The source program of high-level programming languages uses readable English-like syntax so that users can concentrate on the problem rather than on the underlying machine architecture of the computer. High-level programming languages are independent of a particular type of computer. Programs written for one machine can be used for other machines. They are easier to read, write, and maintain. For example, the following statement in the C language

```
a = a + 8;
```

means adding the value for variable a and integer value 8 and storing the result in variable a by replacing its previous value. For comparison, to accomplish this task in a Rabbit 3000 8-bit microprocessor, four machine instructions are needed as shown in Table 1.2. The first column in the table lists the addresses in main memory in hexadecimal format for each instruction. The details about hexadecimal numbers are described in Chapter 3. The second column contains the machine code with its corresponding assembly code in the third column. For the first instruction, the control unit of the CPU loads integer 8 represented in a hexadecimal number into register "de". For the second instruction, the control unit fetches the value for the variable a from main memory with its address calculated using the value in the stack pointer register "sp" and loads the value into register "hl". The stack pointer register "sp" contains the address in main memory reserved for

Table 1.2 The memory addresses, machine code, and assembly code corresponding to a C statement `a = a + 8` for the Rabbit 3000 8-bit microprocessor.

Memory addresses	Machine code	Assembly code	
0X1EA1	000100010000100000000000	ld	de, 0×0008
0X1EA4	1100010000000000	ld	hl, (sp+0)
0X1EA6	00011001	add	hl, de
0X1EA7	1101010000000000	ld	(sp+0), hl

Table 1.3 High-level programming languages.

Languages	Application areas	Inventor
	Compiled languages	
FORTRAN	Numerical and scientific programming	John W. Backus
C	System programming and embedded systems	Dennis M. Ritchie
C++	Object-oriented system programming	Bjarne Stroustrup
Java	Network and system programming	James Gosling
C#	Network and system programming	Anders Hejlsberg
	Scripting languages	
BASIC	Windows application scripting	John Kemeny Thomas Kurtz
Tcl/TK	GUI development and embedded scripting	John Ousterhout
Perl	System administration and CGI programming	Larry Walls
Python	Object-oriented programming	Guido van Rossum
PHP	Web programming	Rasmus Lerdorf
MATLAB	Numerical computing and plotting	Cleve Moler
Mathematica	Numerical computing and plotting	Stephen Wolfram
Ch (C/C++)	Numerical computing, plotting, shell programming, embedded scripting, and teaching	Harry H. Cheng

variables of a program. For the third instruction, the control unit presents two integers in registers `"hl"` and `"de"` to the ALU of the CPU along with directions to add them and store the result in the destination register `"hl"`. The ALU then performs the task of adding two integers. Finally, for the last instruction, the control unit takes the result in the destination register `"hl"` and stores it back into main memory for variable `a`.

The high-level programming languages FORTRAN, C, C++, Java, and C# are commonly used by engineers and scientists. The application areas of these languages and their original inventors or contributors are listed in Table 1.3.

FORTRAN was the first general-purpose high-level computer programming language ever developed. It was invented for FORmula TRANslation in the late 1950s by John Bakus at IBM. Although some people think that it has lived considerably beyond its time, it is still one of the primary languages used for high-performance numerical computing. **FORTRAN 77**, a standard ratified in 1977, was widely used. The new versions **Fortran 90/95** and **Fortran 2003** (using lowercase for the name) added many new features for array programming, module-based programming, and object-oriented programming. Many programming features, such as pointers and classes, in C and C++ are now available in Fortran.

C was invented by Dennis M. Ritchie at AT&T in the 1970s for writing the Unix operating system and its utility programs. It was named "C" because many of its features were derived from an earlier language called "B," which was a simplified version of the BCPL programming language. For many years, Brian Kernighan & Dennis M. Ritchie's book, *The C Programming Language*, published in 1978, served as an informal specification for the language. The version of C described in their book is commonly referred to as K&R C.

In 1983, the American National Standards Institute (ANSI) formed a committee, X3J11, to establish a standard specification for C. The standard was ratified in 1989 and is often referred to as **ANSI C** or **C89**. In 1990, the ANSI C standard, with a few minor modifications, was adopted by the International Organization for Standardization (ISO). This version is sometimes called **C90**. The terms C89 and C90 refer to the same language. The lastest C standard was started in 1991, completed in 1999, and ratified in 2000. This standard is commonly referred to as **C99**.

C is most popularly used for system programming to write system software such as operating systems, utility programs, compilers, interpreters, and libraries. Because C can provide precise control over machines in the same manner as assembly languages, it is commonly considered as a *mid-level* language. C is the language of choice for embedded system applications. It is also widely used to implement applications for end-users.

C's user base and popularity are continuously growing. C99 is a milestone in C's evolution into a viable programming language for numerical and scientific computing. It significantly simplifies writing programs for applications in engineering and science. In this book, all features in C89 and major numerical features in C99 are used to solve problems in engineering and science.

C++ was invented by Bjarne Stroustrup in 1979 at Bell Labs as an enchancement to C for object-oriented programming. The language was first named "C with Classes." In 1983, it was renamed C++ (++ being the increment operator in C and C++). Object-oriented programming is a programming paradigm that uses *objects* and their interactions to design applications at a much higher level. It is suitable for large-scale software projects. C++ is a lot more complicated than C. Unfortunately, without a solid foundation in C, it is impossible to fully master object-oriented features in C++. However, some features, such as references and classes, are relatively simple and very useful for solving problems in engineering and science. A subset of C++ features will be presented in Part II of this book for solving problems in engineering and science. C++ was standardized in 1999. The latest standard was ratified in 2003. C++ was a superset of C until the latest C standard, C99, was introduced. C++ currently does not support many new features such as variable length arrays in C99. However, some of the new C99 features will very likely be included in the next version of the C++ standard.

Like C++, many other so-called modern computer languages, such as **Java** developed by Sun Microsystems and **C#** by Microsoft, are also based on C. They were designed for object-oriented programming. Java can also be used more conveniently for Web-based network computing with graphical user interfaces.

Execution of a Program Written in a High-Level Compiled Language

The CPU of a computer can execute only machine code. A *compiler*, which is a computer program, translates a program written in a high-level language into a lower-level language such as assembly language or machine code. The original text is called the *source code* or *source file* and the output called the *object code* or *object file*. By default, a compiler compiles source code directly into machine code. For a C program, some header files in the form of source code can be included automatically in another source file by the compiler. A *linker* is a computer program that takes one or more objects generated by compilers and assembles them into a single executable program. A linker can also accept *libraries*, which are a collection of compiled object files. Figure 1.4(a) shows the process of developing an executable program using the C language in Windows. First, a C source code named `hello.c` is created and edited using a text editor such as Notepad in Windows. The source code is compiled by a compiler program named **cl.exe**. Some header files are automatically included by the compiler. The compiler compiles the source code into an object file `hello.obj`. Afterward, a linker program, **link.exe**, links the object code and some libraries to create a single executable program named `hello.exe`. Program `hello.exe` is stored in external memory. If it is not executed, it does nothing. The program can be executed from a command shell by typing the program name, or started from a GUI,

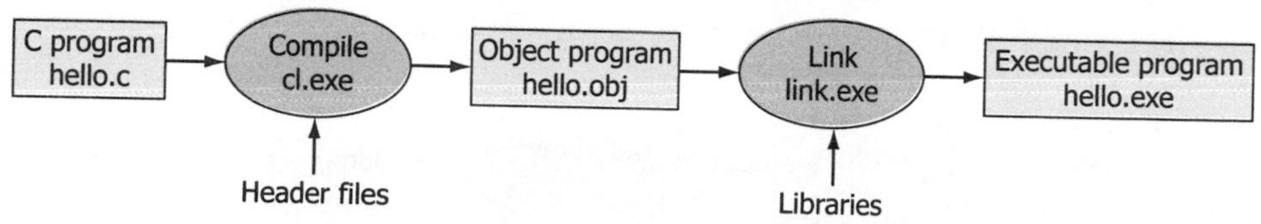

(a) Creating an executable program from a C program using compiler and linker.

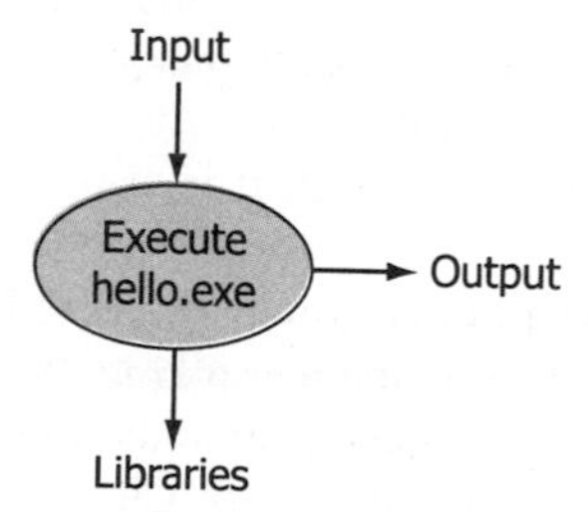

(b) Executing the created executable program.

Figure 1.4: Creating an executable program from a C program using compiler and linker, and executing it.

which loads the program and required runtime libraries into main memory. When program `hello.exe` is executed as shown in Figure 1.4(b), based on the design of the source code, it can take the user's input and produce the output.

Most programs are compiled, linked, and executed in the same platform, such as Windows in PCs. However, this is not the case for many embedded systems. An embedded system, such as a microwave oven, uses a tiny computer or *microcontroller*, which is a computer-on-a-chip, containing a CPU, memory, and input/output functions. A tiny computer or microcontroller has extremely limited resources. It does not have enough memory or powerful CPU to run a compiler. In this case, C programs are cross-compiled by a cross compiler, which is a compiler capable of creating object code and executable program for a platform other than the one on which the compiler is executed. For example, a C program for control of microwave ovens can be cross-compiled in a PC to create an executable. The created executable program is then *burned in* the ROM of an embedded computer in a microwave oven. When a microwave oven is turned on, the program in ROM is executed. It reads input from its touchpad and door sensors, provides output to a digital display and speaker, and controls the machinery for cooking food.

Because C compilers are widely available for almost any computer platform, some high-level languages may be translated into the C language first. The translated C code is then compiled using a C compiler. C++ uses this execution model in its earlier implementations. Today, C++ programs can be compiled into machine code directly without intermediate C code.

For some high-level languages, the source code is compiled into an intermediate representation called *bytecode*, which are instruction sets that can be executed by a program called *virtual machine*. Java uses this execution model. Now, Java programs can also be compiled into machine code directly for more efficient execution.

A program written in a high-level language can also be read and then executed directly by an interpreter, with no compilation and linking stages. This will be described in the next section.

1.3.3 High-Level Scripting Languages

An *interpreter* is a program that executes programs written in a programming language directly without intermediate code such as bytecode. A language interpreted at runtime is called an *interpreted language*

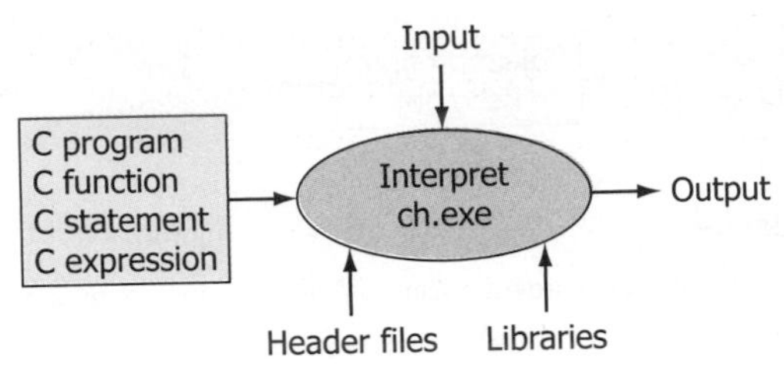

Figure 1.5: Executing a C program, function, statement, or expression using an interpreter.

or *scripting language*. Many languages can be implemented using both compilers and interpreters. So the designation of compiled language and scripting language in Table 1.3 is applied purely because of common implementation practices. For example, C was traditionally considered as a compiled language. With the availability of the C interpreter, Ch, C can now be considered as a scripting language.

The execution of C programs using the C interpreter, Ch, is shown in Figure 1.5. C programs such as `hello.c`, functions, statements, and expressions can be directly interpreted by Ch at runtime without the compilation and linking stages. Header files and libraries used by a C program are loaded automatically by the interpreter. Compared to Figure 1.4, the process of executing a program using an interpreter is much simpler than using compilers and linkers. The program is easier to use and maintain because there is no intermediate object file and executable file.

The main shortcoming of an interpreter is that when a program is interpreted, it typically runs slower than if it had been compiled, especially for a program with a large number of iteration statements. However, since CPU processing power nearly doubles every two years, execution speed is no longer an issue for many applications. Programmers' time becomes more expensive than CPU time. On the other hand, most interpreters allow interpreted code and compiled code to work together. Most computation time of a program is spent on 20 percent of the code. The part of a program that takes the most computation time can be compiled into machine code for fast execution.

Scripting languages were available in the early days of computers. Commonly used scripting languages are listed in Table 1.3. The original **BASIC** (Beginner's All-purpose Symbolic Instruction Code) was designed in 1964 by John Kemeny and Thomas Kurts at Dartmouth College to provide access for nonscience students to computers. It remains popular through its dialect Microsoft Visual Basic in Windows and applications in a large number of microcontrollers. Programs written in command shells in Table 1.1 are called *shell scripts* because they are interpreted by command shells. Shell scripts relieve the users from the tedious task of re-entering sequences of commands by automating tasks in a program. Shell languages are considered as very high-level languages (VHLLs) because commands can be invoked directly from shell scripts. **Tcl/TK** is typically embedded into application programs for scripting. **Perl**, with powerful text processing facilities, is mainly used in system administration and Common Gateway Interface (CGI) for processing fill-out forms of Web pages. **PHP** is used for writing scripts to control Web pages. **Python** is used for object-oriented scripting. **MATLAB** and **Mathematica** have high-level numerical features and graphical plotting. They can be used conveniently to solve problems in engineering and science.

Ch is an embeddable cross-platform C/C++ interpreter. It was originally designed and implemented to make C more suitable for applications so that programmers could use one language for all programming tasks. Ch has the following major capabilities that cannot be served by a C compiler. First, C programs can be interpreted by Ch across different platforms. C programs developed in one machine can be executed in other machines without the burden of compiling and linking the code. It is ideal for scripting applications such as Common Gateway Interface (CGI) for processing fill-out forms of Web pages. An interpreter is especially appealing for teaching and learning computer programming in C. For example, all run-time error messages can refer to the source code, which makes it easier for beginners to find mistakes in the program. Programs using object-based programming features in C++ can also be interpreted in Ch. Second, Ch extends C with high-level numerical and plotting features used in other languages such as Fortran and MATLAB for applications in engineering and science. Some extensions in Ch have already been added in C99. Third, Ch is a VHLL for shell programming with high productivity. Finally, Ch can be seemlessly embedded into compiled programs written in C and C++ to make applications and embedded systems *in situ* programmable using C/C++ scripts. In Part I of this book, some C features are succinctly demonstrated using this interpreter. Major numerical extensions in Ch are presented in Part III. Using Ch as a command shell is briefly demonstrated in section 2.2.2 in Chapter 2. Program 15.26 in Chapter 15 is an example of using Ch as a VHLL for shell programming. However, embedding the Ch interpreter into applications is beyond the scope of this book.

Exercises

1. What are the major hardware components for a computer?
2. What is the function of the ALU in a CPU?
3. Which language can a computer directly understand?
4. What is firmware?
5. What level of computer language is most convenient to the programmer for writing programs?
6. How can the user interact with a computer?
7. Is it possible to obtain assembly code from machine code? Is it possible to obtain a high-level program such as a C program from its machine code or assembly code?
8. Can an object code compiled from a C program be directly executed?
9. How do you create executable programs for embedded systems with extremely limited resources?
10. If a C program is executed by an interpreter, does the C program need to be compiled first?
11. How many versions of the C standard are there? What are their abbreviations?
12. The *clock rate* is the fundamental rate in *cycles per second* (measured in hertz) at which a computer performs its most basic operations such as adding two integers. The clock rate of a computer is used to refer to the speed of a CPU. A CPU with a clock rate of 3 GHz (3 billion cycles/second) is much faster than a CPU with 2 MHz (2 million cycles/second). Assume that the speed of the current CPU is 2.5 GHz, according to Moore's law, predict the speed of the CPU after (a) 2 years, (b) 4 years, (c) 6 years, (d) 8 years, (e) 10 years.

CHAPTER 2

Getting Started

The C programming language requires a disciplined approach to computer program design. In this chapter, we introduce C programming and its applications. We will use two sample C programs to present some important and basic features of the C language. Each statement of the sample programs will be carefully examined. Editing and executing C programs using an integrated development environment (IDE) called ChIDE is introduced. Executing C programs, statements, and expressions interactively in Ch is described. This chapter also shows how to compile and link a C source file to create a binary executable program in both command shell and ChIDE in different platforms with different C compilers. Commonly used portable commands for handling source files are presented so that you will be able to get your C programs to work in different platforms, regardless of whether you use Windows, Linux, or Mac OS X. The C interpreter Ch will make your learning experience more enjoyable.

2.1 The First C Program

Let's get started with C through a simple program that will display the following output on the screen when it is executed:

```
Hello, world
```

The text output from a program is displayed with the grey background in this book as shown in the above output for clarity. The first C program that we will introduce is shown in Program 2.1, which will produce the above output on the screen. This program contains the source code in plain text, which can be created using a text editor such as Notepad in Windows. Programs in this book are displayed with the light blue background as shown in Program 2.1.

To run the code in Program 2.1, source code in plain text is first edited and saved with a file name. In this case, the code is saved in the file `hello.c`. The program `hello.c` is then processed by a C compiler. A C compiler is a separate computer program which can recognize the syntax of the C language. A C compiler can process a C source code and generate an executable program. When the executable program is run, it will produce the desired result based on the code in the C program. On the other hand, a C interpreter is a computer program that can also recognize the syntax of C. But, it can execute the C source code directly to obtain the desired result without producing and using an intermediate executable program. All programs presented in Part I to III in this textbook can run in Ch, a C/C++ interpreter. A C program can also be edited and executed in an IDE, in which program editing and execution can be performed within the same user interface. How to edit and run C programs from an IDE will be described in the next section.

We will explain each line in Program 2.1 in detail. Contents that begin with `/*` and end with `*/` are comments. When comments are processed by C compilers or interpreters, they are ignored and no action is

```
/* File: hello.c
   Print 'Hello, world' on the screen. */
#include <stdio.h>

int main()
{
    printf("Hello, world\n");
    return 0;
}
```

Program 2.1: The first C program.

taken relating to the comments. Comments are used to document a program to make the code more readable by human beings. The first two lines

```
/* File: hello.c
   Print 'Hello, world' on the screen */
```

in Program 2.1 are comments. They document that the file name of the program is *hello.c* and the purpose of the program is to print the message `Hello, world` on the screen. All programs presented in this textbook are available in the distribution of the source code for this textbook. Programs presented in each chapter are located in a separate directory for the chapter. A C program's source file typically ends with `.c`, which is called the *file extension.*

In Program 2.1, the line

```
#include <stdio.h>
```

is a preprocessing directive. This line appears in many C programs. A line that starts with a # has a special meaning, depending on the symbol following it. A preprocessing directive is processed by either a preprocessor of a C compiler or interpreter directly. This specific line with the **include** directive instructs a compiler or interpreter to include the contents of the header **stdio.h** in the program. The contents made available via the **#include** preprocessing directive is called a *header* or *header file*. The header file **stdio.h** contains information such as function declarations related to the standard input/output library. A *library* consists of a collection of functions and relevant information. They are part of the C language. A header file typically ends with the file extension `.h`. Standard C header files, such as **stdio.h**, are distributed together with C compilers or interpreters. Normally, users do not need to worry about the contents inside these standard header files. They are implementation dependent, i.e., for different compilers and interpreters, the contents of these standard C header files are different. Each C compiler or interpreter has its own set of standard header files. The purpose of including the header file **stdio.h** in Program 2.1 is to use the standard output function **printf()** in the subsequent line.

Function is the basic executable module in a C program. Asking a function to perform its assigned tasks is known as *calling* the function. A C program contains one or more functions, one of which must be **main()**, which returns a value of **int** type. Details about the **int** type will be described in Chapter 3. The line

```
int main()
```

is part of every C program. The parenthesis after the symbol **main** indicates that it is a function. A set of identifier-like tokens, which have predefined meanings and are reserved by the C language, are called *reserved keywords*. The complete list of reserved keywords is available in Appendix A. The symbol **int** is one of the reserved keywords in C. In this case, it is used to declare that the function **main**() returns a value of type int. A C program starts to execute at the function **main**().

A function may expect arguments and produce a return value. One communication method between functions is for the calling function to provide a list of values, called *arguments*, to the called function. The argument list is surrounded by the parentheses after the function name when it is called. In this example, the function **main**() does not have any argument, as indicated by the empty list ().

A function consists of *statements* that specify actions to be taken. For a function definition, the statements of the function are enclosed in a pair of braces '{' and '}'. The left brace '{' begins the body of the function. The corresponding right brace '}' ends a function definition. This pair of braces and statements between the braces are called a *block*, which is an important unit in C.

The function **main**() in this example contains two statements. Statement

```
printf("Hello, world\n"); /* display output */
```

calls the function **printf**() to print out `Hello, world` on the screen. In this case, the function **printf**() is referred to as the *called function* whereas the function **main**() is referred to as the *calling function*. A function can be called using the function name followed by an argument list within a pair of parentheses. The function **printf**() is a standard function in the standard input/output C library. The argument of the function **printf**() in this example is a character string. A sequence of characters enclosed in a pair of double quotes, such as `"Hello, world"`, is called a *character string*, *string literal*, or *string constant*. The function **printf**() can take multiple arguments. In this example, only one argument of the string data type is passed to it. When a string is passed to the function **printf**(), it will normally be printed out on the screen exactly as it appears in the program. However, the character sequences `\n` will not be printed on the screen. The backslash '\' is called an *escape character*. When a compiler or interpreter encounters an escape character inside a string, it looks ahead at the next character and combines it to form an escape character. In this case, the escape character `\n` means a *newline character*, which will advance the next output to the left margin of the next line on the screen. One cannot use a `Return` or `Enter` key from a keyboard inside a string literal. For example, a compiler or interpreter will generate an error message for a C program with the code below:

```
printf("Hello, world
        ");
```

Note that the escape character `\n` is a single character. The escape sequence provides a general mechanism for representing characters that cannot be typed or are invisible. A complete list of escape characters can be found in Chapter 3.

Each statement in C must end with a semicolon. The blank spaces, except when inside a string, are ignored by compilers or interpreters. For readability and software maintenance, statements inside a function shall be properly indented, typically with a fixed number of blank spaces. Indentations of four blank space characters is recommended as shown in Program 2.1.

Like **int**, the symbol **return** is also a reserved keyword in C. Line

```
return 0;
```

is included at the end of the function **main**(). When this statement is executed, the value 0 indicates that the program terminated successfully. Depending on how the program is executed, this exit value will be passed to the executing environment. As an example, sections 2.2.1 and 2.2.3 describe how this exit value is passed to the executing environment when the program is executed in Ch. Chapter 6 will further discuss details about functions and this return statement.

2.2 Making It Work

C is a portable language. The same program, such as Program 2.1, can be compiled by different C compilers from different developers to run in different platforms. (However, running the C standard–compliant code is platform and implementation dependent.) There are many different C compilers from different developers for different platforms. Each has its own quirks and extensions to get the code to work.

Most chapters in Parts I and II in this book contain a section titled **"Making It Work,"** in which platform and implementation dependent issues are described. Although they are not part of the C standard, it is important to get your C program to work correctly to get the desired output. We have tested all code presented in this book using a cross-platform C/C++ interpreter Ch, Visual C++ **cl** in Windows, GNU C compiler **gcc** in Linux, GNU C++ compiler **g++** in Linux, Sun C compiler **cc** in Solaris, and Sun C++ compiler **CC** in Solaris. In this section, how to use Ch, Visual C++, GNU C, Sun C Compiler to run C programs in both Windows and Unix (including Linux and Mac OS X) is described in detail. After you understand how to get your C programs to work in these interpreter and compilers, you will be able to use almost any platform and compiler to develop your C programs.

2.2.1 Editing and Executing C Programs in ChIDE

An IDE can be used to develop C programs. It can edit programs with added features of automatic syntax highlighting and execute the programs within the IDE. ChIDE is a user-friendly IDE to edit, debug, and run C/Ch/C++ programs in Ch. It is especially designed for beginners to learn computer programming.

After Ch is installed from the companion CD, ChIDE can be launched by running the program **chide**. ChIDE can also be launched conveniently by double-clicking its icon, shown in Figure 2.1 on the desktop in Windows.

Editing Program Source Code

Text file or program source code editing in ChIDE works similarly to most Macintosh or Windows editors such as Notepad with the additional feature of automatic syntax styling. The user interface can be in one of 30 local languages such as German, French, Chinese, Japanese, and Korean. ChIDE can hold multiple files in memory at one time, but only one file will be visible. By default, ChIDE allows up to 20 files to be in memory at once.

As an example, open a new document and type Program 2.1 in the *editing pane*, as shown in Figure 2.2. The program appears colored on the screen due to syntax highlighting.

For the classroom presentation, the font size of the displayed program can be enlarged by clicking the command `View | Change Font Size`, and then make changes by selecting the desired font size.

Save the document as a file named `hello.c`, as shown in Figure 2.3. The program `hello.c`, located in `CHHOME/demos/bin/hello.c`, can also be loaded using the `File | Open` command. Here `CHHOME` is the home directory for Ch. By default, the home directory for Ch in Windows is `C:/Ch` in the `C` drive. In

Figure 2.1: A ChIDE icon on a desktop in Windows.

```
/* File: hello.c
   Print 'Hello, world' on the screen. */
#include <stdio.h>

int main()
{
    printf("Hello, world\n");
    return 0;
}
```

Figure 2.2: The program edited inside the editing pane in ChIDE.

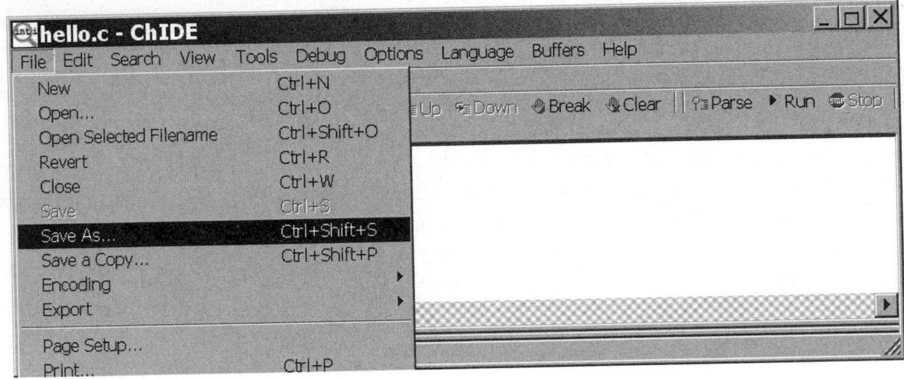

Figure 2.3: Saving the edited program in ChIDE.

this case, the program is located in `C:/Ch/demos/bin/hello.c`. In other platforms, the default home directory for Ch is `/usr/local/ch`.

Running Programs and Stopping Their Execution

Perform the `Run` or `Tools | Run` command, as shown in Figure 2.4, to execute the program `hello.c`. Instead of performing the `Run` or `Tools | Run` command, pressing the function key `F2` will also execute the program.

You may use the command `Parse` or `Tools | Parse` to just check the syntax error of the program without executing it.

If the command execution has failed or it is taking too long to complete, then the `Stop` or `Tools | Stop Executing` command can be used to stop the program.

Output from Execution of Programs

There are four panes in ChIDE: the editing pane, the debug pane, the debug command pane, and the output pane. The *editing pane*, on the top is for editing a program source file or any text file. The *debug pane* is

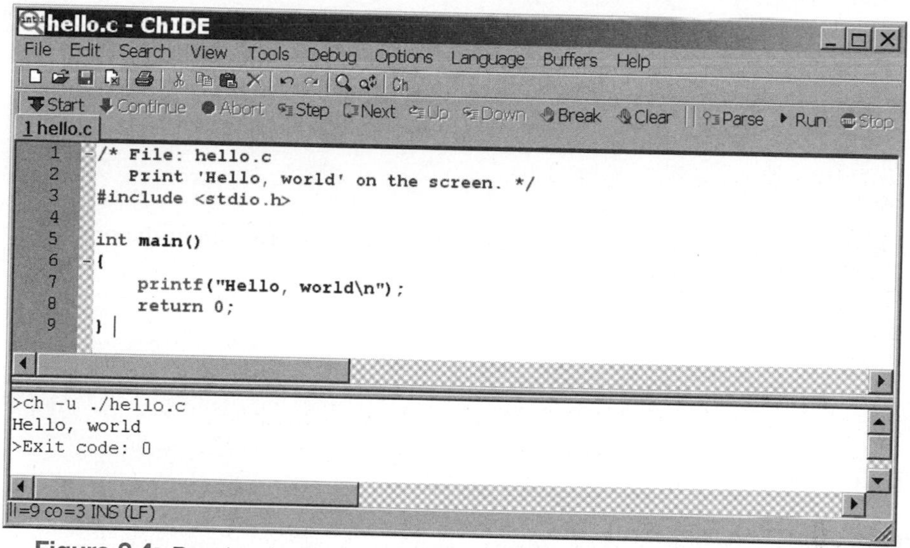

Figure 2.4: Running the program inside the editing pane in ChIDE and its output.

located below the editing pane. Initially it is of zero size, but it can be made larger by dragging the divider between it and the editing pane. The *debug command pane* is located below the debug pane. The debug pane and debug command pane will be opened when the program is executed in debug mode, which will be described in section 3.16.3 in Chapter 3. The *output pane* also is located below the debug pane, but on the left of the debug command pane. Initially it is of zero size, but it can also be made larger by dragging the divider between it and the debug pane. By default, the output from the program is directed into the output pane, when it is executed using the command `Run`.

When the program `hello.c` is executed, the output pane will be made visible if it is not already visible and will display the following three lines

```
>ch -u ./hello.c
Hello, world
>Exit code: 0
```

as shown in Figure 2.4. The first line (displayed in the blue color on the screen),

```
>ch -u ./hello.c
```

from ChIDE shows that it uses Ch to execute the program `hello.c` in the current working directory. The next line (displayed in the black color on the screen),

```
Hello, world
```

is the output from running the Ch program. The last line (displayed also in the blue color on the screen),

```
>Exit code: 0
```

is from ChIDE showing that the program has finished. This line displays the exit code for the program. An exit code of 0 indicates that the program is terminated successfully by the statement

```
return 0;
```

or

```
exit (0);
```

in the program. If a failure had occurred during the execution of the program or the program is terminated with a non-zero value for a return or exit statement such as

```
return -1;
```

or

```
exit(-1);
```

the exit code would be `-1`.

Detecting Program Syntax Errors

ChIDE understands the error messages produced by Ch. To see this, add a mistake to the program by changing the line

```
printf("Hello, world\n");
```

to

```
printf("Hello, world\n";
```

Perform the `Run` or `Tools | Run` command for the modified program. The results should look similar to those below

```
ERROR: missing ')'
ERROR: syntax error before or at line 7 in file C:\Ch\demos\bin\hello.c
  ==>:    printf("Hello, world\n";
  BUG:    printf("Hello, world\n"; <== ???
ERROR: cannot execute command 'C:\Ch\demos\bin\hello.c'
```

as shown in Figure 2.5. Because the program fails to execute, the exit code `-1` is displayed at the end of the output pane as

```
Exit code: -1
```

If you double-click the error message with a line number (displayed in the red color on the screen) in the output pane shown in Figure 2.5 with the left button of your mouse, the line with incorrect syntax and the error message in the output pane will be highlighted (displayed in the yellow background on the screen) as shown in Figure 2.6. The caret is moved to this line and the pane is scrolled automatically if needed to show the line. While it is easy to see where the problem is in this simple case, with a large file, the `Tools | Next Message` command can be used to view each of the reported errors. Upon performing `Tools | Next Message`, the first error message in the output pane and the appropriate line in the editing pane are highlighted (displayed in the yellow background on the screen).

```
hello.c - ChIDE
File Edit Search View Tools Debug Options Language Buffers Help
Start Continue Abort Step Next Up Down Break Clear Parse Run Stop
1 hello.c
1  /* File: hello.c
2     Print 'Hello, world' on the screen. */
3  #include <stdio.h>
4
5  int main()
6  {
7      printf("Hello, world\n";
8      return 0;
9  }

>ch -u ./hello.c
ERROR: missing ')'
ERROR: syntax error before or at line 7 in file C:\Ch\demos\bin\hello.c
  ==>:     printf("Hello, world\n";
  BUG:     printf("Hello, world\n";<== ???
ERROR: cannot execute command 'C:\Ch\demos\bin\hello.c'
>Exit code: -1
li=7 co=28 INS (LF)
```

Figure 2.5: The error line in output from executing program `hello.c`.

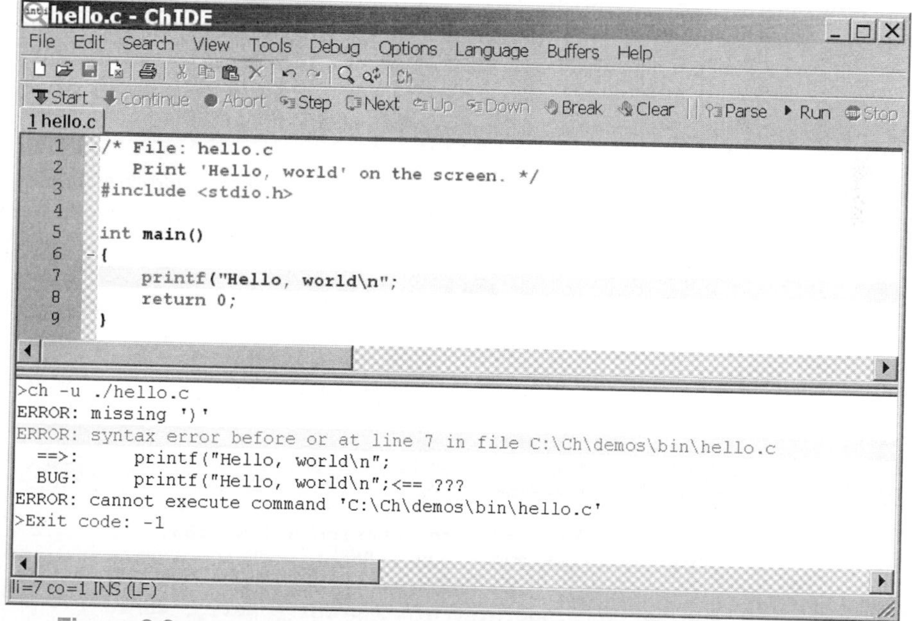

Figure 2.6: Finding the error line in output from executing program `hello.c`.

Errors in computer programs are called *bugs*. The process of finding and reducing the number of bugs is called *debug* or *debugging*. ChIDE is especially helpful for testing and debugging a program. You can set breakpoints, run a program step by step, watch and change values of variables during the program execution, among other things. Using ChIDE for debugging with the debug pane will be described in sections 3.16.3

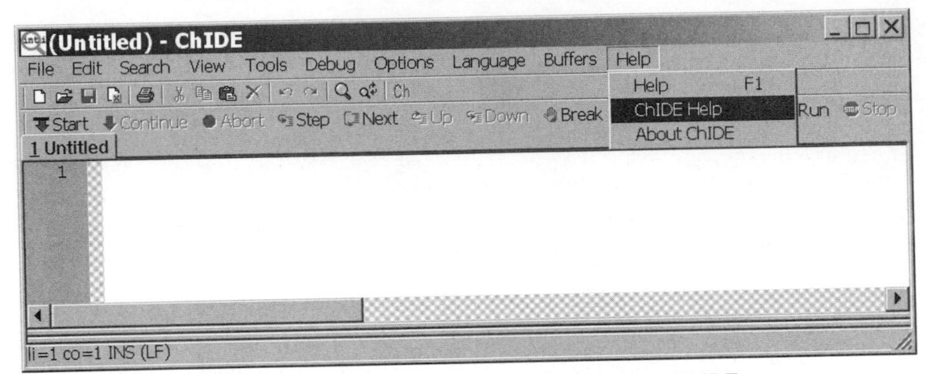

Figure 2.7: Getting online help on how to use ChIDE.

and 6.13.3. More information about running C and C++ programs in Ch using ChIDE can be obtained online by clicking `ChIDE Help` from the `Help` menu, as shown in Figure 2.7.

2.2.2 Using Portable Commands to Handle Files in a Command Shell

Ch can be used as a command shell in which commands are processed. Like other commonly used shells such as MS-DOS shell and C shell, commands can be executed in a Ch shell.

A Ch shell can be launched by running the command **ch**. In Windows, a Ch command shell can also be conveniently launched by clicking the **Ch** icon (displayed in the red color on the screen), shown in Figure 2.8, on the desktop or on the toolbar of the ChIDE.

Assume the user account is the administrator, after a Ch shell is launched in Windows, by default, the screen prompt of the shell window becomes

```
C:/Documents and Settings/Administrator>
```

where `C:/Documents and Settings/Administrator` is the user's *home directory* on the desktop, as shown in Figure 2.9. The prompt, command, and output from a command, and interactive execution of

Figure 2.8: A Ch icon on a desktop in Windows.

Figure 2.9: A Ch command shell.

a command in a command shell are displayed with the dark blue background in this book as shown in the previous prompt for clarity. The colors of the text and background as well as the window size and font size of the shell window shown in Figure 2.9 can be changed by right-clicking the Ch icon at the upper left corner of the window, and selecting the Properties menu to make changes. Note that for Windows Vista, you need to run ChIDE with the administrative privilege to make such a change. The displayed directory `C:/Documents and Settings/Administrator` is also called the *current working directory*. If the user account is not the administrator, the account name *Administrator* shall be changed to the appropriate user account name.

In Unix, such as Linux and Mac OS X, when Ch is launched, the prompt may show

```
/home/harry>
```

where `/home/harry` is the home directory for the user with the account name `harry`.

The prompt > indicates that the system is in a Ch shell and is ready to accept the user's terminal keyboard input. The default prompt in a Ch shell can be reconfigured if it is preferred to use another prompt symbol. If the input typed in is syntactically correct, it will be executed successfully. Upon completion of the execution, the system prompt > will appear again. If an error occurs during the execution of the program or expression, the Ch shell prints out the corresponding error messages to assist the user to solve the problem.

There are hundreds of commands along with their respective online documentation in the system. No one knows all of them. Every computer wizard has a small set of working tools that are used all the time, plus a vague idea of what else is out there. In Windows, Ch supports all MS-DOS commands such as **dir, copy,** and **move**. But, Ch also contains over 250 Unix commands such as **ls, vi, find, sed,** and **awk**. In this section, we will describe through examples how to use the most commonly used commands, listed in Table 2.1, for handling files. It should be emphasized again that these commands running in the Ch shell are portable across different platforms such as Windows, Linux, and Mac OS X. Using these commands, a user can effectively manipulate files on almost any major platform to run C programs. The command **vi** is a portable program for text editing. It can be used to edit source files when you remotely log in to a computer. Although beyond the scope of this book, many resources on how to use **vi** are available on the Internet. They are linked at the author's Web site.

Table 2.1 Portable commands for handling files.

Command	Usage	Description
cd	cd	changes to the home directory
	cd *dir*	changes to the directory *dir*
cp	cp *file1 file2*	copies *file1* to *file2*
ls	ls	lists contents in the working directory
mkdir	mkdir *dir*	creates a new directory *dir*
pwd	pwd	prints (displays) the name of the working directory
rm	rm *file*	removes *file*
chmod	chmod +x *file*	changes the mode of *file* to make it executable
chide	chide *file.c*	launches Ch IDE for editing and executing *file.c*
vi	vi *file*	edits *file*
man	man *cmd*	shows the usage and syntax of command *cmd*

Assume that Ch is installed in `C:/Ch` in Windows, the default installation directory. The current working directory is `C:/Documents and Settings/Administrator`, which is also the user's home directory. The application of portable commands for file handling can be illustrated by interactive execution of commands in a Ch shell as shown below.

```
C:/Documents and Settings/Administrator> mkdir eme5
C:/Documents and Settings/Administrator> cd eme5
C:/Documents and Settings/Administrator/eme5> pwd
C:/Documents and Settings/Administrator/eme5
C:/Documents and Settings/Administrator/eme5> cp C:/Ch/demos/bin/hello.c hello.c
C:/Documents and Settings/Administrator/eme5> ls
hello.c
C:/Documents and Settings/Administrator/eme5> chide hello.c
```

It is desirable to keep all homework related to a course in a separate folder, that is, directory. In the above example, we assume that eme5 is a course name. As shown in *Usage* in Table 2.1, the command **mkdir** takes an argument as a directory (folder) to be created. We first create a directory called `eme5` using the command

```
> mkdir eme5
```

Then, we change to this new directory, `C:/Documents and Settings/Administrator/eme5`, using command

```
> cd eme5
```

Next, we display the current working directory with the command

```
> pwd
```

In Windows, a C program `hello.c`, shown in Figure 2.2 in the directory `C:/Ch/demos/bin`, is copied to the working directory with the same file name using the command

```
> cp C:/Ch/demos/bin/hello.c hello.c
```

If you are using Unix with Ch installed in the default directory `/usr/local/ch`, the command

```
> cp /usr/local/ch/demos/bin/hello.c hello.c
```

can be used to copy program `hello.c` to the current working directory. Files in the current working directory are listed using the command

```
> ls
```

At this point, there is only one file, `hello.c`, in the directory `C:/Documents and Settings/Administrator/eme5`. It is recommended that you save all your developed C programs in this directory so that you may find all programs easily later. Finally, the program **chide** is launched by the command

```
> chide hello.c
```

to edit and execute program `hello.c` in ChIDE, as shown in Figure 2.2. For a classroom presentation, sometimes, it is more convenient to open multiple source files by a single command as shown below:

```
> chide file1.c file2.c header.h
```

The command below opens all files in the current working directory:

```
> chide *
```

To use a command dealing with a path with white space, the path needs to be placed inside a pair of double quotation marks, as shown below, to remove file `hello.c`.

```
> rm "C:/Documents and Settings/Administrator/eme5/hello.c"
```

The command **man** can be used to show the usage and syntax of a command. For example, the command

```
> man ch
```

will show the usage and command-line options for **ch**.

2.2.3 Executing C Programs, Statements, and Expressions in Ch

Unlike other command shells, C programs, functions, statements, and expressions can be readily executed in a Ch command shell, as shown in Figure 1.5. An instructor can use Ch interactively in classroom presentations with a laptop to illustrate programming features quickly, especially when answering students' questions. You can also try out different features of C/C++ quickly as shown in this section.

Interactive Execution of C Programs

It is very simple and easy to run C programs interactively without compilation in a Ch shell. For example, assume that `C:/Documents and Settings/Administrator/eme5` is the current working directory as presented in the previous section. The program `hello.c` in this directory can be executed in Ch to get the output of `Hello, world` as shown below:

```
C:/Documents and Settings/Administrator/eme5> hello.c
Hello, world
C:/Documents and Settings/Administrator/eme5> _status
0
```

The exit code from executing the statement

```
return 0;
```

in Program 2.1 in a Ch command shell is kept in the system variable **_status**. Because the program `hello.c` has been executed successfully, the exit code is 0, as shown in the above output, when **_status** is typed in the command line.

A C program can also be executed in the command line as an input file for command **ch** as shown below:

```
C:/Documents and Settings/Administrator/eme5> ch hello.c
Hello, world
```

In Unix or Mac OS X, to readily use the C program `hello.c` as a command, the file has to be executable. The command **chmod** can be used to change the mode of a file. The command

```
chmod +x hello.c
```

makes the program `hello.c` executable so that it can run in a Ch command shell as shown below:

```
/home/harry/eme5> chmod +x hello.c
/home/harry/eme5> hello.c
Hello, world
```

Set-up Paths and Finding Commands in Ch

When a command is typed into a prompt of a command shell for execution, the command shell will search for the command in prespecified directories. In a Ch shell, the system variable **_path** of string type contains the directories to be searched for the command. Each directory is separated by a semicolon inside the string **_path**. When a Ch command shell is launched, the system variable **_path** contains some default search paths. For example, in Windows, the default search paths are

```
C:/Ch/bin;C:/Ch/sbin;C:/Ch/toolkit/bin;C:/Ch/toolkit/sbin;
C:/WINDOWS;C:/WINDOWS/SYSTEM32;
```

The directory `C:/Documents and Settings/Administrator/eme5` is not in the search paths for a command. If you try to run program `hello.c` in this directory when the current working directory is `C:/Documents and Settings/Administrator`, the Ch shell will not be able to find this program, as shown below, and gives two error messages.

```
C:/Documents and Settings/Administrator> hello.c
ERROR: variable 'hello.c' not defined
ERROR: command 'hello.c' not found
```

To make this work, the user needs to add the directory `C:/Documents and Settings/Administrator`, to the search paths for the command shell, which will be discussed in detail later.

When Ch is launched or a Ch program is executed, by default, it will execute the start-up file **.chrc** in Unix or **_chrc** in Windows in the user's home directory if the start-up file exists. In the remaining presentation, it is assumed that Ch is used in Windows with a start-up file **_chrc** in the user's home directory. This start-up file typically sets up the search paths for commands, functions, header files, etc. In Windows, a start-up file **_chrc** with default set-up is created in the user's home directory during installation of Ch. However, there is no start-up file in a user's home directory in Unix by default. The system administrator may add such a start-up file in a user's home directory. However, the user can execute Ch with the option -d as follows

```
> ch -d
```

to copy a sample start-up file from the directory `CHHOME/config` to the user's home directory if there is no start-up file in the home directory yet. Note that `CHHOME` is not the string `"CHHOME"`; instead, it uses the

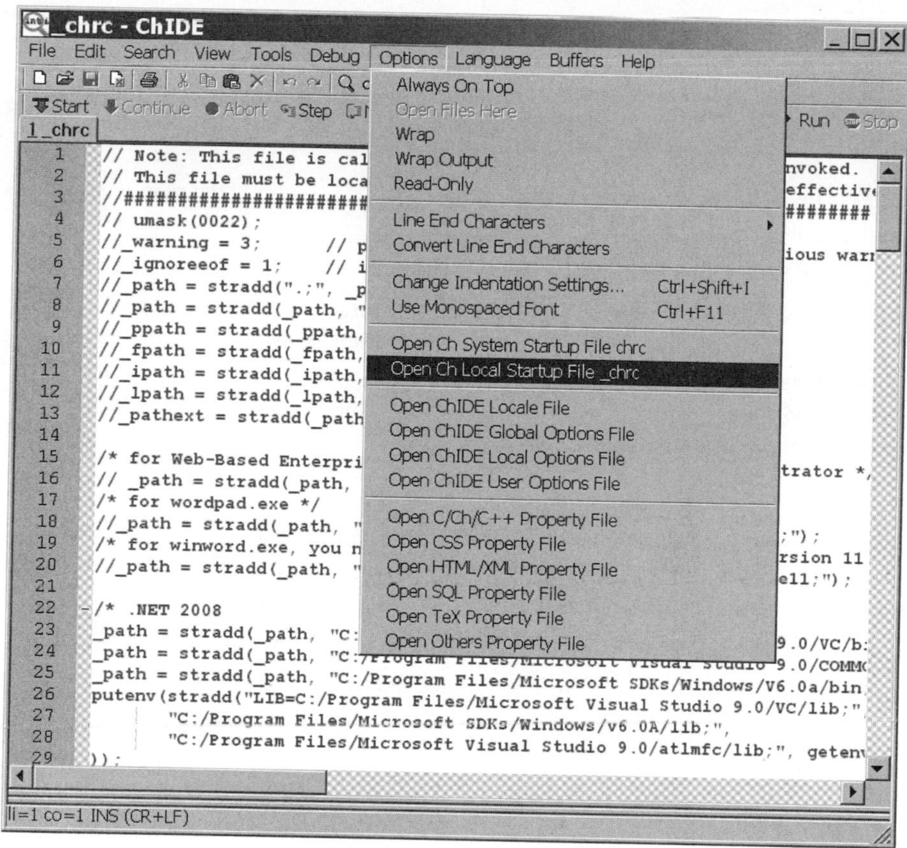

Figure 2.10: Opening the local Ch initialization start-up file for editing.

file system path under which Ch is installed. For example, by default, Ch is installed in `C:/Ch` in Windows and `/usr/local/ch` in Unix.

In Windows, the command in a Ch shell below

```
C:/Documents and Settings/Administrator> ch -d
```

will create a start-up file **_chrc** in the user's home directory `C:/Documents and Settings/Administrator`. This local Ch initialization start-up file **_chrc** can be opened for editing the search paths by ChIDE editor as shown in Figure 2.10.

To include the directory `C:/Documents and Settings/Administrator/eme5` in the search paths for a command, the following statement

```
_path = stradd(_path, "C:/Documents and Settings/Administrator/eme5;");
```

needs to be added to the start-up file **_chrc** in the user's home directory so that the command `hello.c` in this directory can be invoked regardless of what the current working directory is. The function **stradd()** adds arguments of string type and returns it as a new string. After the directory `C:/Documents and Settings/Administrator/eme5` has been added to the search path **_path**, you need to restart a Ch command shell. Then, you will be able to execute the program `hello.c` in this directory as shown below:

```
C:/Documents and Settings/Administrator> hello.c
Hello, world
```

In Unix or Mac OS X, to include the directory `/home/harry/eme5` in the search paths for a command, the following statement

```
_path = stradd(_path, "/home/harry/eme5;");
```

needs to be added to the start-up file **.chrc** in the user's home directory `/home/harry`.

Ch shell is quite compatible with MS-DOS shell and C-shell. Most features in C-shell are available in Ch. Details about using Ch as a command shell are beyond the scope of this book. Alias, one of the useful features as a command shell, is presented here. *Alias* is a shorthand for a command or series of commands with the following syntax as an alias definition:

```
alias("name", "value");
```

It provides a string value that replaces a command name when it is encountered. For example, you may want to go to the directory `C:/Documents and Settings/Administrator/eme5` often when you develop C programs. This can be facilitated by adding the alias definition

```
alias("go", "cd C:/Documents and Settings/Administrator/eme5");
```

in the start-up file in your home directory. This will make the name `go` as the shorthand for the command

```
cd C:/Documents and Settings/Administrator/eme5
```

You may replace `go` in the alias definition with another name, such as `eme5`. With this alias definition, you can change the current working directory to `C:/Documents and Settings/Administrator/eme5` quickly from any other directory as shown below:

```
C:/Ch> pwd
C:/Ch
C:/Ch> go
C:/Documents and Settings/Administrator/eme5> pwd
C:/Documents and Settings/Administrator/eme5
```

Interactive Execution of C Statements and Expressions

All statements and expressions of C can be executed in Ch interactively. In Ch, if there is any output from the system resulting from executing an expression, statement, or command, it will be displayed on the screen. For example, the output `Hello, world` can be obtained by calling the function **printf**() interactively as shown below and as seen in Figure 2.9:

```
C:/Documents and Settings/Administrator> printf("Hello, world")
Hello, world
```

In comparison with Figure 2.9, the last prompt `C:/Documents and Settings/Administrator>` is omitted to save space in the presentation of this book. Note that the semicolon at the end of a statement in a C program is optional when the corresponding statement is executed in a Ch command shell. There is no semicolon in calling the function **printf()** in the above execution. For simplicity, only the prompt > in a Ch command shell will be displayed in the remaining presentation of this book.

The newline character `\n` can be illustrated by

```
> printf("Hello, world\nWelcome to C!")
Hello, world
Welcome to C!
```

After the newline character, the string `Welcome to C!` is displayed starting from the left margin of the next line on the screen.

If a C expression is typed in, it will be evaluated by Ch. The result will then be displayed on the screen. For example, if the expression `1+3*2` is typed in, the output will be 7 as shown below:

```
> 1+3*2
7
```

Any valid C expression can be evaluated in the Ch shell. Therefore, Ch can be conveniently used as a calculator. The expression `1+3*2` contains three operands 1, 3, 2 and two operators '+' and '*'. The arithmetic operators in C '+', '-', '*', and '/' for addition, subtraction, multiplication, and division, respectively, follow the conventional rules of arithmetic. They are all binary operators with two operands. For example, the arithmetic operators are right-associative and the multiplication operator has higher precedence than the addition and subtraction operators. For the expression `1+3*2`, the multiplication expression 3*2, which contains a binary operator '*' and two operands 3 and 2, will be calculated first. The result of this multiplication operation will then be used as one of the two operands of binary addition operator '+'. The other operand of the addition operator is 1.

As another example, one can declare a variable at the prompt. Then, use the variable in subsequent calculations as shown below:

```
> int i
> i = 10
10
> i*i
100
```

In the above C statements, variable `i` is declared as type int using the keyword **int** as the type specifier. The variable `i` is then assigned the value of 10. The variable is used as operands in the multiplication operation.

Throughout this textbook, many programming features will be succinctly presented by executing C statements and expressions in Ch interactively.

2.2.4 Compiling, Linking, and Executing C Programs in a Command Shell

How to compile and link a C program in a command shell, such as Ch or MS-DOS command shell, as shown in Figure 1.4(a), is described in this section. All programs described in this book with the `.c` file extension can be compiled and linked using a C compiler. Developing an executable program from a C source code mainly involves two separate compiling and linking processes.

In the compiling process, a C source code is typically processed first by a preprocessor, which deals with the directives beginning with the symbol '#', such as

```
#include <stdio.h>
```

At this phase, comments in the source code are also removed. The details about preprocessing directives are described in Chapter 7. Depending on implementation, a compiler may invoke a separator program as a preprocessor. Next, the modified file is processed by a compiler, which checks for syntax errors of the program. If the program is syntactically correct, depending on the implementation, a compiler may generate an intermediate code. When a source code of different languages such as Fortran is compiled, the same type of intermediate code is generated. This intermediate code is then optimized for performance. Based on this intermediate code, typically, an assembly code is generated. The assembly code is then processed by an assembler, which generates an object code, i.e., machine instructions. The object code has the file extension of `.o` in Unix and `.obj` in Windows. The compiling process usually refers to all the above tasks to generate an object code from a C source code.

The linking process uses a linker to link the object file with additional code, including libraries, such as an input and output library containing the function **printf()**, to create a complete executable program. The user can then run the executable program to get the result of the program based on the instructions on the source code as shown in Figure 1.4(b).

However, a single program can combine all the above steps for compiling and linking together to create an executable program from a C source code.

Using Visual C++ to Compile C Programs in Windows

The program **cl.exe** is a C compiler in Visual C++ in Windows. It can be used to compile and link both C and C++ programs. The compiler command **cl.exe** can be invoked either as **cl.exe** or **cl** from a command shell such as MS-DOS or Ch shell. If Visual C++ has been installed in your computer before Ch is installed, installation of Ch will modify the start-up file **_chrc** in the user's home directory to support Visual C++ automatically. If you install Ch first, then install Visual C++, you can edit the start-up file **_chrc** by uncommenting the code related to Visual C++ based on the instructions inside the file. The start-up file **_chrc** can be opened for editing, as shown in Figure 2.10.

After a proper setup, the source code `hello.c` can be compiled by the command

```
> cl /c hello.c
```

in a Ch command shell to create an object code `hello.obj`. The command-line option `/c` for the program **cl** compiles the source code only without linking. The object code can in turn be linked by the command

```
> cl hello.obj
```

or using the command **link**

```
> link hello.obj
```

with the standard C library containing input and output functions such as the function **printf()** to create an executable program `hello.exe` with the file extension `.exe` in the current working directory.

We can combine both compiling and linking processes in a single command

```
> cl hello.c
```

In this case, both the object file `hello.obj` and executable program `hello.exe` are generated. The executable program `hello.exe` can be executed by typing either

```
> hello.exe
Hello, world
```

or

```
> hello
Hello, world
```

in a command shell. The program `hello.exe` can also be invoked through other methods such as Windows Explorer or start-up menus.

By default, the name of the executable program is the same as the source file, but with the `.exe` file extension. You can change the file name of the executable using the command-line option `/Fe` immediately followed by your program name without a blank spacc. For example, to name the binary executable file as `myhello.exe`, use the command below:

```
> cl /Femyhello.exe hello.c
```

By default, the command **cl** assumes that files with the .c extension are C source files. The `/TC` or `/Tc` option specifies that the following input file is a C source file, even if it does not have a `.c` extension. Using this option, a C program `hello.ch` with a `.ch` extension can be compiled as follows:

```
> cl /TC hello.ch
```

Section 8.5.1 describes how to compile a program with multiple source files.

Using C Compilers in Unix

Most C compilers in Unix are distributed as a command **cc**. For example, under a Ch command shell in Unix, the command

```
> cc -c hello.c
```

with the option `-c` compiles the C source code `hello.c` in Program 2.1 to generate an object code `hello.o` only without linking. The object code can be linked with othe additional modules such as the C standard input and output library by the command

```
> cc hello.o
```

to create an executable program. By default, the executable program is **a.out**. You can also combine both compiling and linking processes and change the file name of the executable using the command-line option

-o followed by your program name. For example, to name the binary executable as myhello, use the command

```
> cc -o myhello hello.c
```

to compile and link the program hello.c.

By default, the GNU C compiler is distributed as a command **gcc**. In Linux, it is often symbolically linked as the command **cc** so that both commands **gcc** and **cc** share the same copy of the program. To use the GNU C compiler **gcc**, the command

```
> gcc hello.c
```

can be used to create a binary executable program. After compiling and linking, Program 2.1 can be executed by typing the command a.out in a command shell. The output Hello, world will be displayed on the screen, as shown below:

```
> a.out
Hello, world
```

The -x c option specifies that following input file is a C source file, regardless of its file extension. Using this option, a C program hello.ch can be compiled as follows:

```
> gcc -x c hello.ch
```

Invoking gcc with a Language Standard of C89, C90, and C99

The GNU C compiler supports different versions of the C standard. You can select the version of the C standard to use on the command line using the -std option. The options that support different versions of the C standard are as follows:

```
-std=c89 or -std=iso9899:1990
```

for the ISO C89 standard;

```
-std=iso9899:199409
```

for the ISO C90 standard as modified in Amendment 1;

```
-std=c99 or -std=iso9899:1999
```

for the ISO C99 standard. The default is not any version of the standard, but rather, the GNU C language, with the option

```
-std=gnu89
```

for the ISO C90 standard plus its own extensions and some C99 features.

To compile a program, say funcname.c, with C99 features, using the GNU C compiler **gcc**, the program needs to be compiled with the command-line option -std=c99 as follows:

```
> gcc -std=c99 funcname.c
```

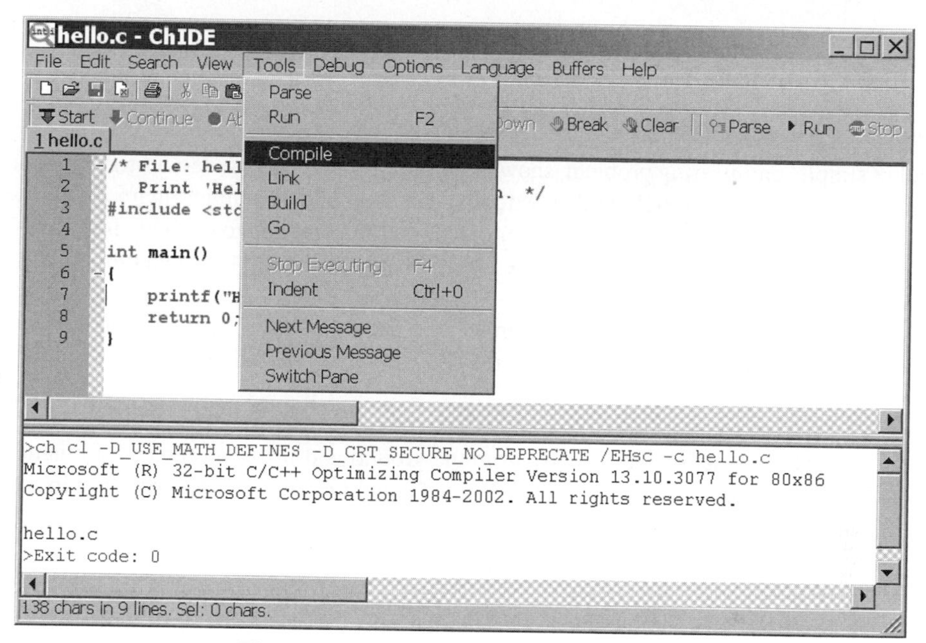

Figure 2.11: Compiling a C/C++ program.

Please note that Visual C++ supports very few new features in C99. Major new features for applications in engineering and science, such as variable-length arrays in C99, which will be described later, are not supported in Visual C++. Therefore, C99 features presented in this book are mainly tested in GNU C and Ch.

2.2.5 Editing, Compiling, Linking, and Executing C Programs in ChIDE

ChIDE can also compile and link an edited C/C++ program in the editing pane using C and C++ compilers. By default, the ChIDE is configured to use the latest Visual C++ installed in your Windows operating system to compile C and C++ programs. The environment variables and commands for the Visual C++ can be modified in the individual start-up configuration file **_chrc** in the user's home directory, which can be opened for editing as shown in Figure 2.10. In Linux, ChIDE uses compilers **gcc** and **g++** to compile C and C++ programs, respectively. The default compiler can be changed by modifying the C/Ch/C++ property file `cpp.properties`, which can be opened under the command Options.

The command `Tools | Compile` as shown in Figure 2.11 can be used to compile a program. The output and error messages for compiling a C or C++ program are displayed in the output pane of the ChIDE. In Windows, compiling a program will create an object file with the file extension `.obj`. The object file can be linked using the command `Tools | Link` to create an executable program. The executable in Windows has the file extension `.exe`. If a make file is available in the current directory, the command `Tools | Build` will invoke the default make file `makefile` or `Makefile` to build an application. A make file can be useful for managing a large program with many source files. How to use a make file for software development is described in section 8.5.2 in Chapter 8. The command `Tools | Go` will execute the developed executable program.

An Application Example

Acceleration of a Moving Body

A practical, but simple, engineering problem, shown in Figure 2.12, is used to demonstrate applications of various programming features throughout this textbook. The dynamic system in Figure 2.12 consists of a single body with mass m moving on a horizontal surface. The force applied to the body is p. The freebody diagram for the body is shown in Figure 2.12. The nomenclature related to the modeling of the system is listed in Table 2.2.

When the body moves along the horizontal surface, the friction force f acting on the rigid body from the ground surface is proportional to the normal force and can be calculated by the following formula:

$$f = \mu N \tag{2.1}$$

where N is the normal force acting on the body from the ground and μ the coefficient of kinetic friction. To keep the body on the surface, the normal force N must equal the gravitational force mg in the vertical direction as shown below:

$$N = mg \tag{2.2}$$

where m is the mass of the body and g is the gravitational acceleration which is 9.81 meters per second squared (m/s^2) at sea level.

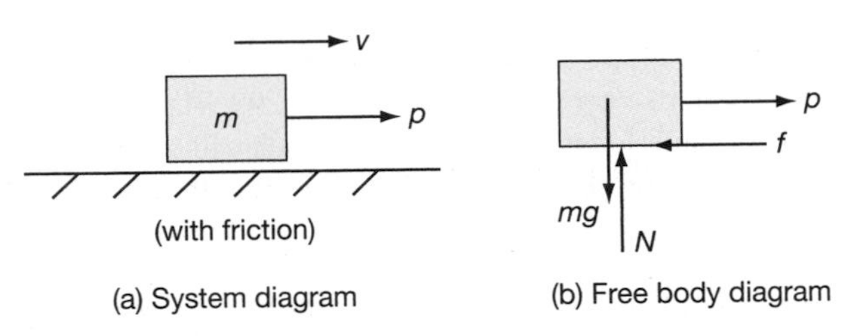

Figure 2.12 The system and freebody diagram.

Table 2.2 Nomenclature for calculating acceleration of the rigid body.

m	mass of the body
x	position of the body
v	velocity of the body
a	acceleration of the body
g	gravitational acceleration
μ	coefficient of kinetic friction
f	friction force
N	normal force
p	applied external force

Newton's second law of motion states that *the acceleration of a particle is proportional to the resultant force acting on it and is in the direction of this force.* When the body moves along the horizontal direction, the following equation of motion of the dynamic system can be derived based on Newton's second law:

$$p - f = ma \tag{2.3}$$

where $p - f$ is the resultant force applied on the body in the direction of the motion. From equations (2.1) to (2.3), the formula for calculating the acceleration of the rigid body moving horizontally can be derived as follows:

$$a = (p - \mu mg)/m \tag{2.4}$$

Equation (2.4) for calculating the acceleration of the rigid body in Figure 2.12 is used to demonstrate applications of various programming features throughout this textbook, as shown in the following problem.

Problem Statement:
For the mechanical system shown in Figure 2.12, given mass $m = 5$ kilograms (kg), coefficient of kinetic friction $\mu = 0.2$, and applied force $p = 20$ Newtons, calculate the resulting acceleration of the rigid body.

This is an introductory textbook for a first course on programming. It is assumed that the readers have only an elementary mathematical background. For those who do not fully understand the derivation of equation (2.4), the above problem statement can be treated as if it was written as follows.

Problem Statement:
Given $m = 5$, $\mu = 0.2$, and $p = 20$, calculate the function $a(p, \mu, m)$ defined in equation (2.4), where g has a constant value of 9.81.

We will try to solve this simple problem using different approaches to demonstrate various programming features.

First, this problem can be most easily solved interactively in a Ch command shell without any programming. Based on formula (2.4), the acceleration can be calculated by the expression $(20 - 0.2 * 5 * 9.81)/5$ in an interactive execution session below.

```
> (20-0.2*5*9.81)/5
2.0380
```

As shown in the displayed result of the expression $(20-0.2*5*9.81)/5$, the acceleration is 2.0380 meters per second squared (m/s^2). Note that the expression $20 - 0.2 * 5 * 9.81$ inside a pair of parentheses is calculated first, before it is used as one of the two operands for the binary division operator. By default, integers such as 20 and 5 are treated as **int** data types in C. The floating-point constants for real numbers such as 0.2 and 9.81 are treated as **double** data types. The double data type will be described further in Chapter 3. In arithmetic operations, when two operands are of the same data type, the data type of the result is the same as the operands. In an operation with mixed data types, the operand of lower precision will be promoted to a data type of higher precision for the operation. For example, in the multiplication expression 0.2*5, the integer operand 5 will be promoted to a floating-point number 5.0 first, before it is used for multiplication with the operand 0.2 of double type. The result of the multiplication operation will be a double data type. In the end, the expression $(20 - 0.2 * 5 * 9.81)/5$ is of the double type. When a value of a double type is displayed in a Ch prompt, it will have four digits after the decimal point.

```
/* File: accel.c
   Calculate acceleration. */
#include <stdio.h>

int main() {
    /* calculate and display acceleration */
    printf("Acceleration a = %f (m/s^2)\n", (20-0.2*5*9.81)/5);
    return 0;
}
```

Program 2.2: Calculating the acceleration at a specified time.

Alternatively, we can write a simple program shown in Program 2.2 to solve the problem. In Program 2.2, the statement

```
printf("Acceleration a = %f (m/s^2)\n", (20-0.2*5*9.81)/5);
```

calls the function **printf()** to print the string literal `Acceleration a =` , followed by the numerical value of the expression $(20 - 0.2 * 5 * 9.81)/5$, the string literal `(m/s^2)`, and a newline character on the terminal screen. In this example, the function **printf()** has two arguments, `"Acceleration a = %f (m/s^2)\n"` and `(20-0.2*5*9.81)/5`. The first argument is the format control string. It contains a string literal to be displayed and it also contains the conversion specifier `%f` indicating that a floating-point value for real number will be printed. More details about conversion specifiers for the function **printf()** will be presented in section 3.15.1 in Chapter 3 and Chapter 9. The second argument specifies the value to be printed. The calculated result of the expression `(20-0.2*5*9.81)/5` with a data type of double, instead of the expression itself, will be passed to the function **printf()** when the program is executed. The output of Program 2.2 can be obtained by executing the source file `accel.c` in Ch as follows:

```
> accel.c
Acceleration a = 2.038000 (m/s^2)
```

When a floating-point number is printed out using function **printf()** with a conversion specifier `%f`, it will have six digits after the decimal point. The function **printf()** in Program 2.2 can also be executed interactively in Ch shell as shown below:

```
> printf("Acceleration a = %f (m/s^2)\n", (20-0.2*5*9.81)/5)
Acceleration a = 2.038000 (m/s^2)
```

Exercises

1. Install C/C++ interpreter Ch Student Edition for Windows from the companion CD or download the latest version for different platforms from the Internet at http://www.softintegration.com.
2. Download GNU Image Manipulation Program (GIMP) from http://www.gimp.org/windows/ for Windows or http://www.gimp.org/macintosh/ for Mac OS X. GIMP can be used to acquire an image from the screen

using the following procedure: Click the menu `File`, click the menu `Create`, click the menu `Screen Shot`, and click `Grab`. Then move the cursor to a window to be aquired.

3. In a Ch command shell, type the command

```
> cd
```

It will display your home directory. What's your home directory? Create a directory (folder) called `eme5`, or other course name you are taking using this textbook, under your home directory by the command

```
> mkdir eme5
```

4. In a Ch command shell, type

```
> ch -d
```

to copy the start-up configuration file **_chrc** in Windows or **.chrc** in Unix from `CHHOME/config` directory to your home directory, where `CHHOME` is the home directory for Ch, such as `C:/Ch` for Windows or `/usr/local/ch` for Unix.

5. Add the directory `HOME/eme5` in the command search path and make an alias `eme5` to quickly change the current working directory to this directory in a Ch command shell. `HOME` is your home directory such as `C:/Documents and Settings/harry` in Windows or `/home/harry` in Unix. Modify the start-up file **_chrc** for Windows and **.chrc** for Unix in your home directory using ChIDE by clicking `Open Ch Local Initialization File` under the `Option` menu or any other text editor. Hand in your startup file.

   a. If you use Windows, this can be done by adding

   ```
   _path = stradd(_path, "C:/Documents and Settings/harry/eme5;");
   alias("eme5", "cd C:/Documents and Settings/harry/eme5");
   ```

   in your start-up file. Change `harry` to your user account name.

   b. If you use Mac, Linux, or Unix, also add the current working directory to the command search path. This can be done by adding

   ```
   _path = stradd(_path, "/home/harry/eme5;");
   alias("eme5", "cd /home/harry/eme5");
   ```

   in your start-up file. Change `harry` to your user account name.

6. Use ChIDE or other text editor to create a C program called `myhello.c` in the directory `eme5` under your home directory with the following statements:

```
/* File: myhello.c
   developed by yourFirstName LastName for homework1 for course EME5.
   Print mutiple lines on the screen */
#include <stdio.h>

int main() {
    printf("Hello, World\n");
    printf("This is my first C program\n");
    return 0;
}
```

7. Write two C programs, `welcome.c` and `welcome2.c`, that will print out

```
Hello, world.
Welcome to C!
```

One program calls the function **printf()** once. The other program calls the function **printf()** twice, one for each output line.

8. For the mechanical system shown in Figure 2.12, given mass $m = 6$ kg, coefficient of kinetic friction $\mu = 0.3$, the applied force p is constant at 10 N. Write a program called `accel.c` to calculate the acceleration of the system.

9. Write a program `rectangle.c` to calculate the area of a rectangle with its width of 3.58 meters and height of 5.4 meters. The output shall be displayed as follows:

```
The area of the rectangle is = 19.332000 m^2
```

10. One mile is 1.6093 kilometers. Write a program `mile2km.c` to convert 23.5 miles to kilometers with the output shown below:

```
23.5 miles is = 37.818550 meters
```

11. Write a program `temperature.c` to convert the temperature from 38.5 degrees in Celsius to degrees in Fahrenheit. The relationship is as follows:

$$f = \frac{9c}{5} + 32$$

where c is the temperature in Celsius and f the temperature in Fahrenheit.

12. The formula for the area of a circle is πr^2, where r is the radius of the circle. Given r of 5 meters, write a program `circle.c` to calculate the area of the circle.

13. The formula for the surface area of a sphere is $4\pi r^2$, where r is the radius of the sphere. Given r of 5 meters, write a program `spherearea.c` to calculate the surface area of the sphere.

14. The formula for the volume of a sphere is $\frac{4\pi r^3}{3}$, where r is the radius of the sphere. Given r of 5 meters, write a program `spherevol.c` to calculate the volume of the sphere.

15. In a Ch command shell, interactively calculate the results for the problems listed in (1) Exercise 8, (2) Exercise 9, (3) Exercise 10, (4) Exercise 11, (5) Exercise 12, (6) Exercise 13, and (7) Exercise 14.

16. For developed programs in (1) Exercise 6, (2) Exercise 7, (3) Exercise 8, (4) Exercise 9, (5) Exercise 10, (6) Exercise 11, (7) Exercise 12, (8) Exercise 13, and (9) Exercise 14:

    a. Execute the program in ChIDE.

    b. Execute the program in a Ch command shell. If the program `filename.c` is executed in Mac OS X or Linux, use the command

    ```
    > chmod +x filename.c
    ```

    to make the program `filename.c` executable.

    c. Compile and link the program using **cc** or **gcc** in a Unix machine, then run the created executable binary program in a command shell.

    d. If you have installed Visual C++ in Windows, compile and link the program using the command **cl**, then run the created executable binary program in a command shell.

    e. If you have installed Visual C++ in Windows, compile and link the program using a compiler in ChIDE, then run the created executable binary program in ChIDE.

The execution and output on the screen can be captured using GIMP or other software package.

CHAPTER 3

Number Systems, Scalar Types, and Input/Output

C is a loosely typed language with a rich set of data types. Unlike other languages such as Pascal, which prohibits automatic type conversion, one data type in C can be converted automatically to another data type if it makes sense in context. The format of a value stored in the computer memory depends on the machine architecture in use. The meaning of a value in the memory is determined by the type of the expression used to access it. How variables of scalar types are declared, and how their values are internally represented in a computer system for manipulation inside C, are described in this chapter. Integer number systems are introduced first. Then, integral, floating-point, complex, and pointer types are presented. Other data types, such as function, void, enum, union, reference, as well as aggregate types array, structure, and class, are presented in the remaining chapters. Finally, how to use predefined functions for data input and output are described.

3.1 Integer Number Systems

3.1.1 Decimal Numbers

Numbers are usually represented in the decimal, or base 10, format. The reason is that there are 10 elements, 0 through 9, which can be used to create numbers. For example, consider the number 4261. It can be thought of as

$$(4 \times 1000) + (2 \times 100) + (6 \times 10) + (1 \times 1) = 4261$$

which is also equal to

$$(4 \times 10^3) + (2 \times 10^2) + (6 \times 10^1) + (1 \times 10^0) = 4261$$

3.1.2 Binary Numbers

For a digital computer, a high voltage can represent 1 whereas a low voltage can stand for 0. Therefore, computers internally use the binary format to represent a number. This representation of numbers is also known as base 2 representation because the binary format consists of only 2 elements, 0 and 1, that represent numbers. For example, the following expressions hold:

$$10_2 = 2_{10}$$

$$11_2 = 3_{10}$$

$$100_2 = 4_{10}$$

$$1000010100101_2 = 4261_{10}$$

This means that the binary number on the left is equivalent to the decimal number on the right. The subscripts 2 and 10 specified previously indicate that the numbers are in binary and decimal formats, respectively. A number without a subscript, by default, is in decimal format.

In Ch, the prefix '`0b`' or '`0B`,' such as `0b1000010100101`, can be used to indicate a binary number. A *bit* refers to a digit in a binary number. The binary number `0b100` is 3 bits long.

Binary to Decimal Conversion

The first step in converting a binary number to its decimal equivalent is to label the binary digit, or bit, to the farthest right as the zero position. Each digit to the left is subsequently labeled as a position number incremented by 1. For example, binary number 1000010100101 can be labeled as follows:

```
 1  0  0 0 0 1 0 1 0 0 1 0 1
 |  |  | | | | | | | | | | |
12 11 10 9 8 7 6 5 4 3 2 1 0   (position number)
```

Next, the values of the binary digits are then multiplied by 2 raised to the power specified by the position number. The sum of all these values is the decimal equivalent of the binary number. For the binary number above, the expression would be

$$\begin{aligned} 1000010100101_2 &= (1 \times 2^{12}) + (0 \times 2^{11}) + (0 \times 2^{10}) + (0 \times 2^9) + (0 \times 2^8) \\ &\quad + (1 \times 2^7) + (0 \times 2^6) + (1 \times 2^5) + (0 \times 2^4) + (0 \times 2^3) \\ &\quad + (1 \times 2^2) + (0 \times 2^1) + (1 \times 2^0) \\ &= 4261_{10} \end{aligned}$$

‡Decimal to Binary Conversion

The conversion of a decimal number to its binary equivalent begins by dividing the number by 2. The remainder is placed as the rightmost bit of the binary representation, and the quotient is divided again by 2 to obtain the value of the next bit, which is also the remainder (either 0 or 1). The process is repeated until the quotient is zero. The result is the binary representation of the decimal number. For example, the process to determine the binary representation of 13 is shown below.

$$\begin{aligned} 13 \div 2 &= 6, & R &= 1 \\ 6 \div 2 &= 3, & R &= 0 \\ 3 \div 2 &= 1, & R &= 1 \\ 1 \div 2 &= 0, & R &= 1 \end{aligned}$$

where `R` in each row is the remainder of the division operation on the left. Thus the binary equivalent of 13 is 1101_2. As another example, the binary representation 1000010100101_2 of 4261 can be obtained as follows:

$$\begin{aligned} 4261 \div 2 &= 2130, & R &= 1 \\ 2130 \div 2 &= 1065, & R &= 0 \\ 1065 \div 2 &= 532, & R &= 1 \\ 532 \div 2 &= 266, & R &= 0 \\ 266 \div 2 &= 133, & R &= 0 \\ 133 \div 2 &= 66, & R &= 1 \\ 66 \div 2 &= 33, & R &= 0 \\ 33 \div 2 &= 16, & R &= 1 \end{aligned}$$

$$
\begin{aligned}
16 \div 2 &= 8, & \mathrm{R} &= 0 \\
8 \div 2 &= 4, & \mathrm{R} &= 0 \\
4 \div 2 &= 2, & \mathrm{R} &= 0 \\
2 \div 2 &= 1, & \mathrm{R} &= 0 \\
1 \div 2 &= 0, & \mathrm{R} &= 1
\end{aligned}
$$

Binary Two's Complement

To represent both positive and negative numbers consistently, integral numbers can be stored in a computer in the *binary two's complement representation*. The leftmost bit is called the *most significant bit*, whereas the rightmost bit is the *least significant bit*. *Byte* is commonly used as a unit to measure the storage or the size of a data type. One byte equals 8 bits. Similarly, the leftmost 8 bits is called the *most significant byte*, whereas the rightmost byte is the *least significant byte*. In this representation, the most significant bit is referred to as the *sign bit*. If this bit is set to 1, then the binary number is negative; otherwise, it is positive. The positive values are the same as the normal binary numbers. The process of converting a negative number to its binary two's complement representation begins first by writing the absolute value of the negative number in binary form. Then, complement the number by reversing each bit. All 0 bits are set to 1, whereas all 1 bits are set to 0. Finally, add 1 to the complemented binary number. In other words, given any decimal number x, its binary two's complement representation can be found as follows:

1. If x is positive, simply convert x to binary.
2. If x is negative, follow the steps below:
   a. Write the absolute value of x in binary.
   b. Complement the binary number by reversing each bit.
   c. Add 1 to the complemented number.

For example, the 32-bit binary two's complement representation of -2 can be obtained as follows:

```
0b00000000000000000000000000000010 (absolute value of -2)
0b11111111111111111111111111111101 (binary complement)
                                +1 (add 1)
0b11111111111111111111111111111110 (two's complement representation of -2)
```

Given a binary number written in two's complement representation for a negative number, the decimal equivalent can be obtained. First, take the complement of the binary number in two's complement representation. Then, add 1 to it. The result is the absolute value of the negative number. For example, the absolute value of 2 of the binary two's complement representation of -2 can be obtained as shown below.

```
0b11111111111111111111111111111110 (two's complement representation of -2)
0b00000000000000000000000000000001 (binary complement)
                                +1 (add 1)
0b00000000000000000000000000000010 (absolute value of -2)
```

Using binary two's complement representation, subtraction of a value can be treated as addition of its two's complement. For example, the subtraction of expression $2-2$ in binary two's complement representation can be performed as $2 + (-2)$ as follows:

```
0b00000000000000000000000000000010 (binary representation of 2)
0b11111111111111111111111111111110 (two's complement representation of -2)
0b00000000000000000000000000000000 (2+(-2))
```

When adding the most significant bits, the one that would be carried over is discarded in the process. We get zero as a result.

In the binary two's complement representation, the value of -1 is represented with 1 for all its bits. The largest positive value occurs when all its bits, except the sign bit, are set to 1. For a representation with n bits, this value is $2^{(n-1)} - 1$. When n is 8, this value is 127. The largest negative value is $-2^{(n-1)}$ when all bits, except the sign bit, are set to 0. When n is 8, this value is -128.

3.1.3 ‡Binary Fraction Numbers

Fractions are ordinarily represented with the denominator increasing by powers of 10. In binary fractions, the denominators increase by powers of 2. For example, the fraction 0.625 is represented in decimal as

$$\frac{6}{10} + \frac{2}{100} + \frac{5}{1000} = 0.625$$

In binary, however, it would be represented as $.101_2$:

$$\begin{aligned} 0.625_{10} &= 0.500 + 0.125 \\ &= \frac{1}{2} + \frac{0}{4} + \frac{1}{8} \\ &= 0.101_2 \end{aligned}$$

Binary Fraction to Decimal Conversion

Converting binary fractions to decimal equivalents is similar to converting regular binary numbers. First, consider the bit closest to the right of the decimal point as the -1 position, where the labels for the subsequent bits to the right are decrements of 1. Next, multiply the value at each position, either 0 or 1, by 2 raised by the power of the position number. The sum of all these values is the decimal equivalent. For example, the decimal conversion of binary fraction .1011 is shown below.

$$\begin{aligned} 0.1011_2 &= (1 \times 2^{-1}) + (0 \times 2^{-2}) + (1 \times 2^{-3}) + (1 \times 2^{-4}) \\ &= \frac{1}{2} + \frac{0}{4} + \frac{1}{8} + \frac{1}{16} \\ &= 0.6875 \end{aligned}$$

Decimal to Binary Fraction Conversion

Converting a decimal fraction to a binary fraction involves the process of multiplying the decimal fraction by 2 and recording the digit in the ones place (the digit to the immediate left of the decimal point). For the first multiplication process, the digit in the ones place is recorded as the leftmost bit in the binary fraction (immediately after the decimal point). Next, this digit is ignored and the resulting fraction is multiplied by 2. Again, the digit in the ones place is stored as the subsequent bit of the binary fraction. This process is repeated until the fraction is reduced to zero. For example, the process for the binary conversion of 0.625 is shown in Figure 3.1. The binary fraction equivalent of 0.625_{10} is 0.101_2. Note that since binary fraction representation uses powers of 2, a small loss in precision may take place in the conversion process, due to truncation.

3.1.4 Octal Numbers

Octal representation is base 8. That is, it is a system that uses 8 elements, 0 through 7, to create numbers. For example, the decimal number 4261 is represented in base 8 as 10245_8. In C, a leading `0` (zero) indicates that the following digits, such as 10245 in `010245`, are in octal format.

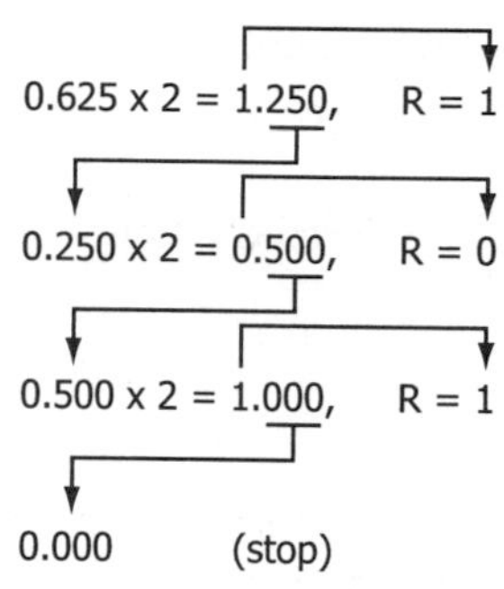
0.625 x 2 = 1.250, R = 1
0.250 x 2 = 0.500, R = 0
0.500 x 2 = 1.000, R = 1
0.000 (stop)

Figure 3.1: Converting the decimal fraction 0.625_{10} to its binary fraction, 0.101_2.

Octal to Decimal Conversion

The conversion of an octal number to its decimal representation begins with labeling the rightmost bit as the zero position and incrementing the label of each subsequent bit by 1. Next, the value of each bit is multiplied by 8 raised to the position number. The sum of all these values is the decimal equivalent of the octal number. For example, the octal number 10245_8 can be converted to its decimal equivalent by the following expressions:

$$\begin{aligned} 10245_8 &= (1 \times 8^4) + (0 \times 8^3) + (2 \times 8^2) + (4 \times 8^1) + (5 \times 8^0) \\ &= 4261_{10} \end{aligned}$$

‡*Decimal to Octal Conversion*

Similar to decimal-to-binary conversion, converting a decimal number to its octal equivalent involves the process of dividing the decimal number by 8 and storing the remainder as a digit of the octal representation. This process is repeated until the the quotient is 0. The remainder values are recorded from left to right, such as the following process for converting 10245_8 to its decimal equivalent:

$$\begin{aligned} 4261 \div 8 &= 532, & R &= 5 \\ 532 \div 8 &= 66, & R &= 4 \\ 66 \div 8 &= 8, & R &= 2 \\ 8 \div 8 &= 1, & R &= 0 \\ 1 \div 8 &= 0, & R &= 1 \end{aligned}$$

Thus the equivalent of 4261_{10} is 10245_8, which corresponds with the statements above.

Binary to Octal Conversion

Converting a binary number to its octal representation involves the process of separating the binary number, from right to left, into 3-bit sections. Each section is then converted to its decimal value, which represents one digit of the octal equivalent. Combining all the values results in the octal representation of the binary number. For example, the octal equivalent of $4261_{10} = 0001000010100101_2$ is 10245_8. The steps for determining the octal value 10245_8 are illustrated below.

```
001 000 010 100 101
\|/ \|/ \|/ \|/ \|/
 1   0   2   4   5   ==>  10245 (octal representation)
```

Octal to Binary Conversion

Converting octal numbers to its binary equivalent involves performing the opposite of the procedure previously described. Each octal digit is treated as a decimal number and broken down to its binary representation. For example, 10245_8 can be converted to its binary form as follows:

```
 1   0   2   4   5
/|\ /|\ /|\ /|\ /|\
001 000 010 100 101  ==>  1000010100101 (binary representation)
```

3.1.5 Hexadecimal Numbers

Hexadecimal numbers involve a base 16 system. For this system, there are 16 elements, ranging from 0 to 15, which are used to create numbers. Because there are no single-digit values to represent the values 10 through 15, the letters A through F are used to represent them. So the decimal number 4261 is represented in base 16 as $10A5_{16}$. In C, the prefix '`0x`' or '`0X`' indicates that the following value, such as 10A5 in `0x10A5`, is in hexadecimal format.

Hexadecimal to Decimal Conversion

Similar to conversions of other base representations to decimal, converting a hexadecimal number begins with the labeling of each digit of the hexadecimal number. The bit farthest to the right is considered the zero position, while each subsequent bit to the left of it is in a position number incremented by 1. The sum of all the digits, each of which are multiplied by 16 raised to the power of its position number, is considered to be the decimal equivalent of the hexadecimal number. For example, the decimal representation of $10A5_{16}$ is

$$\begin{aligned} 10A5_{16} &= (1 \times 16^3) + (0 \times 16^2) + (10 \times 16^1) + (5 \times 16^0) \\ &= 4261_{10} \end{aligned}$$

Note that the letter A is replaced by the number 10 in the above expression.

‡*Decimal to Hexadecimal Conversion*

The process of converting a decimal number to its hexadecimal representation involves the repetitive division of the number and resulting quotients by 16 and recording the remainder as digits of the hexadecimal equivalent. The remainder of the first division represents the zero position digit, while each subsequent remainder is the digit to the left of this position. Note that any remainder greater than 9 is converted to its corresponding alphabetical value. For example, the process of converting 4261_{10} to its hexadecimal equivalent is shown below.

$$\begin{aligned} 4261 \div 16 &= 266, && \text{R} = 5 \\ 266 \div 16 &= 16, && \text{R} = 10 (\text{or A}) \\ 16 \div 16 &= 1, && \text{R} = 0 \\ 1 \div 16 &= 0, && \text{R} = 1 \end{aligned}$$

Thus, the hexadecimal representation of 4261_{10} is $10A5_{16}$.

Binary to Hexadecimal Conversion

For conversion from binary to hexadecimal representation, the binary number is separated into 4-bit sections starting with the bits farthest to the right. Each 4-bit segment is then converted to its hexadecimal equivalent.

Combining all these values results in the hexadecimal form of the binary number. For example,

```
0001 0000 1010 0101
\||/ \||/ \||/ \||/
  1    0    A    5   ==>  10A5 (hexadecimal representation)
```

Hexadecimal to Binary Conversion

Hexadecimal to binary conversion involves converting each digit of the hexadecimal, regarded as a decimal number, to its binary representation. The combination of all the binary numbers is the binary equivalent of the hexadecimal number. For example,

```
  1    0    A    5
/||\ /||\ /||\ /||\
0001 0000 1010 0101  ==>  1000010100101 (binary representation)
```

Hexadecimal to Octal Conversion

Probably the best method to convert a hexadecimal number to its octal representation is to first perform hexadecimal to binary conversion and then binary to octal conversion. For 0x10A5, the conversion steps are as follows:

```
  1    0    A    5
/||\ /||\ /||\ /||\
0001 0000 1010 0101  ==>  1000010100101 (binary representation)

001 000 010 100 101
\|/ \|/ \|/ \|/ \|/
 1   0   2   4   5  ==>  10245 (octal representation)
```

Octal to Hexadecimal Conversion

Converting an octal number to its hexadecimal equivalent requires the opposite procedures of hexadecimal to octal conversion. First, the octal number is written in binary form. Then binary to hexadecimal conversion is performed on the binary number to obtain the hexadecimal representation of the octal number. For example,

```
 1   0   2   4   5
/|\ /|\ /|\ /|\ /|\
001 000 010 100 101  ==> 1000010100101 (binary representation)

0001 0000 1010 0101
\||/ \||/ \||/ \||/
  1    0    A    5  ==> 10A5 (hexadecimal representation)
```

3.2 Character Set

A C source file is a sequences of characters selected from a character set. The character set in C includes the following members: the 26 uppercase letters of the Latin alphabet,

```
A B C D E F G H I J K L M
N O P Q R S T U V W X Y Z
```

the 26 lowercase letters of the Latin alphabet,

```
a  b  c  d  e  f  g  h  i  j  k  l  m
n  o  p  q  r  s  t  u  v  w  x  y  z
```

the 10 decimal digits,

```
0  1  2  3  4  5  6  7  8  9
```

the following 31 graphic characters,

```
!  "  #  %  &  '  (  )  *  +  ,  -  .  /  :
;  <  =  >  ?  [  \  ]  ^  _  {  |  }  ~
```

the space character, and control characters representing horizontal tab, vertical tab, and form feed, as well as control characters representing alert, backspace, carriage return, and new line.

A *token* is a fundamental unit of source code in a program. It is sometimes also referred to by the name *lexical element*. A token is formed by a sequence of characters. *Keywords, identifiers, constants, punctuators, strings*, and *operators* are tokens for a program. For example, in Program 2.1 in Chapter 2, tokens **int** and **return** are keywords; Tokens **main** and **printf** are identifiers for function names; token 0 is an integral constant, token `';'` is a punctuator to terminate a statement; and token `"hello, world"` is a string literal. Tokens also include operators, such as addition operator + for an addition operation. A compiler or interpreter processes tokens in a program based on the rules for the C programming language.

3.2.1 ‡Trigraphs

In some scenarios, some special characters may not be available in an input device. In this case, trigraph sequences can be used to represent special characters. In C, all occurrences in a source file of the following sequences of three characters (called *trigraph sequences*), introduced by two consecutive question mark characters, are replaced with the corresponding single character shown below, so that the users can write C programs using ISO 646-1083 Invariant Code Set.

```
??=    #        ??)    ]        ??!    |
??(    [        ??'    ^        ??>    }
??/    \        ??<    {        ??-    ~
```

For example,

```
> printf("??!")
|
```

The trigraph form `"??!"` represents the character `|`. No other trigraph sequences exist. Each **?** that does not begin one of the trigraphs listed above is not changed. For example,

```
> printf("?")
?
> printf("??%")
??%
```

The string `"??%"` is not a trigraph; hence, each character is treated normally.

To prevent interpretation of the sequence of three characters listed above as a trigraph for its replaced character, use the character escape code '`\?`' for character '`?`'. For example,

```
> printf("?\?!")
??!
```

The string `"?\?!"`, which includes the character escape code '`\?`', can be used to represent the string `"??!"`.

3.3 Comments

Comments of a C program can be enclosed within a pair of delimiters `/*` and `*/` as shown in the first line in Program 2.1 in the previous chapter. Except within a character constant, a string literal, or a comment, the characters `/*` introduce a comment. The contents of a comment are examined by a compiler or interpreter only to identify characters and to find the characters `*/` that terminate the comment. Therefore, the comments can span multiple lines. The two comment delimiters, however, cannot be nested. For example,

```
/* Starts comment /* this nested one is bad */ Ends comment */
```

Added in C99, the symbol `//` comments out a subsequent text terminated at the end of a line. Except within a character constant, a string literal, or a comment, the characters // introduce a comment that includes all characters up to, but not including, the next newline character. The contents of such a comment are examined only to identify characters and to find the terminating newline character. For example,

```
printf("hello, world\n"); // this part is a comment
```

A `//` can be used to comment out `/*` or `*/`, and delimiters `/*` and `*/` can be used to comment out `//`. For example,

```
// example 1: /* is commented out
// example 2: */ is commented out
// example 3: /* and */ are commented out
/* example 4: // is commented out */
```

3.4 Declaration

An *identifier* is a sequence of lowercase and uppercase letters, digits, and underscores. Lowercase and uppercase letters are distinct. The initial character of an identifier shall not be a digit. A reserved word, such as **int** and **return**, cannnot be used as an identifier. An identifier starting with two underscores or one underscore followed by an uppercase letter are reserved by the C language to implement the features of the language. To make the code more readable and portable, standard identifiers used for implementation of the C standard features shall not be redefined by the user. For example, the identifier **printf** for the printing function name in the C standard input/output library shall not be redefined by the user. Table 3.1 shows some invalid identifiers for the user.

Generally, a variable has to be declared before it can be used inside a program. A variable is declared by specifying its data type and identifier in the form

```
type name;
```

Table 3.1 Examples of invalid identifiers.

Invalid identifier	Reason
`int`	reserved word
`double`	reserved word
`for`	reserved word
`2times`	starts with a digit
`integer#`	character # not allowed
`girl&boy`	character & not allowed
`class1+class2`	character + not allowed
Identifiers reserved for C implementation	
`__name`	starts with two underscores __
`_SIG`	starts with an underscore and capital letter S
`printf`	standard function name

where `type` is one of the valid data types such as **int** and `name` is a valid identifier. For example, the statements

```
int i;     /* index variable */
int num;   /* total number of elements */
```

declare variables `i` and `num` of type int. In this case, **int** is a keyword as a declarator for an integer data type and `i` and `num` are identifiers as variable names.

Multiple variables of the same type can be declared in a single statement by a list of identifiers, each separated by a comma, as shown below for two variables `i` and `num` of int type.

```
int i, num;
```

However, when using the former method of declaring only one variable in each declaration statement, it is easier to add user comments.

For a software project, typically about 80 percent of the effort and cost are spent on the maintenance (updating and modifying) of the program after the original development is finished. A program is often maintained by someone other than the original developers. Using meaningful and consistent identifiers for variable names makes a program easier to understand, develop, and maintain. A variable name typically uses lowercase letters. For example, to calculate the acceleration of a rigid body, one may use the identifier `a` for acceleration to be consistent with the symbol used in the diagram and mathematical formula if the program is small. For a large program with many variable names, one may use the identifier `accel` or `acceleration` for the acceleration. For a variable declared with a short name, a comment can be added to make the code more readable. A function name, such as **printf**, typically contains more than four characters to make the meaning of the function more descriptive at the point where the function is called. If an identifier contains two or multiple words, one can use an underscore to separate words or use an uppercase letter for the first character of the subsequent words. For example, to distinguish the acceleration for a train from that for a bus, one may use `accelTrain`, `accel_train`, `trainAccel`, or `train_accel` for the acceleration of a train. An identifier consisting of all uppercase letters and underscores, such as `M_G`, shall only be used for macros, which will be described in detail in Chapter 7.

In C99, a variable can be declared almost anywhere, even after executable statements. For example, in this program

```
int main() {
    int i;
    i = 90;
    int j;
    j = 20;
    return 0;
}
```

the variable j is declared by the declaration statement

```
int j;
```

after the execution statement

```
i = 90;
```

3.5 32-Bit and 64-Bit Programming Models

In addition to the data type **int**, C provides sevaral other basic data types for integral values, including **char, short, long, long long** as well as the pointer type shown in Table 3.2. These basic data types, as well as data types for floating-point numbers, are described in detail in the subsequent sections in this chapter.

The 32-bit computer architecture is commonly used nowadays. Most desktop and laptop computers are based on this architecture. In the 32-bit architecture, the memory addresses are at most 32 bits. The registers in a 32-bit central processing unit (CPU) have 32 bits. 32-bit addresses are capable of selecting one of 4 gigabytes (GB) of memory. According to Moore's law, the CPU processing power continues to increase by about 50 percent every two years and provides the power to process ever larger quantities of data. Computers with 64-bit architecture are increasingly getting more popular and widely available. The 64-bit architecture provides direct addressing of the uniform address space larger than 4 GB.

There are different data models for 32-bit and 64-bit programming in C. The commonly used data models are shown in Table 3.2. ILP32 is the most commonly used 32-bit programming model. Windows and most Unix computers follow this data model. The notation describes the width assigned to the basic data types. ILP32 denoted **int, long,** and pointer as 32-bit types. Windows 3.1, an early version of Windows, and some microprocessors use an IP32 model with 16 bits for **int** and 32 bits for **long** and pointer.

Table 3.2 32-bit and 64-bit programming models.

Data type	LP32	ILP32	LP64	LLP64	ILP64
char	8	8	8	8	8
short	16	16	16	16	16
int	16	32	32	32	64
long	32	32	64	32	64
long long	64	64	64	64	64
pointer	32	32	64	64	64

There are three basic models, LP64, ILP64, and LLP64, for 64-bit programming. LP64 (also known as 4/8/8) denotes **long** and pointer as 64-bit types; LLP64 (also known as 4/4/8) uses **long long** and pointer as 64-bit types; and ILP64 (also known as 8/8/8) uses **int, long**, and pointer as 64-bit types. Most Unix computers use the LP64 model. Windows uses the LLP64 model. Cray computers support both LP64 and ILP64 models.

Other programming models exist, in addition to ones listed in Table 3.2. For example, the size of type char varies in different machines. The older PDP-7 machines use 7 bits, and older DEC machines use 9 bits. However, most machines nowadays use 8 bits for char. The integer type **short** in Cray machines can be 32 bits. For embedded systems using 8-bit or 16-bit mircoprocessors, the size of type **int** is typically 16 bits.

In this book, it is assumed that the programming models of ILP32, LP64, and LLP64 are used. Because the type **long** is not portable among these three data models and can be replaced by either **int** or **long long** in the code, the use of type **long** shall be avoided. In these three models, the size of pointer type presents a major issue in writing portable programs across 32-bit and 64-bit computer architectures. Whenever there is such a portability issue related to 32-bit and 64-bit computer architectures, it will be pointed out in the book.

3.6 Integer Types

An integral value is represented internally as a binary number. We have previously used the data type **int** to represent an integer. Depending on the number of bits for a binary number, the built-in basic integer types **char, short, int, long,** and **long long** are available in C. The data type **long long** was added in C99.

The C language standard does not specify the actual sizes of the basic data types listed in Table 3.2. However, based on the programming models ILP32, LP64 and LLP64 in Table 3.2, **char, short, int,** and **long long** types are 8, 16, 32, and 64 bits, respectively. Representing in the unit of bytes, **char, short, int,** and **long long** types are 1, 2, 4, and 8 bytes, respectively.

The **sizeof** operator gives the size of a type or expression in bytes. For example, the statements

```
> int i
> sizeof(int)
4
> sizeof(i)
4
> sizeof(long long)
8
```

calculate the sizes of data type **int** and the variable `i` with the value of 4 bytes. The **long long** data type has 8 btyes.

3.6.1 The int Type

An *integer* is a whole number that can be negative, positive, or zero. The data type **int** is one of the most commonly used data types. A variable of **int** type in C can be used to represent an integer. In the programming models ILP32, LP64, and LLP64 listed in Table 3.2, an **int** constant or variable occupies 4 bytes (32 bits) of unit memory. Bit 32 is a sign bit. When bit 32 is 0, it is a positive integer. Otherwise, it is a negative integer. The maximum positive integer for a signed 4-byte representation is 2,147,483,647 ($2^{31} - 1$), approximately 2 billion, or 0b01111111111111111111111111111111 in binary form. A negative number is stored in binary complement form. The minimum integer values for a signed char is −2,147,483,648 (2^{31}), or

0b10000000000000000000000000000000 in binary form. The range of integers for an **int** type with 4 bytes is thus −2,147,483,648 to 2,147,483,647. A *macro* is a symbolic constant. The macros **INT_MIN** and **INT_MAX** are defined for the minimum and maximum values for a signed integer of **int** type in the C standard header **limits.h**. How a macro is defined will be described in Chapter 7. For an **int** type fewer 4 bytes, the values of **INT_MIN** and **INT_MAX** are −2,147,483,648 and 2,147,483,647, respectively. If the **int** type is implemented with fewer or more than 4 bytes, the values for these macros are different.

Program 3.1 prints out the maximum and minimum values of type **int**. To use macros **INT_MIN** and **INT_MAX** inside a program, the processing directive

```
#include <limits.h>
```

needs to be added at the beginning of a program to include the header file **limits.h**. The format specifier `"%d"` is used to print signed integers, whereas `"%u"` is for unsigned integers. The output from Program 3.1 is as follows:

```
INT_MAX = 2147483647
INT_MIN = -2147483648
UINT_MAX= 4294967295
```

```
/* File: limits.c
   Display maximum and minimum limits of int */
#include <stdio.h>
#include <limits.h> /* for macros INT_MIN, INT_MAX, UINT_MAX */

int main() {
    printf("INT_MAX = %d\n", INT_MAX);
    printf("INT_MIN = %d\n", INT_MIN);
    printf("UINT_MAX= %u\n", UINT_MAX);
    return 0;
}
```

Program 3.1: Printing maximum and minimum values of type char.

The values of two macros **INT_MAX** and **INT_MIN** are important characteristics of an **int** type. If an integer number is larger than **INT_MAX**, it cannot be represented as an **int** type in a program, causing an *overflow*. In this case, one may use **long long** to represent the integer number. A variable of type **long long** can contain much larger integer numbers. On the other hand, for computations involving small integer numbers, one may use the data type **short** for integer variables to save memory space.

3.6.2 The short Type

A **short** integer ranges from **SHRT_MIN** to **SHRT_MAX**. The macros **SHRT_MIN** and **SHRT_MAX** defined in the C standard header **limits.h** are system constants. Using the programming models ILP32, LP64, and LLP64 in Table 3.2, a **short** data type uses 2 bytes (16 bits) for storage with 1 bit for the sign in C. Negative numbers are stored in 2-byte two's complement plus 1. Therefore, the parameters **SHRT_MIN** and **SHRT_MAX** are −32,768 (2^{15}) and 32,767 ($2^{15} - 1$), respectively.

3.6.3 The long long Type in C99

The **long long** integral type added in C99 contains 8 bytes (64 bits). It has the similar representation as the data type of **int**. A **long long** integer ranges from **LLONG_MIN** to **LLONG_MAX**.The macros **LLONG_MIN** and **LLONG_MAX** are system constants defined in header file **limits.h**. A **long long** data type uses 8 bytes of memory for storage with 1 bit for the sign. Negative numbers are stored in 8-byte two's complement plus 1. Therefore, the macros **LLONG_MIN** and **LLONG_MAX** contain −9,223,372,036,854,775,808 (-2^{63}) and 9,223,372,036,854,775,807 ($2^{63} - 1$), respectively. The suffix `LL` for a constant indicates that the constant is **long long** type. The details about integer constants will be described at the end of this section.

Although Visual C++ in Windows does not support types **long long** in C99, an equivalent type **__int64** can be used. Section 7.4 in Chapter 7 describes how to write portable code using 64-bit integers in Windows and Unix.

3.6.4 The long Type

The **long**, or **long int**, type has 4 bytes (32 bits) in the 32-bit programming model. Depending on the 64-bit programming model, it has either 4 bytes (32 bits) or 8 bytes (64 bits) as shown in Table 3.2. The macros **LONG_MIN** and **LONG_MAX** define the minimum and maximum of **long** type, respectively. If the **long** type has 4 bytes, **LONG_MIN** and **LONG_MAX** have the values of −2,147,483,648 to 2,147,483,647, respectively. Otherwise, their values are the same as macros **LLONG_MIN** and **LLONG_MAX**.

In the 32-bit world, **long** is a portable data type and **int** is not a portable data type, as shown in Table 3.2 for 32-bit programming models LP32 and ILP32. Therefore, the type **long** used to be recommended to write portable programs. However, the situation has changed with the emergence of 64-bit computers. The data type **long** is no longer portable and is a source of major headaches for mixed 32-bit and 64-bit programming. Even for 64-bit programming, different programming models use different sizes for type **long**. Therefore, the user should stay away from type **long** for writing new programs. For cross-platform programming, it is recommended to use **int** for 32-bit integers and **long long** for 64-bit integers. The unsigned integer type **size_t** can be used for mixed 32-bit and 64-bit programming. It is typically 32 bits in a 32-bit programming model and 64 bits in a 64-bit programming. Details about the unsigned integer type **size_t** are described in section 3.12.

3.6.5 Type Specifiers signed and unsigned

By default, the integer data types are signed, that is, the bit for the sign is used to specify a positive or negative number. Type specifier **signed** can also be used to indicate that the variable declared is signed. In contrast, the **unsigned** specifier indicates that the variable is always a positive number so that the sign bit can be used to represent a larger unsigned integer. For example, the statement

```
unsigned int u;
```

declares the variable `u` as an unsigned int. Adding the type specifier **signed** in the front of one of the signed integer types **int, short, long**, and **long long** has no effect on the declaration. However, it can be useful for declaration of type char, which will be described in section 3.8.

If the computation involves only positive numbers, one can use **unsigned** variables to represent integer numbers. The **unsigned int** variable has a range from 0 to **UINT_MAX**, where macro **UINT_MAX** is a system constant defined in the C standard header file **limits.h**. Typically, an **unsigned int** variable occupies 4 bytes of memory without the sign bit, so that the macro **UINT_MAX** is 4,294,967,295 ($2^{32} - 1$) or 11111111111111111111111111111111 in binary form. The value for macro **UINT_MAX** is larger than that for macro **INT_MAX**. Similarly, the **unsigned short** variable ranges from 0 to **USHRT_MAX**, which is also defined in header file **limits.h**. The macro **USHRT_MAX** is 65,535 ($2^{16} - 1$). The **unsigned long long** integer variable ranges from 0 to **ULLONG_MAX**, which is 18,446,744,073,709,551,615ULL ($2^{64} - 1$). The **unsigned long** integer variable ranges from 0 to **ULONG_MAX**. Similar to **long**, the **unsigned long** type has either 4 or 8 bytes depending on the programming data model. If it has 4 bytes, **ULONG_MAX** is 4,294,967,295; otherwise, the value for **ULONG_MAX** is the same as that for **ULLONG_MAX**.

Although Visual C++ in Windows does not support **unsigned long long** in C99, an equivalent type **unsigned __int64** can be used.

3.6.6 Integer Constants

By default, a decimal integer constant like 12345 is an **int** type. An integer can also be specified in binary, octal, or hexadecimal instead of decimal form. A leading 0 (zero) on an integer constant indicates an octal integer, whereas a leading 0x or 0X means hexadecimal. Note that expressions like 029 and 8AB2 are illegal. A decimal integer constant such as 1234 is an **int**. A decimal number with suffix `l` or `L` like `1234L` is a **long** type. The suffix `u` or `U` is for **unsigned int** integer constants. The suffix `ul` or `UL` is for **unsigned long** constants. A **long long** integer constant is written with a terminating `ll` or `LL`, such as 1234ll and 1234LL. The suffix `ull` and `ULL` is for **unsigned long long** integer constants.

Ch also supports binary constants with leading 0b or 0B. For example, decimal 30 can be written as 036 in octal, 0X1e or 0x1E in hexadecimal, and 0b11110 or 0B11110 in binary form.

For example,

```
> int i1 = 4261
> i1
4261
> int i2 = 010245
> i2
4261
> int i3 = 0x10A5
> i3
4261
> int i4 = 0b1000010100101
> i4
4261
```

3.7 Boolean bool Type in C99

In *boolean* algebra, there are only two values: 1 and 0, or **true** and **false**. C99 supports a boolean data type for relational comparisons and logical operations described in Chapter 4. Keyword **bool** in header file **stdbool.h** in C99 can be used to declare variables of boolean type to represent boolean values. For example, the statement

```
bool b;
```

declares variable `b` of boolean type. Variable `b` can be one of two boolean values: 1 for true or 0 for false. Two macros, **true** and **false**, are defined in the header file **stdbool.h**. The boolean type is typically implemented as an unsigned char. Therefore, it has 1 byte in most implementations.

3.8 Character char Type

The **char** data type is a special integer data type. The keyword **char** stands for character. It is also used to store characters such as letters and punctuation. An array of **char** can be used to store a string.

Using the programming models ILP32, LP64, and LLP64 in Table 3.2, a **char** constant or variable occupies 1-byte of unit memory with 8 bits. Bit 8 is a sign bit. The maximum positive integer for a signed 1-byte representation is 127 or 0b01111111 in the binary form. The minimum integer values for a signed char is −128 or 0b10000000 in the binary form. The range of integers for a char is thus −128 to +127. The macros **CHAR_MIN** and **CHAR_MAX**, defined in the C standard header **limits.h**, are system constants for the minimum and maximum values of **char** type. The **unsigned char** variable is similar to an unsigned int ranging from 0 to **UCHAR_MAX**. The macro **UCHAR_MAX** defined in the C standard header **limits.h**, is a system constant. Typically, an **unsigned char** variable occupies 1-byte unit memory without the sign bit, so that the macro **UCHAR_MAX** is 255 or 11111111 in binary form.

The **int, short, long**, and **long long** are signed integer types. However, the C standard does not specify whether the **char** type is signed or unsigned. By default, the **char** type is signed in most implementations. However, some implementations use **char** as an unsigned char by default. For example, Linux running on an ARM architecture-based CPU for embedded computer systems uses an unsigned char for **char** type by default to generate faster and more efficient code. The IRIX on the SGI Mips architecture also uses unsigned char for **char** by default. This may lead to some unexpected results if the **char** type is treated by mistake as a signed char. For example, the code

```
int main() {
    char i = -1;          /* if char is signed char, i is -1 */
                          /* if char is unsigned char, i becomes 255 */
    printf("%d\n", i);
    return 0;
}
```

prints out 255, instead of −1. When a negative integer is assigned to a variable of unsigned integer type, it is converted based on the implicit conversion rules, which will be described in section 4.3 in Chapter 4. In this case, the internal representation of −1 in an 8-bit signed integer is 11111111, which is 255 for an 8-bit unsigned integer. To obtain −1, the statement

```
char i = -1;
```

needs to be changed to

```
signed char i = -1;
```

to declare variable `i` a type **signed char** explicitly.

Character Constants

A program can be developed to process not only numerical data, but also characters and strings. A character constant, stored as an integer, can be written as one character within a pair of single quotes similar to `'a'`. A character constant can be assigned to a variable of type **char**. For example,

```
> char c = 'a'
> c
x
```

Character constants containing more than a single character or escape character are called *multibyte characters*. The apostrophe, backslash, and some characters that might not be easily readable in the source program, such as newline characters, shall be included in character constants by using escape characters as described below. More information about characters can be found in Chapter 12.

A character is actually stored as an integer according to certain numerical codes, such as the ASCII code found in Appendix D. Under this code, certain integers represent certain characters. The standard ASCII code ranges from 0 to 127, which only needs 7 bits to represent. The following example assumes that internal representations of characters are in ASCII code:

```
> char c
> int i
> c = 'a'   // c becomes 'a'
a
> i = c     // i becomes 97, ASCII value for 'a' is 97
97
> c = i+1   // c becomes 'b', ASCII value for 'b' is 98
b
```

In this interactive session, variables `c` of char type and `i` of int type are declared first. The character constant ‘a’, with the ASCII value 97 as shown in Appendix D, is assigned to the variable `c`. Internally, the variable `c` contains the integral value 97 of the ASCII value for the character ‘a’. When the value for variable `c` is assigned to the variable `i` of int type, its ASCII value 97 is assigned to `i`. Therefore, `i` becomes 97. The variable `c` can also be assigned with an ASCII value. In the third assignment, the value 98 of expression `i+1` is assigned to the variable `c`. The ASCII value 98 stands for the character ‘b’, as shown in Appendix D.

Escape Characters

Some special characters and particular behaviors of the output device are impossible to be typed directly in a source program. C uses *escape characters*, which are *escape codes* beginning with the backslash character ‘\’, to represent these characters and behaviors. Escape codes could be *character escape code*, which are characters listed in Table 3.3, and *numeric escape code*, which are up to three octal digits or any number of hexadecimal digits.

Typically the character escape code `\a` produces a beep from the speaker as an alert. The *active position* is the location on a display device, such as a screen, where the next character of output would appear. The intent of writing a printing character to a display device is to display a graphic representation of that character at the active position and then advance the active position to the next position on the current line. The code `\b` moves the active position to the previous position on the current line. The code `\f` represents a *form feed*, which moves the active position to the initial position at the start of the next logical page. The code `\n`, the most commonly used escape code, moves the active position to the initial position of the next line, whereas `\r` moves the active position to the initial position of the current line. The codes `\t` and `\v` move the active position to the next horizontal tabulation position and the next vertical tabulation position, respectively. The code `\\` represents a backslash that is not the preceding character of an escape code. Note that two forward slashes `//` are used to comment out a subsequent text terminated at the end of a line. The single quote appearing in a character constant might be mistaken as the ending apostrophe of the character constant. If this is the case, the code `\'` can be used to represent a single quote in a character constant. Similarly, the code

Table 3.3 Character escape code.

Escape code	Translation
\a	(alert) Produces an audible or visible alert. The active position shall not be changed.
\b	(backspace) Moves the active position to the previous position on the current line. If the active position is at the initial position of a line, the behavior is unspecified.
\f	(form feed) Moves the active position to the initial position at the start of the next logical page.
\n	(newline) Moves the active position to the initial position of the next line.
\r	(carriage return) Moves the active position to the initial position of the current line.
\t	(horizontal tab) Moves the active position to the next horizontal tabulation position on the current line. If the active position is at or past the last defined horizontal tabulation position, the behavior is unspecified.
\v	(vertical tab) Moves the active position to the initial position of the next vertical tabulation position. If the active position is at or past the last defined vertical tabulation position, the behavior is unspecified.
\\	(backslash) Produces a backslash character \. The active position is moved to the next character.
\'	(single quote) Produces a single quote character '. The active position is moved to the next character.
\"	(double quote) Produces a double quote character ". The active position is moved to the next character.
\?	(question mark) Produces a question mark character ?. The active position is moved to the next character.

`\"` can represent a double quote in a string constant. The code `\?` can be used to produce a question mark in circumstances in which it might be mistaken as part of a trigraph described in section 3.2.1. The codes shown below illustrate how character escapes can be used.

```
> printf("abcdefd")
abcdefd
> printf("abcd\befd")  // backspace
abcefd
> printf("abcd\tefd")  // horizontal tab
abcd    efd
> printf("abcd\"efd")  // double quote
abcd"efd
> printf("%c", '\'')   // single quote
'
> printf("%c", '\\')   // a backslash
\
> printf("??!")          // trigraph
|
> printf("?\?!")         // question mark
??!
```

The numeric escape codes come in two varieties: *octal escape codes* and *hexadecimal escape codes*. An *octal escape code* consists of up to three octal digits following the backslash character `\`. For example, under the ASCII encodings in Appendix D. the character `'a'` may be written as `'\141'`; the *null character*, used to terminate strings, can be written as `'\0'`. A *hexadecimal escape code* consists of any number of hexadecimal digits following characters `'\x'`. For example, the character `'a'` can be written in hexadecimal escape code as `'\x61'`.

Each of these escape sequences produces a unique value which can be stored in a single char object. An octal escape code terminates when the first character that is not an octal digit is encountered or when three octal digits have been used. Therefore, the string `"\1111"` represents two characters, `'\111'` and `'1'`, and the string `"\182"` represents three characters, `'\1'`, `'8'`, and `'2'`. Because a hexadecimal escape sequences can be of any length and terminated only by a nonhexadecimal character, to stop a hexadecimal escape in a string, break the string into pieces. It can be used to represent a multibyte character for some languages such as Chinese. For example, the codes `'\x61'` and `'a'` are two characters; however, the hexadecimal escape code `'\x61a'` contains only one multibyte character, rather than two characters of `'a'`.

Array of char as String

Because a string is a sequence of characters, it can easily be represented by an array of **char**. Arrays in C can be declared and its elements can be accessed by operand `[]`. A character array can be declared in the following format:

```
char str[6];
```

Here, variable `str` is a *six-element* character array, which means that it can hold up to six characters to form a string. However, the last element of the array has to be the terminating null character '`\0`' to indicate the end of a string. For example, if the **char** array `str` contains the string `"Hello"`, then the array would hold the characters `'H'`, `'e'`, `'l'`, `'l'`, and `'o'` along with '`\0`'. Additional information about characters and strings can be found in Chapter 12. White spaces and tab characters, such as the ones in the statement `i = c[ 0 ]`, are ignored in the C program except when they are characters within a string, such as `"ab cd"`.

String Literals

A character string literal is a sequence of characters enclosed in double quotes, as in `"xyz"`. The same considerations apply to each element of the sequence in a character string literal as if it were in an integer character constant except that the single quote ' is representable either by itself or by the escape sequence \', but the double quote " shall be represented by the escape sequence \".

A byte with a value of zero with the code `'\0'` is appended to each multibyte character sequence that results from a string literal or literals. The multibyte character sequence is then used to initialize an array of static storage duration and length just sufficient to contain the sequence. For example, in the interactive execution of the C statements below, array `str1` of six elements contains string `"abcde"`, which has six characters including the trailing null character. Array `str2` is allocated enough memory to hold the string `"This is a string"`.

```
> char str1[6] = "abcde"      // The last one is '\0'.
> char str2[] = "This is a string"
```

For character string literals, the array elements have type **char** and are initialized with the individual bytes of the multibyte character sequence. These arrays of static storage duration are distinct. More information about strings can be found in Chapter 12.

3.9 Real Floating-Point Types

The integer data type serves well for some software development projects, especially for system programming. However, for scientific computing, floating-point numbers are extensively used. Floating-point numbers correspond to real numbers that include the numbers between integers. These numbers are defined in C as **float**, **double**, or **long double** types. Floating-point numbers are analogous to the representations of numbers in scientific notion. The internal representation of floating point numbers is described in Chapter 16. Floating-point arithmetic is more complicated than integer arithmetic.

3.9.1 The float Type

Typically, the **float** data type uses 4 bytes (32 bits) for its storage. The macro **FLT_MAX**, defined as the maximum representable finite floating-point number in the **float** data type in the C standard header file **float.h**, is a precalculated system constant. If a number is larger than **FLT_MAX**, which is called an *overflow*, it is represented by the symbol of **Inf**, which corresponds to the mathematical infinity ∞. This is the result of many operations, such as division of a finite number by zero, although an inexact exception may be raised in an IEEE machine. In the same manner, if a number is less than −**FLT_MAX**, it is represented by −**Inf**, which is equivalent to negative infinity, $-\infty$. Table 3.4 lists the metanumbers for floating-point numbers and their mathematical equivalent.

The value of the macro **FLT_MIN** is defined in the C standard library header file **float.h** as a minimum normalized positive floating-point float number. The expressions '0.' and .0 are the same as 0.0. In the same token, the floating-point constant expressions '−0.' and −.0 are equivalent. Mathematically, divisions of zero by zero of 0.0/0.0 and infinity by infinity of ∞/∞ are indeterminate. The results of these operations are represented by the symbol of **NaN**, which stands for Not-a-Number.

The value of 0 in C means that it is the integer zero. Unlike real numbers, there is no 0_- in **int**. Therefore, the integer value of −0 equals 0. The domain [−**FLT_MAX, FLT_MAX**] of real numbers is larger than the domain [−**INT_MIN, INT_MAX**] of integer numbers.

3.9.2 The double and long double Types

For a large range of representable floating-point numbers, a **double** data type can be used. Typically, the **double** data type uses 8 bytes (64 bits) as its storage. Note that there is no external distinction between float Inf and double Inf, although their internal representations differ, which will be described in Chapter 16. This is also true for −Inf and NaN. Similar to float, macros **DBL_MIN** and **DBL_MAX** defined in the header file **float.h** are the minimum and maximum values of type **double**, respectively.

Table 3.4 Table of metanumbers.

Metanumbers	Mathematical representation
`-0.0`	0_-
`+0.0`	0_+
`-Inf`	$-\infty$
`+Inf`	$+\infty$
`NaN`	Not-a-Number (invalid value)

The type specifier **long** can be used to declare variables of type **long** with the number of bits listed in Table 3.2. However, the specifier **long** can also be added in a declaration to increase the storage capacity of a floating-point variable. The data type **long double** is at least as wide as that of **double**. For example, for 32-bit programming model, type **long double** has 8 bytes in Windows, 12 bytes in Linux, and 16 bytes in Solaris. For 64-bit programming, type **long double** has 16 bytes in Linux and Solaris, and 8 bytes in Windows. The macros **LDBL_MIN** and **LDBL_MAX** defined in the header file **float.h** are the minimum and maximum values of type **long double**, respectively. Note that due to the finite precision of the floating-point number representation, the exact values of irrational numbers such as π are not representable in a computer system whether they are represented in **float**, **double**, or **long double**. Similarly, a very large integral value cannot be represented exactly in a floating-point number. Typically a **float** type with 32 bits has 7 significant digits whereas a **double** type with 64 bits has 15 significant digits.

3.9.3 Floating-Point Constants

A floating-point constant contains a decimal point, such as 3.14, or an exponent, such as 2e3 for $2 * 10^2$, or both, such as 3.14e2 for $3.14 * 10^2$. The exponent letter can be a either `e` or `E` and be a negative number such as 3.14E-2 for $3.14 * 10^{-2}$. For example, the macros **FLT_MAX, FLT_MIN, DBL_MAX,** and **DBL_MIN** in the header file **float.h** in a 32-bit machine might be defined as `3.402823466E+38F`, `1.175494351E-38F`, `1.7976931348623158E+308`, and `2.2250738585072014E-308`, respectively. By default, a floating-point constant is of type **double**. To create a floating-point constant of type **float**, add a suffix `f` or `F` such as 3.14F. The suffix `l` or `L` indicates a long double.

An Application Example

Acceleration of a Moving Body

Problem Statement:

For the mechanical system shown in Figure 2.12, given mass $m = 5$ kilograms (kg), coefficient of kinetic friction $\mu = 0.2$, the applied force p is constant at 20 Newtons (N). Write a program to calculate the acceleration of the system.

The solution to the above problem statement involves the use of Equation (2.4) in Chapter 2. Equation (2.4) provides the formula for solving the acceleration of the dynamic system, which is incorporated in Program 3.2. For simplicity and consistence with the mathematical notations, the variables `a`, `mu`, `m`, and `p` represent the acceleration, coefficient of friction μ, mass, and force values, respectively. Comments for these variables are added in the declaration of these variables to make their intended use more clear. For a large program, we could declare variables with the names `accel, mu, mass`, and `force` to make them more descriptive. Because these variables are used to hold decimal numbers, represented internally as floating-point numbers, they are declared with double type. They could also be declared as either float or long double type. However, double type is more commonly used because it provides higher precision than float and most computers can handle it efficiently. After the acceleration has been calculated, it is displayed using the function **printf()**. Using variables to represent mathematical notations make a program easier to modify and more readable. It is especially helpful for solving problems with complicated logic.

The gravity constant $9.81 m/s^2$ is explicitly specified in the acceleration equation in Program 3.2. It is a common programming practice in C to replace a constant by a more descriptive macro. A macro can be defined using the preprocessor directive **#define**, which will be described in detail in Chapter 7.

```
/* File: accelvar.c
   Calculate the acceleration using variables */
#include <stdio.h>

int main() {
    /* declare variables */
    double a,     /* acceleration */
           mu,    /* friction coefficient */
           m,     /* mass */
           p;     /* external force */

    /* initialize variables */
    mu = 0.2;
    m = 5.0;
    p = 20.0;

    /* calculate the acceleration */
    a = (p-mu*m*9.81)/m;

    /* display output */
    printf("Acceleration a = %f (m/s^2)\n", a);
    return 0;
}
```

Program 3.2: Calculating the acceleration using variables.

```
/* File: acceldef.c
   Calculate the acceleration using variables
   and a defined macro for the gravitational acceleration */
#include <stdio.h>

/* define M_G as a macro for the gravitational acceleration */
#define M_G   9.81

int main() {
    /* declare variables */
    double a;    /* acceleration */
    double mu;   /* friction coefficient */
    double m;    /* mass */
    double p;    /* external force */

    /* initialize variables */
    mu = 0.2;
    m = 5;
    p = 20;

    /* calculate the acceleration */
    a = (p-mu*m*M_G)/m;

    /* display output */
    printf("Acceleration a = %f (m/s^2)\n", a);
    return 0;
}
```

Program 3.3: Calculating the acceleration using a macro for a constant.

For example, the statement

```
#define M_G 9.81
```

defines M_G as a macro to represent the gravity constant 9.81. Using the above definition, M_G can now be used to imply the value 9.81. By convention, macros are typically capitalized to distinguish themselves from normal data variables. Macros are often prefixed with a certain symbol to distinguish themselves from other macros. In this example, the prefix M_ is used to avoid potential conflict with the symbol 'G' and to indicate that it is a mathematical constant. Program 3.3 is equivalent to Program 3.2. However, the macro M_G is used to replace constant 9.81 in the acceleration equation. To illustrate an alternative of declaration of multiple variables of the same type, each variable for a, mu, m, and p is declared in a single declaration statement. The output of both programs is the same and is as follows:

```
Acceleration a = 2.038000 (m/s^2)
```

3.10 Complex Types in C99

The complex number, an extension of the real number, has wide applications in science and engineering. The complex number is a new feature added in C99. The variables of three complex types can be declared by the type specifiers **float complex**, **complex** or **double complex**, and **long double complex**. The type specifier **complex** and the macro **I** for representing an imaginary number are defined in the header file **complex.h**. A complex variable uses two floating-point values of type **float, double,** or **long double** to represent its real and imaginary parts. Therefore, the size of a complex number of type **float complex** is 8 bytes, 4 bytes for the real part and 4 bytes for the imaginary part. A complex number of double complex type uses 16 bytes, 8 bytes for the real part and 8 bytes for the imaginary part. Depending on the implementation, the long double complex type has a width at least as wide as the double complex type.

A complex number can be created similar to the following statement `z = x + I*y;`, where z is a complex variable and x and y are the respective real and imaginary parts of the complex number. For example, the statements below declare z1 as a **float complex** variable, and z2 and z3 as **double complex** variables. Variable z1 is assigned the complex number $1 + i2$.

```
#include <complex.h> // define complex and I
float complex z1;    // declare a float complex variable
double complex z2;   // declare a double complex variable
complex z3;          // declare a double complex variable
z1 = 1 + I*2;        // z assigned a complex value
```

Chapter 17 gives a detailed description of complex numbers, including input/output operations, data conversion rules, and functions.

The real floating-point and complex types are collectively called the *floating types*. The type char, the signed and unsigned integer types, and the floating types are collectively called the *basic types*.

3.11 The Pointer Type

Details about pointers are described in Chapter 11. In this section, we give a brief introduction about pointers. A pointer is defined as a variable that contains the address of another variable or dynamically allocated memory. Variables of pointer type can be declared similar to variables of other data types. At declaration, a pointer type can be distinguished by an asterisk '`*`' preceding the variable name. When the unary operator '`&`' is applied to an operand of a variable, it gives the "address of the variable." For example, in Program 3.4, the variable `i` is declared as int and `p` as a pointer to int. The variable `i` is assigned with 10. The expression `&i` gives the address of the variable i. Therefore, the variable `p` is assigned with the address of `i`. In short, `p` points to `i`. A pointer can be printed out using the function **printf**() with the format specifier `"%p"`. The address is displayed as a hexadecimal number. The address of a variable, such as `i`, of a program is typically different in different machines. A sample run of Program 3.4 produces the following output:

```
The value of i is 10
The address of i is 00E81E20
The value of p is 00E81E20
```

```
/* File: pointer.c
   Obtain the address of a variable
   and assigned it to a pointer */
#include <stdio.h>

int main() {
    int i, *p; /* declare i as int, p as pointer to int */

    i = 10;     /* i is assigned with 10 */
    p = &i;     /* p is assigned with the address of i.
                   p points to i */
    printf("The value of i is %d\n", i);
    printf("The address of i is %p\n", &i);
    printf("The value of p is %p\n", p);
    return 0;
}
```

Program 3.4: Assigning the address of a variable to a pointer variable.

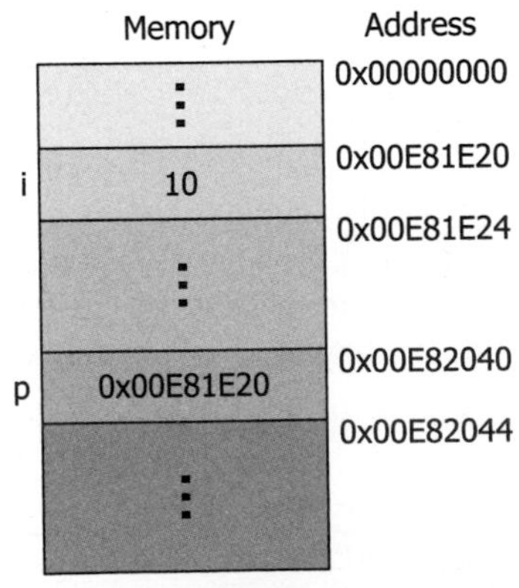

Figure 3.2: A sample memory layout for an integer and a pointer in Program 3.4.

The result corresponds to the memory layout shown in Figure 3.2. The addresses of variables `i` and `p` are `0x00E81E20` and `0x00E82040`, respectively. The value of `p` is `0x00E81E20`, which is the address of the variable `i`. The value at that address for the variable `i` is 10.

The constants 0 or NULL, defined in header file **stdio.h**, can be assigned to a pointer variable as a null pointer.

Pointers also provide another way to declare a string. For example, in the code below,

```
char *str = "This is a string";
```

`str` is a pointer to the first character 'T' of the string `"This is a string"`. The value of `str` is the address of the first character.

3.12 Typedefs

C provides a mechanism for creating new data type names. Declaring a new data type name is similar to declaring a variable except that the declaration is preceded by the keyword **typedef**. For example, according to the C standard, **size_t** is the unsigned integer type of the result of the **sizeof** operator, which gives the size of a data type or an expression in bytes. The details about the **sizeof** operator is described in section 4.11 in Chapter 4. The type **size_t** is declared in the header file **stddef.h**. In 32-bit programming, **size_t** can be declared by

```
typedef unsigned int size_t;
```

as a new type, which is a synonym for the **unsigned int**. In 64-bit programming, it can be declared by

```
typedef unsigned long long size_t;
```

as a synonym for the **unsigned long long**. An implementation, however, may use a built-in data type to define **size_t** for different programming models. The type specifier **size_t** can be used to declare variables of either **unsigned int** type for 32-bit programming or **unsigned long long** type for 64-bit programming. The statement

```
size_t n;
```

declares the identifier `n` of type **size_t**. The type **size_t** is very useful for writing programs that are portable to run in 32-bit and 64-bit computer architectures. For example, it can be used to declare variables for addressing the memory space, which have different limits for 32-bit and 64-bit architectures. A variable of type **size_t** can be used as an argument for memory allocation functions such as **malloc()** and memory manipulation functions such as **memcpy()** as described in Chapters 11 and 12.

Although not required by the C standard, most implementations support the signed version **ssize_t**. For practical purposes, the typedefed data type **ptrdiff_t** in the C standard, instead of **ssize_t**, can be used. Details about data type **ptrdiff_t**, and memory allocation and memory manipulation functions will be described in Chapters 11 and 12.

Note that data type names created by **typedef** are often suffixed with `_t` to distinguish them from regular variable names.

3.13 Determining the Programming Data Model of a Computer

Program 3.5 can be used to obtain the size of basic data types in C89. You may compare the results with values in Table 3.2 to determine the programming data model of your computer. The operator **sizeof** gives the size of a data type in the number of bytes. Details about the operator **sizeof** are described in section 4.11. When

```
/* File: typesize.c
   Obtain the sizes of basic data types in C89 */
#include <stdio.h>
#include <stddef.h>     /* for size_t */

int main() {
    printf("sizeof(char) = %d\n", sizeof(char));
    printf("sizeof(short) = %d\n", sizeof(short));
    printf("sizeof(int) = %d\n", sizeof(int));
    printf("sizeof(long) = %d\n", sizeof(long));
    printf("sizeof(float) = %d\n", sizeof(float));
    printf("sizeof(double) = %d\n", sizeof(double));
    printf("sizeof(long double) = %d\n", sizeof(long double));
    printf("sizeof(pointer) = %d\n", sizeof(int *));
    printf("sizeof(size_t) = %d\n", sizeof(size_t));
    return 0;
}
```

Program 3.5: Obtaining the sizes of basic data types in C89.

Program 3.5 is executed in Windows in the 32-bit programming model ILP32, the output is shown below:

```
sizeof(char) = 1
sizeof(short) = 2
sizeof(int) = 4
sizeof(long) = 4
sizeof(float) = 4
sizeof(double) = 8
sizeof(long double) = 8
sizeof(pointer) = 4
sizeof(size_t) = 4
```

Program 7.3 in Chapter 7 can be used to print the sizes of all basic types in C99.

A binary executable compiled and linked in a 64-bit machine typically cannot run on a 32-bit machine. 64-bit machines, however, will run 32-bit code, 64-bit code, and mixtures of the two. Therefore, a program compiled and linked in a 32-bit machine generally runs in a corresponding 64-bit machine. When the binary executable is executed in a 64-bit machine, it will still use a 32-bit programming model as if it ran in a 32-bit machine. With this interoperability, a 32-bit binary executable can be distributed to run across a large installed base with both 32-bit and 64-bit architectures.

3.14 Initialization

The declaration of a variable may be accompanied by an initializer that specifies the value that that variable should have at the beginning of its lifetime. For example, in the declaration statement

```
int i = 3;
```

the value 3 is the initializer for the variable `i`.

If an object that has static storage duration is not initialized explicitly, it will be initialized according to the following rules:

- If it is a pointer type, it is initialized to a null pointer.
- If it is a arithmetic type, i.e, if the variable can be used as an operand of an arithmetic operation such as addition '+', it is initialized to positive or unsigned zero.

The initial value of an object is that of the expression after conversion. For example, in the code below,

```
int i = 6/3;
double d = 12.345;
char c = 'a';
```

the variable `i` is initialized by the result of the expression `6/3`, which is equal to 2. Variable `d` is initialized to floating-point value `12.345` and character `c` is initialized to `'a'`.

A character array type may be initialized using a string literal. Each element of the character array is correspondingly initialized to each character in the string literal, including the terminating null character. If there is no room for the null character, i.e., the string literal is larger than the array size, it is an error. For example, the array `str1`, with the size of 80 bytes, is initialized by a string literal `"this is a string"` as follows:

```
> char str1[80] = "this is a string"
> printf("%s", str1)
this is a string
```

If an array of unknown size is initialized, its size is determined by the largest indexed element with an explicit initializer. At the end of its initializer list, the array no longer has incomplete type. For example,

```
> char str2[] = "this is a string"
> printf("%s", str2)
this is a string
```

The size of the array of **char** is the same as the length of string "`this is a string`" plus 1, which is for the terminating null character.

3.15 Introduction to Formatted Input and Output

3.15.1 The printf() Function

The function **printf()** can be used to print out text and data to the standard output stream, which is typically the computer terminal. The function **printf()** is defined in the header file **stdio.h**. The format specifiers listed in Table 3.5 can be used to print out variables of different data types and integers in the number representations described earlier.

For example, the integer 4261 can be printed in various formats, as shown below.

```
> printf("%d", 4261)          // decimal integer
4261
> printf("%lld", 4261LL)      // decimal long long integer
4261
```

Table 3.5 Format specifiers for the function printf().

Data type	Format
binary number	"%b" (in Ch only)
char	"%c"
signed integer (char, short, int)	"%d"
unsigned integer (char, short, int)	"%u"
long long	"%lld"
unsigned long long	"%llu"
octal number	"%o"
hexadecimal number	"%x"
float	"%f"
double	"%f" or "%lf"
string	"%s"
pointer	"%p"

```
> printf("%o", 4261)          // octal number
10245
> printf("%x", 4261)          // hexadecimal number
10a5
> printf("%b", 4261)          // binary number (in Ch only)
1000010100101
```

Note that `4261LL` indicates an integer of **long long** data type. The following command-line statements

```
> printf("%f", 15.0F)         // print out a float
15.000000
> printf("%f", 15.0)          // print out a double float
15.000000
> printf("%lf", 15.0)
15.000000
> printf("%c", 'a')
a
> printf("%s", "This string")
This string
```

are examples of printing a floating-point number, character, and string, respectively. Format specifier `"%f"` can be used to print out floating-point numbers of both **float** and **double** types.

Multiple numerical values can be printed out in a single printing statement with multiple format specifiers. Each format specifier corresponds to an argument. For example, one integer and one floating-point number are printed in a single statement below:

```
> printf("integer is %d, floating-point number is %f", 10, 12.34)
integer is 10, floating-point number is 12.340000
```

The *precision* of a floating-point number specifies the number of digits after the decimal point character. The precision typically takes the form of a period (.) followed by an decimal integer. For example, the format `"%.2f"` specifies the precision with two digits after the decimal point, as shown as follows:

```
> printf("%.2f", 12.1234)
12.12
> printf("%.2f", 12.5678)
12.57
```

The fractional part after the specified precision number is rounded to the nearest value. For example, the floating-point number 12.1234 is printed as 12.12 with the precision value of 2, whereas 12.5678 is printed as 12.57.

A floating-point number of float type with 4 bytes typically has 7 significant digits, whereas double type has 15 significant digits. Numerical values after these significant digits are meaningless. For the same floating-point number, different systems may show different values after the significant digits. For example, there are 15 significant digits for double type in Windows. In the following interactive execution of C statements

```
> float f1 = 0.2, f2 = 0.3
> printf("%f", f1)
0.200000
> printf("%f", f2)
0.300000
> printf("%f", f1*f2)
0.060000
> printf("%.20f", f1)
0.20000000298023224000
> printf("%.20f", f2)
0.30000001192092896000
> printf("%.20f", f1*f2)
0.06000000238418579100
> printf("%.20f", 0.06)
0.05999999999999999800
```

variables `f1` and `f2` are assigned with values 0.2 and 0.3, respectively. When the values for variables `f1` and `f2`, and multiplication expression `f1*f2` are printed out using the format specifier `"%f"`, the results look fine. These variables and expression are then printed out with 20 digits after the decimal point using the format specifier `"%f"`. The results indicate that a floating-point number typically cannot be represented exactly inside a computer system. Numerical numbers after 7 significant digits are meaningless for variables and constants of float type. For a variable or constant of double type, it has only 15 significant digits. The interactive execution also displays the floating-point constant number 0.06 of double type with 20 digits after the decimal point. For `f1` of 0.2 and `f2` of 0.3, the expression `f1*f2` does not equal 0.06. We need to keep in mind that the accumulation of such relative errors of expressions in the computation has a significant effect on some numerical algorithms.

The *field width* is considered to be the size of a field in which data are printed. If the number has fewer characters than the field width, then it is padded with space on the left (right-justified) to match the field width. If the field width is too small, it is automatically increased to fit the data. An integer width may be inserted between % and the conversion specifier to indicate a field width. For example, `%6d` specifies a field width of 6 for an integer. `%8.4f` specifies a field width of 8 with 4 digits after the decimal point, as shown below.

```
> printf("%f", 5.12345)
5.123450
> printf("%.4f", 5.12345)
5.1235
> printf("%8.4f", 5.12345)
  5.1235
> printf("%d", 12)
12
> printf("%6d", 12)
    12
```

More information about precision, field width, and other format for output can be found in Chapter 9.

3.15.2 The scanf() Function

The function **scanf()**, also defined in the header file **stdio.h**, is used to input data from the standard input, which is usually the keyboard. The format specifiers for the function **scanf()** are listed in Table 3.6.

Table 3.6 Format specifiers for the function scanf().

Data type	Format
binary number	`"%b"` (in Ch only)
char	`"%c"`
short	`"%hd"`
unsigned short	`"%hu"`
int	`"%d"`
unsigned int	`"%u"`
long long	`"%lld"`
unsigned long long	`"%llu"`
float	`"%f"`
double	`"%lf"`
string	`"%s"`
pointer	`"%p"`

For example, an **int**, **double**, and **char** can be input as shown below.

```
> int i
> float f
> double d
> char c
> scanf("%d", &i)
10
> i
10
> scanf("%f", &f)
15
> f
15.00
> scanf("%lf", &d)
15
> d
15.0000
> scanf("%c", &c)
a
> c
a
```

Note that the address operator '`&`' preceding each variable name is used to obtain its address so that the input value can be stored in the variables. The format specifier `"%d"` can be used for both **short** and **int** data types in output function **printf()**. However, it cannot be used as a format specifier for a variable of **short** data type for input function **scanf()**. Similarly, the format specifier `"%f"` can be used for both **float** and **double** data types in output function **printf()**. The format specifier `"%lf"` has to be used for a variable of **double** type for input function **scanf()**. It is a common mistake to use the format specifier `"%f"` to obtain a value for a variable of type **double**, as shown below.

```
double d;
scanf("%f", &d);
```

The command-line statements below illustrate how to input 4261 in various formats.

```
> int i
> scanf("%d", &i)          // input number in decimal
4261
> long long l
> scanf("%lld", &l)        // input into long long
4261
> l
4261
> scanf("%o", &i)          // input number in octal
10245                      // or '010245'
```

```
> i
4261
> scanf("%x", &i)          // input number in hexadecimal
10A5                       // or '0x10A5' or '0X10A5'
> i
4261
> scanf("%b", &i)          // input number in binary (for Ch only)
1000010100101              // or '0b1000010100101'
> i
4261
```

Program 3.6 illustrates the usage of the functions **printf()** and **scanf()**. A single function call of **scanf()** is used to obtain two input values. The input numbers and their product are then printed on the terminal. If a program is used interactively, it is important that a message should be displayed before the function **scanf()** is called so that the user of the program is prompted to input data accordingly. However, if the program reads input data from a data file using the input/output redirection described in the next section, the prompt message is not necessary. An interactive execution of Program 3.6 is shown below.

```
> scanfc.c
Please input one integer and one floating-point number
10 12.3456
Input values are 10 and 12.345600, their product is 123.456000
```

In this execution, the values 10 and 12.12345 are entered at the prompt.

```
/* File: scanfc.c
   Input to the program from the terminal */
#include <stdio.h>

int main() {
    int num;     /* declare num as an int */
    double d;    /* declare d as a double */

    /* prompt the user for input */
    printf("Please input one integer and one floating-point number\n");
    /* wait for the user to input an integer for num,
       and a floating-point number or integer for d */
    scanf("%d%lf",&num, &d);
    /* display the user's input */
    printf("Input values are %d and %f, their product is %f\n", num, d, num*d);
    return 0;
}
```

Program 3.6: Using pointer for the function **scanf()**.

An Application Example

Acceleration of a Moving Body

Problem Statement:
For the mechanical system shown in Figure 2.12, the applied force p is expressed as a function of time t in

$$p(t) = 4(t - 3) + 20$$

Write a program to calculate the acceleration based on the user input values for `m`, μ, and `t`.

The solution to the above problem involves the use of the formatted input function **scanf()** to obtain values for mass, coefficient of friction, and time from the user interactively. Program 3.7 calculates the

```
/* File: accelio.c
   Interactively calculate the acceleration based on the mass,
   friction coefficient, and time from the terminal */
#include <stdio.h>
#define M_G   9.81   /* gravitational acceleration constant g */

int main() {
    /* declare variables */
    double a, mu, m, p, t;

    /* prompt the user for input of m, mu, and t */
    printf("***** Acceleration Calculator *****\n\n");
    printf("Please enter value for mass in kilogram\n");
    scanf("%lf", &m);
    printf("mass is %lf (kg)\n\n", m);
    printf("Please enter value for friction coefficient\n");
    scanf("%lf", &mu);
    printf("friction coefficient is %lf\n\n", mu);
    printf("Please enter value for time in second\n");
    scanf("%lf", &t);
    printf("time is %lf (s)\n\n", t);

    /* calculate the acceleration based on the user input */
    p = 4*(t-3)+20;
    a = (p-mu*m*M_G)/m;

    /* display output */
    printf("Acceleration a = %f (m/s^2)\n", a);
    return 0;
}
```

Program 3.7: Calculating the acceleration interactively.

acceleration of the system after storing the user input values in variables m, mu, and t. Without the declaration of variables, the values from the user input cannot be processed. An interactive execution of the program with the user input values for mass $m = 5$ kilograms (kg), coefficient of kinetic friction $\mu = 0.2$, and time $t = 2$ seconds, is shown below.

```
> accelio.c
***** Acceleration Calculator *****

Please enter value for mass in kilogram
5
mass is 5.000000 (kg)
Please enter value for friction coefficient
0.2
friction coefficient is 0.200000

Please enter value for time in second
2
time is 2.000000 (s)

Acceleration a = 1.238000 (m/s^2)
```

3.15.3 Redirecting Input from and Output into Files

Normally, the standard output of a program, such as from the function **printf()**, is displayed on the terminal screen. The standard input to a program, such as the function **scanf()**, is from the keyboard. In Unix and Windows, you can redirect input from a file and output also into a file when the program is executed in a command shell. The content described in this section is not part of the C standard, but it is useful and works across different platforms.

You can redirect the standard output into a file by the *output redirection symbol* '>' in a command line. For example, in a Ch command shell, you can redirect the output from program accelvar.c listed in Program 3.2 into the file accelvar.out using the command

```
> accelvar.c > accelvar.out
```

After the execution of the above command, the file accelvar.out shall be created and contains

```
Acceleration a = 2.038000 (m/s^2)
```

By using the symbol '>', when the user redirects output into a file that already exists, the output redirection removes the current contents of that file and replaces them with the output of the command. The user can avoid overwriting the contents of a file by using another redirection symbol '>>', which is called the *append redirection symbol*. Command

```
> accelvar.c >> accelvar.out
```

adds the standard output from program accelvar.c to the end of file accelvar.out, rather than replacing the file. If the user appends output to a file which doesn't exist, the symbol '>>' acts like '>', creating the file and redirecting the output of a command into it.

The standard input to a program can be redirected by the *input redirecting symbol* '<' from a file. For example, if the file scanfc.dat contains

```
10 12.3456
```

the program scanfc.c listed in Program 3.6 can be executed to use these numbers as its input as shown below.

```
> scanfc.c < scanfc.dat
Please input one integer and one floating-point number
Input values are 10 and 12.345600, their product is 123.456000
```

With input indirection, the input to a program can be installed in a file. This can be convenient for testing a program with many input data. You need to enter the data only once in a file and can use it many times for testing and running the program. It can also be useful to run a program with different sets of input data. As mentioned before, if Program 3.6 is used with input values only from data files through the input/output redirection, the statement

```
printf("Please input one integer and one floating-point number\n");
```

could be removed to make the output more clear.

The standard input and output also be redirected to different files at the same time. For example, for the command

```
> scanfc.c < scanfc.dat > scanfc.out
```

Program scanfc.c reads the standard input from the file scanfc.dat and writes the standard output into the file scanfc.out.

As a sample application, the redirection of both standard input and output can be used to write a script in Ch to grade students' homework automatically. The grading system can check the submitted homework with different sets of testing data and save the output from the program. It then compares the output with the standard solution using the command **diff** in the following form:

```
> diff scanfc.out solutionFile
```

which compares the contents of files scanfc.out and solutionFile and writes to the standard output a list of changes necessary to convert scanfc.out into solutionFile.

The redirection of standard input and output described in this section is a feature of the operating system, not a feature in C. In section 14.4 in Chapter 14, using functions in C for input and output redirection is presented.

3.15.4 Pipeline to Redirect the Input and Output of Programs, and Handling Archival Files

Pipeline, available in both Unix and Windows, is another method for redirecting input and output. A pipeline is a sequence of one or more commands separated by the *pipeline symbol* '|'. The standard output of each command except the last one is connected by a pipe to the standard input of the next command. Each command runs as a separate process. Users can regard it as running the first command with its output redirected to a temporary file, then running the second command with its input redirected from the temporary file, and so on.

Commands presented below are commonly used to deal with distributed software packages with C source code. A command with pipeline is used to uncompress and extract files in a distributed archival file.

To distribute multiple source files in a directory, say `program`, one can package and compress them as a single zip file using the command **zip**:

```
> zip -rq program.zip program
```

The option `-rq` packages all files in the directory `program` and its subdirectories *recursively* and *quietly* without displaying file names on the terminal. The command **unzip**:

```
> unzip program.zip
```

can be used to extract the compressed files in the zip file `program.zip`.

Multiple source files can also be combined as a single archival file `program.tar` by the command **tar**:

```
> tar -cvf program.tar program
```

The command option `-c` is for creating an archival file, `-v` for displaying information for files in the archival, and `-f` for file name. The archival file `program.tar` can be compressed by the command **gzip**:

```
> gzip -f program.tar
```

with the option `-f` to create the compressed file `program.tar.gz`. The following command with pipe,

```
> gzip -cd program.tar.gz | tar -xvf -
```

can be used to uncompress and extract files from the archival file `program.tar.gz`. The option `-d` for the command **gzip** decompresses the file `program.tar.gz` and the option `-c` writes the output on the standard output. The option `-x` for command **tar** is for extracting files from the archival. If the name of the tar file is `'-'`, **tar** writes to the standard output or reads from the standard input, whichever is appropriate. In this case, it reads the standard input from the standard output of **gzip**.

In some platforms, such as Linux, the option `-z` for the command **tar** is available to compress a created archival file as shown below.

```
> tar -xvfz  program.tgz program
```

The compressed archival file `program.tgz.` can be uncompressed and extracted by the command

```
> gzip -cd program.tgz | tar -xvf -
```

3.16 Making It Work

3.16.1 Changing Default Standard Output Formats for Floating-Point Numbers in Ch

The default output format for values of float and double types in Ch are `".2f"` and `".4lf"`, respectively. These default formats can be changed by resetting the system variables **_formatf** and **_formatd** inside the startup configuration file **_chrc** in Windows and **.chrc** in Unix in the user's home directory. For example, statements

```
_formatf = ".4f";
_formatd = ".6lf";
```

inside a startup configuration file, change the default output format for values of type **float** with four digits after the decimal point and six digits for type **double**. For example,

```
>10.123456+ 10
20.123456
> 10.123456F + 10
20.1234
```

3.16.2 Running Programs with Standard Input through scanf() in ChIDE

The input and output of a program in ChIDE are handled in the same manner as in a command shell. When a program is executed in ChIDE using the command `Run` or `Tools | Run`, the standard output from the function **printf()** is displayed in the output pane, as shown in Figure 2.4. When the function **scanf()** is called in a program, the input can also be entered in the output pane.

3.16.3 Debugging Programs in ChIDE

Nobody can write perfect code on the first try, especially for a complicated program. A large part of programming is finding and fixing errors. There are three kinds of errors in a program. One is the *syntax error*, which can be detected by a compiler or interpreter, when the code is processed as shown in Figure 2.5. Multiple error messages may be generated for one syntax error. In this case, the first error message is the most relevant for fixing the error.

The other error is the *runtime error*. A runtime error occurs during the execution of a program. For example, dividing an integer by zero is a runtime error. Runtime errors are harder to find than syntax errors because they occur only under certain conditions. A runtime error may also crash the running program and destroy any information about the cause of the error.

The another error is the *algorithmic error* or *logic error*, which cannot be detected by a compiler or interpreter. For example, you might, by mistake, have typed in a wrong value or formula in an equation for calculation. As a result, the output from the program execution is incorrect or is not what you would expect. If a program has either a runtime or logic error, the program has a *bug*. The process of finding and fixing bugs is called *debugging*. A syntax error in a program is relatively easy to fix after you have learned a programming language. Debugging is more difficult, especially for a large program. It requires patience and experience. Sometimes it takes a long time to fix a bug.

A debugger is a tool for debugging programs. To fix a bug in a small program, you can step through the program line by line using a debugger. At each step, you can examine the values of all variables and expressions, or even change values of variables. To fix a bug in a large program, you need to isolate the problem by setting breakpoints. Once the program execution hits a breakpoint, you can examine and change values of variables at that point and execute the program line by line.

ChIDE can be used not only to edit and execute programs, but also as a debugger. As described in section 2.2.1 in Chapter 2, ChIDE has four panes: the editing pane, debug pane, debug command pane, and output pane as shown in Figure 3.3. The menus labeled `Start` to `Clear` in the *debug bar* in Figure 3.3 are *debug commands*. Figure 3.3 indicates that Program 3.2 is being executed and stopped at a breakpoint at line 21. The current executing line 21 is highlighted (displayed in the green color on the screen).

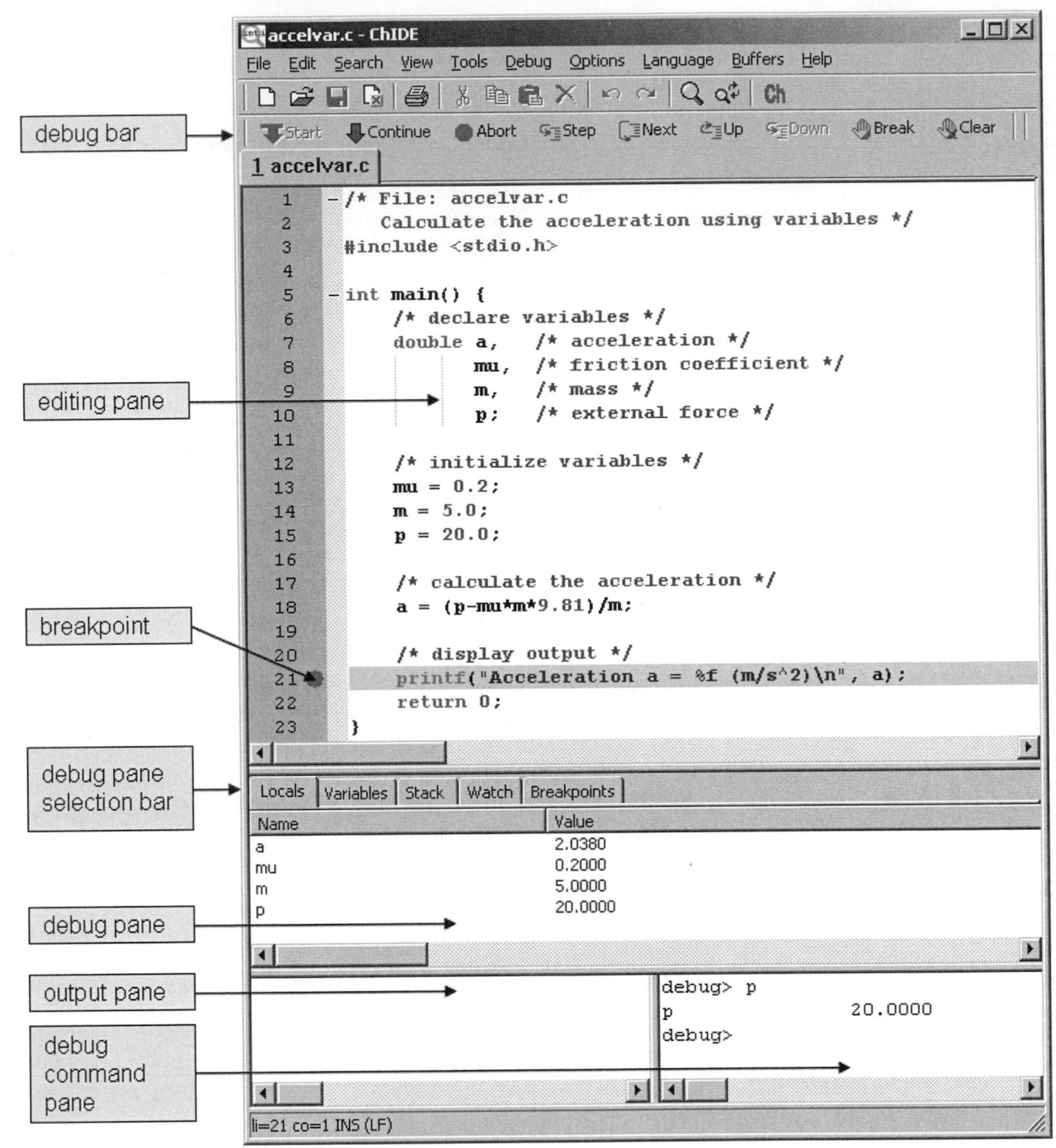

Figure 3.3: Debugging `accelvar.c` in Program 3.2 showing values for all variables in the function **main()** in ChIDE.

Executing Programs in Debug Mode

The user can execute the program in the editing pane in debug mode by the `Start` command. The program will stop when a breakpoint is hit. The user can execute the program line by line either by using the command `Step` or `Next`. For simple statements, the command `Step` is the same as `Next`. They are different when a function call is executed, which will be described in section 6.13.3 in Chapter 6. During debugging, the command `Continue` can be invoked to continue the execution of the program until it hits a breakpoint or the program ends.

If the program execution has failed and is taking too long to complete, then the command `Abort` can be used to stop the program.

Setting and Clearing Breakpoints

Before program execution or during the debugging of an executed program, new breakpoints can be added to stop the program execution when they are hit. A breakpoint for a line can be added by clicking the left margin of the line, as shown at line 21 in Figure 3.3. To clear the breakpoint, click the highlighted mark on the left margin of the line (displayed in the red color on the screen). Breakpoints in the debugger can be examined by clicking the menu `Breakpoints` on the *debug pane selection bar* which is located above the debug pane. The debug pane will display the breakpoint number and its location for each breakpoint. A breakpoint for the current line can also be added by clicking the menu `Break` on the debug bar. It can also be deleted by clicking the menu `Clear`. A breakpoint cannot be set in a declaration statement; however, a breakpoint can be set for a declaration statement with initialization such as

```
int i = 10;
```

The program must not be edited when it is being executed and debugged. Otherwise, the message

> *Warning: Any changes made to the file during debugging will not be reflected in the current debugging session.*

will be displayed. However, when a program has finished its execution, it can be edited. When a program is edited by deleting or adding new code, the breakpoints set for the program will be updated automatically.

Monitoring Local Variables and Their Values in the Debug Pane

When a program is executed line by line by the command `Step` or `Next`, names and their corresponding values of variables in the current stack can be examined in the debug pane by clicking the menu `Locals` on the debug pane selection bar. When control of the program execution is inside a function, the command `Locals` displays the values of local variables and arguments of the function. When control of the program execution is not in a function of a Ch script, the command `Locals` displays the values of global variables of the program. Functions and global variables will be described in Chapters 6 and 8. As shown in Figure 3.3, when the program `accelvar.c` is executed at the highlighted line 21 (displayed in the green color on the screen), local variables `a`, `mu`, `m`, and `p`, and their values 2.0380, 0.2000, 5.0000, and 20.000, respectively, are displayed in the debug pane.

Using the Debug Console Window for Input and Output

When a program in ChIDE is parsed, if there is any syntax error, an error message is displayed in the output pane. When a program is executed in the debug mode, the standard input, output, and error streams are redirected in a separate *Debug Console Window*, as shown in Figure 3.4, for output when the program `accelvar.c` is executed in ChIDE, as shown in Figure 3.3. By default, the console window always stays on the top of other windows. This default behavior can be turned off or on with the command `View | Debug Console Window Always on Top`. The console window can be opened and closed with the command `View | Debug Console Window`. The contents of the console window can be cleared with the command `View | Clear Debug Console Window`. The colors of the background and text as well as the window size and the font size can be changed by right-clicking the ChIDE icon on the upper-left

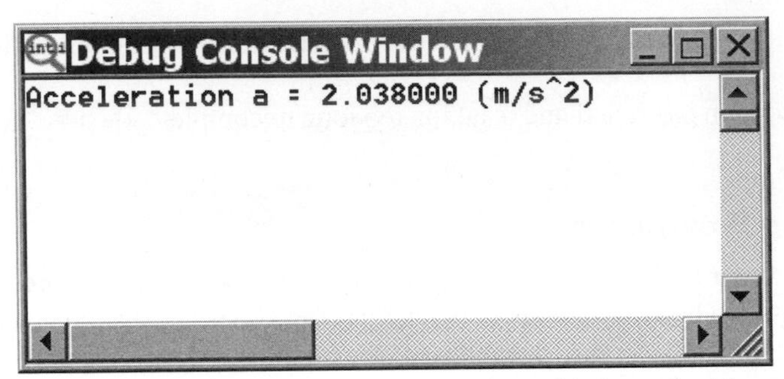

Figure 3.4: Debug Console Window for input/output in debugging, with the output from program `accelvar.c` in ChIDE.

corner of the window and selecting the `Properties` menu. Note that for Windows Vista, you need to run ChIDE with the administrative privilege to make such a change.

Using Debug Commands in the Debug Command Pane

Many debug commands in the debug command pane are available during the debugging of a program. A prompt

```
debug>
```

inside the debug command pane indicates that the debugger is ready to accept debug commands. Type the command `help`, and it will display all available commands. The menu on the left before a colon shows a command, and the description on the right explains the action taken for the command. All commands in the debug bar are available interactively as debug commands in the debug command pane. However, some features are available only through the debug commands in the debug command pane. The command `start` begins debugging a program. Details using these can be found online by clicking `ChIDE Help` from the Help menu, as shown in Figure 2.7 in Chapter 2.

One of the most important features of debug commands in the debug command pane is to obtain and modify values for variables of the debugged program at runtime. One can also just type an expression as a debug command; the expression is displayed on the left and its value is displayed on the right. For example, when the program `accelvar.c` is stopped at line 21 as shown in Figure 3.3, the debug command pane will be able to accept debug commands and expressions. You can obtain the values of expressions using the variables `mu, m, p`, and `a`. You can also change the values of these variables. The interactive session inside the debug command pane is shown below.

```
debug> p
p                          20.0000
debug> 2*p
2*p                        40.0000
debug> p = 30.0
p = 30.0                   30.0000
debug> p
p                          30.0000
```

In these debug commands, the original value 20 for the variable p is displayed first, the expression `2*p` is evaluated, then `p` is changed to 30, and finally its new value is displayed. At this point, if the program execution is continued by one of the commands `Continue`, `Step`, or `Next` on the debug bar, the variable `p` has the value 30.

Exercises

1. Write the octal, decimal, and hexadecimal equivalents of the following binary numbers:
   - **a.** 0b00110011
   - **b.** 0b01101100
   - **c.** 0b01110111
   - **d.** 0b00111101
   - **e.** 0b11111011 (assume binary two's complement notation)
   - **f.** 0b11111111 (assume binary two's complement notation)
   - **g.** 0b0010001000101101O
   - **h.** 0b1010001000101101O (assume binary two's complement notation)
2. Find the binary representation for positive integers and binary two's complement representation for negative integers using 32 bits for the following integral numbers:
   (a) 1, (b) −1, (c) 2, (d) −2, (e) 4, (f) −4, (g) 5, (h) −5, (i) 8, (j) −8, (k) 9, (l) −9, (m) 10, (n) −10, (o) 64, (p) −64, (q) 65, (r) 127, (s) 128, (t) −128, (u) 255, (v) 256, (w) −256, (x) 0xFFFF, (y) 0x7F00
3. Some poor choices for program identifiers are shown below. What makes them poor choices?
   (a) inputfrompipe (b) Int (c) ABC (d) o77U (e) abc$input (f) __id
4. State whether the following statement is true or false. If false, explain why.
   All variables in C must be declared before they are used.
5. Find the error(s) in each of the following program segments. Explain how each error can be corrected.
   - **a.** `printf("%s\n", 'Happy Birthday');`
   - **b.** `printf("\%c\n", 'Hello');`
   - **c.** `printf("%c\n", "This is a string);`
   - **d.** The following statement should print `"Good bye"` (including the quotes):
     ```
     printf(""%s"", "Good bye");
     ```
   - **e.**
     ```
     char c = 'a';
     printf("%s\n", c);
     ```
   - **f.** `printf('Enter your name: ');`
   - **g.** `printf( %f, 123.456);`
   - **h.** The following statement should print the characters `'O'` and `'K'` (excluding the quotes):
     ```
     printf("%s%s\n", 'O', 'K');
     ```
   - **i.**
     ```
     char c;
     scanf("%c", c);
     ```
   - **j.**
     ```
     double d;
     scanf("%f", &d);
     printf("%f", d);
     ```
   - **k.**
     ```
     int d;
     scanf("%f", &d);
     printf("%f", d);
     ```
   - **l.** The following statement should print out 123.456780:
     ```
     double x = 123.45678, y;
     int d;
     d = x;
     y = d;
     printf("%f\n", y);
     ```

6. When printing a floating-point number of float or double using the function **printf()** with the format specifier `"%f"`, how many digits are after the decimal point? Does **printf()** round or truncate the value?
7. Write a program to print out the results of the following integral and floating-point expressions. For floating-point expressions, print out the results with both 6 and 20 digits afer the decimal point.
(a) 2*3, (b) 1/5, (c) 1/2, (d) 3/2, (e) 1/3, (f) 2/3, (g) 1.0/5, (h) 1.0/2, (i) 3.0/2, (j) 1.0/3, (k) 2.0/3, (l) 1/5.0, (m) 1/2.0, (n) 3/2.0. (o) 1/3.0, and (p) 2/3.0.
8. What do `printf("?\?=")` and `printf("??=")` print?
9. What is the output from the following program?

```
#include<stdio.h>

int main() {
    int i = 10;              /* integer */
    double d = 10.0, d2;     /* floating-point values */

    /* %d for integer and floating-point number */
    printf("format %%d for 10   is %d %d\n", 10, i);
    printf("format %%d for 10.0 is %d %d\n", 10.0, d);
    /* %f for integer and floating-point number */
    printf("format %%f for 10 is %f %f\n", 10, i);
    printf("format %%f for 10.0 is %f %f\n", 10.0, d);
    /* result of integer division */
    d  = 1/3;
    d2 = 3/2;
    printf("format %%f for d = %f and d2 = %f\n", d, d2);
    return 0;
}
```

10. Write a program that prints the numbers 1 to 4 on the same line. Write the program using the following methods:

    a. Calling the function **printf()** once with four format specifiers.
    b. Calling the function **printf()** four times.

11. Write a program that will convert the temperature from degrees in Celsius to degrees in Fahrenheit. The user input is the temperature in Celsius. The relationship is as follows:

$$f = \frac{9c}{5} + 32$$

where c is the temperature in Celsius and f is the temperature in Fahrenheit. Check your program with the input values 38.5 and 40 Celsius.

12. One mile equals 1.609 kilometers. Write a program to take the user input distance in miles and convert it to kilometers and print it out. Check your program with the value 38 miles. (a) The program accepts the user input for miles from the terminal and displays the result on the standard output. (b) Redirect your input from file `temperature.dat` and output to file `temperature.out` in a command shell.
13. The formula for the area of a circle is πr^2, where r is the radius of the circle. Write a program to compute the area of a circle. Check your program with a radius of 5 meters. (a) The program accepts the user input for the radius of the circle from the terminal and displays the result on the standard output. (b) Redirect your input from file `circle.dat` and output to file `circle.out` in a command shell.

14. The formula for the surface area of a sphere is $4\pi r^2$, where r is the radius of the sphere. Write a program to compute the surface area of a sphere. The user inputs the radius of the sphere. Check your program with a radius of 5 meters. (a) The program accepts the user input for the radius of the circle from the terminal and displays the result on the standard output. (b) Redirect your input from file `spherearea.dat` and output to file `spherearea.out` in a command shell.
15. The formula for the volume of a sphere is $\frac{4}{3}\pi r^3$, where r is the radius of the sphere. Write a program to compute the volume of a sphere. Check your program with a radius of 5 meters. (a) The program accepts the user input for the radius of the circle from the terminal and displays the result on the standard output. (b) Redirect your input from the file `sphere.dat` and output to the file `sphere.out` in a command shell.
16. For the mechanical system shown in Figure 2.12, write a program to calculate the acceleration of the system with the user input of mass m in kg, the coefficient of kinetic friction μ, the applied constant force p in Newtons. Check your program with $m = 6$, $\mu = 0.3$, and $p = 10$.
17. What are the minimum and maximum values for an integer with n bits in signed representation. What is the maximum value for an integer with n bits in unsigned representation: Express these values in both decimal and binary representations. For a negative value in binary, use binary two's complement representation.

    (a) n is 8. (b) n is 16. (c) n is 32. (d) n is 6. (c) n is 10.

18. Print the following floating-point numbers with 20 digits after the decimal point.

    a. `0.1 0.2 0.3 0.4 0.5 0.6 0.7 0.8 0.9 0.1`
    b. `1.1 1.2 1.3 1.4 1.5 1.6 1.7 1.8 1.9 1.1`

19. Write a program to compute the volume of three different rooms. Assume that each room is a rectangle. The height, width, and length for each room are stored in a line in the file `rooms.dat` as follows:

```
1 2 3
10.0 20.0 30.0
10.0 20.0 300.0
```

    The program reads these data using input redirection and prints out the volume of each room as well as the total volume of all three rooms.

20. Create an archival zip file `eme5.zip`, with contents in the directory `eme5` (or other course name you are taking using this textbook) in your home directory. Copy this file to a different directory. Then uncompress it and extract files. Do the same for an archival file, `eme5.tar.gz`.
21. Download the source code for programs presented in this book at the Web site `http://iel.ucdavis.edu/cfores`. The source code can be downloaded in either file `cfores_code.zip` or file `cfores_code.tar.gz`. What are the commands to uncompress and extract the contents from these two files?
22. Write a Ch program that prompts the user for an unsigned integer and prints the integer's corresponding binary representation.

CHAPTER 4

Operators and Expressions

C is commonly used for scientific numerical computation. A numerical expression may consist of many operations. In C, an *operator* is one or more tokens that, when taken together, specifies an operation to be performed on one or more operands to produce a value. We have seen some operators already in this book, such as the addition operator + and the multiplication operator *. For example, in the expression `i+2`, `i` and `2` are the operands and + is the addition operator. The addition operator + has a single token, whereas the incremental operator ++, which will be described later in this chapter, consists of two tokens. In this chapter, some concepts related to operators and expressions are introduced first. More operators are then described in the subsequent sections.

An operator that has two operands, such as the addition operator, is called a *binary operator*. A *unary operator*, such as `!`, has only one operand. Likewise, a *ternary operator* has three operands.

An *expression* consists of a valid sequence of operators and operands that specifies how to compute a value. An *integral expression* produces a result in one of the integer types. For example, the expression $(3 * 5 + i)$, with `i` declared as an integral type, is an integral expression.

A *floating-point expression* produces a result in one of the floating-point types: **float**, **double**, and **long double**. For example, `3.3+ 4.5` is a floating-point expression of type double. A *constant expression* contains only constant values including macros. A *pointer expression* evaluates to an address value. For example, the expression `&i` gives the address of the variable `i`.

An *expression statement* takes the form of

```
expression;
```

Most C statements are expression statements. For example,

```
printf("Hello, world\n");
a = b + c;
```

4.1 Assignment Operator

The assignment operator is one of the most commonly used operators. An *lvalue* is any object that occurs on the left-hand side of an assignment statement. The lvalue refers to a memory such as a variable or pointer, not a function or constant. On the other hand, the *rvalue* refers to the value of the expression on the right-hand side of an assignment statement. In assignment operations, the data type of the rvalue is converted to the data type of the lvalue, based on the implicit conversion rule which will be described in section 4.3, if they are not of the same types.

When a floating-point number is assigned to an integer variable, the fractional part will be discarded as shown below.

```
> int i
> double d = 10.123
> i = d
10
> i = 10.789
10
```

One may round up a positive floating-point number by adding 0.5 to it before it is assigned to an integer variable. For rounding down a negative floating-point number, one may subtract -0.5 from it. The mathematical function **round()** in C99, defined in the header file **math.h**, can be used to round a floating-point number conveniently, as shown below.

```
> double d = 10.789
> i = d+0.5
11
> i = (-d-0.5)
-11
> i = round(d)
11
> i = round(-d)
-11
```

An assignment operation may run into a problem if the lvalue cannot support the value being assigned to it. For example, a value of int type greater than what can be stored in a variable of short data type will produce a problem because a variable of short type can hold only 2 bytes of memory while an int can hold 4 bytes. This is an example of an *overflow* and may occur with floating-point data types of variable sizes as well. Overflow is also possible when assigning an integral value that is too large to a floating-point variable and vice versa. The following assignment statements may all cause problems in a program.

```
short s;
int i;
float f;

s = 32800;
i = 99999999999;
f = 2147483649;
```

For an integer of int type with 4 bytes, the maximum value defined by the macro **INT_MAX** is 2,147,483,647. For an integer of short type with 2 bytes, the maximum value defined by the macro **SHRT_MAX** is 32,767. In the above example, all three assignment statements will produce an overflow condition. For variables `s` and `i`, their assigned integer values are greater than the maximum integer number supported by the short and int data types. In addition, the integral value `2,147,483,649` is too large to be held as a value of int type before it is converted to a float data type for variable `f`.

4.2 Arithmetic Operators

Arithmetic operations involve negation, addition, subtraction, multiplication, and division as shown in Table 4.1. For the negation operation (-), the data type of the result is the same as the data type of the operand. The sign of a number changes with the use of the negation operator. The use of a unary plus operator (+) in an expression such as $+55 - x$ has no effect and will be ignored. The addition (+), subtraction (-), multiplication (*), and division (/) operations follow mathematical conventions.

Note that even for multiplication of a variable with a constant such as `5*i`, the multiplication operator `'*'` is still needed. When dividing two integers, the remainder is dropped, which results in a possible loss of data. The division of two floating-point zeros is undefined; the result of 0.0/0.0 is NaN, which stands for Not-a-Number. The division of nonzero floating-point number by zero is infinity, which is represented as Inf. Details about these metanumbers in operations and elementary functions are described in Chapter 16.

The expression `i%j` would result in the remainder of `i` divided by `j`. The remainder is zero when `i` can be divided by `j` exactly. The modulus operation can be used to find if an integer is odd or even, which is useful for many applications. If `n` is an odd number, the remainder integer divided by 2, `n%2`, is 1. Otherwise, `n%2` is 0.

The modulus operator (`%`) can be used only with integer operands. All other operators can be applied to operands of the arithmetic type, which consists of integer, floating-point, or complex types. The addition and subtraction operators can be used for pointer arithmetic when the operand is a pointer type. For the subtraction operator, both operands can be pointer types. Details about pointer arithmetic will be described in Chapter 11.

The algorithms and resultant data types of operations depend on the data types of operands. A data type that occupies less memory can be converted to a data type that occupies more memory space without losing any information, which will be described in detail in section 4.3. For example, an integer of char type can be cast into int or float without problems. However, a reverse conversion may result in loss of information. The char data type is the lowest and long double is the highest, as shown in Figure 4.1 for the hierarchy of basic data types. For binary operations, such as addition, subtraction, multiplication, and division, the resultant data type will take the higher order data type of two operands, according to the data type hierarchy shown in Figure 4.1. For example, the addition of two numbers of type float will result in a number of type float, whereas the addition of a number of type float and a number of type double will become a number of type double.

Table 4.1 Arithmetic operations.

Operator	Operation	Description
-	$-x$	negation
+	$+x$	unary plus
+	$x + y$	addition
-	$x - y$	subtraction
*	$x * y$	multiplication
/	x / y	division
%	$i \% j$	modulus

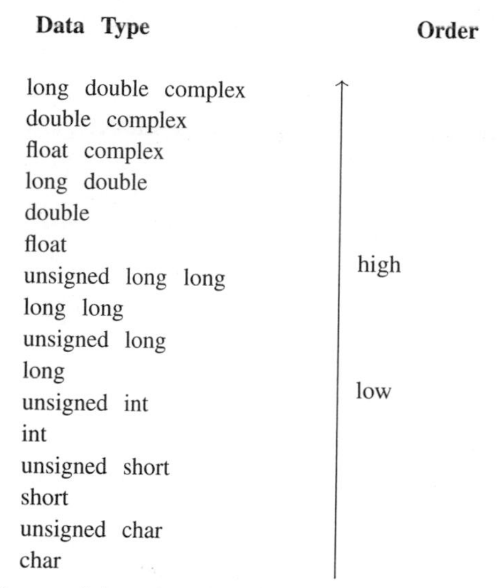

Figure 4.1: The hierarchy of basic data types.

Examples of arithmetic operations are shown below.

```
> int i = 10
> 5*i
50
> 4 + 5.0F
9.00
> 8 - 3.5
4.5000
> 2 * 3
6
> 19/5
3                            // remainder is lost
> 19%5
4                            // remainder is 4
> 19.0/5
3.800
> 19/5.0
3.800
> 0.0/0.0                    // 0.0/0.0 is undefined
nan
> 1.0/0.0                    // 1.0/0.0 is infinity
inf
```

4.3 Implicit Type Conversions

As stated earlier, C is a loosely typed language. All the data types of operands for an operation are checked for compatibility. If the data types do not match, the system signals an error and prints out some informative messages for the convenience of program debugging. However, unlike other programming languages such as Pascal, which prohibits automatic type conversion, some data type conversion rules have been implemented so that they can be invoked whenever necessary. For example, the addition (2.5 + 5) for the floating-point number 2.5 and the integer 5 is performed in floating-point arithmetic after 5 is converted to a floating-point number of double type as shown below.

```
> 2.5 + 5
7.5000
```

The char is the lowest data type and long double complex the highest data type as shown in Figure 4.1. The *implicit conversion* or *automatic conversion* of data types is dependent on the data type hierarchy and conversion rules. The conversion rules related to complex numbers will be described in section 17.3 in Chapter 17. The default conversion rules for real numbers in C are given as follows:

1. When any scalar value is converted to **bool**, the result is 0 if the value compares equal to 0; otherwise, the result is 1.
2. When a value with integer type is converted to another integer type other than **bool**, if the value can be represented by the new type, it is unchanged. Otherwise, if the new type is unsigned, the value is converted by repeatedly adding or subtracting one more than the maximum value that can be represented in the new type until the value is in the range of the new type. Otherwise, the new type is signed and the value cannot be represented in it; the result is implementation-defined.
3. When a finite value of real floating type is converted to an integer type other than **bool**, the fractional part is discarded (i.e., the value is truncated toward zero). If the value of the integral part cannot be represented by the integer type, the behavior is undefined.
4. When a value of integer type is converted to a real floating type, if the value being converted is in the range of values that can be represented but cannot be represented exactly, the result is either the nearest higher or nearest lower value, chosen in an implementation-defined manner. If the value being converted is outside the range of values that can be represented, the behavior is undefined.
5. When a **float** is promoted to **double**, its value is unchanged.
6. When a **double** is demoted to **float** or a value being represented in greater precision and range than required by its semantic type is explicitly converted to its semantic type, if the value being converted is outside the range of values that can be represented, the behavior is undefined. If the value being converted is in the range of values that can be represented but cannot be represented exactly, the result is either the nearest higher or nearest lower representable value, chosen in an implementation-defined manner.
7. In assignment operations, the value of the data type of the right-hand side is converted to the data type of the variable on the left-hand side, if they are not the same types.
8. In binary operations, such as addition, subtraction, multiplication, and division with mixed data types, the result of the operation carrys the higher data type of the two operands.

The implicit conversion of data type, however, may be dangerous because unexpected conversions can occur if the programmer is not careful. For example, when a floating-point number 2.9 is converted to an integer, the fractional part is discarded:

```
> int i
> i = 2.9
2
```

As another example, the expression $2.5 + 1/2$ evaluates to 2.5, not 3.0, as it would be expected, as shown below.

```
> 2.5 + 1/2
2.5000
```

Although $1/2$ is equal to 0.5 mathematically, both `1` and `2` are of **int** types, so the result of $1/2$ is also an **int** type. Thus, the fractional part of 0.5 is truncated to result in the value 0; hence the expression $2.5 + 1/2 = 2.5+0 = 2.5$ in C. To avoid such an unexpected result, one may use the expression $2.5+1.0/2.0$ in a program.

4.4 Precedence and Associativity of Operators

Operators used in C and Ch are summarized in Table 4.2. We have described assignment operator and arithmetic operators so far.

In sections 3.11 and 3.15.2 in Chapter 3, the use of the unary operator `&` to obtain the address of a variable has been presented. Details about the use of the unary address operator `&` and indirection operator `*` will be described in Chapter 11. The member operator `.` and indirect member operator `->` are associated with data types of structures and classes, which will be described in Chapters 13 and 19. The functional type cast operator and scope resolution operator '`::`' are available in C++ and Ch. They will be described in Chapter 18.

Table 4.2 Precedence and associativity of operators.

<table>
<tr><th>Operators</th><th>Associativity</th></tr>
<tr><td>::</td><td></td></tr>
<tr><td>function_name ( ) type()</td><td>right to left</td></tr>
<tr><td>. -></td><td>left to right</td></tr>
<tr><td>' ! ++ -- + - * & (type) sizeof</td><td>right to left</td></tr>
<tr><td>* / % .* ./</td><td>left to right</td></tr>
<tr><td>+ -</td><td>left to right</td></tr>
<tr><td><< >></td><td>left to right</td></tr>
<tr><td>< <= > >=</td><td>left to right</td></tr>
<tr><td>== !=</td><td>left to right</td></tr>
<tr><td>&</td><td>left to right</td></tr>
<tr><td>^</td><td>left to right</td></tr>
<tr><td>|</td><td>left to right</td></tr>
<tr><td>&&</td><td>left to right</td></tr>
<tr><td>^^</td><td>left to right</td></tr>
<tr><td>||</td><td>left to right</td></tr>
<tr><td>?:</td><td>right to left</td></tr>
<tr><td>= += -= *= /= %= &= |= ^= <<= >>=</td><td>right to left</td></tr>
<tr><td>,</td><td>left to right</td></tr>
</table>

The exclusive-or operator `^^`, command substitution operator `` ` ``, element-wise array multiplication operator '`.*`', and element-wise array division operator '`./`' operator are available in Ch only. The operators '`.*`', and '`./`' for computational arrays are described in Chapter 21. All other operators will be described in the remaining sections of this chapter.

An operator at the higher level has higher precedence than operators at the lower level. Operators at the same level have the same precedence. The precedence for arithmetic operators in C is the same as that for arithmetic. For example, a multiplication operator has higher precedence than an addition operator. For the expression $2 + 3 * 4$, the multiplication operation $3 * 4$ will be performed (with the result of 12) before the addition operation of $2 + 12$. A pair of parentheses can be used to specify a particular grouping order. For example, for the expression $(2 + 3) * 4$, the addition operation $2 + 3$ will be performed (with the result of 5) before the multiplication operation $5 * 4$. As another example, the expression `a == b && c != 5` will be evaluated as if they were grouped in the order of `((a == b) && (c != 5))` because the relational operators `==` and `!=` have higher precedence than the logical operator `&&`. Details about operators `==`, `!=`, and `&&` will be described in later sections.

Operators with the same precedence will associate the operands according to their associativities. Unary operators, ternary conditional operators, assignment operators, and comma operators are right associative; all others are left associative. For example, for the expression $2+3-4$, both addition and subtraction operations have the same precedence, and they are left associative. The addition operation 2+3 will be performed first. The result then has 4 subtracted from it. For the statement

```
a = b = c;
```

the value of `c` will be assigned to `b`, then be assigned to `a` because the assignment operator is right associative.

Complicated Expressions and Expression Evaluation Trees

For complicated arithmetic expressions, parentheses `()` could be used to specify which particular group(s) of operands and operations should be considered first or make an expression more readable. As an example, the mathematical formula

$$y = \frac{5 - x}{2} + 2x - 4$$

can be programmed in the C statement as follows.

```
y = (5-x)/2+(2*x)-4;
```

For a division operation, if the numerator or denominator contains an operation with a lower precedence than the division operation, it needs to enclosed in a pair of parentheses. The first pair of parentheses is required to specify that the subtraction operation $x - 5$ is evaluated before the division operation. Otherwise, the first half of the above expression would become `5 - x/2`, in which case the expression $x/2$ is evaluated before the result is subtracted from 5. Although the second pair of parentheses is redundant, it clearly shows that the multiplication operation `2*x` for the mathematical expression $2x$ is performed before the subtraction of 4. When x is 3, the evaluation tree and step-by-step evaluation for the expression `y = (5-x)/2+(2*x)-4` are shown in Figure 4.2. In an evaluation tree, the number inside a circle above an operation indicates the sequence of the operation during the evaluation. The number below an operation is the result of the operation.

When a complicated arithmetic expression is encountered in a program, it is divided into simplier subexpressions. Each subexpression will consist of one operator and one or more operands. For example, expression `2*(1/2 + (3.0 - 5))`, such that `3.0 - 5` for `-2.0`, will be calculated first, followed by `1/2 + (-2.0)` for `-2.0` (expression `1/2 = 0`), and finally `2*(-2.0)` for `-4.0`. Again, the result is different

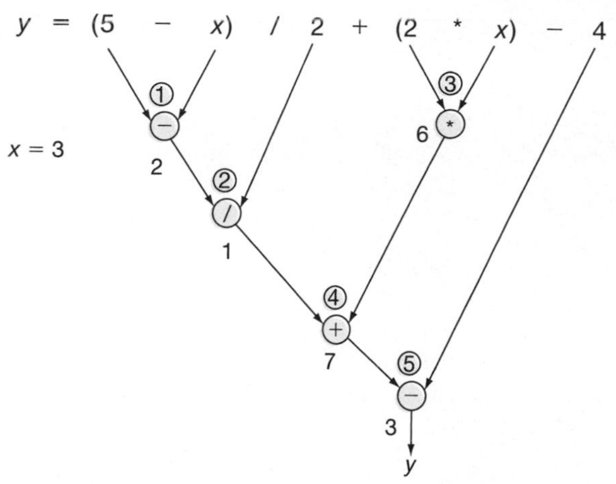

Figure 4.2: The evaluation tree for `y = (5-x)/2+(2*x)-4`.

from the equivalent mathematical expression due to the implicit data type conversions taking place. In general, one should be cautious with mixing different data types when performing assignment or arithmetic operations. As illustrated above, the mixing of floating-point data types with integral data types for arithmetic operations might result in undesirable answers.

Application Examples

Solving Quadratic Equations

A quadratic (a second-order polynomial) equation

$$ax^2 + bx + c = 0 \tag{4.1}$$

can be solved by the formulas

$$x_1 = \frac{-b + \sqrt{b^2 - 4ac}}{2a} \tag{4.2}$$

$$x_2 = \frac{-b - \sqrt{b^2 - 4ac}}{2a} \tag{4.3}$$

According to the formulas (4.2) and (4.3), two solutions of $x_1 = 2$ and $x_2 = 3$ for equation

$$x^2 - 5x + 6 = 0$$

with $a = 1$, $b = -5$, and $c = 6$, can be obtained by Program 4.1.

A multiplication operation has higher precedence than an addition operation, the mathematical expression $b^2 - 4ac$ can be translated into the C expression `(b*b-4*a*c)`, which is the same as `((b*b)-(4*a*c))`.

The commonly used mathematical expression $\sqrt{x}$ for the square root of x can be calculated by the mathematical function **sqrt**`(x)`. This mathematical function takes one argument `x` and returns a value of double type for the square root of `x`. A program using this function needs to include the header file **math.h**, in which function **sqrt**`(x)` is declared. Details about functions in C are described in Chapter 6.

```
/* File: quadratic.c
   Solve for two roots of the quadratic equation x^2-5x+6 = 0  */
#include <stdio.h>
#include <math.h>   /* for sqrt() */

int main() {
    /* declare variables for the coefficients
       of the quadratic equation and roots;
       initialize the coefficients */
    double a = 1.0, b = -5.0, c = 6.0, x1, x2;

    /* solve for two roots of the quadratic equation */
    x1 = (-b+sqrt(b*b-4*a*c))/(2*a);   /* first branch */
    x2 = (-b-sqrt(b*b-4*a*c))/(2*a);   /* second branch */

    /* display two roots */
    printf("x1 = %f\n", x1);
    printf("x2 = %f\n", x2);
    return 0;
}
```

Program 4.1: The solution for $x^2 - 5x + 6 = 0$.

Using the mathematical function **sqrt()**, the formula (4.2) is translated into the C expression as

```
x1 = (-b+sqrt(b*b-4*a*c))/(2*a);
```

The expression $-b + \sqrt{b^2 - 4ac}$ is enclosed in a pair of parentheses to make sure that this numerator is calculated before it is divided by the denominator of the expression $2a$.

Note that there is no exponential operator in C. The mathematical function **pow**(x,y) with two arguments can be used to calculate the exponential expression x^y. The mathematical expression b^2 can be translated into the C expression either in the form of `b*b` or `pow(b,2.0)`. The former is more efficient because each function call, such as `pow(b,2.0)`, has some computational overhead. A less-efficient C statement for equation (4.2) is as follows:

```
x1 = (-b+sqrt(pow(b,2.0)-4*a*c))/(2*a);
```

Given $a = 1.0$, $b = -5.0$, $c = 6.0$, the evaluation tree and step by step evaluation for `x1` in Program 4.1 are shown in Figure 4.3. The output of Program 4.1 is as follows:

```
x1 = 3.000000
x2 = 2.000000
```

The square root of a negative value is a complex number. If the result is constrained in the real domain, the value is NaN. Programs 17.5 and 17.7 in Chapter 17 solve a general quadratic equation using complex numbers in the complex domain.

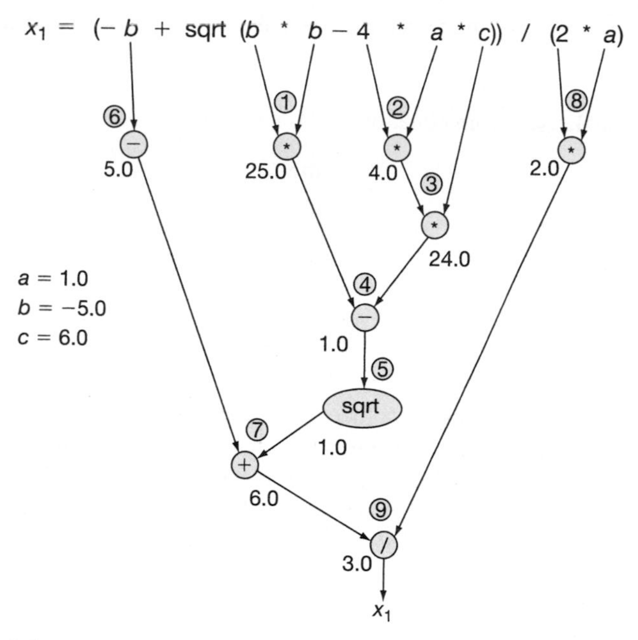

Figure 4.3 The evaluation tree for `x1 = (-b+sqrt(b*b-4*a*c))/(2*a)`.

Using the Law of Sines

Most elementary mathematical functions, including trigonometric functions, are readily available in C. They are also declared in the header file **math.h**. The commonly used trigonometric functions **sin(), cos(),** and **tan()** meaning sine, cosine, and tangent respectively, return a value of double type. The unit for the angular argument of these trigonometric functions is in radians, not in degrees. These mathematical functions are very useful for applications in engineering and science.

For example, for the triangle shown in Figure 4.4, the sides of the triangle are a, b, and c and the angles opposite to those sides are α, β, and γ. The law of sines states

$$\frac{a}{\sin\alpha} = \frac{b}{\sin\beta} = \frac{c}{\sin\gamma} \tag{4.4}$$

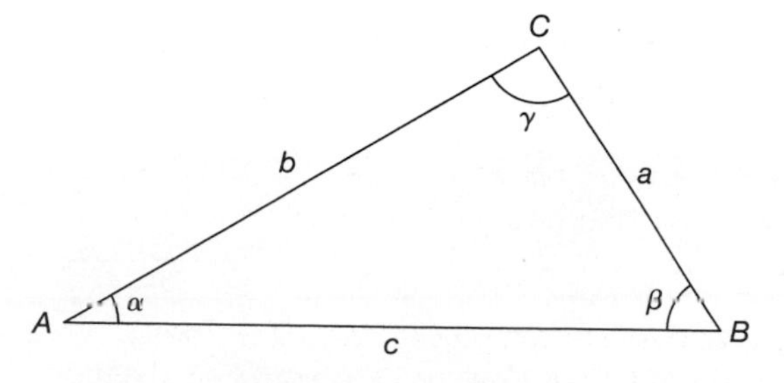

Figure 4.4 A triangle.

The sine law is useful when computing the remaining sides of a triangle if two angles and a side are known. It can also be used when two sides and one of the non-enclosing angles are known. As an example, given the side $a = 10$, angles $\alpha = 90$ degrees, and $\gamma = 60$ degrees, we can obtain the side c. The formula for calculating the side c can be derived from equation (4.4) as follows:

$$c = \frac{a \sin \gamma}{\sin \alpha} \tag{4.5}$$

Based on this formula, Program 4.2 computes the side c with the output as follows:

```
c = 8.660254
```

To use the function **sin()**, a program needs to include the header file **math.h**. Because the unit for angles used in trigonometric functions is the radian, we need to change angles α and γ (given in degrees) into radians first, before they are passed to the function **sin()**. Note that the macro **M_PI** for π is not part of the C standard. However, it is defined in the header file **math.h** in most implemetations. In case it is not available in a system, you may add the following macro inside the code.

```
#define M_PI  3.14159265358979323846
```

Alternatively, define macro **M_PI** in the command line as described in section 4.14 of Chapter 4 for compiling Program 4.2 using Visual C++ in Windows.

```
/* File: sinelaw.c
   Calculate side c based on the sine law,
   given side a and two angles alpha and gamma */
#include <stdio.h>
#include <math.h>  /* for macro M_PI and function sin()
                      in the C standard math lib */

int main() {
    /* declare variables for sides and angles of a triangle */
    double a, c, alpha, gamma;

    a = 10.0;                /* side a */
    alpha = 90.0*M_PI/180; /* change 90 degrees into radian */
    gamma = 60.0*M_PI/180; /* change 60 degrees into radian */

    /* compute side c based on sine law and display the result */
    c = a*sin(gamma)/sin(alpha);
    printf("c = %f\n", c);
    return 0;
}
```

Program 4.2: Computing side c based on the sine law.

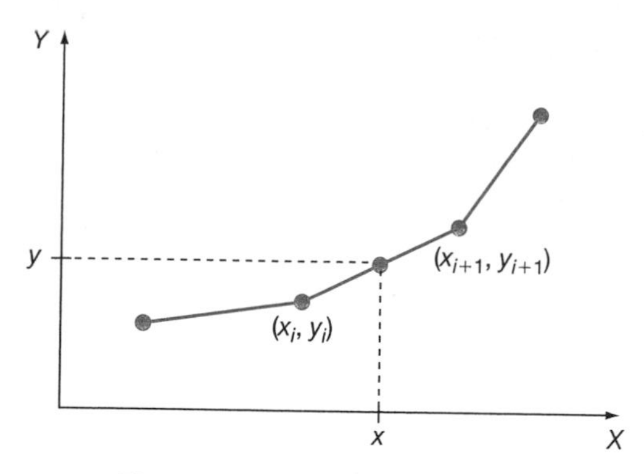

Figure 4.5 Linear interpolation.

Linear Interpolation

Interpolation is for estimation of values between data points. The simplest method of interpolation is called linear interpolation, shown in Figure 4.5. In this case, every two adjacent points are connected with a straight line. The value of y for any x between two adjacent points (x_i, y_i) and (x_{i+1}, y_{i+1}) can be obtained by the equation for the straight line connecting these two points as follows:

$$y = y_i + \frac{y_{i+1} - y_i}{x_{i+1} - x_i}(x - x_i) \tag{4.6}$$

In a linear interpolation, a straight line of a first-order polynomial is used to connect the two adjacent points. For a smoother interpolation, a second- or third-order polynomial or cubic spline can be used to interpolate for the values between every two points. The coefficients of the polynomial or cubic spline are determined by using additional data points that are adjacent to the two data points. The theoretical background for the determination of coefficients of cubic spline is beyond the scope of this book. However, the numerical function **interp1()** in Ch is implemented using cubic splines. It can be used conveniently for the interpolation of data. Similarly, the function **interp2()** can be used for two-dimensional interpolation.

As an application example of linear interpolation, consider a moving body. Its position y is measured at various times t and is recorded in Table 4.3. These data points are plotted with straight lines connecting the adjacent points shown in Figure 4.6. Using linear interpolation, we can find the position 11.90 m of the body at the time of 11 seconds based on the two adjacent data points (10, 10.4) and (12, 13.4) for time and position using Program 4.3. The multiplication and division operators have the same precedence. Therefore, the linear interpolation formula (4.6) can be translated into a programming statement either in the form

```
y = y1 + (y2-y1)*(t-t1)/(t2-t1);
```

Table 4.3 Time and position for a moving body.

t (seconds)	0	3	5	8	10	12	15	18
y (meters)	2	5.2	6	10	10.4	13.4	14.8	18

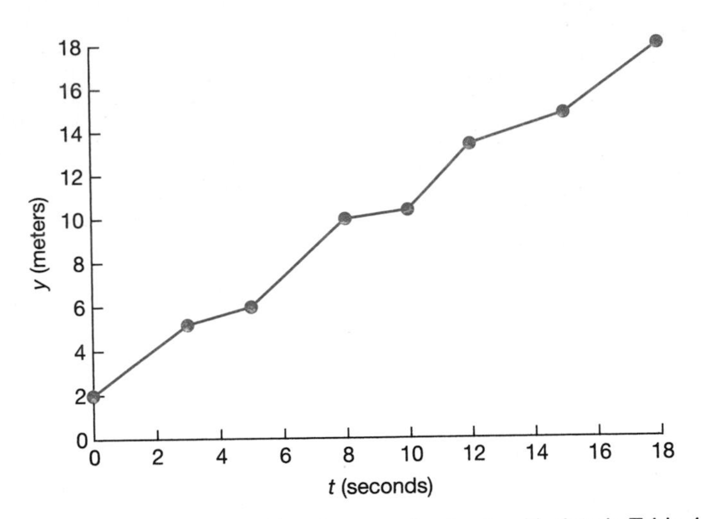

Figure 4.6 Position versus time for a moving body with data in Table 4.3.

```
/* File: interp.c
   Calculate the position y of a moving body when time t
   is 11 seconds based on linear interpolation,
   given two points (t1, y1) and (t2, y2). */
#include <stdio.h>

int main() {
    /* declare variables for times and positions */
    double t1, t2, y1, y2, t, y;

    /* assign two data points */
    t1 = 10.0;
    y1 = 10.4;
    t2 = 12.0;
    y2 = 13.4;

    /* Assign the time at which the position is to be found */
    t  = 11.0;

    /* interpolate the data to get the position y at t=11 */
    y = y1 + (y2-y1)*(t-t1)/(t2-t1);
    /* or y = y1 + (y2-y1)/(t2-t1)*(t-t1); */

    /* display output */
    printf("y = %f (m) at t = %f (second)\n", y, t);
    return 0;
}
```

Program 4.3: Calculating the position at 11 seconds using linear interpolation.

or

```
y = y1 + (y2-y1)/(t2-t1)*(t-t1);
```

In the first case, the product `(y2-y1)*(t-t1)` will be calculated first. It is then divided by `(t2-t1)`. In the second case, the division of `(y2-y1)/(t2-t1)` will be performed first. The quotient is then multiplied by `(t-t1)`. Because the addition operator has higher precedence than the assignment operator, the addition operation with `y1` and assignment operation are performed afterwards in both cases. The output of Program 4.3 is as follows:

```
y = 11.900000 (m) at t = 11.000000 (second)
```

4.5 Relational Operators

For operations using relational operators given in Table 4.4, the result is always an integer with a logic value of 1 or 0 corresponding to **true** or **false**, which are predefined system constants in the header file **stdbool.h** as described in section 3.7 in Chapter 3. The result is true if the comparison is correct, and false otherwise. For example,

```
> int i = 5, j = 3
> i < j
0                    // false
> i <= j
0                    // false
> i == j
0                    // false
> j == j
1                    // true
> i > j
1                    // true
> i >= j
1                    // true
> i != j
1                    // true
```

Table 4.4 Relational operators.

Operator	Operation	Description
<	$x < y$	less than comparison
<=	$x <= y$	less or equal comparison
==	$x == y$	equal comparison
>=	$x >= y$	greater or equal comparison
>	$x > y$	greater comparison
!=	$x != y$	not equal comparison

```
> i != i
0                           // false
```

A floating-point number typically cannot be represented exactly in a computer. The relative errors of floating-point expressions are accumulated during the calculation. Therefore, relational operators == and != for comparison of two floating-point numbers should be used with caution. As we presented in section 3.15 in Chapter 3, the result of the floating-point multiplication expression `f1*f2` for variables `f1` and `f2` of type float, with `f1` of 0.2 and `f2` of 0.3, does not equal the floating-point constant 0.06 of double or float type as shown below.

```
> float f1 = 0.2, f2 = 0.3
> printf("%f", f1*f2)
0.060000
> printf("%f", 0.06)
0.060000
> printf("%.20f", f1*f2)
0.06000000238418579100
> printf("%.20f", 0.06)
0.05999999999999999800
> f1*f2 == 0.06
0
> f1*f2 != 0.06               // 0.06  is type double
1
> f1*f2 != 0.06F              // 0.06F is type float
1
```

Rather than comparing two floating-point numbers `x` and `y` with data types float or double equal to each other as `x == y` or `x - y == 0`, it is better to compare if the absolute value of the difference of these two numbers are smaller than a very small number say, in the order of 10^{-7}. The code below determines if the floating-point values of `x` and `y` are equal or very close to each other.

```
#include <math.h>   /* for use fabs() */
#include <float.h> /* for use FLT_EPSILON */
double x, y, error;
...
error = x - y;   /* error is defined as (x-y) */
if(fabs(error) < FLT_EPSILON) {
   /* error is close to 0.0 */
}
```

where the mathematical function **fabs()** for calculating the absolute value of its argument of double type is declared in the header file **math.h**. The machine epsilon **FLT_EPSILON**, described in detail in section 16.5 of Chapter 16, is the difference between 1 and the smallest value greater than 1 that is representable in float. The macro **FLT_EPSILON** defined in the header file **float.h** typically has the value of 1.19209290E-07 when the size of the float type is 4 bytes. It is commonly used in a convergence criterion for numerical algorithms as shown in Programs 5.14, 5.17, and 6.18 for calculating e^x, the square root of numbers, and roots of nonlinear equations, respectively. Details about the **if** statement will be described in Chapter 5.

4.6 Logical Operators

There are three logical operators in Table 4.5. Table 4.6 summarizes all the logical operations available. The logical negation operator (`!`), also called the logical NOT operator, is a unary operator, whereas `&&` and `||` are binary operators.

If the operand of the unary logical negation operator `!` is nonzero, the result is true. Otherwise, the result is false. The operand can be either an integral or floating point value, as shown in Program 4.4. The output from Program 4.4 is as follows:

```
!0 = 1
!1 = 0
!0.0 = 1
!0.1 = 0
!x = 0
!y = 1
y > x = 0
!(y > x) = 1
```

The logical AND operator (`&&`) can be used to check to see whether both the conditions of its two operands are true. If both conditions are true, then the operation returns true. Otherwise, the operation is false. For the logical OR (`||`), either one or both of its operands has to be true for the operation to be true. For example,

```
> int i = 6, j = 3
> (i > 0) && (i < 5)
0        // false: 2nd condition is false
> (i > 0) || (i < 5)
1        // true: 1st condition is true, 2nd is false (not checked)
```

Logical operators are typically used to form more complex conditions for a loop or **if** statement. Using logical operators in this way eliminates the need for nested **if** statements. For example,

```
if((a < b) && (c < d))
    statement
```

Table 4.5 Logical operators.

Operator	Operation	Description
!	!x	logic negation operator
&&	x && y	logic AND operator
||	x || y	logic inclusive OR operator

Table 4.6 Logical operations.

x	y	!x	x && y	x || y
0	0	1	0	0
0	1	1	0	1
1	0	0	0	1
1	1	0	1	1

```
/* File: notop.c
   Demonstrate working principle of the negation operator ! */
#include <stdio.h>

int main() {
   double x = 4.0, y = 0;

   /* when the operand is an integer */
   printf("!0 = %d\n", !0);
   printf("!1 = %d\n", !1);

   /* when the operand is a floating-point number */
   printf("!0.0 = %d\n", !0.0);
   printf("!0.1 = %d\n", !0.1);

   /* when the operand is a variable */
   printf("!x = %d\n", !x);
   printf("!y = %d\n", !y);

   /* when the operand is an expression */
   printf("y > x = %d\n", y > x);
   printf("!(y > x) = %d\n", !(y > x));
   return 0;
}
```

Program 4.4: Example of a logical negation operator.

is equivalent to

```
if(a < b) {
  if(c < d)
    statement
}
```

The details about **if** statements will be described in Chapter 5.

The `&&` and `||` operations have a "short circuit" behavior. The right operand of the `&&` operation will be evaluated only if the left operand evaluates to **true**. But, the right operand of the `||` operation will be evaluated only if the left operand evaluates to **false**. For example, one may write the code

```
if(x != 0 && y/x < 10)
   statement
```

to test a condition if the expression y/x is less than 10. The short circuit behavior of the logical AND operation `&&` ensures that when x is 0, the division by 0 will not be performed.

An Application Example

Determining a Leap Year

Problem Statement:

A given year is a leap year if one of the following two conditions are satisfied: (a) if it divides exactly by four, but cannot be divided exactly by 100 or (b) if it divides exactly by 400. For example, 2012 is a leap year because it can be divided exactly by four, but cannot be divided exactly by 100. 2000 is also a leap year because it divides exactly by 400. On the other hand, neither 2100 nor 2200 is a leap year. Write a program to determine if a given year read from the user input is a leap year or not.

A given year can be represented using a variable `year` of int type. The modulus operator `%` can be used to determine if an integer can be divided exactly by another integer. The remainder of the modulus operation `year%4` is zero if `year` can be divided exactly by four. The remainder of the modulus operation `year%100` is not zero if `year` cannot be divided exactly by 100. Therefore, the condition (a) for a leap year can be expressed using the relational operators `==` and `!=` along with the logical AND operator `&&` in the following C expression:

```
(year%4 == 0) && (year%100 != 0)
```

If a given year satisfies the condition (a) as a leap year, the above expression evaluates to 1 (true). The parentheses in the above expression are just for clarity. The modulus operator `%` has higher precedence than relatonal operators as shown in Table 4.2. The relational operators `==` and `!=` have higher precedence than the logic AND operator `&&`. Therefore, the above expression can be written wthout parentheses as follows:

```
year%4 == 0 && year%100 != 0
```

Although white spaces in an expression are ignored by a compiler or interpreter, they can make the code more readable. For example, the following expression will be less readable than the previous two expressions:

```
year % 4 == 0 && year % 100 != 0
```

If a year divides exactly by 400 for the condition (b) for a leap year, the relational expression

```
year%400 == 0
```

evaluates to 1. If either the condition (a) or condition (b) is true, the value of the following C expression evaluates to 1 (true):

```
year%4 == 0 && year%100 != 0 || year%400 == 0
```

Program 4.5 is designed using the above logical expression as the conditional expression of an **if** statement. If the conditional expression evaluates to 1 (true) for a given year, it is displayed as a leap year. Otherwise, it is displayed as a non-leap year. An interactive execution of Program 4.5 is shown below:

```
> leapyear.c
Please input a year
2012
2012 is a leap year.
```

```c
/* File: leapyear.c
   Determine if a year input from the terminal is a leap year */
#include <stdio.h>

int main() {
   int year;    /* year (input from the user) */

   /* prompt the user for input */
   printf("Please input a year\n");
   scanf("%d", &year);

   /* determine if the year is a leap year or not, and display the output */
   if(year%4 == 0 && year%100 != 0 || year%400 == 0)
     printf("%d is a leap year.\n", year);
   else
     printf("%d is not a leap year.\n", year);
   return 0;
}
```

Program 4.5: Determining if a given year is a leap year.

4.7 ‡Bitwise Operators

The six bitwise operators are shown in Table 4.7. These operators can be applied only to integral data types. The returned data type depends on the data types of the operands. The result of the unary operator ~ keeps the data type of its operand. The results of binary operators &, |, and ^ will have the higher data type of two operands. The binary operators << and >> return the data type of the left operand.

Table 4.7 Bitwise operators.

<table>
<tr><th>Operator</th><th>Operation</th><th>Name</th><th>Description</th></tr>
<tr><td>&</td><td>i&j</td><td>bitwise inclusive AND</td><td>The result bit is set to 1 if the corresponding bits in i and j are both 1.</td></tr>
<tr><td>|</td><td>i|j</td><td>bitwise inclusive OR</td><td>The result bit is set to 1 if at least one of the corresponding bits in i and j is 1.</td></tr>
<tr><td>^</td><td>i^j</td><td>bitwise exclusive OR</td><td>The result bit is set to 1 if exactly one of the corresponding bits in i and j is 1.</td></tr>
<tr><td><<</td><td>i<<j</td><td>left shift</td><td>Shifts the bits of i by the number of bits specified by j; fill from right with 0 bits.</td></tr>
<tr><td>>></td><td>i>>j</td><td>right shift</td><td>Shifts the bits of i by the number of bits specified by i; the filling from the left is implementation dependent.</td></tr>
<tr><td>~</td><td>~i</td><td>bitwise one's complement</td><td>Sets all 0 bits of i to 1, and all 1 bits to 0.</td></tr>
</table>

The bitwise AND (&), inclusive OR (|), and exclusive OR (^) operators are used to compare two operands bit by bit. The bitwise AND (&) sets each bit of the result to 1 if the corresponding bits in the two operands are both 1. The bitwise inclusive OR (|) sets each bit of the result to 1 if at least one of the corresponding bits in the converted operands is set to 1, whereas the bitwise exclusive OR (^) sets each bit of the result to 1 if exactly one of the corresponding bits in the converted operands is set to 1.

The left shift operator (<<) shifts the first operand to the left by the number of bits specified by the second operand. The shifted bits on the right are filled with 0 bits. When a lvalue is shifted by 1 bit, it is equivalent to multiplying it by 2. On the other hand, the right shift operator (>>) right-shifts the first operand by the number of bits specified by the second operand. The C standard does not specify the method of filling from the left; it is implementation dependent. In most implementations, however, it follows *arithmetic right shift*, in which the most significant bit (MSB) is shifted in. Thus, if a number with 8 bits is 0b00000110 and we right-shift by 1, we get 0b00000011. However, for a signed number with 8 bits of 0b10000110, we would get 0b11000011. However, for an unsigned number with 8 bits of 0b10000110, we would still get 0b00000011. In the *arithmetic right shift*, when a lvalue is shifted to the right by 1 bit, it is equivalent to dividing by 2. The sign of the value is preserved. If a zero is shifted in, it is called a *logical right shift*.

The bitwise one's complement operator (~) sets all the 0 bits of the operand to 1 and all the 1 bits to 0.

The following example using binary constants in Ch illustrates how bitwise operators can be used.

```
> int i
> i = 0b00000101 & 0b00001111
5                       // i = 0b00000101
> i = 0b00000011 | 0b00000111
7                       // i = 0b00000111
> i << 1                // left shift 1 bit
14                      // 0b00001110, fill from right with 0
> i >> 2                // right shif 2 bits
1                       // 0b00000001, fill from left with 0
> ~i
-2                      // 0b11111111111111111111111111111110
```

Note that the result of the shift operations have no effect on the the left operand. To change the value of a shifted variable, an assignment operation can be used to change the value of the left operand. For example,

```
> i = (i << 1)
```

will shift the variable `i` by 1 bit.

Program 4.6 is another example of bitwise operations. In this program, operations are performed on binary numbers `a = 0b10110100` and `b = 0b11011001` of char type with 8 bits. Note that to print out a character with a field width of 8 bits, even when the value of the leading bit is 0, the format specifier `"%8b"` is used. The details about the field width of format specifiers for input and output functions are described in section 3.15.1 in Chapter 3 and Chapter 9. When the char type is signed by default, the output of Program 4.6 is as follows:

```
a =        0b10110100
b =        0b11011001
a & b =    0b10010000
```

```
/* File: bitop.ch (run in Ch only)
   Apply bitwise operators to variables with 1 byte.
   Ch features used: the printing format "%b" and binary constant 0bxxxx */
#include <stdio.h>

int main() {
    /* declare variables and initialize with binary numbers */
    char a = 0b10110100;
    char b = 0b11011001, c;

    /* apply bitwise operators to variables a and b
       and display the result */
    printf("a =      0b%8b\n", a);
    printf("b =      0b%8b\n", b);
    c = a & b;
    printf("a & b =  0b%8b\n", c);
    c = a | b;
    printf("a | b =  0b%8b\n", c);
    c = a ^ b;
    printf("a ^ b =  0b%8b\n", c);
    c = b << 1;
    printf("b << 1 = 0b%8b\n", c);
    c = a >> 1;
    printf("a >> 1 = 0b%8b\n", c);
    c = ~a;
    printf("~a =     0b%8b\n", c);
    return 0;
}
```

Program 4.6: Demonstrating bitwise operations using a Ch program.

```
a | b =  0b11111101
a ^ b =  0b01101101
b << 1 = 0b10110010
a >> 1 = 0b11011010
~a =     0b01001011
```

If the char type were unsigned by default or the data type of variable `a` were declared as an unsigned char in Program 4.6 with initialization in the form

```
unsigned char a = 0b10110100;
```

the output of the statement

```
printf("a >> 1 = 0b%8b\n", c);
```

would become

```
a >> 1 = 0b01011010
```

Program 4.6 uses the printing format `%b` for binary numbers and binary constants starting with the prefix `0b` in Ch. Because the program runs only in Ch right now, the file extension .ch is used. Throughout this book, if a program runs only in Ch, the source has the file extension `.ch`. Program 4.6 and Program 10.30 in Chapter 10 with the file extension `.ch` are the only two programs in Part I of this book that use the features solely available in Ch. All other programs in Part I can be compiled using either C or C++. The features of the printing format `%b` for binary numbers and binary constants starting with the prefix `0b` are good candidates for consideration as new features in the future version of the C standard.

An equivalent program to Program 4.6 (but more complicated) is shown in Program 4.7, which is ISO C standard compliant. Program 4.7, like all other programs presented in this book, runs fine in Ch. The output from Program 4.7 is the same as that from Program 4.6. Program 4.7 uses the function `printbits()` to print bits for the passed character `c` in binary numbers. Inside the function, a **for** loop is used to print all 8 bits. Details about using a **for** loop for repetition will be described in Chapter 5. Functions are presented in Chapter 6. After reading these two chapters, you can then fully understand the techniques used to print the binary representation of a character in the function `printbits()`.

Assume that a variable of char is 1 byte with 8 bits. The position for the leftmost bit is eighth and the rightmost bit is first. The **for** loop inside function `printbit()` prints 8 bits starting with the leftmost bit. The statements in Program 4.7

```
mask = 1 << (i-1);
bit = (c & mask) != 0;
```

```
/* File: bitop.c
   bitop.c is an equivalent C program for the Ch program bitop.ch
   without using the printing format "%b" and binary constant 0bxxxx.
   Apply bitwise operators to variables with 1 byte */
#include <stdio.h>

/* function printbits() prints each bit of the passed argument 'c' */
int printbits(char c) {
    int mask,     /* declare mask */
        num,      /* num of bits for the passed variable */
        i,        /* index variable for the for-loop */
        bit;      /* the binary value 1 or 0 for a bit */
    num = sizeof(char)*8;/* number of bits for a char, 8 bits for a byte */
    /* Assume bit positions are [8 7 6 5 4 3 2 1].  Obtain the binary
       value 1 or 0 at each position, starting with the most left bit */
    for(i=num; i>=1 ; i--) {
        mask = 1 << (i-1); /* (i)th bit of mask is 1
        /* (i)th bit of (c & mask) is 1 only if (i)th bit of c is 1,
           (c & mask) != 0 is 1; Otherwise, it is 0. */
```

Program 4.7: Demonstrating bitwise operations using a C program, the equivalent of Program 4.6. *(Continued)*

```
        bit = (c & mask) != 0;
        printf("%d", bit); /* print either 1 or 0 for the value of bit */
    }
    printf("\n");
    return 0;
}
int main() {
    /* declare variables and initialize with hexadecimal numbers */
    char a = 0xB4;      /*  0xB4 is 0b10110100 */
    char b = 0xD9, c; /*  0xD9 is 0b11011001 */

    /* apply bitwise operators to variables a and b */
    printf("a =       0b");
    printbits(a);
    printf("b =       0b");
    printbits(b);
    c = a & b;
    printf("a & b =  0b");
    printbits(c);
    c = a | b;
    printf("a | b =  0b");
    printbits(c);
    c = a ^ b;
    printf("a ^ b =  0b");
    printbits(c);
    c = b << 1;
    printf("a <<b =  0b");
    printbits(c);
    c = a >> 1;
    printf("a >>b =  0b");
    printbits(c);
    c = ~a;
    printf("~a =      0b");
    printbits(c);
    return 0;
}
```

Program 4.7: *(Continued)*

inside the **for** loop obtains the binary value 1 or 0 for the ith bit of variable `c`. To obtain information for a specific bit of an integral value, a bit-mask is typically used. A bit-mask is often defined as a macro. For example, the bit-mask `MASKBIT3` below can be used to obtain the third bit of integer `c`.

```
#define MASKBIT3 0x0004   /* 0b00000100 */
bit = c & MASKBIT3;
```

The third bit of integral variable `bit` is 1 if the third bit of integer `c` is 1. Otherwise, it is 0. In Program 4.7, the *i*th bit of `mask` is 1 based on the the left shift operation `1 << (i-1)`. The *i*th bit of the result for the bitwise-and operation `(c & mask)` is 1 if and only if the *i*th bit of `c` is 1. Using the relational operator `!=`, the result of the *i*th bit for `c` is assigned to the variable `bit`.

An application example using bitwise-inclusive-or and bitwise-and operations with bit-masks to obtain the information for files and directories is presented in Program 14.22 in section 14.8 of Chapter 14.

4.8 Compound Assignment Operators

Besides the regular assignment operator =, there are ten compound assignment operators: `+=`, `-=`, `*=`, `/=`, `%=`, `&=`, `|=`, `^=`, `<<=`, and `>>=`, which are listed in Table 4.8.

The expression with an assignment operator `op=`, such as

```
lvalue op= rvalue
```

is defined as

```
lvalue = lvalue op rvalue
```

where `lvalue` is any valid lvalue, including complex numbers, and it is evaluated only once. For example, `i += 3` is equivalent to `i = i+3`, as shown below.

```
> int i = 2
> i += 3
5
```

The operators of `+`, `-`, `*`, `/`, `%`, `&`, `|`, `^`, `<<`, and `>>` follow the operation rules discussed in the previous sections.

Table 4.8 Assignment operators.

<table>
<tr><th>Operator</th><th>Operation</th><th>Description</th></tr>
<tr><td>+=</td><td>x += y</td><td>Addition assignment operator</td></tr>
<tr><td>-=</td><td>x -= y</td><td>Subtraction assignment operator</td></tr>
<tr><td>*=</td><td>x *= y</td><td>Multiplication assignment operator</td></tr>
<tr><td>/=</td><td>x /= y</td><td>Division assignment operator</td></tr>
<tr><td>%=</td><td>x %= y</td><td>Modulus assignment operator</td></tr>
<tr><td>=</td><td>x = y</td><td>Assignment operator</td></tr>
<tr><td>&=</td><td>x &= y</td><td>Bitwise AND assignment operator</td></tr>
<tr><td>|=</td><td>x != y</td><td>Bitwise inclusive OR assignment operator</td></tr>
<tr><td>^=</td><td>x ^= y</td><td>Bitwise exclusive OR assignment operator</td></tr>
<tr><td><<=</td><td>x <<= y</td><td>Right shift assignment operator</td></tr>
<tr><td>>>=</td><td>x >>= y</td><td>Left shift assignment operator</td></tr>
</table>

4.9 Increment and Decrement Operators

C is well known for the succinctness of its syntax. The increment operator ++ adds 1 to its operand, whereas the decrement operator -- subtracts 1. If ++ or -- is used as a prefix operator, the expression increments or decrements the operand before its value is used, respectively. If it is used as a postfix operator, the operation will be performed after its value has been used. The operand shall be a valid lvalue. As an example, consider the following:

```
> int i = 5, j
> j = ++i                    // prefix, i++; j = i
6
> i
6
> j = i++                    // postfix, j = i; i++
6
> i
7
```

4.10 Cast Operators for Type Conversions

When the data types of two operands of an arithmetic or assignment operation are different, one of the data types is converted automatically based on the implicit conversion rules, before the operation is performed. Sometimes, it is necessary to convert a value of one type explicitly to a value of another type. For example, based on the conversion rule, when one of the operands for a division operation is a floating-point number and the other is an integer, the operation is performed using a floating-point division. The result of the division is a floating-point number. However, when two variables of int type are divided, the integer result may lose the fractional part of the quotient. Depending on the application, it might be desirable to convert one of the operands into a floating-point number explicitly before the division is performed.

Converting a value of one type explicitly to a value of another type can be achieved by the cast operation

```
(type)expr
```

where `expr` is an expression and `type` is a data type such as int, double, or pointer such as `char *`, `double *`, etc. For example, `(int)9.3`, `(double)9`, `(double *)&i`, and `(double *)iptr` are valid expressions. For example,

```
> int i = 2, j = 3;
> double d
> 2/3
0
> i/j
0
> d = i/j
0.0000
> d = 2.0/3
0.6667
```

```
> d = (double)2/3
0.6667
> d = (double)i/j
0.6667
```

When two integers of constants or variables are divided, the result is an integer. The remainder is discarded as shown for the division of 2 by 3. To keep the remainder for the division of two integers, one of the operands is cast to a floating-point number first. The division of floating-point numbers is then performed, which keeps the remainder. The result of the expressions `(double)2` and `(double)i` with a cast operation is the floating point number 2.0.

4.11 Sizeof Operator

The **sizeof** operator yields the size (in bytes) of its operand. The **sizeof** operator can be applied to any data type to determine the number of bytes required to store that particular data type in memory. It can be applied to either built-in or user-defined data types through **typedef** as described in section 3.12 in Chapter 3 or data structures or classes which will be discussed in Chapters 11, 13, and 19. For example,

```
> sizeof(char)
1
> sizeof(int)
4
> sizeof(float)
4
> sizeof(double)
8
```

It takes 1 byte to store a data of char type. It takes 4 bytes to store either **int** or **float** data. It takes 8 bytes for **double** data. The **sizeof** operator is often used in dynamically allocating memory because it can be used to determine the bytes required for a particular data type.

The operand of the **sizeof** operator can also be a variable or an expression. For example,

```
> int i
> sizeof(i)
4
> sizeof(1)
4
> sizeof(5.0*i)
8
> sizeof(123LL)
8
```

The size of the data type for variable `i` of int type and integer constant 1 is 4. The result of expression `5.0*i` is double type with 8 bytes. The integer constant 123LL of long long type has 8 bytes.

The **sizeof** operator can also be used to determine the size of pointer types and pointer variables. Although the sizes of variables of different types are different, the sizes of variables of different pointer data types, for storing the addresses of different variables, are the same. The size of a variable of pointer data type in 32-bit programming is 4 bytes (32 bts). For 64-bit programming, it is 8 bytes (64 bits), as shown in Table 3.2. For example, in a 32-bit computer,

```
> sizeof(int *)
4
> sizeof(double *)
4
> double *p;
> sizeof(p)
4
```

The result of the operator **sizeof** is an unsigned integer with the type **size_t** defined in the header file **stddef.h**, as described in section 3.12. The result of **sizeof** operation is type unsigned int with 4 bytes in 32-bit machines, as shown below.

```
> sizeof(sizeof(char))
4
```

The type of `sizeof(char)` is **size_t** for unsigned int with 4 bytes for 32-bit programming. In 64-bit machines, the result of the **sizeof** operation is type unsigned long long with 8 bytes, as shown below.

```
> sizeof(sizeof(char))
8
```

4.12 Conditional Operator

The ternary conditional operator '`?:`' introduces a conditional expression in the form of

```
op1 ? op2 : op3
```

In a conditional expression, the first and second operands are separated by a question mark '`?`' and the second and third operands separated by a colon '`:`'. The execution of a conditional expression proceeds as follows:

1. The first operand of the scalar type is evaluated.
2. The second operand is evaluated only if the first does not evaluate to 0. The third operand is evaluated only if the first evaluates to 0.
3. The result is the value of the second or third operand, whichever is evaluated.

For example, the conditional expression 5?1 : 2 will give the value of 1.

```
> 5 ? 1 : 2
1
```

The first operand with the value of 5 is not equal to 0, the second operand with the value of 1 will be the result of the expression. As another example, if x is larger than 3, the conditional expression

```
(x>3) ? 10*x:(x+20)
```

will give the value of $10x$ in the second operand. Otherwise, the expression has the value of $(x + 20)$ in the third operand.

```
> int x = 2
> (x>3) ? 10*x:(x+20)
22
```

As another example, the rounded integer of a floating-point number d can be obtained using a conditional operation directly, as shown below.

```
printf("The rounded integer is %d\n", (int)(d>0?(d+0.5):(d-0.5)));
```

In this case, the rounded integer can be printed out directly without assigning it to a variable of integral type first.

The statement with a conditional expression

```
r = op1 ? op2 : op3;
```

is equivalent to the **if-else** statement below.

```
if(op1 != 0)
  r = op2;
else
  r = op3;
```

The details about the **if-else** statement will be described in Chapter 5.

For the conditional expression

```
op1 ? op2 : op3
```

The first operand of a conditional expression shall have scalar type. For the second and third operands, one of the following shall hold:

1. Both operands have arithmetic type. The result type is determined by the usual arithmetic conversions.
2. Both operands have compatible class, structure, or union types, which will be described in later chapters. The result is the class, structure, or union type.
3. Both operands have type void, which will be described in Chapter 6. The result has type void.
4. Both operands are pointers to compatible types. The result is a pointer to the compatible type.
5. One operand is a pointer and the other is NULL. The result has the type of the operand which is not NULL. NULL is a special value related to pointers, which will be described later in Chapter 11.
6. One operand is a pointer to an object or incomplete type and the other is a pointer to void. The result is a pointer to void.

Conditional expressions are right-associative. For example,

```
op1 ? op2 : op3 ? op4 : op5 ? op6: op7
```

is handled as

```
op1 ? op2 : (op3 ? op4 : (op5 ? op6: op7))
```

For example,

```
> int x = 2
> x>5 ? 1 : x<1 ? 3 : 4 // right-association
4
> x>5 ? 1.0 : 2          // data type conversion
2.0000
> double y
> y = x>5 ? 1.0 : 2
2.0000
```

The expression `x>5 ? 1 : x<1 ? 3 : 4` is treated as `(x>5) ? 1 : ((x<1) ? 3 : 4)`.

More practical application examples of using the conditional operator are given in Program 11.11 in Chapter 11 and in Program 14.4 in Chapter 14.

4.13 ‡Comma Operator

The comma operator '`,`' introduces comma expressions. The comma expression consists of two expressions separated by a comma. For example,

```
a = 1, b = 2;
```

assigns 1 to the variable `a` and 2 to `b`. Two assignment operations are separated by a comma operator. A comma operator is often used in expressions of the for-loop control structure described in Chapter 5.

The comma operator is syntactically left-associative. The following expression

```
a = 1, ++a, a + 10;
```

is equivalent to

```
((a = 1), ++a), a + 10;
```

The left operand of a comma operator is evaluated as a void expression first. Then the right operand is evaluated; the result has its type and value. For example,

```
> a = 1, ++a, a + 10
12
```

The comma operator cannot appear in contexts where a comma is used as a separator, such as the argument list of a function. In these cases, it can be used within parentheses. For example, the exponential function **pow**`(x,y)` has two arguments for exponential expression x^y. It can be used as follows:

```
> double x = 2, y = 3
< pow(x,y)
8.0000
> pow((x=2, x+3), y)          // pow(5, 3)
125.0000
```

where the expression `(x=2, x+3)` is used as the first argument of the function **pow()**.

4.14 Making It Work

4.14.1 Defining a Macro During Compilation for Programs Using M_PI in Visual C++

Program 4.2 uses the macro **M_PI** for π. Although it is not a part of the C standard, it is commonly defined in the header file **math.h**. It is readily available in Unix. However, to expose this macro in Visual C++ in Windows, the program needs to define the macro **_USE_MATH_DEFINES** before including **math.h**, as shown below.

```
#define _USE_MATH_DEFINES
#include <math.h>
```

For most C compilers, a macro can be defined in the command-line option during the compilation with the syntax

```
-DMACRO1 -DMACRO2=value
```

which is equivalent to

```
#define MACRO1 1
#define MACRO2 value
```

inside a C program to be compiled.

By defining a macro during compilation, we can compile Program 4.2 using Visual C++ in Windows in one of two commands below:

```
> cl -D_USE_MATH_DEFINES sinelaw.c
> cl -DM_PI=3.14159265358979323846 sinelaw.c
```

without modifying the code.

4.14.2 Using the C Standard Math Library in GNU C

When a C program is compiled and linked to create a binary executable program, the standard C library, which contains standard functions such as **printf()**, is automatically linked. In Windows, the standard math library is also linked. However, in Unix, the user needs to link the math library explicitly if a program uses math functions, such as **sqrt(), cos(),** and **sqrt()**, by adding the command-line option `-lm` when the binary executable is created. For example, Program 4.2 can be compiled and linked to create a binary executable program `a.out` using the following command:

```
> cc sinelaw.c -lm
```

Without the command-line option `-lm`, the error message

```
sinelaw.c:(.text+0x33): undefined reference to 'sin'
```

or a similar one, will be generated when the object file is linked.

Exercises

1. State whether the following are true/false. If false, briefly explain why.

   a. C operators are evaluated from left to right.

   b. The expression `(x<5 || a>b==1)` is true only if both `x<5` and `a>b` are true.

2. Enclose the following C expressions in parentheses the way a compiler or interpreter would evaluate them. Draw a corresponding evaluation tree for each expression.

   a. `a = b + c`
   b. `a == b || c == d`
   c. `a == b && c > d`
   d. `a = f(x) && a > g(x)`
   e. `a = b >> 2 + 4`
   f. `a == b && x != y`
   g. `a == b || x != y`
   h. `a = b -= 2 + f(2)`
   i. `a = b && a > z ? x : z`
   j. `a = b | c & d ^ e`

3. Given binary numbers `a = 0b1101` and `b = 0b0111`, what are the results of the following expressions in the binary numbers?

   a. `a | b`
   b. `a || b`
   c. `a & b`
   d. `a && b`
   e. `a ^ b | a`
   f. `a < 2 & b > 1`

4. For the following code fragment, what's the output?

```
float f1 = 0.2, f2 = 0.5;
printf("(f1*f1 == 0.1) = %d", f1*f1 == 0.1);
printf("(f1+f1 == 0.07) = %d", f1+f1 == 0.07);
```

5. Function $f(x) = x^2 - 3$ for $x \geq 0$ and its inverse function $f^{-1}(x) = g(x)$ is $\sqrt{x+3}$ with $x \geq -3$ are shown in Figure 4.7. Write a program to calculate $f(4)$ and $g(13)$.

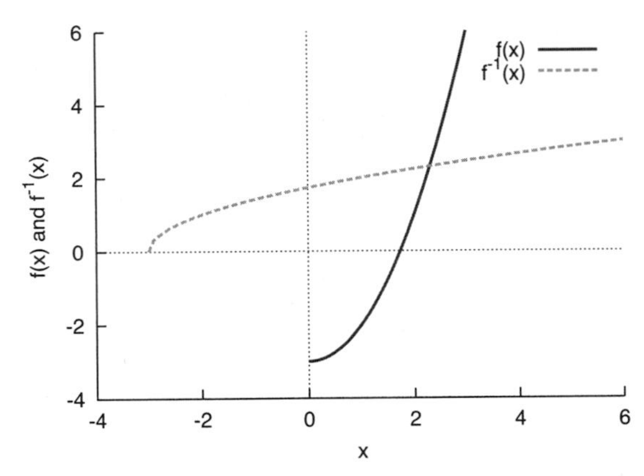

Figure 4.7: Function $f(x)$ and its inverse function $f^{-1}(x)$.

6. Write a program that reads two positive integers x and n of the unsigned int type from the terminal. The program prints out the value of x before and after rotated to the right by n bit positions in binary (The bit in the rightmost position will be moved to the bit in the leftmost position). Test your program using 5 and 3 for x and n, respectively.
7. Write a program that right-shifts an integer variable 3 bits. The program should print the integer in bits before and after the shift operation.
8. Left-shifting an unsigned integer by 1 bit is equivalent to multiplying the value by 2. Write a program `power2.c` that reads two integer arguments *number* and *p* and calculates

$$number * 2^p$$

Use the shift operator to calculate the result. The program should print the values as integers and as bits.

9. Write a program to print out the 7th bit of the following integers:

90, 0X32A, −89, 3563.

10. Computers perform a subtraction such as

```
y = x - value;
```

by adding the binary two's complement of `value` to `x` as follows:

```
y = x +  (~value+1);
```

If `x` is 28 and `value` is 15, use the above formula to calculate `y`. Print out the values of `y, x, value, ~value` and `(~value+1)` as binary numbers.

11. For the following expressions in C, write their corresponding mathematical expressions. You may add proper parentheses to avoid any confusion.

a. `(4/3.0)*3.14*r*r*r`
b. `4/3*3.14*r*r*r`
c. `(9.0/5.0)*c + 32`
d. `9.0/5.0*c + 32`
e. `9.0/5.0*(c + 32)`
f. `9.0+5.0*(c + 32)/(x+y)*3`
g. `9.0+5.0*(c + 32)/(3*(x+y))`
h. `9.0+5.0*c + 32/3*x+y`

12. For the following mathematical expressions, write their corresponding C expressions. You may add proper parentheses to avoid any confusion.

a. $\frac{x+4}{y+5}$
b. $9+5\frac{x+4}{y+5}$
c. $(4/3)3.14r^3$
d. $x < y$
e. $x \geq y$ and $y \leq z$
f. $x \geq y$ and $x \geq 0$
g. $x \leq 1$ or $x > 20$
h. $1 < x \leq 20$
i. $1 < x \leq 20$ or $3 \geq y \geq 1$

13. Write a program to compute the rim area of a washer with the diameters for the inner and outer circles of 3 and 5 centimeters, respectively.

14. The formula for the area of a circle is πr^2, where r is the radius of the circle. If the area of a circle is 20 m^2, write a program to calculate the radius of the circle.

15. The formula for the surface area of a sphere is $4\pi r^2$, where r is the radius of the sphere. If the area of a sphere is 25 m^2, write a program to calculate the radius of the sphere.

16. The straight-line distance of two points (x_1, y_1) and (x_2, y_2) in a Cartesian plane can be calculated by the formula

$$d = \sqrt{(x_1 - x_2)^2 + (y_1 - y_2)^2}$$

a. Write a program to calculate the distance for the points (2, 3) and (4, 5) in a plane.
b. Write a program to calculate the distance for the points (4, 3) and (6, 5) in a plane.
c. Write a program to calculate the distance for the points (1, 3) and (4, 2) in a plane.

17. Solve the following quadratic equations. If there is no solution in the real domain, the result of NaN, which stands for Not-a-Number, might be printed out.

a. $2x^2 - 4x + 1 = 0$
b. $x^2 + 2x + 1 = 0$
c. $5x^2 + 2x - 3 = 0$
d. $4x^2 + 3x + 7 = 0$
e. $x^2 - 4x + 4 = 0$

18. The mathematical formula for the total amount of the money invested with the interest compounded annually is

$$y = p(1 + r)^n$$

where y is the total amount, p the principal invested, r the interest rate, and n the number of years. Write a program to calculate the total amount of the money after 30 years for the invested principal of $10,000 with an 8 percent interest rate.

19. Calculate the values of the following functions for each one at $x = 3.5$.

a. $g_1(x) = 2x\sin(x) + \cos(x) + \dfrac{4x + 3}{3x^2 + 2x + 4}$

b. $g_2(x) = x^2\sqrt{2x}$

c. $g_3(x) = 2x\sin(x) + \cos(x^2\sqrt{2x})$

d. $g_4(x) = \dfrac{3x^2 + 4x + 3}{5\sin(x^2) + 4x^2 + 3}$

20. Calculate the values of the following functions for each one at $x = 3.5$ and $y = 4.2$.

a. $g_5(x, y) = 2x\sin(y) + \cos(x) + \dfrac{4x + 3}{3x^2 + 2y + 4}$

b. $g_6(x) = x^2\sqrt{2y}$

c. $g_7(x) = 2x\sin(y) + \cos(y^2\sqrt{2x})$

d. $g_8(x, y) = \dfrac{3x^2 + 4y + 3}{5\sin(y^2) + 4x^2 + 6}$

21. Given the lengths a, b, and c of the sides of a triangle shown in Figure 4.4, the area of the triangle can be calculated by the formula

$$area = \sqrt{s(s - a)(s - b)(s - c)}$$

where s is the semiperimeter of the triangle defined as

$$s = \frac{a + b + c}{2}$$

Write a program to calculate the area of a triangle with the lengths a, b, and c given as follows:

a. $a = 2\text{cm}, b = 3\text{cm}, c = 4\text{cm}$
b. $a = 3\text{m}, b = 4\text{m}, c = 5\text{m}$
c. $a = 4\text{in}, b = 5\text{in}, c = 6\text{in}$

22. For a triangle with lengths a, b, and c and inner angles α, β, and γ shown in Figure 4.4, the law of cosines states that

$$c^2 = a^2 + b^2 - 2ab\cos(\gamma)$$

or, equivalently,

$$b^2 = a^2 + c^2 - 2ac\cos(\beta)$$

$$a^2 = b^2 + c^2 - 2bc\cos(\alpha)$$

If the angle γ is a right angle, the law of cosines reduces to

$$c^2 = a^2 + b^2$$

which is the Pythagorean theorem.

a. Write a program to calculate the length a when $b = 3$, $c = 5$, and $\alpha = 30°$.
b. Write a program to calculate the length b when $a = 4$, $c = 6$, and $\beta = 45°$.
c. Write a program to calculate the length c when $a = 5$, $b = 7$, and $\gamma = 60°$.
d. Write a program to calculate the angle α when $a = 2.83$, $b = 3$, and $c = 5$.
e. Write a program to calculate the angle β when $a = 4.83$, $b = 4$, and $c = 5$.
f. Write a program to calculate the angle γ when $a = 3.83$, $b = 5$, and $c = 6$.

23. An automatic screw machine produces a right circular cylindrical surface with a diameter of 0.25 in. The setup proof part had a diameter of 0.2482 in. After 600 parts have been produced, the final diameter was 0.2516 in. Some data for this production run are shown below.

n	0	100	200	300	400	500	600
y (in)	0.2482	0.2485	0.2495	0.250	0.2506	0.2511	0.2516

Find the diameter of the part at the point where 350 parts have been produced using linear interpolation as specified.

24. The table gives the disposable personal income (personal income less income tax) in the United States in billions of dollars between 1990 and 2000 (Source: Bureau of Economic Analysis, U. S. Department of Commerce).

Year	1990	1992	1994	1996	1998	1999	2000
Disposable personal income	4166.8	4613.7	5018.9	5534.7	6320.0	6618.0	7031.0

Find the disposable personal income in 1997 using linear interpolation.

25. The table gives the annual profit in dollars made by a company.

Year	1970	1975	1980	1985	1990	1995	2000	2005
Profit	52,500	56,700	59,800	63,500	67,700	68,700	72,000	75,400

Find the profit of the company in 1998 using linear interpolation.

26. Puma 560 (shown in Figure 4.8) is one of the earliest industrial robot manipulators developed for industrial automation. The robot has six degrees of freedom. The end-effector of the robot arm can reach a point within its workspace from any direction. The robot arm mimics a human arm and has eight different configurations in total. The configuration of the robot arm can be left or right arm, above or below elbow, and flip or no-flip wrist. To control the robot, it is often necessary to figure out the configuration of the arm for motion planning, trajectory generation, and collision avoidance. As shown in the code below, three bit-masks, `RIGHT`, `BELOW`, and `FLIP`, corresponding to the right arm, below elbow, and flip wrist are defined. For the convenience of programming, masks `LEFT`, `ABOVE`, and `NOFLIP`, corresponding to the left arm, above elbow, and no-flip wrist are also defined. A configuration for the robot is given in an integer variable `puma_conf` as right arm, above elbow, and no-flip wrist has been specified by bitwise-inclusive-or operations. Write a program to find the configuration of the arm based on the configuration variable `puma_conf` and print out the robot configuration.

```
/* define bit-masks for configuration of Puma 560 */
#define RIGHT   0x0001 /* 0b0001 right arm      */
```

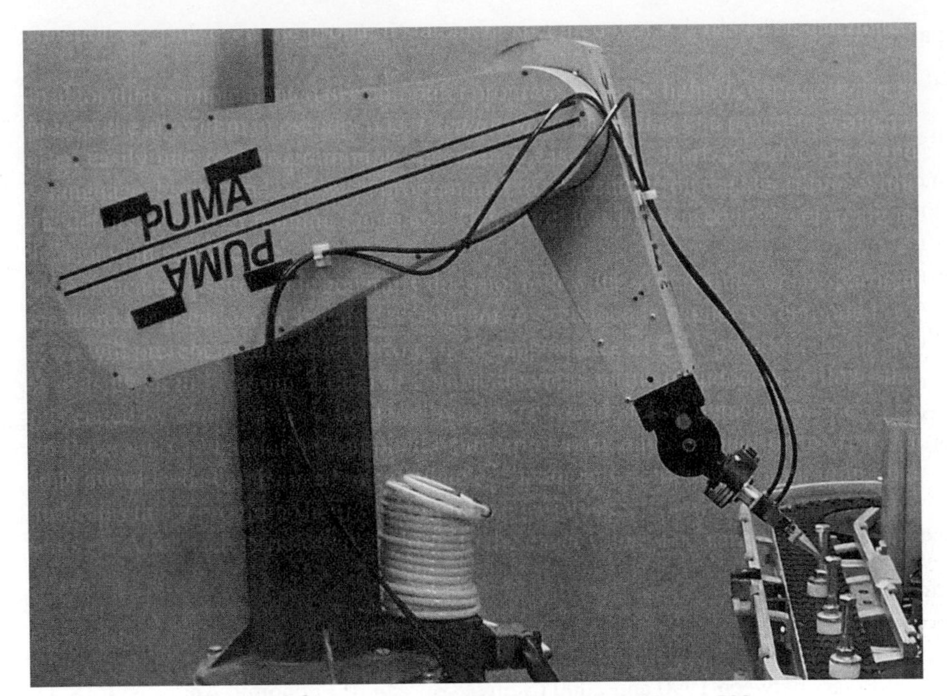

Figure 4.8: An industrial robot manipulator, Puma 560.

```
#define LEFT    0x0000 /* 0b0000 left arm      */
#define BELOW   0x0002 /* 0b0010 below elbow   */
#define ABOVE   0x0000 /* 0b0000 above elbow   */
#define FLIP    0x0004 /* 0b0100 flip wrist    */
#define NOFLIP 0x0000 /* 0b0000 no flip wrist */

int puma_conf = RIGHT|ABOVE|NOFLIP; /* robot configuration */
```

27. Write the output of the following Ch program when it is executed.

```
#include <stdio.h>
int main() {
    int i1 = 0b00001001;
    int i2 = 0b0001111;
    printf("i1 | i2 + 4 = %b\n", i1 | i2+4);
    printf("i1 & i2 + 4 = %b\n", i1 & i2+4);
    return 0;
}
```

28. In serial data transmission, a parity bit is added to make sure that the number of 1s in the transmitted data is either even or odd. In the even-parity transmission, the parity bit is set to either 1 or 0 to make sure the total number of 1s in the transmitted data is even. If an odd number of bits is changed in transmission, the total number of 1s in the received data will not be even, which indicates that an error in transmission has occurred. Write a program to read a character. Print out the input character as a binary number with

8 bits. Determine the number of 1s in its binary representation using bit masks

```
#define MASKBIT1 0x0001 /* 0b00000001 */
...
#define MASKBIT8 0x0080 /* 0b10000000 */
```

Test input characters '3' and '4'.

29. The temperature c in Celsius and the temperature f in Fahrenheit are related by the formula

$$f = \frac{9c}{5} + 32$$

Correct the error below for converting the temperature 40 degrees in Celsius to Fahrenheit.

```
printf("40 degrees in Celsius is %f degrees in Fahrenheit\n", 9*40/5+32);
```

30. The formula for the volume of a sphere is $\frac{4}{3}\pi r^3$, where r is the radius of the sphere. Correct the error below for calculating the volume of a sphere with a radius of 5 meters.

```
printf("volume of a sphere with a radius 5 m is %f (m^3)\n",
       4/3*3.1415926*5*5*5);
```

CHAPTER 5

Statements and Control Flow

The programs we have written so far are pretty simple. They all consist of a series of actions performed in sequence. But more complicated problems may require that certain steps are taken if a condition is true or not, or that an action be repeated a number of times. Writing a program to do this calls for the use of an algorithm. An *algorithm* consists of a set of actions and the order in which they are to be performed. Algorithms can be defined in terms of certain control structures in C, which are classified as sequential, selective, or repetitive. Sequential statements, as we have written so far for most programs, are executed in the order they are written. Selection statements, such as **if** statements used in Program 4.5 in Chapter 4 and **switch** statements, are executed if a condition is met. Repetition statements such as **while** statements, **do-while** statements, and **for** statements, are executed until a condition is no longer true. In this chapter, details about *structured programming* using selection and repetition statements are presented. How to use flowcharts, procedures, and pseudocode for algorithm development is also described.

5.1 Flowcharts for Algorithm Development

To organize structured programs, programmers often use flowcharts, which are visual depictions of algorithms. They indicate what to do and when. A typical flowchart consists of a collection of steps, connected by arrows called flowlines, that indicate which direction the algorithm is to proceed. Each of these steps is denoted using special symbols to describe the type of action. Common flowchart symbols are shown in Figure 5.1. For example, an oval shape is used to represent the beginning or end of a program. A step in which a computation or initialization is to be performed should be enclosed by a rectangle. For input or output steps, the statement is inside a parallelogram. Perhaps the most important symbol is the diamond, which indicates a decision expression. There are two flowlines out of a diamond, and the path taken depends on whether the expression contained within is true or false. A connector can be used to show the continuation of the flowchart from one page to another, or from a decision diamond to another page. When the flow reaches the bottom of a page or needs to jump to another place for clarity, draw a flowchart connector symbol and connect it to a symbol on the chart. A label, typically beginning with a letter *A*, should be placed inside the circle of a connector symbol. Together, these allow you to organize your thoughts in a graphical manner, and once this is done, writing a C program is much easier.

5.2 Simple and Compound Statements

A *statement* specifies an action to be performed. Except as indicated, statements are executed in sequence. A *full expression* is an expression that is not part of another expression or declarator. Each of the

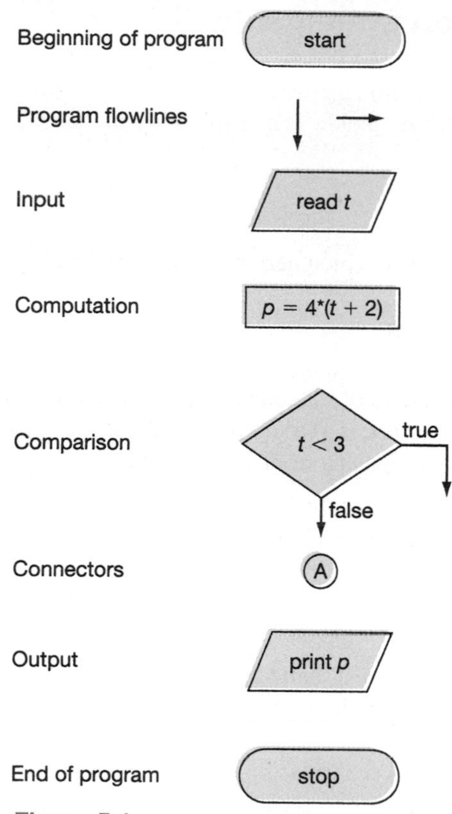

Figure 5.1: Common flowchart symbols.

following is a full expression: an initializer; the expression in an expression statement; the controlling expression of a selection statement (**if** or **switch**); the controlling expression of a **while** statement or **do-while** statement; each of the (optional) expressions of a **for** statement; the (optional) expression in a **return** statement, which will be described in the next chapter. The end of a full expression is a sequence point.

A *compound statement* is a block enclosed with a pair of braces. A *block* allows a set of declarations and statements to be grouped into one syntactic unit. The initializers of objects that have automatic storage duration, and the variable length array declarators of ordinary identifiers with block scope, are evaluated and the values are stored in the objects (including storing an indeterminate value in objects without an initializer) each time the declaration is reached in the order of execution, as if it were a statement, and within each declaration in the order that declarators appear. For example:

```
int i;   // simple statement
{        // compound statement
  int i;
  i =90;
  ...
}
```

5.3 Null and Expression Statements

The semicolon is a statement terminator. An *expression statement* contains an expression followed by a semicolon. For example, each statement below is an expression statement.

```
x = 10;
i++;
printf("hello world\n");
```

A *null statement* consisting of just a semicolon performs no operation.

5.4 Selection Statements

A selection statement selects among a set of statements depending on the value of a controlling expression. A selection statement is a block whose scope is a strict subset of the scope of its enclosing block. Each associated substatement is also a block whose scope is a strict subset of the scope of the selection statement.

5.4.1 The if Statement

The syntax of an **if** statement is as follows:

```
if(expression)
  statement
```

The controlling expression of an **if** statement shall have scalar type. The statement is executed if the expression compares unequal to 0. The relational and logical operations are often used in the controlling expression.

A flowchart illustrating the path of control of a single selection **if** statement is shown in Figure 5.2. The two flowlines coming out of the decision expression indicate the possible directions to be taken. Notice that the statement enclosed in the rectangle is executed only if the decision expression is true.

The variable of boolean type **bool** in C99, as described in section 3.7 in Chapter 3, can be used in a conditional expression as shown below.

```
#include <stdbool.h>
/* ... */
bool b = true;
/* ... */
if (b) {
  b = false;
}
```

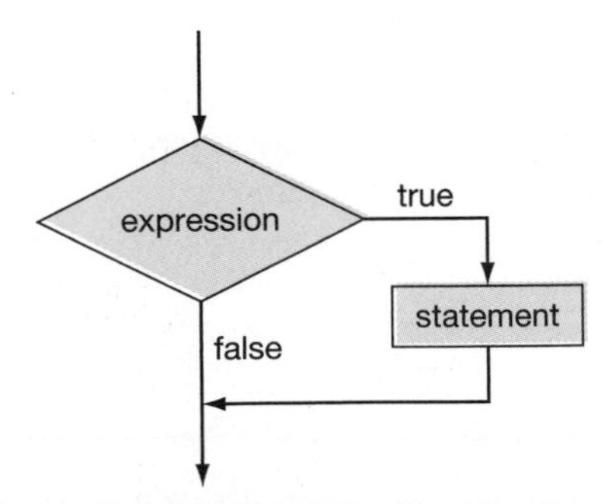

Figure 5.2: The flowchart of an **if** structure.

One of the common mistakes made by beginners in using the **if** statement is to write

```
if(i=5)
```

instead of

```
if(i==5)
```

The result of the conditional expression of the former is 5. Therefore, the condition is always true for the **if** statement.

5.4.2 The if-else Statement

The syntax of an **if-else** statement is as follows:

```
if(expression)
  statement1
else
  statement2
```

The controlling expression of an **if** statement shall have scalar type. The first substatement is executed if the expression compares unequal to 0. The second substatement is executed if the expression compares equal to 0. If the first substatement is reached via a label, then the second substatement is not executed. Figure 5.3 shows the flow of control for an **if-else** statement. Notice that both flowlines out of the decision expression result in an action being taken.

As an example, when a positive floating-point number is cast into an integer, the number can be rounded up by adding 0.5. When the number is negative, it can be rounded down by subtracting 0.5. This rounding operation, depending on the sign of the number, can be implemented using **if-else** statements as shown below.

```
int i;
double d;
...
if(d > 0)
    i = d+0.5;
else
    i = d-0.5;
printf("rounded integer of %f is %d\n", d, i);
```

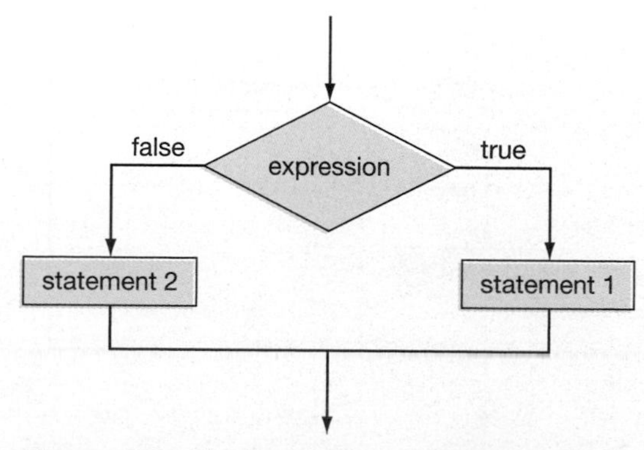

Figure 5.3: The flowchart of an **if-else** structure.

5.4.3 The else-if Statements

The syntax of the **else-if** statement is as follows:

```
if(expression1)
  statement1
else if (expression2)
  statement2
else if (expression3)
  statement3
else
  statement4
```

Semantically, the syntax of the **else-if** statement is an extension of the previous **if-else** statement. The flow of control for an **else-if** statement is shown in Figure 5.4. An **else** is associated with the lexically nearest preceding **if** that is allowed by the syntax. The above statement can be rearranged as

```
if(expression1)
  statement1
else
   if (expression2)
      statement2
```

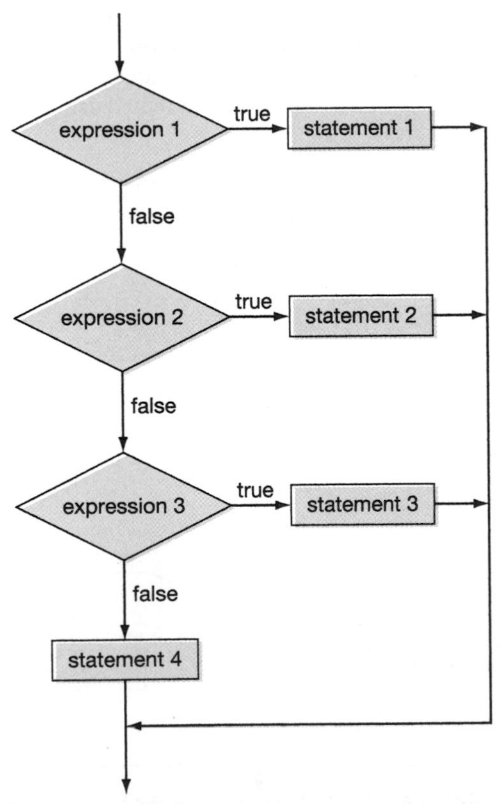

Figure 5.4: The flowchart of an **else-if** structure.

```
else
   if (expression3)
      statement3
   else
      statement4
```

Application Examples

Force of a Moving Body

Problem Statement:
For the mechanical system shown in Figure 2.12, given mass $m = 5$ kilograms (kg) and coefficient of kinetic friction $\mu = 0.2$, the applied force p is expressed as a function of time t in

$$p(t) = \begin{cases} 20 & \text{if} \quad t \le 3 \\ 4(t+2) & \text{if} \quad t > 3 \end{cases}$$

Calculate and print the force dependent on the time provided by the user at the prompt.

This problem can be solved with Program 5.1, which uses an **if-else** statement to determine how the force `p` is calculated. The flowchart for Program 5.1 is shown in Figure 5.5. First, the program uses the function **scanf()** to read in the time. Based on the value of the input time, the force will be calculated using different formulas. If the specified time is less than or equal to 3 seconds, `p` is 20. Otherwise, `p` is equal to $4(t+2)$. The result is then printed out. Program 5.1 can be executed as shown below.

```
> force.c
Please input time in seconds
4
Force p = 24.000000 (N)
```

The problem statement can be modified slightly by changing the formula for the external force `p` as follows.

$$p(t) = \begin{cases} 20 & \text{if} \quad 0 \le t \le 3 \\ 4(t+2) & \text{if} \quad t > 3 \end{cases}$$

```
/* File: force.c
   Calculate the force based on the input time.
   The formulas for the force depend on whether time t
   is less or equal to 3 seconds */
#include <stdio.h>

int main() {
    double p, t;
```

Program 5.1: Calculating the force using the **if-else** structure. (*Continued*)

```
    printf("Please input time in seconds\n");
    scanf("%lf", &t);

    if(t <= 3) { /* when time t is less or equal to 3 s */
        p = 20;
    }
    else {       /* when time t is larger than 3 s */
        p = 4*(t+2);
    }

    /* display the output */
    printf("Force p = %f (N)\n", p);
    return 0;
}
```

Program 5.1: *(Continued)*

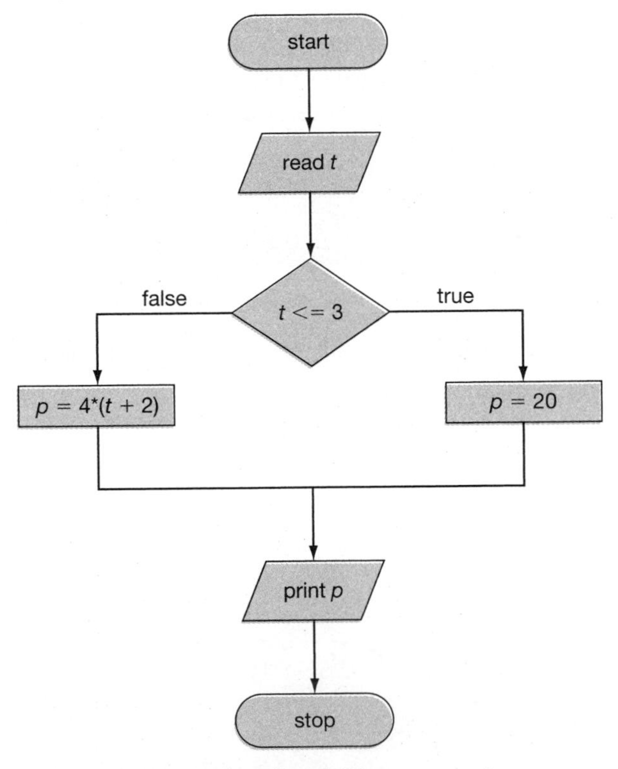

Figure 5.5 The flowchart for the program `force.c`.

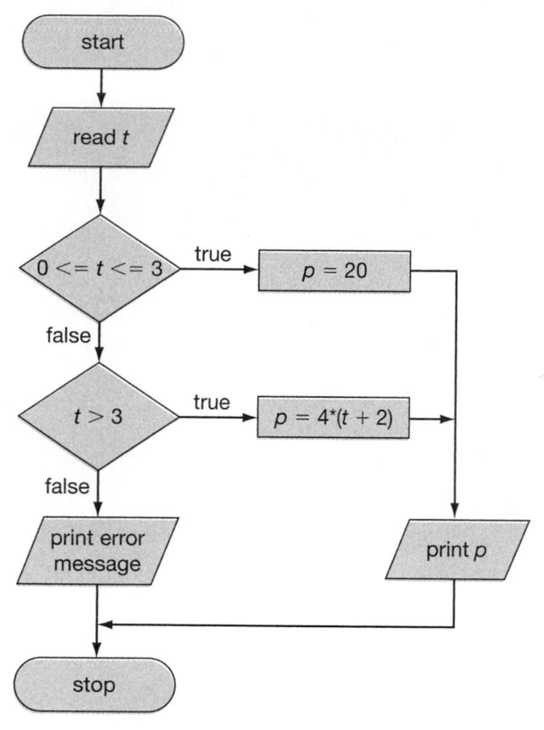

Figure 5.6 The flowchart for the program `force2.c`.

In this case, if the input for time `t` is a negative value, it is an invalid input. The flowchart for solving the problem is shown in Figure 5.6. The algorithm is implemented in Program 5.2 using an **if-else-if-else** structure. The mathematical condition $0 \leq t \leq 3$ for `t` larger than 0 and less than 3 is translated into C code as `(0 <= t && t <= 3)`. When the input time is less than 0, the program will print out an error message and exit. In this case, the value shall not be printed out.

Associating Grades with Scores

Problem Statement:
The valid grades for a class are A, B, C, D, and F corresponding to the scores 4, 3, 2, 1, and 0, respectively. Write a program to print out the score on the terminal when the user enters a grade.

Program 5.3 can be used to handle this program. The grade from the user input is saved in the variable `grade` of char type. The score for a grade can be handled either using an integer or a floating-point number. However, if taking other possible grades such as A- and B+ into consideration, the variable `score` of double type for floating-point number is used for the score. The score is assigned based on the grade using **if-else-if-else** statements. If the user inputs an invalid grade, such as E, the score is assigned with value -1 and an error message is printed. After the **if-else-if-else** statements, the score for the corresponding grade is displayed if the user inputs a valid grade.

```
/* File: force2.c
   Calculate the force based on the input time.
   The formulas for the force depend on whether time t
   is 0<= t <= 3 or t > 3. */
#include <stdio.h>

int main() {
    double p, t;

    printf("Please input time in seconds\n");
    scanf("%lf", &t);
    if(0 <= t && t <= 3)  { /* when 0<= t <= 3 */
        p = 20;
        printf("Force p = %f (N)\n", p);
    }
    else if(t > 3) {        /* when t > 3 */
        p = 4*(t+2);
        printf("Force p = %f (N)\n", p);
    }
    else {                  /* when t < 0 */
        printf("Invalid input\n");
    }
    return 0;
}
```

Program 5.2: Calculating the force using an **if-else-if-else** structure.

```
/* File: ifgrade.c
   The program enter a grade in one of alphabetic letters A, B,
   C, D, F, it prints the corresponding score the numerical value.
   The program uses an if-else if-else statement */

#include <stdio.h>

int main() {
    char grade;         /* grade */
    double score;       /* score */

    /* prompt the user to enter a grade */
    printf("Enter a grade [A, B, C, D, F]: ");
    scanf("%c", &grade);
    if(grade == 'A')        /* entered A */
        score = 4.0;
    else if(grade == 'B') /* entered B */
        score = 3.0;
```

Program 5.3: Displaying the score corresponding to a grade using an **if-else-if-else** structure. (*Continued*)

```
    else if(grade == 'C') /* entered C */
        score = 2.0;
    else if(grade == 'D') /* entered D */
        score = 1.0;
    else if(grade == 'F') /* entered F */
        score = 0.0;
    else {                /* entered any other character */
        score = -1;
        printf("Invalid grade '%c'\n", grade);
    }

    /* display the grade and score */
    if(score != -1)
        printf("The score for the grade '%c' is %.2f\n", grade, score);
    return 0;
}
```

Program 5.3: *(Continued)*

In Program 5.3, it is assumed that the grade is case sensitive. If the grade is case insensitive, such as that the letter `'a'` is treated the same as `'A'`, the logical expressions inside **if-else-if-else** statements need to be changed. For example, for the case insensitive grades `'a'` and `'A'`, the logical expression

```
if(grade == 'A')
```

in Program 5.3 should be changed to

```
if(grade == 'A' || grade == 'a')
```

An interactive execution of Program 5.3 is shown as follows:

```
> ifgrade.c
Enter a grade [A, B, C, D, F]: B
The score for the grade 'B' is 3.00
```

5.4.4 The switch Statement

In Program 5.3, the user input grade is tested against a number of valid constant integers represented as characters. Depending on the grade, the program assigns a corresponding score. The **switch** statement is more commonly used to handle such decisions. It tests whether an expression matches one of a number of `constant` integer values, and the program flow then branches accordingly.

The syntax of a **switch** statement is as follows:

```
switch(expression) {
  case const-expr1:
     statement1
     break;
  case const-expr2:
```

```
        statement2
        break;
    default:
        statement
        break;
}
```

The controlling expression of a **switch** statement shall have integer type. The expression of each **case** label shall be an integer constant expression and no two **case** constant expressions in the same **switch** statement shall have the same value after conversion. There may be at most one **default** label in a **switch** statement. A **switch** statement causes control to jump into or past the statement that is the *switch body*, depending on the value of a controlling expression, and on the presence of a **default** label and the values of any **case** labels on or in the switch body. A **case** or **default** label is accessible only within the closest enclosing **switch** statement. The number of **case** values in a switch statement is not limited.

The integer promotions are performed on the controlling expression. The constant expression in each **case** label is converted to the promoted type of the controlling expression. If a converted value matches that of the promoted controlling expression, control jumps to the statement following the matched **case** label. Otherwise, if there is a **default** label, control jumps to the labeled statement. If no converted **case** constant expression matches and there is no **default** label, no part of the switch body is executed.

The flowchart of a **switch** structure is shown in Figure 5.7. Notice that if any of the **case** statements evaluate as true, the rest are ignored as the **break** statement causes the program to exit the **switch.** If none of the **case** statements are true, then the **default** statement is executed.

As an example, the **if-else-if-else** structure in Program 5.3 can be replaced by a **switch** statement as shown in Program 5.4. The integer expression, `grade`, is evaluated and compared with the constant integer

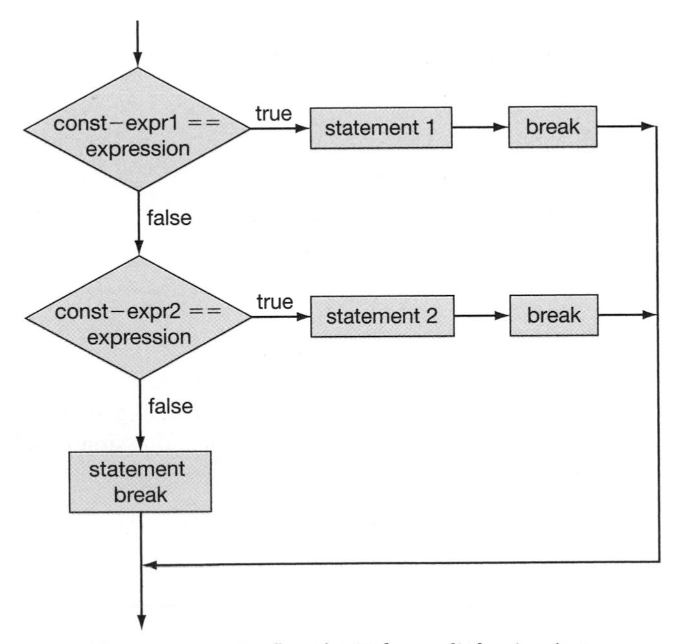

Figure 5.7: The flowchart of a **switch** structure.

```
/* File: switchgrade.c
   The program enter a grade in one of alphabetic letters A, B,
   C, D, F, it prints the corresponding score the numerical value.
   The program uses a swith-statement */
#include <stdio.h>

int main() {
    char grade;         /* grade */
    double score;       /* score */

    /* prompt the user to enter a grade */
    printf("Enter a grade [A, B, C, D, F]: ");
    scanf("%c", &grade);
    switch(grade) {
        case 'A': /* entered A */
            score = 4.0;
            break;
        case 'B': /* entered B */
            score = 3.0;
            break;
        case 'C': /* entered C */
            score = 2.0;
            break;
        case 'D': /* entered D */
            score = 1.0;
            break;
        case 'F': /* entered F */
            score = 0.0;
            break;
        default: /* entered any other character */
            score = -1;
            printf("Invalid grade '%c'\n", grade);
            break;
    }

    /* display the grade and score */
    if(score != -1)
       printf("The score for the grade '%c' is %.2f\n", grade, score);
    return 0;
}
```

Program 5.4: Displaying the score corresponding to a grade using a **switch** statement.

values 'A', 'B', 'C', 'D', and 'F'. The branch for the **else** statement in Program 5.3 is handled by the corresponding default case in the **switch** statement in Program 5.4. If the grade is case insensitive, such as the case insensitive grades 'a' and 'A', multiple case statements can be used as shown below

```
case 'A': /* entered A */
case 'a': /* entered a */
```

for Program 5.4.

Another application example of using a **switch** statement is presented in Program 5.18 later in this chapter.

5.5 Repetition Statements

A repetition or iteration statement causes a statement called the *loop body* to be executed repeatedly until the controlling expression compares equal to 0. The loop body of an iteration statement is a block.

5.5.1 The while Loop

The syntax of a **while** loop is as follows:

```
while(expression)
  statement
```

The evaluation of the controlling expression takes place before each execution of the loop body. The loop body is executed repeatedly until the controlling expression compares equal to 0. The loop body may be a single statement or a compound statement.

The control flow of a **while** loop is shown in the flowchart of Figure 5.8. Notice that the flowline out of the decision expression loops around and the expression is evaluated repeatedly until it is false. For example, the following code fragment

```
int i =0;
while(i<5) {
     printf("%d ", i);
    i++;
}
```

will output

```
0 1 2 3 4
```

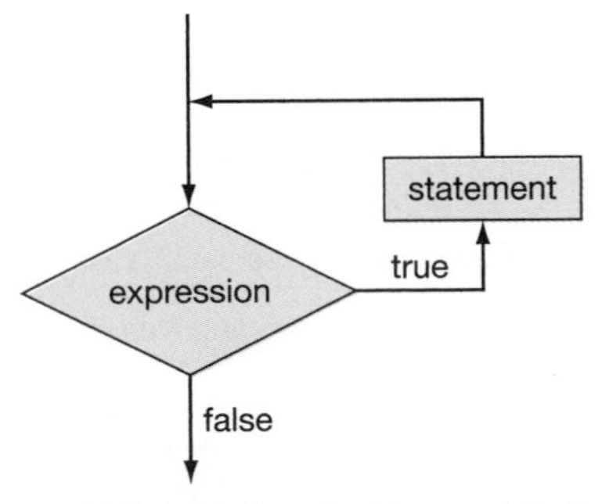

Figure 5.8: The flowchart for a **while** loop.

```
/* File: whilec.c
   Calculate a factorial using a while-loop */
#include <stdio.h>

int main() {
    /* declare variables of unsigned integers */
    unsigned int i, f, n;


    /* initialization */
    i = 1;
    f = 1;

    /* prompt the user to input an integer */
    printf("Please input a number\n");
    scanf("%d", &n);

    /* calculate factorial */
    while(i <= n) {
        f *= i;
        i++;
    }

    /* display output and termination */
    printf("factorial %u! = %u\n", n, f);
    return 0;
}
```

Program 5.5: Calculating factorials using a **while** loop.

To demonstrate the usefulness of a **while** loop, the factorial of an integer n, or $n!$, is calculated. The factorial $n!$ is defined as $n * (n - 1)!$. Program 5.5 calculates the factorial of an integer n input by the user. As shown in the flowchart in Figure 5.9, Program 5.5 assigns the value 1 to variables f and i first, then multiplies f by i at each execution of the loop by the statement

```
f *= i;
```

After each execution of the loop, i is incremented until it becomes equal to n, at which point the loop is exited and the value of f is printed out. The format specifier `"%u"` is used for printing output of unsigned int integers. An example of the execution of Program 5.5 is given below.

```
> whilec.c
Please input a number
4
factorial 4! = 24
```

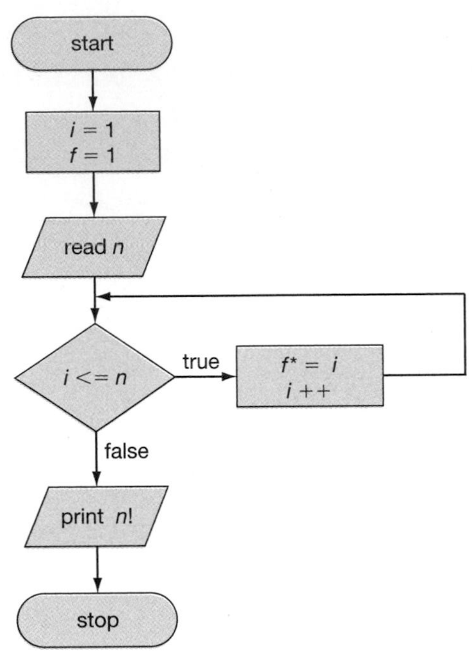

Figure 5.9: The flowchart for Program 5.5.

5.5.2 Major Sections of a Program and Control of Repetition

Major Sections of a Program and Counter-Controlled Repetition

As shown in Program 5.5, a structured program in C typically consists of four sections, namely, *declaration, initialization, processing,* and *termination*. Variables are first declared and initialized. In some applications, the memory for variables of pointer type are dynamically allocated in the initialization phase, which will be described later in Chapter 11. They are then used for data processing and computation using proper algorithms. Finally, in the termination phase, the result will be printed out. The memory allocated for variables of pointer type will be released. A flowchart typically does not include the declaration phase.

As another example, consider the following problem statement.

> *A student takes four courses in a quarter. Each course will be assigned a grade with the score from 0 to 4. Develop a C program to calculate the grade point average (GPA) for the quarter.*

The algorithm for this problem needs to input grades first. Then, save the grade for each class to a variable representing the total points. Next, calculate the GPA, which is the sum of the grades divided by the number of classes taken. Finally, print out the GPA. The flowchart of the algorithm is shown in Figure 5.10. Program 5.6 is the implementation of the algorithm in C. Program 5.6 also contains four phases of *declaration, initialization, processing,* and *termination*. By the convention, the constant in a program is often defined as a macro so that it can easily be changed and the code is more readable. The total number of classes taken is fixed in this program. Therefore, it is defined as a macro `NUM`. The variable `count` of int type is used to count the number of grades entered. The grade for each class is entered and saved in the variable `grade` of double type because it is a decimal number. The variable `total` of double type for a floating point number is used to accumulate the sum of a series of grades which are decimal numbers. The variables `total` and `count` have

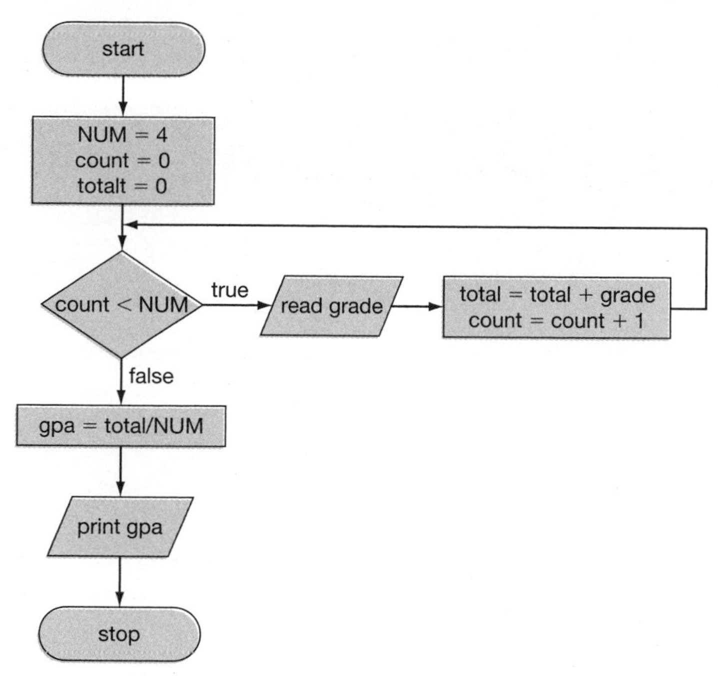

Figure 5.10: The flowchart for Program 5.6.

to be initialized. Otherwise, the result will be incorrect. An uninitialized variable may contain a "garbage" value in C. To obtain a GPA with significant digits after a decimal point, the variable `gpa` of double type is also used. The division of two variables `total` and `count`, one in double and the other in int, results in a floating-point value of double type. A sample execution of Program 5.6 is given below.

```
> gpa.c
Enter a grade:
4
Enter a grade:
3.7
Enter a grade:
3.3
Enter a grade:
4
The GPA is: 3.750000
```

If grades for courses are from a data file, the GPA can be calculated by Program 5.7 using the input/output redirection. For example, if data file `gpa.dat` contains the four grades

```
4 3.7 3.3 4
```

```
/* File: gpa.c
   Calculate the GPA for NUM grades entered from the terminal */
#include <stdio.h>

/* number of grades entered from the terminal */
#define NUM 4

int main() {
    /* declaration */
    int count;
    double grade, total, gpa;

    /* initialization */
    count = 0;
    total = 0;

    /* processing input grades and calculate the GPA */
    while(count < NUM) {
       printf("Enter a grade:\n");
       scanf("%lf", &grade);
       total += grade;
       count++;
    }
    gpa = total/NUM;

    /* display output and termination */
    printf("The GPA is: %f\n", gpa);
    return 0;
}
```

Program 5.6: Calculating the GPA with grades for four courses.

the GPA for these grades can be obtained as follows using the input redirection:

```
> gpa.c < gpa.dat
Enter a grade:
Enter a grade:
Enter a grade:
Enter a grade:
The GPA is: 3.750000
```

If Program 5.6 is designed to process only grades from a data file, the code

```
printf("Enter a grade:\n");
```

```
/* File: gpa2.c
   Calculate the GPA for grades entered from the terminal
   until a sentinel number -1 is entered. */
#include <stdio.h>

#define SENTINELNUM -1    /* sentinel number */
#define HIGHESTMARK 4.0   /* highest mark for grade */

int main() {
    /* declaration */
    int count;
    double grade, total, gpa;

    /* initialization */
    count = 0;
    total = 0;

    /* processing input grades and calculate the GPA */
    printf("Enter a grade [0, %g] or %d to end:\n", HIGHESTMARK, SENTINELNUM);
    scanf("%lf", &grade);
    while((int)grade != SENTINELNUM) {
        /* a valid grade should 0<= grade <= 4 */
        if(0 <= grade && grade <= HIGHESTMARK) {
          total += grade;
          count++;
        }
        else {
          printf("Invalid grade %c\n", '\a');
        }
        printf("Enter a grade [0, %g] or %d to end:\n",HIGHESTMARK,SENTINELNUM);
        scanf("%lf", &grade);
    }

    /* display output and termination */
    if(count != 0) {
        gpa = total/count;
        printf("The GPA is: %f\n", gpa);
    }
    else
      printf("No grade entered.\n");
    return 0;
}
```

Program 5.7: Calculating the GPA with grades for an arbitrary number of courses.

for the prompt could be removed. The output from the program `gpa.c` can also be redirected into a file `gpa.out` as follows.

```
> gpa.c < gpa.dat > gpa.out
>
```

In Programs 5.5 and 5.6, the repetition is controlled by a counter. In this ***counter-controlled repetition***, an integer variable, `i` in Program 5.5 and `count` in Program 5.6, is used to specify the number of times that a set of statements inside a loop should be executed. In this counter-controlled repetition, there are definite repetitions. The number of repetitions is known in advance before the loop begins execution. In Program 5.5, the repetition terminates when the counter exceeds the number entered by the user, whereas in Program 5.6, the repetition ends when the counter equals NUM, defined as 4.

Sentinel-Controlled Repetition

In some applications, the number of repetitions might be not known in advance. For example, consider the following problem statement.

> *Develop a GPA calculation program that will process grades with scores in the range of [0, 4] for an arbitrary number of courses.*

In Program 5.6, the number of courses is known in advance. In this example, the number of courses is not known. The program needs to process grades for an arbitrary number of courses. How can the program determine when to stop the input of grades and calculate and print out the GPA?

To solve this problem, a special value called a *sentinel value* or *signal value* can be used to indicate the end of data entry. In this case, the user enters all grades first. Then, enter the sentinel value to indicate the end of data entry. The sentinel value should be carefully chosen so that it will not be confused with the acceptable input value. To use relational operator == or != in a loop-controlling expression, the sentinel value is typically an integer value. Because grades are in the range of [0, 4], any number outside this range can be used. The sentinel value −1 will be used to solve this problem. The flowchart of the algorithm for this problem is shown in Figure 5.11 for Program 5.7. The sentinel value of constant value in the program is defined as a macro called `SENTINELNUM`. The highest mark is not hard-coded inside a program. Rather, it is defined as a macro called `HIGHESTMARK` because some grading systems may use scores in the range of [0, 5] or [0, 100]. By changing the defined value for the macro `HIGHESTMARK`, the program can be adapted easily to other grading systems. Like Program 5.6, in the declaration phase, Program 5.7 will first declare variables `count` of int type; `grade, total`, and `gpa` of double type. In the initialization phase, the variables `count` and `total` are initialized to 0. In the data-processing phase, the program then enters a **while** loop for indefinite repetition. In this ***sentinel-controlled repetition***, the number of repetition is not known before the loop begins execution. The user enters a grade for each course. If the input value is within the valid range for a grade, the score will be added to the `total` value. Otherwise, an error message will be displayed and a beep will be produced from the speaker of the computer as an alert to the output of the escape character `'\a'`. When the user enters the sentinel value of −1, the program will terminate the repetition. To avoid using the *not equal* relational operator `!=` for comparison of floating-point numbers, the variable `grade` is cast to the int type before it is compared with the sentinel value in the controlling expression of the **while** loop. Upon the completion of execution of statements in the loop, the program enters the termination phase. If valid grades have been entered, the GPA will be calculated and displayed. Otherwise, a message of `"No grade entered"` will be displayed. The sentinel value, −1 in this case, should not be used in the calculation. A sample execution of Program 5.7 is given following.

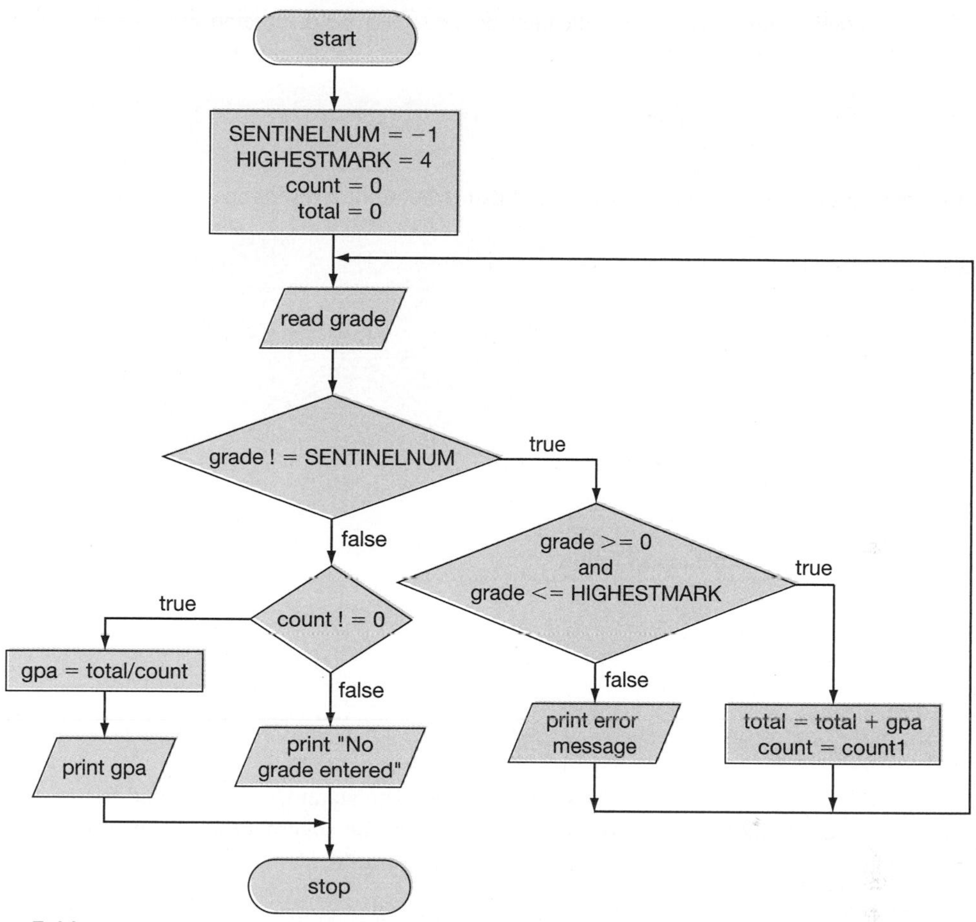

Figure 5.11: The flowchart for Program 5.7 for calculating the GPA with grades for an arbitrary number of courses.

```
> gpa2.c
Enter a grade [0, 4] or -1 to end:
4
Enter a grade [0, 4] or -1 to end:
3.7
Enter a grade [0, 4] or -1 to end:
10
Invalid grade
Enter a grade [0, 4] or -1 to end:
4
Enter a grade [0, 4] or -1 to end:
-1
The GPA is: 3.750000
```

If grades for courses are saved in a data file, the GPA can be calculated by Program 5.7 using the input/output redirection. For example, if the data file `gpa2.dat` contains the following grades with the sentinel number -1 at the end,

```
4 3.7 4 -1
```

the GPA for these grades can be obtained as follows using the input redirection:

```
> gpa2.c < gpa2.dat
Enter a grade [0, 4] or -1 to end:
Enter a grade [0, 4] or -1 to end:
Enter a grade [0, 4] or -1 to end:
Enter a grade [0, 4] or -1 to end:
The GPA is: 3.900000
```

5.5.3 The do-while Loop

The syntax of a **do-while** statement is as follows:

```
do
  statement
while(expression);
```

The evaluation of the controlling expression takes place after each execution of the loop body. The loop body is executed repeatedly until the controlling expression compares equal to 0.

Figure 5.12 illustrates the structure of a **do-while** loop. The statement is executed before the decision expression is evaluated. If the decision expression is true, then the statement is executed until the decision expression evaluates to false. For example, the following code fragment

```
int i =0;
do {
    printf("%d ", i);
    i++;
} while(i<5);
```

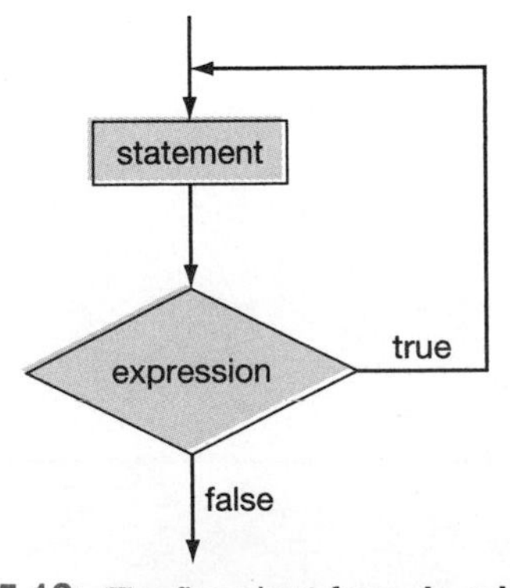

Figure 5.12: The flowchart for a **do-while** loop.

will output

```
0 1 2 3 4
```

The following code fragment

```
int i = 10;
do {
    printf("%d ", i++);
} while(i<5);
```

will output

```
10
```

As shown in this example, the loop body is executed before the controlling expression is evaluated. The following code fragment with a **while** loop will have no output, because the controlling expression of the **while** statement is evaluated first with a value of 0.

```
int i =10;
while(i<5) {
  printf("%d ", i++);
}
```

5.5.4 The for Loop

The syntax of a **for** statement is as follows:

```
for(expression1; expression2; expression3)
  statement
```

The expression *expression1* is evaluated as a void expression before the first evaluation of the controlling expression. The expression *expression2* is the controlling expression that is evaluated before each execution of the loop body. The expression *expression3* is evaluated as a void expression after each execution of the loop body. Both *expression1* and *expression3* can be omitted. An omitted *expression2* is replaced by a nonzero constant.

The structure of a **for** loop is illustrated in Figure 5.13. As shown, after *expression1* is evaluated, the program evaluates *expression2*, and if *expression2* is true, the statement is executed and *expression3* is evaluated. The **for** loop continues until *expression2* is no longer true.

The **for** loop is semantically equivalent to the following **while** loop

```
expression1;
while(expression2) {
  statement
  expression3;
}
```

For example, the following code fragment

```
int i;
for(i=0; i<5; i++) {
  printf("%d ", i);
}
```

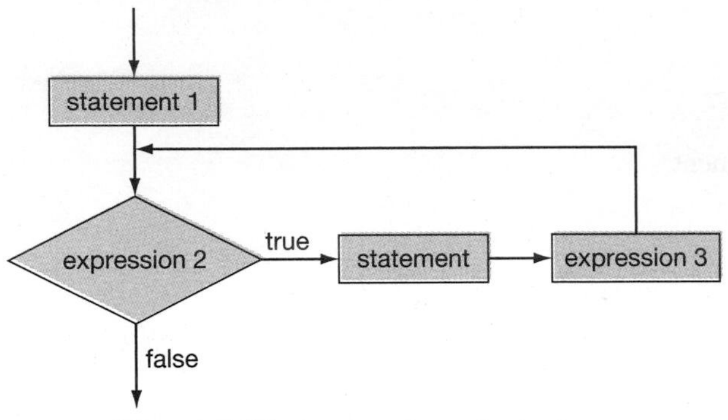

Figure 5.13: The flowchart of a **for** loop.

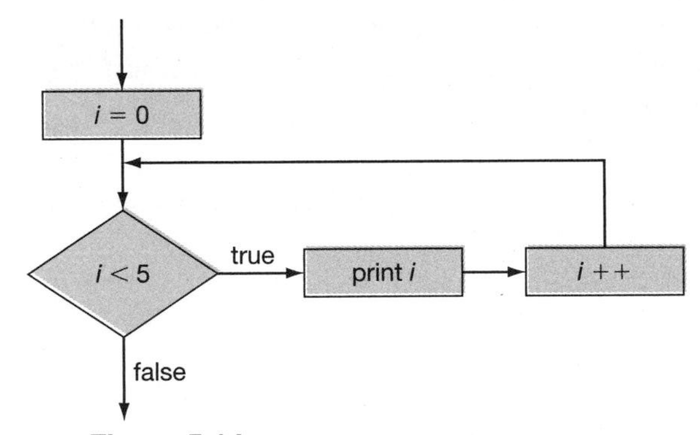

Figure 5.14: The flowchart using a **for** loop.

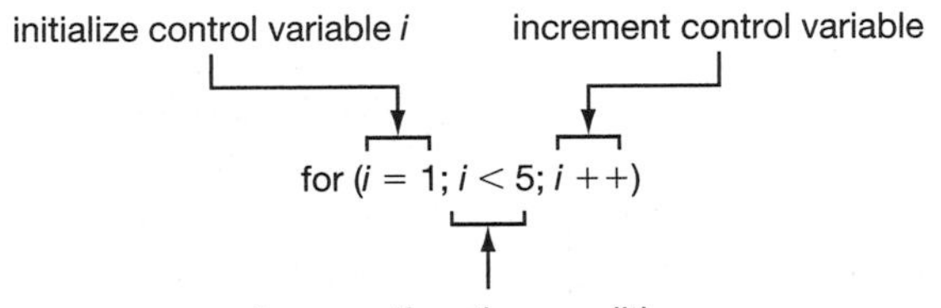

Figure 5.15: A typical **for** loop construct.

has a flow of control as shown in Figure 5.14. In this example, the first expression, `i=0`, initializes the loop control variable `i` with 0, as shown in Figure 5.15. The second expression, `i<5`, is the loop continuation condition. The loop iterates when the control variable `i` is less than 5. The third expression, `i++`, increments the control variable after the loop body

```
printf("%d ", i);
```

is executed. The above code fragment will produce the same output of

```
0 1 2 3 4
```

as in a **while** loop of

```
int i =0;
while(i<5) {
  printf("%d ", i);
  i++;
}
```

More complicated expressions can be used in a **for** loop statement as shown below.

```
int i, j;
for(i=0, j=10; i<10&&j>0; i++, j--) {
  printf("i=%d\n", i);
  printf("j=%d\n", j);
}
```

In this example, the expression `i=0, j=10` with a comma operator as described in section 4.13 in Chapter 4 initializes both control variables `i` and `j`. The loop iterates if `i` is less than 10 and `j` is larger than 0. The expression `i++, j--`, also with a comma operator, increments `i` and decrements `j` after the loop body is executed.

Here's an example that demonstrates the usefulness of a **for** loop. Program 5.8 modified the previous Program 5.5 by using initialize variables f and i as 1, then multiplies f by i during each execution of the loop. After each execution of the loop, i is incremented until it becomes equal to n, at which point the loop is exited and the value of f is printed out.

```
/* File: forloop.c
   Calculate a factorial using a for-loop */
#include <stdio.h>

int main() {
    /* declare variables of unsigned integers */
    unsigned int i, f, n;

    /* prompt the user to input an integer */
    printf("Please input a number\n");
    scanf("%d", &n);

    /* calculate factorial */
    for(i=1, f=1; i<=n; i++) {
       f = f*i;
    }

    /* display the output and termination */
    printf("factorial %u! = %u\n", n, f);
    return 0;
}
```

Program 5.8: Calculating factorials using a **for** loop.

Iterative statements are useful for numerical computations. This can be illustrated by calculating the values of the function sinc(x) in equation (5.1)

$$\text{sinc}(x) = \frac{\sin(x)}{x} \tag{5.1}$$

in the range of $-10 \leq x \leq 10$ with a step size of 5. To use the standard C function **sin()** declared in the header file **math.h** to compute the function sinc(), Program 5.9 includes this header file at the beginning. The output from Program 5.9 is displayed in Figure 5.16.

In general, to divide x linearly in the range of $\mathtt{x0} \leq x \leq \mathtt{xf}$, where `x0` is the initial value and `xf` the final value, with a step size of `xstep`, the number of data points can be calculated by the formula

$$\mathtt{n} = (\mathtt{xf} - \mathtt{x0})/\mathtt{xstep} + 1 \tag{5.2}$$

```
/* File: forsinc.c
   Calculate function sinc(x)=sin(x)/x
   for x from -10 to 10 with step size 5 */
#include <stdio.h>
#include <math.h>    /* for sin() and fabs() */
#include <float.h>   /* for FLT_EPSILON */


int main() {
    double x, x0, xf, xstep, result;
    int i, n;

    printf("    x       sinc(x)\n");
    printf(" ----------------\n");
    x0 = -10.0;                 /* initial value for x */
    xf = 10.0;                  /* final value for x */
    xstep = 5.0;                /* step size for x */
    n  =  (xf - x0)/xstep + 1;  /* number of points */
    for(i = 0; i < n; i++) {
       x = x0 + i*xstep;        /* calculate value x */
       /* if x is a value less than epsilon, sinc(x) is 1 */
       if(fabs(x) < FLT_EPSILON)
          result = 1.0;
       else
          result = sin(x)/x;

       /* display the result */
       printf("%8.4f %8.4f\n", x, result);
    }
    return 0;
}
```

Program 5.9: Computing the function `sinc()` in equation (5.1).

```
       x       sinc(x)
  ----------------
  -10.0000   -0.0544
   -5.0000   -0.1918
    0.0000    1.0000
    5.0000   -0.1918
   10.0000   -0.0544
```

Figure 5.16: The output from Programs 5.9 and 6.6.

Each data point can then be calculated using the formula

$$\texttt{x} = \texttt{x0} + \texttt{i} * \texttt{xstep} \tag{5.3}$$

for x-coordinates and a given equation for y-coordinates inside a loop with i from 0 to $(n-1)$. To calculate equation (5.1) for x in the range of $-10 \leq x \leq 10$ with a step size of 5, a **for** loop is used in Program 6.6. The inital value `x0`, final value `xf`, and step size `xstep` are -10, 10, and 5, respectively. The values for the function sinc() can be easily computed in the entire real domain, except at the origin. When $x = 0$, sin(0)/0 for sinc(0) is indeterminant. Therefore, the expression sin(0)/0 would give the symbol NaN, which stands for Not-a-Number. Unlike taking a square root of a negative number in the real domain, which is invalid, it can be proved in calculus that sinc(0) is 1. Therefore, in Program 5.9, the absolute value of x calculated by the function **fabs()** is a very small value, less than the machine epsilon **FLT_EPSILON** defined in the header file **float.h**, the result for sinc(x) replaced by 1. At the end of each iteration inside the **for** loop in Program 5.9, values for variable x and function sinc(x) are printed out using the format specification `"%8.4f"`, which specifies a field width of 8 with 4 digits following the decimal point.

5.5.5 Nested Loops

Loops can be nested. A *nested loop* is a loop inside another loop. For nested loops, the inner loops must finish before the outer loop can resume iteration. For example, Program 5.10 prints a multiplication table up to 10 shown in Figure 5.17. Program 5.10 uses nested loops. For each value of index `i` from 1 to 10 for the outer loop, the program first prints i, then loops through an inner loop with index `j` from 1 to i and prints $i * j$ for each iteration, and finally prints a new line character. It is important to indent the program with nested loops properly so that the program will be easier to maintain. It is recommended to place the body of a loop inside a pair of braces even if it has only a single statement. For example, with proper indentation and braces, it is clear that the statement

```
printf("%4d", i*j);
```

belongs to the innermost **for** loop. The multiplication table is aligned properly using the format specifier `"%4d"`, which forces the function **printf()** to use a field width of 4 for each integer.

Nested loops can be used to handle a mathematical the function or formula with multiple variables conveniently. For example, the function sinr(x, y) in equation (5.4) has two arguments, x and y.

$$\text{sinr}(x, y) = \frac{\sin(r)}{r}, \text{ with } r = \sqrt{x^2 + y^2} \tag{5.4}$$

```
/* File: nestedloop.c
   Make a multiplication table using two nested loops  */
#include <stdio.h>

int main() {
    int i, j;

    printf("        1   2   3   4   5   6   7   8   9  10\n");
    printf("    ----------------------------------------\n");

    /* for multiplication of i*j, with both i and j from 1 to 10 */
    for(i=1; i<= 10; i++) {          /* outer loop in i */
      /* for each i, calculate i*j for j from 1 to 10 */
      printf("%4d|", i);
      for(j=1; j<=i; j++) {          /* inner loop in j */
        printf("%4d", i*j);
      }
      printf("\n");          /* a newline for each i */
    }
    printf("    ----------------------------------------\n");
    return 0;
}
```

Program 5.10: Printing a multiplication table using nested loops.

```
        1   2   3   4   5   6   7   8   9  10
    ----------------------------------------
   1|   1
   2|   2   4
   3|   3   6   9
   4|   4   8  12  16
   5|   5  10  15  20  25
   6|   6  12  18  24  30  36
   7|   7  14  21  28  35  42  49
   8|   8  16  24  32  40  48  56  64
   9|   9  18  27  36  45  54  63  72  81
  10|  10  20  30  40  50  60  70  80  90 100
    ----------------------------------------
```

Figure 5.17: The multiplication table as output from Program 5.10.

The standard C function **sqrt()**, declared in the header file **math.h**, can be used to calculate the square root of a value. Program 5.11 calculates the values of the function sinr(x, y) when the variables x and y both vary in the range of [−10, 10] with a step size of 10. Because there are two variables, two nested **for** loops are used. Each loop has its own control variable. The control variable `i` for variable `x` is used for the outer loop

```
/* File: forsinr.c
   Calculate function sinr(x, y)=sin(sqrt(x*x + y*y))/sqrt(x*x + y*y)
   for x from -10 to 10 with step size 10,
   and for y from -10 to 10 with step size 10. */
#include <stdio.h>
#include <math.h>    /* for sin() and sqrt() */

int main() {
    double x, x0, xf, xstep,
           y, y0, yf, ystep, result, r;
    int i, j, nx, ny;

    printf("      x          y     sinr(x,y)\n");
    printf("  ----------------------------\n");
    x0 = -10.0;                   /* initial value for x */
    xf = 10.0;                    /* final value for x */
    xstep = 10.0;                 /* step size for x */
    nx = (xf - x0)/xstep + 1;     /* num of points for x */
    y0 = -10.0;                   /* initial value for y */
    yf = 10.0;                    /* final value for y */
    ystep = 10.0;                 /* step size for y */
    ny = (yf - y0)/ystep + 1;     /* num of points for y */

    /* use nested two for-loops for x and y variables */
    for(i = 0; i < nx; i++) {
      x = x0 + i*xstep;           /* calculate value for x */
      /* for each x value, y varies from y0 to yf with ystep */
      for(j = 0; j <ny; j++) {
        y = y0 + j*ystep;         /* calculate value for y */

        /* calculate sinr(x, y) and display the result */
        r = sqrt(x*x + y*y);
        result = sin(r)/r;
        printf("%10.4f %10.4f %8.4f\n", x, y, result);
      }
    }
    return 0;
}
```

Program 5.11: Computing the function `sinr()` in equation (5.4).

whereas the control variable `j` for variable `y` is used for the inner loop. In this case, however, the inner loop and outer loop can be exchanged. The output from Program 5.11 is displayed in Figure 5.18. Note that, like the function sinc(0), at the origin (0, 0), the function sinr(0, 0) is indeterminant. The floating-point division of zero by zero gives the symbol `nan` for NaN, as shown in Figure 5.18. However, we can also use calculus

```
       x          y     sinr(x,y)
------------------------------
-10.0000   -10.0000    0.0707
-10.0000     0.0000   -0.0544
-10.0000    10.0000    0.0707
  0.0000   -10.0000   -0.0544
  0.0000     0.0000       nan
  0.0000    10.0000   -0.0544
 10.0000   -10.0000    0.0707
 10.0000     0.0000   -0.0544
 10.0000    10.0000    0.0707
```

Figure 5.18: The output from Program 5.11 and Program 6.7 in Chapter 6.

to prove that function sinr(0, 0) is 1. Similar to Program 5.9, Program 5.11 could be modified to handle this special case when the value of r (defined as $\sqrt{x^2 + y^2}$) is less than a very small value. In such a case, sinr(x, y) can be replaced with the value 1.

5.6 Jump Statements

A jump statement causes an unconditional jump to another place. To jump from one function to another function, functions **setjmp()** and **longjmp()** in the header file **setjmp.h** should be used.

5.6.1 The break Statement

The **break** statement provides an early exit from the **for**, **while**, and **do-while** loops and the **switch** statements. A break causes the innermost enclosing loop or switch to be exited immediately. A **break** statement shall appear only in a switch body or loop body. For example, the following code fragment

```
int i;
for(i=0; i<5; i++) {
   if(i == 3) {
       break;
   }
   printf("%d \n", i);
}
```

will produce the output of

```
0 1 2
```

5.6.2 The continue Statement

The **continue** statement causes the next iteration of the enclosing the **for**, **while**, or **do-while** loop to begin. For example, for the following code fragment

```
int i;
for(i=0; i<5; i++) {
```

```
        if(i == 3) {
            continue;
        }
        printf("%d \n", i);
    }
```

when the iteration index i is 3, the remaining body of the **for** loop is skipped. The code fragment produces the output of

```
0 1 2 4
```

5.6.3 ‡The goto Statement

A **goto** statement causes an unconditional jump to the statement prefixed by the named label in the enclosing function. A **goto** statement can transfer control either forward or backward within a function. For example,

```
for (/* ... */)
   for(/* ... */) {
      /* ... */
      if(emergency)
          goto hospital;
}
/* ... */
hospital:
    emergenceaction();
```

In the above fragment of the code, if the value of the variable emergency is not zero, the control of the flow will transfer to the labeled statement

```
hospital:
    emergenceaction();
```

where the identifier hospital, followed by a colon, is a label name. Label names shall be unique within a function. Any statement may be preceded by a prefix that declares an identifier as a label name. Labels in themselves do not alter the flow of control. Label names have function scope.

A null statement may also be used to carry a label just before the closing brace '}' of a compound statement, as follows:

```
while(loop1) {
   /* ... */
   do {
      /* ... */
      if(want_out)
          goto end_loop1;
      /* ... */
   } while (loop2);
   /* ... */
   end_loop1: ;
}
```

It should be noted that the logic of a program using **goto** statements is difficult to understand. The code with **goto** statements is also more difficult to optimize by a compiler. Therefore, the **goto** statement is generally not recommended for programming.

5.7 Pseudocode and Procedures for Algorithm Development

To solve various problems in engineering and science, different numerical algorithms often need to be developed. In this section, developing numerical algorithms using pseudocode, flowcharts, and procedures is described by solving the following problem.

Problem Statement:

The exponential function can be expanded as a Taylor series as follows:

$$e^x = 1 + \frac{x}{1!} + \frac{x^2}{2!} + \frac{x^3}{3!} + \frac{x^4}{4!} + \ldots$$
$$= \sum_{i=0}^{\infty} \frac{x^i}{(i)!}. \tag{5.5}$$

The approximate value of e^x can be obtained by the formula

$$\sum_{i=0}^{n} \frac{x^i}{(i)!}$$

Calculate e^x with $x = 0.5$ using a Taylor series until the last term is less than a small machine epsilon defined as a macro **FLT_EPSILON** in the header file **float.h**.

The mathematical function **exp()** defined in the header file **math.h** can readily be used to calculate the exponential function e^x. However, the problem statement specified that $e^{0.5}$ has to be calculated by a Taylor series.

Before an algorithm is implemented in a computer program, it can be helpful, especially for a complicated program, to present the algorithm in pseudocode. *Pseudocode* is an outline of a program written in a form that can be converted easily into real programming statements. Like a flowchart, pseudocode is independent of programming language. Pseudocode allows a programmer to concentrate on the algorithms without worrying about syntactic details of a programming language. Therefore, it is often used to develop algorithms before they are implemented in actual code.

As the name indicated, pseudocode generally does not follow the syntax rules of any particular language. There is no standard for pseudocode because a program in pseudocode cannot be compiled or executed. In this textbook, we will present pseudocode borrowing the appearance of C. A pseudocode for straightforward calculation of e^x is given in Program 5.12. The comment syntax in the pseudocode follows the C standard. A **while** loop is ended by `endwhile`, a **for** loop by `endfor`, and an **if** statement by `endif`. Although the pseudocode in Program 5.12 cannot be compiled or interpreted by any compiler or interpter, the algorithm presented in this pseudocode can be used to calculate $e^{0.5}$ using any computer programming languages. The pseudocode indicates that a program should first initialize variables `x`, `expx`, `term`, and `i`. The variable `expx` represents e^x. After each iteration, it is closer to the exact value. The variable `term` contains a term

$$\frac{x^i}{i!}$$

```
// File: expx.p
// Pseudocode for straightforward computation of exp(x)
// expx contains exp(x) and term is pow(x,i)/i!

x = 0.5
expx = 1.0
term = 1.0
i = 1
while(term>FLT_EPSILON)   // continue if pow(x,i)/i! > epsilon
   // calculate factorial i!
   factorial = 1
   for j = 1, ..., i
        factorial = factorial*j
   endfor

   term = pow(x, i)/factorial
   expx = expx + term
   i = i + 1
endwhile
print expx and exp(x)
```

Program 5.12: The pseudocode for calculating an approximate value for $e^{0.5}$.

of the Taylor series. A **while** loop is used to summarize each term in the Taylor series when the control expression is true, i.e., when the next term is larger than **FLT_EPSILON**. At each iteration, a factorial for $i!$ is calculated using a **for** loop. Afterward, a new term is calculated and added to `expx` by the statements

```
term = pow(x, i)/factorial
expx = expx + term
```

It is assumed that a function such as **pow()** or an operation can be used to calculate x^i. At the end of each iteration, the index variable `i` is incremented for calculating the next term. Finally, the value in the variable `expx` for e^x in comparison with the result from the math function **exp()** is printed out.

According to equation (5.5), term i is related to term $(i - 1)$ by the formula

$$\text{term}_i = \text{term}_{i-1}\frac{x}{i}$$

Using this recursive relation, we can refine our algorithm for calculating the exponential value based on the pseudocode in Program 5.13. The new algorithm neither uses the function **pow()** nor calculates a factorial starting from scratch for each term. Therefore, it is more efficient than the original one.

A flowchart can be considered as a graphical alternative to pseudocode. A flowchart corresponding to the pseudocode in Program 5.13 is shown in Figure 5.19.

In addition to pseudocode and flowchart, procedures can be used to describe algorithms and program logic. *Procedures* are succinct statements used to describe an algorithm in logical steps. It is especially useful for presentation and description of complicated algorithms. As an example, we can describe the numerical

```
// File: expx2.p
// Pseudocode for recursive computation of exp(x)
// expx contains exp(x) and term is pow(x,i)/i!

x = 0.5
expx = 1.0
term = 1.0
i = 1
while(term>FLT_EPSILON)   // continue if pow(x,i)/i! > epsilon
   term = term*x/i
   expx = expx + term
   i = i+1
endwhile
print expx and exp(x)
```

Program 5.13: The pseudocode for calculating an approximate value for $e^{0.5}$ recursively.

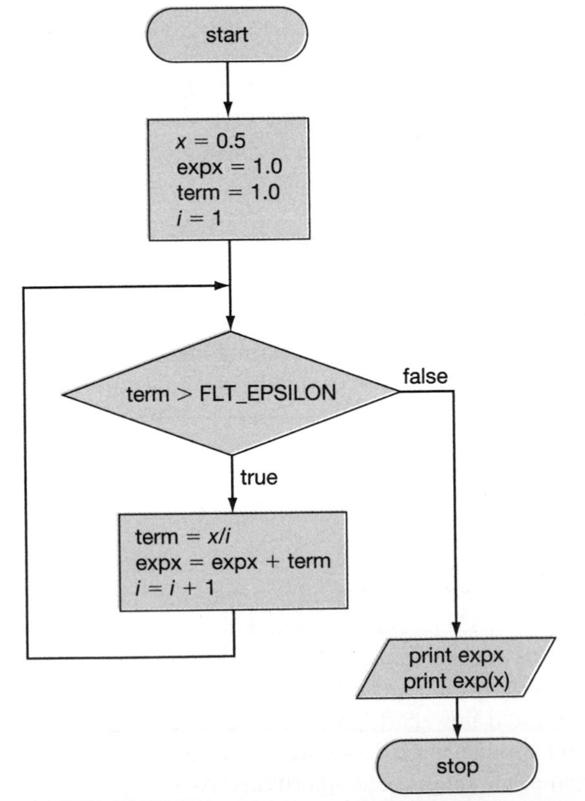

Figure 5.19: The flowchart for calculating $e^{0.5}$ recursively.

algorithm for calculating the exponential value presented in the pseudocode in Program 5.13 in the following procedures:

1. Initialize x = 0.5, expx = 1.0, term = 1.0, and i = 1.
2. If term > FLT_EPSILON, continue at step 3. Otherwise, print expx and **exp**(x), then stop.
3. Update term = term * x/i, expx = expx + term, and i = i+1.
4. Repeat step 2.

After an efficient algorithm has been designed in a pseudocode, a computer program can be more conveniently developed. In this example, Program 5.14 written in C can solve the program based on the algorithm presented in the pseudocode in Program 5.13 and the flowchart shown in Figure 5.19. For comparison, $e^{0.5}$ is also calculated by the mathematical function **exp**(). The output from Program 5.14 for $e^{0.5}$ is shown below:

```
expx   = 1.648721
exp(x) = 1.648721
```

In general, as shown in this example, before you implement an algorithm, especially for complicated ones, you may start with a pseudocode first. You may write a sketchy pseudocode on a piece of paper using a pencil before translating it into C code. You can then modify and refine your algorithm conveniently. When the pseudocode is translated into a program, you may need to fix some syntax errors. Often, you need to debug the program, which does not have syntax errors, at runtime to get the correct result. Although flowcharts

```
/* File: expx2.c
   Calculate the approximate value of exp(0.5) recursively */
#include <stdio.h>
#include <math.h>  /* for pow() and exp() */
#include <float.h> /* for FLT_EPSILON */

int main() {
   int i;
   double x, expx, term;

   x = 0.5;
   expx = 1.0;
   term = 1.0;
   i = 1;
   while(term>FLT_EPSILON) { /* continue if pow(x,i)/i! > epsilon  */
      term *= x/(double)i;
      expx += term;
      i++;
   }
   printf("expx   = %f\n", expx);
   printf("exp(x) = %f\n", exp(x));
   return 0;
}
```

Program 5.14: Calculating an approximate value for $e^{0.5}$ recursively.

and procedures can also be used for developing algorithm, they are more commonly used for presenting algorithms. A flowchart can also be used to present the flow of a program by ignoring programming details for a large program. Such an application example can be found in Figure 13.12 in Chapter 13. Flowcharts for functions used in a program can be drawn separately as shown in Figures 13.13 and 13.14 for Program 13.36. The efficiency of different algorithms can be compared by the CPU time of programs implemented with different algorithms. Program 13.25 in Chapter 13 demonstrates how to obtain the CPU time for executing a fragment of code.

Application Examples

Acceleration of a Moving Body

Problem Statement:
For the mechanical system shown in Figure 2.12, given mass $m = 5$ kilograms (kg) and coefficient of kinetic friction $\mu = 0.2$, the applied force p is expressed as a function of time t by

$$p(t) = \begin{cases} 20 & \text{if} \quad t \leq 3 \\ 4(t+2) & \text{if} \quad t > 3 \end{cases}$$

Write a program to calculate and print the resulting accelerations of the rigid body from $t = 0$ to 10 seconds with a step size of 1 second.

This problem can be solved with Program 5.15. The program contains the constant value for gravity and specifies values for μ and m. Program 5.15 then initializes t and uses an **if-else** statement to determine the force p for each instance as the program increments t from 0 to 10 with 11 data points using a **for** loop. With the initial value t_0 of 0, final value t_f of 10, and step size 1, the number of data points can be calculated using equation (5.2) as follows:

$$n = (t_f - t_0)/\text{step} + 1 = 11$$

Based on equation (5.3), the value for t at each iteration is

$$t = t_0 + i * \text{step} = i$$

where variable `i` for the index of the **for** loop is an int type.

This program merges declaration and initialization as one section. Using the calculated force p, the acceleration a is printed out for each corresponding value of t. The output is also displayed in the data processing phase during the program execution. Values for variable t are printed out using the format specification `"%3.0f"`, which specifies a field width of 3 without a decimal point. Values for variable a are printed out using the format specification `"%8.4f"`, which specifies a field width of 8 with 4 digits following the decimal point. In this case, the field width is the total number of spaces for the floating-point number. The flowchart for Program 5.15 is shown in Figure 5.20. For illustrative purposes, a connector with label *A* is used in the flowchart. The flowchart could be broken into two parts at point A and located in different pages. A label of a connector symbol can also contain both the letter and the page number where the process continues. For example, on page 4, label *A/5* on a connector points to point *A* on page 5. On page 4, the label *A/4* would indicate that the process was continued at point *A* on page 4. The output from Program 5.15 is in Figure 5.21. Examples of flowcharts for more complicated programs will be presented in Figure 6.8 for Program 6.18 and in Figures 13.12, 13.13, and 13.14 for Program 13.36, later in this book.

```
/* File: accelmpts.c
   Calculate the acceleration for time t
   from 0 to 10 seconds using a for-loop */
#include <stdio.h>
#define M_G   9.81  /* gravitational acceleration constant g */

int main() {
    /* declaration and initialization */
    double a, mu=0.2, m=5.0, t0=0.0, tf=10.0, step=1.0, p, t;
    int i, n;

    /* display header of the table for time and accel */
    printf("time (s)  accel (m/s^2)\n");
    printf("-----------------------\n");
    n = (tf - t0)/step + 1;       /* number of points, 11 */
    for(i=0; i<n; i++) {
      t = t0 + i*step;            /* calculate value t */
     /* calculate acceleration based on time */
     if(t <= 3) {  /* if time t is less or equal to 3 */
        p = 20;
     }
     else {        /* else time t is larger than 3 */
        p = 4*(t+2);
     }
     a = (p-mu*m*M_G)/m;

     /* display output */
     printf("%3.0f      %8.4f\n", t, a);
    }
    return 0;
}
```

Program 5.15: Calculating accelerations using a **for** loop.

Problem Statement:
For the mechanical system shown in Figure 2.12, the applied force p is expressed as a function of time t by

$$p(t) = 4(t - 3) + 20$$

Write a program to calculate continuously accelerations based on the user input values for `m`, μ, and `t`. The program shall be terminated when the value -1 is entered for mass.

The problem statement is similar to the one solved by Program 3.7. The difference is that the user can now continuously input values for `m`, `mu`, and `t` to calculate various acceleration values until a sentinel value of -1 is entered.

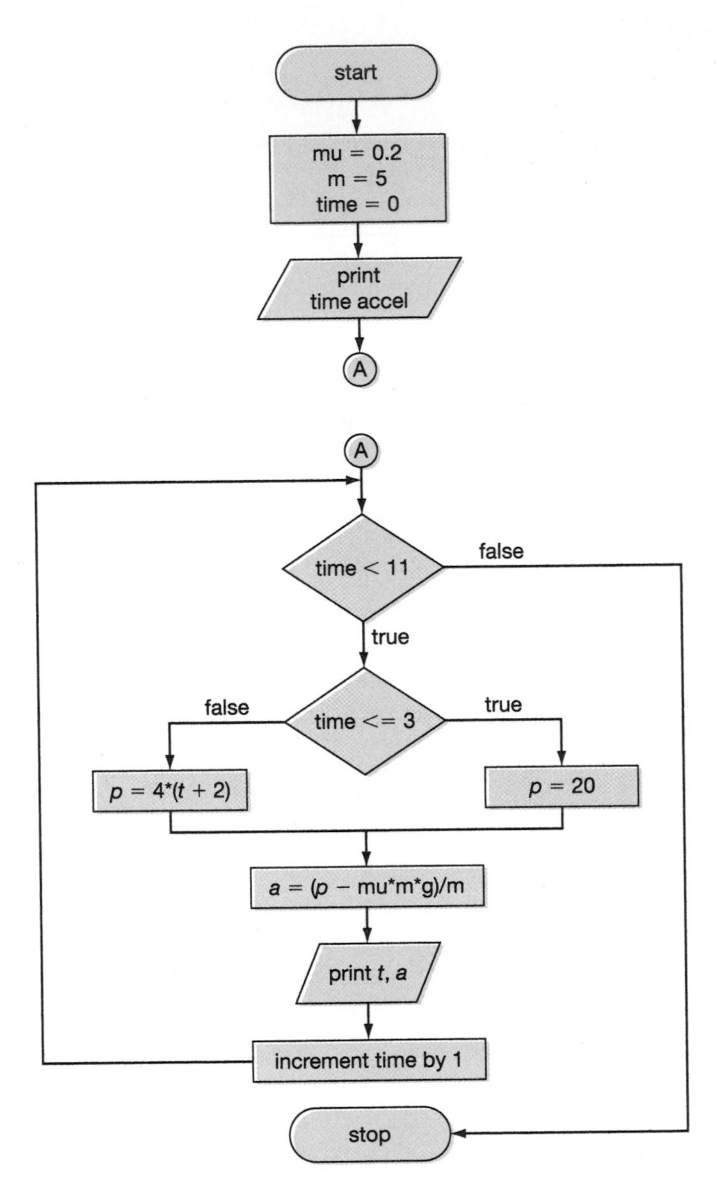

Figure 5.20 The flowchart for Program 5.15.

Program 5.16 is modified from Program 3.7. In programming, a sentinel number is used to indicate that termination of a program is desired. Sentinels are the values that normally do not apply to a given application. For the case of Program 5.16, the sentinel is `-1`. Thus, when `-1` is entered as a value for the mass of the dynamic system, the program terminates. Notice that `-1` would not typically be entered as a value for mass.

```
time (s)  accel (m/s^2)
-----------------------
  0         2.0380
  1         2.0380
  2         2.0380
  3         2.0380
  4         2.8380
  5         3.6380
  6         4.4380
  7         5.2380
  8         6.0380
  9         6.8380
 10         7.6380
```

Figure 5.21: The output from Program 5.15.

```
/* File: accelsentinel.c
   Interactively calculate the acceleration based on the mass,
   friction coefficient, and time from the terminal.
   Terminate until a sentinel number -1 for mass is entered */
#include <stdio.h>
#define M_G   9.81  /* gravitational acceleration constant g */

int main() {
    double a, mu, m, p, t;

    /* prompt the user for input of m, mu, and t */
    printf("***** Acceleration Calculator *****\n\n");
    printf("Please enter value for mass in kilogram\n");
    scanf("%lf", &m);

    /* -1 is a sentinel number for repetition condition */
    while((int)m != -1) {
       printf("mass is %lf (kg)\n\n", m);
       printf("Please enter value for friction coefficient\n");
       scanf("%lf", &mu);
       printf("friction coefficient is %lf\n\n", mu);
       printf("Please enter value for time in seconds\n");
       scanf("%lf", &t);
       printf("time is %lf (s)\n\n", t);
```

Program 5.16: Calculating the acceleration using a sentinel number. *(Continued)*

```
        /* calculate the acceleration based on the user input */
        p = 4*(t-3)+20;
        a = (p-mu*m*M_G)/m;

        /* display output */
        printf("Acceleration a = %f (m/s^2)\n\n", a);
       /* prompt the user for next cycle of input of m, mu, and t */
        printf("Please enter value for mass or -1 to quit the program\n");
        scanf("%lf", &m);
    }
    return 0;
}
```

Program 5.16: *(Continued)*

Calculating the Square Root of a Number Using Newton's Method

Problem Statement:
Based on Newton's method for finding a root of an equation with the mathematical derivation procedure described in Exercise 44 in this chapter, the square root $x = \sqrt{a}$ can be calculated by the formula

$$x_{i+1} = \frac{1}{2}\left(x_i + \frac{a}{x_i}\right) \tag{5.6}$$

In this recursive formula, x_{i+1} is a function of the previous term x_i. It first starts with an initial guess x_0 for a root, then calculates successive approximate roots $x_1, x_2, ..., x_i, x_{i+1}, ...$ A *convergence criterion* for numerical computation is a condition to terminate an iteration. Calculate the square root $\sqrt{3}$ with the initial guess $x_0 = a$ and the convergence criterion $|x_{i+1} - x_i| <$ **FLT_EPSILON**, where **FLT_EPSILON** is a small machine epsilon defined in the header file **float.h**. The program also stops if the number of iterations is larger than 100.

The problem can be solved using Program 5.17. A **for** loop is used for recursive calculation of the square root. Equation (5.6) is translated into the following statement in Program 5.17:

```
x2 = (x1+a/x1)/2.0;
```

If the convergence criterion is met, the control flow of the program will leave the loop by a **break** statement. An iterative algorithm may diverge. In this case, regardless of the number of iterations, no solution can be obtained. The maximum number of iterations in Program 5.17 is 100. If the maximum number of iterations is reached, the program displays an error message to indicate that the algorithm failed to converge. Otherwise, the calculated square root, square root from the math function **sqrt**(), and number of iterations are printed out. The output from Program 5.17 is shown below:

```
sqrtx(3.00) = 1.732051
sqrt(3.00)  = 1.732051
Number of iterations = 5
```

With a good initial guess, Newton's method for calculating the square root of a value is quite efficient. In this case, only five iterations are needed to converge to the square root.

```
/* File: sqrtx.c
   Calculate square root sqrt(a) for a = 3.0 using Newton's method */
#include <stdio.h>
#include <math.h>  /* for fabs() */
#include <float.h> /* for FLT_EPSILON */

#define N 100      /* the maximum number of iteration */

int main() {
   int i;
   double a, x0, x1, x2;

   a = 3.0;           /* sqrt(a) with a = 0.3 */
   x0 = a;            /* an initial guess for x0 */

   x1 = x0;                  /* set x1 to x0 */
   for(i = 1; i <= N; i++) {
      x2 = (x1+a/x1)/2.0;    /* Newton's recursive formula */
      if(fabs(x2-x1) < FLT_EPSILON)
        break;
      x1 = x2;        /* update value x1 for next iteration */
   }
   if(i < N) {        /* number of iteration is less than N */
     printf("sqrtx(%.2f) = %f\n", a, x2);
     printf("sqrt(%.2f)  = %f\n", a, sqrt(a));
     printf("Number of iterations = %d\n", i);
   }
   else {             /* number of iteration equals N */
     printf("sqrtx failed to converge\n");
   }
   return 0;
}
```

Program 5.17: Calculating the square root $\sqrt{3}$ iteratively using Newton's method.

Program 5.17 uses a **break** statement to terminate the iteration of the **for** loop when the convergence criterion is met. For optimization of performance and readability, one may modify the program to get rid of this **break** statement so that the code inside the **for** loop can flow more smoothly. For this purpose, the computational part of Program 5.17 can be modified with the following code fragment:

```
x1 = x0;                     /* set x1 to x0 */
x2 = (x1+a/x1)/2.0;          /* recursive formula */
for(i = 1; i <= N && fabs(x2-x0) >= FLT_EPSILON; i++) {
   x0 = x1;                  /* update x0 for fabs(x2-x0) */
   x2 = (x1+a/x1)/2.0;       /* recursive formula */
   x1 = x2;      /* update value x1 for next iteration */
}
```

The previous code is more readable because the termination condition for the **for** loop is placed at the same place using an AND logic operation. At the end of each iteration for the **for** loop, the values for variables `x1` and `x2` are the same. Therefore, the variable `x0` is used to keep the value for `x1` in the previous iteration for calculating the convergence condition. Program 6.8 in Chapter 6 uses this algorithm to implement a square root function.

Random Number Generation — Rolling a Six-Sided Die

Random numbers are commonly used in game, simulation, and statistical analysis. The header file **stdlib.h** contains functions and definitions useful for generating random numbers. The function **rand()** generates a sequence of *pseudo-random* integers in the range 0 to **RAND_MAX**. The macro **RAND_MAX** is a constant defined in the header file **stdlib.h** and shall be no less than 32767. The function **rand()** has the function prototype

```
int rand(void);
```

which means that **rand()** returns an integer and has no argument. The details about functions and function prototypes are described in Chapter 6. The function **rand()** generates a *pseudo-random* integer. Generating pseudo-random numbers imply that calling the function **rand()** multiple times inside a program produces a sequence of integers that appear to be random. However, executing the program again would produce the same sequence of integers. The pseudo-random feature of the function **rand()** provides a convenient method for debugging programs utilizing random number generation. The repeatability of the sequential integers allows the programmer to anticipate the result of the program. The programmer would be able to make adjustments to obtain the correct output.

Although the pseudo-random feature of the function **rand()** is useful for debugging, generating a different sequence of random numbers for each execution of a program is still desired. To do this, the standard library function **srand()** must be used to *seed* the *random number generator*. The function prototype for the function **srand()** is as follows:

```
void srand(unsigned int seed);
```

The function has no return value. The argument `seed` is an unsigned integer representing the seed to produce a new sequence of random numbers to be returned by subsequent calls to the **rand()** function. Note that the seed value has to be different to generate a new sequence of numbers. That is, if the same seed value is used for a subsequent execution of a program, the sequence of random numbers shall be repeated.

It is often desirable to seed the random number generator with a value corresponding to the current time. Because time is continuously changing, each execution of a program would produce a entirely different sequence of random numbers. Seeding the function **rand()** with a time value can be done with the following statement:

```
srand(time(NULL));
```

where the function **time()** is defined in the header file **time.h**. The **time()** function returns the current calendar time, which is converted to an unsigned integer to seed the random number generator. The details about the function **time()** and other time-manipulating functions are described in detail in section 13.1.17 in Chapter 13.

An interactive execution of these functions in a Ch command shell is shown below.

```
> srand(time(NULL))
> rand()
4497
> rand()
11439
```

Recall that the sequence of random numbers produced by the function **srand()** are between the range of 0 to **RAND_MAX**. Typically, this range is different than the desired range for a given application. For example, the flipping of a coin only requires 0 for "heads" and 1 for "tails." Thus, integers ranging from 0 to 1 are desired for simulating a coin toss. Similarly, the rolling of a six-sided die would require an integer in the range between 1 and 6. Note that the expression `rand() % b` gives an integer in the range of `[0, b-1]`. To scale the random numbers directly generated by the function **rand()**, the following formula can be used:

```
n = a + rand() % b
```

to generate an integer in the range of $[a, a + b - 1]$, where a is considered the shifting value, which is equal to the first number of the desired range. Variable b is the scaling factor and is equal to the width of the desired range of numbers. For the example of simulating the roll of a six-sided die, the formula would be

```
n = 1 + rand() % 6
```

To toss a coin, the formula would be

```
n = 1 + rand() % 2
```

Random floating-point numbers in a specified range are needed for some statistical analysis. The following formula can be used to generate random floating-point numbers in the range `[x1, x2]`:

```
x = x1 + rand()*(x2-x1)/(double)RAND_MAX;
```

For example, the formula below would give uniform random numbers in the range [0, 1].

```
x = rand()/(double)RAND_MAX;
```

Program 5.18 is an example that encapsulates all the above aspects discussed for random number generation. The purpose of this program is to simulate the rolling of a six-sided die 6000 times. If the program is truly random, then each number between 1 and 6 would have an equal likelihood of occurring. The frequency of each occurrence is displayed at the end of the program's execution. Program 5.18 first initializes the counters for recording the frequency of occurrence of each integer. Next, the function **srand()** is called to seed the random number generator with a value corresponding to the current time. A **for** loop is then used to "roll" the die 6000 times, and the counter `rollcount` is incremented accordingly. A **switch** statement is used to record the occurance for one of six faces in each roll in a frequency variable for that face. The output of Program 5.18 is shown following. Notice that occurrence of each face is relatively the same.

```
  Face     Frequency
   1          1003
   2          994
   3          996
   4          1021
   5          990
   6          996
```

```
/* File: srand.c
   Roll a six-sided die 6000 times randomly,
   calculate the frequency for each face. */
#include <stdio.h>
#include <stdlib.h>  /* for using srand() and rand() in the C standard lib */
#include <time.h>    /* for using time() in the C standard lib  */

int main() {
   int face,          /* face in each roll*/
       rollcount,     /* roll count number */
       freq1=0, freq2=0, freq3=0,  /* frequency for each face */
       freq4=0, freq5=0, freq6=0;

   srand(time(NULL)); /* seed the random number generator */
   /* use a loop to roll 6000 times */
   for (rollcount = 1; rollcount <= 6000; rollcount++) {
      /* generate a random number in [1, 6] */
      face = 1 + rand() % 6;
      /* record the face in a frequency variable */
      switch(face) {
        case 1:        /* if face is 1 */
          freq1 += 1; /* increment the frequency variable for face 1 */
          break;
        case 2:        /* if face is 2 */
          freq2 += 1; /* increment the frequency variable for face 2 */
          break;
        case 3:
          freq3 += 1;
          break;
        case 4:
          freq4 += 1;
          break;
```

Program 5.18: Rolling a six-sided die 6000 times. (*Continued*)

```
           case 5:
             freq5 += 1;
             break;
           case 6:           /* if face is 6 */
             freq6 += 1; /* increment the frequency variable for face 6 */
             break;
       }
   }

   /* display the frequency for each face */
   printf(" Face     Frequency\n");
   printf("  1         %d\n", freq1);
   printf("  2         %d\n", freq2);
   printf("  3         %d\n", freq3);
   printf("  4         %d\n", freq4);
   printf("  5         %d\n", freq5);
   printf("  6         %d\n", freq6);
   return 0;
}
```

Program 5.18: *(Continued)*

5.8 Terminating a Loop by End-of-File or End-of-File Key Combination

In section 5.5.2, we described how to use a fixed number of iterations or a special value called sentinel value or signal value to terminate a loop. If the input to a program is entered by the input redirection, for counter-controlled repetition, the number of entries in the data file that can be processed by the program is fixed. For sentinel-controlled repetition in a loop, a data file must contain a sentinel number to terminate the loop. In some applications, it might be desirable to terminate a loop when a program finishes reading the data in a data file. This means to terminate a loop when the end-of-file (EOF) is detected.

Setting the EOF indicator for the standard input involves entering a system-specific key combination. Table 5.1 lists the EOF key combinations for Unix, Linux, Mac OS X, and Windows systems. On Unix, Linux, and Mac OS X systems, the EOF indicator with the key combination

<Ctrl>d

means to press both the *<Ctrl>* key and the *d* key. On Windows, the key combination

<Ctrl>z <return>

means to press both the *<Ctrl>* key and the *z* key, followed by pressing the *Enter* key.

Table 5.1 EOF key combinations for various systems.

Operating system	Key combination
Unix, Linux, Mac OS X	*<Ctrl>d*
Windows	*<Ctrl>z <return>*

As an example, Program 5.19 is the same as Program 5.7 except that the function **feof()** is used instead of a sentinel number −1 to terminate the loop. The statements inside the **while** loop conditioned by

```
while(!feof(stdin))
```

will execute repeatedly until the EOF indicator is set. The expression

```
feof(stdin)
```

can be used to test whether an EOF *indicator* has been set for the console input. The value for the expression is nonzero if the EOF key combination is entered. Details for the function **feof()** are described in section 14.2 in Chapter 14.

An interactive execution of Program 5.19 is as follows:

```
> gpa3.c
Enter a grade [0, 4] or EOF to quit the program
4
Enter a grade [0, 4] or EOF to quit the program
3.7
Enter a grade [0, 4] or EOF to quit the program
4
Enter a grade [0, 4] or EOF to quit the program
(entered <Ctrl>z<return> for Windows) (entered <Ctrl>d for Unix)
The GPA is: 3.750000
```

Suppose that the data file `gpa3.dat` contains the following grades without a sentinel value:

```
4 3.7 3.3
```

In that case, Program 5.19 can be executed with the input data from `gpa3.dat` by the input/output redirection as follows:

```
> gpa3.c < gpa3.dat
Enter a grade [0, 4] or EOF to quit the program
Enter a grade [0, 4] or EOF to quit the program
Enter a grade [0, 4] or EOF to quit the program
Enter a grade [0, 4] or EOF to quit the program
The GPA is: 3.900000
```

Unlike the data files `gpa.dat` for Program 5.6 and `gpa2.dat` for Program 5.7, the number of grades and format of `gpa3.dat` are not constrained. Additional grades for new courses can be appended to the data file to calculate the GPA including new courses. If the program is designed to run with the input/output redirection only, the printing statement for the user prompt can be removed from the program to make the output more clear.

```
/* File: gpa3.c
   Calculate the GPA for grades entered from the terminal.
   Terminate until End-of-File is entered */
#include <stdio.h>

#define HIGHESTMARK 4.0  /* highest mark for grade */

int main() {
    /* declaration */
    int count;
    double grade, total, gpa;

    /* initialization */
    count = 0;
    total = 0;

    /* processing input grades and calculate the GPA */
    printf("Enter a grade [0, %g] or EOF to quit the program\n", HIGHESTMARK);
    scanf("%lf", &grade);
    while(!feof(stdin)) { /* repetition condition */
       /* a valid grade should 0<= grade <= 4 */
       if(0 <= grade && grade <= HIGHESTMARK) {
         total += grade;
         count++;
       }
       else {
         printf("Invalid grade %c\n", '\a');
       }
       printf("Enter a grade [0, %g] or EOF to quit the program\n", HIGHESTMARK);
       scanf("%lf", &grade);
    }

    /* display output and termination */
    if(count != 0) {
       gpa = total/count;
       printf("The GPA is: %f\n", gpa);
    }
    else
      printf("No grade entered.\n");
    return 0;
}
```

Program 5.19: Calculating the GPA using the EOF indicator

5.9 Making It Work

5.9.1 Debugging Programs with Selection and Repetition Statements Using ChIDE

Running a program in the debug mode in ChIDE step by step, as described in section 3.1 in Chapter 3, is very helpful for understanding the working principle of selection and repetition statements. You can examine the conditional expression of the selection statements to see which branch of the selection statements is executed based on the condition. As the body of a repetition statement is executed, you can watch values of a loop index variable at each iteration and a conditional expression for terminating the repetition.

5.9.2 Programming Style and Indenting Programs Using ChIDE

As we described earlier in this book in Chapter 2, for readability and software maintenance, statements inside a function shall be properly indented. Indentation is especially important for a program with many nested loops. Indentation needs to be consistent for a program with a fixed number of blank spaces. Each indentation in most source code presented in this book uses four blank space characters. The use of horizontal tabs for indentation is not recommended because it takes too much space in code with many nested loops and blocks. Also, some word processors treat a horizontal tab as a single white space. Hardcopy of source code without proper indentation is difficult to read.

Programs edited in ChIDE can be properly indented using an indentation utility program. When you click the command `Tools | Indent` on the toolbar, the program in the current editing pane will be properly indented. You can also right-click the file name on the Tab bar, located below the debug bar, and select `Indent` to indent the program in the editing pane. Each indentation has four blank space characters.

Exercises

1. Before submitting your homework, indent programs with four blank space characters for each indentation using ChIDE by clicking the command `Tools | Indent` on the toolbar.
2. State whether the following statement is true or false. If false, explain why.
   The **default** case is required in the **switch** selection structure.
3. Identify and correct the errors in each of the following code blocks. (Note: there may be more than one error.)

   a.
   ```
   if(age >= 65);
     printf("Age is greater than or equal to 65\");
   else
     printf("Age is less than 65\n")
   ```
   b.
   ```
   if(i = 2)
     printf("i is 2\n");
   else
     printf("i is not equal to 2\n");
   ```
   c. The following code should output the odd integers from 999 to 1:
   ```
   for(x = 999; x >= 1; x +=2)
      printf("%d\n", n);
   ```
   d. The following code should output the even integers from 2 to 100:
   ```
   counter = 2;
   Do {
     if(counter % 2 == 0)
   ```

```
        printf("%d\n", counter);
        counter += 2;
    } While(counter < 100)
```

e. The following code should sum the integers from 100 to 150:

```
total = 1;
for(x = 100; x <= 150; x++);
  total += x;
```

4. What does the following program print?

```
#include <stdio.h>

int main() {
  int x = 1, total = 0, y;

  while(x <= 10) {
    y = x * x;
    printf("%d\n", y);
    total += y;
    ++x;
  }
  printf("Total is %d\n", total);
  return 0;
}
```

5. Modify Program 3.5. So that, addition to the sizes of basic data types, if the computer matches one of the programming models listed in Table 3.2, it displays the programming model. Otherwise, it displays the message `unknown programming model`.
6. Write a program using a loop to print out the following sequence exactly, including commas:

```
10, 9, 8, 7, 6,
5, 4, 3, 2, 1
```

7. It is important to write an efficient program with a correct algorithm. Write a program using a loop to add integers from 1 to n with n equal to 1000. Verify the result using the formula $n(n+1)/2$ for the sum from 1 to n, which is more efficient than using a loop.
8. Write a program using a **for** loop to print out the following sequence exactly, including commas:

```
2, 4, 6, 8, 10, 12, 14, 16
```

9. Write a program that utilizes looping to print the following table of values:

```
2N      20*N     200*N     2000*N
2       20       200       2000
4       40       400       4000
6       60       600       6000
8       80       800       8000
10      100      1000      10000
```

The tab character, `\t`, may be used in the printf statement to separate the columns with tabs.

10. Write a program that calculates and prints the average of several integers. Assume that the last value read with **scanf()** is sentinel number 9999. A typical input sequence might be

```
10 8 11 7 9 9999
```

indicating that the average of all the values preceding 9999 is to be calculated. Draw the flowchart for the program.

11. The Fibonacci sequence: 0, 1, 1, 2, 3, 5, 8, 13, ... is defined by the difference equation

$$F_{k+2} = F_{k+1} + F_k$$

Write a program to calculate and print out the Fibonacci sequence with the value k read from the terminal input. Write a pseudocode and draw the flowchart for the program first.

12. Write a program to print out all bits of the following integer numbers with 32 bits without using the format specifier `%b` in Ch.

(a) 90 **(b)** 0X32A **(c)** −89 **(d)** 3563

13. What is the value of `sum` after the code below is executed?

```
int i, sum = 0;
for (i=0; i<10; i++) {
   switch (i) {
      case 0:
      case 1:
      case 3:
      case 5:
         sum++;
      case 4:
         break;
      default:
         break;
   }
}
printf("sum = %d\n", sum);
```

14. Calculate the values of the following statements for x in the range of $-1 \leq x \leq 5$ with a step size of 0.25, and display the output in the format shown in Figure 5.16.

a. $f_1(x) = 2x\sin(x) + \cos(x) + \dfrac{4x+3}{3x^2+2x+4}$

b. $f_2(x) = x^2\sqrt{2x}$

c. $f_3(x) = 2x\sin(x) + \cos(x^2\sqrt{2x})$

d. $f_4(x) = \dfrac{3x^2+4x+3}{5\sin(x^2)+4x^2+3}$

15. Calculate the values of the following statements for x in the range of $-1 \leq x \leq 5$ with a step size of 1 and for y in the range of $2 \leq y \leq 4$ with a step size of 0.5, and display the output in the format shown in Figure 5.18.

a. $f_5(x, y) = 2x\sin(y) + \cos(x) + \dfrac{4x+3}{3x^2+2y+4}$

b. $f_6(x, y) = x^2\sqrt{2y}$

c. $f_7(x, y) = 2x\sin(y) + \cos(y^2\sqrt{2x})$

d. $f_8(x, y) = \dfrac{3x^2 + 4y + 3}{5\sin(y^2) + 4x^2 + 6}$

16. Write a program that reads an integer and determines and prints whether it is odd or even. (Hint: Use the modulus operator `%`. An even number is a multiple of 2. Any multiple of 2 leaves a remainder of zero when divided by 2.)

17. Continue from Exercise 28 in Chapter 4. When characters are represented in ASCII code, only 7 bits are needed. Bit 8 is not used. Write a program to read a character. Print out the input character as a binary number with 8 bits. Determine the number of 1s in its binary representation. If the totol number of 1s in its binary representation is odd, give bit 8 the value 1. Print out the modified value as a binary number with 8 bits. Test characters '3' and '4'.

18. An integer is a *prime* number if it is divisible only by 1 and itself. For example, 2, 3, 5, 7, and 11 are prime numbers. Write a program that reads an integer and determines if it is a prime number. If it is not a prime number, print out the smallest divisor. Otherwise, print out the prime number. Write a pseudocode and draw the flowchart for the program first. Test your program with the numbers -10, 0, 1, 2, 4, 9, 11, and 12. (Hint: Use the modulus operator `%` to determine if a number is divisible by another number. The smallest divisor of even numbers is 2. However, you only need to test up to $\sqrt{n}$ to verify if it is divisible.)

19. Write a program to read in an integer number between 0 and 255. Print out the character corresponding to the input number of the ASCII value as shown in Appendix D. Give an error message if the input number is outside the specified range. The program terminates when the input number is -1. Write a pseudocode and draw the flowchart for the program first.

20. Write a program that will allow the user to convert from the U.S. customary system of units to the International System of metric units (SI). The user can then choose length, volume, or force for the conversion. Note that 1 foot = 0.3048 meter, 1 cubic foot = 0.002817 cubic meter, 1 pound = 4.4482 newtons. Write pseudocode and draw the flowchart for the program first. Test your program by entering the length of 3 feet, 2.5 cubic feet, and 3.5 pounds. The interactive execution of the program shall be as follows:

```
> conversion.c
Enter conversion type(1 = length, 2 = volume, 3 = force): 1
Enter value for conversion: 3
3.000000 ft = 0.914400 m
```

21. Write a program that will display the total amount of money in a bank account with the interest compounded annually from 1 to 30 years. The user enters the principal and rate of interest. The mathematical relationship is as follows:

$$y = p(1 + r)^n$$

where y is the amount, p the principal invested, r the interest rate, and n the number of years. The C function **pow**(x, y) can be used to calculate x^y. Write pseudocode and draw the flowchart for the program first. Test your program with the invested principal of $10,000 and an 8 percent interest rate. The interactive execution of the program shall be as follows:

```
> interest.c
Enter the principal: 10000
Enter the interest rate (%): 8
year  total
1   $10800.00
2   $11664.00
...
```

22. The iteration for calculating a factorial $n!$ starting with `1*2` in Program 5.8. Draw a flowchart, write pseudocode and a program to calculate a factorial $n!$ starting with `n*(n-1)`. Use a **for** loop in the program.
23. Use nested loops to calculate factorials $n!$ for n from 1 to 12 using variables of unsigned int type. Based on **UINT_MAX** defined in the header file **limits.h**, give the maximum n when using unsigned int for calculating $n!$
24. Use nested loops to calculate factorials $n!$ for n from 1 to 20 using variables of unsigned long long type. Based on **ULLONG_MAX** defined in the header file **limits.h**, give the maximum n when using unsigned long long for calculating $n!$
25. Write a program to print the output shown below.

```
     *
    ***
   *****
  *******
 *********
***********
```

Print out one character at a time for a line, not in a string for a line.

26. Draw the flowchart for the algorithm implemented in Program 5.10.
27. Write a program to print out a table, similar to Figure 5.17, for the addition of two integer numbers from 1 to 10.
28. Draw a flowchart and write a program with nested loops to print out the multiplication table shown below:

```
     10   9   8   7   6   5   4   3   2   1
 -------------------------------------------
 10| 100
  9|  90  81
  8|  80  72  64
  7|  70  63  56  49
  6|  60  54  48  42  36
  5|  50  45  40  35  30  25
  4|  40  36  32  28  24  20  16
  3|  30  27  24  21  18  15  12   9
  2|  20  18  16  14  12  10   8   6   4
  1|  10   9   8   7   6   5   4   3   2   1
 -------------------------------------------
```

29. Draw a flowchart and write a program with nested loops to print out the multiplication table shown below:

```
       1   2   3   4   5   6   7   8   9  10
   -----------------------------------------
   1|  1   2   3   4   5   6   7   8   9  10
   2|      4   6   8  10  12  14  16  18  20
   3|          9  12  15  18  21  24  27  30
   4|             16  20  24  28  32  36  40
   5|                 25  30  35  40  45  50
   6|                     36  42  48  54  60
   7|                         49  56  63  70
   8|                             64  72  80
   9|                                 81  90
  10|                                    100
   -----------------------------------------
```

30. What is the output for the programs below?

a.
```
#include <stdio.h>
int main() {
     int i, j;

     for(i=1; i<= 5; i++) {
         for(j=1; j<=i; j++) {
             if(i==3) {
                 continue;
             }
             printf("%d ", i*j);
         }
         printf("\n");
     }
     return 0;
}
```

b.
```
#include <stdio.h>
int main() {
     int i, j;

     for(i=1; i<= 5; i++) {
         for(j=1; j<=i; j++) {
             if(j==3) {
                 continue;
             }
             printf("%d ", i*j);
         }
         printf("\n");
     }
```

```
    return 0;
}
```

c.
```
#include <stdio.h>
int main() {
    int i, j;

    for(i=1; i<= 5; i++) {
       if(i==3) {
          continue;
       }
       for(j=1; j<=i; j++) {
          if(j==3) {
             break;
          }
          printf("%d ", i*j);
       }
       printf("\n");
    }
    return 0;
}
```

31. A company sells five different products with prices shown in the following table:

Product Number	Retail Price
1	2.98
2	4.50
3	9.98
4	4.49
5	6.87

Write a program that reads a series of pairs of numbers in the format of

```
1) Product number
2) Quantity sold for one day
```

Test data in the data file `product.dat` with values

```
4  20
2  30
1  11
5  5
3  23
2  12
```

Your program should use a **switch** statement to help determine the price for each product. Your program should calculate and display the total value of all products sold. Draw the flowchart for the program.

a. Terminate the program when input for the product number is -1.
b. Terminate the program when the input is EOF.

Run the program interactively. Run the program with the data file `product.dat` using the input/output redirection.

32. Develop a GPA calculation program that will process grades with scores of 0, 0.7, 1, 1.3, 1.7, 2, 2.3, 2.7, 3, 3.3, 3.7, and 4 only for an arbitrary number of courses. The user shall input a sequence of scores. The program shall check if each input score is valid or not. Before the program exits, it calculates the GPA based on the previously entered scores. Write a pseudocode and draw the flowchart for the program first.
    a. When the user inputs a value of -1, the program will terminate. Run your program with the testing scores below in the data file `gpa4.dat` by the input/output redirection.
    `4 3.3 3.0 2.7 1.0 1.3 0.0 0.7 4.0 1.7 5 3.7 -1.`
    b. When the user inputs an end-of-file indicator, the program will terminate. Run your program with the testing scores below in the data file `gpa5.dat` by the input/output redirection. Save the GPA as output in the file `gpa4.out`.
    `4 3.3 3.0 2.7 1.0 1.3 0.0 0.7 4.0 1.7 5 3.7.`
33. Develop a GPA calculation program that will process grades A, B, C, D, F or a, b, c, d, f corresponding to scores 4, 3, 2, 1, and 0, respectively. The user shall input a sequence of grades. The program shall check if each input grade is valid or not. When the user inputs the character 'Z', the program will terminate and calculate the GPA based on the previously entered grades. Note that when a character is input from the terminal prompt by typing a character followed by a Return or Enter key, two characters are entered into the input buffer. One is the character and the other is the newline character `'\n'`. You may obtain the input character and get rid of the newline character by using the following statements:

```
char grade, retchar;
scanf("%c%c", &grade, &retchar);
```

Write a pseudocode and draw the flowchart for the program first. Run your program with the testing grades `A B C D F A b c Z` (1) interactively; (2) using testing grades in the data file `gpa6.dat` by the input/output redirection.

   a. Use an **if-else-if-else** structure to test whether the input grade is valid or not, and branch accordingly.
   b. Use a **switch** statement to test whether the input grade is valid or not, and branch accordingly.
34. Modify Exercise 33 to use the EOF indicator, instead of the sentinel value 'Z', to terminate the loop for input of grades. Use the data file `gpa8.dat` containing the grades below. `A B C D F A b c`
35. For the mechanical system shown in Figure 2.12, given mass $m = 6$ kilograms (kg) and coefficient of kinetic friction $\mu = 0.3$, the applied force p is expressed as a function of time t by

$$p(t) = \begin{cases} 20 & \text{if} \quad t \leq 3 \\ 4(t+2) & \text{if} \quad t > 3 \leq 6 \\ 4(t^2+2t) & \text{if} \quad t > 6 \end{cases}$$

   a. Calculate the force dependent on the time provided by the user at the prompt. Check the result when the input time is 2.5 seconds.
   b. Calculate the resulting accelerations of the rigid body from $t = 0$ to 10 seconds with an incremental step value of 1.
36. Print out a temperature conversion table from degrees in Celsius to degrees in Fahrenheit when the temperature varies in the range of [-10, 40] degrees in Celsius with an incremental step size of 1 degree. The relationship is as follows:

$$f = (9/5)c + 32$$

where c is the temperature in Celsius and f the temperature in Fahrenheit.

37. The machine epsilon ε is the difference between 1 and the smallest representable value greater than 1 in the formula below.

$$1.0 + \varepsilon > 1.0$$

The machine epsilon can be calculated by the code fragment

```
epsilon = 1.0;
while(epsilon+1 > 1)
  epsilon /= 2;
epsilon *= 2;
```

Calculate the machine epsilons for float and double. Compare the calculated results with the macros **FLT_EPSILON** and **DBL_EPSILON** defined in the header file **float.h** using the format `"%e"` for output.

38. The value π can be represented by the series as follows:

$$\pi = 4\left(1 - \frac{1}{3} + \frac{1}{5} - \frac{1}{7} + \ldots\right)$$
$$= 4\sum_{i=0}^{\infty} \frac{(-1)^i}{(2i+1)}.$$

Calculate the approximate values for π with the formula below:

$$f(j) = 4\sum_{i=0}^{j} \frac{(-1)^i}{(2i+1)}$$

using a loop for j from 10 to 100 with an incremental step size of 10. Calculate also the approximate value for π when j is 10,000.

39. For the exponential function expanded as a Taylor series in equation (5.5), calculate e^x with $x = 0.5$ and the irrational exponential number e using the algorithm in Program 5.12. Display the number of terms of Taylor series used in the calculation. Compare the result using the above formula with the result using the function **exp**() defined in the header file **math.h** with 15 digits after the decimal point.

40. The sine function can be expanded as a Taylor series as follows:

$$\sin x = x - \frac{x^3}{3!} + \frac{x^5}{5!} - \frac{x^7}{7!} + \ldots$$
$$= \sum_{i=0}^{\infty} \frac{(-1)^i x^{(2i+1)}}{(2i+1)!}.$$

When $-1 \leq x \leq 1$, we can calculate the approximate value $\sin(x)$ by the formula

$$\sum_{i=0}^{n} \frac{(-1)^i x^{(2i+1)}}{(2i+1)!}$$

When $x < -1$ or $x > 1$, formula $\sin(2n\pi + x) = \sin(x)$ or a more robust algorithm may be needed to compute the result for a sine function. Calculate $\sin(x)$ with $x = 0.5$ and $n = 10$. Compare the result using the above formula with the result using the function **sin**() defined in the header file **math.h** with 15 digits after the decimal point. Write a pseudocode and draw its flowchart for the following cases.

a. Write a program to compute each term of the Taylor series straightforwardly with a factorial.
b. Write a program to compute each term of the Taylor series recursively.

41. The cosine function can be expanded as a Taylor series as follows:

$$\cos x = 1 - \frac{x^2}{2!} + \frac{x^4}{4!} - \frac{x^6}{6!} + \ldots$$
$$= \sum_{i=0}^{\infty} \frac{(-1)^i x^{2i}}{(2i)!}$$

When $-1 \leq x \leq 1$, we can calculate the approximate value of $\cos(x)$ by the formula

$$\sum_{i=0}^{n} \frac{(-1)^i x^{2i}}{(2i)!}$$

When $x < -1$ or $x > 1$, formula $\cos(2n\pi + x) = \cos(x)$ or a more robust algorithm may be needed to compute the result for a cosine function. Calculate $\cos(x)$ with $x = 0.5$ and $n = 10$. Compare the result using the above formula with the result using the function **cos()** defined in the header file **math.h** with 15 digits after the decimal point. Write a pseudocode and draw its flowchart for the following cases.

a. Write a program to compute each term of the Taylor series straightforwardly with a factorial.
b. Write a program to compute each term of the Taylor series recursively.

42. Write pseudocode and procedures, and draw a flowchart for Newton's method for calculating a square root shown in Program 5.17.

43. Based on Newton's method, write a program to calculate the square roots $x = \sqrt{a}$ with an initial guess of $x_0 = a$ for a from 1 to 10 with the output shown below. Write pseudocode and draw a flowchart for the program first.

```
    a    square root
-----------------
 1.00    1.000000
 2.00    1.414214
 ...
 9.00    3.000000
10.00    3.162278
```

44. Newton's method for finding a root of an equation $f(x)$ is formulated as

$$x_{i+1} = x_i - \frac{f(x_i)}{f'(x_i)} \tag{5.7}$$

where $f'(x_i)$ is the derivative of function $f(x)$ evaluated at $x = x_i$. The method starts with an initial guess of x_0 for a root and then generate successive approximate roots $x_1, x_2, \ldots, x_i, x_{i+1}, \ldots$ The value x_{i+1} is a function of the previous one, x_i.

a. For function $f(x) = x^2 - a$ and its derivative $f'(x) = 2x$, verify that Newton's formula (5.7) is the same as equation (5.6).
b. For function $f(x) = x^3 - a$ and its derivative $f'(x) = 3x^2$, based on Newton's method, verify that the cubic root $x = \sqrt[3]{a}$ can be calculated by the formula

$$x_{i+1} = \frac{1}{3}\left(2x_i + \frac{a}{x_i^2}\right) \tag{5.8}$$

Calculate the following cubic roots with the initial guess $x_0 = a$ and the convergence criterion $|x_{i+1} - x_i| < $ **FLT_EPSILON**. The program also stops if the number of iterations is larger than 100. Write pseudocode and draw a flowchart for the program first.

i. Calculate the cubic root $\sqrt[3]{3}$.

ii. Calculate the cubic root $\sqrt[3]{a}$ for a from 1 to 10 with the output formatted similarly as that in Exercise 43.

45. Generate 20 random integer numbers in the range [6, 15] and print them out.

46. Generate 20 random floating-point numbers in the range [−2.0, 2.0] and print them out.

47. Write pseudocode and draw flowcharts before writing the following programs.

a. Write a program to generate two random integers ranging from 1 to 10 using the functions **rand()** and **srand()**. The random numbers generated by the program shall be different at each run. Then prompt the user to enter the sum of the two numbers. If the user enters the right answer, print `"Correct!"` If it is wrong, print `"Incorrect. Please try again."` and allow the user to enter another answer until it is right.

b. Modify the program to ask the user a total of 10 addition problems. At the end of the 10th question, print a message to tell the user how many problems were answered correctly. If the user has more than 8 correct solutions, give a complimentary comment. For less than 6 correct solutions, give an encouraging statement. Note that the user should only have one chance to answer each question.

48. In Exercise 47, two random numbers in the range from 1 to 10 are added. Do the same for the subtraction of two random numbers in the range from 1 to 100.

49. In Exercise 47, two random numbers in the range from 1 to 10 are added. Do the same for the multiplication of two random numbers in the range from 1 to 9.

50. Write pseudocode and draw flowcharts before writing the following programs.

a. Write a program to generate two random integers ranging from 1 to 10 using the functions **rand()** and **srand()**. The random numbers generated by the program shall be different at each run. A random operation of either addition or subtraction for these two numbers will be selected. Then prompt the user to enter the result of the operation. If the user enters the right answer, print `"Correct!"` If it is wrong, print `"Incorrect!"` Ask the user a total of 10 problems. At the end of the 10th question, print a message to tell the user how many problems were answered correctly. If the user has more than 8 correct solutions, give a complimentary comment. For less than 6 correct solutions, give an encouraging statement. Note that the user should only have one chance to answer each question.

b. Modify the program to select a random operation of addition, subtraction, or multiplication.

51. The price for one copy of a software package is $399. The discount for the software depends on the volume as shown in a table below.

Number of copies	Discount
num $<$ 5	no discount
num $<$ 20	10%
num $<$ 50	15%
num $\geq$ 50	20%

Write a program to calculate the cost with the number of copies of the software package provided by the user at the prompt. What are the costs when the number of copies purchased is 20 and 25?

52. For the quadratic equation (4.1) in Chapter 4, if its discriminant ($b^2 - 4ac$) is zero, the equation has two identical real roots. If the discriminant is positive, the equation has two distinct real roots shown in equations (4.2) and (4.3). If the discriminant is negative, the equation has the following two complex conjugate roots:

$$x_1 = \frac{-b + i\sqrt{4ac - b^2}}{2a}, \quad x_2 = \frac{-b - i\sqrt{4ac - b^2}}{2a}$$

where i is the imaginary number. Write a program to read the values for coefficients a, b, and c of the quadratic equation from the terminal, and calculate its roots. You may check if the absolute value of the distriminant ($b^2 - 4ac$) is smaller than **FLT_EPSILON** to deminine if the equation has two identical roots. Write pseudocode and draw a flowchart for the program first. Test your program using equations $x^2 - 4x + 4 = 0$ with two identical roots $x = 2$, $x^2 - 5x + 6 = 0$ with two distinct roots $x = 2$ and $x = 3$, and $x^2 - 2x + 5 = 0$ with two complex roots $x = 1 + i2$ and $x = 1 - i2$.

CHAPTER 6

Functions

A C program is generally formed by a set of functions, which subsequently consist of many programming statements. Using functions, a large computing task can be broken into smaller ones; a user can develop application programs based upon what others have done instead of starting from scratch. For example, we have used standard C functions **printf()** for output, **sin()** for calculating the sine function, and **rand()** and **srand()** for generating random numbers. This chapter describes how functions are handled in C and how to write your own functions for your application programs. For user convenience, one may collect all relevant functions as a library. A *library* consists of a set of functions. For example, C provides a standard mathematical library. All C standard libraries are highlighted in this chapter. In addition, a simple plotting library is introduced for graphical visualization, which is important for many applications in engineering and science.

6.1 Function Definitions

A function can be defined in the form of

```
return_type function_name(argument_declaration)
{
  statements
}
```

Parts of the above function definition may be absent. Each argument in the argument declaration is separated not by a semicolon, but by a comma. The `return_type` can be any valid type specifier.

In Program 6.1, the function `addition()` has two arguments of int type. It calculates and returns the sum of the values of two passed arguments. The return type of the function is int. The function `addition()` is called inside the function **main()**. In this case, the function **main()** is the *calling function*, whereas the function `addition()` is the *called function*. The number of arguments in a function call shall match the number of arguments in the function definition, except for functions declared with a variable number of arguments described in section 6.11. The function `addition()` has two arguments. When the function `addition()` is called by the statement

```
sum = addition(3, 4);
```

the memory for variables `a` and `b` in the arguments of of the function `addition()` is allocated. The values of 3 and 4 are then assigned to variables `a` and `b`, respectively.

A **return** statement terminates execution of the current function and returns control to its caller. A function may have any number of **return** statements. If a **return** statement with an expression such as

```
return expression;
```

```c
/* File: addition.c
   Use function addition() to add two integers */
#include <stdio.h>

/* function definition for addition() */
int addition(int a, int b) {
    int s;      /* declare local variable inside function */

    s = a + b;  /* addition of a and b */
    return s;   /* return the sum of a and b */
}

int main() {
    int sum;    /* declare local variable sum */

    /* call function addition() to add 3 and 4, the return
       value from function is assigned to the variable sum */
    sum = addition(3, 4);
    printf("s = %d\n", sum);
    return 0;
}
```

Program 6.1: Using the function addition().

is executed, the value of the expression is returned to the caller as the value of the function call expression. In this example, the statement

```c
return s;
```

returns the value 7 of the variable s. This value is then assigned to the variable sum in the function **main()**. When the control of the program flow leaves the called function, the memory allocated for the variables a and b of the function argument and the local variable s in the called function is freed. The output of Program 6.1 is as follows:

```
s = 7
```

The data type of an actual argument of the calling function can be different from that of the formal argument of the called function so long as they are assignment-compatible. The value of an actual argument will be converted to the data type of its formal definition according to the built-in data conversion rules implicitly at the function interface stage. For example, the function call addition(3.0, 4.0) converts the floating-point numbers 3.0 and 4.0 to integers.

If the expression following the return statement has a type different from the return type of the function in which it appears, the value is converted as if by assignment to an object having the return type of the function. For example:

```c
int func(int a, int b) {
  double d;
  /* ... */
```

```
        d = 4.6;
        return d;
    }
```

The return type of the function `func()` is int. When the expression in the return statement is double type, it will be cast to int implicitly. The digits after the decimal point will be discarded. In this case, the function `func()` returns the value of 4.

Often, a return value of a function may be used as a status to indicate if the function is executed successfully. For a function using return type int as its status indicator, the return value 0 usually indicates that the function is executed successfully, whereas the return value of −1 stands for a failure. If a function returns a pointer type, the return value of NULL, defined in the standard header file **stdlib.h**, but also available in the header file **stdio.h**, is typically reserved for a failure. The calling function may often ignore the returned value. For example, the standard output function **printf()**, with the return type of int, returns the number of characters printed out. This return value is often ignored in a program.

The **void** type is used mainly for void argument lists and functions without return values, as well as pointers to void, which will be discussed in Chapter 11. The keyword **void** appearing in the argument list of a function also indicates that the function has no argument. The function

```
int func1(void)
```

in Program 6.2 has no argument. The keyword **void**, which appears in front of the function name when it is defined, indicates that the function has no return value. A **return** statement without an expression can appear in a function whose return type is void. For example, the function

```
void func2(int i)
```

in Program 6.2 has no return value. It just prints the value of the passed argument if it is positive. It uses a return statement to terminate the function before the print statement is executed when the passed argument is a zero or negative number. The output of Program 6.2 is as follows:

```
func1() is called
status = 0
func1() is called
i in func2() = 10
i in func2() = -10
```

```
/* File: usevoid.c
   Use data type 'void' in function */
#include <stdio.h>

/* use 'void' to indicate that the function has no argument */
int func1(void) {     /* no argument */
    printf("func1() is called\n");
    return 0;          /* function returns 0 */
}
```

Program 6.2: Using **void** in a function. (*Continued*)

```
/* use 'void' to indicate that function has no return value */
void func2(int i) {  /* no return value */
    if(i <= 0) {
      printf("i in func2() = %d\n", i);
      return;          /* no expression following return */
    }
    printf("i in func2() = %d\n", i);
}

int main() {
    int status;         /* declare local variable */

    /* returned value from func1() is assigned to status */
    status = func1();
    printf("status = %d\n", status);
    func1();            /* returned value from func1() is ignored */
    func2(10);          /* no return value from func2() */
    func2(-10);         /* no return value from func2() */
    return 0;
}
```

Program 6.2: *(Continued)*

An Application Example

Force and Acceleration of a Moving Body

Problem Statement:

For the mechanical system shown in Figure 2.12, where mass $m = 5$ kilograms (kg) and coefficient of kinetic friction $\mu = 0.2$, the applied force p is expressed as a function of time t in

$$p(t) = 4(t - 3) + 20$$

write a program to calculate the acceleration when $t = 2$ seconds with the following specifications: (a) Use a function to calculate the external force with an independent variable for time. (b) Use a function to calculate the acceleration with three independent variables for time, kinetic friction coefficient, and mass.

Program 6.3 meets specification (a). The function `force()` has one input argument for time and returns the external force. Because time and force have to be represented using floating-point numbers, the argument for a given time and return value for the force uses double type.

For specification (b), Program 6.4 calculates the acceleration using two functions. The function `accel()` has three input arguments for time, kenetic friction coefficient, and mass. The function `accel()` calls the function `force()` to calculate the applied force. The output of Programs 6.3 and 6.4 are the same, as shown below:

```
Acceleration a = 1.364823 (m/s^2)
```

```
/* File: accelfun.c
   Calculate the acceleration.
   The force is calculated using a function */
#include <stdio.h>
#define M_G   9.81  /* gravitational acceleration constant g */
/* definition of the function for force
   The data type of the argument and return value of
   the function is double */
double force(double t) {
    double p;           /* declare local variable */

    p = 4*(t-3)+20;
    return p;           /* return force p */
}

int main() {
    double a, mu, m, p, t; /* declare local variables */

    /* initialize mu, m, t */
    mu = 0.2;
    m = 5.0;
    t = 2.0;

    /* calculate the force by calling a function */
    p = force(t);
    a = (p-mu*m*M_G)/m;
    printf("Acceleration a = %f (m/s^2)\n", a);
    return 0;
}
```

Program 6.3: Calculating the acceleration using a function for force.

```
/* File: accelfunm.c
   Calculate the acceleration.
   Both force and acceleration are calculated using functions */
#include <stdio.h>
#define M_G   9.81  /* gravitational acceleration constant g */

/* definition of the function force()
   The data type of the argument and return value of
   the function is double */
double force(double t) {
    double p;           /* declare local variable */
```

Program 6.4: Calculating the acceleration using functions with multiple arguments. (*Continued*)

```
    p = 4*(t-3)+20;
    return p;          /* return force p */
}

/* function accel() has multiple arguments for t, mu, and m */
double accel(double t, double mu, double m) {
    double a, p;      /* declare local variables */

    /* calculate force by calling function force() */
    p = force(t);
    a = (p-mu*m*M_G)/m;
    return a;          /* return acceleration a */
}

int main() {
    double a, mu, m, t; /* declare local variables */

    mu = 0.2;
    m = 5.0;
    t = 2.0;
    /*  call function accel() to calculate acceleration;
        inside function accel(), it calls another function force() */
    a = accel(t, mu, m);
    printf("Acceleration a = %f (m/s^2)\n", a);
    return 0;
}
```

Program 6.4: *(Continued)*

6.2 Function Prototypes

In Program 6.4, the function `accel()` calls function `force()`, which returns a value of double type. Therefore, the function `force()` needs to be defined before it is called by the function `accel()`. For the same reason, the function `accel()`, which returns a value of double type, appears before the **main()** function. To move functions `force()` and `accel()` after **main()** in a program as shown in In Program 6.5, or in another file, function prototypes are needed.

A *function prototype* is a declaration of a function that declares the return type and types of its parameters. A function prototype contains no function definition, but it has the essential information for interface with the function. A function prototype is required if the return type of the function is not int and the function is called before its definition is processed, or if the function definition is located in a different file or in a library.

For example, Program 6.5 is similar to Program 6.4 with the same output. It also utilizes functions to calculate the force and acceleration values. The difference is that function prototypes

```
double force(double t);
double accel(double t, double mu, double m);
```

```
/* File: accelprot.c
   Calculate the acceleration.
   Both force and acceleration are calculated using functions.
   With function prototypes, main() function is at the beginning */
#include <stdio.h>
#define M_G   9.81  /* gravitational acceleration constant g */

/* function prototypes for force() and and accel() */
double force(double t);
double accel(double t, double mu, double m);

/* main() function appears before the definitions of
   called functions force() and accel() are defined */
int main() {
    double a, mu, m, t;
    int i;

    mu = 0.2;
    m = 5.0;
    t = 2.0;
    a = accel(t, mu, m);
    printf("Acceleration a = %f (m/s^2)\n", a);
    return 0;
}

double force(double t) {
    double p;

    p = 4*(t-3)+20;
    return p;
}

double accel(double t, double mu, double m) {
    double a, p;

    p = force(t);
    a = (p-mu*m*M_G)/m;
    return a;
}
```

Program 6.5: Calculating the acceleration using function prototypes.

for `force()` and `accel()` are used at the beginning, thus allowing the definitions for these two functions to be placed at the end of the program rather than at the beginning.

The data types for the same argument in different function prototypes for the same function shall be the same even in different files. Likewise, the return types of different function prototypes for the same function shall be the same.

Parameter names must appear in function definitions, but the parameter names for arguments of function prototypes need not be included, although they can help in documenting functions and improving the readability of the program. For example, the following two function prototypes for the function `accel()` are the same.

```
double accel(double, double, double);
double accel(double t, double mu, double m);
```

If there is no argument in a the function prototype, such as

```
double accel();
```

the argument type compatibility checking will be turned off. However, the return type of the function will still be checked.

A function requiring no argument can be prototyped with the single type specifier **void**. For example:

```
int func(void);
```

A program may call functions defined in a library or other source file compiled separately. In this case, a function prototype needs to be declared with type qualifier **extern** to indicate that the function is an externally defined function in another module. Function prototypes for functions in a library are typically included in a header file. For example, function prototypes for commonly used mathematical functions are declared in the header file **math.h**, which contains the function prototype

```
extern double sin(double x);
```

for the sine function. Therefore, a program can include the header file **math.h** to use the sine function **sin()**. On the other hand, it might be desirable to make a function available only in a single source file so that it will not conflict with variable names in other modules. To limit the scope of a function, say `func()`, in a single file, it can be declared with the type qualifier **static** as follows:

```
static double func(double x);
```

Detailed information about external and static variables and functions is given in Chapter 8.

Functions can occur in any order in a program. However, in C89, if a function is called before it is defined, the return type of the function is assumed to be int. In other words, when a function, say `funct()`, has not been defined before it is invoked, it will act as if it had been prototyped by

```
int funct();
```

with a return type of int, whether or not it has a function argument. Therefore, if the return value of a function is not int, a function prototype or function definition must be declared before the function can be called. This is the case for Program 6.5, in which the return type of functions `force()` and `accel()` is not int.

The C99 standard no longer allows the implicit function declaration with return type int for functions if they are called before they were declared. Therefore, it is a good practice to declare a function or function prototype before it is called.

The function prototypes can be used multiple times so long as they are compatible each time. Function prototypes are typically placed in a header file for a project or library. How to place function prototypes, such as those in Program 6.5, in a header file will be described in Chapter 7.

6.3 Calling Functions: Call-by-Value versus Call-by-Reference

In general, arguments can be passed to functions in one of two models: *call-by-value* and *call-by-reference*. In the call-by-value model, the values of the actual parameters are copied into formal parameters local to the called function. When a formal parameter is used as an lvalue (the object that can occur at the left side of an assignment statement), only the local copy of the parameter will be altered. In the call-by-reference method, however, the address of an argument is copied into the formal parameter of a function. Inside the called function, the address is used to access the actual argument used in the calling function. This means that when the formal parameter is used as an lvalue, the parameter will affect the variable used to call the function. FORTRAN uses the call-by-reference model, whereas the convention in C is call-by-value. If it is desired that the called function alter its actual parameters in the calling function in C, the addresses of the parameters shall be passed explicitly, which will be described in section 11.3 in Chapter 11. However, in C++ and Ch, arguments can be passed by reference with reference types, as described in Chapter 18.

6.4 Standard C Header Files and Libraries

Header files typically contain function prototypes for performing operations that are related to one another. They may also include macros and type definitions required by some of the functions. Table 6.1 lists all the header files corresponding to the C standard libraries. These header files contain function prototypes and other resources for the functions available in the standard libraries. For example, the header file **math.h** for the standard C mathematical library contains the function prototypes

```
extern double sin(double x);
extern double exp(double x);
```

for the sine function $\sin(x)$ and the natural exponential function e^x. You may look at the header file **math.h** to find function prototypes for all mathematical functions in the standard C library.

Each C compiler and C interpreter has its own header files for the standard C libraries. For example, for C/C++ interpreter Ch, header files such as **math.h** for the standard C libraries are located in the directory `C:/Ch/include` in Windows and `/usr/local/ch/include` in Unix by default. For the C compiler **gcc** in Unix, header files for the standard C libraries are located in the directory `/usr/include`. The C/C++ compiler for Visual C++ in Microsoft Visual Studio .NET 2008, header files for the standard C libraries are located in `Program Files/Microsoft Visual Studio 9/VC/include` by default.

6.5 Mathematical Functions and Type Generic Functions in C99

Functions in C can be used to represent mathematical functions and formulas. Elementary mathematical functions, such as **sin**() for the sine function and **sqrt**() for the square root function, declared in the header file **math.h** for real numbers can be used for scientific computing. In C99, these functions are type generic when the header file **tgmath.h** is included. They can also be used to handle arguments of complex numbers as described in Chapter 17. Because the header file **tgmath.h** contains **math.h**, there is no need to include both header files in an application. A list of type generic mathematical functions in C99 defined in the header file **tgmath.h** is as follows: **abs**(), **acos**(), **acosh**(), **asin**(). **asinh**(), **atan**(), **atan2**(), **atanh**(), **ceil**(), **conj**(), **cos**(), **cosh**(), **exp**(), **fabs**(), **floor**(), **fmod**(), **frexp**(), **log**(), **log10**(), **max**(), **min**(), **modf**(), **pow**(), **real**(), **sin**(), **sinh**(), **sqrt**(), **tan**(), **tanh**().

Table 6.1 C standard header files.

Header file	Description
assert.h	Defines a macro that puts diagnostic tests into programs.
complex.h	Defines macros and declares functions that support complex arithmetic; added in C99.
ctype.h	Declares several functions useful for testing and mapping characters.
errno.h	Defines several macros related to the reporting of error conditions.
fenv.h	Declares two types and several macros and functions to provide access to the floating-point environment; added in C99.
float.h	Defines several macros that expand to various limits and parameters of the standard floating-point types.
inttypes.h	Includes header file **stdint.h** and extends it with additional facilities provided by hosted implementations; added in C99.
iso646.h	Defines macros that correspond to tokens for logical operations; added in C99.
limits.h	Defines several macros that expand to various limits and parameters of the standard integer types.
locale.h	Declares two functions and one type, and defines several macros to allow a program to be modified for the current locale on which it is running.
math.h	Declares two types and several functions and defines several macros for general mathematical operations.
setjmp.h	Defines the macro **setjmp**() and declares one function and one type for bypassing the normal function call and return discipline.
signal.h	Declares a type and two functions and defines several macros for handling various signals, which are conditions that may be reported during program execution.
stdarg.h	Declares a type and defines four macros for advancing through a list of arguments whose number and types are not known to the called function when it is translated.
stdbool.h	Defines macros for boolean operations; added in C99.
stddef.h	Declares several types and defines several macros for performing certain calculations.
stdint.h	Declares sets of integer types having specified widths and defines corresponding sets of macros as well as macros that specify limits of integer types corresponding to types defined in other standard headers.
stdio.h	Declares types, macros, and functions for standard input and output.
stdlib.h	Declares several types, macros, and functions for general utility, such as conversion of numbers to text and text to numbers, memory allocation, and generation of random numbers.
string.h	Declares one type and several functions and defines one macro useful for string manipulation and processing.
tgmath.h	Includes header files **math.h** and **complex.h** and defines several type-generic macros corresponding to the functions in **math.h** and **complex.h** for mathematical operations; added in C99.
time.h	Defines macros and declares several types and functions for manipulating time and date.
wchar.h	Declares several types and one tag and defines several macros and functions for extended multibyte and wide-character utilities.
wctype.h	Declares data types, one macro, and many functions for wide-character classification and mapping utilities.

A type generic function acts like a built-in system function. It can handle different data types of the arguments gracefully. The output data type of a function depends on the data types of the input arguments, which is called *polymorphism*. Like arithmetic operators, the commonly used generic mathematical functions are polymorphic. The returned data type of a function depends on the data types of the input arguments. For example, for the polymorphic function **abs()**, if the data type of the input argument is int, it will return an int as the absolute value. If the input argument of **abs()** is a float or double, the output will return the same data type of float or double, respectively. For a complex number input, the result of **abs()** is a float with the value of the modulus of the input a complex number. Similarly, the type generic function **sin()** can be used to calculate the sine of numerical values in float, double, complex, or double complex types, as shown below.

```
#include<tgmath.h>
int main() {
    float f;
    double df;
    complex z;
    double complex dz;
    ...
    f = sin(f);
    df = sin(df);
    z = sin(z);
    dz = sin(dz);
}
```

6.6 Functions for Mathematical Formulas

Functions in C are well suited to handle numerical computation with equations and formulas. This can be illustrated by an example. Program 5.9 in Chapter 5 computes the function $\mathrm{sinc}(x)$ in equation (6.1)

$$\mathrm{sinc}(x) = \frac{\sin(x)}{x} \tag{6.1}$$

inside a **for** loop in the range of $-10 \leq x \leq 10$ with a step size of 5. For comparison, we will use a C function for the function sinc() to obtain the same result. Equation (6.1) is translated into a C the function. The function should have one argument. Because the variable x for this the function uses real numbers, the argument and return type of the corresponding C function should use either float or double. As computer hardware is becoming cheaper and faster with a large memory, double data type is more commonly used than float for scientific numerical computing. Equation (6.1) is translated into the function `sinc()` shown in Program 6.6 with the following function prototype:

```
double sinc(double x);
```

Inside the **for** loop in Program 6.6, the function `sinc()` is called in each iteration. The output from Program 6.6 is the sam as one shown in Figure 5.16.

A mathematical function or formula with multiple variables can also be translated into a function in C conveniently. For example, the function $\mathrm{sinr}(x, y)$ in equation (6.2) has two arguments x and y.

$$\mathrm{sinr}(x, y) = \frac{\sin(r)}{r}, \text{ with } r = \sqrt{x^2 + y^2} \tag{6.2}$$

```
/* File: sinc.c
   Calculate function sinc(x)=sin(x)/x
   for x from -10 to 10 with step size 5 using a function sinc() */
#include <stdio.h>
#include <math.h>    /* for sin() and fabs() */
#include <float.h>   /* for FLT_EPSILON */

/* definition of function sinc()   */
double sinc(double x) {
    double retval;

    /* if x is a value less than epsilon, sinc(x) is 1 */
    if(fabs(x) < FLT_EPSILON)
       retval = 1.0;
    else
       retval = sin(x)/x;
    return retval;
}

int main() {
    double x, x0, xf, xstep, result;
    int i, n;

    printf("    x     sinc(x)\n");
    printf(" ----------------\n");
    x0 = -10.0;                      /* initial value for x */
    xf = 10.0;                       /* final value for x */
    xstep = 5.0;                     /* step size for x */
    n  =  (xf - x0)/xstep + 1;       /* number of points */
    for(i = 0; i < n; i++) {
       x = x0 + i*xstep;             /* calculate value x */
       /* call function sinc() to calculate sin(x)/x */
       result = sinc(x);

       /* display the result */
       printf("%8.4f %8.4f\n", x, result);
    }
    return 0;
}
```

Program 6.6: Using the function `sinc()` for mathematical equation (6.1).

It can be translated into the function `sinr()` with two arguments in Program 6.7. The function has the following function prototype

```
double sinr(double x, double y);
```

The data type of the returned value and two arguments of the function is double. The standard C function **sqrt()**, with the function prototype:

```
extern double sqrt(double x);
```

declared in the header file **math.h**, is used to calculate the square root of a value. Similar to Program 5.11, Program 6.7 calculates the values of the function sinr(x, y) when the variables x and y both vary in the range of $[-10, 10]$ with a step size of 10. Because there are two variables, two nested **for** loops are used. Inside the inner loop, the function `sinr()` is called in each iteration. The output from Program 6.7 is the same as one shown in Figure 5.18.

```
/* File: sinr.c
   Calculate function sinr(x, y)=sin(sqrt(x*x + y*y))/sqrt(x*x + y*y)
   using function sinr() for x from -10 to 10 with step size 10,
   and for y from -10 to 10 with step size 10. */
#include <stdio.h>
#include <math.h>    /* for sin() and sqrt() */

/* function definition for sinr() */
double sinr(double x, double y) {
    double r, retval;

    r = sqrt(x*x + y*y);
    retval = sin(r)/r;
    return retval;
}

int main() {
    double x, x0, xf, xstep,
           y, y0, yf, ystep, result;
    int i, j, nx, ny;

    printf("      x          y     sinr(x,y)\n");
    printf("    ----------------------------\n");
    x0 = -10.0;                    /* initial value for x */
    xf = 10.0;                     /* final value for x */
    xstep = 10.0;                  /* step size for x */
    nx = (xf - x0)/xstep + 1;      /* num of points for x */
    y0 = -10.0;                    /* initial value for y */
    yf = 10.0;                     /* final value for y */
    ystep = 10.0;                  /* step size for y */
    ny = (yf - y0)/ystep + 1;      /* num of points for y */
```

Program 6.7: Using the function `sinr()` for mathematical equation (6.2). (*Continued*)

```
    /* use nested two for-loops for x and y variables */
    for(i = 0; i < nx; i++) {
        x = x0 + i*xstep;           /* calculate value for x */
        /* for each x value, y varies from y0 to yf with ystep */
        for(j = 0; j <ny; j++) {
            y = y0 + j*ystep;       /* calculate value for y */

            /* calculate sinr(x, y) by a function and display the result */
            result = sinr(x, y);
            printf("%10.4f %10.4f %8.4f\n", x, y, result);
        }
    }
    return 0;
}
```

Program 6.7: (*Continued*)

An Application Example

A Square Root Function Based on Newton's Method

Taking the square root for a given number is a commonly used mathematical operation in engineering and science. The standard math library contains such a function, which is called **sqrt()**. In this application example, we create our own square root function to illustrate how math functions are developed. Program 5.17 in Chapter 5 calculates the square root for a given number based on Newton's method in equation (5.6). Based on Program 5.17, we can develop a general square root function using Newton's method, as shown in Program 6.8. The function `sqrtx()` has the following function prototype:

```
double sqrtx(double x);
```

If successful, the function returns $\sqrt{x}$. Otherwise, it prints out an error message and returns -1. Argument `x` is used as the initial guess for the recursive formulation in Newton's method. The output from Program 6.8 is shown below:

```
sqrtx(3.00) = 1.732051
sqrtx() failed to converge
sqrtx(-3.00) = -1.000000
```

If the argument for `sqrtx()` is negative, Not-a-Number (NaN), or Inf, as shown in Table 3.4 in Chapter 3, the function prints an error message and returns -1.0. This error handling is not ideal. An error message to the standard output may break some applications, such as processing Web-based filled-out forms. The return value -1.0 may also lead to an incorrect numerical result. The most desirable return value in these situations is a quiet NaN as shown in Program 16.4. Handling metanumbers NaN and Inf is described in Chapter 16.

```
/* File: sqrtf.c
   Function sqrtx() based on Newton's method for calculating a square root */
#include <stdio.h>
#include <math.h>  /* for fabs() */
#include <float.h> /* for FLT_EPSILON */

#define N 100       /* the maximum number of iteration */

double sqrtx(double x) {
   int i;
   double x0, x1, x2;

   x0 = x;          /* an initial guess for x0 */
   x1 = x0;                      /* set x1 to x0 */
   x2 = (x1+x/x1)/2.0;           /* recursive formula */
   for(i = 1; i <= N && fabs(x2-x0) >= FLT_EPSILON; i++) {
     x0 = x1;                    /* update x0  for fabs(x2-x0) */
     x2 = (x1+x/x1)/2.0;        /* Newton's recursive formula */
     x1 = x2;      /* update value x1 for next iteration */
   }

   if(i < N) {      /* number of iteration is less than N */
     return x2;
   }
   else {           /* number of iteration equals N */
     printf("sqrtx() failed to converge\n");
     return -1.0;
   }
}

int main() {
   double a;

   a = 3.0;          /* for sqrt(3.0) */
   printf("sqrtx(%.2f) = %f\n", a, sqrtx(a));
   a = -3.0;         /* for sqrt(-3.0) */
   printf("sqrtx(%.2f) = %f\n", a, sqrtx(a));
   return 0;
}
```

Program 6.8: Developing a square root function `sqrtx()` using Newton's method.

6.7 Plotting Functions for Graphical Display

A picture is worth thousands of words. Graphical plotting is useful for visualization and understanding many problems in engineering and science. There is no standard C function for graphical plotting. However, plotting can be accomplished by some functions in a library. For example, SIGL (SoftIntegration Graphical Library) is a high-level graphical C++ library available from SoftIntegration, Inc. SIGL is compatible with the graphical functions in Ch. To make sure that a program using the plotting features can be compiled using a C++ compiler, all programs using the functions in SIGL have the file extension `.cpp`. A program using the plotting features in SIGL needs to include the header file **chplot.h**. Like any other C programs, programs using SIGL are ready to run in Ch and ChIDE. How to compile programs with SIGL using a C++ compiler in Windows and Unix in a command shell is described in sections 18.7.1 in Chapter 18 and 20.5.1 in Chapter 20. The compilation options have already been set up in ChIDE. Therefore, a program using SIGL can also be readily compiled and linked using compilers invoked from ChIDE.

In this section, two simple functions for two- and three-dimensional graphical plotting and their applications are presented.

6.7.1 Two-Dimensional Plotting

The function **fplotxy()** is a high-level plotting function with its prototype defined in the header file **chplot.h**. The function **fplotxy()** is useful for generating two-dimensional plots. The function **fplotxy()** can be treated as if it had the following function prototype:

```
int fplotxy(double func(double), double x0, double xf, int num,
            char *title, char *xlabel, char *ylabel);
```

It plots a function with the variable x in the range $x0 \le x \le xf$. The function to be plotted, `func`, is specified as a pointer to a function that takes an argument of double type and returns a double type. The details for pointer to function will be described in section 11.11 in Chapter 11. A function with the function prototype of

```
double func(double x);
```

can be passed as the first argument of the function **fplotxy()**. The argument `num` specifies how many points in the range are to be plotted. The title and labels for x and y axes are specified by the arguments `title`, `xlabel`, and `ylabel`, respectively.

Program 6.9 uses the plotting function **fplotxy()** to plot the mathematical function sinc(x) of equation (6.1) in section 6.6. The generated plot for function sinc(x) in the range of $-10 \le x \le 10$ with 80 points is shown in Figure 6.1. Section 20.3 in Chapter 20 and describes how to copy a displayed plot on a screen in Windows into a Word or PowerPoint file for documentation and presentation.

```
/* File: sinc_fplotxy.cpp
   Plot function sinc(x)= sin(x)/x for -10<=x<=10 with 80 points */
#include <math.h>
#include <chplot.h>   /* for using fplotxy() in the plotting library */
```

Program 6.9: A program to plot the function sinc() using the plotting function **fplotxy()**. *(Continued)*

```
/* function definition for sinc() to be plotted */
double sinc(double x) {
    double retval;

    retval = sin(x)/x;
    return retval;
}

int main() {
    double x0 = -10.0, xf = 10.0; /* initial and final values for x */
    int num = 80; /* number of data points for (x, y) for plotting */

    /* plot sinc from x0 to xf with num points,
       title of the plot is "function sinc()",
       x label of the plot is "x",
       y label of the plot is "sinc(x)" */
    fplotxy(sinc, x0, xf, num, "function sinc(x)", "x", "sinc(x)");
    return 0;
}
```

Program 6.9: *(Continued)*

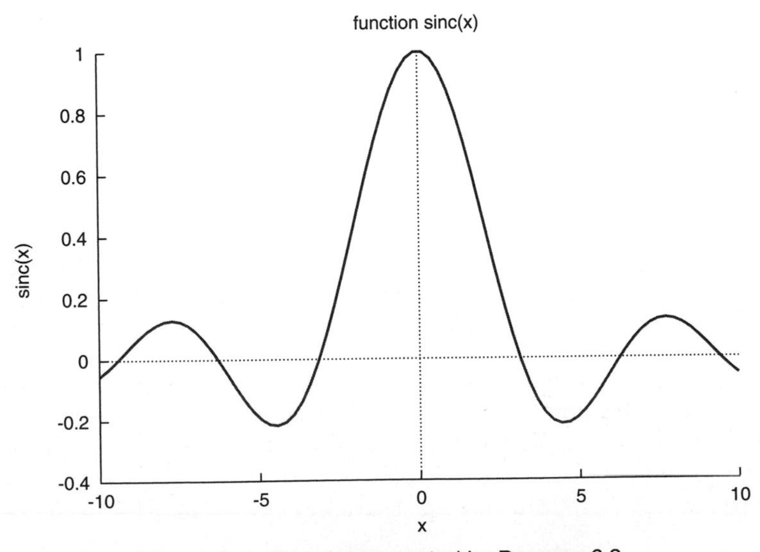

Figure 6.1: The plot generated by Program 6.9.

Application Examples with Graphical Plotting

Plotting the Trajectory of a Projectile

Problem Statement:
A projectile is fired into the air with an initial speed v_0 of 35 m/s and initial projection angle of $\theta_0 = 15°$. Plot its trajectory with 100 points.

Note that the total distance traveled in the x direction is

$$x_f = \frac{v_0^2 \sin(2\theta_0)}{g} \tag{6.3}$$

where v_0 is the initial speed θ_0 the initial projection angle, and g the gravitational acceleration. The trajectory can be expressed in x and y coordinates as

$$y = \tan(\theta_0)x - \left(\frac{g}{2v_0^2 \cos^2\theta_0}\right)x^2 \tag{6.4}$$

with x in the range of $0 < x < x_f$. The trajectory function y in terms of x is implemented as the function `func()` in Program 6.10. To use the standard mathematical functions **sin()** and **tan()**, the header file **math.h** is included in the program. The unit for the initial projection angle needs to be converted from degrees to radians for calculation. The function **fplotxy()** is used to plot the trajectory shown in Figure 6.2 for x in the range of $0 < x < x_f$ with 100 points. The macro **M_PI** for π, typically defined in the header file **math.h**, as previously pointed out in Chapter 4, is used for the conversion of an angle from degrees to radians.

```
/* File: projectilefunc.cpp
   Plot a projectile based on the function y(x). */
#include <math.h>
#include <chplot.h>   /* for fplotxy() */
#define M_G   9.81   /* gravitational acceleration constant g */

/* function for the y-coordinate of the projectifle */
double func(double x) {
   double theta0,          /* initial velocity */
          v0,              /* projection angle */
          y;               /* y coordinate */

   v0 = 35.0;              /* set the initial velocity */
   theta0 = 15*M_PI/180; /* calculate the projection angle in radians */
   /* calculate the y coordinate */
   y = tan(theta0)*x - M_G*x*x/(2*v0*v0*cos(theta0)*cos(theta0));
   return y;
}
```

Program 6.10: A program to plot the trajectory of a projectile. *(Continued)*

```
int main() {
    double theta0, v0;               /* projection angle and initial velocity */
    double x0 = 0, xf;               /* initial and final distances, x0 is 0 */
    int num = 100;                   /* number of points for plotting */

    /* calculate the final distance xf for x based on v0 and theta0 */
    v0 = 35.0;                       /* initial velocity */
    theta0 = 15*M_PI/180;            /* projection angle in radians */
    xf = v0*v0*sin(2*theta0)/M_G; /* the distance in the x direction */
    /* plot y version x for x from 0 to xf with num points */
    fplotxy(func, x0, xf, num,
            "A projectile with the initial projection angle of 15 degrees",
            "x (m)", "y (m)");
    return 0;
}
```

Program 6.10: (*Continued*)

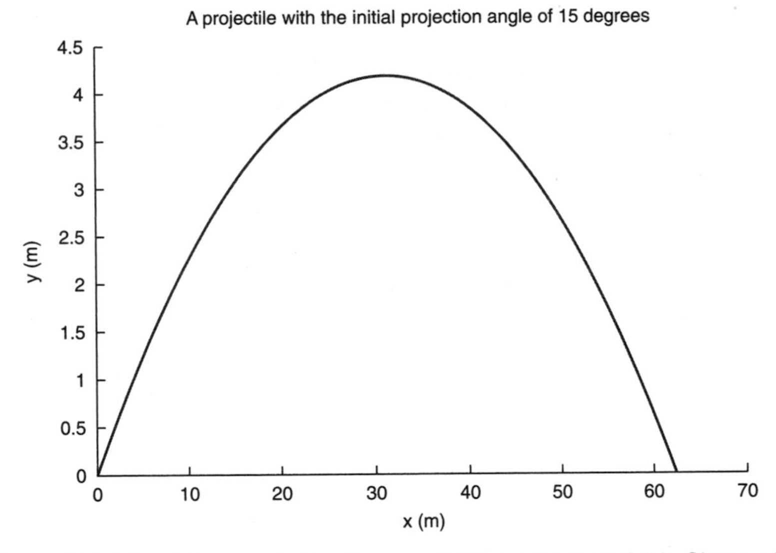

Figure 6.2 The plot generated by Program 6.10 and Program 8.3 in Chapter 8.

Plotting the Acceleration for a Moving Body

As another example, we can plot the accelerations of a mechanical system presented previously.

Problem Statement:
For the mechanical system shown in Figure 2.12, where mass $m = 5$ kilograms (kg) and coefficient of kinetic friction $\mu = 0.2$, the applied force p is expressed as a function of time t in

$$p(t) = 4\sin(t - 3) + 20$$

Write a program to plot the accelerations **a** for $t = 0$ to $t = 10$ seconds with 11 points. Modify the program to plot the accelerations with 100 points.

Program 6.11 uses the function **fplotxy()** to plot the acceleration of the system with 11 data points shown in Figure 6.3. To use the mathematical function **sin()**, the header file **math.h** is included. Because the function passed to the first argument of the function **fplotxy()** must have only one argument, we have modified the function `accel()` with one argument for time. The variables `m` for mass and `mu` for the coefficient of kinetic friction are inside the function `accel()`. Because we only used 11 points, the acceleration curve is not smooth. If we change the program with 100 points for the variable `num` in Program 6.11, the acceleration curve will be smooth, as shown in Figure 6.4.

```
/* File: accelsinplot.cpp
   Plot acceleration versus time for time from 0 to 10 seconds.
   It uses 11 points of data for the plotting */
#include <stdio.h>
#include <math.h>
#include <chplot.h>
#define M_G   9.81   /* gravitational acceleration constant g */

double force(double t) {
    double p;
    p = 4*sin(t-3)+20;
    return p;
}

double accel(double t) {
    double mu, m, a, p;

    mu = 0.2;
    m = 5.0;
    p = force(t);
    a = (p-mu*m*M_G)/m;
    return a;
}

int main() {
    double t0 = 0, tf = 10.0;
    int num = 11;

    /* plot function accel() from t0 to tf with 11 points.
       The curve in the plot is not smooth for 11 points.
       The value for num can be changed to 100 to get a smooth curve.
       The title of the plot is "Acceleration Plot".
       the label for x-coordinate is "time (s)",
       the label for y-coordinate is "accel (m/s^2)" */
    fplotxy(accel, t0, tf, num, "Acceleration Plot",
            "time (s)", "accel (m/s^2)");
    return 0;
}
```

Program 6.11: Plotting accelerations with the force of the sine function using 11 points.

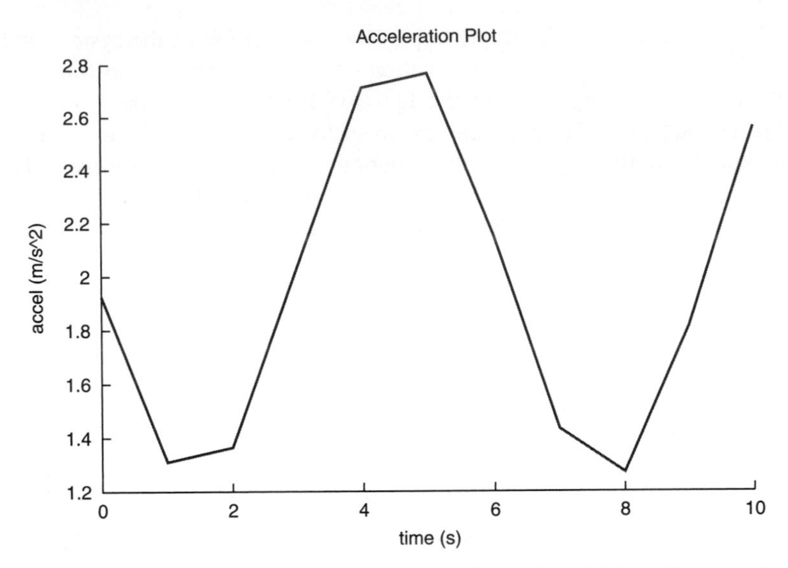

Figure 6.3 The acceleration plot for external force $p = 4\sin(t-3)+20$ from Program 6.11 with num = 11, and Programs 21.11, 21.12, and 21.13 in Chapter 21 for N1 with 11 data points.

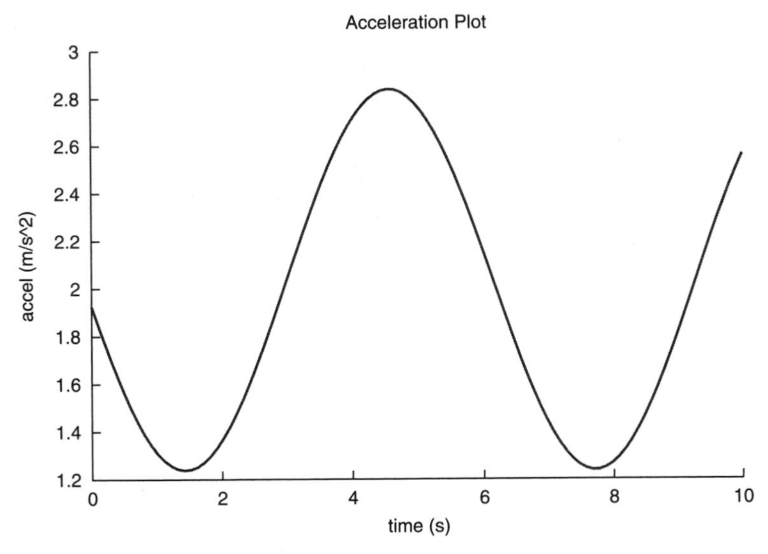

Figure 6.4 The acceleration plot for external force $p = 4\sin(t-3)+20$ from Program 6.11 with num = 100, and Program 10.17 in Chapter 10 and 13.12 in Chapter 13, and Programs 21.11, 21.12, and 21.13 in Chapter 21 for N2 with 100 data points.

6.7.2 Plotting Multiple Curves in a Single Plot

It would be nice to merge two curves in Figures 6.3 and 6.4 into a single plot for comparison. To have multiple curves in a single plot, we need to use the plotting class **CPlot**. Details about class in C++ and plotting class **CPlot** are described in Chapters 19 and 20, respectively. A class is a user defined data-type. The data associated with the declared class can be processed conveniently by its member functions. As an example, the function call

```
fplotxy(func, x0, xf, num, title. xlabel, ylabel);
```

can be replaced by the following code using a plotting class **CPlot**:

```
CPlot plot;
plot.title(title);
plot.label(PLOT_AXIS_X, xlabel);
plot.label(PLOT_AXIS_Y, ylabel);
plot.func2D(x0, xf, num, func);
plot.plotting();
```

The first statement declares the variable `plot` of the class **CPlot** and allocates the necessary memory for the class object. The declarator **class** is a keyword in C++. The class **CPlot** is defined in the header file **chplot.h**. The remaining statements call its member functions of the class **CPlot** to process the data for the object `plot`. The first function call adds a title to the plot. The subsequent two function calls add labels for the x and y coordinates. The function call

```
plot.func2D(x0, xf, num, func);
```

generates the data for plotting by using the function `func()` in the range of `[x0, xf]` with `num` of points. Multiple data set can be added to a plot by calling this function multiple times. The last function call processes the data and displays the plot. Details for these member functions are described in Chapter 20.

Using these member functions of the plotting class **CPlot**, Program 6.12 plots two acceleration curves in a single plot shown in Figure 6.5. In Program 6.12, the member function **func2D()** is called twice to add two sets of plotting data for the object `plot`. The first curve has 11 points and the second one has 100 points. To distinguish these two curves, the member function **legend()** is called to add legends to the plot. The first argument is a string for the legend. The second argument is the number of data set associated with the legend. The numbering of the data set starts with zero.

```
/* File: accelfunc2D.cpp
   Plot acceleration curves on the same figure with 11 and 100 points each. */
#include <stdio.h>
#include <math.h>
#include <chplot.h>    /* for class CPlot for plotting */
#define M_G   9.81     /* gravitational acceleration constant g */

/* function accel() to be plotted */
double accel(double t) {
    double mu, m, a, p;

    mu = 0.2;
    m = 5.0;
    p = 4*sin(t-3)+20;
    a = (p-mu*m*M_G)/m;
    return a;
}
```

Program 6.12: Plotting two acceleration curves in a single plot. (*Continued*)

```
int main() {
    double t0 = 0, tf = 10.0;    /* time t from t0 to tf */
    int num1 = 11, num2 = 100;   /* with 11 and 100 points */
    CPlot plot;                  /* instantiate a plotting class */

    /* use a plotting class plot two curves on the same figure */
    /* set title of the plot */
    plot.title("Acceleration Plot");
    /* set the label on the x-axis */
    plot.label(PLOT_AXIS_X, "time (s)");
    /* set the label on the y-axis */
    plot.label(PLOT_AXIS_Y, "accel (m/s^2)");
    /* set the 1st function accel() to be plotted
       from t0 to tf with num1 points */
    plot.func2D(t0, tf, num1, accel);
    /* set the legend for the 1st curve */
    plot.legend("11 points", 0);
    /* set the 2nd function accel() to be plotted
       from t0 to tf with num2 points */
    plot.func2D(t0, tf, num2, accel);
    /* set the legend for the 2nd curve */
    plot.legend("100 points", 1);
    /* after the above setup, ready and go, plot and display it! */
    plot.plotting();
    return 0;
}
```

Program 6.12: (*Continued*)

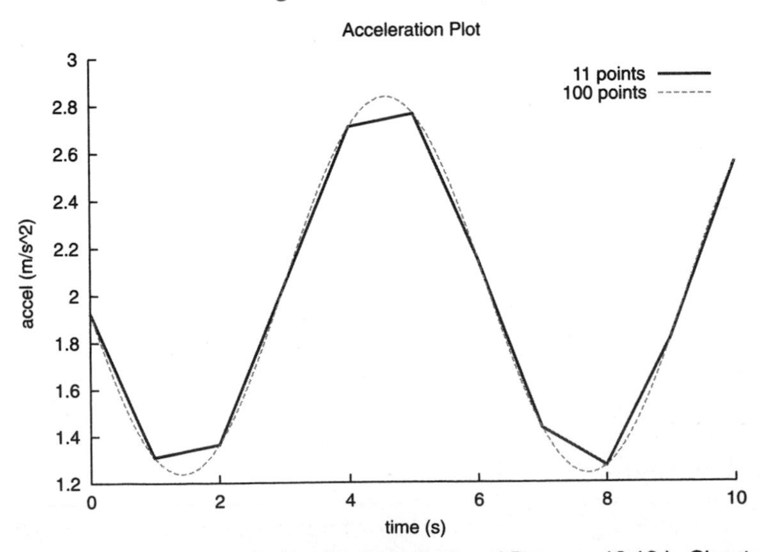

Figure 6.5: The plot generated by Program 6.12 and Program 10.18 in Chapter 10.

6.7.3 Three-Dimensional Plotting

Functions with two variables for three-dimensional plotting can be plotted using the plotting function **fplotxyz()**, which has the following prototype:

```
int fplotxyz(double func(double, double), double x0, double xf,
             double y0, double yf, int numx, int numy, char *title,
             char *xlabel, char *ylabel, char *zlabel);
```

It plots a function with two variables x and y in the range $x0 \le x \le xf$ and $y0 \le y \le yf$. The function to be plotted, `func`, is specified as a pointer to a function that takes two arguments of type double and returns a value of type double. A function with the function prototype of

```
double func(double x, double y);
```

can be passed as the first argument of the function **fplotxyz()**. The arguments `numx` and `numy` specify how many points in the x and y ranges to be plotted, respectively. The remaining four arguments label the title and x, y, and z axes of a plot.

As an example, Program 6.13 uses the plotting function **fplotxyz()** to plot the mathematical function sinr(x, y) of equation (6.2) in section 6.6. It plots the function sinr(x, y) in the ranges of $-10 \le x \le 10$ and $-10 \le y \le 10$ with 80 points for the x-coordinates and 100 points for the y-coordinates. The generated plot is displayed in Figure 6.6. The plotting functions ignore the value of NaN in the data for plotting. The total number of points plotted in Figure 6.6 is $80 \times 100 = 8100$. If one chooses 1000 points in the x and y dimensions, it will have 1 million points in total, which needs extensive computational time and memory for plotting.

Similar to the function **fplotxy()**, the function call

```
fplotxyz(func, x0, xf, y0, yf, numx, numy, title. xlabel, ylabel);
```

```
/* File: hat.cpp
   Plot a 3D surface for sinr(x,y)=sin(sqrt(x*x + y*y))/sqrt(x*x + y*y). */
#include <math.h>
#include <chplot.h>   /* for 3D plotting function fplotxyz() */

/* function sinr() with two variables to be plotted */
double sinr(double x, double y) {
    double r, retval;

    r = sqrt(x*x + y*y);
    retval = sin(r)/r;
    return retval;
}

int main() {
    /* plotting  with -10<=x<=10, -10<=y<=10 */
    double x0 = 10.0, xf = 10.0, y0 = -10.0, yf = 10.0;
```

Program 6.13: A program to plot a three-dimensional surface for the function `sinr()` by the plotting function **fplotxyz()**. (*Continued*)

```
    /* use 80 points for x-coordinate, 100 points for y-coordinate */
    int numx = 80, numy = 100;

    /* plot sinr() for x from x0 to xf with numx points,
       y from y0 to yf with numy points.
       The title, labels for x, y, and z coordinates are
       "function sinr(x, y)", "x", "y", "sinr", respectively. */
    fplotxyz(sinr, x0, xf, y0, yf, numx, numy,
             "function sinr(x, y)", "x", "y", "sinr");
    return 0;
}
```

Program 6.13: *(Continued)*

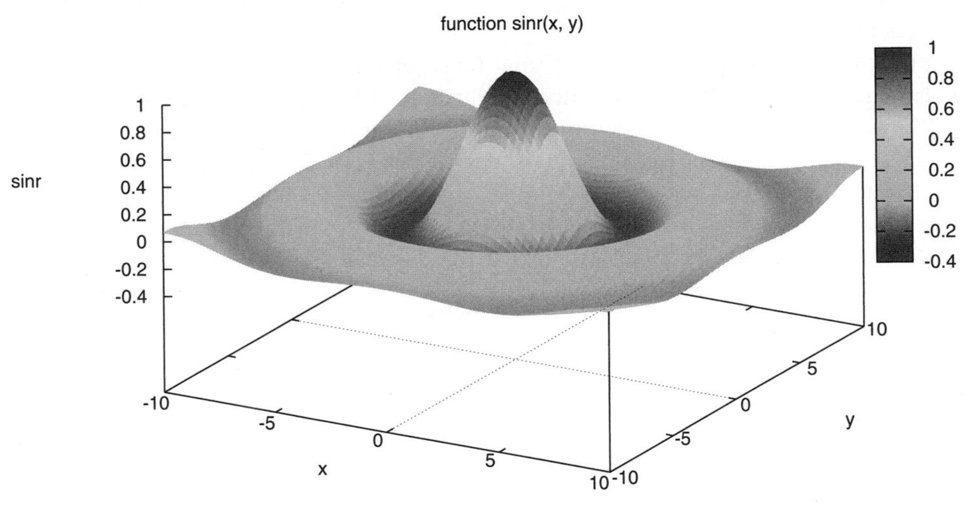

Figure 6.6: The plot generated by Programs 6.13.

can be replaced by the following code using a plotting class **CPlot**:

```
CPlot plot;
plot.title(title);
plot.label(PLOT_AXIS_X, xlabel);
plot.label(PLOT_AXIS_Y, ylabel);
plot.func3D(x0, xf, y0, yf, numx, numy, func);
plot.plotting();
```

The function call

```
plot.func3D(x0, xf, y0, yf, numx, numy, func);
```

generates the data for plotting by using the function `func()` in the range of [`x0, xf`] with `numx` of points for the x-axis and the range of [`y0, yf`] with `numy` of points for the y-axis. Multiple data sets can be added to a plot by calling this function multiple times.

6.8 Recursive Functions

Functions can be used recursively. That is, a function can directly call itself. When a function calls itself recursively, each function call will have a new set of local automatic variables. Inside a recursive function, conditional statements, such as **if-else**, are normally needed to exit the function and return the control flow of a program to the calling function.

Program 5.5 in Chapter 5 calculates the factorial of an integer n input by the user. In Program 6.14, the function `factorial()` with a **for** loop is used to calculate the factorial for an integer passed as its argument. Note that the factorial n! is defined as $n * (n-1)!$. Program 6.14 utilizes the function `factorial()` to calculate all the factorials up to 5!. Another method to calculate the factorial of an integer is to use a recursive function. Program 6.15 is equivalent to Program 6.14, except that the function `factorial()` is now a recursive function. It calls itself until the condition `n <= 1` is met. The output of Programs 6.14 and 6.15 is shown below:

```
0! = 1
1! = 1
2! = 2
3! = 6
4! = 24
5! = 120
```

```
/* File: factorloop.c
   Calculate the factorial using a loop in a function */
#include <stdio.h>

/* function prototype for factorial() with return type unsigned int */
unsigned int factorial(int n);

int main() {
    int i;

    /* calculate factorials 0!, 1!, 2!, 3!, 4!, 5! */
    for(i=0; i<=5; i++)
       printf("%d! = %u\n", i, factorial(i));
    return 0;
}

/* function call factorial(n) returns the factorial n! */
unsigned int factorial(int n) {
    unsigned int i, f; /* declare variables of unsigned int */

    /* using a recursive formula n! = n*(n-1)! for calculating f = n! */
    for(i=1, f=1; i<=n; i++) {
       f *= i;
    }
    return f;
}
```

Program 6.14: Calculating factorials using a function with a **for** loop.

```
/* File: factorrecursive.c
   Calculate the factorial using a recursive function */
#include <stdio.h>

/* function prototype for factorial() with return type unsigned int */
unsigned int factorial(int n);
int main() {
    int i;

    /* calculate factorials 0!, 1!, 2!, 3!, 4!, 5! */
    for(i=0; i<=5; i++)
       printf("%d! = %u\n", i, factorial(i));
    return 0;
}

/* factorial(n) returns the factorial n!; function is recursive. */
unsigned int factorial(int n) {
    if(n <=  1) {  /* termination condition for this recursive function */
      return 1;
    }
    else {          /*  using a recursive formula n! = n*(n-1)! */
      return n*factorial(n-1);
    }
}
```

Program 6.15: Calculating factorials using a recursive function.

A practical application of recursive functions will be given in section 13.5 in Chapter 13, where a function recursively searches for a student based on the student ID and name in a database using a GPA library.

6.9 Predefined Identifier __func__ in C99

The predefined identifier **__func__**, with two underscores before and after the symbol `func`, can be used to obtain the function name within a function. The identifier **__func__** is implicitly declared by as if, immediately following the opening brace of each function definition, the declaration

```
static const char __func__[] = "function-name";
```

appeared, where `function-name` is the name of the lexically enclosing function or member function of a class. For example, consider Program 6.16. The purpose of the function `funcname()` is to use **__func__** to print the name of the function.

To compile Program 6.16 with the C99 feature of the predeclared identifier **__func__**, using the GNU C compiler gcc, the program needs to be compiled with the command-line option `-std=c99` as follows:

```
gcc -std=c99 funcname.c
```

```
/* File: funcname.c (run in C99 and Ch only)
   Compile in gcc, use command 'gcc -std=c99 funcname.c'
   Demonstrate that each function has an implicitly declared
   identifier __func__ */
#include <stdio.h>

/* function uses __func__ to refer its function name */
void funcname(void) {
    printf("The function name is %s\n", __func__);
}

int main() {
    funcname();
    return 0;
}
```

Program 6.16: Using __func__ to get a function name.

The output of Program 6.16 is as follows:

```
The function name is funcname
```

This predefined variable of function name in conjunction with the file name and line number of a program is useful for debug. An example will be given in Program 7.2 in Chapter 7.

6.10 Algorithm Development and Implementation: Finding Roots of Equations Using the Bisection Method

Many problems in engineering and science require that you find roots of equations. For a value r, if $f(r)$ is zero, r is a root of equation $f(x) = 0$. If function $f(x)$ is plotted, the roots of the equation are the points where the curve of the function intersects with the x-axis. The y-coordinates for these interception points are zero. Therefore, the roots of equation $f(x) = 0$ are also called the zeros of function $f(x)$.

As an example, the projectile expressed by the function $y(x)$ in equation (6.4) is shown in Figure 6.2. There are two zero points for the function $y(x)$; one is at the origin and the other is somewhere between 60 and 70. These two zero points, or roots, correspond to the original and landing positions of the projectile. In this example, we have an explicit formula to find the second root by equation (6.3). However, in many other applications, we may not be fortunate enough to have explicit formulas for calculating roots. For example, there are no explicit solutions for finding two roots of the humps function shown in Figure 6.11.

In this section, we introduce a numerical method called the *bisection method* to find roots of equations. To use this method, we first have to identify an approximate interval at which a root is located. This can typically be accomplished by plotting the function and examining the generated curve for interceptions with the x-axis. You may adjust the range of the x-axis for plotting to narrow down an approximate interval with a zero point. For example, a root is located between 60 and 70 in the projectile shown in Figure 6.2. One root for the humps function shown in Figure 6.11 is located between -0.5 and 1, and the other is between 1 and 1.5.

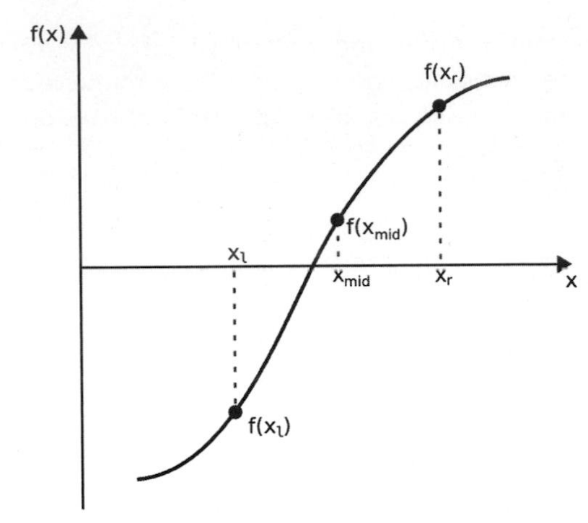

Figure 6.7: The working principle of the bisection method, halving the interval to reach the root.

Algorithm of the Bisection Method

Assume that there is an approximate interval $x_l \le x \le x_r$ where a zero exists for a continuous function $f(x)$, as shown in Figure 6.7. In this case, the function at these two end points of the interval changes the sign, therefore $f(x_l)f(x_r) \le 0$. If we can use a method to move the two end points of the interval closer to each other while maintaining the condition $f(x_l)f(x_r) \le 0$, we can get the approximate root. The bisection method uses the formula

$$x_{mid} = \frac{x_l + x_r}{2} \tag{6.5}$$

to calculate its midpoint x_{mid}. If $f(x_l)f(x_{mid}) \le 0$, the zero is located on the interval $x_l \le x \le x_{mid}$; otherwise, the zero is on the interval $x_{mid} \le x \le x_r$. Use the midpoint x_{mid} as either x_l or x_r of a new interval, we can iteratively bisect the interval to obtain a new midpoint.

Convergence Criteria for Bisection Method

The above algorithm for bisection method can iteratively calculate a new midpoint. The algorithm is very robust. The more iteration, the closer the midpoint is to the zero point. A *convergence criterion* for numerical computation is a condition to terminate an iteration. Below are two commonly used convergence criteria for finding roots of equations.

$$|f(x_i)| < tolerance \tag{6.6}$$

$$|x_i - x_{i-1})| < tolerance \tag{6.7}$$

The first convergence criterion in equation (6.6) states that when the absolute value of $f(x_i)$ is smaller than a specified small value, *tolerance*, the value x_i is a good approximate root of equation $f(x) = 0$. The second convergence criterion in equation (6.7) means that x_i is a good approximate root of of equation $f(x) = 0$ if it is very close to the previous value x_{i-1}. In other words, more iterations will not be able to gain much accuracy for the approximate root.

Numerical Algorithms of the Bisection Method in Procedures, Flowcharts, and Pseudocode

In the previous chapter, we have shown how to use procedures, flowcharts, and pseudocode to describe algorithms and program logic. In this section, these different methods are used to develop algorithms of the bisection method for calculating roots of functions. Assume that the initial end points are $x_l = x_0$ and $x_r = x_f$.

The convergence criterion (6.6) is used. We can describe a numerical algorithm for the bisection method in the following procedures.

Procedures for the initial numerical algorithm for the bisection method

1. Initialize $x_l = x_0$ and $x_r = x_f$.
2. If $f(x_l)f(x_r) > 0$, print an error message and then stop. Otherwise, continue to step 3.
3. Calculate $x_{mid} = (x_l + x_r)/2$ and $f_{mid} = f(x_{mid})$.
4. If $|f_{mid}| > tolerance$, continue to step 5. Otherwise, print the root x_{mid} and $f(x_{mid})$, and then stop.
5. If $f(x_l)f_{mid} \le 0$, set $x_r = x_{mid}$. Otherwise, set $x_l = x_{mid}$.
6. Update $x_{mid} = (x_l + x_r)/2$ and $f_{mid} = f(x_{mid})$ with new x_l or x_r.
7. Repeat step 4.

In this algorithm, step 7 brings the control flow of the program back to step 4. This can be accomplished using a loop in the implementation. In the above algorithm, at each iteration for steps 4 to 7, the function `f()` is called twice, the first time in step 5 for $f(x_l)$ and the second time in step 6 for $f(x_{mid})$. There is a significant overhead in each function call in comparison with an operation. We can refine the above algorithm to have only one function call at each iteration as described in the following procedures for the refined algorithm.

Procedures for the refined numerical algorithm for the bisection method

1. Initialize $x_l = x_0$, $x_r = x_f$, $f_{left} = f(x_l)$.
2. If $f_{left}f(x_r) > 0$, print an error message and then stop. Otherwise, continue to step 3.
3. Calculate $x_{mid} = (x_l + x_r)/2$ and $f_{mid} = f(x_{mid})$.
4. If $|f_{mid}| > tolerance$, continue to step 5. Otherwise, print the root x_{mid} and $f(x_{mid})$, and then stop.
5. If $f_{left}f_{mid} \le 0$, set $x_r = x_{mid}$, Otherwise, set $x_l = x_{mid}$ and $f_{left} = f_{mid}$.
6. Update $x_{mid} = (x_l + x_r)/2$ and $f_{mid} = f(x_{mid})$ with new x_l or x_r.
7. Repeat step 4.

In this refined algorithm, the variable `fleft` is used to keep the value of the function at the left point of the root so that the function is called only once at each iteration.

Flowchart for the refined numerical algorithm for the bisection method

A flowchart corresponding to this refined algorithm is shown in Figure 6.8. Speaking of flowcharts, examples of drawing flowcharts for functions and recursive functions are shown in Figures 13.12, 13.13, and 13.14 for Program 13.36 in Chapter 13.

Pseudocode for the refined numerical algorithm for the bisection method

The pseudocode for the refined algorithm for the bisection method is given in Program 6.17. As shown in the pseudocode, the values for two end points at the left and right of a root are initialized by the statements

```
xleft  = x0
xright = xf
```

It is possible that the two end values x_0 and x_f are invalid such that $f(x_0)f(x_f) > 0$. This is checked by the condition expression

```
fleft * f(xright) > 0.0
```

in the **if** statement.

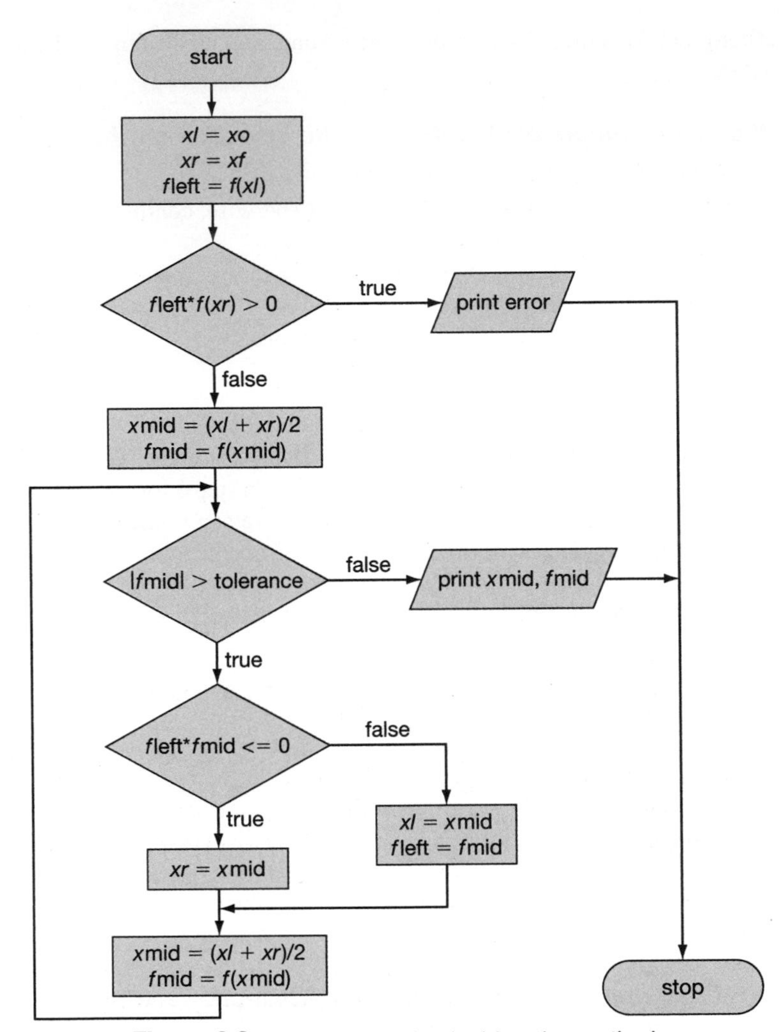

Figure 6.8: The flowchart for the bisection method.

```
// File: bisectmethod.p
// Pseudocode for Bisection Method

// initialize xleft and xright with initial end points
xleft  = x0
xright = xf

// The signs of f(xleft) and f(xright) must be different
// to guarantee there is a root
fleft = f(xleft)
```

Program 6.17: The pseudocode for the bisection method. (*Continued*)

```
if(fleft * f(xright) > 0.0)
    print error message
endif

// caclculate the mid point and its function value
xmid = (xleft+xright)/2.0;
fmid = f(xmid);
while(fabs(fmid) > tolerance)
    // f(xleft)*f(mid) to determine the updating of left or right point
    if(fleft*fmid <= 0.0) // mid point becomes the right point
        xright = xmid
    else                  // mid point becomes the left point
        xleft = xmid
        fleft = fmid
    endif
    // update the mid point and its function value
    xmid = (xleft+xright)/2.0
    fmid = f(xmid)
endwhile
print xmid and fmid
```

Program 6.17: *(Continued)*

Before iteration using a **while** loop, the midpoint is calculated. The convergence criterion in equation (6.6) is used as the conditional expression for the **while** loop. The **if-else** statement inside the **while** loop updates one end point using the midpoint based on the condition $f(x_l)f(x_{mid}) \le 0$ as described in the algorithm of the bisection method. We have saved the value for $f(x_{mid})$ in $f(x_l)$ by the statement

```
fleft = fmid
```

so that the function $f()$ is called only once at each iteration. Before the next iteration, the midpoint and function value at this midpoint are calculated at the end of the **while** loop. The **while** loop finishes when the convergence criterion is met. The calculated root, the value for the last midpoint x_{mid}, and the residual value of the function at this point are printed out.

Implementation of the Bisection Method

Based on the pseudocode in Program 6.17 for the refined algorithm, we can easily implement the bisection method in C to find a root for a function. As an example, with an initial speed v_0 of 35 m/s and initial projection angle of $\theta_0 = 15°$, the projectile function $y(x)$ in equation (6.4) has a root somewhere between 60 meters and 70 meters as shown in Figure 6.2. Program 6.18 uses the above algorithm for the bisection method to calculate this root numerically. Program 6.18 looks quite similar to the pseudocode in Program 6.17. Equation (6.4) is implemented as the function `func()` in Program 6.18.

Variables `xleft`, `xright`, `xmid`, `fleft`, and `fmid` are for the symbols x_l, x_r, x_{mid}, $f(x_l)$, and $f(x_{mid})$ shown in Figure 6.7. The values for two end points are initialized by the statements

```
xleft  = x0;
xright = xf;
```

with x0 = 60.0 and xf = 70.0. The *tolerance* used in the convergence criterion is **FLT_EPSILON** which is first presented in section 4.5 in Chapter 4. This macro for the machine epsilon of type float is defined in the header file **float.h**. The output from Program 6.18 is shown below:

```
x = 62.436290 m, func(x) = -7.68432e-08
```

Based on the algorithm for the bisection method in this section, general-purpose root-finding functions are developed in sections 11.11.2 and 11.12 in Chapter 11. An alternative root-finding method called Newton's method is described in Exercise 42.

```
/* File: bisectmethod.c
   Find a root for projectile funct using bisection method in range [60, 70] */
#include <stdio.h>
#include <math.h>              /* for fabs() */
#include <float.h>             /* for FLT_EPSILON */
#define M_G   9.81             /* gravitational acceleration constant g */

/* function for the y-coordinate of the projectifle */
double func(double x) {
   double theta0,              /* initial velocity */
          v0,                  /* projection angle */
          y;                   /* y coordinate */
   theta0 = 15*M_PI/180; /* set the projection angle in radian */
   v0 = 35.0;                  /* set the initial velocity */
   y = tan(theta0)*x - M_G*x*x/(2*v0*v0*cos(theta0)*cos(theta0));
   return y;
}

int main() {
   double xleft, fleft;            /* x and f(x) on the left of the root */
   double xright;                  /* x on the right of the root */
   double xmid, fmid;              /* x and f(x) on the mid of xleft and xright */
   double tolerance;               /* convergence tolerance */
   double x0 = 60.0, xf = 70.0; /* initial end points */

   /* initialize xleft and xright with initial end points */
   xleft  = x0;
   xright = xf;
   /* use machine epsilon for float type as convergence tolerance */
   tolerance=FLT_EPSILON;

   /* The signs of f(xleft) and f(xright) must be different
      to guarantee there is a root */
   fleft = func(xleft);                /* calculate f(xleft) */
```

Program 6.18: Finding a root of the projectile using the bisection method.

```
    if(fleft * func(xright) > 0.0) {     /* invalid x0 and xf */
        printf("Error: invalid end points\n");
        return -1;              /* return -1 for invalid xleft and xright */
    }
    xmid = (xleft+xright)/2.0;          /* mid point */
    fmid = func(xmid);                  /* f() in the mid point */
    while(fabs(fmid) > tolerance) {/* convergence criterion to terminate loop */
        /* f(xleft)*f(mid) to determine the updating of left or right point */
        if(fleft*fmid <= 0.0) {         /* mid point becomes the right point */
            xright = xmid;              /* update the right point */
        }
        else {                          /* mid point becomes the left point */
            xleft = xmid;               /* update the left point */
            fleft = fmid;               /* update f(xleft) */
        }
        xmid = (xleft+xright)/2.0;      /* update the mid point */
        fmid = func(xmid);              /* f() in the mid point */
    }
    printf("x = %f m, func(x) = %g\n", xmid, fmid);
    return 0;
}
```

Program 6.18: *(Continued)*

6.11 ‡Variable Number Arguments in Functions

C allows a variable number of arguments to be passed to a function. In some applications, the number of arguments passed to a function is unknown in advance and could be different for different cases. With this feature, one function could handle argument lists with different lengths for different cases. A typical function that takes a variable number of arguments is defined as follows:

```
#include <stdarg.h>
type1 funcname (arg_list, type2 paramN, ...) {
  va_list ap;
  type3 v;                  // first unnamed argument
  va_start(ap, paramN);     // initialize the list
  v = va_arg(ap, type3);    // get 1st unnamed argument from the list
  ...                       // get the rest of the list
  va_end(ap);               // clean up the argument list
  ...
}
```

where `arg_list` is the argument list of the named argument, `paramN` is the last named argument, and `v` is the first unnamed argument of type `type3`. The standard header file **stdarg.h** contains a set of macro definitions for handling a variable argument list. These macros are listed in Table 6.2. Besides these macros, the type **va_list** is also defined in the header file **stdarg.h**. It is used to declare an object that can hold information of

Table 6.2 Macros defined in the header file stdarg.h for handling the variable argument list.

Macro	Description
VA_NOARG	The second argument for **va_start**(), if no argument is passed to function (in Ch only).
va_arg	Expands to an expression that has the specified type and the value of the next argument in the calling function.
va_arraydim	Obtains array dimension of the variable argument (in Ch only).
va_arrayextent	Obtains the extent for a specified dimension in the array of variable argument (in Ch only).
va_arraytype	Determines if the next argument is an array (in Ch only).
va_arraynum	Obtains the number of elements in the array of variable argument (in Ch only).
va_copy	Makes a copy of the **va_list**(in C99 and Ch only).
va_count	Obtains the number of variable arguments (in Ch only).
va_datatype	Obtains the data type of variable argument (in Ch only).
va_end	Facilitates a normal return from the function.
va_start	Initializes *ap* for subsequent use by other macros.

the argument list and refer to each argument in turn. This object is typically referred to as `ap` according to the C notational convention.

The macro **va_start** initializes `ap` to point to the first unnamed argument. It shall be called before `ap` is used. The rightmost named parameter, which plays a special role in accessing a variable argument list, is designated `paramN` here. It is used by **va_start** to get started. After that, each call of **va_arg**() returns one unnamed argument and steps `ap` to the next one. The macro **va_arg** takes a type name as an argument to determine what type to return and the location of the next unnamed argument to get. The data type can be a simple data type, such as **int**, pointer, or an aggregate data type, such as class, computational array. Finally, after all of the arguments have been read and before returning from the function, macro **va_end** must be called to clean up the argument list.

Program 6.19 defines a function `area()` with a variable argument list. Depending on the shape specified by the argument `type`, the `area()` function calculates the area of a circle, square, or rectangle. The object `ap` and a **switch** statement are used to determine the desired shape and calculate the area of the object. The output of Program 6.19 is shown in Figure 6.9.

```
The area of circle with radius 2 meters is 12.57 (m^2)
The area of square with side 2 meters is 4.00 (m^2)
The area of rectangle with length 3 meters and width 2 meters is 6.00 (m^2)
```

Figure 6.9: The output from Program 6.19 and Program 13.29 in Chapter 13

```
/* File: vararg.c
   Calculate areas of different shapes using a function
   with a variable number of arguments. */
#include <stdio.h>
```

Program 6.19: Using a function with a variable number of arguments. (*Continued*)

```
#include <stdarg.h>   /* for va_list, va_start(), va_arg(), va_end() */
#include <math.h>     /* for M_PI */

/* define macros for circle, square, and rectangle */
#define CIRCLE        1
#define SQUARE        2
#define RECTANGLE     3

/* function area() with a variable number of arguments */
double area (int type, ...) {
    va_list ap;            /* variable used for handling ... */
    double radius;         /* radius of a circle */
    double side;           /* side of a square */
    double length, width; /* length and width of a rectangle */
    double a = 0.0;        /* area of a shape, default is 0 */

    va_start(ap, type); /* use the argument type to start ap */
    /* depending on the type of shape,
       obtain the passed argument(s) and calculate the area */
    switch(type) {
        case CIRCLE:
          /* for a circle, obtain the passed radius  */
          radius = va_arg(ap, double);
          a = M_PI*radius*radius;
          break;
        case SQUARE:
          /* for a square, obtain the passed side */
          side = va_arg(ap, double);
          a = side*side;
          break;
        case RECTANGLE:
          /* for a rectanle, obtain the passed length and width */
          length = va_arg(ap, double);
          width  = va_arg(ap, double);
          a = length*width;
          break;
        default:
          /* in case a mistake is made by passing an unknown shape */
          printf("Error: unknown shape\n");
          break;
    }
    va_end(ap); /* end the processing of the variable number of arguments*/

    return a;
}
```

Program 6.19: *(Continued)*

```
int main() {
    /* The unit for lengths is meter */
    double radius = 2.0;                      /* radius of a circle */
    double side = 2.0;                        /* side of a square */
    double length = 3.0, width = 2.0; /* length and width of a rectangle */
    double a;                                 /* area of a shape */

    /* calculate and display areas for shapes circle, square, and rectangle */
    a = area(CIRCLE, radius);
    printf("The area of circle with radius 2 m is %.2f (m^2)\n", a);
    a = area(SQUARE, side);
    printf("The area of square with side 2 m is %.2f (m^2)\n", a);
    a = area(RECTANGLE, length, width);
    /* A single long line of output is broken into two printf() statements */
    printf("The area of rectangle with length 3 m and width 2 m");
    printf(" is %.2f (m^2)\n", a);
    return 0;
}
```

Program 6.19: *(Continued)*.

6.12 ‡Old-Style Function Definitions

Although obsolete, the old-style function definition, known as K&R function definition, is still supported in C. In this notation, parameter identifiers in a function definition are separated by the declaration list as shown below.

```
return_type function_name(argument)
argument_declaration
{
  statements
}
```

Each argument in this function definition is separated by a comma. Arguments are declared as if they were in declaration statements. For example, the function `addition()` in Program 6.1 can be defined in the following notation:

```
int addition(a, b)
int a;
int b;
{
    int s;
    s = a + b;
    return s;
}
```

or

```
int addition(a, b)
int a, b;
{
    return a + b;
}
```

6.13 Making It Work

6.13.1 Interactive Execution of Functions in a Ch Command Shell

All functions in the C standard libraries can be executed interactively and can be used inside user-defined functions in a Ch command shell. For example:

```
> sin(3.14)
0.0016
> sin(3.14/2)
1.0000
> double add(double a, double b) {double c; return a+b+sin(1.5);}
> double c
> c = add(10.0, 20)
30.9975
```

The function `add()`, which calls the type-generic mathematical function **sin()** is defined at the prompt and then used.

6.13.2 Using Function Files in Ch

A *function file* in Ch is a file that contains only one function definition. The name of a function file ends in `.chf`, such as `force.chf`. The names of the function file and the function definition inside the function file must be the same. The functions defined using function files are treated as if they were system built-in functions in Ch.

Similar to the system variable **_path** for commands described in section 2.2.3 in Chapter 2, a function is searched based on the search paths in the system variable **_fpath** for function files. Each path is delimited by a semicolon. By default, the variable **_fpath** in Windows contains the following search paths:

```
C:/Ch/lib/libc;C:/Ch/lib/libch;C:/Ch/lib/libopt;C:/Ch/libch/numeric;
```

If the system variable **_fpath** is modified interactively in a Ch shell, it will be effective only for functions invoked in the current shell interactively. For running scripts, the setup of function search paths in the current shell will not be used and inherited in subshells. In this case, the system variable **_fpath** can be modified in the start-up file **_chrc** in Windows or **.chrc** in Unix at the user's home directory.

Use the function `force()` in Program 6.3 as an example. If a file named `force.chf` contains the program shown in Program 6.20, the function `force()` will be treated as a system built-in function, which can be called to compute the force based on the input argument of time. Assume that the function file `force.chf` is located at `C:/Documents and Settings/Administrator/eme5/force.chf`, the directory

```
/* File: force.chf */
double force(double t) {
    double p;

    p = 4*(t-3)+20;
    return p;
}
```

Program 6.20: The function file for the function `force()` used by the program `accelfuncfile.ch`.

`C:/Documents and Settings/Administrator/eme5` should be added to the function search path in the start-up file **.chrc** in Unix or **_chrc** in Windows in the user's home directory with the following statement:

```
_fpath=stradd(_fpath, "C:/Documents and Settings/Administrator/eme5;");
```

As illustrated in Figure 1.5 in Chapter 1, the function `force()` then can be used either interactively in command mode as shown below,

```
> double p;
> p = force(3)
20.0000
```

or inside programs. In Program 6.21, the function `force()` is called without a function prototype in the **main()** function. However, to be C-compatible, one can also add a function prototype for force() in Program 6.21. The output of Program 6.21 is the same as that of Program 6.3. If the search paths for function files have not been properly set up, an error message such as

```
ERROR: function 'force()' not defined
```

will be displayed when the function `force()` is called.

```
/* File: accelfuncfile.ch */
#include <stdio.h>
#define M_G   9.81

int main() {
    double a, mu, m, p, t;

    mu = 0.2;
    m = 5.0;
    t = 2.0;
    p = force(t);
    a = (p-mu*m*M_G)/m;
    printf("Acceleration a = %f (m/s^2)\n", a);
    return 0;
}
```

Program 6.21: Calculating the acceleration using the function file `force.chf` for force.

When a function is called interactively in a Ch shell, the function file will be loaded. If you modify a function file after the function has been called, the subsequent calls in the command mode will still use the old version of the function definition that had been loaded. To invoke the modified version of the new function file, you can either remove the function definition in the system using the command **remvar** followed by a function name or start a new Ch shell by typing **ch** at the prompt. For example, the command

```
> remvar force
```

removes the definition for the function `force`(). The command **remvar** can also be used to remove a declared variable.

6.13.3 Debugging Programs with Functions in ChIDE

Using ChIDE to debug programs was introduced in section 3.16.3 in Chapter 3. In this section, debugging programs with functions is described.

The command `Step` on the debug bar in ChIDE will step into a function, whereas the command `Next` will step over the function to the next line. Figure 6.10 shows the execution of the program `accelfun.c` listed in Program 6.3 in ChIDE. The program stops in the function `force()` at line 14 with a breakpoint when it is called by the calling function **main()** at line 26. The current executing line 14 is highlighted (displayed in the green color on the screen). Unlike previously displayed interfaces for ChIDE, ChIDE in Figure 6.10 is displayed in vertical mode so that the debug pane can show more information. The command `Options | Vertical Split` can be used to change the display in the vertical mode. In the vertical mode,

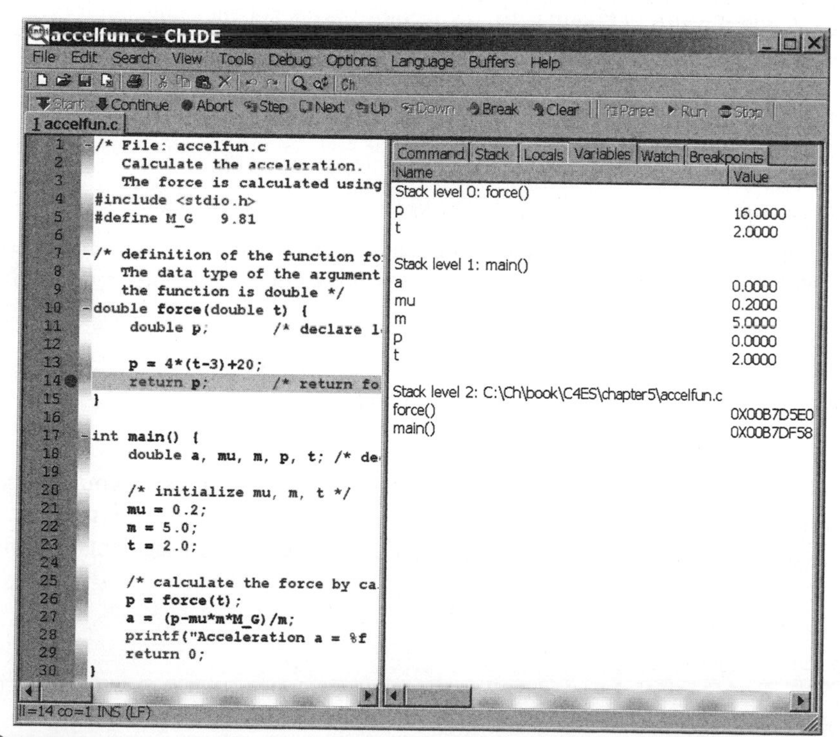

Figure 6.10: Debugging `accelfun.c` in Program 6.3, showing values for all variables in different stacks in ChIDE.

the editing pane is on the left, debug pane in the middle, output pane in the upper-right, and debug command pane in the lower-right. Only the editing and debug panes are shown in Figure 6.10.

Variable names and their corresponding values in all stacks can be displayed by clicking the menu `Variables` on the debug pane selection bar, as shown in Figure 6.10. In this case, the program is stopped at line 14. Local variable names and their values of called function `force()` and calling function **main()** as well as global variables are displayed in the debug pane. The current running function has stack level 0, whereas level $n + 1$ is the function that has called a function with stack level n. Function `force()`, the current running function, has stack level 0. The variables `p` and `t` inside this function have values of 16.0 and 2.0. The values for variables `a, mu, m, p,` and `t` in the function **main()** with stack level 1, which calls the function `force()` with stack level 0, are also displayed. Note that both functions `force()` and **main()** have their own variable named `p` with their own memory. Their values are different at this point. The variable `p` in the function **main()** is 0, whereas a variable `p` in the function `force()` is 16.0. Function names `force` and `main` are variables of function type. Their addresses are displayed in the debug pane as variables for the program `accelfun.c` at the stack level 2, which invokes the function **main()** at stack level 1. The details about global variables will be described in Chapter 8.

When you click the menu `Stack` on the debug pane selection bar, functions and program names with the corresponding stack level will be displayed in the debug pane.

The user can change the function stack during debugging. It can go `Up` to its calling function or move `Down` to the called function so that the variables within its scope can be displayed or accessed in the debug pane. For example, when you click the command `Up` on the debug bar in Figure 6.10, the control flow of the program moves to its calling function **main()** at line 26. Both lines 14 and 26 would be highlighted (displayed in the green color on the screen). In Figure 6.10, the menu `Down` is not clickable, but it is clickable once the current stack is moved up to the function **main()** after clicking the menu `Up`. Then, the debug pane would only show the function **main()** at stack level 1 and the program `accelfun.c` at stack level 2 and their variables and corresponding values.

Exercises

1. Add the directory `HOME/eme5` to the function file search paths in Ch. `HOME` is your home directory, such as `C:/Documents and Settings/harry` in Windows or `/home/harry` in Unix. In Windows, add

   ```
   _fpath = stradd(_fpath, "C:/Documents and Settings/harry/eme5;");
   ```

   to the start-up file _chrc in your home directory. In Unix, add

   ```
   _fpath = stradd(_fpath, "/home/harry/eme5;");
   ```

   to the start-up file .chrc in your home directory. Change `harry` to your user account name, and `eme5` to the name of the course that you are taking using this textbook. Hand in your start-up file.
2. Identify and correct the errors, if there are any, in the following program segments. Briefly explain why.

   a.
   ```
   int func(double a);
   int func(int a) {
       return 10*a;
   }
   ```

   b.
   ```
   int func(int a) {
       return 2*;
   }
   func(2, 3);
   ```

c.
```
void func1(int a);
int func1(int a) {
    int b;
    b = 2*a;
    return b;
}
```

d.
```
void func1(int a) {
    return 2*a;
}
```

e.
```
double sum(doubl a, double b) {
    return a+b;
}
void func(double a, double b) {
    double sum;
    sum = sum(a, b);
}
```

f.
```
int funct1(int i){return i*i;}
int funct1();
int funct1(int j);
int funct2();
int funct2(int);
int funct2(int i);
```

g.
```
int funct3(int i) {
     return i*i
};
int i;

i = (int)funct3(i);
funct3(i);
i = funct3(8);
```

h.
```
double cube(float);                /* function prototype */
       ...
cube(float number)                 /* function definition */
{
  return number * number * number;
}
```

i.
```
/* add integers from 1 to n by the recursive function sum()  */
int sum(int n)
{
  if(n == 0)
    rcturn 0;
  else
    return n + sum(n);
}
```

3. Give the output of the following code:

```
#include <stdio.h>
void func(int a, int b, double c) {
    printf("a = %d\n", a);
    printf("b = %d\n", b);
    printf("c = %f\n", c);
}
int main() {
    func(3.3, 3.7, 4);
    return 0;
}
```

4. Solve each of the following problems:

   a. Write the function header for the function `funct()`, which takes parameters `arg1` of double type and `arg2` of int type and does not return a value.

   b. Write the function prototype for the function in part (a).

5. Write a function that converts miles to kilometers. Note that 1 mile equals 1.6093440 km.

6. Calculate the values of the following functions using a C function for each one at $x = 3.5$.

   a. $g_1(x) = 2x\sin(x) + \cos(x) + \dfrac{4x+3}{3x^2+2x+4}$

   b. $g_2(x) = x^2\sqrt{2x}$

   c. $g_3(x) = 2x\sin(x) + \cos(x^2\sqrt{2x})$

   d. $g_4(x) = \dfrac{3x^2+4x+3}{5\sin(x^2)+4x^2+3}$

7. Calculate the values of the following functions using a C function for each one at $x = 3.5$ and $y = 4.2$.

   a. $g_5(x, y) = 2x\sin(y) + \cos(x) + \dfrac{4x+3}{3x^2+2y+4}$

   b. $g_6(x, y) = x^2\sqrt{2y}$

   c. $g_7(x, y) = 2x\sin(y) + \cos(y^2\sqrt{2x})$

   d. $g_8(x, y) = \dfrac{3x^2+4y+3}{5\sin(y^2)+4x^2+6}$

8. Calculate the values of the following functions using a C function for x in the range of $-1 \le x \le 5$ with a step size of 0.25, and display the output in the format shown in Figure 5.16. Plot each function using the plotting function **fplotxy()** with 100 points.

   a. $f_1(x) = 2x\sin(x) + \cos(x) + \dfrac{4x+3}{3x^2+2x+4}$

   b. $f_2(x) = x^2\sqrt{2x}$

   c. $f_3(x) = 2x\sin(x) + \cos(x^2\sqrt{2x})$

   d. $f_4(x) = \dfrac{3x^2+4x+3}{5\sin(x^2)+4x^2+3}$

9. Calculate the values of the following functions using a C function for x in the range of $-1 \le x \le 5$ with a step size of 1 and for y in the range of $2 \le y \le 4$ with a step size of 0.5, and display the output in the

format shown in Figure 5.18. Plot each function using the plotting function **fplotxyz()** with 100 points for the x and y coordinates.

a. $f_5(x, y) = 2x\sin(y) + \cos(x) + \dfrac{4x+3}{3x^2+2y+4}$

b. $f_6(x, y) = x^2\sqrt{2y}$

c. $f_7(x, y) = 2x\sin(y) + \cos(y^2\sqrt{2x})$

d. $f_8(x, y) = \dfrac{3x^2+4y+3}{5\sin(y^2)+4x^2+6}$

10. Calculate the values of the function

$$f_9(x, y) = \frac{3x^2+4y+3}{5\sin(y^2)+4x^2+3}$$

using a C function for x in the range of $-1 \leq x \leq 5$ with a step size of 1 and for y in the range of $2 \leq y \leq 4$ with a step size of 0.5, and display the output in the format shown in Figure 5.18. Plot each function using the plotting function **fplotxyz()** with 100 points for the x and y coordinates. Please explain why the plot is not smooth. This exercise further illustrates the value of visualization to identify some potential pitfalls.

11. The function

$$f_{10}(x) = x^2 + 5\sin(10x)$$

is a superposition of a parabolic function and a harmonic function. Calculate the values of the function using a C function for x in the range of $-4 \leq x \leq 4$ with a step size of 0.5, and display the output in the format shown in Figure 5.16. Plot the function using **fplotxy()** with 200 points.

12. Modify Program 4.7 to print out all bits of the following integers with 32 bits without using the format specifier `%b` in Ch.

a. 90, 0X32A, −89, 3563
b. 35, 0X12C, −35, 3344.

13. Write a function `rightrot(x, n)` that returns the value of the positive integer x rotated to the right by n bit positions (the bit in the rightmost position will be moved to the bit in the leftmost position). Test your program using 5 and 3 for x and n, respectively.

```
int rightrot(int x, int n) {
    ...
}
```

14. The formula for the volume of a sphere is $\frac{4}{3}\pi r^3$, where r is the radius of the sphere. Write a function to return the volume of a sphere with the input argument for the radius of the sphere. Test your program with a radius of 5 meters.

15. Write a program that calculates the area and perimeter of a rectangle. The area and perimeter are calculated using two separate functions, which both take two arguments of double type for the width and length of the rectangle. Calculate the area and perimeter using these two functions in the main program for a rectangle with width and length of 2 cm and 5.5 cm, respectively.

16. The Fibonacci series

```
0, 1, 1, 2, 3, 5, 8, 13, 21, ...
```

begins with 0 and 1. It has the property that each subsequent Fibonacci number is the sum of the previous two Fibonacci numbers; that is, the Fibonacci series is defined by the equation

$$F_{k+2} = F_{k+1} + F_k$$

Write the function

```
int fibonacci(int n);
```

to calculate a Fibonacci number with an argument for the series number. Calculate all Fibonacci numbers in a program called `fibonacci.c` when k is 10, with the following constraint:

a. Function `fibonacci()` should be nonrecursive.
b. Function `fibonacci()` should be recursive.

17. Exercise 18 in Chapter 5 wrote a program to test if an integer is a prime number. Write a function to return the smallest divisor for an integer. Use this function to determine and print all the prime numbers between 1 and 1000.

18. Write a C program that uses the function **rand()** to generate an integer randomly in the range of 1 to 50. The random number generated by the program shall be different at each run. The program then prompts the user to guess the number by displaying the following messages:

```
I have a number between 1-50.
Can you guess what it is?
Enter your initial guess.
```

After the user's initial guess, the program should display one of the following responses:

```
(1) Correct!  That's the number.
    Would you like to play again (y or n)?
(2) Too low.  Guess again.
(3) Too high.  Guess again.
```

The program should loop until the user guesses the correct answer. Use the "Too low" and "Too high" messages to help the user guess the number. Once the user guesses the right number, the program should ask whether he or she would like to play again. Describe your algorithm in procedures, pseudocode, and flowcharts. (Note: write a function called `guessGame()` to play this "guessing game.")

19. Use the random number generation functions **rand()** and **srand()** defined in the header file **stdlib.h** for each problem below. Describe your algorithm in procedures, pseudocode, and flowcharts.

a. Write a program that generates two random integers ranging from 1 to 10. The random numbers generated by the program shall be different at each run. Then prompt the user to enter the sum of the two numbers. If the user enters the right answer, it prints a correct comment. If it is wrong, print an incorrect comment and allow the user to enter another answer until it is right. Correct or incorrect comments are randomly printed out. Use two functions, one for handling correct answers and the other for incorrect answers. The response to a correct answer may be `"Correct!"`, `"Good Job!"`, or `"Great!"`. The response to an incorrect answer may be `"Incorrect. Please try again."`, `"Wrong. Try again."`, or `"No. Enter another answer."`.

b. Modify the program to ask the user a total of 10 addition problems. At the end of the 10th question, print a message to tell the user how many problems were answered correctly. If the user has more than 8 correct solutions, give a complimentary comment. For less than 6 correct solutions, give an encouraging statement. Note that the user should have only one chance to answer each question.

20. In Exercise 19, two random numbers in the range from 1 to 10 are added. Do the same for the subtraction of two random numbers in the range from 1 to 100.
21. In Exercise 19, two random numbers in the range from 1 to 10 are added. Do the same for the multiplication of two random numbers in the range from 1 to 9.
22. Use the random number generation functions **rand()** and **srand()** defined in the header file **stdlib.h** for each problem below. Describe your algorithm in procedures, pseudocode, and flowcharts.

    a. Write a program to generate two random integers ranging from 1 to 10 using functions **rand()** and **srand()**. The random numbers generated by the program shall be different at each run. A random operation of either addition or subtraction for these two numbers will be selected. Then prompt the user to enter the result of the operation. If the user enters the right answer, it prints a correct comment. If it is wrong, print an incorrect comment and allow the user to enter another answer until it is right. Correct or incorrect comments are randomly printed out. Use two functions, one for handling correct answers and the other for incorrect answers. The response to a correct answer may be `"Correct!"`, `"Good Job!"`, or `"Great!"`. The response to an incorrect answer may be `"Incorrect."`, `"Wrong."`, or `"Bad answer."`. Ask the user a total of 10 problems. At the end of the 10th question, print a message to tell the user how many problems were answered correctly. If the user has more than 8 correct solutions, give a complimentary comment. For less than 6 correct solutions, give an encouraging statement. Note that the user should have only one chance to answer each question.

    b. Modify the program to select a random operation of addition, subtraction, or multiplication.
23. The temperature in Fahrenheit can be expressed in Celsius as follows:

$$f(c) = (9/5)c + 32$$

where c is the temperature in Celsius and f the temperature in Fahrenheit. Plot the relation when the temperature varies in the range of $[-10, 40]$ degrees in Celsius using 50 points.
24. A projectile is fired into the air with an initial speed v_0 of 35 m/s and initial projection angle $\theta_0 = 45°$. Plot its trajectory with 50 points. The trajectory can be expressed in X- and Y-coordinates using equations (6.3) and 6.4.
25. For the mechanical system shown in Figure 2.12, given mass $m = 6$ kilograms (kg) and coefficient of kinetic friction $\mu = 0.3$, the applied force p is expressed as a function of time t in

$$p(t) = \begin{cases} 20 & \text{if} \quad t \le 3 \\ 4(t+2) & \text{if} \quad 3 < t \le 6 \\ 4(t^2 + 2t) & \text{if} \quad t > 6 \end{cases}$$

Plot the accelerations of the rigid body from $t = 0$ to 10 seconds with 100 points.
26. Calculate factorials $n!$ for n from 1 to 20 using a factorial function with return type of unsigned long long.

    a. Use a **for** loop in the factorial function.

    b. Use a recursive factorial function.
27. Based on the algorithm presented in Program 5.14, write an exponential function with the function prototype

```
double expx(double x);
```

Test your function by computing $e^{0.5}$ and e.

28. Based on the algorithm presented in Exercise 40 in Chapter 5, write a sine function with the function prototype

```
double sine(double x);
```

Test your function by computing `sine(0.5)`.

29. Based on the algorithm presented in Exercise 41 in Chapter 5, write a cosine function with the function prototype

```
double cosine(double x);
```

Test your function by computing `cosine(0.5)`.

30. Based on the algorithm presented in Exercise 44 in Chapter 5, write a cubic root function with the function prototype

```
double cbrtx(double x);
```

Use this function to solve Exercise 44(b) in Chapter 5.

31. The humps function (shown in Figure 6.11) is defined as

$$humps(x) = \frac{1}{(x-0.3)^2+0.01} + \frac{1}{(x-0.9)^2+0.04} - 6 \tag{6.8}$$

The function has maxima near $x = 0.3$ and $x = 0.9$. Plot the function for the variable x in the range of $-1 \leq x \leq 2$. Calculate the value of the function at $x = 0.3$ and $x = 0.9$.

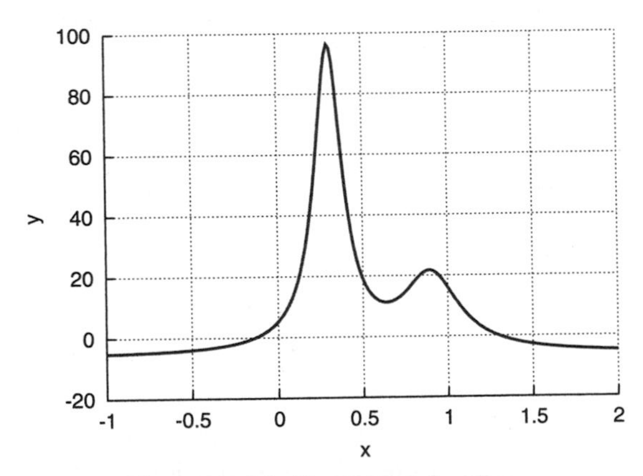

Figure 6.11: The humps function.

32. The peaks function with two variables is defined as

$$peaks(x, y) = 3(1-x)^2 e^{-x^2-(y+1)^2} - 10\left(\frac{x}{5} - x^3 - y^5\right)e^{-x^2-y^2} - \frac{1}{3}e^{-(x+1)^2-y^2} \tag{6.9}$$

Plot the function for the variables x and y in the ranges of $-3 \le x \le 3$ and $-4 \le y \le 4$, respectively as shown in the illustration. Calculate the value of the function at $x = 1.5$ and $y = 2.5$.

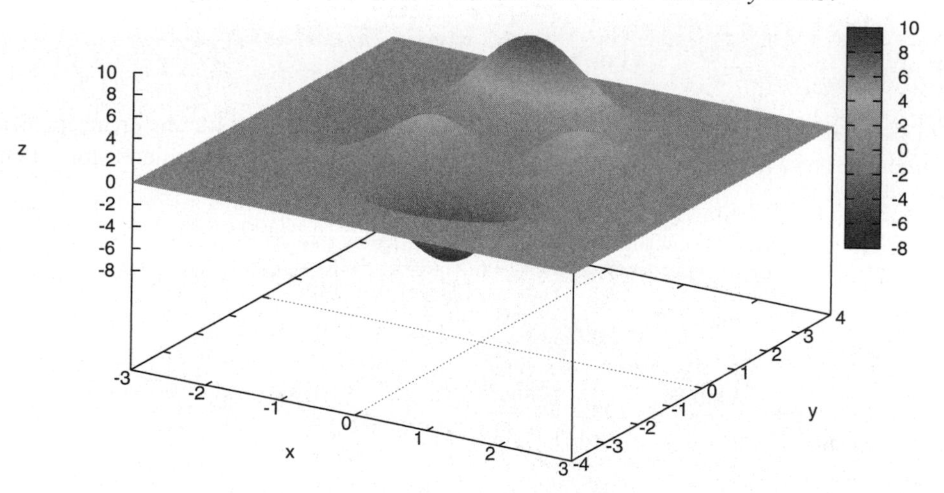

33. A random variable x with probability density function

$$f_X(x;\mu,\sigma) = \frac{1}{\sqrt{2\pi}\sigma} e^{\frac{-(x-\mu)^2}{2\sigma^2}} \tag{6.10}$$

shown in Figure 6.12 for $-\infty < x < \infty$ has a *normal distribution* with parameters μ and σ. The normal distribution is also called a *Gaussian distribution*. The values of μ and σ, which are in the range of $-\infty < \mu < \infty$ and $\sigma > 0$, determine the shape of the probability density function. The value of μ determines the center of the probability density function, and the value of σ determines the dispersion. The function $f_X(x;\mu,\sigma)$ is nonnegative. The area under $f_X(x;\mu,\sigma)$ from $-\infty < x < \infty$ is 1. The maximum value of the probability density function is $(\sqrt{2\pi}\sigma)^{-1}$, which occurs at $x = \mu$. A normal random variable with $\mu = 0$ and $\sigma^2 = 1$ is called a *standard normal random variable*.

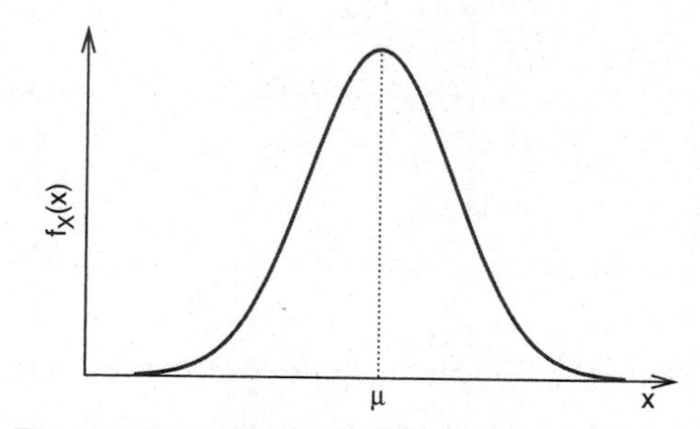

Figure 6.12: The probability density function.

a. Plot the probability density function for a standard normal random variable x in the range $-6 \le x \le 6$. Calculate $(\sqrt{2\pi}\sigma)^{-1}$.

b. Plot the probability density function for x in the range $-4 \le x \le 8$ with $\mu = 2$ and $\sigma = 3$. Calculate $(\sqrt{2\pi}\sigma)^{-1}$.

c. Plot two separate probability density functions in Exercises 33 (a) and 33 (b) in the same figure with x in the range $-10 \le x \le 10$. Use the member function **func2D()** of the plotting class **CPlot**.

34. A piecewise continuous function $f(x)$ with period 2π can be represented using a Fourier series. The analytic representation of the periodic function $f(x)$ shown in the figure is

$$f(x) = \begin{cases} -k & \text{when} \quad -\pi < x < 0 \\ k & \text{when} \quad 0 < x < \pi \end{cases}$$

with $f(x+2\pi) = f(x)$. This type of function may occur as external forces acting on mechanical systems, electromotive forces in electric circuits, etc. the function $f(x)$ can be represented using a Fourier series below.

$$f(x) = 4k \sum_{i=0}^{\infty} \frac{\sin(2i+1)x}{(2i+1)}$$

The first four terms are

$$s1 = \frac{4k \sin x}{\pi}, \quad s2 = \frac{4k \sin 3x}{3\pi}, \quad s3 = \frac{4k \sin 5x}{5\pi}, \quad s4 = \frac{4k \sin 7x}{7\pi}$$

The partial sums are

$$f_1(x) = \frac{4k \sin x}{\pi}$$
$$f_2(x) = \frac{4k \sin x}{\pi} + \frac{4k \sin 3x}{3\pi}$$
$$f_3(x) = \frac{4k \sin x}{\pi} + \frac{4k \sin 3x}{3\pi} + \frac{4k \sin 5x}{5\pi}$$
$$f_4(x) = \frac{4k \sin x}{\pi} + \frac{4k \sin 3x}{3\pi} + \frac{4k \sin 5x}{5\pi} + \frac{4k \sin 7x}{7\pi}$$

The function $f(x)$ and $f_4(x)$ versus x are shown in the illustration below.

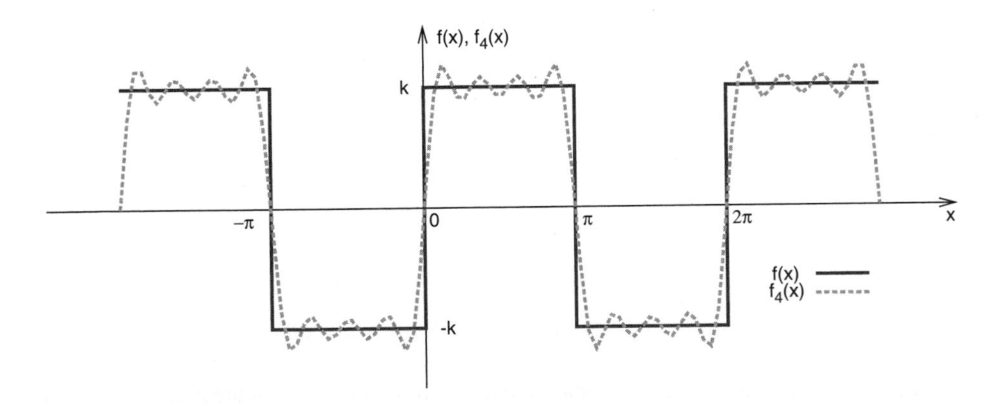

With $k = 1$, plot the first four terms and partial sums $f_1(x)$, $f_2(x)$, $f_3(x)$, $f_4(x)$ of the Fourier series for the periodic function for x in the range of $-\pi$ to π in the same figure.

35. Vibration or oscillation occurs often in mechanical systems or electric circuits. A sample mechanical system of damped free vibration is shown in the following illustration.

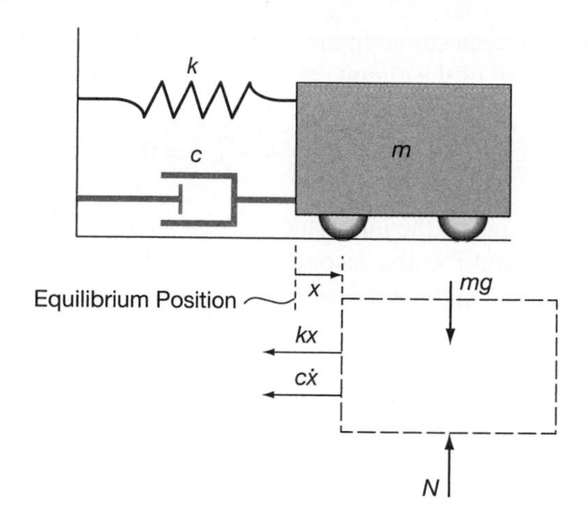

The system consists of mass, a spring, and a dashpot or viscous damper. The damper consists of a cylinder filled with a viscous fluid and a piston with holes or other passages by which the fluid can flow from one side of the piston to the other. The purpose of the damper is to limit or retard the vibration. When the mass m in kilograms is moved the distance x in meters toward the right from the equilibrium position, the spring exerts the force $-kx$ on the body as shown in the diagram. The constant of proportionality k is known as the *spring constant, modulus,* or *stiffness* and has the unit Newton/meter or N/m for short. The dashpot also inserts a force on the body. The magnitude of the damping force from the dashpot is proportional to the velocity of the mass as shown in the diagram. The constant of proportionality c is know as the *viscous damping coefficient* with unit Newtion-second/meter or N·s/m for short. The direction of the damping force applied to the mass is opposite to that of the velocity $\dot{x}$, the first derivative of the distance x. Based on Newton's second law, the equation of motion for the damped free vibration of the body is

$$-kx - c\dot{x} = m\ddot{x} \quad \text{or} \quad m\ddot{x} + c\dot{x} + kx = 0$$

where $\ddot{x}$ is the acceleration of the mass, the second derivative of the distance x. The above equation can be rewritten in the *standard form* of a second-order differential equation as

$$\ddot{x} + 2\zeta\omega_n\dot{x} + \omega_n^2 x = 0 \tag{6.11}$$

where ω_n defined as $\sqrt{k/m}$ is called the *undamped natural frequency*. The nondimensional value ζ (zeta) defined as $c/(2m\omega_n)$ is called the *viscous damping factor* or *damping ratio*. It is a measure of the severity of the damping.

For a source-free parallel RLC circuit shown in the illustration below,

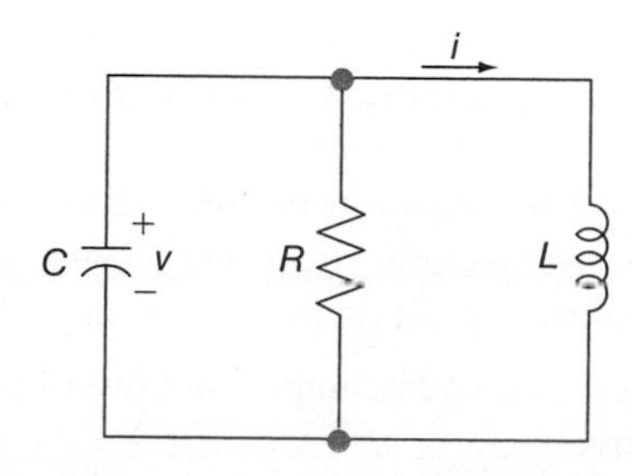

assume that the the energy has been stored in the circuit by a previous connected source. The governing equation for the voltage v in volt of the circuit can be derived as follows:

$$\ddot{v} + \frac{1}{RC}\dot{v} + \frac{1}{LC}v = 0$$

where R is the resistance in ohms, L the inductance in henrys, and C the capacitance in farads, $\dot{v}$ is the first derivative of the voltage, and $\ddot{v}$ is the second derivative of the voltage, If we define the *undamped natural frequency* $\omega_n = 1/\sqrt{LC}$ and the *damping ratio* $\zeta = \sqrt{L}/(3R\sqrt{C})$, the above equation can be simplified as the *standard form* of a second-order differential equation

$$\ddot{v} + 2\zeta\omega_n\dot{v} + \omega_n^2 v = 0 \tag{6.12}$$

Equation (6.12) is in the same form as equation (6.11). Therefore, the solution method and analysis for the distance of the damped free vibration can also be applied to the voltage oscillation of the source-free parallel RLC circuit.

The general solution of equation (6.11) is

$$x = Ae^{(-\zeta+\sqrt{\zeta^2-1})\omega_n t} + Be^{(-\zeta-\sqrt{\zeta^2-1})\omega_n t} \tag{6.13}$$

where constants A and B can be determined by the initial condition of the system. Because $0 < \zeta < \infty$, depending on whether the radicand $(\zeta^2 - 1)$ is positive, negative, or zero, the damped motion can be classified into three different categories.

a. Overdamped with $\zeta > 1$. The radicand $(\zeta^2 - 1)$ is positive. A sample solution for the distance x is

$$x(t) = 4.2e^{-1.57t} - 0.2e^{-54.2t} \tag{6.14}$$

In this case, there is no oscillation. The motion decays and x approaches zero for large values of time as shown in the illustration.

b. Critically damped with $\zeta = 1$. The radicand $(\zeta^2 - 1)$ is zero. A sample solution for the distance x is

$$x(t) = 4(1 - 3t)e^{-3t} \tag{6.15}$$

The motion is also nonperiodic for a critically damped system. The mass will also reach the equilibrium position rapidly.

c. Underdamped with $\zeta < 1$. The radicand $(\zeta^2 - 1)$ is negative. A sample solution for the distance x is

$$x(t) = 4e^{-0.5t}\sin(3t + 2) \tag{6.16}$$

In this case, there is oscillation as shown in the illustration on next page. The solution is an exponentially decreasing harmonic function. However, because it is a damped motion, the mass will eventually approach the equilibrium position for large values of time t.

The overdamped, critically damped, and underdamped motions of a system are represented by equations (6.14), (6.15), and (6.16), respectively.

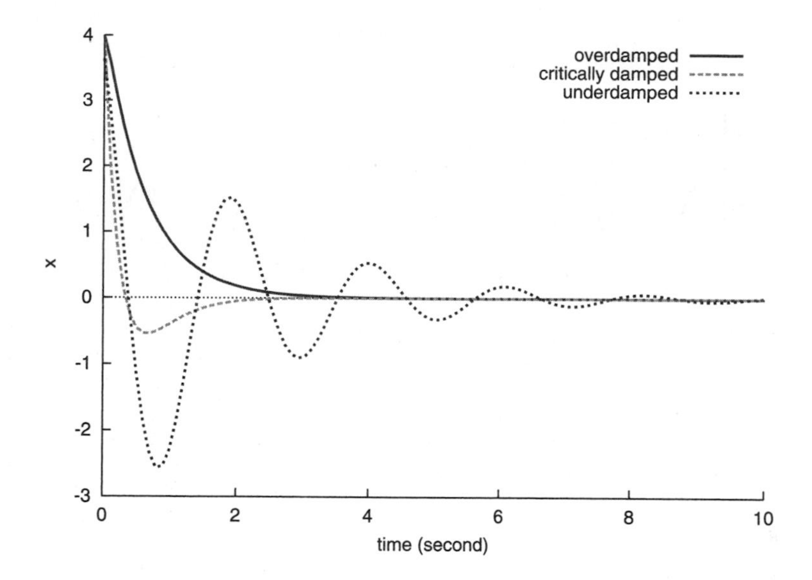

a. Calculate the distances x when time t = 2 seconds.

b. Plot the responses of distance x versus time for $0 \leq t \leq 10$ in the same plot as shown in the illustration, which is the same as one on the cover page of this book.

c. One may consider the motion of an elevator approaching a stop. It would be very uncomfortable to ride if it were underdamped, and very slow to ride if it were overdamped. Critical damping provides the fastest and smoothest ride. The *settling time* is defined as the time for the response to reach and stay within a certain amount from the final value. Obtain the approximate settling time for the response to reach and stay within 2 percent of the displacement between the initial and final values for these three motions.

36. A sine function is a periodic function of an angle in the domain $[-1, 1]$. The period of the function is 2π. A *sinusoid* is a sine function of time expressed in the form of

$$s(t) = A \sin(2\pi f t + \phi) \tag{6.17}$$

where A is the amplitude, f the frequency in cycles per second or hertz, t the time in seconds, and ϕ the *phase angle* in radians. The period of a sinusoid is $1/f$ in seconds.

$$s_1(t) = 5 \sin(2\pi t)$$
$$s_2(t) = 3 \sin(\pi t + \pi)$$

The function $s_1(t)$ has an amplitude 5, a frequency of 1 Hz and a period of 1, and phase shift of zero. The function $s_2(t)$ has an amplitude 3, a frequency of 0.5 Hz and a period of 2, and phase angle of π. It is known that a sum of two sinusoids is also a periodic signal with the period equal to the *least common multiple* of the periods of the two separate sinusoids. For example, if the period for s_1 is 1 and the period for s_2 is 2, the sum

$$s = s_1 + s_2$$

has the period 2. Plot sinusoids $s_1(t)$ and $s_2(t)$, and signal s shown in the illustration on next page.

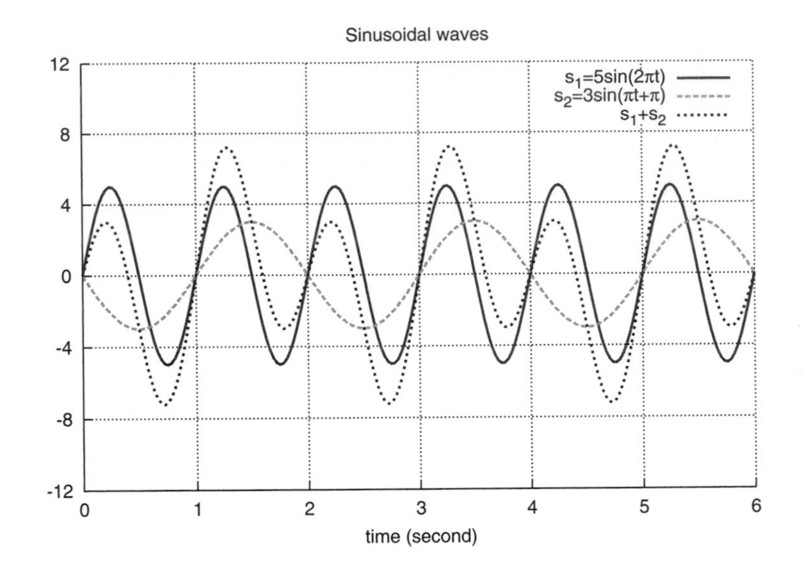

37. Modify Program 6.18 to find zeros for the following functions. Also, plot the functions over a proper range containing the zeros.

a. Function cos(x) in the range $1 < x < 2$.
b. Find the first zero for the humps function shown in Figure 6.11.
c. Find the second zero for the humps function shown in Figure 6.11.

38. The formula for the volume of a sphere is $\frac{4}{3}\pi r^3$, where r is the radius of the sphere. If the volume of a sphere is 90 m^3, write a program to calculate the radius of the sphere using the bisection method. Plot the function $f(r) = \frac{4}{3}\pi r^3 - 90$ in the range $-5 \le x \le 5$.

39. Modify Program 6.18 to print the number of iterations.

40. Modify Program 6.18 based on the procedures for the first numerical algorithm for the bisection method. Also write a pseudocode and draw the corresponding flowchart.

41. Modify Program 6.18 to use the convergence criterion 2 in equation (6.7) for the bisection method. Describe the algorithm in procedures. Write a program in pseudocode and draw the corresponding flowchart.

42. Newton's method for finding a root of an equation $f(x)$ is formulated as

$$x_{i+1} = x_i - \frac{f(x_i)}{f'(x_i)} \tag{6.18}$$

where $f'(x_i)$ is the derivative of function $f(x)$ evaluated at $x = x_i$. The method starts with an initial guess x_0 for a root and then generate successive approximate roots $x_1, x_2, \ldots, x_i, x_{i+1}, \ldots$ The value x_{i+1} is a function of the previous one x_i. The convergence criteria in equations (6.6) and (6.7) can be used to stop the iteration. A good initial guess is often important for the convergence of Newton's method. If there are multiple roots, a different initial guess may lead to a different solution. Sometimes, Newton's method may fail to converge to a root. Therefore, a program should terminate the iteration after a large number of trials. Write programs to solve the following problems with the convergence criterion in equation (6.7) and a maximum number of iterations 100. Write pseudocode and draw flowcharts for programs first.

a. Find two roots for function $f(x) = x^2 - 3$ with its derivative $f'(x) = 2x$ using initial guesses of $x_0 = 2$ and $x_0 = -2$. Plot function $f(x)$ in the range $-5 \le x \le 5$.

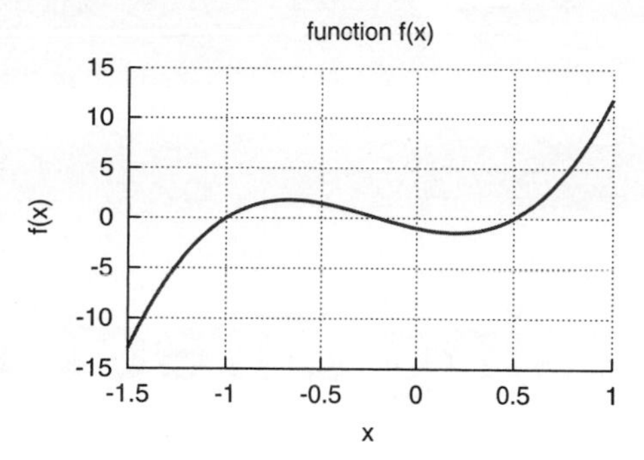

Figure 6.13: A third-order polynomial function $f(x) = 10x^3 + 7x^2 - 4x - 1$.

b. Find a root for function $f(x) = x^3 - 3$ with its derivative $f'(x) = 3x^2$ using an initial guess of $x_0 = 2$. Plot function $f(x)$ in the range $-5 \le x \le 5$.

c. Plot the third-order polynomial function $f(x) = 10x^3 + 7x^2 - 4x - 1$ in the range $-1.5 \le x \le 1$ shown in Figure 6.13. The function has three roots near $-1, 0.2$, and 0.5. The derivative of the function is $f'(x) = 30x^2 + 14x - 4$. Find these three roots with initial guesses -2, 0.5, and 2.

CHAPTER 7

Preprocessing Directives

When a C program is processed by a compiler, it typically takes several stages of translation. Preprocessing of a program occurs before the program is compiled. Actions of preprocessing consist of inclusion of other files in the file being compiled, replacement of symbolic constants and macros, and conditional inclusion of the code block. When a C program is interpretively executed, the preprocessing and program parsing typically take place at the same time. A preprocessing directive consists of a sequence of preprocessing tokens that begins with a pound sign '#'. For example, we have used the preprocessing directive

```
#define M_G 9.81
```

to define the macro M_G for the gravitational acceleration constant 9.81 in previous applications. All available preprocessing directives and preprocessing operators in C are listed in Table 7.1. The details about these directives and operators are described in this chapter.

Unlike C statements ending with a semicolon, a preprocessing directive ends with a new line. To span a preprocessing directive over more than one line, enter a backslash immediately before the newline character. For example, the definition of the macro MACRO_OVER_TWO_LINES below spans over two lines.

```
#define MACRO_OVER_TWO_LINES "This is a very very long macro \
                              that spans over two lines."
```

7.1 Macro Replacement

A preprocessing directive of the form

```
#define identifier replacement-list newline
```

defines an object-like macro that causes each subsequent instance of the macro name to be replaced by the replacement list of preprocessing tokens that constitute the remainder of the directive. The newline is a character that terminates the **#define** preprocessing directive.

The identifier immediately following the **#define** is called the *macro name*. The *macro name* is followed by a sequence of tokens called a replacement list. Two replacement lists are identical if and only if the preprocessing tokens in both have the same number, ordering, spelling, and white-space separation, where all white-space separations are considered identical.

The simple form of macro is particularly useful for introducing named constants into a program, so that some numbers (such as the length of a table) may be written in exactly one place and then referred to elsewhere by name. This makes it easier to change the number later. Named constants typically consist of all capital letters and underscores. For example, given the macro

```
#define BLOCK_SIZE 0x100
```

we can write

```
int size = BLOCK_SIZE;
```

Table 7.1 Preprocessing directives and operators.

Directive	Description
`#`	Null directive.
`#define`	Defines a preprocessor macro.
`#elif`	Includes some text based on the value of another expression,
	if the previous `#if`, `#ifdef`, `#ifndef`, or `#elif` test failed.
`#else`	Includes some text, if the previous
	`#if`, `#ifdef`, `#ifndef`, or `#elif` test failed.
`#endif`	Terminates conditional text.
`#error`	Produces a compile-time error with a designated message.
`#if`	Conditionally includes text, based on the value of an expression.
`#ifdef`	Conditionally includes text, based on whether a macro name is defined.
`#ifndef`	Conditionally includes text, based on if a name is not a defined macro.
`#include`	Inserts text from another source file.
`#line`	Gives a line number for a message.
`#pragma`	Implementation-dependent features.
`#undef`	Removes a preprocessor macro definition.
Operator	**Description**
`#`	Replaces a maco parameter with a string constant containing the parameter's value.
`##`	Creates a single token out of two adjacent tokens.
`defined`	Preprocessing operator that yields 1 if a name is defined as
	a preprocessing macro and 0 otherwise; used in `#if` and `#elif`.

instead of

```
int size = 0x100;
```

A preprocessing directive of the form

```
#define identifier( identifier-list-opt ) replacement-list newline
```

defines a function-like macro with arguments, similar syntactically to a function call. The parameters are specified by the optional list of identifiers, whose scope extends from their declaration in the identifier list until the newline character that terminates the **#define** preprocessing directive. Each subsequent instance of the function-like macro name followed by an open parenthesis '(' as the next preprocessing token introduces the sequence of preprocessing tokens that is replaced by the replacement list in the definition (an invocation of the macro). The replaced sequence of preprocessing tokens is terminated by the matching closing parenthesis ')' preprocessing token, skipping intervening matched pairs of left and right parentheses preprocessing tokens. Within the sequence of preprocessing tokens making up an invocation of a function-like macro, newline is considered a normal white-space character. The name for a macro for a constant typically contains capital letters, underscores, and numerical digits. A function type macro may use small letters.

For example, if macros `mul` and `add` with two arguments are defined by

```
#define mul(x,y) ((x)*(y))
#define add(x,y) ((x)+(y))
```

then the source program line

```
result = mul(5, a+b)*add(x,y);
```

is replaced with

```
result = ((5)*(a+b))*((x)+(y));
```

Note that the parentheses are important in the macro definition. If the macros `mul()` and `add()` were defined without parentheses as

```
#define mul(x,y) x*y
#define add(x,y) (x)+(y)
```

the statement

```
result = mul(5, a+b)*add(x,y);
```

would become

```
result = 5*a+b*(x)+(y);
```

A defined macro can be removed and then redefined later. For example, one may remove a previously defined macro `M_G` by

```
#undef M_G
```

A variable argument list macro is introduced in C99. It uses the ellipsis notation in the arguments. The identifier **__VA_ARGS__**, that occurs in the replacement list, is treated as if it were a parameter, and the variable arguments form the preprocessing tokens used to replace it. For example, the code fragment

```
#define debug(...)      printf(__VA_ARGS__)
#define debug2(fp, ...)    fprintf(fp, __VA_ARGS__)
debug("x = %d\n", x);
debug2(stderr, "x = %d\n", x);
```

results in

```
printf("x = %d\n", x);
fprintf(stderr,  "x = %d\n", x);
```

An Application Example

Acceleration of a Moving Body

Problem Statement:
For the mechanical system shown in Figure 2.12, given mass $m = 5$ kilograms (kg) and coefficient of kinetic friction $\mu = 0.2$, the applied force p is expressed as a function of time t in

$$p(t) = 4\sin(t - 3) + 20 \qquad \text{when } t \geq 0$$

```
/* File: accelmacro.c
   Calculate the acceleration using a macro */
#include <stdio.h>
#include <math.h>              /* for sin() */

/* define macros for g, force, and acceleration */
#define M_G   9.81
#define FORCE(t)               (4*(sin((t)-3))+20)
#define ACCEL(p, mu, m)        (((p)-(mu)*(m)*M_G)/(m))

int main() {
    double a, p, mu, m, t; /* declare variables */

    mu = 0.2;              /* set mu */
    m = 5.0;               /* set mass to 5 kg */
    t = 2.0;               /* set time to 2 seconds */
    p = FORCE(t);          /* use macro to calculate the force */
    a = ACCEL(p, mu, m);   /* use macro to calculate the accel */
    printf("Acceleration = %f (m/s^2)\n", a);
    return 0;
}
```

Program 7.1: Calculating accelerations using a macro.

Write a program to calculate the acceleration a when $t = 2$ seconds. Solve for the acceleration using macros for formulas of force p and acceleration a.

This problem can be solved with Program 7.1. A constant value for gravitational acceleration g is defined as a constant macro using the preprocessing directive **#define**. The formulas for the force and the acceleration are defined as macros `FORCE(t)` and `ACCEL(p, mu, m)`, respectively. These macros are used to compute the force and acceleration at $t = 2$ seconds. The acceleration at $t = 2$ seconds is then printed out. The output of Program 7.1 is the same as that of Program 6.3.

A macro can also be used as an argument of another macro. For example, the statement

```
a = ACCEL(p, mu, m);
```

for calculating of the acceleration in Program 7.1 can be replaced by

```
a = ACCEL(FORCE(t), mu, m);
```

In general, a macro for a constant usually uses all capital letters. However, for a function like macro with arguments, lowercase can be used for macro names. In this example, the function type macros `FORCE()` and `ACCEL()` are defined with capital letters. They can also be defined with lowercase letters.

Macros can also be defined during compilation as command-line options as described in section 4.14.1 in Chapter 4.

7.2 Predefined Macros

The macro names predefined in C are listed in Table 7.2. The **__LINE__** macro refers to the presumed line number within the current source file of the current source line, whereas **__FILE__** is the presumed name of the current source file. Using macros **__LINE__** and **__FILE__**, and the predefined variable **__func__** for the function name described in section 6.9 in Chapter 6, a new macro can be used to obtain the information of a program for debugging. Note that the variable **__func__** is not part of the preprocessor specifications. In Program 7.2, the macro `printerror()` is invoked inside a function to print out the information. The output from Program 7.2 is as follows:

```
Error in printerror.c:funcname1():14
Error in printerror.c:funcname2():17
```

Table 7.2 Predefined macros in C.

Macro name	Description
`__LINE__`	The line number of the current source program line, which is expressed as a decimal integral constant.
`__FILE__`	The name of the current source file, which is expressed as a string constant.
`__DATE__`	The calendar date of the translation, which is expressed as a string constant in the form of `Mmm dd yyyy`.
`__TIME__`	The current time expressed as a string constant in the form of `"hh:mm:ss"`.
`__STDC__`	The decimal constant 1 for a C standard–conforming implementation.
`__STDC_VERSION__`	The decimal constant 199901L for C99 standard–conforming implementation.

```
/* File: printerror.c (run in C99 and Ch only)
   Compile in gcc, use command 'gcc -std=c99 pointerror.c'
   A generic macro to print out file name, function, and line number.
   The program uses C99 feature __func__ */
#include <stdio.h>

/* define the macro printerror() to print out file name,
   function, and line number */
#define printerror()  printf("Error in %s:%s():%d\n", \
                          __FILE__, __func__, __LINE__);

/* two functions using the define macro */
void funcname1() {
    printerror();        /* Line 14 */
}
void funcname2() {
    printerror();        /* Line 17 */
}
```

Program 7.2: Using macros to obtain information about a program. (*Continued*)

```
int main() {
    /* call functions that invokes the macro */
    funcname1();
    funcname2();
    return 0;
}
```

Program 7.2 *(Continued)*

Program 7.4 in section 7.9 also uses macros **__LINE__** and **__FILE__** to print out the current line number and file name of the program, respectively.

The macro **__DATE__** specifies the date of translation of the source file and is in the form of `"Mmm dd yyyy"`. The Macro **__TIME__** specifies the time of translation of the source file in the form `"hh:mm:ss"`. Both the **__DATE__** and **__TIME__** macros return the date and time in the forms as if they were generated by the **asctime()** function described in section 13.1.17 in Chapter 13. For example, the results of one sample command-line execution of macros **__DATE__** and **__TIME__** are as follows:

```
> __DATE__
Mar 11 2008
> __TIME__
10:57:42
```

The **__STDC__** macro is the decimal constant 1, which is used to indicate a conforming implementation. For a C99 conforming implementation, the macro **__STDC_VERSION__** is defined with the decimal constant 199901L. This macro can be used for conditional inclusion of the code using C99 features, which will be described in section 7.4.

Note that the values of the predefined macros, except for **__LINE__** and **__FILE__**, remain constant throughout the translation unit. Also, none of the macro names in Table 7.2, nor the identifier defined, shall be the subject of a **#define** or a **#undef** preprocessing directive. Predefined macro names beginning with a leading underscore followed by an uppercase letter or a second underscore are reserved for C standard macros. The user shall not define macros with such names in application programs.

Almost all implementations of C compilers and interpreters have their own extensions and special cases. An implementation-specific predefined macro is often defined. For example, the macro **_WIN32** is predefined for Visual C++, whereas the macro **_CH_** is predefined for Ch. In Windows, the macro **_WIN32_** is defined in Ch. Using these macros, a program can be written to work in different platforms and compilers. An example of using the macro **_WIN32** is given in the next section and Program 14.22 in Chapter 14. Macro **_CH_** is used to run programs with multiple source files in Program 8.7 in Chapter 8.

7.3 Source File Inclusion

A **#include** directive identifies a header or source file that can be processed by the compiler or interpreter. A header file typically contains function prototypes, macros, external global variable type declarations, structure definitions, typedefed data types, etc. A header file can be included by different source files to facilitate the program development.

A preprocessing directive of the form

```
#include <header.h>
```

searches for a header file `header.h` between the < and > delimiters and causes the replacement of that directive by the entire contents of the header. Each compiler and interpreter searches such a header file in its system include directories. System include directories for different implementations are presented in section 7.11.

The header files for C standard libraries, such as **math.h**, are typically located in the system include directories for header files. Therefore, it is used in the form of

```
#include <math.h>
```

The user-developed header file typically uses a preprocessing directive of the form

```
#include "header.h"
```

It causes the replacement of that directive by the entire contents of the source file identified by the specified sequence between the " delimiters. The named source file is searched for in the current directory first. It is then searched as if the header file was specified within the delimiters < and >.

7.4 Conditional Inclusion

Preprocessing directives of the forms

```
#if   expr1
#elif expr2
#else
#endif
```

is equivalent to the **if-else if-else** statement. It checks whether the controlling expression evaluates to nonzero. The expression that controls conditional inclusion shall be an integer expression except that it shall not contain declared identifiers. It may contain the preprocessing operation

```
defined (identifier)
```

which evaluates to 1 if the identifier is currently defined as a macro name, 0 if it is not. Sample code using the preprocessing operator **defined()** can be found in Program 8.7 in Chapter 8.

Preprocessing directives of the forms

```
#ifdef  identifier
#ifndef identifier
```

check whether the identifier is or is not currently defined as a macro name. Their conditions are equivalent to

```
#if defined(identifier)
#if !defined(identifier)
```

Each directive's condition is checked in order. If it evaluates to false (zero), then the group that it controls is skipped: directives are processed only through the name that determines the directive to keep track of the level of nested conditionals; the rest of the directives' preprocessing tokens are ignored, as are the other preprocessing tokens in the group. Only the first group whose control condition evaluates to true (nonzero) is processed. If none of the conditions evaluates to true, and there is a **#else** directive, then the group controlled by the **#else** is processed; if lacking a **#else** directive, then all the groups until the **#endif** are skipped.

As an example, Program 7.3 prints the sizes of all basic types in C99. Comparing Program 3.5 in Chapter 3, Program 7.3 uses conditional inclusion to include code blocks related to new features added in C99. If the code

```
/* File: basictypesize.c
   Obtain the sizes of basic data types in C99
   if C99 is supported. Otherwise, exclude new data types in C99.
   Compile in gcc, use command 'gcc -std=c99 basictypesize.c' */
#include <stdio.h>
#include <stddef.h>   /* for size_t */
/* this code block using C99 features
   is included only for C99 comforming inplementation */
#if __STDC_VERSION__==199901L
#include <stdbool.h>  /* for bool */
#include <complex.h>  /* for complex */
#endif

int main() {
    printf("sizeof(char) = %d\n", sizeof(char));
    printf("sizeof(short) = %d\n", sizeof(short));
    printf("sizeof(int) = %d\n", sizeof(int));
    printf("sizeof(long) = %d\n", sizeof(long));
    printf("sizeof(float) = %d\n", sizeof(float));
    printf("sizeof(double) = %d\n", sizeof(double));
    printf("sizeof(long double) = %d\n", sizeof(long double));
    printf("sizeof(pointer) = %d\n", sizeof(int *));
    printf("sizeof(size_t) = %d\n", sizeof(size_t));
/* this code block is included only for C99 comforming inplementation */
#if __STDC_VERSION__==199901L
    printf("sizeof(bool) = %d\n", sizeof(bool));
    printf("sizeof(long long) = %d\n", sizeof(long long));
    printf("sizeof(float complex) = %d\n", sizeof(float complex));
    printf("sizeof(complex) = %d\n", sizeof(complex));
    printf("sizeof(double complex) = %d\n", sizeof(double complex));
    printf("sizeof(long double complex) = %d\n", sizeof(long double complex));
#endif
    return 0;
}
```

Program 7.3: Obtaining the sizes of basic data types in C99.

is compiled using a C99 conforming compiler, it prints out sizes of all basic data types in C99, including the new types **bool, long long, float complex, double complex**, and **long double complex**. The code can also be compiled using an old C compiler, which does not support C99 features. In this case, the output from Program 7.3 is the same as that from Program 3.5. For a C99 compiler, the macro **__STDC_VERSION__** is predefined with 199901L as described in section 7.2. Therefore, the controlling expression `__STDC_VERSION__==199901L` in the preprocessing directive

```
#if __STDC_VERSION__==199901
```

evaluates to 1. The code block

```
#include <stdbool.h>   /* for bool */
#include <complex.h>   /* for complex */
```

before the terminating directive

```
#endif
```

is included. Similarly, the code block related to the C99 features near the end of Program 3.5 in Chapter 3 for printing the sizes of new data types in C99 is included only when a C99 conforming compiler is invoked.

An example of using the structure of preprocessing directives **#if-#elif-#endif** is given below. As described in section 3.6.3, data types **long long** and **unsigned long long** in C99 are not supported in Visual C++. Instead, it uses the type declarators **_int64** and **unsigned _int64**. To write a portable code that can be compiled in a C99-conforming compiler and VC++, we can define new data types using **typedef**, as presented in section 3.12. New data types `long64_t` and `ulong64_t` for signed and unsigned 64-bit integers, respectively, can be defined as follows:

```
#ifde _WIN32
typedef __int64 long64_t;
typedef unsigned  __int64 long64_t;
#else
typedef long long long64_t;
typedef unsigned long long ulong64_t;
#endif
```

If this code fragment is placed in a header file for a project, the user-defined data types `long64_t` and `ulong64_t` can then be used in all source code for the project. Another example of using the preprocessing directives **#if-#elif-#endif** is given in Program 14.22 in Chapter 14.

To include a header file in a program only once, you typically handle it by using the combination of the preprocessing directives **#ifndef**, **#define**, and **#endif**. For example, a header file `header.h` typically consists of code fragments similar to ones shown below at the beginning and end of the file.

```
#ifndef HEADER_H
#define HEADER_H
 ...
#endif
```

If the header file `header.h` is first processed, the macro `HEADER_H` is not defined. Therefore, the contents of the header file will be included. At the subsequent inclusion of the file, the macro has already been defined. The contents of the header file will not be included again.

7.5 ‡Converting Tokens to Strings

The # token appearing within a macro definition is recognized as a unary stringization operator. If, in the replacement list, a parameter is immediately preceded by a # preprocessing token, both are replaced by a single character string literal preprocessing token that contains the spelling of the preprocessing token sequence for the corresponding argument. For example,

```
> #define TEST(a) #a
> printf("%s",TEST(abcd))
abcd
```

The macro parameter abcd has been converted to the string constant "abcd".

Each occurrence of white space between the argument's preprocessing tokens becomes a single space character in the character string literal. White space before the first preprocessing token and after the last preprocessing token composing the argument is deleted. Otherwise, the original spelling of each preprocessing token in the argument is retained in the character string literal. The spelling of string literals and character constants: a \ character is inserted before each " and \ character of a character constant or string literal (including the delimiting " characters), is specially handled. For example,

```
> #define TEST(a) #a
> printf("1%s2",TEST(   a     b   ))
1a b2
```

Here the argument is turned into the string constant "a b". The white spaces before a and after b are deleted, and the sequence of white spaces between a and b is replaced by a single character.

7.6 ‡Token Merging in Macro Expansions

The merging of tokens to form new tokens is controlled by the presence of the merging operator ## in macro definitions. For both objectlike and functionlike macro invocations, before the replacement list is re-examined for more macro names to replace, each instance of a ## preprocessing token in the replacement list (not from an argument) is deleted and the preceding preprocessing token is concatenated with the following preprocessing token. The new token might be the name of a function, variable or type, or a keyword; it might even be the name of another macro, in which case it will be expanded. The common use of concatenation is concatenating two names into a longer name. It is also possible to concatenate two numbers, or a number and a name, such as '1.5' and 'e3', into a number. In addition, multicharacter operators such as '+=' can be formed by concatenation. For example,

```
> #define CONC2(a, b) a ## b
> #define CONC3(a, b, c) a ## b ## c
> CONC2(1, 2)
12
> CONC3(3, +, 4)
7
```

The macro CONC2(1, 2) concatenates two numbers, 1 and 2, into 12, and CONC2(3, +, 4) concatenates these three arguments into 3+4, which generates 7 in command line.

C converts comments to white spaces before macros are even considered. Any "/* comment sequence */" sequence will be interpreted as a number of blank spaces. The user can use comments next to a "##" in a macro definition, or in actual arguments that will be concatenated because the comments will be initially converted to blank spaces that will later be discarded by the concatenation operation. For example,

```
> #define CONC2(a, b) a ## b
> CONC2(1, /*this is a comment */2)
12
```

The comment in the second argument is discarded in concatenation.

A ## preprocessing token shall not occur at the beginning or at the end of a replacement list for either form of macro definition.

7.7 ‡Error Directive

A preprocessing directive of the form

```
#error pp-tokens-opt newline
```

causes the implementation to produce a diagnostic message that includes the specified sequence of preprocessing tokens and the interpretation to cease.

For example, when Program 7.4 is executed, it gives the output as follows:

```
ERROR: #error:  This is an error, the code here is reached
ERROR: syntax error before or at line 8 in file error.c
  ==>: #error This is an error, the code here is reached
  BUG: #error This is an error, the code here is reached<== ???
ERROR: cannot execute command 'error.c'
```

```
/* File: error.c
   Demonstrate the usage of the directive #error */
#include <stdio.h>
#define SOMEMACRO

int main() {
#ifdef SOMEMACRO
#error This is an error, the code here is reached
    /* the code here will not be processed */
    printf("bad \n");
#else
    printf("ok \n");
#endif
    return 0;
}
```

Program 7.4: Using the directive **#error**.

7.8 ‡Null Directive

A preprocessing directive of the form

```
#newline
```

has no effect on the program. The line is ignored.

7.9 ‡Line Control

The **#line** directive can be used to alter the line numbers assigned to the source code. This directive gives a newline number to the following line, which is then incremented to derive the line numbering of subsequent lines. The directive can also specify a new file specification for the program source file. This is useful for referring to original source files that are preprocessed into C code by other programs.

A preprocessing directive of the form

```
#line digit-sequence newline
```

causes the implementation to behave as if the following sequence of source lines begins with a source line that has a line number as specified by the digit sequence (interpreted as a decimal integer). The line number is stored in the predefined macro **__LINE__** internally.

A preprocessing directive of the form

```
#line digit-sequence "s-char-sequence-opt" newline
```

sets the presumed line number similarly and changes the presumed name of the source file to be the contents of the character string literal. The name of the source file is stored in the predefined macro **__FILE__** internally. For example, in Program 7.4, before the line directive

```
#line 200 "newFileName"
```

the line number is counted from the beginning of the line starting with line 1. The file name is `linefile.c`. After this line directive, the line number is set to 200 and the file name becomes `newFileName`. The output from Program 7.4 is given as follows:

```
The predefined macro __FILE__ = linefile.c
Before line directive, line number is 8
The predefined macro __FILE__ = newFileName
After line directive, line number is 201
```

7.10 Pragma Directive

A preprocessing directive of the form

```
#pragma pp-tokens-opt newline
```

is called a pragma directive. The C standard defines **#pragma** as a means to implement platform-dependent functionality. According to the C standard, if the preprocessing token **STDC** does not immediately follow pragma in the directive prior to any macro replacement (**#pragma STDC**), implementation-defined features can be added. The **#pragma** statements implemented in Ch will be used as examples in Chapter 8 to illustrate how the pragma directive can be used.

An Application Example

Acceleration of a Moving Body

As pointed out in section 5.5.2 in Chapter 5, a structured program in C typically consists of four sections of *declaration, initialization, processing,* and *termination*. In addition to system header files such as **stdio.h**, a program often includes the user's local header files at the beginning, which is illustrated by an example.

Problem Statement:
For the mechanical system shown in Figure 2.12 given mass $m = 5$ kilograms (kg) and coefficient of kinetic friction $\mu = 0.2$, the applied force p is expressed as a function of time t in

$$p(t) = 4\sin(t - 3) + 20 \qquad \text{when} t \geq 0$$

Develop functions for calculating force p and acceleration a. The function prototypes shall be defined in the header file `accel.h`. Write a program to calculate the acceleration a when $t = 2$ seconds.

Programs 7.5 and 7.6 are the solution for the problem statement above. For some software packages, there might be hundreds of functions. It is inconvenient to keep function prototypes for these functions in an application program. Typically, macros and function prototypes are placed in header files for convenient

```
/* File: accel.h
   The header file for calculation of acceleration */

/* These two lines are included so that this header file
   can be included multiple times in a source file.
   If ACCEL_H is not defined, define it so that next time
   when the file is included, the contents will not be included again */
#ifndef ACCEL_H
#define ACCEL_H

/* define macro M_G for the gravitational acceleration */
#define M_G   9.81

/* function prototypes */
double force(double t);
double accel(double t, double mu, double m);

#endif /* end for ACCEL_H */
```

Program 7.5: Header file for calculating accelerations with function prototypes and macro.

```
/* File: accelhead.c
   Calculate the acceleration with a header file */
#include <stdio.h> /* system header file for the standard input/output lib */
#include <math.h>  /* system header file for the standard math lib */
#include "accel.h" /* user's local header file */

int main() {
    /* declare variables */
    double a, p, mu, m, t;

    /* Initialize variables */
    mu = 0.2;
    m = 5;
    t = 2;

    /* processing */
    a = accel(t, mu, m);

    /* display output and termination */
    printf("Acceleration = %f (m/s^2)\n", a);
    return 0;
}

/* function definition for calculating force */
double force(double t) {
    double p;

    p = 4*sin(t-3)+20;
    return p;
}

/* function definition for calculating acceleration */
double accel(double t, double mu, double m) {
    double a, p;

    p = force(t);
    a = (p-mu*m*M_G)/m;
    return a;
}
```

Program 7.6: Calculating accelerations with the header file `accel.h`.

code development and maintenance. Thus, Program 7.5 is a header file that contains the function prototypes for the `force()` and `accel()` functions as well as the definition for the macro `M_G`, which represents the gravitational acceleration constant `9.81`. Program 7.6 is the application program which defines functions force() and accel() and uses them in the function **main()** to determine the acceleration of the dynamic system described in the problem statement. The output of Program 7.5 is the same as that of Program 6.3.

Note that the header file listed as Program 7.5 contains the preprocessing directives **#ifndef**, **#define**, and **#endif** to check and see whether the corresponding header file has previously been loaded. For example, the code fragment

```
#ifndef ACCEL_H
#define ACCEL_H
...
#endif  /* ACCEL_H */
```

checks to determine whether the header file accel.h has been loaded. If it has, then the header file does not need to be loaded again. Otherwise, the contents within the header file represented by the ellipses "..." will be loaded for use within an application file. This prevents the continuous reloading of the header file if it has already been loaded somewhere else by the **#include** preprocessing directive.

7.11 Making It Work

7.11.1 Default Directories for Header Files

When a header file, such as headerfile.h, is included through the preprocessing directive

```
#include <headerfile.h>
```

it is searched in the default directories for header files.

Default Directories for Header Files in Ch

In Ch, the system includes directories for header files are specified by the system variable **_ipath** of the string type. Each directory is delimited by a semicolon. By default, CHHOME/include and CHHOME/toolkit/include are included in the search paths for header files, where CHHOME is the home directory of Ch (such as C:/Ch in Windows and /usr/local/ch in Unix). By default, Ch is installed in C:/Ch in Windows. The value for **_ipath** is "C:/Ch/include;C:/Ch/toolkit/include;". In Unix, by default, the value for **_ipath** is "/usr/local/ch/include;/usr/local/ch/toolkit/include;".

Similar to **_path** for the search paths for commands and **_fpath** for the search paths for function files, the variable **_ipath** for system include directories for header files can be set up in a start-up file **_chrc** in Windows and **.chrc** in Unix in the user's home directory. For example, the statement below

```
_ipath = stradd(_ipath, "C:/Documents and Setting/Administrator/eme5;");
```

adds C:/Documents and Setting/Administrator/eme5 to the search paths for system include directories for header files.

Default Directories for Header Files in Visual C++ and GNU C

The Visual C++ compiler in Windows searches the header file based on the paths in the environment variable **INCLUDE**. For example, the environment variable **INCLUDE** can be set to Program Files/Microsoft Visual Studio 9/VC/include for Visual C++ 2008. Similar to Ch, each directory is also delimited by a semicolon. Using environment variables in C is described in section 8.4 of Chapter 8.

The GNU C compiler **gcc** searches a header file in the system include directory `/usr/include`.

For Visual C++ and GNU C compilers, additional directories can be added during the compilation by the command-line option

```
-Idir
```

The compiler will look for header files in the directory `dir` first, before the system include directories. If the directory contains a white space, include it in a pair of double quotes. For example, to compile program `accelhead.c`, with the command

```
> cl accelhead.c -I"C:/Documents and Setting/Administrator/eme5"
```

program **cl** in Visual C++ looks for header files in the directory `C:/Documents and Setting/Administrator/eme5` first, before directories specified by the environment variable **INCLUDE**. Using the command

```
> gcc accelhead.c -I/home/harry/eme5 -lm
```

GNU C compiler searches header files in `/home/harry/eme5`, then in `/usr/include`. The command-line option `-lm` is for linking the math library as described in section 4.14.2 in Chapter 4.

Exercises

1. Add the directory `HOME/eme5` to header file search paths in Ch. `HOME` is your home directory such as `C:/Documents and Settings/harry` in Windows or `/home/harry` in Unix. In Windows, add

   ```
   _ipath = stradd(_ipath, "C:/Documents and Settings/harry/eme5;");
   ```

   to the start-up file _chrc in your home directory. In Unix, add

   ```
   _ipath = stradd(_ipath, "/home/harry/eme5;");
   ```

   to the start-up file .chrc in your home directory. Change `harry` to your user account name, and `eme5` to the name of the course that you are taking using this textbook. Hand in your start-up file.
2. What are the two convenient methods to comment out a section of codes?
3. The macro below is supposed to double its numeric argument. What is wrong with it? Rewrite the macro correctly.

   ```
   #define DOUBLE(a) 2*a
   ```

4. The macro below is supposed to triple its numeric argument. What is wrong with it? Rewrite the macro correctly.

   ```
   #define TRIPLE(a) 3*a
   ```

5. Write a macro ABS(x), using a conditional operation, to expand to the absolute value of its argument `x`.
6. Write a program that defines the macro `MINIMUM2(x,y)` using a conditional operator and use this macro to return the smallest of two numerical values. Input the values from the keyboard.
7. Write macros to perform the following tasks:

   a. Set the *n*th element of array of `buf` to `val`:

   ```
   SETBIT(buf, n, val)
   ```

b. Get the value of the *n*th element of **int** array `buf`:

```
GETBIT(buf, n)
```

8. Write a program to obtain the user input for the radius of a disc.

a. Use a macro to compute the area of the disc.
b. Use a macro to compute the circumference of the disc.

Check your program with the user input of a radius of 5 meters.

9. Write a program to obtain the user input for the radius and height of a solid cylinder.

a. Use a macro to compute the volume of the cylinder.
b. Use a macro to compute the surface area of the cylinder.

Check your program with the user input of a radius of 5 meters and height of 3.5 meters.

10. Write a program that defines a macro with one argument to compute the area of a disc. The program should compute the areas for discs with radii ranging from 1 to 10 meters and print the results in the following tabular format:

```
radius (m) area (m^2)
-----------------------
    1         3.14
    2        12.57
...
```

11. Write a program to compute the areas for discs of radius 1 to 10 meters and print the results in the tabular format shown in the previous exercise. The program defines a function with one argument for the radius to compute the area of a disc. The function prototype shall be included in the header file `disc.h` which can be included multiple times in a program.

12. Write a program that defines a macro with one argument to compute the volume of a sphere. The program should compute the volumes for spheres with radiuses ranging from 1 to 10 meters and print the results in the following tabular format:

```
radius (m) volume (m^3)
-----------------------
    1         4.19
    2        33.51
...
```

13. Write a program to compute the volumes for spheres with radii ranging from 1 to 10 meters and print the results in the tabular format shown in the previous exercise. The program defines a function with one argument for the radius to compute the volume of a sphere. The function prototype shall be included in the header file `sphere.h` which can be included multiple times in a program.

14. For the code fragment below, what are the expansions of `L(L)(a,a)` and `L(L)(a,ABC)`?

```
#define L(x)        L ## x
#define LL(L, y)    L = # y
```

CHAPTER 8

Storage Classes and Program Structure

A program in a single source file can be used to solve a simple problem. For a complicated problem, many functions need to be developed. These functions might call each other and return values of different data types. To make the matter simple, a header file can be created, which contains all function prototypes, as shown in Chapter 7. For a large-scale project, it will be more manageable to break a program into separate source files. Each file contains relevant functions. A header file can then be included by all other source files. In some applications, it might be desirable to share some variables with all functions in a single source file and share other variables with functions in all source files.

For example, Program 6.10 in section 6.7 in Chapter 6 plots the trajectory for a projectile. The initial speed v_0 and projection angle θ_0 are used in both functions `func()` and **main()**. They are used to calculate the y-coordinate in the function `func()` and the final position `xf`. If the values for these variables are changed, they need to be changed in both functions. Using global variables for the initial velocity and projection angle, they can be shared in different functions. Therefore, changes can be made more conveniently. For a complicated problem, variables often need to be shared by multiple functions. In this chapter, we will describe relevant features in C for solving complicated problems.

8.1 Global and Local Variables

A *global variable* is one that is defined outside any programming block in a file. When a global variable is defined, any function that follows the variable definition may reference it. Although not recommended, global variables shared by different functions can be used to communicate between functions. In contrast, a *local variable* may be used only within the function or block in which it is defined.

Program 8.1 illustrates both the application of global and local variables. In the **main()** function, functions `func1()`, `func2()`, and `func3()` are called to increment variable `g` and display its value. Note that although functions `func1()` and `func2()` increment global variable `g` by 1, the function `func3()` only increments its local variable, which is also defined as `g`. This shows that a global variable cannot be accessed within a function if a local variable is defined with the same name. The output of Program 8.1 is as follows:

```
g in func1() = 11
g in func2() = 12
g in func3() = 1
g in main() = 12
```

```
/* File: global.c
   Demonstrate the usage of global variables   */
#include <stdio.h>

int g = 10;        /* declare global variable g */

void func1(void) {
     g++;          /* use global variable g */
     printf("g in func1() = %d\n", g);
}

void func2(void) {
     g++;          /* use global variable g */
     printf("g in func2() = %d\n", g);
}

void func3(void) {
     int g = 0;        /* declare and initialize local variable g */

     g++;
     printf("g in func3() = %d\n", g);
}

int main() {
     func1(); /* use global variable g */
     func2(); /* use global variable g */
     func3(); /* use local variable g */
     printf("g in main() = %d\n", g);
     return 0;
}
```

Program 8.1: Using a global variable.

8.1.1 Scopes of Identifiers

An identifier can denote an object; a function; a tag or a member of a class, structure, union, or enumeration; a typedef name; a label name; a macro name; or a macro parameter. Details about structure, union, and enumeration will be presented in Chapter 13. Classes will be described in detail in Chapter 19. The same identifier can denote different entities at different points in the program.

For each different entity that an identifier designates, the identifier is *visible* (i.e., can be used) only within a region of program text called its *scope*. Different entities designated by the same identifier either have different scopes or are in different name spaces. There are five kinds of scopes: function, file, block, function prototype, and program. A *function prototype* is a declaration of a function that declares the types of its parameters. The other scopes for identifiers in a program are illustrated in Figure 8.1.

A label name is the only kind of identifier that has *function scope*. It can be used in a **goto** statement anywhere in the function in which it appears and is declared implicitly by its syntactic appearance followed by a colon and a statement, as described in section 5.6.3 in Chapter 5.

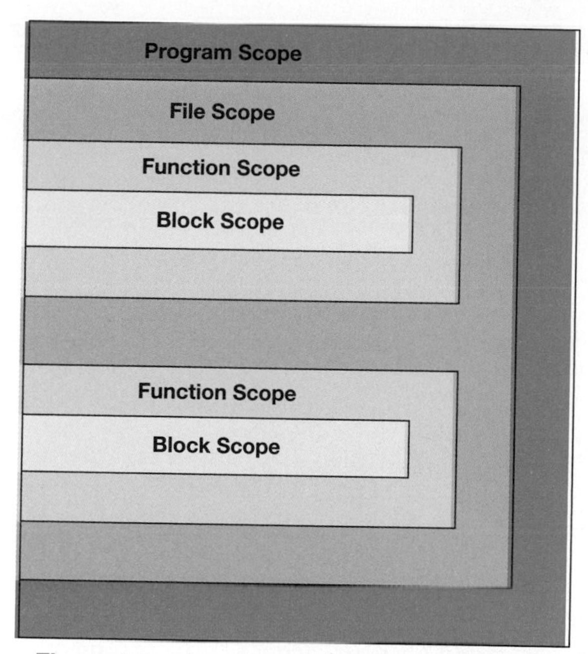

Figure 8.1: The scope of identifiers in a program.

Every other identifier has its scope determined by the placement of its declaration (in a declarator or type specifier). If the declarator or type specifier that declares the identifier appears outside of any block, the identifier has *program scope*. If the identifier is declared outside of any block with storage-class qualifier **static** as a static variable, the identifier has *file scope*. If the declarator or type specifier that declares the identifier appears inside a block or within the list of parameter declarations in a function definition, the identifier has *block scope*, which terminates at the end of the associated block. If the declarator or type specifier that declares the identifier appears within the list of parameter declarations in a function prototype (not part of a function definition), the identifier has *function prototype scope*, which terminates at the end of the function declarator. If an identifier designates two different entities in the same name space, the scopes might overlap. If so, the scope of one entity (the *inner scope*) will be a strict subset of the scope of the other entity (the *outer scope*). Within the inner scope, the identifier designates the entity declared in the inner scope; the entity declared in the outer scope is *hidden* (and not visible) within the inner scope. Two identifiers have the same scope if and only if their scopes terminate at the same point.

A program may consist of multiple files. A file may contain multiple functions. A function may have multiple blocks or nested blocks. Because of the above scope rules, a variable declared inside a block cannot be accessed outside its block. A variable declared inside a function cannot be accessed outside the function. This allows you to write a block or function of the code without worrying about whether the declared variable names conflict with names used in other parts of the program.

Program 8.2 is an example of the use of scopes for identifiers. As their names imply, the variable `program_i` has program scope and `file_i` has file scope. For variables `function_i` and `block_i`, they have function and block scope, respectively. The output of Program 8.2 is as follows:

```
program_i in main() = 10
file_i in main() = 20
program_i in func() = 10
```

```
file_i in func() = 20
function_i in func() = 30
program_i in block = 10
file_i in block = 20
function_i in block = 30
block_i in block = 40
```

```
/* File: scopeid.c
   Demonstrate the scope of identifiers */
#include <stdio.h>

int program_i = 10;       /* declare a global variable with program scope */
/* extern int otherfile_i; if otherfile_i is declared in other file */
static int file_i  = 20; /* declare a static variable with file scope */
void func(void) {
    int function_i = 30; /* declare a variable with function scope */

    /* display values of variables accessible inside this function */
    printf("program_i in func() = %d\n", program_i);
    printf("file_i in func() = %d\n", file_i);
    printf("function_i in func() = %d\n", function_i);
    {
        int block_i = 40; /* declare a variable with block scope */
        /* display values of variables accessible inside this block */
        printf("program_i in block = %d\n", program_i);
        printf("file_i in block = %d\n", file_i);
        printf("function_i in block = %d\n", function_i);
        printf("block_i in block = %d\n", block_i);
    }

}
int main() {
    /* variables in program or file scope can be accessed
       in any function in a file;
       display values of variables accessible inside this function */
    printf("program_i in main() = %d\n", program_i);
    printf("file_i in main() = %d\n", file_i);
    /* call function func() to display values of variables
       accessible inside the function */
    func();
    return 0;
}
```

Program 8.2: Different scopes of variables with the same name.

```
/* File: projectileglobal.cpp
   Plot a projectile based on the function y(x) using global variables
   for theta0 and v0 */
#include <math.h>
#include <chplot.h> /* for fplotxy() */

#define M_G   9.81 /* gravitational acceleration constant g */
double theta0, v0; /* declare global variables */

double func(double x) {
    double y;

    /* calculate the y coordinate */
    y = tan(theta0)*x - M_G*x*x/(2*v0*v0*cos(theta0)*cos(theta0));
    return y;
}

int main() {
    double x0 = 0, xf;                  /* initial and final distances, x0 is 0 */
    int num = 100;                      /* number of points for plotting */

    v0 = 35.0;                          /* initial velocity */
    theta0 = 15*M_PI/180;               /* projection angle in radian  */
    xf = v0*v0*sin(2*theta0)/M_G;  /* the distance in the x direction */
    fplotxy(func, x0, xf, num,
            "A projectile with the initial projection angle of 15 degrees",
            "x (m)", "y (m)");
    return 0;
}
```

Program 8.3: A program to plot the trajectory of a projectile using global variables.

As another example, Program 6.10 in section 6.7 in Chapter 6 plots the trajectory for a projectile. The initial speed v_0 and initial projection angle θ_0 are calculated in both functions `func()` and **main()**. If the variables `v0` and `theta0` for initial speed and projection angle, respectively, are declared as global variables, they can be shared in different functions and need to be calculated only once as shown in Program 8.3. The output from Program 8.3. is the same as the one shown in Figure 6.2 in section 6.7 in Chapter 6.

Unless explicitly stated otherwise, where this book uses the term *identifier* to refer to some entity (as opposed to the syntactic construct), it refers to the entity in the relevant name space whose declaration is visible at the point the identifier occurs.

Class, structure, union, and enumeration tags, which will be described in Chapters 13 and 19, have a scope that begins just after the appearance of the tag in a type specifier that declares the tag. Each enumeration constant has a scope that begins just after the appearance of its defining enumerator in an enumerator list. Any other identifier has a scope that begins just after the completion of its declarator.

8.1.2 Name Spaces of Identifiers

If more than one declaration of a particular identifier is visible at any point in a program, the syntactic context disambiguates uses that refer to different entities. The separate *name spaces* categorized for various identifiers are given as follows:

- *Macro names* (the macros defined using the preprocessing directive **#define**);
- *Label names* (disambiguated by the syntax of the label declaration and use);
- The *tags* of classes, structures, unions, and enumerations (disambiguated by following any of the keywords **class**, **struct**, **union**, or **enum**);
- The *members* of classes, structures or unions; each class, structure or union has a separate name space for its members (disambiguated by the type of the expression used to access the member via the **.** or -> operator);
- All other identifiers, called *ordinary identifiers* (declared in ordinary declarators or as enumeration constants).

8.2 Storage Classes

8.2.1 Storage Duration of Objects

An object has a *storage duration* that determines its lifetime. There are three storage durations: static, automatic, and allocated. The valid storage-class specifiers are given in Table 8.1.

An object whose identifier is declared with external or internal linkage with the storage-class specifier **static** has *static storage* duration. For such an object, storage is reserved and its stored value is initialized only once, prior to program start-up. If an object whose identifier with the static storage duration is declared without an initializer, its initial value of the object is zero. The object exists, has a constant address, and retains its last-stored value throughout the execution of the entire program. Details about linkages of identifiers are described in section 8.3.1.

An object whose identifier is declared with no linkage and without the storage-class specifier **static** has *automatic storage duration*. For an object that does not have a variable length array type, storage is guaranteed to be reserved for a new instance of the object on each entry into the block with which it is associated; the initial value of the object is indeterminate in C and zero in C++ and Ch. If an initialization is specified for the object, it is performed each time the declaration is reached in the execution of the block; otherwise, the value becomes indeterminate in C or zero in C++ and Ch each time the declaration is reached. Storage for the object is no longer guaranteed to be reserved when execution of the block ends in any way. Note that entering an enclosed block or calling a function suspends, but does not end, execution of the current block.

For an object that does have a variable length array type in C99, described in section 10.7 in Chapter 10, storage is guaranteed to be reserved for a new instance of the object each time the declaration is reached in

Table 8.1 Storage-class specifiers.

Specifier	Function
auto	local automatic variable
extern	external variable
register	register variable
static	static variable

the execution of the program. The initial value of the object is indeterminate in C and zero in Ch. Storage for the object is no longer guaranteed to be reserved when the execution of the program leaves the scope of the declaration.

If an object is referred to when storage is not reserved for it, the behavior is undefined. The value of a pointer that referred to an object whose storage is no longer reserved is indeterminate. During the time that its storage is reserved, an object has a constant address.

The storage can be *allocated* dynamically at runtime by the functions **calloc(), malloc()**, and **realloc()** and subsequently freed by the function **free()**. Details about memory allocation and pointers are described in Chapter 11. The storage can also be dynamically *allocated* and deallocated by the operators **new** and **delete**, respectively, in C++ and Ch, which are presented in Chapter 18.

A declaration of an identifier for an object with a storage-class specifier **register** suggests that access to the object be as fast as possible. However, the extent to which such suggestions are effective is implementation-defined. Some implementations may even ignore the suggestion, executing a program based on its own optimization scheme.

8.2.2 Static Variables Inside a Function

Local variables declared inside a function with the keyword **static** have static duration rather than automatic duration. The difference between an automatic variable and a **static** local variable is that the latter retains its value even when the function is exited. For initialization of a variable, a static variable is initialized only once, whereas a variable of automatic storage duration is initialized each time the function is called. When the function is called the next time, the **static** local variable contains the value it had prior to the last function exit. Program 8.4 illustrates the difference between automatic and static durations. The static variable `x` is initialized only once. Its value is retained for use the next time the function is entered. The automatic variable `y` is initialized each time the function `func()` is called. The output of this program is as follows:

```
x = 10 y = 10
x = 11 y = 11
x = 11 y = 10
x = 12 y = 11
```

```
/* File: staticf.c
   Use 'static' variable inside a function */
#include <stdio.h>

/* function func() has a static variable inside */
int func(void) {
    static int x=10; /* static variable x is initialized only once */
    int y=10;        /* automatic variable y is initialized  */
                     /* each time  when func() is called */
    printf("x = %d y = %d\n", x, y);
    x++; y++;
    printf("x = %d y = %d\n", x, y);
    return 0;
}
```

Program 8.4: A static variable inside a function. (*Continued*)

```
int main() {
    /* x inside func() in the second call retains the value
       in the first call. */
    func(); /* first call func() */
    func(); /* second call func() */
    return 0;
}
```

Program 8.4: (*Continued*)

A function with static variables depends on the values stored in the static variables; the result of each function call may be different. Therefore, a function with static variables is generally not suitable for multi-threading applications with re-entry.

The function `daystr()` in Program 11.11 in Chapter 11 uses a static variable to handle strings for each day of a week. A comprehensive application example using functions `gpa_monthString()` and `obtainGPA()` with static variables and related flowcharts will be presented in section 13.5 in Chapter 13 using a GPA library.

8.2.3 Static Variables Outside a Function

A variable declared outside a function with the keyword **static** has *file scope* instead of *program scope*. This means that the variable can be referenced only from its declaration point to the end of the file in which it is defined. Programs 8.5 and 8.6 illustrate this point. The static variable `x` and static function `func2()` can be accessed only inside the file `staticfile.c` and not in the file `staticprog.c`. Only the global variable `x` in the file `staticprog.c` may be accessed and modified in the file `staticprog.c`. The output of this example is shown below:

```
global x in main() = 20
static x in func2() = 10
static x in func1()  = 11
global x in main() = 21
```

```
/* File: staticfile.c
   Use 'static' specifier for variables in file scope */
#include <stdio.h>

/* variables x and function func2() in file scope
   are accessible only in this file 'staticfile.c' */
static int x = 10;  /* declare static variable x */
static int func2(void); /* declare static function func2() */

/* function func1() in program scope.
   func1() uses variables and call function func2() in file scope */
int func1(void) {
    func2();   /* call static function */
```

Program 8.5: A program with static variables in the file scope. (*Continued*)

```
    /* use variable x in file scope */
    printf("static x in func1()  = %d\n", x);
    x++;
    return 0;
}

static int func2(void) {
    /* use variable x in file scope */
    printf("static x in func2() = %d\n", x);
    x++;
    return 0;
}
```

Program 8.5: (*Continued*)

```
/* File: staticprog.c
   Use a function in a different file */
#include <stdio.h>

/* load code from file staticfile.c for Ch */
#if defined(_CH_)
#pragma importf <staticfile.c>
#endif

/* declare 'extern' function func1() so that func1()
   in file staticfile.c can be be used in in this file */
extern int func1(void);
/* declare global variable x; */
int x = 20;

int main() {
    /* use global variable x in this file */
    printf("global x in main() = %d\n", x);
    x++;
    func1(); /* call function func1() in staticfile.c,
                it has also a variable x in file scope */
    printf("global x in main() = %d\n", x);
    return 0;
}
```

Program 8.6: A program using code with static variables in file scope.

Note that the lines

```
#if defined(_CH_)
#pragma importf <staticfile.c>
#endif
```

are used in Ch to include the contents of the file `staticfile.c`, primarily static variable `x` and static function `func1()`, to be accessed in the file `staticprog.c`. In other C compilers, this segment of the code is ignored. Details about using this pragma directive to load multiple files in Ch are described in section 8.5.1. As an application example, the function `highestLowestGPA()` in Program 13.34 in Chapter 13 is defined as a static function in a file scope.

8.3 External Variables and Functions

8.3.1 Linkages of Identifiers

An identifier declared in different scopes or in the same scope more than once can be made to refer to the same object or function by a process called *linkage*. There are three kinds of linkage: external, internal, and none.

In the set of source files that constitutes an entire program, each declaration of a particular identifier with *external linkage* denotes the same object or function. Within a source file, each declaration of an identifier with *internal linkage* denotes the same object or function. Each declaration of an identifier with *no linkage* denotes a unique entity.

If the declaration of a file scope identifier for an object or a function contains the storage-class specifier **static**, the identifier has internal linkage.

For an identifier declared with the storage-class specifier **extern** in a scope in which a prior declaration of that identifier is visible, if the prior declaration specifies internal or external linkage, the linkage of the identifier at the later declaration is the same as the linkage specified at the prior declaration. If no prior declaration is visible, or if the prior declaration specifies no linkage, then the identifier has external linkage.

If the declaration of an identifier for a function has no storage-class specifier, its linkage is determined exactly as if it were declared with the storage-class specifier **extern**. If the declaration of an identifier for an object has file scope and no storage-class specifier, its linkage is external.

The following identifiers have no linkage: an identifier declared to be a function parameter; a block scope identifier for an object declared without the storage-class specifiers **extern**.

It is a syntax error if the same identifier appears with both internal and external linkage.

Variables and functions with external linkage can be used outside files in which they are defined. Programs 8.7, 8.8, and 8.9 demonstrate how the keyword **extern** is used to declare external variables and functions. The global variable `x` and the function `func1()` are defined in the file `externfile.c`. They are declared in the header file `externprog.h`. To access them in the file `externprog.c`, the keyword **extern** is used to declare the external variable `x` and the function `func1()` in the file `externprog.h` by the declaration statements

```
extern int x;
extern int func1(void);
```

In this case, the storage-class specifier **extern** is mandatory for the declaration of the variable `x`. But it is optional for the function prototype `func1()` because, by default, a function has external linkage.

Program 8.7 uses the following preprocessing directive **pragma:**

```
#if defined(_CH_)
#pragma importf <externfile.c>
#endif
```

```
/* File: externprog.h
   Define declare external functions and variables */
#ifndef EXTERNPROG_H
#define EXTERNPROG_H

/* declare extern variable x */
extern int x;
/* declare extern function func1() */
extern int func1(void);

/* load code from file externfile.c for Ch */
#if defined(_CH_)
#pragma importf <externfile.c>
#endif

#endif /* EXTERNPROG_H */
```

Program 8.7: A header file with the declaration of external variables.

```
/* File: externfile.c
   Declare global variable x and function func1() */
#include <stdio.h>
#include "externprog.h"

int x = 10;  /* declare global variable */

/* declare global function func1(). It uses global variable x */
int func1(void) {
    printf("global x in func1()  = %d\n", x);
    x++;
    return 0;
}
```

Program 8.8: The program with the definition of an external variable.

```
/* File: externprog.c
   Program uses global variable x and function func1() in file externfile.c */
#include <stdio.h>
#include "externprog.h"  /* header file for external functions and variable */

int main() {
    /* use global variable x and function func1() in file externfile.c */
    printf("global x in main() = %d\n", x);
```

Program 8.9: A program using an external variable. (*Continued*)

```
    x++;
    func1();
    printf("global x in main() = %d\n", x);
    return 0;
}
```

Program 8.9: (*Continued*)

to include the definitions of the global variable x and the function func1() in Program 8.8 if the program runs in Ch. The output of Program 8.9, which also uses the source code listed in Program 8.8, is as follows:

```
global x in main() = 10
global x in func1()  = 11
global x in main() = 12
```

8.3.2 Selection of Methods for Communication Between Functions

A C program generally consists of many functions. Selection of methods for communication is important. Methods for communication between functions can be summarized as follows.

Functions can communicate through return values, arguments, and global variables. The input to a function can be obtained from its arguments or using the variables at higher lexical levels. The output of a function can be a return value, its arguments, and variables at higher lexical levels. To pass results back to the calling function from the called function, one can use pointers for pass-by-value, which will be described in Chapter 11. In C++ and Ch, the results in a called function can also be passed back to the calling function using pass-by-reference, which will be described in Chapter 18. If a function is used as an operand in expressions, the result from the function should be implemented as a return value. If a large number of variables must be shared among different functions, variables at higher lexical levels are more convenient than long argument lists. For better readability, a function shall not be defined across multiple files; hence, local variables inside a function are not visible outside the file within which the function is defined. Variables at higher lexical levels are useful for communicating between functions, especially if functions must share some data yet neither calls the other. To avoid too many data connections between functions, a function that is self-containing should communicate with other functions through its arguments and return value.

For functions in a reusable library, however, global or local static variables should be avoided inside a function. A function with a global variable may not be suitable for a multi-thread application, in which the function might be called by different threads simultaneously.

8.4 ‡Environment Variables

An environment variable, typically consisting of capital letters, is a system variable that can be shared by different processes and programs. Environment variables are handled differently from the variables in C. They do not need to be declared. The functions **putenv()** and **getenv()** can be used to handle environment variables.

The function **putenv()** can add an environment variable to the system. It takes an argument of a string in the form of name=value. It makes the value of the environment variable name equal to value by altering an existing variable or creating a new one. The function **putenv()** returns a nonzero valuc if it was unable to obtain enough space for an expanded environment. Otherwise, 0 is returned.

The function **getenv()** with an argument `name` of string type for an environment variable searches the environment list for a string of the form `name=value` and, if the string is present, returns a pointer to the value in the current environment. Otherwise, it returns a null pointer.

It was pointed out section 7.11.1 in Chapter 7 that the environment variable **INCLUDE** contains the default directories for header files for Visual C++ in Windows. Each directory is separated by a semicolon. The environment variable **INCLUDE** is set up in the start-up file in **_chrc** in the user's home directory. For example, the statement

```
putenv("INCLUDE=C:/Program Files/Microsoft Visual Studio 9.0/VC/include;");
```

sets `C:/Program Files/Microsoft Visual Studio 9.0/VC/include` as the default directory for header files for Visual C++.

The functions **remenv()** and **isenv()** with an argument `name` of string type for an environment variable are added in Ch. The function **remenv()** can remove an environment variable. The function **isenv()** can test if a symbol is an environmental variable. As a command shell, Ch can also handle environment variables interactively. The interactive command execution below demonstrates their application.

```
> putenv("ENVVAR=value")
0
> getenv("ENVVAR")
value
> isenv("ENVVAR")
1
> remenv("ENVVAR")
> isenv("ENVVAR")
0
```

In the above execution, the environment variable **ENVVAR** is assigned with `value`. It is then obtained by the function **getenv()**. Before the environment variable is removed, the function **isenv()** returns 1. After it is removed by the function **remenv()**, the function **isenv()** returns 0.

You can log in remotely to another workstation, which acts as a client. However, your local workstation may refuse connection to the client; the remote client fails with an error message. A proper communication has to be established so that the client will be able to determine which server receives the graphical output of the client. At the same time, your workstation's X server will allow the remote system to send the output. This is accomplished by setting the environment variable **DISPLAY** on the client and adding the client to the name list of remote systems on your workstation's X server by the command **xhost**. For example, if you log in to the remote machine *mouse* from the local machine *cat* and want the graphical output of *mouse* to be sent to *cat*, you should execute the command

```
cat> xhost mouse
```

on the local machine *cat* to add the remote machine *mouse* to the list of the remote systems of the local X server. You also need to execute

```
mouse> putenv("DISPLAY=cat:0.0")
```

on the remote machine *mouse*. After this proper set-up, many applications executed in a remote host with graphical output can be displayed in the local machine. For example,

```
mouse> xcalc
```

will execute the command **xcalc**, a scientific calculator, in the machine `mouse`, and display the output in the local machine `cat`.

If the machine *mouse* is often used remotely, the command `putenv("DISPLAY=cat:0.0")` can be placed in the start-up file **.chrc** in the user's home directory of the machine *mouse*.

An Application Example

Acceleration of a Moving Body

External variables, static variables in file scope, and header files are primarily used to develop large application programs. Here, a practical example is used to demonstrate their working principles. A more comprehensive application example using these concepts is presented in section 13.5 in Chapter 13.

Problem Statement:

For the mechanical system shown in Figure 2.12, given mass $m = 5$ kilograms (kg) and coefficient of kinetic friction $\mu = 0.2$, the applied force p is expressed as a function of time t in

$$p(t) = 4\sin(t - 3) + 20$$

Write a program to calculate the acceleration **a** when $t = 2$ seconds with the following features: Use the global variable `g_a` and the function `accel()` for acceleration; and the static variable `p` and the static function `force()` for force. Initialize the static and the global variables using the global function `initialize()`. The function prototypes, global variable, and macros shall be defined in the header file `accelextern.h`. The source code for functions are contained in the function file `accelexternfunc.c`.

Programs 8.10, 8.11, and 8.12 provide the solution for this application problem. The header file in Program 8.10 defines the macro `M_G` as the gravitational acceleration constant, declares the functions `initialize()` and `accel()`, and the variable `g_a` as an external variable with the keyword **extern**. Program 8.12 contains the definitions for the functions `force()`, `initialize()`, and `accel()`. The function `force()` and the external function `accel()` are defined to calculate the force and acceleration,

```
/* File: accelextern.h
   Define macros, and declare external functions and variables */
#ifndef ACCELEXTERN_H
#define ACCELEXTERN_H

#define M_G   9.81        /* define the gravitatonal accel constant */

/* declare external functions and variable */
extern void initialize(void);
```

Program 8.10: The header file for calculating accelerations with external and static functions. (*Continued*)

```
extern void accel(double t, double mu, double m);
extern double g_a;  /* declare extern global variable g_a */

/* load code from file accelexternfunc.c when the program runs in Ch */
#if defined(_CH_)
#pragma importf <accelexternfunc.c>
#endif


#endif /* ACCELEXTERN_H */
```

Program 8.10: *(Continued)*

```
/* File: accelextern.c
   Calculate the acceleration use global variable g_a and global functions
   initialize() and accel(). */
#include <stdio.h>
/* header file "accelextern.h" contains declarations of external
   variables and function prototypes */
#include "accelextern.h"

int main() {
    double mu, m, t; /* declare variables */

    mu = 0.2;          /* set mu */
    m = 5.0;           /* set mass */
    t = 2.0;           /* set time */
    /* initialize global variable g_a and static variable p */
    initialize();
    accel(t, mu, m); /* calculate acceleration and get it back using g_a */
    printf("Acceleration = %f (m/s^2)\n", g_a); /* display output */
    return 0;
}
```

Program 8.11: Calculating accelerations with external and static functions.

```
/* File: accelexternfunc.c
   Define global variable g_a and functions initialize() and accel()
   used by the source file accelextern.c. Static variable p and
   function force() with scope is used for implementation of accel(). */
#include <math.h>
/* header file "accelextern.h" contains declarations of external
   variables and function prototypes */
#include "accelextern.h"
```

Program 8.12: External and static functions for calculating accelerations. *(Continued)*

```
/* declare global variable and function prototype with file scope */
double g_a;          /* declare global variable g_a */
static double p;     /* declare static variable p  with file scope */
static void force(double t); /* static function force() with file scope */

/* static function with file scope. It uses static variable p */
static void force(double t) {
    p = 4*sin(t-3)+20;
}

/* a global function using static variable p and global variable g_a */
void initialize(void) {
    p = 0;
    g_a = 0;
}

/* a global function calling static function and using
   global variable g_a and static variable p */
void accel(double t, double mu, double m) {
    force(t);
    g_a = (p-mu*m*M_G)/m;
}
```

Program 8.12: *(Continued)*

respectively. Because the variable `p` and the function `force()` are used only in the file `accelexternfunc.c` in Program 8.12, they are declared as static variables in the file scope with the keyword **static** to avoid possible namespace collision with the same variable or function names in other source files. The function `initialize()` sets the default values for the static variable `p` and global variable `g_a`.

Program 8.11 uses the following preprocessing directive **pragma** to include the declarations and definitions of global variables in the file `accelexternfunc.c` in Program 8.12 if the program runs in Ch:

```
#if defined(_CH_)
#pragma importf <accelexternfunc.c>
#endif
```

In other C compilers, this segment of the code is ignored. In Program 8.11, the function: `initialize()` is called to initialize variables `p` and `g_a` before the function `accel()` is called to calculate the acceleration. Because the static variable `p` and the static function `force()` in the file `accelexternfunc.c` are in file scope, the output of Program 8.11 is the same as that of Programs 6.3, 6.4, and 6.5.

Programs 8.10, 8.11, and 8.12 represent a typical style of software engineering in C. A developer of a software package typically develops and maintains functions and header files. The user of the software package typically uses the header files and provided functions either in source code or binary libraries to create their own applications. For this example, a developer might develop and maintain the header file in Program 8.10 and functions in Program 8.12. The developer often uses many internal functions for a software package such as the static function in Program 8.12. The user will use the header file in Program 8.10

and functions to develop their own applications such as Program 8.11. The application program typically needs to call an initialization function, such as `initialize()` in Program 8.12, to set up global variables used in a software package.

8.5 Making It Work

8.5.1 Running C Programs with Multiple Files

Running C Programs with Multiple Files in Ch

To run a C program with multiple source files in Ch, the source file with function **main()** is the application program. Other source files, such as `filename1.c` and `filename2.c`, can be loaded in a header file using the **pragma** preprocessing directive as follows.

```
#pragma importf <filename1.c>
#pragma importf <filename2.c>
```

The previous application program consists of multiple files listed in Programs 8.10, 8.11, and 8.12. When the program `accelextern.c` is executed in Ch, the source code in the file `accelexternfunc.c` is loaded by a preprocessing directive **pragma** inside the header file `accelextern.h` as follows.

```
#if defined(_CH_)
#pragma importf <accelexternfunc.c>
#endif
```

The preprocessing directive **pragma** followed by the token **importf** loads the file `accelexternfunc.c`, specified inside the pair of brackets, in the location where **#pragma** is placed. The file is searched based on the search paths in the system variable **_fpath** for function files. The system variable **_fpath** can be modified in a start-up file as described in section 6.13.2 in Chapter 6. With the preprocessing directive **pragma**, the program `accelextern.c` can be simply executed in Ch by the command

```
> accelextern.c
```

Running C Programs with Multiple Files in Visual C++

To run the same program in Windows compiled in Virtual C++, the following command can be entered:

```
> cl accelextern.c accelexternfunc.c
```

to create the executable program `accelextern.exe`. However, you can also compile each file separately and then link them together. This way, you can fix all the compile problems in each individual source file before compiling the next one. For example, commands with the command-line option `/c`

```
> cl /c accelexternfunc.c
> cl /c accelextern.c
```

compile source code `accelexternfunc.c` and `accelextern.c` to create object code `accelexternfunc.obj` and `accelextern.obj`, which can then be linked to creat an executable `accelextern.exe` by the command:

```
> cl accelextern.obj accelexternfunc.obj
```

You can also mix source code and object code on the same command for compiling and linking as shown below:

```
> cl accelextern.obj accelexternfunc.c
```

to create the executable `exterprog.exe`.

Running C Programs with Multiple Files in GNU C

For GNU C, the command

```
> cc -o accelextern accelextern.c accelexternfunc.c
```

or

```
> gcc -o accelextern accelextern.c accelexternfunc.c
```

can be used to create the executable file `accelextern`. You can also compile each source file separately using the command line option `-c` and then link them together, or mix source code and object code on the same command as shown below to create the executable `accelexter`:

```
> gcc -c accelexternfunc.c
> gcc accelextern.c accelexternfunc.o
```

8.5.2 ‡Maintaining Programs with make

A large program typically consists of many source files. If some individual files are changed, the program using the latest code can readily run in Ch. However, to build a binary executable, it will be desirable to compile only those changed files and files depending on those changed files. The **make** program can be used to keep track of the dependency for a large program with many source files. Looking at the dates of relevant files, only the modified source files and files depending on them are recompiled to recreate the executable file. It also allows you to keep different commands and options in a documented file so that you do not have to remember different commands with different options. This is especially useful for development of application programs across different platforms.

Structure of a Make File

The **make** program executes commands based on dependency rules specified by the developer in a special make file. When the **make** command is executed, it looks in the current directory for the default make file `makefile` first. If it does not exist, **make** next looks for `Makefile`, the alternative default make file. The

```
# comments
target: dependent files
[Tab]    command 1
[Tab]    command 2
...
[Tab]    command n
```

Program 8.13: The basic structure of a make file.

basic structure of a make file is shown in Program 8.13. A comment line starts with a pound sign '#'. The **make** ignores comment lines. A dependency line, which specifies a dependency rule, contains a target immediately followed by a colon, then followed by the dependent files. After a dependency line, a series of tab-indented command lines define actions to be taken, if the dependent files have been modified more recently than the target. It should be noted that a command line *must* begin with an invisible Tab, followed by a command. A dependency line and its tab-indented commands are the basic building block of a make file, which contains multiple such building blocks.

Variables can be defined. By convention, variable names use capital letters, such as `VARI`, and they are defined at the beginning of a make file. The value of a variable can be obtained later by enclosing the variable inside a pair of parentheses and preceded by a dollar sign such as `$(VARI)`.

A Make File for the Application Program in Unix

Program 8.14 is a `Makefile` that can be used to build the executable `accelextern` in Unix, as described in the previous section. Line

```
CC = cc
```

```
# File: Makefile
# Type 'make' in a command shell to build 'accelextern' in Unix

CC = cc
CFLAG = -c
LFLAG = -lm

target: accelextern

accelextern: accelextern.o accelexternfunc.o
	$(CC) -o accelextern $(LFLAG) accelextern.o accelexternfunc.o
accelextern.o: accelextern.c accelextern.h
	$(CC) $(CFLAG) accelextern.c -I./
accelexternfunc.o: accelexternfunc.c accelextern.h
	$(CC) $(CFLAG) accelexternfunc.c -I./
clean:
	rm -f *.o accelextern
```

Program 8.14: A make file for creating program `accelextern` in Unix.

defines variable CC as a compiler command used for compilation. In some platforms, one may use the command **gcc**, instead of **cc**. Line

```
CFLAG = -c
```

defines variable CFLAG as an optional flag for compilation to produce an object code only. Line

```
LFLAG = -lm
```

defines variable LFLAG as an optional flag for linking with the math library.

The dependency line

```
target: accelextern
```

specifies an executable file accelextern. There is no command following this dependency line.

The block

```
accelextern: accelextern.o accelexternfunc.o
        $(CC) -o accelextern $(LFLAG) accelextern.o accelexternfunc.o
```

contains a dependency line and its command line. The file accelextern depends on the object files accelextern.o and accelexternfunc.o. When one of these two files is modified, the command for the dependency line will be executed to create an updated executable accelextern. A dependency line and its command lines can be placed in any place in a make file. Trace the chain of dependencies, the object file accelextern.o depends on the source files accelextern.c and accelextern.h as shown below:

```
accelextern.o: accelextern.c accelextern.h
        $(CC) $(CFLAG) accelextern.c -I./
```

If the object file accelextern.o does not exist or when one of them is changed, the source code accelextern.c will be recompiled to create the object file. Similarly, accelexternfunc.o depends on the source files accelexternfunc.c and accelextern.h. If one of them is changed, the source code accelexternfunc.c will be recompiled. Both source files with the file extentsion .c depend on the header file accelextern.h. If the header file is changed, both source files will be recompiled.

When the make file in Program 8.14 is invoked by the **make** command, executed commands are displayed as shown below:

```
> make
cc -c accelextern.c -I./
cc -c accelexternfunc.c -I./
cc -o accelextern -lm accelextern.o accelexternfunc.o
```

The object files and executable accelextern are created by the above make command.

Files are not necessarily compiled and linked in the exactly the same order as they appear in the make file. The **make** command determines which files should be compiled first based on dependency lines.

If the file accelexternfunc.c is modified, it needs to be recompiled. However, the file accelextern.c does not need to be recompiled. The object files for this application program can be linked with the updated object file accelexternfunc.o to create the executable using the latest code for accelexernfunc.c. Once the modification is finished, all you need to do is to type the command **make** as shown below:

```
> make
cc -c accelexternfunc.c -I./
cc -o accelextern -lm accelextern.o accelexternfunc.o
```

Compared with the previous case, the following command is not executed this time:

```
cc -c accelextern.c -I./
```

After the executable `accelextern` is built with the latest source code, if no change has been made to files, the **make** command will not execute any tab-indented commands. In Linux, the command displays a message shown below.

```
> make
make: Nothing to be done for 'target'.
```

The target `clean` in the make file shown below

```
clean:
        rm -f *.o accelextern
```

does not depend on any file. It is an *empty dependency*. When the **make** command is executed, by default, the first target is invoked. Other target can be invoked explicitly as a command argument of the **make** command as shown below for the target `clean`:

```
> make clean
rm -f *.o accelextern
```

Its tab-indented command removes object files with `.o` file extension and the executable `accelextern`.

A Make File for the Application Program in Windows

The make file `Makefile.win` in Program 8.15 for Windows corresponds to `Makefile` for Unix in Program 8.14. The commands for building the executable `accelextern.exe` described in the previous section are organized in dependency and command lines. The variable `CLFAG` is defined as a compilation flag. The Visual C++ 2008 compiler generates warning messages for many standard C functions such as **scanf()** for the security reason described in section 12.5 in Chapter 12. The option `-D_CRT_SECURE_NO_DEPRECATE` suppresses these warning messages.

The **make** command option `-f` *filename* can be used to find an alternative make file, instead of the default make file `makefile` or `Makefile`. The make file `Makefile.win` for Windows can be invoked as follows:

```
> make -f Makefile.win
```

with the **make** command provided in Ch. Visual C++ has its own make command called **nmake** with some new features such as commands not starting with a Tab. The **nmake** command can be used to process the make file `Makefile.win` as follows:

```
> nmake -f Makefile.win
```

```
# File: Makefile.win
# Type 'make -f Makefile.win' in a command shell
# to build 'accelextern.exe' in Windows

CC = cl
# create .obj file and disable warning message for using scanf()
CFLAG = /c -D_CRT_SECURE_NO_DEPRECATE
LFLAG =

target: accelextern.exe

accelextern.exe: accelextern.obj accelexternfunc.obj
	$(CC) $(LFLAG) accelextern.obj accelexternfunc.obj
accelextern.obj: accelextern.c accelextern.h
	$(CC) $(CFLAG) accelextern.c -I./
accelexternfunc.obj: accelexternfunc.c accelextern.h
	$(CC) $(CFLAG) accelexternfunc.c -I./
clean:
	del *.obj
	del *.exe
```

Program 8.15: A make file for creating program `accelextern.exe` in Windows.

An example of using make files for building libraries across different platforms can be found in section 15.6.3 in Chapter 15.

Using Make Files in Ch and ChIDE

ChIDE can be used to edit make files with syntax highlighting. When editing C programs, ChIDE changes a tab into four white spaces by default. But ChIDE preserves tabs for make files.

There are three ways to use a make file in Ch and ChIDE. First, a make file can be invoked by the command **make** in a Ch command shell. Second, the command **make** and its options can be typed in the output pane in ChIDE. Finally, the default make file `makefile` or `Makefile` can be invoked by the command `Tools | Build` in ChIDE as described in section 2.2.5 in Chapter 2.

8.5.3 Debugging Programs with Global Variables in ChIDE

The method for debugging programs with functions in ChIDE, described in section 6.13.3, is also applicable to programs with global variables. Selecting the menu `Variables` on the debugging pane selection bar, all variables, including global variables, and their corresponding values in the scope will be displayed.

As an instructor, it will be convenient to load multiple source files in ChIDE on the command line as shown below:

```
> chide accelextern.c accelexternfunc.c accelextern.h
```

for a classroom presentation. This will also be the case for programs with structures and classes, typically having multiple files, which will be described later.

Exercises

1. The code below declares three variables named *x* with types int, float, and double. On which lines is each of the variables declared and used?

```
int x;
void f(float x) {
    float f = x;
    {
        double x;
        x = 3.4;
    }
    f = x+2;
}
int i = x;
```

2. The definition of function `f()` is shown below. What will be the value of `f(10)` if the function has never been called before? What will `f(10)` be the second time it is called?

```
int f(int x) {
    static int i = 0, j = 1;
    i = i+1;
    j += i+1;
    return x*i*j;
}
```

3. Write the output of the following program when it is executed:

```
#include <stdio.h>
float func(int i) {
  static float f = 10;
  f += i;
  return f;
}
int main() {
  printf("func(5) = %f\n", func(5));
  printf("func(15) = %f\n", func(15));
  return 0;
}
```

4. Write a function with the function prototype

```
int f(void);
```

that prints out *n* asterisks, where *n* represents the number of times it has been called. If it is called three times, for instance, the output will be

```
*
* *
* * *
```

Test the function by calling it five times.

a. Use a static variable inside the function.
b. Use a global variable inside the function.

5. Write a program to calculate the areas of different shapes. The areas of a square, rectangle, triangle, and circle shall be calculated and returned from separate functions located in the file `func.c`. The function prototypes are placed in the header file `area.h`. In the main program `area.c`, the user shall be asked to select a shape first, then enter the necessary parameters for the shape. The calculated area will then be displayed.
6. A projectile is fired into the air with an initial speed v_0 of 35 m/s. Write a program to plot the trajectory of y versus x with different initial projection angles. The user shall input an initial angle. It can be proved that, when the initial projection angle is 45 degrees, the projectile travels the longest distance in the x direction. Plot the trajectory of the proejctile with initial projection angles of 15, 30, 45, and 60 degrees.

   a. Plot each trajectory in a separate plot.
   b. Plot all trajectories with different initial projection angles in a single plot using the member function **func2D()** of the plotting class **CPlot**.

7. The value of $\sigma > 0$ in equation (6.10) in Exercise 33 determines the shape of the probability density functions shown in Figure 6.12. Given $\mu = -2$, plot the probability density functions for σ equal to 0.5, 1, 2, and 3 in a single plot, with x in the range $-10 \leq x \leq 10$. The variable for σ shall be declared as a global variable so that only one function needs to be defined and passed as an argument to the member function **func2D()** of the plotting class **CPlot**.

CHAPTER 9

‡Formatted Input and Output

The functions **scanf()** and **printf()** are the primary methods for reading data into, and writing data out of, a program. The function **scanf()** inputs data from the standard input stream, whereas the function **printf()** outputs data to the standard output stream. The format of both functions has been briefly introduced in section 3.15 in Chapter 3. This chapter provides a more in-depth discussion of the formatting features of functions **scanf()** and **printf()** to handle more sophisticated input and output. The features presented are applicable to a large family of other relevant input and output functions. In addition, the function **getnum()** is introduced as a convenient method to obtain a floating-point number from the terminal.

9.1 Formatting Output for Functions in the printf Family

Precisely formatted output is accomplished using the output function **printf()**. The function **printf()** has the following form:

```
printf(format-control-string, arguments);
```

where `format-control-string` contains literal text and conversion specifications. Characters (other than %) in the literal text are sent to the output unchanged. Each specification begins with a percent sign '%' and ends with a conversion specifier. Each specification results in fetching zero or more subsequent arguments, converting them, if applicable, according to the corresponding conversion specifier, and then writing the result to the output. Examples of conversion specifications are flags, field widths, and precisions. The function **printf()** can perform rounding, column alignment, right and left justification, literal character insertion, fixed width, etc. Some examples of using the function **printf()** to display output are shown below.

```
> int = 5
> float f = 1.234
> double d = 123.4567
> printf("i = %d\n", i)
i = 5
> printf("f = %f\n", f)
f = 1.234000
> printf("d = %lf\n", d)
d = 123.456700
> printf("i = %d, f = %f, d = %lf\n", i, f, d)
i = 5, f = 1.234000, d = 123.456700
```

The format specifiers described in this section are applicable to the other output functions **fprintf()** described in Chapter 14 and **sprintf()** in Chapter 12 in the **printf** family.

9.1.1 Printing Integers

Table 9.1 lists the integer conversion specifiers available for the function **printf()**. The table also provides a short description of each conversion specifier. The format specifier `"%i"` is exactly the same as `"%d"` for the output. As an example of using some of the integer conversion specifiers listed in Table 9.1, consider Program 9.1. Program 9.1 prints out the character representation `j` for the ASCII number 106 as well as its decimal, octal, and hexadecimal representations. For variables `i1` and `i2`, the hexadecimal values are converted to decimal values. The output of Program 9.1 is as follows:

```
j
106
-106
106
152
6a
6A
32
536870912
536870912
536870912
```

Table 9.1 Conversion specifiers for integers.

Type	Description
b	Displays a binary number (in Ch only).
d, i	Displays a signed decimal integer in the style *[-]dddd*.
o	Displays an unsigned octal integer in the style dddd.
x or **X**	Displays an unsigned hexadecimal integer in the style dddd. The letters **abcdef** are used for **x** conversion, and the letters **ABCDEF** for **X** conversion.
h or **l** or **ll**	Places before any integer conversion identifier to indicate **short** or **unsigned short**, **long** or **unsigned long**, and **long long** or **unsigned long long** integer, respectively.
u	Displays an unsigned decimal integer, such as *%u*, *%hu*, *%lu*, and *%llu*.

```
/* File: intio.c
   Print output of integer numbers with different output format specifiers. */
#include <stdio.h>

int main() {
    short i1 = 0x20;      /* declare and initialize a short int */
```

Program 9.1: Formatted output for an int type. (*Continued*)

```
    int i2 = 0x20000000; /* declare and initialize an int */
    long long l2 = 0x20000000; /* declare and initialize an long long */

    printf("%c\n", 106);   /* print the corresponding char for ASCII value 106 */
    printf("%d\n", 106);   /* print decimal number */
    printf("%d\n", -106);  /* print a negative decimal number */
    printf("%i\n", 106);   /* print decimal number */
    printf("%o\n", 106);   /* print an octal number for 106 */
    printf("%x\n", 106);   /* print a hexadecimal number for 106 */
    printf("%X\n", 106);   /* print a hexadecimal number using capital letters */
    printf("%hd\n", i1);   /* print a short integer */
    printf("%ld\n", i2);   /* print a long long int using %ld */
    printf("%d\n", i2);    /* print a long long int using %d */
    printf("%lld\n", i2);  /* print a long long int using %lld */
    return 0;
}
```

Program 9.1 *(Continued)*

Examples of the conversion specifier `%b` in Ch for binary numbers are shown below. For the binary conversion specifier, an integer number between the symbol **%** and the character **b** specifies how many bits starting with bit 0 will be printed. If without the integer number, the default format will print data of type int without leading zeros (as in the example below), data of type float in 32 bits, and data of type double in 64 bits.

```
> int i = 106
> printf("i = 0b%b", i)
i = 0b1101010
> printf("i = 0b%8b", i)
i = 0b01101010
> printf("%b", 2.0F)
01000000000000000000000000000000
```

Note that the internal IEEE floating-point representation of 2.0 in type float is obtained by printing out the memory layout in binary format.

9.1.2 Printing Floating-Point Numbers

The conversion specifiers for floating-point values are listed in Table 9.2. Note that the length modifier `l` placed before any of the floating-point conversion specifiers is ignored. Program 9.2 illustrates the use of floating-point conversion specifiers. Floating-point variables `f` and `d` are displayed in both floating-point and exponential forms in this example. For the conversion specifier **g** or **G**, the display style used is depends on the value to be converted. An exponential display is used if the exponent resulting from such a conversion is less than −4 or greater than or equal to the precision. Thus, for floating-point 12.345, the value displayed is in floating-point form. For value 12.0, the output is represented in an integer. For value 12345678.9, however, the printed value is in exponential form because the exponent is greater than the default precision. The output

Table 9.2 Conversion specifiers for floating-point values.

Type	Description
f or **F**	Displays floating-point values in the style *[-]ddd.ddd*. An infinity value is converted to either *[-]***inf** or *[-]***infinity**. For NaN, it is converted to either *[-]***nan** or *[-]***nan**(*n-char-sequence)*. The meaning of any *n-char-sequence* is implementation-dependent. The **F** conversion specifier produces **INF**, **INFINITY**, or **NAN** instead of **inf**, **infinity**, or **nan**, respectively.
a or **A**	A **double** argument representing a floating-point number in the style *[-]0xh.hhhhp±d*, where there is one hexadecimal digit (which is nonzero if the argument is normalized floating-point number and is otherwise unspecified) before the decimal-point character and the number of hexadecimal digits after it is equal to the precision. The exponent always contains at least one digit, and then it has only as many more digits necessary to represent the exponent of 2. If the value is zero, the exponent is zero. A **double** argument representing an infinity or NaN is converted in the style of **f** or **F** conversion specifier.
e or **E**	Displays a floating-point value in exponential form. The value is rounded to the appropriate number of digits. The **E** conversion specifier produces a number with **E** instead of **e** introducing the exponent. The exponent always contains at least two digits, and only as many more digits as necessary to represent the exponent. If the value is zero, the exponent is zero. An infinity or NaN value is converted in the style of an **f** or **F** conversion specifier.
g or **G**	Displays a floating-point value in either the floating-point form **f** or the exponential form **e** (or **E**). The conversion form used depends on the value. Style **e** (or **E**) is used only if the exponent resulting from such a conversion is less than −4 or greater than or equal to the precision. For infinity or NaN, the value is converted in the style of an **f** or **F** conversion specifier.

of Program 9.2 is as follows:

```
10.123000
12.345000
12.345000
1.234500e+01
-1.234500e+01
1.234500E+01
12.345
12.345
12
12
1.23457e+07
1.23457E+07
```

```
/* File: doubleio.c
   Print output of floating point numbers with different
   output format specifiers. */
#include <stdio.h>

int main() {
    float f = 10.123;
    double d = 12.345;
```

Program 9.2: Formatted output for a double type. *(Continued)*

```
    printf("%f\n", f);              /* use f for float */
    printf("%f\n", d);              /* use f for double */
    printf("%lf\n", d);             /* use lf for double */
    printf("%e\n", 12.345);         /* use e for double */
    printf("%e\n", -12.345);        /* use e for double of a negative value */
    printf("%E\n", 12.345);         /* use E for double */
    printf("%g\n", 12.345);         /* use g for double */
    printf("%G\n", 12.345);         /* use G for double */
    printf("%g\n", 12.0);           /* use g with 0 for fractional part */
    printf("%G\n", 12.0);           /* use g with 0 for fractional part */
    printf("%g\n", 12345678.9);     /* use g with a large integral part */
    printf("%G\n", 12345678.9);     /* use g with a large integral part */
    return 0;
}
```

Program 9.2: *(Continued)*

9.1.3 Printing Characters and Strings

Table 9.3 lists the conversion specifiers for printing characters and strings. The **c** conversion specifier requires an argument of type char, whereas **s** requires an array of type char or string literal. For example, the following commands display the character `'a'` and string `"hello"` as outputs.

```
> printf("%c", 'a')
a
> printf("%s", "hello")
hello
```

9.1.4 Miscellaneous Conversion Specifiers

The remaining conversion specifiers are listed in Table 9.4. The specifier **p** displays a pointer value of an object in an implementation-defined manner. Program 9.3 uses the **s** and **p** conversion specifiers to display

Table 9.3 Conversion specifiers for characters and strings.

Type	Description
c	Displays a character.
s	Displays a string.

Table 9.4 Miscellaneous conversion specifiers.

Type	Description
p	Displays an address stored in a pointer.
n	Stores the number of characters written to the output stream by function **printf()**.
%	Displays the `'%'` character.

```
/* File: strio.c
   Print output of strings and pointer with
   different output format specifiers. */
#include <stdio.h>

int main() {
    /* declare variables for strings, int, and pointer to int */
    char string[] = "String 2 is printed by an array of characters.";
    char *strPtr = "String 3 is printed by a pointer of char.";
    int i = 106;
    int *ptr;

    printf("%s\n", "String 1 is printed directly.");
    printf("%s\n", string);
    printf("%s\n", strPtr);
    ptr = &i;   /* p points to the address of i */
    printf("The value of i is %d.\n", i);
    printf("The address of i is %p.\n", ptr);
    return 0;
}
```

Program 9.3: Formatted output for strings and pointers.

strings from the arguments `string` and `strPtr` as well as the address of the argument `i`. The output of Program 9.3 is shown below:

```
String 1 is printed directly.
String 2 is printed by an array of characters.
String 3 is printed by a pointer of char.
The value of i is 106.
The address of i is 0x81a425c.
```

The two other conversion specifiers are **n** and **%**. The **n** conversion specifier stores the number of characters written to the output stream by the function **printf()**. A pointer to int is required for the corresponding argument; however, no argument is converted and nothing is displayed. If the **n** conversion specifier includes any flags, a field width, or precision, the behavior is undefined. For example,

```
> int i
> printf("The address of n is %p", &i)
The address of i is 0x81a38a4
> printf("# of printed characters:%n", &i)
# of characters:
> i
24
```

The statement

```
printf("# of printed characters:%n", &i)
```

prints out 24 characters.The number of characters printed is stored in the variable `i` using the format specifier `%n`.

The % conversion specifier simply prints the `'%'` character to the output. Again, no argument is converted. The complete conversion specification shall be `%%`. For example,

```
> printf("The percent sign: %%")
The percent sign: %
```

9.1.5 Printing with Field Widths and Precisions

In C, the *field width* is the size of a field in which data are printed. The field width takes the form of either an asterisk (*) or a decimal number. If the converted value has fewer characters than the field width, then it is padded with space on the left (if it's right-justified) or right (if it's left-justified) to match the field width. If the field width is too small, it is automatically increased to fit the data. An integer width may be inserted between % and the conversion specifier to indicate a field width. For example, `%4d` specifies a field width of 4. Also consider Program 9.4, which illustrates the key points mentioned above. The output of Program 9.4 is as follows:

```
12345
   12345
12345
   12345
```

The precision of a data to be printed out may also be specified in C. The meaning of the word *precision* varies depending on the data type. For example, the precision of an integer refers to the minimum number of digits to print. For floating-point numbers, the precision specifies the number of digits to appear after the decimal-point character. This is valid for conversion specifiers **e**, **E**, and **f**. The precision corresponding to conversion specifiers **g** and **G** relates to the maximum number of significant digits. For string conversions, the precision specifies the maximum number of characters to be written from a string.

```
/* File: field.c
   Print output for integer numbers with different field widths. */
#include <stdio.h>

int main() {
    int i = 12345;

    printf("%d\n", i);      /* automatic field width  */
    printf("%8d\n", i);     /* field width of 8  */
    printf("%4d\n", i);     /* specified field width is less than
                               the required one  */
    printf("%*d\n", 8, i); /* equivalent to printf("%8d\n", i) */
    return 0;
}
```

Program 9.4: Field width in formatted output.

The precision takes the form of a period (.) followed by either an asterisk `'*'` or by an optional decimal integer. The precision and field width may be combined as in `%8.5f`, which specifies a field width of 8 with 5 digits following the decimal point. Program 9.5 provides some examples of printing data with specified precision as well as field widths. It prints out data of various precisions for the integer `i`, the floating-point number `d`, and the string `str`. The output of Program 9.5 is as follows:

```
Precision for integers.
5678
005678

Precision for floating-point number.
123.457
123.457
  123.457
1.235e+02

Precision for g and G conversion.
123.5

Precision for strings.
Hello, students.
         Hello, students.
```

```
/* File: precision.c
   Print output for integer and floating-point numbers, and strings
   with different precisions. */
#include <stdio.h>

int main() {
    int i = 5678;
    double d = 123.45678;
    char *str = "Hello, students.";

    printf("Precision for integers.\n");
    printf("%.3d\n", i);
    printf("%.6d\n", i);

    printf("\nPrecision for floating-point number.\n");
    printf("%5.3f\n", d);
    printf("%7.3f\n", d);
    printf("%9.3f\n", d);
    printf("%.3e\n", d);
```

Program 9.5: Precisions in formatted output. (*Continued*)

```
    printf("\nPrecision for g and G conversion.\n");
    printf("%.4g\n", d);

    printf("\nPrecision for strings.\n");
    printf("%s\n", str);
    printf("%25s\n", str);

    return 0;
}
```

Program 9.5: *(Continued)*

As noted above, a field width, precision, or both may be indicated by an asterisk. In this case, an **int** argument supplies the field width or precision. The arguments specifying field width and precision shall appear (in that order) before the argument (if any) to be converted. If the precision takes the form of `.` followed by an asterisk such as `%3.*f`, it can be specified by an integer argument. For example,

```
> int i = 3
> printf("%*.*d", 5, i, 2)    // equivalent to printf("%5.3d", 2)
  002
> i = 6
> printf("%*.3f", i, 2.0)     // equivalent to printf("%6.3f", 2.0)
2.000
```

9.1.6 Using Flags in a Format-Control String

Adjustment *flags* are also available to supplement the output-formatting capabilities of the function **printf()**. They are placed immediately to the right of the percent sign. Multiple flags can be used in one conversion specification. The five available flag characters along with a description of each are listed in Table 9.5. These five flags provide additional control for the output format.

Program 9.6 provides several examples of using flags for specially formatting output. The output is shown below. Note that unless the plus sign flag is used, positive values do not display a + before the number.

```
Using minus sign flag.
     123.456000
123.456000

Using plus sign flag.
123.456000
-123.456000
+123.456000
-123.456000

Using space flag.
425
```

```
-425
 425
-425

Using # flag.
0142
0x62
0X62
12
12.0000

Using 0 flag.
00098
```

Table 9.5 Flag characters for the function printf().

Type	Description
– (minus sign)	The result of the conversion is left-justified within the field. It is right-justified if this flag is not specified.
+ (plus sign)	The result of a signed conversion always begin with a plus or minus sign. Displays a plus sign before positive values and a minus sign before negative values.
space #	Prints a space before a positive value not printed with the + flag. The result is converted to an "alternative form." For **o** conversion, prefix 0 to the output. For **x** (or **X**) conversion, prefix 0x (or 0X) to a nonzero result. For **e**, **E**, **f**, **g**, or **G** conversions, the result of converting a floating-point number always contains a decimal-point character, even if no digits follow it. For **g** and **G** conversions, trailing zeros are not removed from the result. For other conversions, the behavior is undefined.
0 (zero)	Leading zeros are used to pad the field width rather than blank spaces, except when converting infinity of NaN. If the **0** and – flags both appear, the **0** flag is ignored. For **d**, **i**, **o**, **u**, **x**, and **X**, if a precision is specified, then the **0** flag is ignored. For other conversions, the behavior is undefined.

```
/* File: flag.c
   Print output for integer and floating-point numbers with different flags. */
#include <stdio.h>

int main() {
    double d = 123.456;
    int i = 98;

    printf("\nUsing minus sign flag.\n");
    printf("%15f\n", d);
    printf("%-15f\n", d);
```

Program 9.6: Flags in formatted output. (*Continued*)

```
    printf("\nUsing plus sign flag.\n");
    printf("%f\n%f\n", d, -d);
    printf("%+f\n%+f\n", d, -d);

    printf("\nUsing space flag.\n");
    printf("%d\n%d\n", 425, -425);
    printf("% d\n% d\n", 425, -425);

    printf("\nUsing # flag.\n");
    printf("%#o\n", i);
    printf("%#x\n", i);
    printf("%#X\n", i);
    printf("%g\n", 12.0);
    printf("%#g\n", 12.0);

    printf("\nUsing 0 flag.\n");
    printf("%05d\n", i);

    return 0;
}
```

Program 9.6: *(Continued)*

9.2 Formatting Input for Functions in the scanf Family

Precise formatting input is accomplished by using the input function **scanf()**. The function **scanf()** has the following form:

```
scanf(format-control-string, arguments);
```

where `format-control-string` contains specifications to describe input format. Each specification begins with a percent sign (%), ends with a conversion specifier, and is enclosed in quotation marks. The *format-control-string* for the function **scanf()** is similar to the format-control-string discussed for the function **printf()**. The `arguments` are pointers to variables in which the input values will be stored. The conversion specifiers for the function **scanf()** are similar to the ones described for the function **printf()**. The format specifiers described in this section are applicable to the other input functions **fscanf()** and **sscanf()** in the **scanf** family.

If a conversion specification is invalid, the behavior is undefined. The conversion specifiers **A, E, F, G**, and **X** are also valid and behave the same as **a**, **e**, **f**, **g**, and **x**, respectively. If end-of-file (EOF) is encountered during input, conversion is terminated. If EOF occurs before any characters matching the current directive have been read (other than leading white space, where permitted), execution of the current directive terminates with an input failure; otherwise, unless execution of the current directive is terminated with a matching failure, execution of the following directive (other than **%n**, if any) is terminated with an input failure.

Trailing white space (including newline characters) is left unread unless matched by a directive. The success of literal matches and suppressed assignments is not directly determinable other than via the **%n** directive. If conversion terminates on a conflicting input character, the offending input character is left unread in the input stream.

9.2.1 Inputting an Integer

Table 9.6 lists the format specifiers for integer input using the function **scanf()**. Integers may be input as decimal, octal, or hexadecimal values. For example, the decimal integer 106 is input using different formats below.

```
> int i;
> scanf("%d", &i);         // decimal integer input
106
> i
106
> scanf("%i", &i);         // decimal integer input
106
> i
106
> scanf("%o", &i);         // octal integer input
152
> i
106
> scanf("%x", &i);         // hexadecimal integer input
                           // or 0x6A or 0X6A
6A
> i
106
```

Table 9.6 Conversion specifiers for integer input using the function scanf().

Type	Description
b	Matches an optionally signed binary integer. The corresponding argument shall be a pointer to unsigned integer (for Ch only).
d	Matches an optionally signed decimal integer. The corresponding argument shall be a pointer to signed integer.
i	Matches an optionally signed integer. The corresponding argument shall be a pointer to signed integer. It can be used to handle decimal, octal, and hexadecimal integers.
o	Matches an optionally signed octal integer. The corresponding argument shall be a pointer to unsigned integer.
u	Matches an optionally signed decimal integer. The corresponding argument shall be a pointer to unsigned integer.
x or **X**	Matches an optionally signed hexadecimal integer. The corresponding argument shall be a pointer to unsigned integer.

```
> scanf("%b", &i);       // binary integer input
1101010
> i
106
```

There is no difference in output when the format specifiers `"%d"` and `"%i"` are used in the output function **printf()**. However, these format specifiers are different when they are applied to the input function **scanf()**. The format specifier `"%d"` can be used only to obtain a signed decimal integer, whereas specifier `"%i"` can also be used to obtain an integer in octal or hexadecimal format. In the example below, a hexadecimal integer is input through the function **scanf()** with the `"%i"` conversion specifier.

```
> int i
> scanf("%i", &i)
0x6A
> i
106
```

For the input of an integral variable of short type, the modifier '**h**' has to be placed before the type conversion specifiers '**d**' or '**i**'. For example,

```
> short s
> scanf("%hd", &s)
18
> s
18
```

9.2.2 Inputting a Floating-Point Number

Similar to printing floating-point numbers, the conversion specifiers shown in Table 9.7 can be used to input a floating-point number with the function **scanf()**. Note that a length modifier `l` preceding a conversion specifier such as `"%lf"` specifies type double, whereas a preceding `L` is for type long double. Unlike the

Table 9.7 Conversion specifiers for floating-point input using the function scanf().

Type	Description
a	Matches an optionally signed floating-point number whose format is in the style *[-]0xh.hhhhp±d*, or an infinity or NaN.
e	Matches an optionally signed floating-point number in exponential form, or an infinity or NaN.
f	Matches an optionally signed floating-point number in decimal format, or an infinity or NaN.
g	Matches an optionally signed floating-point number in either decimal or exponential form, or an infinity or NaN.

function **printf()**, the format specifier "%f" cannot be applied to the function **scanf()** to get a floating-point number for a variable of type double. Below are examples of inputting floating-point number 123.45 in various formats.

```
> float f
> scanf("%f", &f);          // float input
123.45
> f
123.45
> double d
> scanf("%lf", &d);         // double input decimal form
123.4500
> scanf("%le", &d);         // double input in exponential form
1.2345e+02
> d
123.45
```

9.2.3 Inputting Characters and Strings

Table 9.8 lists the format conversion specifiers for inputting characters and strings. Specifier **c** is for characters and **s** is for strings. Program 9.7 is an interactive program that prompts the user to enter a character and string to print the values entered. Executing the program with input character 'a' and input string "This" would produce the following result:

```
> scanfstr.c
Please enter a character: a
The input character was: a
Please enter a string: This
The input string was: This
```

The string length for the variable str is 4 without a carriage return character at the end.

Table 9.8 Conversion specifiers for characters and strings input using the function scanf().

Type	Description
c	Matches a sequence of characters of exactly the number specified by the field width (1 if no field width is present in the directive). If no **l** length modifier is present, the corresponding argument shall be a pointer to the initial element of a character array large enough to accept the sequence. No null character is added. If an **l** length modifier is present, the input shall be a sequence of multibyte characters.
s	Matches a sequence of non-white-space characters. If no **l** length modifier is present, the corresponding argument shall be a pointer to the initial element of a character array large enough to accept the sequence and a terminating null character, which will be added automatically. If an **l** length modifier is present, the input shall be a sequence of multibyte characters.

```
/* File: scanfstr.c
   Demonstrate how to input characters and strings */
#include <stdio.h>

int main() {
    char c, str[50];

    printf("Please enter a character: ");
    scanf("%c", &c);
    printf("The input character was: %c\n", c);

    printf("Please enter a string: ");
    scanf("%s", str);
    printf("The input string was: %s\n", str);

    return 0;
}
```

Program 9.7: Formatted input for characters and strings.

9.2.4 Miscellaneous Input Conversion Specifiers

Table 9.9 lists the remaining conversion specifiers available for the function **scanf()**. The specifier **p** is used to read in the address of a variable. The specifier **n** is used to count and store the number of characters input thus far in the function **scanf()**. The conversion specifier **%** allows for a percent sign to be skipped in the input. Examples of using the above conversion specifiers for the function **scanf()** is as follows:

```
> int i = 5
> int *iptr
> &i
0x81a42c4
> scanf("%p", &iptr)
0x81a42c4
> iptr
0x8142c4
> int n
> char str[10]
> scanf("%d%n", &i, &n)
1234
> i
1234
> n
4
> scanf("%%%s", str)
%sign
> str
sign
```

Table 9.9 Miscellaneous input conversion specifiers.

Type	Description
p	Matches an implementation-defined set of sequences, which should be the same as the set of sequences that may be produced by the **%p** conversion of the function **fprintf**(). The corresponding argument shall be a pointer to pointer to **void**. The input item is converted to a pointer value in an implementation-defined manner. If the input item is a value converted earlier during the same program execution, the pointer that results shall be equal to that value; otherwise, the behavior of the **%p** conversion is undefined.
n	No input is consumed. The corresponding argument shall be a pointer to signed int into which is to be written the number of characters read from the input stream so far by this call to the function **scanf**(). Execution of a **%n** directive does not increment the assignment count returned at the completion of executing of the **scanf**() function. No argument is converted, but one is consumed. If the conversion specification includes an assignment-suppressing character or a field width, the behavior is undefined.
%	Matches a single % character; no conversion or assignment occurs. The complete conversion specification shall be %%.
[] (*scanset*)	Matches a nonempty sequence of characters from a set of expected characters (the scanset). If no **l** length modifier is present, the corresponding argument shall be a pointer to the initial element of a character array large enough to accept the sequence and a terminating null character, which will be added automatically.
[^] (*inverted scanset*)	Matches a nonempty sequence of characters that does not appear in the list of characters (scanlist) between the circumflex (^) and the right bracket. If no **l** length modifier is present, the corresponding argument shall be a pointer to the initial element of a character array large enough to accept the sequence and a terminating null character, which will be added automatically.

The function **scanf()** also allows for the input of a sequence of characters through the use of a *scan set*, which is a set of characters enclosed in square brackets [] and preceded by a percent sign (%). The scan set causes the function **scanf()** to search for characters in the input stream that matches those in the scan set. Only those matching characters are stored in the corresponding argument for a scan set; that is, a pointer to **char**. The scan set operation terminates once a character not contained in the scan set is encountered. For example,

```
> char s[10], r[10]
> scanf("%[abcde]%s", s, r)
acbdxyze
> s
acbd
> r
xyze
```

Notice that only `"acbd"` are written into the variable `s`. The remaining string is written into the variable `r`.

Aside from the scan set, the *inverted scan set* can also be used for character input. The inverted scan set does the exact opposite of a regular scan set. This means that only characters not appearing within the square brackets are stored inside the **char *** argument. An inverted scan set may be identified by a caret ^ within the square brackets and preceding the character sets. For example,

```
> char s[10]
> scanf("%[^aeiou]", s)
xyzdefabc
> s
xyzd
```

Here, the list for the inverted scanset contains all the vowels in the alphabet. The function **scanf()** stores only the characters up to the first occurrence of any of one of the vowels.

9.2.5 Assignment Suppression

Within the format-control-string, the *assignment suppression character* * allows the function **scanf()** to ignore any unnecessary characters from the input. For example,

```
> int hr, min, sec
> scanf("%d%*c%d%*c%d", &hr, &min, &sec)
3:15:25
> hr
3
> min
15
> sec
25
```

In the above example, the assignment suppression character was used in conjunction with the **%c** conversion specifier to indicate that a character, **:** in this case, should be read but not stored in a variable. The results of inputting a time are stored in integer variables `hr`, `min`, and `sec`.

When a character such as `'c'` is typed as an input from a keyboard, there are two characters in the input stream: one is 'c' and the other is the newline character `'\n'`. The ASCII value of the character `'\n'` is 10, as listed in Appendix D. The *assignment suppression character* * can be used to suppress the newline character as shown in Program 9.8. A sample interactive execution of Program 9.8 is shown below.

```
> scanfchar.c
Please enter a character: a
The input character is: a
Please enter a character: b
The input character is: b
The ASCII value of the second character is: 10
```

```
/* File: scanfchar.c
   Demonstrate how to suppress a newline character in the input */
#include <stdio.h>

int main() {
    char c, c2;

    printf("Please enter a character: ");
    /* suppress the newline character using '%*c' */
    scanf("%c%*c", &c);
    printf("The input character is: %c\n", c);

    printf("Please enter a character: ");
    /* the input newline character is received in c2 */
    scanf("%c%c", &c, &c2);
    printf("The input character is: %c\n", c);
    printf("The ASCII value of the second character is: %d\n", c2);
    return 0;
}
```

Program 9.8: Suppressing the newline character in the input.

Not only characters, but also numerical values, can be suppressed. For example,

```
> int i
> float x
> char name[10], name2[10]
> scanf("%2d%f%*d %[0123456789]%s", &i, &x, name, name2)
56789 0123 34a72
> i
56
> x
789.00
> name
34
> name2
a72
```

where `56` is stored in `i` of type int with the specifier `"%2d"`; `789` is stored in `f` of type float with the specifier `"%f"`; `0123` is suppressed with `"%*d"`; `"34"` is stored into the character array `name` using a scanset in the function **scanf**(): the remaining string `"a72"` is stored in `name2`. The white space inside the control format of the function **scanf**() is used to skip the space before 34 in the input string. Without this white space, no character would be read into the string `name` and the value for the string `name2` would be `"34a72"`.

As another example, if a student's identification number, name, the year of birth, and GPA (grade point average) are input in the format

```
101, John, 1985,· 3.33
```

or

```
101,   John,   1985,   3.33
```

it can be processed with the format string shown below:

```
> int id;
> char name[32];
> short year;
> double gpa;
> scanf("%d%*[, ]%[^,]%*c%hd%*c%lf", &id, name, &year, &gpa);
101,   John,   1985,   3.33
> name
John
> gpa
> 3.3300
```

where the format specifier `"%*[, ]"` suppresses the comma and multiple white spaces before the name, the specifier `"%[^,]"` reads the name excluding a comma, and the commas in the input are suppressed by the specifier `"%*c"`. Note that for an integer of short type such as the variable `year`, the format specifier has to be `"%hd"` or `"%hi"` with a modifier `h`. On the other hand, for a variable of type double, the format specifier has to be `"%lf"` with a modifier `l` for type double. The white space in the front of a numerical number is skipped when it is read using the function **scanf**().

9.3 Inputting Numbers Using getnum()

The function **getnum**() with the prototype of

```
double getnum(char *msg, double d);
```

obtains a real number as a return value from the console through the standard input stream. If no value is entered by just hitting the carriage return key, then the default value passed from the second argument is returned. The first argument is a message string that can be used to prompt the user to enter an input value. For example,

```
> double d
> d = getnum("Please enter a number[10.0]: ", 10);
Please enter a number[10.0]:
90
> d
90.0000
```

Notice that `10.0` is shown in the message string between two square brackets to indicate that it is a default value. The C source code for the function **getnum**() is presented in Program 12.6 in Chapter 12. The function is available in Ch by default.

Exercises

1. Identify and correct the errors, if there are any, in the following programs. If there are any, briefly explain why they are wrong.

   a.
```
#include <stdio.h>
int main () {
  printf("str = %f\n", "ABCD");
}
```
   b.
```
#include <stdio.h>
int main () {
  double d = 10;
  printf("d = %f\n", d);
  scanf("%f", &d);
  printf("d = %f\n", d);
}
```
   c.
```
#include <stdio.h>
int main () {
  int i,
  for(i=0, i<10; i++)
     printf("i = %f\n", i);
}
```

2. Write a program with three variables of double type. The format specifiers **lf**, **le**, and **lg** are used for **scanf()** to read the user input of three floating-point numbers with the value 1.234. Print the values of each variable using these format specifiers for the function **printf()** as well.
3. Show what is printed by each of the following statements. If a statement is incorrect, explain why.

   a. `printf("%-10d\n", 10000);`
   b. `printf("%c\n", "This is a string");`
   c. `printf("%*.*lf\n", 8, 3, 1024.978654);`
   d. `printf("%\#o\n%#X\n%#e\n", 17, 17, 1008.83689);`
   e. `printf("% ld\n%+ld\n", 1000000, 1000000);`
   f. `printf("%10.2E\n", 444.93738);`
   g. `printf("%10.2g\n", 444.93738);`
   h. `printf("%g\n", 444.0);`
   i. `printf("%10g\n", 444.0);`
   j. `printf("%10.2g\n", 444.0);`
   k. `printf("%d\n", 10.987);`

4. Write a statement calling the function **printf()** or **scanf()** for each of the following:

   a. Print the unsigned integer 40000 left-justified in a 15-digit field.
   b. Print 12.3456 left-justified in a 15-digit field with 3 digits after the decimal point.
   c. Read a hexadecimal value into the variable `hex`.
   d. Print 200 with and without a plus sign.
   e. Print 100 in hexadecimal form preceded by `0x`.
   f. Read characters into the array `s` until the letter `p` is encountered.

g. Print 1.234 in a 9-digit field with preceding zcros.
h. Read a time of the form `hh:mm:ss`, storing the parts of the time in the integer variables `hour`, `minute`, and `second`. Skip the colons (`:`) in the input stream. Use the assignment-suppression character.
i. Read a string of the form `"characters"` from the standard input. Store the string in character array `s`. Eliminate the quotation marks from the input stream.
j. Read a time of the form `hh:mm:ss`, storing the parts of the time in the integer variables `hour`, `minute`, and `second`. Skip the colons (`:`) in the input stream. Do not use the assignment-suppression character.

5. Write a program using a loop to print out the the following sequence:

```
10.0, 9.5, 9.0, 8.5, 8.0, 7.5, 7.0, 6.5, 6.0, 5.5,
5.0, 4.5, 4.0, 3.5, 3.0, 2.5, 2.0, 1.5, 1.0
```

6. Write a program that calculates the area and perimeter of a rectangle. The area and perimeter are calculated using two separate functions that both take two arguments of double type for the width and length of the rectangle. Calculate the area and perimeter using these two functions in the main program with the width and length of the rectangle typed in as a standard input from the command-line prompt.
7. Write a function `printTriangle()` using a **for** loop to print out a triangle. The argument of the function `printTriangle()` is the number of lines for the triangle to be printed out. The following code fragment

```
void printTriangle(int n);
int main() {
    printTriangle(4);
    printTrianglc(8);
    return 0;
}
```

shall print out the output shown below:

```
   *
  ***
 *****
*******
       *
      ***
     *****
    *******
   *********
  ***********
 *************
***************
```

8. Write a program with a **for** loop, but without an **if** or **switch** statement, to display each output shown below.

a.

```
    1      0.1234
   10      1.2340
  100     12.3400
 1000    123.4000
10000   1234.0000
```

b.

```
    1   1.234E-01
   10   1.234E+00
  100   1.234E+01
 1000   1.234E+02
10000   1.234E+03
```

c.

```
 2N   20N   200N       2000N
---------------------------
  2    20    200     2000.00
  4    40    400     4000.00
  6    60    600     6000.00
  8    80    800     8000.00
 10   100   1000    10000.00
```

d.

```
2N     20N    200N    2000N
-------------------------
2      20     200     2000.00
4      40     400     4000.00
6      60     600     6000.00
8      80     800     8000.00
10     100    1000    10000.00
```

9. Write the output of the following program when it is executed:

```
#include <stdio.h>
#include <stdbool.h>
int main() {
    int i1 = 0b0110;
    int i2 = 0b1101;
    int i3 = 0X1A;
    printf("i1 = %d\n", i1);
    printf("i2 = %d\n", i2);
    printf("i3 = %d\n", i3);
    printf("i2 = %x\n", i2);
    printf("i2 = %X\n", i2);
```

```
    printf("i1 | i2 = %b\n", i1 | i2);
    printf("i1 & i2 = %b\n", i1 & i2);
    return 0;
}
```

10. As in Exercise 36 in Chapter 5, use a variable of double type for temperatures in Celsius. Print out temperatures in Celsius without decimal points and temperatures in Fahrenheit with only two digits after the decimal point in the temperature conversion table.

11. The information for a student includes student ID, name, birthday (month, day, and year), and GPA. Write a program to obtain the student information from the terminal in the following three formats:

a. `101 John 12 11 1985 3.33`
b. `101, John, 12, 11, 1985, 3.33`
c. `101:John:12:11:1985:3.33`

The ID shall be saved in a variable of int type, the name in an array of char, the birthday in variables of type short, and GPA in a variable of type double.

12. As in Exercise 33 (a) and (b) in Chapter 5, use an assignment suppression character * to suppress the newline character entered from the terminal.

13. Modify Program 3.7 in Chapter 3 to use the function **getnum()** with default values of 5 kg for mass, 0.2 for kinetic friction coefficient, and 2 seconds for time.

CHAPTER 10

Arrays

Arrays are commonly used programming features for computation with large sets of data in engineering and science. An *array* is an aggregate data structure consisting of related data items that extend in one or more dimensions to represent columns, planes, cubes, etc. All elements in an array have the same name and data type. In this chapter, arrays and its applications are presented first. Next, vectors and matrices are briefly introduced because arrays are often associated with vector and matrix analysis. Finally, using arrays in scientific computation is illustrated by solving linear systems of equations numerically.

10.1 Declaration of Arrays

10.1.1 One-Dimensional Arrays

A one-dimensional array is declared with the following format:

```
type name[expr];
```

where the symbol `type` contains the declaration specifiers that specify a data type of each array element, such as int. The symbol `name` is a declarator that contains an identifier. The delimiters `[` and `]` delimit an optional integral expression `expr` that specifies the number of elements of the array. If `expr` is a constant integral expression, it shall have a value greater than zero. In C99, `expr` does not have to be a constant expression. If it is not a constant expression, it is evaluated at program execution time and shall evaluate to a value greater than zero. An array whose size is determined at program execution time is called a *variable length array* (VLA), which will be discussed in section 10.7. If the integral size expression `expr` is not present, the array type is incomplete. An incomplete array occurs in array declaration, function arguments, and external declaration. They are completed by array initialization, a function call, and a declaration, which will be described later in this chapter.

For example, the statement

```
int a[6];
```

declares a one-dimensional array named `a`. Array `a` consists of six elements, which have an integer data type. The elements of an array can be referred by the following format:

```
name[position_number]
```

where `position_number` is also known as an array *subscript*. Note that the first element of an array is by default at position 0, not at position 1. For example, the six elements of array `a` can be represented as `a[0]`, `a[1]`, `a[2]`, `a[3]`, `a[4]`, and `a[5]` and used as shown following.

```
> int a[6], i
> a[0] = 10
10
> a[5] = 2*a[0]
20
> i = a[0]+a[5]
30
```

In this example, element `a[0]` is assigned the value 10 first. Its value is then multiplied by 2 and assigned to the element `a[5]`. The sum of elements `a[0]` and `a[5]` is assigned to the variable `i`.

The input and output for an element `a[i]` of array `a` can be treated as if `a[i]` is a simple variable, as shown below.

```
> scanf("%d", &a[2]);
20
> printf("a[2] = %d", a[2]);
a[2] = 20
```

10.1.2 Two-Dimensional Arrays

Two-dimensional arrays require two expressions in their declarations: one for the row size and one for the column size. Similar to a one-dimensional array, a two-dimensional array can be declared using the following format:

```
type name[expr1][expr2];
```

where `expr1` and `expr2` are integral expressions. The value of `expr1` specifies the number of rows of the array, whereas the value of `expr2` specifies the number of columns of the array. For example, the statement

```
int b[2][3];
```

declares a 2×3 array. This means that array `b` consists of two rows and three columns. The elements of a two-dimensional array can be referred by the following format:

```
name[row_subscript][column_subscript]
```

where `row_subscript` specifies the row position of the element and `column_subscript` specifies the column position. By default, each subscript also begins with 0, such that `b[0][0]` is the first element in the first row of array `b` in the above example.

10.1.3 Definitions Related to Arrays

The number of dimensions in an array is referred to as the *rank* of the array. The number of elements in a dimension is called the *extent* of the array in that dimension. The *shape* of an array is a vector where each element of the vector is the extent in the corresponding dimension of the array. The *size* of an array is the number of bytes used to store the total number of elements of the array. For example: consider the array declaration below.

```
int c[3][4];
```

The rank of array c is 2, and the extents corresponding to the first and second dimensions are 3 and 4, respectively. The shape of the array is a vector with two elements 3 and 4, that is, (3, 4). The size of the array is `sizeof(int)*3*4 = 4*3*4 = 48` bytes.

10.1.4 The Size of an Array

The size of an array can be calculated by the **sizeof** operator in bytes. For example:

```
> int a[6]
> sizeof(a)
24
> int c[3][4]
> sizeof(c)
48
> double d[3][4]
> sizeof(d)
96
> char s[6]
> sizeof(s)
6
```

10.2 How Arrays Are Stored in Memory

When an array is declared, memory is allocated automatically with respect to its type and extent(s). Arrays are grouped in consecutive memory locations. For example, a sample memory layout for the one-dimensional array a of six elements of **int** type declared below

```
int a[6];
```

is shown in Figure 10.1. Thus array a occupies 24 consecutive bytes of memory, because each integer element takes up 4 bytes. For example, memory location 0x2008 refers to element a[2] of the array.

Sample memory layout for the two-dimensional array b of **int** type declared below

```
int b[2][3];
```

is shown in Figure 10.2. Array b as shown in Figure 10.2 (a) has six elements with two horizontal rows and three vertical columns. From a programming point of view, it is a block of memory with each row of the array lying in a contiguous block of memory as shown in Figure 10.2 (b). The memory layout for the two-dimensional array b is similar to that of the one-dimensional array a as shown in Figure 10.1. In general, for a two-dimensional array c declared as

```
int c[M][N];
```

the expression c[i][j] refers to the element [i][j] in row i and column j of the array c. The offset of the memory for this element of type int from the beginning of the memory for the array is `(i*N+j)*sizeof(int)` in bytes. It is the $(i * N + j + 1)$th element of the array starting from the beginning in row-by-row order. As an example, for the two-dimensional array b, M is 2 and N is 3. The expression b[1][0], with 1 for i and 0 for j, refers to the element [1][0] in the second row (row 1) and

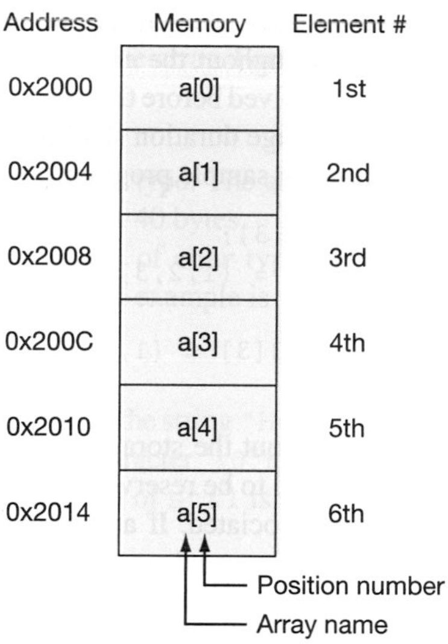

Figure 10.1: A one-dimensional array and its sample memory layout starting at the sample memory address 0x2000.

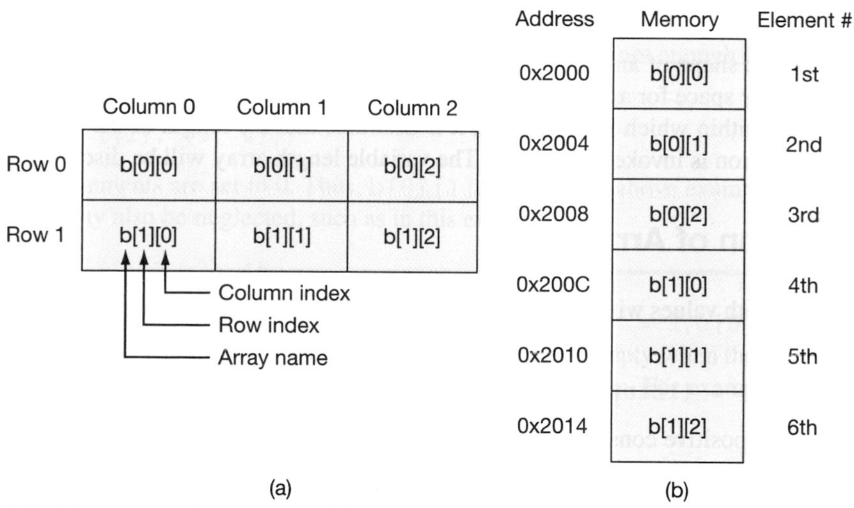

Figure 10.2: A 2x3 two-dimensional array and its row-wise memory layout starting at the sample memory address 0x2000.

first column (column 0). The offset for element `b[1][0]` from the beginning of the memory for the array is 12 bytes, calculated by the expression `((1*N+0)*sizeof(int))`. Assume that the address for array `b` starts at 0x2000 and the address for element `b[1][0]`, the fourth element of the array, is 0x200C.

Storage duration determines the lifetime of an object as described in section 8.2.1 in Chapter 8. An array declared with external linkage (global variable) or internal linkage (static variable in the file scope), or with the storage-class specifier **static** (static variable inside a function), has *static storage duration.* For such an array,

```
    /* calculate the mean value. */
    meanval = sum / N;
    printf("The mean value of the array is %f\n", meanval);
    return 0;
}
```

Program 10.2: *(Continued)*

Minimum and Maximum

Program 10.3 finds the minimum value in the array `a`. The variable `minval` is first assigned with the value of the first element `a[0]` of the array. It is then compared with all other elements one by one in a **for** loop. The index variable `i` for the loop starts with 1 so that the first element will be compared with the second element `a[1]` in the first iteration. If the value for a new element is smaller than the value saved in the variable `minvalue`. The value for the new element will be assigned to the variable `minval`. At the end of the iteration, the variable `minval` contains the minimum value of the array. If there are multiple copies of the minimum value in the array, `minval` contains the first minimum value of the array.

To find the maximum value in an array, the conditional expression of the **if** statement in Program 10.3

```
a[i] < minval
```

```
/* File: minimum.c
   Find the minimum value in an array */
#include <stdio.h>

#define N 8   /* number of elements for array a */

int main() {
    /* declare array a with initialization */
    double a[N] = {3.0, 21.0, 0.0, -3.0, 34.0, -14.0, 45.0, 18.0};
    double minval;  /* minimum value */
    int i;          /* variable for array index */

    minval = a[0];  /* initialize to the first element */
    /* loop through the array starting with the second element */
    for(i= 1; i < N; i++) {
        if(a[i] < minval) {  /* if a[i] < minval, set new minval */
            minval = a[i];
        }
    }
    printf("The minimum value of the array is %f\n", minval);
    return 0;
}
```

Program 10.3: Finding the minimum value for elements in an array.

needs to be changed to

```
a[i] > maxval
```

The output of Program 10.3 is given below:

```
The minimum value of the array is -14.000000
```

Sorting

Sorting data is an important function of computers. For example, one may sort a student record in a class based on the midterm or final examination scores of the students for the class. Program 10.4 lists the pseudocode for sorting the values in an array with N elements into ascending order. The sorting algorithm used in Program 10.4 is called the *bubble sort* illustrated in Figure 10.3. As the algorithm is processed, the smaller values will gradually propagate toward the top of the array like air bubbles rising in the water, whereas the larger values will sink to the bottom of the array. The algorithm processes the array through several iterations. After the first iteration, the smallest number will be sorted out and placed at the top of the array. After the second iteration, the second smallest number will be sorted out and placed at the second element of the array. At each iteration, the largest number in the remaining elements of the array will be sorted out.

Program 10.4 uses nested **for** loops to implement the algorithm for a bubble sort. During each iteration in the outer loop with the loop control variable `i`, a smaller number in the array will be propagated toward the top. For an N-element array, there are only N-1 iterations needed. In the first iteration with `i` equal to 0, the program compares `a[i]` with `a[1]`, then with `a[2]`, until it finishes comparison with `a[N-2]`. This comparison is performed by the inner **for** loop with the loop control variable `j` incrementing from `i+1` to N−1.

```
// File: sort.p
// Pseudocode for bubble sort

declare array a[N] with index from 0 to N-1

// find the smallest value in the remaining part of
// the array in each iteration starting with a[i]
for i = 0, 1, ..., N-2
    // compare a[i] with a[j] for j from i+1 to N-1
    for j = i+1, ..., N-1
        // when a[i] > a[j], swap their values
        if(a[i] > a[j])
            temp = a[i]
            a[i] = a[j]
            a[j] = temp
        endif
    endfor
endfor
```

Program 10.4: Pseudocode for sorting an array in ascending order using the bubble sort.

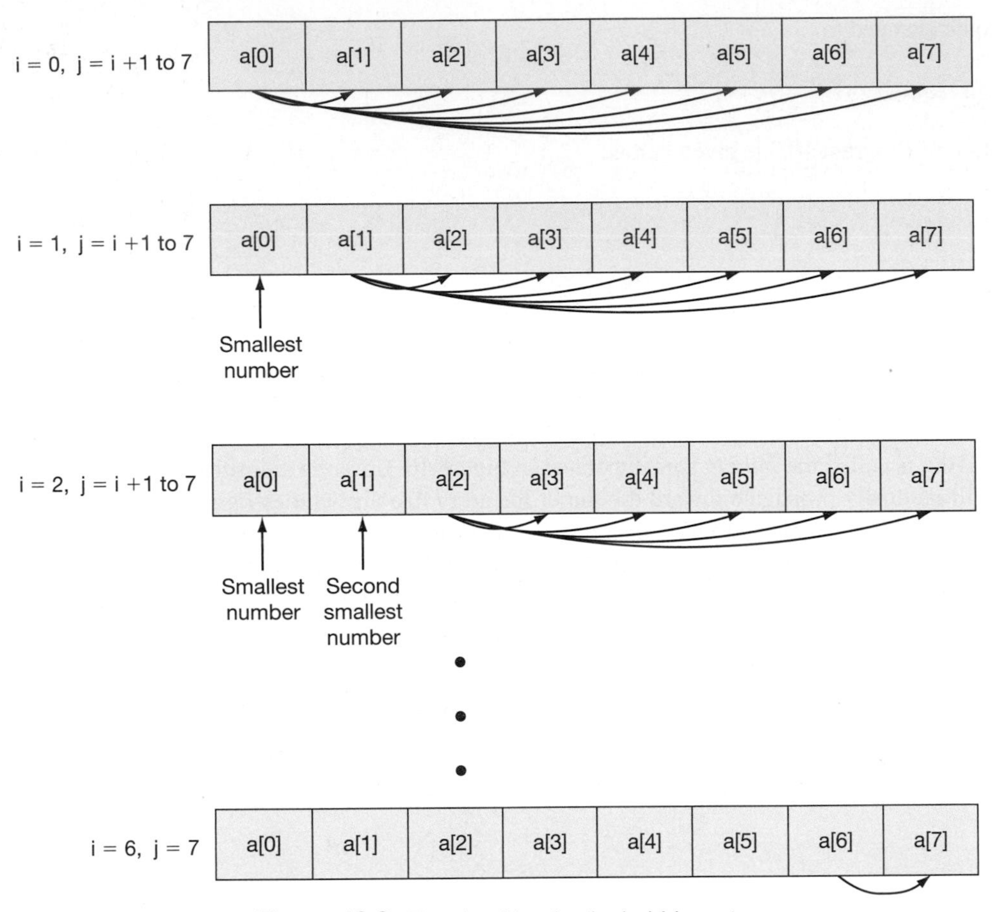

Figure 10.3: The algorithm for the bubble sort.

The value of the loop control variable `i` for the outer loop is used as the initial value `i+1` of the loop control variable `j` of the inner loop at each iteration. If `a[i]` is larger than `a[j]`, the swap is necessary, which is performed using the following three assignment operations:

```
temp = a[i]
a[i] = a[j]
a[j] = temp
```

The variable `temp` holds the value `a[i]` temporarily for swapping. After the first iteration, element `a[0]` contains the smallest value. In the second iteration, we only need to compare `a[1]` with the remaining elements from `a[2]` to `a[N-1]`. After the second iteration, element `a[1]` contains the second smallest number in the array. At the last iteration, elements `a[6]` and `a[N-1]` will be compared. The largest number will sink to element `a[N-1]`.

Program 10.5 is an implementation of the pseudocode in Program 10.4 in C. It sorts the values in an eight-element array into ascending order. The sorted array is printed at each iteration in the outer **for** loop. When Program 10.5 is executed, the values in the original array and at each iteration are printed out as shown in Figure 10.4.

To sort the array in descending order, only the conditional expression of the **if** statement in Programs 10.4 and 10.5 needs to be changed to

```
a[i] < a[j]
```

The bubble sort is not efficient for sorting a large list. To sort a large number of data, the quicksort algorithm is more efficient. The strategy of the quicksort is to divide a list into two sublists, then recursively sort two sublists. C provides a standard function **qsort()** for sorting lists based on the quicksort algorithm, which will be presented in section 11.12 in Chapter 11.

```
/* File: sort.c
   Sort an array using the bubble sort algorithm */
#include <stdio.h>

#define N 8    /* number of elements for array a */

int main() {
    /* declare array a with initialization */
    double a[N] = {3.0, 21.0, 0.0, -3.0, 34.0, -14.0, 45.0, 18.0};
    double temp;   /* temporary for swap */
    int i, j;      /* variables for array index */

    printf("The original data:\n");
    for(i = 0; i < N; i++) {  /* print the original array */
        printf("%g ", a[i]);
    }
    printf("\nThe sorted data in each iteration:\n");
    /* find the smallest value in the remaining part of
       the array in each iteration staring with a[i] */
    for(i = 0; i < N-1; i++) {
        /* compare a[i] with a[j] for j from i+1 to N-1 */
        for(j = i+1; j < N; j++) {
            if(a[i] > a[j]) {  /* when a[i] > a[j], swap their values */
                temp = a[i];
                a[i] = a[j];
                a[j] = temp;
            }
        }
        for(j = 0; j < N; j++) { /* print the array in each iteration */
            printf("%g ", a[j]);
        }
        printf("\n");
    }
    return 0;
}
```

Program 10.5: Sorting an array in ascending order with the bubble sort.

```
The original data:
3 21 0 -3 34 -14 45 18
The sorted data in each iteration:
-14 21 3 0 34 -3 45 18
-14 -3 21 3 34 0 45 18
-14 -3 0 21 34 3 45 18
-14 -3 0 3 34 21 45 18
-14 -3 0 3 18 34 45 21
-14 -3 0 3 18 21 45 34
-14 -3 0 3 18 21 34 45
```

Figure 10.4: The output from Program 10.5.

Application Examples

Acceleration of a Moving Body

Problem Statement:
For the mechanical system shown in Figure 2.12, given mass $m = 5$ kilograms (kg) and coefficient of kinetic friction $\mu = 0.2$, the applied force p is expressed as a function of time t in

$$p(t) = \begin{cases} 20 & \text{if} \quad t \leq 3 \\ 4(t+2) & \text{if} \quad t > 3 \end{cases}$$

Write a program to calculate and print the acceleration **a** when $t = 0$ to $t = 10$ seconds with a step size of 1 second.

Program 10.6 provides a simple solution to the above problem statement. A program should be as portable as possible and the size of particular arrays may depend upon the application. To change many array sizes for a large program would be a time-consuming and error-prone task. It is a common practice to define a macro for a constant. Then use this macro as the size of arrays in the declaration. The macro `N` is defined with the value of 11. Arrays `a` and `t` with `N` elements each are declared to store values for the respective acceleration and time values at intervals of 1 second. A **for** loop is used to calculate the acceleration value at each time step. Inside the loop, the formula (10.1) is used to calculate each element of array `t` for time in the range from 0 to 10 seconds. Another **for** loop is used to display the time and acceleration. We could have placed this printing statement near the end of the first **for** loop. For clarity, we use a separate **for** loop to display the result. The output of Program 10.6 is shown in Figure 10.5.

```
/* File: accelarray.c
   Calculate the acceleration using arrays for accel and time
   using 11 points  */
#include <stdio.h>
#include <math.h>
#define M_G   9.81   /* gravitational acceleration constant g */
#define N     11     /* num of points for arrays a and t*/
```

Program 10.6: Calculating accelerations and time using arrays. (*Continued*)

```
int main() {
    double a[N], t[N];          /* arrays a for accel and t for time */
    double mu, m, p;            /* mu, m for mass, and p for force */
    double t0, tf;              /* initial and final times */
    int i;                      /* variable for array index */

    /* set mu, mass, initial time, and final time */
    mu = 0.2;                   /* set mu */
    m = 5.0;                    /* set mass to 5 kg */
    t0 = 0.0;                   /* initial time 0 */
    tf = 10.0;                  /* final time 10 seconds */
    /* processing data */
    for(i=0; i<N; i++) {         /* using a for-loop to set t[i] and a[i] */
        t[i] = t0+i*(tf - t0)/(N-1); /* calculate t[i] */
        p = 4*sin(t[i]-3)+20;        /* use t[i] to calculate p */
        a[i] = (p-mu*m*M_G)/m;       /* calculate a[i] */
    }

    /* display the output */
    printf(" time (s)  accel (m/s^2)\n");
    printf("-------------------------\n");
    for(i=0; i<N; i++) {
        printf("%8.4f    %8.4f\n", t[i], a[i]);
    }
    return 0;
}
```

Program 10.6: *(Continued)*

```
  time    accel (m/s^2)
-----------------------
  0.0000     1.9251
  1.0000     1.3106
  2.0000     1.3648
  3.0000     2.0380
  4.0000     2.7112
  5.0000     2.7654
  6.0000     2.1509
  7.0000     1.4326
  8.0000     1.2709
  9.0000     1.8145
 10.0000     2.5636
```

Figure 10.5: The output from Program 10.6 and Program 11.10 in Chapter 11 when n is 11.

Evaluation of Polynomial Functions

Problem Statement:
Evaluate the polynomial function

$$p(x) = 2x^5 - 5x^4 + 10x^3 - 10x^2 + 5x - 1 \tag{10.3}$$

at $x = 0.1$.

Polynomial functions are commonly used in engineering and science. There is no exponential operator in C. The function **pow()** with the function prototype

```
extern double pow(double x, double y);
```

declared in the header file **math.h**, can be used to calculate the exponential expression. The mathematical expression x^5 can be translated into the C expression `x*x*x*x*x` or using a function call `pow(x, 5)`. However, for calculating x^5, the expression `x*x*x*x*x` is more efficient than the function call `pow(x, 5)` because of the overhead in calling a function.

Therefore, a straightforward method for evaluation of a polynomial would sum up as

```
2*x*x*x*x*x - 5*x*x*x*x + 10*x*x*x - 10*x*x + 5*x - 1
```

which involves 15 multiplications and 5 additions and subtractions. This method is error-prone for a high-order polynomial because of the accumulation of relative errors in each operation.

A better approach is to evaluate the polynomial using

```
(((((2*x-5)*x+10)*x-10)*x)+5)*x-1
```

with only 5 multiplications and 5 additions and subtractions. For a high-order polynomial, the saving of multiplications is significant. For example, for a 100th-order polynomial, the first method would use 5050 multiplications versus 100 multiplications for the second one.

For a high-order polynomial, a recursive approach using an array can simplify the modeling and evaluation. For the numerical computation, a polynomial of

$$p(x) = c_0x^n + c_1x^{n-1} + \cdots + c_{n-1}x + c_n$$

can be represented by an array `c` with $(n+1)$ elements of $[c_0, c_1, \ldots, c_{n-1}, c_n]$ using its coefficients. Then, use a loop to evaluate it recursively as shown below.

```
p = c[0];
for(i=1; i<=n; i++)
    p = p*x + c[i];
```

For example, Program 10.7 evaluates the 5th polynomial in equation (10.3) at $x = 0.1$. The coefficients of the polynomial are presented in an array with six elements. The output from Program 10.7 is as follows:

```
x=0.10  p=-0.590480
```

A large number of numerical analysis functions related to polynomials is available in Ch. They can readily be used for the polynomial evaluation **ployeval()**, multiplication **conv()**, division **deconv()**, curve-fitting **polyfit()**, etc.

```
/* File: polynomial.c
   Evaluate a polynomial recursively    */
#include <stdio.h>

#define N 6  /* 5th order polynomial with 6 coefficients */

int main() {
    /* 5th order polynomial 2x^5 - 5x^4 + 10x^3 - 10x^2 + 5x - 1 */
    double c[N]={2, -5.0, 10.0, -10.0, 5.0, -1.0}, /* polynomial coefficients */
           p,        /* polynomial value */
           x;        /* x in the polynomial */
    int i;           /* variable for array index */

    x=0.1;           /* set x value */
    p = c[0];        /* initialize p for recursive evaluation */
    for(i=1; i<N; i++) {
       p = p*x + c[i];  /* recursive evaluation of polynomial */
    }
    printf("x=%.2f  p=%f\n", x, p);
    return 0;
}
```

Program 10.7: Evaluating a polynomial recursively using an array.

Random Number Generation: Rolling a Six-Sided Die

Problem Statement:
Simulate the rolling of a six-sided die 6000 times and record the number of times it falls on each face.

Program 5.18 in Chapter 5 simulates the rolling of a six-sided die 6000 times and records the number of times it falls on each face. The frequency for each face is kept in a variable. Six variables `freq1` to `freq6` are used for six different faces. Program 5.18 can be modified to use a single variable of array type for frequencies of six different faces. Program 10.8 uses a six-element array `freq` as a counter for each face of the die. Using the variable `face` as an array index for the array `freq`, the switch statement in Program 5.18 is replaced by a single-assignment expression statement

```
freq[face-1] += 1;
```

Because the array elements are from `freq[0]` to `freq[5]`, whereas the values for the variable `face` ranges from 1 to 6, the subscript of the array is offset by 1. Using an array, the frequency for each face can be printed out using a loop conveniently. For alignment of the output, the format specification with a field width of 12 is used to print out the string `"Frequency"` and counters for each face of the die. Because Programs 5.18 and 10.8 are supposed to simulate the random rolling of the die 6000 times, the output of either program will be different for every program execution. The result of one run-time execution of

Program 10.8 is shown below.

```
Face    Frequency
  1          978
  2         1060
  3          972
  4         1028
  5          962
  6         1000
```

```
/* File: sranda.c
   Roll a six-sided die 6000 times randomly,
   calculate the frequencies for each face.
   Use an array to keep frequency for each face */
#include <stdio.h>
#include <stdlib.h>  /* for using srand() and rand() */
#include <time.h>    /* for using time() */

int main() {
   int face,            /* face in each roll*/
       rollcount,       /* roll count number */
       freq[6]={0};     /* array of frequencies for each face,
                           initialize each element with 0 */

   srand(time(NULL)); /* seed the random number generator */
   /* use a loop to roll 6000 times */
   for (rollcount = 1; rollcount <= 6000; rollcount++) {
      /* generate a random number in [1, 6] */
      face = 1 + rand() % 6;
      /* the corresponding frequency for the face is incremented.
         array index for freq[] ranges from 0 to 5 */
      freq[face-1] += 1;
   }

   /* display the result */
   printf("%s%12s\n", "Face", "Frequency");
   for(face = 1; face <= 6; face++ ) {
      printf("  %d%12d\n", face, freq[face-1]);
   }
   return 0;
}
```

Program 10.8: Rolling a six-sided die 6000 times using an array.

Statistical Values for Accessing a Web Page

Problem Statement:
Calculate the mean value for the number of times that a Web page was accessed in a given period of time. Also calculate the mean values for the number of times that a Web page was accessed weekly.

The daily hit numbers of a Web page for a given five-week period are stored in a 5 × 7 two-dimensional array `a` in Program 10.9. Seven columns represent seven days a week. Each row stands for a week. An element in array `a` in Program 10.9 contains the number of times a Web page was accessed for a given day. The array is declared with fixed sizes for both dimensions. If the variable declaration `a[WEEK][DAY]` is replaced by `a[][DAY]`, array `a` would be declared as an incomplete array with the first dimension completed by the number of rows in initialization. The values of all elements are summarized in the variable `dailytotal`. The variable `dailytotal` is initialized at the declaration. Two nested loops with index `i` for the first dimension for the week and `j` for the second dimension for a day are used to access an element of the array. The variable `weektotal` for a weekly total has to be initialized for each week in the outer loop. The weekly total in each row is summarized in the inner loop with seven iterations. The mean value is calculated using a floating-point number and saved in the variable `meanval` before it is printed out.

```
/* File: weeklyhit.c
   Calculate the mean value for weekly hit and daily hit of a Web page */
#include <stdio.h>
#define WEEK 5          /* 5 rows for a total number of 5 weeks in the data */
#define DAY 7           /* 7 columns for each day in each week */

int main() {
    /* The daily hit is recorded in an array with row for a week and column
       for each day in week. Alternatively, the array can be declared as
       int a[][DAY] = {367, 654, 545, 556, 565, 526, 437, */
    int a[WEEK][DAY] = {367, 654, 545, 556, 565, 526, 437,
                        389, 689, 554, 526, 625, 537, 468,
                        429, 644, 586, 626, 652, 546, 493,
                        449, 689, 597, 679, 696, 568, 522,
                        489, 729, 627, 729, 737, 598, 552};
    /* array indexes, weekly total num of hits, and daily total num of hits.
       initialize dailytotal to 0 */
    int i, j, weektotal, dailytotal = 0;
    double meanval; /* a floating-point number for the mean value */

    printf("Week Mean hit\n");
    printf("-------------\n");
    for(i = 0; i < WEEK; i++) { /* loop through the row for each week */
        weektotal = 0;          /* initialize weektotal to 0 for each week */
```

Program 10.9: Calculating the mean values for daily and weekly accessing a Web page in a given five-week period. (*Continued*)

```
        /* loop through the column for each day in a week */
        for(j = 0; j < DAY; j++) {
            weektotal += a[i][j];  /* add daily hit number to weektotal */
            dailytotal -= a[i][j]; /* add daily hit number to dailytotal */
        }
        meanval =  (double)weektotal/(double)DAY; /* mean weekly hit */
        printf(" %d%10.2f\n", i+1, meanval);      /* output mean weekly hit */
    }
    meanval =  (double)dailytotal/(double)(WEEK*DAY); /* mean daily hit */
    printf("The mean value for daily hit is %.2f\n", meanval); /* output */
    return 0;
}
```

Program 10.9: (*Continued*)

```
Week Mean hit
-------------
 1     521.43
 2     541.14
 3     568.00
 4     600.00
 5     637.29
The mean value for daily hit is 573.57
```

Figure 10.6: The output from Programs 10.9 and 10.15.

The output from Program 10.9 for the mean value for all elements of a two-dimensional array and mean values for elements in each row of the array are displayed in Figure 10.6. Viewing the mean values for the number of times that a Web page was accessed weekly, the trend is very clear. The number of page hits is steadily increasing. Program 11.12 in Chapter 11 calculates the mean value for each day of the week in the given five-week period.

10.5 Passing Arrays to Functions

As described in Chapter 6, arguments can be passed to functions in one of two models: *call-by-value* and *call-by-reference*. In the call-by-value model, the values of the actual parameters are copied into formal parameters local to the called function. When a formal parameter is used as an lvalue, only the local copy of the parameter will be altered. In the call-by-reference method, however, the address of an argument is copied into the formal parameter of a function. Inside the called function, the address is used to access the actual argument used in the calling function. This means that when the formal parameter is used as an lvalue, the parameter will affect the variable used to call the function. Arrays are passed to an argument of a function by call-by-reference in C. The mechanism for passing arrays to functions will be described in this section.

10.5.1 Passing One-Dimensional Arrays to Functions

When an array is passed to a function, what is actually passed is the address of the first element of the array. Thus, only the array name needs to be specified in the called function. For example, on the calling side, it can be invoked as

```
type name[10];
...
function(name);
```

where type is the data type for array name. The array name is passed to the function. On the receiving end, the function header can be declared in the form of

```
returnType function(type name[])
```

where returnType is the return type of the function. The size of the array is omitted because no memory is allocated for the array. The memory for the array shall be created in the calling function. If a pointer is used, the function can be declared as

```
returnType function(type *name)
```

which will be described in sections 11.6 and 11.15 in Chapter 11. If the number of elements of the array passed to the function is fixed, say 10, the function can be declared as

```
returnType function(type name[10])
```

Even though the size of the passed array is specified, there is still no memory allocated for the array. The size information might be used by the compiler to check the compatibility of the passed array against the function declaration.

Often, the number of elements of the array is passed as another argument of the function. In this case, the function header can be declared as

```
returnType function(int n, type name[])
```

or

```
returnType function(int n, type *name)
```

The function can be called by

```
function(10, name);
```

A formal parameter of array type in a function is effectively a pointer type. Therefore, the actual parameter in a function call is a pointer. An array name itself is actually a pointer type and it is the address of its first element, which will be explained further in Chapter 11. Because the address of the element name[i] of the array name can be obtained by the expression &name[i]. Therefore, the above function call is the same as

```
function(10, &name[0]);
```

which passes the address of the first element of the array name to the second argument of the function. Because the memory for a two-dimensional array is organized row-wise, as described in section 10.2, a row of a two-dimensional array can be passed as an array to a function. For example, if the array name2 is declared as

```
type name2[5][10];
```

the address of the first element of the *i*th row of the array `name2` is `&name2[i][0]`. Therefore, the *i*th row of the array `name2` can be passed to `function` as follows:

```
function(10, &name2[i][0]);
```

An example of passing rows of a two-dimensional array to a function will be given in Program 10.15, later in this chapter.

Using the feature of VLA in C99, it can be declared as

```
returnType function(int n, type name[n])
```

which will be described in section 10.7.

As an example, Program 10.10 adds one-dimensional arrays `d1` and `d2`, each with five elements of **double** data type, and stores the result in the array `d1` element-wise using the function `oneDadd()`. The result is shown below:

```
2.00 4.00 6.00 8.00 10.00
```

```
/* File: passarray.c
   Pass one dimensional arrays of variable length to a function */
#include <stdio.h>

/* add dd1 and dd2, store the result in array dd1 element-wise. */
void oneDadd(int n, double dd1[], double dd2[]) {
    int i;

    for(i = 0; i <= n-1; i++) { /* loop through the entire array */
        dd1[i] += dd2[i];       /* add element by element */
    }
}

int main() {
    /* declare and initialize two arrays */
    double d1[5] = {1.0, 2.0, 3.0, 4.0, 5.0};
    double d2[5] = {1.0, 2.0, 3.0, 4.0, 5.0};
    int i;

    oneDadd(5, d1, d2);         /* call function to add arrays d1 and d2 */
    for(i = 0; i < 5; i++) {  /* display the modified array d1 */
        printf("%.2lf ", d1[i]);
    }
    printf("\n");
    return 0;
}
```

Program 10.10: Passing one-dimensional arrays to a function.

In the function definition of `oneDadd()` in Program 10.10,

```
void oneDadd(int n, double dd1[], double dd2[])
```

both `dd1` and `dd2` are defined as variables of **double** array type in function parameter scope. They are incomplete arrays, completed by a function call. They are in fact pointers to **double**. Thus, one-dimensional arrays of variable length can be passed to the function `oneDadd()`. as shown in the program. In general, the size of an array is not available to the called function. For example, the sizes of the arrays in the function `oneDadd()` are passed in by the parameter `n` in the program. An exception would be a string. Strings are zero-terminated so that their sizes can be computed directly by the **strlen**() function as described in section 12.8 in Chapter 12.

If expressions such as `dd1[-2]` or `dd1[20]` were used inside the function `oneDadd()` in Program 10.10, they would refer to objects outside the bounds of the passed array. Because no extents are specified in the declaration of the formal arrays, the statement `dd1[-2] += dd2[20+n]` would be syntactically legal if it were in the function `oneDadd()`. even if it may be problematic. It is not possible to generate any warning or error message for this kind of statement. It is the programmer's responsibility to make sure that each element of the formal array in the called function is within the bounds of actual arrays in the calling function.

However, if the extents of the arrays to be passed in the calling functions are known, the formal array arguments in the function can be declared with specified extents, such as

```
void oneDadd(int n, double dd1[5], double dd2[5])
```

Furthermore, because the extent has been specified in the formal argument, error messages would be generated in Ch at runtime due to the array boundary error if the statement of `dd1[-2] += dd2[20]` were used in the function `oneDadd()`. To avoid a likely crash of the system if an array index is smaller than zero, the lower bound of zero will be used as the array index in Ch. Similarly, if an index is greater than the upper bound of the formal array, the upper bound of the formal array will be used as the index. Therefore, the assignment statement `dd1[-2] += dd2[20]` would be handled as the statement `dd1[0] += dd2[4]`.

Searching

An array may contain a large number of data. In many applications in engineering and science, it is necessary to search an array for a particular value and its location in the array. The simplest algorithm for searching is *linear search* or *sequential search*, which checks every element of a list one at a time in sequence until a match is found. The function `lsearch()` with the prototype

```
int lsearch(int n, double data[], double val);
```

in Program 10.11 searches the array `data` with `n` using a **for** loop for the value `val`. If the value is found in the array, the function `lsearch()` returns the index of the element. Otherwise, it returns -1. In the function `lsearch()`, the search value `val` is compared with elements of the array `data` using the equal comparison relational operator `'=='`. For some applications, such as those involving experimental data, it is better to compare if the absolute value of the difference of two numbers is smaller than a very small number **FLT-EPSILON** as described in section 4.4 in Chapter 4. Inside the function **main**(), the function `lsearch()` is called to search for value -14.0 in the array `a` with 8 elements. The function can be called by either

```
lsearch(N, &a[0], value);
```

or

```
lsearch(N, a, value);
```

```c
/* File: search.c
   Linear search for a value in an array */
#include <stdio.h>

#define N 8   /* number of elements for array a */

/* linear search for val in data[]. return index of element
   if there is a match; otherwise, return -1 */
int lsearch(int n, double data[], double val) {
    int i;

    for(i = 0; i < n; i++) { /* search through each element */
        if(val == data[i]) { /* or use fabs(val - data[i]) < FLT_EPSILON */
            return i;        /* return location (index) for the value */
        }
    }
    return -1;               /* return -1 if no match */
}

int main() {
    /* declare array a with initialization */
    double a[N] = {3.0, 21.0, 0.0, -3.0, 34.0, -14.0, 45.0, 18.0};
    double value = -14.0; /* the value to be searched */
    int loc;              /* location of the value in an array */
    int i;

    printf("The original data:\n");
    for(i = 0; i < N; i++) {  /* print the original array */
        printf("%g ", a[i]);
    }

    /* search value in a */
    loc = lsearch(N, &a[0], value);
    /* or loc = lsearch(N, a, value);  */

    if(loc != -1) {                /* found it */
        printf("\nFind %g in element %d\n", value, loc);
    }
    else {                         /* did not find it */
        printf("\nCannot find %g in array\n", value);
    }

    return 0;
}
```

Program 10.11: Searching a value in an array.

The output from Program 10.11 is shown below.

```
The original data:
3 21 0 -3 34 -14 45 18
Find -14 in element 5
```

It is simple to find a particular value in an unsorted list by using a linear search. However, it is not efficient for searching a particular value in large amounts of data. A binary search algorithm is more efficient for finding a particular value in a sorted list, especially for a large list. The algorithm of binary search is similar to that of the bisection method for finding a root of an equation described in section 6.10 in Chapter 6. Beginning with an entire sorted list, it repeatedly divides the search interval in half. If the value to be found is less than the element in the middle of the interval, narrow the interval to the lower half. Otherwise, narrow it to the upper half. The process is repeated until the value is found or the interval is empty. C provides a standard function **bsearch()** for performing a binary search of sorted lists. Because binary searches can be only applied to a sorted list, the function **qsort()** for quicksort is often used to sort data first. Then, the function **bsearch()** is called to search a particular value in the sorted list. These two generic functions can be used to sort and search lists of objects with the same type. An example using the functions **qsort()** and **bsearch()** will be presented in Program 11.21 in section 11.12 in Chapter 11.

10.5.2 An Example of a Statistical Library

One of the primary purposes of computer programming is to process data, such as experimental data, weather temperatures, stock prices, and geometric data. Numeric data can be conveniently stored in arrays and then processed. In section 10.4, we described how to calculate the mean value for elements in an array, find the minimum and maximum values, and sort elements of an array. In this section, we introduce other commonly used statistical measurements. We also develop a library of statistical functions, which can be used for analyzing data for different applications.

Median

For a data set **x** of n elements sorted in ascending order, The element x_0 denotes the smallest value, x_1 denotes the second smallest value, . . . , x_{n-1} denotes the largest value. The *median* $\overline{x}$ is the value in the middle of the sorted data set. It is defined as the middle or $([n+])/2)th$ element if n is odd, and halfway between the two middle elements (the $[n/2]th$ and $[n/2+1]th$) if n is even. Mathematically, the median is expressed as follows:

$$\overline{x} = \begin{cases} x_{[n+1]/2} & n \text{ is odd} \\ \dfrac{x_{[n/2]} + x_{[n/2]+1}}{2} & n \text{ is even} \end{cases} \tag{10.4}$$

The median is not influenced very much by extreme values. For example, for an array sorted in ascending order with elements

```
-10, 2, 4, 5, 6, 7, 90
```

the median is 5.

Variance and Standard Deviation

The very simple measure of variability is *sample range*, which is defined as the difference between the largest and smallest sample observations. Although the sample range is easy to calculate, it ignores all the information in the sample between the smallest and largest observations.

The most important measures of variability of data are *variance* and *standard deviation*. Mathematically, the sample variance is defined as

$$\sigma^2 = \frac{\sum_{i=0}^{n-1}(x_i - \mu)^2}{n-1} \tag{10.5}$$

where n is the number of observations of data set **x**, and μ is the mean of data set **x** defined in equation (10.2).

The *standard deviation* σ of the data set is defined as the square root of the variance

$$\sigma = \sqrt{\sigma^2} \tag{10.6}$$

The unit of measurement for the variance is the square of the original unit of the variable. For example, if x is measured in meters, the unit for the variance is meter^2. The standard deviation has the desirable property of measuring variability in the original unit of the variable of interest for the data set **x**. The term $x_i - \mu$ is the difference between x_i and the mean value μ, or the deviation of x_i from the mean. The standard deviation is the most common measure of statistical dispersion, measuring how widely spread the values in a data set are. If many data points are close to the mean, then the standard deviation is small; if many data points are far from the mean, then the standard deviation is large. If all the data values are equal, then the standard deviation is zero.

A library of functions for statistical analysis has been developed. The header file `statlib.h` in Program 10.12 contains the function prototypes for this library. Each function is prototyped using the

```
/***************************************************************************
 * File: statlib.h
 * This header file contains function prototypes for the statistics library.
 ***************************************************************************/
#ifndef STATLIB_H
#define STATLIB_H

#include <math.h> /* for sqrt() used in stdDeviation() */

/* function prototypes for statlib */
extern double mean(int totnum, double data[]);
extern double minimum(int totnum, double data[]);
extern double maximum(int totnum, double data[]);
extern double median(int totnum, double data[]);
extern double variance(int totnum, double data[]);
extern double stdDeviation(int totnum, double data[]);
extern int aboveVal(int totnum, double data[], double val);
extern void sort(int totnum, double data[]);

/* load functions in the statlib for Ch */
#ifdef _CH_
#pragma importf "statlib.c"
#endif

#endif /* STATLIB_H */
```

Program 10.12: The header file `statlib.h` for a statistical library.

storage-class specifier **extern** as an external function explicitly as described in section 8.3 in Chapter 8. Function definitions for this library are given in Program 10.13. It is assumed that the data for analysis are stored in an array. The first argument of these functions is the number of elements for the array passed in the second argument. The second argument is an array of double type. The function `mean()` calculates and returns the mean for an array passed in the second argument and is based on Program 10.2. The functions `minimum()` and `maximum()` for calculating the minimum and maximum are based on Program 10.3.

```
/***********************************************************************
 * File: statlib.c
 * This function file contains function definitions for
 * the statistics library.
 ***********************************************************************/
#include "statlib.h"    /* header file for statlib */

/* calculate the mean value of the data in the list */
double mean(int totnum, double data[]) {
    double meanval, sum;
    int i;

    sum = 0.0;
    for(i=0; i<totnum; i++) {
        sum += data[i];
    }
    meanval = sum/totnum;
    return meanval;
}

/* find the minimum value of the data in the list */
double minimum(int totnum, double data[]) {
    double minval;
    int i;

    minval = data[0];
    for(i= 1; i < totnum; i++) {
        if(data[i] < minval)
            minval = data[i];
    }
    return minval;
}

/* find the maximum value of the data in the list */
double maximum(int totnum, double data[]) {
    double maxval;
    int i;
```

Program 10.13: The function file `statlib.c` for a statistical library. *(Continued)*

```
    maxval = data[0];
    for(i = 1; i < totnum; i++) {
        if(data[i] > maxval)
            maxval = data[i];
    }
    return maxval;
}

/* find the median value of the data in the sorted list;
   the passed array data should have been sorted by function sort() */
double median(int totnum, double data[]) {
    double medianval;

    if(totnum%2) /* odd total number */
        medianval = data[totnum/2];
    else         /* even total number */
        medianval = (data[totnum/2-1] + data[totnum/2])/2.0;
    return medianval;
}

/* calculate the variance of data in the list */
double variance(int totnum, double data[]) {
    double meanval, sum, var;
    int i;

    meanval = mean(totnum, data);
    sum = 0.0;
    for(i=0; i<totnum; i++) {
        sum += (data[i] - meanval)*(data[i] - meanval);
    }
    var = sum/(totnum-1);
    return var;
}

/* calculate the standard deviation of data in the list */
double stdDeviation(int totnum, double data[]) {
    double var, std;

    var = variance(totnum, data);
    std = sqrt(var);
    return std;
}
```

Program 10.13: *(Continued)*

```
/* number of elements above 'val' */
int aboveVal(int totnum, double data[], double val) {
    int i, num;
    for(i = 0, num=0; i < totnum; i++) {
        if(data[i] >= val) {
            num++;
        }
    }
    return num;
}

/* sort the data in the ascending order using the bubble sort algorithm */
/* passed array data[] in the calling function will be changed */
void sort(int totnum, double data[]) {
    int i, j;
    double temp;

    /* find the smallest value in the remaining part of
       the array in each iteration staring with data[i] */
    for(i = 0; i < totnum-1; i++) {
        /* compare with data[i] with data[j] for j from i+1 to N-1 */
        for(j = i+1; j < totnum; j++) {
            /* when data[i] > data[j], swap their values */
            if(data[i] > data[j]) {
                temp = data[i];
                data[i] = data[j];
                data[j] = temp;
            }
        }
    }
}
```

Program 10.13: *(Continued)*

Based on Program 10.5, the function `sort()` sorts an array passed in from its second argument in ascending order using the bubble sort algorithm illustrated in Figure 10.3. Unlike all other functions in the library, changes are made to elements of the array inside the function `sort()`. These changes are reflected in its calling function.

The function `median()` returns the median for all elements of the sorted array in either ascending or descending order, passed from its second argument. The array passed to the function `median()` is typically sorted by the function `sort()` first. When there is an even number of elements, the median is calculated as the mean of the two middle elements. The modular operation '%' is used to determine if the number of elements is an odd or even number. If n is an odd number, n % 2 is 1. Otherwise, n % 2 is 0.

The function `variance()` calculates the variance using equation (10.5). It calls the function `mean()` to find the mean of the data set. The function `stdDeviation()` calculates the standard deviation based on equation (10.6). It calls the function `variance()`.

The function `aboveVal()` calculates the number of elements with their values at or above the value passed in its last argument.

The application of the statistical library `statlib` is illustrated by two examples. The first example uses the library to process the GPA with the problem stated as follows.

Problem Statement:
Given the GPA (grade point average) for students in a class as follows:

```
3.33, 3, 3.1, 3.93, 2.3, 2.31, 3.99, 2.8, 2.9, 3.7.
```

Calculate the average GPA for students in the class, highest and lowest GPAs, standard deviation of the GPAs, and the number of students with a GPA of 3.0 or above. Sort student GPAs in ascending order and calculate the median of the GPAs.

The statistical library can be used to solve this problem. Program 10.14 includes the header file `statlib.h` to use functions in the library. The GPAs for students are stored in the array `data` in the main function in Program 10.14. The total number of elements of the array is calculated by the expression

```
totnum = sizeof(data)/sizeof(double);
```

This number of elements and data for GPAs are passed as two arguments to each function to process the data. The GPA functions are called in the main function. When Program 10.14 is executed, the output is shown in Figure 10.7.

```
/* File: gpa.c
   Calculate statistical info for a list of GPA's
   using the statistics library statlab.h and statlib.c */
#include <stdio.h>
#include "statlib.h" /* the header file for statistics lib */

int main() {
    /* the database for students' GPA in a class */
    double data[] = {3.33, 3, 3.1, 3.93, 2.3, 2.31, 3.99, 2.8, 2.9, 3.7};
    double gpa;
    int i, totnum, num;

    /* find the total number of elements in array 'data' */
    totnum = sizeof(data)/sizeof(double);
    printf("The total number of students is %d\n", totnum);

    /* use the statlib to get the result, and then disply it */
    gpa = mean(totnum, data);
    printf("The average GPA for all students is %.2f\n", gpa);
    gpa = maximum(totnum, data);
    printf("The highest GPA for all students is %.2f\n", gpa);
    gpa = minimum(totnum, data);
    printf("The lowest GPA for all students is %.2f\n", gpa);
```

Program 10.14: A program using functions in the statistical library `statlib`. *(Continued)*

```
    gpa = stdDeviation(totnum, data);
    printf("The standard deviation of GPA for all students is %.2f\n", gpa);
    num = aboveVal(totnum, data, 3.0);
    printf("The number of students with GPA 3.0 or above is %d\n", num);
    sort(totnum, data);
    printf("The student record sorted in ascending GPA:\n");
    for(i=0; i< totnum; i++) {
        printf("%.2f ",data[i]);
    }
    printf("\n");
    gpa = median(totnum, data);
    printf("The median GPA for all students is %.2f\n", gpa);
    return 0;
}
```

Program 10.14: (*Continued*)

```
The total number of students is 10
The average GPA for all students is 3.14
The highest GPA for all students is 3.99
The lowest GPA for all students is 2.30
The standard deviation of GPA for all students is 0.60
The number of students with GPA 3.0 or above is 6
The student record sorted in ascending GPA:
2.30 2.31 2.80 2.90 3.00 3.10 3.33 3.70 3.93 3.99
The median GPA for all students is 3.05
```

Figure 10.7: The output from Program 10.14.

The second example uses the library to calculate the mean value for each row of a two-dimensional array as well as the mean value for all elements of the array. Program 10.9 calculated the mean values for the number of times that a Web page was accessed weekly as well as the mean value for the number of times that a Web page was accessed daily in a given period of time. Program 10.15, modified from Program 10.9, calls the function `mean()` in the library to calculate the mean value for each row of array `a` by the statement

```
meanval = mean(DAY, &a[i][0]);
```

As described in section 10.5.1, the address of the first element of each row is passed to the second argument of the function `mean()`. Unlike passing a scalar to a function, the data type of the passed array must match with the data type of the formal array. Arrays processed by functions in the statistical library are of type double. Therefore, array `a` in Program 10.9 is declared as type double. The mean values for each row are accumulated in the variable `meanvals` to calculate the mean value for daily visits to the Web page. The output from Program 10.15, shown in Figure 10.6, is the same as that from Program 10.9.

```
/* File: weeklyhit2.c
   Calculate the mean value for weekly hit and daily hit of a Web page
   using a statistic lib */
#include <stdio.h>
#include "statlib.h" /* header file for statistics lib */
#define WEEK 5       /* 5 rows for a total number of 5 weeks in the data */
#define DAY 7        /* 7 columns for each day in each week */

int main() {
    /* The daily hit is recorded in an array with row for a week and column
       for each day in week. Alternatively, the aray can be declared as
       double a[][DAY] = {367, 654, 545, 556, 565, 526, 437, */
    double a[WEEK][DAY] = {367, 654, 545, 556, 565, 526, 437,
                          389, 689, 554, 526, 625, 537, 468,
                          429, 644, 586, 626, 652, 546, 493,
                          449, 689, 597, 679, 696, 568, 522,
                          489, 729, 627, 729, 737, 598, 552};
    /* array index */
    int i;
    double meanval;/* a floating-point number for the mean value for each row */
    double meanvals = 0.0; /* mean values for all rows */

    printf("Week Mean hit\n");
    printf("-------------\n");
    for(i = 0; i < WEEK; i++) { /* loop through the row for each week */
        meanval = mean(DAY, &a[i][0]);
        meanvals += meanval;                   /* add a row of mean value */
        printf(" %d%10.2f\n", i+1, meanval);  /* output mean weekly hit */
    }
    meanval =  meanvals/WEEK; /* mean daily hit */
    printf("The mean value for daily hit is %.2f\n", meanval); /* output */
    return 0;
}
```

Program 10.15: Calculating the mean values for daily and weekly visits to a Web page in a given five-week period using the statistical library.

10.5.3 Passing Two-Dimensional Arrays to Functions

One-dimensional arrays can be passed to functions conveniently in C, as described in the previous section. This section will continue the discussion and describe how to pass multidimensional arrays of fixed shape to functions. Although there are some differences, passing two-dimensional arrays to functions is somewhat similar to passing one-dimensional arrays. For example, a function can be called in the form of

```
type name[2][3];
...
function(2, 3, name);
```

where `type` is the data type of the array `name`. Both numbers of rows and columns of a two-dimensional array are typically passed into a function along with the array.

If a two-dimensional array of fixed length is to be passed to a function, the parameters of the array definition in the arguments of the function should also include the number of columns (i.e., the second dimension of the array) along with the number of rows. For the above function call, on the receiving end, the function header can be declared in one of the following forms:

```
returnType function(int m, int n, double name[2][3])
returnType function(int m, int n, double name[][3])
returnType function(int m, int n, double (*name)[3])
returnType function(int m, int n, double [name][m][n])
```

where `returnType` is the return type of the function. The first two forms are similar to the format for passing one-dimensional arrays to a function. The third method, using a pointer to array to pass two-dimensional arrays to a function, will be described in section 11.13 in Chapter 11. The fourth method uses VLA in C99, which is described in section 10.7.

As an example, Program 10.16 illustrates passing two-dimensional arrays to a function. The function `twoDadd()` in Program 10.16 is used to add two two-dimensional arrays. Different declaration formats for formal two-dimensional array arguments are demonstrated below for the declaration of the function `twoDadd()` in Program 10.16.

```
double twoDadd(int m, int n, double dd1[][3], double dd2[][3],
                    double dd3[2][3])
```

```
/* File: passarray2d.c
   Pass two dimensional arrays of fixed length to a function */
#include <stdio.h>

/* The column of arrays is fixed with 3. */
double twoDadd(int m, int n, double dd1[][3], double dd2[][3], double dd3[2][3])
{
   int i, j;          /* variable for loop indexes */
   double sum = 0; /* declare and initialize sum to 0 */

   for(i = 0; i < m; i++) {
      for(j = 0; j < n; j++) {
         /* add arrays dd2 and dd3 element wise, and save the result
            in array dd1 */
         dd1[i][j] = dd2[i][j]+dd3[i][j];
         sum += dd1[i][j]; /* add each element of array dd1 */
      }
   }
   return sum; /* return the sum for all elements of arrays dd2 and dd3 */
}
```

Program 10.16: Passing two-dimensional arrays to a function. (*Continued*)

```
int main() {
    /* declare arrays and initialize them */
    double d1[2][3],
                 d2[2][3]={{1.0, 2.0, 3.0}, {4.0 ,5.0 ,6.0}},
                 d3[2][3]={{1.0, 2.0, 3.0}, {4.0 ,5.0 ,6.0}},
                 sum; /* sum for all elements of arrays dd2 and dd3 */
    int i, j;    /* variable for array indexes */

    sum =twoDadd(2, 3, d1, d2, d3); /* call function for d1 = d2 + d3 */
    /* display sum and array d1 with d1 = d2 + d3 */
    printf("sum = %.2f\n", sum);
    printf("d1 = \n");
    for(i = 0; i < 2; i++) {
        for(j = 0; j < 3; j++) {
            printf("%8.2f", d1[i][j]);
        }
        printf("\n");
    }
    return 0;
}
```

Program 10.16: *(Continued)*

The missing extents of the row dimensions for formal arguments `dd1` and `dd2` indicate that arrays of variable row size, but with a fixed column size of 3, can be passed into these arguments. The Argument `dd3`, however, is limited to a row size of 2. If the number of rows of the array passed in as the argument `dd3` is not 2, the system may generate a warning message.

In general, when passing arrays to functions, the ranks of actual arrays shall match with the rank of the formal array argument in the function definition and function prototypes. Otherwise, the system may produce a warning message. If the extent for a dimension of an array is given in the function definition or function prototypes, the extent of the actual array shall match with the corresponding extent of the array in the formal definition. Otherwise, the system may also produce a warning message. The shapes of the array in the function definition and its function prototypes shall be the same as well. Otherwise, it is a syntax error.

Program 10.16 calls the function `twoDadd()` to add the corresponding elements of the arrays `d2` and `d3` and store the results in the array `d1`. The sum of all these elements (i.e. the sum of the elements of d1) is also calculated as the return value of the function `twoDadd()`. The output of Program 10.16 below displays the result of the return value from the function as well as the values for array `d1`:

```
sum = 42.00
d1 =
    2.00    4.00    6.00
    8.00   10.00   12.00
```

Multidimensional arrays that are greater than two dimensions can be handled in the same manner. In general, only the size of the first dimension of an array can vary; all others shall be specified in the function definition and function prototypes.

10.6 Plotting Data in Arrays for Graphical Display

Section 6.7 in Chapter 6 describes how to use the high-level functions **fplotxy()** and **fplotxyz()** to plot two- and three-dimensional functions, respectively. However, in some applications, such as data acquisition, we may need to visualize the experimental data which are not represented in analytic functions. In this section, we will introduce simple functions in the SftIntegetration Graphical Library (SIGL) and Ch that can be used to plot data in arrays.

10.6.1 Two-Dimensional Plotting

The function **plotxy()** is a high-level function to plot data in arrays. The function **plotxy()** is useful for generating two-dimensional plots. Its function prototype is defined in the header file **chplot.h**. The function **plotxy()** can be treated as if it had the following function prototype:

```
int plotxy(double x[], double y[], int n,
           char *title, char *xlabel, char *ylabel);
```

The array `x` stores data for the x-axis, while array `y` stores data for the y-axis. Both arrays `x` and `y` shall have the same number of elements, which is specified by the third argument `n` of integral value. The title and labels for axes are specified by the remaining three arguments: `title`, `xlabel`, and `ylabel`, respectively. Like using the function **fplotxy()**, a program using the function **plotxy()** needs to include the header file **chplot.h**.

Often, arrays of data for plotting need to be generated using a loop. Assume that the variables `x0` and `xf` represent the initial and final values of x with n data points in total, respectively. For the x-coordinates of the plot, equation (10.1) can be used inside a repetition loop to fill an array with n elements linearly in the range of $x0 \le x \le xf$ for i from 0 to $(n-1)$. For each element `x[i]`, the y-coordinate can be calculated accordingly inside the loop.

An Application Example

Acceleration of a Moving Body

Problem Statement:
For the mechanical system shown in Figure 2.12, given mass $m = 5$ kilograms (kg) and coefficient of kinetic friction $\mu = 0.2$, the applied force p is expressed as a function of time t in

$$p(t) = 4\sin(t-3) + 20$$

Write a program to calculate and plot the accelerations **a** for $t = 0$ to $t = 10$ seconds with 100 data points.

Program 10.17, which is being used to solve this problem is similar to Program 10.6. The difference is that the function **plotxy()** is used to plot the acceleration of the system with 100 data points, instead of printing out the value with 11 data points. The output plot is the same as the one shown in Figure 6.4 in Chapter 6. The acceleration plot allows for a better visualization of the behavior of the system due to an applied load. In Program 10.17, the variable `t0` is for the initial time of 0 and `tf` for the final time of 10 seconds. Based on the formula in equation (10.1), the statement

```
t[i] = t0+i*(tf - t0)/(N-1);
```

will create array `t` with `t[0]` equal to `t0` and `t[N-1]` equal to `tf`.

```
/* File: accelsinmpts.cpp
   Plot accelereration versus time with 100 points */
#include <stdio.h>
#include <math.h>
#include <chplot.h>     /* for plotxy() */

#define M_G   9.81      /* gravitational acceleration constant g */
#define N     100       /* num of points for plotting */

int main() {
    /* declare variables for accel, time, mu, mass, force */
    double a[N], t[N], t0, tf;
    double mu, m, p;
    int i;

    /* set mu, mass, initial time, and final time */
    mu = 0.2;
    m = 5.0;
    t0 = 0.0;
    tf = 10.0;

    for(i=0; i<N; i++) {                   /* go through the loop N times */
        t[i] = t0+i*(tf - t0)/(N-1); /* calculate element t[i] for time */
        p = 4*sin(t[i]-3)+20;          /* calculate force p */
        a[i] = (p-mu*m*M_G)/m;         /* calculate element a[i] for accel */
    }

    /* call plotting function in the plotting library */
    plotxy(t, a, N, "Acceleration Plot", "time (s)", "accel (m/s^2)");
    return 0;
}
```

Program 10.17: Calculating and plotting accelerations with force of the sine function using arrays.

10.6.2 Plotting Multiple Curves in a Single Plot

Similar to **fplotxy**(), the function **plotxy**() can be replaced by member functions of the plotting class **CPlot**. The function call

```
plotxy(x, y, n, title. xlabel, ylabel);
```

can be replaced by the following code using a plotting class **CPlot**:

```
CPlot plot;
plot.title(title);
plot.label(PLOT_AXIS_X, xlabel);
```

```
plot.label(PLOT_AXIS_Y, ylabel);
plot.data2DCurve(x, y, n);
plot.plotting();
```

The data of arrays `x` and `y` with `n` elements are added to the plotting object by the member function call

```
plot.data2DCurve(x, y, n);
```

Detailed information about the member function **data2DCurve**() can be found in section 20.1 in Chapter 20. Multiple sets of data stored in arrays can be added to the plot by this member function. For example, Program 10.18 plots two acceleration curves with data stored in arrays. Arrays `t1` and `a1` contain 11 points of data for time and acceleration, respectively. Arrays `t2` and `a2` have 100 elements. Similar to Program 6.12, a legend for each curve is added by the member function **legend**(). The plot generated by Program 10.18 is the same as the one shown in Figure 6.5.

```
/* File: acceldata2DCurve.cpp
   Plot accelereration versus time with 11 and 100 points on the same figure */
#include <stdio.h>
#include <math.h>           /* for sin() */
#include <chplot.h>         /* for class CPlot for plotting */

#define M_G    9.81         /* gravitational acceleration constant g */
#define N1     11           /* num of points for the 1st curve */
#define N2     100          /* num of points for the 2nd curve */

int main() {
    /* declare two sets of arrays for plottting for a versus t */
    double a1[N1], t1[N1], a2[N2], t2[N2];
    double t0, tf, mu, m, p;
    int i;
    CPlot plot;             /* instantiate a plotting class */

    /* set mu, mass, initial time, and final time */
    mu = 0.2;
    m = 5.0;
    t0 = 0.0;
    tf = 10.0;

    /* calculate t1[i] and a1[i] with N1 points */
    for(i=0; i<N1; i++) {
        t1[i] = t0+i*(tf - t0)/(N1-1);
        p = 4*sin(t1[i]-3)+20;
        a1[i] = (p-mu*m*M_G)/m;
    }
```

Program 10.18: Plotting two acceleration curves in a single plot with data in arrays. (*Continued*)

```
    /* calculate t2[i] and a2[i] with N2 points */
    for(i=0; i<N2; i++) {
        t2[i] = t0+i*(tf - t0)/(N2-1);
        p = 4*sin(t2[i]-3)+20;
        a2[i] = (p-mu*m*M_G)/m;
    }

    /* use a plotting class plot two curves on the same figure */
    /* set title of the plot */
    plot.title("Acceleration Plot");
    /* set the label on the x-axis */
    plot.label(PLOT_AXIS_X, "time (s)");
    /* set the label on the y-axis */
    plot.label(PLOT_AXIS_Y, "accel (m/s^2)");
    /* add data a1[] and t1[] for plotting in the 1st curve */
    plot.data2DCurve(t1, a1, N1);
    /* set the legend for the 1st curve */
    plot.legend("11 points", 0);
    /* add data a2[] and t2[] for plotting in the 2nd curve */
    plot.data2DCurve(t2, a2, N2);
    /* set the legend for the 2nd curve */
    plot.legend("100 points", 1);
    /* after the above setup, ready and go, plot and display it! */
    plot.plotting();
    return 0;
}
```

Program 10.18: *(Continued)*

An Application Example

Linear Regression

In many problems in engineering and science, two or more variables are inherently related. *Regression analysis* is a statistical technique to model and explore the relationship of two or more variables. Based on data points gathered for variables, either through experimental or other means, regression analysis can be used to build an analytical model for variables. The simplest form of regression analysis is *linear regression* for two variables. In this model, one variable is expressed as a linear function of another variable.

As an example, positions of a moving body at various times are measured and recorded in Table 4.3 in section 4.2 in Chapter 4. These data are plotted in Figure 4.6 where the points lie approximately on a straight line. Suppose that a body is traveling with a constant velocity v. The relation between the time t and the position reached by the body y is given by the linear equation

$$y = b + vt \tag{10.7}$$

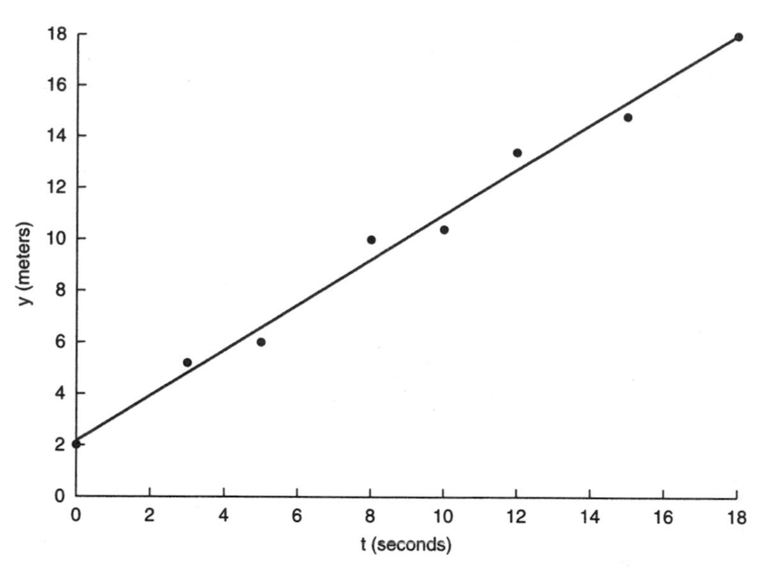

Figure 10.8 Straight-line fitting of data. This is also the plot generated by Program 10.19 and Program 21.9 in Chapter 21.

where b is the initial position y_0. In regression analysis, the intercept b and slope v of the straight line are called *regression coefficients*. We assume that the reason why the points do not lie exactly on a straight line is due to errors of measurement. Because measurements are subject to experimental error, the linear equation is not satisfied exactly by the measured values y and t. It is not possible to deduce the exact values v and y_0 from the data in Table 4.3. The problem is how to derive the best possible values of v and y_0 from the data, in other words, how do you fit the best straight line to the data plotted in Figure 10.8? The most commonly used approach to determine the slope v and intercept b of this straight line is to use the *least squares method*. The theoretical derivation of the formulas for the linear regression coefficients v and intercept b are beyond the scope of this book. But they can be calculated by formulas as follows:

$$v = \frac{\sum_{i=0}^{n-1}(t_i - t_\mu)(y_i - y_\mu)}{\sum_{i=0}^{n-1}(t_i - t_\mu)^2} \tag{10.8}$$

$$b = y_\mu - vt_\mu \tag{10.9}$$

where n is the number measurements of position y, y_i the position measured at time t_i, t_μ the mean value of the times, and y_μ the mean value of the positions.

For measured positions at various times in Table 4.3, Program 10.19 calculates linear regression coefficients v and b using formulas (10.8) and (10.9), respectively. These coefficients are handled as two global variables so that they can be accessed in both functions `func()` for equation (10.7) and `main()`. Data points are stored in the arrays `y` and `t` with n elements. The variables `t_mean` and `y_mean` for the mean values t_μ and y_μ are calculated using the function `mean()` in the statistical library. The variable `sumty` contains the value for

$$\sum_{i=0}^{n-1}(t_i - t_\mu)(y_i - y_\mu)$$

```
/* File: linreg.cpp
   Perform linear regression analysis for a set of data.
   Plot the fitted line in comparison with the original scattered data points */
#include <stdio.h>
#include <chplot.h>    /* for class CPlot for plotting */
#include "statlib.h"   /* for mean()  in the statistical lib */
#define NUM   100      /* number of points for plotting */
double b, v;           /* linear regression coefficients */

/* linear function y = b + v*t */
double func(double t) {
    double y;
    y = b + v*t;
    return y;
}
int main() {
    /* declare and initialize the original data */
    double t[] = {0.0, 3.0, 5.0, 8.0,  10.0, 12.0, 15.0, 18.0};
    double y[] = {2.0, 5.2, 6.0, 10.0, 10.4, 13.4, 14.8, 18.0};
    /* mean values and sums in the formulas for regression analysis */
    double t_mean, y_mean, titm, sumty, sumts;
    int i, n, num=0; /* index, number of data points, data set number */
    CPlot plot;      /* instantiate a plotting class */

    n = sizeof(t)/sizeof(double); /* calculate the number of data points */
    /* calculate the linear regression coefficients based on the formulas */
    t_mean = mean(n, t);
    y_mean = mean(n, y);
    for(i=0; i<n; i++) {
       titm = t[i] - t_mean;
       sumty = titm*(y[i]-y_mean);
       sumts = titm*titm;
    }
    v = sumty/sumts;
    b = y_mean - v*t_mean;
    /* display the linear regression coefficients v and b, and find y(11.0) */
    printf("v = %.2f\n", v);
    printf("b = %.2f\n", b);
    printf("y is = %.2f (m) at time t = 11 (s)\n", func(11.0));

    /* set the label on the x-axis */
    plot.label(PLOT_AXIS_X, "t (second)");
    /* set the label on the y-axis */
```

Program 10.19: A program for straight-line fitting of data. (*Continued*)

```
    plot.label(PLOT_AXIS_Y, "y (meter)");
    /* set the range for x-axis from 0 to 18 */
    plot.axisRange(PLOT_AXIS_Y, 0.0, 18.0);
    /* add data t[] and y[] as the 1st set of data for plotting */
    plot.data2DCurve(t, y, n);
    /* set the scattered point plot type for the 1st set of data */
    plot.plotType(PLOT_PLOTTYPE_POINTS, num);
    /* set function func2D() plotted from t[0] to t[n-1] with NUM points */
    plot.func2D(t[0], t[n-1], NUM, func);
    /* after the above setup, ready and go, plot and display it! */
    plot.plotting();
    return 0;
}
```

Program 10.19: *(Continued)*

```
v = 0.88
b = 2.17
y is = 11.84 (m) at time t = 11 (s)
```

Figure 10.9: The output from Program 10.19 and Program 21.9 in Chapter 21.

The variable `sumts` contains the value for

$$\sum_{i=0}^{n-1}(t_i - t_\mu)^2$$

After the regression coefficients v and b are calculated, they will be printed on the terminal. The position at 11 seconds is also calculated. The output from Program 10.19 is in Figures 10.8 and 10.9.

Note that, using linear interpolation, Program 4.3 obtains the position 11.90 m of the body at the time of 11 seconds based on the two adjacent data points (10, 10.4) and (12, 13.4). However, a linear model provides more flexibility for analysis. For example, it can be used to calculate the position beyond the specified data points. The model also gives the velocity v.

Program 10.19 also plots the original data in scattered points and the straight line that best fits the data points shown in Figure 10.8. The range of the y-axis is specified from 0 to 18 meters by the statement

```
plot.axisRange(PLOT_AXIS_Y, 0, 18);
```

The plot type of scattered points for the first data set, 0 for `num`, is specified by the statement

```
plot.plotType(PLOT_PLOTTYPE_POINTS, num);
```

The statement

```
plot.func2D(t[0], t[n-1], 100, func);
```

plots the straight line in equation (10.7) from t_0 to t_{n-1} with 100 points. By default, data points are connected by straight lines.

Linear regression analysis is a commonly used data analysis technique. To make application development easier, one may add the linear regression analysis function `linearreg()` as shown in Program 10.20 to the statistical library `statlib.c`. The following function prototype needs to be added to the header file `statlib.h`.

```
extern void linearreg(int n, double t[], double y[], double coeff[2]);
```

`n` is the number of elements for the passed arrays `t` and `y` for data to be fitted in the linear regression model. The linear regression coefficients for the intercept and slope are passed to the calling function by the argument `coeff`, an array with two elements.

Program 21.9 in Chapter 21 solves the same problem using matrix notation.

It should be noted that a linear model may not be a good fit for a data set. Before a linear model is used, one should plot data points in scattered points to see if it is a good fit. Besides the linear equation, which is a first-order polynomial, higher-order polynomials can be used to fit a data set. In addition, a combination of elementary functions, such as polynomial, sine, and exponential functions, can also be used to fit a curve. These can be conveniently accomplished using numerical functions **polyfit**() for polynomial fit and **curvefit**() for a general curve fit in Ch.

```
/* File: linearreg.c
   A linear regression analysis function using
   function mean() in statlib.h and statlib.c */
#include "statlib.h"  /* for mean()  in the statistical lib */

/* A linear regression function, n is the size for arrays t and y of input data.
   coeff[2] is the output array with TWO elements for regression coefficients */
void linearreg(int n, double t[], double y[], double coeff[2]) {
    /* mean values and sums in the formulas for regression analysis */
    double t_mean, y_mean, titm, sumty, sumts;
    int i;

    /* calculate the linear regression coefficients based on the formulas */
    t_mean = mean(n, t);
    y_mean = mean(n, y);
    for(i=0; i<n; i++) {
       titm = t[i] - t_mean;
       sumty = titm*(y[i]-y_mean);
       sumts = titm*titm;
    }
    coeff[1] = sumty/sumts;
    coeff[0] = y_mean - coeff[1]*t_mean;
}
```

Program 10.20: A linear regression function.

10.6.3 Three-Dimensional Plotting

The function **plotxy()** can be used to generate a two-dimensional plot with data in arrays. To generate a three dimensional plot with data in arrays, the function **plotxyz()** can be used. A three-dimensional plot can be either a surface, such as one shown in Figure 6.6 in Chapter 6, or a curve. For the user's convenience, the same function **plotxyz()** can be used to handle both types of three-dimensional plots. In C++, the function **plotxyz()** is overloaded, a mechanism of using the same function name but with a different function prototype. In Ch, the function **plotxyz()** is implemented with a variable number of arguments. We present this function using different function prototypes to handle different plot types.

For generating a three-dimensional surface plot, the function **plotxyz()** can be treated as if it had the following function prototype:

```
int plotxyz(double x[], double y[], double z[], int nx, int ny,
            char *title, char *xlabel, char *ylabel, char *zlabel);
```

The arrays `x` and `y`, with their number of elements specified by the arguments `nx` and `ny`, store data for the x-axis and y-axis, respectively. The array z contains the data for the `z` coordinate for each point on the surface. Therefore, the number of elements for the array `z` is $nx * ny$. The title and labels for axes are specified by the remaining four arguments `title`, `xlabel`, `ylabel`, and `zlabel`, respectively. Like using the function **plotxy()**, a program using the function **plotxyz()** needs to include the header file **chplot.h**.

As an example, in section 6.7.3, the function **fplotxyz()** is used to plot the function

$$\text{sinr}(x, y) = \frac{\sin(r)}{r}, \text{ with } r = \sqrt{x^2 + y^2}$$

with variables x and y as shown in Figure 6.6. The plot uses 80 points for the x-coordinates and 100 points for the y-coordinates in the ranges of $-10 \leq x \leq 10$ and $-10 \leq y \leq 10$, respectively. The same plot can be generated using the function **plotxyz()** as shown in Program 10.21. The data for x and y coordinates are stored in arrays of 80 and 100 elements, respectively. The array z with 80×100 elements is used to hold the data for plotting. Two nested loops are used to generate the data for the z-coordinates of the surface corresponding to each point in the x and y coordinates.

```
/* File: hatarray.cpp
   Plot function sinr(x, y)=sin(sqrt(x*x + y*y))/sqrt(x*x + y*y)
   using function sinr() for x from -10 to 10 80 points,
   and for y from -10 to 10 with step size 100. */

#include <math.h>
#include <chplot.h>

#define NUMX 80
#define NUMY 100

int main() {
    /* declare and initialize with variables for x0, xf, y0, yf */
    double x0 = -10.0, xf = 10.0, y0 = -10.0, yf = 10.0, r;
```

Program 10.21: A program to plot a three-dimensional surface using data in arrays by the plotting function **plotxyz()**. *(Continued)*

```
    /* declare arrays for x, y, and z coordinates. Number of elements for
       z is related to number of points for x and y by NUMX*NUMY */
    double x[NUMX], y[NUMY], z[NUMX*NUMY];
    int i, j;

    /* fill array y with values in the range [y0, yf] linearly */
    for(j=0; j<NUMY; j++)
       y[j] = y0 + j*(yf-y0)/(NUMY-1);
    for(i=0; i<NUMX; i++) {
       /* fill array x with values in the range [x0, xf] linearly */
       x[i] = x0 + i*(xf-x0)/(NUMX-1);
       /* fill array z with values in the ranges [x0, xf] and [y0, yf] */
       for(j=0; j<NUMY; j++) {
          r = sqrt(x[i]*x[i] + y[j]*y[j]);
          z[i*NUMY+j] = sin(r)/r;
       }
    }
    /* plot 3D surface using plotxyz() */
    plotxyz(x, y, z, NUMX, NUMY, "function sinr(x, y)", "x", "y", "sinr");
    return 0;
}
```

Program 10.21: *(Continued)*

Similar to **plotxy**(), the function **plotxyz**() can be replaced by member functions of the plotting class **CPlot**. The function call

```
plotxyz(x, y, z, nx, ny, title, xlabel, ylabel, zlabel);
```

can be replaced by the following code using a plotting class **CPlot**:

```
CPlot plot;
plot.title(title);
plot.label(PLOT_AXIS_X, xlabel);
plot.label(PLOT_AXIS_Y, ylabel);
plot.data3DSurface(x, y, z, nx, ny);
plot.plotting();
```

The plotting data of arrays `x`, `y`, and `z` are added to the plotting object by the member function call

```
plot.data3DSurface(x, y, z, nx, ny);
```

Detailed information about the member function **data3DSurface**() can be found in section 20.1 in Chapter 20.

For generating a three-dimensional curve, the function **plotxyz**() can be treated as if it had the following function prototype:

```
int plotxyz(double x[], double y[], double z[], int n,
            char *title, char *xlabel, char *ylabel, char *zlabel);
```

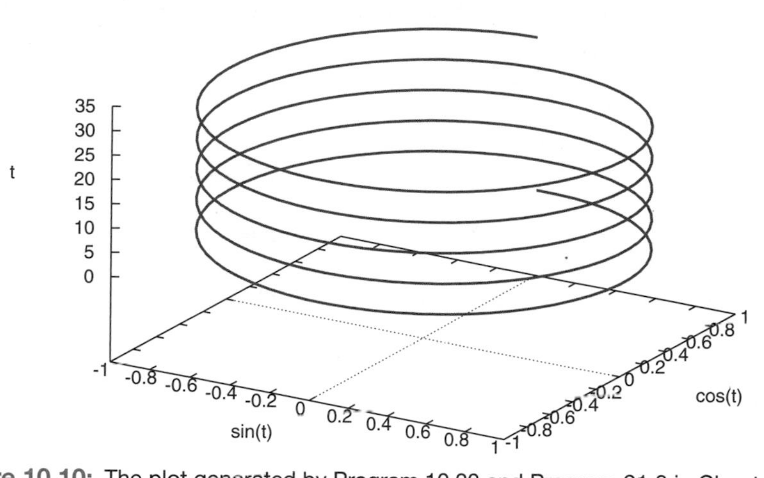

Figure 10.10: The plot generated by Program 10.22 and Program 21.8 in Chapter 21.

In this case, arrays `x`, `y`, and `z` shall have the same number of elements specified by the fourth argument, `n`. The remaining four arguments specify the title and labels of three axes.

As an example, the three-dimensional curve shown in Figure 10.10 is modeled by the parametric functions in terms of parameter t below:

$$x = \sin(t) \tag{10.10}$$

$$y = \cos(t) \tag{10.11}$$

$$z = t \tag{10.12}$$

Figure 10.10 is generated by Program 10.22 with 300 points for the curve for t from 0 to 10π.

```
/* File: helix.cpp
   Plot 3D curve using plotxyz() */
#include <math.h>
#include <chplot.h> /* for plotxyz() */

#define N 300        /* number of data points for the 3D curve */

int main() {
    /* declare arrays for plotting, t is coordinates in z-axis  */
    double t[N], x[N], y[N];
    int i;

    /* fill the array with the data based on the formula for the helix curve */
    for(i=0; i<N; i++) {
```

Program 10.22: A program to plot three-dimensional data in arrays using the plotting function **plotxyz()**. (*Continued*)

```
        t[i] = 10*M_PI*i/(N-1); /* data in time for z-axis */
        x[i] = sin(t[i]);        /* data in x-axis */
        y[i] = cos(t[i]);        /* data in y-axis */
    }
    /* plot 3D curve using plotxyz() */
    plotxyz(x, y, t, N, "Helix", "sin(t)", "cos(t)", "t");
    return 0;
}
```

Program 10.22: (*Continued*)

Similar to a surface, the data for plotting a three-dimensional curve in the function call

```
plotxyz(x, y, z, n, title. xlabel, ylabel, zlabel);
```

can be replaced by the the member function **data2DCurve**() of the class **CPlot** as follows:

```
CPlot plot;
plot.title(title);
plot.label(PLOT_AXIS_X, xlabel);
plot.label(PLOT_AXIS_Y, ylabel);
plot.data3DCurve(x, y, z, n);
plot.plotting();
```

10.7 Variable Length Arrays (VLAs) in C99

Because C was not originally designed for numerical computing, handling multidimensional arrays in C is cumbersome in many situations. For example, contrary to the fame of C for its conciseness and clarity, passing VLAs to functions in C89 is neither intuitive nor easy to understand; it is quite complicated in comparison with other features, as will be described in Chapter 11. Adding VLAs to C is a critical step in evolving C as a leading programming language for applications in science and engineering. VLAs whose size is known only at program execution time have been added in C99. Details about VLAs in C99 are described in this section.

10.7.1 Passing VLAs to Functions

The VLA in a function parameter is a formal argument which takes the shape of the actual argument passed to it. That is, the arrays for actual and formal arguments have the same rank and extent in each dimension. The bounds of the array shall be an integral variable declared in the same function prototype prior to the array argument, as shown in Program 10.23 with the function prototype

```
double func(int m, int n, double a[m][n]);
```

The array bounds for a VLA, such as m and n, have to be declared before an array definition. Without VLA in C99, one would have to use the function

```
double func(int m, int n, double **a);
```

where a is a pointer to pointer to double, to pass two-dimensional arrays of different length, which will be described in section 11.15 in Chapter 11.

```
/* File: pass2Dcarrayvla.c (run in C99 and Ch only)
   Compile in gcc, use command 'gcc -std=c99 pass2Dcarrayvla.c'
   Calculate the sum of all elements of two-dimensional arrays
   by passing of variable length to a function using VLA in C99.
   It can be compiled by a C compiler/interpreter which
   supports this new feature in C99, such as Ch and gcc */
#include <stdio.h>
#include <stdlib.h>

/* define macro for different extents of arrays */
#define M1 2
#define N1 3
#define M2 3
#define N2 4

/* possible function prototype for VLA */
double func(int m, int n, double a[m][n]);
/* or double func(int m, int n, double a[*][*]); */
/* or double func(int, int, double [*][*]); */

int main() {
    /* declare and initialize arrays a1 and a2 with different extents */
    double a1[M1][N1]={1.0, 2.0, 3.0, 4.0, 5.0, 6.0};
    double a2[M2][N2]={1.0, 2.0, 3.0, 4.0, 5.0, 6.0,
                       7.0, 8.0, 9.0, 10.0, 11.0, 12.0};
    double sum; /* sum for all elements of an array */

    sum = func(M1, N1, a1);     /* calculate the sum for array a1 */
    printf("sum = %f\n", sum); /* display sum for array a1 */

    sum = func(M2, N2, a2);     /* calculate the sum for array a2 */
    printf("sum = %f\n", sum); /* display sum for array a2 */
    return 0;
}

/* function to calculate the sum of two-dimensional arrays with
   different extents */
double func(int m, int n, double a[m][n]) {
    double sum = 0;             /* declare and initialize sum */
    int i, j;                   /* declare index variables for loops */
```

Program 10.23: Using VLAs to pass two-dimensional arrays of different sizes. (*Continued*)

```
    for(i=0; i<m; i++) {
        for(j=0; j<n; j++) {
            sum += a[i][j];       /* sum all elements one by one */
        }
    }
    return sum;                   /* return the sum */
}
```

Program 10.23: *(Continued)*

Program 10.23 is an example of passing a VLA as a function argument. The extents of the rows and columns for the formal array argument `a` depends on integral variables `m` and `n`, respectively. Arrays `a1` and `a2` of different shape in the function main() are passed to the same argument `a` of variable length of the function `func()`. The function adds all the elements of the passed array and returns the sum. The main function prints out the returned sums for arrays `a1` and `a2`. The following command

```
gcc -std=c99 pass2Dcarrayvla.c
```

compiles Program 10.23 with VLAs in C99 using the GNU C compiler. The output of Program 10.23 is as follows:

```
sum = 21.000000
sum = 78.000000
```

In a function prototype, the size of an array can be replaced by the symbol '`*`', as shown in Program 10.23 as

```
double funct(int m, int n, double a[*][*]);
```

or without variable names as

```
double funct(int, int, double [*][*]);
```

The shape of a VLA cannot be determined until execution time. The rank of the array is equal to the number of brackets in the array specification.

An Application Example

Sorting Two-Dimensional Arrays

Problem Statement:
Write a function to sort each row of a two-dimensional array in ascending order and to pass medians for each row to the calling function.

The function `sort()` in Program 10.13 for a statistical library can sort a one-dimensional array. Using a VLA, the function prototype for `sort()` in Program 10.13 could be changed to

```
void sort(int n, double a[n]);
```

Program 10.15 uses the function `sort()` to sort each row of a two-dimensional array. The median for each sorted row is then calculated by the function `median()` in the library. However, this statistical library cannot be used for statistical analysis for each column of two-dimensional arrays.

As an application example of passing two-dimensional arrays of different lengths to a function, a function for sorting two-dimensional arrays is developed. The example also shows how to use triple-nested loops. For two-dimensional arrays, there are multiple values for median, one for each row. Therefore, an argument of arrays needs to be used to pass back these medians in floating-point numbers. A proper function prototype for sorting two-dimensional arrays is

```
void sortArray2d(int m, int n, double a[m][n], double medians[m]);
```

as shown in Program 10.24. There is no return value from this function. The sorted array and its medians for each row are passed back to the calling function through its argument `a` and `medians` of array type. There

```
/* File: sortarray2d.c (run in C99 and Ch only)
   Compile in gcc, use command 'gcc -std=c99 sortarray2d.c'
   Sort two-dimensional arrays of different sizes in row-wise ascending
   order by the same function with arguments of variable length arrays */
#include <stdio.h>

/* function prototypes for sorting and printing arrays */
void sortArray2d(int m, int n, double a[m][n], double median[m]);
void printArray2d(int m, int n, double a[m][n]);
void printArray(int n, double a[n]);

/* extents for arrays a1 and a2 in function main() */
#define M1 2
#define N1 3
#define M2 3
#define N2 4

int main() {
    /* declare two arrays a1 and a2 with different sizes */
    double a1[M1][N1] = {3.0, 21.0, -3.0,
                         8.0, -9.0, 10.0};
    double a2[M2][N2] = {3.0,   21.0,  0.0, -3.0,
                        34.0, -14.0, 45.0, 18.0,
                         8.0,  -9.0,  4.0, 10.0};
    double median1[M1], median2[M2]; /* medians for arrays a1 and a2 */

    /* display the original and sorted data for array a1 */
    printf("The original data:\n");
    printArray2d(M1, N1, a1);
    sortArray2d(M1, N1, a1, median1);
    printf("The sorted data in row-wise ascending order:\n");
    printArray2d(M1, N1, a1);
```

Program 10.24: Using a function to sort each row of an array in ascending order and calculate medians for each row of the array. *(Continued)*

```
    printf("The medians in each row:\n");
    printArray(M1, median1);

    /* display the original and sorted data for array a2 */
    printf("\nThe original data:\n");
    printArray2d(M2, N2, a2);
    sortArray2d(M2, N2, a2, median2);
    printf("The sorted data in row-wise ascending order:\n");
    printArray2d(M2, N2, a2);
    printf("The medians in each row:\n");
    printArray(M2, median2);
    return 0;
}

/* function to sort array a in row-wise ascending order using bubble sort.
   argument median[] contains the medians for each row */
void sortArray2d(int m, int n, double a[m][n], double median[m]) {
    int i, j, k; /* array indices */
    double temp; /* temporary variable for swap */

    /* outer loop for each row of array a */
    for(k = 0; k < m; k++) {
        /* sort each row based on the column index of array a */
        for(i = 0; i < n-1; i++) {
            /* sort one row at a time, the row index k for array a is fixed
               inside this i-loop */
            for(j = i+1; j < n; j++) {
            /* if(a[k][i] > a[k][j]), swap the values for these two elements */
                if(a[k][i] > a[k][j]) {
                    temp = a[k][i];
                    a[k][i] = a[k][j];
                    a[k][j] = temp;
                }
            }
        }
        /* calculate the median for the sorted row */
        if(n%2) /* the total number of elements is odd */
           median[k] = a[k][n/2];
        else    /* the total number of elements is even */
           median[k] = (a[k][n/2-1] + a[k][n/2])/2.0;
    }
}
```

Program 10.24: *(Continued)*

```
/* function to print elements of a two-dimensional array */
void printArray2d(int m, int n, double a[m][n]) {
     int i, j;
     for(i = 0; i < m; i++) {
          for(j = 0; j < n; j++) {
              printf("%4g", a[i][j]);
          }
          printf("\n");
     }
}

/* function to print elements of a one-dimensional array */
void printArray(int n, double a[n]) {
     int i;
     for(i = 0; i < n; i++) {
          printf("%4g", a[i]);
     }
     printf("\n");
}
```

Program 10.24: *(Continued)*

are three nested loops in the function `sortArray2d()`. Similar to the function `sort()`, Program 10.24 uses the bubble sort algorithm to sort each row. The inner two loops with indices `i` and j are the same as those in the function `sort()` in Program 10.13. The outer loop with index `k` is for each row. Within the inner loops, two elements, `a[k][i]` and `a[k][j]`, have the same first index for a given row. The median for each row is calculated in this outer loop.

The function `printArray2d()` in Program 10.24 prints out each element of the passed two-dimensional array of variable lengths.

```
void printArray2d(int m, int n, double a[m][n]);
```

The format control string for each element is `"%4g"` with a field width 4 and flexible `g` format which displays a floating-point number in either the floating-point form or the exponential form. The function `printArray()` prints out each element of the passed one-dimensional array of variable lengths.

```
void printArray(int n, double a[n]);
```

Because it is used to display medians for each row, a floating-point number is displayed with a field width 6 and 2 digits after the decimal point. The output often Program 10.24 is show in Figure 10.11.

Two-dimensional arrays `a1` and `a2` in Program 10.24 are different sizes. The functionk `printArray2d()` is called to display the original data in array `a1` first. Next, the function `sortArray2d()` is called to sort the array `a1` in row-wise ascending order. Then, the function `printArray2d()` is called again to to display the sorted data in array `a1`. Finally, the medians for each row are printed out by calling the function `printArray()`. The process is repeated for the array `a2`.

```
The original data:
   3  21  -3
   8  -9  10
The sorted data in row-wise ascending order:
  -3   3  21
  -9   8  10
The medians in each row:
  3.00  8.00

The original data:
   3  21   0  -3
  34 -14  45  18
   8  -9   4  10
The sorted data in row-wise ascending order:
  -3   0   3  21
 -14  18  34  45
  -9   4   8  10
The medians in each row:
  1.50 26.00  6.00
```

Figure 10.11: The output from Program 10.24.

10.7.2 Deferred-Shape Arrays

Declaration

A *deferred-shape array* has its shape value determined at runtime. It can be declared in the form of

```
type name[expr]
```

where `type` specifies the data type of array `name`. The nonconstant integral expression `expr` gives the size of the array at execution time. Because the size of a deferred-shape array is obtained at program execution time, it is useful for applications when the size of the array cannot be specified beforehand.

The size of a deferred-shape array type shall not change until the execution of the block containing the declaration has ended. Therefore, at least one of the size expressions is a nonconstant integral expression for deferred-shape arrays. The variables used in the size expression must be declared beforehand. For example, arrays `a`, `b`, `c`, `d`, and `e` in Program 10.25 are valid declarations of deferred-shape arrays, whereas arrays `f`, `g`, and `h` are not. The expression `n3` had not been defined yet when the array `f` was declared. The sizes of arrays `g` and `h` are not positive integral values. A deferred-shape array `p` cannot be declared with the **static** storage class specifier. Because the size of a deferred-shape array is unknown until the execution time, the size of the deferred-shape array often is different at each invocation. Therefore, the deferred-shape array such as `q` cannot be initialized.

When the built-in **sizeof** operator is applied to an operand that has array type, the result is the total number of bytes allocated for storing the elements of the array. For deferred-shape arrays, the result is not a constant expression and is computed at program execution time.

```
/* File: declaredefer.c
   Demonstration of declaration of deferred-shape arrays */
int n1;          /* declare global variable n1 with allocation of memory */
extern int n2; /* declare extern variable n2 without allocation of memory */

int funct1(int i) {  /* function definition */
    return i*i;
}

void funct2(int m, int n) {
    int i = 8*n;
    int j = 0, k = -9;
    int a[i][4];           /* OK */
    int b[m][3];           /* OK: mix fixed-extent with deferred extent */
    int c[n*m][n];         /* OK */
    int d[funct1(n)][3*funct1(i)]; /* use function in the array size */
    int e[n1][n2*n];                /* OK, n1 declared, n2 declared */
    int f[n3];            /* ERROR: n3 has not been defined yet */
    int g[j];             /* ERROR: zero size (j is 0) */
    int h[k];             /* ERROR: negative size (k is -9) */
    static int p[m];      /* ERROR: static VLA */
    int q[m] = {1, 2}; /* ERROR: initialize VLA  */
}
int n2 = 10, n3 = 20;  /* declare n2 and n3 with allocation of memory */
```

Program 10.25: Declaration of deferred-shape arrays.

An Application Example

Acceleration of a Moving Body

Problem Statement:
For the mechanical system shown in Figure 2.12, given mass $m = 5$ kilograms (kg) and coefficient of kinetic friction $\mu = 0.2$, the applied force p is expressed as a function of time t in

$$p(t) = 4\sin(t - 3) + 20$$

Write a function to print the acceleration and force versus time from $t = 0$ to $t = 10$. Arrays for acceleration and time are declared and used in the main function. These arrays, along with their size, are passed to the function. An array for forces shall be allocated dynamically inside the function. The function is called twice, one with arrays of 11 elements and the other with 6.

The solution to the problem statement is given in Program 10.26. The program calls the function `accel()` to calculate and print the acceleration of the system for both 11 and 6 data points. Note that VLAs of `t` and `a` are used as function arguments, as shown in the function header

```
int accel(int n, double t[n], double a[n])
```

to use the same function for arrays of variable sizes. Inside the function, the array `p` is declared as a deferred-shape by

```
double p[n];
```

Its size `n` is determined at runtime. The output generated by Program 10.26 is shown in Figure 10.12.

```
/* File: accelvla.c (run in C99 and Ch only)
   Compile in gcc, use command 'gcc -std=c99 accelvla.c -lm'
   Calculate acceleration, force, and time using VLA in C99.
   The array for force is also a deferred-shape array */
#include <stdio.h>
#include <math.h>     /* for sin() */

#define M_G   9.81    /* gravitational acceleration constant g */
#define N1    11      /* number of points for a, p, and t */
#define N2     6      /* number of points for a, p, and t */

/* pass arrays t and a of variable length */
int accel(int n, double t[n], double a[n]) {
    double p[n];              /* declare deferred-shape array p */
    double mu, m, t0, tf;
    int i;

    /* set mu, mass, initial time, and final time */
    mu = 0.2;
    m = 5.0;
    t0 = 0.0;
    tf = 10.0;

    /* calculate t[i], pi[i], a[i] */
    for(i=0; i<n; i++) {
        t[i] = t0+i*(tf - t0)/(n-1);
        p[i] = 4*sin(t[i]-3)+20;
        a[i] = (p[i]-mu*m*M_G)/m;
    }

    /* post processing of the data by printing out or plotting.
       Here, data for t, p, and a are printed out */
    printf(" time (s) force (N) accel (m/s^2)\n");
```

Program 10.26: Calculating accelerations and forces using VLAs. (*Continued*)

```
    printf("---------------------------------\n");
    for(i=0; i<n; i++) {
        printf("%8.4f  %8.4f  %8.4f\n", t[i], p[i], a[i]);
    }
    printf("\n");  /* a newline to separate each function call */
    return 0;
}

int main() {
    double t1[N1], a1[N1]; /* declare array t1 and a1 with N1 points */
    double t2[N2], a2[N2]; /* declare array t2 and a2 with N2 points */

    accel(N1, t1, a1);      /* pass arrays with N1 points */
    accel(N2, t2, a2);      /* pass arrays with N2 points */
    return 0;
}
```

Program 10.26: *(Continued)*

```
 time (s) force (N) accel (m/s^2)
----------------------------------
  0.0000   19.4355    1.9251
  1.0000   16.3628    1.3106
  2.0000   16.6341    1.3648
  3.0000   20.0000    2.0380
  4.0000   23.3659    2.7112
  5.0000   23.6372    2.7654
  6.0000   20.5645    2.1509
  7.0000   16.9728    1.4326
  8.0000   16.1643    1.2709
  9.0000   18.8823    1.8145
 10.0000   22.6279    2.5636

 time (s) force (N) accel (m/s^2)
----------------------------------
  0.0000   19.4355    1.9251
  2.0000   16.6341    1.3648
  4.0000   23.3659    2.7112
  6.0000   20.5645    2.1509
  8.0000   16.1643    1.2709
 10.0000   22.6279    2.5636
```

Figure 10.12: The output from Program 10.26.

10.8 Introduction to Vector and Matrix Analysis

Vectors and matrices are used in a wide variety of engineering applications. Two- and three-degree vectors are commonly used to represent physical properties such as position, velocity, and force with magnitudes and directions in two- and three-dimensional space. Matrices can be used to represent systems of linear equations, stress tensors in a loaded material, etc. This section describes the representation of mathematical vectors and matrices as one- and two-dimensional arrays in C. It also illustrates some basic mathematical vector and matrix operations and their C counterparts.

10.8.1 Introduction to Vectors

A mathematical *vector* is simply a list of numbers. For instance, $\boldsymbol{v} = (1, 3, 3)$ describes a three-dimensional vector and $\boldsymbol{b} = (b_1, b_2, b_3, b_4)$ stands for a four-dimensional vector. In C, one-dimensional arrays are perfectly suitable to represent vectors. For instance, the line of code

```
double v[3];
```

declares a one-dimensional array v suitable to represent a three-dimensional vector. Note that there is a disparity for word *dimension* in the mathematical terminology and C terminology. The *dimension* for a vector in mathematics refers to the number of elements. An n-dimensional vector is represented as a one-dimensional array with n elements in C.

The Scalar Product of Two Vectors

The scalar product (or dot product) of two vectors $\boldsymbol{a}$ and $\boldsymbol{b}$ with the same size is defined as

$$s = \boldsymbol{a} \cdot \boldsymbol{b} \tag{10.13}$$

$$s = a_1 b_1 + a_2 b_2 + a_3 b_3 + \cdots + a_n b_n \tag{10.14}$$

The scalar product is used in many different applications. For instance, when the vectors are being used to represent magnitudes and directions, the dot product between two vectors is

$$\boldsymbol{a} \cdot \boldsymbol{b} = ab \cos \theta \tag{10.15}$$

where θ is the angle between the two vectors, and a and b are the magnitudes of each vector.

The sample code for calculating the scalar product of two vectors is shown below.

```
#define N 20

double s, a[N], b[N];
int i;
...
s = 0;
for(i=0; i<N; i++) {
    s += a[i]*b[i];
}
```

10.8.2 Introduction to Matrices

A matrix is a mathematical entity that is a rectangular collection of numbers. Matrices and matrix operations are commonly used in engineering to analyze systems of linear equations and in many other applications. The following matrix $\boldsymbol{A}$ is an example of a matrix with $m \times n$ numbers arranged in m rows and n columns.

$$\boldsymbol{A}_{m\times n} = \left[a_{ij}\right] = \begin{bmatrix} a_{11} & a_{12} & \cdots & a_{1n} \\ a_{21} & a_{22} & \cdots & a_{2n} \\ \cdots & \cdots & \cdots & \cdots \\ a_{m1} & a_{m2} & \cdots & a_{mn} \end{bmatrix} \tag{10.16}$$

where the symbol a_{ij} denotes the number in the ith row and jth column.

Two-dimensional arrays are used to represent matrices in C. For instance,

```
double a[3][4];
```

declares a two-dimensional array suitable for representing a 3×4 matrix, with three rows and four columns.

Matrix Addition and Subtraction

Two matrices $\boldsymbol{A}$ and $\boldsymbol{B}$ can be added if and only if they have the same number of rows and the same number of columns. When adding matrices, each entry in the resultant matrix is the sum of the entries in the corresponding positions in the matrices being added.

$$\boldsymbol{C}_{m\times n} = \boldsymbol{A}_{m\times n} + \boldsymbol{B}_{m\times n} \tag{10.17}$$

$$\begin{bmatrix} c_{11} & c_{12} & \cdots & c_{1n} \\ c_{21} & c_{22} & \cdots & c_{2n} \\ \cdots & \cdots & \cdots & \cdots \\ c_{m1} & c_{m2} & \cdots & c_{mn} \end{bmatrix} = \begin{bmatrix} a_{11} & a_{12} & \cdots & a_{1n} \\ a_{21} & a_{22} & \cdots & a_{2n} \\ \cdots & \cdots & \cdots & \cdots \\ a_{m1} & a_{m2} & \cdots & a_{mn} \end{bmatrix} + \begin{bmatrix} b_{11} & b_{12} & \cdots & b_{1n} \\ b_{21} & b_{22} & \cdots & b_{2n} \\ \cdots & \cdots & \cdots & \cdots \\ b_{m1} & b_{m2} & \cdots & b_{mn} \end{bmatrix} \tag{10.18}$$

where the element c_{ij} in the position (i, j) of the resultant matrix $\boldsymbol{C}$ is defined as

$$c_{ij} = a_{ij} + b_{ij} \tag{10.19}$$

Sample code for the addition of two matrices is given below.

```
#define M 10
#define N 20

double a[M][N], b[M][N], c[M][N];
int i, j;
...
for(i=0; i<M; i++) {
    for(j=0; j<N; j++) {
        c[i][j] = a[i][j]+b[i][j];
    }
}
```

The Multiplication of a Matrix and a Scalar Value

When a matrix $\boldsymbol{A}$ is multiplied by a scalar value, each element of the matrix is multiplied by the scalar value. The size of the resultant matrix is the same size as the original one.

$$\boldsymbol{B}_{m\times n} = s\boldsymbol{A}_{m\times n} \tag{10.20}$$

$$\begin{bmatrix} b_{11} & b_{12} & \cdots & b_{1n} \\ b_{21} & b_{22} & \cdots & b_{2n} \\ \cdots & \cdots & \cdots & \cdots \\ b_{m1} & b_{m2} & \cdots & b_{mn} \end{bmatrix} = s \begin{bmatrix} a_{11} & a_{12} & \cdots & a_{1n} \\ a_{21} & a_{22} & \cdots & a_{2n} \\ \cdots & \cdots & \cdots & \cdots \\ a_{m1} & a_{m2} & \cdots & a_{mn} \end{bmatrix} \tag{10.21}$$

where the element of the resultant matrix $\boldsymbol{B}$ for the product of matrix $\boldsymbol{A}$ and scalar value s is defined as

$$b_{ij} = sa_{ij} \tag{10.22}$$

The sample code for the multiplication of a matrix and a scalar value is shown below.

```
#define M 10
#define N 20

double a[M][N], b[M][N], s;
int i, j;
...
for(i=0; i<M; i++) {
     for(j=0; j<N; j++) {
          b[i][j] = s*a[i][j];
     }
}
```

The Multiplication of Matrix and Vector

A matrix $\boldsymbol{A}$ and a vector $\boldsymbol{v}$ can be multiplied in the order of $\boldsymbol{Av}$ if and only if the number of columns of the matrix equals the number of elements of the vector. The result is a vector with the number of elements equal to the number of rows in the matrix.

$$\boldsymbol{b}_m = \boldsymbol{A}_{m\times n}\boldsymbol{v}_n \tag{10.23}$$

$$\begin{bmatrix} b_1 \\ b_2 \\ \vdots \\ b_m \end{bmatrix} = \begin{bmatrix} a_{11} & a_{12} & \cdots & a_{1n} \\ a_{21} & a_{22} & \cdots & a_{2n} \\ \cdots & \cdots & \cdots & \cdots \\ a_{m1} & a_{m2} & \cdots & a_{mn} \end{bmatrix} \begin{bmatrix} v_1 \\ v_2 \\ \vdots \\ v_n \end{bmatrix} \tag{10.24}$$

The element b_i in the resultant vector is the scalar product of the ith row of the matrix $\boldsymbol{A}$ and the vector $\boldsymbol{v}$. It is calculated by the following formula:

$$b_i = \boldsymbol{a}_{i\alpha} \cdot \boldsymbol{v} \tag{10.25}$$

where $\boldsymbol{a}_{i\alpha}$ represents the ith row of the matrix as a vector. In other words,

$$b_i = a_{i1}v_1 + a_{i2}v_2 + \cdots + a_{in}v_n \tag{10.26}$$

As an example, if we multiply the matrix

$$A = \begin{bmatrix} 3 & 5 & 6 \\ 4 & 2 & 1 \\ 0 & 7 & 1 \end{bmatrix} \tag{10.27}$$

by the vector on the right

$$v = \begin{bmatrix} 2 \\ 1 \\ -2 \end{bmatrix} \tag{10.28}$$

the vector b for the product Av is

$$b = \begin{bmatrix} -1 \\ 8 \\ 5 \end{bmatrix} \tag{10.29}$$

which can be calculated by Program 10.27 with its output as follows:

```
b = -1 8 5
```

```
/* File: matrixv.c
   Calculate matrix equation b = Ax */
#include <stdio.h>

#define M 3     /* number of rows */
#define N 3     /* number of columns */

int main() {
    /* declare and initialize matrix A and vector v, declare b */
    double a[M][N] = {3, 5, 6,
                      4, 2, 1,
                      0, 7, 1};
    double v[N] = {2, 1, -2}; b[M];
    int i, j;

    /* multiply row-by-row */
    for(i=0; i<M; i++) {
        b[i] = 0;
        for(j=0; j<N; j++) {
            b[i]+= a[i][j]*v[j];
        }
    }
    printf("b = %g, %g, %g\n", b[0], b[1], b[2]); /* printing vector b */
    return 0;
}
```

Program 10.27: Multiplication of a matrix by a vector.

Using VLAs in C99, we can also write a function `matvecmul()`, as shown in Program 10.28 with the following function prototype:

```
void matvecmul(int m, int n, double a[m][n], double v[n], double b[m]);
```

to perform the multiplication of a matrix by a vector in equation (10.23). In this function, argument `m` is the number of rows for matrix `a` and the number of rows for vector `b`, `n` represents the number of columns for matrix `a` and the number of rows for vector `v`. The output from Program 10.28 is the same as that from Program 10.27.

```
/* File: matvecmul.c
   Calculate matrix equation b = Ax using function matvecmul() using
   VLA in C99. Compile in gcc, use command 'gcc -std=c99 matvecmul.c' */
#include <stdio.h>

#define M 3    /* number of rows */
#define N 3    /* number of columns */

void matvecmul(int m, int n, double a[m][n], double v[n], double b[m]) {
   int i, j;  /* array indices */

   /* multiply row-by-row */
   for(i=0; i<m; i++) {
       b[i] = 0;
       for(j=0; j<n; j++) {
           b[i]+= a[i][j]*v[j];
       }
   }
}

int main() {
   /* declare and initialize matrix A and vector x, declare b */
   double a[M][N] = {3, 5, 6,
                     4, 2, 1,
                     0, 7, 1};
   double x[N] = {2, 1, -2}, b[M];

   matvecmul(M, N, a, x, b);
   printf("b = %g, %g, %g\n", b[0], b[1], b[2]); /* printing vector b */
   return 0;
}
```

Program 10.28: Multiplication of a matrix by a vector using the function `matvecmul()`.

The Multiplication of Two Matrices

Two matrices $\boldsymbol{A}$ and $\boldsymbol{B}$ can be multiplied in the order of $\boldsymbol{AB}$ if and only if the number of columns in the first equals the number of rows in the second:

$$\boldsymbol{C}_{m\times p} = \boldsymbol{A}_{m\times n}\boldsymbol{B}_{n\times p} \tag{10.30}$$

$$\begin{bmatrix} c_{11} & c_{12} & \cdots & c_{1p} \\ c_{21} & c_{22} & \cdots & c_{2p} \\ \cdots & \cdots & \cdots & \cdots \\ c_{m1} & c_{m2} & \cdots & c_{mp} \end{bmatrix} = \begin{bmatrix} a_{11} & a_{12} & \cdots & a_{1n} \\ a_{21} & a_{22} & \cdots & a_{2n} \\ \cdots & \cdots & \cdots & \cdots \\ a_{m1} & a_{m2} & \cdots & a_{mn} \end{bmatrix} \begin{bmatrix} b_{11} & b_{12} & \cdots & b_{1p} \\ b_{21} & b_{22} & \cdots & b_{2p} \\ \cdots & \cdots & \cdots & \cdots \\ b_{n1} & b_{n2} & \cdots & b_{np} \end{bmatrix} \tag{10.31}$$

The element c_{ij} in the position (i, j) of the resultant matrix is the scalar product of the ith row of the first matrix and the jth column of the second matrix.

$$\begin{bmatrix} & \vdots & \\ & \vdots & \\ \cdots & c_{ij} & \cdots\cdots \\ & \vdots & \end{bmatrix} = \begin{bmatrix} \cdots\cdots\cdots\cdots \\ \cdots\cdots\cdots\cdots \\ a_{i1}\ a_{i2} \cdots a_{in} \\ \cdots\cdots\cdots\cdots \end{bmatrix} \begin{bmatrix} \cdots b_{1j} \cdots\cdots \\ \cdots b_{2j} \cdots\cdots \\ \cdots\cdots\cdots\cdots \\ \cdots b_{nj} \cdots\cdots \end{bmatrix} \tag{10.32}$$

The element c_{ij} is calculated by

$$c_{ij} = a_{i1}b_{1j} + a_{i2}b_{2j} + a_{i3}b_{3j} + \cdots + a_{in}b_{nj} \tag{10.33}$$

Sample code for the multiplication of two matrices is shown below.

```
#define M 10
#define N 20
#define P 30

double a[M][N], b[N][P], c[M][P];
int i, j, k;
...
for(i=0; i<M; i++) {
     for(j=0; j<P; j++) {
          c[i][j] = 0;
          for(k=0; k<N; k++) {
              c[i][j] += a[i][k]*b[k][j];
          }
     }
}
```

The Transpose of a Matrix

The transpose of an $m \times n$ matrix $\boldsymbol{A}$ is the following $n \times m$ matrix, denoted by $\boldsymbol{A}^T$, obtained by interchanging the rows and columns of $\boldsymbol{A}$:

$$\boldsymbol{A} = \begin{bmatrix} a_{11} & a_{12} & \cdots & a_{1n} \\ a_{21} & a_{22} & \cdots & a_{2n} \\ \cdots & \cdots & \cdots & \cdots \\ a_{m1} & a_{m2} & \cdots & a_{mn} \end{bmatrix} \tag{10.34}$$

$$B = A^T = \begin{bmatrix} a_{11} & a_{21} & \cdots & a_{m1} \\ a_{12} & a_{22} & \cdots & a_{m2} \\ \cdots & \cdots & \cdots & \cdots \\ a_{1n} & a_{2n} & \cdots & a_{mn} \end{bmatrix} \tag{10.35}$$

For example, if a 3 × 2 matrix is

$$M = \begin{bmatrix} 1 & 2 & 3 \\ 4 & 5 & 6 \end{bmatrix} \tag{10.36}$$

then the transpose of the M, M^T becomes

$$M^T = \begin{bmatrix} 1 & 4 \\ 2 & 5 \\ 3 & 6 \end{bmatrix} \tag{10.37}$$

Sample code for obtaining the transpose of a matrix is given below.

```
#define M 10
#define N 20

double a[M][N], b[N][M]
int i, j;
...
for(i=0; i<M; i++) {
    for(j=0; j<N; j++) {
        b[j][i] = a[i][j];
    }
}
```

The Identity Matrix

The identity matrix, denoted by I, is a square matrix whose diagonal elements are all unity and off-diagonal elements are all zeroes.

$$I = \begin{bmatrix} 1 & 0 & \ldots & 0 \\ 0 & 1 & \ldots & 0 \\ \vdots & \vdots & \ddots & \vdots \\ 0 & 0 & \ldots & 1 \end{bmatrix} \tag{10.38}$$

A matrix multiplied by an identity matrix either on the left or right remains the same. That is,

$$A = IA \tag{10.39}$$

$$A = AI \tag{10.40}$$

where A is a square matrix. If v is a vector, the vector remains the same if it is multiplied by an identity matrix on the left. That is,

$$v = Iv \tag{10.41}$$

Sample code for creating an identity matrix is given below.

```
#define N 20

double a[N][N]={0};
int i;
...
for(i=0; i<N; i++) {
    a[i][i] = 1;
}
```

Each element of array a is initialized with zeros first. The diagonal elements are then set to 1.

As an example, matrices $\boldsymbol{A}$, $\boldsymbol{B}$, $\boldsymbol{C}$, and vector $\boldsymbol{v}$ are given as follows:

$$\boldsymbol{A} = \begin{bmatrix} 1 & 2 & 3 \\ 4 & 5 & 6 \end{bmatrix}, \boldsymbol{B} = \begin{bmatrix} 4 & 5 & 6 \\ 7 & 8 & 9 \end{bmatrix}, \boldsymbol{C} = \begin{bmatrix} 1 & 2 \\ 3 & 4 \\ 5 & 6 \end{bmatrix}, \boldsymbol{v} = \begin{bmatrix} 1 \\ 2 \\ 3 \end{bmatrix} \tag{10.42}$$

$\boldsymbol{A}$ and $\boldsymbol{B}$ are 2×3 matrices, $\boldsymbol{C}$ is a 3×2 matrix, and $\boldsymbol{v}$ is a column vector with three elements. The vector $\boldsymbol{x}$ with two elements and 2×2 matrix $\boldsymbol{Y}$, defined by the equations below

$$\boldsymbol{x} = (\boldsymbol{A} + \boldsymbol{B})\boldsymbol{v} \tag{10.43}$$

$$\boldsymbol{Y} = 3\boldsymbol{AC} \tag{10.44}$$

can be calculated by Program 10.29. Arrays a, b, c, v, x, and y in Program 10.29 represent the matrices or vectors $\boldsymbol{A}$, $\boldsymbol{B}$, $\boldsymbol{C}$, $\boldsymbol{v}$, $\boldsymbol{x}$, and $\boldsymbol{Y}$, respectively. Arrays a, b, c, and v are declared and initialized with values specified in equation (10.42). The sum $(\boldsymbol{A} + \boldsymbol{B})$ for matrices $\boldsymbol{A}$ and $\boldsymbol{B}$ is saved in a temporary array d by the statement

```
d[i][j] = a[i][j]+b[i][j];
```

inside two nested loops. The array d is then multiplied by the array v for the expression $(\boldsymbol{A} + \boldsymbol{B})\boldsymbol{v}$ using two nested loops by the statement

```
x[i] += d[i][j]*v[j];
```

When an element for vector $\boldsymbol{x}$ is calculated in the inner loop with the index j, it is printed out as the statement

```
printf("%d", x[i]);
```

Each element for matrix $\boldsymbol{Y}$ from the matrix expression $3\boldsymbol{AC}$ is obtained by three nested loops with the statement

```
y[i][j] += 3*a[i][k]*c[k][j];
```

The output from Program 10.29 is given in Figure 10.13.

```
/* File: matrixexpr.c
   Calculate matrix formulas x = (A+B)v and y = 3A*C */
#include <stdio.h>

/* for multiplication A[M1][N1]*C[M2][N2], N1 must equal M2 */
#define M1 2 /* number of rows for A, B, v */
#define N1 3 /* number of columns for A, B */
#define M2 3 /* number of rows for C */
#define N2 2 /* number of columns for C */

int main() {
  /* declare and initialize matrices A, B, C and vector v */
  double a[M1][N1] = {{1,2,3},{4,5,6}};
  double b[M1][N1] = {{4,5,6},{7,8,9}};
  double c[M2][N2] = {{1,2},{3,4},{5,6}};
  double v[N1] = {1,2,3};
  /* declare x and y, and temporary variable D for (A+B) */
  double x[M1], y[M1][N2], d[M1][N1];
  int i, j, k;

  for(i=0; i<M1; i++) {
     for(j=0; j<N1; j++) {
        d[i][j] = a[i][j]+b[i][j]; /* calculate D = (A + B) */
     }
  }
  printf("x = \n");
  /* calculate D*v for (A+B)v */
  for(i=0; i<M1; i++) {
     x[i] = 0;
     for(j=0; j<N1; j++) {
        x[i] += d[i][j]*v[j]; /* calculate D*v */
     }
     printf("%g ", x[i]);
  }
  printf("\n");

  printf("y = \n");
  for(i=0; i<M1; i++) {
     for(j=0; j<N2; j++) {
        y[i][j] = 0;
        for(k=0; k<N1; k++) {
           y[i][j] += 3*a[i][k]*c[k][j]; /* calculate 3A*C */
        }
```

Program 10.29: Calculating matrix and vector expressions $(\boldsymbol{A} + \boldsymbol{B})\boldsymbol{v}$ and $3\boldsymbol{AC}$. (*Continued*)

```
            printf("%g ", y[i][j]);
        }
        printf("\n");
    }
    return 0;
}
```

Program 10.29: *(Continued)*

```
x =
46 82
y =
66 84
147 192
```

Figure 10.13: The output from Program 10.29 and Program 21.1 in Chapter 21.

10.8.3 Solving Systems of Linear Equations Using linsolve() in Ch

For a vector equation

$$\boldsymbol{A}\boldsymbol{x} = \boldsymbol{b} \tag{10.45}$$

if $\boldsymbol{A}$ and $\boldsymbol{x}$ are known, the product $\boldsymbol{A}\boldsymbol{x}$ for the vector $\boldsymbol{b}$ can be easily obtained by multiplying the matrix by the vector. In Program 10.27, we multiply the matrix

$$\boldsymbol{A} = \begin{bmatrix} 3 & 5 & 6 \\ 4 & 2 & 1 \\ 0 & 7 & 1 \end{bmatrix} \tag{10.46}$$

by the vector on the right

$$\boldsymbol{x} = \begin{bmatrix} 2 \\ 1 \\ -2 \end{bmatrix} \tag{10.47}$$

to obtain the vector

$$\boldsymbol{b} = \begin{bmatrix} -1 \\ 8 \\ 5 \end{bmatrix} \tag{10.48}$$

On the other hand, if we know the matrix $\boldsymbol{A}$ and vector $\boldsymbol{b}$, how can we find the vector $\boldsymbol{x}$ so that when it is multiplied on the left by $\boldsymbol{A}$, it produces the vector $\boldsymbol{b}$? The problem is to find the three unknowns x_1, x_2, and x_3 in the equation

$$\begin{bmatrix} 3 & 5 & 6 \\ 4 & 2 & 1 \\ 0 & 7 & 1 \end{bmatrix} \begin{bmatrix} x_1 \\ x_2 \\ x_3 \end{bmatrix} = \begin{bmatrix} -1 \\ 8 \\ 5 \end{bmatrix} \tag{10.49}$$

If we expand the above matrix, it becomes

$$3x_1 + 5x_2 + 6x_3 = -1 \tag{10.50}$$

$$4x_1 + 2x_2 + x_3 = 8 \tag{10.51}$$

$$7x_2 + x_3 = 5 \tag{10.52}$$

Therefore, the problem becomes solving a system of three linear equations for three unknowns x_1, x_2, and x_3. This problem of solving a linear system of equations arises in many applications in engineering and science.

There are many numerical algorithms available to solve a linear system of equations. We will not discuss numerical algorithms in this book. They are discussed in any textbook on numerical analysis. A system of linear equations can be conveniently solved by a high-level numerical function **linsolve()**, defined in the header file **numeric.h** in Ch, described in section 22.5 in Chapter 22. The first argument of the function **linsolve()** passes back the result for the unknown vector $\boldsymbol{x}$, the remaining two arguments are for the square matrix $\boldsymbol{A}$ and the known vector $\boldsymbol{b}$. Program 10.30 solves the system of linear equations (10.50)-(10.52) using the function **linsolve()** with the output shown in Figure 10.14.

10.8.4 ‡ Solving Systems of Linear Equations Using CLAPACK

LAPACK (Linear Algebra PACKage) written in FORTRAN 77 is one of the most popular packages for solving systems of linear equations. It provides routines for solving systems of linear equations, least-squares

```
/* File: linearsys.ch
   Solve a system of linear equations Ax=b for x using linsolve() */
#include <stdio.h>
#include <numeric.h>    /* for linsolve() */

int main() {
    /* declare and initialize 3x3 matrix A and vector, declare x */
    double a[3][3] = {3, 5, 6,
                      4, 2, 1,
                      0, 7, 1};
    double b[3] = {-1, 8, 5}, x[3];

    linsolve(x, a, b); /* solve for x in Ax=b */
    printf("x = %g, %g, %g\n", x[0], x[1], x[2]); /* print vector x */
    return 0;
}
```

Program 10.30 Solving a system of linear equations using **linsolve()** in Ch.

```
x = 2, 1, -2
```

Figure 10.14 The output from Program 10.30 and Program 10.31.

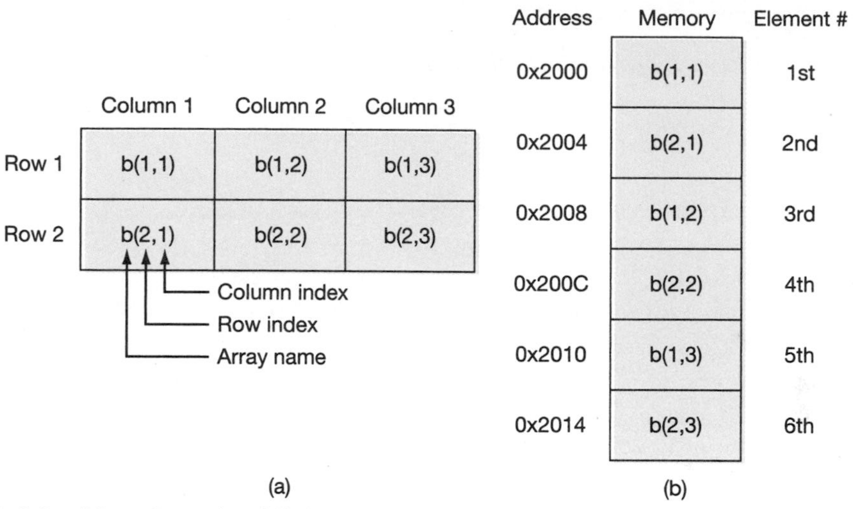

Figure 10.15: A 2 × 3 two-dimensional Fortran array and its column-wise memory layout starting with the sample memory address 0x2000.

solutions of linear systems, and many other linear system related problems such as eigenvalue problems and singular value problems. There are two major differences between arrays in C and arrays in Fortran and MATLAB. The subscript for a Fortran or MATLAB array starts with 1, whereas in C, it starts with 0. Arrays in Fortran and MATLAB are assigned and stored *column-wise*, whereas arrays in C are associated *row-wise*. For example, a 2 × 3 two-dimensional array in Fortran can be declared as follows:

```
INTEGER, DIMENSION (2,3) :: b
```

The array `b` can be accessed by `b(i,j)` with subscript `i` from 1 to 2 and `j` from 1 to 3, as shown in Figure 10.15. The second element in the memory is `b(2,1)`, not `b(1,2)`. You may compare the memory layout with that for an equivalent two-dimensional C array shown in Figure 10.2.

LAPACK is used as a numerical engine in most mathematical software packages such as MATLAB, Mathematica, and Ch. To call functions in LAPACK from C programs, CLAPACK is more commonly used. CLAPACK is translated from LAPACK in FORTRAN 77 to C automatically by a conversion utility program **f2c**. Because internally, functions in the CLAPACK library were originally written in FORTRAN 77. Arrays inside these functions are associated column-wise. Therefore, C arrays need to be transposed before they are passed to numerical functions in CLAPACK. For example, Program 10.31 solves the system of linear equations (10.50), (10.51), and (10.52) using the function **dgesv_()** in CLAPACK. The transpose `at` for array `a` is passed to the third argument of the function **dgesv_()**. Array `b` for vector $\boldsymbol{b}$ is passed to the function for calculating the solution vector $\boldsymbol{x}$. The result for the solution vector $\boldsymbol{x}$ is passed back to the calling function through the same array `b`. Therefore, if the contents of the original array `b` are needed later, one may save it in a different array first. As commented in Program 10.31, other arguments of the function need to be properly set up and passed to the function **dgesv_()**. The output from Program 10.31 is shown in Figure 10.14.

CLAPACK is supported in Ch by default. A program using functions in CLAPACK can be compiled using a C compiler or readily executed in Ch interpretively.

```
/* File: linearsys.c
   Solve a system of linear equations Ax=b for x using CLAPACK */
#include <stdio.h>
#include <clapack.h>   /* definitions for CLAPACK */

/*
int dgesv_(int *n, int *nrhs, double *a, int *lda, int *ipiv,
           double *b, int *ldb, int *info);
*/

/* define the size of matrix and vector */
#define N 3

int main() {
    /* declare and initialize 3x3 matrix A and vector b */
    double a[N][N] = {3, 5, 6,
                      4, 2, 1,
                      0, 7, 1};
    double at[N][N];              /* transpose of matrix A */
    double b[N] = {-1, 8, 5}; /* original vector b and solution x */

    int n = N;      /* number of columns of matrix A  */
    int nrhs = 1;   /* number of columns of b, usually 1  */
    int lda = N;    /* number of rows (Leading dimension of A) of A  */
    int ipiv[N];    /* pivot indices  */
    int ldb = N;    /* number of rows of b  */
    int info;       /* status of the calling the function */
    int i, j;       /* array indices */

    /* obtain transpose of matrix A */
    for(i=0; i<N; i++) {
        for(j=0; j<N; j++) {
            at[j][i] = a[i][j];
        }
    }

    /* solve for x in Ax=b  using function dgesv_() in CLAPACK */
    dgesv_(&n, &nrhs, &at[0][0], &lda, ipiv, b, &ldb, &info);

    if(info == 0) /* succeed */
       printf("x = %g, %g, %g\n", b[0], b[1], b[2]); /* print vector x */
    else
       printf("dgesv_() failed %d\n", info);
    return 0;
}
```

Program 10.31: Solving a system of linear equations using the function **dgesv_()** in CLAPACK.

10.9 Making It Work

10.9.1 Debugging Programs with Arrays in ChIDE

The method for debugging programs, described in sections 3.16.3 and 6.13.3, is also applicable to programs with arrays. If you select the menu `Locals` or `Variables` on the debugging pane selection bar, each element of the array for a variable of array type in the scope, will be displayed. When an element of an array is modified, the entire array will be updated when the array is displayed.

Exercises

1. Identify and correct the errors, if there are any, in the following program. If there are errors, briefly explain them.

```
int main() {
    int a[3] = {1, 2};
    printf("a[1] = %f\n", a[1]);
}
```

2. Find the error(s) in each of the following program segments, and explain how each error can be fixed.

a.
```
char str[5];
scanf("%s", str);      /* User types hello */
```
b.
```
int a[3];
printf("%d  %d  %d\n", a[1], a[2], a[3]);
```
c.
```
double f[3] = {1.1, 10.01, 100.001, 1000.001};
```
d.
```
double d[2][10];
d[1,9] = 2.345;
```

3. Find the errors in the following code and explain them.

```
void funct( int n, int a[n] ){
    extern int m;
    static int b[n][n];
    double d[][n]={{1, 2, 3}, {4,5,6}};
}
```

4. Identify and correct the errors in the following code. Briefly explain them.

```
int N;
int M=90;

int funct4(int n){
  int i;
  int m = n;
  int a[n][n];
  int b[n][m];
  int c[printf("%d\n", n)][n];
  int d[n][N];
  int e[n][M];
```

```
    int f[n] = {1, 2, 3, 4};
    static int g[n];

    for(i=0; i<n; i++)
      a[i][i] = 3+b[i][i];

  }
  funct4(4);
```

5. What is the output of the following program?

```
#include <stdio.h>
int a1[5], a2[10];
void funct(int n, int a[n]) {
   int i;
   a[0] = 0;
   for(i=1; i<n; i++) {
      a[i] = i+a[i-1];
   }
}
int main() {
   funct(5, a1);
   funct(10, a2);
   printf("a1[2] = %d\n", a1[3]);
   printf("a2[6] = %d\n", a2[6]);
   return 0;
}
```

6. When an array is passed to a function, what is actually passed?
7. The array `a` in Program 10.9 contains the daily page accessing numbers for a Web page in a given five-week period. Write a program to calculate the mean value for the number of accesses for each day of the week.
8. Write a function with the function prototype of

```
int compare(double a[], double b[], int npts);
```

It will compare values in two arrays of the same size. If the corresponding values in each element of the two arrays are the same, the function returns 1. Otherwise, it returns 0. Test the function with function calls `compare(a, a)` and `compare(a, b)` with the arrays $a = [1, 2, 3, 4]$, $b = [1, 3, 4, 5]$.

9. Write a function `decimate_by3()` with the prototype

```
void decimate_by3(int n, int a1[], int a2[]);
```

that copies every third element in an input array `a1[]` of length `n` to an output array `a2[]` and discards all the other values. For example, if `a1[]` contains 7, 12, 13, 16, 19, 22, 16, 9, then the output array `a2[]` should contain 7, 16, 16. (Hint: use the modulus operation `'%'`.)

10. A pixel consists of a two-dimensional location and an associated light intensity. In an array of pixels (e.g., a digital camera), let $p_1, p_2, \ldots, p_n$ be the `n` two-dimensional points and $g_1, g_2, \ldots, g_n$ be their associated light intensities. If g is the sum of the individual light intensities, the centroid C (a 2-D vector

in the x, y plane) is found as

$$C_x = (g_1x_1 + g_2x_2 + \cdots + g_nx_n)/g$$
$$C_y = (g_1y_1 + g_2y_2 + \cdots + g_ny_n)/g$$

An array of pixel locations and an associated array of light intensities are initialized below.

```
void comp_c(int nrows, double p[][2], const double g[],
            double centr[2]);
int main() {
     double p[][2] = { {5.0, -4.0},
                       {4.0, 3.0},
                       {-1.0, 6.0},
                       {-9.0, 5.0} };
    double g[]= {0.25, 0.57, 0.63, 0.1};
```

Write and call the function `comp_c()` using nested **for** loops to compute the centroid in each dimension, given the locations and light intensities. In the function **main()**, display the centroid using the following format:

```
centroid = x.xxx y.yyy
```

11. Write a function `makefib()` with the prototype

```
void makefib(int n, int a[]);
```

that sets an integer array `a[]` to the first `n` elements in the Fibonacci series defined by

$$F_{k+2} = F_{k+1} + F_k$$

Let n be an input parameter, which you may assume is at least 2. The first two elements in the Fibonacci series are 1 and 1. Thereafter the next element is computed as the sum of the last two elements. For example, if `n` were 6, the array `a[]` would be set to: 1, 1, 2, 3, 5, 8.

12. Write a function `insert0()` with the following prototype:

```
void insert0(int n, int a1[], int a2[]);
```

that has as input an integer array `a1[]` of length `n` and as output an integer array `a2[]` of length `2n`. The function copies the input array to the output array, inserting the value 0 between each copied value. Thus, if `a1[]` contains the values −9, 16, 0, 2, the output array `a2[]` should have the values −9, 0, 16, 0, 0, 0, 2, 0.

13. A binary bar code scan is a bit pattern that contains only 1s and 0s. To find the edges of light and dark regions, process an input bit pattern in the following manner:

- Assign a 1 to the output bit pattern whenever two consecutive bits are different.
- Assign a 0 to the output bit pattern whenever two consecutive bits are the same.

For example, input and output bit patterns of a bar code edge detection program might look like the following:

```
0000111100001100001100 (input bit pattern)
0000100010001010001010 (output bit pattern)
```

Write a program that reads an input bit pattern of up to 1024 bits from a file using input redirection and writes the output bit pattern to a file using output redirection. Read input bits until the end of the file is encountered, counting the total number of bits read. As part of the solution, write and call the function `edge()` with the prototype

```
void edge(int n, int a1[], int a2[]);
```

to perform edge detection. The arguments of the function `edge()` contain the length of the input and output arrays with the same size, input array, and output array. Inside the function, you should assign 0 to the first bit of the output array.

14. Write a function `merge()`

```
void merge(int n1, int arr1[], int n2, int arr2[], int arr3[]);
```

to merge the contents of two sorted (ascending-order) integer arrays. For example, if `arr1[]` of length `n1` has values −10, −2, 4, 6, 7 and `arr2[]` of length `n2` has values −2, 3, 5, then make `arr3[]` equal to −10, −2, −2, 3, 4, 5, 6, 7. Nothing is returned.

15. Ten measurements were made on the inside diameter of forged piston rings used in an automobile engine. The data measured in millimeters are 75.001, 75.003, 75.002, 75.004, 75.000, 75.015, 75.005, 75.004, 75.002, and 75.003. A dot diagram for these measured data is shown in Exercise 7 in Chapter 20. Compute the sample range, sample variance, and sample standard deviation using the statistical library developed in section 10.5.

16. For the piston ring data in Exercise 15, if the largest observation, 75.015, is removed. Compute the sample range, sample variance, and sample standard deviation. Compare the results with those obtained in Exercise 15. How sensitive are the sample range, sample variance, and sample standard deviation to this particular measurement?

17. Extend Programs 10.13 and 10.14 by adding the function

```
int belowVal(int totnum, double data[], double val);
```

to calculate the number of students with a GPA below the specified value 3.0 in its third argument.

18. In Program 10.13, the total number of elements in an array is passed to each function. Assume that the statistical library is used for processing GPA. Because a GPA value is always positive, one can append a sentinel number in the array of data for GPA values. Modify Program 10.13 so that functions are declared without passing the total number of arguments with the code shown below.

```
#define EOD -1
double mean(double data[]) {
    double meanval, sum;
    int i;

    sum =0.0;
    for(i=0; data[i] != EOD; i++) {
        sum += data[i];
    }
    meanval = sum/i;
    return meanval;
}
int main() {
   double data[] = {3.33, 3, 3.1, 3.93, 2.3, 2.31, 3.99, 2.8, 2.9,
                    3.7, EOD};
   ...
}
```

19. The grades A, A-, B+, B, B-, C+, C, C-, D+, D, D-, and F are assigned with the points 4, 3.7, 3.3, 3, 2.7, 2.3, 2, 1.7, 1.3, 1, 0.7, and 0, respectively. A student has grades of

```
3.0 4.0 3.3 3.7 4.0 3.7 3.3 3.7 4.0 3.3
```

for courses taken so far. Draw flowcharts and write pseudocode and computer programs to perform the following tasks:

a. Calculate the GPA for the student.

b. Students with GPAs of 3.5 and higher are on the Dean's List. The student will take four courses next semester. Calculate the GPA that the student needs next semester to make the Dean's List.

c. Before the end of the year, the student will take six more courses. What's the highest possible GPA that the student can earn by the end of the year? If the student is able to reach a cumulative GPA of 3.8 by the end of the year, calculate the GPA that the student needs in the remaining six courses to reach a cumulative GPA of 3.8.

20. Draw a flowchart and write succinct procedures for the pseudocode listed in Program 10.4.

21. Assume that an array contains length in the unit of miles. Write a function that converts the length to kilometers. Assume that the function prototype is as follows:

```
void mile2kilometer(double a[], int npts);
```

Note that 1 mile equals 1.6093440 kilometers.

22. Write a program to sort the following arrays in ascending order. Also find the mean and median for the values of these arrays. Do it in the following two ways: (1) Do not use the statistical library. (2) Use the statistical library.

a. [1, 4, 6, 4, 9, 5]

b. [1, 4, 6, 4, 9, 5, 12]

c. [1.3, 4.4, 5.4, 4, 9.5, 5, 6.2, 2.5]

d. [1.3, 4.4, 5.4, 4, 9.5, 5, 6.2, 2.5, 10]

23. Write a program to read 10 integer numbers from the standard input at the prompt. Sort these numbers in descending order and then print them out through the standard output. Do not use the statistical library.

24. What is the output of the following program?

```
int a[3][4] = {{1,2,3,4},
               {5,6,7,8},
               {9,10,11,12}};
int funct(int b[]) {
   printf("b[0] = %d\n", b[0]);
   printf("b[1] = %d\n", b[1]);
}
funct(&a[1][2]);
```

25. The monthly sales (x1,000 dollars) of a product in the last two years are as follows:

	Jan	Feb	Mar	Api	May	Jun	Jul	Aug	Sep	Oct	Nov	Dec
Year 1	367	654	545	556	565	526	437	389	689	554	526	625
Year 2	429	644	586	626	652	546	449	689	597	679	696	568

The file monthsale.dat contains only the sale data, e.g, 367 654 ... Write a program to read the sales data from the file monthsale.dat and calculate the monthly average of the sale for each year in the last two years using the function mean() in the statistical library and print the result in the following format:

```
Year          Average Monthly Sales (x1,000 $)
-------------------------------------------
  0                  xxx.yy
  1                  xxx.yy
```

a. Sales data are read from the file monthsale.dat to a one-dimensional array year by year using the input/output redirection.
b. Sales data are read from the file monthsale.dat to a two-dimensional array using the input/output redirection.

26. Temperature measurements in degrees in Fahrenheit are recorded every two hours for a week, as shown in the table below.

Day	12 AM	2 AM	4 AM	6 AM	8 AM	10 AM	12 PM	2 PM	4 PM	6 PM	8 PM	10 PM
Sunday	36.7	35.7	34.5	38.5	40.5	42.0	43.7	40.9	38.9	38.4	37.6	36.5
Monday	37.3	36.4	37.4	39.5	41.3	43.0	44.8	42.8	39.3	40.3	38.3	38.2
Tuesday	38.5	37.3	38.5	40.8	42.2	44.0	46.4	46.9	42.4	41.4	39.6	39.5
Wednesday	39.7	39.2	39.5	41.5	43.5	45.0	47.7	47.9	43.9	42.2	40.1	40.3
Thursday	40.6	40.4	40.5	42.9	44.1	46.0	47.2	48.4	45.5	43.4	41.8	41.8
Friday	41.4	41.1	41.5	42.5	44.5	46.0	48.1	48.9	45.9	43.5	42.6	41.2
Saturday	42.7	42.4	42.5	43.0	44.8	45.0	46.7	47.2	46.1	45.4	44.9	43.9

Write a program to read in the two-dimensional arrays of temperatures from the file temperature.dat using input/output redirection. The file temperature.dat contains only temperatures, e.g, 36.7 35.7 ... Find the maximum and minimum temperatures for each day (row of data). In the function **main()**, display the results on the screen:

```
Day   Max   Min
----------------
 0    43.7  34.5    <--  Day 0 corresponds to Sunday
 1    44.8  36.4
...
 6    47.2  42.4    <--  Day 6 corresponds to Saturday
```

a. The function **main()** calls a function find_max_min() with the function prototype

```
#define HOURS 12
void find_max_min(int n, double temps[][HOURS],
                  double max[], double min[]);
```

to find the maximum and minimum temperatures for each day, storing the results in 1-D arrays, max[] and min[].

b. The function **main()** calls the functions `maximum()` and `minimum()` in the statistical library to find the maximum and minimum temperatures for each day, respectively.

27. Modify the function `sortArary2d()` in Program 10.24 to use the functions `sort()` and `median()` in the statistical library to sort each row of the passed array and calculate the median of the sorted row.

28. Write a function with the following function prototype:

a. `void sortarray2(int m, int n, int a[m][n], double median[m]);`
b. `void sortarray2(int m, int n, double a[m][n], double median[m]);`

that sorts each column of a two-dimensional array in ascending order and passes medians for each column to the calling function. Test the function using two arrays `a1` and `a2` with elements in Program 10.24 in the function main().

29. Given a matrix such as

$$\begin{bmatrix} 1 & 9 & 6 \\ 5 & 9 & 7 \\ 4 & 8 & 4 \end{bmatrix}$$

a. sort each row of the matrix in ascending order.
b. sort each column of the matrix in ascending order.

30. Write the function `binsearch()` for a binary search with the function prototype

```
int binsearch(int n, double data[], double val);
```

The arguments and return value of the function are the same as that for the function `lsearch()` in Program 10.11. Write the pseudocode and draw a flowchart for the algorithm. Modify Program 10.11 to test the function `binsearch()`.

31. Use a one-dimensional array to solve the following problem. Draw a flowchart and write pseudocode and a computer program. Read in 10 numbers one at a time. Each input number should be in the range of [1, 100]. As each number is read, print it out immediately only if it is not a duplicate of numbers already read. At the end, print all nonduplicated numbers. Provide for the "worst case," in which all 10 numbers are different. Use the smallest possible array to solve this problem.

32. Write a program to verify that the straightforward evaluation of a 100th-order polynomial needs 5050 multiplications.

33. Evaluate the following polynomials at $x = 2.5$ using the recursive method with an array for the coefficients of a polynomial.

a. $x^5 - 15x^4 + 10x^3 + 5x - 1$
b. $3x^6 + x^5 - 15x^4 - 20x^2 + 5x - 1$
c. $2x^7 + 5x^6 + x^5 + 10x^3 - 20x^2 + 5x - 1$
d. $3x^8 + 2x^7 + x^6 + x^5 - 15x^4 - 3x^2 + 2x - 1$

34. Write the function `evalpoly()` for evaluation of polynomials with the function prototype below:

```
double evalpoly(double c[], int n, double x);
```

where `c` is the array for the coefficients of a polynomial, `n` the number of elements of array `c`, and `x` the value to be evaluated for the polynomial.

a. Use this function to evaluate polynomial (a) in Exercise 33.
b. Use this function to evaluate polynomials (a) and (b) in a single program in Exercise 33.
c. Use this function to evaluate polynomials (c) and (d) in a single program in Exercise 33.

35. Write a function with the following function prototype

```
int f(int a[3][3]);
```

that transposes a 3×3 rectangular matrix. For example, given this matrix:

$$\begin{bmatrix} 1 & 2 & 3 \\ 4 & 5 & 6 \\ 7 & 8 & 9 \end{bmatrix}$$

your function should change its contents to the following transpose matrix:

$$\begin{bmatrix} 1 & 4 & 7 \\ 2 & 5 & 8 \\ 3 & 6 & 9 \end{bmatrix}$$

36. Write a function with the following function prototype:

```
int f(int m, int m, int a[m][n], int t[n][m]);
```

that transposes an $m \times n$ matrix. Test the function with a given matrix a of

$$\begin{bmatrix} 1 & 2 & 3 \\ 4 & 5 & 6 \end{bmatrix}$$

the following transpose matrix t shall be created by the function

$$\begin{bmatrix} 1 & 4 \\ 2 & 5 \\ 3 & 6 \end{bmatrix}$$

37. Plot the functions below for x from 1 to 8 with 50 points using arrays.

a. $\sin(x)$ **b.** $\sin(x)x$ **c.** $1/x^2$ **d.** $\dfrac{3x^2 + 4x + 3}{5\sin(x^2) + 4x^2 + 3}$

38. Given matrix

$$\boldsymbol{A} = \begin{bmatrix} 1 & 2 & 3 \\ 4 & 5 & 6 \\ 7 & 8 & 9 \end{bmatrix}, \boldsymbol{B} = \begin{bmatrix} 1 & 4 & 7 \\ 2 & 5 & 8 \\ 3 & 6 & 9 \end{bmatrix}, \boldsymbol{v} = \begin{bmatrix} 1 \\ 2 \\ 3 \end{bmatrix}$$

write a program to calculate the following vector and matrix expressions:
a. $\boldsymbol{v} \cdot \boldsymbol{v}$ **b.** $\boldsymbol{A} + \boldsymbol{B}$ **c.** $\boldsymbol{A} - \boldsymbol{B}$ **d.** $10\boldsymbol{A}\boldsymbol{v}$ **e.** $\boldsymbol{A}\boldsymbol{B}$ **f.** $\boldsymbol{A}\boldsymbol{B}\boldsymbol{v}$ **g.** $5\boldsymbol{A}\boldsymbol{B}\boldsymbol{A}\boldsymbol{B}$
h. $\boldsymbol{A}\boldsymbol{B}\boldsymbol{A}\boldsymbol{B} + \boldsymbol{A}\boldsymbol{B}$ **i.** $\boldsymbol{A}\boldsymbol{B}(\boldsymbol{A}\boldsymbol{B} + \boldsymbol{I})\boldsymbol{v}$ where **I** is an identity matrix

39. Given matrix

$$\boldsymbol{A} = \begin{bmatrix} 5 & 2 & 3 \\ 3 & 5 & 7 \\ 5 & 6 & 9 \end{bmatrix}, \boldsymbol{B} = \begin{bmatrix} 1 & 4 & 7 \\ 6 & 7 & 5 \\ 8 & 6 & 9 \end{bmatrix}, \boldsymbol{v} = \begin{bmatrix} 4 \\ 5 \\ 6 \end{bmatrix}$$

write a program to calculate the expressions given in Exercise 38.

40. Given

$$\boldsymbol{A} = \begin{bmatrix} 1 & 2 & 3 \\ 4 & 5 & 6 \\ 7 & 8 & 9 \end{bmatrix}, \boldsymbol{B} = \begin{bmatrix} 7 & 8 & 9 \\ 1 & 2 & 3 \\ 4 & 5 & 6 \end{bmatrix}, \boldsymbol{C} = \begin{bmatrix} 7 & 8 \\ 1 & 2 \\ 4 & 5 \end{bmatrix}, \text{ and } \boldsymbol{b} = \begin{bmatrix} 1 \\ 4 \\ 7 \end{bmatrix}$$

calculate the following matrix expressions.

a. $\mathbf{x} = \mathbf{AC}$
b. $\mathbf{y} = 2\mathbf{ABb} + \mathbf{Ab}$
c. $\mathbf{z} = A(2\mathbf{B} + \mathbf{I})\mathbf{b}$ where **I** is an identity matrix

41. Write a matrix-vector library with the following functions:

```
/* matrix addition: C = A + B */
void matmatadd(int m, int n, double a[m][n], double b[m][n], double c[m][n]);
/* matrix subtraction: C = A - B */
void matmatsub(int m, int n, double a[m][n], double b[m][n], double c[m][n]);
/* matrix multiplication: C = A * B */
void matmatmul(int m, int n, int p, double a[m][n], double b[n][p],
                                    double c[m][p]);
/* matrix multiply by vector: b = A v */
void matvecmul(int m, int n, double a[m][n], double v[n], double b[m]);
/* matrix multiply by scalar: B = A s */
void matsmul(int m, int n, double a[m][n], double s, double b[m][n]);
/* matrix transpose: B = transpose(A); */
void mattranspose(int m, int n, double a[m][n], double b[n][m]);
/* identity matrix: A = I  */
void matidentity(int n, double a[n][n]);
/* vector multiply scalar: b = v s */
double vectsmul(int n, double v[n], double s, double b[n]);
/* scalar product for vectors a and b */
double vectorprod(int n, double a[n], double b[n]);
```

Similar to the statistical library with files `statlib.h` and `statlib.c`, the header file `matveclib.h` includes function prototypes, whereas the source code `matveclib.c` contains the definitions of these functions. A sample implementation of the function `matvecmul()` is available in Program 10.28. Use this library to solve the following problems.

a. Exercise 38 **b.** Exercise 39 **c.** Exercise 40 **d.** Calculate vector $\boldsymbol{x}$ in equation (10.43) and matrix $\boldsymbol{Y}$ in equation (10.44) with matrices $\boldsymbol{A}$, $\boldsymbol{B}$, $\boldsymbol{C}$, and vector $\boldsymbol{v}$ given in equation (10.42).

42. Modify Program 10.31 using array `a` only, without its transpose `at`.

43. Write a program to solve the system of linear equations:

a.
$$\begin{aligned} 3x_1 + 5x_2 + 6x_3 &= 2 \\ 4x_1 + 2x_2 + x_3 &= 9 \\ 7x_2 + x_3 &= 5 \end{aligned}$$

b.
$$\begin{aligned} 3x_1 + 5x_2 + 6x_3 + x_4 &= 2 \\ 4x_1 + 2x_2 + x_3 &= 9 \\ 7x_2 + x_3 &= 5 \\ 7x_1 + x_4 &= 8 \end{aligned}$$

44. The illustration shows a bridged-T circuit, where i_s is the current source. When R is 1 ohm, the node voltage v_A, v_B, and v_C can be solved by the equation

$$\begin{aligned} 2.5v_A - 0.5v_B - 2v_C &= i_s \\ -0.5v_A + 3v_B - 0.5v_C &= 0 \\ -2v_A - 0.5v_B + 3.5v_C &= 0 \end{aligned}$$

Given $i_s = 5$ amperes, calculate the node voltage v_A, v_B, and v_C in volts.

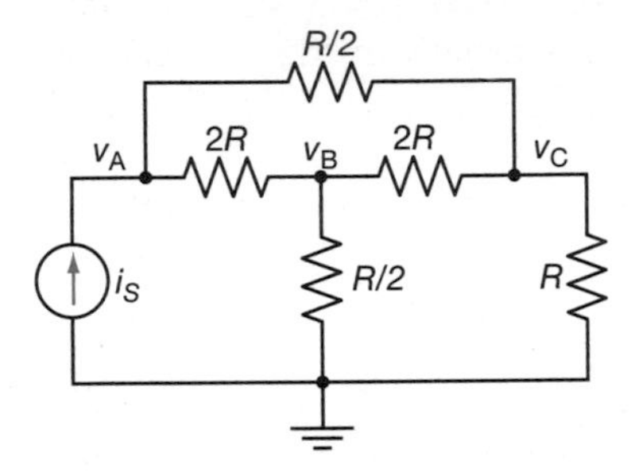

45. For the circuit shown in the illustration, the four mesh-current equations can be written in a single matrix form

$$\begin{bmatrix} 13/12 & -1 & 0 & 0 \\ -1 & 4/3 & 5/6 & -1/2 \\ 0 & 1 & -1 & 0 \\ 0 & 0 & 0 & 1 \end{bmatrix} \begin{bmatrix} i_1 \\ i_2 \\ i_3 \\ i_4 \end{bmatrix} = \begin{bmatrix} 14 \\ 0 \\ 6 \\ -6 \end{bmatrix}$$

where the left-hand matrix is called the *mesh transformation matrix*. Calculate the currents i_1, i_2, i_3, and i_4 shown in the network.

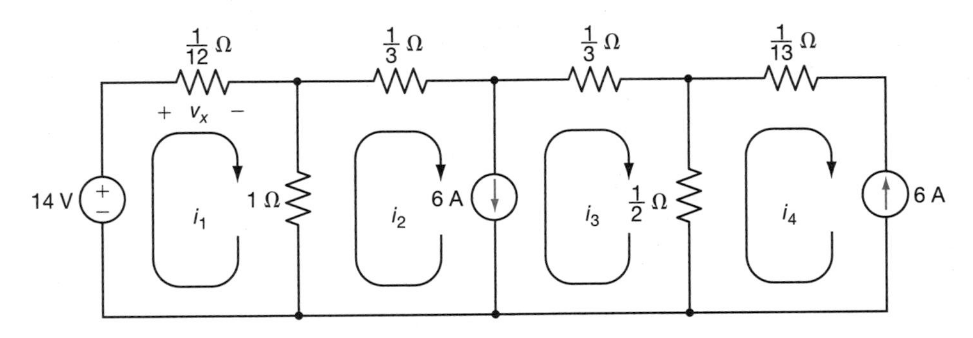

46. The temperature in degrees Fahrenheit can be expressed in degrees Celsius as follows:

$$f(c) = (9/5)c + 32$$

where c is the temperature in degrees Celsius and f the temperature in degrees Fahrenheit. Plot the relation when the temperature varies in the range of $[-10, 40]$ degrees Celsius using arrays with 50 points.

47. For the mechanical system shown in Figure 2.12, given mass $m = 6$ kilograms (kg) and coefficient of kinetic friction $\mu = 0.3$, the applied force p is expressed as a function of time t in

$$p(t) = \begin{cases} 20 & \text{if } t \le 3 \\ 4(t+2) & \text{if } t > 3 \le 6 \\ 4(t^2+2t) & \text{if } t > 6 \end{cases}$$

Plot the accelerations of the rigid body from $t = 0$ to 10 seconds with 100 points using the function **plotxy()**.

48. A projectile is fired into the air with an initial speed v_0 of 35 m/s and initial projection angle of $\theta_0 = 15°$. Plot its trajectory of y versus x using arrays for x and y with 100 points. The trajectory can be expressed in x- and y-coordinates using equations (6.3) and 6.4 in section 6.7.

49. Plot the humps function shown in Figure 6.11 in Chapter 6 for x in the range $-1 \le x \le 2$. Use an array for x with 100 points.

50. Plot the peaks function defined in equation (6.9) for x in the range $-3 \le x \le 3$ and y in the range $-4 \le x \le 4$ using the function **plotxyz()**. Use arrays for x with 60 points and y with 80 points.

51. Plot the probability density function shown in Figure 6.12 for x in the range $-4 \le x \le 8$ with $\mu = 2$ and $\sigma = 3$. Use arrays for x and f with 100 points.

52. Plot the first four terms and the partial sums $f_1(x)$, $f_2(x)$, $f_3(x)$, $f_4(x)$ of the Fourier series for the periodic function defined in Exercise 34 in Chapter 6 for x in the range of $-\pi$ to π in a single plot. Use arrays for x, the first four terms s_i, and the partial sums f_i with 100 points.

53. Plot the responses of distance versus time for the overdamped, critically damped, and underdamped mechanical systems defined in Exercise 35 in Chapter 6 using arrays for distance x and time t with 100 points.

54. Plot sinusoids $s_1(t)$ and $s_2(t)$, and signal $s = s_1(t) + s_2(t)$ defined in Exercise 36 in Chapter 6 using arrays for signals s_1, s_2, s, and time t with 200 points.

55. The curvelinear motion of a particle is defined by

$$x = 50t - 8t^2$$
$$y = 100 - 4t^2$$

where x and y are in meters and t is in seconds. Find the position when t is 2 seconds. Plot the path of the particle for $0 \le t \le 5$.

56. The harmonic motion of a particle is defined by

$$x = \sin(t)$$
$$y = \cos(t)$$

where x and y are in meters and t is in seconds. Plot the path of the particle for $0 \le t \le 7$.

57. The three-dimensional motion of a particle is defined by

$$x = \mathrm{e}^{-0.02t} \sin(t)$$
$$y = \mathrm{e}^{-0.02t} \cos(t)$$
$$z = t$$

As the time t varies from 0 to 10π, the sine and cosine functions will vary through five cycles. The absolute values of x and y become smaller as t increases. The trajectory of the particle follows a spiral curve. Plot the path of the particle for $0 \le t \le 10\pi$.

58. Plot the positions of a moving body shown in Figure 4.6 using the data points in Table 4.3 in section 4.2 in Chapter 4.

59. Write a linear regression function shown in Program 10.20 with the function prototype

```
void linearreg(double t[], double y[], int n, double coeff[2]);
```

where `t` and `y` are arrays of data to be fitted in the linear regression model, and `n` is the number of elements for the passed arrays `t` and `y`. The linear regression coefficients for the intercept and slope are passed to the calling function by the argument `coeff` of array with two elements. Modify Program 10.19 to use this function.

60. Using the data for diameters of a right circular cylindrical surface at different production runs in Exercise 23 in Chapter 4, perform the following tasks.

a. Draw a plot with scattered points for diameters at different production runs.
b. Assuming that a simple linear regression model is appropriate, obtain the least squares fit relating diameters to production run. Overlay the fitted straight line on the plot with scattered points.
c. Find the diameter of the part at production run 350.
d. Find the fitted diameter corresponding to production run 300.
e. Calculate the diameter of the part at production run 300. Find the *residual*, which is defined as the error in the fit of the model to the observed value.

61. Using the data for U.S. disposable personal income in Exercise 24 in Chapter 4, perform the following tasks.

a. Draw a plot with scattered points for disposable personal income in each year.
b. Assuming that a simple linear regression model is appropriate, obtain the least squares fit relating disposable personal income to year. Overlay the fitted straight line on the plot with scattered points.
c. Find the disposable personal incomes in 1997 and 2020.
d. Find the fitted disposable personal income in 1998.
e. Calculate the disposable personal income in 1998. Find the *residual*, which is defined as the error in the fit of the model to the observed value.

62. Using the data for the annual profit of a company in Exercise 25 in Chapter 4, perform the following tasks.

a. Draw a plot with scattered points for the profit in each year.
b. Assuming that a simple linear regression model is appropriate, obtain the least squares fit relating company profit to year. Overlay the fitted straight line on the plot with scattered points.
c. Find the company profits in 1998 and 2020.
d. Find the fitted profit in 2000.
e. Calculate the company profit in 2000. Find the *residual*, which is defined as the error in the fit of the model to the observed value.

CHAPTER 11

Pointers

The pointer is one of the most powerful features in C. A pointer is defined as a variable that contains the address of another variable or dynamically allocated memory. If we have a pointer variable of type *pointer to int*, it can point to the address of a variable of type int. Pointers are often used to pass results in the called function to the calling function. Pointers and arrays in C are closely related to each other. In some cases, they are interchangeable. Pointers can be used to create dynamic data structures. Through a pointer, a program can also easily access a specified memory location. It can be used to read and modify the value in the memory. Therefore, C is commonly used for interfacing hardware.

However, the pointer is also the most difficult capability to master. It is easy to make programming errors related to pointers. Unlike a syntax error, programming errors related to pointers are often difficult to debug. Most bugs in a C program are related to pointers. This chapter explains basic concepts related to pointers and their applications.

11.1 Pointer Variables

Variables of pointer type can be declared similar to variables of other data types, as described in section 3.11 in Chapter 3. A pointer declaration can be distinguished by an asterisk '*' preceding the variable name. For example,

```
int *p, i;
```

declares `p` as a pointer to int and `i` as an int type. Pointers of any data type can be declared. An integer constant expression with the value 0, or such an expression cast to type of pointer to void (**void** *), is called a null pointer constant. The macro **NULL** is defined in the standard header file **stddef.h** as a null pointer constant. But it is typically also available when the header file **stdio.h** is included. Aside from the address of a memory location, pointers may also be initialized to a null pointer constant. Initializing a pointer to **NULL** is usually preferred over initializing it to 0. For example, the pointer variable p below is initialized to a null pointer constant **NULL**.

```
int *p=NULL;
```

The variable of a pointer type is used to store the memory address of a variable. It is independent of the variable type that it points to, such as char or double. As presented in Table 3.2, in Chapter 3 for 32-bit programming, the size of pointer variables is 4 bytes (32 bits). For 64-bit programming, it is 8 bytes (64 bits). Section 4.11 in Chapter 4 shows how to obtain the size of pointer types and variables using the operator **sizeof** portably in 32-bit and 64-bit programming.

One may use **typedef** as described in section 3.12 in Chapter 3 to create new pointer types, typically in a header file, and then use them in other source code. For example, the statement

```
typedef int *intptr_t;
```

declares a new data type `intptr_t` of pointer int. It can be used to declare variables `p1` and `pt2` of type pointer to int as shown below:

```
intptr_t p1, pt2;
```

The above two declaration statements are equivalent to the following single declaration statement:

```
int *p1, *p2;
```

11.1.1 Pointer Operators

There are two basic operators for pointers. They are the *indirection*, or *dereferencing operator*, '`*`', and the *address operator* '`&`'. They are used in the following context:

1. To declare a variable of pointer, add the operator '`*`' in front of the identifier.
2. To obtain the address of a variable, add the address operator '`&`' in front of the variable name.
3. To obtain the value pointed by a variable of pointer type, add the indirection operator '`*`' in front of the variable name.

The unary operator '`&`' gives the *address of a variable*. The expression `&i` means the address of variable `i`. The operator `&` can be applied only to a valid lvalue. The indirection or dereference operator '`*`' gives the *contents of an object pointed to by a pointer*. The expression `*p` represents the value stored in the location pointed to by variable `p`. It is different from the multiplication operator and is also different from its use in the declaration of variables of pointer type.

For example, Program 11.1 declares variables `i` and `j` of int type and `p` of pointer to int. Before the indirection operator is used, variable `i` is assigned with 10 and j with 0. Variable `p` is assigned with the address of variable `i` by the statement

```
p = &i;
```

At this point, pointer `p` points to the address of `i`. If the addresses of variables `i`, `j`, and `p` are assumed to be `0x00E81E20`, `0x00E81E24`, and `0x00E82040`, respectively, the value of `p` is `0x00E81E20` as shown on the left side of Figure 11.1. Once a linkage has been established between a variable and another variable of pointer type, they can be used interchangeably. After the above assignment operation, the object pointed to by pointer `p` can be accessed by the indirection operator `*`, so that the expression `*p` and the variable `i` refer to the same object with the value 10. *The expression* `(*p)` *and the variable* `i` *can be used interchangeably.* When the object pointed to by `p` is changed to the value 20 by the statement

```
*p = 20;
```

it effectively changes the value of the variable `i`, pointed by pointer `p`, to 20. In the next statement

```
j = *p;
```

the indirection operator '*' is used to obtain the value pointed by the pointer `p` and assigned to variable `j`. The memory layout after the above two statements with indirection operations is shown on the right side of Figure 11.1. The value for `p`, which is the address of `i`, remains the same. A sample output of Program 11.1 is shown in Figure 11.2.

```
/* File: poperators.c
   Demonstrate pointer, indirection operation, and address operation */
#include <stdio.h>

int main() {
    int i, j, *p; /* declare i and j as int, p as pointer to int */

    i = 10;     /* i is assigned with 10 */
    j = 0;      /* j is assigned with 0 */
    p = &i;     /* p is assigned with the address of i.
                   p points to i, *p <==> i */
    printf("The value of i is %d\n", i);
    printf("The value of j is %d\n", j);
    printf("The address of i is %p\n", &i);
    printf("The value of p is %p\n", p);
    printf("The value of *p is %d\n", *p);

    *p = 20;     /* The memory pointed by p is assigned with 20;
                    effectively, i is assigned with 20 */
    j = *p;      /* j is assigned with the value pointed by p,
                    effectively, j is assigned with the value of i */
    printf("After indirection operations\n");
    printf("The value of i is %d\n", i);
    printf("The value of j is %d\n", j);
    printf("The address of i is %p\n", &i);
    printf("The value of p is %p\n", p);
    printf("The value of *p is %d\n", *p);
    return 0;
}
```

Program 11.1: Pointer operations.

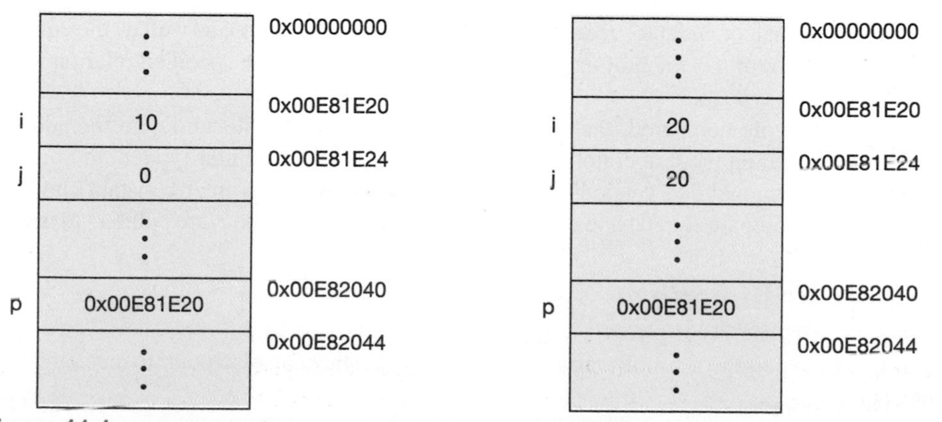

Figure 11.1: A sample memory layout before and after indirection operations in Program 11.1.

```
The value of i is 10
The value of j is 0
The address of i is 00E81E20
The value of p is 00E81E20
The value of *p is 10
After indirection operations
The value of i is 20
The value of j is 20
The address of i is 00E81E20
The value of p is 00E81E20
The value of *p is 20
```

Figure 11.2: A sample output of Program 11.1.

Like variables of other data type, a variable of pointer type can also be initialized during declaration as shown below.

```
> int i
> int *p = &i          // initialization
> i = 10
10
> *p                   // dereference
10
```

The asterisk in a declaration statement with the following initialization

```
int *p = &i;
```

is not treated as a dereference operator of a pointer type. It is used only to declare that variable `p` is a pointer to int. It is assigned the value of the address of variable `i`. After declaration, the asterisk in `*p` is treated as a dereference operator.

11.1.2 Relational Operators with Pointers

Variables of pointer type can be used as operands for the relational operators `<`, `>`, `<=`, `>=` (meaning less than, greater than, less than or equal to, greater than or equal to, respectively), as well as the equality operator `==` and nonequality operator `!=`. Each of these operators shall yield 1 if the specified relation is true and 0 if it is false. The result has type int.

When two pointers are compared, the result depends on the relative locations in the address space of the objects pointed to. When these operators are applied to variables of pointer type, both operands shall be pointers to qualified or unqualified versions of compatible types. A null pointer constant can be used as an operand. Two pointers compare equal if and only if both are null pointers or both are pointers to the same object.

11.2 Pointer Arithmetic

Pointers do not have to point to a simple variable of scalar type. They can also point to an element of an array. For example,

```
int a[6], *p;
p = &a[3];
```

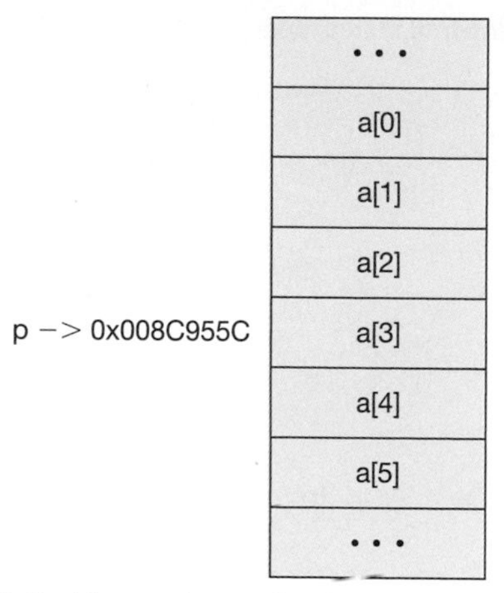

Figure 11.3: Memory layout for the six-element array `a`.

	. . .
0x008C9550	a[0]
p−2 −> 0x008C9554	a[1]
0x008C9558	a[2]
p −> 0x008C955C	a[3]
0x008C9560	a[4]
p+2 −> 0x008C9564	a[5]
	. . .

Figure 11.4: Using pointer arithmetic on the pointer `p`.

In this example, the address of `a[3]` is assumed at the memory location `0x008C955C`. The last statement has `p` pointing at the fourth element `a[3]` of the array `a`, as shown in Figure 11.3. Note that, by default, the array index starts at `0`, instead of `1`. The pointer `p` can be used just like the one in the previous section. The expression `*p` gives what `p` points to, which in this case is the value of `a[3]`.

Once we have a pointer pointing at an element of an array or dynamic allocated memory, we can perform pointer arithmetic. Given that `p` is a pointer to `a[3]`, we can add `i` to `p`.

```
p + i
```

In C, adding `i` increments pointer `p` to point to the *ith* element beyond its current location with the address of `p` plus `i*sizeof(*p)` bytes. For example, if `p` points to the fourth element of an integral array `a` with six elements, which has the address `0x008C9550`, `p+2` (or `p += 2`) points to

```
0x008C955C+2*sizeof(int) = 0x008C9564
```

and is illustrated in Figure 11.4. For subtracting an integer from a pointer, the expression `p-2` (or `p -= 2`) points to

```
0x008C955C-2*sizeof(int) = 0x008C9950
```

as shown in Figure 11.4 as well.

Consider the following command-line statements:

```
> int a[6]={100,200,300,400,500,600}, *p;
> p = &a[0]           // p = 0x008C9550, p points to a[0]
> *p
100
> p += 3              // p = 0x008C955C, p points to a[3]
> *p
400
> *(p+1)              // p+1 points to a[4]
500
> *(p-1)              // p-1 points to a[2]
300
> *p+1
401
> *p = 10             // set a[3] = 10
> *(p+2) = 20         // set a[5] = 20
> *(p-2) = 30         // set a[1] = 30
```

The array `a` with six elements is initialized with values from 100 to 600 at the declaration. It is assumed that the array `a` starts at the address 0x008C9550. The pointer `p` first points to the address of the array `a` by the statement

```
p = &a[0];
```

The indirection operation `*p` gives the value of the element `a[0]` pointed by the pointer `p`. The pointer arithmetic is then performed to reassign the pointer `p` to point to the element `a[3]` by the statement

```
p += 3;
```

At this point, the expression `*p` gives the value of 400 for the element `a[3]`. For pointer arithmetic, an integral number can be either added to or subtracted from a pointer. For example, the expression `(p+1)` points to the element `a[4]`, whereas the expression `(p-1)` points to `a[2]`. The indirecton operations `*(p+1)` and `*(p-1)` have the values 500 and 300 for elements `a[4]` and `a[2]`, respectively. The unary operator `*` has a higher precedence than the addition operator. The expression `*p + 1`, without the parentheses, gives 401. The expression first fetches the value of 400, pointed to by `p`, then adds 1 to that value.

An indirection expression can also be used as an lvalue to change the content of the memory pointed by a pointer. In the above interactive execution of statements, the statements

```
*p = 11;
*(p+2) = 12;
*(p-2) = 13;
```

set elements `a[3]`, `a[5]`, and `a[1]` with values of 11, 12, and 13, respectively. Note that the expression `*p + 1`, with the value of 401, cannot be used as an lvalue because it does not refer to a valid memory address. The content of the array `a` after the above assigment statements is shown in Figure 11.5.

If a pointer is incremented or decremented by 1, the increment operator `++` and decrement operator `--` can be used. If `p` is a pointer to some element of an array, then `++p` (equivalent to `p = p + 1` or `p += 1`)

Address	Content
0x008C9550	a[0] = 100
p−2 -> 0x008C9554	a[1] = 13
0x008C9558	a[2] = 300
p -> 0x008C955C	a[3] = 11
0x008C9560	a[4] = 500
p+2 -> 0x008C9564	a[5] = 12

Figure 11.5: The content of the array `a` after execution of assignment statements using pointer arithmetic.

increments `p` to point to the next element, whereas `--p` (equivalent to `p = p - 1` or `p -= 1`) decrements `p` to point to the previous element. For example, if `p` points to the fourth element of an integral array `a`, which has the address of 0x008C9550,

- `++p` points to $0x008C955C + \textbf{sizeof(int)} = 0x008C9560$
- `--p` points to $0x008C955C - \textbf{sizeof(int)} = 0x008C9558$

As an example, Program 11.2 asks the user to input a six-letter word, then prints the word reversely. The functions **getchar()** and **putchar()** are used to handle input and output for a character, respectively. They are declared in the header file **stdio.h**. The function **getchar()** with prototype

```
int getchar(void);
```

returns the character read as an unsigned char from the standard input and cast to an int. The function **putchar()** with the prototype

```
int putchar(int c);
```

writes the character `c` to the standard output. It returns the character written as an unsigned char cast to an int. Details about handling characters in C are described in Chapter 12.

In Program 11.2, the array `word` of type char has six elements. The pointer `p` points to the first element of the array. A **for** loop is used to fill six elements of the array, each with a character. At each iteration, a character is read and assigned to an element pointed by the pointer `p` using the statement

```
*p = getchar();
```

The pointer `p` is then advanced to point to the next element using an increment operation `p++`. At the end of the first **for** loop, `p` points to the element `word[N]` which is outside the memory allocated for the array `word` with *N* elements.

The second **for** loop in Program 11.2 prints each character in the array `word`, starting from the element `word[N-1]`. At each iteration, `p` is moved back to point to the previous element by a decrement operation `p--`. The element is then accessed and printed out as the following statement.

```
putchar(*p);
```

```
/* File: reverseword.c
   Input a word with six characters, print it reversely. */
#include <stdio.h>      /* for getchar() and putchar() */

#define N        6      /* number of elements for an array */
int main() {
    char word[N];       /* an array for N characters */
    char *p;            /* pointer to char */
    int i;

    p = &word[0];       /* p points to the first element of array word */
    printf("Please input a six-letter word\n");
    for(i=0; i<N; i++) {
       /* get a character from the standard input and assign it to *p */
       *p = getchar();
       p++;             /* p points to the next element */
    }

    /* print the word in reverse order, p now points to word[N] (outside
       the memory for array word from word[0] to word[N-1]) */
    for(i=0; i<N; i++) {
       p--;             /* p points to the previous element */
       /* access a character by *p and print it to the standard output */
       putchar(*p);
    }
    putchar('\n');      /* print a newline character for the prompt */
    return 0;
}
```

Program 11.2: A program to input a six-letter word and print it reversely using the pointer arithmetic.

After printing six letters using the **for** loop, a newline character is printed. An interactive execution of Program 11.2 is shown below,

```
> reverseword.c
Please input a six-letter word
number
rebmun
```

The increment and decrement operators also allow for performing two actions at once. The post-increment expression `*p++` accesses what `p` points to, while simultaneously incrementing `p` so that it points to the next element. The pre-increment form `*++p` increments `p`, then accesses what it points to. The working principle is the same for the post-decrement expression `*p--` and pre-decrement expression `*--p`. As an example, statements

```
*p = getchar();
p++;
```

in Program 11.2 can be replaced by a single statement with a post-increment expression as follows:

```
*p++ = getchar();
```

Similarly, statements

```
p--;
putchar(*p);
```

can be substituted by a statement with a pre-decrement expression

```
putchar(*--p);
```

Note that `(*p)++` increments what `p` points to. The increment operator `++` has a higher precedence than a cast operator. The statement `(int *)p++` is interpreted as `(int *)(p++)`.

The increment and decrement operations have side effects. For example, the statement `*ptr++ += 2` is different from the statement `*ptr++ = *ptr++ +2` because lvalue `*ptr++` contains an increment operation.

Pointers can also be subtracted from each other, such as `p2 - p1`. When doing so, pointers `p1` and `p2` shall have the same data type. The expression `p2 - p1` results in the number of elements between `p1` and `p2`. The result of pointer subtraction can be assigned to a variable of signed integer type **ptrdiff_t** defined in the file **stddef.h**. For 32-bit programming, the signed integer type **ptdidiff_t** can be defined by

```
typedef int ptrdiff_t;
```

For 64-bit programming, it can be defined by

```
typedef long long ptrdiff_t;
```

An implementation, however, may use a built-in data type to define **ptrdiff_t** for different programming models.

For example, in the code fragment below, the array `a` has six elements of type int, and the pointers `p1` and `p2` of pointer to int point to the second and fifth elements of the array, respectively. The result of the subtraction operation of two pointers $(p2 - p1)$ is assigned to the variable `i` of type **ptdidiff_t**. The value for `n` is 3, as shown below.

```
#include <stddef.h>
int a[6], *p1, *p2;
ptrdiff_t n;
p1 = &a[1];
p2 = &a[4];
n = p2 - p1; // n is 3
```

A possible memory layout for this example is as shown in Figure 11.6.

Pointer to char is often treated as a string. The following example illustrates how pointers can be used to handle strings.

```
char dest[100], src[100] = "original string";
char *dp = &dest[0], *sp = &src[0];

/* copy src to dest */
while(*sp != '\0') {
    *dp++ = *sp++;
}
*dp = '\0';
```

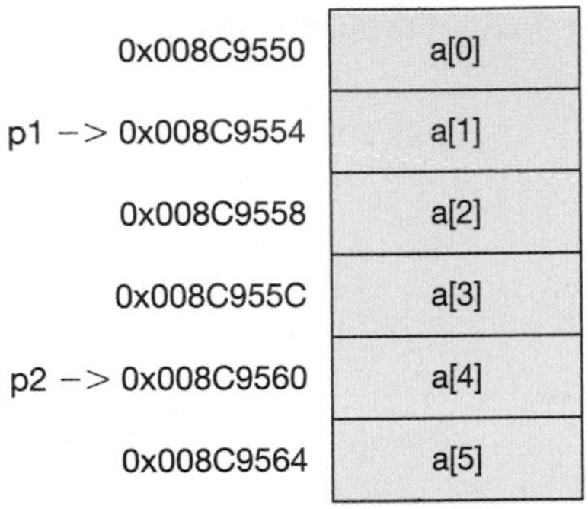

0x008C9550	a[0]
p1 -> 0x008C9554	a[1]
0x008C9558	a[2]
0x008C955C	a[3]
p2 -> 0x008C9560	a[4]
0x008C9564	a[5]

Figure 11.6: Subtracting pointers from each other.

In the above example, variables `dp` and `sp` of pointers to char are used to copy a string in the array `src` to the array `dest`. The pointers `dp` and `sp` are first pointed to the memory for the arrays `dest` and `src`, respectively. Then a **while** loop is used to copy the content in the array `src` to the array `dest` element-by-element by statement

```
*dp++ = *sp++;
```

until a null-terminating character `'\0'` for a string is reached. The above statement is equivalent to

```
*dp = *sp;
 dp++;
 sp++;
```

When pointer arithmetic is performed, it should be within the valid range. For example, if the array `a` has 10 elements, the valid subscript for a 10-element array ranges from 0 to 9. The expressions `a[10]` and `a[-1]` would refer to the object outside the memory allocated for the array `a`.

Pointers of different data types are also possible. They are similar to pointers to int, and the pointer arithmetic discussed applies to them as well. For example, the command-line examples below declare pointers `dptr`, `zp1`, and `zp2` of double, complex, and double complex types, respectively.

```
> double d[10], *dptr
> dptr = &d[0]
00E815F0
> dptr = dptr + 1
00E815F8
> *dptr = 10
> d[1]
10.000000
> complex z1[5], *zp1
> zp1 = &z1[0]
00E87E60
> zp1 = zp1 + 1
00E87E68
> double complex z2[5], *zp2
```

```
> zp2 = &z2[0]
00E87B00
> zp2 = zp2 + 1
00E87B10
```

The pointers are first assigned to point to the first elements of their corresponding arrays, and then pointer arithmetic is used to have them point to the second elements. For example, the pointer `dptr` initially points to the first element of array `d` of type double with statement `dptr = &d[0]`. Then the pointer `dptr` is incremented by 1 with the statement `dptr = dptr + 1` pointing to element `d[1]`. The expressions `*dptr` and `d[1]` will have the same value.

A more thorough discussion of the relationship between pointers and arrays can be found in section 11.5.

11.3 Calling Functions by Reference Using Pointers

When Ch passes arguments to functions, it passes them by value. In many cases, however, it is desirable to alter the passed argument in the function. For example, assume that a sorting routine is trying to exchange two out-of-order elements `a` and `b` with the function `swap()`. The following statement from Program 11.3 will not be able to swap the values for `a` and `b` in the function **main**().

```
swap(a, b);
```

The output of Program 11.3 is as follows:

```
a = 5, b = 6
```

```
/* File: noswap.c
   Demonstrate call-by-value in C */
#include <stdio.h>

/* a function was supposed to swap passed x and y  in the calling function,
   but, it failed to swap. */
void swap(int x, int y) {
    int temp;     /* temporary variable */

    /* swap inside this function for x and y */
    temp = x;
    x = y;
    y = temp;
}

int main() {
    int a = 5, b = 6;                    /* declare and initialize a and b */
```

Program 11.3: A program that failed to swap values. (*Continued*)

```
    swap(a, b);                          /* try to swap a and b */
    printf("a = %d, b = %d\n", a, b); /* output is a = 5, b = 6, no swap! */
    return 0;
}
```

Program 11.3: (*Continued*)

Because of call-by-value, the function `swap()` cannot affect the arguments `a` and `b` in the calling function. As illustrated in Figures 11.7 and 11.8, variables `a` and `b` occupies 4 bytes apiece. When the function `swap()` is called, variables `x` and `y`, each occupying 4 bytes, are allocated. The values for `a` and `b` are copied to the local variables `x` and `y`. The swap operations affect only the values of the local variables `x` and `y`. It only swaps `x` and `y` inside the function `swap()`. When the function call is completed, the memory for local variables will be released. Note that the value of a noninitialized temporary variable `temp` is unknown before it is assigned a value in the swap operation.

To remedy the problem, pointers can be used to pass the addresses of variables to functions and access variables through their addresses indirectly. With this method, it is possible to write a new swap function to alter arguments passed into them. The `swap()` function in Program 11.4 can be called using pointers to swap values explicitly inside a calling function. The function call to `swap()` is modified as

```
swap(&a, &b);
```

The operator '`&`' gives the address of a variable; thus, expression `&a` is a pointer to the address of `a`, and `&b` is a pointer to the address of `b`. In this case, the `swap()` function should use the addresses rather than the copies of values `a` and `b`. In the function definition for `swap()` in Program 11.4, the parameters are declared as pointers `pa` and `pb`, and the variables `a` and `b` in the calling function are accessed indirectly through these pointers. The output of executing Program 11.4 is shown below with values for `a` and `b` swapped:

```
a = 6, b = 5
```

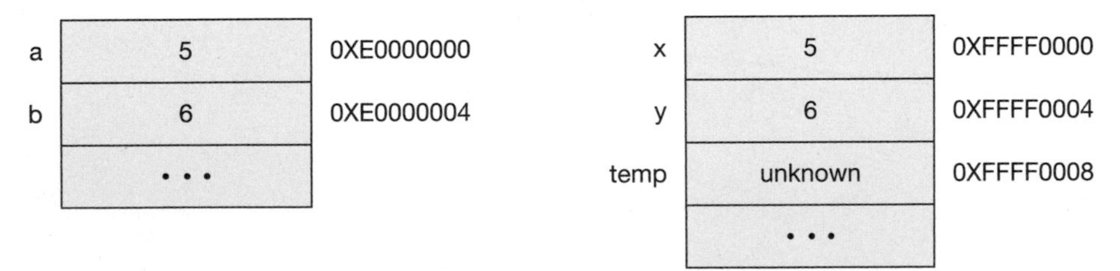

Figure 11.7: The contents of variables before swapping operations in Program 11.3.

a	5	0XE0000000
b	6	0XE0000004
	• • •	

x	5	0XFFFF0000
y	5	0XFFFF0004
temp	5	0XFFFF0008
	• • •	

Figure 11.8: The contents of variables after swapping operations in Program 11.3.

```
/* File: swap.c
   A call-by-reference through indirection operation of pointers in C */
#include <stdio.h>

/* a function to swap objects pointed by pa and pb
   in the calling function by indirection operations */
void swap(int *pa, int *pb) {
    int temp;     /* temporary variable */

    /* swap values pointed by pa and pb in the calling function
       by indirection operations */
    temp = *pa;
    *pa = *pb;
    *pb = temp;
}

int main() {
    int a = 5, b = 6;     /* declare and initialize a and b */

    swap(&a, &b);         /* swap a and b by passing the addresses of a and b */
    printf("a = %d, b = %d\n", a, b); /* output is a = 6, b = 5, swap! */
    return 0;
}
```

Program 11.4: Swapping values in the calling function using pointers.

Figures 11.9 and 11.10 illustrate how values for variables a and b in the main function are swapped by calling the function swap(). Before the swap operations, variables pa and pb inside the swap() contain the addresses of the variables a and b in the main function. In this example, the address of the variable a is 0XE0000000. The address of the local variable pa of pointer to int type is 0XFFFF0000. The expressions *pa and *pb with indirection operation inside the function swap() refer to the variables a and b in the main function, respectively. Therefore, the swap operations

```
temp = *pa;
*pa = *pb;
*pb = temp;
```

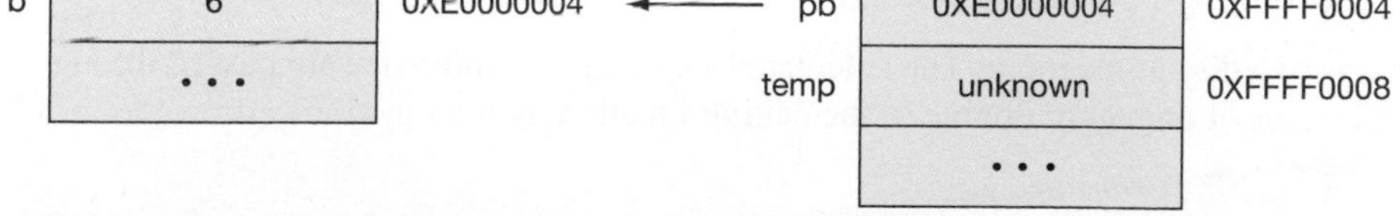

Figure 11.9: The contents of variables before swapping operations in Program 11.4.

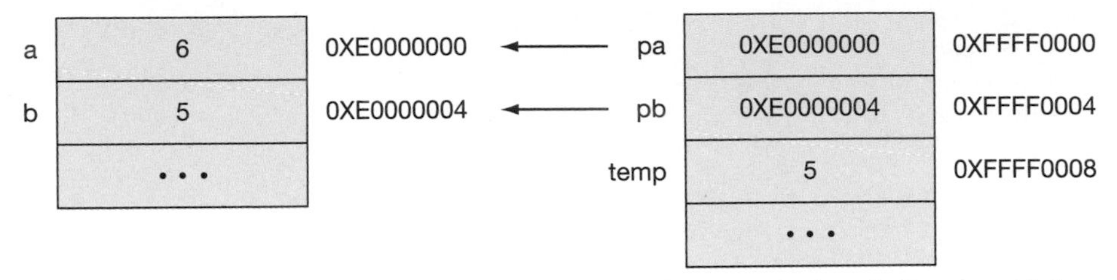

Figure 11.10: The contents of variables after swapping operations in Program 11.4.

inside the function `swap()` are equivalent to performing the operations

```
temp = a;
a = b;
b = temp;
```

for variables `a` and `b` inside the main function. After swap operations, the values of variables `pa` and `pb` remain the same. The allocated memory for variables `pa` and `pb` inside the function `swap()` will be released when the function returns.

One of the major applications of pointers in C is to pass the results of a function to its calling function. Recall that the function **scanf()** as shown in Program 3.6 in Chapter 3 uses pointers to pass results through its argument to the calling function.

Application Examples of Passing Values from a Function Using Pointers

Two examples are presented to demonstrate the application of passing arguments by reference using pointers.

Calculating the Area and Circumference of a Metal Disc

The first example uses a function to calculate the area and circumference of a metal disc with a given radius. Because a function can return only one argument, we could not return both area and circumference from a function. We could use global variables to keep the calculated area and circumference of a disc. However, names of global variables could conflict with other names. Therefore, it is more desirable to write a function to calculate the area and circumference of a disc and pass these results back to the calling function through pointers, as shown in Program 11.5.

In Program 11.5, the function `disc()` with the prototype

```
void disc(double radius, double *area, double *circum);
```

takes the radius of a disc as the input. The calculated area and circumference are passed through variables `area` and `circum` of pointer to double to the calling function by the function call

```
disc(radius, &area, &circum);
```

```
/* File: disc.c
   Use a function to calculate the area and circumference of a disc.
   Pass the results by reference using pointers.  */
#include <stdio.h>
#include <math.h>    /* for M_PI */

/* function disc() calculates area and circumference
   of a disc with a given radius. */
void disc(double radius, double *area, double *circum) {
    *area = M_PI * radius *radius;
    *circum = 2*M_PI*radius;
}

int main() {
    double radius;          /* radius of the disc */
    double area, circum;    /* area and circumference of the disc */

    /* printf("Enter the radius for the disc (m): ");
       scanf("%lf", &radius); */
    radius = 3.5;           /* radius is 3.5 meters */

    disc(radius, &area, &circum);
    printf("area = %f (m^2)\n", area);
    printf("circumference = %f (m)\n", circum);
    return 0;
}
```

Program 11.5: Passing both area and circumference of a metal disc to the calling function using pointers.

With a given radius of 3.5 meters, the output from Program 11.5 is given in Figure 11.11.

```
area = 38.484510 (m^2)
circumference = 21.991149 (m)
```

Figure 11.11: The output from Programs 11.5, Program 18.6 in Chapter 18, and Program 23.15 in Chapter 23.

Decomposing a Floating-Point Number into Integral and Fractional Parts

Program 11.6 is another application example of using a pointer to pass the result to its calling function. A floating-point number of type double from the user input in the function **main()** is passed to the function `decompose()` as the first argument `x`. The function `decompose()` decomposes this floating-point number into an integral part and a fractional part. The function returns the fractional part. The integral part is passed back to the calling function **main()** through the argument `iptr` of pointer to double. Both

```
/* File: decompose.c
   Decompose a floating-point number into integral part and fractional part */
#include <stdio.h>
#include <limits.h>    /* INT_MAX */

/* function decomposes x into integral and fractional parts. The integral part
   is passed by pointer iptr and the fractional part is returned. */
double decompose(double x, double *iptr) {
   int i;

   i = (int) x;    /* get the integral part, it must be smaller than INT_MAX */
   *iptr  = (double)i; /* pass back to the calling function */
   return x - i;       /* return the fractional part */
}

int main() {
    /* variables for x, integral and fractional parts */
    double x, intpart, fracpart;

    printf("Please input a floating-point number smaller than %d\n", INT_MAX);
    scanf("%lf", &x);

    fracpart = decompose(x, &intpart);
    printf("The integral part of %f is %.f, and fractional part is %f\n",
           x, intpart, fracpart);
    return 0;
}
```

Program 11.6: Decomposing a floating-point number into an integral part and a fractional part.

the original floating-point number, integral part, and fractional part are then printed out. The format `%.f` is used to print the integral part, without a decimal point and fractional part, of the variable `intpart` of type double. Note that the function `decompose()` in Program 11.6 is a simplified version of the C standard math function **modf()** because the integral part of the floating-point number in this implementation must be less than or equal to **INT_MAX**. To implement the function **modf()**, you need to understand how floating-point numbers are represented inside a computer system, which is described in Chapter 16. An interactive execution of Program 11.6 is shown below:

```
> decompose.c
Please input a floating-point number smaller than 2147483647
123.456789
The integral part of 123.456789 is 123, and fractional part is 0.456789
```

11.4 Using the const Qualifier with Pointers

A pointer can be used to change the object it points to. There are situations in a program in which an object cannot be modified. In this case, the type qualifier **const** can be used to inform the compiler that a particular variable cannot be modified. This also makes the code more readable with clear intention. For example, the code below

```
const char *str = "this is a constant string";
```

declares the variable `str` as a pointer to a const-qualified char. The contents that `str` points to cannot be modified. As another example of this application, a function parameter of pointer type can be const-qualified so that the function is not allowed to modify the passed object. Based on the algorithm described in section 11.2, the function `strcopy()` in Program 11.7 copies the string from `sp` to the memory pointed to by the variable `dp`. Using a **while** loop, the string `sp` is copied to the character array `dp` element by element until the null-terminating character is reached in the string `sp`. The statement

```
*dp++ = *sp++;
```

```
/* File: strcopy.c
   Copy a string. The source string is const-qualified */
#include <stdio.h>

/* Function copying string from sp to dp.
   string pointed to by sp is not modified inside the function.
   To make this intention clear, it is const-qualified so that
   it cannot be modified inside the function.  */
char *strcopy(char *dp, const char *sp) {
    char *retp = dp;
    while(*sp != '\0') { /* copy each character in the string
                            till the null terminating character is reached */
      /* copy a character, advance pointers dp and sp to the next elements */
      *dp++ =  *sp++;
    }
    *dp = '\0'; /* fill the last element with the null terminating character */
    return retp;  /* return the passed dp */
}

int main() {
     const char *src = "original string"; /* original string */
     char dest[100];                      /* destination string */

     strcopy(dest, src);                  /* copy src to dest */
     printf("dest = %s\n", dest);         /* display the copied string */
     return 0;
}
```

Program 11.7: Using const-qualified pointers in the string copying function.

assigns the value pointed to by `sp` to the address pointed to by `dp` and then increments the pointers `sp` and `dp` to point to their next elements. Then the character '`\0`' is appended to the copy `dp` to indicate the end of the string. The resulting copied string is returned by the function `strcopy()`. The string pointed to by the variable `sp` of pointer type cannot be modified inside the function because `sp` is const-qualified. On the other hand, because the memory pointed by the pointer `dp` is modified inside the function, it cannot be const-qualified. In the function main(), the string `src` is also const-qualified. The output from Program 11.7 is as follows:

```
dest = original string
```

The function `strcopy()` in Program 11.7 is a sample implementation of the string function **strcpy()** in the C standard string library with the header file **string.h**, which will be described in detail in Chapter 12. The function `strcopy()` performs the same function as **strcpy()** described in section 12.8.2 in Chapter 12.

The **const** qualifier can also be applied to other data types. Because this type qualifier was introduced in C89, some compilers may not enforce it rigorously.

11.5 Relation Between Pointers and Arrays

Arrays and pointers are intimately tied. Not only can a pointer be used to access an array, but also the variable name of an array itself can be treated as a pointer. An array name acts as a constant pointer. Its value is the address of the first element of the array. So if `a` is an int array of six elements and `p` is a pointer to int, then the statement

```
p = a;
```

is equivalent to

```
p = &a[0];
```

Pointers can also perform array-subscripting operations. If `p` points to the first element of array `a`, the expressions `a[1]`, `*(a+1)`, `*(p+1)`, and `p[1]` all refer to the same second element of the array. They can be used as both lvalue and rlvalue. For example,

```
> int a[6] = {1,2,3,4,5,6}, *p
> p = a            // p = &a[0]
> a[1]
2
> *(a+1)
2
> *(p+1)
2
> p[1]
2
```

Assume that `a1` is a one-dimensional array of int type with a length of 10 and `p` is a pointer to int, elements of `a1` can be accessed by four methods illustrated in the interactive execution in a Ch shell as follows:

```
> int i
> int a1[10], *p
> a1[3]=3         // method 1
> for(i=0; i<10; i++) printf("%d ", a1[i])
0 0 0 3 0 0 0 0 0 0
> *(a1+4)=4       // <==> a1[4]=4, method 2
> for(i=0; i<10; i++) printf("%d ", a1[i])
0 0 0 3 4 0 0 0 0 0
> p = a1
> *(p+5)=5        // <==> a1[5]=5, method 3
> p[6] = 6;       // <==> a1[6]=6, method 4
> for(i=0; i<10; i++) printf("%d ", a1[i])
0 0 0 3 4 5 6 0 0 0
```

According to the pointer arithmetic described in section 11.2, `p+5` points to the sixth element of `a1`. The variable name `a1` in statement

```
*(a1+4)=4
```

is actually treated as a pointer to int. On the other hand, a pointer can also be treated as an array, as `p[6]` refers to the same memory for the element `a[6]`.

As a special case, the address of an array is the array itself. For example, for the array `a`, the expressions `&a[0]`, `a`, and `&a` all refer to the address of the array with the same value. Therefore, if *s* is an array of char, such as

```
char s[100];
```

the statement

```
scanf("%s", s);
```

is the same as

```
scanf("%s", &s);
```

For a multi-dimensional array, a pointer can also be used to access its memory. For example, the variable `a2` is a two-dimensional array of int type with size (3×4) and `p` is a pointer to int as declared below:

```
> int i, j
> int a2[3][4] ={1,2,3,4,5,6,7,8,9,10,11,12}, *p
> p = &a2[1][0]
> p[0] = 15              // a2[1][0]=15
> p[1] = 16              // a2[1][1]=16
> p = a2                 // p = &a2[0][0]
> *(p+1*4+2)=17          // a2[1][2]=17
> for(i=0; i<3; i++) for(j=0; j<4; j++) printf("%d ", a2[i][j]);
1 2 3 4 15 16 17 8 9 10 11 12
```

The assignment operation

```
p = &a2[1][0]
```

assigns the address of the fifth element `a2[1][0]` to the variable `p` of pointer to int. Then, the expressions `p[0]` and `*p` refer to the same element `a2[1][0]`. The expression `p[1]` refers to the element `a2[1][1]`. After the assignment operation

```
p = a2
```

the value of `p+1*4+2` points to the address of the seventh element of array `a2` at `a2[1][2]`. The expression `*(p+1*4+2)` refers to the element `a2[1][2]`.

11.6 Using Pointers to Pass One-Dimensional Arrays to Functions

As described in section 10.5.1 in Chapter 10, when an array is passed to a function, what is actually passed is the address of the first element of the array. In the called function, this argument is a local variable of pointer type, pointing to the first element of the passed array. That is why pointers can be used to pass one-dimensional arrays to functions. Program 11.8 is an example that uses a pointer to pass one-dimensional arrays of variable lengths to calculate the sum of the elements in the arrays. The function definition and prototype

```
double func(int n, double *a);
```

```
/* File: pass1Dcarray.c
   Calculate the sum of an array using a function by passing arrays
   as an argument. */
#include <stdio.h>
#include <stdlib.h>
double func(int n, double *a);

int main() {
    /* declare and initialize arrays of diff dimensions and extents */
    double a[5] = {1.0, 2.0, 3.0, 4.0, 5.0};          /* 1D with 5 elements */
    double b[6] = {1.0, 2.0, 3.0, 4.0, 5.0, 6.0};     /* 1D with 6 elemtns */
    double c[2][3] = {1.0, 2.0, 3.0, 4.0, 5.0, 6.0}; /* 2D array */
    double sum; /* declare sum */

    sum = func(5, a);             /* calculate the sum for array a */
    printf("sum = %f\n", sum); /* display sum for array b */

    sum = func(6, b);             /* calculate the sum for array b */
    printf("sum = %f\n", sum); /* display sum for array b */

    /* sum = func(2*3, c); may get warning in some C/C++ compilers */
    sum = func(2*3, &c[0][0]); /* calculate the sum for array c */
    printf("sum = %f\n", sum); /* display sum for array c */
    return 0;
}
```

Program 11.8: Passing arrays to a function. (*Continued*)

```
/* a function to calculate the sum of one-dimensional arrays with
   different extents using a pointer  */
double func(int n, double *a) {
    double sum = 0;                 /* declare and initialize sum */
    int i;                          /* declare index variable for loop */

    for(i=0; i<n; i++) {
        sum += (a+i);                /* sum all alements one by one */
    }
    return sum;                      /* return the sum */
}
```

Program 11.8: (*Continued*)

in Program 11.8 can be replaced by the following code with an argument of incomplete array type:

```
double func(int n, double a[]);
```

Similarly, the statement

```
sum += *(a+i);
```

using the indirection operation `*(a+i)` to access an element of an array in the called function can be replaced by the statement

```
sum += a[i];
```

using the array reference expression `a[i]` without changing the function prototype. Typically, for a function argument of pointer type, the passed memory in the calling function is accessed using an indirection operation in the called function. For an argument of array type, the memory is accessed by an array reference expression.

In Program 11.8, the address for array `c` with the dimension of 2×3 is passed to the function by the statement

```
sum = func(2*3, &c[0][0]);
```

The output of Program 11.8 is as follows:

```
sum = 15.000000
sum = 21.000000
sum = 21.000000
```

Another example of passing a two-dimensional array to an argument of a one-dimensional array is given in Program 11.23.

It should be pointed out that the declaration

```
double data[]
```

for an argument of incomplete array type in Programs 10.12 and 10.13 for functions of the statistical library could simply be replaced by

```
double *data
```

without affecting the library and its application programs.

For a function argument of array type, regardless of a fully specified array, incomplete array, or variable length array, when an array is passed to this argument, only its address is passed. Therefore, the size of this array argument calculated by the **sizeof** operator inside the function is the result for the size of a pointer type. For example, for the function `func2()` with the the prototype

```
void func2(int n, double a[10], double b[], double c[n]);
```

the **sizeof** operations `sizeof(a)`, `sizeof(b)`, and `sizeof(c)` inside the function `func2()` all give 4 bytes for 32-bit programming or 8 bytes in 64-bit programming.

The relation between multi-dimensional arrays and pointers to arrays will be described in section 11.13.

11.7 Dynamic Allocation of Memory

One problem with using a fixed-size array is that either it is too small to handle special cases, or it is too big and resources are wasted. Without using variable length arrays (VLAs) in C99, this problem can be solved by dynamically allocated memory. As another example, data structures are often used to develop large-scale software projects. A data structure typically allows a system to be able to adjust automatically to a dynamically changing condition. For example, a robot in a field may need to track random targets. When a new target appears, it needs to be recorded in the system. Because the number of targets cannot be predetermined, a dynamic data structure is needed. To implement such a dynamic data structure, a program typically needs to allocate memory dynamically described in this section.

The memory can be dynamically allocated using the standard functions **malloc()**, **calloc()**, or **realloc()**. The order and contiguity of storage allocated by successive calls to these dynamic memory allocation functions **malloc()**, **calloc()**, and **realloc()** are unspecified.

The function **malloc()** prototyped with

```
void *malloc(size_t size);
```

is used to dynamically allocate memory for an object whose size in the number of bytes is specified by the argument `size`. The data type **size_t** is defined as the unsigned integer type for the **sizeof** operator as described in section 3.12 in Chapter 3. The type **size_t** is a synonym for the **unsigned int** for 32-bit programming and **unsigned long long** for 64-bit programming as described in section 3.12 in Chapter 3. Therefore, the same function prototype can be used for **malloc()** for both 32-bit and 64-bit programming. The pointer returned from the **malloc()** function if the allocation succeeds is suitably aligned so that it may be assigned to a pointer to any type of object and then used to access such an object or an array of such objects in the memory allocated (until the memory is explicitly freed or reallocated). Each such allocation shall yield a pointer to an object separate from any other object. The pointer returned points to the start (lowest byte address) of the allocated memory. If the memory cannot be allocated, the function **malloc()** returns a null pointer **NULL**. If the size of the memory requested is zero, the behavior is platform-dependent: either a null pointer is returned or the behavior is as if the size were some nonzero value, except that the returned pointer shall not be used to access an object.

The value of a pointer that refers to freed memory is indeterminate according to the C standard. Typically, it will result in the crash of a program either immediately or later when the other part of the program is executed.

The return type of the function **malloc()** is pointer to void, which is a generic pointer. Although it is not required by the C standard, it is a common practice to cast the returned value to the pointer type of the lvalue in an assignment statement.

The **sizeof** operator can be used to compute the size, in bytes, of a variable or type. It is useful to allocate memory for variables whose sizes are unknown to the users. To allocate memory for 100 numbers of type int, the following statement can be used:

```
int *p = (int *)malloc(100 * sizeof(int));
```

The returned type of pointer to void by the function **malloc()** is cast to the type of pointer to int. The following call to the function **calloc()** is equivalent to the above statement.

```
int *p = calloc(100, sizeof(int));
```

The function **calloc()** with the prototype

```
void *calloc(size_t nelem, size_t elsize);
```

allocates memory for an array with the number of elements specified by its first input argument, `nelem`. The second input argument, `elsize` specifies the number of bytes to be allocated for each element. Unlike the function **malloc()**, the memory allocated by the function **calloc()** is initialized to zeros.

Obviously, no computer has an infinite amount of memory available. If the function call `malloc (1000000000)` is used, or if `malloc(10)` is called 100,000,000 times, the system will probably run out of memory. When the **malloc()** function is unable to allocate the requested memory, it returns a **NULL** pointer. Therefore, for every function call to **malloc()**, it is important to check the returned value before using it. A typical call to the function **malloc()** with an error check is shown below.

```
int *p = (int *)malloc(100 * sizeof(int));
if(p == NULL)
{
    printf("Error: no memory\n");
    exit(1);
}
```

If the function **malloc()** returns a null pointer constant determined by the equality operation `p==NULL`, the code should return to its caller or exit from the program entirely after printing the error message. It cannot proceed with the code that would have used the memory pointed to by `p`.

Unlike variables of automatic storage duration, dynamically allocated memory does not automatically disappear when a function returns. Just as one can use the function **malloc()** to control exactly when and how much memory to allocate, one can also control exactly when to deallocate it. In fact, many programs use memory on a transient basis. They allocate some memory, use it for a while, but then reach a point where they do not need that particular piece of memory anymore. Because memory is not inexhaustible, it is a good idea to deallocate (that is, release or free) memory when it is no longer required.

Dynamically allocated memory is deallocated with the function **free()** with the prototype

```
void free(void *ptr);
```

The argument to **free()** is a pointer to a block previously allocated by **malloc(), calloc(),** or **realloc()**. For example, if `p` contains a pointer previously returned by the function **malloc()**, the statement

```
free(p);
```

can be used to release the memory dynamically allocated. After **free()** is executed, this memory is made available for further allocation by the application, though it is not returned to the system. Memory is returned to the system only upon termination of the application. If `ptr` is a null pointer, no action occurs.

Freeing the memory that is still in use causes *memory corruption*. This might happen if a random number is passed to **free()** or the memory pointed by `ptr` is freed more than once by calling `free(ptr)` multiple times. A program with the corrupted memory may result in a crash at a later time when a memory allocation function is called.

On the other hand, not freeing the memory that is no longer in use causes *memory leak*. For some programs, such as your homework assignment, that run in a fixed or bounded period of time, not freeing the memory no longer in use is not a concern, especially for programs that do not consume a large memory. When such a program finishes, it automatically releases all its memory. For other programs such as the operating system, Web server, and calendar manager, that have to run for days or months at a time, the memory leak can cause serious problems. The computer typically first becomes slower and slower, and finally the program with the memory leak crashes when memory cannot be allocated anymore.

The memory corruption and memory leak in C are among the most difficult bugs to fix. To avoid these memory bugs, for each memory allocation function call, such as **malloc()** or **calloc()**, there must be a corresponding function call **free()**. However, for a large program or when the logic of a program becomes complicated, it takes considerable time and effort to avoid and fix such memory bugs. Before a software product is released, one of major tasks is to find and fix the memory bugs. Exercise 53 describes simple methods to find if a program has a memory leak in different platforms.

Dynamically allocated memory can also be reallocated with the function **realloc()**. Its function prototype is as follows:

```
void *realloc(void *ptr, size_t size);
```

The function **realloc()** changes the size of the memory block pointed to by `ptr` to `size` bytes. If `ptr` is NULL, then the call `realloc(ptr, size)` is equivalent to `malloc(size)`. If `size` is equal to zero, then the call is equivalent to `free(ptr)`. The **realloc()** function returns a pointer to the newly allocated memory, which may be different from `ptr`, or **NULL** if the request fails. If the function call to **realloc()** fails, the original block is left untouched. For example, if the pointer `ptr` was allocated memory for an integer array of 10 elements, the following statement will reallocate memory for the pointer to reduce the size of the array to 5 elements. Memory for the last 5 elements are returned to the system's memory for reuse.

```
ptr = realloc(ptr, 5*sizeof(int));
```

Similar to functions **malloc()** and **calloc()**, the memory allocated by the function **realloc()** needs to be freed by the function **free()**.

Application Examples

Copying Strings

In Program 11.7, a fixed memory of 100 bytes is allocated for the array `dest` as a string inside function **main()**. If the string that needs to be copied to is more than 100 characters, the allocated memory is not enough. On the other hand, for a shorter string, some memory is wasted. To accommodate the dynamic nature of an application, the memory can be dynamically allocated at runtime, as illustrated in Program 11.9. The statement

```
dest = (char *) malloc(sizeof(char)*(strlen(src) + 1));
```

allocates the memory for the pointer `dest` to contain a copy of the string `src`. The standard C function **strlen()** with the prototype

```
size_t strlen(const char *s);
```

```
/* File: strcopymem.c
   Copy a string. The source string is const-qualified */
#include <stdio.h>
#include <stdlib.h>      /* for malloc() and free() */
#include <string.h>      /* for strlen() */

/* Function copying string from sp to dp.
   string pointed to by sp does not need to be modified inside the function.
   To make this intention clear, it is const-qualified so that
   it cannot be modified inside the function.  */
char *strcopy(char *dp, const char *sp) {
    while(*sp != '\0') { /* copy each character in the string
                            till the null terminating character is reached */
      /* copy a character, advance pointers dp and sp to the next elements */
      *dp++ =  *sp++;
    }
    *dp = '\0'; /* fill the last element with the null terminating character */
    return dp;  /* return dp */
}

int main() {
     const char *src = "original string"; /* original string */
     char *dest;                           /* destination string */

     /* allocate memory for string dest */
     dest = (char *) malloc(sizeof(char)*(strlen(src) + 1));
     if(dest == NULL) {  /* when mallc() failed */
        printf("Error: no memory\n");
        return -1;
     }
     else {
        strcopy(dest, src);               /* copy src to dest */
        printf("dest = %s\n", dest);      /* display the copied string */
        free(dest);                       /* free allocated memory */
        return 0;
     }
}
```

Program 11.9: Using dynamically allocated memory to hold a string.

returns the length of the string; i.e, the number of characters before the null character '`\0`' in the string `s`. Details about the function **strlen()** are further described in section 12.7.1 in Chapter 12. All strings have a terminating '`\0`' character, which is not included by the **strlen()** function. The number of bytes of the required memory for the string `src` is `strlen(src)+1`, not `strlen(src)`. To use the string function **strlen()**, the header file **string.h** needs to be included. The result from the function **malloc()** is cast to the type of pointer to char. Before the program exits, the allocated memory for `dest` is released by the function call

```
free(dest);
```

The output of Program 11.9 is the same as that of Program 11.7.

Acceleration of a Moving Body

As another example, the function `accel()` in Program 11.10 is used to calculate the acceleration of the system described in the above problem statement. It has one input argument that specifies the number of acceleration points to calculate between the interval $t = 0$ to 10 seconds. As the problem statement required, the function **malloc()** is used to allocate memory for array variables `a` and `t`. Notice that the memory for `a` and `t` are freed at the end of the function.

```
/* File: acceldynmemory.c
   Calculate acceleration, force, and time using arrays.
   The memory for array for force is dynamically allocated. */
#include <stdio.h>
#include <math.h>     /* for sin() */

#define M_G   9.81    /* gravitational acceleration constant g */
#define N1    11      /* number of points for a, p, and t */
#define N2     6      /* number of points for a, p, and t */

/* pass arrays t and a as pointers */
int accel(int n, double *t, double *a) {
    double *p;          /* declare p as a pointer */
    double mu, m, t0, tf;
    int i;

    /* set mu, mass, initial time, and final time */
    mu = 0.2;
    m = 5.0;
    t0 = 0;
    tf = 10.0;

    /* allocate memory for array p */
    p = (double *) malloc(sizeof(double)*n);
    if(p == NULL) {
       printf("Error: not enough memory\n");
       return -1;
    }

    /* calculate t[i], pi[i], a[i] */
    for(i=0; i<n; i++) {
        t[i] = t0+i*(tf - t0)/(n-1);
```

Program 11.10: Calculating accelerations using dynamically allocated memory. (*Continued*)

```
        p[i] = 4*sin(t[i]-3)+20;
        a[i] = (p[i]-mu*m*M_G)/m;
    }

    /* post processing of the data by printing out or plotting.
       Here, data for t, p, and a are printed out */
    printf(" time (s) force (N) accel (m/s^2)\n");
    printf("--------------------------------\n");
    for(i=0; i<n; i++) {
        printf("%8.4f  %8.4f  %8.4f\n", t[i], p[i], a[i]);
    }
    printf("\n");   /* a newline to separate each function call */
    free(p);        /* free memory allocated for p */
    return 0;
}

int main() {
    double t1[N1], a1[N1]; /* declare array t1 and a1 with N1 points */
    double t2[N2], a2[N2]; /* declare array t2 and a2 with N2 points */

    accel(N1, t1, a1);     /* pass arrays with N1 points */
    accel(N2, t2, a2);     /* pass arrays with N2 points */
    return 0;
}
```

Program 11.10: *(Continued)*

For our familiar mechanical problem in section 10.7.2, Program 10.26 uses C99 features of VLAs to calculate and display accelerations and forces versus time. We can solve the same problem without using VLAs using Program 11.10. The function `accel()` in Program 10.26 with the prototype

```
int accel(int n, double t[n], double a[n])
```

for VLAs `t` and `a` can be modified to use pointers either in the form of

```
int accel(int n, double t[], double a[])
```

or

```
int accel(int n, double *t, double *a)
```

In Program 11.10, the latter form is used. The deferred-shape array `p` for forces declared by the statement

```
double p[n];
```

is replaced by a pointer to double in the form of

```
double *p;
```

The memory for the array p is allocated dynamically at runtime using the function **malloc()**. The allocated memory for p is released at the end of the function. The data-processing parts of Programs 11.10 and 10.26 are the same. The output of Program 11.10 is the same as that of Program 10.26, as shown in Figure 10.12 in section 10.7.2.

For one-dimensional arrays, VLAs in C99 do not seem to simplify the program too much. However, for multidimensional arrays, VLAs simplify the passing of multidimensional arrays of different lengths to a function significantly, which will be described in section 11.15 in this chapter.

11.8 Functions Returning Pointers

A function can return a pointer type. For example, the C standard function **malloc()** returns the allocating memory with the type of pointer to void. Functions returning a pointer are commonly used in C programs, especially for large-scale applications, which often use some data structures.

For a function with return type of pointer, it typically returns the memory associated with the dynamically allocated memory, memory of the passed arguments, memory for variables of static storage duration, and **NULL**. For lower-level programming to interface with hardware, a pointer can also associate with a specific memory and address of the hardware. The function `strcopy()` in Programs 11.7 and 11.9 returns a pointer to the memory associated with its argument. The memory associated with global or static variables with static storage duration can also be returned from a function, which will be illustrated in section 11.10.

For a function with return value of pointer type, typically, if the function call is successful, it returns a valid pointer. Otherwise, it returns **NULL**.

When a function passes or returns a pointer, the pointer shall point to a valid memory. Otherwise, when the data pointed to by the pointer is accessed by the indirection operation, a segmentation or bus error might occur to crash the program. For example, a variable of automatic storage duration has local scope. The variable of automatic duration and its associated memory will not be available when the program control is out of scope. Therefore, the code below has a hidden bug.

```
int *func() {
     int localvar;
     /* code ... */
     /* Error: return the address of the local variable localvar */
     return &localvar;
}
```

The function `func()` returns the address of the local variable `localvar` of automatic storage duration. When the function `func()` returns, the memory for the variable `localvar` will be deallocated automatically. Any attempt to access the memory address return by the function `func()` may get an unexpected result. Depending on the state of the system, sometimes it may give the value of the variable `localvar` of the previously called function; it may give a garbage value; in the worst case, it may cause the program to crash. Accessing freed memory is one of the most difficult problems to debug in a C program, especially for a large program.

11.9 Pointers to Pointers

Because a pointer of a different type is a variable itself, it has an address in memory. *A pointer to pointer*, sometimes called *double pointer*, is defined as a variable that contains the address of another pointer. A variable of pointer to pointers can be declared by preceding the variable name with two successive asterisks. For example, a variable pp of pointer to pointer to int can be declared as follows.

```
int **pp;
```

The interactive Ch shell is especially useful for understanding how a pointer works, as shown in the following interactive execution of programming statements with a pointer and a pointer to pointers.

```
> int i, *p, **pp
> p = &i                    // assign address of i to p
00E81E20
> *p = 10
10
> printf("i = %d\n", i)
i = 10
> pp = &p                   // assign address of p to pp
00E82040
> printf("**pp = %d\n", **pp)
**pp = 10
```

The command-line statements declare variables i, p, and pp of type int, pointer to int, and pointer to pointer to int, respectively. Given that the addresses of i, p, and pp are 0x00E81E20, 0x00E8240, and 0x00E83060, respectively, Figure 11.12 shows the memory layout of these three variables, where the address of variable i of type int is assigned to the variable p of pointer to int. The expression *p and variable i share the same memory with the same value. The pointer to pointers pp is pointed to the address of the pointer variable p. Then the expression **pp and variable i also share the memory with the same value. The expression **pp and its equivalent forms are shown as follows:

```
**pp == *(*pp) == *p == i
```

The relation of the variable i of int type, pointer of p and pointer to pointers pp is shown in Figure 11.13.

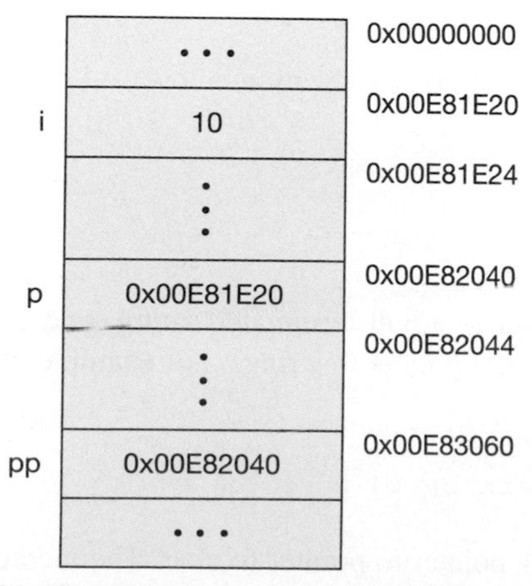

Figure 11.12: Memory layout for variables i, p, and pp.

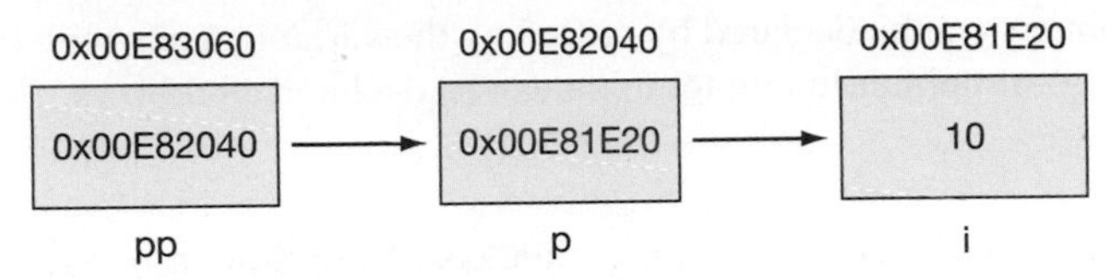

Figure 11.13: The relation between the variable `i` and pointers `p` and `pp`.

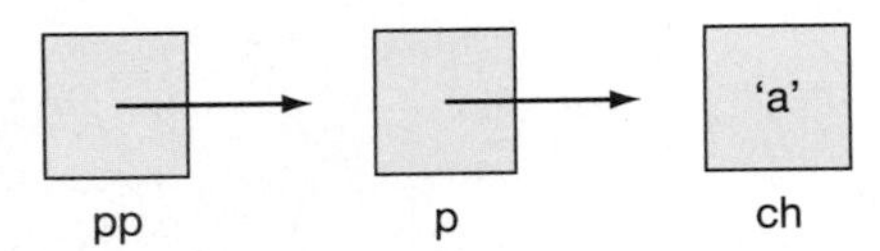

Figure 11.14: A pointer (`pp`) to a pointer (`p`) that points to a char.

As another example, consider the following code and its illustration in Figure 11.14:

```
char ch, *p, **pp;
ch = 'a';
p = &ch;
pp = &p;
```

where variable `ch` is declared as type char, variable `p` is a pointer to char, and variable `pp` is a pointer to pointer to char. The variable `ch` is assigned the character constant `'a'`. The variable `p` is pointed at the address of variable `ch`. The variable `pp` is pointed at the address of variable `p`, which is a pointer type. The indirection operation `*p` gives the value `'a'` at the address pointed by `p`. The expression `*pp` gives the value pointed by `pp`, which is the address of variable `ch`. The double indirection operation `**pp`, therefore, gives the value `'a'` of the variable `ch`, as shown in Figure 11.14.

Without changing the semantics, the above declaration and assignment statements can be replaced by a single declaration statement with initialization as follows:

```
char ch = 'a', *p = &ch, **pp = &p;
```

or multiple declaration statements with the initialization below.

```
char ch = 'a';
char *p = &ch;
char **pp = &p;
```

Because **char *** is used to refer to a null-terminated string, one common and convenient notion is to declare a pointer to pointer to char as a pointer to strings. For example, the code below

```
char *p = "ab"; // a string
char **pp = &p; // a pointer to p
```

declares `p` as a pointer and `pp` as a pointer to pointer to char. The memory layout for variables `p` and `pp` is shown in Figure 11.15.

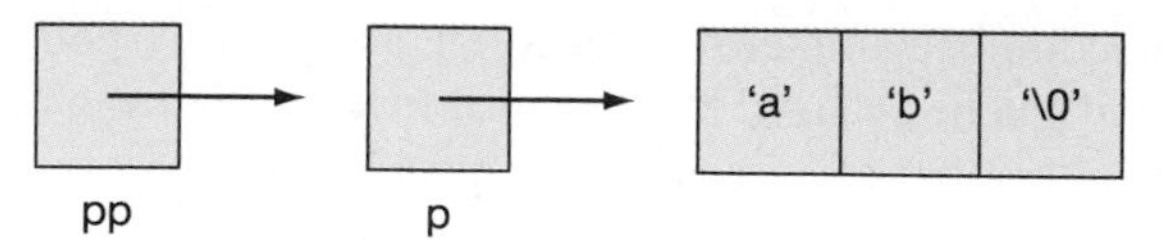

Figure 11.15: The pointer pp points to a string.

Handling an array of strings using a pointer to pointer is shown in the commands below.

```
> char *s1 = "ab";
> char *s2 = "py";
> char **pp;
> pp = (char**)malloc(3*sizeof(char*));
4006c8d0
> pp[0] = s1;
ab
> pp[1] = s2;
py
> pp[2] = NULL;
00000000
> pp[1][1]
y
```

The memory layout for the above code is illustrated in Figure 11.16. The pointer to pointer pp is allocated a memory with three elements of pointer to char. The variable pp can be treated as an array of pointer to char. The first element pp[0] of pointer to char points to the string "ab", pointed by variable s1. The second element pp[1] points to the string "py", pointed by the variable s2. Because pp[1] is a pointer to char, the expression pp[1][1] refers to the second character 'y' in the string s2. The last element pp[2] is assigned to a null pointer. The individual strings can be referred to as pp[0] and pp[1]. Semantically, this is similar to the declaration of an array of pointer to char with initialization, as shown below.

```
char *pp[] = {"ab",
              "py",
              NULL
             };
```

Details about arrays of pointers will be described in the next section.

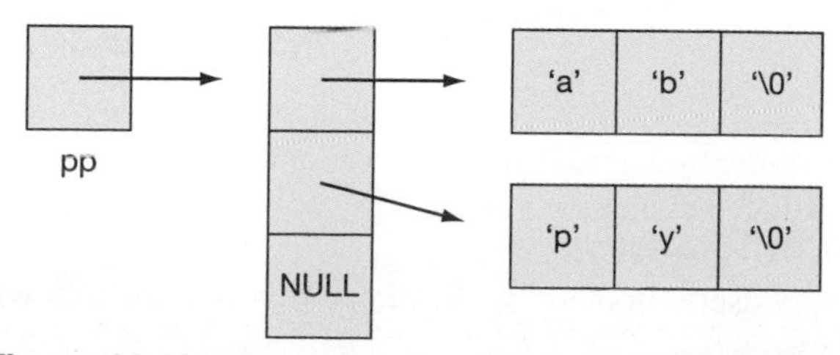

Figure 11.16: The pointer pp points to an array of strings.

If an argument of a function is a pointer to pointer, the address of a pointer can be passed to it. The pointer in the calling function can be changed by the called function. For example, the address of a pointer can be passed to the first argument of the function `allocMemory()` below to allocate a memory of `n` bytes specified in the second argument.

```
int allocMemory(void **pp, size_t n) {
    *pp = malloc(n);              /* allocate memory */
    if(*pp == NULL) {             /* failed to allocate memory */
       printf("Error: no memory\n");
       return -1;
    }
    else
       return 0;
}
```

If the function is called by

```
int *p;
allocMemory(&p, 100);
```

the statement

```
    *pp = malloc(n);              /* allocate memory */
```

inside the function `allocMemory()` modifies the pointer `p` to make it point to the allocated memory of 100 bytes. Often, for a function with return type of int, the return value indicates the status of the function call. If the function call is successful, it returns 0. Otherwise, it returns -1. In this case, if the memory allocation fails, the function `allocMemory()` returns -1.

The pointer to pointer is useful to pass multiple dimensional array of variable lengths to a function which is described in section 11.15. It is also useful for command-line user interfaces through the arguments of the function **main()**, which will be presented in section 12.10 of Chapter 12.

11.10 Arrays of Pointers

Because pointers are variables themselves, an array of pointers can be declared. For example, in the statements

```
char *s1 = "abc";
char *s2 = "123";
char *p[3];
p[0] = s1;
p[1] = s1;
p[2] = NULL;
```

The variables `s1` and `s2` are pointer to char as strings. The variable `p` is declared as an array with three elements of pointer to char. The first and second elements of the array point to the strings `s1` and `s2`, respectively. The last element is assigned with the value NULL.

Arrays of pointers are very useful in many applications. Consider the following code fragment:

```
char day1[7][10] = {"Sunday", "Monday", "Tuesday", "Wednesday",
                    "Thursday", "Friday", "Saturday"};
```

```
char *day2[7] =     {"Sunday", "Monday", "Tuesday", "Wednesday",
                     "Thursday", "Friday", "Saturday"};
```

The variable day1 is a two-dimensional array of type char, whereas day2 is an array of pointer to char. The memory layout for day1 and day2 are shown in Figures 11.17 and 11.18, respectively. Like a two-dimensional array, an element in a string can be accessed by an expression for an array element with two indices. For example, the expression day2[1][3] refers to the character 'd' in the string "Monday". The advantage of using day2 is that each pointer can point to arrays with different lengths rather than the fixed length of 10 bytes. The function daystr() in Program 11.11 contains a static array of constant strings, as described in section 8.2.2 in Chapter 8, and returns a pointer to the proper one based on its argument. Each element of the array day is const-qualified with the data type const char *, a pointer to const char. The valid range for an argument of the function daystr() is from 0 to 6, with 0 for Sunday, 1 for Monday, 6 for

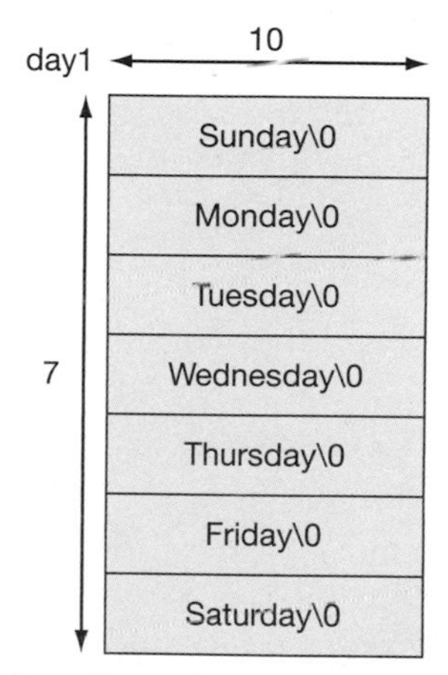

Figure 11.17: A two-dimensional array for each day of a week.

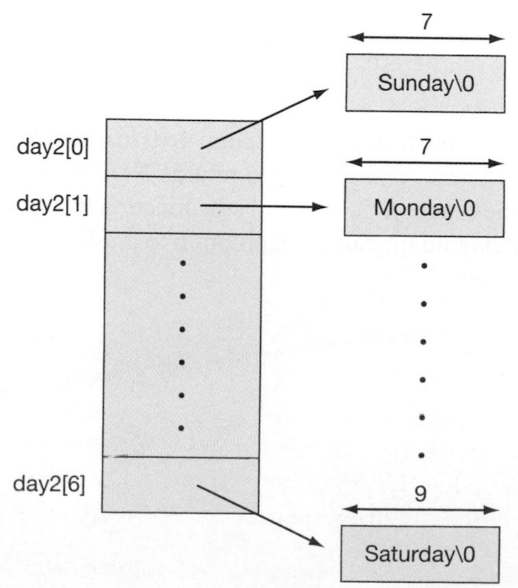

Figure 11.18: An array of pointers for each day of a week.

```
/* File: daystr.c
   Use array of pointers */
#include <stdio.h>
#define DAY 7

/* function returns a pointer to char which points to
   a string for each day of the week */
const char *daystr(int n) {
    /* a static variable with the static storage duration.  Even after
       the function is called, the memory for day is still valid */
    static const char *day[7] = {"Sunday", "Monday", "Tuesday",
                  "Wednesday", "Thursday", "Friday", "Saturday"};
    /* Use a conditional operator to return either NULL or a valid string
       depending on the passed argument. */
    return (n < 0 || n > 6) ? NULL : day[n];
}

int main() {
    int i;
    const char *p;

    /* print the string for each day of a week */
    for(i = 0; i < DAY; i++) {
        p = daystr(i);
        printf("%s\n", p);
    }
    return 0;
}
```

Program 11.11: The function returns a static string.

Saturday, etc. A conditional expression described in section 4.10 in Chapetr 4 is used in the return statement. If the argument is outside the valid range, the function returns **NULL**. Without the type specifier **static** for declaration of the array `day` in the function `daystr()`, the function would return a pointer to the memory of automatic duration. This hidden bug might cause the program to crash at an unexpected location. The output from Program 11.11 is shown below:

```
Sunday
Monday
Tuesday
Wednesday
Thursday
Friday
Saturday
```

Program 11.12 shows how an array of pointers can be used in an application. Program 10.9 in Chapter 10 calculates the mean values for the number of times that a Web page was accessed weekly. It also calculates the mean value for "hits" on a Web page each day. Program 11.12 calculates the mean value for accessing a Web page for each day of the week in a given five-week period. The daily hit numbers of a Web page for a given five-week period are stored in the array a in Program 11.12. If the number of rows of the array a in the first dimension is determined by the number of rows in initialization. There are five rows for the array a. The

```
/* File: dayhit.c
   Calculate the mean value for accessing a Web site each day in a week */
#include <stdio.h>
#define WEEK 5          /* 5 rows for a total number of 5 weeks in the data */
#define DAY 7           /* 7 columns for each day in each week */

/* declare 'day' as an array of pointer to const char as
   string for each day in a week, day has a static storage duration. */
const char *day[] = {"Sunday", "Monday", "Tuesday", "Wednesday",
                     "Thursday", "Friday", "Saturday"};

int main() {
   /* The daily hit is recorded in an array with row for a week and
      column for each day in week. */
    int a[][DAY] = {367, 654, 545, 556, 565, 526, 437,
                    389, 689, 554, 526, 625, 537, 468,
                    429, 644, 586, 626, 652, 546, 493,
                    449, 689, 597, 679, 696, 568, 522,
                    489, 729, 627, 729, 737, 598, 552};
    /* array indexes, day total num of hits */
    int i, j, daytotal;
    double meanval; /* a floating-point number for the mean value */


    printf("%-10s%-10s\n", "Day", "Mean hit");
    printf("------------------\n");
    for(j = 0; j < DAY; j++) { /* loop through the column for each day */
        daytotal = 0;          /* initialize daytotal to 0 for each day */
        for(i = 0; i < WEEK; i++) {
            daytotal += a[i][j]; /* add day hit number to daytotal */
        }
        meanval =  (double)daytotal/(double)WEEK; /* mean day hit */
        printf("%-10s%8.2f\n", day[j], meanval);  /* output day hit */
    }
    return 0;
}
```

Program 11.12: Calculating the mean value for accessing a Web page for each day of the week in the given five-week period.

program uses two nested loops to access each element of the array. The variable `daytotal` for each day of the week is initialized with zero in the outer loop with the index variable `j` and summarized in the inner loop with the index variable `i`. The mean value for each day of the week in a given five-week period is calculated using floating-point numbers and displayed in the outer loop at each iteration. The strings for the names of each day of the week are stored in an array `day` of pointer to char. The size of the array `day` is not specified. The compiler or interpreter counts the number of initializers and fills the number 7. The element `day[j]` is a pointer to char and is used inside the outer loop. The output for string is left-justified using the format specification `"%-10s"` with a field width of 10 spaces.

The output for the mean value for accessing a Web page for every day of the week in a given five-week period in Program 11.12 is shown below:

```
Day        Mean hit
------------------
Sunday       424.60
Monday       681.00
Tuesday      581.80
Wednesday    623.20
Thursday     655.00
Friday       555.00
Saturday     494.40
```

From this result, some plausible explanations might be offered. It appears that the network traffic is light on weekends.

As another example, Program 11.13 demonstrates how an array of pointers can be used to eliminate complicated storage management and overhead of moving lines. The original strings of different lengths

```
/* File: arrayofpointer.c
   Swap the elements in array of pointers */
#include <stdio.h>

int main() {
    /* array of pointer to char */
    char *p[3] = {"ABC", "HIJKL", "EF"};
    char *tmp; /* temporary variable for swap */

    printf("Before swap: %s, %s, %s\n", p[0], p[1], p[2]);
    /* swap the value for elements p[1] and p[2] */
    tmp = p[1];
    p[1] = p[2];
    p[2] = tmp;
    printf("After swap: %s, %s, %s\n", p[0], p[1], p[2]);
    return 0;
}
```

Program 11.13: Using an array of pointers to char as an array of strings.

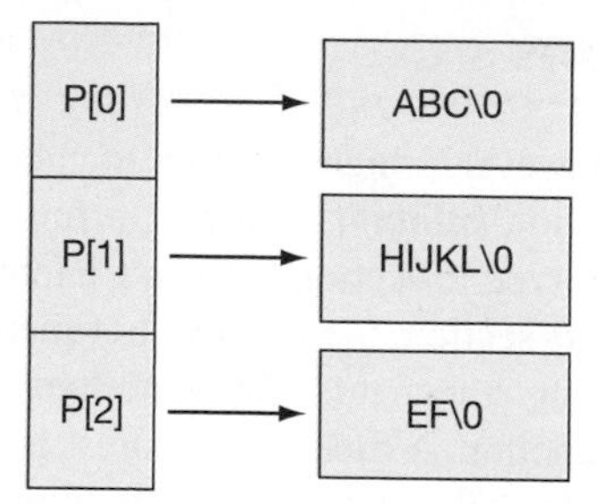

Figure 11.19: The original values for each element of an array of pointer to char before swapping texts.

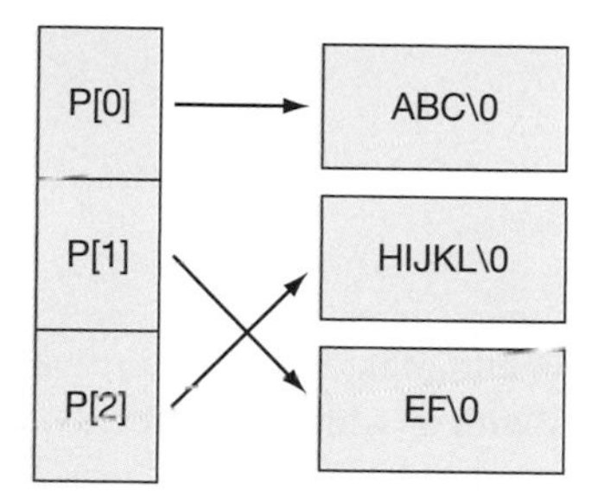

Figure 11.20: The final values for each element of an array of pointer to char after swapping texts.

pointed to by pointers `p[0]`, `p[1]`, and `p[2]` in Program 11.13, are shown in Figure 11.19. Without moving and copying characters in these strings, the contents pointed to by pointers `p[1]` and `p[2]` are exchanged by swapping values of pointers, as shown in Figure 11.20. The output of Program 11.13 is shown below.

```
Before swap: ABC, HIJKL, EF
After swap: ABC, EF, HIJKL
```

In the previous example, the exact number of elements was specified for the array of pointers to char `p`. As an alternative method, **NULL** can also be used to indicate the end of an array of strings. For example, an array of strings can be usd to hold a list of names terminated by **NULL**.

```
char *p[] = {"John",
             "Doe",
             "Peter",
             NULL};
int i;
for(i = 0; p[i] != NULL; i++) {
    printf("p[i] = %s\n", p[i]);
}
```

Once **NULL** is encountered, the **for** loop terminates; thus, the result of the above code fragment is as follows:

```
John
Doe
Peter
```

11.11 Pointers to Functions

A function can call other functions. However, which function to call may not be determined until program execution time. For example, the function **fplotxy()** can plot a function by passing a function to its first argument, as shown in its function prototype in section 6.7.1 in Chapter 6. The first argument of the function **fplotxy()** is a pointers to function. In this section, the pointers to functions in C is described.

Each function contains programming statements which are located in memory. A function pointer is a variable containing the address of the function. A function's address is the entry point of the function. In other words, a function pointer can be used to call a function. Furthermore, a function pointer can be assigned, placed in arrays, passed to functions, returned by functions, etc. The declarations of some function pointers are shown below:

```
void (*pf1) (void);
int  (*pf2) ();
int  (*pf3) (double f);
```

where `pf1` is declared as a pointer to function that has no return value or arguments; `pf2` is declared as a pointer to function that returns an integer with or without arguments; `pf3` is declared as a pointer to function that returns an integer and takes an argument of type double.

Program 11.14 illustrates how a pointer to function is used. The function `fun()` is a regular function that has the same prototype as the function pointed to by `pf`. After the declaration and assignment of `pf`,

```
/* File: funptr.c
   Use a pointer to function */
#include <stdio.h>

/* a function with an argument of type double and return type int */
int fun(double f) {
    printf("f = %f\n", f);
    return 0;
}

int main() {
    /* declare pf as a pointers to function with an argument of
       type double and return type int */
    int (*pf)(double f);

    fun(10.0);    /* call function fun() */
    pf = fun;     /* pf points to fun() */
    pf(20.0);     /* call fun() indirectly using pf() */
    return 0;
}
```

Program 11.14: Using a pointer to function.

the `fun()` function can be called by using `pf`. The output of Program 11.14 is as follows:

```
f = 10.000000
f = 20.000000
```

Note that, similar to an array name, a function name also represents the address of a function. The address operator '`&`' before a function is ignored. For example, the statement

```
pf = &fun;
```

is treated as

```
pf = fun;
```

Like other data types, a pointer to function can be defined as a user-defined data type using the keyword **typedef** described in section 3.12 in Chapter 3. For example, the data type `FUNCPTR` of Program 11.15 can be defined by the statement

```
typedef int (*FUNCPTR)(double);
```

as a pointer to function that returns a value of int type and takes an argument of double type. It can then be used as a type declarator. For example, `pf` in the **main()** function is declared a variable of the type `FUNCPTR` (i.e., a pointer to function). The output of Program 11.15 is the same as that of Program 11.14.

```
/* File: funptrtypedef.c
   Use typedef to declare a data type of pointers to function */
#include <stdio.h>

/* declare FUNCPTR as a data type of pointers to function
   with an argument of type double and return type int */
typedef int (*FUNCPTR)(double f);

/* a function with an argument of type double and return type int */
int fun(double f) {
    printf("f = %f\n", f);
    return 0;
}

int main() {
    /* declare pf as a pointers to function with an argument of
       type double and return type int */
    FUNCPTR pf;

    fun(10.0);      /* call function fun() */
    pf = fun;       /* pf points to fun() */
    pf(20.0);       /* call fun() indirectly using pf() */
    return 0;
}
```

Program 11.15: Using typedef for pointers to function.

Two pointers to function can be compared like other pointers. For example, given

```
int fun (double f) {
    printf("f = %f\n", f);
    return 0;
}
int (*pf1)(double f);
int (*pf2)(double f);

pf1 = fun;
pf2 = fun;
```

the equality comparison operation `pf1 == pf2` gives 1.

11.11.1 Functions with Arguments of Pointers to Functions

Pointers to functions can also be passed as arguments to functions, which is commonly used to set callback functions. Program 11.16 is an example of using a pointer to function as a function argument. The variable `FUNCPTR` is declared by

```
typedef int (*FUNCPTR)(double);
```

as a data type of pointer to function that takes one argument of double type and returns a value of int type. The function `f2` with the prototype

```
int f2(FUNCPTR pf, double f);
```

takes two arguments: the first one, `pf`, is a pointer to function and the second `f` is double type. When a pointer to function is used as a parameter of a function, it can be written using a regular function header without an asterisk in front of the variable name and a pair of opening and closing parentheses. Therefore, alternatively, the function header for `f2()` can be changed to one of the following two forms:

```
int f2(int (*pf)(double), double f);
int f2(int pf(double), double f);
```

The first form is more commonly used because it clearly indicates that `pf` is a pointer. Inside the function `f2`, the function pointer argument `pf` is used to call a function which takes an argument of double type. In the **main()** function, the name of the function `f1()` is passed to `f2()` as a function pointer. The execution and output of Program 11.16 is as follows:

```
i = 5.000000
```

```
/* File: funptrarg.c
   Function with an argument of pointers to function */
#include <stdio.h>

/* declare FUNCPTR as a data type of pointer to function
   with an argument of type double and return type int */
typedef int (*FUNCPTR)(double);
```

Program 11.16: Passing a function pointer as an argument to function. (*Continued*)

```
/* function prototype using FUNCPTR */
int f2(FUNCPTR pf, double f);

/* a function with an argument of type double and return type int */
int f1(double f) {
    printf("f = %f\n", f);
    return 0;
}

/* function with an argument of pointers to function
   with an argument of type double and return type int.
   These two are alternative function headers
      int f2(int (*pf)(double), double f)
      int f2(int pf(double), double f) */
int f2(FUNCPTR pf, double f)
{
    pf(f);
    return 0;
}

int main() {
    f2(f1, 5.0); /* pass f1 to f2(). Inside f2(), f1() is called
                    indirectly through pf(). */
    return 0;
}
```

Program 11.16: *(Continued)*

11.11.2 Developing a Function to Find Roots of Equations Using the Bisection Method

In section 6.10 in Chapter 6, we presented an algorithm to find roots of equations based on the bisection method. The algorithm is implemented in Program 6.18 to calculate a root of a projectile equation. Because finding roots of nonlinear equations is a common problem in engineering and science, it will be desirable to implement the bisection method as a function in C. The function can then be reused to find roots of equations for different applications. We can implement such a general-purpose root-finding function effectively using pointers.

Designing of a Root-Finding Function Based on the Bisection Method

Based on the algorithm for the bisection method developed in 6.10, a root-finding function `bisect()` can be designed with the following function prototype:

```
int bisect(double *x, double x0, double xf, double tolerance,
           double (*func)(double));
```

Arguments x_0 and x_f are two end points of the approximate interval on which a root is located. The value *epsilon* for the convergence condition is passed as the argument `tolerance`. We could use an additional argument of the function to select the convergence criteria. However, for simplicity, we implement the bisection method using only the first convergence criterion in equation (6.6). The function `bisect()` can be used to find zeros of different functions. Therefore, the argument `func` of pointer to function is used to pass different functions to `bisect()`. The passed function shall have the prototype of

```
double func(double);
```

The argument and return types of the function are the same. Both are type double.

The function `bisect()` could return the calculated root. However, for error handling, the function `bisect()` returns an integer value for the status of the computation of the algorithm. If successful, the function returns 0. If the passed value for the argument `tolerance` for the convergence condition, by mistake or numerical computation, is less than or equal to 0, it returns −1. Because of the finite representation of a floating-point number, in general, the value for *epsilon* cannot be 0 or negative. It is possible that the user may input two end values x_0 and x_f such that $f(x_0)f(x_f) > 0$. In this case, the function returns −2 to indicate this possible error. The only ways to get the approximate root from the function `bisect()` in C are to pass it to the calling function through a pointer or use a global variable. Using a global variable is not desirable for implementing a general-purpose reusable function. As we mentioned before in section 8.3.2 in Chapter 8, a function using variables of static storage duration is not reentrant for multithread applications. Therefore, the argument `x` of type pointer to double is used to pass the calculated approximate root from the function `bisect()`.

Implementation of the Function bisect() with the Bisection Method

The function `bisect()` in Program 11.17 is implemented based on the above design. Variables `xleft`, `xright`, `xmid`, `fleft`, and `fmid` are for the symbols x_l, x_r, x_{mid}, $f(x_l)$, and $f(x_{mid})$ shown in Figure 6.7. The arguments `x0` and `tf` are assigned to `xleft` and `xright` as initial values. The `tolerance` is an argument of the function. The **while** loop for implementation of the algorithm in the function `bisect()` is the same as that in Program 6.18. When the convergence criterion is met, the value for the last midpoint point is passed as an approximate root through the argument `x`. The function finally returns 0 for successful completion of the calculation of a root based on the bisection method.

Using the Function bisect()

As shown in Figure 20.1 in Chapter 20 for the sine function sin(x), there is a root between 2 and 4. The exact value for the root in the interval $2 < x < 4$ for the function sin(x) is π, which is approximately

```
/* File: bisect.c
   Find a root for func() using function bisect() with bisection method
   in the range [x0, xf]. The signs of f(x0) and f(xf) must be diff
   to guarantee there is a root */
#include <stdio.h>
#include <math.h>                  /* for fabs() */
#include <float.h>                 /* for FLT_EPSILON */

/* function to find a root using bisection method */
int bisect(double *x, double x0, double xf, double tolerance,
           double (*func)(double)) {
   double xleft = x0, fleft;   /* x and f(x) on the left of the root */
```

Program 11.17: Finding a root of an equation using the bisection method. (*Continued*)

```
    double xright = xf;          /* x on the right of the root */
    double xmid, fmid;           /* x and f(x) on the mid of xleft and xright */

    if(tolerance <= 0.0)         /* invalid tolerance */
       return -1;                /* return -1 for invalid tolerance */

    fleft = func(x0);                 /* calculate f(xleft) */
    if(fleft * func(xf) > 0.0) {      /* invalid x0 and xf */
       return -2;                     /* return -2 for invalid x0 and xf */
    }

    xmid = (xleft+xright)/2.0;        /* mid point */
    fmid = func(xmid);                /* f() in the mid point */
    while(fabs(fmid) > tolerance) {/* convergence criterion to terminate loop */
       /* f(xleft)*f(mid) to determine the updating of left or right point */
       if(fleft*fmid <= 0.0) {        /* mid point becomes the right point */
          xright = xmid;              /* update the right point */
       }
       else {                         /* mid point becomes the left point */
          xleft = xmid;               /* update the left point */
          fleft = fmid;               /* update f(xleft) */
       }
       xmid = (xleft+xright)/2.0;     /* update the mid point */
       fmid = func(xmid);             /* f() in the mid point */
    }
    *x = xmid;                        /* pass xmid to the calling function */
    return 0;                         /* return 0 for successful */
}

int main() {
    /* find the root at M_PI for sin(x) specified in the range [2.0, 4.0].
       use machine epsilon for float type as convergence tolerance */
    double x, x0=2.0, xf=4.0, tolerance=FLT_EPSILON;
    int status;

    status = bisect(&x, x0, xf, tolerance, sin);
    if(status == -1)  /* calling bisect() failed */
       printf("Error: bisect() failed, invalid tolerance\n");
    else if(status == -2)  /* calling bisect() failed */
       printf("Error: bisect() failed, invalid end points\n");
    else             /* calling bisect() successfully */
       printf("x = %f, sin(x) = %g\n", x, sin(x));
    return 0;
}
```

Program 11.17: (*Continued*)

3.141593. Program 11.17 uses the function `bisect()` to find this root numerically. The *epsilon* used in the convergence criterion is **FLT_EPSILON**. The output from Program 11.17 is shown below:

```
x = 3.141593, sin(x) = -8.74228e-08
```

11.11.3 ‡Functions Returning Pointers to Functions

Like regular pointers, function pointers not only can be used as arguments of functions, but also as returned values of functions, as shown in Program 11.18. The return type of the function `fun2()` is `FUNCPTR`, a pointer to function with an argument of type double and return type of int. Without using **typedef**, the function can be defined with the function prototype as follows:

```
int (*fun2(int i))(double f);
```

In the function **main()**, the function `fun2()` is called to return the function `fun()`. The function `fun()` is then indirectly called by the pointer to the function `pf`, which is a user-defined type. The two statements

```
pf = fun2(1);
pf(20);
```

in Program 11.18, the use of `pf` can be replaced by a single statement `fun2(1)(20)` because the value returned from `fun2(1)` is not **NULL**. If `fun2(1)` return NULL, then `fun2(1)(20)` and `pf(20)` result in undefined behavior. Using a function returning a pointer to function, the output of Program 11.18 is as follows:

```
f = 20.000000
```

```
/* File: returnfunptr.c
   Function returns a pointer to functions */
#include <stdio.h>

/* declare FUNCPTR as a data type of pointer to functions
   with an argument of type double and return type int */
typedef int (*FUNCPTR)(double f);

/* a function with an argument of type double and return type int */
int fun(double f) {
    printf("f = %f\n", f);
    return 0;
}

/* function returns a pointer to function with an argument of
   type double and return type int. The alternative function header is
      int (*fun2(int i))(double f) */
FUNCPTR fun2(int i)
```

Program 11.18: A function returning a pointers to function. (*Continued*)

```
{
    if(i)              /* if i is not zero, return fun */
      return fun;
    else
      return NULL;
}

int main() {
     FUNCPTR pf;      /* declare pf as a pointer to function */

     pf = fun2(1);    /* fun2() returns 'fun' */
     pf(20.0);        /* call function 'fun()' indirectly by pf() */
     return 0;
}
```

Program 11.18: *(Continued)*

11.11.4 ‡Callback Functions for Event-Driven Programming

Programs we have developed so far are based on procedure (function) calls. In this *procedural programming*, a function is called at any given point during a program's execution, including by other functions or itself. The program is in control, asking for certain types of input at certain times.

On the other hand, in *event-driven programming*, the flow of a program is determined by events such as sensor inputs, user actions like mouse clicks or key presses, or messages from other programs. Events of many different types can occur at any time and in any order. They are placed on a queue in the order they are received and then processed. The need to handle events is a major difference between procedural programming and event-driven programming. There are mainly three components for event-driven programming. First, it needs *event handlers*, also referred as *callback functions*, that handle events. For example, a GUI (graphical user interface) program is typically event-driven. When the user clicks a menu to open a file, an event handler is invoked to open the file. Second, an event handler needs to bind to an event first, which is also referred to as *registering a callback function*. This is typically accomplished by passing a function to the system through a pointer to function. Some applications may use an array of pointers to function or a structure containing members of pointers to function to register callback functions. Details about structures are described in Chapter 13. Third, it needs a *main loop*, a function that checks for events and then invokes the matching event handlers.

Although event-driven programming is beyond the scope of this book, an example is used to demonstrate the concept of registering a callback function. The C standard function **atexit()** with a prototype in the file **stdlib.h**

```
int atexit(void (*func)(void));
```

has a single argument which is a pointer to function. This pointer to function has no return value and requires no argument. The **atexit()** function registers the function pointed to by `func` to be called at normal program termination. The function returns 0 if successful. Otherwise, it returns 0. In Program 11.19, the function **atexit()** is called twice by

```
atexit(f1);
atexit(f2);
```

```
/* File: atexit.c
   Register callback functions which are called at the exit */
#include <stdlib.h>  /* for atexit() */
#include <stdio.h>

void f1(void) {       /* callback function */
    printf("f1() is called\n");
}

void f2(void) {       /* callback function */
    printf("f2() is called\n");
}

int main(void) {
    /* register callback functions */
    printf("Register callback functions f1() and f2()\n");
    atexit(f1);
    atexit(f2);

    /* this part of code is executed before callback functions are called */
    printf("Before callbacks are called\n");
    return 0;
}
```

Program 11.19: Registering callback functions called at the program termination through **atexit**().

to register callback functions `f1()` and `f2()`. Afterwards, the function **printf()** is called. Upon the program termination, callback functions `f1()` and `f2()` are called in the reverse order of their registration. The messages from the functions `f1()` and `f2()` are displayed at the end of the program. The message from the function `f2()` is displayed before that from the function `f1()`. The output of Program 11.19 is as follows:

```
Register callback functions f1() and f2()
Before callbacks are called
f2() is called
f1() is called
```

11.12 ‡Generic Pointer for Passing Arguments with Different Data Types

Generally, a pointer is associated with a particular type. The exception is a *pointer to void*. It is a generic pointer which can be used to hold any data type. Any pointer to other types may be assigned to and from pointers to void, and may be compared with them. Furthermore, the pointer to any object can be converted to the type of pointer to void without loss of information. However, a pointer to void cannot be dereferenced by the indirection operator as described below. To access the object pointed to by the original pointer properly, the converted pointer has to be converted back to the original pointer type. We used the pointer to void in section 11.7. The dynamic memory allocation functions **malloc(), calloc()**, and **realloc()** return the allocated memory in the type of pointer to void. It can be assigned to an lvalue of any pointer type. On the other hand, a pointer of any data type can be passed to the function **free()**, which has an argument of pointer to void, to free the allocated memory. The memory manipulation functions, such as **memcpy()** presented in section 12.9 in Chapter 12 use the pointer to void to manipulate, compare, and search blocks of memory. In section 14.5 of Chapter 14, the functions **fread()** and **fwrite()** use the pointer to void to handle input and output of binary objects.

In this section, we will show how to use the pointer to void to pass values of different data types to the same argument of a function for different applications. As a simple example, the function below

```
void func(int num, void *param) {
     int i;
     double d;

     if(num == 1) { /* obtain the passed value of int type */
        i = *(int*)param;
        printf("Passed integer is %d", i);
     }
     else {           /* obtain the passed value of double type */
        d = *(double*)param;
        printf("Passed floating-point number is %f", d);
     }
}
```

obtains a value passed from the second argument based on the data type specified in the first argument. If the first argument `num` is 1, the passed value of type int is obtained by the statement

```
i = *(int*)param;
```

which is equivalent to

```
int *p;
p = (int*)param;
i = *p;
```

The parameter `param` of pointer to void is cast to pointer to int first, the object pointed to by the pointer `param` is then accessed using the indirection operation. Similarly, if `num` is not equal to 1, the passed floating-point number of type double is obtained by the statement

```
d = *(double*)param;
```

The function can be called in a calling function as shown below.

```
int i = 10;
double d = 20.0;
func(1, &i);
func(2, &d);
```

The function `bisect()` in Program 11.17 can find a zero for the function $f(x)$ in a given interval. In some applications, it will be more convenient to find a zero for a function with one or multiple parameters. The bisection function can then be called multiple times with different parameters for different zeros. This can be implemented using the generic pointer to void to handle a function with one variable, but with parameters of different types. Let's name such a modified function using the bisection method as `bisect2()` with the function prototype

```
int bisect2(double *x, double x0, double xf, double tolerance,
            double (*func)(double, void*), void *param);
```

The implementation of the function `bisect2()` is the same as the function `bisect()` in Program 11.17, except that the function calls `func(x0), func(xf)`, `func(xmid)` should be replaced by `func(x0, param), func(xf, param)`, `func(xmid, param)`, respectively.

To use the function `bisect2()`, consider equation (6.4) as the projectile function of distance x with the projection angle as a parameter shown below.

$$y(x, \theta_0) = \tan(\theta_0)x - \left(\frac{g}{2v_0^2 \cos^2 \theta_0}\right) x^2 \tag{11.1}$$

Program 11.20 uses the function `bisect2()` to find zeros of the projectile function with the initial speed v_0 of 35 m/s, and two different initial projection angles of $\theta_0 = 15°$ and $\theta_0 = 45°$ in the range $1 < x < 200$. When the function `bisect2()` is called by

```
status = bisect2(&x, x0, xf, tolerance, traj, &theta0);
```

```
/* File: bisect2.c
   Find roots for the projectile function using the bisection method
   in the range [1, 200] with the initial projection speed of 35m/s and
   projection angles 15 degrees and 45 degrees. */
#include <stdio.h>
#include <math.h>          /* for fabs() */
#include <float.h>         /* for FLT_EPSILON */

#define M_G   9.81         /* gravitational acceleration constant g */

/* function prototype for bisect2() */
int bisect2(double *x, double x0, double xf, double tolerance,
            double (*func)(double, void*), void *param);

/* function for the y-coordinate of the projectifle with the projection angle
   as a parameter */
double traj(double x, void *param) {
   double theta0,          /* projection angle */
          v0,              /* initial velocity */
          y;               /* y coordinate */

   theta0 = *(double*)param; /* calculate the projection angle in radians */
   v0 = 35.0;              /* set the initial velocity */
   /* calculate the y coordinate */
```

Program 11.20: Finding zeros of the projectile function with the initial projection angle as a parameter using the bisection method. (*Continued*)

```
    y = tan(theta0)*x - M_G*x*x/(2*v0*v0*cos(theta0)*cos(theta0));
    return y;
}

int main() {
   /* find the root of projectile function y(x) specified in the range
   [60.0, 70.0]. use machine epsilon for float type as convergence tolerance */
   double x, x0=1.0, xf=200.0, tolerance=FLT_EPSILON,
          theta0 = 15*M_PI/180; /*  the projection angle in radians */
   int status;

   theta0 = 15*M_PI/180;  /* the projection angle in radians */
   status = bisect2(&x, x0, xf, tolerance, traj, &theta0);
   if(status < 0)    /* calling bisect2() failed */
      printf("Error: bisect2() failed, status = %d\n", status);
   else              /* calling bisect2() successfully */
      printf("x = %f m, traj(x) = %g\n", x, traj(x, &theta0));

   theta0 = 45*M_PI/180; /* the projection angle in radians */
   status = bisect2(&x, x0, xf, tolerance, traj, &theta0);
   if(status < 0)  /* calling bisect2() failed */
      printf("Error: bisect2() failed, status = %d\n", status);
   else              /* calling bisect2() successfully */
      printf("x = %f m, traj(x) = %g\n", x, traj(x, &theta0));
   return 0;
}
```

Program 11.20: *(Continued)*

the address of the variable `theta0` for the projection angle θ_0 is passed as the last argument using a pointer to void. This pointer is passed as the second argument inside the function `bisect2()` through function calls such as `func(x0, param)` to function `traj()`. Inside the function `traj()`, the projection angle θ_0 is retrieved by the statement

```
theta0 = *(double*)param;
```

The output from Program 11.20 is shown below:

```
x = 62.436290 m, traj(x) = -5.68794e-08
x = 124.872579 m, traj(x) = 4.94892e-08
```

In Program 11.20, we calculated roots of the projectile equation twice for different initial projection angles. The projectile function has a parameter of type double. The same function `bisect2()` can also be used to find zeros of functions with parameters of other types. If multiple parameters, such as both projection angle `theta0` and initial velocity `v0`, need to be passed, an array or a pointer to structure with multiple members can be passed as shown in Program 13.13 described in Chapter 13. When the function `bisect2()` is called to find a zero for a function without a parameter, the null pointer **NULL** can be used as the last argument for `param`.

```
/* File: pointer2array.c
   Use pointer to arrays  */
#include <stdio.h>

int main() {
  /* declare two two-dimensional arrays with three columns */
  int a[2][3] = {1,2,3,4,5,6};
  int b[2][3] = {10,20,30,40,50,60};
  int (*p)[3]; /* declare p as a pointer to arrays of three elements */

  /* p points to a, p <==> a, p[i][j] is the same as a[i][j] */
  p = a;
  printf("p[1][1] = %d\n", p[1][1]);
  p[1][2] = 100;
  printf("a[1][2] = %d\n", a[1][2]);

  /* p points to b, p <==> b, p[i][j] is the same as b[i][j] */
  p = b;
  printf("p[1][1] = %d\n", p[1][1]);
  p[1][2] = 200;
  printf("b[1][2] = %d\n", b[1][2]);
  return 0;
}
```

Program 11.22: Using a pointer to arrays to point to different arrays.

and access the various elements of the array it points to. The output of Program 11.22 is shown below:

```
p[1][1] = 5
a[1][2] = 100
p[1][1] = 50
b[1][2] = 200
```

The size of pointer to arrays of X type is the same as that of pointer to X type. In the above example, the size of `p2` for a pointer to three elements of type int is 4 bytes for 32-bit programming or 8 bytes for 64-bit programming.

A pointer to array can also be used as a function argument to pass arrays to the function. For an argument of multi-dimensional array, the variable name of the array is treated as a pointer to array. For example, the function definition

```
double twoDadd(int m, int n, double dd1[][3], double dd2[3][3],
               double dd3[2][3]);
```

in Program 10.16 can be replaced by the function definition

```
double twoDadd(int m, int n, double (*dd1)[3], double (*dd2)[3],
               double dd3[2][3]);
```

In this case, the variables dd1 and dd2 are declared as pointers to arrays of three elements of type double. In both function definitions, the **sizeof** operations sizeof(dd1), sizeof(dd2), and sizeof(dd3) inside the function twoDadd() will all give 4 bytes for 32-bit programming or 8 bytes for 64-bit programming.

The relation between pointers and arrays can be further illustrated by the interactive execution of the code below:

```
> int i, j
> int a2[3][4] ={1,2,3,4,5,6,7,8,9,10,11,12}, *p
> p = a2[1]           // p = &a2[1][0]
> p[0] = 100          // a2[1][0]=100
> for(i=0; i<3; i++) for(j=0; j<4; j++) printf("%d ", a2[i][j]);
1 2 3 4 100 6 7 8 9 10 11 12
> sizeof(a2)
48
> sizeof(a2+1)
4
> sizeof(*(a2+1))
16
> sizeof(a2[1])
16
> *(*(a2+1)+3)=200     // *(a2[1]+3)=200 or a2[1][3]=200
> for(i=0; i<3; i++) for(j=0; j<4; j++) printf("%d ", a2[i][j]);
1 2 3 4 100 6 7 200 9 10 11 12
```

The variable a2 is an array of 3×4 elements. The pointer expression (a2+1) or a2[1] gives the address of the fifth element of array a2. It is a pointer to array of 4 elements and contains the address of the second row of array a2. The assignment operation

```
p = a2[1]
```

assigns the address of the fifth element a2[1][0] to the variable p of pointer to int. Then, the expressions p[0] and *p refer to the same element a2[1][0]. The expression sizeof(a2) is 48, the number of bytes for the array a2 with 12 elements of int type. The expression (a2+1) is a pointer to array of 4 elements of type int. The expression sizeof(a2+1) is 4 for 32-bit programming and 8 for 64-bit programming. But, the results for expressions sizeof(*(a2+1)) and sizeof(a2[1]) are 16, the number of bytes for an array of 4 elements of type int. Therefore, both expressions *(*(a2+1)+3) and *(a2[1]+3) refer to the array element a2[1][3].

11.14 ‡Dynamic Allocation of Two-Dimensional Arrays

From a mathematical point of view, a matrix or an array of $(m \times n)$ dimensions is a set of numbers arranged in a rectangular block of m horizontal rows and n vertical columns. From a programming point of view, it is a block of memory with each row of the matrix lying in a contiguous block of memory. Two methods for dynamic memory allocation of two-dimensional arrays will be presented here. In the first method, the memory for the matrix allocated is in a single contiguous block, whereas in the second method, each row of the matrix lies in a contiguous block of memory, but the whole matrix is not in a sequential memory block.

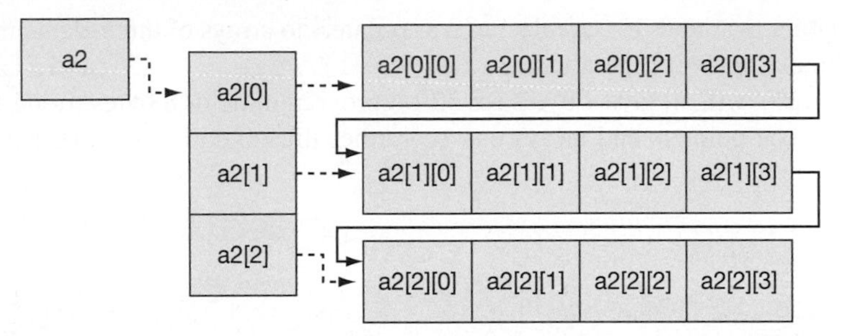

Figure 11.21: Dynamic allocation of two-dimensional arrays (method 1).

Assume that a2 is a two-dimensional array of size ($m \times n$). The values of m and n are determined at runtime. The following code fragment shows how to allocate a single contiguous memory dynamically for the array a2[m][n].

```
int i;
double **a2;
/* ... source code to obtain m and n at runtime */
a2 = (double **)malloc(m * sizeof(double*));
if(a2 == NULL) {
  fprintf(stderr, "ERROR: %s(): not enough memory\n", __func__);
  exit(1);
}
a2[0] = (double *)malloc(m * n * sizeof(double));
if(a2[0] == NULL) {
  fprintf(stderr, "ERROR: %s(): not enough memory\n", __func__);
  exit(1);
}
for(i = 1; i < m; i++) {
  a2[i] = a2[0] + i * n;
}
/* ... source code to handle vector a2 */
free(a2[0]);
free(a2);
/* ... source code no longer uses a2 */
```

First, a2 is declared as a pointer to pointer to double. After obtaining the values of m and n, the memory for m pointers to double is allocated for a2. So, a2 can be considered as a one-dimensional array of pointers with m elements shown in Figure 11.21. Then a single contiguous memory with m * n * sizeof(double) bytes for m * n elements is allocated. Each pointer a2[i] points to a segment in this block. Therefore, a2 becomes a two-dimensional array. In the example following, the elements of an array of size (3×4) are accessed by two different methods.

```
> int i, j
> double **a2
> a2 = (double **)malloc(3 * sizeof(double*))
4006cdc0
```

```
> for(i=0; i<3; i++) printf("%p ", a2[i])
00000000 00000000 00000000
> a2[0] = (double *)malloc(3 * 4 * sizeof(double)); // size (3 X 4)
> a2[1] = a2[0] + 4                          // a2[i] = a2[0] + i * n
> a2[2] = a2[0] + 2*4                        // a2[i] = a2[0] + i * n
> for(i=0; i<3; i++) printf("%p ", a2[i])   // 1-dimension of pointer
4007bee8 4007bf08 4007bf28
> for(i=0; i<3; i++) for(j=0; j<4; j++) printf("%1.1f ", a2[i][j])
0.0 0.0 0.0 0.0 0.0 0.0 0.0 0.0 0.0 0.0 0.0 0.0
> a2[1][1]=3              // method 1
> *(*(a2+1)+2)=4          // <==> a2[1][2]=4, method 2
> for(i=0; i<3; i++) for(j=0; j<4; j++) printf("%1.1f ", a2[i][j])
0.0 0.0 0.0 0.0 0.0 3.0 4.0 0.0 0.0 0.0 0.0 0.0
```

Once a memory block with `m * n * sizeof(double)` bytes is allocated for `a2`, the subscripts `i` and `j` in the form of `a2[i][j]` or `*(*(a2+i)+j)` can go from 0 to `m-1` and 0 to `n-1`, respectively. Any attempt to access `a2[m][n]` gives an unexpected value.

The following code fragment shows the second method for dynamic allocation of the two-dimensional array `a2`. Memory for each row of the matrix is allocated separately. Therefore, the memory block for different rows may not be contiguous. The memory layout for array `a2` is shown in Figure 11.22.

```
int i;
double **a2;
/* ... source code to obtain m and n at runtime */
a2 = (double **)malloc(m * sizeof(double*));
if(a2 == NULL) {
  fprintf(stderr, "ERROR: %s(): not enough memory\n", __func__);
  exit(1);
}
for(i = 0; i < m; i++) {
  a2[i] = (double *)malloc(n * sizeof(double));
  if(a2[i] == NULL) {
    fprintf(stderr, "ERROR: %s(): not enough memory\n", __func__);
    exit(1);
  }
}
```

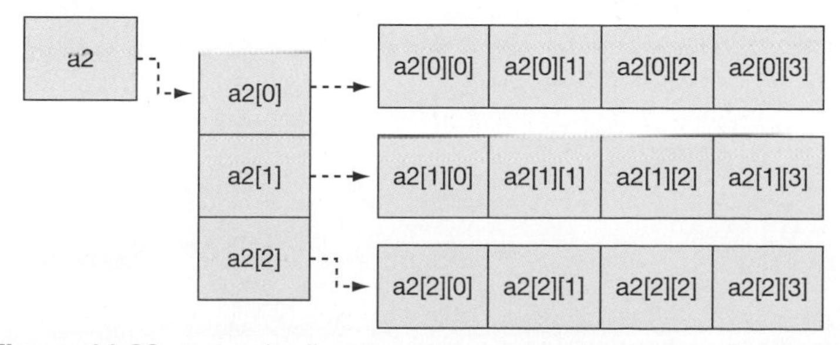

Figure 11.22: Dynamic allocation of two-dimensional arrays (method 2).

```
/* ... source code to handle vector a2 */
for(i = 0; i < m; i++)
  free(a2[i]);
free(a2);
/* ... source code no longer uses a2 */
```

The major difference between the two methods for dynamic allocation of two-dimensional arrays described in this subsection is that the function **malloc()** is called for each row of the matrix in the latter.

If the memory for an array is used, `a2[i]` can point to each row of the array, as shown in the next section.

11.15 ‡Using Pointers to Pass Multidimensional Arrays of Variable Length to Functions

In C, a multidimensional array can be viewed as a one-dimensional array. That is, each element of an array is stored consecutively in the memory. As mentioned before, an array name in an expression is also the pointer to the first element of the array. Because a multidimensional array is stored internally as a one-dimensional linear array, it is easy to pass the address of the first element of a multidimensional array to a function using a pointer as shown in Program 11.8. Program 11.23 uses a pointer to pass a (2×3) integer array `a` to function `printArray()`. A **for** loop inside the function `printArray()` displays the content of the two-dimensional array row-by-row. The element `a[i][j]` of $(m \times n)$ array `a` in the function **main()** can be accessed by the pointer indirection operation `*(a+i*n+j)` in the function `printArray()`. Inside the function `printArray()`, the expression `a[i][j]` is invalid. For example, the element `a[1][2]` of (2×3) array `a` can be accessed by the expression `*(a+1*3+2)`. The output from Program 11.23 is as follows:

```
Array a =
1 2 3
4 5 6
a[1][2] = 6
```

```
/* File: pass2Das1D.c
   Pass two-dimensional arrays as one-dimensional arrays */
#include <stdio.h>

/* print the passed array, treat is a two-dimensional array */
void printArray(int m, int n, int *a) {
    int i, j;  /* loop indexes */

    for(i = 0; i < m*n; i++) {
        if(i == n)              /* print a line when each row */
            printf("\n");
        printf("%d ", *(a+i)); /* print element by element in the array */
    }
```

Program 11.23: Passing a two-dimensional array as a one-dimensional array using pointers. (*Continued*)

```
    printf("\n");

    /* access element a[i][j] for mxn array a using *(a+i*n+j) */
    i = 1;
    j = 2;
    printf("a[%d][%d] = %d\n", i, j, *(a+i*n+j));
}

int main() {
    int a[2][3] = {1, 2, 3,    /* declare array of 2x3 */
                   4, 5, 6};

    printf("Array a = \n");
    printArray(2, 3, &a[0][0]); /* pass array a of 2x3 to printArray() */
    return 0;
}
```

Program 11.23: *(Continued)*

The technique of passing multidimensional arrays of different sizes to functions as one-dimensional arrays obscures the dimensionality of arrays, however. To preserve the dimensionality of multidimensional arrays in called functions, one can use multiple indirections of pointers in C. Program 11.24 is an example that uses a pointer to pointer to pass two-dimensional array to a function.

The functionality of Program 11.24 is the same as Program 10.23. The program passes two arrays of the same dimensions, but with different lengths, to the same argument of the function `func()`, which adds all the elements of the passed array and returns the sum. Program 10.23 uses a two-dimensional VLA rather than a pointer to pointers. It is much simpler. However, the feature of VLAs, only available in C99, might

```
/* File: pass2Dcarray.c
   Calculate the sum of all elements of two-dimensional arrays by
   passing of variable length to a function using pointers to pointers. */
#include <stdio.h>
#include <stdlib.h>  /* for malloc() and free() */
/* define macro for different extents of arrays */
#define M1 2
#define N1 3
#define M2 3
#define N2 4
double func(int m, int n, double **aa); /* function prototype */

int main() {
    /* declare and initialize arrays a1 and a2 with different extents */
    double a1[M1][N1]={1.0, 2.0, 3.0, 4.0, 5.0, 6.0};
```

Program 11.24: Passing two-dimensional arrays of different dimensions. *(Continued)*

```
    double a2[M2][N2]={1.0, 2.0, 3.0, 4.0, 5.0, 6.0,
                       7.0, 8.0, 9.0, 10.0, 11.0, 12.0};

    /* declare pointers to pointers for passing arrays of diff length */
    double **pa1, **pa2, sum;  /* also declare sum */
    int i;                     /* index variable for for-loop */

    /* allocate array of pointers for each row */
    pa1 = (double **)malloc(M1*sizeof(double*));
    for(i=0; i<M1; i++) {
        pa1[i] = a1[i];        /* pa1[i] points to i-th row of a1 */
    }
    printf("a1[1][1] = %f, pa1[1][1] = %f\n", a1[1][1], pa1[1][1]);
    sum = func(M1, N1, pa1);   /* calculate the sum for array a1 */
    printf("sum = %f\n", sum); /* display sum for array a1 */
    free(pa1);                 /* free allocated array  */

    /* allocate array of pointers for each row */
    pa2 = (double **)malloc(M2*sizeof(double*));
    for(i=0; i<M2; i++) {
        pa2[i] = a2[i];        /* pa2[i] points to i-th row of a2 */
    }
    printf("a2[1][1] = %f, pa2[1][1] = %f\n", a2[1][1], pa2[1][1]);
    sum = func(M2, N2, pa2);   /* calculate the sum for array a2 */
    printf("sum = %f\n", sum); /* display sum for array a2 */
    free(pa2);                 /* free allocated array */
    return 0;
}

/* function to calculate the sum of two-dimensional arrays with
   different extents */
double func(int m, int n, double **a) {
    double sum = 0;            /* declare and initialize sum */
    int i, j;                  /* declare index variables for loops */

    for(i=0; i<m; i++) {
        for(j=0; j<n; j++) {
            sum += a[i][j];    /* sum all alements one by one */
        }
    }
    return sum;                /* return the sum */
}
```

Program 11.24: *(Continued)*

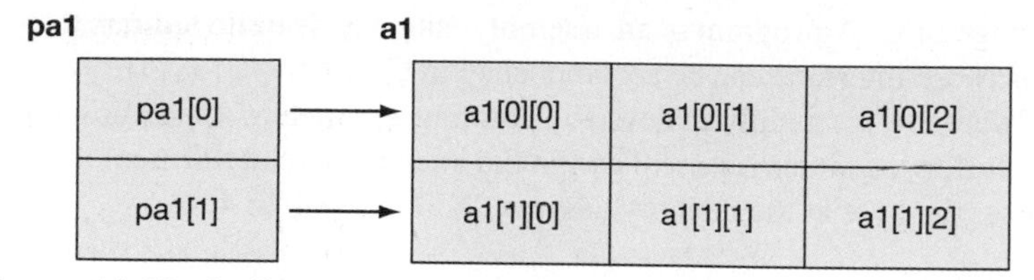

Figure 11.23: An illustration of the pointer to pointer `pa1` in Program 11.24.

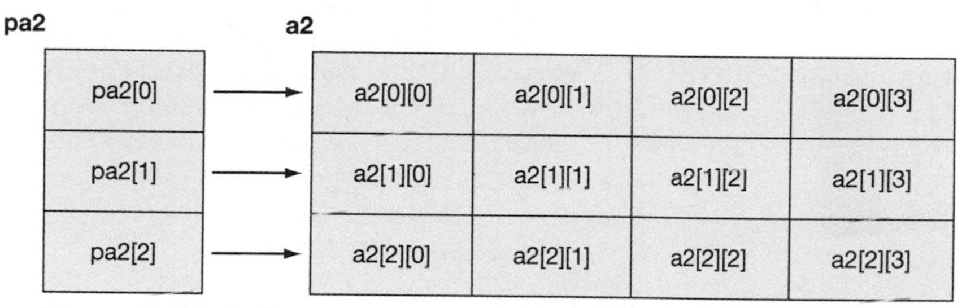

Figure 11.24: An illustration of the pointer to pointer `pa2` in Program 11.24.

not be available in all C compilers. The method of using multiple indirections of pointers in Program 11.24 is available in all C89-compliant compilers.

In Program 11.24, `pa1`, a pointer to pointers is assigned to point to the two-dimensional array `a1`. `pa2`, another pointer to pointers is assigned to point to two-dimensional array `a2` of different size from `a1`. Note that memory has to be allocated for each pointer to pointers. The pointers to pointers are then used to pass the two-dimensional arrays into the function `func()` to sum all the elements of the array. Figures 11.23 and 11.24 illustrate the interactions between the pointers to pointer and arrays. After allocating memory, `pa1` can be considered as an array of pointers to double, which is shown in Figure 11.23. Each element of the array `pa1` points to a row of the array `a1`. The pointer `pa1[0]` points to address `&a1[0][0]`, whereas the pointer `pa1[1]` points to `&a1[1][0]`. Note that the array elements `pa1[i][j]` and `a1[i][j]` share the same memory as shown for the values for the elements `pa1[1][1]` and `a1[1][1]`. Similarly, the elements `pa2[i][j]` and `a2[i][j]` share the same memory as well. The pointer `pa2[0]` also points to `&a2[0][0]`, `pa2[1]` points to `&a2[1][0]`, and `pa2[2]` points to `&a2[2][0]`. The output from Program 11.24 is similar to that from Program 10.23 as shown below:

```
a1[1][1] = 5.000000, pa1[1][1] = 5.000000
sum = 21.000000
a2[1][1] = 6.000000, pa2[1][1] = 6.000000
sum = 78.000000
```

11.16 ‡Using Pointers for Interfacing Hardware

A computer program written for a mechatronic, embedded, or microcontroller system often needs to deal with input and output signals by accessing specific memory locations or registers associated with input/output devices in an embedded computer. For such a lower-level hardware interface, one can write a program either in an assembly language or C. A program in an assembly language is quite tedious to write and debug. Most applications with hardware interface can be accomplished in C.

Interfacing hardware in C, is mainly achieved by pointing a pointer to a specific memory location or register. For example, the following statements will assign the integer value at the memory location 0XFFF68FFE to the variable i and set the byte at the memory address 0XFFFFF000 to 4.

```
char *cptr;
int i, *iptr;
float *fptr;
size_t j;
iptr = (int *)0XFFF68FFE;        // point to the memory at 0XFFF68FFE
i = *iptr;                       // i equals the value at 0X68FFE;
cptr = (char *)0XFFFFF000;       // point to the memory at 0XFFFFF000
*cptr = 4;                       // 4 is assigned to 0XFFFFF000
fptr = (float *)cptr + 1;        // fptr points to 0XFFFFF004
j = (size_t)cptr;                // j becomes 0XFFFFF004
```

An integral value cannot be assigned to a pointer variable without an explicit type cast, and vice versa. The cast operator `(int *)` first casts the integer value 0XFFF68FFE as a pointer to int with the value of 0XFFF68FFE in hexadecimal numeration. The variable `iptr` of pointer to int is then pointed to the address 0XFFF68FFE by the assignment statement

```
iptr = (int *)0XFFF68FFE;
```

Using a pointer indirection operator, variable `i` is assigned the value at the address pointed by the pointer variable `iptr`. Similarly, the variable `cptr` of pointer to char is pointed to the address of 0XFFFFF000 by the statement

```
cptr = (char *)0XFFFFF000;
```

The memory location of 0XFFFFF000 pointed to by `cptr` is then assigned the value 4. Because the variable `cptr` is a pointer to char, `cptr+1` is 0XFFFFF001. However, `(float *)cptr+1` will give the address of 0XFFFFF004, not 0XFFFFF001, because after the casting operation, the address for the next element of a floating-point number is 4 bytes apart.

Note that the lower segment of the memory in an embedded computer system or workstation is usually reserved for the operating system and system programs. An application program will be terminated with exception handling if the values in these protected segments of memory are changed by pointers.

Exercises

1. Identify and correct the errors, if there are any, in the following program segments. If there are errors, briefly explain them.

   a.
   ```
   int *number;
   printf("%d\n", *number);
   ```
   b.
   ```
   float *realPtr;
   int *integerPtr;
   integerPtr = realPtr;
   ```
   c.
   ```
   int *x, y;
   x = y;
   ```

d.
```
char s[] = "this is a character array";
for( ; *s != '\0'; s++)
  printf("%c ", *s);
```

e.
```
short *numPtr, result;
void *genericPtr = numPtr;
result = *genericPtr + 7;
```

f.
```
float x = 19.34;
float xPtr = &x;
printf("%f\n", xPtr);
```

g.
```
char *s;
printf("%s\n", s);
```

h.
```
int funct1(int *p){
  int i=-1;
  int *pp;
  pp = p+i;
  return &i;
}

int main() {
  int i = 5;
  funct1(i);
}
```

2. State whether the following are true or false. If false, explain why.

  a. Two pointers that point to different arrays cannot be compared meaningfully.

  b. Because the name of an array is a pointer to the first element of the array, array names may be manipulated in precisely the same manner as pointers.

3. For each of the following, write a single statement that performs the indicated task. Assume that the variables `value1` and `value2` of type long long int have been declared and that `value1` has been initialized to 100,000.

  a. Declare the variable `llptr` to be a pointer to an object of type long long int.

  b. Assign the address of the variable `value1` to the pointer variable `llptr`.

  c. Print the value of the object pointed to by `llptr`.

4. Use the function **malloc()** to do the following:

  a. For the integer pointer `p`, allocate memory for a 10-element array. Fill each element with the value of 5, then free the memory.

  b. Suppose the variable `str` is declared as a pointer to char, allocate enough memory to store the string `"This string"`.

5. Write a function called `swapp()` to interchange pointers `p` and `q` so that after the function is called, `p` points to the object to which `q` formerly pointed, and vice versa.

6. A string is an array of characters terminated by the character `'\0'`. Write a function that copies string s1 to string s2 using pointers. Its function prototype should be:

```
void str_cpy(const char *s1, char *s2);
```

Do not use the function **strcpy()** in the standard C library.

7. Write a function that compares the strings s1 and s2 using pointers. It should return a value of 0 if the strings are identical, greater than 0 if the boolean expression `(*s1>*s2)` is 1, and less than 0 if the boolean expression `(*s2>*s1)` is 1. The sign of a nonzero return value is determined by the sign of the difference between the values of the first pair of bytes that differ in the strings being compared. Its function prototype should be:

```
int str_cmp(const char *s1, const char *s2);
```

Do not use the function **strcmp**() in the standard C library.

8. What does this program do?

```
#include<stdio.h>

void mystery1(char *, const char *);
int main() {
   char string1[80], string2[80];

   printf("Enter two strings: ");
   scanf("%s%s", string1, string2);
   mystery1(string1, string2);
   printf("%s", string1);
   return 0;
}

void mystery1(char *s1, const char *s2) {
  /* makes s1 pointing to the end of string s1 */
   while(*s1 != '\0')
      ++s1;
   while(*s1 = *s2) {
      s1++;
      s2++;
   )
}
```

9. What does this program do?

```
#include<stdio.h>

int mystery2(const char *);
int main() {
   char string[80];

   printf("Enter a string: ");
   scanf("%s", string);
   printf("%d\n", mystery2(string));
   return 0;
}

int mystery2(const char *s) {
   int x;
```

```
    for(x = 0; *s != '\0'; s++)
        ++x;
    return x;
}
```

10. Using **typedef** to define a data type of *pointer to function with two arguments of double type and returning pointer to int*. Write a declaration statement of a variable of pointer to function using the data type defined by the **typedef** definition. Also write an actual function of that type that can be pointed to by the declared pointer variable.

11. If `a` has type `int [4]`, and `b` has type `int [6][8]`, rewrite the following expressions using the variable name and indirection operator `'*'`, but without using the subscript operator `[]`.

a. a[i]

b. b[i][j]

12. Give the output of the following program when it is executed.

```
#include <stdio.h>
typedef int *INTP;
int main() {
    int i =10;
    INTP p1, p2;
    p1 = &i;
    *p1 *= 2;
    p2 = p1;
    printf("i = %d\n", i);
    printf("*p2 = %d\n", *p2);
}
```

13. Give the output of the following program.

```
#include <stdio.h>
#include <stdlib.h>
#define M1 2
#define N1 3
int main() {
    double a1[M1][N1]={1, 2, 3, 4, 5, 6};
    double **pa1;
    int i;

    pa1 = (double **)malloc(M1*sizeof(double*));
    for(i=0; i<M1; i++) {
        pa1[i] = a1[i];
    }
    printf("a1[1][2] = %f\n", a1[1][2]);
    printf("pa1[1][1] = %f\n", pa1[1][1]);
    free(pa1);
    return 0;
}
```

14. What is the output of the following program?

```
#include <stdio.h>
char c[4][6] = {
   'a', 'b', 'c', 'd', 'e', '\0',
   'f', 'g', 'h', 'i', 'j', '\0',
   'k', 'l', 'm', 'n', 'o', '\0',
   'p', 'q', 'r', 's', 't', '\0'
};
int main() {
     int n=4, m=6;
     int i=2, j=3;
     printf("1 %c\n",  c[i][j]);
     printf("2 %c\n", *(c[i]+j));
     printf("3 %c\n", *(*(i+c)+j));
     printf("4 %c\n", *(*(c+i)+j));
     printf("5 %c\n", *(&c[0][0]+i*m+j));
     printf("6 %c\n", *((char *)c[i]+j));
     printf("7 %c\n", *((char *)(c+i)+j));
     printf("8 %c\n", *((char *)c+i*m+j));
     printf("9 %s\n",  c[i]);
     printf("10 %s\n",  *(c+i));
     return 0;
}
```

15. Given the following declarations and assignments, what do these expressions evaluate to?

```
int a1[10] = {9, 8, 7, 6, 5, 4, 3, 2, 1, 0};
int *p1, *p2;
p1 = a1+3;
p2 = *a1[2];
```

```
(a) *(a1+4)   (b) a1[3]   (c) *p1   (d) *(p1+5)   (e) p1[-2]
(f) *(a1+2)   (g) a1[6]   (h) *p2   (i) *(p2+3)   (j) p2[-1]
```

16. Given the following declarations and assignments, what do these expressions evaluate to?

```
int a2[3][4] = {1,2,3,4,
                5,6,7,8,
                9,10,11,12}
int *p, (*p2)[4];
p = a2[1];
p2 = a2;
```

```
(a) *(p+1*4+2)   (b) *(*(a2+1)+2)   (c) a2[2][3]   (d) *p
(e) p[-1]        (f) p[2]           (g) *(p+2)     (h) p2[1][3]
```

17. Complete the following program with the function `monthstr()`, which returns the name of a month using an array of pointers according to its argument with a value from 1 to 12 corresponding to January to December, respectively.

```
const char *monthstr(int month);
/* add code here */
```

```
int main() {
    int i;
    for(i = 1; i <= 12; i++) {
        printf("%s\n", monthstr(i));
    }
    return 0;
}
```

18. The monthly sales (× $1000) of a product in the last two years are as follows:

	Jan	Feb	Mar	Api	May	Jun	Jul	Aug	Sep	Oct	Nov	Dec
Year 1	367	654	545	556	565	526	437	389	689	554	526	625
Year 2	429	644	586	626	652	546	449	689	597	679	696	568

Write a program to calculate the monthly average of the sales for each month for the last two years. Display full names for months using an array of pointer to char in the following format:

```
Month           Sales (x1,000 $)
-------------------------- ---
January         398.00
...
```

19. For Exercise 26 in Chapter 10, display the name for each day of a week using an array of pointer to char in the following format:

```
Day          Max    Min
-----------------------
Sunday       43.7   34.5
...
Saturday     47.2   42.4
```

20. Given the following declarations and assignments, what do these expressions evaluate to?

```
double a[2][3] = {1, 2, 3, 4, 5, 6};
complex *zp;
char *c[] = {"jkfghjdsf",
             "jgkdfjg",
             "gdfknbcvml",
             NULL
            };
char **p;
zp = (complex *)a[1];
p = c;

(a) a[0][1]   (b) a[1][0]   (c) ++a[1][2]   (d) a[1] - a[0]
(e) zp[0]     (f) *--zp     (g) c[1][2]     (h) *(*p +4)
(i) p[1][2]   (j) p[1]      (k) p[0][2]     (l) **p
```

21. If the array a is defined as `int a[3][5]`, which of the following expressions are equivalent to `a[j][k]`?

```
(a) *(a[j]+k)            (b) **(a[j+k])            (c) *(*(a+j)+k)
(d) **(a+j)+k            (e) *(&a[0][0] +j*5 +k)   (f) **a+j+k
(g) *(&a[j]+k)           (h) *((int *)a[j] +k)     (i) *((int *)(a)+j*3+k)
(j) *((int *)(a+j)+k)    (k) *(a+j*5+k)            (l) *((int *)(a)+j*5+k)
(m) *((int *)(a)+j+k)    (n) *((int *)(a)+2*j+k)   (o) *(&a[0][0]+4*j+k)
(p) *(a+4*j+k)           (q) *(&a[0][0]+6*j+k)
```

22. Identify and correct the errors in the following code. If there are errors, briefly explain them.

a.

```
double *A1;
double A2[3][4];

A2[2][3] = 5.0;
*(A1+1) = A2[2][3];
A1 = A2[2];
*(A2[2]) = 3;
A1 += 1;
*(A1) = 4;
```

b.

```
double **A1;
double A2[3][4];
int i,j;
int m=3, n=4;

A1 = (double**)malloc( m*n*sizeof(double));
for(i = 0; i < m; i++)
  for(j = 0; j < n; j++)
    A1[i][j] = i+j;
A1[2] = A2[2];
printf("%f %f\n", *(A2[2]), A2[2])
```

c.

```
double **A1;
double A2[3][4];
int m = 3, n = 4;
int i,j;

A1 = (double **)malloc(m*sizeof(double*));
A1[0] = (double *)malloc(m*n*sizeof(double));
for(i=0; i<m; i++){
  for(j=0; j<n; j++){
    A1[i][j] = i+j;
  }
}
A1[m]=A2[3];
...
free(A1);
```

23. Point out the errors in the following C code, and briefly explain them.

```
int main() {
  char c = '5';
  int 5i, k;
  int l1; l2;
  int m, *p;
  double d ='c';
  int *ipp = malloc(sizeof(int*));
  char *cpp = "abcdebf"
  m++; --m;
  m = 0xABGCE;
  m = 08321;
  *p = 90;
  ipp = 0x12345;
  c = '\123';
  c = '\70';
  c = '\782';
  c = '\0123';
  k = ipp - cpp;
  p = &m+1;
  k = (int)p+k;
}
```

24. Write a program to dynamically allocate contiguous memory for `double **A2` with size of 3×4.

25. Write a program to dynamically allocate noncontinuous memory for `double **A2` with size of 3×4.

26. What does the following program do?

```
int main(){
  double A1[4][5], A2[4][5], A3[4][5];
  double B1[5][6], B2[5][6], B3[5][6];
  int i;
  void Dmultiple(double (*D1)[5], double D2[][5], double D3[4][5],
                     int m, int n);

  Dmultiple(A1, A2, A3, 4, 5);
  Dmultiple(B1, B2, B3, 3, 5);

}
void Dmultiple(double (*D1)[5], double D2[][5], double D3[4][5],
                     int m, int n){
  int i,j;
  for(i=0; i<m; i++){
    for(j=0; j<n; j++){
      D1[i][j] = D2[i][j]*D3[i][j];
    }
  }
}
```

27. Complete the following program

```
#define M 3
#define N 6
void fun(int **A, int m, int n);
int main() {
    int a[M][N] = { 1, 2, 3, 4,  5,  6,
                    7, 8, 9, 10, 11, 12,
                    1, 2, 3, 4,  5,  6};
    int **A;
    /* add code for passing a through A to fun() here*/
    fun(A, M, N);
    /* add any code necessary here */
}

void fun(int **A, int m, int n) {;
    /* add code for print out, using A[0][0], ..., A[m-1][n-1] */
}
```

The output of the program becomes:

```
A =
1 2 3 4  5  6
7 8 9 10 11 12
1 2 3 4  5  6
```

28. Complete the following program so that the output of the program is the same as in the previous problem.

```
#define M 3
#define N 6
void fun(int *A, int n, int m);
int main() {
    int a[M][N] = { 1, 2, 3, 4,  5,  6,
                    7, 8, 9, 10, 11, 12,
                    1, 2, 3, 4,  5,  6};
    /* add any necessary code here */
    fun(a, M, N);
    /* add any necessary code here */
}

/* add code for print out */
void fun(int *A, int m, int n)
    /* add any necessary code here */
}
```

29. With the declaration statements below,

```
void funct( int n, int a[n] ){
    extern int m;
    typedef int T[n];
```

explain whether the following declaration statements can be attached to this code. If not, explain why.

a. `int (*p1)[n];`
b. `int (*p2)[4];`
c. `T **cc;`

30. What are the differences in the following declarations?

a.
```
int *p2[3];
int (*p1)[3];
```
b.
```
int **p3[3][4];
int (*p5)[3][4];
int *(*p4)[3][4];
```

31. Write a function `findmax2d()` with the prototype

```
void find_ijmax(int nrow, int ncol,  double a[nrow][ncol],
                int *i_maxp, int *j_maxp);
```

The array `a` is passed as an input argument with its number of rows and number of columns specified by the arguments `nrow` and `ncol`, respectively. The output arguments `i`-maxp and `j`-maxp contain the indices, `i` and `j`, for the element of the array with the maximum value.

32. Write a function with the following function prototype

```
double sortArrayptr(int n, int *a);
```

that sorts an array with *n* elements in ascending order. Arrays of different dimensions can be passed in this function. For a two-dimensional array, the sorted array is in row-by-row ascending order for the entire matrix. The function returns the median for all elements of the array. Test the function using the array `a` in Program 10.5 and `a2` in Program 10.24, and print out the sorted arrays.

33. Modify Program 10.5 to sort the array `a` in descending order using the function **qsort()**.

34. Modify Program 10.24 to sort the array `a2` using the function **qsort()** in the following ways:

a. In row-wise descending order for the entire array.
b. In row-wise descending order for each row.
c. In column-wise descending order for each column.

35. Using VLAs in C99, Program 10.24 sorts and displays two-dimensional arrays of different sizes. Modify these programs to replace VLAs by pointers to pointer. The modified functions shall have the function prototypes as follows:

```
void sortArray2d(int m, int n, double **a, double median[]);
void printArray2d(int m, int n, double **a);
void printArray(int n, double a[]);
```

or

```
void sortArray2d(int m, int n, double **a, double *median);
void printArray2d(int m, int n, double **a);
void printArray(int n, double *a);
```

36. Write a C program called `linearsys1.c` to perform the following operation $B = A + 2 * \sin(A)$ for the following two matrices: $A_1 = \begin{bmatrix} 1 & 2 & 2 & 5 \\ 7 & 8 & 9 & 3 \\ 5 & 7 & 3 & 2 \end{bmatrix}$ $A_2 = \begin{bmatrix} 1 & 5 & 3 \\ 5 & 6 & 7 \end{bmatrix}$

The program `linearsys1.c` shall contain two top-level functions, **main()** and `linear1()`. The function `linear1()` should be implemented to evaluate the expression $B = A + 2 * \sin(A)$. The function prototype for `linear1()` is as follows:

```
void linear1(double **B, double **A, int n, int m);
```

where A is an n × m matrix. The function `linear1()` is called twice in the program linearsys1.c, as shown below:

```
int main() {
  double **b1, **a1, B1[3][4], A1[3][4] = {...};
  double **b2, **a2, B2[2][3], A2[2][3] = {....};
  /* add code here, use memory for B and A */
  linear1(b1, a1, 3, 4);
  linear1(b2, a2, 2, 3);
  /* print out the results of B1 and B2 here */
}
```

37. Modify Program 11.2 with the following restrictions:

   a. Using only the array word.

   b. The program reads an integer for the number of letters in a word, allocates memory dynamically for `word`, reads a word with the specified number of letters, and prints it reversely.

   c. The program reads an integer for the number of letters in a word, declares the array `word` as a VLA in C99, reads a word with the specified number of letters, and prints it reversely.

38. Write a program to read a list of numbers entered from the terminal. Before this list of numbers is entered, the program first prompts the user to specify how many numbers are going to be entered. Based on this number, the memory will be allocated dynamically for an array, which will be used to store the entered data. Print the original entered data. Sort the data using the function `sort()` in Program 10.13. Print the sorted data. Calculate the median of the data using the function `median()` in Program 10.13. Print the median. Test the function using the array `a` in Program 10.5 and the array `a2` in Program 10.24.

39. Modify Exercise 38 to use a VLA in C99, instead of dynamically allocating the memory for an array.

40. Write a program that reads the values for the width and length of a rectangle using two variables of double type. Pass values of these variables to a function, which calculates the area and perimeter of the rectangle. The area and perimeter of the rectangle passed back from two other arguments of this function are printed out in the function **main()**. Check your program with the user input for the width and length of 4 and 5 meters, respectively.

41. Write a program that reads the values for the width, length, and height of a rectangular box using three variables of double type in the function **main()**. Pass values of these variables to a function, which calculates the volume and surface area for six sides of the box. The volume and surface area of the box passed back from two other arguments of this function are printed out in the function **main()**. Check your program with the user input for the width, length, and height of 2, 3, and 4 meters, respectively.

42. Write a program that reads the value for the radius of a sphere using a variable of double type in the function **main()**. Pass the value of this variable to a function, which calculates the volume and surface area for the sphere. The volume and surface area of the sphere passed back from two other arguments of this function are printed out in the function **main()**. Check your program with the user input for the radius of 5 meters.

43. Write a program that reads the values for the radius and height of a solid cylinder using two variables of type double. Pass the values for the radius and height to function `cylinder()`, which calculates the surface area and volume of the cylinder. The area and volume of the cylinder passed back from two other arguments of this function are printed out in the function **main**(). Check your program with the user input for a radius of 5 meters and a height of 3.5 meters.

44. Write a linear regression function with the function prototype

```
void linearreg(double t[], double y[], int n, double *b, double *v);
```

where `t` and `y` are arrays of data to be fitted in the linear regression model, `n` is the number of elements for the passed arrays `t` and `y`. The linear regression coefficients for the intercept `b` and slope `s` are passed to the calling function by pointers. Modify Program 10.19 to use this function.

45. Use the function `bisect()` in Program 11.17 to find zeros for the following functions. Also, plot the functions over a proper range containing the zeros.

   a. Function cos(x) in the range $1 < x < 2$.
   b. Projectile function $y(x)$ in equation (6.4) in the range $60 < x < 70$ with an initial speed v_0 of 35 m/s and initial projection angle of $\theta_0 = 15°$. Compute the difference of the result using the function `bisect()` with that using equation (6.3).
   c. Find two zeros for the humps function shown in Figure 6.11.

46. The formula for the volume of a sphere is $\frac{4}{3}\pi r^3$, where r is the radius of the sphere. If the volume of a sphere is 90 m^3, write a program to calculate the radius of the sphere using the function `bisect()` in Program 11.17. Plot the function $f(r) = \frac{4}{3}\pi r^3 - 90$ in the range $-5 \leq x5$.

47. Modify Program 11.17 to use the convergence criterion 2 in equation (6.7) for the bisection method in the function `bisect()`.

48. Modify the function `bisect()` in Program 11.17 to pass the number of iterations for bisection to the calling function. Print also the number of iterations in the function **main**().

49. Modify the function `bisect()` in Program 11.17 with a maximum number of iterations for bisection as part of the convergence criteria. If the number of iterations exceeds this maximum number, the function `bisect()` returns -3. Add an argument `num` for the number of iterations for the function `bisect()`. By default, the maximum number of iterations is 20. If the passed value through `num` is larger than the default maximum number of iterations, use the passed value as the maximum number in the bisection algorithm. Pass the number of iterations for bisection to the called function also using this argument. Inside the function **main**(), first call the modified function `bisect()` with the maximum number of iterations 10. Next call it with the maximum number of iterations 100. Print out the actual number of iterations passed back from the function `bisect()`.

50. Modify Program 11.17 to find the zeros of the projectile function with the initial speed v_0 of 35 m/s, and initial projection angle θ_0 with four different values of 15°, 35°, 45°, and 65° in the range $10 < x < 150$.

51. Based on Newton's method described in Exercise 42 in Chapter 6, write a function `newton()` to find a root of an equation. The algorithm in the function `newton()` uses the convergence criterion in equation (6.7) with a maximum number of iterations 100. The function `newton()` has the following prototype

```
int newton(double *x, double x0, double tolerance,
           double (*f)(double), double (*fprime)(double));
```

The argument `x` of pointer to double passes the calculated approximate root to the calling function. The argument x_0 is the initial guess, `tolerance` is the small *epsilon* for the convergence condition in equation (6.7), `f` of pointer to function for function $f(x)$ with its root to be found, and `fprime` of pointer to function is for the derivative $f'(x)$. If successful, the function returns 0. Otherwise, it returns -1. Use this function to solve the following problems.

a. Find two roots for the function $f(x) = x^2 - 3$ using the initial guesses $x_0 = 2$ and $x_0 = -2$.
b. Find a root for the function $f(x) = x^3 - 3$ with the initial guess $x_0 = 2$.
c. Find three roots for the function $f(x) = 10x^3 + 7x^2 - 4x - 1$ with the initial guesses -2, -0.5, and 2.

52. For the mechanical system shown in Figure 2.12, given mass $m = 5$ kilograms (kg) and coefficient of kinetic friction $\mu = 0.2$, the applied force p is a function of time t expressed as one of the following two formulas:

$$p_1(t) = 4\sin(t - 3) + 20$$
$$p_2(t) = 4(t^2 - 3) + 20$$

Write two functions with the prototypes

```
double force1(double t);
double force2(double t);
```

for the forces $p_1(t)$ and $p_2(t)$, respectively. The function `accel()` calculates and plots the accelerations **a** using the function **plotxy()** from $t = 0$ to $t = 10$ seconds with a variable number of points.

a. The function `accel()` has the prototype

```
void accel(int n, int num);
```

where `n` is for the number of data points and `num` for selecting one of the above external force formulas.

b. The function `accel()` has the prototype

```
void accel(int n, double (*force)(double t));
```

where `n` is for the number of data points and `force` for selecting one of the above external force formulas.

Write a program to call the function `accel()` twice with the value 100 for `n`, such that the first time, it plots acceleration using $p_1(t)$, and the second time, it uses $p_2(t)$.

53. Copy the program `leak.c` below

```
/* File: leak.c */
#include <stdlib.h>   /* for malloc() and free() */

int main() {
    void *p;

    while(1) {   /* an infinite loop to test the memory leak */
       p = malloc(64);
       free(p);   /* comment this line to leak 64 bytes in each iteration */
    }
    return 0;
}
```

to the program `leak2.c` and comment out the statement

```
free(p);
```

so that `leak2.c` has a memory leak. If a program is compiled to run in a binary executable, check the memory leak for the process of the binary executable. If a program runs in Ch or ChIDE, check the memory leak for the process of the binary executable **ch** or **chide**. In Unix, you may type the commands `man ps` and `man grep` to find the detailed information about the commands **ps** and **grep**. You may kill a program executed in a command shell by typing the command Ctrl-C. Compare the memory usage for programs `leak.c` and `leak2.c`. Find the memory size used by the program `leak.c` at runtime. Execute programs `leak.c` and `leak2.c` in two separate windows.

a. In Windows, type Ctrl-Alt-Delete key combination to bring up the Windows Task Manager, and check the memory size used by **ch** in the column of `Mem Usage`.

b. In Linux and Solaris, type the command below in another window several times over the period of one minute.

```
> ps -elf | grep leak
```

c. In Mac OS X, type the command below in another window several times over the period of one minute.

```
> ps -u    | grep leak
```

CHAPTER 12

Characters and Strings

A string in C consists of a sequence of characters. It is a null-terminated array of characters. C has a rich set of standard library functions to process characters and strings. These functions can also be used to process lines of text or text in a file. In this chapter, using C standard library functions for handling characters and strings is described first. The techniques are then used to process command-line arguments.

12.1 Character Code

Characters such as letters and punctuation are stored as integers according to a certain numerical code, such as American Standard Code for Information Interchange (ASCII) code that ranges from 0 to 127 listed in Appendix D. Only 7 bits are required to represent a character in ASCII code. For example, the ASCII value for `'a'` is 97. Although ASCII code is the most popular, there are other codes to represent characters. Extended Binary Coded Decimal Interchange Code (EBCDIC) is another popular codes that is used mainly in IBM mainframes and computers from some other vendors. It uses 8-bit character encoding instead of 7-bit. The integer 97 in EBCDIC code represents the character `'/'`.

As described in section 3.8 in Chapter 3, type **char** is used to define variables of characters. The value of a variable of type char is a single character, as in `'x'` or escape sequence enclosed in single quotes, as in `'\n'`. The statement below is an example of declaring and initializing a character variable.

```
char c = 'a';
```

It declares the variable `c` with type char and initializes it with the character `'a'`. The code works regardless of the internal integer representations of characters. If the system uses the ASCII code, the above statement is equivalent to

```
char c = 97;
```

However, the above code is not portable. The variable `c` contains `'a'` in ASCII code, whereas in EBCDIC code, `c` becomes `'/'`. Therefore, a symbolic name should be used for a character for portable C programs.

Furthermore, we cannot assume that a particular group of characters is always contiguous. In ASCII code, lowercase letters, uppercase letters, and digits are in three contiguous groups as shown in Appendix D. For example, the ASCII values for characters `'a'` to `'z'` range from 97 to 122 contiguously. However, in EBCDIC code, only digits are in a contiguous group. Therefore, using the relational and logical expression

```
c >= 'a' && c <= 'z'
```

to test whether the variable `c` of char type contains a lowercase letter works only in ASCII code. It does not work in EBCDIC code. For a portable program, the function call

```
islower(c)
```

should be used to check if the variable `c` contains a lowercase letter. Portable character-handling functions, including **islower()**, will be described in section 12.3.

12.2 Character Input and Output

Some functions in the standard input/output library defined in the header file **stdio.h** are specifically for manipulating characters. The character input function **getchar()** and output function **putchar()** have been described in section 11.2 in Chapter 11. In Program 11.2, the function **getchar()** is used to read a character from the standard input and the function **putchar()** for writing a character to the standard output.

The functions **scanf()** and **printf()** can also be used for input and output of characters. In these functions, the conversion specifier `"%c"` is used to specify a character. Consider Program 12.1 as an example. This program first reads a character value using the function **getchar()**. It then uses the function **printf()** to display the character's internal integer representation value, such as ASCII code, and alphabetical character. It also uses the function **putchar()** to display the character. Note that when the user types in a character and hits the carriage return key, a newline character is also entered in the standard input stream buffer beside the character. Next, it gets the newline character `'\n'` and prints out its internal integer representation value as well. An Interactive execution of Program 12.1 with an input character `'a'` in a machine using ASCII code

```
/* File: charget.c
   Get characters from the terminal keyboard */
#include <stdio.h>

int main() {
    char c;

    printf("Please input a character\n");
    c = getchar();              /* get a char from the keyboard */
    /* print the ASCII value and character */
    printf("ASCII c = %d, c = %c\n", c, c);
    putchar(c);                 /* print character c */
    printf("\n");               /* print a newline character '\n' */
    /* print the ASCII value for the newline character '\n' and character */
    printf("Note: ASCII '\\n' = %d, '\\n' = %c\n", '\n', '\n');

    /* obtain the newline character '\n' in the buffer */
    c = getchar();
    /* print the ASCII value and character for the newline character */
    printf("ASCII c = %d, c = %c\n", c, c);
    /* print the newline character */
    putchar(c);
    return 0;
}
```

Program 12.1: Getting input characters.

is shown below.

```
> charget.c
Please input a character
a
ASCII c = 97, c = a
a
Note: ASCII '\n' = 10, '\n' =

ASCII c = 10, c =
```

12.3 Character-Handling Functions

The character-handling library defined in the header file **ctype.h** has many portable functions to perform tests and manipulate characters. Accessing this library requires the header file **ctype.h**. Each function defined in **ctype.h** has a character input argument represented as an int type. The value of this argument may be an **unsigned char** or the equivalent of the macro **EOF**, typically with a value of −1, defined in the header file **stdio.h**. Each function that performs a test on the input character returns a nonzero value for true and zero for false. These functions can be identified by the prefix “is” associated to its name. Similarly, functions for character manipulation have names that begin with “to.” A summary of functions in the character-handling library is listed in Table 12.1.

Program 12.2 is an example that uses the function **isdigit()** to determine whether or not the input argument `c` is a digit. The output of Program 12.2 is shown below.

```
isdigit('A') returns 0
'A' is not a digit.
isdigit('2') returns 1
'2' is a digit.
```

```
/* File: isdigit.c
   Demonstration of using character function isdigit() */
#include <ctype.h>    /* for character functions such as isdigit() */
#include <stdio.h>

int main() {
    char c = 'A';   /* character 'A' is not a digit */

    printf("isdigit('%c') returns %d\n", c, isdigit(c));
    if(isdigit(c))
        printf("'%c' is a digit.\n", c);
```

Program 12.2: Using character functions. (*Continued*)

```
    else
        printf("'%c' is not a digit.\n",c);

    c = '2';        /* character '2' is a digit */
    printf("isdigit('%c') returns %d\n", c, isdigit(c));
    if(isdigit(c))
        printf("'%c' is a digit.\n",c);
    else
        printf("'%c' is not a digit.\n",c);
    return 0;
}
```

Program 12.2: *(Continued)*

Table 12.1 Functions in ctype.h.

Function	Description
int isascii(int `c`**)**	Returns **true** if `c` is an ASCII character and **false** otherwise.
int isalnum(int `c`**)**	Returns **true** if `c` is a digit or letter and **false** otherwise.
int isalpha(int `c`**)**	Returns **true** if `c` is a letter and **false** otherwise.
int isdigit(int `c`**)**	Returns **true** if `c` is a digit and **false** otherwise.
int isxdigit(int `c`**)**	Returns **true** if `c` is a hexadecimal digit character and **false** otherwise.
int islower(int `c`**)**	Returns **true** if `c` is a lowercase letter and **false** otherwise.
int isupper(int `c`**)**	Returns **true** if `c` is an uppercase letter and **false** otherwise.
int isspace(int `c`**)**	Returns **true** if `c` is a white-space character: newline (`'\n'`), space (`' '`), form feed (`'\f'`), carriage return (`'\r'`), horizontal tab (`'\t'`), or vertical tab (`'\v'`); and **false** otherwise.
int iscntrl(int `c`**)**	Returns **true** if `c` is a control character and **false** otherwise.
int ispunct(int `c`**)**	Returns **true** if `c` is a printing character other than a space, digit, or letter and **false** otherwise.
int isprint(int `c`**)**	Returns **true** if `c` is a printing character including space (`' '`) and **false** otherwise.
int isgraph(int `c`**)**	Returns **true** if `c` is a printing character other than space (`' '`) and **false** otherwise.
int toascii(int `c`**)**	If `c` is an ASCII character, **toascii()** returns `c` as the equivalent ASCII number. Otherwise, **toascii()** returns the argument unchanged.
int tolower(int `c`**)**	If `c` is an uppercase letter, **tolower()** returns `c` as a lowercase letter. Otherwise, **tolower()** returns the argument unchanged.
int toupper(int `c`**)**	If `c` is a lowercase letter, **toupper()** returns `c` as an uppercase letter. Otherwise, **toupper()** returns the argument unchanged.

12.4 Strings

As described in section 3.8 in Chapter 3, a string is a set of sequential characters. It can include letters, digits, and certain special characters such as `*`, `/`, and `$`. A *string literal*, or *string constant*, is a series of multibyte characters enclosed in double quotes, such as `"Hello"`. Furthermore, the *null character* `'\0'` is automatically appended to a string literal to designate the end of a string. Thus, all strings need to be terminated by the null character. A string may be declared as a character array or pointer to char as **char** *. Some examples are shown below.

```
> char str1[7] = {'S', 't', 'r', 'i', 'n', 'g', '\0';
> char str2[] = {'S', 't', 'r', 'i', 'n', 'g', '\0'}
> char str3[] = "String"
> char *strp = "String"
> sizeof(str1)
7
> sizeof(str2)
7
> sizeof(str3)
7
> sizeof(strp)
4
```

Note that when allocating the size of the character array for a string, an extra array element is required for the null character `'\0'`. The number of bytes for the string `"String"` is 7 because of the extra null character. The variables `str1`, `str2`, and `str3` are arrays of seven characters. They are initialized with the same value. The size of the array `str1` is fixed. The size of the array `str2` is determined by the number of elements in the initialization. The array `str3` is initialized using an alternative form for string. The variable `strp` is a pointer to char, which has 4 bytes for 32-bit programming or 8 bytes for 64-bit programming. The memory for the string pointed by `strp` is allocated by the compiler or interpreter.

12.5 String Input and Output

Similar to characters, the standard input/output library with the header file **stdio.h** contains functions specifically for handling strings. For example, the function **gets()**, whose prototype is shown below, can be used to input characters from the standard input into buffer `s` until a newline or end-of-file (EOF) character is encountered.

```
char *gets(char *s);
```

The function **fgets()** with prototype

```
char *fgets(char *s, int n, FILE *stream);
```

is similar to the function **gets()**. The **fgets()** function reads bytes from the input `stream` into the array pointed to by `s`, until $n - 1$ bytes are read, or a newline character is read and transferred to `s`, or an EOF condition is encountered. The argument `stream` specifies the input stream to obtain the string and does not have to be the standard input stream. Note that for both functions, a terminating null character is automatically appended to the buffer `s`.

For string output, the function **puts()** with the prototype

```
int puts(const char *s);
```

can be used to print out the string `s` followed by a newline character.

The functions **scanf()** and **printf()** may also be used to read and print strings. For either case, the string conversion specifier `"%s"` is required. The function **sscanf()** is equivalent to **scanf()** except that the input string is read from a character array instead of the standard input. Likewise, the function **sprintf()** stores the output into a character array instead of printing it to the standard output. The prototypes for both functions are shown below.

```
int sscanf(const char *s, const char *format, ...);
int sprintf(char *s, const char *format, ...);
```

It is recommended that the function **fgets()** be used for string input instead of the functions **scanf()** and **gets()**. The functions **scanf()** and **gets()** do not restrict the number of characters entered into the buffer, which may lead to buffer overflow. The *buffer overflow* is a common programming flaw exploited often by computer hackers to break into a system. Because of a potential security flaw caused by buffer overflow, the function **gets()** is obsolete in C and should not be used. The function **fgets()** should be used in C programs. As described in section 8.5.2 in Chapter 8, the Visual C++ 2008 compiler gives a warning message for programs using the function **scanf()** because it is vulnerable for string input.

Program 12.3 uses some of the standard input and output functions to get a string from the standard input and print it out. The function **strlen()** is used to obtain the length of the string and the detail about **strlen()** will be discussed is section 12.8.1. The newline character in `str` is replaced by a null character using the statement

```
str[strlen(str)-1] = '\0';
```

The interactive execution of Program 12.3 is shown below.

```
> getputstr.c
Please input a string.
This is a string
string len = 17, str= This is a string
```

```
/* File: getputstr.c
   Get strings from the terminal keyboard and and print out */
#include <stdio.h>     /* for printf(), fgets(), puts() */
#include <string.h>    /* strlen() */

int main() {
    char str[32];

    printf("Please input a string.\n");
    fgets(str, sizeof(str), stdin); /* obtain a string from the keyboard */
    /* print the string  */
    printf("string len = %d, str= %s\n", strlen(str), str);
    puts(str);

    /* remove the return character at the end of string */
    str[strlen(str)-1] = '\0';
    printf("string len = %d, str= %s\n", strlen(str), str);
    puts(str);
    return 0;
}
```

Program 12.3: Formatted input and output for strings.

```
This is a string

string len = 16, str= This is a string
This is a string
```

The format specifier "%s" for **scanf()** can be used to obtain an input string. But the function will match only a sequence of bytes that are not white-space characters. It cannot be used to handle strings with white spaces. Program 12.4 illustrates the difference of these two functions when handling the input of strings. The format specifier "*c" in the statement

```
scanf("%d*c", &id);
```

is used to skip the carriage return character entered by the user when an identification number is typed in. Otherwise, the subsequent statement for a user name would retrieve only a return character of '\n' in the input buffer. The interactive execution of Program 12.4 is shown below.

```
> scanfgets.c
Please input a string, num, and string
John
name = John
1234
id = 1234
Doe Smith
name = Doe Smith
```

```
/* File: scanfgets.c */
#include <stdio.h>

int main() {
    int id;
    char name[32];

    printf("Please input a string, num, and string.\n");
    scanf("%s", name);
    printf("name = %s\n", name);
    scanf("%d%*c", &id);
    printf("id = %d\n", id);
    fgets(name, sizeof(name), stdin);
    name[strlen(name)-1] = '\0';      /* replace the newline char by '\0' */
    printf("name = %s\n", name);
    return 0;
}
```

Program 12.4: Using **scanf**() and **fgets**() for the input string.

12.6 The Continuation Character

The continuation character '\' can be used to span a string over multiple lines. For example, the following print statement will print a string that takes three lines of code.

```
printf("This is a very very very very very very \
long string that is taking up multiple lines of \
text to write.");
```

Adjacent string literals are treated as a single string literal. For example, the pair of adjacent character string literals

```
"A" "3"
```

produces a single character string literal containing the two characters whose values are 'A' and '3'. Therefore, one can extend a long string across multiple lines by separating the string into shorter ones. For example,

```
printf("This is also a very very very very very"
       "long string, but it is separated into"
       "three shorter strings.");
```

Although the indentations in the above example aid in the readability of the print statement, using the continuation character is more explicit.

12.7 Converting Strings to Numerical Values

In some applications, such as processing the user input from a fill-out form through a Web page, numerical values are typically transferred as strings to a program. The program needs to convert strings to numerical values. String conversion functions are available from the general utilities library defined in the header file **stdlib.h**. These functions can be used to convert a string of digits to integers and floating-point numbers. Table 12.2 lists the string conversion functions and a brief description of their functionality. Note that integer and floating-point values can be converted to strings by the function **sprintf()**.

Program 12.5 illustrates how strings are converted to numerical values and vice versa. First, strings `stri` and `strd` are converted to integer and floating-point values with the functions **atoi()** and **atof()**, respectively. Then these values, stored as int variable `i` and double variable `d`, are inputted into string `str` with the function

Table 12.2 String-conversion functions in stdlib.h.

Function	Description
double atof(const char *s)	Converts string s to **double**.
int atoi(const char *s)	Converts string s to **int**.
long atol(const char *s)	Converts string s to **long int**.
double strtod(const char *s, **char** **endptr)	Converts string s to **double**.
long strtol(const char *s, **char** **endptr, **int** base)	Converts string s to **long**.
unsigned long strtoul(const char *s, **char** **endptr, **int** base)	Converts string s to **unsigned long**.

```
/* File: strtonum.c
   Demonstrate how to convert a string to a numerical number.
   Demonstrate how to a numerical number to a string. */
#include <stdio.h>          /* for printf(), sprintf(), and puts() */
#include <stdlib.h>         /* for atoi() and atof() */

int main() {
    /* declare variables of different types */
    char *stri = "1234";    /* string with an integer number */
    char *strd = "12.34";   /* string with a floating-point number */
    char str[50];           /* string to hold the numbers */
    int i;                  /* variable of int type */
    double d;               /* variable of double type */

    /* convert a string to integer and floating-point numbers */
    i = atoi(stri);          /* convert a string to int */
    printf("i = %d \n",i);
    d = atof(strd);          /* convert a string to double */
    printf("d = %f \n",d);

    /* convert integer and floating-point numbers into a string */
    sprintf(str, "i = %d d = %f", i, d);
    puts(str);
    return 0;
}
```

Program 12.5: Converting strings to numerical values.

sprintf(). The output of Program 12.5 is as follows:

```
i = 1234
d = 12.340000
i = 1234 d = 12.340000
```

As stated in Table 12.2, the function **strtod()** converts the initial portion of string `s` to a numerical value of type double. A pointer to the remaining string is stored in the object pointed to by `endptr`, provided that `endptr` is not a null pointer. Similarly, the function **strtol()** converts the initial portion of the string pointed to by `s` to **long int** representation. Again, provided that `endptr` is not a null pointer, it is assigned the remainder of the string `s`. Integer argument `base` specifies the base of the value converted. The value of `base` can be either 0 or between 2 and 36. A base value of 0 means that the value to be converted can be in octal, decimal, or hexadecimal format. If the value is between 2 and 36, the expected form of the subject sequence is a sequence of letters and digits representing an integer with the radix specified by `base`. The letters from *a* (or *A*) through *z* (or *Z*) are ascribed the values 10 to 35; only letters whose ascribed values are less than that of `base` are permitted. If the value of `base` is 16, the characters *0x* or *0X* may precede the sequence of letters and digits. As an example, consider the following.

```
> double x
> char *endptr
> x = strtod("123abc", &endptr)
123.0000
> x
123.0000
> endptr
abc
> long l
> l = strtol("3456789defghij", &endptr, 0)
3456789
> l
3456789
> endptr
defghij
> l = strtol("1111zzzzzzzz", &endptr, 2)
15
> l
15
> l = strtol("1111zzzzzzzz", &endptr, 16)
4369
> l
4369
```

In the above example, the function **strtod()** converted the numerical portion of the string `"123abc"` to a floating-point value `123.0000` and stored the remainder of the string as `endptr`. Similarly, the function **strtol()**, with the argument `base` equal to 0, converted the string `"3456789defghij"` to a long integer value and remainder `"defghij"`. For a base of 2, the function **strtol()** only reads in numbers less than 2 and converts it into binary. Thus, a base value of 16 would specify a hexadecimal number.

As another example, Program 12.6 contains the source code for the function **getnum()** described in section 9.3 in Chapter 9. The **getnum()** function is used to obtain a number from the console through the

```
/************************************************************
 *  File:          getnum.c
 *  Description: Function returns default number (when RETURN
 *                 or ENTER is entered) or new number from stdin
 *  Input:
 *    msg:         displayed message
 *    d:           default number
 *  Output:        return default or new number
 *  Note:          this file is the same as getnum.chf in Ch
 ***********************************************************/
#include <stdio.h>  /* for NULL, printf(), fgets(), BUFSIZ */
#include <stdlib.h> /* for strtod() */
```

Program 12.6: Get a number from the standard input device. (*Continued*)

```
#include <string.h> /* for strlen() */

double getnum(char *msg, double d) {
  char buf[BUFSIZ],*endptr, *chp;
  int gettingNum = 1; /* initialize to 1 for true */

  if(msg!=NULL)             /* when there is a message, display it */
     printf("%s\n", msg);
  while (gettingNum) {  /* infinite loop, until valid number is entered*/
     chp = fgets(buf, BUFSIZ, stdin); /* get the user input */
     if(strlen(chp)==1)   /* if just hit ENTER, return default value */
        return d;
     buf[strlen(chp)-1] = '\0';/* get rid of the newline char '\n' */
     d = strtod(buf, &endptr); /* change string to double */
     if (strlen(endptr)>0)     /* when invalid number is entered */
        printf("\a%s: invalid number, try again: ",buf);
     else                      /* got a valid number, quit while-loop */
        gettingNum = 0;        /* set to 0 to quit while-loop */
  }
  return d;                    /* return the user entered number */
}
```

Program 12.6: *(Continued)*

standard input stream **stdin**. It utilizes the **fgets()** function to obtain the user's input. The argument `msg` is a string that prompts the user to enter a number, and the argument `d` is the default value. If the user does not specify a number, then `strlen(chp) == 1` is true for the return character `'\n'`, and the default value is returned. If the user types in a number, it is treated as a string. This string is then converted to a numerical value of type double using the function **strtod()**. Note that the statement

```
buf[strlen(chp)-1] = '\0';
```

removes the return character `'\n'` by replacing it with the terminating null character `'\0'`. The macro **BUFSIZ** for the default size is defined in the header file **stdio.h**.

12.8 String Manipulation

The header file **string.h** has several functions useful for manipulating strings. These functions could be used to determine a string's length, compare and manipulate strings, and search and tokenize them. This section will discuss how these string functions in **string.h** and some other miscellaneous ones are used.

12.8.1 Determining String Length

The function **strlen()** is prototyped as follows:

```
size_t strlen(const char *s);
```

This function returns the number of characters before the null character `'\0'` in string `s`. The return data type **size_t** is defined as an unsigned integer type as described in section 3.12 in Chapter 3. As an example of using the function **strlen()**, consider the following:

```
> char str[10] = "Hello"
> str
Hello
> sizeof(str)
10
> strlen(str)
5
```

The size of the character array `str` is 10. Although the number of bytes for the string `"Hello"` is 6, the length of the string is only 5 because the null-terminating character is not included.

12.8.2 Copying Strings

The functions for copying strings in the header file **string.h** are listed in Table 12.3. The functions **strcpy()** and **strncpy()** are used for copying strings. A sample C standard compliant implementation of the function **strcpy()** is shown in Program 11.7 as the function `strcopy()`. Examples of these string copying functions are shown below.

```
> char str1[80] = "abcdefghijk"
> str1
abcdefghijk
> strcpy(str1, "efghij")
efghij
> str1
efghij
> strncpy(str1, "klmnopqrs", 3)
klmhij
> str1
klmhij
> strncpy(str1, "tuv", 5)
tuv
> str1
tuv
```

Table 12.3 String-copying functions.

Function	Description
char *strcpy(char `*s1`**, const char** `*s2`)	Copies string `s2` into `s1`. The value of `s1` is returned.
char *strncpy(char `*s1`**, const char** `*s2`**, size_t** `n`)	Copies at most `n` characters of string `s2` into `s1`. If there are fewer than `n` characters in `s2` before the null terminating character, then null characters are added into `s1` as padding until the specified number has been written. The value of `s1` is returned.

```
/* File: strcpy.c
   Copy a string using the C standard function */
#include <stdio.h>
#include <string.h>                /* for strcpy() */
#include <stdlib.h>                /* for malloc(), free(), exit() */

int main() {
    char *name, str[10];           /* declare strings */

    /* allocate the memory dynamically for string 'name' */
    name = (char *)malloc(sizeof(char)*(strlen("John")+1));
    if(name == NULL) {
      printf("Error: no memory\n");
      exit(EXIT_FAILURE);          /* exit with failure status */
    }
    strcpy(name, "John");          /* copy string "John" to name */
    printf("name = %s\n", name);/* print string name */

    strcpy(str, name);             /* copy string name to str */
    printf("str = %s\n", str);     /* print string str */
    free(name);                    /* free memory allocated for name */
    return 0;
}
```

Program 12.7: Using the function **strcpy**().

Program 12.7 first allocates the memory for `name` using the function **malloc()** by the statement below.

```
name = (char *)malloc(sizeof(char)*(strlen("John")+1));
```

The length of the string to be copied is obtained by the function **strlen()**. Note that an extra byte is added to hold the terminating null character of the string. Allocating the memory for the new string without adding this extra byte is a common mistake.

Typically, a successful program execution terminates after the return statement is reached inside the function **main()**. Another method to cause normal program termination for either successful or unsuccessful execution is to use the function **exit()**. Calling this function returns control to the host environment. The prototype for the function **exit()** is as follows:

```
void exit(int status);
```

The value of status is either **EXIT_SUCCESS** for a successful termination to the calling environment or **EXIT_FAILURE** for an unsuccessful termination. The two macros **EXIT_SUCCESS** and **EXIT_FAILURE** are typically defined as 0 and 1, respectively, in the header file **stdlib.h**. Thus for the example of Program 12.7 the program execution will be terminated if the function **malloc()** fails to allocate the memory.

Using the function **strcpy()**, the string `"John"` is copied to the memory pointed by `name`. The string pointed by `name` is then copied to array `str`, which can hold up to 10 characters. Before the program exits,

```
/* File: stringvla.c (run in C99 and Ch only)
   Compile in gcc, use command 'gcc -std=c99 stringvla.c'
   Allocate memory for a string using VLA in C99 */
#include <stdio.h>
#include <string.h>   /* for strcpy() */

int main() {
    /* allocate memory for name using VLA.
       NOTE: 1 extra byte for the null terminating character '\0' !!! */
    char name[strlen("John")+1];

    strcpy(name, "John");          /* copy string "John" to name */
    printf("name = %s\n", name); /* print string name */
    return 0;
}
```

Program 12.8: Copying a string using a VLA of characters.

the allocated memory is freed. The output of Program 12.7 is as follows:

```
name = John
str = John
```

Program 12.8 is similar to Program 12.7. A function call to **strcpy()** copies the string `"John"` to the buffer `name`. The difference is that a variable length array (VLA) of deferred-shape type array in C99 is used to hold the string. The memory allocated at runtime has enough space to store the characters for `"John"` and the null-terminating character. The output for Program 12.8 is shown below:

```
name = John
```

12.8.3 Appending Strings

The functions **strcat()** and **strncat()**, listed in Table 12.4, append a string to the end of another string. Note that the first character of the appending string `s2` overwrites the null-terminating character for the string-concatenating functions. Also for the function **strncat()**, if the null character is encountered in the string `s2` before `n` characters have been appended, then the null-terminating character is the last to be copied.

Table 12.4 String-concatenating functions.

Function	Description
char *strcat(char `*s1`, **const char** `*s2`)	Appends a copy of string `s2` to `s1`. The value of `s1` is returned.
char *strncat(char `*s1`, **const char** `*s2`, **size_t** `n`)	Appends at most `n` characters of string `s2` to `s1`. The value of `s1` is returned.

An example of using the function **strcat()** is shown below:

```
> char str2[80] = "abcd"
> strcat(str2, "efg")
abcdefg
> str2
abcdefg
```

Program 12.9 allocates memory for the string `s` and prints out values stored in the the string. The program first copies the string `s1` to `s` before appending the string `s2`. Both the lengths of the strings `s1` and `s` are displayed as well. The output is shown below:

```
s = ABCD
s = ABCDabcd
strlen(s1) = 4
strlen(s) = 8
```

```
/* File: strmemory.c
   Dynamically allocate memory for a string */
#include <stdio.h>
#include <string.h>    /* for strcpy(), strcat(), strlen() */
#include <stdlib.h>    /* for malloc(), free(), exit() */

int main() {
    char s1[10]="ABCD", s2[10]="abcd"; /* declare strings */
    char *s;                           /* string needs memory */

    /* Allocate memory for string s to hold s1, s2, and '\0' */
       NOTE: add 1 byte for the null terminating character '\0' !!! */
    s = (char *)malloc(sizeof(char)*(strlen(s1)+strlen(s2)+1));
    if(s==NULL) {
        printf("Error: no memory\n");
        exit (EXIT_FAILURE);
    }
    strcpy(s, s1);              /* copy string s1 to s */
    printf("s = %s\n", s);      /* print string s */
    strcat(s, s2);              /* append string s2 to string s */
    printf("s = %s\n", s);      /* print string s again */
    printf("strlen(s1) = %d\n", strlen(s1)); /* calculate strlen for s1 */
    printf("strlen(s) = %d\n", strlen(s));   /* calculate strlen for s2 */
    free(s);                    /* free the allocated memory for s */
    return 0;
}
```

Program 12.9: Using the function **malloc**() for strings.

```
/* File: strmemoryvla.c (run in C99 and Ch only)
   Compile in gcc, use command 'gcc -std=c99 strmemoryvla.c'
   Allocate memory for a string using VLA in C99 */
#include <stdio.h>
#include <string.h>     /* for strcpy(), strcat(), strlen() */

int main() {
      char s1[10]="ABCD", s2[10]="abcd"; /* declare strings */
      /* NOTE: add 1 byte for the null terminating character '\0' !!! */
      char s[strlen(s1)+strlen(s2)+1];

      strcpy(s, s1);             /* copy string s1 to s */
      printf("s = %s\n", s);  /* print string s */
      strcat(s, s2);             /* append string s2 to string s */
      printf("s = %s\n", s);  /* print string s again */
      printf("strlen(s1) = %d\n", strlen(s1)); /* calculate strlen for s1 */
      printf("strlen(s) = %d\n", strlen(s));   /* calculate strlen for s2 */
      return 0;
}
```

Program 12.10: Using a VLA for strings.

The above result may also be obtained with Program 12.10. The difference between this program and Program 12.9 is that it uses a VLA in C99, a deferred-shape array `s` in this case, to allocate the memory at runtime to store both strings `s1` and `s2`. The function **strlen()** is used to determine the length of the two strings, and the extra byte is for the null-terminating character.

12.8.4 Comparing Strings

Functions for comparing strings are listed in Table 12.5. If the strings are equal, then the functions return zero. If the first string `s1` in the comparison is less than the second string `s2`, a negative number is returned. In contrast, if the first string is greater than the second, a positive number is returned. For example,

```
> char s1[5] = "abcd", s2[5] = "abce", s3[5] = "aacd"
> strcmp(s1, s1)
0
> strcmp(s1, s2)
-1
> strcmp(s2, s1)
1
> strcmp(s1, s3)
1
> strncmp(s1, s2, 3)
0
```

Table 12.5 String-comparison functions.

Function	Description
int strcmp(const char *s1, **const char** *s2)	Compares string s1 with s2.
int strncmp(const char *s1, **const char** *s2, **size_t** n)	Compares up to n characters of string s1 with s2.

In the above example, the strings s1 and s2 are identical up to the third character. Because the ASCII value of character 'd' is less than that of 'e', the string s1 is less than 'e'. Similarly, comparing the strings s1 and s3 shows that there is a difference at the second character position. With 'b' having a greater value than 'a', the string s1 is thus greater than s3. Using the function **strncmp()**, it was found that the first three characters of the strings s1 and s2 are identical.

12.8.5 ‡Searching Strings

The header file **string.h** also contains functions for performing searches on strings. They can be used to search for a character or group of characters in a string. Likewise, search for string within a string is also possible.

Searching a Character in a String

Functions for locating a character inside a string can be found in Table 12.6. The difference between the two listed functions is that the function **strchr()** searches for the first occurrence of the character in a string, whereas the function **strrchr()** searches for the last occurrence. For example,

```
> char str1[80] = "abcdefgdef"
> strchr(str1, 'd')
defgdef
> strchr(str1, 'w')
0000000
> strrchr(str1, 'd')
def
```

In the above example, the function **strchr()** was used to find the first occurrence of character 'd' in the string str1 and return a pointer to that location. However, for the second call to the function **strchr()**, a null pointer is returned because the character 'w' does not appear in the string str1. With the function call to **strrchr()**, a pointer to the last occurrence of character 'd' in the string str1 is returned.

Searching Characters in a String

The functions in Table 12.7 all perform searches on a string, s1, to determine occurrences of characters specified by whether or not they are included in another the string, s2. For example, the following commands

Table 12.6 Functions for searching a character.

Function	Description
char *strchr(const char *s, **int** c)	Finds the first occurrence of character c in string s. If c is found, a pointer to c in s is returned. Otherwise, a NULL pointer is returned.
char *strrchr(const char *s, **int** c)	Finds the last occurrence of c in string s. If c is found, a pointer to c in string s is returned. Otherwise, a NULL pointer is returned.

Table 12.7 Function for searching characters.

Function	Description
size_t strcspn(const char *s1, **const char** *s2)	Returns the length of the initial segment of string s1 consisting of characters not contained in string s2.
size_t strspn(const char *s1, **const char** *s2)	Returns the length of the initial segment of string s1 consisting only of characters contained in string s2.
size_t strpbrk(const char *s1, **const char** *s2)	Finds the first occurrence in string s1 of any character in string s2. If a character from string s2 is found, a pointer to the character in string s1 is returned. Otherwise, a NULL pointer is returned.

show how to use these functions for searching strings.

```
> strcspn("this is a test", "ab")
8
> strspn("this is a test", "sith ")
8
> strpbrk("this is a test" " absj")
s is a test
```

In the above example, the function call to **strcspn()** searches the string "this is a test" to find the first occurrence of either 'a' or 'b'. The value 8 is returned because it is the number of characters skipped to reach character 'a'. In contrast, the call to function **strspn()** returns the length of the string before the search reaches a character not specified in the second string argument "siht". The function **strpbrk()** is similar to the function **strcspn()**, except that it returns a pointer to the first occurrence of a character found in the string argument "absj". That is why "s is a test" is returned.

Searching a String in Another String

The function **strstr()** in the header file **string.h** is used to search for a string within another string. It is prototyped as follows:

```
char *strstr(const char *s1, const char *s2);
```

where s2 is the string to be searched in s1. If the string s2 is found, then a pointer to that place in s1 is returned. Otherwise, a NULL pointer is returned. For example, the command below returns the last part of the string "this is a test" where the substring "a" is found.

```
> strstr("this is a test", "a")
a test
```

12.8.6 ‡Tokenizing Strings

A string may be broken up into *tokens*. A token in this context is a series of characters separated by certain characters described as *delimiting characters*, which are usually spaces or punctuation marks. (The definition of token here for the function **strtok()** is different from that used as a lexical element of the C language described in section 3.2 in Chapter 3.) The function **strtok()** is usually used to tokenize a string. Its prototype is as follows:

```
char *strtok(char *s1, const char *s2);
```

The argument s1 is the string to be tokenized, whereas the argument s2 contains the specified delimiters. To tokenize an entire string, the first function call to **strtok()** will use s1 as the first argument, while each subsequent call will use NULL. The function **strtok()** returns a pointer to the current token. If there are no more tokens, the function returns NULL. At the exit of the **while** loop, the content pointed to by s1 will be changed. As an example, consider Program 12.11, which tokenizes the string "Comma, colon: and space are delimiters". The output is shown below:

```
token = Comma
token = colon
token = and
token = space
token = are
token = delimiters
str = Comma
```

The function **strtok()** is implemented using a static variable inside the function. It is not thread-safe; i.e., the function cannot be called simultaneously by different threads. The function cannot also not be called inside nested loops to obtain tokens from different strings. For applications in multithreads or nested loops, the function **strtok_r()** shall be used. The function **strtok_r()**, prototyped as

```
char *strtok_r(char *s1, const char *s2, char **lasts);
```

```
/* File: strtok.c
   Get tokens from a string */
#include <stdio.h>
#include <string.h> /* for strtok() */

int main() {
    /* declare the original string */
    char *str = "Comma, colon: and space are delimiters";
    char *delimit = " ,:";  /* delimiters ' ', ':', and ',' */
    char *token;            /* contain a token */

    token = strtok(str, delimit);    /* initial call to strtok() */
    while(token!= NULL) {            /* looping, till all tokens are obtained */
        printf("token = %s\n", token);   /* print a token */
        token = strtok(NULL, delimit);   /* get the next token */
    }
    printf("str = %s\n", str); /* see, original string has been messed up! */
    return 0;
}
```

Program 12.11: Using the function **strtok()**.

```
/* File: strtok_r.c
   Get tokens from a string using thread-safe reentrant function strtok_r() */
#include <stdio.h>
#include <string.h>
#include <string.h> /* for strtok_r() */

int main() {
    /* declare the original string */
    char *str = "Comma, colon: and space are delimiters";
    char *delimit = " ,:";   /* delimiters ' ', ':', and ',' */
    char *token, *endptr = NULL; /* contain a token, and a pointer
                                    to save the end of string */

    token = strtok_r(str, delimit, &endptr); /* initial call to strtok() */
    while(token!= NULL) {           /* looping, till all tokens are obtained */
        printf("token = %s\n", token);   /* print a token */
        token = strtok_r(NULL, delimit, &endptr); /* get the next token */
    }
    printf("str = %s\n", str); /* see, original string has been messed up! */
    return 0;
}
```

Program 12.12: Using the function **strtok_r**().

is similar to the function **strtok**(). It can be used to tokenize the string `s1` with delimiters specified by `s2`. The difference is that the `lasts` pointer can keep track of the next substring in which to search for the next token and allows reentry into the function **strtok_r**(). Program 12.12 is almost the same as Program 12.11 except that the function **strtok_r**() is used instead of **strtok**(). The output of Program 12.12 is the same as that of Program 12.11.

‡An Application Example

Obtaining Web Addresses

In this section, an example will be used to demonstrate how string functions are used in applications. Many search engines index Web pages in a database. To do this, it is necessary to find all other hyperlinks from a Web page. A complete hyperlink in a Web page typically is enclosed in a pair of double quotation marks starting with `http://`. For example, the statement

```
Click <a href="http://www.ucdavis.edu">here</a>
```

in a Hyphertext Markup Language (HTML) file contains a hyperlink to the universal resource locator (URL) Web address `http://www.ucdavis.edu`.

Program 14.7 in Chapter 14 can obtain all Web addresses hyperlinked from an HTML file. Program 12.13 can obtain all hyperlinked Web addresses entered by the user. For example, the program `geturl.c` can be executed interactively as follows:

```
> geturl.c
Please input a string with URL address such as
"http://www.softintegration.com"
Click <a href="http://www.ucdavis.edu">here</a>
http://www.ucdavis.edu
```

At the prompt, the user types

```
Click <a href="http://www.ucdavis.edu">here</a>
```

The program processes the user input and displays

```
http://www.ucdavis.edu
```

Program 12.13 uses the function **fgets()** to save the user input into the string `line`. The **while** loop in Program 12.13 is used to retrieve multiple URL addresses in the same line. If the **while** loop is replaced

```
/* File: geturl.c
   Get the URL web address from the terminal input */
#include <stdio.h>        /* printf(), fgets() */
#include <string.h>       /* for strstr(), strchr(), strcpy(), strncpy() */
#define LINESIZE 1024     /* the maximum input line length */

int main() {
    /* declare strings line for the input string, url for URL address
       beginptr for the beginning of the URL address,
       endptr for the end of the URL address */
    char line[LINESIZE], url[LINESIZE], *beginptr, *endptr;
    int len;  /* the len of the URL address */

    printf("Please input a string with URL address such as\n");
    printf("\"http://www.softintegration.com\"\n");
    fgets(line, LINESIZE, stdin); /* get the user input */
    /* find "http:// in the string */
    /* There might be multiple URL addresses in the user input line */
    while (beginptr = strstr(line, "\"http://"))
    {
        beginptr++; /* skip " in "http:// */
        /* find the closing " */
        endptr = strchr(beginptr, '"');
        if(endptr != NULL)  /* when there is " */
        {
            len = endptr - beginptr; /* calculate the length of URL address */
            strncpy(url, beginptr, len); /* copy URL address to url */
```

Program 12.13: Retrieving a Web address from an input line. *(Continued)*

```
            url[len] = '\0';           /* append a null character for url */
            printf("%s\n",url );       /* got a URL, print it */
            strcpy(line, endptr);      /* update string line to find next URL */
        }
        else { /* set line to a null terminating character to quit while-loop */
            line[0] = '\0';
        }
    }
    return 0;
}
```

Program 12.13: *(Continued)*

with a compound **if** statement, the program will obtain only one Web address even if there are multiple addresses in the same input line. It first locates the string token `"http://` in the input line by the following expression

```
beginptr = strstr(line, "\"http://")
```

A double quotation mark character is escaped inside a string.

Within the body of the **while** loop, the expression

```
beginptr++;
```

advances the pointer `beginptr` to the next character by skipping the double quotation mark character. The variable `beginptr` then points to the first character of the URL address. The statement

```
endptr = strchr(beginptr, '"');
```

looks for the enclosing double quotation mark starting from the beginning of the URL address. If there is an enclosing double quotation mark, the variable `endptr` points to the enclosing double quotation mark, as shown in Figure 12.1. The total length of the URL address is obtained by the statement

```
len = endptr -beginptr;
```

The subtraction of two pointers gives the number of elements between two pointers. Both variables `endptr` and `beginptr` are pointers to char. The above expression gives the number of characters between `endptr` and `beginptr`, which is the length of the URL address. The function call

```
strncpy(url, beginptr, len);
```

copies the URL address from the input line pointed by `beginptr` to the array `url`. Unlike the function **strcpy()**, the function **strncpy()** does not copy a null-terminating character for a string. The statement

```
url[len] = '\0';
```

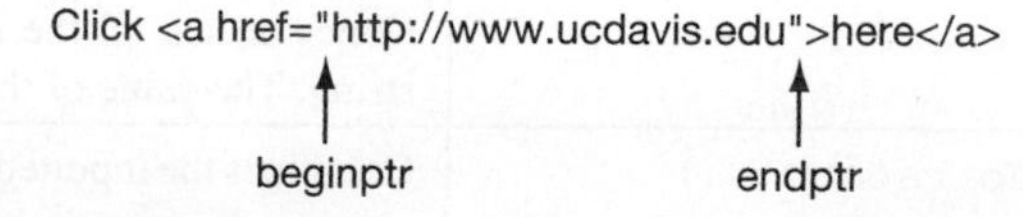

Figure 12.1 Pointers point to the beginning and end of a Web address.

assigns a null character to the element `url[len]` to terminate the string. After a valid URL address is printed out on the screen, the buffer `line` is updated with the remaining contents in the original string by the function call

```
strcpy(line, endptr);
```

The **while** loop starts the next iteration. The conditional expression of the **while** loop will process the contents in the buffer `line` again. If there is no enclosing double quotation mark, the buffer `line` is cleaned up by setting its first character as a null-terminating character. The **while** loop will then terminate.

12.8.7 ‡Additional String Manipulation Functions

Although not part of the C standard library, the C functions listed in Table 12.8 are available in many platforms and in Ch.

For example, consider the code below.

```
> char *buffer
> char test[90] = "abcd"
> buffer= strdup("John")
John
> buffer
John
> free(buffer)
> buffer = strconcat(test, "efgh", "ijk")
abcdefghijk
> test
abcd
> free(buffer)
> buffer = strjoin("+", test, "efgh", "ijk")
abcd+efgh+ijk
```

Table 12.8 Additional functions for string manipulation.

Function	Description
char *strdup(const char *`s`)	Duplicates a string pointed to by `s`. This function returns a pointer to the duplicated string.
int strcasecmp(const char `*s1`, **const char** `*s2`)	Compares the two strings `s1` and `s2` similar to function **strcmp()**, except that case is ignored.
int strncasecmp(const char `*s1`, **const char** `*s2`, **int** `n`)	Compares up to `n` characters of strings `s1` and `s2`. This function is also case insensitive.
char *strconcat(const char `*s1, ...`)	Concatenates all the inputted strings into a single string. The value of the new string is returned.
char *strjoin(const char `*separator, ...`)	Combines the inputted strings to a single string separated by the specified delimiter string `separator`.

```
> free(buffer)
> strcasecmp("this", "THIS")
0
```

The function **strdup()** is used to duplicate a string. Note that the memory allocated by this function needs to be deallocated by the function **free()** later.

The function **strconcat()** is used to append the string `"efgh"` to the string `test` and then append `"ijk"` to the result. The function **strjoin()** is also used to combine the three strings, but they are separated by `"+"`. The memory allocated inside the functions **strconcat()** and **strjoin()** shall be allocated by the function **free()**.

Using the case-insensitive function **strcasecmp()**, the strings `"this"` and `"THIS"` are equivalent.

12.9 ‡Memory Functions in a String-Handling Library

The memory functions in the header file **stdlib.h** can be used to manipulate, compare, and search blocks of memory. They are listed in Table 12.9. The parameters for these functions use generic pointers to void. This allows functions to be passed with arguments of pointers to any data type, as described in section 11.12 in Chapter 11. Because a void pointer cannot be dereferenced, each function has to receive a size argument specifying the number of bytes, or characters, to process. The argument for the number of characters of these functions is of unsigned integer type **size_t** as described in section 3.12 in Chapter 3. It can be used to address the memory space for both 32-bit and 64-bit computers.

Table 12.9 Memory functions.

Function	Description
void *memcpy(void `*s1`, **const void** `*s2`, **size_t** `n`)	Copies `n` characters from the object pointed to by `s2` into the object pointed to by `s1`. A pointer to the resulting object is returned.
void *memmove(void `*s1`, **const void** `*s2`, **size_t** `n`)	Copies `n` characters from the object pointed to by `s2` into the object pointed to by `s1`. For this function, the characters in `s2` are first copied into a temporary space before they are copied to `s1`. `s1` and `s2` can overlap. A pointer to the resulting object is returned.
int memcmp(const void `*s1`, **const void** `*s2`, **size_t** `n`)	Compares the first `n` characters of the objects pointed to by `s1` and `s2`. The function returns 0, less than 0 or greater than 0 if `s1` is equal to, less than, or greater than `s2`, respectively.
void *memchr(const void `*s`, **int** `c`, **size_t** `n`)	Finds the first occurrence of `c`, converted to **unsigned char**, in the first `n` characters of the object pointed to by `s`. If `c` is found, a pointer to `c` in the object is returned. Otherwise, NULL is returned.
void *memset(void `*s`, **int** `c`, **size_t** `n`)	Copies `c`, converted to **unsigned char**, into the first `n` characters pointed to by `s`. A pointer to the resulting object is returned.

```
/* File: memcopy.c
   Copy contents in the memory using memcpy() */
#include <stdio.h>
#include <string.h>  /* for memcpy() */

int main() {
  /* declare strings */
  char s1[10]="ABCD1234", s2[10];
  char *p;  /* declare p as a pointer to char */
  /* declare variables d1 and d2 of double type, dp of pointer to double */
  double d1 = 12.1234, d2, *dp;

  /* for strings, memcpy() is the same as strcpy() */
  p = memcpy(s2, s1, 6);       /* copy 6 characters from s1 to s2 */
  printf("s1 = %s\n", s1);     /* print s1 */
  s2[6] = '\0';                /* append a null terminating character */
  printf("s2 = %s\n", s2);     /* print string s2 */
  printf("p = %s\n", p);       /* print string s2 through p */

  /* memcpy() can be used to copy objects of other types */
  /* copy an object of double, form d1 to d2 */
  dp = (double *)memcpy((void*)&d2, (void *)&d1, sizeof(double));
  printf("d2 = %f\n", d2);     /* print d2 */
  printf("*dp = %f\n", *dp);   /* print d2 through dp */
  return 0;
}
```

Program 12.14: Using the function **memcpy**().

Program 12.14 is an example to illustrate how to use the function **memcpy()**. This program first copies the string `s1` into the string `s2`. Then it copies the value of the variable `d1` in `d2`. The output of Program 12.14 is as follows:

```
s1 = ABCD1234
s2 = ABCD12
p = ABCD12
d2 = 12.123400
*dp = 12.123400
```

12.10 The main() Function and Command-Line Arguments

The main routine **main()** is a special function. Command-line arguments or parameters can be passed to a program through the arguments of the function **main()** with the function prototype, as shown below.

```
int main(int argc, char *argv[]);
```

The first argument, conventionally called `argc` for argument count, is the number of the command-line arguments; the second, called `argv` for argument vector, is a pointer to an array of character strings of variable length. Each string contains one argument of the command line. Therefore, the argument `argv` can also be considered as a pointer to pointer to char. Then, the function **main()** can be written alternatively as

```
int main(int argc, char **argv);
```

When a program is invoked, values for the arguments `argc` and `argv` of the function **main()** are passed to the program by the host environment. The string expression `argv[0]` is the name of the program so that the value of `argc` is at least 1. If `argc` is 1, there are no command-line argument after the program name. In addition, the value of `argv[argc]` is a null pointer.

For example, Program 12.15 will print out the number of command-line arguments and all the arguments of the command line. This program can be executed in the command-line mode as follows.

```
> mainarg.c arg1 arg2
argc = 3
argv[0] = mainarg.c
argv[1] = arg1
argv[2] = arg2
```

When the command

```
mainarg.c arg1 arg2
```

is processed, the system will create an array of pointer to char shown in Figure 12.2. This array has four elements. The first element points to the command string `"mainarg.c"`, the subsequent elements point to the remaining arguments in the command line, and the last one is assigned a null pointer. This array of pointer to char is then passed to the second argument `argv` of the function **main()**.

```
/* File: mainarg.c
   Obtain the command line arguments through function main() */
#include <stdio.h>

/* argc contains the number of arguments in the command line,
   including the program name. argv is an array of strings,
    each string contains an argument */
int main(int argc, char *argv[])
/* or int main(int argc, char **argv) */
{
    int i;

    printf("argc = %d\n", argc); /* print the number of argument */
    for(i=0; i<argc; i++) {      /* print each command line argument */
        printf("argv[%d] = %s\n", i, argv[i]);
    }
    return 0;
}
```

Program 12.15: Arguments of the function **main**().

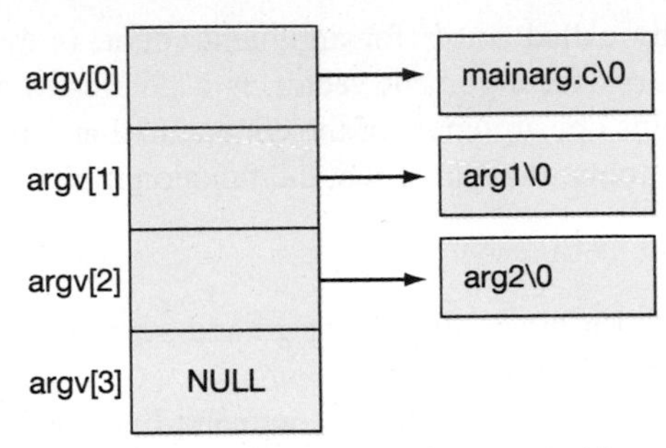

Figure 12.2: The array of pointer to char created for a command.

12.10.1 ‡Handling Option Flags in Command-Line Arguments

One of the conventions of Unix-style commands, as shown in Table 2.1 in Chapter 2 and section 3.15.4 in Chapter 3, is that the argument beginning with a minus sign `'-'` indicates an option flag. As another example, the program **which.ch** in Ch can take two valid options, `-a` and `-v`. The command

```
which -a name
```

finds all commands, including function files, environment variables, and header files with `name`. The command

```
which -v name
```

sends out search messages if the `name` is not found. These two options can be used at the same time in the form of

```
which -a -v name
```

or

```
which -va name
```

For example, the command **which.ch** executed in Windows with the option `-a pwd` may produce the following output.

```
> which -a pwd
C:/Ch/bin/pwd.exe
C:/Ch/include/pwd.h
```

Program 12.16 is the code for handling command-line arguments, which is extracted from the program **which.ch**. Here, the variables `a_option` and `v_option` indicate whether the options `-a` and `-v` are on or

```
/* File: commandline.c
   Process command line argument with options -a or -av etc. */
#include <stdio.h>
#include <stdlib.h>   /* for exit() */

#define TRUE  1          /* define boolean value true */
#define FALSE 0          /* define boolean value false */
```

Program 12.16: Handling command-line options. (*Continued*)

```
int main(int argc, char *argv[]) {
  char *s, *cmd;          /* declare variables s and cmd */
  int a_option = FALSE; /* default, no -a option */
  int v_option = FALSE; /* default, no -v option */

  cmd = argv[0];          /* save cmd in argv[0] */
  if(argc == 1){          /* no argument */
     printf("Usage: %s [-av] names \n", cmd);
     exit(EXIT_FAILURE);
  }

  argc--; argv++;  /* skip the command, the 1st one in the argument list */
  /* process each argument beginning with - */
  while(argc > 0 && **argv == '-') {
     /* empty space is not valid option */
     /* use a for-loop to handle multiple options followed
        with '-' such as as '-av', "s = argv[0]+1" skips '-'   */
     for(s = argv[0]+1; *s!='\0'; s++)
     {
        switch(*s) /* compare the character */
        {
          case 'a':            /* if it is 'a' in '-a', '-av', or '-va' */
             a_option = TRUE;
             break;
          case 'v':             /* if it is 'v' in '-v', '-av', or '-va' */
             v_option = TRUE;
             break;
          default:               /* unknown character such as 'w' in '-w' */
             printf("Warning: invalid option %c\n", *s);
             printf("Usage: %s [-av] names \n", cmd);
             break;
        }
     }
     argc--; argv++;             /* move to the next argument */
  }

  /* when options -a and/or -v is on the command line, print it */
  if(a_option)
     printf("option -a is on\n");
  if(v_option)
     printf("option -v is on\n");
  while(argc > 0) { /* print out the remaining arguments  */
     printf("%s\n",  *argv);
```

Program 12.16: *(Continued)*

```
        argc--; argv++;
    }
    return 0;
}
```

Program 12.16: *(Continued)*

not. Their values are `false` by default. If there is no command-line argument, the program will print out the error message because the program **which.ch** has at least one argument, that is, the name to be searched for. Two loops are needed to process command-line options: one for each option starting with the minus sign `'-'`, and the other for each option letter following the symbol `'-'`. The **while** loop in this program handles all arguments that begin with the symbol `'-'`. The address for the first argument in a string `argv[0]` for the command name is saved in the variable `cmd`. At each iteration, the number of unprocessed arguments increments 1 by the expression `argc--` and the current argument becomes `argv[0]` by the expression `argv++`. If the argument begins with the minus sign, the equality

```
**argv == '-'
```

equivalent to `argv[0][0] == '-'`, holds. A **for** loop is used to obtain multiple option letters following the symbol `'-'`, such as `-av`, in the current string argv[0]. The expression

```
s = argv[0]+1
```

equivalent to `*argv+1 == '-'`, makes `s` point to the second character of this argument. More information about pointers to pointers is available in section 11.9 in Chapter 11. The loop continuation condition expression

```
*s != '\0'
```

allows the iteration of the **for** loop to continue till the end of the current string argv[0]. If the characters `'a'` and `'v'` are found in these arguments, the variables `a_option` and `v_option` are both set to true, respectively, within a switch statement. If other characters following the option character `'-'` are found, the error messages will be printed out. At the end of Program 12.16, options and the remaining command-line arguments are printed out.

Assuming that the file name of Program 12.16 is `commandline.c`, the results from executing Program 12.16 with different options are shown below.

```
> commandline.c -a -v arg1
option -a is on
option -v is on
arg1
> commandline.c -av arg1
option -a is on
option -v is on
arg1
> commandline.c -v arg1 arg2
option -v is on
arg1
arg2
```

```
> commandline.c
Usage: commandline.c [-av] names
```

The program expects at least one argument from the command line. If there is not at least one argument, the proper usage of the command will be displayed.

An Application Example

Force of a Moving Body

Problem Statement:

For the mechanical system shown in Figure 2.12, given mass $m = 5$ kilograms (kg), gravitational acceleration constant $g = 9.81m/s^2$ and coefficient of kinetic friction $\mu = 0.2$, the applied force p is expressed as a function of time t in

$$p(t) = 4\sin(t - 3) + 20$$

Write a program to calculate the force p and acceleration a with time entered at the command line. The force p will be printed only when the program is invoked with the command-line option `-p`.

The solution to the above problem is shown in Program 12.17. The function `force()` calculates the external force applied on the system at time `t`. The function **main()** performs a check to determine whether

```
/* File: acceloption.c
   Calculate accelerations with time from the command line.
   When the command line has an option -p, print force. */
#include <stdio.h>
#include <stdlib.h>        /* for exit() */
#define TRUE  1            /* define boolean value true */
#define FALSE 0            /* define boolean value false */
#define M_G   9.81         /* gravitational acceleration constant g */

double force(double t) { /* function for force */
    double p;
    p = 4*(t-3)+20;
    return p;
}
int main(int argc, char **argv) {
    char *s, *cmd;          /* declare variables s and cmd */
    int p_option = FALSE; /* default, no -p option */
    double a, mu, m, p, t; /* declare a, mu, m, p, t for calculating accel */

    cmd = argv[0];          /* save cmd in argv[0] */
    if(argc < 2 || argc > 3) {   /* not enough or extra argument */
```

Program 12.17: Calculating acceleration with command-line options. (*Continued*)

```
        printf("Usage: %s [-p] time \n", cmd);
        printf("        -p will print out the force.\n");
        exit(EXIT_FAILURE);
    }

    argc--; argv++;  /* skip the command, the 1st one in the argument list */
    /* process each argument beginning with - */
    while(argc > 0 && **argv == '-') {
       /* empty space is not valid option */
       /* use a for-loop to handle multiple options followed
          with '-' such as as '-p', "s = argv[0]+1" skips '-'   */
       for(s = argv[0]+1; *s != '\0'; s++) {
         switch(*s) {
           case 'p':                     /* if *s is 'p' in '-p' */
             p_option = TRUE;            /* print out force   */
             break;
           default:
             printf("Warning: invalid option %c\n", *s);
             printf("Usage: %s [-p] time \n", cmd);
             printf("        -p will print out the force.\n");
             exit(EXIT_FAILURE);
         }
       }
       argc--; argv++;                /* move to the next argument */
    }
    /* convert string to double for time entered in command line,
       then calculate and display the acceleration */
    t = atof(argv[0]);                /* convert a string to double */
    mu = 0.2; m = 5.0; p = force(t);
    a = (p-mu*m*M_G)/m;
    if(p_option)                      /* if has -p option , print force */
      printf("Force p = %f\n", p);
    printf("Acceleration a = %f\n", a);
    return 0;
}
```

Program 12.17: *(Continued)*

the command-line option `-p` is specified for the program execution. If this is the case, then the program displays both the force and acceleration values. If the option `-p` is not specified, then only the value for the acceleration is printed out. The time entered at the command-line input is converted from a string to a floating-point number using the function **atof()**. The conditional statement

```
if(argc < 2 || argc > 3)
```

will make sure that the program is invoked with either two or three arguments, including the program name itself. For example,

```
> acceloption.c 2
Acceleration a = 1.238000
> acceloption.c -p 2.0
Force p = 16.000000
Acceleration a = 1.238000
```

12.11 Making It Work

12.11.1 Debugging Programs with Command-Line Arguments in ChIDE

There are three different methods to run a program with command-line arguments in ChIDE.

1. You can preset program parameters. Click the command `View | Parameters`; you can input your parameter values. It allows up to four parameters in total. Then run the program in the editing pane.
2. You can type the command, such as

   ```
   ch filename.c arg1 arg2 arg3 arg4 arg5 arg6
   ```

   in the output pane to run the program `filename.c`.
3. To run the program in the editing pane in the debug mode, type

   ```
   debug> start arg1 arg2 arg3 arg4 arg5 arg6
   ```

   inside the debug command pane.

Exercises

1. Identify and correct the errors in the following code. If there are errors, briefly explain them.

   a.
   ```
   char *s1 = "abcdefg", *s2;
   s2 = (char *)malloc(strlen(s1));
   strcpy(s2, s1);
   printf("%s\n", s);
   ```

   b.
   ```
   char *s1 = "abcdefg", *s2;
   s2 = (char *)malloc(sizeof(s1)+1);
   strcpy(s2, s1);
   printf("%s\n", s);
   ```

   c.
   ```
   #include <stdlib.h>
   #include <string.h>
   int main() {
       char s1[4] = "abcd";
       char s2[]  = "1234";
       char *s3;

       s3 = (char*) malloc(sizeof(char)*(strlen(s1)+sizeof(s2)));
       strcpy(s3, s1);
   ```

```
    strcat(s3, s2);
    printf("s3 = %c\n", s3);
    return 0;
}
```

d.
```
char *s1 = "abcd", s2[] = "ABCD", *s3, s4[5];
s3 = s1;
printf("s3 = %s\n", s3);
s3 = s2;
printf("s3 = %s\n", s3);
s4 = s1;
printf("s4 = %s\n", s4);
s4 = s2;
printf("s4 = %s\n", s4);
```

2. In some programming languages, strings are entered and surrounded by either single or double quotation marks. Write a program that reads the three strings `suzy`, `"suzy"`, and `'suzy'`. Are the single and double quotes ignored by C or read as part of the string?
3. What is the output of the following program?

```
char c[4][6] = {
   'a', 'b', 'c', 'd', 'e', '\0',
   'f', 'g', 'h', 'i', 'j', '\0',
   'k', 'l', 'm', 'n', 'o', '\0',
   'p', 'q', 'r', 's', 't', '\0'
  };
int n=4, m=6;
int i=2, j=3;
printf("%c\n", *(c[i]+j));
printf("%c\n", *((char *)c+i*m+j));
printf("%s\n", c[i]);
printf("%s\n", *(c+i+1));
```

4. What is the output of the following program?

```
char *c[] = {
           "ARRAY",
           "OF",
           "POINTERS",
           "TO",
           "CHAR",
           NULL
          };

char **cp[] = {(char **)c+3, (char **)c+2, (char **) c+1, (char **)c};
char ***cpp = cp;

int main() {
```

```
    printf("%s ", **++cpp);      /* **++cpp    <==> **(++cpp)    */
    ++cpp;
    printf("%s\n", *--*cpp+2); /* *--*cpp+2 <==> (*(--(*cpp)))+2 */
}
```

5. Write a function `countchars()` with the prototype

```
int countchars(const char *str, char ch);
```

that returns how many times a certain character is found in a string. For example, if the input string is `"Under the sun"` and the input character is `'u'`, the returned value is 1.

6. Write a function `reversestring()` with the prototype

```
void reversestring(const char *s1, char *s2);
```

The string `s1` is the input and the string `s2` is the output. They are the same except that the letters in the string are in reverse order. For example, if `s1` is `"letter"`, the function changes `s1` to `"rettel"`.

7. Write a program that uses the function **strcmp()** to compare two strings input by the user. The program should state whether the first string is less than, equal to, or greater than the second string.
8. Write a program that uses the function **strncmp()** to compare two strings input by the user. The program should input the number of characters to be compared. The program should state whether the first string is less than, equal to, or greater than the second string.
9. Write a program that reads four strings and prints only those strings beginning with the letter `'b'`.
10. Write a program that inputs four lines of text and uses **strtok()** to count the total number of words. Assume that the words are separated by either spaces or newline characters.
11. Write a program that inputs four strings that represent integers, converts the strings to integers, sums the values, and prints the total of the four values.
12. Write a program that inputs four strings that represent floating-point values, converts the strings to double values, sums the values, and prints the total of the four values. Input the strings `"2", "10.5", "12", "12.5"` to test your program.
13. Write a C function called `printToken()`, which will print out the tokens

```
abc ABC ABCD
123 456 789 abc
```

based on the value in its argument of pointer to char. Use the function strtok() with delimiters of `" *,;:"`.

```
#include<stdio.h>
#include<string.h>
void  printToken(char *s);
int main(){
    char s1[] = "abc*ABC ABCD";
    char s2[] = "123:456,789;abc";
    printToken(s1);
    printToken(s2);
}
void  printToken(char *s) {
```

14. Complete the function `my_strncpy()` in the program below. The function `my_strncpy()` copies the string, which can be no more than `n` bytes long, pointed to by `s2` (including the terminating `'\0'`

character) to the array pointed to by s1. If there is no null byte among the first n bytes of s2, the result will not be null-terminated. In the case where the length of s2 is less than n, the remainder of s1 will be padded with nulls. The function returns s1.

```
#include <stdio.h>
/* #include <string.h> */
char *my_strncpy(char *s1, char *s2, size_t n) {
   /* add your code here */
}
int main() {
      char *p, s[10]="123456789", s2[]="abcd";

      p = my_strncpy(s, s2, 2);
      printf("s = %s\n", s);
      printf("p = %s\n", p);
      my_strncpy(s, s2, 10);
      printf("s = %s\n", s);
      return 0;
}
```

15. Write a program to read the radius of a circle in meters from the command line. The program prints out the radius and area of the circle. Test your program with the command-line option shown below.

```
> circle.c 3.5
```

16. Write a program to read the radius of a sphere in meters from the command line. The program prints out the radius and volume of the sphere. Test your program with the command-line option shown below.

```
> sphere.c 3.5
```

17. Write a program to read a radius from the command line. The program will print out the value of the radius. The command-line option -c will print out the area of the circle whereas the option -s will print out the volume of the sphere. Test your program with the command-line options shown below.

```
> radius.c 5
> radius.c -c 5
> radius.c -s 5
> radius.c -c -s 5
> radius.c -cs 5
```

18. Write a program to extract Web addresses starting with www. and ending with .edu. The program displays Web addresses contained in the input entered by the user. Test your program with the following two lines.

```
http://www.mit.edu
<a href="http://www.ucdavis.edu"> UC Davis </a>
```

19. Write a program to remove comments in each of the following C statements, which is stored in a string. Print out each modified statement without comments.

a. Remove a comment in the following statement:

```
int i;   /* comment */
```

b. Remove comments in the following statement:

```
int i;   /* comment1 */ i = 90; /* comment2 */
```

20. Modify Program 11.2 to perform the following tasks:

a. To reverse an input word up to 10 characters. Test your program with the input words `number` and `numbers`.

b. To reverse input characters with no limit on the number of characters. The program first allocates 10 bytes to hold characters from the user input. If the allocated memory is not enough to hold the input characters, the function **realloc()** can be called repeatedly to reallocate the memory. Test your program with the input word `experimental`.

21. The *cryptography* studies information hiding. An ordinary plain text can be encrypted into an unintelligible gibberish cipher text. To encode and decode messages, a *key* is typically used for replacement of certain characters. Write the program `encode.c` with 26 elements of the encoding key shown below:

```
char key[27] ="efghijklmnopqrstuvwxyzabcd";   /* encoding key */
```

The first character in the array `key` contains the character that replaces the letter 'a', the second character replaces the letter 'b', and so forth. In this case, each character is replaced by another character that is four positions away in the alphebetic sequence. The letter 'a' is replaced by the letter 'e', 'b' by 'f', 'c' by 'g', and so on. The program reads a string, encodes the input string, and displays the encoded string. The program shall be executed as follows:

```
> encode.c
Please input a string
America
The encoded string is: Aqivmge
```

22. Write the program `decode.c` to read a string that was encoded by the program `encode.c` described in Exercise 21, decode the input string, and display the decoded string. Test the program using the encoded string `Aqivmge`.

CHAPTER 13

Structures, Enumerations, Unions, and Bit Fields

13.1 Structures

In previous chapters, we have shown how to represent numbers and characters, and arrays of these objects in C. Some problems cannot be conveniently modeled using these simple objects. Structures in C are used to model complex objects for solving complicated problems in engineering and science. *Structures* may be thought of as a collection of components, known as *members* or *member fields*, that can have different data types. Unlike arrays, which represent a set of data with the same type, structures usually are used to store a set of related data of different types. For example, records of an individual's personal information are typically categorized by their name, identification number (such as social security number), and date of birth. So for electronic records, these values may be stored as individual variables, such as an integer value for the person's identification number and a character array for the name. Thus, two variables, `id` of type int and `name` of type array of chars, might be used to create a person's record:

```
int id;
char name[32];
```

Using separate variables, such as `id` and `name`, is suitable for storing one person's information. Arrays of separate variables for identification number and names may be utilized for a small group of people. But if a list of records contains hundreds or thousands of individuals, then it would be more difficult to access and maintain a person's information because the data are scattered. It is preferable to create a single variable to store all relevant data for a person. In the above case, a structure can be used to group a set of data storing an individual's identification number and name. The structure can be used to store all information of an individual. At the end of this chapter, a GPA (grade point average) library will be developed to illustrate applications and various features of structures in software development.

Structures described in this chapter are also useful to implement dynamic data structures such as linked lists, stacks, queues, and trees, which will be described in Chapter 15. Many problems can be more conveniently solved using these dynamic data structures.

13.1.1 Structure Definition

The *structure type* is a collection of members that can have different data types. The following is an example of a simple structure.

```
struct Student {
    int id;
```

	id	name
Bytes	4	32

Figure 13.1: Memory storage for `struct Student`.

```
    char name[32];
};
```

where the keyword **struct** introduces the definition for the structure `Student` with a list of declarations enclosed in braces. The structure `Student`, following the keyword **struct**, is referred to as the *structure name*, or the tag of the structure, and it is used to declare variables of that structure type. The structure `Student` contains two members, or member fields, of type int and array of type char. The two members, `id` and `name`, are used to hold the student identification number and name, respectively. Memory storage for the structure `Student` is shown in Figure 13.1, with 4 bytes for the member `id` of type int and 32 bytes for `name` of type array of chars.

13.1.2 Declaration of Structure Type

The syntax of a structure declaration may be fairly complex. The common methods for declaring structures are described as follows.

1. Declaring a tag name and then using the tag name to declare actual variables. An example is shown below.

```
struct Student {
    int id;
    char name[32];
};
...
struct Student s;
```

   Note that `s` is declared as a variable of type `struct Student` with two members, `id` and `name`.
2. Declaring a structure without using a tag name. This method of declaration is useful if the structure is used only in one place. An example is shown below.

```
struct {
    int id;
    char name[32];
} s;
```

3. Declaring a structure with a tag name and variables. From the declaration below, it can be seen that `s1` and `s2` are variables of type `struct Student` type.

```
struct Student {
    int id;
    char name[32];
} s1, s2;
```

The first form of declaration is more commonly used, especially for a large program. The structure definition is often placed in a header file, which might be included by different source files. Then, each source file can use the same structure definition.

Typedef for Structure Type

A structure may also be defined by using a **typedef** declaration as described in section 3.12 in Chapter 3. Declaring a structure by a **typedef** name can be done in one of two ways, either

```
typedef struct {
   int id;
   char name[32];
} student_t;
...
student_t s;
```

or

```
struct Student {
   int id;
   char name[32];
};
...
typedef struct Student student_t;
...
student_t s;     // struct Student s;
```

where student_t is of the type struct Student. For a large program, the structure definitions and **typedef** declared data types are often placed in a header file.

For a more complete example using **typedef** for structures, consider Program 13.1, which displays the following output:

```
s.id   = 101
s.name = John
```

Details about accessing members of a structure will be described in section 13.1.4.

```
/* File: typedefs.c
   Use typdef to declare a structure data type */
#include <stdio.h>
#include <string.h>

typedef struct Student { /* define student_t as a data type */
    int id;
    char name[32];
} student_t;

int main() {
    student_t s;         /* use data type student_t */

    s.id = 101;
    strcpy(s.name, "John");
```

Program 13.1: Defining a new data type of structure type using **typedef**. *(Continued)*

```
    printf("s.id   = %d\n", s.id);
    printf("s.name = %s\n", s.name);
    return 0;
}
```

Program 13.1: (*Continued*)

13.1.3 Pointer to Structures

Declaring a pointer to structure is the same as declaring pointers to other objects or types. For example, the following code declares s as a structure type and three different structure pointers sp1, sp2, and sp3. Both sp1 and sp2 are pointers to struct Student, and they point to the address of the variable s. The variable sp3 is a pointer to pointer to struct Student, and it points to the address of the variable sp2 of type pointer to structure.

```
struct Student {
   int id;
   char name[32];
} s, *sp1;

int main () {
   struct Student *sp2, **sp3;
   sp1 = &s;
   sp2 = sp1;
   sp3 = &sp2;
   /* ... */
}
```

One may also declare a pointer to a structure by a **typedef** name as well. This is done in a similar way to the declaration of structure type using **typedef**. For example,

```
typedef struct Student {
   int id;
   char name[32];
} student_t, *studentptr_t;
...

student_t s;            // struct Student s;
studentptr_t sptr;      // struct Student *sptr;
```

which declares student_t as the type of struct Student and studentptr_t as the type of pointer to struct Student.

If we declare a new data type studentPtr_t using **typedef** as pointer to struct Student, the declaration statement

```
struct Student *sp2, **sp3;
```

can be replaced by

```
typedef struct Student *studentPtr_t;
studentPtr_t sp2, *sp3;
```

13.1.4 Accessing Structure Members

There are two methods to access structure members. The first method is to access a structure member by the structure name, which is achieved by using the structure variable name, *member operator* or *dot operator* '.', and the name of the member, as shown by the following statement in both Programs 13.1 and 13.2:

```
s.id = 101;
```

The address of a member can be obtained by the address operator '&'. For example, the address of the member `id` can be obtained by `&s.id`. Note that the dot operator '.' has higher precedence than the address operator '&', as shown in Table 4.2 in Chapter 4. The expression `&s.id` is the same as the expression `&(s.id)`. Recall that a variable of type array is also the address of the array, as described in section 11.5 in Chapter 11. Therefore, the result of the expression `s.name` is a pointer to char.

For a more complete example of accessing structure members by structure name, refer to Program 13.2. The interactive execution of Program 13.2 is shown below.

```
> accessmember.c
s.id   = 101
s.name = John
Please input id and name
102
Doe
s.id   = 102
s.name = Doe
```

Program 13.2 first defines a `Student` structure and declares the variable `s` of type `struct Student`. Then it inputs data into the members of the structure and displays these values. The members `s.id` and `s.name` are then filled with the user input `102` and `Doe` using the function **scanf()**.

```
/* File: accessmember.c
   Access members of a structure  */
#include <stdio.h>
#include <string.h>

struct Student {     /* define struct Student */
    int id;
    char name[32];
};

int main() {
    struct Student s;

    s.id = 101;      /* access members using member operator '.' */
    strcpy(s.name, "John");
    printf("s.id   = %d\n", s.id);
    printf("s.name = %s\n", s.name);
```

Program 13.2: Accessing members of a structure. (*Continued*)

```
    /* get user input from the terminal keyboard */
    printf("Please input id and name\n");
    scanf("%d", &s.id);
    scanf("%s", s.name);
    printf("s.id   = %d\n", s.id);
    printf("s.name = %s\n", s.name);
    return 0;
}
```

Program 13.2: *(Continued)*

The second method to access a structure member is through a pointer to the structure. This can be done by using a pointer to a structure, the *indirect member operator* or *arrow operator* `'->'`, and the name of the member. An example is as follows:

```
struct Student s, *sp;
sp = &s;
...
printf("sp->id = %d\n", sp->id);
```

The address of a member pointed to by a pointer to structure can also be obtained by the address operator `'&'`. Program 13.3, a modified version of Program 13.2, now utilizes a pointer to structure to access the structure's members. Although Program 13.3 does not show the advantage of using a pointer, it illustrates important working principles of a pointer to structure. The advantages of using pointers to structure will be presented in the subsequent sections of this chapter, such as passing information in a structure to functions and other applications.

The input string of the function **scanf()** with the format specifier `"%s"` cannot be separated by white spaces. To input a name with both first and last names separated by a white space from a standard input stream, the function **fgets()** is called in Program 13.3 as follows:

```
fgets(sp->name, sizeof(sp->name), stdin);
```

as in Program 13.3. The newline character obtained by the function **fgets()** at the end of the string `sp->name` is relaced with the null terminating character `'\0'` by the statement

```
sp->name[strlen(sp->name)-1] = '\0';
```

as described in section 12.5 in Chapter 12.

In this example, the size of array `sp->name` is 32 bytes. Similar to Program 12.4 in Chapter 12, the format specifier `"*c"` in the statement

```
scanf("%d*c", &sp->id);
```

is used to skip the carriage return character entered by the user when an identification number is typed in. Otherwise, the subsequent statement for a user name would retrieve only a return character of `'\n'` in the input buffer. In Program 13.2, the function **scanf()** in

```
scanf("%s", s.name);
```

will skip the return character in the input buffer when obtaining a string. The interactive execution of Program 13.3 is shown on next page.

```
/* File: spointer.c
   Use a pointer to structure */
#include <stdio.h>
#include <string.h>

struct Student {
    int id;
    char name[32];
};

int main() {
    struct Student s, *sp;

    sp = &s;                      /* sp pointer to s */
    sp->id = 101;                 /* access a member using arrow operator */
    strcpy(sp->name, "John");
    printf("sp->id   = %d\n", sp->id);
    printf("sp->name = %s\n", sp->name);

    /* obtain the user input from the keyboard */
    printf("Please input id and name\n");
    scanf("%d%*c", &sp->id);   /* skip the newline character */
    fgets(sp->name, sizeof(sp->name), stdin);
    sp->name[strlen(sp->name)-1] = '\0'; /* replace the newline char by '\0' */
    printf("sp->id   = %d\n", sp->id);
    printf("sp->name = %s\n", sp->name);
    return 0;
}
```

Program 13.3: Accessing members of a structure using a pointer to structure.

```
> spointer.c
sp->id   = 101
sp->name = John
Please input id and name
102
Doe Smith
sp->id   = 102
sp->name = Doe Smith
```

13.1.5 Structure Initialization

If an object of structure type has static storage duration, which is not initialized explicitly, it will be initialized according to the following rules:

- Every member of the structure is initialized recursively.

- If a member is pointer type, it is initialized to a null pointer.
- If a member is arithmetic type, it is initialized to positive zero.

There are two common ways to initialize a structure explicitly. The first way is to initialize the structure in the structure's declaration, as in the following:

```
struct Student {
   int id;
   char name[32];
} s = {101, "John"};
```

The other way to initialize a structure is similar to initializing an array. That is, the structure's variable name should be followed by the assignment operator '=' and then a list of initializers enclosed in braces. This method is shown below.

```
struct Student s = {102, "Doe"};
```

One should note that each initializer type must match with the type of its corresponding member in the structure. Program 13.4 is an example that uses the two methods mentioned to initialize two variables of type `struct Student` and then prints out the following results:

```
s.id    = 101
s.name = John
s2.id   = 102
s2.name = Doe
```

Notice that the variable `s` is a global variable and `s2` is a local variable.

```
/* File: initial.c
   Initialize variables of structure type */
#include <stdio.h>

struct Student {
    int id;
    char name[32];
} s={101, "John"};     /* initialize a global variable s */

int main() {
    struct Student s2 = {102, "Doe"}; /* initialize variable s2 */

    printf("s.id    = %d\n", s.id);
    printf("s.name = %s\n", s.name);
    printf("s2.id   = %d\n", s2.id);
    printf("s2.name = %s\n", s2.name);
    return 0;
}
```

Program 13.4: Initializing variables of structure type.

13.1.6 Size of Structures

The size of a structure can be determined by the **sizeof** operator. The argument of the **sizeof** operator can be either the struct type or a variable of struct type. Like other pointer types, the size of a pointer to a structure is 4 bytes (32 bts) for 32-bit machines and 8 bytes (64 bits) for 64-bit machines based on the programming data models listed in Table 3.2 in Chapter 3. If a structure contains a member of pointer type, the size of the same structure in a 32-bit programming model is typically different from that in a 64-bit programming model. Program 13.5 prints out the sizes of `struct Student` and its pointer type. When the program runs in a 32-bit computer, the result is shown below:

```
sizeof(struct Student) = 36
sizeof(s) = 36
sizeof(struct Student*) = 4
sizeof(sp) = 4
```

It should be noted that the size of a structure may not be the sum of the sizes of each member of the structure due to the alignment of the structure members, which will be described in section 13.1.16.

C statements with structure types can also be conveniently executed in a Ch shell interactively as shown below.

```
> struct Student { int id; char name[32];} s1 = {101, "John"}, s2;
> s1
.id = 101
.name = John
```

```
/* File: sizeofs.c
   Calculate the size of a structure */
#include <stdio.h>

struct Student {
    int id;
    char name[32];
} s, *sp;

int main() {
    /* calculate  the size of structure type  */
    printf("sizeof(struct Student) = %u\n", sizeof(struct Student));
    printf("sizeof(s) = %u\n", sizeof(s));

    /* The size of a pointer to structure is the same as the size
       of a pointer to other data types */
    printf("sizeof(struct Student*) = %u\n", sizeof(struct Student*));
    printf("sizeof(sp) = %u\n", sizeof(sp));
    return 0;
}
```

Program 13.5: Determining the size of a structure.

```
> s2.id = 102
> strcpy(s2.name, "Doe")
> s2
.id = 102
.name = Doe
> sizeof(struct Student)
36
> sizeof(s1)
36
```

When a value of structure type is displayed interactively, all members and their values of the structure are displayed. In this case, members `id` and `name` of structure `Student` are displayed.

13.1.7 Assigning and Comparing Structures

The assignment operator `'-'` can be applied to variables of a structure and to pointers to structure types. A structure can be assigned to a structure variable, provided that they are of the same structure type. The value of each member of the structure of the rvalue will be assigned to the corresponding member of the lvalue. For example, Program 13.6 assigns `s1` to `s`, both of which share the same structure type, `Student`.

```
/* File: assign.c
   Assign structure type to a variable  */
#include <stdio.h>
#include <string.h>

struct Student {
    int id;
    char name[32];
} s1 = {101, "John"};

int main() {
    struct Student s, *sp, *sp1;

    s = s1;    /* assigning structure s1 to  structure s,
                  the entire structure is copied from s1 to s2 */
    printf("s.id = %d\n", s.id);
    printf("s.name = %s\n", s.name);
    sp = &s;   /* assigning the address of s to a pointer to structure sp,
                  only the address is copied */
    sp1 = &s1; /* only address of s1 is copied to sp1 */
    if(sp == sp1) { /* compare pointers to structures */
        printf("sp and sp1 point to the same object.\n");
    }
    else {
```

Program 13.6: Assignment of structure. (*Continued*)

```
        printf("sp and sp1 point to different objects.\n");
    }
    /* Compare two structures, all members shall be compared */
    if(s.id == s1.id && !strcmp(s.name, s1.name)) {
        printf("The contents of s and s1 are the same.\n");
    }
    return 0;
}
```

Program 13.6: *(Continued)*

The relational operators `'=='` and `'!='` can be applied to variables of pointer to structure type. These two relational operators can be used to check if two variables of pointer to structure type point to the same object, as for pointers to simple data types such as int. A variable of pointer to structure can also be compared to a NULL pointer. Variables of structure type cannot be used as operands of the relational operators `'=='` and `'!='` to compare if they are the same structure. To compare variables of the same structure type, their corresponding members have to be compared. In Program 13.6, the variables `sp` and `sp1` point to `s` and `s1` of different objects, respectively. The contents of `s1` are assigned from `s`. The corresponding members `id` and name of `s` and `s1` are compared. The function **strcmp**() is used to compare two strings. The output of Program 13.6 is as follows:

```
s.id = 101
s.name = John
sp and sp1 point to different objects.
The contents of s and s1 are the same.
```

13.1.8 Arrays of Structures

Because a structure is a data object, it is possible to create arrays of structures. Each element of the array has a structure data type. An array of structures can be declared by the same method for declaring a structure variable. Program 13.7 is an example that first declares and initializes an array of structures with three elements. The

```
/* File: arrays.c
   Use array of structure */
#include <stdio.h>

struct Student {
    int id;
    char name[32];
};

int main() {
    /* declare s as an array of structure */
    struct Student *p, s[3] = {{101, "John"},
                               {102, "Doe"},
                               {103, "Peter"}};
    int i, num; /* index variable and num of elements for array s */
```

Program 13.7: An array of structures. *(Continued)*

```
    /* obtain the number of elements in array s */
    num = sizeof(s)/sizeof(struct Student);
    printf("number of elements is %d\n", num);
    /* access each member for each element of the array */
    for(i=0; i<num; i++) {
       printf("s[%d].id   = %d\n", i, s[i].id);
       printf("s[%d].name = %s\n", i, s[i].name);
    }
    return 0;
}
```

Program 13.7: *(Continued)*

memory layout for the structure array `s` is shown in Figure 13.2. Each element occupies 36 bytes: 4 bytes for `id` and 32 bytes for `name`. The data for the first student are stored in the structure `s[0]`. The individual data items are `s[0].id` and `s[0].name`, with values of 101 and `"John"`, respectively, as shown in Figure 13.3. Like an array of integers, the expression `&s[1]` gives the address of the second element of the array `s`. Like an array of other simple data types, the expression

```
sizeof(s)/sizeof(struct Student)
```

gives the number of elements in the array `s` of type `struct Student`. The output for the values of the elements of the array from executing Program 13.7 is shown below:

```
number of elements is 3
s[0].id   = 101
s[0].name = John
s[1].id   = 102
s[1].name = Doe
s[2].id   = 103
s[2].name = Peter
```

Like arrays of scalar types, a variable of an array of structures is also converted to a pointer to a structure. A pointer to a structure can also be treated as an array of structures. In Program 13.8, the variable `sp` is a pointer to the type `struct Student`. It is first assigned to point to the array `s`. Then `sp` is treated as an array and the ith element of the array `s` is accessed by the expression `sp[i]` in the **for** loop in Program 13.8.

	s[0].id	s[0].name	s[1].id	s[1].name	s[2].id	s[2].name
Bytes	4	32	4	32	4	32

Figure 13.2: The memory layout for the structure array `s`.

	.id	.name
s[0]	101	"John"
s[1]	102	"Doe"
s[2]	103	"Peter"

Figure 13.3: The contents of the structure array `s`.

```
/* File: arraysp.c
   Handle an array of structure using a pointer */
#include <stdio.h>

struct Student {
    int id;
    char name[32];
};

int main() {
    struct Student *sp, s[3] = {{101, "John"},
                                {102, "Doe"},
                                {103, "Peter"}};
    int i;

    sp = s; /* sp points to the array of structure */
    for(i=0; i<3; i++) { /* at the end of for-loop, sp remains the same */
       printf("sp[%d].id   = %d\n", i, sp[i].id);
       printf("sp[%d].name = %s\n", i, sp[i].name);
    }
    /* at the end of this for-loop, sp advanced beyond the last element
       of the array */
    for(i=0; i<3; i++, sp++) {
       printf("id   = %d\n", sp->id);
       printf("name = %s\n", sp->name);
    }

    return 0;
}
```

Program 13.8: An array of structures as a pointer.

At the end of the execution of the first **for** loop, the variable sp still points to the address for the first element of the array s. In the second **for** loop in Program 13.8, the variable sp of pointer type is also used to access each element of the array s. In each iteration, the pointer expression sp++ changes the value of sp to point to the next element in the array. At the end of this **for** loop, the variable sp does not point to any element of the array. The output from executing Program 13.8 is shown as follows:

```
sp[0].id   = 101
sp[0].name = John
sp[1].id   = 102
sp[1].name = Doe
sp[2].id   = 103
sp[2].name = Peter
id   = 101
name = John
id   = 102
```

```
name = Doe
id   = 103
name = Peter
```

13.1.9 Passing Structures as Function Arguments

There are two methods to pass structures as arguments of a function: *passing by value* or *passing by reference*. *Passing by value* refers to passing a copy of the entire structure, while *passing by reference* only passes the address of the structure. Thus, passing by reference is usually the faster, more convenient method. In most cases, passing structures as function arguments should be done by using pass by reference. There are only a few circumstances when one would want to pass a structure by value: (1) the structure is very small and (2) you want to make sure that the called function does not change the structure being passed in any way. Program 13.9 illustrates both methods. The structure `s1` is passed to the argument `s` by value whereas the address of the structure `s2` is passed to the argument `sp` by reference. When Program 13.9 runs, output is as follows:

```
s.id = 101
s.name = John
sp->id   = 102
sp->name = Doe
```

```
/* File: funcstructarg.c
   Function arguments contain structure and pointer to structure */
#include <stdio.h>

struct Student {
    int id;
    char name[32];
} s1={101, "John"};

/* when a structure is passed, each member of the structure is copied.
   similar to assignment */
void func(struct Student s, struct Student *sp) {
    printf("s.id = %d\n", s.id);
    printf("s.name = %s\n", s.name);
    printf("sp->id   = %d\n", sp->id);
    printf("sp->name = %s\n", sp->name);
}

int main() {
    struct Student s2 = {102, "Doe"};

    func(s1, &s2); /* passed structure s1 and address of s2 to func() */
    return 0;
}
```

Program 13.9: A function with arguments of structure type.

In some applications, an array of structures needs to be passed as an argument to a function for processing. In comparison with previous examples, the structure `Student` in Program 13.10 contains an additional member `gpa` of double type to hold the GPA for a student. The argument `s` for the function `func1()` is a one-dimensional array of structures. The number of iterations for the **for** loop is passed as an argument. In the **for** loop, the variable `s` is treated as an array and the ith element of the array is accessed by the expression `s[i]`. In the **while** loop, the variable `s` is treated as a pointer to a structure. The pointer `s` advances to the next element by the pointer expression `s++`. Unlike the **for** loop with a fixed number of interactions, the loop is terminated by a sentinel number −1 defined as the macro `EOD` for the end of data for the member `id`. The array `s` in the function **main()** is initialized with four elements. The member `id` for the last element is initialized with the sentinel number `EOD`. The array `s` is directly passed to the function `func1()` by the function call `func1(s)`. The same array is also passed to the function `func1()` indirectly by the function call `func1(sp)`. The variable `sp` is a pointer to structure that points to the array `s`.

The function `func2()` in Program 13.10 has an argument `sp` of the type pointer to a structure. Both array of structures and pointer to a structure can be passed to it. Similar to the function `func1()`, the variable `sp` inside the function `func2()` can be treated either as an array of structures or a pointer to a structure.

```
/* File: funcstructargarray.c
   pass an array of structures to a function */
#include <stdio.h>

#define EOD -1        /* define a sentinel number for end of data */

struct Student {
    int id;
    char name[32];
    double gpa;
};

void func1(int n, struct Student s[]) { /* argument as an array */
    int i;

    for(i=0; i<n; i++) {    /* treat s as an array */
       printf("id = %d ", s[i].id);
       printf("name = %5s ", s[i].name);
       printf("GPA = %.2f\n", s[i].gpa);
    }
    while(s->id != EOD) {  /* treat s as a pointer */
       printf("id = %d ", s->id);
       printf("name = %5s ", s->name);
       printf("GPA = %.2f\n", s->gpa);
       s++;
    }
}
```

Program 13.10: A function with arguments of array of structures and pointer to structure. *(Continued)*

```
void func2(int n, struct Student *sp) { /* argument as a pointer */
    int i;

    for(i=0; i<n; i++) {    /* treat sp as an array */
       printf("id = %d ", sp[i].id);
       printf("name = %5s ", sp[i].name);
       printf("GPA = %.2f\n", sp[i].gpa);
    }
    while(sp->id != EOD) {  /* treat sp as a pointer */
       printf("id = %d ", sp->id);
       printf("name = %5s ", sp->name);
       printf("GPA = %.2f\n", sp->gpa);
       sp++;
    }
}

/* calculate average GPAs for all students */
double averageGPA(struct Student *sp) {
    double gpa, totalval;
    int i;

    totalval=0.0; /* initialize the totalval */
    for(i=0; sp[i].id != EOD; i++) {
        totalval += sp[i].gpa;  /* add a GPA to totalval */
    }
    gpa = totalval/(double)i;     /* calculate GPA */
    return gpa;                   /* return the GPA */
}

int main() {
    struct Student s[] = {{101, "John",  3.33},
                          {102, "Doe",   3},
                          {103, "Peter", 3.1},
                          {EOD, NULL, EOD}}; /* terminating element */
    struct Student *sp;   /* pointer to structure */

    sp = s;               /* sp pointer to s */
    func1(3, s);          /* pass s to func1() */
    func1(3, sp);         /* pass sp to func1() */
    func2(3, s);          /* pass s to func2() */
    func2(3, sp);         /* pass sp to func2() */
    printf("GPA for students in the list is %.2f\n", averageGPA(s));
    return 0;
}
```

Program 13.10: *(Continued)*

The function `averageGPA()` calculates the average GPA of the students in the array of `Student` structures. The expression `sp[i].gpa` accesses the GPA of a student in the ith element of the array. The result will remain the same if the declaration of the function argument is changed as follows:

```
double averageGPA(struct Student sp[]);
```

When Program 13.10 is executed, the following output

```
id = 101 name =  John GPA = 3.33
id = 102 name =   Doe GPA = 3.00
id = 103 name = Peter GPA = 3.10
```

will appear eight times. Then, the output

```
GPA for students in the list is 3.14
```

is displayed.

Application Examples

Acceleration of a Moving Body Modeled Using a Structure

Problem Statement:
For the mechanical system shown in Figure 2.12, given mass $m = 5$ kilograms (kg) and coefficient of kinetic friction $\mu = 0.2$, the applied force p is expressed as a function of time t in

$$p(t) = 4\sin(t - 3) + 20 \qquad \text{when } t >= 0$$

Write a program to

1. Calculate the resulting acceleration of the rigid body at $t = 2$ seconds.
2. Plot the accelerations a from $t = 0$ to 10 seconds with the number of points N equal to 100.

Note: Use a structure with members for the mass and coefficient of kinetic friction. The structure should be defined in the header file `accel.h`. Two macros for g and N, as well as function prototypes, are also placed in the header file.

This problem may be solved with Programs 13.11 and 13.12. Program 13.11 is a header file that contains the constant value for gravity, the number of data points to be plotted, and `struct Body`, which is used to specify the parameters of the body. The `struct Body` structure has two members of double type, `mu` for the friction coefficient between the surface and body, and `m` for the mass of the body. The size of the structure is 16 bytes, 8 bytes for each member. Program 13.12 contains three functions to help solve the problem. The function `force()` calculates the external force acting on the system at a specified time, while `accel()` determines the body's acceleration at time t. Finally, the function `plotAccel()` is used to plot the acceleration of the system for $t = 0$ to 10 seconds. The function **main()** declares the variable `b`

```
/* File: accel.h
   Header file for calculating and plotting accelerations
   using a structure */
#ifndef ACCEL_H
#define ACCEL_H

#define M_G   9.81  /* gravitational acceleration constant g */
#define N     100   /* num of points for plotting */

struct Body {       /* structure for a body */
      double mu;    /* friction coefficient */
      double m;     /* mass */
};

/* function prototypes */
extern double force(double t);
extern double accel(const struct Body *b, double t);
extern void plotAccel(const struct Body *b, double t0, double tf);

#endif
```

Program 13.11: The header file for calculating accelerations with structure type.

```
/* File: accelstruct.cpp
   Use a structure to calculate and plot accelerations */
#include <stdio.h>
#include <math.h>      /* for sin() */
#include <chplot.h>    /* for plotxy() */
#include "accel.h"     /* local header file */

double force(double t) {  /* function to calculate the force */
    double p;

    p = 4*(sin(t-3))+20;
    return p;
}

double accel(const struct Body *b, double t) { /* for acceleration */
    double a, p;
    p = force(t);
```

Program 13.12: Calculating accelerations with structure type. (*Continued*)

```
    a = (p-b->mu*b->m*M_G)/b->m;
    return a;
}

/* plot accelerations */
void plotAccel(const struct Body *b, double t0, double tf) {
    double a[N], t[N];    /* define arrays for plotting */
    int i;

    for(i=0; i<N; i++) {
      t[i] = t0 + i*(t0-tf)/(N-1);
      a[i] = accel(b, t[i]);
    }
    plotxy(t, a, N, "Acceleration Plot", "time (s)", "accel (m/s^2)");
}

int main() {
    /* declare accel, force, time, initial time, final time, mu, mass */
    double a, p, t, t0, tf, mu, m;
    struct Body b;        /* declare a body with mu and m */

    t = 2.0;              /* set time at 2 seconds */
    t0 = 0.0;             /* initial time 0 second */
    tf = 10.0;            /* final time 10 seconds */
    b.mu = 0.2;           /* mu */
    b.m = 5.0;            /* mass */
    p = force(t);         /* calculate force */
    a = accel(&b, t);     /* calculate acceleration by passing address of b */
    printf("External force p = %f (N)\n", p);
    printf("Acceleration a = %f (m/s^2)\n", a);
    plotAccel(&b, t0, tf); /* plot accelerations by passing address of b */
    return 0;
}
```

Program 13.12: *(Continued)*

of type structure `Body`. The address of the variable `b` is passed to an argument of pointer to structure for the functions `accel()` and `plotAccel()`. The variable `b` inside these two functions contain the address of the variable `b` in the main function. The address of the variable `b` in the function `plotAccel()` is in turn passed to the function `accel()`. For time t at 2 seconds, the external force and acceleration values are shown below. The acceleration plot for part 2 of the problem is shown in Figure 6.4 in Chapter 6.

```
External force p = 16.634116 (N)
Acceleration a = 1.364823 (m/s^2)
```

‡Passing Multiple Variables to an Argument of Function Using a Generic Pointer and Structure

As described in section 11.12 in Chapter 11, the contents of a structure can also be passed to a function through an argument of a generic pointer to void. For example, Program 11.20 can be modified to use the structure `InitCond` with two members to pass both projection angle `theta0` and initial velocity `v0` from the main function to the callback function for the bisection method `bisect2()`, as shown in Program 13.13. The address of the structure `initc` is passed from the function **main()** through the last argument of the function `bisect2()`, to the generic pointer `param` of the callback function `traj()`. The values for members of the structure are retrieved inside the function `traj()` by casting the generic pointer `param` to a pointer to structure `InitCond` using

```
initcptr = (struct InitCond *)param;
```

```
/* File: bisect3.c */
#define M_G   9.81          /* gravitational acceleration constant g */

struct InitCond {          /* define struct InitCond */
   double theta0;          /* initial velocity   */
   double v0;              /* member for initial velocity */
};


double traj(double x, void *param) {
   double theta0,           /* projection angle  */
          v0,               /* initial velocity */
          y;                /* y coordinate */
   struct InitCond *initcptr;

   /* cast from (void *) for param to (struct InitCond *) for initcptr */
   initcptr = (struct InitCond *)param;
   theta0 = initcptr->theta0; /* projection angle */
   v0 = initcptr->v0;         /* initial velocity */
   y = tan(theta0)*x - M_G*x*x/(2*v0*v0*cos(theta0)*cos(theta0));
   return y;
}

int main() {
    ...
    struct InitCond initc;
    initc.theta0 = 15*M_PI/180; /*  the projection angle in radians */
    initc.v0 = 35.0;             /* set the initial velocity */
    status = bisect2(&x, x0, xf, tolerance, traj, &initc);
    ...
}
```

Program 13.13: Passing contents in a structure to a callback function through a generic pointer to void.

13.1.10 Functions Returning Structures

Similar to returning arrays from functions, it is also possible to return structures from functions. Note that the return type of the function must match the actual returned value, as with the following code fragment, which returns a structure type of `struct tag`:

```
struct tag funct1(void) {
   struct tag s;
   ...
   return s;
}
```

One advantage of returning a structure is the ability to return more than one value, because the **return** statement can return only one expression to the calling routine. If the expression happens to be a structure, then a large number of values can be indirectly returned. However, functions using arguments of pointer to structure to pass values for members of the structure is more commonly used than functions returning structures. Program 13.14 utilizes a function that returns a structure. The output of the program is shown below:

```
s1.id = 102
s1.name = Doe
```

```
/* File: returns.c
   Function returns a structure */
#include <stdio.h>
#include <string.h>          /* for strcpy() */

struct Student {
    int id;
    char name[32];
};

/* function returns a structure */
struct Student func(int id) {
    struct Student s1;

    s1.id = id + 1;          /* s1.id becomes 101+1 */
    strcpy(s1.name, "Doe");
    return s1;               /* return a structure */
}

int main() {
    struct Student s = {101, "John"}, s1;
```

Program 13.14: A function returning a value of structure type. (*Continued*)

```
    s1 = func(s.id); /* assign the returned structure to s1 */
    printf("s1.id = %d\n", s1.id);
    printf("s1.name = %s\n", s1.name);
    return 0;
}
```

Program 13.14: (*Continued*)

As another example, the functions **div()** and **ldiv()** in the header file **stdlib.h** perform integer and long integer division, respectively. The function prototypes for these functions are as follows:

```
div_t div(int n, int d);
ldiv_t ldiv(long n, long d);
```

These two division functions compute both the quotient and the remainder of the argument n divided by the argument d. The results are stored in either structure **div_t** or **ldiv_t**, depending on which function is used. Note that if d is equal to 0, the result is undefined. The structure **div_t** is defined in the header file **stdlib.h** as follows:

```
typedef struct {
  int quot;
  int rem;
} div_t;
```

The structure **ldiv_t** has similar members, but with **long** data types. Applications of these structure types are shown interactively in a Ch shell below. For example,

```
> div(10, 3)
.quot = 3
.rem = 1
> ldiv(15L, 2L)
.quot = 7
.rem = 1
```

The members quot and rem of the structures **div_t** and **ldiv_t** contain the quotient and the remainder for a division operation 10/3.

13.1.11 Functions Returning a Pointer to Structures

Because returning a structure from a function is possible, it is only reasonable to be able to return a pointer to structure from a function. Similar to returning a structure, the return type of the function must agree with the actual returned value.

When returning a structure from a function, it is also desirable to return a pointer to a structure, just like when passing structures as function arguments. Note that when a function passes or returns a pointer, the pointer should point to a variable of static duration, such as a global or static variable, dynamically allocated memory, or valid memory for a variable of automatic storage duration. For example, the function `func2()` below returns the address of the global variable `s` of static storage duration.

```
struct tag s;
struct tag *funct2(void) {      /* define a function that */
                                /* returns a pointer to structure. */
    ...
    return &s;
}
```

In Program 13.15, the function `func()` returns the address of the structure passed as its argument. The output of Program 13.15 is as follows:

```
sp->id = 102
sp->name = John
```

The execution of Program 13.16, however, would produce an error. The reason is that the return value for the function `func()`, `s1`, is a variable of automatic storage duration. This means that the memory allocation for the variable only exists within the scope of the function `func()`. Once control is returned to the function **main()**, the variable `s1` would no longer exist. When a structure is passed to a function or returned, the contents of the structure are copied. When the size of a structure is larger than the size of a pointer to structure, it is more efficient to pass or return a pointer to structure, rather than the structure itself.

```
/* File: returnsptr.c
   Function returns a pointer to structure */
#include <stdio.h>

struct Student {
    int id;
    char name[32];
};

struct Student *func(struct Student *sp) {
    sp->id = 102;
    return sp;   /* return a pointer to structure   */
}

int main() {
    struct Student *sp, s={101, "John"};

    sp = func(&s);    /* sp points to s */
    printf("sp->id = %d\n", sp->id);
    printf("sp->name = %s\n", sp->name);
    return 0;
}
```

Program 13.15: A function returning a value of pointer to structure type.

```
/* File: returnsptr_err.c
   Function incorrectly returns a pointer to structure
   that points to the memory of automatic storage duration. */
#include <stdio.h>

struct Student {
    int id;
    char name[32];
} s={101, "John"};

struct Student *func(void) {
    struct Student s1;

    s1 = s;
    s1.id = 102;
    return &s1;    /* Error: return a pointer to local variable */
}

int main() {
    struct Student *sp;

    sp = func();
    printf("sp->id = %d\n", sp->id);
    printf("sp->name = %s\n", sp->name);
    return 0;
}
```

Program 13.16: A function incorrectly returning a pointer pointing to the memory of automatic storage duration.

13.1.12 Dynamic Allocation of Memory for Structures

As described in section 11.7 in Chapter 11, memory can be dynamically allocated at runtime. For example, the function **malloc()** with the prototype

```
void *malloc(size_t size);
```

can allocate the memory space for an object whose size is specified by the argument and returns a generic pointer to void. The size of a structure might be different for diffferent platforms and machine architectures. To allocate the memory space properly for a structure, the size of the structure shall be calculated first with the **sizeof** operator. The return value of this function is cast to a pointer to structure. The code fragment below illustrates how to allocate memory dynamically for a structure of type `struct Student`.

```
struct Student *sp;
sp = (struct Student *)malloc(sizeof(struct Student));
```

```
/* File: dynmemory.c
   Dynamically allocate memory for a structure */
#include <stdio.h>
#include <string.h>          /* for strcpy() */
#include <stdlib.h>          /* for malloc() and free() */

struct Student {
    int id;
    char name[32];
};

struct Student *func(int id, char *name) {
    struct Student *sp; /* local variable sp is diff from sp in main() */
    /* allocate the memory for sp */
    sp = (struct Student *)malloc(sizeof(struct Student));
    sp->id = id;             /* fill the first 4 bytes with id */
    strcpy(sp->name, name);  /* fill the subsequent ones with name */
    return sp;   /* return dynamically allocated memory for structure */
}

int main() {
    struct Student *sp;

    sp = func(101, "John"); /* sp pointer to dynamically allocated memory */
    printf("sp->id = %d\n", sp->id);
    printf("sp->name = %s\n", sp->name);
    free(sp);               /* free the allocated memory */
    return 0;
}
```

Program 13.17: Using pointer to structure and dynamically allocated memory.

Program 13.17 is an example of dynamically allocating memory for a structure. Note that the local variable `sp` of the function `func()` is different from the `sp` in the function **main()**. The output for this program is shown below:

```
sp->id = 101
sp->name = John
```

13.1.13 Handling Members of Pointer Type

If a member of a structure is of a pointer type, then memory has to be allocated for this member for it to be used. The functions **malloc()** and **calloc()** can be used to allocate the memory space dynamically. The return value of these two functions can be assigned to a structure member of pointer type. Note that the memory allocated by these two functions needs to be freed by the function **free()**. Program 13.18 is an example of

```
/* File: memberptr.c
   Structure with member of pointer type */
#include <stdio.h>
#include <string.h>    /* for strcpy() */
#include <stdlib.h>    /* for malloc(), free(), exit() */

struct Student {
     int id;
     char *name;         /* name is a pointer to char */
};

int main() {
     struct Student s;

     s.id = 101;
     /* allocate memory for the member 'name' */
     s.name = (char *)malloc(sizeof(char)*(strlen("John")+1));
     if(s.name == NULL) {
       printf("Error: no memory\n");
       exit(EXIT_FAILURE);
     }
     strcpy(s.name, "John"); /* use the allocated memory */

     printf("s.id   = %d\n", s.id);
     printf("s.name = %s\n", s.name);
     free(s.name);              /* free the allocated memory */
     return 0;
}
```

Program 13.18: A structure with a member of pointer type.

how to use the function **malloc()** to allocate the memory for a structure member of pointer type. The output is shown below:

```
s.id   = 101
s.name = John
```

Dynamic allocation of memory is useful in many ways. For Program 13.18, `char *name` is used instead of `char name[32]` in the structure `Student`. This allows the structure to handle names longer than 31 characters as well as save memory with names less than 31 characters in length. Comprehensive application examples of structures with such members of pointer types are presented in Chapter 15.

13.1.14 Nested Structures

A nested structure is defined as a structure in which one of its members is also a structure. Nested structures are useful because they allow for the creation of data hierarchies. For example, consider the following structure declaration for `Student`. The structure `Student` is considered a nested structure because the member *birthday* is a structure of `struct Birthday` type.

```
struct Birthday {
   short day, month, year;
};

struct Student {
   int id;
   char name[32];
   struct Birthday birthday;
} s, *sp;
```

The members for the structure `Birthday`, used to store a student's birthday, use data of type short to save memory space. In fact, the member `id`, identification number, can also use data type of short. The members of `struct Birthday` inside the variable `s` of type `struct Student` can be accessed by the following format:

```
s.birthday.day
s.birthday.month
s.birthday.year
```

The address for the day of the birthday can be obtained by the expression `&s.birthday.day`. The members of `struct Birthday` inside the variable `sp` of type pointer to `struct Student` can be accessed by the following format:

```
sp->birthday.day
sp->birthday.month
sp->birthday.year
```

Similarly, the address for the day of the birthday can be obtained by the expression `&sp->birthday.day`.

Program 13.19 is an example using the nested structure `Student` defined above to store and display information about a student. Note that the student's year is accessed by a pointer to structure, `sp`, and the

```
/* File: nested.c
   Use a nested structure */
#include <stdio.h>
#include <string.h>               /* for strcpy() */

struct Birthday {                 /* define struct Birthday */
    short day, month, year;
};

struct Student {                  /* define struct Student */
    int id;
    char name[32];
    struct Birthday birthday;   /* contain a nested structure */
};

int main() {
    struct Student s, *sp; /* declare variables */
```

Program 13.19: Nested structures with a member of structure type. (*Continued*)

```
    /* set s for John */
    sp = &s;       /* sp points to s, so "sp->" is the same as "s." */
    s.id = 101;
    strcpy(s.name, "John");
    /* Set birthday for John September 16, 1990 */
    s.birthday.day = 16;          /* set day */
    s.birthday.month = 8;         /* set month */
    sp->birthday.year = 1990; /* set year, equivalent to s.birthday.year=1990 */
    /* print the information for John in s */
    printf("id   = %d\n", s.id);
    printf("name = %s\n", s.name);
    printf("birthday = %d\n", s.birthday.day);
    printf("birth month = %d\n", s.birthday.month);
    printf("birth year = %d\n", sp->birthday.year);
    return 0;
}
```

Program 13.19: *(Continued)*

```
id   = 101
name = John
birthday = 16
birth month = 8
birth year = 1990
```

Figure 13.4: The output from Programs 13.19, 13.20, and 13.21.

arrow operator (`->`) was used to point to the member structure `Birthday` instead of the dot operator. The output of Program 13.19 is shown in Figure 13.4.

The member `birthday` in the structure `Staff` in Program 13.20 is a pointer to structure `Birthday`. For the variable `s` of structure type declared by

```
struct Staff s;
```

the pointer `s.birthday` is a pointer to an object `bday` of type structure `Birthday` by the statement

```
s.birthday = &bday;
```

Because the member `birthday` is a pointer to structure, its members need to be accessed by the arrow operator `'->'`. The date of birth for the object `s` of `Staff` can be accessed as follows:

```
s.birthday->day
s.birthday->month
s.birthday->year
```

The same memories can also be accessed correspondingly by the variable `bday` as follows:

```
bday.day
bday.month
bday.year
```

The output of Program is shown in Figure 13.4.

```
/* File: nestedpointer.c
   Use a nested pointer to structure */
#include <stdio.h>
#include <string.h>             /* for strcpy() */

struct Birthday {               /* define struct Birthday */
    short day, month, year;
};

struct Staff {                  /* define struct Staff */
    int id;
    char name[32];
    struct Birthday *birthday; /* contain a nested pointer to structure */
};

int main() {
    struct Staff s;             /* declare variable of struct Staff */
    struct Birthday bday;       /* declare variable of struct Birthday */

    /* set s for John */
    s.id = 101;
    strcpy(s.name, "John");
    s.birthday = &bday;        /* s.birthday points to bday */
    /* set John's birthday */
    s.birthday->day = 16;
    s.birthday->month = 8;
    s.birthday->year = 1990;

    /* print the information for John in s */
    printf("id   = %d\n", s.id);
    printf("name = %s\n", s.name);
    printf("birthday = %d\n", s.birthday->day);
    printf("birth month = %d\n", s.birthday->month);
    printf("birth year = %d\n", s.birthday->year);
    return 0;
}
```

Program 13.20: Nested structures with a member of pointer to structure type.

The nested structure `Staff` in Program 13.21 is the same as that in Program 13.20. However, the variables `sp` and `bday` in Program 13.21 are pointer to structures. Their memory are dynamically allocated at runtime. The birthday can be accessed through either variable `sp` by

```
sp->birthday->day
sp->birthday->month
sp->birthday->year
```

```
/* File: nestedpointer2.c
   Use a nested pointer to structure with dynamically allocation
   for the memory */
#include <stdio.h>
#include <string.h>                /* for strcpy() */

struct Birthday {                  /* define struct Birthday */
    short day, month, year;
};

struct Staff {                     /* define struct Staff */
    int id;
    char name[32];
    struct Birthday *birthday; /* contain a nested pointer to structure */
};

int main() {
    struct Staff *sp;              /* declare a pointer to struct Staff */
    struct Birthday *bday;         /* declare a pointer to struct Birthday */


    /* allocated memory for John */
    sp = (struct Staff *)malloc(sizeof(struct Staff));
    sp->id = 101;                   /* set John's id */
    strcpy(sp->name, "John");       /* set John's name */
    /* allocate memory for holding John's birthday */
    bday = (struct Birthday*)malloc(sizeof(struct Birthday));
    /* set John's birthday */
    bday->day = 16;
    bday->month = 8;
    bday->year = 1990;
    sp->birthday = bday;

    /* print the information for John in sp */
    printf("id   = %d\n", sp->id);
    printf("name = %s\n", sp->name);
    printf("birthday = %d\n", sp->birthday->day);
    printf("birth month = %d\n", sp->birthday->month);
    printf("birth year = %d\n", sp->birthday->year);
    /* free allocated memory, you must free sp->birthday first,
    before free sp. However, memory birthday can also be freed by free(bday) */
    free(sp->birthday); /* or free(bday); */
    free(sp);
    return 0;
}
```

Program 13.21: Nested structures with a member of pointer to structure type with memory dynamically allocated.

or directly through the variable `bday` by

```
bday->day
bday->month
bday->year
```

Both `sp->birthday` and `bday` in Program 13.21 refer to the same memory. The dynamically allocated memory for the object of `struct Birthday` can be released by either

```
free(sp->birthday);
```

or

```
free(bday);
```

Alternatively, the temporary variable `bday` is not necessary in Program 13.21 if the code

```
bday = (struct Birthday*)malloc(sizeof(struct Birthday));
bday->day = 16;
bday->month = 8;
bday->year = 1990;
sp->birthday = bday;
```

is replaced by

```
sp->birthday = (struct Birthday*)malloc(sizeof(struct Birthday));
sp->birthday->day = 16;
sp->birthday->month = 8;
sp->birthday->year = 1990;
```

In this case, the memory has to be freed by the function call

```
free(sp->birthday);
```

In this case, the memory of `sp->birthday` of the structure `Birthday` is indirectly accessible only through the variable `sp`. The memory for `sp->birthday` has to be freed before the memory for `sp` is released. The output of Program 13.21 is shown in Figure 13.4.

13.1.15 ‡Macro offsetof

The **offsetof** macro defined in the header file **stddef.h** can be used to determine the integral byte offset of any non-bitfield structure members. Bit-field will be described in section 13.4. The macro takes two input arguments. The first argument is a structure, while the second is the name of the member, as shown below:

```
offsetof(structure-type, member-name);
```

The result of the macro **offsetof** is an integral byte offset between the specified member and the beginning of the structure. The result is of type **size_t**, which is defined in the header file **stddef.h**. For `struct Student` below,

```
struct Student {
   int id;
   char name[32];
}
```

```
/* File: offsetofs.c
   Obtain the offsets for members of a structure */
#include <stdio.h>
#include <stddef.h>     /* for macro offsetof() */

struct Student{
    int id;
    char name[32];
};

int main() {
    size_t offset;     /* offset is declared with data type size_t */

    /* obtain and display the offsets for members of struct Student */
    printf("sizeof(struct Student) = %u\n", sizeof(struct Student));
    offset = offsetof(struct Student, id);
    printf("offset id in struct Student = %u\n", offset);
    offset = offsetof(struct Student, name);
    printf("offset name in struct Student = %u\n", offset);
    return 0;
}
```

Program 13.22: Using the macro **offsetof**().

the structure contains two members, `id` and `name`. The memory storage for `struct Student` was shown in Figure 13.1. As the figure shows, the offset of the member `id` is 0, and the offset of the member `name` is 4. Program 13.22 shows how to obtain the offset of the members of `struct Student`. The results are as follows:

```
sizeof(struct Student) = 36
offset id in struct Student = 0
offset name in struct Student = 4
```

13.1.16 ‡Alignment of Structures

Some platforms require that any data element larger than a character must be assigned an address that is a multiple of a power of 2. The alignment is treated differently on different platforms. Even on the same platform, the alignment could be different because of the different order of the members of a data object. Although alignment restrictions are invisible to the programmer, they may create *gaps* in a structure. Program 13.23 is used to show how gaps can be created inside structures. The structure `tag1` in Program 13.23 has a gap between the members `s` and `d` (as shown in Figure 13.5) for the memory storage of the structure. It is consistent in most platforms. The structure `tag2` in Program 13.23 also has gaps (as shown in Figures 13.6 and 13.7) for the memory storage of the structure. Figure 13.6 is the alignment for each member of the structure `tag2` in Windows and Solaris on both 32-bit and 64-bit machines as well as in Linux on 64-bit machines. Figure 13.7 is the alignment for each member of the same structure `tag2` in Linux on 32-bit machines. This example shows that the alignment for the same structure in the 32-bit programming model can be different from that in the 64-bit programming model. When Program 13.23 is executed in Windows or Solaris on both 32-bit and

```
/* File: alignment.c
   Demonstrate alignment of structures */
#include <stdio.h>
#include <stddef.h> /* for macro offsetof() */

struct tag1 {         /* 1st structure with int, short, double */
    int i;
    short s;
    double d;
};
struct tag2 {         /* 2nd structure with int, double, short */
    int i;
    double d;
    short s;
};

int main() {
    size_t offset; /* offset for members of a structure *.

    /* obtain the size and offsets for members of 1st structure */
    printf("sizeof(struct tag1) = %u\n", sizeof(struct tag1));
    offset = offsetof(struct tag1, i);
    printf("offset i in struct tag1 = %u\n", offset);
    offset = offsetof(struct tag1, s);
    printf("offset s in struct tag1 = %u\n", offset);
    offset = offsetof(struct tag1, d);
    printf("offset d in struct tag1 = %u\n\n", offset);

    /* obtain the size and offsets for members of 2nd structure */
    printf("sizeof(struct tag2) = %u\n", sizeof(struct tag2));
    offset = offsetof(struct tag2, i);
    printf("offset i in struct tag2 = %u\n", offset);
    offset = offsetof(struct tag2, d);
    printf("offset d in struct tag2 = %u\n", offset);
    offset = offsetof(struct tag2, s);
    printf("offset s in struct tag2 = %u\n", offset);
    return 0;
}
```

Program 13.23: Finding alignment of structures.

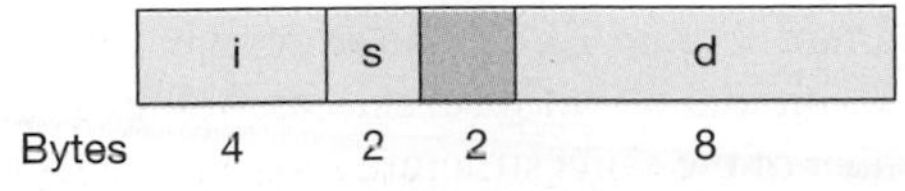

Figure 13.5: Memory storage for `struct tag1`.

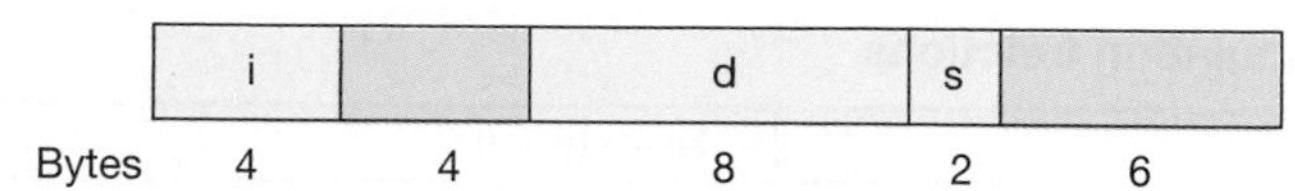

Figure 13.6: Memory storage for `struct tag2` in Windows and Solaris for both 32-bit and 64-bit machines, and in Linux for 64-bit machines.

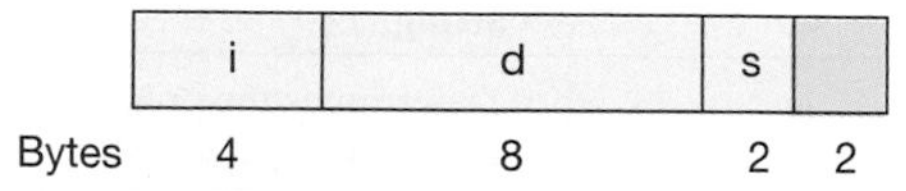

Figure 13.7: Memory storage for `struct tag2` in Linux for 32-bit machines.

64-bit machines, or in Linux on 64-bit machines, the output is shown below:

```
sizeof(struct tag1) = 16
offset i in struct tag1 = 0
offset s in struct tag1 = 4
offset d in struct tag1 = 8

sizeof(struct tag2) = 24
offset i in struct tag2 = 0
offset d in struct tag2 = 8
offset s in struct tag2 = 16
```

However, when this program is executed in Linux on 32-bit machines, the output is as follows:

```
sizeof(struct tag1) = 16
offset i in struct tag1 = 0
offset s in struct tag1 = 4
offset d in struct tag1 = 8

sizeof(struct tag2) = 16
offset i in struct tag2 = 0
offset d in struct tag2 = 4
offset s in struct tag2 = 12
```

13.1.17 ‡Time-Manipulating Functions and Their Applications

As more in-depth examples of using structures such as functions returning a pointer to structure, the time functions in the standard C libraries will be introduced in this section.

Time-Manipulating Functions

The time functions listed in Table 13.1 are defined in the header file **time.h**. Program 13.24 uses some time-manipulating functions in C. The header file **time.h** contains declarations for a few new data types: **clock_t**, **time_t**, and **struct tm**. Types **clock_t** and **time_t** are arithmetic types, declared as **size_t** as described in section 3.12 in Chapter 3, capable of representing time. The structure **tm** holds the components of a

Table 13.1 Time-manipulating functions.

Type	Description
char *asctime(const struct tm*`timeptr`)	Converts the broken-down time in the structure pointed to by `timeptr` into a string in the form: *weekday month day hour:min:sec year*`\n\0`. The return value is a pointer to the string.
clock_t clock(void)	Determines the processor time used by a program in units of **CLOCKS_PER_SEC**.
char *ctime(const time_t `*timer`)	Converts the calendar time pointed to by `timer` to local time in the form of a string. Return a pointer to that string.
double difftime(time_t `time1`**, time_t** `time0`)	Computes the number of seconds elapsed between two calendar times, `time1` and `time0`.
struct tm *gmtime(const time_t *`timer`)	Converts the calendar time pointed to by `timer` into a broken-down time, expressed in Coordinated Universal Time (UTC).
struct tm *localtime(const time_t `*timer`)	Converts the calendar time pointed to by `timer` into a broken-down time, expressed as local time, which is the return value.
time_t mktime(struct tm*`timeptr`)	Converts the broken-down time, expressed as local time, in the structure pointed to by `timeptr` into calendar time with the same encoding as that of the values returned by the **time()** function. Returns the specified calendar time encoded as a value of type **time_t**. If the calendar time cannot be represented, the function returns the value −1.
size_t strftime(char *`s`**, size_t** `max`, **const char ***`format`, **const struct tm ***`tm`)	Formats the broken-down time `tm` according to the format specification `format` and places the result in the character array `s` of size `max`.
time_t time(time_t *`timer`)	Determines the current calendar time. Return the implementation's best approximation to the current calendar time. If that time is not available, the value −1 is returned. The return value is also assigned to the object pointed to by `timer`, provided that it is not a null pointer.

```
/* File: time.c
   Use time functions with structure tm */
#include <stdio.h>
#include <time.h> /* for time_t, struct tm, and time functions */

/* define an array of pointers for names of each day */
const char *wday[] = {
      "Sunday", "Monday", "Tuesday", "Wednesday",
      "Thursday", "Friday", "Saturday", "-unknown-"
};
```

Program 13.24: Time functions using structures. (*Continued*)

```
int main() {
    time_t timer;                 /* declare timer */
    struct tm *timeptr, ts;  /* declare timeptr and ts of structure type */
    char *timestr;                /* time string */

    timer = time(NULL);           /*  get the current calendar time */
    printf("timer = %d\n", timer); /* print it */

    timeptr = localtime(&timer);    /* convert calendar time to local time */
    /* print local time in broken-down time */
    printf("year = %d\n", timeptr->tm_year+1900);
    printf("month = %d\n", timeptr->tm_mon+1);
    printf("day = %d\n", timeptr->tm_mday);
    printf("wday = %d\n", timeptr->tm_wday);
    /* use wday[] to convert an integer into a string for a day */
    printf("wday = %s\n", wday[timeptr->tm_wday]);
    printf("hour = %d\n", timeptr->tm_hour);
    printf("minute = %d\n", timeptr->tm_min);
    printf("second = %d\n", timeptr->tm_sec);
    printf("Daylight Saving Time flag = %d\n", timeptr->tm_isdst);

   /* convert the broken-down time into a time string */
    timestr = asctime(timeptr);
    printf("time = %s", timestr); /* print time string */
   /* convert the calendar time into a time string */
    timestr = ctime(&timer);
    printf("time = %s", timestr); /* print time string */

    /* obtain one year from the current time in the broken-down time */
    timeptr->tm_year += 1;
    /* conver in the broken-down time into the calendar time */
    timer = mktime(timeptr);
    printf("timer = %d\n", timer);  /* print the calendar time */
    return 0;
}
```

Program 13.24: (*Continued*)

calendar time, called the *broken-down time*. The structure contains at least the following members, in any order, shown following:

```
struct tm {
    int tm_sec;    // seconds after the minute [0, 59]
    int tm_min;    // minutes after the hour [0, 59]
    int tm_hour;   // hours since midnight [0, 23]
    int tm_mday;   // day of the month [1, 31]
    int tm_mon;    // months since January [0, 11]
    int tm_year;   // years since 1900
```

```
        int tm_wday;   // days since Sunday [0, 6]
        int tm_yday;   // days since January 1 [0, 365]
        int tm_isdst; // Daylight Saving Time flag
    };
```

Note that the value of tm_isdst is positive if Daylight Standard Time is in effect, zero if it is not in effect, and negative if the information is not available. Additionally, the header file **time.h** also defines the macro **CLOCKS_PER_SEC**, which corresponds to the number of *clock ticks* equal to 1 second.

Program 13.24 uses the function **time()** to obtain the current calendar time in seconds since 00:00:00 UTC, January 1, 1970. This calendar time is then converted to local time as an object pointed to by the **struct tm** timeptr. The individual members of timeptr are then displayed. Notice that the integer value corresponding to the weekday can be converted to its actual name, "Thursday" in this case, with an array of strings containing the name of the weekday. The same method can be used to label the months with their respective names. Keep in mind that in the output for month, an integer 1 is added to the member tm_mon so that January corresponds to the integer value 1, not 0. The function **asctime()** converts the data stored in timeptr into a string with the weekday and month displayed by their names. The function call to **ctime()**

```
timestr = ctime(&timer);
```

is equivalent to the following code fragment:

```
timeptr = localtime(&timer);
timestr = asctime(timeptr);
```

The broken-down time in the structure can be conveniently manipulated. For example, we can easily add one year to the broken-down time by incrementing the value for the member tm_year. However, the calendar time is useful for applications that need to represent the time using a single variable. In Program 13.24, the final time-manipulating function **mktime()** is used to convert the broken-down time of the structure pointed to by timeptr, which was incremented by 1 year, into the corresponding calendar time. The output of Program 13.24 is shown below:

```
timer = 1211061652
year = 2008
month = 5
day = 17
wday = 6
wday = Saturday
hour = 15
minute = 0
second = 52
Daylight Saving Time flag = 1
time = Sat May 17 15:00:52 2008
time = Sat May 17 15:00:52 2008
timer = 1242597652
```

Note that the output will be different for subsequent executions of Program 13.24. This is due to the change in time.

The **clock()** function returns the implementation's best approximation to the central processing unit (CPU) time used by the program since the beginning of an implementation-defined era related only to the

```
/* File: clock.c
   Use clock() to find the CPU time for a segment of the code */
#include <stdio.h>
#include <time.h>      /* for clock_t, clock(), CLOCKS_PER_SEC */

int main() {
    int i;
    clock_t t;         /* declare variable t for processor time */

    clock();           /* first call clock() */
    for(i = 0; i<1000;i++) {}; /* an empty loop */
    /* return the time between first call and this call */
    t = clock();
    printf("The CPU time for 1000 loop iterations is %.2f seconds.\n",
           (double)t/(double)CLOCKS_PER_SEC);
    return 0;
}
```

Program 13.25: Using the **clock**() function.

program invocation. To determine the time in seconds, the value returned by the clock function should be divided by the value of the macro **CLOCKS_PER_SEC**. If the processor time used is not available or its value cannot be represented, the function returns the value `(clock_t)-1`. To measure the time spent in a program, the function **clock()** should be called at the start of the program and its return value subtracted from the value returned by subsequent calls. For example, Program 13.25 calls the function **clock()** twice to compute the time it takes for a program to count from 0 to 1000 in increments of 1 using a **for** loop. For one runtime execution of Program 13.25, the output is as follows:

```
The CPU time for 1000 loop iterations is 0.01 seconds
```

The function **time()** determines the current calendar time, whereas the function **difftime()** computes the difference between two calendar times in seconds. These two functions are normally used in conjunction with one another. For example, Program 13.26 calls the function **time()** once before the **for** loop and then again after the loop. Function **difftime()** is then called to compute the time it takes for the **for** loop to complete. The output of Program 13.26 is shown below:

```
The elapsed time for 100000 loop iterations is 4.000000 seconds
```

The function **gmtime()** converts the calendar time given as an input argument of type **time_t** * into a broken-down time, expressed as UTC. Program 13.27 illustrates the difference between the functions **gmtime()** and **localtime()** described above. The output of Program 13.27 below shows that the time converted by the function **localtime()** is in the 12-hour format, whereas the function **gmtime()** converted the current time in the 24-hour format.

```
Local time and date: Tue Jun 17 14:45:26 2008
Coordinated Universal Time and date: Tue Jun 17 21:45:26 2008
```

```
/* File: difftime.c
   Use difftime() to find the difference to system time */
#include <stdio.h>
#include <time.h>              /* for time_t, time(), difftime() */

int main() {
    time_t time0, time1;       /* declare variables for system time */
    int i;

    time0 = time(NULL);        /* return system time */
    for(i = 0;i<100000;i++) {};
    time1 = time(NULL);        /* return system time */
    printf("The elapsed time for 100000 loop iterations is %f seconds.\n",
            difftime(time1,time0));
    return 0;
}
```

Program 13.26: Computing the time difference.

```
/* File: gmtime.c
   Use gmtime() to get Coordinated Universal Time (UTC) */
#include <stdio.h>
#include <time.h>  /* for struct tm, time_t, time(), localtime(), asctime() */

int main() {
    struct tm *local_time, *gm; /* variables for broken-down time */
    time_t t;                   /* variable for calendar time */

    t = time(NULL);             /* get the current calendar time */
    /* convert the calendar time to a broken-down local time */
    local_time = localtime(&t);
    /* convert broken-down local time into a string and print it */
    printf("Local time and date: %s",asctime(local_time));
    gm = gmtime(&t); /* convert the calendar time into UTC time */
    printf("Coordinated Universal Time and date: %s",asctime(gm));
}
```

Program 13.27: Converting calendar time into a broken-down time.

The function **strftime()** writes a broken-down time into a character array according to a specified format. Table 13.2 lists the format specifiers available for the function **strftime()**. These format specifiers utilize the appropriate fields of **struct tm** pointed to by the last argument of the function **strftime()**. For example, Program 13.28 uses the function **strftime()** along with time format specifiers `"%H"`, `"%M"`, and `"%p"` to print out the current time. For a specific execution of Program 13.28, the output is as follows:

```
It is now 09:16 AM.
```

Table 13.2 Time format specifiers for function strftime().

Format	Description
%a, %A	Abbreviated weekday name, full weekday name (`tm_wday`)
%b, %B	Abbreviated month name, full month name (`tm_mon`)
%c	Date and time
%C	Year specified as a decimal number between 00 and 99 (`tm_year`)
%d	Day of the month as a decimal number between 01 and 31 (`tm_mday`)
%D	Equivalent to `"%m/%d/%y"` (`tm_mon, tm_mday, tm_year`)
%e	Day of the month as a decimal number between 1 and 31; a single digit is preceded by a space (`tm_tmday`)
%F	Equivalent to `"%Y-%m-%d"`, the ISO 8601 date format (`tm_year, tm_wday, tm_yday`)
%g, %G	The last 2 digits of the week-based year as a decimal number between 00 and 99, the week-based year as a decimal number (`tm_year, tm_wday, tm_yday`)
%h	Equivalent to `"%b"` (`tm_mon`)
%H	The 24-hour clock hour as a decimal number between 00 and 23 (`tm_hour`)
%I	The 12-hour clock hour as a decimal number between 01 and 12 (`tm_hour`)
%j	The day of the year as a decimal number between 001 and 366 (`tm_yday`)
%m	The month as a decimal number between 01 and 12 (`tm_mon`)
%M	The minute as a decimal number between 00 and 59 (`tm_min`)
%n	A newline character
%p	Equivalent of the AM/PM designations associated with the 12-hour clock (`tm_hour`)
%r	The locale's 12-hour clock time (`tm_hour, tm_min, tm_sec`)
%R	Equivalent to `"%H:%M"` (`tm_hour, tm_min`)
%S	The second as a decimal number between 00 and 60 (`tm_sec`)
%t	The horizontal-tab character
%T	Equivalent to `"%H:%M:%S"`, the ISO 8601 time format (`tm_hour, tm_min, tm_sec`)
%u	The ISO 8601 weekday as a decimal number between 1 and 7, where Monday is 1 (`tm_wday`)
%U	The week number of the year as a decimal number between 00 and 53, where the first Sunday is the first day of week 1 (`tm_year, tm_wday, tm_yday`)
%V	The ISO 8601 week number of the current year as a decimal number between 01 and 53, where week 1 is the first week that has at least 4 days in the current year and with Monday as the first day of the week (`tm_year, tm_wday, tm_yday`)
%w	The weekday as a decimal number between 0 and 6, where Sunday is 0 (`tm_wday`)
%W	The week number of the year as a decimal number between 00 and 53, where the first Monday is the first day of week 1 (`tm_year, tm_wday, tm_yday`)
%x, %X	The appropriate date representation with the time, the appropriate time representation without the date
%y, %Y	The year as a decimal number without a century between 00 and 99, the year as a decimal number with the century (`tm_year`)
%z	The offset from UTC in the ISO 8601 format, such as `"-0430"`, which means 4 hours 30 minutes behind UTC, west of Greenwich, or no characters if no time zone is determinable (`tm_isdst`)
%Z	The time zone name or abbreviation, or no characters if no time zone is determinable (`tm_isdst`)
%%	The character `'%'`

```
/* File: strftime.c
   Use strftime() to convert a broken-down time into a string time */
#include <stdio.h>
#include <stdlib.h>
#include <time.h>  /* for struct tm, time_t, time(), localtime(), strftime() */

int main() {
    struct tm *ptr;           /* variable for broken-down time */
    time_t ltime;             /* variable for calendar time */
    char str[80];             /* time string */

    ltime = time(NULL);       /* get the current calendar time */
    /* convert the calendar time to a broken-down local time */
    ptr = localtime(&ltime);
    /* get the time string based on the broken-down local time ptr */
    strftime(str,80,"It is now %H:%M %p.",ptr);
    printf("%s\n",str);       /* print time string */
    return 0;
}
```

Program 13.28: Using the function **strftime**() and time format specifiers.

13.2 Enumerations

An enumerated type comprises a set of named integer constant values. For example, the declaration with the keyword **enum**

```
enum datatypes {
    inttype,       // 0
    floattype,     // 1
    doubletype,    // 2
} d1, d2;
```

creates a new enumerated type, `enum datatypes`, whose values are `inttype`, `floattype`, and `doubletype` enclosed in braces. It also declares two variables of the enumerated type `d1` and `d2`, which can be assigned enumeration constants with the following assignment statement:

```
d1 = inttype;
d2 = doubletype;
```

The first enumeration constant receives the value 0 by default and the subsequent enumeration constants receive an integer value 1 greater than the previous enumeration constant. The values of `d1` and `d2` will be 0 and 2, respectively.

An explicit integer value can be associated with an enumeration constant in the definition. For example, given the declaration

```
enum datatypes {
    inttype,           // 0
```

```
    floattype = 10,    // 10
    doubletype         // 11
};
```

the value of `inttype`, `floattype`, `doubletype` will be 0, 10, and 11, respectively.

Enumerated types can be used to replace the **#define** directive in some applications. The following code fragment uses a variable of enum type in a **switch** statement:

```
enum datatypes {
    inttype,
    floattype,
    doubletype
};
enum datatype dtype;
/* some code ... */
switch(dtype) {
    case inttype:
      /* some code ... */
      break;
    case floattype:
        /* some code ... */
      break;
    case doubletype:
      /* some code ... */
      break;
}
/* some code ... */
```

As an example, in Program 6.19 in Chapter 6, we used a function with a variable number of arguments to calculate the area of various shapes. The shape types are defined as macros in Program 6.19. We can rewrite the program using an enumerated type shown in Program 13.29 to calculate the area of various shapes. In this program, the enumerated type `shapes` has three values corresponding to a circle, square, and rectangle. The enumerated value along with the required dimension(s) are passed into the function `area()`, where a **switch** statement is used to determine the shape of the object and calculate its area. The function `area()` returns the area of the shape, and the function **main()** prints the results. The output from Program 13.29 is the same as that from Program 6.19 shown in Figure 6.9 in Chapter 6.

```
/* File: enums.c
   Calculate areas of different shapes using a function
   with a variable number of arguments using enumerates */
#include <stdio.h>
#include <stdarg.h>    /* for va_list, va_start(), va_arg(), va_end() */
#include <math.h>      /* for M_PI */
```

Program 13.29: Using the enumerate type. (*Continued*)

```
/* declare enumerates for circle, square, and rectangle */
enum shapes {
    CIRCLE,
    SQUARE,
    RECTANGLE
};

/* function area() with a variable number of arguments */
double area (enum shapes type, ...) {
    va_list ap;             /* variable used for handling ... */
    double radius;          /* radius of a circle */
    double side;            /* side of a square */
    double length, width; /* length and width of a rectangle */
    double a=0.0;           /* area of a shape */

    va_start(ap, type); /* use the argument type to start ap */
    /* depending on the type of shape,
       obtain the passed argument(s) and calculate the area */
    switch(type) {
        case CIRCLE:
          /* for a circle, obtain the passed radius  */
          radius = va_arg(ap, double);
          a = M_PI*radius*radius;
          break;
        case SQUARE:
          /* for a square, obtain the passed side */
          side = va_arg(ap, double);
          a = side*side;
          break;
        case RECTANGLE:
          /* for a rectangle, obtain the passed length and width */
          length = va_arg(ap, double);
          width  = va_arg(ap, double);
          a = length*width;
          break;
        default:
          /* in case a mistake is made by passing an unknown shape */
          printf("Error: unknown shape\n");
          break;
    }
    va_end(ap); /* end the processing of the variable number of arguments*/
    return a;
}
```

Program 13.29: *(Continued)*

```
int main() {
    /* The unit for lengths is meter */
    double radius = 2.0;                  /* radius of a circle */
    double side = 2.0;                    /* side of a square */
    double length = 3.0, width = 2.0; /* length and width of a rectangle */
    double a;                             /* area of a shape */

    /* calculate and display areas for shapes circle, square, and rectangle */
    a = area(CIRCLE, radius);
    printf("The area of circle with radius 2 m is %.2f (m^2)\n", a);
    a = area(SQUARE, side);
    printf("The area of square with side 2 m is %.2f (m^2)\n", a);
    a = area(RECTANGLE, length, width);
    /* A single long line of output is broken into two printf() statements */
    printf("The area of rectangle with length 3 m and width 2 m");
    printf(" is %.2f (m^2)\n", a);
    return 0;
}
```

Program 13.29: *(Continued)*

13.3 ‡Unions

A union type describes an overlapping nonempty set of member objects, each of which has an optionally specified name and possibly distinct type. Like structures, unions can have members. Unlike structures, a union can hold only one of its members at a time. The members are conceptually overlaid in the same memory. Each member of a union is located at the beginning of the union.

For example, below is a declaration of the union `data` introduced by the keyword **union** with two members `i` and `d` inside braces.

```
union data {
    int i;
    double d;
} obj, *p = &obj;
```

The variable `obj` is decalared as a union `data`, whereas the variable `p` is a pointer to the union `data` and it points to `obj`. The memory layout for the union `data` is shown in Figure 13.8. The offset for both members `i` and `d` is zero. The following equalities for the address of the object `obj` of union type hold.

```
(union data*)&(p->i) == (union data*)(p->d) == p
```

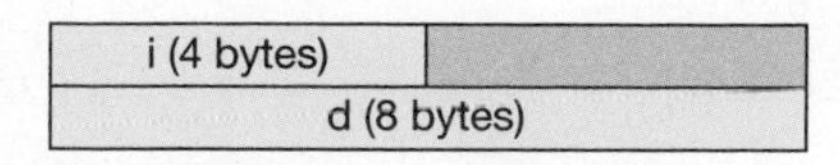

Figure 13.8: The memory storage for `union data`.

Because a union holds only one member at a time, if two or more members are used without casting, the result could be strange. For example, the following code fragment

```
obj.i = 10;
printf("obj.d = %f\n", obj.d);
```

will print out zero or a tiny value instead of 10, because of the differences in the representation of an int and a double variable.

The size of an instance of a union is the amount of memory necessary to represent the largest member, plus the padding that raises the length up to an appropriate alignment boundary. In this example, the size of the union `data` is 8, which is the result of the expression `sizeof(union data)`. However, because of the alignment for double type, the size of the union `data2` below

```
union data2{
        int i;
        double d;
        char c[12];
};
```

is 16, although the largest member `c` occupies only 12 bytes of memory.

Program 13.30 is an example of declaring a union and accessing its members. The memory layout for the union `data` of Program 13.30 is shown in Figure 13.8. The output is given below. Note that the size of `data` is 8, and the offset for both members is zero.

```
sizeof(union data) = 8
sizeof(u) = 8
offsetof(union data, i) = 0
offsetof(union data, d) = 0
u.i = 10
u.d = 0.000000
u.i = 1077149696
u.d = 20.000000
```

```
/* File: union1.c
   Demonstrate the concept of the union */
#include <stdio.h>
#include <stddef.h>  /* for offsetof() */

union data {          /* define a union */
    int i;            /* a member of int type */
    double d;         /* a member of double type */
};

int main() {
    union data u; /* declare variable u of union type */
```

Program 13.30: Using unions. (*Continued*)

```
    /* the size of union is the memory for the largest member, double */
    printf("sizeof(union data) = %u\n", sizeof(union data));
    printf("sizeof(u) = %u\n", sizeof(u));
    /* the offset for each member of the union is the same, 0 */
    printf("offsetof(union data, i) = %u\n", offsetof(union data, i));
    printf("offsetof(union data, d) = %u\n", offsetof(union data, d));

    /* assign the member i with an integer, use 4 bytes */
    u.i = 10;
    printf("u.i = %d\n", u.i);     /* u.i is 10 */
    printf("u.d = %f\n", u.d);     /* u.d is undefined */

    /* assign the member d with a floating point number, use 8 bytes */
    u.d = 20.0;
    printf("u.i = %d\n", u.i);     /* u.i is undefined */
    printf("u.d = %f\n", u.d);     /* u.d is 20.0 */
    return 0;
}
```

Program 13.30: *(Continued)*

Unions are often associated with a *data tag* of enumerated type, which is an object used to indicate which component is currently stored in the union. Unions and their data tags are usually enclosed in a common structure. For example, the structure `struct tag` below contains a union variable `data` and an enumerated variable `datatype`.

```
union data {
   int i;
   float f;
   double d;
};

enum datatype {
   inttype,
   floattype,
   doubletype
};

struct tag {
   datatype dtype;
   union data u;
};
```

The *data tag* is an enumerated list for int, float, and double types. Thus, if data type `inttype` is specified for `struct tag`, then it is easily recognizable that an integer is currently stored in the union `data`. Program 13.31 shows an example using the union and data tag defined above. The function `storeData()`

```
/* File: union2.c
   How a union is typically used in an application. */
#include <stdio.h>

union data {        /* define a union */
    int i;          /* a member of int type */
    float f;        /* a member of float type */
    double d;       /* a member of double type */
};

enum datatype {     /* define an enumerate type */
    inttype,        /* int type */
    floattype,      /* float type */
    doubletype      /* double type */
};

struct tag {        /* define a structure */
    enum datatype dtype; /* this enumerate type associates the data
                            inside union n. */
    union data u;  /* union contains the data specified by dtype */
};

/* function prototypes */
void storeData(enum datatype, struct tag *, const void *); /* store data */
void printData(const struct tag *);                        /* print data */

int main() {
    /* declare and initialize variables of different types */
    int i = 10;         /* declare i of int type */
    float f = 20.0;     /* declare f of float type */
    double d = 30.0;    /* declare d of double type */
    struct tag s;       /* declare s of structure tag */

    storeData(inttype, &s, &i); /* store i inside s based on inttype */
    printData(&s);      /* print the stored data based on dtype inside s */
    storeData(floattype, &s, &f); /* store f inside s based on inttype */
    printData(&s);      /* print the stored data based on dtype inside s */
    storeData(doubletype, &s, &d); /* store d inside s based on inttype */
    printData(&s);      /* print the stored data based on dtype inside s */
    return 0;
}
```

Program 13.31: A program using unions with an enumerate type. (*Continued*)

```
/* store data passed by the generic pointer in the memory pointed by sp
   with data type specified by dtype, object pointed by sp WILL BE modified */
void storeData(enum datatype dtype, struct tag *sp, const void *data) {
    sp->dtype = dtype;  /* save the stored data type in sp */
    switch(dtype) {     /* check the data type of the passed data */
      case inttype:              /* int type  */
       /* cast data from the generic pointer into 'int *',
          obtain the data by *((int*) data), store it in sp->u.i */
        sp->u.i = *(int*)data;
        break;
      case floattype:             /* do the same for float type */
        sp->u.f = *(float*)data;
        break;
      case doubletype:            /* do the same for double type */
        sp->u.d = *(double*)data;
        break;
      default:                    /* in case a mistake is made */
        printf("Error: unknown data type\n");
        break;
    }
}

/* print the stored data in sp, object pointed by sp
   WILL NOT BE modified. sp is const-qualified. */
void printData(const struct tag *sp) {
    switch(dtype) {     /* check the data type of the stored data */
      case inttype:                        /* int type  */
        printf("data = %d\n", sp->u.i); /* print int */
        break;
      case floattype:                      /* float type */
        printf("data = %f\n", sp->u.f); /* print float */
        break;
      case doubletype:                     /* double type */
        printf("data = %f\n", sp->u.d); /* print double */
        break;
      default:                             /* in case a mistake is made */
        printf("Error: unknown data type\n");
        break;
    }
}
```

Program 13.31: *(Continued)*

may be used to input data into the data structure `tag`, while `printData()` may access and print the data stored in the union based on the data type in the union. The output of Program 13.31 is as follows:

```
data = 10
data = 20.000000
data = 30.000000
```

If an object of union type has static storage duration, which is not initialized explicitly, it will be initialized according to the following rules:

- The first named member is initialized recursively.
- If the first member is pointer type, it is initialized to a null pointer.
- If the member is arithmetic type, it is initialized to positive zero.

13.4 ‡Bit-Fields

A member of a structure or union may be declared to consist of a specified number of bits (including a sign bit, if any). Such a member is called a *bit-field*; its number of bits is preceded by a colon. Bit-fields have the capability of defining and accessing directly within a word. Therefore, it saves the memory space at runtime, especially for programs that use structures or unions with many members extensively.

In Program 13.32, the size of `tag` is 12 because there are three integers inside the structure. However, the size of `bitfield` is 4 because three members only take 12 bits of memory, plus padding. Therefore,

```
/* File: bitfield.c
   Demonstrates bit-fields */
#include <stdio.h>

struct tag1 {                /* define a regular structure */
    int a;                   /* declare a as a member of int */
    unsigned int b;          /* declare b as a member of unsigned int */
    unsigned int c;          /* declare c as a member of unsigned int */
} s1 = {1, 2, 3};            /* declare s1 as struct tag1 */

struct tag2 {                /* declare a structure with bitfields */
    int a : 4;               /* declare a as a bit-field of int with 4 bits */
    unsigned int b : 4;      /* b as a bit-field of unsigned int with 4 bits */
    unsigned int c : 4;      /* c as a bit-field of unsigned int with 4 bits */
} s2 = {1, 2, 3};            /* declare s2 as struct tag2 */

int main() {
    s2.c = 4;                 /* assign 4 to bit-field c of s2 */

    /* print and compare ssize of struct tag1 and struct tag2 */
    printf("sizeof tag1 is %u\n", sizeof(struct tag1));
```

Program 13.32: Using a bit-field. *(Continued)*

```
    printf("sizeof tag2 is %u\n", sizeof(struct tag2));

    /* print out each members of bit-fields of structure tag2 */
    printf("s2.a = %d\n", s2.a);
    printf("s2.b = %d\n", s2.b);
    printf("s2.c = %d\n", s2.c);
    return 0;
}
```

Program 13.32: *(Continued)*

if the memory is a concern for an application, the use of bit-fields inside a structure can be considered. The selection operator "." can be used to access the members of a bit-field. The output of Program 13.32 is shown below.

```
sizeof tag1 is 12
sizeof tag2 is 4
s2.a = 1
s2.b = 2
s2.c = 4
```

Bit-fields can be signed or unsigned. The bit-field `a` in Program 13.32 is signed, whereas bit-fields `b` and `c` are unsigned. For a 4-bit bit-field, the range for a signed bit-field is from −8 to 7 and the range for an unsigned one is from 0 to 15.

There are certain constraints for bit-fields. We cannot take the address of a bit-field. Besides, bit-fields are machine-dependent. Consider the bit field below.

```
struct eeh_type {
  uint16 u1: 10;    /* 10 bits */
  uint16 u2:  6;    /* 6 bits */
};
```

This might actually be implemented as

```
<10-bits><6-bits>
```

or as

```
<6-bits><10-bits>
```

depending on the machine and operating system.

13.5 Design of a GPA Library and Its Applications

In this section, a practical example is used to illustrate the application of various features of structures. It also shows how to design a library containing multiple functions that can then be used in different application programs. The top-down and bottom-up design of programs are illustrated

Assume that data for a class of students are available. The data include the identification number, name, birthday, and GPA for each student. They are stored in an array of student structures. We need to write a program to calculate the total number of students, average GPA, highest GPA, and lowest GPA for the class. The program should also be able to find the number of students above a certain GPA, as well as sort the list of students based on their GPA. The program should be interactive, allowing the user to select which statistical result will be calculated and displayed dynamically.

13.5.1 Design and Implementation of a GPA Library

In section 10.5.2, we used functions in a statistical library to process student GPAs. However, that statistical library cannot be used conveniently to process information including student ID, name, and GPA. To develop a menu-driven interactive program to process student information, we will first develop a GPA library containing a set of functions. The functions in the GPA library can then be used within the interactive program. The header file `student.h` for the GPA library is shown in Program 13.33. The macro `GPA_EOD` defined as

```
#define GPA_EOD -1
```

in Program 13.33 is used as a sentinel number. Macros defined in the header file `student.h` will also be used in application programs that use the GPA library.

```
/**************************************************************
* File: student.h
* This header file contains macros, data structures and
* function prototypes for the GPA library. Macro names with
* prefix GPA_,  variable names with prefix gpa_, symbols
* Birthday, Student, student_t are reserved for this lib.
**************************************************************/
#ifndef STUDENT_H
#define STUDENT_H

/* define End Of Data */
#define GPA_EOD -1

/* define boolean numbers */
#define TRUE 1
#define FALSE 0

struct Birthday {                /* structure for birthday */
    short day, month, year;      /* day, month, year */
};

typedef struct Student {         /* structure for a student */
    int id;                      /* student id */
    char name[32];               /* student name */
    struct Birthday birthday;    /* student birthday */
    double gpa;                  /* student GPA */
} student_t;
```

Program 13.33: The header file `student.h` for a GPA library. *(Continued)*

```
/* function prototypes for a single student */
extern void gpa_printStudent(const student_t *sp);
extern int gpa_getId(const student_t *sp);
extern char *gpa_getName(const student_t *sp);
extern struct Birthday gpa_getBirthday(const student_t *sp);
extern double gpa_getGPA(const student_t *sp);

/* function prototypes for a list of students */
extern int gpa_totnum(const student_t *head);
extern void gpa_printList(const student_t *head);
extern double gpa_averageGPA(const student_t *head);
extern student_t *gpa_highestGPA(const student_t *head);
extern student_t *gpa_lowestGPA(const student_t *head);
extern student_t *gpa_find(const student_t *head, int id, const char *name);
extern int gpa_aboveGPA(const student_t *head, double gpa);
extern void gpa_sortGPA(student_t *head);

/* utility function */
extern const char *gpa_monthString(int month);

/* load code from file studentfunc.c for Ch */
#ifdef _CH_
#pragma importf "studentfunc.c"
#endif

#endif /* STUDENT_H */
```

Program 13.33: (*Continued*)

Two macros, TRUE and FALSE, for boolean values 1 and 0, respectively, are also defined in the header file student.h. These two boolean values are used for the implementation of GPA functions and applications using these functions. We could have used the C99 feature of the boolean type and macros **true** and **false** by including the header file **stdbool.h** here. But, for the illustrative purpose of writing the C89-compatible code, we use our own defined macros TRUE and FALSE in this GPA library.

The structures Birthday and Student

```
struct Birthday {
    short day, month, year;
};

typedef struct Student {
    int id;
    char name[32];
    struct Birthday birthday;
    double gpa;
} student_t;
```

will be used to hold the information of a given student. For programming convenience, a new data type `student_t` is defined for the `Student` structure.

Functions with function prototypes of

```
extern void gpa_printStudent(const student_t *sp);
extern int gpa_getId(const student_t *sp);
extern char *gpa_getName(const student_t *sp);
extern struct Birthday gpa_getBirthday(const student_t *sp);
extern double gpa_getGPA(const student_t *sp);
```

handle a single student. For argument-passing efficiency, information for a student is passed using a pointer to the structure of that student. Because the data in the structure is not modified by these functions, the type-specifier **const** is used to specify the pointers. Based on the input argument for a student, these functions will either print out the information for the student or return the identification number, name, birthday, or GPA of the student.

Functions with function prototypes of

```
extern int gpa_totnum(const student_t *head);
extern void gpa_printList(const student_t *head);
extern double gpa_averageGPA(const student_t *head);
extern student_t *gpa_highestGPA(const student_t *head);
extern student_t *gpa_lowestGPA(const student_t *head);
extern student_t *gpa_find(const student_t *head, int id, char *name);
extern int gpa_aboveGPA(const student_t *head, double gpa);
extern void gpa_sortGPA(student_t *head);
```

handle a list of students. Information for a list of students are stored in an array of student structures. Different from other functions, the function `gpa_sortGPA()` modifies the structure pointed by the pointer `head`. Therefore, there is no type specifier **const** in the declaration of its function argument. Although the first argument of these functions is a pointer to the student structure, it is the address of the first element of an array of students. The function parameter can be changed to an array of student structures as

```
extern int gpa_totnum(student_t head[]);
```

without affecting the result. These functions can be used to calculate the total number of students; print out all students in the list; calculate the average GPA, highest GPA, and lowest GPA for the class; find a student based on an identification number and name; find the number of students above a certain GPA; and sort the list of students based on GPA in descending order using the bubble sort algorithm presented in section 10.4 in Chapter 10. The functions `gpa_highestGPA()`, `gpa_lowestGPA()`, and `gpa_find()` return a pointer to a structure that points to a desired student element in a list. The function `gpa_find()` returns NULL if the list does not contain a student with the specified id and name.

The utility function

```
extern const char *gpa_monthString(int month);
```

returns a string containing the month based on the integral argument for the month in the range from 1 to 12 for the twelve months. The returned constant string has static duration. This function is similar to the function `daystr()` in Program 11.11 described in section 11.10 in Chapter 11.

To avoid any namespace conflicts, macros in this GPA library start with the prefix `GPA_`. This convention of macro naming is typically used for library development. All external functions in the GPA library that can be used in application programs start with the prefix `gpa_`. Using a prefix for all external functions in a library is also a common practice in library development. Because the header file `student.h` will be used in applications, the symbols `Birthday`, `Student`, and `student_t`, and the variables starting with `GPA_` and `gpa_` are reserved for this GPA library. Application programs, such as `student.c` and `studentmenu.c` described later in this section, using this GPA library shall not define macros or variables with these reserved symbols. By convention, a macro shall consist of capital letters, digits, and underscores. There are different conventions for naming external functions for a library. For example, it would be acceptable to use the following prefixes for the function `gpa_getName()` in the GPA library.

```
gpa_getName()
gpaGetName()
gpa_get_name()
gpa_Get_Name()
GPA_get_name()
GPA_Get_Name()
```

The function definitions of the GPA library are in the file `studentfunc.c` shown in Program 13.34. The function

```
static student_t *highestLowestGPA(const student_t *head, int isFindHighest);
```

is a static function within a file scope, as described in section 8.2.3 in Chapter 8. It returns a student from a list of students in `head` with the highest or lowest GPA, depending on the value of the second argument. If the second argument is `TRUE`, which is defined in the header file `student.h`, the function returns the student with the highest GPA. Otherwise, it returns the student with the lowest GPA. The implementation of the function assumes that the lowest GPA value is positive and the highest GPA is 5.0. This function is used to implement functions

```
extern student_t *gpa_highestGPA(const student_t *head);
extern student_t *gpa_lowestGPA(const student_t *head);
```

Because internal functions, such as `highestLowestGPA()`, will not be used in application programs, they typically do not start with the reserved symbol `gpa_`, as with external functions of the GPA library.

Functions dealing with a single student in Program 13.34 are quite straightforward. The identification number of the last element of the array of students is `GPA_EOD`. This sentinel number is used in functions that handle an array of students, such as the function `gpa_totnum()`, and that calculate the total number of elements in an array of student structures. Note that functions that use global or static variables are nonreentrant and cannot be called concurrently in a multithread application. Therefore, global or static variables should be avoided in developing a library.

The variable `head` in all functions in `studentfunc.c`, except in the function `gpa_sortGPA()`, points to an array of student structures. The expression `head++` advances the pointer to the next element of the array. In the function `gpa_sortGPA()` for sorting the GPA in descending order, the expression `head[i].gpa` accesses the GPA of the *i*th element. Based on the comparison of the GPA values `head[i].gpa` and `head[j].gpa`, the values for elements `head[i]` and `head[j]` may be swapped in the bubble sort.

```
/************************************************************
* File: studentfunc.c
* This file contains function definitions for the GPA library
************************************************************/
#include <stdio.h>
#include <string.h>    /* for strcmp() */
#include "student.h"   /* header file GPA lib */

/* static function in file scope */
static
student_t *highestLowestGPA(const student_t *head, int isFindHighest);

/* external functions */

/* Code block 1: functions for a single student */
void gpa_printStudent(const student_t *sp) { print info for a student */
    if(sp == NULL) {
        printf("Error: invalid argument passed to printStudent()\n");
        return;
    }
    printf("  id: %d; name: %6s; birthday: %8s %2d, %d; GPA: %.2f\n",
          sp->id, sp->name, gpa_monthString(sp->birthday.month),
          sp->birthday.day, sp->birthday.year, sp->gpa);
}

int gpa_getId(const student_t *sp) {      /* get student ID */
    return sp->id;
}

char *gpa_getName(const student_t *sp) {  /* get student name */
    return (char *)sp->name;
}

struct Birthday gpa_getBirthday(const student_t *sp) { /* get birthday */
    return sp->birthday;
}

double gpa_getGPA(const student_t *sp) {  /* get student GPA */
    return sp->gpa;
}


/* Code block 2: functions for a list of students */
/* get total number of students in the list */
```

Program 13.34: The function file `studentfunc.c` for a GPA library. (*Continued*)

```
int gpa_totnum(const student_t *head) {
    int totnum = 0;
    while(head->id != GPA_EOD) {
        totnum++;
        head++;
    }
    return totnum;
}

/* print info for all students in the list */
void gpa_printList(const student_t *head) {
    while(head->id != GPA_EOD) {
        gpa_printStudent(head);
        head++;
    }
}

/* calculate the average of the GPA for students in the list */
double gpa_averageGPA(const student_t *head) {
    double gpa, totalval;
    int i;

    totalval=0.0;
    for(i=0; head->id != GPA_EOD; head++, i++) {
        totalval += head->gpa;
    }
    gpa = totalval/i;
    return gpa;
}

/* find the student with the highest GPA in the list */
student_t *gpa_highestGPA(const student_t *head) {
    return highestLowestGPA(head, TRUE);
}

/* find the student with the lowest GPA in the list */
student_t *gpa_lowestGPA(const student_t *head) {
    return highestLowestGPA(head, FALSE);
}

/* find the student based on the id and name */
student_t *gpa_find(const student_t *head, int id, const char *name) {
    while(head->id!=GPA_EOD && !(!strcmp(head->name, name) && head->id == id)) {
       head++;
    }
```

Program 13.34: *(Continued)*

```
    if(head->id == GPA_EOD)
       return NULL;
    else
       return (student_t *)head;
}

/* print out the students with GAP above 'gpa' */
int gpa_aboveGPA(const student_t *head, double gpa) {
    int num;
    for(num=0; head->id != GPA_EOD; head++) {
        if(head->gpa >= gpa) {
            gpa_printStudent(head);
            num++;
        }
    }
    return num;
}

/* sort students with GPA in descending order using bubble sort */
void gpa_sortGPA(student_t *head) {
    int i, j, totnum; /* declare indexes i and j, total num of students */
    student_t tmp;    /* declare a temporary student element for swap */

    totnum = gpa_totnum(head); /* get the total number of students to sort */
    /* find the student with highest GPA in the remaining part of list
       in each iteration staring with head[i]  */
    for(i = 0; i < totnum-1; i++) {
        /* compare with head[i].gpa with head[j].gpa for j from i+1
           to totnum-1 */
        for(j = i+1; j < totnum; j++) {
            /* when head.gpa[i] < head.gpa[j], swap their values */
            if(head[i].gpa < head[j].gpa) {
                tmp = head[i];
                head[i] = head[j];
                head[j] = tmp;
            }
        }
    }
}

/* Code block 3: utility functions */
/* The function returns a string of a month based on the
   argument in the range of 1 to 12. If the value of the
```

Program 13.34: (*Continued*)

```
   argument is outside this range, the function returns NULL. */
const char *gpa_monthString(int month) {
    static const char *monthName[] = {"January", "February", "March",
            "April", "May", "June", "July", "August", "September",
            "October", "November", "December"};

    return (month < 1 || month > 12) ? NULL : monthName[month-1];
}

/* Code block 4: internal functions */
/* find the student with the highest or lowest GPA in the list */
static student_t *highestLowestGPA(const student_t *head, int isFindHighest) {
    student_t *sp;
    double gpa;

    gpa = head->gpa;        /* initial gpa */
    sp = (student_t *)head; /* initial sp */
    while(head->id != GPA_EOD) {  /* search through the list */
        /* if isFindHighest is TRUE, find the student with the
           highest GPA, else find the student with the lowest GPA */
        if(isFindHighest == TRUE && head->gpa > gpa) {
            gpa = head->gpa;
            sp= (student_t *)head;
        }
        else if(isFindHighest == FALSE && head->gpa < gpa) {
            gpa = head->gpa;
            sp = (student_t*)head;
        }
        head++;  /* move the next element */
    }
    return sp;
}
```

Program 13.34: *(Continued)*

13.5.2 Testing the GPA Library

Two programs will be developed to illustrate how the GPA library can be used to handle the GPA of a class. The first program is very simple for testing purposes. The second program presented in the next section illustrates how to design and implement user-friendly application programs using libraries.

Program 13.35 first calculates the total number of students in the list and the average GPA of the list. Then it finds the students with the highest and lowest GPA. Next, it finds Peter's GPA and all students with a GPA above 3.0. Finally, it sorts and displays the students in descending GPA order. The flowchart for the program is shown in Figure 13.9, and the source code is given in Program 13.35.

```
/************************************************************
* File: student.c
* This program tests the GPA library with data in an array
************************************************************/
#include <stdio.h>
#include "student.h"   /* header file for GPA library */

/* the database for students' GPA,
   more students can be added */
student_t data[] = {
    {101, "John",   12, 11, 1985, 3.33},
    {102, "Doe",    13, 3,  1988, 3},
    {103, "Peter",  21, 4,  1984, 3.1},
    {104, "Mary",   8,  2,  1985, 3.93},
    {105, "Ron",    30, 12, 1986, 2.3},
    {106, "George", 9,  1,  1987, 2.31},
    {107, "Mike",   10, 8,  1986, 3.99},
    {108, "Steve",  17, 5,  1989, 2.8},
    {109, "Jone",   25, 4,  1990, 2.9},
    {110, "Ron",    6,  11, 1988, 3.7},
    {GPA_EOD, "", GPA_EOD, GPA_EOD, GPA_EOD, GPA_EOD} /* terminating element */
};

int main() {
    student_t *head, *sp; /* head of the list and a single student */
    double gpa;           /* GPA value */
    struct Birthday b;    /* b for birthday */
    int num; /* number of students with GPA above a specified value */

    head = data;          /* head of the list */
    printf("The total number of students is %d\n", gpa_totnum(head));
    gpa = gpa_averageGPA(head); /* GPA for all students */
    printf("The GPA for all students is %.2f\n", gpa);
    sp = gpa_highestGPA(head); /* find the student with the highest GPA */
    b = gpa_getBirthday(sp);   /* get the birthday of this student */
    printf("%s who was born on %s %d, %d has the highest GPA %.2f\n",
           gpa_getName(sp), gpa_monthString(b.month), b.day, b.year,
           gpa_getGPA(sp));
    printf("The student with the lowest GPA:\n");
    sp = gpa_lowestGPA(head);  /* find the student with the lowest GPA */
    gpa_printStudent(sp);      /* print infor for this student */
    /* find the student with ID 103 and named 'Peter' */
```

Program 13.35: A program `student.c`, using functions in a GPA library. (*Continued*)

```
    sp = gpa_find(head, 103, "Peter");
    if(sp) {   /* if Peter is in the list, get and print his GPA */
      printf("Peter's GPA is %.2f\n", gpa_getGPA(sp));
    }
    printf("Students with GPA 3.0 or above:\n");
    /* get the number of students with GPA above 3.0 and print them out */
    num = gpa_aboveGPA(head, 3.0);
    printf("%d students with GPA 3.0 or above.\n", num);
    gpa_sortGPA(head);    /* sort students in the list based on GPA */
    printf("The student record sorted in descending GPA:\n");
    gpa_printList(head); /* print info for students in the sorted list */
    return 0;
}
```

Program 13.35: (*Continued*)

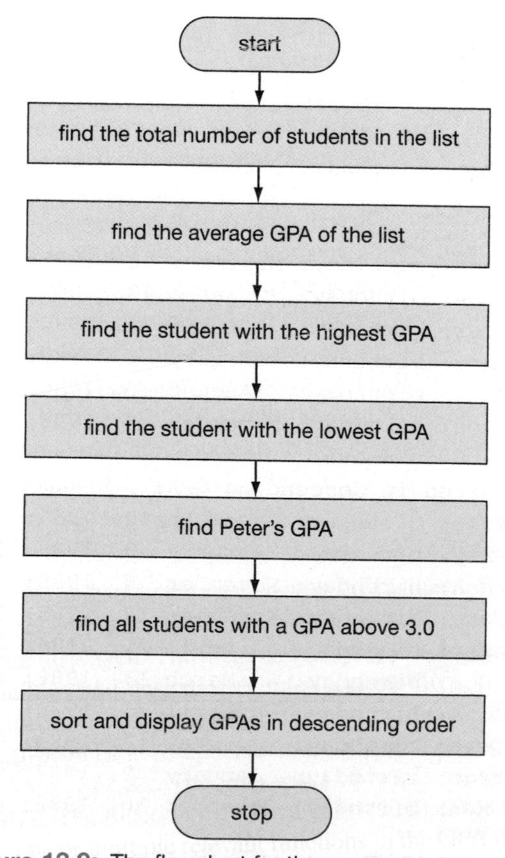

Figure 13.9: The flowchart for the program `student.c`.

```
************************ GPA Menu ************************
av, average: display the average of GPAs for all students
h,  highest: display the student with the highest GPA
l,  lowest:  display the student with the lowest GPA
ab, above:   display students with GPA above a value
s,  sort:    display the record sorted in descending GPA
o,  obtain:  obtain a student's GPA
q,  quit:    quit the system
..........................................................

GPA> h
Mike who was born on August 10, 1986 has the highest GPA 3.99

************************ GPA Menu ************************
av, average: display the average of GPAs for all students
h,  highest: display the student with the highest GPA
l,  lowest:  display the student with the lowest GPA
ab, above:   display students with GPA above a value
s,  sort:    display the record sorted in descending GPA
o,  obtain:  obtain a student's GPA
q,  quit:    quit the system
..........................................................

GPA>
```

Figure 13.11: The user interface of an interactive GPA calculation program.

in our implementation. The control variable `act` of the **switch** statement, which contains the returned value from the function `getActionMenu()`, can be an integral value. For readability, macros can be defined or an enumerated type can be created. For example, the macro or enumerate value `AVERAGEGPA` indicates that the user wants to obtain the average GPA of the class. Macros or enumerated data with the prefix `GPA_` are reserved for the development of the GPA library, which might be developed and maintained by a different developer. The application program shall not define macros with the prefix `GPA_`. In our implementation, an enumerated type will be introduced. (As this flowchart demonstrates, for a large program, some details are omitted in flowcharts so that they can highlight the most important algorithms and program logic.)

Based on the desired user interface and program logic flowchart, a menu-driven interactive GPA calculation program, `studentmenu.c`, has been developed as shown in Program 13.36. The program first includes proper header files. The header file **string.h** contains functions for string comparison and the header file. The macro `MAX_TRY_NUM` for the maximum number of tries is defined as 3. The program needs to receive the user input from the prompt. The macro `MAX_PROMPT_STR` contains the maximum length of the user input string. The enumerated type `action_t` is defined as the return type for the function `getActionMenu()`. In addition to the function **main()**, the program has two user functions, `getActionMenu()` and `obtainGPA()`. The prototypes for these functions are placed at the beginning of the program so that these functions can be called inside the function **main()** when their definitions are placed at the end of the program. Like Program 13.35, student information is stored in the variable `data` of type array of `Student` structure in Program 13.36.

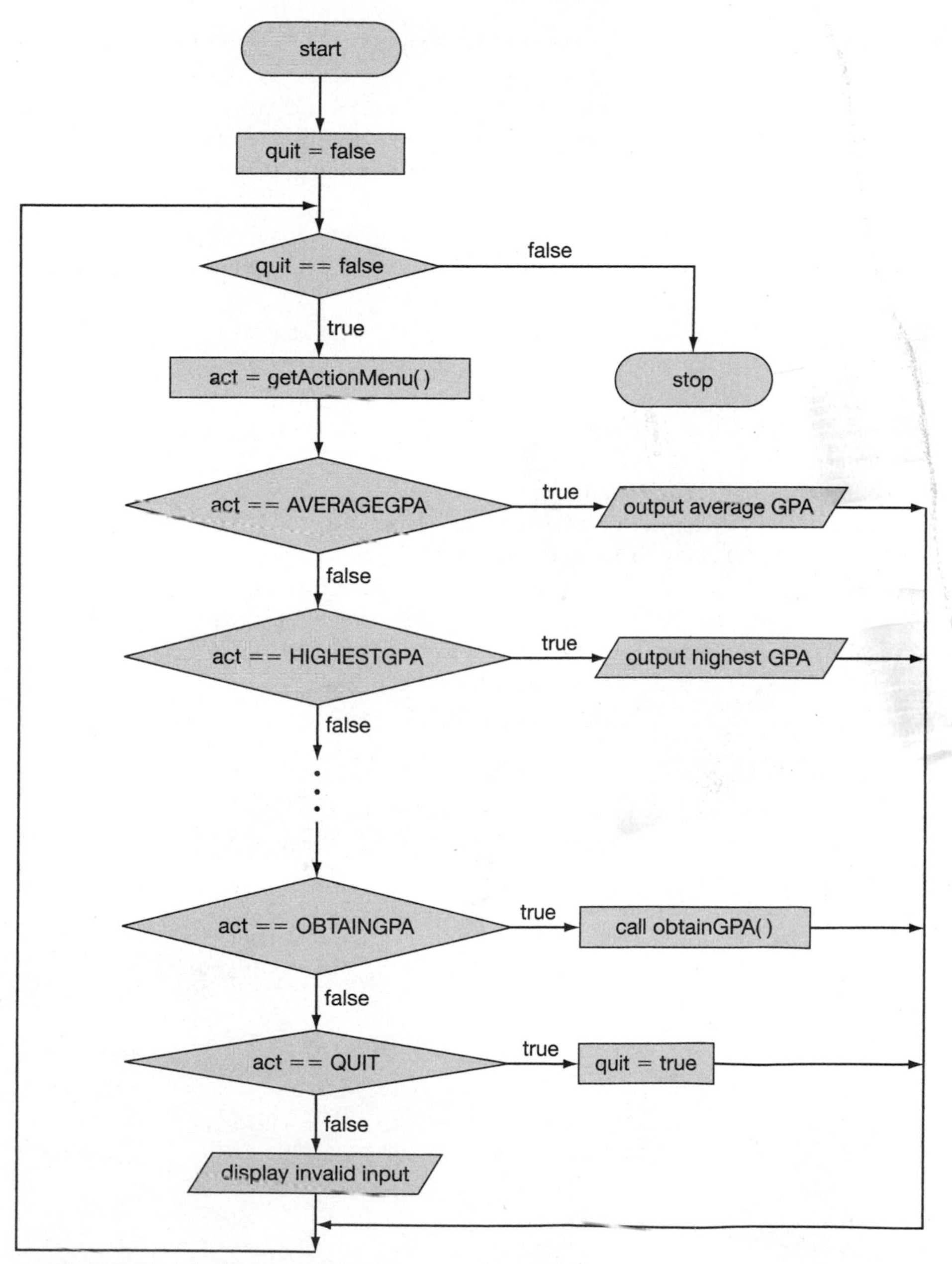

Figure 13.12: The flowchart for the menu-driven GPA program `studentmenu.c`.

```
/*************************************************************
 * File: studentmenu.c
 * This application program uses the GPA library to process
 * GPA of students in the database. The application is menu driven.
 *************************************************************/
#include <stdio.h>
#include <string.h>          /* for strcmp()   */
#include "student.h"         /* the header file for GPA lib */

#define MAX_TRY_NUM  3       /* maximum number of tries */
#define MAX_PROMPT_STR  128 /* maximum prompt string length */

/* enumerated type for actions from the menu driven user input */
typedef enum Action {
    UNDEFINED,    /* undefined action */
    AVERAGEGPA,   /* find the average of GPAs for all students */
    HIGHESTGPA,   /* find the student with the highest GPA */
    LOWESTGPA,    /* find the student with the lowest GPA */
    ABOVEGPA,     /* find students with GPA above a given value */
    SORTGPA,      /* sort the students based on GPA in descending order */
    OBTAINGPA,    /* obtain the GPA for a student based on id and name */
    QUIT          /* quit the program */
} action_t;

/* function prototypes for this application only */
extern action_t getActionMenu(void);  /* action menu */
/* obtain the GPA for a student */
extern void obtainGPA(student_t *head);

/* the database of students processed by the GPA library */
/* members of the student structure: id, name, {day, month, year}, gpa */
student_t data[] = {
    {101, "John",   12, 11, 1985, 3.33},
    {102, "Doe",    13, 3,  1988, 3},
    {103, "Peter",  21, 4,  1984, 3.1},
    {104, "Mary",   8,  2,  1985, 3.93},
    {105, "Ron",    30, 12, 1986, 2.3},
    {106, "George", 9,  1,  1987, 2.31},
    {107, "Mike",   10, 8,  1986, 3.99},
    {108, "Steve",  17, 5,  1989, 2.8},
    {109, "Jone",   25, 4,  1990, 2.9},
    {110, "Ron",    6,  11, 1988, 3.7},
    /* the last one is terminating element */
    {GPA_EOD, "", GPA_EOD, GPA_EOD, GPA_EOD, GPA_EOD}
};
```

Program 13.36: A menu-driven program `studentmenu.c`, using functions in a GPA library. (*Continued*)

```
int main() {
    student_t *head, *sp; /* head of the list and a single student */
    double gpa;           /* GPA value */
    struct Birthday b;    /* b for birthday */
    int num; /* number of students with GPA above a specified value */
    action_t act;         /* action in the menu */
    int quit = FALSE;     /* flag for quit or continue the menu */
    head = data;          /* head points to the data base */
    while(quit==FALSE) {  /* continue the menu if not quit */
        act = getActionMenu();  /* get an action */
        switch(act) {     /* take an action based on the value of 'act' */
            case AVERAGEGPA:  /* obtain the average of all GPAs */
              printf("The GPA for all students is %.2f\n",gpa_averageGPA(head));
              break;
            case HIGHESTGPA: /* find the student with the highest GPA */
              sp = gpa_highestGPA(head);
              b = gpa_getBirthday(sp);
              printf("%s who was born on %s %d, %d has the highest GPA %.2f\n",
                     gpa_getName(sp), gpa_monthString(b.month), b.day, b.year,
                     gpa_getGPA(sp));
              break;
            case LOWESTGPA:  /* find the student with the lowest GPA */
              sp = gpa_lowestGPA(head);
              b = gpa_getBirthday(sp);
              printf("%s who was born on %s %d, %d has the lowest GPA %.2f\n",
                     gpa_getName(sp), gpa_monthString(b.month), b.day, b.year,
                     gpa_getGPA(sp));
              break;
            case ABOVEGPA: /* find students with GPA above a given value */
              printf("please input GPA\n");
              scanf("%lf%*c", &gpa);
              printf("Students with GPA %.2f or above:\n", gpa);
              num = gpa_aboveGPA(head, gpa);
              printf("%d students with GPA %.2f or above.\n", num, gpa);
              break;
            /* sort the students based on GPA in descending order */
            case SORTGPA:
              gpa_sortGPA(head);  /* sort in descending order */
              printf("The student record sorted in descending GPA:\n");
              gpa_printList(head);/* print all students */
              break;
            /* obtain the GPA for a student based on id and name */
            case OBTAINGPA:
              obtainGPA(head);    /* using a function in this program */
              break;
```

Program 13.36: *(Continued)*

```
            case QUIT:                 /* quit the program */
              quit = TRUE;             /* set flag quit to TRUE */
              break;
            default:                   /* in case a mistake is made */
              printf("\aInvalid input!\n");
              break;
        }
    }
    return 0;
}

/*-------------------------------------------------------------------
* Function getActionMenu() gets the action item from user' menu.
* The function returns a proper enum in enum Action, if successful.
*                       UNDEFINED                    , if failed.
*-------------------------------------------------------------------*/
action_t getActionMenu(void) {
    action_t act;                    /* action to be taken */
    const char *prompt = "GPA> ";    /* prompt for the menu */
    char str[MAX_PROMPT_STR];        /* place holder for the user input */

    printf("\n");
    printf("*********************** GPA Menu **********************\n");
    printf("av, average: display the average of GPAs for all students\n");
    printf("h,  highest: display the student with the highest GPA\n");
    printf("l,  lowest:  display the student with the lowest GPA\n");
    printf("ab, above:   display students with GPA above a value\n");
    printf("s, sort:     display the record sorted in descending GPA\n");
    printf("o, obtain:   obtain a student's GPA\n");
    printf("q, quit:     quit the system\n");
    printf("......................................................\n\n");

    printf("%s", prompt);               /* print the prompt "GPA> " */
    fgets(str,MAX_PROMPT_STR,stdin);  /* get the user input */
    str[strlen(str)-1] = '\0';  /* get rid of '\n' in the input string */
    /* set act based on the user input */
    /* if the user input 'av' or 'average' */
    if(!strcmp(str, "av") || !strcmp(str, "average")) {
        act = AVERAGEGPA;
    }
    /* else if the user input 'h' or 'highest' */
    else if(!strcmp(str, "h") || !strcmp(str, "highest")) {
        act = HIGHESTGPA;
    }
```

Program 13.36: *(Continued)*

```
    else if(!strcmp(str, "l") || !strcmp(str, "lowest")) {
        act = LOWESTGPA;
    }
    else if(!strcmp(str, "ab") || !strcmp(str, "above")) {
        act = ABOVEGPA;
    }
    else if(!strcmp(str, "s") || !strcmp(str, "sort")) {
        act = SORTGPA;
    }
    else if(!strcmp(str, "o") || !strcmp(str, "obtain")) {
        act = OBTAINGPA;
    }
    else if(!strcmp(str, "q") || !strcmp(str, "quit")) {
        act = QUIT;
    }
    else { /* none of the above valid input */
        act = UNDEFINED;
    }
    return act;
}

/*---------------------------------------------------------------------
* Function obtainGPA() Obtains the GPA for a student from the database.
* Make sure the student with id and name is in the database.
* The user can input id and name up to 3 times defined in
* MAX_TRY_NUM. After three failed tries, the function will quit.
* The static variable try_count is used for implementation.
*---------------------------------------------------------------------*/
void obtainGPA(student_t *head) {
    student_t *sp;           /* a student */
    int id;                  /* student id */
    char name[32];           /* student name */
    static try_count = 0;    /* track the number of tries using static var */

    printf("please input student id\n");
    /* get the student id and suppress the newline character '\n' */
    scanf("%d%*c", &id);
    printf("please input student name\n");
    fgets(name, sizeof(name), stdin); /* the user input string */
    /* get rid of the newline character '\n' in the input string */
    name[strlen(name)-1] = '\0';
    sp = gpa_find(head, id, name); /* find the student based on id and name */
```

Program 13.36: (*Continued*)

```
    if(sp) { /* when the student is found, print his GPA */
        printf("%s's GPA is %.2f\n", name, gpa_getGPA(sp));
        try_count = 0;        /* reset the count for next action */
    }
    else {   /* when the student is not found, try it again */
        printf("%s with id %d is not in the database.\n", name, id);
        try_count++; /* increment the count for number of failed try */
        if(try_count < MAX_TRY_NUM) { /* if less than specified num of tries */
            obtainGPA(head); /* call the function recursively, up to 3 times */
        }
        else {                 /* exit the function after three failed tries */
            printf("You have tried %d times, nice try!\n", try_count);
            try_count = 0;     /* reset the count for next action */
        }
    }
}
```

Program 13.36: *(Continued)*

Inside the function **main()** in Program 13.36, the variable `head` of type pointer to `student_t` points to the first element of `data`. The controlling variable `quit` is used in a **while** loop in Program 13.36. This variable is initialized to `FALSE`, and it is changed to `TRUE` when the user wants to quit the program. When the user input is invalid, the statement

```
printf("\aInvalid input!\n");
```

makes a sound through the character `'\a'` before the string `"Invalid input!"` is printed out.

When the user wants to display all students with a GPA above a certain value, the function `getActionMenu()` returns the value `ABOVEGPA`. For the case of `ABOVEGPA` inside the **switch** statement, the user input GPA value is obtained by the function **scanf()**. However, the carriage return character `'\n'` remains in the input buffer. This carriage return character, which might affect the subsequent function for the user input, is suppressed by the format specifier `'*c'` in the statement

```
scanf("%lf%*c", &gpa);
```

The function `gpa_aboveGPA()` in the GPA library is used to find the number of students with their GPA above a given value.

During the development of the function **main()**, the function `getActionMenu()` could just return a fixed value for testing. Once the top-level funcion **main()** has been designed and coded, we can then work out the details of the lower-level functions. The flowchart for the function `getActionMenu()` is shown in Figure 13.13. It first displays the action option menu shown in Figure 13.11, and then it takes in the input from the user. Based on the user input, an enumerated value will be returned for the variable `act`. The user input will be compared with the defined character or strings. Whenever there is no conflict for using a character to stand for a string of commands, the character will be used. For example, the character `'h'` stands for the highest GPA. Both `average` and `above` have the same first character, so we need two characters to distinguish these two actions. For example, the input will be compared with string `"av"` or `"average"` to identify if the user wants to find the average GPA. The function `getActionMenu()` returns the enumerated value `UNDEFINED`, if the user input is not defined as an action option.

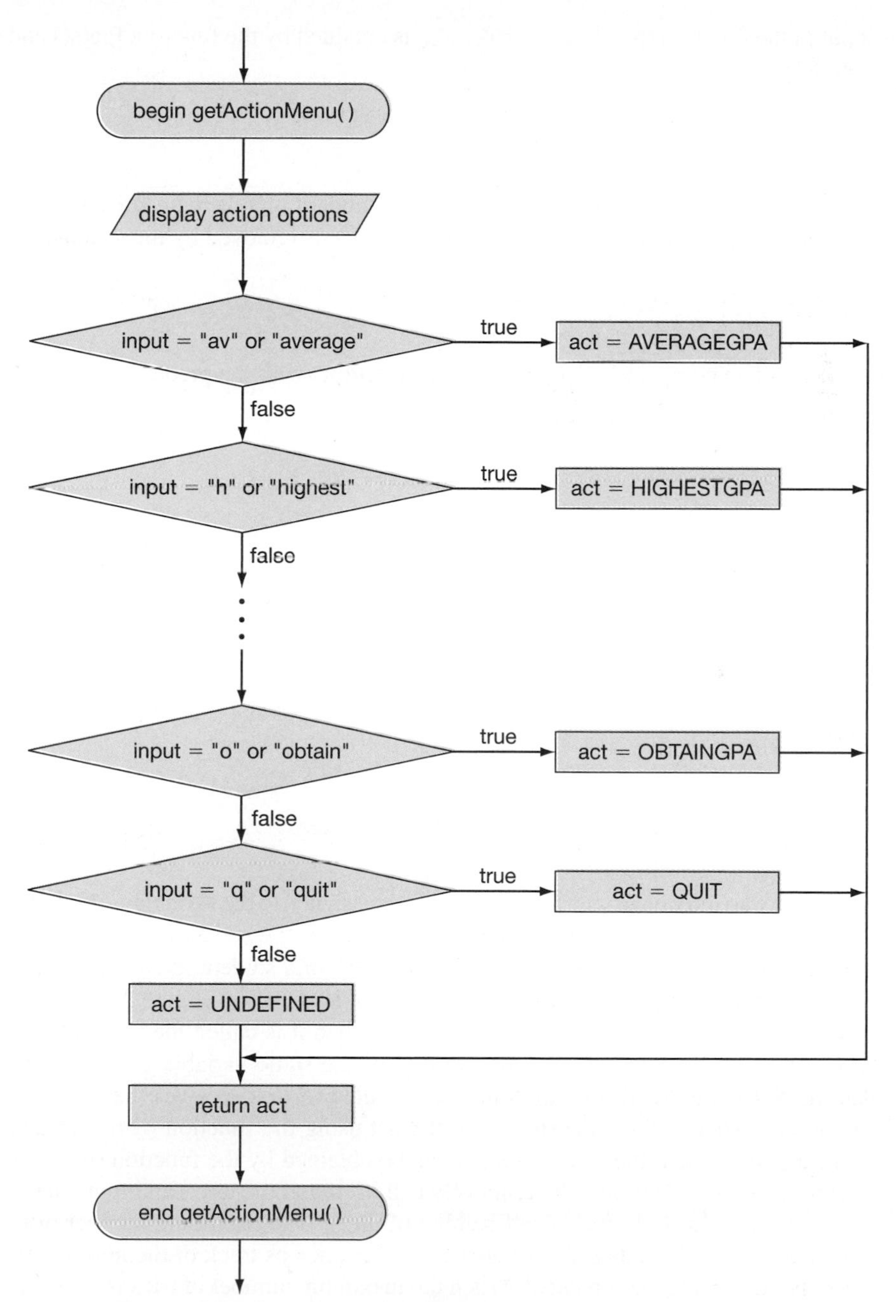

Figure 13.13: The flowchart for the function `getActionMenu()`.

The user input in the function getActionMenu() is obtained by the function **fgets()** and saved in the string str as follows:

```
fgets(str,MAX_PROMPT_STR,stdin);
```

The function **fgets()** can also obtain a string from a file. The standard input stream **stdin** is used to obtain the input from the prompt. The last return character in the string str is removed by the statement

```
str[strlen(str)-1] = '\0';
```

The user input string is then compared using the function **strcmp()** with the predefined action string such as "av" and "average", as shown below.

```
if(!strcmp(str, "av") || !strcmp(str, "average")) {
    act = AVERAGEGPA;
}
```

Note that in some interactive application programs, the carriage return character, characters 'y' and 'Y', and strings yes and Yes are all taken as if the user has input the "yes". In this case, the comparison expression can be written as follows:

```
if(str[0] == '\n' || str[0] == 'y' || str[0] == 'Y' ||
   !strncmp(str, "yes") || !strcmp(str, "Yes")) {
     ...
}
```

The returned value from the function getActionMenu() is assigned to the variable act of type action_t. It is used as a control variable for a **switch** statement.

As shown in Figure 13.12, if the user wants to find the GPA of a student, the function obtainGPA() will be called. The flowchart for the function obtainGPA() is shown in Figure 13.14. The initialization of a static variable inside a function is performed only once when it is called the first time, as described in section 8.2.2 in Chapter 8. Therefore, the function initializes the static variable try_count to zero once when it is called the first time. Each time the function is called, it first receives the identification number and name from the user. Then it finds the student in the list using the function gpa_find() in the GPA library. If the student is in the list, the student's GPA can be obtained by the function gpa_getGPA() and then displayed. Otherwise, the function will recursively call itself and the user can input a new Id and name. The user can repeat this process only for a fixed number of times. The maximum number of tries is defined by the macro MAX_TRY_NUM. The integral variable try_count keeps track of the number of tries. In each recursive call, this counter will be incremented. When the maximum number of tries is exceeded or a student is found, this counter will be reset to 0. This counter is implemented using a static variable inside the function obtainGPA(). We could have used a global variable to keep track of the counter. But a global variable might cause a potential namespace collision. The function is easier to maintain and self-contained when a static variable inside the function is used.

In this example, the student information for a class are stored in an array of Student structures in the application program. This is inconvenient to use. In section 14.3 in Chapter 14, this application example will be modified with the student information stored in a file.

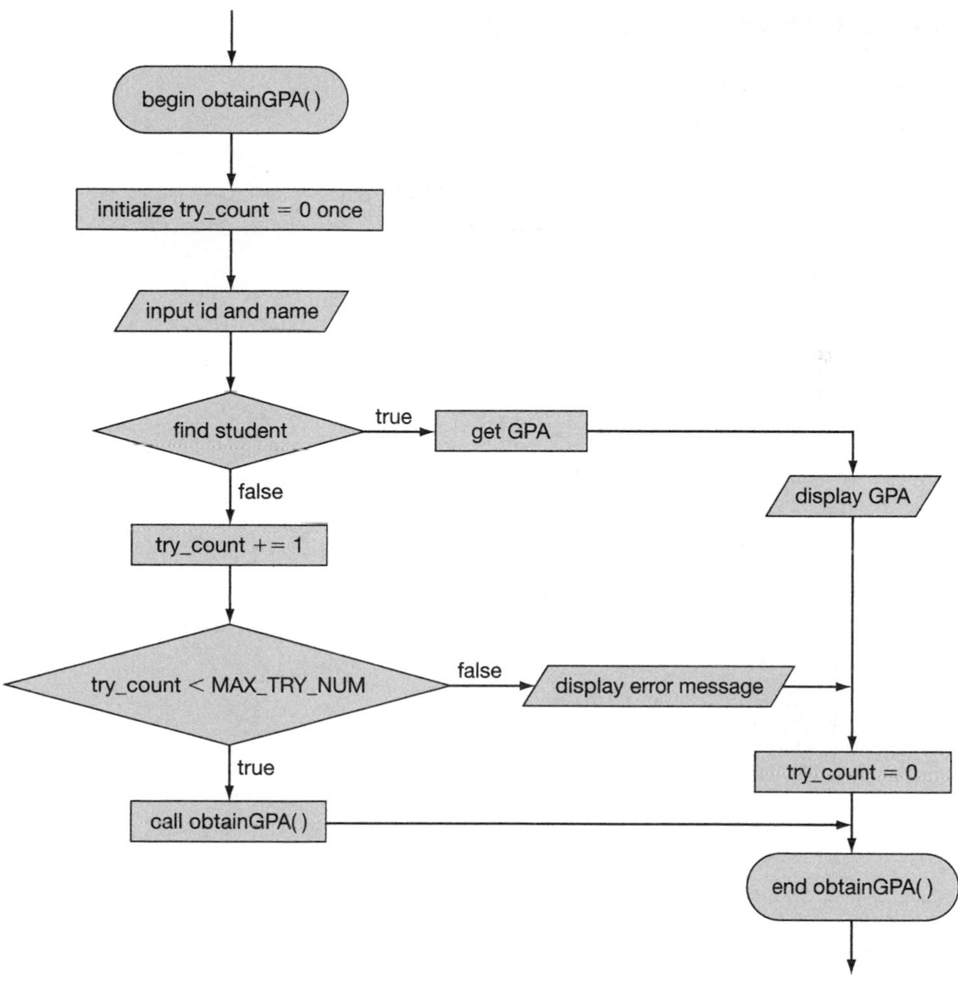

Figure 13.14: The flowchart for the function `obtainGPA()`.

13.6 Making It Work

13.6.1 Debugging Programs with Structures in ChIDE

The method for debugging programs, described in sections 3.16.3 and 6.13.3, is also applicable to programs with structures. Selecting the menu `Locals` or `Variables` on the debugging pane selection bar, for a variable of structure type in the scope, each member of the structure will be displayed. When a member of a structure is modified, the entire structure will be updated when the structure is displayed.

Exercises

1. State whether the following statements are true or false. If false, briefly explain why.

  a. Members of a structure must have the same type.
  b. Structures cannot be compared using operator == or !=.
  c. Values in enumerations begin with a 1.

d. Members of different structures can use the same name.
e. It is not necessary to have a tag name for a structure.
f. Call by reference is the only way to pass structures to functions.

2. Give the output of the following program:

```
#include<stdio.h>
struct tag{
    int i;
    char name[32];
} s1={10, "ABCD"};

int main() {
    struct tag s2;

    s2.i = 2*s1.i;
    strcpy(s2.name, s1.name);
    strcat(s2.name, "1234");
    printf("s2.i = %d\n", s2.i);
    printf("s2.name= %s\n", s2.name);
    return 0;
}
```

3. Give the output of the following program:

```
#include<stdio.h>
struct tag{
    int i;
    int j;
} s1;
struct tag funct(int a) {
    static int i =10;
    int j = a+i;
    i++;
    s1.i = i;
    s1.j = j;
    return s1;
}

int main() {
    struct tag s;

    s = funct(1);
    printf("s.i = %d\n", s.i);
    printf("s.j = %d\n", s.j);
    s = funct(2);
    printf("s.i = %d\n", s.i);
    printf("s.j = %d\n", s.j);
    return 0;
}
```

4. Give the output of the following program:

```
#include <stdio.h>
typedef struct data {
    int a;
    float b[10];
} DATA;
int main() {
    DATA d;
    struct data *p;

    d.a = 10;
    d.b[2] = 10;
    p = &d;
    p->a = d.a;
    p->b[1]= 2*d.b[2];
    printf("p->a= %d\n", p->a);
    printf("p->b[1]= %f\n", p->b[1]);
    return 0;
}
```

5. Provide the definition of each of the following structures and unions:

a. The structure `inventory`, containing the character array `partName[30]`, the integer `partNumber`, the floating point number `price`, the integer `stock`, and the integer `reorder`.
b. The union `data`, containing `char c`, `short s`, `long l`, `float f`, and `double d`.
c. A struct called `address`, containing character arrays `streetAddress[25]`, `city[20]`, `state[3]`, and `zipCode[6]`.

6. The daily sales of a grocery store are saved in the file `sale.dat`. Each line contains the record for a product name, price per pound in dollars, and total number of pounds sold. A comment line for the record starts with the symbol `'#'`. If the file `sale.dat` contains the following data:

```
# product name, unit price ($), units (pound) sold
orange  1.2   506.21
apple   1.25  944.23
grape   2.25  393.5
cherry  4.25  234.56
```

write a program using a structure to read the data using the input/output redirection. Find the products with the largest sale volume in terms of weight and in terms of dollars. Calculate the total sales for a day.

7. Below is the definition of a structure type and a variable of that type. Write a series of statements that assign a valid value to each component of the structure. If some components of the structure overlap, assign the value to only one of the overlapping components.

```
struct tag {
  int i;
  union tag2 {
    int i;
    double a;
    char b[8];
```

```
        int *c;
    } u;
    struct tag3 {
        int i;
        unsigned m: 1;
        unsigned n: 8;
        unsigned l: 16;
    } s;
} x;
```

8. What is the main difference between a structure and a union?
9. What does the colon and the integer in `unsigned int a : 4` mean?
10. Is an array or a structure preferable to store all the student IDs enrolled in a computer class and a student's personal information?
11. Create the union `integer` with members `char c`, `short s`, `int i`, and `long b`. Write a program that inputs a value of type char, short, int, and long and stores the values in union variables of type `union integer`. Each union variable should be printed as a char, short, int, and long. Are the values always printed correctly?
12. Write a program using a structure that allows the user to enter the information of company name, address, phone number, and credit rating (`good` or `bad`) for a customer. At the end, the program displays the input from the user.
13. What does the following program print?

```
#include <stdio.h>

struct tag {
    char *p;
    char name[32];
} s = {"abcd", "ABCD"};

int main() {
    printf("s.p    = %s\n", s.p);
    printf("s.p[1]    = %c\n", s.p[1]);
    printf("s.name    = %s\n", s.name);
    printf("s.name[0]    = %c\n", s.name[0]);
    printf("s.name[1]    = %c\n", s.name[1]);
    printf("*s.name    = %c\n", *s.name);
    return 0;
}
```

14. Modify the function `averageGPA()` in Program 13.10 using the pointer operator `sp->`, instead of using the array reference `s[i]`, to access each element of the passed array.
15. What does the following program print?

```
#include <stdio.h>
#include <stdlib.h>
#include <string.h>

struct tag {
```

```
        int i;
        char *p;
        char name[32];
    } s;

    int main() {
        struct tag *sp;
        struct tag sa[2]={{100, "abcd", "ABCD"},
                          {200, "xyz", "XYZ"}};

        sp = &s;
        s.i = 123;
        strcpy(s.name, "abcd");
        sp->p = (char *)malloc(sizeof(char)*strlen("ABCD1234")+1);
        strcpy(sp->p, "ABCD1234");
        printf("sp->i     = %d\n", sp->i);
        printf("sp->name    = %s\n", sp->name);
        printf("s.p     = %s\n", s.p);
        sa[1] = s;
        printf("sa[0].i    = %i\n", sa[0].i);
        printf("sa[0].p    = %s\n", sa[0].p);
        printf("sa[1].p    = %s\n", sa[1].p);
        return 0;
    }
```

16. Write a program that will print out the current date and time when the program is executed and the date and time after 30 days.
17. The **offsetof()** macro is defined in the header file **stddef.h** as follows:

```
#define offsetof(s, m)   (size_t)(&(((s *)0)->m))
```

    Explain why the code above produces the offset of a structure member in bytes.
18. Find the size of the following structures. Draw the memory layout for each member of the structures.
    a. `struct type1 {int i; char a[5]; short s; double d;}`
    b. `struct type2 {int i; char a[2]; double d; short s;}`
19. What integer value is returned by the function `f()` below? Is the cast to type int in the return statement necessary?

```
enum color {red, blue=12, green, white};
int f() {
    return (int) green;
}
```

20. Write a program that prints the 12 *numerals* and names of the months using enumeration.
21. Extend Programs 13.33, 13.34, and 13.35 by adding the following functions:
    a. `int gpa_belowGPA(const student_t *head, double gpa);`
    to display students with a GPA below the specified value in its second argument. The function returns the number of students with a GPA below the specified value.

b. `double gpa_stdDeviation(const student_t *head);`
to return the standard deviation of GPA.

c. `void gpa_sortGPAascending(student_t *head);`
to sort students with a GPA in ascending order.

d. `void gpa_sortAge(student_t *head);`
to sort students in descending age.

e. `void gpa_sortName(student_t *head);`
to sort students in alphebatical order based on the first letter of their name.

22. Write a linear regression function with the function prototype

```
void linearreg(double t[], double y[], int n, struct refcoeff *coeff);
```

where `t` and `y` are arrays of data to be fitted in the linear regression model, `n` is the number of elements for the passed arrays `t` and `y`. The linear regression coefficients for the intercept and slope are passed to the calling function by the argument `coeff` of pointer to structure type defined below.

```
/* structure for the coefficients of linear regression */
struct regcoeff {
    double b;    /* intercept */
    double v;    /* slope */
};
```

Modify Program 10.19 in Chapter 10 to use this function.

23. Programs developed in Exercises 19, 20, and 21 in Chapter 6 can be used for testing arithmetic skills. Write an interactive menu-driven mathematical examination program that allows the user to choose one of three tests:

a. Addition of two integers ranging from 1 to 10,
b. Addition of two integers ranging from 1 to 100,
c. Multiplication of two integers ranging from 1 to 10.

Use an enumerated type to implement these three choices. For each topic, 10 questions will be asked. The user should have only one chance to answer each question. At the end of the 10th question, print a message to tell the user how many problems were answered correctly.

24. Write an interactive menu-driven program to calculate areas for different shapes. Use an enumerated type to implement choices for square, rectangle, and circular shapes. It prompts the user to input necessary parameters for a shape to calculate its area.

25. Write an interactive menu-driven program to calculate volumes for different shapes. Use an enumerated type to implement choices for rectangle, sphere, and cylinder shapes. It prompts the user to input necessary parameters for a shape to calculate its volume.

26. Modify Program 11.20 in Chapter 11 to pass both the projectile angle `theta0` and the initial velocity `v0` using a structure to the function `traj()` through the last argument of the function `bisect2()`. Find zeros of the projectile function with the initial speed v_0 of 35 m/s and initial projection angle θ_0 of 15°, and v_0 of 25 m/s and θ_0 of 45°.

27. Use the function **qsort()** to sort the students in Program 13.35 based on their GPAs in ascending order. Then find the student with a GPA of 3.1 using the function **bsearch()**. Print out all information for this student.

28. Based on the GPA library example, write a program to handle a small library of books in a lab. The program allows a user to borrow and return books.

CHAPTER 14

File Processing

In the previous chapters, data were stored in variables and arrays in main memory for a program. However, once the program terminates, all the data are lost because the variables and arrays are temporary and exist only during program execution. To overcome this problem, data in a program can be saved into files. The input and output redirection described in section 3.15.3 in Chapter 3 depends on a command shell and has limited capabilities to deal with only two files, one for input and the other for output. In this chapter, we will describe how to create, update, and process files in C. The GPA library presented in Chapter 13 will be extended to handle student information stored in data files. We will introduce both text and binary files and explain how to obtain various information related to files in a system.

14.1 Opening and Closing Files

Input and output in C, whether to or from physical devices such as terminals and tape drives, or whether to or from files supported on structured storage devices, are mapped into logical data *streams* whose properties are more uniform than their various inputs and outputs. Two forms of mapping are supported, mapping for *text streams* and for *binary streams*. A text stream is an ordered sequence of characters composed into *lines*, each line consisting of zero or more characters plus a terminating newline character. A binary stream is an ordered sequence of characters that can record internal data transparently.

A file is the most common I/O facility that can be used as a stream in C. Data type **FILE**, defined in the header file **stdio.h**, maintains information about the stream. An object of type **FILE ***, created by calling some functions such as **fopen()**, is used to access the file by other file manipulation functions such as **fscanf()**. The function **fopen()** opens a file. Its function prototype is

```
FILE *fopen(const char *filename, const char *mode);
```

It returns a pointer to the object controlling the stream on success. If the open operation fails, a null pointer constant, NULL, is returned. The name of the file that will be opened and associated with a stream is specified by the first argument, `filename`. The second argument, `mode`, specifies the reason behind opening the file. Its valid values are described in Table 14.1. Opening a file with read mode '**r**' as the first character in the argument `mode` causes the file to be opened only for read operations. Opening a file with write mode '**w**' as the first character in the argument `mode` causes the file to be opened only for write operations. Opening a file with append mode '**a**' as the first character in the argument `mode` causes all subsequent writes to the file to be forced to the then-current end-of-file (EOF). A `mode` argument of '**b**' is used to handle binary files.

When a file is opened with update mode '**+**' as the second or third character in the above list of *mode* argument values, both input and output may be performed on the associated stream. However, output shall not be directly followed by input without an intervening call to the function **fflush()** or to one of the file

Table 14.1 Opening modes for function fopen().

Mode	Meaning
r	Opens text file for reading
w	Truncates to zero length or creates text file for writing
a	Appends; opens or creates text file for writing at the EOF
rb	Opens binary file for reading
wb	Truncates to zero length or creates binary file for writing
ab	Appends; opens or creates binary file for writing at the EOF
r+	Opens text file for update (reading and writing)
w+	Truncates to zero length or creates text file for update
a+	Appends; opens or creates text file for update, writing at the EOF
r+b *or* **rb+**	Opens binary file for updating (reading and writing); data can be read anywhere in the file, but it can be written only at the EOF
w+b *or* **wb+**	Truncates to zero length or creates binary file for updating
a+b *or* **ab+**	Appends; opens or creates binary file for update; data can be read anywhere in the file, but it can only be written at the EOF

positioning functions **fseek()**, **fsetpos()**, and **rewind()**, which will be described in a later session. Similarly, input shall not be directly followed by output without an intervening call to a file positioning function, unless the input operation encounters the EOF. Opening (or creating) a text file with update mode may instead open (or create) a binary stream on some platforms.

When opened, a stream is fully buffered if and only if it can be determined not to refer to an interactive device. The error and EOF indicators for the stream are cleared. Buffering of input and output will be described in section 14.6.

All files that are opened and associated with streams shall be closed before the program exits. The number of files that can be opened at the same time is limited. For example, some systems may allow up to 256 files to be opened for a process. An opened file should be closed if it is no longer used. The function **fclose()** can be used to close a file. Its prototype is

```
int fclose(FILE *stream);
```

The function **fclose()** returns zero if the stream was successfully closed, or the value of macro **EOF** defined in the header file **stdio.h** if any errors were detected. The **fclose()** function causes the stream pointed to by *stream* to be flushed and the associated file to be closed. Any unwritten buffered data for the stream is delivered to the host environment to be written to the file; unread buffered data are discarded. The stream is disassociated from the file. If the associated buffer was automatically allocated, it is deallocated.

The following code fragment illustrates how the functions **fopen()** and **fclose()** are used.

```
FILE *fp;
if((fp = fopen("filename","r")) == NULL) {
   printf("Error: cannot read the file 'filename'\n");
}
...
fclose(fp);
```

Both variable names `stream` and `fp` are commonly used to represent file streams. The above code opens the text file `filename` for reading. Afterwards, the file stream is closed. Note that the parentheses around

```
fp = fopen("filename","r")
```

are necessary because the comparison operator == has higher precedence than the assignment operator =. Without the parentheses, the boolean result of the expression

```
fopen("filename","r")) == NULL
```

will be assigned to `fp`. This is a common programming mistake.

When a C program begins execution, there are three text streams **stdin**, **stdout**, and **stderr** predefined and opened. The stream **stdin** stands for standard input, **stdout** stands for standard output, and **stderr** stands for standard error. They are defined in the header file **stdio.h**. For example, the function **fprintf()** with the following function prototype

```
int fprintf(FILE *stream,  char  *format,  /* args */ ...);
```

places output on the named output `stream` with the format control string `format`. The function **fscanf()** with the following function prototype

```
int fscanf(FILE*stream, const char *format, /* args */ ...);
```

reads from the named input `stream` with the format control string `format`.

The function **printf()** uses the standard output stream. Using the preopened file stream **stdout**, the function call

```
printf(format, arglist);
```

is equivalent to

```
fprintf(stdout, format, arglist);
```

The control format for the function **printf()** described in section 9.1 in Chapter 9 is applicable to function **fprintf()**. The function **scanf()** uses the standard input stream **stdin**. The function call

```
scanf(format, arglist);
```

is equivalent to

```
fscanf(stdin, format, arglist);
```

Similarly, the control format for the function **scanf()** described in section 9.2 in Chapter 9 is applicable to the function **fscanf()**.

14.2 Reading and Writing Sequential Files

After a file is opened and associated with a stream, it can perform read or write operations according to the opening mode. Functions presented in Chapters 9 and 12 for standard input and output have corresponding versions associated with a file stream.

The function **fgetc()** with the function prototype

```
int fgetc(FILE *stream);
```

corresponds to the function **getchar()** introduced in section 12.2 in Chapter 12. It obtains the next byte as an unsigned char converted to an int, from the input stream pointed to by `stream`, and advances the associated file position indicator for the stream. The function **getc()** is functionally identical to **fgetc()**, except that it is implemented as a macro. It may run faster than **fgetc()**, but its name cannot be passed as an argument to a function call.

Each input function above that is used to read from files has a corresponding output function that is used to write to files. The function **fputc()** with the function prototype

```
int fputc(int c, FILE *stream);
```

corresponding to the function **putchar()**, writes the byte specified by `c` (converted to an unsigned char) to the output stream pointed to by `stream`, at the position indicated by the associated file-position indicator for the stream, and advances the indicator appropriately. Similar to **getc()**, the macro **putc()** is functionally identical to **fputc()**.

As an example, the function `copyfile()` in Program 14.1 copies one file to another character by character using the functions **fgetc()** and **fputc()**. The function **feof()**, first introduced in section 5.8 in Chapter 5, is used in a **while** loop to determine whether there is still data to be read from the input file and continues to read from the file until the EOF indicator is reached. The function **feof()** with its prototype

```
int feof(FILE *stream);
```

```
/* File: copyfile.c
   Copy a file character by character */
#include <stdio.h> /* for fopen(), fclose(), fgetc(), fputc(), feof() */

int copyfile(const char *inputfile, const char *outputfile) {
    FILE *fp1, *fp2; /* declare FILE pointers for input and output files */
    char c;          /* the buffer for a character */

    /* Treat file as a binary file. */
    /* open the input file for reading */
    if((fp1 = fopen(inputfile, "rb")) == NULL)
        return -1; /* if failed to open the file for reading, return -1  */
    /* open the output file for writing */
    if((fp2 = fopen(outputfile, "wb")) == NULL) {
        fclose(fp1); /* close the opened file for reading */
        return -1; /* if failed to open the file for writing, return -1 */
    }
    c  = fgetc(fp1);        /* read a character */
    while(!feof(fp1)) {     /* while not end-of-file */
       fputc(c, fp2);       /* write a character to the output file */
       c  = fgetc(fp1);     /* read a new character from the input file */
    }
    fclose(fp1);            /* close the file stream for the input file */
    fclose(fp2);            /* close the file stream for the output file */
    return 0;
}
```

Program 14.1: Copying a file character by character.

returns a nonzero value when the *end-of-file indicator* (EOF) has previously been detected reading the named input stream. It returns 0 otherwise. The function `copyfile()` returns 0 if file copying is successful. Otherwise, it returns −1.

Note that if the code fragment

```
c  = fgetc(fp1);
while(!feof(fp1)) {
   c  = fgetc(fp1);
   fputc(c, fp2);
}
```

in the function `copyfile()` was changed to

```
while(!feof(fp1)) {
   c  = fgetc(fp1);
   fputc(c, fp2);
}
```

or

```
while(!feof(fp1)) {
   fputc(fgetc(fp1), fp2);
}
```

an extra erroneous character would have been copied. However, if the same code fragment is changed to

```
while((c = fgetc(fp1)) != EOF) {
   fputc(c, fp2);
}
```

the function `copyfile()` will remain the same, as if the file had an extra character of EOF at the end.

Depending on the system, the line orientation is different. In Windows, when a newline character `'\n'` is written to a text file by the function **fputc()**, two characters, one for a carriage return character `'\r'` and one for a newline character `'\n'`, are written. On the other hand, when two adjacent characters `'\r'` and `'\n'` in a text file are read by the function **fgetc()**, they are treated as a single newline character `'\n'`. To avoid this confusion of the file's line structure in different systems, files are opened in binary mode for reading with `"rb"` and writing with `"wb"` in the function `copyfile()`.

File copying in the function `copyfile()` in Program 14.1 is implemented using character-oriented functions. The same function can also be implemented using the line-oriented functions **fgets()** and **fputs()** as shown in Program 14.2. In the function `copyfile2()`, a file is copied line by line. Like the function `copyfile()`, to avoid the confusion of a file's line structure, files are opened in binary mode in the function `copyfile2()`.

The function **fgets()** was previously introduced in Chapter 12 to read a string from the standard input. However, it can also be used to read a line from a file. The function **fgets()**, with its prototype

```
char *fgets(char *s, int n, FILE *stream);
```

reads bytes from `stream` into the array pointed to by `s`, until `n-1` bytes are read, or a newline character is read and transferred to `s`, or an EOF condition is encountered. The string is then terminated with a null byte. If an EOF is encountered and no bytes have been read, no bytes are transferred to `s`, and a null pointer is returned. If a read error occurs, such as trying to use these functions on a file that has not been opened for

```
/* File: copyfile2.c
   Copy a file line by line*/
#include <stdio.h>
#include <stdio.h> /* for fopen(), fclose(), fgets(), fputs(), feof() */
#define BUFSIZE 1024   /* the maximum line size */

int copyfile2(const char *inputfile, const char *outputfile) {
    FILE *fp1, *fp2;    /* declare FILE pointers for input and output files */
    char line[BUFSIZE]; /* the buffer for a line */

    /* open input file for reading and output file for writing
       in binary mode */
    if((fp1 = fopen(inputfile, "rb")) == NULL)
        return -1; /* if failed to open the file for reading */
    if((fp2 = fopen(outputfile, "wb")) == NULL) {
        fclose(fp1);
        return -1; /* if failed to open the file for writing */
    }
    fgets(line, BUFSIZE, fp1); /* read a line */
    while(!feof(fp1)) {  /* while not end-of-file */
       fputs(line, fp2); /* write a line into the output file */
       fgets(line, BUFSIZE, fp1); /* read a newline from the input file */
    }
    fclose(fp1);          /* close the file stream for the input file */
    fclose(fp2);          /* close the file stream for the output file */
    return 0;
}
```

Program 14.2: Copying a file line by line.

reading, a null pointer is returned and the error indicator for the stream is set. If an EOF is encountered, the EOF indicator for the stream is set. Otherwise, s is returned.

On the other hand, the function **fputs()**, with its prototype

```
int fputs(const char *s, FILE *stream);
```

writes the null-terminated string pointed to by s to the named output stream. The terminating null byte is not written. On successful completion, the function returns the number of bytes written; otherwise, it returns EOF and sets **errno**, declared in the header file **errno.h**, to indicate the error.

Using the return value of the function **fgets()**, the block of code for copying a file

```
fgets(line, BUFSIZE, fp1);
while(!feof(fp1)) {
   fputs(line, fp2);
   fgets(line, BUFSIZE, fp1);
}
```

can be replaced by the code below:

```
while(fgets(line, BUFSIZE, fp1) != NULL) {
   fputs(line, fp2);
}
```

The functions **fscanf()** and **fprintf()**, using a format control string, are more flexible to use for some applications. All input and output associated with file streams can also be performed interactively in a Ch command shell, as shown below.

```
> FILE *fp
> fp = fopen("testfile", "w")
> fprintf(fp, "This is output to testfile\n");
> fclose(fp)
> more testfile
This is output to testfile
```

In the above interactive execution, a file pointer is declared with the type specifier **FILE**. The function **fopen()** then opens the file `testfile` for writing. Next, data are written into this file using the function **fprintf()**. After this is done, the function **fclose()** is called to close the file. Finally, the command **more** is used to display the content of `testfile`.

Application Examples

Acceleration of a Moving Body

Problem Statement:
For the mechanical system shown in Figure 2.12, given mass $m = 5$ kilograms (kg), gravitational acceleration constant $g = 9.81 m/s^2$, and coefficient of kinetic friction $\mu = 0.2$, the applied force p is expressed as a function of time t in

$$p(t) = 4\sin(t - 3) + 20$$

Write a program to calculate the accelerations a during $t = 0$ to $t = 10$ with time step 1 and save the accelerations into a text file, when

1. The file name is `accel.txt`
2. The file name is specified by the command-line argument.

Then write another program to read the accelerations from file `accel.txt` and print them out.

The solutions to this problem are Programs 14.3 and 14.4. Program 14.3 first opens the file `accel.txt` using the function **fopen()** with the option `"w"` to store the output of the program. If the file fails to open, the program terminates with an error message describing the problem. On a successful opening of the file, the program proceeds to calculate the acceleration of the system from $t = 0$ to 10 seconds for every 1 second. These acceleration values are written to the file `accel.txt`. The function **fclose()** at the end of the program is used to close the file. The final contents of the file `accel.txt` are shown in Figure 14.1.

```
/* File: accelo.c
   Write accelerations into file accel.txt */
#include <stdio.h>  /* for fopen(), fclose(), fprintf(), printf() */
#include <stdlib.h> /* for exit() */
#define M_G   9.81  /* gravitational acceleration constant g */

int main() {
    /* declaration and initialization */
    double a, mu=0.2, m=5.0, t0=0.0, tf=10.0, step=1.0, p, t;
    int i, n;
    FILE *stream;  /* a file stream */

    /* open file accel.txt for writing */
    stream = fopen("accel.txt", "w");
    if(stream == NULL) {
      printf("Error: cannot open 'accel.txt'\n");
      exit(EXIT_FAILURE);
    }
    n = (tf - t0)/step + 1;          /* number of points, 11 */
    for(i=0; i<n; i++) {
       t = t0 + i*step;              /* calculate value t */
       p = 4*sin(t-3)+20;            /* use t to calculate p */
       a = (p-mu*m*M_G)/m;           /* calculate a */
       fprintf(stream, "%f\n", a);/* write acceleration into the file */
    }
    fclose(stream);                  /* close the file stream */
    printf("Done! Finished writing data to file accel.txt\n");
    return 0;
}
```

Program 14.3: Writing accelerations into a file.

```
/* File: accelfile.c
   Write accelerations into a file  with the user specified file name */
#include <stdio.h>  /* for fopen(), fclose(), fprintf() */
#include <stdlib.h> /* for exit() */
#define M_G   9.81  /* gravitational acceleration constant g */

char dfilename[] = "accel.txt"; /* default file name */

int main(int argc, char **argv) {
    /* declaration and initialization */
    double a, mu=0.2, m=5.0, t0=0.0, tf=10.0, step=1.0, p, t;
```

Program 14.4: Writing accelerations into a file with the user-specified name. (*Continued*)

```
    int i, n;
    FILE *stream;               /* a file stream */
    char *cmd, *filename;       /* cmd and file name */

    cmd = argv[0];              /* save the command */
    if(argc >= 3){              /* extra argument */
        fprintf(stderr, "Usage: %s [filename]\n", cmd);
        exit(EXIT_FAILURE);
    }
    /* get the user specified or default file name */
    filename = (argc == 2 ? argv[1]:dfilename);
    /* open the file for writing */
    stream = fopen(filename, "w");
    if(stream == NULL) {
        printf("Error: cannot open '%s'\n", filename);
        exit(EXIT_FAILURE);
    }
    n = (tf - t0)/step + 1;          /* number of points, 11 */
    for(i=0; i<n; i++) {
       t = t0 + i*step;              /* calculate value t */
       p = 4*sin(t-3)+20;            /* use t to calculate p */
       a = (p-mu*m*M_G)/m;           /* calculate a */
       fprintf(stream, "%f\n", a);/* write acceleration into the file */
    }
    fclose(stream);                  /* close the file stream */
    printf("Done! Finished writing data to file %s\n", filename);
    return 0;
}
```

Program 14.4: (*Continued*)

```
1.925104
1.310562
1.364823
2.038000
2.711177
2.765438
2.150896
1.432558
1.270861
1.814468
2.563589
```

Figure 14.1: The contents of the file `accel.txt` and the output of Program 14.5.

Program 14.4 has the same functionality as Program 14.3. Instead of storing the acceleration values into the file `accel.txt`, however, the file name for the program to write to is specified by the user as a command-line argument. If no file name is entered, then the default name is `accel.txt`. For example, the command

```
> accelfile.c
```

creates `accel.txt` as the default file, whereas the command

```
> accelfile.c file.txt
```

writes the data generated by running Program 14.4 to the file `file.txt`. Whether the default file name or a user-defined file name is used is determined by the statement

```
filename = (argc == 2 ? argv[1]:dfilename);
```

This statement checks to see whether there is a file name specified as a command-line argument when the program is executed. If the expression `argc == 2` is true, then a user-defined name is present and the string variable `filename` is assigned this name, which is stored in `argv[1]`. However, if the expression is false, then the default file name `accel.txt` in the variable `dfilename` is assigned to `filename`. If more than one file name is specified at the command line, an error occurs to stop execution of the program, as illustrated below.

```
> accelfile.c file1.txt file2.txt
Usage: accelfile.c [filename]
```

Program 14.5 reads the contents of the file `accel.txt` and prints them out. In this program, the function **fopen()** with the option `"r"` opens the file `accel.txt`. If the file does not exist in the current directory or cannot be read, then the program displays an error message and stops execution. If no problem occurs while opening the file, Program 14.5 proceeds to read the acceleration values stored in the file `accel.txt` and prints them out as shown in Figure 14.1. The **while** loop uses the function **feof()** to determine whether there is still data to be read from the file `accel.txt` and continues to read from the file until the EOF indicator is reached.

```
/* File: acceli.c
   Read accelerations from file accel.txt */
#include <stdio.h>  /* for fopen(), fclose(), fscanf(), printf() */
#include <stdlib.h> /* for exit() */

int main() {
    double a;         /* acceleration */
    FILE *stream;     /* a file stream */

    /* open file accel.txt for reading */
    stream = fopen("accel.txt", "r");
```

Program 14.5: Reading accelerations from a file. (*Continued*)

```
    if(stream == NULL) {
      printf("Error: cannot open 'accel.txt'\n");
      exit(EXIT_FAILURE);
    }
    fscanf(stream, "%lf", &a);    /* read an acceleration */
    while(!feof(stream)) {        /* while not end-of-file */
      printf("%f\n", a);          /* print the acceleration */
      fscanf(stream, "%lf", &a); /* read the next acceleration */
    }
    fclose(stream);               /* close the file stream */
    return 0;
}
```

Program 14.5: (*Continued*)

Processing Student Information in Files

Problem Statement:
For the GPA library in section 13.5 in Chapter 13, student information is contained in an application program. If the information of identification number, name, birthday, birth month, birth year, and GPA for a student is kept in a file `rwstudent.data`, shown below

```
101 John 12 11 1985 3.33
```

read this information into a program and save the information in a new file called `rwstudent-New.data`.

Program 14.6 uses `Birthday` and `Student` structures described in section 13.5 in Chapter 13 to keep the information for a student. The function `readData()` uses **fscanf()** to read the information from the file `rwstudent.data`. The function `writeData()` uses **fprintf()** to write the information stored in `Birthday` and `Student` structures to the file `rwstudentNew.data`. Note that for variables of type short, the format specifier `"hd"` is used for reading and writing the data.

In some applications, each entry in a data file might be separated by commas or other symbols. For example, the student information might be stored in a file with each entry separated by a comma and a single or multiple white spaces, as shown below

```
101,  John, 12, 11, 1985,  3.33
```

In this case, the function call of **fscanf()** in Program 14.6 can be replaced by the following statement:

```
fscanf(stream, "%d%*[, ]%[^,]%*c%hd%*c%hd%*c%hd%*c%lf",
               &sp->id, sp->name, &sp->birthday.day,
               &sp->birthday.month, &sp->birthday.year, &sp->gpa);
```

As described in section 9.2.5 in Chapter 9, the format specifier `"%*[, ]"` suppresses the comma and multiple white spaces before the name. The specifier `"%[^,]"` reads the name excluding a comma, while the commas in the input are suppressed by the specifier `"%*c"`. To read in a number for a variable of type

```
/* File: rwstudent.c
   Read student information from file "rwstudent.data" and
   write it into another file "rwstudentNew.data" */
#include <stdio.h>  /* for fopen(), fclose(), fprintf(), fscanf(), printf() */

struct Birthday {             /* define structure for birthday */
    short day, month, year;
};

typedef struct Student {      /* define structure for student */
    int id;
    char name[32];
    struct Birthday birthday;
    double gpa;
} student_t;

/* read student information in filename into the buffer pointed by sp */
int readData(student_t *sp, const char *filename) {
    FILE *stream;

    stream = fopen(filename, "r");
    if(stream == NULL) {
        fprintf(stderr, "Error: cannot open file '%s' for reading\n", filename);
        return -1;
    }
    fscanf(stream, "%d%s%hd%hd%hd%lf", &sp->id, sp->name,
              &sp->birthday.day, &sp->birthday.month, &sp->birthday.year,
              &sp->gpa);
    fclose(stream);
    return 0;
}

/* write student information in the buffer pointed by sp into filename */
int writeData(const student_t *sp, const char *filename) {
    FILE *stream;

    stream = fopen(filename, "w");
    if(stream == NULL) {
        fprintf(stderr, "Error: cannot open file '%s' for writing\n", filename);
        return -1;
    }
    fprintf(stream, "%d %s %hd %hd %hd %g\n", sp->id, sp->name,
        sp->birthday.day, sp->birthday.month, sp->birthday.year, sp->gpa);
```

Program 14.6: Reading student information from a file and writing it into another file. (*Continued*)

```
    fclose(stream);
    return 0;
}

int main() {
    const char *rfilename = "rwstudent.data";    /* read this data file */
    const char *wfilename = "rwstudentNew.data"; /* write into ths file */
    student_t s;     /* declare a student_t to hold the information */
    int status;      /* status for writing */

    readData(&s, rfilename);                 /* read data in rfilename into s */
    status = writeData(&s, wfilename); /* write data from s into wfilename */
    /* demonstrate how a return value should be used,
       give a message in stdout  */
    if(status)
       printf("writeData() failed\n");
    else
       printf("writeData() is successful\n");
    return 0;
}
```

Program 14.6: *(Continued)*

short, the format specifier `"%hd"` is used. If there is only a single white space between each entry, the format specifier can be simplied as follows:

```
"%d%*2c%[^,]%*c%hd%*c%hd%*c%hd%*c%lf"
```

where the format specifier `"%*2c"` is used to suppress the comma and white space following the student ID.

‡Obtaining Web Addresses from HTML Files

> **Problem Statement:**
> Display all Web addresses hyperlinked from a Hypertext Markup Language (HTML) file. The HTML file is specified in the command-line option. By default, the HTML file is `geturlfile.html`.

Program 12.13 in Chapter 12 can obtain a hyperlinked Web address from the user input. Program 14.7 can process an HTML file to display all Web addresses hyperlinked from an HTML file. A sample HTML file is shown in Program 14.8. An HTML file can be processed by a Web browser to access the information stored in Web servers on the World Wide Web. Like Program 14.4, Program 14.7 takes an optional command-line argument as a filename for the HTML file to be processed. Similar to Program 14.4, the variable `filename` for file name is a pointer to char. If there is no optional argument, the variable `filename` points to the default file name `geturlfile.html`. Otherwise, the command-line argument is used as a file name. The program then opens the file for processing. Like Program 14.5, a **while** loop is used to read each line of the HTML file until it is terminated when the function **feof()** returns the EOF indicator. Each input line is processed by using the same code described in Program 12.13. Finally, the

```
/* File: geturlfile.c
   Get URL Web addresses from an HTML file */
#include <stdio.h>       /* for fopen(), fclose(), fgets(), feof(), printf() */
#include <string.h>      /* for strstr(), strchr(), strcpy(), strncpy() */
#include <stdlib.h>      /* for exit() */
#define LINESIZE 1024    /* the maximum input line length */

int main(int argc, char *argv[]) {
    /* declare strings line for the input string, url for URL address
       beginptr for the beginning of the URL address,
       endptr for the end of the URL address */
    char line[LINESIZE], url[LINESIZE], *beginptr, *endptr;
    int len;                 /* the len of the URL address */
    FILE *stream;            /* declare a file stream */
    /* declare variables for cmd, file name, and default file name */
    char *cmd, *filename, dfilename[] = "geturlfile.html";

    cmd = argv[0];           /* save the command */
    if(argc > 2){            /* extra argument */
        fprintf(stderr, "Usage: %s [filename]\n", cmd);
        exit(EXIT_FAILURE);
    }
    /* get the user specified or default file name */
    filename = (argc == 2 ? argv[1]:dfilename);
    stream = fopen(filename, "r"); /* open the file for reading */
    if(stream == NULL) {
        printf("Error: cannot open '%s'\n", filename);
        exit(EXIT_FAILURE);
    }

    fgets(line, LINESIZE, stream); /* read a line from the file */
    while(!feof(stream)) {         /* read the file till EOF */
      /* find "http:// in the string */
      /* There might be multiple URL addresses in the user input line */
      while (beginptr = strstr(line, "\"http://")) {
         beginptr++; /* skip " in "http:// */
         /* find the closing " */
         endptr = strchr(beginptr, '"');
         if(endptr != NULL)  /* when there is " */
         {
             /* calculate the length of the URL address */
             len = endptr - beginptr;
             strncpy(url, beginptr, len); /* copy URL address to url */
```

Program 14.7: Retrieving Web addresses from an HTML file. (*Continued*)

```
            url[len] = '\0';            /* append a null character for url */
            printf("%s\n",url );        /* got a URL, print it */
            strcpy(line, endptr);       /* update string line to find next URL */
         }
         else {/* set line to a null terminating character to quit while-loop */
            line[0] = '\0';
         }
      }
      fgets(line, LINESIZE, stream); /* read a line from the file */
   }
   fclose(stream);                     /* close the file stream */
   return 0;
}
```

Program 14.7: (*Continued*)

```
<html>
<head>
<title>
Using Ch for Interactive Web Applications
</title>
</head>

<a href="http://www.softintegration.com"> C/C++ Interpreter Ch </a> <br>
<a href="http://www.softintegration.com/webservices/index.html">
Web-Based Computing</a> <br>
Click <a href="http://www.ucdavis.edu">here</a>
or <a href="http://www.ucdavis.edu">here</a> <br>
<a href="http://iel.ucdavis.edu"> URL http://iel.ucdavis.edu</a>
</html>
```

Program 14.8: A sample HTML file.

HTML file is closed before the program exits. When Program 14.7 is executed, the following output for Web addresses in file `geturlfile.html` will be displayed as follows:

```
http://www.softintegration.com
http://www.softintegration.com/webservices/index.html
http://www.ucdavis.edu
http://www.ucdavis.edu
http://iel.ucdavis.edu
```

Note that the second occurrence of the Web address `http://iel.ucdavis.edu` is not displayed in the output because it is not enclosed within a pair of double quotation marks.

14.2.1 ‡Differences in Binary Mode for Reading and Writing Sequential Files

When Program 14.3 is executed in Unix, the output file `accel.txt` has 11 lines; each line has 9 characters, including a newline character. The program **wc** can be used to print the number of newlines, words, and bytes in a text file such as `accel.txt`, as shown below.

```
> wc accel.txt
11 11 99 accel.txt
```

The first three columns show the number of lines, words, and bytes for the file `accel.txt` in the fourth column. Because the stream to the output file `accel.txt` is opened as a text file with the option `"w"`, the output is subject to different line orientations.

In Windows, when a newline character `'\n'` is written to the output file, two characters `'\r'` and `'\n'` are written. There would be an extra byte in each line in the output `accel.txt` from Program 14.3. The output from executing the program **wc** for the file `accel.txt`, as shown below

```
> wc accel.txt
11 11 110 accel.txt
```

has 110 bytes instead of 99 bytes.

If we open the file for writing as a binary file by

```
stream = fopen("accel.txt", "wb");
```

there is no effect on the output when the program is executed in Unix. On Windows, however, each line of the output file `accel.txt` will be terminated by a single newline character `'\n'`, instead of the two characters `'\r'` and `'\n'`. In this case, the output file will be consistent with 99 bytes in different platforms. However, some application programs in Windows such as Notepad will display such an output file in a single line, because only the combination of two adjacent characters `'\r'` and `'\n'` is treated as a newline.

Program 14.5 is able to read the text file `accel.txt` created by Program 14.3, regardless whether it is created in Unix or Windows. The format specifier `"%lf"` in the function call

```
fscanf(stream, "%lf", &a);    /* read an acceleration */
```

in Program 14.5 ignores input white-space characters, including `'\r'` and `'\n'`.

The program named `accelichar.c` is distributed along with other programs for the testing purpose. It reads the text file `accel.txt` character by character using the code

```
char c;
int i=0;
FILE stream = fopen("accel.txt", "r");
fscanf(stream, "%c", &c);    /* read a character */
while(!feof(stream)) {       /* while not end-of-file */
  i++;                       /* count number of char read */
  printf("%c", c);           /* print the acceleration */
  fscanf(stream, "%c", &c); /* read next character */
}
```

Similar to writing a newline character, in Windows, two adjacent characters '\r' and '\n' are read as a single newline character. In Unix, they are treated as two separate characters. To treat these two adjacent characters as two separate characters in Windows, the file for reading needs to be opened in binary mode to suppress the line orientation by

```
stream = fopen("accel.txt", "rb");
```

14.3 Design of a GPA Library Using Data Files and Its Applications

To use the functions in the GPA library in section 13.5 in Chapter 13, the student information is stored in an array of Student structure. This is not convenient for applications when data are stored in files or a database. In this section, we will design a GPA library to use student information stored in a file as shown in Figure 14.2. In this data file, a line starting with the symbol # is a comment. A program should ignore comment lines in a data file. The information for a student is stored in a line with the first entry for the student identification number, followed by student name, birthday, birth month, birth year, and GPA. Each valid line contains the information for a student. Therefore, the data file in Figure 14.2 contains the student information in an array of structures in Program 13.35 in Chapter 13.

14.3.1 Development of a GPA Library Using Data Files

In our new GPA library, all functions in the previous GPA library remain the same. We only add a few functions to process student information in a data file. Program 14.9 is an application program using functions in the new GPA library. This program is similar to Program 13.35. When Program 14.9 is executed, it will display the same output on the screen, as shown in Figure 13.10 in Chapter 13. In Program 14.9, the student information pointed to by the variable head is obtained by the function call

```
head = gpa_readData(filename);
```

where the argument filename contains the data file student.data shown in Figure 14.2. Similar to Program 13.35, the program calculates the total number of students in the list, average GPA, highest GPA, lowest GPA, and students with GPAs above 3.0. It then displays the sorted list with GPAs in descending order.

```
# comment starts with '#' as the 1st character
101 John 12 11 1985 3.33
102 Doe 13 3 1988 3
103 Peter 21 4 1984 3.1
104 Mary 8 2 1985 3.93
105 Ron 30 12 1986 2.3
106 George 9 1 1987 2.31
# Note: Mike has the highest GPA.
107 Mike 10 8 1986 3.99
108 Steve 17 5 1989 2.8
109 Jone 25 4 1990 2.9
110 Ron 6 11 1988 3.7
```

Figure 14.2: A data file student.data with student information in a class.

```
/*************************************************************
* File: studentfile.c
* This program tests the GPA library with data in a file
*************************************************************/
#include <stdio.h>
#include <stdlib.h>       /* for exit(EXIT_FAILURE) */
#include "studentfile.h"  /* header file for GPA library */

int main() {
   student_t *head, *sp; /* head of the list and a single student */
   double gpa;           /* GPA value */
   struct Birthday b;    /* b for birthday */
   int num; /* number of students with GPA above a specified value */
   const char filename[] = "student.data"; /* student data file */

   /* read student data file */
   head = gpa_readData(filename);
   if(head == NULL) {
      fprintf(stderr, "Error: failed to read file '%s'\n", filename);
      exit(EXIT_FAILURE);
   }
   printf("The total number of students is %d\n", gpa_totnum(head));
   gpa = gpa_averageGPA(head); /* GPA for all students */
   printf("The GPA for all students is %.2f\n", gpa);
   sp = gpa_highestGPA(head); /* find the student with the highest GPA */
   b = gpa_getBirthday(sp);   /* get the birthday of this student */
   printf("%s who was born on %s %d, %d has the highest GPA %.2f\n",
          gpa_getName(sp), gpa_monthString(b.month), b.day, b.year,
          gpa_getGPA(sp));
   printf("The student with the lowest GPA:\n");
   sp = gpa_lowestGPA(head);  /* find the student with the lowest GPA */
   gpa_printStudent(sp);      /* print infor for this student */
   /* find the student with ID 103 and named 'Peter' */
   sp = gpa_find(head, 103, "Peter");
   if(sp) {  /* if Peter is in the list, get and print his GPA */
     printf("Peter's GPA is %.2f\n", gpa_getGPA(sp));
   }
   printf("Students with GPA 3.0 or above:\n");
   /* get the number of students with GPA above 3.0 and print them out */
   num = gpa_aboveGPA(head, 3.0);
   printf("%d students with GPA 3.0 or above.\n", num);
   gpa_sortGPA(head);   /* sort students in the list based on GPA */
   printf("The student record sorted in descending GPA:\n");
```

Program 14.9: A program `studentfile.c` using functions in a GPA library with data in a file. (*Continued*)

```
    gpa_printList(head); /* print info for students in the sorted list */
    /* write the student data file with sorted GPA */
    gpa_writeData(head, "studentNew.data");
    gpa_clearList(head); /* clear the memory allocated for the data */
    return 0;
}
```

Program 14.9: *(Continued)*

At the end of Program 14.9, the statement

```
gpa_writeData(head, "studentNew.data");
```

saves the sorted student data in descending order in the file `studentNew.data` as shown in Figure 14.3. The statement

```
gpa_clearList(head);
```

deletes the memory allocated by the function `gpa_readData()`.

The header file `studentfile.h` is almost the same as `student.h` in Program 13.33 in Chapter 13 with a few minor changes. To process student information in a data file, the following functions, as they are prototyped in the header file `studentfile.h`, are added in this new GPA library:

```
extern student_t *gpa_readData(const char *filename);
extern int gpa_writeData(const student_t *head, const char *filename);
extern void gpa_clearList(student_t *head);
extern void gpa_setGPA(student_t *sp, double gpa);
```

The source code for these functions shown in Programs 14.10 and 14.11 are located in the source file `studentfilefunc.c`. Because user application programs do not need to use the macro `GPA_EOD`, this macro is defined by the statement

```
#define GPA_EOD -1
```

```
107 Mike 10 8 1986 3.99
104 Mary 8 2 1985 3.93
110 Ron 6 11 1988 3.7
103 Peter 21 4 1984 3.51
101 John 12 11 1985 3.33
102 Doe 13 3 1988 3
109 Jone 25 4 1990 2.9
108 Steve 17 5 1989 2.8
106 George 9 1 1987 2.31
105 Ron 30 12 1986 2.3
```

Figure 14.3: A data file `studentNew.data` with students' GPAs in descending order.

```
/* read student data file and return data in list with the allocated memory */
student_t *gpa_readData(const char *filename) {
    student_t *head, *sp; /* declare head of the list and a single student */
    int i, totnum;        /* declare index i and total number of students */
    FILE *stream;         /* a file stream for reading data from filename */
    char line[BUFSIZE];   /* a buffer to hold the a line from filename */

    stream = fopen(filename, "r");  /* open filename for reading */
    if(stream == NULL) {
        fprintf(stderr, "Error: cannot open file '%s' for reading\n", filename);
        return NULL;
    }
    /* get total number of records */
    totnum = 0;
    fgets(line, BUFSIZE, stream);   /* read a line into the buffer */
    while(!feof(stream)) {
       if(line[0] != '#') { /* excluding the comment line starts with '#' */
          totnum++;
       }
       fgets(line, BUFSIZE, stream); /* read a line into the buffer */
    }
    if(totnum == 0) {                 /* check if there is no data */
        fprintf(stderr, "Error: no valid data in file '%s'\n", filename);
        return NULL;
    }
    /* allocate memory for records, (totnum+1) with an extra one for
       a sentinel element */
    head = (student_t *) malloc((totnum+1)*sizeof(student_t));
    if(head==NULL) {
        fprintf(stderr, "Error: not enough memory\n");
        return NULL;
    }
    sp = head;                        /* sp points to the head of the list */

    rewind(stream);          /* stream points to the beginning of the file */
    for(i=0; i<totnum; i++, sp++) {   /* read records */
        fgets(line, BUFSIZE, stream); /* read a line into the buffer */
        while(line[0] == '#') { /* skip the comment line starts with '#' */
           fgets(line, BUFSIZE, stream); /* read the next line */
        }
        /* read the data for a student from string line and save them in
           the memory pointed by sp */
        sscanf(line, "%d%s%hd%hd%hd%lf", &sp->id, sp->name,
              &sp->birthday.day, &sp->birthday.month, &sp->birthday.year,
```

Program 14.10: The function `gpa_readData()` to read data in a file. *(Continued)*

```
            &sp->gpa);
    }
    fclose(stream);          /* close the file stream */
    /* append a sentinel element */
    sp->id = GPA_EOD;
    sp->name[0] = '\0';
    sp->birthday.day = GPA_EOD;
    sp->birthday.month = GPA_EOD;
    sp->birthday.year = GPA_EOD;
    sp->gpa = GPA_EOD;
    return head;             /* return the head of the list */
}
```

Program 14.10: (*Continued*)

```
/* write student data into a file */
int gpa_writeData(const student_t *head, const char *filename) {
    FILE *stream;     /* a file stream for writing data int filename */

    stream = fopen(filename, "w"); /* open filename for writing */
    if(stream == NULL) {
        fprintf(stderr, "Error: cannot open file '%s' for writing\n", filename);
        return -1;
    }
    while(head->id != GPA_EOD) { /* write until the sentinel element */
        fprintf(stream, "%d %s %hd %hd %hd %g\n", head->id, head->name,
                head->birthday.day, head->birthday.month, head->birthday.year,
                head->gpa);
        head++;          /* advance to the next element */
    }
    fclose(stream);      /* close the file stream */
    return 0;
}

/* clear the list with allocated memory */
void gpa_clearList(student_t *head) {
    if(head) {          /* if the memory had been allocated for head */
        free(head);  /* release the memory */
    }
}

/* set student GPA */
void gpa_setGPA(student_t *sp, double gpa) {
    sp->gpa = gpa;
}
```

Program 14.11: The functions `gpa_writeData()` to write data in a file, `gpa_clearList()` to clear the list, and `gpa_setGPA()` to set a GPA.

in the file `studentfilefunc.c`, limiting its use for implementation of functions in the GPA library only. The source file `studentfilefunc.c` also defines the macro `BUFSIZE` for the size of the input line buffer size by

```
#define BUFSIZE 1024
```

The macro `BUFSIZE` is used in the function `gpa_readData()`. The file `studentfilefunc.c` also contains all source code in the file `studentfunc.c` listed in Program 13.34 in Chapter 13.

We will examine how these four new functions are implemented in the new GPA library. Unlike the function `readData()` in Program 14.6, which reads only a set of data for a single student, the function `gpa_readData()` in Program 14.10 reads multiple sets of data for a list of students. The data are stored in a dynamically allocated array of `Student` structures, one element for a student. The memory pointed by the variable `head` is returned to the calling function and passed to other GPA functions. Before the program exits, this dynamically allocated memory is freed by the function `gpa_clearList()` in Program 14.11. To allocate the memory for a dynamic array, we have to know the total number of elements. In this case, we need to know the total number of valid lines excluding the comment line. After the file is opened, the contents of the file is read line by line using the function **fgets()**. The first **while** loop in the function `gpa_readData()` counts the number of valid lines for student information. The total number of students in a data file is stored in the integer variable `totnum`. Because a sentinel element will be added at the end of the array in the function `gpa_readData()` to indicate the ending of the data, it allocates the memory for `(totnum+1)` elements using the function **malloc()**. Afterwards, the stream is rewinded to point to the beginning of the text file using the function **rewind()**, which has the prototype

```
void rewind(FILE *stream);
```

After rewinding, when the function **fgets()** is called again, it will read the data starting from the beginning. If not using **rewind()**, the stream would have to be closed first by calling **fclose()**, and then a new stream would be opened by calling **fopen()**. The student information in a data file is processed in a **for** loop. Inside this **for** loop, a **while** loop is used to skip comment lines, which start with the symbol `'#'`. Because we have to skip comment lines, unlike the function `readData()` in Program 14.6, we cannot use the function **fscanf()** to read the data directly. Each line in a file is saved in the variable `line` of type string first by the function **fgets()**. The information in the string is then read into each member of the `student_t` structure in the memory pointed by `sp` using the function **sscanf()**. The details about the function **sscanf()** are described in section 12.5 in Chapter 12.

Similar to the function `writeData()` in Program 14.6, the function `gpa_writeData()` in Program 14.11 writes the student information in a program to a file. Inside the function `gpa_writeData()`, a **while** loop is used to process all data in the list.

The function `gpa_setGPA()` in Program 14.11 is used to change the GPA for a student. This function is used in a menu-driven interactive application program.

14.3.2 Development of a Menu-Driven Interactive GPA Program Using Data Files

The user interface of the menu-driven interactive GPA program is shown in Figure 14.4. Similar to Program 13.36 in section 13.5 in Chapter 13, this application allows the user to interactively query and sort the GPAs of students in the list. Comparing with Figure 13.11, there are three new entries: one for changing the GPA of a student, one for reading a new GPA data file, and the last for writing data to a new file, as shown in the interactive user interface in Figure 14.4. Comparing with the previous one in Figure 13.11, this new

```
************************ GPA Menu ************************
av, average: display the average of GPAs for all students
h,  highest: display the student with the highest GPA
l,  lowest:  display the student with the lowest GPA
ab, above:   display students with GPA above a value
s,  sort:    display the record sorted in descending GPA
o,  obtain:  obtain a student's GPA
c,  change:  change a student's GPA
r,  read:    read a new GPA data file
w,  write:   write to a GPA data file
q,  quit:    quit the system
..........................................................

GPA>
```

Figure 14.4: The interactive user interface for the program `studentfilemenu.c`.

interactive GPA application program is more flexible. It contains the following three new entries:

```
c, change:   change a student's GPA
r, read:     read a new GPA data file
w, write:    write to a GPA data file
```

which allow the user to change the GPA of a student, read different GPA data files, and write the result of the program into a file. For example, the user can sort students in the list based on the GPAs and save the sorted list in a file.

The source code for this interactive menu-driven program is shown in Program 14.12. Compared with Program 13.36, Program 14.12 added a macro called `MAX_FILENAME_LENGTH` for the maximum length of a file name used inside the function **main()**. Corresponding to three new entries in the user interface, the new enumerated values `CHANGEGPA, READFILE,` and `WRITEFILE` are added in the enumerated data

```
/*********************************************************************
 * File: studentfilemenu.c
 * This application program uses the GPA library to process GPAs of
 * students in the database of a file. The application is menu driven.
 *********************************************************************/
#include <stdio.h>
#include <string.h>                /* for strcmp()   */
#include <stdlib.h>                /* for exit(EXIT_FAILURE) */
#include "studentfile.h"           /* the header file for GPA lib */

#define MAX_TRY_NUM  3             /* maximum number of tries */
#define MAX_PROMPT_STR  128        /* maximum prompt string length */
#define MAX_FILENAME_LENGTH 128 /* maximum file name length */
```

Program 14.12: A menu-driven program `studentfilemenu.c` using functions in a GPA library. (*Continued*)

```
/* enumerated type for actions from the menu driven user input */
typedef enum Action {
    UNDEFINED,    /* undefined action */
    AVERAGEGPA,   /* find the average of GPAs for all students */
    HIGHESTGPA,   /* find the student with the highest GPA */
    LOWESTGPA,    /* find the student with the lowest GPA */
    ABOVEGPA,     /* find students with GPA above a given value */
    SORTGPA,      /* sort the students based on GPA in descending order */
    OBTAINGPA,    /* obtain the GPA for a student based on id and name */
    CHANGEGPA,    /* change the GPA for a student based on id and name */
    READFILE,     /* read student information from a file */
    WRITEFILE,    /* write student information into a file */
    QUIT          /* quit the program */
} action_t;

/* function prototypes for this application only */
extern action_t getActionMenu(void);  /* action menu */
/* obtain the GPA for a student */
extern void obtainGPA(student_t *head);
/* change the GPA for a student */
extern void changeGPA(student_t *head);
/* initialize the head of the list for students */
extern student_t *initialize(const char *filename);

int main() {
    student_t *head, *sp; /* head of the list and a single student */
    double gpa;           /* GPA value */
    struct Birthday b;    /* b for birthday */
    int num; /* number of students with GPA above a specified value */
    action_t act;         /* action in the menu */
    int quit = FALSE;     /* flag for quit or continue the menu */
    /* declare filename for data file, initialized with the default data file */
    char filename[MAX_FILENAME_LENGTH] = "student.data";

    /* head points to the list of students in default data file student.data */
    head = initialize(filename);
    while(quit==FALSE) {  /* continue the menu if not quit */
        act = getActionMenu();  /* get an action */
        switch(act) {     /* take an action based on the value of 'act' */
            case AVERAGEGPA:  /* obtain the average of all GPAs */
              printf("The GPA for all students is %.2f\n",gpa_averageGPA(head));
              break;
            case HIGHESTGPA: /* find the student with the highest GPA */
              sp = gpa_highestGPA(head);
```

Program 14.12: *(Continued)*

```
      b = gpa_getBirthday(sp);
      printf("%s who was born on %s %d, %d has the highest GPA %.2f\n",
             gpa_getName(sp), gpa_monthString(b.month), b.day, b.year,
             gpa_getGPA(sp));
      break;
    case LOWESTGPA:  /* find the student with the lowest GPA */
      sp = gpa_lowestGPA(head);
      b = gpa_getBirthday(sp);
      printf("%s who was born on %s %d, %d has the lowest GPA %.2f\n",
             gpa_getName(sp), gpa_monthString(b.month), b.day, b.year,
             gpa_getGPA(sp));
      break;
    case ABOVEGPA: /* find students with GPA above a given value */
      printf("please input GPA\n");
      scanf("%lf%*c", &gpa);
      printf("Students with GPA %.2f or above:\n", gpa);
      num = gpa_aboveGPA(head, gpa);
      printf("%d students with GPA %.2f or above.\n", num, gpa);
      break;
    case SORTGPA: /* sort students based on GPA in descending order */
      gpa_sortGPA(head);  /* sort in descending order */
      printf("The student record sorted in descending GPA:\n");
      gpa_printList(head);/* print all students */
      break;
    case OBTAINGPA: /* obtain GPA for a student based on id and name */
      obtainGPA(head);     /* using a function in this program */
      break;
    case CHANGEGPA: /* change GPA for a student based on id and name */
      changeGPA(head);
      break;
    case READFILE: /* read the student information in a data file */
      printf("Please input a GPA data file name\n");
      fgets(filename, MAX_FILENAME_LENGTH, stdin); /* get file name */
      filename[strlen(filename)-1] = '\0';          /* remove '\n' */
      gpa_clearList(head);  /* release the allocated memory for head */
      head = initialize(filename); /* point to the list from filename */
      break;
    case WRITEFILE: /* write student info in the list into data file */
      printf("Please input a GPA data file name\n");
      fgets(filename, MAX_FILENAME_LENGTH, stdin); /* get file name */
      filename[strlen(filename)-1] = '\0';          /* remove '\n' */
      gpa_writeData(head, filename);  /* write list into filename */
      break;
```

Program 14.12: *(Continued)*

```
        case QUIT:              /* quit the program */
          quit = TRUE;          /* set flag quit to TRUE */
          break;
        default:                /* in case a mistake is made */
          printf("\aInvalid input!\n");
          break;
      }
  }
  gpa_clearList(head);  /* release the allocated memory for head */
  return 0;
}

/*---------------------------------------------------------------
* Function initialize() creates a list for student information
* in file filename. The memory allocated for the list needs to
* be released by function gpa_clearList().
*--------------------------------------------------------------*/
student_t *initialize(const char *filename) {
    student_t *head;
    head = gpa_readData(filename);
    if(head == NULL) {
        fprintf(stderr, "Error: failed to read file '%s'\n", filename);
    }
    return head;
}

/*------------------------------------------------------------------------
* Function changeGPA() changes the GPA for a student from the database
* of a file. Make sure the student with id and name is in the database.
* The user can input id and name up to 3 times defined in * MAX_TRY_NUM.
* After three failed tries, the function will quit.
* The static variable try_count is used for implementation.
*-----------------------------------------------------------------------*/
void changeGPA(student_t *head) {
    student_t *sp;           /* a student */
    int id;                  /* student id */
    char name[32];           /* student name */
    static try_count = 0;    /* track the number of tries using static var */
    double gpa;              /* new GPA value from the user input */

    printf("please input student id\n");
    /* get the student id and suppress the newline character '\n' */
    scanf("%d%*c", &id);
    printf("please input student name\n");
```

Program 14.12: (*Continued*)

```
    fgets(name, sizeof(name), stdin); /* the user input string */
    /* get rid of the newline character '\n' in the input string */
    name[strlen(name)-1] = '\0';
    sp = gpa_find(head, id, name); /* find the student based on id and name */
    if(sp) { /* when the student is found, change the GPA */
        printf("please input GPA\n");
        scanf("%lf%*c", &gpa);      /* get GPA and surpress RETURN character */
        gpa_setGPA(sp, gpa);  /* change the GPA in the list for the sutndet */
        printf("%s's GPA has been changed to %.2f\n", name, gpa);
        try_count = 0;
    }
    else {    /* when the student is not found, try it again */
        printf("%s with id %d is not in the database.\n", name, id);
        try_count++; /* increment the count for number of failed try */
        if(try_count < MAX_TRY_NUM) { /* if less than specified num of tries */
            changeGPA(head); /* call the function recursively, up to 3 times */
        }
        else {                /* exit the function after three failed tries */
            printf("You have tried %d times, nice try!\n", try_count);
            try_count = 0;  /* reset the count for next action */
        }
    }
}
```

Program 14.12: *(Continued)*

type `Action`. There are four functions in this program. The function definition for `obtainGPA()`, listed in Program 13.36, is the same in these two programs. Therefore, it is not listed in Program 14.12. The function `getActionMenu()` in these two programs is the same, except that the code fragment

```
else if(!strcmp(str, "c") || !strcmp(str, "change")) {
    act = CHANGEGPA;
}
else if(!strcmp(str, "r") || !strcmp(str, "read")) {
    act = READFILE;
}
else if(!strcmp(str, "w") || !strcmp(str, "write")) {
    act = WRITEFILE;
}
```

for handling cases of `CHANGEGPA, READFILE,` and `WRITEFILE` is added inside `getActionMenu()` in Program 14.12. The function `initialize()` calls the function `gpa_readData()` in the GPA library to allocate an array of `Student` structures dynamically to hold the student information in the default GPA data file `student.data`. The allocated memory is released using the function `gpa_clearList()` in the GPA library before the program exits.

There are three new cases, CHANGEGPA, READFILE, and WRITEFILE, in the **switch** statement inside a **while** loop. To change the GPA of a student, the function changeGPA() is called. Like the function obtainGPA(), based on the student ID and name from the user input, this function finds a student using the function gpa_find() in the GPA library. If the student id and name are invalid, it will ask the user for new input three times by recursively calling the function changeGPA() before the function exits. If the student is in the list, the function changes the student's GPA using the function gpa_setGPA() in the GPA library.

To read a new GPA data file in the case of READFILE, the program will prompt the user for a file name first. It then frees the memory allocated by the previous function call of initialize() using the function gpa_clearList() in the GPA library. Finally, it reads the new data file using the function initialize(). To write the student information in the list inside the program, the user types in the file name. The function gpa_writeData() in the GPA library is then called to write the data into the file.

This example illustrates how previously developed functions in a library can be extended and used for new applications. Although the new GPA library in this section is more flexible than the one in section 13.5 in Chapter 13, it still has limitations. For example, it is not convenient to add or remove a student in the list. The member name for a student name in the structure student has a fixed number of 32 bytes. In Chapter 15, this GPA library will be modified so that it can be used more conveniently to develop applications with a variable number of students.

14.4 ‡Redirecting Input and Output Inside a Program

In section 3.15.3 in Chapter 3, the input and output redirection feature of an operating system for running a program was described. The standard input and output of a program can be redirected to a file when the program is executed.

In this section, a more general file stream redirection scheme in C is presented. The technique can be used to handle the standard input and output redirection.

The standard function **freopen()** allows for the redirection of a file stream in a program. Its function prototype is as follows:

```
FILE *freopen(const char *filename, const char *mode,
              FILE *stream);
```

The function **freopen()** first tries to close the stream pointed to by stream, but it will ignore any error that may occur. It then opens the file given by filename for the purpose specified by mode. The mode argument is similar to that of the corresponding argument for the function **fopen()**. Rather than associating the file stream with a new **FILE *** type, it is now associated with the stream pointed to by stream. The **freopen()** returns the value of stream on success, a null pointer on failure. The function **freopen()** is primarily used to reassociate one of the standard input/output streams (**stdin**, **stdout**, and **stderr**) with a file.

Program 3.6 in Chapter 3 reads one integer and one floating-point number from the standard input. As an example of input redirection, we modified Program 3.6 to redirect its input from file scanfc.dat. The function call

```
stream = freopen("scanfc.dat", "r", stdin);
```

in Program 14.13 associates the standard input stream **stdin** with the file scanfc.dat. That is, function calls that would normally read in data from **stdin** will now read data from the file scanfc.dat. With the **stdin** stream redirected to the file scanfc.dat, the function call to **scanf()** in Program 14.13 obtains the

```
/* File: scanfcin.c
   Input an integer and a floating point number to the program
   from file scanfc.dat using freopen().
   The program is modified from scanfc.c */
#include <stdio.h>  /* for printf(), FILE,  freopen(), fclose() */
#include <stdlib.h> /* for exit() */

int main() {
    int num;        /* declare num as an int */
    double d;       /* declare d as a double */
    FILE *stream; /* declare a file stream */

    /* redirect stdin from to scanfc.dat */
    stream = freopen("scanfc.dat", "r", stdin);
    if(stream ==  NULL) { /* open "scanfc.dat" failed */
        printf("Error: cannot open 'scanfc.dat'\n");
        exit(EXIT_FAILURE);
    }

    /* prompt the user for input */
    printf("Please input one integer and one floating-point number\n");
    /* the user to input an integer for num, and a floating-point number
       or integer for d from file "scanfc.dat" */
    scanf("%d%lf",&num, &d);
    /* display the input from file "freopenstdio.in" */
    printf("Your input values are %d and %f\n", num, d);
    fclose(stream); /* close the file stream */
    return 0;
}
```

Program 14.13: Using the function **freopen**() to redirect the standard input.

data for `num` and `d` from the file `scanfc.dat`. The opened stream should be closed before the program exits. If the file `scanfc.dat` contains

```
10 12.3456
```

the interactive execution of Program 3.6 is shown below.

```
> scanfcin.c
Please input one integer and one floating-point number
Your input values are 10 and 12.345600
```

The result is the same as that from the execution of Program 3.6 with the input redirected from the file `scanfc.dat` shown in section 3.15.3.

Program 3.2 displays the calculated acceleration as the standard output by the function **printf**(). As an example of output redirection, Without modifying the function call using **printf()**, Program 14.14 redirects the standard output to the file `accelvar.out`. The function call

```
stream = freopen("accelvar.out", "w", stdout);
```

```
/* File: accelvarout.c
   Calculate the acceleration using variables.
   Redirect output from stdout to accelvar.out.
   The program is modified based on accelvar.c  */
#include <stdio.h>  /* for printf(), FILE,  freopen(), fclose() */
#include <stdlib.h> /* for exit() */

int main() {
    /* declare variables */
    double a,      /* acceleration */
           mu,     /* friction coefficient */
           m,      /* mass */
           p;      /* external force */
    FILE *stream; /* declare a file stream */

    /* redirect stdout to accelvar.out */
    stream = freopen("accelvar.out", "w", stdout);
    if(stream ==  NULL) { /* open "accelvar.out" failed */
        printf("Error: cannot open 'accelvar.out'\n");
        exit(EXIT_FAILURE);
    }

    /* initialize variables */
    mu = 0.2;
    m = 5.0;
    p = 20.0;

    /* calculate the acceleration */
    a = (p-mu*m*9.81)/m;

    /* the stdout is directed to file "accelvar.out" */
    printf("Acceleration a = %f (m/s^2)\n", a);
    fclose(stream); /* close the file stream */
    return 0;
}
```

Program 14.14: Using the function **freopen**() to redirect the standard ouput.

in Program 14.14 associates the file `accelvar.out` with the standard output stream **stdout**. That is, function calls that would normally print out data in **stdout** will now write to the file `accelvar.out`. The opened stream should also be closed before the program exits. With the **stdout** stream redirected to file `accelvar.out`, the function call to **printf()** in Program 14.14 will write the output

```
Acceleration a = 2.038000 (m/s^2)
```

into the file `accelvar.out`.

For an application in Windows with the graphical user interface (GUI), the standard ouput from function calls such as **printf()** are ignored. To view the standard output, it can be redirected to a file first and then processed. This redirection capability is important for an application using a third-party library that calls functions with the standard output. Otherwise, the output from the library may not be accessible.

14.5 ‡Reading and Writing Random Access Files

Some files support random access, such as files on the hard drive, but some do not, such as **stdout** and **stdin**, which are connected to the console. If a file supports random access, a *file position indicator* can be used to determine the position to read or write the next item. By default, the file position indicator points to the beginning of a file when it is opened. The reading or writing functions mentioned in the preceding section read or write items from the position pointed by the file position indicator and then increment the indicator properly so that it points to the next position to read or write. For example, if the item read or written is a character, the indicator is incremented by 1.

The function **fwrite()** writes a specified number of bytes from a location in memory to a file. It has the function prototype

```
size_t fwrite(const void *ptr, size_t size, size_t nitems,
              FILE *stream);
```

where the argument `ptr` is a pointer to the location of bytes to be written using a generic pointer as described in section 11.12 in Chapter 11, `size` is the number of bytes for each item, `nitems` is the number of items to write, and `stream` is the stream for a destination file. The argument `size` is type `size_t` of unsigned integer type, which is 64 bits for 64-bit programming as described in section 3.12 in Chapter 3.

In contrast, the function **fread()**, with the prototype shown below, reads a specified number of bytes from a file into memory.

```
size_t fread(void *ptr, size_t size, size_t nitems, FILE *stream);
```

The argument `ptr` points to the location for reading the bytes, `size` specifies the number of bytes for each item, `nitems` corresponds to the number of items to be read, and `stream` is the file for reading.

Furthermore, for files supporting random access, the indicator can be set by the function **fseek()**. Its prototype is

```
int fseek(FILE *stream, long int offset, int whence);
```

The function returns nonzero only for a request that cannot be satisfied. It sets the file position indicator for the stream pointed to by the argument `stream`. For a binary stream, the new position, measured in characters from the beginning of the file, is obtained by adding `offset` to the position specified by `whence`. The specified position is the beginning of the file if `whence` is **SEEK_SET**, the current value of the file position indicator if **SEEK_CUR**, or the EOF if **SEEK_END**. For a text stream, `offset` shall either be zero or a value returned by an earlier successful call to the function **ftell()** on a stream associated with the same file and `whence` shall be **SEEK_SET**. After a successful **fseek** call, the next operation on an update stream may be either input or output.

Besides the function **fseek()**, file positioning functions also include the function **fgetpos()**, which stores the current value of the file position indicator; **fsetpos()**, which sets the file position indicators according to the value of an object of type **fpos_t**; the function **ftell()**, which obtains the current value of the file position indicator for the stream; and the function **rewind()**, which sets the file position indicator to the beginning of the file. The function **rewind()** is used in an application example in section 14.3.

An Application Example

Acceleration of a Moving Body

Problem Statement:

For the mechanical system shown in Figure 2.12, given mass $m = 5$ kilograms (kg), gravitational acceleration constant $g = 9.81 m/s^2$, and coefficient of kinetic friction $\mu = 0.2$, the applied force p is expressed as a function of time t in

$$p(t) = 4\sin(t - 3) + 20 \qquad \text{when } t >= 0$$

Write a program to calculate the accelerations a during $t = 0$ to $t = 10$ with time step 1 and save the accelerations into a binary file `accel.bin` using the function **fwrite()**.

The solution to the above problem is Program 14.15. It initially calculates the acceleration of the system from $t = 0$ to 10 seconds and stores these values into the 11-element array `a`. The program uses the function call

```
fopen("accel.bin", "wb");
```

with the mode of `"wb"` to create a binary file `accel.bin` and uses function **fwrite()** to write the stored acceleration values to the file. If the file `accel.bin` cannot be opened, then an error message is displayed and the program terminates. The result of executing Program 14.15 is the binary file `accel.bin`. If you open this binary file using a text editor, the output looks like gibberish, although you may see some recognizable characters.

```
/* File: accelbino.c
   Write an entire array of acceleration in binary mode into a file */
#include <stdio.h>   /* for fopen(), fclose(), fwrite(), printf() */
#include <stdlib.h> /* for exit() */
```

Program 14.15: Writing a binary file using the function **fwrite()**. (*Continued*)

```
#define M_G   9.81   /* gravitational acceleration constant g */
#define N     11     /* number of elements for array a */

int main() {
    /* declaration and initialization */
    double mu=0.2, m=5.0, t0=0.0, tf=10.0, step=1.0, p, t;
    double a[N];       /* declare an array for accelerations */
    int i;             /* index variable */
    FILE *stream;      /* a file stream for writing */

    /* calculate acceleration */
    for(i=0; i<N; i++) {
        t = t0+i*(tf - t0)/(N-1); /* calculate t */
        p = 4*sin(t-3)+20;         /* use t to calculate p */
        a[i] = (p-mu*m*M_G)/m;
    }
    /* open file "accel.bin" for writing in binary mode */
    stream = fopen("accel.bin", "wb");
    if(stream == NULL) {
        printf("Error: cannot open 'accel.bin'\n");
        exit(EXIT_FAILURE);
    }
    /* write an entire array of a in binary mode into the file accel.bin */
    fwrite(a, sizeof(double), N, stream);
    fclose(stream);                /* close the file stream */
    printf("Done! Finished writing data to file accel.bin\n");
    return 0;
}
```

Program 14.15: *(Continued)*

Problem Statement:
Write a program to perform the following functions:

1. Read all the accelerations from the binary file `accel.bin` using the **fread()** function and print them out.
2. Read the fifth acceleration in the file and print it out.
3. Read the sixth acceleration and print it out.

A sample solution to this problem is Program 14.16. The function **fopen()** with the option `"rb"` is used to open the binary file `accel.bin` for reading. Similar to the other application programs, execution is terminated if the file fails to open. If the function call to **fopen()** is successful, the function **fread()** reads the data from the file `accel.bin` and stores it in the array `a`. A **for** loop is then used to print out all the values in the array. To solve problems 2 and 3, the function **fseek()** is called in conjunction with the function **fread()**. The function **fseek()** first moves the file position indicator to the fifth value stored in the file `accel.bin` starting from the beginning by using the macro **SEEK_SET**. A call to **fread()** reads this value and saves it into the variable `d`, which is then printed out. The function call **fread()** advances the file stream to the next element. Another call to the function **fread()** obtains the value of the sixth element to be printed. The result of Program 14.16 is shown in Figure 14.5.

```
/* File: accelbini.c
   Read the binary file accel.bin written by program accelbino.c */
#include <stdio.h>  /* for fopen(), fclose(), fread(), fseek(), printf() */
#include <stdlib.h> /* for exit() */
#define N     11    /* number of elements for array a */

int main() {
    double a[N];       /* declare an array for accelerations */
    double d;          /* one element of array for accelerations */
    int i;             /* index variable */
    FILE *stream;      /* a file stream for reading */

    /* open binary file accel.bin */
    stream = fopen("accel.bin", "rb");
    if(stream == NULL) {
      printf("Error: cannot open 'accel.bin'\n");
      exit(EXIT_FAILURE);
    }
    /* read N numbers of double type in binary mode */
    fread(a, sizeof(double), N, stream);
    printf("Data from file accel.bin.\n");
    for(i=0; i<N; i++) {
      printf("a[%d] = %f\n", i, a[i]);
    }

    /* reset file stream to the 5th element */
    fseek(stream, 4*sizeof(double), SEEK_SET);
    /* read the 5th element */
    fread(&d, sizeof(double), 1, stream);
    printf("The 5th element of acceleration is %f\n", d);
    /* read the next in the file pointed by stream, 6th element */
    fread(&d, sizeof(double), 1, stream);
    printf("The 6th acceleration is %f\n", d);
    fclose(stream); /* close the file stream */
    return 0;
}
```

Program 14.16: Reading a binary file using the functions **fread** and **fseek()**.

```
Data from file accel.bin.
a[0] = 1.925104
a[1] = 1.310562
a[2] = 1.364823
a[3] = 2.038000
a[4] = 2.711177
a[5] = 2.765438
a[6] = 2.150896
a[7] = 1.432558
a[8] = 1.270861
a[9] = 1.814468
a[10] = 2.563589
The 5th element of acceleration is 2.711177
The 6th acceleration is 2.765438
```

Figure 14.5: The output of program `accelbini.c`.

14.5.1 Reading and Writing Random Access Files with Structures

A structure is a data object. Its values can be written to a file or read from a file by the functions **fwrite()** and **fread()**. As previously mentioned, the functions **fwrite()** and **fread()** are used to write and read a block of data. To write the data of a structure to a file, the first argument can be specified by the address of a structure, while the second argument is the size of the structure. The size of the structure can be calculated by the **sizeof()** operator.

Program 14.17 illustrates how the functions **fwrite()** and **fread()** can be used to write and read data of a structure to or from a file. After the structure `s1` is initialized, a binary file `student.bin` is created to store the data contained in the structure. The file `student.bin` is then closed before it is opened for reading purposes. Using the function **fread()**, the data from the binary file is stored into the structure `s2`. The members of the structure `s2` are then displayed. The created file `student.bin` is removed by the function **remove()**, which is described in section 14.9. The output of this program is as follows:

```
s2.id   = 101
s2.name = John
```

```
/* File: fwrites.c
   Read and write a binary with using a structure */
#include <stdio.h>  /* for fopen(), fclose(), fread(), fwrite(), remove() */
#include <stdlib.h> /* for exit() */

struct Student {   /* define a structure for students */
    int id;
    char name[32];
};
```

Program 14.17: Reading and writing a random access file using a structure. (*Continued*)

```
int main() {
    /* declare s1 and s2,  initialize s1 */
    struct Student s1 = {101, "John"}, s2;
    FILE *stream;    /* a file stream for writing and reading */

    /* open a binary file student.bin for writing */
    stream = fopen("student.bin", "wb");
    if(stream == NULL) {
      printf("Error: cannot open 'student.bin' for writing.\n");
      exit(EXIT_FAILURE);
    }
    /* write s1 into file student.bin */
    fwrite(&s1, sizeof(struct Student), 1, stream);
    fclose(stream);    /* close the file stream */

    /* open the binary file student.bin for reading,
       re-use the variable stream */
    stream = fopen("student.bin", "rb");
    if(stream == NULL) {
      printf("Error: cannot open 'student.bin' for reading.\n");
      exit(EXIT_FAILURE);
    }
    /* read the contents in file student.bin in s2 */
    fread(&s2, sizeof(struct Student), 1, stream);
    fclose(stream);    /* close the file stream */

    /* print out the contents of structure s2 */
    printf("s2.id   = %d\n", s2.id);
    printf("s2.name = %s\n", s2.name);
    remove("student.bin"); /* remove file student.bin */
    return 0;
}
```

Program 14.17: *(Continued)*

14.5.2 Byte Order of Integral and Floating-Point Numbers in the Memory

As described in section 14.2.1, although subject to different line orientations, the output text file `accel.txt`, created by Program 14.3, can be read by Program 14.5 across different platforms. This will not be the case for binary files created by the function **fwrite()** because of different byte orders for representing integral and floating-point numbers in computers. For example, the output binary file `accel.bin`, created by Program 14.15 in Windows with Intel's x86 processors, cannot read by Program 14.16 in a Sun SPARC workstation or Apple computer with PowerPC. This section describes byte ordering used to store integral and floating-point numbers in computers.

Like human languages, some are read and written from left to right, others from right to left. Similarly, data in a computer system can be read and written differently. *Endianness* refers to the *byte ordering* used to represent integral and floating-point numbers in the memory. There are two forms of endianness: one is *big endian* and the other is *little endian*. Big endian means that the most significant byte, as described in section 3.1 in Chapter 3, is stored at the lowest memory address, whereas the least significant byte is at the highest memory address. Therefore, big endian implies "big end first." On the other hand, the little endian means that the least significant byte is stored at the lowest memory address whereas the most significant byte is at the highest memory address. Little endian implies "little end first." The memory layout for an integer with 4 bytes on big and little endian machines is shown in Table 14.2.

As an example, for a hexadecimal integer 0x12345678 with 4 bytes, the most significant byte (byte 3) is 0x12 and the least significant byte (byte 0) is 0x78. On a big endian machine, 0x12 is at the lowest memory address and 0x78 at the highest memory address as shown in Table 14.3. For the same integer on a little endian machine, 0x78 is at the lowest memory address and 0x12 at the highest memory address.

Well-known proccessor architectures that use the big endian format include Motorola 68000, PowerPC, SPARC, and HP-UX 11i. Intel x86 uses little endian. Some architectures, such as ARM and SPARC version 9, feature switchable endianness. For some systems, the default endianness is selected by hardware on the motherboard. Others can select the specific endian format via software, typically at the startup of the computer. Program 14.18 can be used to determine the endianness of a computer. The hexadecimal integer 0x1234567 is assigned to the variable `i` of type int. The value in the lowest byte of the memory for the variable `i` can be used to determine the endianness of the computer. The expression

```
*(char *)&i == (char)0x12
```

compares the integer value in the lowest byte for the variable `i` with the integer 0x12 of type char to determine if the machine is big endian. For a little endian machine, the expression `*(char *)&i` equals 0x78.

Program 14.19 illustrates how the endianness of a computer affects different data stored in a binary file. Values in the variables `c1` and `c2` of type char, `s` of type short, `i` of type int, and `f` of float type are written into the file `byteorder.bin` using the function **fwrite()**.

As we mentioned before, a binary file typically cannot be handled by a text editor. However, the content of a binary file can be examined by a hexadecimal viewer. A hexadecimal viewer program called **hexdump** is bundled in Linux and Mac OS X. If the output file `byteorder.bin` is created by Program 14.19 in a big endian machine such as Mac OS X with PowerPC, Solaris with SPARC, or HP-UX, the content of the file can be examined by this program in Linux or Mac OS X with PowerPC as follows:

```
> hexdump -C byteorder.bin
00000000  61 7a 43 58 12 34 56 78  3f 80 00 00   |azCX.4Vx?...|
```

Table 14.2 Memory layout of an int on big endian and little endian machines.

Endianness	Low address		High address	
Big endian	Byte 3	Byte 2	Byte 1	Byte 0
Little endian	Byte 0	Byte 1	Byte 2	Byte 3

Table 14.3 Integer 0x12345678 on big endian and little endian machines.

Memory offset (byte)	0	1	2	3
Memory content for big endian	0x12	0x34	0x56	0x78
Memory content for little endian	0x78	0x56	0x34	0x12

```c
/* File: endian.c
   Determine the endianness of a computer */
#include <stdio.h>

int main () {
    int i = 0x12345678;                     /* declare and initialize i */

    if (*(char *)&i == (char)0x12)          /* computer is big endian */
        printf ("big endian\n");
    else if (*(char *)&i == (char)0x78)     /* computer is little endian */
        printf ("little endian\n");
    else       /* it should not reach here normally, just in case */
        printf ("unknown endian (maybe middle endian or mixed endian)\n");
    return 0;
}
```

Program 14.18: Determining the endianness of a computer.

```c
/* File: byteorder.c
   Write chars, short, int, and float into a binary file. The byte order of
   the data in the binary file can be examined using the program hexdump */
#include <stdio.h>  /* for fopen(), fclose(), fwrite(), printf() */
#include <stdlib.h> /* for exit() */

int main() {
    /* declaration and initialization */
    char c1 = 0x61;        /* ASCII value for decimal value 97 and 'a' */
    char c2 = 0x7a;        /* ASCII value for decimal value 122 for 'z'   */
    short s = 0x4358;      /* ASCII value 0x43 is 'C', 0x58 is 'X' */
    int i = 0x12345678;    /* ASCII value 0x12 is not printable character.
                              0x34 is '4', 0x56 is 'V', 0x78 is 'x' */
    float f = 1.0;         /* binary representation of 1.0 is 0x3F800000,
                              ASCII value 0x3F is '?', ASCII values 0x80 and
                              0x00 are not printable character */
    FILE *stream;          /* a file stream for writing */

    /* open file "byteorder.bin" for writing in binary mode */
    stream = fopen("byteorder.bin", "wb");
    if(stream == NULL) {
        printf("Error: cannot open 'byteorder.bin'\n");
        exit(EXIT_FAILURE);
    }
    /* write c1, c2, s, i and f into the file byteorder.bin */
    fwrite(&c1, sizeof(char), 1, stream);
```

Program 14.19: Writing data in char, short, int, and float into a binary file. (*Continued*)

```
    fwrite(&c2, sizeof(char), 1, stream);
    fwrite(&s, sizeof(short), 1, stream);
    fwrite(&i, sizeof(int), 1, stream);
    fwrite(&f, sizeof(float), 1, stream);
    fclose(stream);                  /* close the file stream */
    printf("Done! Finished writing data to file byteorder.bin\n");
    return 0;
}
```

Program 14.19: *(Continued)*

The option `-C` displays both hex and ASCII characters. The first entry is the offset in hexadecimal, followed by 16 space-separated, two-column, hexadecimal bytes, then followed by the same 16 bytes of ASCII characters enclosed in symbols `'|'`. In this case, the offset is 0. The file `byteorder.bin` has 12 bytes. The hexadecimal value for the first byte for the variable `c1` of type char is 0x61 with the corresponding ASCII character `'a'`. The second byte for the hexadecimal value for the second byte `c2` of type char is 0x7a with the corresponding ASCII character `'z'`. The subsequent two bytes are for the variable `s` of type short with the value 0x4358. The ASCII characters corresponding to the internal representations of 0x43 and 0x58 are `'C'` and `'X'`, respectively. The next four bytes are for the variable `i` of type int with the value 0x12345678. A nonprintable character, such as one corresponding to the ASCII value 0x12, is displayed as '.'. The ASCII characters corresponding to hexadecimal values 0x34, 0x56, and 0x78 are `'4'`, `'V'`, and `'x'`, respectively. The internal representation for floating-point numbers is presented in Chapter 16. The memory layout for the floating-point number 1.0F of type float with four bytes can be represented using hexadecimal number 0x3F800000, as shown in Table 16.1 in Chapter 16. Except for the first byte with 0x3F for the character '?', the ASCII representation of other three bytes are not printable.

On the other hand, if the output file `byteorder.bin` is created by Program 14.19 in a little endian machine such as Windows, Linux, Mac OS X with Intel x86, the output from the program **hexdump** in Linux or Mac OS X with Intel x86 is as follows:

```
> hexdump -C byteorder.bin
00000000  61 7a 58 43 78 56 34 12  00 00 80 3f    |azXCxV4....?|
```

The hexadecimal values and their corresponding ASCII characters for the first two bytes for the variables `c1` and `c2` of type char are the same. For the short integer `s` with the value 0x4358, due to the little endian format, the hexadecimal value 0x58 is displayed as the third byte before 0x43. Similarly, for the integer `i` and the floating-point number 1.0, the least significant bytes are displayed first and the most significant bytes are displayed last.

There is no hexadecimal viewer program in Windows by default. Ch contains a small utility program called **hexdump**, which is a Ch shell script written in C by Eric Raymond. The program, with about 300 lines of C code, is available at `CHHOME/bin/hexdump`. If the file `byteorder.bin` is created by Program 14.19 in a little endian machine, it can be examined by this utility program as follows:

```
> hexdump byteorder.bin
0000  61 7a 58 43 78 56 34 12  00 00 80 3f    azXCxV4. ...?
```

Unlike the program in Linux and Mac OS X, this utility program displays both hexadecimal values and ASCII characters by default. The first entry is the offset in hexadecimal, followed by 16 space-separated, two-column, hexadecimal bytes, and then followed by the same 16 bytes of ASCII characters separated in the middle by a space.

Now let's get back to the issue raised at the beginning of this section. The byte ordering for binary files will be an issue when a file system is shared by computers with different endianness. The binary output file `accel.bin`, generated by Program 14.15, can be read by Program 14.16 only when both programs run in computers with the same endianness. The design and implementation of binary file formats and software for processing these files, such as image file formats JPEG and PNG, also need to take the endianness into consideration.

Byte ordering is also an important issue when data are sent through the network for computers with different endianness. For network programming, the functions **htonl()**, **htons()**, **ntohl()**, and **ntohs()** are commonly used to convert 16-bit and 32-bit integers between the host and network byte order in conjunction with Internet addresses and ports as returned by **gethostent()** and **getservent()**. Details about network programming is beyond the scope of this book.

14.6 ‡Buffered and Unbuffered Input/Output

A stream can be *buffered* or *unbuffered*. When a stream is unbuffered, characters are intended to appear from the source or at the destination as soon as possible. Otherwise, characters may be accumulated and transmitted to or from the host environment as a block.

Furthermore, a buffered stream can be *fully buffered* or *line buffered*. When a stream is fully buffered, characters are intended to be transmitted to or from the host environment as a block when a buffer is filled. When a stream is line buffered, characters are intended to be transmitted to or from the host environment as a block when a newline character is encountered.

By default, output to a terminal is line buffered and all other input/output is fully buffered, but the stream **stderr** is unbuffered. The functions **setbuf()** and **setvbuf()** can be used to assign stream buffers. The prototypes of these two functions are shown below.

```
void setbuf(FILE *stream, char *buf);
int setvbuf(FILE *stream, char *buf, int type, size_t size);
```

The function **setbuf()** can be used after a stream has been opened but before it is read or written. It causes the buffer pointed to by `buf` to be used instead of an automatically allocated buffer. If `buf` is not NULL, input/output will be fully buffered. Otherwise, it will be completely unbuffered. The size of the buffer is specified by the macro **BUFSIZ**, which is defined in the **stdio.h** header file. For example,

```
char buf[BUFSIZ];
FILE *fp = fopen("testfile", "w");
if(fp)
  setbuf(fp, buf);  // set user-defined buffer
```

The function **setvbuf()** provides more flexibility to assign stream buffers. Like the function **setbuf()**, it may be used only after the stream pointed to by `stream` has been associated with an open file and before any other operation is performed on the stream. The argument `type` determines how `stream` will be buffered. The applicable macros for `type` defined in **stdio.h** are listed in Table 14.4. The size of the buffer pointed to

Table 14.4 Buffering type for function setvbuf().

Type	Description
_IOFBF	Causes input/output to be fully buffered
_IOLBF	Causes input/output to be line buffered
_IONBF	Causes input/output to be unbuffered

by `buf` is specified by `size` instead of **BUFSIZ**. The **setvbuf()** function returns zero on success, or nonzero if an invalid value is given for the argument `type` or if the request cannot be satisfied. The expression

```
setbuf(stream, buf);
```

is equivalent to the conditional expression

```
((buf == NULL) ?
 (void) setvbuf(stream, NULL, _IONBF, 0) :
 (void) setvbuf(stream, buf, _IOFBF, BUFSIZ))
```

C programs are commonly used for Web CGI (Common Gateway Interface) programming to process the user-entered data in fill-out forms. It is important that a proper content type is sent to Web browsers in correct sequences when multiple processes are involved. The standard output is typically set to unbuffered by the function call

```
setbuf(stdout, NULL);
```

so that the output from the current process will be sent immediately before the output from other processes is delivered.

The function **fflush()** with a prototype of

```
int fflush(FILE *stream);
```

can also be used to explicitly flush a buffer of a file *stream*. For example, when Program 5.1 in Chapter 5 is executed in an Integrated Development Environment (IDE) with a GUI, the output from the **printf()** function might appear after the input value for the **scanf()** function is displayed, even though the **printf()** function is called before the function **scanf()**. To display the output and input in the proper sequence in an output window, the standard output stream from the function **printf()** can be flushed out immediately by the function call

```
fflush(stdout);
```

which can be inserted right after a **printf()** statement. However, using

```
setbuf(stdout, NULL);
```

will have the same effect of flushing out the output for all functions, such as **printf()**, that send output to the standard output stream.

A file may be disassociated from a controlling stream by closing the file. Output streams are flushed before the stream is disassociated from the file. The value of a pointer to a file object becomes NULL after the associated file is closed.

14.7 ‡Error Handling and Program Debugging

14.7.1 Functions for Error Detection for Files

Two functions available to aid in detecting file reading errors are **feof()** and **ferror()**. The function **feof()** was introduced in Chapter 9. It tests an input file stream for an EOF indicator. It returns a nonzero value when the end of a file has been reached. The function prototype for the function **ferror()** is as follows:

```
int ferror(FILE *stream);
```

Similar to the **feof()** function, it tests the input stream specified by the argument `stream` for any possible errors. If the error indicator has been set (i.e., an error occurred), the **ferror()** function returns a nonzero value. Therefore, the functions **feof()** and **ferror()** could be used to distinguish whether an EOF occurred due to an end-of-file or error.

Once the EOF or error indicator has been set, they can be cleared only by the functions **rewind()** or **clearerr()**, or when the file is closed. Because the **rewind()** function has been discussed in the previous sections, only the function **clearerr()** will be described here. The function prototype for **clearerr()** is as follows:

```
void clearerr(FILE *stream);
```

Calling the function **clearerr()** clears the EOF and error indicators for the stream pointed to by the argument `stream`.

14.7.2 Functions for Handling Error Messages

The function **strerror()**, prototyped as

```
char *strerror(int errornum);
```

converts an error specified by the **int** variable `errornum` into a text string. This message is system-dependent, and the function **strerror()** returns a pointer to this string. For example, consider Program 14.20 and its output shown below:

```
fopen(): No such file or directory
```

```
/* File: strerror.c
   Handling error messages  */
#include <stdio.h>     /* for fopen() and perror() */
#include <string.h>    /* for strerror() */
#include <errno.h>     /* for errno */
#include <stdlib.h>    /* for exit() */

int main() {
    FILE *fp;                 /* declare a file pointer */
    char *errmessage;         /* pointer to error message */

    fp = fopen("UnknownFile", "r");  /* a failed statement */
    if(fp==NULL) {    /* cannot open the file by fopen() */
```

Program 14.20: Error handling with strings. (*Continued*)

```
        /* get the error message based on errno */
        errmessage = strerror(errno);
        printf("fopen(): %s\n", errmessage);
        /* Altenratively, use perror("fopen()"); */
        exit(EXIT_FAILURE);
    }
    exit(EXIT_SUCCESS);
}
```

Program 14.20: (*Continued*)

The function **fopen()** can be used to open a file. If a file to be opened exists, the function will return a non-NULL value. If it fails to open the specified file, the function returns NULL and the error number **errno** of a system variable will be set to a proper integral value defined in the header file **errno.h**. Program 14.20 attempts to open a file named "UnknownFile" reading by the function **fopen()**, but it fails because the file does not exist. As a result, the error number **errno** will be set. The function **strerror()** is used to obtain this error message corresponding to its argument **errno**. Additionally, the function **perror()** declared in the header file **stdio.h** may also be used for displaying the error message. Its function prototype is as follows:

```
void perror(const char *s);
```

The function **perror()** maps the error number of **errno** to the corresponding error message. If the argument s is not a null pointer and the character pointed to by s is not the terminating null character, the **perror()** function prints out the string pointed to by s followed by a colon and then the error message. Thus the statements

```
errmessage = strerror(errno);
printf("fopen(): %s\n", errmessage);
```

can be replaced by the following line:

```
perror("fopen()");
```

In Program 14.20, the program execution will be terminated once an error occurs when the program attempts to open a file that does not exist. If the file exists, however, a successful program termination would have occurred.

14.7.3 Using the Macro assert() for Debugging

The **assert()** macro is a useful tool for program debugging, particularly during software development. It is defined, using the predefined system macros **__FILE__** and **__LINE__**, in the header file **assert.h** with the function prototype as follows:

```
void assert(int expr);
```

The **assert()** macro takes in an integer or relational expression as its argument. Depending on whether the **NDEBUG** macro is defined, the **assert()** macro can be either active or inactive. If the **NDEBUG** macro is defined prior to the point when the header file **assert.h** is loaded with the preprocessing directive **#include**, then the **assert()** macro is disabled within the program. However, if **NDEBUG** is not defined, then the effects of the macro **assert()** depend on its integral argument. If the value of expr is 0, or false, the **assert()** macro displays an error message to the standard output stream and terminates the program by calling the **abort()**

function, which causes abnormal program termination. The error message displayed should include the text of the argument `expr`, the file name, and the line number.

To debug a program, one may need to flush out the output from the standard output stream by the function call

```
fflush(stdout);
```

after the inserted `printf()` function is called. Setting the standard output stream without buffering at the beginning of a program by the function call

```
setbuf(stdout, NULL);
```

will have a global effect for the entire program. As an example, consider Program 14.21. Because the definition for the macro **NDEBUG** is commented out, the assertion facilities are active. No buffer is used for the standard output stream. The first call to the macro **assert()** is okay because the variable `val` is equal to 1. However, the second call to **assert()** provides a problem because `val` is now set to 0.

The output of Program 14.21 is as follows:

```
assert(1)
assert(0)
Assertion failed: val, file assert.c, line 15
Abort
```

As stated earlier, the **assert()** macro is useful for debugging during software development. Once the software is ready for distribution, the macro **NDEBUG** can be defined to disable the assertion tests. Thus the lines where the macro **assert()** are called do not need to be deleted. Furthermore, the assertion lines can also serve as additional program documentation.

```
/* File assert.c
   Debug a program using NDEBUG and assert()   */
#include <stdio.h>
/* #define NDEBUG */
#include <assert.h>            /* for assert() */

int main() {
    int val = 1;

    setbuf(stdout, NULL);      /* set no buffer */
    printf("assert(1)\n");
    assert(val);               /* val is 1 */
    printf("assert(0)\n");
    val = 0;
    assert(val);               /* val is 0 */
    return 0;
}
```

Program 14.21: Using the macros **assert**() and **NDEBUG** for debugging.

14.8 ‡Obtaining Information about Files and Directories

There is a lot of information associated with a directory, which may contain many other files and subdirectories. Obtaining information about files and directories will be described in this section. It also further illustrates how structures are applied in the standard C library.

The function **access()** checks the accessibility of a file. The function **access()** is not a part of the C standard library. But it is a part of the POSIX (Portable Operating System Interface) standard, which is supported in most Unix systems. Based on the POSIX standard, the function is declared in the header file **unistd.h**. In Windows, which is not POSIX-compliant, it is defined in the header file **io.h**. The function is prototyped as

```
int access(const char *name, int mode);
```

The first argument is a file name. Based on the POSIX standard, the value of the second argument, which is of type int, is either the bitwise-inclusive-or of the access permissions to be checked (**R_OK**, **W_OK**, and **X_OK**) or the existence test (**F_OK**). These symbolic constants of bit-masks are presented in Table 14.5. In Windows, the users may define these macros on their own for the function **access()**. If the requested access is permitted, the function returns 0. Otherwise, it returns −1 and **errno** is set to indicate the error.

The prototype of the function **stat()** is also a part of the POSIX standard. The function is declared in the header file **sys/stat.h** as follows:

```
int stat(const char * name, struct stat *stbuf);
```

The first argument of the function **stat()** is a file name and the second argument will pass back all information about that file in an object of **stat** structure. If the file is searchable, upon successful completion, the function returns 0. Otherwise, it returns −1 and **errno** is set to indicate the error. The structure describing the value passed in the second argument of the function **stat()** is typically defined as follows:

```
struct stat {
    dev_t    st_dev;     /* block device inode is on */
    ino_t    st_ino;     /* inode number */
    mode_t   st_mode;    /* protection and file type */
    nlink_t  st_nlink;   /* hard link count */
    uid_t    st_uid;     /* user id */
    gid_t    st_gid;     /* group id */
    dev_t    st_rdev;    /* the device number for a special file */
    off_t    st_size;    /* number of bytes in a file */
    time_t   st_atime;   /* time of last access */
```

Table 14.5 Macros and typical bit-mask constants for the function access() in the POSIX standard.

Macros	Binary Constants	Hexadecimal Constants	Description
F_OK	0b0000	0x0000	Tests for existence of file
X_OK	0b0001	0x0001	Tests for execute or search permission
R_OK	0b0010	0x0002	Tests for read permission
W_OK	0b0100	0x0004	Tests for write permission

```
    time_t  st_mtime;   /* time of last modify */
    time_t  st_ctime;   /* time of last status change */
}
```

The meanings of these members of structure are explained by the comment following the member. All typedefed types, such as **dev_t** and **mode_t**, are defined in **sys/types.h**. The member `st_mode` is used to test whether a file is of the specified type.

Based on the POSIX standard, the macros below can be used to test the file type.

```
S_ISDIR(m)     // Test macro for a directory file.
S_ISCHR(m)     // Test macro for a character special file.
S_ISBLK(m)     // Test macro for a block special file.
S_ISREG(m)     // Test macro for a regular file.
S_ISFIFO(m)    // Test macro for a pipe or a FIFO special file.
```

The value `m` supplied to the macro is the value of the member `st_mode` from the variable `stbuf` of **stat** structure. The macro evaluates to a nonzero value if the test is true, and zero if the test is false.

In Windows and most Unix systems, the macros for bit masks below can be used to find the file type in the `st_mode` field of the **stat** structure.

```
Macros    Meaning
---------------------------------------------------
S_IFMT    File type mask
S_IFDIR   Directory
S_IFCHR   Character special (indicates a device if set)
S_IFREG   Regular
S_IREAD   Read permission, owner
S_IWRITE  Write permission, owner
S_IEXEC   Execute/search permission, owner
---------------------------------------------------
```

Program 14.22 uses the functions **access()** and **stat()** to obtain information for the file `fileinfo.c` portably across Unix and Windows platforms. The macro _WIN32 is predefined in the Visual C++ in Windows. When the program is compiled using Visual C++, the macros **F_OK**, **R_OK**, **W_OK**, and **X_OK** are defined and the header file **io.h** is included. In other platforms, the header file **unistd.h** is included. Whether the file `fileinfo.c` exists and has read permission or not are checked by the function calls

```
access(name, F_OK)
access(name, R_OK)
```

where `name` is a string containing the file name. The subsequent call

```
access(name, W_OK|X_OK)
```

to the function **access()** determines the write and execution permissions. The result of the bitwise-inclusive-or operation of the second argument, based on the value for bit-masks **W_OK** and **X_OK**, is 0b0110. Next, information about the file is obtained using the function **stat()** by the function call

```
stat(name, &stbuf)
```

```
/* File: fileinfo.c
   Obtain information about file fileinfo.c */
#include <stdio.h>
#ifdef _WIN32              /* if compiled using Visual Studio .NET */
#define F_OK    0          /* define F_OK for existence of File */
#define X_OK    1          /* define X_OK for eXecute permission */
#define W_OK    2          /* define W_OK for Write permission */
#define R_OK    4          /* define R_OK for Read permission */
#include <io.h>            /* for access() */
#else                      /* all other platforms */
#include <unistd.h>        /* for X_OK, F_OK, R_OK, W_OK and access() */
#endif
#include <sys/stat.h>      /* for struct stat, stat() */

int main() {
    const char *name = "fileinfo.c"; /* file name */
    struct stat stbuf;   /* declare a variable of a stat structure */

    if(!access(name, F_OK)) { /* check if file exists */
        printf("fileinfo.c exists\n");
    }
    if(!access(name, R_OK)) { /* check if file has read permission */
        printf("fileinfo.c is readable \n");
    }
    /* check if file has write and execute permissions */
    if(!access(name, W_OK|X_OK)) {
        printf("fileinfo.c is writable and executable\n");
    }
    if(!stat(name, &stbuf)) { /* check if file is searchable */
       /* print the size of the file */
       printf("fileinfo.c has %d bytes\n",  stbuf.st_size);
       /* print the last modification time */
       printf("fileinfo.c was modified at %d\n",  stbuf.st_mtime);
       printf("fileinfo.c was modified at %s",  ctime(&(stbuf.st_mtime)));
       /* chech if it is a directory or not */
       /* or if(S_ISDIR(stbuf.st_mode)) for POSIX implementation */
       if((stbuf.st_mode & S_IFMT) == S_IFDIR)
           printf("fileinfo.c is a directory\n");
       else
           printf("fileinfo.c is not a directory\n");
    }
    return 0;
}
```

Program 14.22: Obtaining file information.

The member `st_size` of the variable `stbuf` of **stat** structure gives the file size in the number of bytes. The member `st_mtime` gives the last modification time of the file. The function **ctime()**, defined in the header file **time.h** and presented in section 13.1.4 in Chapter 13, is used to convert the calendar time stored in the member `st_mtime` to the local time. The result of the bitwise-and operation of the member `st_mode` with the file type mask `S_IFMT` can be compared with other defined constants to determine the file type. The expression

```
(stbuf.st_mode & S_IFMT) == S_IFDIR
```

determines if the file is a directory or not. For a POSIX-standard-compliant implementation, the above operation can be replaced by

```
S_ISDIR(stbuf.st_mode)
```

The output for a sample run of Program 14.22 is given below:

```
fileinfo.c exists
fileinfo.c is readable
fileinfo.c is writable and executable
fileinfo.c has 1804 bytes
fileinfo.c was modified at 1206862592
fileinfo.c was modified at Sat Mar 29 23:36:32 2008
fileinfo.c is not a directory
```

In Programs 14.1 and 14.2, a file is copied to another one piece by piece. If the size of a file is known in advance, using the functions **fread()** and **fwrite()**, an entire file can be copied once as shown in Program 14.23. The structure member `st_size` gives the size of an input file. The memory for the buffer is allocated and deallocated dynamically using the functions **malloc()** and **free()**, respectively. However, the buffer for the contents of the file could also be declared as a deferred-shape array of type char at runtime, the feature available in C99. The input file is opened in binary mode. Its contents are read into the buffer first, then written to an output file, also in binary mode. Because both input and output files are opened in binary mode, they are not concerned with the file's line structure. This function will work for all files regardless of the data format stored in the files.

```
/* File: copyfile3.c
   Copy a file once in an entire file */
#include <stdio.h>    /* for fopen(), fclose(), fread(), fwrite(), feof() */
#include <sys/stat.h> /* for struct stat, stat() */

int copyfile3(const char *inputfile, const char *outputfile) {
    FILE *fp1, *fp2;    /* declare FILE pointers for input and output files */
    struct stat stbuf;  /* declare stbuf for file status structure */

    /* open input file for reading and output file for writing
       in binary mode */
    if((fp1 = fopen(inputfile, "rb")) == NULL)
```

Program 14.23: Copying an entire file. *(Continued)*

```
        return -1; /* if failed to open the file for reading */
    if((fp2 = fopen(outputfile, "wb")) == NULL) {
        fclose(fp1);
        return -1; /* if failed to open the file for writing */
    }

    if(!stat(inputfile, &stbuf)) { /* if the input file exists */
        /* allocate the memory to hold the contents of the file */
        char *contents = (char *)malloc(sizeof(stbuf.st_size));
        if(contents) {
           fread(contents, stbuf.st_size, 1, fp1);   /* read the entire file */
           fwrite(contents, stbuf.st_size, 1, fp2);  /* write the entire file */
           free(contents);  /* free the allocated memory */
        }
        else {
           printf("Error: not enough memory\n");
           return -1; /* if failed to allocate memory */
        }
    }
    else {
        printf("Error: call stat() failed\n");
    }
    fclose(fp1);             /* close the file stream for the input file */
    fclose(fp2);             /* close the file stream for the output file */
    return 0;
}
```

Program 14.23: *(Continued)*

14.9 ‡Removing and Renaming Files and Directories

It is often desirable to rename a file or remove it completely. Renaming a file makes it possible to have a new file name that better describes the content of the file. The option to delete a file allows for the removal of obsolete files and frees up memory. The functions **remove()** and **rename()** discussed in this section can be used to perform such tasks. Note, however, that these functions have to be used outside the **fopen()/fclose()** sequence. Also, some files may not be modified due to their permission status. For example, a file may be write-protected so it cannot be renamed or deleted.

The functions **remove()** and **rename()** can be used to delete or change the name of a directory. Similar to files, directories cannot be removed or renamed if the user does not have write permission. In addition, a directory has to be emptied before it can be deleted.

The remove() Function

The **remove()** function is prototyped as follows:

```
int remove(const char *name);
```

Calling this function deletes the file or directory specified by the argument `name`. Any subsequent attempt to access the file or directory would fail, provided that a new file or directory with the same name has not been created. If the file to be deleted is currently open when the function **remove()** is called, the behavior is implementation-defined. The return value is 0 upon success and nonzero for failure. As an example, Program 14.17 uses the function **remove()** to remove the temporary file `student.bin`.

The rename() Function

The function **rename()**, with the prototype

```
int rename(const char *oldfile, const char *newfile);
```

can be used to change the name of a file or directory. Calling this function changes the name of the file or directory specified by the string pointed to by `oldfile` to the one specified by `newfile`. Afterwards, the file or directory will no longer be accessible by the old name. If a file or directory with the same name as that specified by `newfile` already exists prior to the call to the function **rename()**, the behavior is implementation-defined. The return value is 0 for a successful operation and nonzero for failure.

14.10 ‡Temporary Files

For the user's convenience, there are a couple of functions defined in the header file **stdio.h** for handling temporary files. The function **tmpfile()** is prototyped as follows:

```
FILE *tmpfile(void);
```

It creates a temporary file for reading and writing (`"wb+"`). A pointer pointing to the temporary file is returned unless the **tmpfile()** function cannot create or open the temporary file. In this case, NULL is returned. The temporary file will be deleted automatically when it is closed by the **fclose()** function or the program terminates.

The function **tmpnam()**, with the function prototype

```
char *tmpnam(char *name);
```

generates a unique temporary filename that can be used as the name of a temporary file. If the input argument `name` is NULL, the function **tmpnam()** returns the address of an internal static area which holds the filename, which is overwritten by subsequent calls to the function **tmpnam()**. If `name` is not NULL, the filename is passed back in the argument `name`. Note that a file opened with the filename generated by the function **tmpnam()** needs to be removed by a function call to **remove()**. Otherwise, they will still exist after the program termination. As an example, the following interactive code will create and delete a set of temporary files.

```
> FILE *fptr
> fptr = tmpfile()
> fclose(fptr)                // close and delete temporary file
> char *filename
> filename = tmpnam(NULL)
/tmp/fileECDGnP
> fptr = fopen(filename, "w")  // open temp file "/tmp/fileECDGnP"
> fclose(fptr)                // close temporary file
> remove(filename)            // delete file "/tmp/fileECDGnP"
```

Exercises

1. Write a program that inputs a line of text with the function **fgets()** into the **char** array `s[100]`. Output the line in both uppercase and lowercase letters. Input the string `"abcd1234ABCD"` to test your program.
2. Write a program using a **for** loop to put the following numbers to a file named `record.dat`.
   `1 2 3 4 5 6 7 8 9 10`
3. Write a program to read the file `record.dat` created in the above problem and print it out as standard output.
4. Write a program to save the following sequence of numbers in a file named `number.dat`. Then read the data in this file and display the numbers on the screen.

   `1 3 5 7 9 11`

5. Solve Exercise 19 in Chapter 3 without using the input/output redirection.
6. Solve Exercise 32 in Chapter 5 without using the input/output redirection.
7. Solve Exercise 33 in Chapter 5 without using the input/output redirection.
8. Solve Exercise 34 in Chapter 5 without using the input/output redirection.
9. Solve Exercise 25 in Chapter 10 without using the input/output redirection.
10. Solve Exercise 26 in Chapter 10 without using the input/output redirection.
11. Solve Exercise 6 in Chapter 13 without using the input/output redirection.
12. Write a program that searches the input file for every occurrence of a word. The input file name and search word shall be specified on the command line as follows:

```
> search.c filename word
```

   Print out the filename, word, and number of occurrence. Try the word `numpoints` in the file `CHHOME/demos/lib/libch/plot/ref/plotxy.ch`, where `CHHOME` is the home directory for Ch, such as `C:/Ch` for Windows and `/usr/local/ch` for Unix.
13. Write a program that makes a list of all words found in an input file. Sort the list based on the value of the first characters of all words. Write the sorted list to an output file, along with the number of times each word appears in the input file.
14. Write a program that reads an input file and tabulates the number of times that each of the 128 ASCII characters appears.
15. Write a program that analyzes the input data file. The input file contains only integer values and white space. The program should print the number of lines in the file and the number of integer values (not integer digits). The program and the input file name shall be specified on the command line as follows:

```
> analyze.c filename
```

16. Write a program that counts the number of characters, words, and lines in a file, similar to the command **wc**. Try the file `CHHOME/demos/lib/libch/plot/ref/plotxy.ch`, where `CHHOME` is the home directory for Ch, such as `C:/Ch` for Windows and `/usr/local/ch` for Unix.
17. Write a program `info.c` to obtain the file or directory from the command line. If the input is a file, print out its permission mode and file size. If the file is a directory, print out only its permission mode. Otherwise, give an error message.
18. Write a program to check the permission status (read, write, and execute) for files and directories in the Ch home directory. For files, print out the file sizes.

19. If a student's information is saved in the file `rwstudent1.data` with the following format:

```
101, John, 12, 11, 1985, 3.33
```

modify Program 14.6 to read the student information in this file.

a. Use the function **fscanf**() to read the data file.

b. Use the function **fgets**() to read the data file first. Then process the input string using the function **sscanf**().

20. If a student's information is saved in the file `rwstudent1.data` with the following format:

```
101:John:12:11:1985:3.33
```

modify Program 14.6 to read the student information in this file.

a. Use the function **fscanf**() to read the data file.

b. Use the function **fgets**() to read the data file first. Then process the input string using the function **sscanf**().

21. Student records in a class are stored in a student data file with the following data formats.

```
1 John Smith 101 3.4
2 Mary Jones 102 3.2
3 Bill Bush 103 2.4
4 Peter Clinton 104 2.8
(more data)
```

The first field in a row is the student number of the class, the second is the student name, the third is the student ID, and the last one is the GPA. Write a program called `prog.c` to read a student data file specified at the command line and calculate and display the average GPA of the class. For example, the command

```
> prog.c data.txt
```

will handle the student data file `data.txt`.

a. Use the function **fscanf**() to read the data file.

b. Use the function **fgets**() to read the data file.

22. The grades A, A-, B+, B, B-, C+, C, C-, D+, D, D-, F are assigned with the points 4, 3.7, 3.3, 3, 2.7, 2.3, 2, 1.7, 1.3, 1, 0.7, 0, respectively. The data files `grade1.data` and `grade2.data` with the contents

```
3.0 4.0 3.3 3.7 4.0 3.7 3.3 3.7 4.0 3.3
```

and

```
2.0 3.0 2.7 3.3 3.0 2.3 2.7 2.7 3.3 3.7
```

respectively, contain grades of ten subjects for two different students. Write a computer program with the GPA data file as an input in the command line, to do the following:

a. Calculate the GPA for the student.

b. Students with a GPA of 3.5 or greater are on the Dean's honor list. The student will take four courses next quarter. What's the GPA the student needs to earn for the next quarter to be eligible for the Dean's honor list.

c. Before the end of the year, the student will take six more courses. What's the highest possible GPA that the student can earn by the end of the year? If the student can reach the GPA of 3.7 by the end of the year, what's the minimum GPA for the remaining six courses?

23. Write a program that will process a file and extract Web addresses starting with a token `www.` and ending with `.edu`. The program displays Web addresses inside the file with the file name entered as a command option. The default file name for processing is `getwwwfile.html`. Test the program using the HTML file in Program 14.8.

24. The comment for a data file for the GPA library starts with the symbol `'#'` as the first character in a line. Modify the function `gpa_readData()` in Program 14.10 so that white spaces can precede the comment symbol.

25. Modify Program 14.12 with the function `readFile()`. When the user fails to read a data file, give the user three chances to enter a new name for the data file. Draw the flowchart for the function `readFile()`.

26. Modify Program 14.12 with a command-line option to read a data file from the command line in the following ways:

- **a.** Without a default data file.
- **b.** With the default data file `student.data`.

27. Write the program `rmcomment.c` to remove all comments in a program with a command-line user interface. The first command argument is the original program and the second argument is the new program without comment.

- **a.** Use the function **fgetc()** to get the contents from the original file.
- **b.** Use the function **fgets()** to get the contents from the original file.
- **c.** Use the function **stat()** to find the size of the file, obtain the file into a buffer, and finally process the file in the buffer.

For example, the command

```
> remcomment.c hello.c newhello.c
```

will remove all comments inside the program `hello.c` below and save the new program without comment in the file `newprog.c`.

```
/* File: hello.c */
#include <stdio.h>

int main() {        /* this is comment */
    printf("Hello, world\n");  /* Comment across
                                  multiple lines */
    return 0;
}
```

28. Modify Exercise 28 in Chapter 13 to process the database of a library of books in a file `book.dat`.

29. Write the program `encode2.c` to encode a data file based on the encoding method described in Exercise 21 in Chapter 12. Both the original data file and encoded file shall be specified on the command line as follows:

```
> encode2.c originalFileName encodedFileName
```

30. Write the program `decode2.c` to decode a data file that was encoded by the program `encode2.c` described in Exercise 29. Both encoded file and decoded original data file shall be specified on the command line as follows:

```
> decode2.c encodedFileName decodedFileName
```

CHAPTER 15

‡Dynamic Data Structures and Cross-Platform Software Development

In section 14.3 in Chapter 14, the information for students is stored in a file. Based on the number of students, an array of structure for student is dynamically allocated. Each element stores the information for a student. The Grade Point Average (GPA) library is then used to process the information for students in the array. An array is a static data structure. Once a contiguous block of memory for an array is allocated, the array size is fixed during the execution of the program. Therefore, Program 14.12 cannot be easily modified to allow the user to process information for new students not in the original data file. One could allocate the array to be sufficiently bigger than the number of students in the original data file. But this would waste the memory. *Dynamic data structures* can grow and shrink with the memory allocated and freed at runtime. In this chapter, commonly used dynamic data structures, which are the foundations for building large-scale flexible software programs, are presented. To illustrate their practical applications, the previous GPA library is modified to use dynamic data structures to handle a variable number of students. Although C contains standard libraries, the C standard does not specify how to build libraries. Building libraries is platform-dependent. It is a difficult topic, ignored by most textbooks. However, building libraries is important for serious software projects. In this chapter, details on building static and dynamic libraries for modular programming and using make files for across-platform software development are described using examples.

15.1 Self-Referencing Structures

Although a structure cannot contain instances of itself, it can contain pointers to instances of itself. For example, the following structure, `Teacher`, contain a member `next` of pointer to structure `Teacher`.

```
struct Teacher {
    int id;
    char name[32];
    struct Teacher *next;
};
```

This structure is called a *self-referencing structure*, which contains a member of pointer to an instance of itself. This self-referencing structure can be used to implement dynamic data structures.

Programs 15.1 and 15.2 are examples of using self-referencing structures to store and display sets of data. The output from Programs 15.1 and 15.2 are the same, as shown in Figure 15.1. Both Programs 15.1 and 15.2

```
/* File: selfref.c
   Use a self-referencing structure */
#include <stdio.h>
#include <stdlib.h>  /* for malloc() and free() */

struct Teacher {
    int id;
    char name[32];
    struct Teacher *next;  /* link to the next node */
};

struct Teacher *addTeacher(int id, char *name) {
    struct Teacher *tp;
    tp = (struct Teacher *)malloc(sizeof(struct Teacher));
    tp->id = id;            /* set member id */
    strcpy(tp->name, name); /* set member name */
    tp->next = NULL;        /* set member next, point to NULL */
    return tp;
}

int main() {
    struct Teacher *head;

    head = addTeacher(101, "John");       /* first node */
    head->next = addTeacher(102, "Doe"); /* link two nodes */

    printf("id = %d\n", head->id);       /* print 1st node */
    printf("name = %s\n", head->name);
    printf("id = %d\n", head->next->id); /* print 2nd node */
    printf("name = %s\n", head->next->name);
    free(head->next);                    /* free 2nd node */
    free(head);                          /* free 1st node */
    return 0;
}
```

Program 15.1: Using a self-referencing structure for multiple nodes.

```
/* File: selfrefloop.c
   Use while-loops to process nodes of
   self-referencing structure in a linked list */
#include <stdio.h>
#include <stdlib.h>  /* for malloc() and free() */
```

Program 15.2: Processing multiple nodes using loops. (*Continued*)

```
struct Teacher {
    int id;
    char name[32];
    struct Teacher *next;  /* link to the next node */
};

struct Teacher *addTeacher(int id, char *name) {
    struct Teacher *tp;
    tp = (struct Teacher *)malloc(sizeof(struct Teacher));
    tp->id = id;              /* set member id */
    strcpy(tp->name, name); /* set member name */
    tp->next = NULL;          /* set member next, point to NULL */
    return tp;
}

int main() {
    struct Teacher *head, *node;

    head = addTeacher(101, "John");
    head->next = addTeacher(102, "Doe");

    node = head;  /* point to the head */
    while(node != NULL) {  /* process all nodes */
      printf("id = %d\n", node->id);
      printf("name = %s\n", node->name);
      node = node->next;
    }

    while(head != NULL) {   /* remove memory for each node */
      node = head;          /* node points to the head */
      head = node->next;    /* head points to the next node */
      free(node);           /* free the previous head through node */
    }
    return 0;
}
```

Program 15.2: *(Continued)*

```
id = 101
name = John
id = 102
name = Doe
```

Figure 15.1: The output from Programs 15.1 and 15.2.

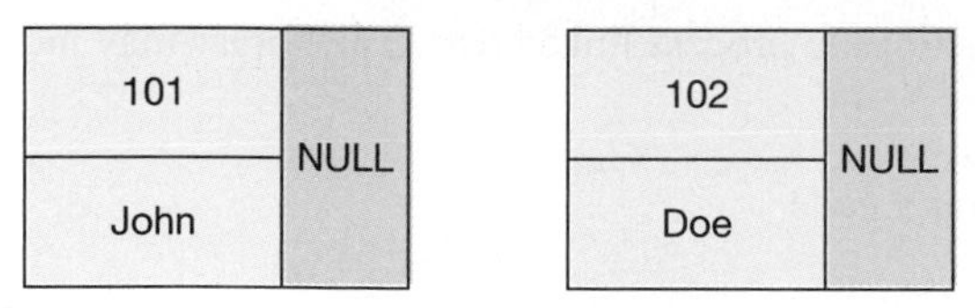

Figure 15.2: Two nodes created by addTeacher().

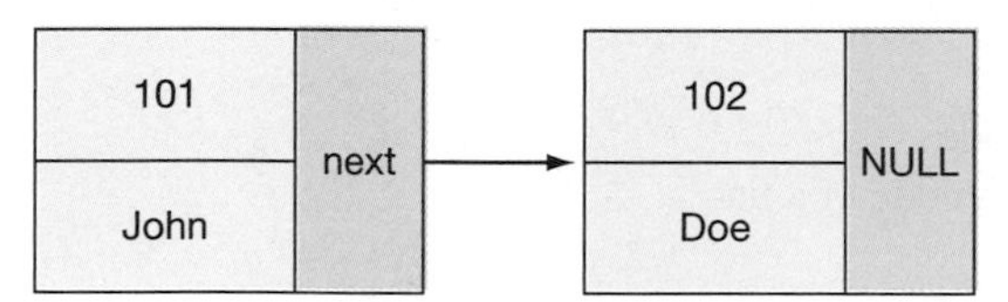

Figure 15.3: Two linked nodes.

call the function addTeacher() twice to create the two nodes shown in Figure 15.2. The arguments id and name of the function addTeacher() are the values for two members of the structure Teacher. The memory for a node is dynamically allocated by the statement

```
tp = (struct Teacher *)malloc(sizeof(struct Teacher));
```

The other member next of pointer to structure is set to NULL in this function. This null pointer can be used as a sentinel value for a node at the end of a list. The assignment statement

```
head->next = addTeacher(102, "Doe");
```

links these two nodes, as shown in Figure 15.3.

If there are multiple nodes in a linked list, it is more convenient to use loops to handle each node in the loop, as shown in Program 15.2. A temporary variable node is used to obtain a node of the linked list through a **while** loop. The sentinel value NULL for the member next of the last node is used to stop the iteration of the loop. At each iteration, the variable node points to the next node in the list. The contents, such as the id and name of the node, can be accessed through its members. A **while** loop is also used to free the memory allocated in the function addTeacher(). In the first **while** loop, we only need one variable node to travel through the entire list to print out the values of id and name in each node. In the second **while** loop, we need to use two variables, head and node, to travel through the entire list to free the memory allocated for each node. The variable node first holds the previous head. The variable head then points to the next node in the list. Finally, the previous head is freed through node, as shown in the code fragment below.

```
node= head;           /* node points to the head */
head = node->next;    /* head points to the next node */
free(node);           /* free the previous head through node */
```

At the end of the iteration of the loop, head is NULL.

15.2 Singly Linked Lists

Program 15.2 illustrates the basic concept of a linked list. A *linked list* consists of *nodes*. Adjacent nodes are linked to each other. In this section, general working principles and operations of linked lists are presented.

We can write a library of functions to process linked lists. The library may include the following functions:

1. Create a node
2. Free memory allocated for a node
3. Prepend a node
4. Append a node
5. Insert a node
6. Find a node
7. Remove a node
8. Print information in a node
9. Print information in each node of a list
10. Clear a list

These list-processing functions are implemented in the source code `list.h` and `listlib.c`. The header file `list.h` in Program 15.3 defines a self-referencing structure `ListNode` for each node and prototypes of functions for linked lists. The data structure `ListNode` for a node of a linked list is shown below.

```
struct ListNode {
    int id;                  /* id number */
    char *name;              /* name */
    struct ListNode *next; /* link to the next node */
};
typedef struct ListNode *Node; /* define type Node */
```

```
/* File: list.h
   header file for singly linked list */
#ifndef LIST_H_
#define LIST_H_

/* a self-referencing structure for a list node */
struct ListNode {
    int id;                  /* id number */
    char *name;              /* name */
    struct ListNode *next; /* link to the next node */
};
typedef struct ListNode *Node; /* define type Node */

/* function prototypes for list processing */
/* create a node */
extern Node createNode(int id, const char *name);
/* free an elment */
extern void freeNode(Node nd);
/* prepend to the list at the beginning */
```

Program 15.3: The header file for the example of a singly linked list. (*Continued*)

```
extern void prepend(Node *head, Node nd);
/* append to the list at end */
extern void append(Node *head, Node nd);
/* insert to the list at pos */
extern int insert(Node *head, Node nd, int pos);
/* find the node with id and name */
extern Node find(Node head, int id, const char *name);
/* remove a node from the list */
extern void remov(Node *head, Node nd);
/* print id and name in a node */
extern void print(Node nd);
/* print id and name in each node of the list */
extern void printList(Node head);
/* clear all nodes attached to the list */
extern void clearList(Node head);

/* import definitions of list processing functions for Ch */
#ifdef _CH_
#pragma importf <listlib.c>
#endif

#endif /* LIST_H_ */
```

Program 15.3: *(Continued)*

where the member `next` is called a *link*. It contains an address of another node of type structure `ListNode`. So `ListNode` is a self-referencing structure. With this structure, we can have an unspecified number of such structures linked together. The members `id` and `name` are data for a node. In this example, the members `id` and `name` can be used to hold the ID number and name of a student, respectively. The data structure can also be expanded with the birthday, address, GPA, and so forth. Depending on an application, data of a node can be different. The defined data type `Node`, which is a pointer to `struct ListNode`, can be used more conveniently to process a linked list. The source file `listlib.c` contains function definitions defined in the header file `list.h` for manipulating a linked list.

Program 15.4 demonstrates how list-manipulating functions are used to handle a linked list. This example first creates four nodes (`nd1`, `nd2`, `nd3`, and `nd4`), and then puts them in a linked list by various methods

```
/* Fil: list.c
   Create and manipulate a singly linked list */
#include <stdio.h>
#include "list.h"   /* header file for singly linked list */
```

Program 15.4: An application program using a singly linked list. *(Continued)*

```
int main() {
    Node head, nd;   /* head and a node of the list */
    /* create four nodes of a list */
    Node nd1 = createNode(101, "John"),
         nd2 = createNode(102, "Doe"),
         nd3 = createNode(103, "Peter"),
         nd4 = createNode(104, "Mary");

    head = NULL;             /* initialize head of the list */
    prepend(&head, nd1);     /* prepend node nd1 to head of the list */
    printf("List with one node:\n");
    printList(head);         /* print the list 1st time */
    prepend(&head, nd2);     /* prepend node nd2 to the head of the list */
    printf("List with node for Doe prepended in head:\n");
    printList(head);         /* print the list 2nd time */
    append(&head, nd3);      /* append node nd3 to the list */
    printf("List with node for Peter appended:\n");
    printList(head);         /* print the list 3rd time */
    insert(&head, nd4, 2);/* insert node nd4 at 2nd place of the list */
    printf("List with node for Mary at the 2nd place:\n");
    printList(head);        /* print the list 4th time */

    nd = find(head, 102, "Doe"); /* find node with id 102 and name Doe */
    remov(&head, nd);        /* remove this node from the list */
    printf("List without node for Doe:\n");
    printList(head);        /* print the list 5th time */
    nd = find(head, 101, "John");/* find node with id 101 and name John */
    remov(&head, nd);        /* remove this node from the list */
    printf("List without node for John:\n");
    printList(head);         /* print the list 6th time */
    clearList(head);         /* clear the list */
    return 0;
}
```

Program 15.4: *(Continued)*

with the functions `prepend()`, `append()`, and `insert()`. Whenever the list is modified, the function `printList()` is called to display the data in each node of the list. Next, two nodes in the list are found using the function `find()` and removed by the function `remov()`. Finally, the function `clearList()` is used to clear the entire linked list.

Execution of the program `list.c` in Program 15.4 produces the output shown in Figure 15.4. In the remainder of this section, each function for list processing is presented in conjunction with the description for Program 15.4. Using a singly linked list in a GPA library to handle a variable number of students is presented in section 15.5.

```
List with one node:
id  = 101, name = John
List with node for Doe prepended in head:
id  = 102, name = Doe
id  = 101, name = John
List with node for Peter appended:
id  = 102, name = Doe
id  = 101, name = John
id  = 103, name = Peter
List with node for Mary at the 2nd place:
id  = 102, name = Doe
id  = 104, name = Mary
id  = 101, name = John
id  = 103, name = Peter
List without node for Doe:
id  = 104, name = Mary
id  = 101, name = John
id  = 103, name = Peter
List without node for John:
id  = 104, name = Mary
id  = 103, name = Peter
```

Figure 15.4: The output of Program 15.4.

15.2.1 Creating and Freeing a Node

The source file `listlib.c` contains the list-processing functions. It includes the following header files at the beginning:

```
#include <stdio.h>
#include <string.h> /* for strdup() and strcmp() */
#include <stdlib.h> /* for malloc() and free() */
#include "list.h"   /* header file for singly linked lists */
```

The `createNode()` function in the source code `listlib.c` is listed in Program 15.5. It is used to create a node of a list. The function `createNode()` is similar to `addTeacher()` in Program 15.2. The arguments `id` and `name` are the values for members of the structure `ListNode`. The memory for a node is dynamically allocated by the statement

```
nd = (Node) malloc(sizeof(struct ListNode));
```

The function `createNode()` returns NULL if **malloc()** failed to allocate the memory. Otherwise, a node with the type of pointer to structure is returned. The memory for the member `name` of a node is dynamically allocated by the function **strdup()**.

The `freeNode()` function, also defined in Program 15.5, is used to free the memory for a node created by the function `createNode()`. It frees the memory allocated for the member `name` by the function **strdup()** and for the node itself.

```
/************************************************
 *  File: listlib.c
 *  Definitions of functions for singly linked lists
 ************************************************/
#include <stdio.h>
#include <string.h> /* for strdup() and strcmp() */
#include <stdlib.h> /* for malloc() and free() */
#include "list.h"   /* header file for singly linked lists */

/* create a node of a list */
Node createNode(int id, const char *name) {
    Node nd;

    nd = (Node) malloc(sizeof(struct ListNode));
    if(nd == NULL) {
        fprintf(stderr, "Error: not enough memory.\n");
        return NULL;
    }
    nd->id = id;              /* set member id */
    nd->name = strdup(name);/* set member name */
    nd->next = NULL;          /* set member next, point to NULL */
    return nd;
}

/* free a node of a list */
void freeNode(Node nd) {
    if(nd) {
        if(nd->name) {        /* if name is not NULL */
            free(nd->name);
        }
        free(nd);
    }
}
```

Program 15.5: The function `createNode()` for creating a node, and the function `freeNode()` for freeing memory for a node allocated in the function `createNode()`.

The following declaration statement with initialization in Program 15.4

```
Node nd1 = createNode(101, "John"),
     nd2 = createNode(102, "Doe"),
     nd3 = createNode(103, "Peter"),
     nd4 = createNode(104, "Mary");
```

creates four nodes (`nd1, nd2, nd3,` and `nd4`), as shown in Figure 15.5. When these nodes are created, they are not linked. Other functions are required for linking two adjacent nodes to form a linked list.

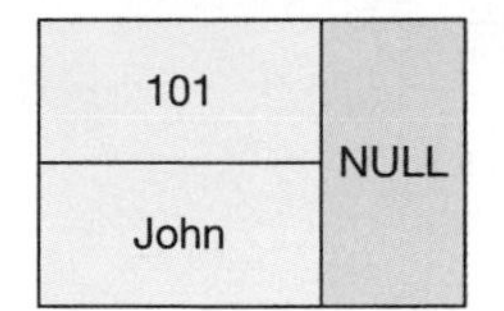

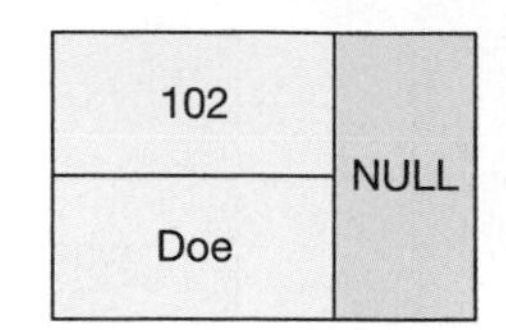

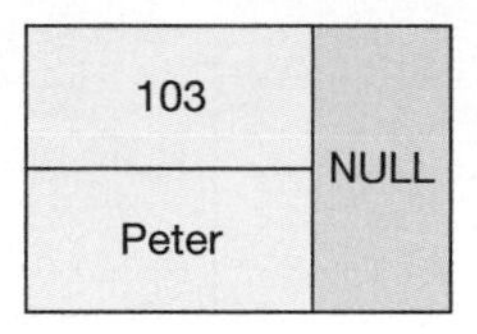

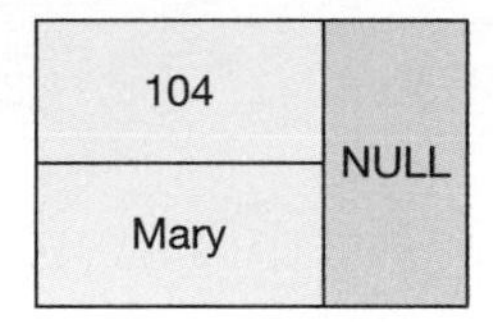

Figure 15.5: Creating four nodes: `nd1`, `nd2`, `nd3`, and `nd4`.

15.2.2 Prepending a Node to a List

The function `prepend()` is used to add a node to the beginning of a linked list. Its definition is shown in Program 15.6, where `head` is a pointer that points to the beginning of the list. The result of the pointer indirection operation `*head` gives the first node of a linked list. The argument `nd` is the node to be prepended. The member `next` of the node `nd` points to the first node of the linked list by the statement

```
nd->next = *head;
```

This step links the node `nd` to the one that was previously first on the list. The next statement

```
*head = nd;
```

makes the pointer `head` point to the new *head* of the linked list.

The statements

```
head = NULL;
prepend(&head, nd1);
```

in Program 15.4 would result in a linked list shown in Figure 15.6. The head of the list is first initialized to NULL. The node `nd1` is then prepended by the function `prepend()`. The above two statements could be replaced by the following single statement

```
head = nd1;
```

The statement

```
prepend(&head, nd2);
```

prepends `nd2` as the first node of the list, as shown in Figure 15.7.

```
/* prepend to the list at the beginning */
void prepend(Node *head, Node nd) {
    nd->next = *head;/* head becomes the next node of the new node */
    *head = nd;      /* the new node becomes the new head */
}
```

Program 15.6: The function `prepend()` to prepend a node at the beginning of the list.

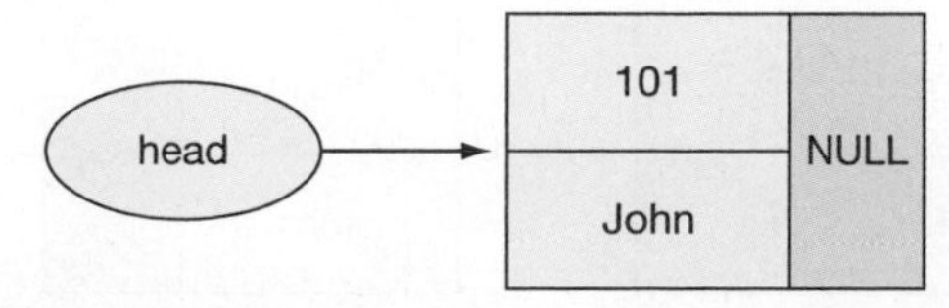

Figure 15.6: Using `prepend(&head, nd1)` to begin a singly linked list.

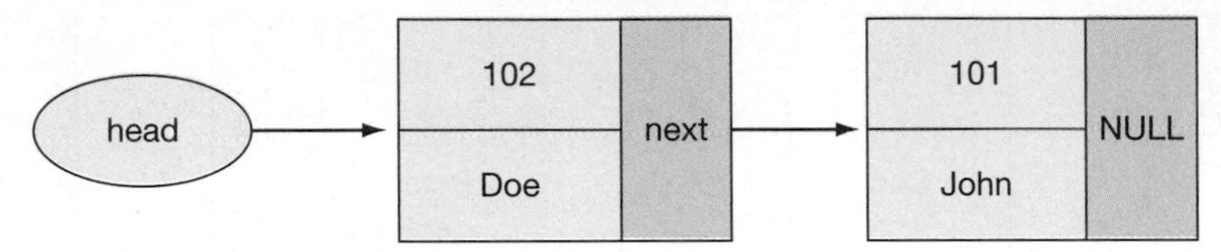

Figure 15.7: Prepending node `nd2` to the linked list by `prepend(&head, nd2)`.

15.2.3 Appending a Node to a List

Similar to the function `prepend()`, the function `append()` can also be used to add a node to a linked list. The difference is that `append()` adds the node to the end of the list rather than the beginning. Its definition is shown in Program 15.7, where `head` points to the beginning of the linked list and `nd` is the new node. The function `append()` first checks to see whether there is already a node in the linked list. If the list is empty, the passed node becomes the first one on the list. If a linked list already exists, the function performs a search to determine the end of the list, or *tail*. Once the tail is found, the new node is then added to the end of the list. In Program 15.4, the node `nd3` is appended to the linked list by the statement

```
append(&head, nd3);
```

as shown in Figure 15.8 for the updated list.

```
/* append to the list at end */
void append(Node *head, Node nd) {
    Node tmp = *head; /* tmp is the head of the list */

    if(*head == NULL) /* no node in linked list */
      *head = nd;
    else {
      /* get the tail of the linked list */
      while(tmp->next)
        tmp = tmp->next;
      /* add the new one to the end of the list */
      tmp->next = nd;
    }
}
```

Program 15.7: The function `append()` to append a node to the list.

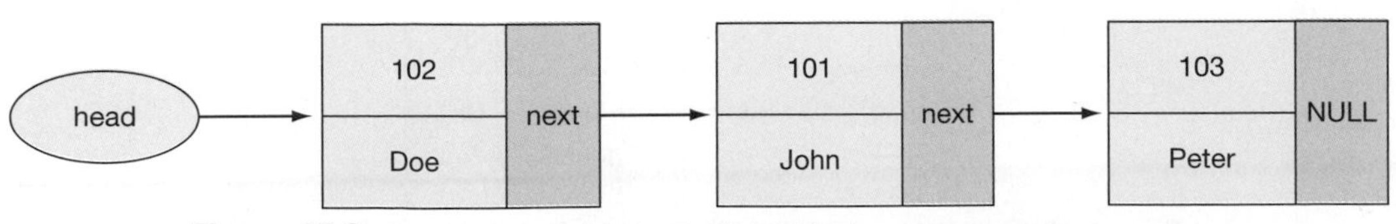

Figure 15.8: Appending a node to the linked list by `append(&head, nd3)`.

15.2.4 Inserting a Node into a List

Perhaps one of the most complicated functions to perform on a linked list is to insert a node anywhere in the list. Inserting a node involves searching for the place where the new node will be added and manipulating the `next` pointers so that the link is not broken. The definition for the function `insert()` is shown in Program 15.8. Its arguments are similar to the arguments for the functions `prepend()` and `append()`, except for the addition of the argument `pos`. This argument specifies the position in the list where the new node should be inserted.

From Program 15.8, one could see that the easiest insertion point is handled first. If *pos* is 1, the new node is inserted at the head of the linked list. The process is the same as that for the function `prepend()`, although the function `insert()` uses a temporary variable `tmp` to hold the original head. If the insertion point is elsewhere, the function `insert()` performs a search to determine where the new node should be inserted using the following **while** loop:

```
while(tmp) {
  if(++i >= pos-1) /* match or invalid position */
    break;
```

```
/* insert to the list at pos */
int insert(Node *head, Node nd, int pos) {
    int i = 0;
    Node tmp = *head; /* tmp is the head of the list */

    /* insert to the first position */
    if(pos == 1) {
      *head = nd;
      (*head)->next = tmp;
      return 0;
    }

    /* get position */
    while(tmp) {
      if(++i >= pos-1) /* match or invalid position */
        break;
      tmp = tmp->next;
    }
    if(i != pos-1) { /* can not get that position */
      fprintf(stderr, "Error: Wrong position for insert(). \n");
      return -1;
    }
    /* update links */
    nd->next = tmp->next;
    tmp->next = nd;
    return 0;
}
```

Program 15.8: The function `insert()`, to insert a node into the list.

```
    tmp = tmp->next;
  }
```

The iteration of the **while** loop stops if i equals `pos-1`. At this point, the variable `tmp` becomes the node where the new node follows. The iteration also stops if `pos` is invalid, such as −2. If `pos` is too large, the iteration will finish until `tmp` is NULL. If the insertion position does not exist for the linked list, an error message is sent to the standard error stream and function returns −1. Otherwise, the function returns 0. One could also choose to implement the insertion operation in such a way that, at this point, the function ignores the insertion operation and returns silently. The calling function can use the returned value from the function **insert**() to check if the function call is successful. If an insertion point is found, the link (the `next` pointer), needs to be directed to the appropriate node. The link that originally pointed to this node must be detached and attached to the new node by the following statements at the end of the function.

```
nd->next = tmp->next;
tmp->next = nd;
```

The new node `nd` is the next node of node `tmp`. Refer to Figure 15.9 for `nd->next = tmp->next` and Figure 15.10 for `tmp->next = nd` for illustrations of the insertion process. Note that these two figures represent the process for inserting the node `nd4` between the nodes `nd1` and `nd2` in Program 15.4 by the function call

```
insert(&head, nd4, 2);
```

In this case, inside the function `insert()` in Program 15.8, the node `nd` is for Mary and the node `tmp` is for Doe.

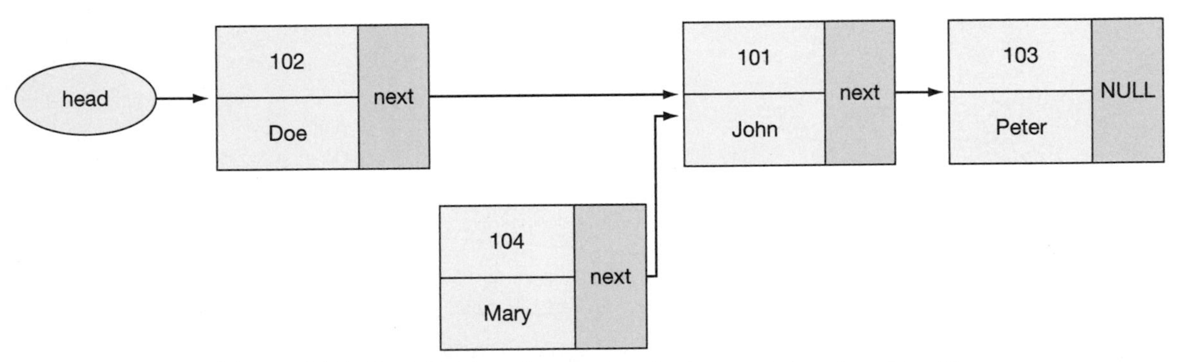

Figure 15.9: The initial insertion process for `insert(&head, nd4, 2)`.

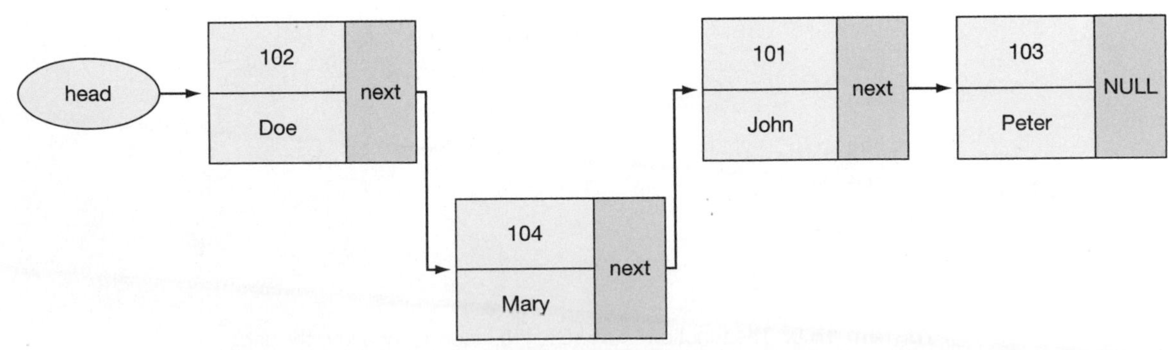

Figure 15.10: The final insertion process for `insert(&head, nd4, 2)`.

15.2.5 Finding and Removing a Node from a List

Not only can we insert a node into a linked list, but we also can remove a node from it. The function `find()` in Program 15.9 finds a node based on its `id` and `name` and returns the node. If there is no match, the function returns NULL. Unlike the functions `prepend()`, `append()`, and `insert()`, the head of the linked list is not changed in the function `find()`. Therefore, the type of argument `head` is `Node`, instead of pointer to `Node`.

The function `remov()` removes a node from the list. Because the function **remove()** is a standard C function for removing a file from the system, as described in section 14.9 in Chapter 14, the function name `remov` is used for removing a node from the list. From Program 15.10, one can see that `remov()` requires two arguments, `head` for the linked list and `nd` for the node to be removed.

```
/* find a node with id and name */
Node find(Node head, int id, const char *name) {
     while(head!=NULL &&
        !(head->id == id && !strcmp(head->name, name))) {
        head = head->next;
     }
     return head;
}
```

Program 15.9: The function `find()`, to find a node in the list.

```
void remov(Node *head, Node nd) {
     Node tmp = *head; /* tmp is the head of the list */

     if (*head == NULL)          /* empty list */
       return;
     else if (*head == nd) {   /* nd is the head */
       *head = (*head)->next;
       freeNode(nd);          /* free the memory for the node */
     }
     else {
       while (tmp->next) {
         if (tmp->next == nd) {  /* found the node */
           tmp->next = tmp->next->next; /* detach the node */
           freeNode(nd);         /* free the memory for the node */
           return;
         }
         tmp = tmp->next;
       }
     }
}
```

Program 15.10: The function `remov()`, to remove a node from the list.

According to Program 15.10, if `head` points to NULL, the list is empty and the function just returns. However, if the list is not empty, the function first checks if the node to be removed is the head of the list. If the head is the node to be removed, the head is updated. The second node in the list becomes the new head. Otherwise, the function searches for the node in the list using a **while** loop. Once the desired node `tmp->next` is found, the `next` pointer of the previous node `tmp` must be reassigned to point to the node after the one to be removed by the statement

```
tmp->next = tmp->next->next;
```

The memory allocated in the function `createNode()` for the removed node from the list is freed by the function call

```
freeNode(nd);
```

Figures 15.11 to 15.14 illustrate the removal of the nodes `nd2` and `nd1`, respectively, according to the following code fragment in Program 15.4:

```
nd = find(head, 102, "Doe");
remov{&head, nd);
nd = find(head, 101, "John");
remov(&head, nd);
```

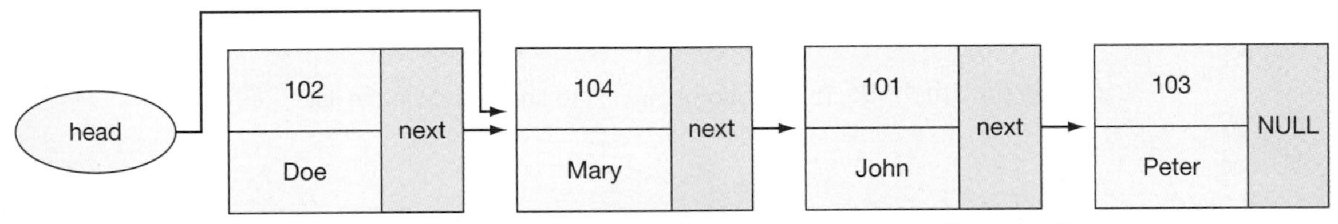

Figure 15.11: The initial process for removing a node with $id = 102$.

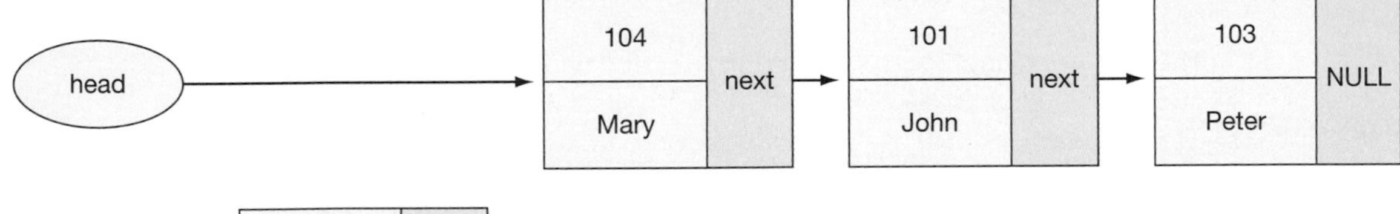

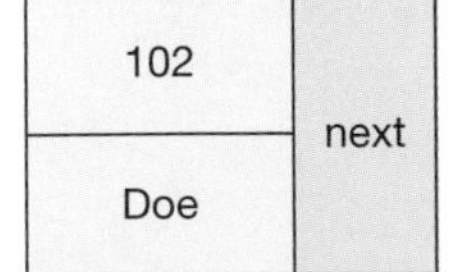

Figure 15.12: The final process for removing a node $id = 102$.

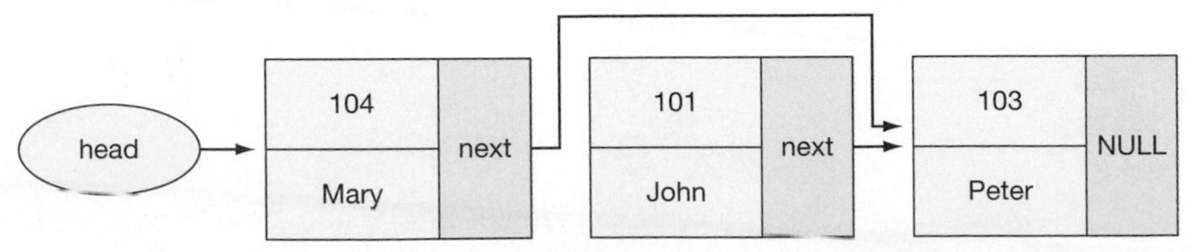

Figure 15.13: The initial process for removing a node with $id = 101$.

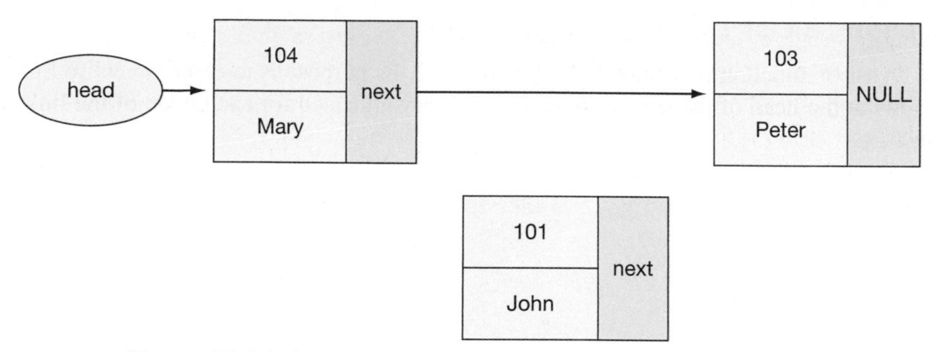

Figure 15.14: The final process for removing a node with $id = 101$.

Based on the list-processing functions in the library, we can also write the function `remov2()` to remove a node from a list based on the ID and name directly, as shown below.

```
void remov2(Node *head, int id, const char *name) {
    Node nd;
    nd = find(*head, id, name);
    remov(head, nd);
}
```

The function `remov2()` calls `find()` to find the node to be removed in the list first, then uses the function `remov()` to remove it from the list.

15.2.6 Printing Information of a Node and List

The `print()` function in Program 15.11 prints the `id` and `name` of a node. Using a **while** loop, the function `printList()` displays the information for each node in the entire list.

```
/* print id and name in a node */
void print(Node nd) {
    if(nd) {
      printf("id   = %d, name = %s\n", nd->id, nd->name);
    }
}

/* print id and name in each node of the list */
void printList(Node head) {
    while(head) {
      print(head);
      head = head->next;
    }
}
```

Program 15.11: The function `print()` to print the ID and name of a node, and the function `printList()` to print each node in the list.

15.2.7 Clearing a List

The `clearList()` function is defined in Program 15.12. Its purpose is to clear the entire linked list. The function begins at the head of the list and frees the memory allocated for each node of the linked list using the function `freeNode()`.

```
/* delete all nodes and their associated memory of the list */
void clearList(Node head) {
    Node nd;

    while(head) {
        nd = head;
        head = head->next;
        freeNode(nd);
    }
}
```

Program 15.12: The function `clearList()`, to clear the list.

15.3 Doubly Linked Lists

As described in the previous section, a node in a singly linked list is linked to the next one. One can access nodes in a list from the beginning to the end. In some applications, it is desirable to access nodes in a list backward, starting from the end or the middle towards the beginning of the list. This would require a *doubly linked list*, in which nodes can be accessed from the beginning to the end and vice versa. Thus, a doubly linked list would have two members that point to the next and previous nodes. As an application example, each statement in a C program is parsed and saved as a node in a doubly linked list in the C/C++ interpreter Ch. The size of the list can grow dynamically. Therefore, the interpreter can handle a program without a limit on the number of lines of the code, other than the limit on the memory imposed by a machine. To process a loop in a C program, such as a **for** loop or **while** loop, the information for previous statements can be accessed through the doubly linked list.

In this section, a library for doubly linked lists is presented. The header file `dlist.h` contains the structure `ListNode` below for each node of a doubly linked list.

```
struct ListNode {
    int id;                 /* id number */
    char *name;             /* name */
    struct ListNode *next;  /* link to the next node */
    struct ListNode *prev;  /* link to the previous node */
};
typedef struct ListNode *Node; /* define type Node */
```

In this self-referencing structure, the two variables `next` and `prev` are pointers to structure `ListNode`. One points to the next node and the other points to the previous node. The function prototypes for doubly linked lists in the header file `dlist.h` are the same as ones for singly linked lists in the header file `list.h` shown in Program 15.3. Function definitions for processing doubly linked lists are located in the source file `dlistlib.c`.

Program 15.13 shows how a doubly linked list is used. Similar to Program 15.4, Program 15.13 first creates four nodes (nd1, nd2, nd3, and nd4) using the function createNode(). These four nodes are then linked as a doubly linked list using the functions prepend(), append(), and insert(). A node with the ID 104 and name Mary in the middle of the doubly linked list is then found by the function find(). After the node is found, Program 15.13 traverses forward through the list from the middle node until the end, using the link next in each node, and prints the information for each node using the function print(). Afterward, Program 15.13 traverses backward through the list from the middle node until the beginning, using the link prev in each node, and also prints the information for each node. This shows that a doubly linked list can be easily traversed back and forth. Next, the node with the ID 101 for John is removed using the function remov(). Finally, the list is cleared and the allocated memory freed. The output of Program 15.13 is shown in Figure 15.15.

```
/* File: dlist.c
   Create and manipulate a doubly linked list */
#include <stdio.h>
#include "dlist.h"    /* header file for doubly linked list */

int main() {
    Node head, nd, node;   /* head and nodes of the list */
    /* create four nodes of a list */
    Node nd1 = createNode(101, "John"),
         nd2 = createNode(102, "Doe"),
         nd3 = createNode(103, "Peter"),
         nd4 = createNode(104, "Mary");

    head = NULL;             /* initialize head of the list */
    prepend(&head, nd1);   /* prepend node nd1 to head of the list */
    prepend(&head, nd2);   /* prepend node nd2 to the head of the list */
    append(&head, nd3);    /* append node nd3 to the list */
    insert(&head, nd4, 2);/* insert node nd4 at 2nd place of the list */
    printf("A doubly linked list:\n");
    printList(head);      /* print the list */

    /* find node with id 104 and name Mary */
    node = find(head, 104, "Mary");
    nd = node;           /* save node */
    printf("Travel list forward starting with node for Mary:\n");
    while(nd != NULL) {
      print(nd);
      nd = nd->next;
    }
    nd = node;           /* set nd to node */
    printf("Travel list backbard starting with node for Mary:\n");
```

Program 15.13: A program with a doubly linked list using a structure. (*Continued*)

```
    while(nd != NULL) {
      print(nd);
      nd = nd->prev;
    }

    nd = find(head, 101, "John");/* find node with id 101 and name John */
    remov(&head, nd);      /* remove this node from the list */
    printf("List without node for John:\n");
    printList(head);       /* print the list */
    clearList(head);       /* clear the list */
    return 0;
}
```

Program 15.13: (*Continued*)

```
A doubly linked list:
id  = 102, name = Doe
id  = 104, name = Mary
id  = 101, name = John
id  = 103, name = Peter
Travel list forward starting with node for Mary:
id  = 104, name = Mary
id  = 101, name = John
id  = 103, name = Peter
Travel list backbard starting with node for Mary:
id  = 104, name = Mary
id  = 102, name = Doe
List without node for John:
id  = 102, name = Doe
id  = 104, name = Mary
id  = 103, name = Peter
```

Figure 15.15: The output of Program 15.13.

Function definitions for `freeNode()`, `find()`, `print()`, `printList()`, and `clearList()` are the same as the ones for singly linked lists presented in the previous section. In the remainder of this section, only the functions `createNode()`, `prepend()`, `append()`, `insert()`, and `remov()` for processing doubly linked lists are presented in conjunction with Program 15.13.

With the addition of a pointer to the previous node in `struct ListNode` for doubly linked lists, some functions for manipulating a linked list must be redefined accordingly. When adding or deleting a node, not only does the `next` pointer have to point to the correct memory address, but the `prev` pointer has to do the same as well. Otherwise, the doubly linked list would be broken.

The function `createNode()` in Program 15.14 is the same as that in Program 15.5, except that the link to the previous node a doubly linked list is set to NULL by the statement

```
nd->prev = NULL;
```

```
/***************************************************
 *  File: dlistlib.c
 *  Definitions of functions for doubly linked lists
 ***************************************************/
#include <stdio.h>
#include <string.h> /* for strdup() and strcmp() */
#include <stdlib.h> /* for malloc() and free() */
#include "dlist.h"  /* header file for doubly linked lists */

/* create a node of a list */
Node createNode(int id, const char *name) {
    Node nd;

    nd = (Node) malloc(sizeof(ListNode));
    if(nd == NULL) {
        fprintf(stderr, "Error: not enough memory.\n");
        return NULL;
    }
    nd->id = id;                /* set member id */
    nd->name = strdup(name);/* set member name */
    nd->next = NULL;            /* set member next, point to NULL */
    nd->prev = NULL;            /* set member prev, point to NULL */
    return nd;
}
```

Program 15.14: The function `createNode()`, to create a node for a doubly linked list.

The function `prepend()` in Program 15.15 prepends a node to a doubly linked list. The original head becomes the `next` node of the new node by the statement

```
nd->next = *head;
```

Because there is no other node before the prepended node, its `prev` pointer will be NULL as it is set in the function `createNode()` in Program 15.14. Also, note that the new node becomes the previous node of the original head via the statement

```
(*head)->prev = nd;
```

```
/* prepend to the list at the beginning */
void prepend(Node *head, Node nd) {
    nd->next = *head;/* head becomes the next node of the new node */
    if(*head) {      /* the new node becomes head's previous node */
      (*head)->prev = nd;
    }
    *head = nd;      /* the new node becomes the new head */
}
```

Program 15.15: The function `prepend()` to prepend a node at the beginning of a doubly linked list.

if the list is not empty, i.e., (*head) is not NULL. Finally, the new node becomes the new head by the statement

```
(*head) = nd;
```

The statements

```
head = NULL;
prepend(&head, nd1);
```

in Program 15.13 create a doubly linked list with one node, as shown in Figure 15.16. The statement

```
prepend(&head, nd2);
```

prepends nd2 as the first node of the list, as shown in Figure 15.17.

The function append() shown in Program 15.16 is similar to that in Program 15.7. The only difference is that the link to the previous node of the appended node points to the last node in the original list by the statement

```
nd->prev = tmp; /* update the link to the previous node */
```

In Program 15.13, the node nd3 is appended to the list by the statement

```
append(&head, nd3);
```

The statement

```
tmp->next = nd; /* new nd becomes the last one */
```

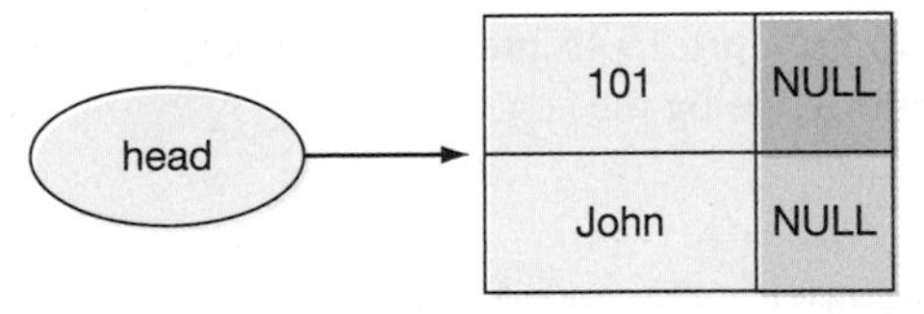

Figure 15.16: Using prepend(&head, nd1) to start a doubly linked list.

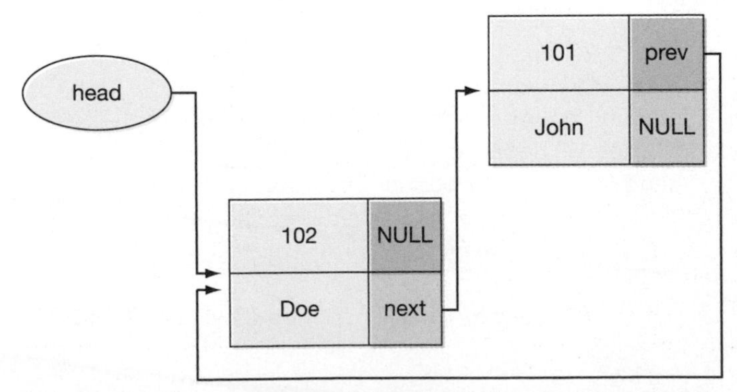

Figure 15.17: Prepending the node nd2 to the list by prepend(&head, nd2).

```
/* append to the list at end */
void append(Node *head, Node nd) {
    Node tmp = *head; /* tmp is the head of the list */

    if(*head == NULL) /* no node in linked list */
        *head = nd;
    else {
       /* get the tail of the linked list */
       while(tmp->next)
          tmp = tmp->next;
       /* add the new one to the end of the list */
       tmp->next = nd; /* new nd becomes the last one */
       nd->prev = tmp; /* update the link to the previous node */
    }
}
```

Program 15.16: The function `append()`, to append a node for a doubly linked list.

in Program 15.16 would result in the list shown in Figure 15.18. The statement

```
nd->prev = tmp; /* update the link to the previous node */
```

in Program 15.16 completes the appending process with the updated list shown in Figure 15.19.

The addition of the `prev` pointer into `struct ListNode` in a doubly linked list also increases the complexity of the function `insert()` in Program 15.17. Similar to `insert()` for a singly linked list in Program 15.8, a temporary pointer `tmp` is pointed to the head of the list initially. If the node is inserted at the beginning of the list, the new node `nd` becomes the head by the assignment expression `*head = nd`. Its `next` node is the original head, which is pointed to by `tmp`. Finally, the `prev` pointer of `tmp` points to the newly inserted node to preserve the doubly linked list.

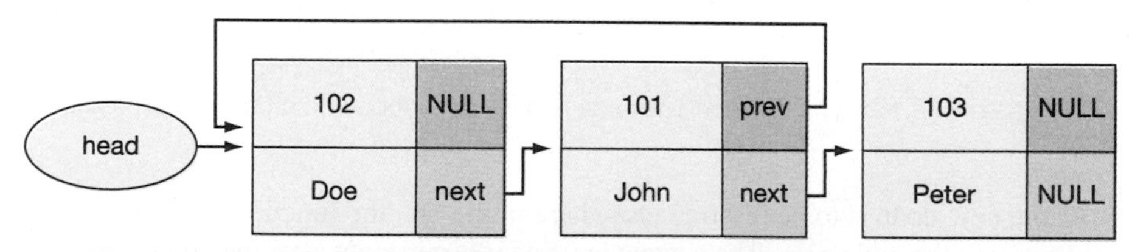

Figure 15.18: The initial process of the function call `append(&head, nd3)`.

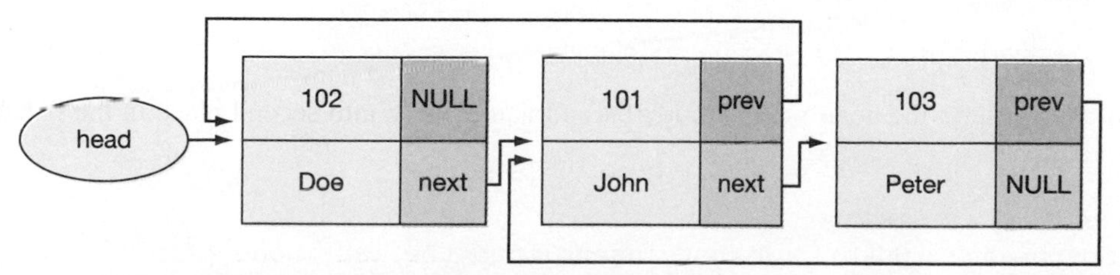

Figure 15.19: The final process of the function call `append(&head, nd3)`.

```
/* insert to the list at pos */
int insert(Node *head, Node nd, int pos) {
    int i = 0;
    Node tmp = *head; /* tmp is the head of the list */

    /* insert to the first position */
    if(pos == 1) {
       *head = nd;
       nd->next = tmp;
       tmp->prev = nd;
       return 0;
    }

    /* get position */
    while(tmp) {
      if(++i >= pos-1) /* match or invalid position */
        break;
      tmp = tmp->next;
    }
    if(i != pos-1) { /* can not get that position */
      fprintf(stderr, "Error: Wrong position for insert(). \n");
      return -1;
    }
    /* update links */
    nd->next = tmp->next;
    if(tmp->next != NULL)    /* not insert into the last node */
      tmp->next->prev = nd;
    tmp->next = nd;
    nd->prev = tmp;
    return 0;
}
```

Program 15.17: The function `insert()` to insert a node into a doubly linked list.

However, if the new node is to be inserted elsewhere in the list, the function `insert()` would find the insertion point first with the node `tmp`. The new node `nd` is inserted right after the node `tmp`. As an example, the function call

```
insert(&head, nd4, 2);
```

in Program 15.4 inserts the node `nd4` with id 104 and name Mary into second place in the list. When the following statements

```
nd->next = tmp->next;
if(tmp->next != NULL)    /* not insert into the last node */
  tmp->next->prev = nd;
```

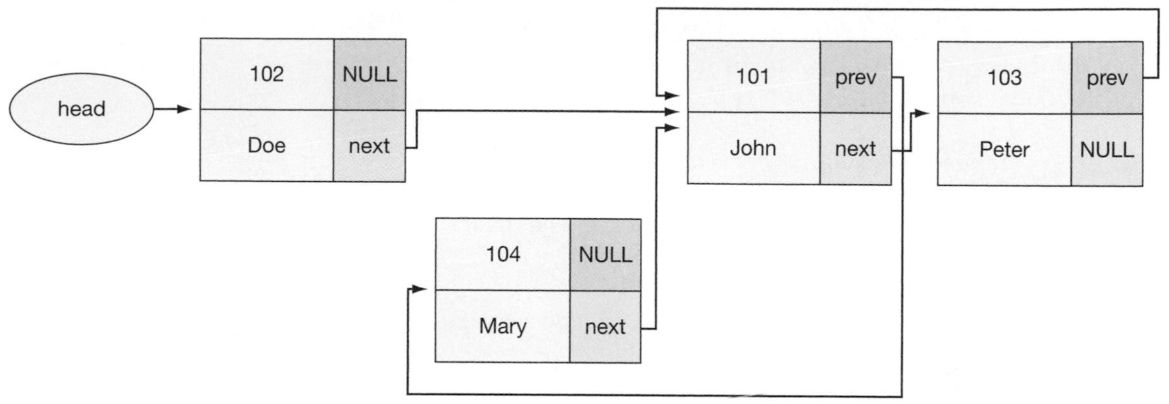

Figure 15.20: The initial process of the function call `insert(&head, nd4, 2)`.

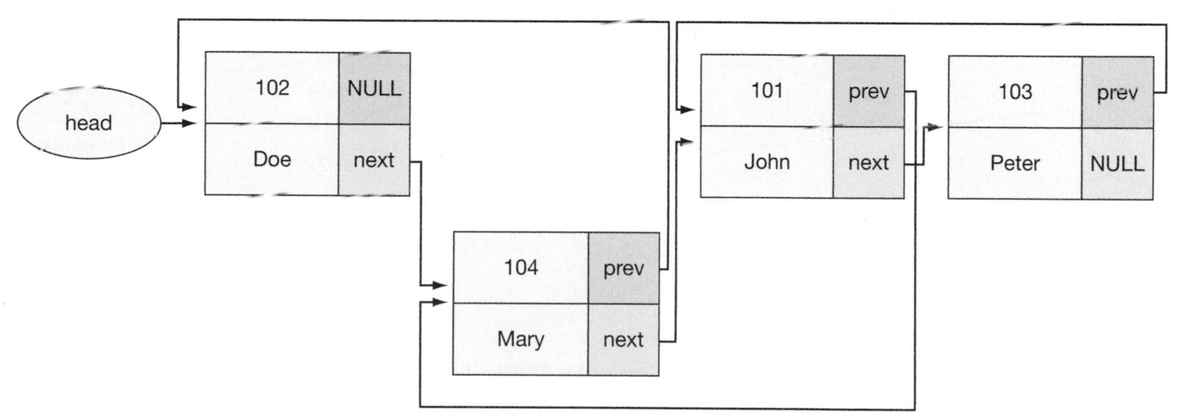

Figure 15.21: The final process of the function call `insert(&head, nd4, 2)`.

in Program 15.17 are executed, `nd` is the node `nd4` for Mary and `tmp` is the node `nd2` for Doe, as shown in Figure 15.20. The next node of the node `tmp` becomes the next node of the inserted node `nd`. If the node `tmp` is not the last node in the list, the previous node of the next node of the node `tmp` points to the inserted node. When the above insertion process is completed, the list is shown in Figure 15.20. The next two statements

```
tmp->next = nd;
nd->prev = tmp;
```

in Program 15.17 further update the links of the doubly linked list. The inserted node `nd` becomes the next node of the node `tmp`. The node `tmp` becomes the pervious node of the inserted node `nd`, as shown in Figure 15.21.

The function `remov()` in Program 15.18 removes a node from a doubly linked list. This function definition is similar to the corresponding one for a singly linked list in Program 15.10. Inside the function `remov()`, a temporary variable `tmp1` is initialized to be the head of the list. If the list is empty, the function just returns. If the first node is to be deleted, the second node becomes the head. In this case, the new head's `prev` pointer is set to NULL. However, if the node to be removed is elsewhere, the function `remov()` searches through the list to find the node and then remove it from the list. As an example, Program 15.4

```
/* remove a node from the list */
void remov(Node *head, Node nd) {
  Node tmp = *head; /* tmp is the head of the list */

  if (*head == NULL)          /* empty list */
    return;
  else if (*head == nd) {   /* nd is the head */
    *head = (*head)->next;
    (*head)->prev = NULL;
    freeNode(nd);             /* free the memory for the node */
  }
  else {
    while (tmp->next) {
      if (tmp->next == nd) {   /* found the node */
        tmp->next = tmp->next->next; /* detach the node */
        if(tmp->next != NULL) /* not remove the last node */
          tmp->next->prev = tmp;      /* detach the node */
        freeNode(nd);         /* free the memory for the node */
        return;
      }
      tmp = tmp->next;
    }
  }
}
```

Program 15.18: The function `remov()` to remove a node from a doubly linked list.

removes the node `nd1` with id 101 and name John from a doubly linked list by the following statements:

```
nd = find(head, 101, "John");
remov(&head, nd);
```

When the statement

```
tmp->next = tmp->next->next;
```

in the function `remov()` is called, both nodes `nd` and `tmp->next` point to the node `nd1` for John. Node `tmp` points to the node for Mary. The `next` pointer of the previous node is reassigned to point to the node after the one to be deleted. The above statement makes the node for Mary point to the node for Peter, as shown in Figure 15.22. When the statement

```
if(tmp->next != NULL) /* not remove the last node */
  tmp->next->prev = tmp;
```

in the function `remov()` is executed, the node `tmp->next` has been updated and points to the node `nd3` for Peter. The `prev` pointer of the next node, that is, the node following the removed node, points to the node preceding the removed node, if the node to be removed is not the last node in the list. In our example, the link `prev` of the node for Peter points to the node for Mary, as shown in Figure 15.23. When a node is detached from the list, the memory allocated in the function `createNode()` is freed by the function call `freeNode(nd)`.

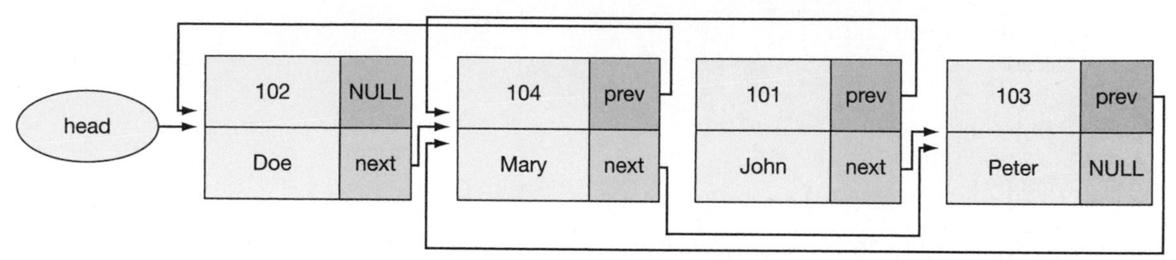

Figure 15.22: The initial process of the function call `remov(&head, nd)`.

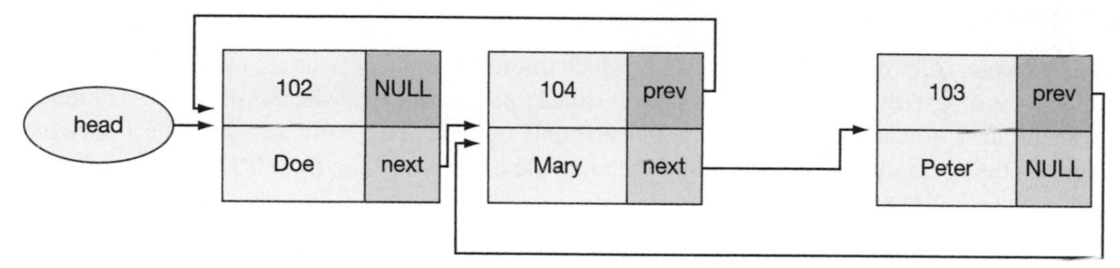

Figure 15.23: The final process of the function call `remov(&head, nd)`.

15.4 Other Dynamic Data Structures

In addition to singly and doubly linked lists, other dynamic data structures are used for various applications. In this section, other commonly used dynamic data structures of circularly linked lists, stacks, queues, and binary trees are briefly introduced.

15.4.1 Circularly Linked Lists

A *circularly linked list* is a special case of a singly or doubly linked list when the last node in the list is linked to the first node, as shown in Figure 15.24. Creating, inserting, and removing a node for a circularly linked list are the same as for singly and doubly linked lists. The `head` of a circular linked list can be treated as the first node. If the list is empty, `head` points to NULL. If there is only one node in the list, `head` points to itself. The `head` is used to determine when the list has been traversed back to the beginning. It can also be used to as the sentinel node to clear the list.

As an example, a three-node circularly linked list can be used for path planning and trajectory generation for motion control of the industrial robot manipulator shown in Figure 4.8 in Chapter 4. Assume that the end-effector of a robot manipulator moves from positions A, B, . . . to F as shown in Figure 15.25. A node of the list contains the necessary information, such as distance, velocity, and acceleration for motion control for a segment. When the end-effector is moving from A to B, three nodes in the list contain information for three segments AB, BC, and CD. When the end-effector finishes the motion for the segment AB, the node, which holds the information for the segment AB, can be used to hold the information for the segment DE. Therefore, when the robot finishes the motion for the segment CD, it will execute the trajectory for the motion of the segment DE.

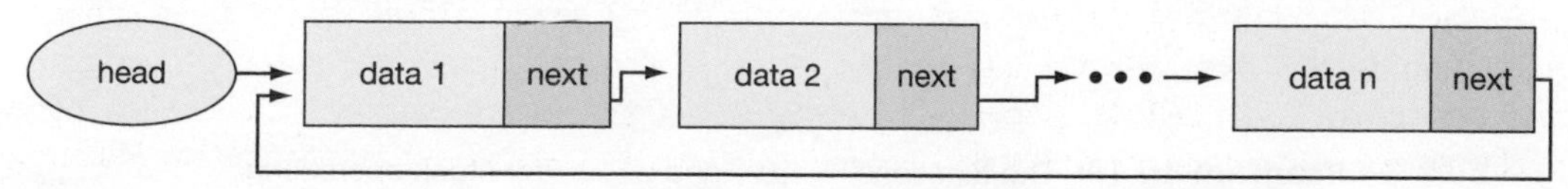

Figure 15.24: A circularly linked list.

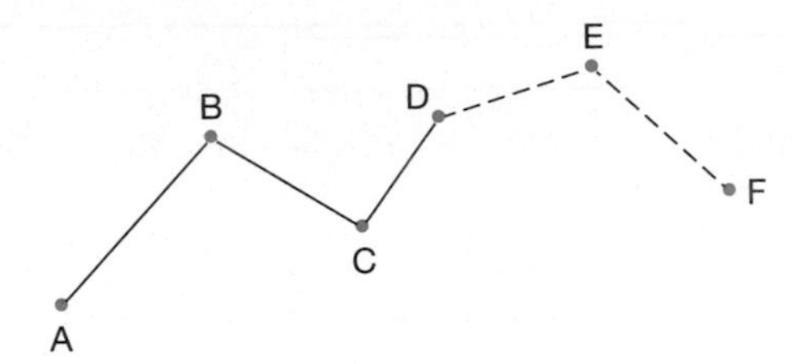

Figure 15.25: The trajectory of the end-effector for a robot manipulator.

15.4.2 Stacks

A *stack* is a special case of a singly linked list, in which insertions and deletions are made at one end called its *top*. The process of inserting a node into the stack is called a *push* operation, whereas the process of removing a node from the stack is called a *pop* operation. Because only one end of the list is affected, like a stack of plates in a cafeteria, the operation of a stack follows the principle of *Last-In-First-Out (LIFO)* or *First-In-Last-Out (FILO)*.

Most operations for singly linked lists are applicable to a stack. However, a stack is a simplified version of a singly linked list. Program 15.19 gives the data structure for a stack and functions for push and pop

```
/* a self-referencing structure for a stack node */
struct StackNode {
    /* data for each node */
    ...
    struct StackNode *next;      /* link to the next node */
};
typedef struct StackNode *Node; /* define type Node */

/* insert a node to the top of the stack */
void push(Node *head, Node nd) {
    nd->next = *head;/* head becomes the next node of the new node */
    *head = nd;      /* the new node becomes the new head */
}

/* delete a node from the top of the stack */
void pop(Node *head) {
    Node tmp = *head;          /* tmp is the head of the list */

    if (*head == NULL)         /* empty node */
      return;
    else {
      *head = (*head)->next;
      freeNode(tmp);           /* free the memory for the head node */
    }
}
```

Program 15.19: The functions `push()` and `pop()` for stack operations.

operations. The function `push()` is the same as the function `prepend()` in Program 15.6. The function `pop()` is a simplified version of the function `remov()` in Program 15.10. It removes the node from the top of the list. A node can be created and freed similarly by functions `createNode()` and `freeNode()` in Program 15.5, respectively.

Stacks are almost ubiquitous in system software. They are used extensively at every level of a modern computer system. For example, a stack is used to process a C expression, such as `2+3*i`. When a parser encounters an operand, the operand is pushed to a stack. When an operator is encountered, based on the precedence of the operator, the pushed operand is popped up. The expression is calculated and the result is pushed into the stack as an operand for the next operation.

15.4.3 Queues

A *queue* is a special case of a singly linked list, in which all additions to the list are made at one end and all deletions from the list are made at the other end. Two main operations for a queue is to add a node to the tail of the queue and remove a node from the head of the queue. Therefore, like a queue in a grocery store, the queue follows the working principle of *First-In-First-Out* (*FIFO*). In this FIFO data structure, the first element added to the queue will be the first one to be removed. The operation of adding a node to a queue is called `enqueue`, whereas the operation of removing a node from a queue is called `dequeue`. Because we need to keep track of both head and tail of a queue, two variables, `head` and `tail`, are needed for enqueue and dequeue operations, as shown in Figure 15.26. The software implementation for the data structure of a queue and these two operations are given in Program 15.20. The **if** statements are used to handle special cases when the queue is empty or there is only one node in a queue.

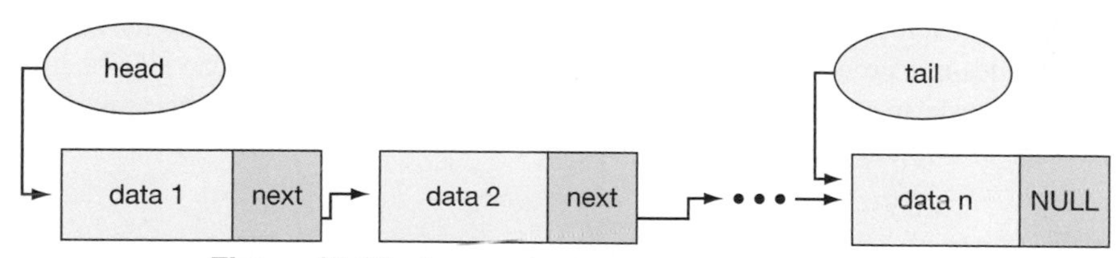

Figure 15.26: A queue implemented using a linked list.

```
/* a self-referencing structure for a queue node */
struct QueueNode {
    /* data for each node */
    ...
    struct QueueNode *next;     /* link to the next node */
};
typedef struct QueueNode *Node; /* define type Node */

/* insert a node at queue tail */
void enqueue(Node *head, Node *tail, Node nd) {
    if(*head == NULL) {    /* no node in queue */
      *head = nd;          /* nd becomes head */
    }
```

Program 15.20: The functions `enqueue()` and `dequeue()` for queue operations. (*Continued*)

```
    else {
      (*tail)->next = nd; /* append nd to tail */
    }
    *tail = nd;             /* update tail */
}

/* delete a node from queue head */
void dequeue(Node *head, Node *tail) {
    Node tmp = *head;       /* tmp is the head of the list */

    if (*head == NULL)      /* empty node */
      return;
    else {
      *head = (*head)->next;
      freeNode(tmp);        /* free the memory for the head node */
      if(*head == NULL)     /* empty queue now */
        *tail = NULL;       /* set tail to NULL also */
    }
}
```

Program 15.20: *(Continued)*

Queues can be very useful for modeling and simulation of many different situations. For example, it can be used to model queues in a grocery store for FIFO or first-come-first-serve. It can also be used to schedule events such as printing tasks in a computer, handling a waiting list in a restaurant or hair salon, and monitoring landings and takeoffs of airplanes in an airport.

15.4.4 Binary Trees

The singly linked list, doubly linked list, circular linked list, stack, and queue are implemented using a linearly linked list. There are dynamic data structures that cannot be represented using a linearly linked list, but they can be conveniently represented by a binary tree as shown in Figure 15.27. A *binary tree* consists of a node called the *root*, with two sub-binary trees called the *left subtree* and *right subtree* of the root. The data structure for a binary tree is given below.

```
/* a self-referencing structure for a binary tree node */
struct TreeNode{
    /* data for each node */
    ...
    struct TreeNode *left;  /* link to the left node */
    struct TreeNode *right; /* link to the right node */
};
typedef struct TreeNode *Node; /* define type Node */
```

Two nodes in the structure are used to hold the left and right subtrees. The binary tree is commonly used for fast binary searching, graph theory, and other applications LIFO. Details about implementation for operations of a binary tree is beyond the scope of this book.

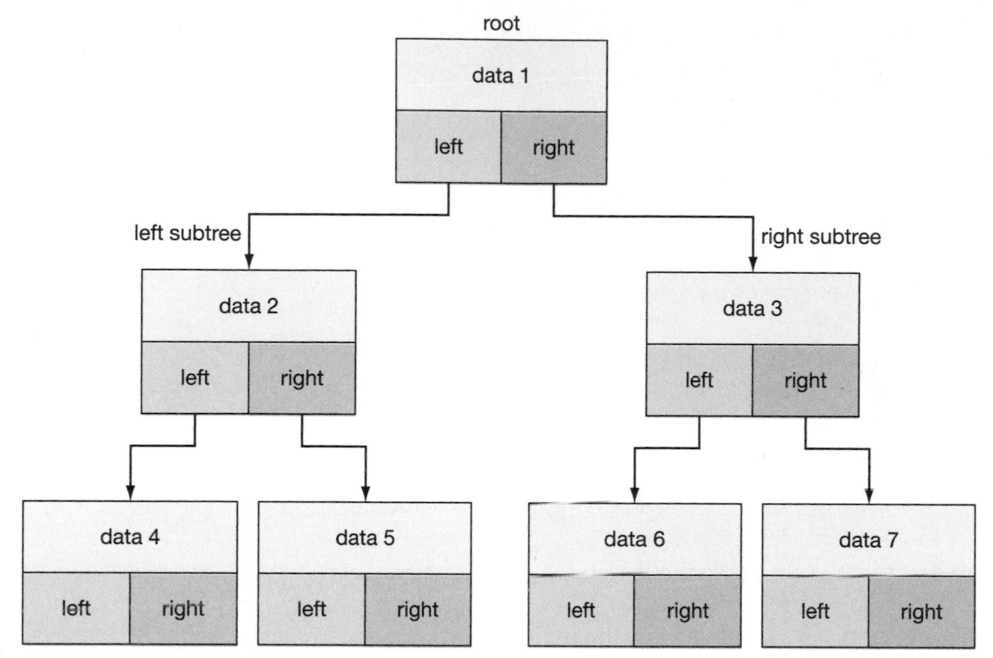

Figure 15.27: A binary tree implemented using a linked list.

15.5 A Case Study for Software Development—Development of a Menu-Driven Interactive GPA Program

This section illustrates the software development using dynamic data structures through a practical application example.

15.5.1 Modular Software Design—Separating Reusable Libraries from Applications

In section 14.3 in Chapter 14, based on a GPA library, a menu-driven GPA program has been developed for an interactive program to process student information, including GPAs, in a data file. In a modular software project, a library might be developed and maintained by different developers or from a third-party vendor. The GPA library could be provided as a static or dynamically linked library. A vendor may distribute the library in the form of the header file `studentfile.h` in Program 15.21 and binary library files. In Unix, a binary library file could be distributed as a static library, `libgpa.a`, or dynamically linked library, `libgpa.so`, based on the source file `studentfilefunc.c` in Program 14.10 in Chapter 14. In Windows, the static binary library could be distributed as `gpa.lib`, or a dynamically linked library as `gpa.lib` and `gpa.dll`. We will describe how to create these binary library files in the next section.

All external functions in a library should be documented for application developers. These external functions in the library are called *application programming interface* (API). The GPA library developer may use Program 14.9 as an example to test the library. This example might be used in the documentation of the APIs of the library to illustrate how the APIs should be used by application developers. Application developers develop and maintain programs using the library, such as Program 14.12, which might be used by staff at universities. A user's guide is typically written for end users, who have no programming experience.

```
*********************** GPA Menu ***********************
av, average: display the average of GPAs for all students
h,  highest: display the student with the highest GPA
l,  lowest:  display the student with the lowest GPA
ab, above:   display students with GPA above a value
s,  sort:    display the record sorted in descending GPA
o,  obtain:  obtain a student's GPA
c,  change:  change a student's GPA
r,  read:    read a new GPA data file
w,  write:   write to a GPA data file
a,  add:     add a student
re, remove:  remove a student
q,  quit:    quit the system
.........................................................

GPA>
```

Figure 15.28: The user interface of an interactive GPA program using the GPA library with a linked list.

Assume that end users have requested that the ability to add and remove students in the system at runtime be added. We could modify the program to retrieve and save student information in a data file at runtime. With such feedback from the end users or customers, application programmers ask the GPA library developer to provide more APIs so that new features (as shown in Figure 15.28) can be implemented. Using a new GPA library, an interaction menu-driven GPA program should allow the user to add new students to the data file or remove students from the data file. Compared with Figure 14.4 in Chapter 14, the new version has interactive menus

```
a,  add:     add a student
re, remove:  remove a student
```

for adding and removing a student from the system.

Based on the feedback from users of the GPA library, the developer of the library would revise and modify the library using a singly linked list. "Do not break existing application programs" is one of the guiding principles for the revision of a library. Application programs 14.9 and 14.12 still work without any modification, although the underlying implementation of the library could have been extensively modified. In the next subsection, such an upward-compatible GPA library based on a singly linked list is developed.

15.5.2 Development of a GPA Library Using a Singly Linked List

The header file `studentfile.h` of the new version of the GPA library using a singly linked list is shown in Program 15.21. The file `studentlistfunc.c` in Program 15.22 contains the source code for functions in the library. Using this new library, application programs 14.9 and 14.12 can run readily without any modification.

The following code fragment in the header file `studentfile.h` in Program 15.21

```
#if defined(_WIN32)  /* for compilation using VC++ in Windows */
#define EXTERN extern __declspec(dllexport)
#else                /* for compilation in Unix or run in Ch */
#define EXTERN extern
#endif
```

```
/*********************************************************
 * File: studentfile.h
 * This header file contains macros, data structures and
 * function prototypes for the GPA library using a linked list.
 * Macro names with prefix GPA_,  variable names with prefix gpa_,
 * symbols Birthday, ListStudent, student_t, StudentNode are reserved
 * for this lib.
 *********************************************************/
#ifndef STUDENTFILE_H
#define STUDENTFILE_H

/* define macros for building a binary GPA library */
#if defined(_WIN32)  /* for compilation using VC++ in Windows */
#define EXTERN extern __declspec(dllexport)
#else                /* for compilation in Unix or run in Ch */
#define EXTERN extern
#endif

/* define boolean numbers */
#define TRUE 1
#define FALSE 0

struct Birthday {
    short day, month, year;
};

struct ListStudent {
    int id;
    char *name;
    struct Birthday birthday;
    double gpa;
    struct ListStudent *next;
};

/* define new data types student_t for compatibility of the
   previous code studentfile.c */
typedef struct ListStudent student_t;
typedef struct ListStudent *StudentNode; /* for linked list */

/* functions for a single student */
EXTERN void gpa_printStudent(StudentNode sn);
EXTERN int gpa_getId(StudentNode sn);
EXTERN char *gpa_getName(StudentNode sn);
EXTERN struct Birthday gpa_getBirthday(StudentNode sn);
EXTERN double gpa_getGPA(StudentNode sn);
```

Program 15.21: The header file `studentfile.h` for a GPA library using a linked list. (*Continued*)

```
EXTERN void gpa_setGPA(StudentNode sn, double gpa);
/* functions for a linked list */
EXTERN StudentNode gpa_createStudent(int id, const char *name,
                    struct Birthday b, double gpa);
EXTERN void gpa_freeStudent(StudentNode sn);

/* functions for a list of students */
EXTERN int gpa_totnum(StudentNode head);
EXTERN void gpa_printList(StudentNode head);
EXTERN double gpa_averageGPA(StudentNode head);
EXTERN StudentNode gpa_highestGPA(StudentNode head);
EXTERN StudentNode gpa_lowestGPA(StudentNode head);
EXTERN StudentNode gpa_find(StudentNode head, int id, const char *name);
EXTERN int gpa_aboveGPA(StudentNode head, double gpa);
EXTERN void gpa_sortGPA(StudentNode head);
EXTERN StudentNode gpa_readData(const char *filename);
EXTERN int gpa_writeData(StudentNode head, const char *filename);
EXTERN void gpa_clearList(StudentNode head);
/* functions for a linked list */
EXTERN void gpa_prepend(StudentNode *head, StudentNode sn);
EXTERN void gpa_append(StudentNode *head, StudentNode sn);
EXTERN int gpa_insert(StudentNode *head, StudentNode sn, int pos);
EXTERN void gpa_remove(StudentNode *head, StudentNode sn);

/* utility functions */
EXTERN const char *gpa_monthString(int month);

/* load code from file studentlistfunc.c for Ch */
#ifdef _CH_
#pragma importf "studentlistfunc.c"
#endif

#endif /* STUDENTFILE_H */
```

Program 15.21: (*Continued*).

```
/************************************************************
* File: studentlistfunc.c
* This file contains function definitions for the GPA library
* using a linked list.
************************************************************/
#include <stdio.h>
#include <string.h>       /* for strcmp() and strdup() */
```

Program 15.22: The function file `studentlistfunc.c` for a GPA library using a linked list. (*Continued*)

```
#include <stdlib.h>        /* for malloc() and free() */
#include "studentfile.h"   /* header file GPA lib */

/* line buffer size */
#define BUFSIZE 1024

#define TRUE 1
#define FALSE 0

/* static function in file scope */
static
StudentNode highestLowestGPA(StudentNode head, int isFindHighest);


/* external functions */

/* Code block 1: functions for a single student */
void gpa_printStudent(StudentNode sn) {
    if(sn == NULL) {
        fprintf(stderr, "Error: invalid argument passed to printStudent()\n");
        return;
    }
    printf("  id: %d; name: %6s; birthday: %8s %2d, %d; GPA: %.2f\n",
           sn->id, sn->name, gpa_monthString(sn->birthday.month),
           sn->birthday.day, sn->birthday.year, sn->gpa);
}

int gpa_getId(StudentNode sn) {
    return sn->id;
}

char *gpa_getName(StudentNode sn) {
    return sn->name;
}

struct Birthday gpa_getBirthday(StudentNode sn) {
    return sn->birthday;
}

double gpa_getGPA(StudentNode sn) {
    return sn->gpa;
}
```

Program 15.22: *(Continued)*

```
void gpa_setGPA(StudentNode sn, double gpa) {
    sn->gpa = gpa;
}

/* create a student node */
StudentNode gpa_createStudent(int id, const char *name,
                     struct Birthday b, double gpa) {
    StudentNode sn;

    sn = (StudentNode) malloc(sizeof(struct ListStudent));
    if(sn == NULL) {
        fprintf(stderr, "Error: not enough memory.\n");
        return NULL;
    }
    sn->id = id;
    sn->name = strdup(name);
    sn->birthday = b;
    sn->gpa = gpa;
    sn->next = NULL;
    return sn;
}

/* free the memory for a student node and related memory */
void gpa_freeStudent(StudentNode sn) {
    if(sn) {
        if(sn->name) {
            free(sn->name);
        }
        free(sn);
    }
}


/* Code block 2: functions for a list of students */
/* get total number of students in the list */
int gpa_totnum(StudentNode head) {
    int totnum = 0;

    while(head != NULL) {
        totnum++;
        head = head->next;
    }
    return totnum;
}
```

Program 15.22: *(Continued)*

```
/* print info for all students in the list */
void gpa_printList(StudentNode head) {
    while(head != NULL) {
        gpa_printStudent(head);
        head = head->next;
    }
}

/* calculate the average of the GPA for students in the list */
double gpa_averageGPA(StudentNode head) {
    double gpa, totalval;
    int i;

    totalval=0.0;
    for(i=0; head != NULL; head = head->next, i++) {
         totalval += head->gpa;
    }
    gpa = totalval/i;
    return gpa;
}

/* find the student with the highest GPA in the list */
StudentNode gpa_highestGPA(StudentNode head) {
    return highestLowestGPA(head, TRUE);
}

/* find the student with the lowest GPA in the list */
StudentNode gpa_lowestGPA(StudentNode head) {
    return highestLowestGPA(head, FALSE);
}

/* find the student based on the id and name */
StudentNode gpa_find(StudentNode head, int id, const char *name) {
    while(head!=NULL && !(!strcmp(head->name, name) &&
          head->id == id)) {
       head = head->next;
    }
    return head;
}

/* print out the students with GAP above 'gpa' */
int gpa_aboveGPA(StudentNode head, double gpa) {
    int num;
```

Program 15.22: (*Continued*)

```
    for(num=0; head != NULL; head=head->next) {
        if(head->gpa >= gpa) {
            gpa_printStudent(head);
            num++;
        }
    }
    return num;
}

/* sort students with GPA in descending order using bubble sort */
void gpa_sortGPA(StudentNode head) {
    struct ListStudent tmp;      /* for contents of a node */
    StudentNode next, sni, snj; /* temporary nodes */

    sni = head; /* start from the beginning for the outer loop */
    snj = head; /* start from the beginning for the inner loop */

    while(sni!= NULL) {
        while(snj!= NULL) {
            if(sni->gpa < snj->gpa) {
               /* swap contents of sni and snj, update next links */
                tmp = *sni;           /* save sni */
                next = sni->next;     /* save pointer next for node sni */
                *sni = *snj;          /* sni is set with the value for snj */
                sni->next = next;     /* update pointer next for node sni */
                next = snj->next;     /* save pointer next for node snj */
                *snj = tmp;           /* snj has the value of sni */
                snj->next = next;     /* update pointer next for node snj */
            }
            snj = snj->next;  /* process the next node */
        }
        /* move to the next node */
        sni = sni->next;
        snj = sni;
    }
}

/* read student data file and return the data in list with the allocated memory */
StudentNode gpa_readData(const char *filename) {
    StudentNode head, sn; /* declare head of the list of students,
                             and a single student */
    FILE *stream;          /* a file stream for reading data from filename */
    char line[BUFSIZE];    /* a buffer to hold the a line from filename */
```

Program 15.22: *(Continued)*

```
    int id;                      /* student id */
    char name[32];               /* student name */
    struct Birthday birthday;    /* student birthday */
    double gpa;                  /* student GPA */

    stream = fopen(filename, "r");  /* open filename for reading */
    if(stream == NULL) {
        fprintf(stderr, "Error: cannot open file '%s' for reading\n", filename);
        return NULL;
    }

    head = NULL;
    fgets(line, BUFSIZE, stream); /* read a line into the buffer */
    while(!feof(stream)) {
        while(line[0] == '#') { /* skip the comment */
           fgets(line, BUFSIZE, stream); /* read a line into the buffer */
        }
       /* read the data for a student from string line and save them in
           the memory pointed by sn, id and name */
        sscanf(line, "%d%s%hd%hd%hd%lf", &id, name,
               &birthday.day, &birthday.month, &birthday.year, &gpa);
        /* create a node with id, name, birthday, and gpa */
        sn = gpa_createStudent(id, name, birthday, gpa);
        gpa_append(&head, sn);         /* append the node into the list */
        fgets(line, BUFSIZE, stream); /* read a line into the buffer */
    }
    fclose(stream);             /* close the file stream */
    return head;                /* return the head of the list */
}

/* write student data into a file */
int gpa_writeData(StudentNode head, const char *filename) {
    FILE *stream;       /* a file stream for writing data int filename */

    stream = fopen(filename, "w");  /* open filename for writing */
    if(stream == NULL) {
        fprintf(stderr, "Error: cannot open file '%s' for writing\n", filename);
        return -1;
    }
    while(head != NULL) {  /* write until the sentinel value for the last link */
        fprintf(stream, "%d %s %hd %hd %hd %g\n", head->id, head->name,
                head->birthday.day, head->birthday.month, head->birthday.year,
                head->gpa);
        head = head->next; /* advance to the next element */
    }
```

Program 15.22: *(Continued)*

```
    fclose(stream);         /* close the file stream */
    return 0;
}

/* delete all nodes and their associated memory of the list */
void gpa_clearList(StudentNode head) {
    StudentNode sn;

    while(head) {
       sn = head;
       head = head->next;
       gpa_freeStudent(sn);
    }
}

/* prepend to the list at the beginning */
void gpa_prepend(StudentNode *head, StudentNode sn) {
    sn->next = *head;/* head becomes the next node of the new node */
    *head = sn;      /* the new node becomes the new head */
}

/* append to the list at end */
void gpa_append(StudentNode *head, StudentNode sn) {
    StudentNode tmp = *head; /* tmp is the head of the list */

    if(*head == NULL) /* no node in linked list */
      *head = sn;
    else {
       /* get the tail of the linked list */
       while(tmp->next)
          tmp = tmp->next;
       /* add the new one to the end of the list */
       tmp->next = sn;
    }
}

/* insert to the list at pos */
int gpa_insert(StudentNode *head, StudentNode sn, int pos) {
    StudentNode tmp = *head; /* tmp is the head of the list */
    int i = 0;

    /* insert to the first position */
    if(pos == 1) {
```

Program 15.22: (*Continued*)

```
        *head = sn;
        (*head)->next = tmp;
        return 0;
    }

    /* get position */
    while(tmp) {
        if(++i >= pos-1) /* match or invalid position */
            break;
        tmp = tmp->next;
    }
    if(i != pos-1) { /* can not get that position */
        fprintf(stderr, "Error: Wrong position for insert().\n");
        return -1;
    }
    /* update links */
    sn->next = tmp->next;
    tmp->next = sn;
    return 0;
}

/* remove a node from the list */
void gpa_remove(StudentNode *head, StudentNode sn) {
    StudentNode tmp = *head; /* tmp is the head of the list */

    if (*head == NULL)        /* empty node */
        return;
    else if ((*head) == sn) {  /* sn is the head */
        *head = (*head)->next;
        gpa_freeStudent(tmp);  /* free the memory for the node */

    }
    else {
        while (tmp->next) {
            if (tmp->next == sn) {   /* found the node */
                tmp->next = tmp->next->next; /* detach the node */
                gpa_freeStudent(sn); /* free the memory for the node */
                return;
            }
            tmp = tmp->next;
        }
    }
}
```

Program 15.22: *(Continued)*

```
/* Code block 3: utility functions */
const char *gpa_monthString(int month) {
    static const char *monthName[] = {"January", "February", "March",
          "April", "May", "June", "July", "August", "September",
          "October", "November", "December"};

    return (month < 1 || month > 12) ? NULL : monthName[month-1];
}


/* Code block 4: internal functions */

/* find the student with the highest or lowest GPA in the list */
static
StudentNode highestLowestGPA(StudentNode head, int isFindHighest) {
    StudentNode sn;
    double gpa;

    gpa = head->gpa;        /* initial gpa */
    sn =  head;             /* initial sn */
    while(head != NULL) {
        if(isFindHighest == TRUE && head->gpa > gpa) {
            gpa = head->gpa;
            sn= head;
        }
        else if(isFindHighest == FALSE && head->gpa < gpa) {
            gpa = head->gpa;
            sn = head;
        }
        head = head->next;
    }

    return sn;
}
```

Program 15.22: *(Continued)*

defines the macro EXTERN for building a binary library. When the header file is processed by Visual C++ in Windows, the macro is defined as extern __declspec(dllexport). The type specifier **__declspec(dllexport)** is needed only to export an external function in a separate library, such as gpa.dll, so that it cannot be invoked in an application program. It is Visual C++–specific. When the program is executed in Unix or Ch, the macro EXTERN is the same as **extern**. Each external function is type-qualified by the macro EXTERN. Details about building a binary library will be described in the next subsection.

The dynamic data structure ListStudent, with a self-referencing pointer and a new data type StudentNode, are defined in the header file. Comparing with the structure ListNode in section 15.2, the structure ListStudent contains additional members for the birthday and GPA of a student. For upward compatibility, the data type student_t is also defined. The APIs for the previous version of the GPA library are modified to use the data type StudentNode. In addition, the prototypes for the list-processing functions

```
EXTERN void gpa_prepend(StudentNode *head, StudentNode sn);
EXTERN void gpa_append(StudentNode *head, StudentNode sn);
EXTERN void gpa_insert(StudentNode *head, StudentNode sn, int pos);
EXTERN void gpa_remove(StudentNode *head, StudentNode sn);
```

for prepending, appending, inserting, and removing a student node in the list, respectively, are added. The definitions of these functions listed in Program 15.22 are the same as the functions prepend(), append(), insert(), and remov() presented in section 15.2.

The following functions

```
void gpa_printStudent(StudentNode sn);
int gpa_getId(StudentNode sn);
char *gpa_getName(StudentNode sn);
struct Birthday gpa_getBirthday(StudentNode sn);
double gpa_getGPA(StudentNode sn);
void gpa_setGPA(StudentNode sn, double gpa);
```

for a single student node in Program 15.22 are the same as those in the previous version of the library shown in Program 13.34 in Chapter 13. The functions

```
StudentNode gpa_createStudent(int id, const char *name,
                        struct Birthday b, double gpa);
void gpa_freeStudent(StudentNode sn);
```

for creating and freeing a student node are similar to the functions createNode() and freeNode() in Program 15.5.

Other functions in Program 15.22 have the same functionality as ones in the previous library. But they are implemented using a singly linked list. For example, the function gpa_totnum() traverses the entire list to obtain the total number of nodes in the list. The functions gpa_printList() and gpa_find() are the same as printList() in Program 15.11 and find() in Program 15.9, respectively.

The function gpa_sortGPA() for sorting the GPA in ascending order using the bubble sort needs special attention. It uses two nested **while** loops for iteration of the sorting algorithm. After the GPA is sorted, the links of the list remain the same. Therefore, when the contents of the two nodes sni and snj need to be swapped, the pointer next is saved first by the statement

```
next = sni->next;    /* save pointer next for node sni */
```

After values for all members of the node snj are assigned to the node sni, the pointer next for sni is updated as follows:

```
*sni = *snj;         /* sni is set with the value for snj */
sni->next = next;    /* update pointer next for node sni */
```

The similar code is used for assigning the value of the temporary node tmp for sn1 to the node snj.

The function gpa_readData() in Program 14.10 in Chapter 14 reads multiple sets of data for a list of students and returns a dynamically allocated array of structure. Similarly, the function gpa_readData() in Program 15.22 reads a data file with the same format. The functions gpa_createStudent() and gpa_append() inside a **while** loop are used to build a singly linked list with each node containing the information for a student. Because the list can grow dynamically, there is no need to know the number of students in the data file in advance. The function returns the head of the singly linked list. The function `gpa_readData()` in both Programs 14.10 and 15.22 returns a pointer to structure. Therefore, they are compatible. The function `gpa_readWrite()` in Program 15.22, similar to the one in Program 14.10, writes student information in the linked list to a data file.

15.5.3 Development of a Menu-Driven Interactive GPA Program Using a Singly Linked List

Using the GPA library with the header file in Program 15.21 and the functions in Program 15.22, the menu-driven interactive GPA program listed in Program 14.12 in Chapter 14 still works without any modification. Because the library now uses dynamic data structures, the linked list for holding the student information can grow and shrink at runtime. We can revise Program 14.12 so that it allows the user to add and remove students to the list. Program 15.23 is similar to Programs 13.36 and 14.12. When Program 15.23 is executed, the user interface of the program is shown previously in Figure 15.28. Corresponding to two new entries in the user interface, the new enumerated values `ADDSTUDENT` and `REMOVESTUDENT` are added in the enumerated data type `Action`.

```
/**********************************************************************
 * File: studentlistmenu.c
 * This application program uses the GPA library with a linked list
 * to process GPAs of students in the database of a file.
 * The application is menu driven.
 **********************************************************************/
#include <stdio.h>
#include <string.h>              /* for strcmp()  */
#include <stdlib.h>              /* for exit(EXIT_FAILURE) */
#include "studentfile.h"         /* the header file for GPA lib */

#define MAX_TRY_NUM  3           /* maximum number of tries */
#define MAX_PROMPT_STR  128      /* maximum prompt string length */
#define MAX_FILENAME_LENGTH 128 /* maximum file name length */

/* enumerated type for actions from the menu driven user input */
typedef enum Action {
    UNDEFINED,     /* undefined action */
    AVERAGEGPA,    /* find the average of GPAs for all students */
    HIGHESTGPA,    /* find the student with the highest GPA */
    LOWESTGPA,     /* find the student with the lowest GPA */
    ABOVEGPA,      /* find students with GPA above a given value */
    SORTGPA,       /* sort the students based on GPA in descending order */
    OBTAINGPA,     /* obtain the GPA for a student based on id and name */
```

Program 15.23: A menu-driven program `studentlistmenu.c` using functions in a GPA library with a linked list. (*Continued*)

```
    CHANGEGPA,    /* change the GPA for a student based on id and name */
    READFILE,     /* read student information from a file */
    WRITEFILE,    /* write student information into a file */
    ADDSTUDENT,   /* add a student into the list */
    REMOVESTUDENT, /* remove a student from the list */
    QUIT          /* quit the program */
} action_t;

/* function prototypes for this application only */
extern action_t getActionMenu(void);  /* action menu */
/* obtain the GPA for a student */
extern void obtainGPA(StudentNode head);
/* change the GPA for a student */
extern void changeGPA(StudentNode head);
/* initialize the head of the list for students */
extern StudentNode initialize(const char *filename);
/* add a student to the list */
extern void addStudent(StudentNode *head);
/* remove a student from the list */
extern void removeStudent(StudentNode *head);

int main() {
    StudentNode head, sn; /* head of the list and a single student */
    double gpa;           /* GPA value */
    struct Birthday b;    /* b for birthday */
    int num; /* number of students with GPA above a specified value */
    action_t act;         /* action in the menu */
    int quit = FALSE;     /* flag for quit or continue the menu */
    /* declare filename for data file, initialized with the default data file */
    char filename[MAX_FILENAME_LENGTH] = "student.data";

    /* head points to the list of students in the default data file student.data */
    head = initialize(filename);
    while(quit==FALSE) {  /* continue the menu if not quit */
        act = getActionMenu();  /* get an action */
        switch(act) {     /* take an action based on the value of 'act' */
            case AVERAGEGPA:  /* obtain the average of all GPAs */
              printf("The GPA for all students is %.2f\n", gpa_averageGPA(head));
              break;

            /* CODE HHER IS THE SAME AS THA IN PROGRAM studentfilemenu.c */
            /* ... */
```

Program 15.23: (*Continued*)

```
        /* add a student to the list */
        case ADDSTUDENT:
          addStudent(&head);
          break;
        /* remove a student from the list */
        case REMOVESTUDENT:
          removeStudent(&head);
          break;
        case QUIT:               /* quit the program */
          quit = TRUE;           /* set flag quit to TRUE */
          break;
        default:                 /* in case a mistake is made */
          printf("\aInvalid input!\n");
          break;
      }
    }
    gpa_clearList(head);  /* release the allocated memory for head */
    return 0;
}

/*----------------------------------------------------------------
* Function addStudent() adds a student to the linked list inside the
* system. Make sure the student with id and name is not in the
* database. The user can input id and name up to 3 times defined in
* MAX_TRY_NUM. After three failed tries, the function will quit.
* The static variable try_count is used for implementation.
*----------------------------------------------------------------*/
void addStudent(StudentNode *head) {
    StudentNode sn;         /* a student */
    int id;                 /* student id */
    char name[32];          /* student name */
    static try_count = 0;   /* track the number of tries using static var */
    double gpa;             /* new GPA value from the user input */
    struct Birthday birthday; /* structure for birthday info */

    sn = *head;             /* get the head of the list */
    printf("please input student id\n");
    /* get the student id and suppress the newline character '\n' */
    scanf("%d%*c", &id);
    printf("please input student name\n");
    fgets(name, sizeof(name), stdin); /* the user input string */
    /* get rid of the newline character '\n' in the input string */
    name[strlen(name)-1] = '\0';
```

Program 15.23: *(Continued)*

```
    sn = gpa_find(*head, id, name); /* find the student based on id and name */
    if(sn) { /* id is already in the database, try MAX_TRY_NUM times */
       printf("Id %d is in the database already.\n", id);
        try_count++; /* increment the count for number of failed try */
        if(try_count < MAX_TRY_NUM) { /* if less than specified num of tries */
           addStudent(head);/* call the function recursively, up to 3 times */
        }
        else {              /* exit the function after three failed tries */
           printf("You have tried %d times, nice try!\n", try_count);
           try_count = 0;   /* reset the count for next action */
        }
    }
    else {
        printf("please input student birthday (day month year) \n");
        scanf("%hd%hd%hd%*c", &birthday.day, &birthday.month, &birthday.year);
        printf("please input GPA\n");
        scanf("%lf%*c", &gpa); /* get the GPA */
        /* create a student node */
        sn = gpa_createStudent(id, name, birthday, gpa);
        gpa_append(head, sn); /* append the new student to the list */
        try_count = 0;        /* reset the count for next action */
    }
}

/*---------------------------------------------------------------------
* Function removeStudent() removes a student from the linked list inside
* the system.  Make sure the student with id and name is in the database
* The user can input id and name up to 3 times defined in
* MAX_TRY_NUM. After three failed tries, the function will quit.
* The static variable try_count is used for implementation.
*--------------------------------------------------------------------*/
void removeStudent(StudentNode *head) {
    StudentNode sn;          /* a student */
    int id;                  /* student id */
    char name[32];           /* student name */
    static try_count = 0;  /* track the number of tries using static var */

    printf("please input student id\n");
    /* get the student id and suppress the newline character '\n' */
    scanf("%d%*c", &id);
    printf("please input student name\n");
    fgets(name, sizeof(name), stdin); /* the user input string */
    /* get rid of the newline character '\n' in the input string */
```

Program 15.23: *(Continued)*

```
    name[strlen(name)-1] = '\0';
    sn = gpa_find(*head, id, name); /* find the student based on id and name */
    if(sn) { /* when the student is found, remove the student data from the list */
        gpa_remove(head, sn);    /* remove the student */
        try_count = 0;    /* reset the count for next action */
    }
    else {  /* when the student is not found, try it again */
        printf("%s with id %d is not in the database.\n", name, id);
        try_count++; /* increment the count for number of failed try */
        if(try_count < MAX_TRY_NUM) { /* if less than specified num of tries */
            removeStudent(head); /* call the function recursively, up to 3 times */
        }
        else {                  /* exit the function after three failed tries */
            printf("You have tried %d times, nice try!\n", try_count);
            try_count = 0;    /* reset the count for next action */
        }
    }
}
```

Program 15.23: *(Continued)*

There are six functions in this program. The definitions for the functions `obtainGPA()`, `changeGPA()`, and `initialize()` are the same as ones in the previous versions. The function `obtainGPA()` is listed in Program 13.36 in Chapter 13. The other two functions are listed in Program 14.12 in Chapter 14. Therefore, they are not listed in Program 15.23. The function `getActionMenu()` is the same as the one used in the previous version in Program 14.12, except that the code fragment

```
else if(!strcmp(str, "a") || !strcmp(str, "add")) {
    act = ADDSTUDENT;
}
else if(!strcmp(str, "re") || !strcmp(str, "remove")) {
    act = REMOVESTUDENT;
}
```

for handling cases of `ADDSTUDENT` and `REMOVESTUDENT` is added inside `getActionMenu()` in Program 15.23.

There are two new cases of `ADDSTUDENT` and `REMOVESTUDENT` in the switch-statement inside a **while** loop. To add a new student to the list, the function `addStudent()` is called. Like the functions `obtainGPA()` and `changeGPA()`, based on the student ID and name from the user input, this function first determines if the student is already in the list or not using the function `gpa_find()` in the GPA library. If the student is already in the list, it asks the user for new input three times by recursively calling the function `addStudent()` before the function exits. If the student is not in the list, the function adds the student to the list using the functions `gpa_createStudent()` and `gpa_append()` in the GPA library. Similarly, the function `removeStudent()` removes a student from the list based on the input ID and name for the student using the function `gpa_remove()` in the GPA library. The user is given up to three opportunities to input the valid student ID and name in the list.

15.5.4 Further Refinement of the GPA Library and Its Application Programs

The updated versions of the GPA library and menu-driven interactive GPA program are more flexible than previous versions. However, they can still be improved in many ways. First, the student information is stored in a data file, which is not secure and flexible. The student information could be stored in a database. The modification would involve only the change of the GPA library. The functions `gpa_readGPA()` `gpa_writeGPA()` could be modified to access information in the database using the C APIs in Open Database Connectivity (ODBC), which provides standard interfaces to various database management systems. Next, the menu-driven user interface of the program can be replaced by a graphical user interface (GUI). As pointed out in section 11.11.4 in Chapter 11, the GUI is typically developed using event-driven programming. Several different APIs can be used for GUI programming. Windows APIs can be used to create a GUI in Windows. APIs in GTK+ can be used for cross-platform GUI programming in Windows and Unix. Finally, it would be more desirable to access student information in a database through a password-protected website. For this purpose, in addition to ODBC, Common Gateway Interface (CGI) or other programming models can be used for Web-based computing. C/C++ interpreter Ch has high-level CGI modules to facilitate Web-based computing. Applications written with APIs in ODBC, Windows API, GTK+, and CGI can run readily in Ch. Like functions in the standard math library or our GPA library, these APIs are just modular and reusable C functions, which can be used to facilitate the development of applications. There are numerous libraries available for various applications and many of them are distributed in the form of open source (meaning that the source code is included).

15.6 Making It Work

15.6.1 Compiling and Linking Applications with the GPA Library Source Code

Program 15.23 uses the GPA library with the header file `studentfile.h` in Program 15.21 and the source code `studentlistmenu.c` for function definitions in Program 15.22. The source code `studentlistmenu.c` can run readily in Ch without compilation. Based on the information presented in sections 7.11.1 and 8.5.1, with the header file in the current directory, the program can be compiled and linked using the command below in Unix

```
> cc studentlistmenu.c studentlistfunc.c -I./
```

to create the default binary executable program `a.out`. Using Visual C++ in Windows, the the executable program `studentlistmenu.exe` can be created by the following command:

```
> cl studentlistmenu.c studentlistfunc.c -I./
```

15.6.2 Building Static and Dynamic Libraries in Windows and Unix

The GPA library with functions presented in the previous section can be built separately and used by different application programs. There are mainly two types of libraries. A *static library* or *statically linked library* is a set of functions and variables which are resolved for calling functions at link time, as shown in Figure 1.4(a) in Chapter 1. It can be merged with other static libraries and object files at link time to form a single binary executable. On the other hand, a *dynamic link library* (DLL) means that the functions in the library are loaded into an application program at runtime as shown in Figure 1.4(b), rather than being linked at link time. When an application is linked with a DLL, it records only what library functions the program needs and the index names or numbers of the functions in the library. In Unix, a DLL is often called a *shared library*, which allows the same library to be used by multiple programs at the same time. When an executable is linked to static libraries, it includes the actual code for the library functions. Therefore, the size of an executable created using static libraries will be large compared to an executable that uses dynamic libraries. An executable can use both static and dynamic libraries. If an executable is created using a dynamic library at link time, the same dynamic library must exist at runtime. This makes distribution of an executable difficult to support in different versions of an operating system, which may not include an older version of dynamic link libraries. However, an executable created using static libraries can avoid such version issues related to dynamic link libraries. In this section, using the GPA library as an example, building and using static and dynamic link libraries in Windows and Unix is described.

Building Static Libraries in Windows

In Windows, the command

```
> cl /c studentlistfunc.c -I./
```

compiles and generates an object file `studentlistfunc.obj`. The command **lib** creates a static library from the input arguments of object files. The output static library file, typically with the `.lib` file extension, can be specified by the option `/OUT:`. The command below creates the static GPA library `gpas.lib`.

```
> lib /OUT:gpas.lib studentlistfunc.obj
```

The static library `gpas.lib` can be used at link time to generate executables. For example, the application `studentfile.c` in Program 14.9 in Chapter 14 can be compiled and linked with this static library to create the executable `studentfile.exe` as follows:

```
> cl /Festudentfile.exe studentfile.c gpas.lib
```

Building Static Libraries in Unix

In Unix, the following commands can be used to create the static GPA library `libgpa.a`:

```
> cc -c studentlistfunc.c -I./
> ar -r libgpa.a studentlistfunc.o
> ranlib libgpa.a
```

The command **cc** compiles the program `studentlistfunc.c` to create the object file `studentlistfunc.o`. The command **ar** creates an archival file `libgpa.a` from the object file `studentlistfunc.o`. If an object file already exists in the archival file, the option `-r` replaces the object file with the new object file. Like the command **lib** in Windows, the command **ar** can take multiple object files. The command **ranlib** makes the archival file `libgpa.a` as a static library. A static library in Unix typically has the `.a` file extension. The static library `libgpa.a` can be used directly with the full name

```
> cc -o studentfile studentfile.c libgpa.a -lm -lc -L./
```

or as the command-line option `-lgpa`:

```
> cc -o studentfile studentfile.c -lgpa -lm -lc -L./
```

to create the executable `studentfile` with the application program `studentfile.c`. The compiler command-line options `-lm` and `-lc` link standard math and C libraries in the default directory `/usr/lib`. To link a library that is not in the default directory, the option `-L` immediately followed by a directory name can be used to specify the directory where the library is located. The option `-L./` instructs the linker to look for a library in the current directory.

Building DLLs in Windows

The DLL in Windows typically uses the `.dll` file extension. The dynamic GPA library `gpa.dll` can be created from the object file `studentlistfunc.obj` by the command

```
> link /DLL /OUT:gpa.dll studentlistfunc.obj
```

By default, the link command **link** creates a binary executable with the `.exe` file extension. With the option `/DLL`, the command **link** creates two DLL files `gpa.dll` and `gpa.lib`. The type qualifier **__declspec(dllexport)** in the header file `studentfile,h` in Program 15.21 allows symbols for external functions to be exported in the output file `gpa.lib`. The link-time DLL file `gpa.lib`, typically with the `.lib` file extension, is used at link time to resolve external symbols for callers using functions in the library. For example, the application `studentlistmenu.c` in Program 15.23 can be compiled and linked with this DLL to create the executable `studentlistmenu.exe` as follows:

```
> cl /Festudentlistmenu.exe studentlistmenu.c gpa.lib
```

The runtime DLL file `gpa.dll`, typically with the `.dll` file extension, must be present in the system when the program `studentlistmenu.exe` is executed. System DLL files are typically located in the system directory `C:\Windows\System32` for 32-bit machines. The user's DLL files can be placed in the same directory where the executable is located or in a directory contained in the value of the environment variable **PATH**.

Building Shared Libraries in Unix

Static libraries typically have the `.lib` file extension in Windows and the `.a` file extension in Unix by default. In Windows, link-time DLLs use `.lib` file extension and runtime DLLs `.dll` file extension. In Unix, the file extension for shared libraries is different in different platforms. The shared library has the `.so` file extension in Linux, Solaris, and FreeBSD. It uses `.dylib` in Mac OS X and `.sl` in HP-UX. Shared libraries are typically located in the directory `/usr/lib`.

To create a shared library in Unix, source files need to be compiled first to create object files. A linker command **ld** is then used to build a shared library. Different platforms typically have different command-line options for generating shared libraries. For example, in Linux, the shared GPA library can be generated by the commands below.

```
> cc -c studentlistfunc.c -I./
> ld -shared -o libgpa.so studentlistfunc.o
```

The compiler **cc** generates an object file `studentlistfunc.o` from the source code `studentlistfunc.c`. The linker **ld** with options "`-shared -o libgpa.so`" creates the shared library `libgpa.so` from the object file `studentlistfunc.o`. A shared library can also be created with multiple separately compiled object files. In Solaris, the shared GPA library `libgpa.so` can be created using the following command, with the option `-G`, instead of `-shared`:

```
> ld -G -o libgpa.so studentlistfunc.o
```

The shared library `libgpa.so` can be used through the command-line option `-lgpa`:

```
> cc -o studentlistmenu studentlistmenu.c -lgpa -lm -lc -L./
```

to create the executable `studentlistmenu` with the application program `studentlistmenu.c`. If both the shared library `libgpa.so` and the static library `libgpa.a` exist in the system, the command-line option `-lgpa` links the application with the shared library by default. To use the static library explicitly, the static library `libgpa.a` can be supplied with the full name as a command argument as follows:

```
> cc -o studentlistmenu studentlistmenu.c libgpa.a -lm -lc -L./
```

Distributing Libraries

For users' convenience or for protection of their intellectual property, developers may distribute developed libraries without source code. For example, the GPA library can be distributed without the source code `studentlistfunc.c`.

In Windows, the header file `studentfile.h`, the static library `gpas.lib`, and the DLL files `gpa.lib` and `gpa.dll` may be distributed. The files `studentfile.h`, `gpas.lib`, and `gpa.lib` are for application developers to build executables with the `.exe` file extension. Header files can be placed in directories specified by the environment variable **INCLUDE**, as described in section 7.11.1 in Chapter 7. The files `gpas.lib` and `gpa.lib` used at link time can be placed in a directory specified by the environment variable **LIB**. The file `gpa.dll` is used at runtime by executables created using the DLL file `gpa.lib`. The file `gpa.dll` can be placed in the system directory `C:\Windows\System32` for 32-bit machines.

In Unix, the header file `studentfile.h`, static library `libgpas.a`, and the DLL file `libgpa.so` may be distributed. The files `studentfile.h`, `libgpa.a`, and `libgpa.so` are for application developers to build executables. The files `studentfile.h` and `libgpa.a` are not needed by executables at runtime. The file `libgpa.so` is needed for executables created using the shared library. Both the library files `libgpa.a` and `libgpa.so` may be placed in the system library directory `/usr/lib`. In Linux and Windows, the environment variable **LD_LIBRARY_PATH** contains the colon-separated search paths for shared libraries. If a shared library is not in the default system library directory, it is searched in the value of the environment variable **LD_LIBRARY_PATH**.

A version number can be used to distinguish different versions of the runtime shared libraries in Unix. For example, a Linux system may contain two versions of GPA shared libraries `libgpa.so.1` and `libgpa.so.2`. The above created shared GPA library `libgpa.so` could be renamed as `libgpa.so.2` for distribution. In the distribution, the default shared library `libgpa.so` is symbolically linked to the latest version of the shared library in the system by the command **ln**:

```
> ln -s libgpa.so.2 libgpa.so
```

so that the latest version of the shared library will be used when an application is linked with the GPA library. However, because of the existence of the shared library `libgpa.so.1`, applications built with an older version of the shared GPA library `libgpa.so.1` are still able to run.

15.6.3 Maintaining Programs with make

How to use the **make** program to keep track of the dependency for a large program with many source files has been described in section 8.5.2 in Chapter 8. Using the GPA library as an example, this section demonstrates how to use make files to conveniently develop and maintain libraries across different platforms.

A Make File for GPA Programs in Linux

Program 15.24 is a `Makefile` that can be used to build GPA libraries and executables in Linux, as described in the previous section. The executable `studentfile` using a static GPA library `libgpa.a` and `studentlistmenu` using a shared GPA library `libgpa.so`. The line

```
DLLFLAG = -shared
```

```
# File: Makefile
# build studentfile using static library libgpa.a in Unix
# build studentlistmenu using dynamic library libgpa.so in Unix
# In Solaris, use command "make DLLFLAG=-G"

# default DLLFLAG for Linux
DLLFLAG = -shared

target: studentfile studentlistmenu

studentfile: studentfile.o libgpa.a
        cc -o studentfile studentfile.o libgpa.a -lm -lc -L./
studentlistmenu: studentlistmenu.o libgpa.so
        cc -o studentlistmenu studentlistmenu.o -lgpa -lm -lc  -L./
studentfile.o: studentfile.c studentfile.h
        cc -c studentfile.c -I./
studentlistmenu.o: studentlistmenu.c studentfile.h
        cc -c studentlistmenu.c -I./
studentlistfunc.o: studentlistfunc.c studentfile.h
        cc -c studentlistfunc.c -I./
libgpa.a: studentlistfunc.o
        ar -r libgpa.a studentlistfunc.o
        ranlib libgpa.a
libgpa.so: studentlistfunc.o
        ld $(DLLFLAG) -o libgpa.so studentlistfunc.o
clean:
        rm -f *.o libgpa.a libgpa.so studentfile studentlistmenu
```

Program 15.24: A make file for creating the programs `studentfile` and `studentlistmenu` in Linux.

defines the variable DLLFLAG as an optional flag for the shared library. The value of this variable is later obtained in the command line following the dependency line for the shared library libgpa.so, as shown below.

```
libgpa.so: studentlistfunc.o
        ld $(DLLFLAG) -o libgpa.so studentlistfunc.o
```

The dependency line

```
target: studentfile studentlistmenu
```

specifies two dependent executable files, studentfile and studentlistmenu. There is no command following this dependency line. The block

```
studentfile: studentfile.o libgpa.a
        cc -o studentfile studentfile.o libgpa.a -lm -lc -L./
```

contains a dependency line and its command line. The file studentfile depends on the object file studentfile.o and the static GPA library libgpa.a. When one of these two files is modified, the command for the dependency line will be executed to create an updated executable studentfile. Trace the chain of dependencies: the object file studentfile.o depends on the source files studentfile.c and studentfile.h as shown below:

```
studentfile.o:  studentfile.c studentfile.h
        cc -c studentfile.c -I./
```

The static GPA library libgpa.a depends on the file studentlistfunc.o for object code, which in turn depends on the source files studentlistfunc.c and studentfile.h, as shown below.

```
studentlistfunc.o: studentlistfunc.c studentfile.h
        cc -c studentlistfunc.c -I./
libgpa.a: studentlistfunc.o
        ar -r libgpa.a studentlistfunc.o
        ranlib libgpa.a
```

The library libgpa.a is built by the commands **ar** and **ranlib**. When the make file in Program 15.24 is invoked by the **make** command, each executed command and its output are displayed as shown below in Linux.

```
> make
cc -c studentfile.c -I./
cc -c studentlistfunc.c -I./
ar -r libgpa.a studentlistfunc.o
ar: creating libgpa.a
ranlib libgpa.a
cc -o studentfile studentfile.o libgpa.a -lm -lc
cc -c studentlistmenu.c -I./
ld -shared -o libgpa.so studentlistfunc.o
cc -o studentlistmenu studentlistmenu.o -lgpa -lm -lc  -L./
```

The object files, static and shared GPA libraries, and the executables `studentfile` and `studentlistmenu` are created by the above make command. The output

```
ar: creating libgpa.a
```

is from the execution of the command **ar** when the archival is created the first time.

If the file `studentlistfunc.c` is modified, it needs to be recompiled. The static library `libgpa.a` and shared library `libgpa.so` also need to be rebuilt. However, the files `studentfile.c` and `studentlistmenu.c` do not need to be recompiled. The object files for these application programs can be linked with the updated GPA library to create executables using the latest code for `studentlistfunc.c`. Once the modification is finished, all you need to do is to type the command **make**, as shown below.

```
> make
cc -c studentlistfunc.c -I./
ar -r libgpa.a studentlistfunc.o
ranlib libgpa.a
cc -o studentfile studentfile.o libgpa.a -lm -lc
ld -shared -o libgpa.so studentlistfunc.o
cc -o studentlistmenu studentlistmenu.o -lgpa -lm -lc  -L./
```

Compared with the previous case, the following two commands are not executed this time:

```
cc -c studentfile.c -I./
cc -c studentlistmenu.c -I./
```

The target `studentlistmenu` can be invoked explicitly to built the executable `studentlistmenu` as follows:

```
> make studentlistmenu
cc -c studentlistmenu.c -I./
cc -c studentlistfunc.c -I./
ld -shared -o libgpa.so studentlistfunc.o
cc -o studentlistmenu studentlistmenu.o -lgpa -lm -lc  -L./
```

For the target `clean`, its tab-indented command removes object files with the `.o` file extension, libraries, and executables as follows:

```
> make clean
rm -f *.o libgpa.a libgpa.so studentfile studentlistmenu
```

Using the Same Make File in Other Unix Platforms

By default, the make file in Program 15.24 works only in Linux. For other platforms, the make file needs to be modified. A make file can contain definitions of variables and even can include other make files. Variables in a make file may be overridden in the command-line arguments passed to the **make** command. Therefore, users can specify different behaviors for commands using the same make file.

Commands such as compilation and linking are quite portable in different Unix platforms, including Linux, Solaris, HP-UX, FreeBSD, Mac OS X, and QNX. A single make file can typically be used for different

Unix platforms. In Solaris, the link option to build a shared library is `-G`, instead of `-shared`. The default link option for building the shared library can be modified by the command

```
> make DLLFLAG=-G
```

The command-line argument `DLLFLAG=-G` overrides the value defined for the variable `DLLFLAG` inside the make file.

A Make File for GPA Programs in Windows

The make file `Makefile.win` in Program 15.25 for Windows corresponds to `Makefile` for Linux in Program 15.24. The commands for building static and dynamic link libraries as well as executables described in the previous section are organized in dependency and command lines.

```
# File: Makefile.win
# build studentfile.exe using static library gpas.lib
# build studentlistmenu.exe using dynamic library gpa.lib and gpa.dll

# create .obj file and disable warning message for using scanf()
CFLAG=/c -D_CRT_SECURE_NO_DEPRECATE

target: studentfile.exe studentlistmenu.exe

studentfile.exe: studentfile.obj gpas.lib
	cl /Festudentfile.exe studentfile.obj gpas.lib
studentlistmenu.exe: studentlistmenu.obj gpa.dll
	cl /Festudentlistmenu.exe studentlistmenu.obj gpa.lib
studentfile.obj: studentfile.c studentfile.h
	cl $(CFLAG) studentfile.c -I./
studentlistmenu.obj: studentlistmenu.c studentfile.h
	cl $(CFLAG) studentlistmenu.c -I./
studentlistfunc.obj: studentlistfunc.c studentfile.h
	cl $(CFLAG) studentlistfunc.c  -I./
gpas.lib: studentlistfunc.obj
	lib /OUT:gpas.lib studentlistfunc.obj
gpa.dll: studentlistfunc.obj
	link /DLL /OUT:gpa.dll studentlistfunc.obj
clean:
	del *.obj
	del *.exp
	del *.lib
	del *.dll
	del *.exe
```

Program 15.25: A make file for creating the programs `studentfile.exe` and `studentlistmenu.exe` in Windows.

The make file `Makefile.win` for Windows can be invoked as follows:

```
> make -f Makefile.win
```

with the **make** command provided in Ch. The **nmake** command in Visual C++ can be used to process the make file `Makefile.win` as follows:

```
> nmake -f Makefile.win
```

15.6.4 Very High-Level Shell Programming

The process of building GPA libraries and executables across different platforms using the make files `Makefile.win` for Windows, and `Makefile` for Unix, can be automated by a Ch script command `makegpa` shown in Program 15.26. The command `makegpa`, like the command **make**, can be used across platforms in different command shells. The command `makegpa` illustrates some important features of Ch for very high-level shell programming. These shell programming features, available in most command shells, are briefly described in this section.

C programs can run not only in a Ch command shell without compilation, but also as commands in other command shells. The shebang `#!` at the first line of the code is used in a script to indicate an interpreter for execution. The Ch shebang

```
#!/bin/ch
```

in the first line of the script command `makegpa` makes the command executable from other command shells such as C-shell, Bourne shell, Korn shell, and BASH. However, the MS-DOS command shell does not recognize shebangs. It recognizes a shell script by its file extension. To make the script executable in MS-DOS shell, change the command name from `makegpa` to `makegpa.ch`, with the `.ch` file extension. The function **main()** is optional in Ch. The system variables **_argc** and **_argv** are equivalent to the arguments `argc` and `arv` of the function **main()**, respectively,

```
int main(int argc, char *argv[])
```

described in section 12.10 in Chapter 12. A variable of string type **string_t** can be used to handle strings. The interpreter manages the memory for strings gracefully, and the user does not need to allocate and deallocate the memory explicitly. The function **stradd()** returns the sum of the strings in its arguments. A macro, predefined for each platform, can be used to identify the running platform for across-platform programming. For example, the macro **_LINUX_** is predefined for Linux and the macro **_WIN32_** is predefined for Windows.

```
#!/bin/ch
/* File: makegpa or makegpa.ch in Windows
   a command to invoke different Makefiles
   with diff command line arguments for diff platforms */

int i;
string_t makecmd, arg;
/*  obtain command-line arguments and passed them to 'make' command */
```

Program 15.26: The command `makegpa` for building GPA libraries and executables. *(Continued)*

```
for(i = 1; i<_argc; i++) {
   arg = stradd(arg, _argv[i], " ");
}

#if (defined(_LINUX_) || defined(_LINUXPPC_)) /* for Linux */
/* or if(!strcmp(`uname`, "Linux")) */
  make -f Makefile $arg
#elif defined(_SOLARIS_)                      /* for Solaris */
/* or if(!strcmp(`uname`, "SunOS")) */
  make DLLFLAG=-G -f Makefile $arg
#elif defined(_WIN32_)                        /* for Windows */
/* or if(!strcmp(`uname`, "windows32")) */
  if(`which.ch nmake` != NULL)    /* if Visual C++ nmake.exe exists */
     makecmd = "nmake";
  else                            /* else use make.exe from Ch */
     makecmd = "make";
  $(makecmd) -f Makefile.win $arg
#else
  printf("Undefined platform\n");
#endif
```

Program 15.26: *(Continued)*

The *command substitution* pipes the output of a command into a variable inside a program. This is accomplished by enclosing the embedded command in a pair of accent grave marks `, which are sometimes called *back quotation marks*. The command substitution operation `` `uname` `` executes the command **uname** and the result of string type is the standard output of the command. If the command has no output, the result of the operation is NULL. Therefore, alternatively, the command **uname** can be used to obtain the operating system of the running platform. For a strict C program, the C function **uname()** can be used. Commands can be used directly in shell programming. The value for a variable can be passed to a command by the *variable substitution*, the variable substitution symbol '$' (a dollar sign) followed by a variable name or an expression enclosed in a pair of parentheses. The command

```
make -f Makefile $arg
```

passes the command-line arguments for the command `makegpa` to the command **make** through the string `arg`.

The operation `` `which.ch nmake` `` returns the command **nmake** with a full path, if the command exists. Otherwise, it returns NULL. For Windows, if the Visual C++ has been installed, the command **nmake** from the Visual C++ is preferred than the **make** command. A proper command is assigned to the variable `makecmd` of string type in Windows. The command is then invoked by the variable substitution as follows:

```
$(makecmd) -f Makefile.win $arg
```

Commands, such as **make**, in a shell script are searched based on the path setup in the system variable **_path** described in section 2.2.3 in Chapter 2. Details about using Ch for shell programming can be found in *Ch User's Guide*.

Exercises

1. The structure `Data` below defines the `id` and `name` for teachers.

```
struct Data {
  int id;
  char name[32];
}data[] ={{101, "John"},
          {102, "Doe"},
          {103, "Peter"},
          {104, "Mary"},
          {-1, NULL}
        };
```

Modify Program 15.2 using a loop to add nodes to the list using the function addTeacher(). The information for each node shall come from an element of `data`. Use the sentinel value −1 of `data[i].id` to terminate the loop.

2. Given that `head` points to the beginning of the singly linked list, `tail` points to the last node of the list, `current` points to the current node, `next` points to the current's next node, and `tmp` points to any node, write statements that would do each of the following. Assume that the pointer `nd` points to a new node that's ready to be linked to the list.

   a. Insert the new node at the end of the list and set `current` to point to it.
   b. Move the last node to the head. Assume that `current` points to the second to the last node.
   c. Assume the node tt tmp follows the node tt current. Insert the new node after `current` and before `tmp`.

3. Modify Program 15.3 and 15.8 to add the following functions:

   a. `void insertAfter(Node *head, Node nd, Node np);`
   to insert the node `np` after the node `nd`.
   b. `void insertBefore(Node *head, Node nd, Node np);`
   to insert the node `np` before the node `nd`.
   c. `void insertBetween(Node *head, Node nd, Node nq, Node np);`
   to insert the node `np` between the node `nd` and the node `nq`.

4. In the following C program, the linked list `head` is made by calling the function `makeList(5)` with the number of elements in the list passed as an argument. The field *i* in the structure em struct tag in each element is stored with a sequential numerical number. The value for the field *i* in the first element of the list is 1. Write a function called `addElement(int n)` that will return the sum of the values of the first *n* elements in the list. The number *n* is passed from the argument of the function.

```
#include<stdlib.h>
#include<stdio.h>
struct tag {
    int i;
    struct tag *next;
} *head, *tmp1, *tmp2;

int main() {
  int sum;
```

```
    makeList(5);                /* make a list with 5 elements */
    sum = addElement(4);        /* add values of the first 4 elements
                                   in the list */

    printf("sum = %d\n", sum);
    return 0;
}

int makeList(int n) {
    int i;
    for (i=1; i<=n; i++) {
        tmp1 = (struct tag * )malloc(sizeof(struct tag));
        if(tmp1 == NULL)
            return -1;
        tmp1->next = NULL;
        tmp1->i = i;
        if(head == NULL){ /* first time */
            head = tmp1;
            tmp2 = tmp1;
        }
        else {
            tmp2->next = tmp1;
            tmp2 = tmp1;
        }
    }
    return 0;
}

int addElement(int n) {
```

5. Write a program that reads 10 floating-point numbers from the standard input, stores them in a linked list, and then searches the list for the largest number and displays it.
6. Write a program with a function

```
int insertElement(struct NodeList *head, int number);
```

that inserts an integer into its correct position in an ordered linked list. Make an ordered linked list with the numbers 6, 14, 28, 31, 46, and 52 in an array. Test the program by inserting the numbers 5, 18, 40, and 58 in an array, one at a time.
7. Write a program with the function

```
int deleteElement(struct ListNode *head, int number);
```

that deletes a node with the specified integral value in an ordered list with an integer in each node described in the previous problem. Test the program by deleting elements with integers 6, 31, and 52.
8. Write a function with two arguments of pointer type, each pointing to a linked list. The function concatenates the two lists by attaching the second list to the first.
9. For Program 15.4, write the function

```
int printId(Node head, int id);
```

to print out the information for a student with identification number `id` in the list. Modify Program 15.4 to call this function by

```
printId(head, 103);
```

after four nodes are added to the list.

10. Solve Exercise 6 in Chapter 13 without using the input/output redirection. Use a linked list to keep the data for each product in a record line in the file `sale.dat`.
11. Extend Programs 15.21, 14.9, and 15.22 by adding the following functions:
    a. `int gpa_belowGPA(StudentNode head, double gpa);`
    to display students with a GPA below the specified value in its second argument. The function returns the number of students with a GPA below the specified value.
    b. `double gpa_stdDeviation(StudentNode head);`
    to return the standard deviation of GPAs.
    c. `void gpa_sortGPAascending(StudentNode head);`
    to sort students with GPAs in ascending order.
    d. `void gpa_sortAge(StudentNode head);`
    to sort students in descending age.
    e. `void gpa_sortName(StudentNode head);`
    to sort students in alphebatical order based on the first letter of their name.
12. Modify Program 15.4 to include the header file `dlist.h` described in section 15.3, which invokes functions in the file `dlistlib.c` for the doubly linked list.
13. Modify Program 11.2 in Chapter 11 to read a string. Use a doubly linked list to store characters of the string. Print the string reversely.
14. Add the Ch shebang to Program 15.1 and run the script in your login shell in Unix.
15. Add the Ch shebang to Program 15.1, change the program name to `selfret.ch`, and run the script command `selfref` in a MS-DOS shell in Windows.
16. Modify Programs 10.12 and 10.13 in Chapter 10 to create the static and shared statistical libraries `libstat.a` and `libstat.so` in Unix, and the static and dynamic link libraries `stats.lib` and `stat.lib` and `stat.dll` in Windows, respectively. (a) Compile and link Program 10.14 to use the static library and Program 10.9 to use the dynamic library. (b) Write a Ch script `makestat` and make files to keep track of the dependency of files and to compile and link programs across different platforms.
17. Modify the programs `list.h` and `listlib.c` to create a shared singly linked list library `liblist.so` in Unix and a DLL with the files `list.lib` and `list.dll` in Windows. (a) Compile and link Program 15.4 to use the shared library in Unix and DLL in Windows. (b) Write a Ch script called `makelist` and make files to keep track of the dependency of files and to compile and link programs across different platforms.
18. Modify the programs `dlist.h` and `dlistlib.c` described in section 15.3 to create a shared doubly linked list library `libdlist.so` in Unix and a DLL with the files `dlist.lib` and `dlist.dll` in Windows. (a) Compile and link Program 15.13 to use the shared library in Unix and DLL in Windows. (b) Write a Ch script called `makedlist` and make files to keep track of the dependency of files and to compile and link programs across different platforms.
19. Modify Exercise 28 in Chapter 14 to process the database of a library of books in a file `book.dat` using a linked list.

CHAPTER 16

‡Scientific Computing in the Entire Real Domain in C99

In this chapter, the scientific computing aspect of C will be addressed. The IEEE 754 standard for binary floating-point arithmetic is a significant milestone on the road to consistent floating-point arithmetic with respect to real numbers. To make the power of the IEEE 754 standard easily available to the programmer, the floating-point numbers of Inf, $-$Inf, and NaN, referred to as *metanumbers*, are introduced in C99. (The symbol NaN stands for Not-a-Number.) These metanumbers are transparent to the programmer. Signed zeros $+0.0$ and -0.0 in C99 behave like correctly signed infinitesimal quantities 0_+ and 0_-, whereas symbols Inf and $-$Inf correspond to mathematical infinities ∞ and $-\infty$, respectively. The commonly used mathematical functions defined in the header file **tgmath.h** are generic, as described in section 6.5 in Chapter 6. They can handle different data types of the arguments gracefully. In this chapter, the representation of floating-point numbers in the IEEE 754 standard is presented first. The floating-point arithmetic and mathematical functions using metanumbers are then described.

16.1 IEEE Floating-Point Numbers and Metanumbers

There are three data types available to represent floating-point numbers in C: **float**, **double**, and **long double** as described in section 3.9 in Chapter 3. The most common implementation of floating-point arithmetic is based upon the IEEE 754 standard. In this standard, a floating-point number is represented in the form of

$$(-1)^{sign} 2^{exponent-bias} 1.f \tag{16.1}$$

where $1.f$ is the significand. The 1 is implicit and f represents the fractional bits of the normalized number. This normalized floating-point number contains a “hidden” bit, ‘1’. Therefore, this representation has one more bit of precision than would otherwise be the case.

16.1.1 The float Data Representation

The float data type has 32 bits of memory for storage. The result of a float data is formulated as

$$(-1)^{sign} 2^{exponent-127} 1.f \tag{16.2}$$

and illustrated in Figure 16.1. Bit 31 is a sign bit; it is 1 for negative numbers. Bits 23 to 30 are the *exponent* bits. The exponent is offset by 127 to allow a range of numbers spanning 1. Cases when all the exponent bits are 0s and all the exponent bits are 1s are reserved for the metanumbers Inf, $-$Inf, and NaN, as shown in Table 16.1. Bits 0 to 22 define the fractional component of the significand. The leading integer of the normalized significand is always 1, so it doesn’t need to be stored. In binary fractions, the most significant bit

31	30 29 28 27 26 25 24 23	22 21 20 19 18 17 16 15 14 13 12 11 10 9 8 7 6 5 4 3 2 1 0
sign bit	exponent	fraction

Figure 16.1: 32-bit representation of the float data type.

Table 16.1 Hexadecimal representations of selected real numbers.

Value	Float	Double
0.0	00000000	0000000000000000
−0.0	80000000	8000000000000000
1.0	3F800000	3FF0000000000000
−1.0	BF800000	BFF0000000000000
2.0	40000000	4000000000000000
−2.0	C0000000	C000000000000000
3.0	40400000	4008000000000000
−3.0	C0400000	C008000000000000
Inf	7F800000	7FF0000000000000
−Inf	FF800000	FFF0000000000000
NaN	7FFFFFFF	7FFFFFFFFFFFFFFF
FLT_MAX	7F7FFFFF	
DBL_MAX		7FEFFFFFFFFFFFFF
FLT_MIN	007FFFFF	
DBL_MIN		000FFFFFFFFFFFFF
FLT_MINIMUM	00000001	
DBL_MINIMUM		0000000000000001

represents 0.5, the next bits representing 0.25, 0.125, etc. Table 16.1. shows the hexadecimal representation of some float numbers.

For example, according to formula (16.2), the float numbers 1.0 and −2.0, can be obtained by $(-1)^0 2^{127-127} 1.0 = 1.0$ and $(-1)^1 2^{128-127} 1.0 = 2.0$, as shown in Figures 16.2 and 16.3, respectively. Remember that the fraction of the normalized significand is stored in a binary fraction. The float number 3.0 can be calculated by $(-1)^0 2^{128-127}(1.1)_2 = 2*(1.1)_2 = 2*(1.5)_{10} = (3.0)_{10}$, as shown in Figure 16.4, where

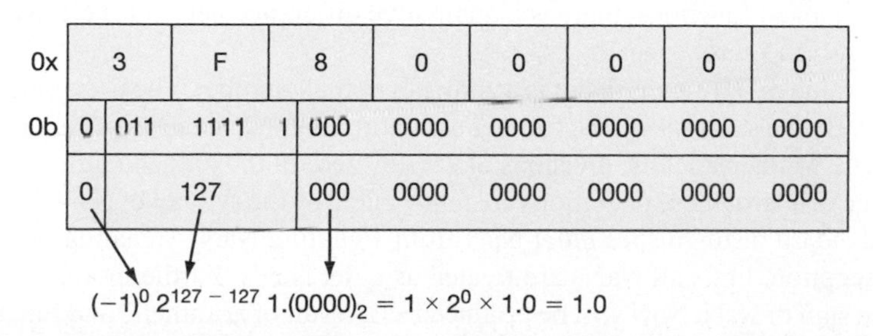

Figure 16.2: The representation of the floating-point number 1.0 in type float.

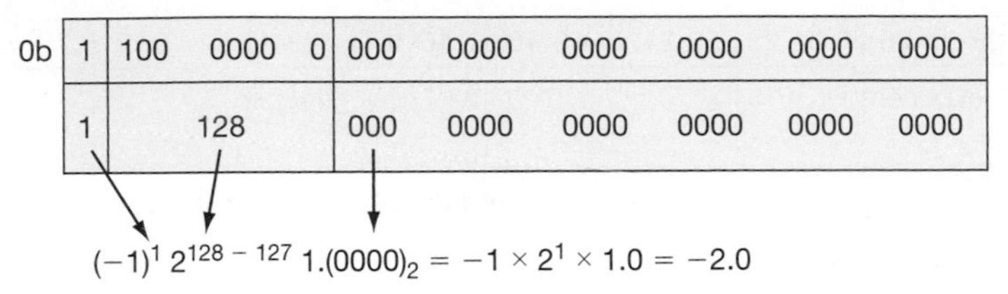

Figure 16.3: The representation of the floating-point number −2.0 in type float.

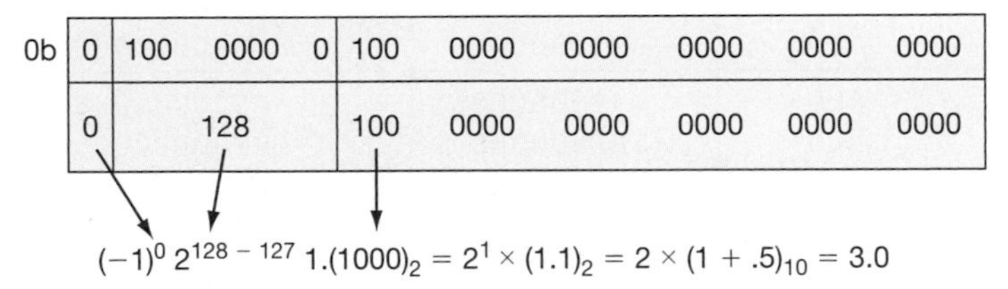

Figure 16.4: The representation of the floating-point number 3.0 in type float.

the subscripts indicate the base of the floating-point number. Note that the IEEE 754 standard distinguishes +0.0 from −0.0 for floating-point numbers.

The macro **FLT_MAX** is defined as the maximum representable finite floating-point number in the float data type in the C standard header file **float.h**. If a number is greater than **FLT_MAX**, it is called an *overflow*. Any number greater than **FLT_MAX** has all eight exponent bits set to 1s. This shall be represented by the metanumber Inf, which corresponds to the mathematical infinity symbol ∞. This is the result of many operations, such as division of a finite number by zero, although an inexact exception may be raised in an IEEE machine. Any number less than −**FLT_MAX** shall be represented by the metanumber −Inf, which corresponds to the mathematical negative infinity symbol $-\infty$.

The value of the parameter **FLT_MIN** is defined in the C standard library header file **float.h** as a minimum normalized positive floating-point float number. If a number is less than **FLT_MIN**, it is called an *underflow*. The IEEE 754 standard provides a *gradual underflow*. When a number is too small for a normalized representation, leading zeros are placed in the significand to produce a denormalized representation. *A denormalized number* is a nonzero number that is not normalized and whose exponent is the minimum exponent for the storage type. In Ch, the maximum representable positive denormalized float is defined as **FLT_MINIMUM**, as shown in Table 16.1. There is only one unit in the last place for **FLT_MINIMUM**, so it is commonly referred to as *ulp*. Almost all floating-point implementations substitute the value zero for a value that is smaller than **FLT_MINIMUM** for IEEE machines, and **FLT_MIN** for non-IEEE machines. However, in arithmetic operations and mathematical functions, there is a qualitative difference between **FLT_MINIMUM**, which is smaller than **FLT_MIN**, and zero.

In this book, the value of 0.0 means that it is a zero, not a small number. The C expressions of 0., 0.00, and .0 are the same as 0.0. By the same token, the following floating-point constant expressions −0.0, −0., −0.00, and −.0 are equivalent. Mathematically, divisions of zero by zero of 0.0/0.0 and infinity by infinity of ∞/∞ are indeterminate. The results of these operations are represented by the symbol of NaN. It should be mentioned that the IEEE 754 standard distinguishes *quiet* NaN from *signaling* NaN. Signaling NaN should generate a signal or raise an exception. In C, all NaNs are treated as quiet NaNs. Furthermore, the IEEE 754 standard does not interpret the sign of NaN. NaN will be produced as a result of arithmetic and functions in C, although it can be created by manipulating the bit pattern of the memory location of a float variable. The expression

−NaN is interpreted as NaN in C. The metanumbers are treated just as regular floating-point numbers. The internal hexadecimal representations of the metanumbers for the float type are also given in Table 16.1.

16.1.2 The double Data Representation

The double data type uses 64 bits as its storage. The result of the double data is formulated as

$$(-1)^{sign} 2^{exponent-1023} 1.f \tag{16.3}$$

Bit 63 is a sign bit; it is 1 if the number is negative. The 11-bit exponent of bits 52 to 62 is biased by 1023; values of all 0s and all 1s are reserved for metanumbers. Bits 0 to 51 are fractional components of normalized significand. Like float, the integral value 1 of the normalized significand is hidden. The hexadecimal representation of some typical double numbers are also given in Table 16.1. Note that the width and bias values of the exponent of double is different from those of float. Therefore, a float cannot be converted into a double just by padding zeros in its fraction. On the other hand, when double data is cast into a float, the result cannot be obtained just by ignoring the values in bits 0 to 31. Note that there is no external distinction between float Inf and double Inf, although their internal representations differ. This is also true for the metanumbers −Inf and NaN. Similar to float, the macros **DBL_MAX** and **DBL_MIN** are defined in the header file **float.h** for the maximum and minimum values in double type, respectively. In Ch, the macro **DBL_MINIMUM** is also defined for the maximum representable positive denormalized value in double type. The internal memory representations of these special finite double floating-point numbers are also given in Table 16.1. Note that due to the finite precision of the floating-point number representation, the exact values of irrational numbers such as π are not representable in a computer system whether they are represented in float, double, or long double type.

16.2 Operators and Expressions with Metanumbers

In Chapter 4, operators and expressions with integral types and regular real numbers have been described. In this section, the arithmetic and relational operators with metanumbers will be presented. The operation rules for regular real numbers and metanumbers are given in Tables 16.2 to 16.12. In Tables 16.2 to 16.12, x, x1, and x2 are regular positive normalized floating-point numbers in float or double; the metanumbers Inf, −Inf, and NaN are constants or the values of float or double variables. By default, constant metanumbers are float constants.

16.2.1 Arithmetic Operations

For the negation operation shown in Table 16.2, the data type of the result is the same as the data type of the operand, and a real number will change its sign by the negation operation. There is no −NaN in C. The leading plus sign '+', a unary plus operator, in an expression such as $+57864 - x$ will be ignored. It should be pointed out that the negation of a positive integer zero is still a positive zero. Based on binary two's complement

Table 16.2 Negation results.

	Negation −						
Operand	−Inf	−x1	−0.0	0.0	x2	Inf	NaN
Result	Inf	x1	0.0	−0.0	−x2	−Inf	NaN

Table 16.3 **Addition results.**

Addition (+)							
Left operand	**Right operand**						
	−Inf	−x1	−0.0	0.0	x2	Inf	NaN
Inf	NaN	Inf	Inf	Inf	Inf	Inf	NaN
y2	−Inf	y2−x1	y2	y2	y2+x2	Inf	NaN
0.0	−Inf	−x1	0.0	0.0	x2	Inf	NaN
−0.0	−Inf	−x1	−0.0	0.0	x2	Inf	NaN
−y1	−Inf	−y1−x1	−y1	−y1	−y1+x2	Inf	NaN
−Inf	−Inf	−Inf	−Inf	−Inf	−Inf	NaN	NaN
NaN	NaN	NaN	NaN	NaN	NaN	NaN	NaN

Table 16.4 **Subtraction results.**

Subtraction (−)							
Left operand	**Right operand**						
	−Inf	−x1	−0.0	0.0	x2	Inf	NaN
Inf	Inf	Inf	Inf	Inf	Inf	NaN	NaN
y2	Inf	y2+x1	y2	y2	y2−x2	−Inf	NaN
0.0	Inf	x1	0.0	0.0	−x2	−Inf	NaN
−0.0	Inf	x1	0.0	−0.0	−x2	−Inf	NaN
−y1	Inf	−y1+x1	−y1	−y1	−y1−x2	−Inf	NaN
−Inf	NaN	−Inf	−Inf	−Inf	−Inf	−Inf	NaN
NaN	NaN	NaN	NaN	NaN	NaN	NaN	NaN

Table 16.5 **Multiplication results.**

Multiplication (*)							
Left operand	**Right operand**						
	−Inf	−x1	−0.0	0.0	x2	Inf	NaN
Inf	−Inf	−Inf	NaN	NaN	Inf	Inf	NaN
y2	−Inf	−y2*x1	−0.0	0.0	y2*x2	Inf	NaN
0.0	NaN	−0.0	−0.0	0.0	0.0	NaN	NaN
−0.0	NaN	0.0	0.0	−0.0	−0.0	NaN	NaN
−y1	Inf	y1*x1	0.0	−0.0	−y1*x2	−Inf	NaN
−Inf	Inf	Inf	NaN	NaN	−Inf	−Inf	NaN
NaN	NaN	NaN	NaN	NaN	NaN	NaN	NaN

Table 16.6 Division results.

Division (/)							
Left operand	**Right operand**						
	−Inf	−x1	−0.0	0.0	x2	Inf	NaN
Inf	NaN	−Inf	NaN	NaN	Inf	NaN	NaN
y2	−0.0	−y2/x1	−Inf	Inf	y2/x2	0.0	NaN
0.0	−0.0	−0.0	NaN	NaN	0.0	0.0	NaN
−0.0	0.0	0.0	NaN	NaN	−0.0	−0.0	NaN
−y1	0.0	y1/x1	Inf	−Inf	−y1/x2	−0.0	NaN
−Inf	NaN	Inf	Inf	−Inf	−Inf	NaN	NaN
NaN	NaN	NaN	NaN	NaN	NaN	NaN	NaN

Table 16.7 Less than comparison results.

Less than comparison (<)							
Left operand	**Right operand**						
	−Inf	−x1	−0.0	0.0	x2	Inf	NaN
Inf	0	0	0	0	0	0	0
y2	0	0	0	0	y2 < x2	1	0
0.0	0	0	0	0	1	1	0
−0.0	0	0	0	0	1	1	0
−y1	0	−y1 < −x1	1	1	1	1	0
−Inf	0	1	1	1	1	1	0
NaN	0	0	0	0	0	0	0

Table 16.8 Less than or equal to comparison results.

Less than or equal to comparison (<=)							
Left operand	**Right operand**						
	−Inf	−x1	−0.0	0.0	x2	Inf	NaN
Inf	0	0	0	0	0	1	0
y2	0	0	0	0	y2 <= x2	1	0
0.0	0	0	1	1	1	1	0
−0.0	0	0	1	1	1	1	0
−y1	0	−y1 <= −x1	1	1	1	1	0
−Inf	1	1	1	1	1	1	0
NaN	0	0	0	0	0	0	0

Table 16.9 Equal comparison results.

Equal comparison (==)							
Left operand	**Right operand**						
	−Inf	−x1	−0.0	0.0	x2	Inf	NaN
Inf	0	0	0	0	0	1	0
y2	0	0	0	0	y2 == x2	0	0
0.0	0	0	1	1	0	0	0
−0.0	0	0	1	1	0	0	0
−y1	0	−y1 == −x1	0	0	0	0	0
−Inf	1	0	0	0	0	0	0
NaN	0	0	0	0	0	0	0

Table 16.10 Greater than or equal to comparison results.

Greater than or equal to comparison (>=)							
Left operand	**Right operand**						
	−Inf	−x1	−0.0	0.0	x2	Inf	NaN
Inf	1	1	1	1	1	1	0
y2	1	1	1	1	y2 >= x2	0	0
0.0	1	1	1	1	0	0	0
−0.0	1	1	1	1	0	0	0
−y1	1	−y1 >= −x1	0	0	0	0	0
−Inf	1	0	0	0	0	0	0
NaN	0	0	0	0	0	0	0

Table 16.11 Greater than comparison results.

Greater than comparison (>)							
Left operand	**Right operand**						
	−Inf	−x1	−0.0	0.0	x2	Inf	NaN
Inf	1	1	1	1	1	0	0
y2	1	1	1	1	y2 > x2	0	0
0.0	1	1	0	0	0	0	0
−0.0	1	1	0	0	0	0	0
−y1	1	−y1 > −x1	0	0	0	0	0
−Inf	0	0	0	0	0	0	0
NaN	0	0	0	0	0	0	0

Table 16.12 Not equal comparison results.

Not equal comparison (!=)							
Left operand	**Right operand**						
	−Inf	−x1	−0.0	0.0	x2	Inf	NaN
Inf	1	1	1	1	1	0	0
y2	1	1	1	1	y2 != x2	1	0
0.0	1	1	0	0	1	1	0
−0.0	1	1	0	0	1	1	0
−y1	1	−y1 != −x1	1	1	1	1	0
−Inf	0	1	1	1	1	1	0
NaN	0	0	0	0	0	0	0

representation of negative integer numbers discussed previously, the metanumbers Inf and NaN cannot be represented in the type int.

For the addition, subtraction, multiplication, and division operations shown in Tables 16.3 to 16.6, the resultant data type will be type double if any one of two operands is double; otherwise, the result is float. Mathematically indeterminate expressions, such as $\infty - \infty$, $\infty * 0.0$, ∞/∞, and $0.0/0.0$, will result in NaNs. The values of ± 0.0 play important roles in the multiplication and division operations. For example, a finite positive value of x2 divided by 0.0 results in a positive infinity $+\infty$, whereas division by −0.0 will create a negative infinity $-\infty$. If any one of the operands of binary arithmetic operations is NaN, the result is NaN.

16.2.2 Relational Operations

For relational operations given in Tables 16.7 to 16.12, the result is always an integer with a logic value of 1 or 0 corresponding to the macros **true** or **false** defined in the header file **stdbool.h**. According to the IEEE 754 standard, there is a distinction between +0.0 and −0.0 for floating-point numbers. In C, the value of 0.0 means that the value approaches zero from positive numbers along the real line, and it is the origin of the real line. The value of −0.0 means that the value approaches zero from negative numbers along the real line, and it is infinitely smaller than 0.0 in many cases. Signed zeros +0.0 and −0.0 in a C program behave like correctly signed infinitesimal quantities 0_+ and 0_-, respectively. Although there is a distinction between −0.0 and 0.0 for floating-point numbers in many operations, according to the IEEE 754 standard, the comparison shall ignore the sign of zeros, so −0.0 equals 0.0 in relational operations. Functions such as **signbit**(x) and **copysign**(x, y) can be used to handle signs of expressions. The value of −0.0 could be regarded differently from 0.0 for comparison operations in C. Zero is unsigned in comparison operations. The equality for metanumbers has different implications in C. Two identical metanumbers Inf are considered to be equal to each other. Comparing a NaN with any number, including Inf and NaN, is false. This is just for the convenience of programming because, mathematically, the infinity of ∞ and not-a-number of NaN are undefined values that cannot be compared with each other. Metanumbers of Inf, −Inf, and NaN in C are treated as regular floating-point numbers consistently in arithmetic, relational, and logic operations.

16.2.3 Logical Operators

Because there are only two values (either **true** or **false**) for logic operations, the values of ±0.0 are treated as logic **false**, while the metanumbers −Inf, Inf, and NaN are considered as logic **true**. For example, evaluations of !(−0.0) and !NaN will get the values of 1 and 0, respectively.

16.3 Type Generic Mathematical Functions with Metanumbers

In this section, the generic mathematical functions of C will be discussed. The input and output of the functions involving the metanumbers will be highlighted. The results of the mathematical functions involving metanumbers are given in Tables 16.13 to 16.16. In Tables 16.13 to 16.16, unless indicated otherwise, x, x_1, x_2 are real numbers with $0 < x, x_1, x_2 < \infty$; and k is an integral value. The value of `pi` is the finite representation of the irrational number π in floating-point numbers. The returned data of a function is float or double, depending on the data type of the input arguments. In Table 16.13, if the order of the data type `x` is less than or equal to float, the returned data type is float. The returned data type is double if `x` is of double type. If the argument `x` of a function in Table 16.13 is NaN, the function will return NaN. In Tables 16.14 to 16.16, the returned data type will be the same as the higher-order data type of two input arguments if any of two arguments is float or double. Otherwise, the float is the default returned data type.

Functions defined in this section will return float or double, except for the functions **abs**() and **pow**(). If the argument of the function **abs**() is an integral value, the returned data type is int. If the arguments of the function **pow**() are integral values, the returned data type is double. For example, **pow**(2,16) will return the value 65536 of double type.

The absolute function **abs**(x) will compute the absolute value of an integer or a floating-point number. The absolute value of a negative infinity $-\infty$ is a positive infinity ∞. The function **labs**() is similar to the function **abs**(), except that its argument and return value is of type long. For example,

```
> abs(-3.0)
3.0
> labs(-15L)
15
```

The **sqrt**(x) function computes the nonnegative square root of `x`. If `x` is negative, the result is NaN, except that **sqrt**(−0.0) = −0.0 according to the IEEE 754 standard. The square root of infinity, **sqrt**(∞), is infinity. The symbols NaN and Inf are predefined in Ch and can be used readily. For example,

```
> sqrt(NaN)
nan
> sqrt(Inf)
inf
```

The **exp**(x) function computes the exponential function of `x`. The following results hold: $e^{-\infty} = 0.0$; $e^{\infty} = \infty$; $e^{\pm 0.0} = 1.0$.

The **log**(x) function computes the natural logarithm of `x`. If `x` is negative, the result is NaN. The value of −0.0 is considered equal to 0.0 in this case. The following results hold: **log**(±0.0) = $-\infty$; **log**(∞) = ∞. The `log10`(x) function computes the base-10 logarithm of `x`. If `x` is negative, the result is a NaN. Like

Table 16.13 Results of real functions for ± 0.0, $\pm\infty$, and NaN.

Function	x value and results						
	−Inf	−x1	−0.0	0.0	x2	Inf	NaN
abs(x)	Inf	x_1	0.0	0.0	x_2	Inf	NaN
sqrt(x)	NaN	NaN	−0.0	0.0	sqrt(x)	Inf	NaN
exp(x)	0.0	e^{-x_1}	1.0	1.0	e^{x_2}	Inf	NaN
log(x)	NaN	NaN	−Inf	−Inf	$\log(x_2)$	Inf	NaN
log10(x)	NaN	NaN	−Inf	−Inf	$\log_{10}(x_2)$	Inf	NaN
sin(x)	NaN	$-\sin(x_1)$	−0.0	0.0	$\sin(x_2)$	NaN	NaN
cos(x)	NaN	$\cos(x_1)$	1.0	1.0	$\cos(x_2)$	NaN	NaN
tan(x)	NaN	$-\tan(x_1)$	−0.0	0.0	$\tan(x_2)$	NaN	NaN
	Note: $\tan(\pm\pi/2 + 2 * k * \pi) = \pm$Inf						
asin(x)	NaN	$-\text{asin}(x_1)$	−0.0	0.0	$\text{asin}(x_2)$	NaN	NaN
	Note: asin(x) = NaN, for $\lvert x\rvert > 1.0$						
acos(x)	NaN	$\text{acos}(x_1)$	pi/2	pi/2	$\text{acos}(x_2)$	NaN	NaN
	Note: acos(x) = NaN, for $\lvert x\rvert > 1.0$						
atan(x)	−pi/2	$-\text{atan}(x_1)$	−0.0	0.0	$\text{atan}(x_2)$	pi/2	NaN
sinh(x)	−Inf	$-\sinh(x_1)$	−0.0	0.0	$\sinh(x_2)$	Inf	NaN
cosh(x)	Inf	$\cosh(x_1)$	1.0	1.0	$\cosh(x_2)$	Inf	NaN
tanh(x)	−1.0	$-\tanh(x_1)$	−0.0	0.0	$\tanh(x_2)$	1.0	NaN
asinh(x)	−Inf	$-\text{asinh}(x_1)$	−0.0	0.0	$\text{asinh}(x_2)$	Inf	NaN
acosh(x)	NaN	NaN	NaN	NaN	$\text{acosh}(x_2)$	Inf	NaN
	Note: acosh(x) = NaN, for $x < 1.0$; acosh(1.0) = 0.0						
atanh(x)	NaN	$-\text{atanh}(x_1)$	−0.0	0.0	$\text{atanh}(x_2)$	NaN	NaN
	Note: atanh(x) = NaN, for $\lvert x\rvert > 1.0$; atanh(±1.0) = ±Inf						
ceil(x)	−Inf	$\text{ceil}(-x_1)$	−0.0	0.0	$\text{ceil}(x_2)$	Inf	NaN
floor(x)	−Inf	$\text{floor}(-x_1)$	−0.0	0.0	$\text{floor}(x_2)$	Inf	NaN
ldexp(x, k)	−Inf	$\text{ldexp}(-x_1, k)$	−0.0	0.0	$\text{ldexp}(x_2, k)$	Inf	NaN
modf(x, &y)	−0.0	$\text{modf}(-x_1, \&y)$	−0.0	0.0	$\text{modf}(x_2, \&y)$	0.0	NaN
y	−Inf	y	−0.0	0.0	y	Inf	NaN
frexp(x, &k)	−Inf	$\text{frexp}(-x_1, \&k)$	−0.0	0.0	$\text{frexp}(x_2, \&k)$	Inf	NaN
k	0	k	0	0	k	0	0

Table 16.14 **Results of the function pow(y, x) for ±0.0, ±∞, and NaN.**

pow(y, x)											
y value	x value										
	−Inf	−x1	$-2k-1$	−2k	−0.0	0.0	2k	$2k+1$	x2	Inf	NaN
Inf	0.0	0.0	0.0	0.0	1.0	1.0	Inf	Inf	Inf	Inf	NaN
y2 > 1	0.0	$y_2^{-x_1}$	y_2^{-2k-1}	y_2^{-2k}	1.0	1.0	y_2^{2k}	y_2^{2k+1}	$y_2^{x_2}$	Inf	NaN
1.0	NaN	1.0	1.0	1.0	1.0	1.0	1.0	1.0	1.0	NaN	NaN
0 < y2 < 1	Inf	$y_2^{-x_1}$	y_2^{-2k-1}	y_2^{-2k}	1.0	1.0	y_2^{2k}	y_2^{2k+1}	$y_2^{x_2}$	0.0	NaN
0.0	Inf	Inf	Inf	Inf	1.0	1.0	0.0	0.0	0.0	0.0	NaN
−0.0	Inf	Inf	−Inf	Inf	1.0	1.0	0.0	−0.0	0.0	0.0	NaN
−y1	NaN	NaN	$-y_1^{-2k-1}$	y_1^{-2k}	1.0	1.0	y_1^{2k}	$-y_1^{2k+1}$	NaN	NaN	NaN
−Inf	NaN	NaN	−0.0	0.0	1.0	1.0	Inf	−Inf	NaN	NaN	NaN
NaN	NaN	NaN	NaN	NaN	NaN	NaN	NaN	NaN	NaN	NaN	NaN

Table 16.15 **Results of the function atan2(y, x) for ±0.0, ±∞, and NaN.**

atan2(y, x)							
y value	x value						
	−Inf	−x1	−0.0	0.0	x2	Inf	NaN
Inf	3*pi/4	pi/2	pi/2	pi/2	pi/2	pi/4	NaN
y2	pi	$\text{atan2}(y_2, -x_1)$	pi/2	pi/2	$\text{atan2}(y_2, x_2)$	0.0	NaN
0.0	pi	pi	pi	0.0	0.0	0.0	NaN
−0.0	−pi	−pi	−3*pi/4	−pi/2	−0.0	−0.0	NaN
−y1	−pi	$\text{atan2}(-y_1, -x_1)$	−pi/2	−pi/2	$\text{atan2}(-y_1, x_2)$	−0.0	NaN
−Inf	−3*pi/4	−pi/2	−pi/2	−pi/2	−pi/2	−pi/4	NaN
NaN	NaN	NaN	NaN	NaN	NaN	NaN	NaN

the function **log**(), the value of −0.0 is considered equal to 0.0. The following results hold: **log10**(±0.0) = −∞; **log10**(∞) = ∞.

The trigonometric functions **sin**(x), **cos**(x), and **tan**(x) compute sine, cosine, and tangent of x measured in radians, respectively. The sine and tangent are odd functions so that **sin**(±0.0) = ±0.0 and **tan**(±0.0) = ±0.0. The cosine is an even function so that **cos**(±0.0) = 1.0. When the value of the argument is positive or negative infinity, all these functions return NaNs. For example, the sine of NaN and Inf are as follows:

```
> sin(NaN)
nan
> sin(Inf)
nan
```

Table 16.16 Results of the function fmod(y, x) for ± 0.0, $\pm\infty$, and NaN.

fmod(y, x)							
y value	**x value**						
	−Inf	−x1	−0.0	0.0	x2	Inf	NaN
Inf	NaN	NaN	NaN	NaN	NaN	NaN	NaN
y2	y_2	fmod($y_2, -x_1$)	NaN	NaN	fmod(y_2, x_2)	y_2	NaN
0.0	0.0	0.0	NaN	NaN	0.0	0.0	NaN
−0.0	−0.0	−0.0	NaN	NaN	−0.0	−0.0	NaN
−y1	y_1	fmod($-y_1, -x_1$)	NaN	NaN	fmod($-y_1, x_2$)	$-y_1$	NaN
−Inf	NaN	NaN	NaN	NaN	NaN	NaN	NaN
NaN	NaN	NaN	NaN	NaN	NaN	NaN	NaN

Theoretically, it is true that **tan**$(\pm\pi/2 + 2 * k * \pi) = \pm\infty$. But, in practice, because the irrational number π cannot be represented exactly in float or double data, the **tan**(x) function will never return infinities of $\pm\infty$. The function **tan**() is not continuous at $\pi/2$, **tan**$(\pi/2 - \varepsilon) = \infty$, and **tan**$(\pi/2 + \varepsilon) = -\infty$, where ε is a very small number. Due to the finite precision and round-off errors of floating-point numbers, one may get a wrong result near the value of $\pi/2$.

The properties of odd functions of sine and tangent are reflected in their inverse functions **asin**(x) and **atan**(x). The **asin**(x) function computes the principal value of the arc sine of x. When the value of x is in the range of [−1.0, 1.0], the **asin**(x) function returns the value in the range of $[-\pi/2, \pi/2]$ radians. When x is outside the range of [−1.0, 1.0], the arc sine is undefined and **asin**(x) returns NaN. The range of the input value for the even function **acos**(x) of arc cosine is the same as that of **asin**(x). The **acos**(x) function computes the principal value of the arc cosine of x. The range of the principal value of the arc cosine is $[0.0, \pi]$ radians. The **atan**(x) function computes the principal value of the arc tangent of x. The **atan**(x) function returns the value in the range of $[-\pi/2, \pi/2]$ radians. The following results hold: **atan**$(\pm\infty) = \pm\pi/2$.

Like the trigonometric functions **sin**(x) and **tan**(x), the hyperbolic functions **sinh**(x) and **tanh**(x) are odd functions. The **sinh**(x) and **tanh**(x) functions compute the hyperbolic sine and tangent of x, respectively. The even function **cosh**(x) computes the hyperbolic cosine of x. The following results hold: **sinh**$(\pm 0.0) = \pm 0.0$; **cosh**$(\pm 0.0) = 1.0$; **tanh**$(\pm 0.0) = \pm 0.0$; **sinh**$(\pm\infty) = \pm\infty$; **cosh**$(\pm\infty) = \infty$; **tanh**$(\pm\infty) = \pm 1.0$;

The inverse hyperbolic sine, cosine, and tangent are defined as **asinh**(x), **acosh**(x), and **atanh**(x), respectively. For the **acosh**(x) function, if the argument is less than 1.0, it is undefined and **acosh**(x) returns NaN. The function call **acosh**(1.0) returns a positive zero. The valid domain for the function **atanh**(x) is [−1.0, 1.0]. The following results hold: **asinh**$(\pm 0.0) = \pm 0.0$; **asinh**$(\pm\infty) = \pm\infty$; **acosh**$(\infty) = \infty$; **atanh**$(\pm 0.0) = \pm 0.0$; **atanh**$(\pm 1.0) = \pm\infty$.

The **ceil**(x) function computes the smallest integral value that is not less than the value of x. The counterpart of **ceil**(x) is the function **floor**(x), which computes the largest integral value that is not greater than the value of x. The following results hold: **ceil**$(\pm 0.0) = \pm 0.0$; **floor**$(\pm 0.0) = \pm 0.0$; **ceil**$(\pm\infty) = \pm\infty$; **floor**$(\pm\infty) = \pm\infty$.

The **ldexp**(x, k) function multiplies the value of the floating-point number x with the value of 2 raised to the power of k. The returned value of $x * 2^k$ keeps the sign of x.

The functions **modf**(x, xptr) and **frexp**(x, iptr) have two arguments. The first argument is the input data and the second argument is a pointer that will store the resulted integral part of the function call. The **modf**(x, xptr) function breaks the argument x into integral and fractional parts, each of which has the same sign as the argument. The **modf**() function returns the fractional part and the integral part is stored to the memory pointed to by the second argument. The basic data types of two arguments must be the same. For example, if the first argument `x` is type float, the second argument `xptr` must be a pointer to float. If the first argument is a metanumber, the integral part will equal the metanumber, whereas the fractional part becomes zero with the sign of the first argument except for NaN. For example,

```
> double d
> modf(12.34, &d)
0.3400                    // return value is fraction part
> d
d = 13.0000               // stores integer part in d
```

The **frexp**(x, iptr) function breaks a floating-point number into a normalized fraction and an integral power of 2 in the form of $x * 2^k$. The **frexp**(x, iptr) function returns the normalized fraction and the integral part is stored to the memory pointed to by the second argument, which is a pointer to int. For example,

```
> int i
> frexp(12.34, &i)
0.7712
> i
4
> 0.7712*(2*2*2*2)          // 0.7712 * 2^4
12.3392
```

If the first argument is a metanumber, the fractional part will equal the metanumber, whereas the integral part becomes zero.

The mathematical functions **pow**(y, x), **atan2**(y,x), and **fmod**(y,x) have two input arguments. The results of these three functions are given in Tables 16.14 to 16.16. The **pow**(y, x) function computes `y` raised to the power of `x`, which is y^x or $e^{x\log(y)}$. If x is negative, y^x becomes $1/y^{|x|}$ with the defined division operation given in Table 16.6. If y is less than zero and x is not an integral value, the function is undefined. The value of -0.0 is considered equal to 0.0 in the evaluation of $\log(-0.0)$ when the value of x is not an integral number. When x is an odd integer number and y is negative, the result is negative. If both y and x are zeros, 0^0 is indeterminate. For a positive value of y, the result depends on the value of y when x is infinity. If y is less than 1, y^∞ is 0.0; 1.0^∞ is indeterminate; if y is greater than 1, y^∞ is infinity. If y is infinity and x is zero, $(\pm\infty)^{\pm 0.0}$ are indeterminate. To ensure the proper flow, a C program shall not stop during the execution due to invalid operations. C is designed to be deterministic; all operations and generic functions deliver correct numerical results, including Inf or NaN. It is a bad design for a computer language if at one point it can deliver a correct numerical result while at another point it returns a wrong numerical result. In general, whenever there is a problem in defining the value for a function or operation mathematically, the corresponding C expression will return NaN. Because C expressions such as 1/**log**(0.0) and **exp**(1/ − 0.0) evaluate to 0.0, **pow**(0.0,0.0) is defined as NaN in C. For the same reason, **pow**(Inf, 0.0) and **pow**(NaN, 0.0) are also defined as NaN. In general, all mathematically indeterminate expressions are defined as NaN in C.

The **atan2**(y, x) function computes the principal value of the arc tangent of `y/x` using the signs of both arguments to determine the returned value in the range of $[-\pi, \pi]$ radians. Given the (x, y) coordinates of a point in the X-Y plane, the **atan2**(y, x) function computes the angle of the radius from the origin to the point. Any positive number that overflows is represented by Inf. The negative overflow is −Inf. The following results hold: **atan2**(±Inf, −Inf) $= \pm 3\pi/4$; **atan2**(±Inf, Inf) $= \pm\pi/4$; **atan2**(±Inf, x) $= \pm\pi/2$;

atan2($\pm y$, Inf) $= \pm 0.0$; and **atan2**($\pm y$, $-$Inf) $= \pm\pi$. When both values of y and x are 0s, the function **atan2**(y, x) will return the results consistent with the manipulation of metanumbers discussed so far. The value of -0.0 is considered to be a negative number less than zero. Therefore, the following results are defined for these special operations: **atan2**(0.0, -0.0) $= \pi$; **atan2**(0.0, 0.0) $= 0.0$; **atan2**(-0.0, -0.0) $= -3\pi/4$; and **atan2**(-0.0, 0) $= -\pi/2$, which is consistent with the treatment of the metanumbers of $\pm$Inf in **atan2**($-$Inf, $-$Inf) $= -3pi/4$. In C, **atan2**(0.0, 0.0) is a specially defined value.

The **fmod**(y,x) function computes the floating-point remainder of `y/x`. The **fmod**(y,x) function returns the value of $y - i * x$ for some integer i. The magnitude of the returned value with the same sign of x is less than the magnitude of x. If x is zero, the function is undefined and returns NaN. When y is infinity, the result is also undefined. If x is infinity and y is a finite number, the result is the same as y.

16.4 Representations of Metanumbers in Programs

In C99, the macros **INFINITY** and **NAN**, defined in the header file **math.h**, can be used in programs. The macro **INFINITY** expands to a constant expression of type float representing infinity, and the macro **NAN** for NaN of type float.

The metanumbers Inf and NaN are treated as regular numbers in input/output (I/O) functions. The default data types for these numbers are float.

Program 16.1 illustrates how the macros **INFINITY** and **NAN** are used to handle metanumbers for variables of float and double types. The program declares two variables, `fInf` and `fNaN`, of type float and two variables, `dInf` and `dNaN`, of type double. They are assigned with the values of metanumbers. When the infinity is printed as a floating-point number with the format specifier `"%f"`, it is displayed in the form of either **inf** or **infinity**, depending on the implementation; for NaN, it is displayed as **nan**. With the format specifier `"%F"`, infinity is displayed as **INF** or **INFINITY**; for NaN, it is displayed as **NAN**. When applied to infinity and NaN values, the $-$, $+$, and space flag characters have their usual meaning; the `#` and 0 flag characters have no effect.

```
/* File: metanums.c (run in C99 and Ch only)
   Compile in gcc, use command 'gcc -std=c99 metanums.c'
   Use metanumbers INFINITY and NAN, and printf() with metanumbers
 */
#include <stdio.h>
#include <math.h> /* for INFINITY and NAN */

int main() {
    float finf, fnan;      /* declare variables of float */
    double dinf, dnan;     /* declare variables of double */

    finf = INFINITY;       /* Inf */
    fnan = NAN;            /* NaN */
    dinf = INFINITY;       /* Inf */
    dnan = NAN;            /* NaN */
    printf("The float   Inf  = %f\n", finf);
    printf("The float  -Inf  = %f\n", -finf);
    printf("The float   NaN  = %f\n", fnan);
```

Program 16.1: Using metanumbers in a program. *(Continued)*

```
    printf("The double  Inf  = %f\n", dinf);
    printf("The double -Inf  = %f\n", -dinf);
    printf("The double  NaN  = %f\n", dnan);
/* If the program runs in Ch, %b format is used to display
   the binary representation of floating-point numbers */
#ifdef _CH_
    printf("The float   Inf  = %b \n", finf);
    printf("The float  -Inf  = %b \n", -finf);
    printf("The float   Nan  = %b \n", fnan);
    printf("The double  Inf  = %b \n", dinf);
    printf("The double -Inf  = %b \n", -dinf);
    printf("The double  NaN  = %b \n", dnan);
    printf("The int     2    = %b \n",   2);   /* only display 2 bits */
    printf("The int     2    = %32b \n",  2); /* display 32 bits */
    printf("The int    -2    = %b \n", -2);   /* display 32 bits */
    printf("The float   0.0F = %b \n", 0.0F);
    printf("The float  -0.0F = %b \n", -0.0F);
    printf("The float   1.0F = %b \n",  1.0F);
    printf("The float  -1.0F = %b \n", -1.0F);
    printf("The float   2.0F = %b \n",  2.0F);
    printf("The float  -2.0F = %b \n", -2.0F);
#endif
    return 0;
}
```

Program 16.1: *(Continued)*

When Program 16.1 runs in Ch, the binary representation of metanumbers are printed using the binary format specifier `"%b"`, which uses the field width 32 for type float and 64 for type double. For comparison, the memory storage for integers of ±2, and float constant ±0.0, ±1.0, ±2.0 are printed. The output of Program 16.1 when it is executed in Ch is as follows:

```
The float   Inf   = inf
The float  -Inf   = -inf
The float   NaN   = nan
The double  Inf   = inf
The double -Inf   = -inf
The double  NaN   = nan
The float   Inf   = 01111111100000000000000000000000
The float  -Inf   = 11111111100000000000000000000000
The float   Nan   = 01111111111111111111111111111111
The double  Inf   = 01111111111100000000000000000000\
                    00000000000000000000000000000000
The double -Inf   = 11111111111100000000000000000000\
                    00000000000000000000000000000000
The double  NaN   = 01111111111111111111111111111111\
                    11111111111111111111111111111111
```

```
The int      2    = 10
The int      2    = 00000000000000000000000000000010
The int     -2    = 11111111111111111111111111111110
The float    0.0F = 00000000000000000000000000000000
The float   -0.0F = 10000000000000000000000000000000
The float    1.0F = 00111111100000000000000000000000
The float   -1.0F = 10111111100000000000000000000000
The float    2.0F = 01000000000000000000000000000000
The float   -2.0F = 11000000000000000000000000000000
```

The output for the binary representation for each metanumber of type double is reformatted in two lines to allow for presentation in this book.

For metanumbers Inf, −Inf, and NaN, there is no difference between float and double types from the user's point of view. It can be easily verified that the bit-mappings of all these numbers in memory match with the data representations given in Table 16.1.

Metanumbers can also be input into a program by the family of **scanf()** functions. The character sequences **inf** or **infinity**, regardless of the case of each character, can be used to represent infinity. Similarly, the character sequences **nan**, regardless of the case of each character, stand for NaN. This can be illustrated interactively in Ch as follows:

```
> double d1, d2
> scanf("%lf%lf", &d1, &d2)
Inf NaN
> printf("d1 = %f, d2 = %f", d1, d2)
d1 = inf, d2 = nan
> printf("d1 = %F, d2 = %F", d1, d2)
d1 = INF, d2 = NAN
```

16.5 Programming Examples

16.5.1 Computation of Extreme Values of Floating-Point Numbers

Due to different machine architectures for representation of floating-point numbers, the extreme values such as the maximum representable floating-point value are different. For two machines with the same representation of floating-point values, the same operations such as adding two values on each machine may produce different results, depending on the schemes for rounding a number that cannot be represented exactly. To aid serious numerically oriented programmers in writing their programs, the C standard added the header file **float.h** as a companion to the existing header file **limits.h** to deal with the machine-dependent integer values only. In this section, examples of how parameters defined in the C standard library **float.h** can be computed in C without knowing the intricate architecture of the computer. A program can depend less on these parameters if a language can support the metanumbers Inf and NaN. The use of metanumbers such as Inf and NaN instead of parameters is recommended.

Minimum Floating-Point Numbers FLT_MIN and FLT_MINIMUM

The parameter **FLT_MIN** is defined in the C standard library header file **float.h** as a minimum normalized positive floating-point float number. If a number is less than **FLT_MIN**, it is called an *underflow*. Because the IEEE 754 standard provides a *gradual underflow*, the minimum denormalized positive floating-point float number is defined as **FLT_MINIMUM**. Because of gradual underflow, the expression `x - y == 0` is 1 if and only if x equals y. This would not be the case for a system that lacks gradual underflow. This parameter is very useful from a programming point of view. As an example, assume that values of **FLT_MINIMUM** and **FLT_MIN** are 1.401298e-45 and 1.175494e-38, respectively. The following code will illustrate subtleties of these two parameters.

```
float f, *flt_minimum;
int minimum, i;
minimum = 1;                          // memory location becomes 00000001
flt_minimum = (float*)&minimum;       // *flt_minimum becomes FLT_MINIMUM
i = *flt_minimum > 0.0;               // i becomes 1
i = FLT_MIN > *flt_minimum;           // i becomes 1
i = fabs(*flt_minimum) > 0.0;         // i becomes 1
f = (*flt_minimum)/(*flt_minimum); // f becomes 1.0; note 0.0/0.0 = NaN
f = f/1.e-46                        // f becomes Inf: 1.e-46 < FLT_MINIMUM
```

Machine Epsilon FLT_EPSILON

The machine epsilon ε, represented by the symbol **FLT_EPSILON** in C, is the difference between 1 and the smallest value greater than 1 that is representable in float in the formula below.

$$1.0 + \varepsilon > 1.0$$

This parameter, defined in the C header file **float.h** as a macro, is a system constant, which can be calculated by the algorithm presented in Exercise 37 in Chapter 5. This parameter is very useful for scientific computing. For example, the iterative error from the calculation of an algorithm is often used as a criterion for testing the convergence of the algorithm. This iterative error is often close to zero, but not exactly zero. This can be tested by the pseudo code below.

```
if(fabs(error) < FLT_EPSILON) {
   /* convergent */
}
```

The function **fabs()**, declared in the header file **math.h**, can be used to obtain the absolute value of a floating point value. As another example, due to the finite precision of the floating-point representation and alignment of addition operation, when a significantly small value and a large number are added together, the small number may not contribute to the summation. Using **FLT_EPSILON**, adding a small positive number x to a large positive number y can capture at least three decimal digits of significance of y that can be tested by

```
if(x < y * FLT_EPSILON * 1000)
```

The following code can calculate and print out the machine epsilon on the screen.

```
float epsilon;
epsilon = 1.0;
while(epsilon+1 > 1)
  epsilon /= 2;
epsilon *= 2;
printf("The machine epsilon FLT_EPSILON is %e", epsilon);
```

The output from the execution of the previous code in one machine is as follows:
The machine epsilon FLT_EPSILON is 1.192093e-07
which matches the value of the parameter **FLT_EPSILON** defined in the C header file **float.h**. Although the above computation of the parameter **FLT_EPSILON** is simple, which uses the default rounding mode of round toward nearest, it may be vulnerable to other rounding modes. A more robust method of obtaining this parameter is to manipulate the bit pattern of the memory of a float variable as shown previously.

Maximum Floating-Point Number FLT_MAX

The parameter **FLT_MAX** defined in the C header file **float.h** is the maximum representable finite floating-point number. Any value that is larger than **FLT_MAX** will be represented as Inf, and any value less than −**FLT_MAX** is represented by −Inf. If the value of **FLT_MAX** is represented as $fltmax * 10^e$, then the following two equations will be satisfied:

$$(fltmax + FLT\_EPSILON) * 10^e = Inf$$

$$(fltmax + FLT\_EPSILON/2) * 10^e = FLT\_MAX$$

where the machine epsilon **FLT_EPSILON** was defined before and the exponential value e is to be calculated. The following two expressions will further demonstrate the difference between **FLT_MAX** and Inf:

$$1/\text{Inf} * \text{FLT\_MAX} = 0.0$$

$$1/\text{FLT\_MAX} * \text{FLT\_MAX} = 1.0$$

Program 16.2 calculates **FLT_MAX**, as well as **FLT_MAX_10_EXP** and **FLT_MAX_EXP** of the machine, and prints them on the screen. The value of **FLT_MAX_10_EXP** is the maximum integer such that 10 raised to its power is in the range of the representable finite floating-point numbers. The value of **FLT_MAX_EXP** is the maximum integer such that 2 raised to its power minus 1 is a representable finite floating-point number. For the illustrative purpose, only the **while** loop control structure is used in this example. The output of Program 16.2 is as follows:

```
FLT_MAX = 3.40282347e+38
FLT_MAX_10_EXP = 38
FLT_MAX_EXP = 128
```

```
/* File: fltmax.c (run in C99 and Ch only)
   Compile in gcc, use command 'gcc -std=c99 fltmax.c -lm'
   Calculate the floating-point constants FLT_MAX, FLT_MAX_10_EXP,
   FLT_MAX_EXP defined in header file float.h  */
#include <stdio.h>
#include <tgmath.h>       /* for INFINITY, pow(), frexp() */

int main() {
    float base=10.0, /* base 10 for exponential value */
          flt_max,   /* for calculating and holding FLT_MAX */
          f;         /* a temporary variable with float type  */
```

Program 16.2: Obtaining the maximum floating-point number. (*Continued*)

```
    int e,          /* for calculating and holding FLT_MAX_10_EXP */
        flt_max_exp, /* FLT_MAX_EXP */
        i;          /* index variable */

    /* calculate exponential number FLT_MAX_10_EXP, '38'in 3.40282347e+38 */
    e = 0;      /* initialize e */
    f = base;   /* initialize f */
    while(f != INFINITY) { /* looping till f == Inf */
      e++;                 /* increment e */
      f *= base;           /* 10^e */
    }
    /* e contains the value for FLT_MAX_10_EXP */
    printf("FLT_MAX_10_EXP = %d \n", e);

    /* calculate FLT_MAX */
    /* step 1, calculate leading nonzero number, '3'in 3.40282347e+38
       at the end of the loop, i becomes 4 */
    i = 0; f = 0.0; /* intialize variables */
    while(f != INFINITY)
      f = ++i * pow(base, e);

    /* step 2, calculate numbers after decimal point,
       40282347 in '3.40282347e+38' */
    flt_max = i;   /* flt_max is 4 to start with */
    while(e != 0)  /* use a loop to calculate FLT_MAX */
    {
      /* 1st iteration, flt_max is 4.0, after this statement, flt_max is 30 */
      /* 2nd iteration, flt_max is 35.0, after this statement,flt_max is 34.0 */
      flt_max = --flt_max * base;
      /* obtain the remaining value */
      e--; i = 0; f = 0.0;
      while(f != INFINITY && i < 10)
      {
        f = ++flt_max * pow(base, e);
        i++;
      }
    }
    printf("FLT_MAX = %.8e \n", flt_max);

    /* calculate FLT_MAX_EXP */
    f = frexp(flt_max, &flt_max_exp);
    printf("FLT_MAX_EXP = %d \n", flt_max_exp);
    return 0;
}
```

Program 16.2: *(Continued)*

The previous values for **FLT_MAX**, **FLT_MAX_10_EXP**, and **FLT_MAX_EXP** are the same as for the parameters defined in the C header file **float.h**. By just changing the declaration of the first statement from float to double, the corresponding extreme values **DBL_MAX**, **DBL_MAX_10_EXP**, and **DBL_MAX_EXP** for type double can be obtained. In this case, the polymorphic arithmetic operators and mathematical functions **pow**() and **frexp**() will return data of type double.

In the above calculation of the extreme floating-point values, the user does not need to know the intricate machine representation of floating-point numbers. If one knows the machine representation of a floating-point number, the calculation of the extreme values can be much simpler. For example, according to Table 16.1, the value of **FLT_MAX** is represented in the hexadecimal form $(0X7F7FFFFF)_{16}$. The following program can be used to obtain the maximum representable finite floating-point number **FLT_MAX**.

```
int i;
float *flt_max;
flt_max = (float *)&i;// flt_max points to the memory of i
i = 0X7F7FFFFF;        // *flt_max becomes FLT_MAX
```

16.5.2 Programming with Metanumbers

C99 distinguishes −0.0 from 0.0 for real numbers. The metanumbers Inf, −Inf, and NaN are very useful for scientific computing. For example, the function $f(x) = e^{\frac{1}{x}}$ is not continuous at the origin, as shown in Figure 16.5. This discontinuity can be handled gracefully in C99. The evaluation of the expression **exp**(1/0.0) will return Inf and **exp**(1/(−0.0)) gives 0.0, which corresponds to mathematical expressions $e^{\frac{1}{0+}}$ and $e^{\frac{1}{0-}}$ or $\lim_{x\to 0_+} e^{\frac{1}{x}}$ and $\lim_{x\to 0_-} e^{\frac{1}{x}}$, respectively. In addition, the evaluation of expressions **exp**(1.0/Inf) and **exp**(1.0/(−Inf)) will get the value of 1.0.

Figure 16.5. is generated by Program 16.3. It draws two curves for the function $f(x) = e^{\frac{1}{x}}$ using a plotting class described in Chapter 20. The data sets of these two curves are calculated using the mathematical

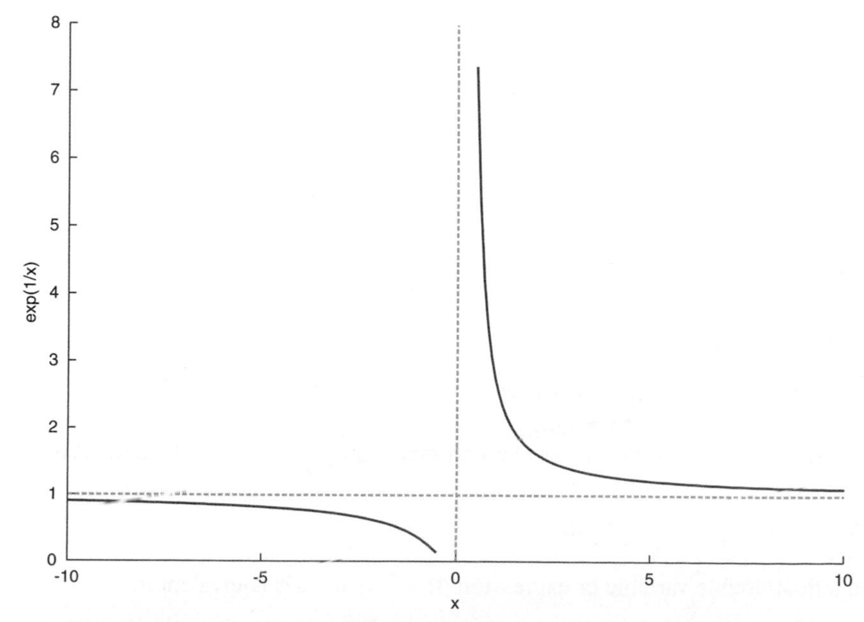

Figure 16.5: The plot generated by Program 16.3 for function $f(x) = e^{\frac{1}{x}}$.

```
/* File: expx.cpp
   Calculate and plot e^(1/x) in the range of [-10, 10].
   Data in the range [-0.5, 0.5] are not plotted */
#include <math.h>
#include <chplot.h>  /* for CPlot */

#define NUM 100       /* number of points for each curve */
int main() {
    /* declare variables */
    double x0, xf, x1[NUM], x2[NUM], f1[NUM], f2[NUM];
    CPlot plot;
    int i;

    x0 = 0.5;    /* initial value, use 0.5 to avoid 0.0 in the plotting */
    xf = 10.0;   /* final value */
    for(i=0; i< NUM; i++) {                  /* use a loop to generate data */
       x1[i] = x0 + i*(xf-x0)/(NUM-1);
       f1[i] = exp(1.0/x1[i]);
       x2[i] = -x1[i];                       /* symetrical about y axis */
       f2[i] = exp(1.0/x2[i]);
    }
    plot.label(PLOT_AXIS_X, "x");             /* x label */
    plot.label(PLOT_AXIS_Y, "exp(1/x)");      /* y label */
    plot.data2DCurve(x1, f1, NUM);            /* curve for x in [0.5, 10] */
    plot.data2DCurve(x2, f2, NUM);            /* curve for x in [-10, -0.5] */
    plot.line(-10, 1, 0, 10, 1, 0);           /* draw a horizontal line */
    plot.line(0, 0, 0, 0, 8, 0);              /* draw a vertical line */
    plot.plotting();                          /* plot it */
    return 0;
}
```

Program 16.3: Plotting the function $e^{1/x}$.

function **exp**(). Two lines, one horizontal and one vertical at the point (0, 1), are drawn using the geometric primitive member function **CPlot**::**line**(). For a member function call of

```
plot.line(x1, y1, z2, x2, y2, z2)
```

The first three arguments are the coordinates for a point at one end of the line. The last three arguments for the coordinates for the other point of the line.

As another example, the function **finite**(x) recommended by the IEEE 754 standard is equivalent to the C expression

```
-INFINITY < x && x < INFINITY
```

where x can be a float/double variable or expression. If x is float, it is equivalent to

```
-FLT_MAX <= x && x <= FLT_MAX
```

If x is double, it is is equivalent to

```
-DBL_MAX <= x && x <= DBL_MAX
```

The mathematical statement "*if* $-\infty < value <= \infty$, *then* y *becomes* ∞" can be programmed easily as follows:

```
if(-INFINITY < value && value <= INFINITY)
    y = INFINITY;
```

However, a computer can only evaluate an expression step by step. Although the metanumbers are limits of the floating-point numbers, they cannot replace mathematical analysis. For example, the natural number *e* equal to 2.718281828 ... is defined as the limit value of the expression

$$\lim_{x \to \infty} \left(1 + \frac{1}{x}\right)^x = e.$$

However, the value of the expression **pow**(1.0 + 1.0/Inf, Inf) is NaN. The evaluation of this expression is carried out as follows:

$$\left(1.0 + \frac{1.0}{Inf}\right)^{Inf} = (1.0 + 0.0)^{Inf} = 1.0^{Inf} = NaN$$

If the value FLT_MAX is used in the above expression instead of Inf, the result is obtained by

$$\left(1.0 + \frac{1.0}{FLT\_MAX}\right)^{FLT\_MAX} = (1.0 + 0.0)^{FLT\_MAX} = 1.0^{FLT\_MAX} = 1.0$$

Because the metanumber NaN is unordered, a program involving relational operations should be handled cautiously. For example, the expression `x > y` is not equivalent to `!(x <= y)` if either x or y is a NaN. As another example, the code fragment

```
if(x > 0.0)
    function1();
else
    function2();
```

is different from the code fragment

```
if(x <= 0.0)
    function2();
else
    function1();
```

The condition of the second **if** statement should be written as `(x <= 0.0 || isnan(x))` for these two code fragments to have the same functionality. The function **isnan()** in C99 tests if its argument is NaN or not. It returns 1 if its argument is NaN; otherwise, it returns 0.

An Application Example: A Square Root Function That Can Handle Metanumbers

Program 6.8 in Chapter 6 presents a version of the square root function `sqrtx()` using Newton's method. In this application example, this square root function is refined, as shown in Program 16.4, so that it can handle metanumbers. Compared to Program 6.8 in Chapter 6, Program 16.4 handles negative numbers and metanumbers NaN and Inf by the following code:

```
if(isnan(x) || x<0.0)
  return NAN;
else if(x == INFINITY)
  return INFINITY;
```

before Newton's recursive formula is used to calculate the square root the passed argument. The square root of a negative number or NaN is NaN. The square root of infinity is infinity. If the algorithm fails to converge to a root in 100 iterations, the function also returns NaN. The output from Program 16.4 is shown below:

```
sqrtx(3.00) = 1.732051
sqrtx(-3.00) = nan
sqrtx(nan) = nan
sqrtx(-inf) = nan
sqrtx(inf) = inf
```

```
/* File: sqrtr.c
   Function sqrtx() based on Newton's method for calculating a square root.
   It can handle -x, NaN, -Inf, Inf
   Use isnan(), NAN, INFINITY in C99 to implement sqrtx().
   Compile in gcc, use command 'gcc -std=c99 sqrtr.c'  */
#include <stdio.h>
#include <math.h>  /* for fabs() */
#include <float.h> /* for FLT_EPSILON */

#define N 100       /* the maximum number of iteration */

double sqrtx(double x) {
   int i;
   double x0, x1, x2;

   /* handle negative and metanumbers */
   if(isnan(x) || x<0.0)
     return NAN;
   else if(x == INFINITY)
     return INFINITY;

   x0 = x;          /* an initial guess for x0 */
   x1 = x0;                    /* set x1 to x0 */
   x2 = (x1+x/x1)/2.0;         /* recursive formula */
   for(i = 1; i <= N && fabs(x2-x0) >= FLT_EPSILON; i++) {
      x0 = x1;                 /* update x0  for fabs(x2-x0) */
      x2 = (x1+x/x1)/2.0;      /* Newton's recursive formula */
```

Program 16.4: The square root function `sqrtx()` using Newton's method, which can handle metanumbers. *(Continued)*

```
        x1 = x2;        /* update value x1 for n
        x1 = x2;        /* update value x1 for next iteration */
    }

    if(i < N) {         /* number of iterations is less than N */
      return x2;        /* return the square root */
    }
    else {              /* number of iterations equals N */
      /* printf("sqrtx() failed to converge\n"); */
      return NAN;       /* return NaN if failed to converge */
    }
}

int main() {
    double a;

    a = 3.0;          /* for sqrtx(3.0) */
    printf("sqrtx(%.2f) = %f\n", a, sqrtx(a));
    a = -3.0;         /* for sqrtx(-3.0) */
    printf("sqrtx(%.2f) = %f\n", a, sqrtx(a));
    a = NAN;          /* for sqrtx(NaN) */
    printf("sqrtx(%.2f) = %f\n", a, sqrtx(a));
    a = -INFINITY; /* for sqrtx(-Inf) */
    printf("sqrtx(%.2f) = %f\n", a, sqrtx(a));
    a = INFINITY;   /* for sqrtx(Inf) */
    printf("sqrtx(%.2f) = %f\n", a, sqrtx(a));
    return 0;
}
```

Program 16.4: *(Continued)*

Exercises

1. Write a program to create a table to display the results of (a) abs(x); (b) sqrt(x); (c) exp(x); (d) log(x); (e) log10(x); (f) sin(x); (g) cos(x); (h) tan(x) when x equals ± 0.0, $\pm\infty$, and NaN.
2. Show the value of x after each of the following statements is performed:
   - **a.** x = fabs(7.5);
   - **b.** x = floor(7.5);
   - **c.** x = fabs(0.0);
   - **d.** x = ceil(0.0);
   - **e.** x = fabs(-6.4);
   - **f.** x = ceil(-6.4);
   - **g.** x = ceil(-fabs(-8 + floor(-5.5)));
   - **h.** x = abs(-Inf)/sqrt(-Inf);

3. The function **sin()** is a type generic function. What does that mean?
4. State whether the following statements are true or false. If false, explain why.

   a. Ch does not distinguish `0.0` from `-0.0`.
   b. It is called an underflow when a number is less than **FLT_MIN**, a macro defined in the C standard library header file **float.h**.

5. Give the internal representation of the following integral and floating-point variables in both binary and hexadecimal representations:

   a. char c1 = '8', c2 = 8;
   b. short s1 = 25, s2 = -25;
   c. int i1 = 25, i2 = -25;
   d. unsigned int ui1 = 24, ui2 = 25;
   e. float f1 = 24, f2 = -25, f4 = NaN, f5 = Inf, f6 = -Inf;
   f. double d1 = 24, d2 = -25, d4 = NaN, d5 = Inf, d6 = -Inf;

6. Give the value of int constants represented in the following binary forms:

   a. `11111111111111111111111111110110`
   b. `00000000000000000000000000011001`
   c. `11111111111111111111111111101110`
   d. `00000000000000000000000000100101`
   e. `11111111111111111111111110001011`

7. Give the value of a float constant represented in the following binary forms:

   a. `01000001001000000000000000000000`
   b. `11000000010111000000000000000000`
   c. `01000000001110100000000000000000`
   d. `01000000001100011000000000000000`
   e. `11000000001010010000000000000000`

8. Implement the function `decompose()` with the function prototype

```
double decompose(double x, double *iptr);
```

   It breaks a floating-point number `x` into an integral part and a fractional part. The function returns the fractional part and passes the integral part through the argument `iptr`. This will be an implementation of the functionalities of the C standard math function **modf()**.

9. Based on the algorithm presented in Exercise 44 in Chapter 5, write a cubic root function with the function prototype

```
double cbrtx(double x);
```

   The function shall be able to handle negative numbers and metanumbers. Call the function to take the cubic root for 3.0, −3.0, **NAN**, **INFINITY**, and −**INFINITY**.

CHAPTER 17

‡Programming with Complex Numbers in C99 and C++

Complex numbers have wide applications in engineering and science. Owing to the importance of complex numbers in scientific programming, numerically oriented programming languages and software packages usually support them one way or another. For example, Fortran, a language designed mainly for scientific computing, has provided complex data types since its earliest days. The early version of C does not have complex data types as a basic feature because numerically oriented scientific computing was not its original design goal. Complex data types were added in C99.

For numerical computing, Ch supports all features related to complex numbers mandated by C99. Furthermore, type generic mathematical functions in Ch are overloaded for handling complex numbers with optional arguments for different branch cuts. C99 provides real metanumbers of Inf, −Inf, and NaN and signed zeros 0.0 and −0.0, which makes the power of the IEEE 754 standard for binary floating-point arithmetic easily available to the programmer. Ch extends the idea of metanumbers to complex numbers not only for arithmetic, but also for commonly used mathematical functions in the spirit of the IEEE 754 standard. Ch treats floating-point real numbers with signed zeros and complex numbers with unsigned zeros, as well as Not-a-Number (NaN) and infinities in an integrated consistent manner.

In this chapter, programming with complex numbers in C99 and C++ is described. Complex numbers are also available in C++, but they are implemented as classes instead of built-in data types. In the last section of this chapter, writing portable programs with complex numbers that can be compiled in both C99 and C++ is described.

17.1 Introduction to Complex Analysis

Complex numbers z can be defined as the ordered pairs

$$z = (x, y) \tag{17.1}$$

with specific addition and multiplication rules. The real numbers x and y are called the *real* and *imaginary parts* of z. If we identify the pair $(x, 0.0)$ as real numbers, real numbers are a subset of complex numbers. If a real number is considered either as x or $(x, 0.0)$ and if i denotes the *pure imaginary number* $(0, 1)$ with $i * i = -1$, complex numbers can be mathematically represented as

$$z = x + iy \tag{17.2}$$

Both equations (17.1) and (17.2) can be used for complex numbers in C.

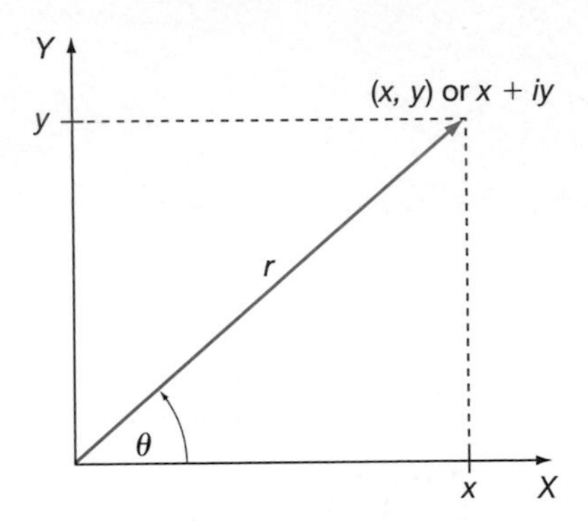

Figure 17.1: A geometrical interpretation of the complex number z.

Like real numbers, arithmetic operations can be performed on complex numbers. For example,

$$(x_1 + iy_1) \pm (x_2 + iy_2) = (x_1 \pm x_2) + i(y_1 \pm y_2) \tag{17.3}$$

$$(x_1 + iy_1) \times (x_2 + iy_2) = (x_1x_2 - y_1y_2) + i(y_1x_2 + x_1y_2) \tag{17.4}$$

The division of a nonzero complex number is defined as $\frac{z_1}{z_2} = z_1z_2^{-1}$, such that $zz^{-1} = 1$. Thus, given $z1 = x_1 + iy_1$ and $z2 = x_2 + iy_2$, the following equation holds:

$$\frac{z_1}{z_2} = \frac{x_1x_2 + y_1y_2}{x_2^2 + y_2^2} + i\frac{y_1x_2 - x_1y_2}{x_2^2 + y_2^2} \tag{17.5}$$

When $z_1 = 1$, then

$$\begin{aligned} z_2^{-1} &= \frac{1}{z_2} \\ &= \frac{1}{x + iy} \\ &= \frac{x - iy}{x^2 + y^2} \end{aligned} \tag{17.6}$$

Two complex numbers are considered to be equal to one another only if both the real and imaginary parts are equal. For example, the complex numbers z_1 and z_2 are equal if $x_1 == x_2$ and $y_1 == y_2$.

Geometrically, the complex number $z = x + iy$ can be interpreted as shown in Figure 17.1, with x representing the coordinate in the x-axis and y for the y-axis. The *modulus* or absolute value of complex z is defined as

$$r = |z| = \sqrt{x^2 + y^2} \tag{17.7}$$

which is the distance between the origin and point (x, y). The *phase angle* or *argument* of z is defined as

$$\theta = \arctan \frac{y}{x} \tag{17.8}$$

Figures 17.2, 17.3, 17.4, and 17.5 illustrate the addition, subtraction, multiplication, and division of the complex numbers z_1 and z_2, respectively.

The *complex conjugate* of $z = x + iy$ is $z = x - iy$ and is illustrated in Figure 17.6.

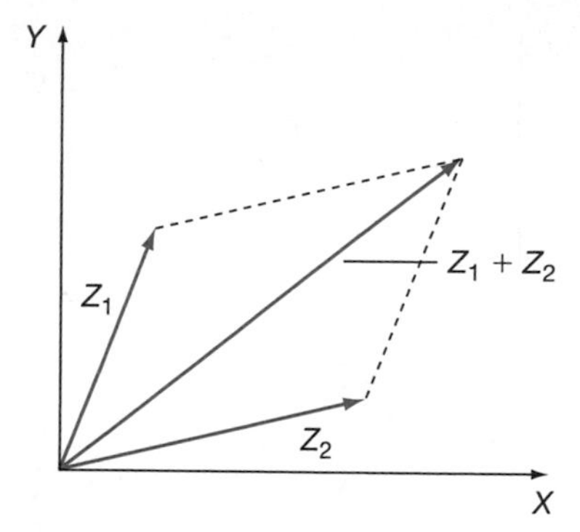

Figure 17.2: Adding complex numbers.

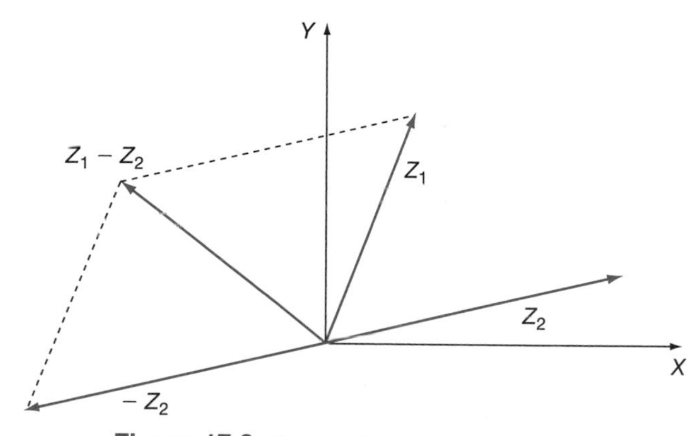

Figure 17.3: Subtracting complex numbers.

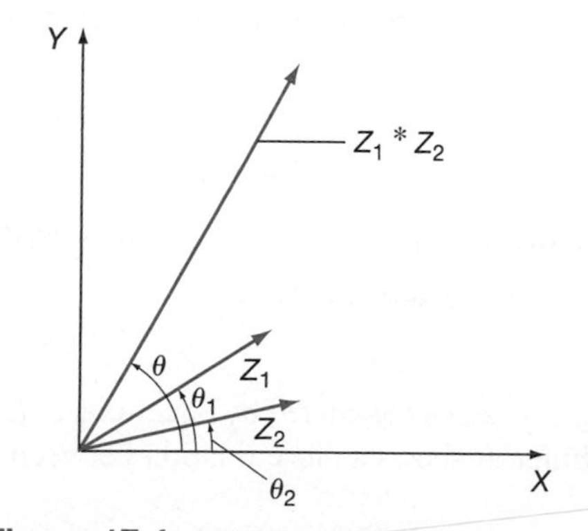

Figure 17.4: Multiplying complex numbers.

So far, the complex number has been represented in the Cartesian coordinate system only in the form (x, y) or $z = x + iy$. However, the complex number z can also be represented in polar form $x = r\cos\theta$ and $y = r\sin\theta$, where r and and θ are the modulus and phase angle of z, respectively. Thus, the complex number z shown in Figure 17.1 can be expressed as follows:

$$z = r\cos\theta + ir\sin\theta \tag{17.9}$$

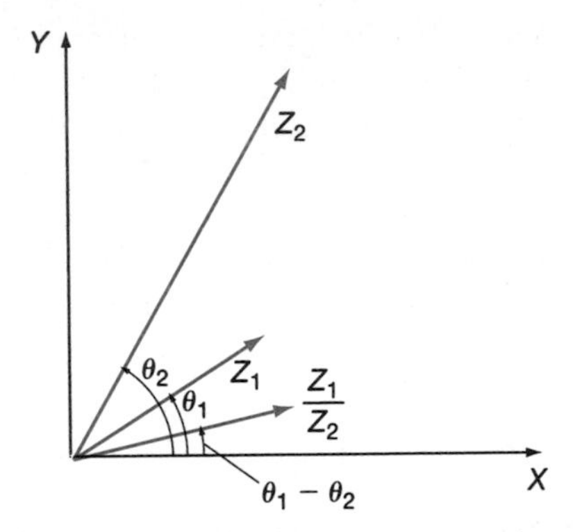

Figure 17.5: Dividing complex numbers.

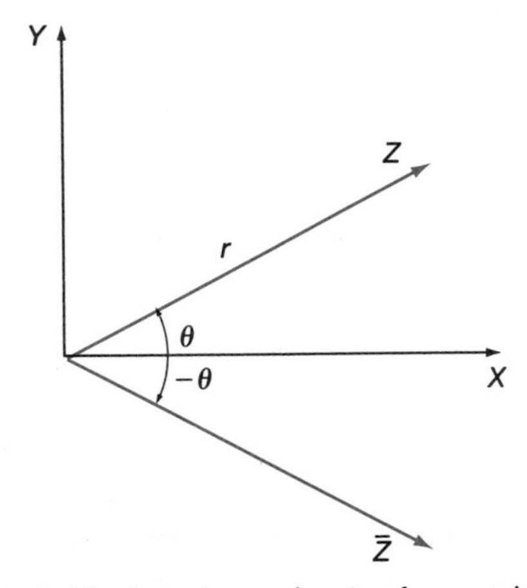

Figure 17.6: The complex conjugate of a complex number.

Similarly, complex numbers can be represented in exponential form according to Euler's formula:

$$e^{i\theta} = \cos\theta + i\sin\theta \tag{17.10}$$

With Euler's formula (17.10), the complex number $z = x + iy$ can be written in polar form as follows:

$$\begin{aligned} z &= r(\cos\theta + i\sin\theta) \\ &= re^{i\theta} \end{aligned} \tag{17.11}$$

where the modulus r and phase angle θ can be calculated by equations (17.7) and (17.8), respectively. Euler's formula is named after Leonhard Euler. It shows a close relation between the complex exponential function and trigonometric functions.

17.2 Introduction to Programming with Complex Numbers

Like floating-point types, complex types are part of basic types in C99. The real and imaginary parts of a complex number are floating-point numbers. To declare a variable of complex type in a C99 program, it needs to include the header file **complex.h**, which defines the keyword **complex**. There are three complex types: **float complex**, **complex** or **double complex**, and **long double complex**. A floating-point complex number of float complex type contains real and imaginary numbers of float type, where the size of the entire float complex type is 8 bytes, 4 bytes for the real part and 4 bytes for the imaginary part. A complex or double complex data type, however, contains real and imaginary numbers of double data type, with a total size of 16 bytes, 8 bytes each for the real and imaginary parts. The long double complex type has at least the number of bytes of type double complex. One can declare not only a *simple complex variable*, but also *pointer to complex*, *array of complex*, and *array of pointer to complex*, etc. Declarations of these complex variables are similar to the declarations for any other basic data types in C. An array of complex numbers are manipulated in the same manner as the floating-point types of float and double. The following code segment illustrates how complex numbers are declared and manipulated:

```
#include <complex.h>       // for complex and I
double complex z;          // z as double complex variable
float complex z1;          // z1 as float complex variable
complex *zptr1;            // zptr1 as pointer to  double complex variable
complex z2[2], z3[2][3]; // z2 and z3 as arrays of double complex
zpt1r = &z1;               // zptr1 points to the address of z1
double x = 3.0, y = 4.0; // real and imaginary parts;
z = x + I*y;               // z = 3+i4
```

The macro **I** is defined as `complex(0.0, 1.0)` in the header file **complex.h** to represent an imaginary number with the unit length. In the code segment above, the variable `z` is assigned the complex number $3+i4$.

In Ch, a complex number $(x + iy)$ can be constructed using a complex constructor **complex(x, y)** as shown below.

```
> double complex z
> z = complex(3.0, 4.0)
complex(3.0000,4.0000)
```

Another method of assigning a complex number to a complex variable is to use the polar coordinates through the **polar()** function. The function **polar()** is available in C++ and Ch. Although it is not defined in C99, it can be easily added or defined as a macro, which will be described in section 17.7. The function **polar()** takes two input arguments, `r` and `theta`. The variable `r` refers to the modulus of the complex number, and `theta` is its phase angle expressed in radians, not in degrees. The functions **creal()**, **cimag()**, **cabs()**, and **carg()** can be used to obtain the real part, imaginary part, modulus, and phase angle of a complex number. For example, the following code fragment assigns a complex number to the variable `z` given $r = 10$ and $\theta = 30^o$. Then obtain the real part, imaginary part, modulus, and phase angle of the complex number:

```
#include <math.h>              // for M_PI
#include <complex.h>           // for complex and I
double r = 10;
double theta = 30*(M_PI/180);// convert degree to radian
double complex z;
z = polar(r, theta);           // complex number r e^(i theta)
x = creal(z);                  // get real part of z;
y = cimag(z);                  // get imaginary part of z;
r = cabs(z);                   // obtain modulus of z;
theta = carg(z);               // obtain phase angle of z;
```

Note that the macro **M_PI**, defined in the header file **math.h**, represents the irrational number π.

Program 17.1 illustrates how complex numbers are handled in a C99 conforming program. The program includes the standard header file **complex.h** so that complex type, imaginary number I, and complex functions can be used. For illustrative purposes, a complex variable z is declared. A complex number $3 + i4$ is constructed and assigned to the variable z by the statement

```
z = 3.0 + I*4.0;            /* construc complex number 3+i4 */
```

The real part, imaginary part, modulus, and phase angle of this complex number are then obtained by the functions **creal**(), **cimag**(), **cabs**(), and **carg**(), respectively, and displayed. The variables preal and pimag of pointers to double are pointed to the real and imaginary parts of the complex variable z by the statements

```
preal = (double *)&z;     /* preal points to real part of z */
pimag = preal+1;          /* pimag points to imag part of z */
```

```
/* File: cexample.c (run in C99 and Ch only)
   Compile in gcc, use command 'gcc -std=c99 cexample.c'
   Handle complex numbers: declaration, complex constructor,
   real and imaginary parts, modulus, phase angle, input and output */
#include <stdio.h>
#include <complex.h> /* for complex, I, creal(), cimag(), cabs(), carg() */

int main() {
    double complex z;          /* declare z as double complex */
    double *preal, *pimag;     /* pointer to real and imaginary parts */

    /* use creal() and cimag() to get real and imag parts of z */
    z = 3.0 + I*4.0;           /* construct complex number 3+i4 */
    printf("z = complex(%f, %f)\n", creal(z), cimag(z));
    printf("modulus(z) = %f, phase angle (z) = %f\n", cabs(z), carg(z));

    /* use pointers to double to change real and imag parts of z */
    preal = (double *)&z;      /* preal points to real part of z */
    pimag = preal+1;           /* pimag points to imag part of z */
    *preal = 10.0;             /* real(z) = 10.0 */
    *pimag = 20.0;             /* imag(z) = 20.0 */
    printf("z = complex(%f, %f)\n", *preal, *pimag);
    printf("z = complex(%f, %f)\n", creal(z), cimag(z));

    /* use preal and pimag to access z for scanf() */
    printf("Please type in real and imaginary parts of complex number:\n");
    scanf("%lf%lf", preal, pimag);
    printf("z = complex(%f, %f)\n", creal(z), cimag(z));
    return 0;
}
```

Program 17.1: A program using complex numbers.

Through pointer indirection operations, the value of the complex variable z is changed to $10 + i20$. Finally, using the two variables preal and pimag of pointer type, the function **scanf()** is called to obtain the user input for real and imaginary parts of the complex variable z. The value of this complex variable is then displayed. The input and output of Program 17.1, when it is interactively executed, is shown below.

```
> cexample.c
z = complex(3.000000, 4.000000)
modulus(z) = 5.000000, phase angle (z) = 0.927295
z = complex(10.000000, 20.000000)
z = complex(10.000000, 20.000000)
Please type in real and imaginary parts of complex number:
5.0 6.0
z = complex(5.000000, 6.000000)
```

17.3 Data Type Conversions

Section 4.3 stated type conversion rules for the data types char, int, float, double, and long double. This section presents the conversion rules related to complex numbers. Note that the **float complex**, **complex** or **double complex**, and **long double complex** data types are of the highest order in the data type hierarchy, as shown in Figure 4.1. The default conversion rules related to complex numbers are as follows:

1. In binary operations, such as addition, subtraction, multiplication, and division with mixed data types, the result of the operation will carry the higher data type of two operands. When one of the two binary operands is complex and the data type of the other operand is a real number, the real number will be cast into a complex before the operation is carried out. This conversion rule is also valid for an assignment statement when data types of the lvalue and rvalue are different.
2. When a value of complex type is converted to another complex type, both the real and imaginary parts follow the conversion rules for the corresponding real types.
3. The memory of a complex variable can be accessed by pointers. If the real or imaginary part of a complex variable is obtained by a pointer indirection operation, the sign of a zero will be carried over.
4. A real number of char, int, float, double, or long double type can be converted to a complex number with its imaginary part being zero. Conversion from double to float complex data type may cause the information to be lost.

   In C, when a real value of Inf, −Inf, or NaN is converted to a complex number, the imaginary part is zero.

   In Ch, when casting a real number into a complex number, the values of Inf and −Inf become ComplexInf, which represents a complex number with the value of Inf for both real and imaginary parts; and the value of NaN becomes ComplexNaN, a special complex number with the value of NaN for both real and imaginary parts.

   The implementation of Ch follows the complex analysis with consistent mathematical results.
5. In C, when a complex number is converted to a real number, the imaginary part is always discarded.

   In Ch, when a complex number is converted to a real number, only its real part is used and the imaginary part will be discarded if the imaginary part is zero. If the imaginary part is not equal to zero, the converted real number becomes NaN. The real and imaginary components of a complex number can be obtained explicitly by the functions **creal**(z) and **cimag**(z), which will be discussed in detail in section 17.6. When a complex number is converted to a real number, either implicitly by an assignment statement such as `f = z` or explicitly by **creal**(z), **cimag**(z), **float**(z), **double**(z), (**float**)z, and (**double**)z, the sign of a zero will not be carried over. Converting a complex number to an integral value such as char and int is equivalent to conversion of **creal**(z) to an integral value if the imaginary part is not identically zero. For example, `i = `**ComplexInf** will make `i` equal to **INT_MAX**. However, if **real**() or **imag**() is used as an lvalue, the sign of zeros from an rvalue will be preserved, which will allow experimentation with signed zeros in computations of complex numbers.

To write a portable code, the function **creal**() may be used to obtain the real part of a complex number.

The following code segment illustrates how data type conversions relating to complex numbers are handled.

```
double d = 4.0;
double complex z;
z = d;            // convert double to complex
z = 3.0 + I*d;    // complex multiply double
d = z;            // convert complex to double
                  // d is 3.0 in C99, d is NaN in Ch
d = creal(z)      // d is the real part of z,    d is 3.0
d = 3.0 + I*0.0;  // convert complex to double, d is 3.0
```

It is recommended to use the function **creal**() to obtain the real part of a complex number to make your code more portable for different implementations.

17.4 Complex Operations

The arithmetic and relational operations for complex numbers are treated in the same manner as those for real numbers in C. This section discusses how these operations are defined and handled.

The negation of a complex number and arithmetic and comparison operations for two complex numbers are defined in Table 17.1, where the complex numbers z, z_1, and z_2 are defined as $x + iy$, $x_1 + iy_1$, and $x_2 + iy_2$, respectively.

The negation of a complex number will change the sign of both the real and imaginary parts of the complex number. The addition of two complex numbers will add the real and imaginary components of two

Table 17.1 The complex operations.

Definition	Syntax	Semantics
Negation	$-$z	$-x - iy$
Addition	z1 + z2	$(x_1 + x_2) + i(y_1 + y_2)$
Subtraction	z1 $-$ z2	$(x_1 - x_2) + i(y_1 - y_2)$
Multiplication	z1 $*$ z2	$(x_1 * x_2 - y_1 * y_2) + i(y_1 * x_2 + x_1 * y_2)$
Division	z1 / z2	$\frac{x_1 * x_2 + y_1 * y_2}{x_2^2 + y_2^2} + i\frac{y_1 * x_2 - x_1 * y_2}{x_2^2 + y_2^2}$
Equal	z1 == z2	$x_1 == y_2$ and $y_1 == y_2$
Not equal	z1 != z2	$x_1 \mathrel{!=} x_2$ or $y_1 \mathrel{!=} y_2$

complex numbers, separately. The subtraction of two complex numbers will subtract the real and imaginary parts of the second complex number from the real and imaginary of the first complex number, respectively. Treating the imaginary number i as a complex number of `complex(0.0, 1.0)`, the multiplication and division of two complex numbers are defined in Table 17.1. For binary operations with real and complex operands, the regular real operand will be cast into a complex before the operation. Complex numbers are not ordered; one cannot compare to see whether one complex number is larger or smaller than the other. But two complex numbers can be tested to see whether they are equal or not. Two complex numbers are equal to each other if and only if both the real and imaginary parts of two complex numbers are equal to each other, separately. If the real or imaginary parts of two complex numbers are not equal to each other, then the two complex numbers are not equal. For example,

```
> double complex z1 = complex(3.0, 4.0), z2
> z2 = z1 + z1
complex(6.0000,8.0000)
> z2 = 2*z1 + 10
complex(16.0000,8.0000)
> z1 == z2
0
> z1 == z1
1
```

An lvalue is any object that occurs on the left-hand side of an assignment statement. The assignment operations `+=`, `-=`, `*=`, `/=`, as well as the increment operation `++` and decrement operation `--`, can be applied to an lvalue of complex type. For example,

```
> double complex z = complex(3.0, 4.0)
> z += complex(2.0, 3.0)
complex(5.0000,7.0000)
> z *= 2.0
complex(10.0000,14.0000)
> z++
complex(10.0000,14.0000)
> z
complex(11.0000,14.0000)
```

17.5 Complex Functions

The functions specifically for complex numbers, defined in the header file **complex.h**, are listed in Table 17.2 along with their definitions. These functions are similar to their equivalent type generic functions except that their expected arguments are complex numbers of type double complex. Aside from the function **cabs()**, **carg()**, **creal()**, and **cimag()**, the return value for these functions are also complex numbers of type double complex. A more detailed discussion of type generic functions relating to complex numbers can be found in the next section. For the functions of type complex, a suffix `'f'` can be added to the functions in Table 17.2. For example, the function **csinf()** accepts an argument and returns its value of sine of type complex. Program 17.2

Table 17.2 The syntax and semantics of complex functions defined in the header file complex.h.

Syntax	Semantics
cabs(z)	$\mathrm{sqrt}(x^2 + y^2)$
creal(z)	x
cimag(z)	y
carg(z)	$\Theta;\ \Theta = \mathrm{atan2}(y, x)$
csqrt(z)	$\mathrm{sqrt}(\mathrm{sqrt}(x^2 + y^2))\left(\cos\frac{\Theta}{2} + i\sin\frac{\Theta}{2}\right);\ \Theta = \mathrm{atan2}(y, x)$
cexp(z)	$e^x(\cos y + i\sin y)$
clog(z)	$\log(\sqrt{x^2 + y^2}) + i\Theta;\ \Theta = \mathrm{atan2}(y, x)$
cpow(z_1, z_2)	${z_1}^{z_2} = e^{z_2 \ln z_1} = \exp(z_2 * \log(z_1))$
csin(z)	$\sin x \cosh y + i \cos x \sinh y$
ccos(z)	$\cos x \cosh y - i \sin x \sinh y$
ctan(z)	$\frac{\sin z}{\cos z}$
casin(z)	$-i\log(iz + \mathrm{sqrt}(1 - z^2))$
cacos(z)	$-i\log(z + i\mathrm{sqrt}(1 - z^2))$
catan(z)	$\frac{1}{2i}\log(\frac{1 + iz}{1 - iz})$
csinh(z)	$\sinh x \cos y + i \cosh x \sin y$
ccosh(z)	$\cosh x \cos y + i \sinh x \sin y$
ctanh(z)	$\frac{\sinh x \cos y + i \cosh x \sin y}{\cosh x \cos y + i \sinh x \sin y}$

```
/* File: cfunction.c (run in C9 and Ch only)
   Compile in gcc, use command 'gcc -std=c99 cfunction.c -lm'
   Use complex mathematical functions */

#include <stdio.h>
#include <complex.h>   /* for complex, I, creal(), cimag(), csin(), csinf() */

int main() {
    /* declare and initialize  complex variables z and dz */
    float complex z = 1.0+I*2.0;
    double complex dz = 1.0+I*2.0;

    /* calculate and print sin() for z and dz */
    z = csinf(z);
```

Program 17.2: Using complex mathematical functions. (*Continued*)

```
    dz = csin(dz);
    printf("z  = complex(%f, %f)\n", creal(z), cimag(z));
    printf("dz = complex(%f, %f)\n", creal(dz), cimag(dz));
    return 0;
}
```

Program 17.2: *(Continued)*

provides an example of using the functions **csinf**() and **csin**() to compute the sine of both float complex and double complex types, respectively. The output of the program is as follows:

```
z  = complex(3.165778, 1.959601)
dz = complex(3.165779, 1.959601)
```

Notice that the real part of dz is slightly different from the real part of z due to rounding.

17.6 Type Generic Mathematical Functions

Aside from the complex functions mentioned above, type generic mathematical functions defined in the header file **tgmath.h** can be used with complex numbers. If a mathematical function has only one argument, and that argument is a complex number, then the function automatically becomes a complex function. Likewise, for a mathematical function with two arguments as a real function, if either one of two input arguments is a complex number, the mathematical function also becomes a complex function.

The type generic functions related to the complex numbers are listed in Table 17.3 along with their definitions. The input arguments of these functions can be complex numbers, variables, or expressions. For presentation purposes, the complex numbers z, z_1, and z_2 are defined as $x + iy$, $x_1 + iy_1$, and $x_2 + iy_2$, respectively. In Ch, a complex function can be used to calculate different branches of the function. The integer values of k, k_1, and k_2 are the branch numbers of the complex functions. If arguments for these branch numbers of the calling function are not integers, they will be cast into integers internally. For mathematical expressions in the second column in Table 17.3, if the arguments of mathematical functions are regular real numbers, the mathematical functions are real mathematical functions. In Table 17.3, the principal value Θ of the argument of a complex number is in the range of $-\pi < \Theta \leq \pi$. The definition of the principal value Θ for various complex numbers is given in Table 17.4. Note that the trigonometric function atan2(y, x) is in the range of $-\pi \leq \text{atan2}(y, x) \leq \pi$. Normally, through complex arithmetic and complex functions, one shall not get a complex number with its real or imaginary part being the value of −Inf, Inf, or NaN and the other part being a regular real number. This kind of result can be obtained only explicitly by the functions **real**(z) and **imag**(z), and the floating-point pointer variables through lvalues.

The first four functions in Table 17.3 return real numbers. The **sizeof** operator gives, in bytes, an integer of the variable, type specifier, or expression that it precedes. Its returned data type is of type **unsigned int** for 32-bit machines and type **unsigned long long** for 64-bit machines. If the operand is of complex type, the **sizeof** operation gives the value of 8, which is the number of bytes required for storing two floats of real and imaginary parts of a complex number. If the operand is of type double complex, it gives 16 bytes—8 bytes each for the real and the imaginary part of the complex number. The **abs**(z) function computes the modulus of a complex number. The returned data type is float. The functions **real**(z) and **imag**(z) return the real and imaginary parts of a complex number, respectively. The results of **real**(z) and **imag**(z) are always float types. If the data type of the argument for **real**() is lower or equal to double, the input data will be cast into float. If the data type

Table 17.3 The syntax and semantics of type generic complex functions. Function calls with argument k, k_1, or k_2 are valid in Ch only.

Syntax	Semantics
sizeof(z)	8 bytes for complex and 16 bytes for double complex
abs(z)	$\text{sqrt}(x^2 + y^2)$
real(z)	x
imag(z)	y
conj(z)	$x - iy$
carg(z)	$\Theta;\ \Theta = \text{atan2}(y, x)$
polar(z)	$\text{sqrt}(x^2 + y^2) + i\Theta;\ \Theta = \text{atan2}(y, x)$
polar(r, $theta$)	$r\cos(theta) + ir\sin(theta)$
sqrt(z)	$\text{sqrt}(\text{sqrt}(x^2 + y^2))\left(\cos\frac{\Theta}{2} + i\sin\frac{\Theta}{2}\right);\ \Theta = \text{atan2}(y, x)$
sqrt(z, k)	$\text{sqrt}(\text{sqrt}(x^2 + y^2))\left(\cos\frac{\Theta + 2k\pi}{2} + i\sin\frac{\Theta + 2k\pi}{2}\right);\ \Theta = \text{atan2}(y, x)$
exp(z)	$e^x(\cos y + i\sin y)$
log(z)	$\log(\sqrt{x^2 + y^2}) + i\Theta;\ \Theta = \text{atan2}(y, x)$
log(z, k)	$\log(\sqrt{x^2 + y^2}) + i(\Theta + 2k\pi);\ \Theta = \text{atan2}(y, x)$
log10(z)	$\frac{\log(z)}{\log(10)}$
log10(z, k)	$\frac{\log(z, k)}{\log(10)}$
pow(z_1, z_2)	$z_1^{z_2} = e^{z_2 \ln z_1} = \exp(z_2 * \log(z_1))$
pow(z_1, z_2, k)	$z_1^{z_2} = e^{z_2 \ln z_1} = \exp(z_2 * \log(z_1, k))$
ceil(z)	$\text{ceil}(x) + i\ \text{ceil}(y)$
floor(z)	$\text{floor}(x) + i\ \text{floor}(y)$
fmod($z1$, $z2$)	$z;\ \ \frac{z_1}{z_2} = k + \frac{z}{z_2},\ k \geq 0$
modf($z1$, &$z2$)	$\text{modf}(x_1, \&x_2) + i\ \text{modf}(y_1, \&y_2)$
frexp($z1$, &$z2$)	$\text{frexp}(x_1, \&x_2) + i\ \text{frexp}(y_1, \&y_2)$
ldexp($z1$, $z2$)	$\text{ldexp}(x_1, x_2) + i\ \text{ldexp}(y_1, y_2)$
sin(z)	$\sin x \cosh y + i\cos x \sinh y$
cos(z)	$\cos x \cosh y - i\sin x \sinh y$
tan(z)	$\frac{\sin z}{\cos z}$
asin(z)	$-i\log(iz + \text{sqrt}(1 - z^2))$
asin(z, k)	$-i\log(iz + \text{sqrt}(1 - z^2, k))$
asin(z, $k1$, $k2$)	$-i\log(iz + \text{sqrt}(1 - z^2, k_1), k_2)$
acos(z)	$-i\log(z + i\text{sqrt}(1 - z^2))$

(Continued)

Table 17.3 *(Continued)*

Syntax	Semantics
acos(z, k)	$-i\log(z + i\text{sqrt}(1 - z^2, k))$
acos(z, $k1$, $k2$)	$-i\log(z + i\text{sqrt}(1 - z^2, k_1), k_2)$
atan(z)	$\frac{1}{2i}\log\left(\frac{1+iz}{1-iz}\right)$
atan(z, k)	$\frac{1}{2i}\log\left(\frac{1+iz}{1-iz}, k\right)$
atan2($z1$, $z2$)	$\frac{1}{2i}\log\left(\frac{1+iz_1/z_2}{1-iz1/z_2}\right)$
atan2($z1$, $z2$, k)	$\frac{1}{2i}\log\left(\frac{1+iz_1/z_2}{1-iz1/z_2}, k\right)$
sinh(z)	$\sinh x \cos y + i \cosh x \sin y$
cosh(z)	$\cosh x \cos y + i \sinh x \sin y$
tanh(z)	$\frac{\sinh x \cos y + i \cosh x \sin y}{\cosh x \cos y + i \sinh x \sin y}$
asinh(z)	$\log(z + \text{sqrt}(z^2 + 1))$
asinh(z, k)	$\log(z + \text{sqrt}(z^2 + 1, k))$
asinh(z, $k1$, $k2$)	$\log(z + \text{sqrt}(z^2 + 1, k_1), k_2)$
acosh(z)	$\log(z + \text{sqrt}(z + 1)\text{sqrt}(z - 1))$
acosh(z, k)	$\log(z + \text{sqrt}(z + 1, k)\text{sqrt}(z - 1, k))$
acosh(z, $k1$, $k2$)	$\log(z + \text{sqrt}(z + 1, k_1)\text{sqrt}(z - 1, k_1), k_2)$
atanh(z)	$\frac{1}{2}\log\left(\frac{1+z}{1-z}\right)$
atanh(z, k)	$\frac{1}{2}\log\left(\frac{1+z}{1-z}, k\right)$

Table 17.4 The principal value Θ $(-\pi < \Theta \leq \pi)$ of the argument for complex(x, y).

	Θ					
y value	**x value**					
	−x1	−0.0	0.0	x2	Inf	NaN
y2	atan2(y_2, $-x_1$)	pi/2	pi/2	atan2(y_2, x_2)		
0.0	pi	0.0	0.0	0.0		
−0.0	pi	0.0	0.0	0.0		
−y1	atan2($-y_1$, $-x_1$)	−pi/2	−pi/2	atan2($-y_1$, x_2)		
Inf					Inf	
NaN						NaN

of the argument for **imag**() is lower than or equal to double, the value of zero will be returned. The sign of a zero will be ignored in **real**(z) and **imag**(z) functions. For example, **real**(complex(−0.0, 0.0)) will return 0.0. These functions are illustrated below.

```
> double complex z = complex(3.0, 4.0)
> sizeof(z)
16
> real(z)
3.0000
> imag(z)
4.0000
```

The **conj**(z) function returns the complex conjugate $\overline{z}$ of z. The complex number $\overline{z}$ represented by the point $(x, -y)$ is the reflection in the real axis of the point (x, y) representing z, as shown previously in Figure 17.6. For example,

```
> double complex z = complex(3.0, 4.0)
> conj(z)
complex(3.0000,-4.0000)
```

The function **carg**() gives the phase angle of a complex number. The function **polar**() is implemented mainly for the convenience of making the transformation between Cartesian and polar representations of a complex number. If there is only one input argument, then a complex number, with its real and imaginary parts being the modulus and argument, respectively, of the input complex number, will be returned. If there are two input arguments, the complex number z in the polar form will be returned. The first and second input arguments are the modulus and argument of z, respectively. According to the definition $re^{i\theta}$ for the polar function, negative values for r are valid. For example,

```
> double complex z
> z = polar(5.0, 0.0)
complex(5.0000,0.0000)
> z = polar(5.0, 0.6)
complex(4.1267,2.8232)
> abs(z)
5.0000
> carg(z)
0.6000
```

The **exp**(z) function will calculate the exponential function of the complex number z.

The function **log**() will calculate the natural logarithmic function of a complex number, whereas for convenience, the function **log10**() will calculate its base-10 logarithmic function.

The exponential function with a complex base can be calculated by the function **pow**(), which is accomplished by the exponential function and logarithmic function shown in Table 17.3. Unlike its corresponding real function, the complex function **pow**() is always well defined. If any one of two arguments of **pow**(z1, z2) is complex, the result is complex, which is obtained by the expression `exp(z2*log(z1))`. The result of the expression y^x equals the real part of the expression `pow(complex(y,0.0), complex(x,0.0))`, with its imaginary part being zero. For example,

```
> complex z = complex(3.0, 4.0)
> exp(z)
complex(-13.1288,-15.2008)
> log(z)
complex(1.6094,0.9273)
> exp(log(z))
complex(3.0000,4.0000)
> pow(z, 2)
complex(-7.0000, 24.0000)
```

For the functions **ceil**(z), **floor**(z), and **ldexp**(z1, z2), the real and imaginary parts are treated as if they were two separate real functions. The functions **modf**(z1, &z2) and **frexp**(z1, &z2) are handled in the same manner. For these two functions, when the data type of the first arguments is complex, the data type of the second argument must be pointer to complex. The **fmod**(z1, z2) function computes the complex remainder of z1/z2.

The complex trigonometric functions **sin**(z), **cos**(z), and **tan**(z) and the complex hyperbolic functions **sinh**(z), **cosh**(z), and **tanh**(z) have unique values. Program 17.3 is similar to Program 17.2. The difference is that Program 17.3 uses type generic function **sin()** rather than complex functions **csinf()** and **csin()** to compute the sine of $1 + i2$. The output of Program 17.3 is the same as Program 17.2.

```
/* File: cgeneric.c  (run in C99 and Ch only)
   Compile in gcc, use command 'gcc -std=c99 cgeneric.c -lm'
   Use generic mathematical functions for complex argument */
#include <stdio.h>
#include <complex.h>    /* for complex, I, creal(), cimag() */
#include <tgmath.h>     /* sin() */

int main() {
    /* declare and initialize  complex variables z and dz */
    complex z = 1.0+I*2.0;
    double complex dz = 1.0+I*2.0;

    /* calculate and print sin() for z and dz */
    z = sin(z);
    dz = sin(dz);
    printf("z  = complex(%f, %f)\n", creal(z), cimag(z));
    printf("dz = complex(%f, %f)\n", creal(dz), cimag(dz));
    return 0;
}
```

Program 17.3: Using generic mathematical functions with an argument of complex type.

An Application Example

Solving Quadratic Equations

In this section, the application of complex numbers will be demonstrated by solving second-order polynomial equations. A second-order polynomial equation (4.1) can be solved by the formulas (4.2) and (4.3) presented in section 4.2 in Chapter 4.

For equation

$$x^2 - 4x + 13 = 0 \tag{17.12}$$

two complex solutions of $x_1 = 2 + i3$ and $x_2 = 2 - i3$ cannot be solved in the real domain. These complex numbers cannot be represented with the data type double and would result in NaN in C. This is illustrated by the output of Program 17.4 shown below:

```
x1 = nan
x2 = nan
```

Using complex numbers, equation (17.12) with the two complex solutions of $x_1 = 2 + i3$ and $x_2 = 2 - i3$ can be solved by Program 17.5 with the output shown below:

```
x1 = complex(2.000000, 3.000000)
x2 = complex(2.000000, -3.000000)
```

```
/* File: quadratic1.c
   Solve for two roots of the quadratic equation
   x^2-4x+13 = 0   */
#include <stdio.h>
#include <math.h>   /* for sqrt() */

int main() {
    /* declare variables for the coefficients
       of the quadratic equation and roots;
       initialize the coefficients */
    double a = 1.0, b = -4.0, c = 13.0, x1, x2;

    /* solve for two roots of the quadratic equation */
    x1 = (-b+sqrt(b*b-4*a*c))/(2*a);   /* first branch */
    x2 = (-b-sqrt(b*b-4*a*c))/(2*a);   /* second branch */

    /* display two roots */
    printf("x1 = %f\n", x1);
    printf("x2 = %f\n", x2);
    return 0;
}
```

Program 17.4: The solution for $x^2 - 4x + 13 = 0$ in the real domain.

In Program 17.5, coefficients a, b, and c as well as solutions x_1 and x_2 are represented as complex numbers.

```
/* File: quadratic2.c   (run in C99 and Ch only)
   Compile in gcc, use command 'gcc -std=c99 quadratic2.c -lm'
   Solve for two complex roots of the quadratic equation
   x^2-4x+13 = 0  in the complex domain */
#include <stdio.h>
#include <tgmath.h>    /* for sqrt() */
#include <complex.h>   /* for complex, I, creal(), cimag() */


int main() {
   /* declare variables of type complex for the coefficients
      of the quadratic equation and roots;
      initialize the coefficients */
   double complex a = 1.0, b = -4.0, c = 13.0, x1, x2;

   /* solve for two roots of the quadratic equation */
   x1 = (-b+sqrt(b*b-4*a*c))/(2*a);   /* first branch */
   x2 = (-b-sqrt(b*b-4*a*c))/(2*a);   /* second branch */

   /* display two roots */
   printf("x1 = complex(%f, %f)\n", creal(x1), cimag(x1));
   printf("x2 = complex(%f, %f)\n", creal(x2), cimag(x2));
   return 0;
}
```

Program 17.5: The solution for $x^2 - 4x + 13 = 0$ in the complex domain.

17.7 Writing Portable C and C++ Programs with Complex Numbers

Both C99 and C++ support programming with complex numbers, but they are handled differently. C++ is not a superset of C in this case. Complex types are built-in data types in C99. They are more naturally integrated with other data types for real numbers. On the other hand, complex types are implemented as classes in C++, which is more flexible for handling functions involving complex numbers. Usually, a C99 conforming program with complex numbers cannot be compiled using a C++ compiler and vice versa. With some disciplines, however, it is possible to write portable programs with complex numbers that can be compiled either in a C99 or C++ compiler. In this section, we describe how to write such portable programs.

Before we present the technique for writing a portable code, we need to point out that the declaration of complex variables used in C99 is not applicable in C++. To be compatible, we define new data types `float_complex` for float complex and `double_complex` for double complex by using **typedef** in C as follows:

```
typedef float  complex float_complex;
typedef double complex double_complex;
```

The function **polar()** is a commonly used feature to form a complex number in the polar coordinates. It is available in both C++ and Ch. We can add this function by defining it as a macro as follows:

```
#define polar(r, theta)   ((r)*cos(theta)+I*(r)*sin(theta))
```

To define this macro, apparently, we need to include the header files **tgmath.h** for the functions **cos()** and **sin()**, and **complex.h** for **I** of the imaginary number.

On the other hand, to make a program with complex numbers to compile in C++, we also need to create the compatible data type `float_complex` for complex and `double_complex` for double complex. C++ uses complex constructor `double_complex(x, y)` to form a complex number $x + iy$. To use the complex constructor of `x+I*y` in C99, the macro `I` can be defined for C++ code by

```
#define I double_complex(0.0, 1.0)
```

Furthermore, the real, imaginary, modulus, and phase angle of a complex number are obtained by the functions **creal(), cimag(), cabs()**, and **carg()** in C99, respectively. In C++, they are obtained by the functions **real(), imag(), abs()**, and **arg()**. Therefore, we need to add the functions **creal(), cimag(), cabs()**, and **carg()** for C++. They can be simply defined by macros as follows:

```
#define creal real
#define cimag imag
#define cabs  abs
#define carg  arg
```

The complex functions **casin()** and **cacos()**, not available in C++ by default, are defined by the macros

```
#define casin(z)   (-I*log(I*(z)+sqrt(1.0-(z)*(z))))
#define cacos(z)   (-I*log((z)+I*sqrt(1.0-(z)*(z))))
```

The above described modifications on C99 and C++ sides can be nicely handled using the header file `ccomplex.h` shown in Program 17.6. The setup for C++ is included under the preprocessing condition of

```
#ifdef __cpluscplus
```

The macro **__cpluscplus** is a predefined macro for a C++ compiler. The setup for C99 is included in the else branch of the preprocessing condition structure. The header file also includes other header files for handling mathematical functions with complex arguments.

```
/* File: ccomplex.h
   A portable header file for using complex in C99 and C++.
   (1) The following features are added in C++
       (a) complex types double_complex and float_complex
       (b) imaginary number I
       (c) functions creal(), cimag(), cabs(), and carg()
   (2) The following features are added in C99 and Ch
       (a) types double_complex and float_complex
   (3) The following feature is added in C99
       (a) function polar()
*/
#ifndef CCOMPLEX_H
#define CCOMPLEX_H
```

Program 17.6: A header file for writing portable C99 and C++ programs with complex numbers. (*Continued*)

```
#ifdef __cplusplus  /* for C++ */
  #include <math.h>                              /* for math functions */
  #include <iostream>                            /* for using namespace std */
  #include <complex>                             /* for complex class */
  using namespace std;                           /* for complex I/O */
  typedef complex<double> double_complex;        /* double complext type */
  typedef complex<float>  float_complex;         /* float complex or complex type */
  #define I double_complex(0.0, 1.0)             /* define pure imaginary number */
  #define creal real                             /* define creal() */
  #define cimag imag                             /* define cimag() */
  #define cabs  abs                              /* define cabs() */
  #define carg  arg                              /* define carg() */
  #define casin(z)   (-I*log(I*(z)+sqrt(1.0-(z)*(z)))) /* define cacos() */
  #define cacos(z)   (-I*log((z)+I*sqrt(1.0-(z)*(z)))) /* define cacos() */

#else                /* for C99 and Ch */
  #include <tgmath.h>                            /* type generic functions */
  #include <complex.h>                           /* complex numbers */
  typedef float complex float_complex;           /* define float complex type */
  typedef double complex double_complex;         /* define double complex type */
  /* function polar() is available in C++ and Ch. Define it for C99 */
  #ifndef _CH_
  #define polar(r, theta)   ((r)*cos(theta)+I*(r)*sin(theta))
  #endif
#endif

#endif /* end CCOMPLEX_H */
```

Program 17.6: *(Continued)*

Using the header file `ccomplex.h` to write portable C99 and C++ programs with complex numbers is demonstrated by Program 17.7, which can be compiled either using a C compiler supporting complex types in C99, such as **gcc**, or a C++ compiler, such as **g++** and Visual C++. Program 17.7 includes the header file `ccomplex.h` to resolve the major differences of C99 and C++. Complex variables of type double complex in the program are declared and initialized by the type specifier `double_complex`. Similar to Program 17.5, Program 17.7 solves for complex roots of equation (17.12). Afterwards, the use of imaginary number **I** and the functions **sin(), creal(), cimag(), cabs(), carg()**, and **polar()** are demonstrated. The output from Program 17.7 is shown below:

```
x1 = complex(2.000000, 3.000000)
x2 = complex(2.000000, -3.000000)
sin(1+i2) = complex(3.165779, 1.959601)
z = complex(3.000000, 4.000000)
modulus(z) = 5.000000, phase angle (z) = 0.927295
z = complex(3.000000, 4.000000)
```

```
/* File: quadratic3.c (run in C99, Ch, and C++)
   Compile in gcc, use command 'gcc -std=c99 quadratic3.c -lm'
   Compile in g++, use command 'g++ quadratic3.c -lm'
   Compile in Visual C++, use command 'cl /TP quadratic3.c'
                        or use command 'cl quadratic3.cpp'

   Solve for two complex roots of the quadratic equation
   x^2-4x+13 = 0  in the complex domain.
   This program is portable and can be compiled in both C99 and C++ */
#include <stdio.h>
#include "ccomplex.h" /* portable header for complex numbers in C99 and C++ */

int main() {
    /* Use double_complex to declare and initialize variables */
    double_complex a = 1.0, b = -4.0, c = 13.0, x1, x2, z;

    x1 = (-b +sqrt(b*b-4.0*a*c))/(2.0*a); /* use math function sqrt() */
    x2 = (-b -sqrt(b*b-4.0*a*c))/(2.0*a);
    printf("x1 = complex(%f, %f)\n", creal(x1), cimag(x1));
    printf("x2 = complex(%f, %f)\n", creal(x2), cimag(x2));

    /* Use I, sin(), creal(), cimag(), cabs(), carg(), and polar() */
    z = 1.0 + I*2.0;                  /* construct a complex number */
    z = sin(z);                       /* use mathematical function sin() */
    /* get real part creal() and imaginary part cimag() of complex z */
    printf("sin(1+i2) = complex(%f, %f)\n", creal(z), cimag(z));
    z = 3.0 + I*4.0;                  /* construct a complex number */
    /* get real part creal() and imaginary part cimag() of complex z */
    printf("z = complex(%f, %f)\n", creal(z), cimag(z));
    /* get modulus cabs() and phase angle carg() of complex z */
    printf("modulus(z) = %f, phase angle (z) = %f\n", cabs(z), carg(z));
    /* form a complex number in the polar form by polar(r, theta) */
    z = polar(cabs(z), carg(z));
    printf("z = complex(%f, %f)\n", creal(z), cimag(z));
    return 0;
}
```

Program 17.7: A portable C99 and C++ program with complex numbers.

There are some other notable differences in dealing with complex numbers in C99 and C++, and beginners need to pay attention to them. In C99, according to the built-in conversion rules described in section 17.3, a binary operation can be mixed with operands of real and complex numbers. For example, multiplication of an integer with a complex number, such as `4*z` with z being a complex variable, is allowed. But this is not valid in C++, which can cause a problem when porting a C99 code to C++. For example, the solution for the first root of the quadratic equation (17.12) in Program 17.7 could be written as

```
x1 = (-b +sqrt(b*b-4*a*c))/(2.0*a);
```

for a C99 program. But the program would give an error message if it were compiled using a C++ compiler. Unfortunately, error messages from C++ are usually very difficult to comprehend, especially for beginners. The error message in this case is so cryptic that it is not clear that all you need to do is to change 4 to 4.0 in the previous statement to pass the compilation by the compiler. On the other hand, the complex constructor `double_complex()` and lvalues of **real**() and **imag**() in C++ and Ch, as shown below

```
double_complex z1 = double_complex(3.0, 4.0);
double_complex z2;
real(z2) = real(z1);
imag(z2) = imag(z1);
```

are not available in a typical C compiler. Nevertheless, using features presented in the header file `ccomplex.h` in Program 17.6, one can write portable programs to solve problems in engineering and science involving complex numbers conveniently.

An Application Example

Unit-Step Responses of a Second-Order System

A *prototype second-order control system* is shown in Figure 17.7. For a unit-step function input, the output response of the system is

$$y(t) = 1 - \frac{e^{-\zeta\omega_n t}}{\sqrt{1-\zeta^2}} \sin(\omega_n \sqrt{1-\zeta^2}\, t + \cos^{-1}\zeta) \tag{17.13}$$

In the design and analysis of control systems, it is important to study the effects of the system parameters ζ and ω_n on the step response $y(t)$ of the prototype second-order control system. One way is to plot the transient response $y(t)$ versus the normalized time $\omega_n t$ for various values of ζ's as shown in Figure 17.8 with ζ of 0.1, 0.5, 0.9, 1.3, and 1.7. The figure shows that as ζ decreases, the response becomes more oscillatory. When $\zeta \geq 1$, the step response does not exceed its final value during the transient.

Figure 17.8 for step responses of the prototype second-order control system is generated by Program 17.8. When $\zeta < 1$, the step response can readily be plotted using equation (17.13) in the real domain. However, when $\zeta \geq 1$, expression $\sqrt{1-\zeta^2}$ and $\cos^{-1}\zeta$ are undefined in the real domain. Therefore, we have to evaluate the function $y(t)$ in the complex domain. To be consistent, the function $y(t)$ is

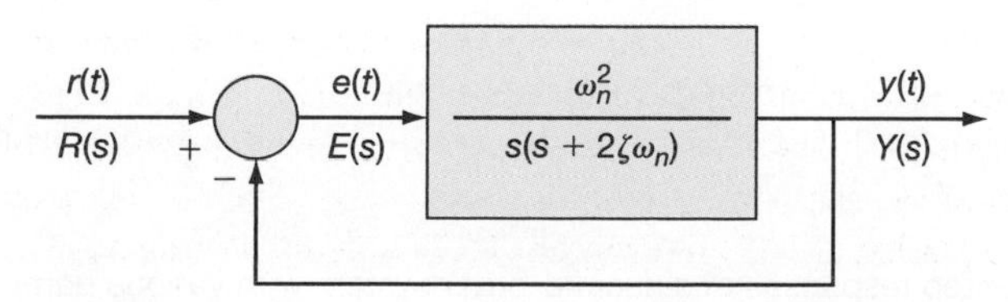

Figure 17.7 The prototype second-order control system.

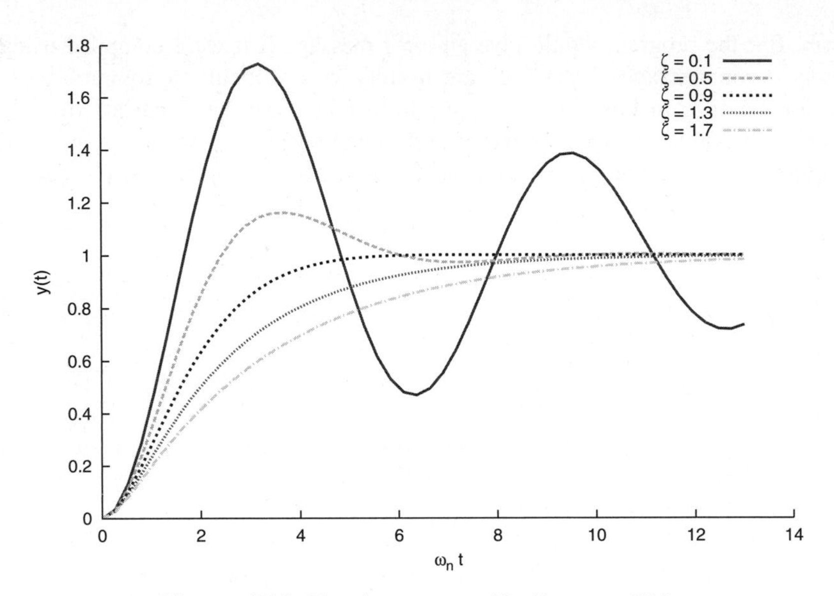

Figure 17.8 The plot generated by Program 17.8.

```
/* File: response.cpp
   Calculate and display unit-step responses of
   a second-order system with various damping ratios.
   Compile in g++, use command
    g++ response.cpp -I/usr/local/silib/include -L/usr/local/silib/lib -lchplot
   Compile in Visual C++, use command
    cl response.cpp -IC:/silib/include C:/silib/lib/libchplot.lib
*/
#include <chplot.h>
#include "ccomplex.h" /* portable header for C99 and C++ */

#define N 50            /* number of points for plotting */

double zeta;            /* parameter zeta */

double response(double t) {
    double wn = 1.0, y;
    double_complex per, damp, res;

    /* when zeta > 1,
       srqt(1-zeta*zeta) and acos(zeta) are complex numbers */
    damp = exp(-zeta*wn*t)/sqrt(1.0-zeta*zeta+0.0*I);
    per = sin(wn*sqrt(1.0-zeta*zeta+0.0*I)*t + cacos(zeta-0.0*I));
    res = damp*per;
```

Program 17.8: The unit-step responses of a second-order system with various damping ratios. (*Continued*)

```
    /* get rid of tiny imaginary part in res */
    y = 1.0 - creal(res);
    return y;
}

int main() {
    double t0=0, tf=13; /* time from 0 to 13 seconds */
    int i;
    class CPlot plot;
    char str[64];          /* string for legend */

    plot.enhanceText(); /* use enhanced text for special symbols */
    plot.label(PLOT_AXIS_X, "{/Symbol w}_n t"); /* for w_n t */
    plot.label(PLOT_AXIS_Y, "y(t)");
    for(i=0, zeta=0.1; zeta <= 2; i++, zeta += 0.4) {
        plot.func2D(t0, tf, N, response);
        sprintf(str, "{/Symbol z} = %.1f", zeta); /* string "zeta = 0.1" */
        plot.legend(str, i);              /* add legend "zeta = 0.1 */
    }
    plot.plotting();
}
```

Program 17.8: (*Continued*)

implemented as `response()` in Program 17.8 using complex numbers for evaluation of equation (17.13) by the following code:

```
damp = exp(-zeta*wn*t)/sqrt(1.0-zeta*zeta+0.0*I);
per = sin(wn*sqrt(1.0-zeta*zeta+0.0*I)*t + cacos(zeta-0.0*I));
res = damp*per;
/* get rid of tiny imaginary part in res */
y = 1.0 - creal(res);
```

The variables `damp`, `per`, and `res` are type double complex, whereas the variable `y` is type double. To use the complex version of the function **sqrt()**, a complex number of zero, 0.0*I, is added to its argument. For the function **cacos()**, a complex zero is subtracted from its argument. Otherwise, an incorrect branch of the complex value from the function **cacos()** will be returned when the code is compiled using the C++ compiler **g++** in Linux. The implementation of complex numbers in Ch is more consistent for complex functions with multiple branches. An optional argument for a branch number for complex functions as shown in Table 17.3 in Ch is also very handy for testing different branches. Alternatively, we can declare the variable `zeta` of type double complex. Then we do not need to add or subtract a complex zero 0.0*I in the expression.

When $\zeta < 1$, the imaginary part of variable `res` is zero. However, when $\zeta \geq 1$, the imaginary part of the variable `res` is a tiny value, smaller than the machine epsilon **DBL_EPSILON** defined in the header file **float.h**. Therefore, only the real part of the variable `res` is used for $y(t)$ by the function **creal()**.

Unit-step responses are plotted using a plotting class. The function `response()` is invoked by the member function **func2D()** inside a **for** loop with different values for ζ. After the member function **enhanceText()** for plotting is called by

```
plot.enhanceText();
```

the special symbols ω_n in the x-axis and ζ in legends can be generated using the enhanced text `"{/Symbol w}_n"` and `"{/Symbol z}"`, respectively.

When $\zeta = 1$, the prototype second-order control system is critically damped. Equation (17.13) is no longer valid. The numerical result for $y(t)$ would become NaN if equation (17.13) is used. When $\zeta = 1$, the derived formula for the unit-step response of the system is as follows:

$$y(t) = 1 - e^{-\omega_n t}(1 + \omega_n t) \tag{17.14}$$

It is left as an exercise at the end of this chapter to add this step response for a critical damped system to Figure 17.8.

Application examples using complex numbers to calculate roots of polynomials, find poles of transfer functions for design and analysis of control systems, and calculate eigenvalues and eigenvectors of matrices can be found in Chapter 22. Complex numbers can also be used conveniently for partial-fraction expansion and residue computation using the function **residue()** in Ch.

17.8 Making It Work

17.8.1 Compiling a Portable C/C++ Program Using C and C++ Compilers

The file `quadratic3.c` in Program 17.7 with the C99 feature of complex numbers, has the `.c` extension. As described in section 2.2.4 in Chapter 2, it can be compiled using the GNU C compiler, which supports most ISO C99 features, and linked with the math library as follows:

```
> gcc -std=c99 quadratic3.c -lm
```

To use the C++ part of the code, the program can be compiled using the GNU C++ compiler, which will be described in section 18.7.1 in Chapter 18, by the command

```
> g++ quadratic3.c -lm
```

The command **cl** in Visual C++ in Windows can be used to compile both C and C++ programs. By default, a file with the `.c` extension is treated as a C source file. The `/TP` option of the command **cl** specifies that the following input file is a C++ source file, even if it does not have a `.cpp` or `.cxx` extension. Using this option, a C++ program `quadratic.c` can be compiled as follows:

```
> cl /TP quadratic3.c
```

Alternatively, we can copy the file `quadratic3.c` to the file `quadratic3.cpp`, and then compile it as a C++ program by

```
> cl quadratic3.cpp
```

Exercises

1. Calculate 5(1+i3)(x+iy)+4 with $x = 2$ and $y = 3$ at the command prompt of a Ch shell.
2. Write a program to calculate the following items:

   a. $z_1 = (3 + i5) + (4 - i2)$
   b. $z_2 = (2 - i) * (i6)$
   c. $z_3 = (7 + i15)/(9 + i30)$
   d. $z_4 = 3e^{i2.3\pi} + 4e^{i3.4\pi}$

   Use the functions **creal()**, **cimag()**, **cabs()**, and **carg()** to determine the real part, imaginary part, magnitudes, and phase angle of z_1, z_2, z_3, and z_4, respectively.
3. Let $z1 = 3 + i4$, $z2 = 5e^{i40^\circ}$, and $z3 = 4 + i4$. Determine the values of $z4$, $z5$, $z6$ given the following:

   a. $z4 = z1 * z2 - z2 * z3$
   b. $z5 = z1/z3 - z1 * z3$
   c. $z6 = z4 - z1 * z5 + z2$

4. Solve the equation

$$5x^2 + 2x + 1 = 0$$

5. Write a program to solve the following second-order polynomial equation:

$$ax^2 + bx + c = 0$$

   interactively using the formula

$$x = \frac{-b \pm \sqrt{b^2 - 4ac}}{2a} \tag{17.15}$$

   The input from the console is obtained by the function **scanf()** with a = 1, b = −7, c = 12; and a = 2, b = 4, c = 8. (i) Use real numbers only. (ii) Use complex numbers.
6. Given $f(z) = z^2 - 3$ and the inverse function $f^{-1}(z)$ is $\sqrt{z + 3}$, write a program to calculate $f(i\sqrt{2})$ and $f^{-1}(-5)$ in the complex domain.
7. Calculate the transient response of a prototype second-order control system $y(t)$ in equation (17.13) for ζ of 0.9 and 1.2 when the normalized time $\omega_n t$ is 2, in the following ways:

   a. Use variables of type double for numerical computation.
   b. Use variables of type double complex for numerical computation. Display real and imaginary parts of the result using the format specifier `"%g"`.

8. Add the unit-step response in equation (17.14) for the critically damped prototype second-order control system in Figure 17.8.
9. Modify Program 17.8 using the member function **funcp2D()** of the plotting class **CPlot** to get rid of the global variable `zeta`. The value of the local variable `zeta` of type double inside the function **main()**, for the parameter ζ, is passed as an argument to the function `func()`. Inside the function `func()`, a variable `zeta` of type double complex is used for numerical computation in complex numbers without an extra term `0.0*I` in function arguments.

PART II

Object-Based Programming in C++

CHAPTER 18

‡Introduction to C++

C++ contains many extensions to features available in C. Most extensions are mainly for object-oriented programming. However, some extensions overcome the shortcomings of C. In this chapter, some simple and useful extensions in C++ are presented. Classes in C++ for object-based programming will be described in Chapter 19.

18.1 The First C++ Program

C++ source files conventionally use either of the suffixes `.cpp` or `.cxx`. A simple example of a C++ program is shown as Program 18.1. It is a modified version of the familiar "Hello World" C program in Program 2.1 in Chapter 2. The difference is that Program 18.1 uses the standard output stream (**cout**) and the stream insertion operator (<<) to display `Hello, world`. To use this simplified output format, the header file **iostream** without a file extension, instead of the header file **stdio.h**, is included at the beginning of the program.

Although Ch does not support all features in C++, C++ features presented in this book are available in Ch. These C++ programs can be executed in Ch in the same manner as C programs. For example, Program 18.1 can be executed in a Ch command shell as follows:

```
> hello.cpp
Hello, world
```

```
/* File: hello.cpp
   Print 'Hello, world' on the screen using C++. */
#include <iostream>      // for I/O in C++
using namespace std;     // for using cout, cin, cerr, endl, ends

int main() {
    cout << "Hello, world\n";
    return 0;
}
```

Program 18.1: A simple C++ program.

or

```
> ch hello.cpp
Hello, world
```

Like C programs, C++ program can be edited and executed in ChIDE.

18.2 Simplified Input and Output

C++ provides three simplified formats for input and output. They are the standard input stream **cin**, which is normally connected to the keyboard, the standard output stream **cout**, which is normally connected to the computer screen, and the standard error stream **cerr**, which is normally connected to the screen. All three streams can be assigned to other devices rather than the default devices.

Furthermore, C++ provides the stream insertion operator "<<", which performs output to the stream **cout**, the stream extraction operator ">>", which performs input from the stream **cin**, and the stream manipulator **endl**, which issues a newline character and flushes the output buffer. However, some systems do not display output immediately due to buffering. Operators "<<" and ">>" are associated from left to right and can be used in a cascaded form. For example,

```
> int i, j
> cin >> i              // <==> scanf(&i)
10
> cout << i             // <==> printf(i)
10
> cerr << i
10
> cin >> i >> j         // <==> scanf(&i, &j)
20 30
> cout << i << j        // <==> printf(i, j)
2030
```

To use the streams **cin, cout**, and **cerr** in a program, it is necessary to include the header file **iostream** and a **using** directive for namespace in input/output (I/O) streams in the form of

```
using namespace std;
```

or

```
using std::cout;
using std::cin;
using std::cerr;
using std::endl;
using std::ends;
```

Programs 18.2 and 18.3 are examples of input and output in C++. Program 18.2 uses **cin** to obtain two numbers for calculating their product. Execution of the source file `cinc.cpp` would result in the following:

```
/* File: cinc.cpp
   Obtain input from the keyboard using cin */
#include <iostream>          // for I/O in C++
using namespace std;         // for using cout, cin, cerr, endl

int main() {
    int a, b, product;

    cout << "Please enter first integer number\n";
    cin >> a;                // scanf("%d", &a);
    cout << "Please enter second integer number" << endl;
    cin >> b;                // scanf("%d", &b);
    cout << "product = " << a*b << endl;
    return 0;
}
```

Program 18.2: Formatted Input using **cin**.

```
> cinc.cpp
Please enter first integer number
2
Please enter second integer number
3
product = 6
```

where 2 and 3 are entered values. Program 18.3, on the other hand, shows the similarity between output with the standard C function, **printf()**, and the C++ output stream, **cout**. The output of Program 18.3 is shown below:

```
Output using C functions:
c = a
i = 10
f = 20.00
d = 30.5000
s = John

Output using C++ features
c = a
i = 10
f = 20.00
d = 30.5000
s = John
```

Program 18.4 uses a different format of the **using** directive. Its output is the same as that from Program 18.2.

```
/* File: coutc.cpp
   Output using cout in C++ in comparison with printf() in C */
#include <stdio.h>            // for I/O in C
#include <iostream>           // for I/O in C++
using namespace std;          // for using cout, cin, cerr, endl

int main() {
    /* declare and initialize variables */
    char c = 'a';
    int i = 10;
    float f  = 20.0;
    double d = 30.5;
    char *s = "John";

    printf("Output using C functions:\n", c);
    printf("c = %c\n", c);
    printf("i = %d\n", i);
    printf("f = %g\n", f);
    printf("d = %g\n", d);
    printf("s = %s\n\n", s);

    cout << "Output using C++ features\n";
    cout << "c = " << c << endl;
    cout << "i = " << i << endl;
    cout << "f = " << f << endl;
    cout << "d = " << d << endl;
    cout << "s = " << s << endl;
    return 0;
}
```

Program 18.3: Formatted output using **cout**.

```
/* File: using.cpp
   Use 'using' directives for input and output streams  */
#include <iostream>     // for I/O in C++

/* Use 'using' directive */
using std::cout;
using std::cin;
using std::endl;
// or using namespace std;

int main() {
    int a, b, product;
```

Program 18.4: A program with **using** directives. (*Continued*)

```
    cout << "Please enter first integer number\n";
    cin >> a;            // scanf("%d", &a);
    cout << "Please enter second integer number" << endl;
    cin >> b;            // scanf("%d", &b);
    cout << "product = " << a*b << endl;
    return 0;
}
```

Program 18.4: *(Continued)*

18.3 Passing Arguments of Function by References

A program written in a procedural computer programming language is generally formed by a set of functions. The user may not need to know the details inside functions that were developed by others. But to use the functions effectively, the user has to understand how to interact functions through their arguments and return values. In general, arguments can be passed to functions in one of two ways: *call-by-value* and *call-by-reference*. C uses call-by-value, whereas Fortran uses call-by-reference. In the call-by-value model in C, when a function is called, the values of the actual parameters are copied into formal parameters local to the called function. When a formal parameter is used as an lvalue (the object that can occur at the left side of an assignment statement), only the local copy of the parameter will be altered. If the user wants the called function to alter its actual parameters in the calling function, the addresses of the parameters must be passed to the called function explicitly, as described in section 11.3 in Chapter 11. In the call-by-reference method available in C++, however, the address of an argument is copied into the formal parameter of a function. Inside the function, the address is used to access the actual argument used in the calling function. This means that when the formal parameter is used as an lvalue, the parameter will affect the variable used to call the function.

The reference type of a function argument can be declared with an ampersand '&' in front of the variable name. The call-by-reference method is illustrated in Program 18.5. Similar to Program 11.4, Program 18.5 swaps the values of the two passed arguments in the calling function. However, the function `swap()` in Program 18.5 with the function prototype

```
void swap(int &x, int &y);
```

```
/* File: swap.cpp
   Use references in C++ to pass arguments of function by reference */
#include <stdio.h>             // for printf()

/* swap values in the passed arguments in the
   calling function using call by reference */
void swap(int &x, int &y) {
    int temp;

    temp = x;
    x = y;
    y = temp;
}
```

Program 18.5: Passing an argument of function by reference. *(Continued)*

```
int main() {
    int a = 5, b = 6;

    swap(a, b);                         // swap a and b
    printf("a = %d  b = %d\n", a, b); // output: a = 6; b = 5;
    return 0;
}
```

Program 18.5: *(Continued)*

has two arguments of reference type. When the function `swap()` is called in the **main()** function by

```
swap(a, b);
```

the variables `x` and `y` inside the function `swap()` refer to the variables `a` and `b` in the **main()** function, respectively. Unlike Program 11.4, no pointer indirection is involved in Program 18.5.

As an application example, recall that in Program 11.5 in Chapter 11, the function `disc()` passes the calculated area and circumference through the variables `area` and `circum` of pointer to double to the calling function. Program 11.5 can be modified to pass the results by references as shown in Program 18.6.

```
/* File: discref.c
   Use a function to calculate the area and circumference of a disc.
   Pass the results by reference using reference types.  */
#include <stdio.h>
#include <math.h>    /* for M_PI */

/* function discref() calculates area and circumference
   of a disc with a given radius. */
void discref(double radius, double &area, double &circum) {
    area = M_PI * radius *radius;
    circum = 2*M_PI*radius;
}

int main() {
    double radius;           /* radius of the disc */
    double area, circum;     /* area and circumference of the disc */

    /* printf("Enter the radius for the disc (m): ");
       scanf("%lf", &radius); */
    radius = 3.5;            /* radius is 3.5 meters */

    discref(radius, area, circum);
    printf("area = %f (m^2)\n", area);
    printf("circumference = %f (m)\n", circum);
    return 0;
}
```

Program 18.6: Passing the area and circumference of a metal disc to the calling function using references.

The function `discref()` with the prototype

```
void discref(double radius, double &area, double &circum);
```

can be called by

```
discref(radius, area, circum);
```

to obtain the area and circumference without using pointers. The output from Program 18.6 is shown in Figure 11.11 in Chapter 11, the same as that from Program 11.5.

18.4 The New and Delete Operators

In C, the dynamic memory allocation and deallocation are normally performed by the functions **malloc()** and **free()**. In C++, the operator pair **new** and **delete** can perform the same function as **malloc()** and **free()** and also provide other benefits.

The operator **new** can calculate automatically the proper size of the memory to be allocated while the function **malloc()** must take an argument as to the size of the memory. The operator **new** can return a pointer of the correct type, while the function **malloc()** only returns a pointer to void.

Program 18.7 is an example of how the operators **new** and **delete** are used. The new operator can also be used to allocate a block of memory with an array syntax. For example, the expression `new int [10]` allocates a memory of 40 bytes for 10 elements of int. The output of Program 18.7 is shown below:

```
*dp1 = 1.2000
dp2[5] = 3.4000
*(dp2+5) = 3.4000
```

```
/* File: newmalloc.cpp
   Use new and delete in C++ in comparison with malloc() and free() in C */
#include <iostream>              // for I/O in C++
using namespace std;             // for using cout, cin, cerr, endl

int main() {
    int *p1 = new int;           // int *p = (int *)malloc(sizeof(int));
    int *p2 = new int[10];       // int *p = (int *)malloc(sizeof(int)*10);
    double *dp1, *dp2;

    dp1 = new double;            // dp1 = (double *)malloc(sizeof(double));
    dp2 = new double[10];        // dp2 = (double *)malloc(sizeof(double)*10);
    *dp1 = 1.2;
    dp2[5] = 3.4;
    cout << "*dp1 = " << *dp1 << endl;
    cout << "dp2[5] = " << dp2[5] << endl;
    cout << "*(dp2+5) = " << *(dp2+5) << endl;
```

Program 18.7: Using the operators new and delete for handling memory. (*Continued*)

```
    delete p1;      // free(p1);
    delete p2;      // free(p2);
    delete dp1;     // free(dp1);
    delete dp2;     // free(dp2);
    return 0;
}
```

Program 18.7: (*Continued*)

If the attempt to allocate memory is successful, the operator **new** returns a pointer to the allocated memory. Otherwise, it calls the handler function pointed to by **_new_handler** if **_new_handler** is not NULL, and then returns a NULL pointer. A program may install different handler functions for the **new** operator during execution, by supplying a pointer to a function defined in the program or the library as an argument to the function **set_new_handler()**. The function **set_new_handler()** is defined in the header file **new** as follows:

```
void (*set_new_handler (void(*)(void)))(void);
```

or

```
typedef void (*FuncHandler_t)(void);
FuncHandler_t set_new_handler(FuncHandler);
```

It establishes the function designated by the argument for the current **_new_handler**, and returns NULL on the first call, or the previous **_new_handler** on subsequent calls. Program 18.8 allocates memory for variable `p` and p1, sets the function `newhandle()` as the handler function for the **new** operator, then tries to allocate a large memory for the variables `p2` and `p3`. The system has enough memory for `p`, but not for `p1, p2`, and `p3`. The function `newhandler()` is called when the **new** operator fails to allocate memory for `p2` and `p3`. By default, the handler for the **new** operator is NULL. When the **new** operator fails to allocate the memory for `p1`, no handler is invoked. The output from executing Program 18.8 is as follows:

```
p = 2be880
p1 = 0
Error: new operator failed
p2 = 0
Error: new operator failed
p3 = 0
```

```
/* File: newhandler.cpp
   Set handler called when the 'new' operator fails
   */
#include <iostream>
#include <new>              // For function set_new_handler()
#include <limits.h>         // for INT_MAX
#include <stdio.h>          // for printf()
using namespace std;
```

Program 18.8: Setting a handler for memory allocation using the operator **new**. (*Continued*)

```
void newhandler(void);    // function prototype

int main() {
    char *p = new char [10];        // Ok
    printf("p = %p\n", p);

    char *p1 = new char [INT_MAX]; // No memory, no error handler
    printf("p1 = %p\n", p1);

    set_new_handler(newhandler);    // set error handler

    char *p2 = new char [INT_MAX]; // No memory, with error handler
    printf("p2 = %p\n", p2);

    char *p3 = new char [INT_MAX]; // No memory, with error handler
    printf("p3 = %p\n", p3);

    /* delete allocated memory */
    if(p)
      delete p;
    if(p1)
      delete p1;
    if(p2)
      delete p2;
    if(p3)
      delete p3;
    return 0;
}

/* error handler for the 'new' operator */
void newhandler(void) {
    printf("Error: new operator failed\n");
    /* exit(1); */
}
```

Program 18.8: *(Continued)*

The most important feature for the operator **new** is that it can invoke the contructor of a class automatically and perform some initialization if necessary, whereas the function **malloc()** cannot. Similarly, the corresponding destructor will be called by the operator **delete**. The details of using these two operators with classes will be presented in Chapter 19.

18.5 The Unary Scope Resolution Operator

C++ provides a unary scope resolution operator '`::`' to access a global variable when a local variable of the same name is in the scope. The format, `::variablename`, may be used to access the global variable `variablename`. For example, in Program 18.9, the variable name `num` is used as both local and global

```
/* File: scope.cpp
   Use scope resolution operator '::' to access variables in the global scope */
#include <iostream>              // for I/O in C++
using namespace std;             // for using cout, cin, cerr, endl

int num = 10;                    // declare a global variable

int main() {
    int num = 20;                // declare a local variable with the same name

    cout << "num = " << num << endl;       // access the local variable
    cout << "::num = " << ::num << endl;   // access the global variable
    ::num = 30;                            // access the global variable
    cout << "num = " << num << endl;       // access the local variable
    cout << "::num = " << ::num << endl;   // access the global variable
    return 0;
}
```

Program 18.9: Using the scope resolution operator.

variables. The unary scope resolution operator is used to access the global variable. The output of Program 18.9 is shown below:

```
num = 20
::num = 10
num = 20
::num = 30
```

Although Program 18.9 shows how the unary scope resolution operator '`::`' may be used to access a global variable in a C++ program, it is often used with classes to define member functions and access static members of a class. The details concerning classes will be presented in Chapter 19.

18.6 Functional Type Cast Operators

There are functional type casting operations in C++ in the form of

```
type(expr)
```

for data types of single object. In this functional type casting operation, `type` shall not be a pointer data type. For example, `int(9.3)` and `double(4)` are valid C++ expressions. Program 18.10 shows how functional type casting is used in a C++ program. The output of Program 18.10 is as follows:

```
i = 10
d = 6.6667
```

```
/* File: cast.cpp
   Use cast operator type(xpr) */
#include <iostream>          // for I/O in C++
using namespace std;         // for using cout, cin, cerr, endl

int main() {
    int i;
    double d;

    i = int(10.6);           // equivalent to i = (int)10.6 in C
    cout << "i = " << i << endl;

    d = double(20)/3;        // equivalent to d = (double)20/3 in C
    cout << "d = " << d << endl;
    return 0;
}
```

Program 18.10: Functional type casting operations.

18.7 Making It Work

18.7.1 Compiling, Linking, and Executing C++ Programs in a Command Shell

A C++ program can be executed in Ch and ChIDE in the same manner as a C program. However, there are differences in compiling C++ programs compared with compiling C programs. The differences are highlighted in this section.

Using Visual C++ to Compile C+ Programs in Windows

The compiler command **cl** in Visual C++ can be used to compile both C and C++ programs. By default, the command **cl** assumes that files with the `.c` extension are C source files, whereas files with the `.cpp` or `.cxx` extension are C++ source files. With the proper setup as described in section 2.2.4, the C++ program `hello.cpp` can be compiled and linked by the command

```
> cl hello.cpp
```

Similar to a C program, both the object file `hello.obj` and the executable program `hello.exe` will be generated. The executable program `hello.exe` can be executed by typing either

```
> hello.exe
```

or

```
> hello
```

in a command shell such as an MS-DOS shell or a Ch shell.

If a source code with the `.c` file extension uses C++ features, when it is compiled using the command **cl**, an error message will be generated. In this case, the `/TP` or `/Tp` option of the command **cl** can be used to compile it as a C++ code. These options specify that the following input file is a C++ source file, even if it does not have a `.cpp` or `.cxx` extension. Using these options, a C++ program `hello.ch` or `hello.c` can be compiled using one of the following commands.

```
> cl /TP hello.ch
> cl /TP hello.c
```

Using C++ Compilers in Unix

In Unix, a C++ compiler program is different from a C compiler. The command **g++** is for the GNU C++ compiler for different platforms. Solaris and HP-UX use the command **CC**, whereas Mac OS X and FreeBSD use the command **c++** for the C++ compiler. Therefore, one of the following commands

```
> g++ hello.cpp
> CC hello.cpp
> c++ hello.cpp
```

can be used to compile the C++ source file `hello.cpp` depending on the system and compiler installed. Similarly, for a C program, the above command compiles the source file and links the resulting object file with the standard C/C++ library to create an executable program called `a.out`. Program 18.1 can then be executed by typing the command

```
> a.out
```

in a command shell.

The GNU C++ compiler treats files with the `.c` extension as C++ source files as well. However, use "`-x c++`" option for GNU C++ compiler specifies that the input file is a C++ source file, regardless of its file extension. Using this option, a C++ program `hello.ch` can be compiled as follows:

```
> gcc -x c++ hello.ch
```

Exercises

1. Give the output of the following program:

```
#include<stdio.h>
int funct(int &i, int j) {
    int temp;
    temp = i;
    i = j;
    j = temp;
```

```
        return i*j;
}
int main() {
        int i =4, j = 5, k;

        k = funct(i, j);
        printf("i = %d\n", i);
        printf("j = %d\n", j);
        printf("k = %d\n", k);
        return 0;
}
```

2. Write a program that reads three integer values (*num1*, *num2*, *num3*) and a string *s* from the terminal. Use reference types to pass these values into a function called `swap_numbers()` that will do one of the following:
   - If string *s* = "LtoR," then the values of *num1*, *num2*, and *num3* will be swapped from left to right.
   - If string *s* = "RtoL," then the values of *num1*, *num2*, and *num3* will be swapped from right to left.

   For example, if `num1 = 7`, `num2 = 8`, `num3 = 9`, and `s = "LtoR"`, then `swap_numbers(num1, num2, num3, s)` will produce the following result: `num1 = 9`, `num2 = 7`, and `num3 = 8`.
3. **a.** Write a program that reads the values for the height and width of a rectangle using two variables of double type in the function **main**(). Calculate the area and perimeter of the rectangle using the function `func()` called as shown in the code below. Print these values in the function **main**().

```
/* add code here */
int main () {
        double height, width, area, perimeter;
        /* add code here */
       func(height, width, area, perimeter);
        /* add code here */
}
```

   b. Write a program that prompts the user to input the radius of a circle. The radius should then be passed into a function that will pass the values of the circle's perimeter and area by reference to the calling function. The perimeter and area of the circle will be printed in the **main()** function.

   c. Modify the function above so that it will pass back both the perimeter and area of an equilateral triangle, square, or pentagon given the number of sides and their relative lengths as two other arguments.
4. Write a program that reads the values for the width, length, and height of a rectangular box using three variables of double type in the function **main**(). Pass values of these variables to a function, which calculates the volume and surface area for six sides of the box. The volume and surface area of the box passed back from two other arguments of this function by reference are printed out in the function **main**(). Check your program with the user input for the width, length, and height of 2, 3, and 4 meters, respectively.
5. Write a program that reads the value for the radius of a sphere using a variable of double type in the function **main**(). Pass the value of this variable to a function, which calculates the volume and surface area for the sphere. The volume and surface area of the sphere passed back from two other arguments of this function by reference are printed out in the function **main**(). Check your program with the user input for the radius of 5 meters.

6. Write a program with the two alternate functions specified following, of which each simply triples the variable `count` defined in the function **main()**. Then compare and contrast the two approaches. These two functions are
   a. The function `tripleCallByValue()`, which passes a copy of `count` call-by-value, triples the copy, and returns the new value.
   b. The function `tripleByReference()`, which passes `count` with true call-by-reference via a reference parameter and triples the original copy of `count` through its alias (i.e., the reference parameter).
7. What is the purpose of the unary scope resolution operator?
8. Write a linear regression function with the function prototype

```
void linearreg(double t[], double y[], int n, double &b, double &v);
```

   where `t` and `y` are arrays of data to be fitted in the linear regression model, `n` is the number of elements for the passed arrays `t` and `y`. The linear regression coefficients for the intercept `b` and slope `s` are passed to the calling function by references. Modify Program 10.19 to use this function.
9. Modify Program 11.6 to pass the integral part from the function `decompose()` by reference.
10. Modify Program 11.17 to pass the calculated root from the function `bisect()` by reference.
11. Modify Program 11.17 to pass the calculated root and number of iterations from the function `bisect()` by reference. Also, print the number of iterations in the function **main()**.
12. Modify Program 11.20 to pass an argument by reference without using pointers. Without generic pointers, the modified function for the bisection method may be able to handle only a parameter of type double.

CHAPTER 19

‡Classes and Object-Based Programming in C++

The class in C++ is a natural evolution of the structure. A class can be used to create user-defined types. Class usage is often referred to as *object-based programming* (OBP). Classes model objects that have both attributes and behaviors. Data members are the attributes of a class, and member functions represent their behaviors. Thus, the data and functions of a class are closely related. Using classes is more convenient than using structures to develop applications for large-scale projects. In this chapter, using classes in C++ for object-based programming is presented.

19.1 Class Definition and Objects

In C, functions cannot be members of a structure. In C++, both class and structure can have *member functions* which are members of function type. The class and structure are the same, except that members of a class are private, whereas members of a structure are public by default.

Figure 19.1 is an example of the definition of a class. The specifier **class** is followed by the class name, then a list of declarations, or *members*, enclosed in braces. Based on the definition, the class `CStudent` has two private data members, `m_id` and `m_name`, and one private member function, `m_checkId()` specified by the keyword **private** followed by a colon. Within the public region specified by the keyword **public** followed by a colon, `CStudent()` and `~CStudent()` are the *constructor* and *destructor*, respectively. The public member function is `print()`. Details about the member-access specifiers, as well as public and private members, are discussed in the next section.

Once a class has been defined, it can be used as a data type to instantiate an *object* or *instance* of the class. For example, an object of class `CStudent` can be instantiated by the following formats:

```
class CStudent s;        // declare an object of class CStudent
CStudent *sp;            // declare a pointer to a CStudent object
CStudent sa[2];          // declare an array of CStudent objects
```

Note that the type specifier **class** is optional in the declaration.

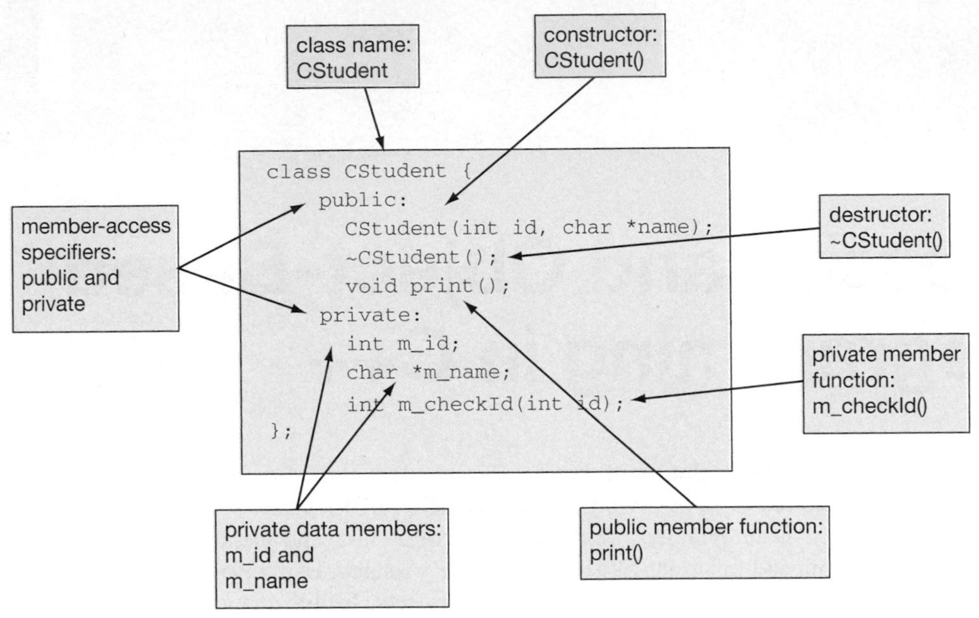

Figure 19.1: A class definition.

19.2 Public and Private Members of a Class

The keywords **public** and **private** in C++ are member access specifiers for a class. They can appear multiple times and in any order in a class definition. By default, members in a class are private, whereas members in a structure are public. For the class `CStudent`, the members `m_id` and `m_name` are considered private members and are not accessible outside the class. Outside the class, they may be accessed only through public member functions. Typically, the data members and utility functions of a class are defined as private members while member functions for a user interface are defined as public members. Having data members such as `m_id` and `m_name` be private and not accessible outside the class is called *information hiding*. In certain situations, however, there may be a need for a public data member. For such cases, a public data member is accessible outside the class by the *member operator* '`.`' and *indirect member operator* '`->`' for a pointer to class. This is also true for public member functions used to access private data members or call private member functions. Program 19.1 is an example of how to access public data members from outside the class. The output of Program 19.1 is shown below.

```
student.m_id   = 101
student.m_name = John
```

```
/* File: publicc.cpp
   Access public members of a class */
#include <stdio.h>   // for printf()
#include <string.h> // for strcpy()
```

Program 19.1: Accessing public members from outside the class. (*Continued*)

```
class CStudent{      // define class CStudent
    public:          // m_id and m_name are public members
      int   m_id;
      char *m_name;
};

int main() {
    CStudent s;      //  instantiate an instance of class CStudent;

    s.m_id = 101;    //  access a member of the class
    s.m_name = new char [strlen("John")+1]; // allocate memory for m_name
    strcpy(s.m_name, "John");
    printf("s.m_id   = %d\n", s.m_id);
    printf("s.m_name = %s\n", s.m_name);
    delete(s.m_name);                          // delete the allocated memory
    return 0;
}
```

Program 19.1: (*Continued*)

In contrast, the result of executing Program 19.2 in Ch, shown below, illustrates what would happen if one were to try to access the private members `m_id` and `m_name` from outside the class.

```
ERROR: access private member CStudent::m_id
ERROR: syntax error before or at line 15 in file private_err.cpp
  ==>:      s.m_id = 101;          // Error: access private member
  BUG:      s.m_id<== ???
ERROR: access private member CStudent::m_name
ERROR: syntax error before or at line 16 in file private_err.cpp
  ==>:      s.m_name = new char [strlen("John")+1];
  BUG:      s.m_name =<== ???
ERROR: expecting an identifier in declaration
ERROR: syntax error before or at line 16 in file private_err.cpp
...
```

```
/* File: private_err.cpp
   Incorrectly access private members of a class */
#include <stdio.h>  // for printf()
#include <string.h> // for strcpy()

class CStudent{      // define class CStudent
    private:         // m_id and m_name are private members
      int   m_id;
      char *m_name;
};
```

Program 19.2: Incorrectly accessing private members of a class. (*Continued*)

```
int main() {
    CStudent s;     //  instantiate an instance of class CStudent;

    s.m_id = 101;    // Error: access private member
    s.m_name = new char [strlen("John")+1]; // Error: access private member
    strcpy(s.m_name, "John");
    printf("s.m_id   = %d\n", s.m_id);
    printf("s.m_name = %s\n", s.m_name);
    delete(s.m_name);
    return 0;
}
```

Program 19.2: *(Continued)*

19.3 Member Functions of a Class

As previously mentioned, a function may also be a member of a class. In the definition of a member function, a function name is preceded by the class name and the scope resolution operator '::', as shown below.

```
ReturnType className::MemberFunctionName(...) {
    ...
}
```

Because different classes can have members with the same name, the scope resolution operator can prevent any confusion. We can redefine the class of `CStudent` to include a couple of member functions. The new definition of the class `CStudent` is as follows:

```
class CStudent {
    int m_id;
    char *m_name;
  public:
    void setId(int id);
    void setName(char *name);
};

void CStudent::setId(int id) {
    m_id = i;
}

void CStudent::setName(char *name) {
    if(name) {
       m_name = new char[strlen(name)+1];
       strcpy(m_name, name);
    }
}
```

The function `setId()` takes the ID number of a student as the argument and then sets the class member `id` to it. The function `setName()` sets the member `name` to a new name. The members `setId()` and `setName()` are called *member functions* or *methods* in C++. One can invoke a member function by using the member operator '`.`', which is just like accessing a member of a structure, as shown below.

```
int main() {
    class CStudent s;
    ....

    s.setId(1);
    s.setName("Jason");
    ....
}
```

If a pointer to class is being used to access a member function, then the indirect member operator '`->`' shall be used. One of the main roles of member functions of a class is to provide a means to access private members of the class.

Program 19.3 is an example of accessing private data members with member functions. Included are the definitions of the class `CStudent` along with the member functions `setId()`, `setName()`, `print()`, and `freeMemory()`. The two new functions, `print()` and `freeMemory()`, prints the data stored in the class `CStudent` and frees the memory dynamically allocated for the data member `m_name`, respectively. Note that in C++ programs, the standard output object **cout** is typically used instead of the function **printf()** to display output. The output of Program 19.3 is shown below:

```
m_id   = 101
m_name = John
```

```
/* File: membercout.cpp
   Use member functions and cout */
#include <string.h>           // for strcpy()
#include <iostream>           // for I/O in C++
using namespace std;          // for using cout, cin, cerr, endl

class CStudent{               // define class CStudent
   public:                    // declare public member functions
     void setId(int id);
     void setName(char *name);
     void print();
     void freeMemory();
   private:                   // declare private data
     int m_id;
     char *m_name;
};
```

Program 19.3: Using member functions with cout. (*Continued*)

```
void CStudent::setId(int id) {                    // set student ID
    m_id = id;
}

void CStudent::setName(char *name) {              // set student name
    if(name != NULL) {
      m_name = new char[strlen(name)+1];          // allocate memory for name
      strcpy(m_name, name);
    }
}

void CStudent::print() {                          // print student info
    cout << "m_id   = " << m_id <<endl;
    cout << "m_name = " << m_name <<endl;
}

void CStudent::freeMemory() {// free the allocated memory by CStudent::setName()
    if(m_name != NULL)
       delete(m_name);
}

int main() {
    CStudent s;          // instantiate an instance of class CStudent;

    s.setId(101);        // set student ID
    s.setName("John");  // allocate memory and set student name
    s.print();           // print student ID and name
    s.freeMemory();      // free the allocated memory for m_name
    return 0;
}
```

Program 19.3: (*Continued*)

19.4 Constructors and Destructors in a Class

When an object of a class is instantiated, data members of the object are initialized to zero by default. However, initialization of data members of an object to different values can be done in a constructor. The constructor and destructor are special member functions that have no return value. The constructor has the same name as the class name. It is invoked automatically each time an object is instantiated and performs some initialization. A constructor can take arguments for initializing its data members. For example, the following statement will instantiate the object `objectName` of the class `classname` using a constructor with two arguments `value1` and `value2`:

```
classname objectName = classname(value1, value2);
```

or

```
class classname objectName = classname(value1, value2);
```

Note that the constructor will be invoked automatically when the **new** operator is used to instantiate an object of a class, which will be presented in section 19.5.

The destructor is also a special member function of a class. It is a compliment of the constructor and often used to free memory allocated for the object of the class. The destructor can be identified by a tilde ~ followed by the class name, such as `~CStudent()` for the class `CStudent`. The destructor has no input arguments or return value. It will be called automatically after the termination of the function **main()** or block where the object of a class is declared. The destructor will also be automatically invoked when the class object is deleted by the operator **delete**, which will be presented in section 19.5.

Program 19.4 is an example that instantiates the two objects `s1` and `s2` of the class `CStudent` and initializes the data members of these two objects with the constructor. The values of the data members are then displayed by the member function `print()`. At the end of the program execution, the destructor frees the memory allocated for the objects `s1` and `s2` of the class `CStudent`. The file `constructor.cpp` of Program 19.4 requires two additional files, `student.h` and `CStudent.cpp` in Programs 19.5 and 19.6,

```
/* File: constructor.cpp
   Use constructor */
#include "student.h"    // header file with class definition for CStudent

int main() {
    CStudent s1 = CStudent(101,"John");  // initialize with constructor
    CStudent s2 = CStudent(102,"Doe");   // initialize with constructor

    s1.print();                          // use member function
    s2.print();                          // use member function
    return 0;
}
```

Program 19.4: Using a constructor.

```
/* File: student.h
   header file with define class CStudent */
#ifndef STUDENT_H
#define STUDENT_H

class CStudent {                         // define class CStudent
    public:     // public method
      CStudent(int id, char *name);    // constructor
```

Program 19.5: The header file for the class `CStudent`. (*Continued*)

```
      ~CStudent();                         // destructor
      void print();                        // member function
    private:  // private data
      int m_id;                            // private data
      char *m_name;                        // private data
};

/* load member function definitions in file CStudent.cpp for Ch */
#ifdef _CH_
#pragma importf <CStudent.cpp>
#endif

#endif /* STUDENT_H */
```

Program 19.5: *(Continued)*

```
/* File: CStudent.cpp
   Definitions of member functions for class CStudent */
#include <string.h>         // for strcpy()
#include <iostream>         // for I/O in C++j
#include "student.h"        // for class CStudent definition
using namespace std;        // for using cout, cin, cerr, endl

CStudent::CStudent(int id, char *name) { // constructor definition
    m_id = id;
    if(name != NULL) {
      m_name = new char[strlen(name)+1]; // allocate memory
      strcpy(m_name, name);
    }
}

CStudent::~CStudent() {                  // destructor definition
    if(m_name != NULL) {
       delete (m_name);                  // free the allocated memory
    }
    cout << "Destructor ~CStudent() is called\n";
}

void CStudent::print() {                 // member function definition
    cout << "m_id   = " << m_id <<endl;
    cout << "m_name = " << m_name <<endl;
}
```

Program 19.6: Definitions of the member functions of the class `CStudent`.

respectively. The header file `student.h` defines the class `CStudent`, whereas the file `CStudent.cpp` defines the member functions of the class. Note that the destructor `~CStudent()` outputs a statement to show that it has been invoked at the end of the program. The output of Program 19.4 is shown below:

```
m_id   = 101
m_name = John
m_id   = 102
m_name = Doe
Destructor ~CStudent() is called
Destructor ~CStudent() is called
```

19.5 The New and Delete Operators

As mentioned in Chapter 18, the **new** and **delete** operators may be used instead of the functions **malloc()** and **free()** for dynamic memory allocation and deallocation. It is often more useful to use the **new** and **delete** operators because **new** can automatically calculate the appropriate size for memory allocation, while the function **malloc()** takes an argument for the size of the memory. Aside from this, the most important feature is that the operator **new** can invoke the constructor of a class automatically and performs the initialization if necessary, whereas the function **malloc()** cannot. The corresponding destructor of the class will be called by the operator **delete**.

Program 19.7 shows how the operators of **new** and **delete** are used with classes. This program is similar to Program 19.4. They both use the same class definition and member functions. The difference is that Program 19.7 utilizes the **new** and **delete** operators. In the example, the **new** operator creates two objects of the class `CStudent`. As stated previously, the **new** operator automatically allocates the proper memory size for each object and returns a pointer to the correct type. After the objects `sp1` and `sp2` have been instantiated, the values of their data members are printed out with the indirect member operator '`->`' followed by the member

```
/* File: newc.cpp
   Use new and delete operators with class */
#include "student.h"  // definition for class CStudent

int main() {
    CStudent *sp1 = new CStudent(101,"John"); // declare and initialize
    CStudent *sp2 = new CStudent(102,"Doe");  // declare and initialize

    sp1->print();
    sp2->print();
    delete (sp1);         // free the allocated memory by new operator
    delete (sp2);         // free the allocated memory by new operator
    return 0;
}
```

Program 19.7: Using pointer to class and the operator **new**.

in Program 19.9 is used in the constructor to check whether the input argument *id* is a valid value. If the value of the input `id` is less than or equal to zero, the member function `m_checkId()` prints out an error message, and the constructor will set the private data member `m_id` to −1. Otherwise, the value of the input will be assigned to the private data member `m_id`. The output of Program 19.9 is as follows:

```
Error: -10 is invalid id
id = 101
id = -1
Destructor ~CStudent() is called
Destructor ~CStudent() is called
```

```
/* File: membercout.cpp
   Use private member function and cout */
#include <string.h>          // for strcpy()
#include <iostream>          // for I/O in C++
using namespace std;         // for using cout, cin, cerr, endl

class CStudent{          // define class CStudent
  public:                // declare public member functions
    CStudent(int id, char *name); // constructor
    ~CStudent();                  // destructor
    void print();                 // member function
    int getId();                  // member function
  private:               // declare private data and member function
    int m_id;                     // private data
    char *m_name;                 // private data
    int m_checkId(int id);        // private member function
};

CStudent::CStudent(int id, char *name) { // constructor definition
    if(!m_checkId(id))
      m_id = id;
    else
      m_id = -1;
    if(name != NULL) {
      m_name = new char[strlen(name)+1]; // allocate memory for name
      strcpy(m_name, name);
    }
}

CStudent::~CStudent() {                           // destructor definition
    if(m_name != NULL) {
```

Program 19.9: Using a private member function. (*Continued*)

```
        delete(m_name);                              // free the allocated memory
    }
    cout << "Destructor ~CStudent() is called\n";
}

void CStudent::print() {                             // print student info
    cout << "m_id   = " << m_id <<endl;
    cout << "m_name = " << m_name <<endl;
}

int CStudent::getId() {                              // get ID
    return m_id;
}

/* private member function definition to check ID */
int CStudent::m_checkId(int id) {
    if(id <= 0) {
       cout << "Error: " << id << " is invalid id\n";
       return -1;
    }
    else
       return 0;
}

int main() {
    CStudent s1 = CStudent(101,"John");
    CStudent s2 = CStudent(-10,"Doe");      // -10 is an invalid ID
    int id;

    id = s1.getId();
    cout << "id = " << id << endl;
    id = s2.getId();
    cout << "id = " << id << endl;
    return 0;
}
```

Program 19.9: *(Continued)*

An Application Example

Force and Acceleration of a Moving Body

Through an example, this section demonstrates how to design programs with classes. It is important to separate the interface from the implementation details of a class.

Problem Statement:
The parameters for the mechanical system shown in Figure 2.12 are $m = 5kg$, $g = 9.81m/s^2$, and $\mu = 0.2$. The external force **p** is expressed as a function of time t:

$$p(t) = 4\sin(t - 3) + 20$$

Write a program to perform the following tasks.

1. Calculate the external force and acceleration when $t = 2$ seconds.
2. Plot the acceleration **a** from $t = 0$ to $t = 10$ seconds with the number of points N equal to 100.

Note: Use a class to represent the object of the body with the mass and friction coefficient of the body as private data members of the class. The class is defined in the header file `accel.h`. The two macros for g and N are also defined in the header file. The application program will interface to the object through the public member function `setSys()` to set the values of friction coefficient and mass, and the functions `force()` and `accel()`. The acceleration plot shall be plotted by a public member function on `plotAccel()`.

The problem may be solved with Programs 19.10 to 19.12. The header file `accel.h` in Program 19.10 contains macros defining `M_G` and `N` as the gravity constant and number of plotting points, respectively, and the definition for the class `CBody`. The class `CBody` has the private data members `m_mu` and `m_m` for the values of coefficient of friction and mass, respectively, and public member functions to perform specific tasks. The member function `setSys()` is used to set the parameters of the system. The functions `force()` and `accel()` determine the external force and acceleration of the system with respect to time, t. The member function `plotAccel()` plots the acceleration versus time from 0 to 10 seconds. Definitions of the class member functions are in the file `CBody.cpp` in Program 19.11. The actual application program is Program 19.12. It is used to perform the analysis on the system and display the results. The external force and acceleration of the system at $t = 2$ seconds are shown below, while the acceleration plot for $t = 0$ to 10 seconds is the same as Figure 6.4 in Chapter 6.

```
External force p = 16.6341 (N)
Acceleration a = 1.3648 (m/s^2)
```

```
/* File: accel.h
   header file for calculate the acceleration using class  */
#ifndef ACCEL_H
#define ACCEL_H

#define M_G   9.81   // gravitational acceleration constant g
#define N     100    // num of points for plotting

class CBody {          // define class CBody
  public:    // public member functions
    CBody();           // constructor
    ~CBody();          // destructor
```

Program 19.10: The header file for calculating accelerations using a class. (*Continued*)

```
      void setSys(double mu, double m);  // member function to set system
      double force(double t);            // member function for force
      double accel(double t);            // member function for accel
      void plotAccel(double t0, double tf);// member function for plotting
    private:  // private data
      double m_mu;  // friction coefficient
      double m_m;   // mass
};

/* load member function definitions in file CBody.cpp for Ch */
#ifdef _CH_
#pragma importf <CBody.cpp>
#endif

#endif
```

Program 19.10: (*Continued*)

```
/* File: CBody.cpp
   Definition of member functions of class CBody */
#include <math.h>      // for sin()
#include <chplot.h>    // for plotxy()
#include "accel.h"     // for class CBody definition

CBody::CBody() {       // constructor
    m_mu = 0;          // initialize mu with 0
    m_m = 0;           // initialize m with 0
}

CBody::~CBody() {      // destructor (empty)
    ;
}

void CBody::setSys(double mu, double m) {  /* set system for mu and m */
    m_mu = mu;
    m_m = m;
}

double CBody::force(double t) {    /* calculate force */
    double p;

    p = 4*(sin(t-3))+20;
    return p;
}
```

Program 19.11: Definitions of member functions for calculating accelerations. (*Continued*)

```
double CBody::accel(double t) {    /* calculate acceleration */
    double a, p;

    p = force(t);
    a = (p-m_mu*m_m*M_G)/m_m;
    return a;
}

/* plotting accel versus time  */
void CBody::plotAccel(double t0, double tf) {
    double a[N], t[N];    /* define arrays for plotting */
    int i;

    for(i; i<N; i++) {
      t[i] = t0 + i*(tf-t0)/(N-1);
      a[i] = accel(t[i]);
    }
    plotxy(t, a, N, "Acceleration Plot", "time (s)", "accel (m/s^2)");
}
```

Program 19.11: *(Continued)*

```
/* File: accelclass.cpp
   Use class CBody to calculate and plot accelerations */
#include <iostream>          // for I/O in C++
#include "accel.h"           // for class CPlot and member functions
using namespace std;         // for using cout, cin, cerr, endl


int main() {
    /* declare accel, force, time, initial time, final time, mu, mass */
    double a, p, t, t0, tf, mu, m;
    CBody b;                 /* CBody b = CBody(); */

    mu = 0.2;                /* mu */
    m = 5.0;                 /* mass */
    t = 2.0;                 /* set time at 2 seconds */
    t0 = 0.0;                /* initial time 0 second */
    tf = 10.0;               /* final time 10 seconds */
    b.setSys(mu, m);         /* set system */
    p = b.force(t);          /* calculate force */
    a = b.accel(t);          /* calculate acceleration */
```

Program 19.12: Calculating accelerations using a class. *(Continued)*

```
    /* display force p and acceleration a, and plot accelerations */
    cout << "External force p = " << p << " (N)" << endl;
    cout << "Acceleration a = " << a << " (m/s^2)" << endl;
    b.plotAccel(t0, tf); /* plot accelerations by passing address of b */
    return 0;
}
```

Program 19.12: Calculating accelerations using a class. (*Continued*)

19.8 The Implicit this Pointer

In C++, every object has an implicit pointer called **this** to point to its own address. Although the pointer **this** is not regarded as a part of the object, that is, it is not reflected in the **sizeof** operation, but rather it is actually used implicitly to reference the data members and member functions of an object. This is particularly useful if the variable name of the argument of a function is the same as that of the member. For example, to avoid confusion in the code below, the private members `m_id` and `m_name` are referenced by the **this** pointer.

```
CStudent::CStudent(int m_id, char *m_name) {
   this->m_id = m_id;
   this->m_name = m_name;
}
```

More practically, one might define private members for the id and name of the `class CStudent` with the identifiers `id` and `name`. In this case, the member constructor above would be implemented as

```
CStudent::CStudent(int id, char *name) {
   this->id = id;
   this->name = name;
}
```

Program 19.13 uses **this** pointers inside both the constructor and destructor to initialize the data members of the class `CStudent` and free up memory, respectively. The output of Program 19.13 is shown below:

```
this->m_id   = 101
this->m_name = John
m_id    = 12.3400
```

```
/* File: thisptr.cpp
   Use 'this' pointer */
#include <string.h>         // for strcpy()
#include <iostream>         // for I/O in C++
using namespace std;        // for using cout, cin, cerr, endl
```

Program 19.13: Using the **this** pointer. (*Continued*)

```
class CStudent{              // define class CStudent
    public:
      CStudent(int id, char *name);
      ~CStudent();
      void print();
    private:
      int m_id;
      char *m_name;
};


CStudent::CStudent(int id, char *name) {
    this->m_id = id;              // Use 'this' pointer
    if(name != NULL) {
      m_name = new char[strlen(name)+1];
      strcpy(m_name, name);
    }
}

CStudent::~CStudent() {
    if(this->m_name != NULL) { // use 'this' pointer
       delete(this->m_name);
    }
}

void CStudent::print() {
    double m_id = 12.34;

    /* use 'this' pointer */
    cout << "this->m_id   = " << this->m_id <<endl;
    cout << "this->m_name = " << this->m_name <<endl;
    cout << "m_id        = " << m_id <<endl;
}

int main() {
    CStudent s = CStudent(101,"John");

    s.print();
    return 0;
}
```

Program 19.13: *(Continued)*

The size of a class does not include member functions and **this** pointer. Note that a static member function has no **this** pointer because it exists independent of any object of a class, which will be described in the next section.

19.9 Static Member of a Class

Typically each object of a class has its own copy of the data members in memory. But in certain cases, different objects of a class need to use some "class-wide" information. That means they have to share the same copy of a variable as if it were a global variable. A static class variable can provide this mechanism. The values of a static member in all objects of a class are the same. The change of its value affects all objects. Even if no object of a class exists, the static member is still there and can be manipulated. Static data members can be accessed by using the scope resolution operator '::', such as in `CStudent::m_count`. The declaration of a static member begins with the keyword **static**. For example, a static member `m_count` can be added to the definition of class `CStudent` as shown below.

```
class CStudent {
  public:
    CStudent(int id, char *name);
    ~CStudent();
    void print();
    int getCount();
  private:
    int m_id;
    char *m_name;
    static int m_count;    //number of objects instantiated
};
```

where the member `m_count` maintains the count of objects of the class `CStudent`. The static data member can be initialized with the following statement, along with definitions of other member functions. A static data member must be initialized once at file scope. For example, in

```
int CStudent::m_count = 0;
```

the member `m_count` can be referenced through any member function of the `CStudent` object. In Program 19.14, the value of `m_count` increases by 1 for every call to the constructor and decreases by 1 for

```
/* File: staticmem.cpp
   Use static member in a class */
#include <string.h>          // for strcpy()
#include <iostream>          // for I/O in C++
using namespace std;         // for using cout, cin, cerr, endl
class CStudent{       // define class CStudent
   public:
     CStudent(int id, char *name);
     ~CStudent();
     void print();
     int getCount();
   private:
```

Program 19.14: Using a static member of a class. *(Continued)*

```
        m_name = new char[strlen(name)+1];
        strcpy(m_name, name);
      }
      m_count++;              // use member m_count
}

CStudent::~CStudent() {
    if(m_name != NULL) {
       delete(m_name);
    }
    m_count--;              // use member m_count
    cout << "Destructor ~CStudent() is called\n";
}

void CStudent::print() {
    cout << "m_id   = " << m_id <<endl;
    cout << "m_name = " << m_name <<endl;
}

int CStudent::getCount() {
    return m_count;   // return m_count;
}

int main() {
    CStudent *sp1 = new CStudent(101,"John");
    cout << "m_count from sp1->getCount() = " << sp1->getCount() << endl;

    CStudent *sp2 = new CStudent(102,"Doe");
    cout << "m_count from sp1->getCount() = " << sp1->getCount() << endl;
    cout << "m_count from sp2->getCount() = " << sp2->getCount() << endl;

    delete (sp1);
    cout << "m_count from sp2->getCount() = " << sp2->getCount() << endl;
    delete (sp2);
    return 0;
}
```

Program 19.15: *(Continued)*

Static members can not only be simple data types, but also static member functions, such as the member function `getCount()` defined below.

```
class CStudent {
   public:
     CStudent(int id, char *name);
     ~CStudent();
     void print();
```

```
    static int getCount();
  private:
    int m_id;
    char *m_name;
    static int m_count;
};

int CStudent::getCount() {
    return m_count;
}
```

The function can be used to get the count of objects currently instantiated, as shown below.

```
int main() {
    CStudent s = CStudent(1, "Jason");
    ....

    cout << "Number of student is "
         << s.getCount() << endl;
    ....
}
```

The static member function can be called even though there is no object instantiated. In other words, `getCount()` can be called using the following statement before `s` is instantiated. For example,

```
int main() {
    ....
    cout << "Number of student is "
         << CStudent::getCount() << endl;
    ....
}
```

Program 19.16 is a complete example that uses the static member function `getCount()` to obtain the current number of objects of the class `CStudent`. As can be seen, the function `getCount()` returns the value of `m_count`, which increases or decreases by 1 when an object is created or destroyed. The output of Program 19.16 is as follows:

```
m_count from CStudent::getCount() = 0
m_count from sp1->getCount() = 1
m_count from CStudent::getCount() = 1
m_count from sp1->getCount() = 2
m_count from sp2->getCount() = 2
m_count from CStudent::getCount() = 2
Destrcutor ~CStudent() is called
m_count from sp2->getCount() = 1
m_count from CStudent::getCount() = 1
Destrcutor ~CStudent() is called
m_count from CStudent::getCount() = 0
```

```
/* File: staticfunc.cpp
   Use static member function in a class */
#include <string.h>          // for strcpy()
#include <iostream>          // for I/O in C++
using namespace std;         // for using cout, cin, cerr, endl

class CStudent{      // define class CStudent
    public:
      CStudent(int id, char *name);
      ~CStudent();
      void print();
      static int getCount(); // declare static member function
    private:
      int m_id;
      char *m_name;
      static int m_count; // declare static member m_count
};
int CStudent::m_count=0;  // allocate memory and initialize static member


CStudent::CStudent(int id, char *name) {
    m_id = id;
    if(name != NULL) {
      m_name = new char[strlen(name)+1];
      strcpy(m_name, name);
    }
    m_count++;              // use static member m_count
}

CStudent::~CStudent() {
    if(m_name != NULL) {
      delete(m_name);
    }
    m_count--;              // use static member m_count
    cout << "Destructor ~CStudent() is called\n";
}

void CStudent::print() {
    cout << "m_id   = " << m_id <<endl;
    cout << "m_name = " << m_name <<endl;
}

int CStudent::getCount() {  // static member function
    return m_count;   // return CStudent::m_count;
}
```

Program 19.16: Using a static member function of a class. (*Continued*)

```
int main() {
    cout << "m_count from CStudent::getCount() = "<<CStudent::getCount() <<endl;
    CStudent *sp1 = new CStudent(101,"John");
    cout << "m_count from sp1->getCount() = " << sp1->getCount() << endl;
    cout << "m_count from CStudent::getCount() = "<<CStudent::getCount() <<endl;

    CStudent *sp2 = new CStudent(102,"Doe");
    cout << "m_count from sp1->getCount() = " << sp1->getCount() << endl;
    cout << "m_count from sp2->getCount() = " << sp2->getCount() << endl;
    cout << "m_count from CStudent::getCount() = "<<CStudent::getCount() <<endl;

    delete (sp1);
    cout << "m_count from sp2->getCount() = " << sp2->getCount() << endl;
    cout << "m_count from CStudent::getCount() = "<<CStudent::getCount() <<endl;
    delete (sp2);
    cout << "m_count from CStudent::getCount() = "<<CStudent::getCount() <<endl;
    return 0;
}
```

Program 19.16: *(Continued)*.

19.10 Nested Classes

Nested classes are classes that are defined within the scope of another class. Classes in which the nested classes are defined are called *surrounding classes* or *enclosing classes*. Another class can be nested at any part of the surrounding class. A nested class is actually considered a member of the enclosing class. So the normal access and visibility rules in classes apply to nested classes as well. If a class is nested in the public section of a class, it is visible outside the surrounding class. If it is nested in the private section, it is visible only for the members of the surrounding class.

Although a nested class is considered a member of the enclosing class, its members are not members of the enclosing class. So member functions of the surrounding class have no special access to members of a nested class. Member functions of a nested class also follow regular access rules and have no special access privileges to members of their enclosing classes.

Program 19.17 shows how to define nested classes in the enclosing class `Encl`. The output of Program 19.17 is as follows:

```
variable = 5
variable1 = 10
```

```
/* File: nested.cpp
   Use nested classes */
#include <iostream>      // for I/O in C++
using namespace std;     // for using cout, cin, cerr, endl
```

Program 19.17: Using nested classes. *(Continued)*

```
class Encl {        // define class Encl
    public:         // public members
        Encl(int);              // constructor
        ~Encl();                // destructor
        int getVar();           // member function
        class nestPub { // define nested class nestPub
            public:
                int getVar1();          // nested public function
                void setVar1(int var); // nested public function
            private:
                int variable1; // nested private function
        } pubelement;
    private:        // private members
        class nestPrv { // define nested class nestPrv
            public:
                int getVar2();          // nested public function
            private:
                int variable2; // nested private function
        } prvelement;
        int variable;           // define private variable
};

Encl::Encl(int var) { // constructor
    variable = var;
}
Encl::~Encl() {         // destructor
}

int Encl::getVar() { // member function
    return variable;
}

int Encl::nestPub::getVar1() { // nested public function
    return variable1;
}

void Encl::nestPub::setVar1(int var) { // nested public function
    variable1 = var;
}

int Encl::nestPrv::getVar2() { // nested private function
    return variable2;
}
```

Program 19.17: *(Continued)*

```
int main() {
    Encl e = Encl(5);
    cout << "variable = " << e.getVar() << endl;
    e.pubelement.setVar1(10);
    cout << "variable1 = " << e.pubelement.getVar1() << endl;
    return 0;
}
```

Program 19.17: *(Continued)*

In this example, the access rules to members of the class and nested classes are defined as follows:

- The public nested class `nestPub` is visible both outside and inside the enclosing class `Encl`.
- The public member functions `getVar1()` and `setVar1()` of the class `nestPub` are also globally visible.
- The private data member `variable1` of the class `nestPub` is accessible only for the members of the class `nestPub`.
- The private class `nestPrv` is visible only inside the surrounding class `Encl`.
- The public members of the class `nestPub` can be used by the members of the public nested class `nestPub`.
- The public member function `getVar2()` of the class `nestPrv` can be accessed only by the members of the enclosing class `Encl` and the members of its nested classes.
- The private data member `variable2` of the class `nestPrv()` is visible only for the members of the class `nestPrv`.

Besides the definition of the nested class, their member functions are defined in Program 19.17. The definitions of member functions of nested classes are similar to the definitions of the member functions of normal classes. The function name is preceded by both the surrounding class name and the nested class name. Two scope resolution operators '`::`' are used because both `nestPub` and `nestPrv` have member functions named `getVar()`. The scope resolution can prevent confusion.

19.11 Making It Work

19.11.1 Interactive Execution of Code with Classes in Ch

Classes can be used conveniently in a Ch command shell interactively, as shown below.

```
> int i = 10
> class tagc {public: void set(int); int get(int &); \
              private: int m_i, m_j;}
> void tagc::set(int i) {m_i = 2*i;}
> int tagc::get(int &i) {i++; return m_i;}
> tagc c
> c.set(20)
> c.get(i)
40
```

```
> i
11
> c
.m_i = 40
.m_j = 0
> sizeof(tagc)
8
```

Similar to structure type, when a value of class type is displayed interactively, all members and their values of the class are displayed. In this case, the members `m_i` and `m_j` of the class `tagc` are displayed. The **sizeof** operation for a class does not include memory for member functions for the class. Therefore, the size of the class `tagc` is 8 bytes, 4 bytes each for `m_i` and `m_j` of type int.

19.11.2 Running C++ Programs with Multiple Files

Typically, C++ programs that use classes contain multiple files. These are the header file with the class definition and prototypes for the member functions, the source file with the member function definitions, and the application program that actually uses the class. For example, to use the class `CStudent` defined in the header file `student.h` in Program 19.5, the application program with the source file in Program 19.4 needs to include the header file. The source file `CStudent.cpp` in Program 19.6, containing the definitions for member functions of the class `CStudent`, needs to be linked to use the member functions.

The method for running a C++ program with multiple source files is implementation-dependent.

Running C++ Programs with Multiple Source Files in Ch

To run a C++ program with multiple source files in Ch, the source file with the function **main()** is the application program. Other source files are usually loaded in a header file using the preprocessing directive

```
#pragma importf <filename.cpp>
```

For example, for a C++ program with the source files `constructor.cpp` and `CStudent.cpp`, the file `constructor.cpp` contains the function **main()**. The application program shall be executed by simply entering its file name at the command prompt in Ch, as shown below.

```
> constructor.cpp
```

or

```
> ch constructor.cpp
```

The source file `CStudent.cpp` containing member function definitions is loaded by the preprocessing directive **pragma** inside the header file `student.h` with the following statements:

```
#if defined(_CH_)
#pragma importf <CStudent.cpp>
#endif
```

The preprocessing directive **pragma** followed by the token **importf** will load the file `CStudent.cpp`, specified inside a pair of brackets, in the location where **#pragma** is placed. The file is searched based on the search paths specified by the system variable **_fpath** for function files. The system variable **_fpath** can be modified in a start-up file as described in section 6.13.2 in Chapter 6.

Running C++ Programs with Multiple Source Files in Windows and Unix

For Visual C++ in Windows, if a C++ program contains multiple source files, they can all be placed in a command line for the compiler. For example, for the C++ program with the source files `constructor.cpp` and `CStudent.cpp`, and the file `constructor.cpp` contains the function **main()**, the executable binary program `constructor.exe` can be created by the command

```
> cl constructor.cpp CStudent.cpp
```

In Unix, the executable binary program `a.out` can be created by one of the following commands:

```
> g++ constructor.cpp CStudent.cpp
> CC constructor.cpp CStudent.cpp
> c++ constructor.cpp CStudent.cpp
```

19.11.3 Debugging Programs with Classes in ChIDE

The method for debugging programs, described in sections 3.16.3 in Chapter 3 and 6.13.3 in Chapter 6, is also applicable to programs with classes. Selecting the menu `Locals` or `Variables` on the debugging pane selection bar, for a variable of class type in the scope, each member of the class, except member functions, will be displayed. When a member of a class is modified, the entire class will be updated when the class is displayed. Inside a member function of a class, all local variables and the implicit **this** pointer for the member function, as well as members of the class (except member functions of the class) and corresponding values are displayed.

Exercises

1. Complete the following program with the member functions `addNum()` and `getSum()`. The function `addNum()` adds the passed value to the private member m_sum. The function `getSum()` obtains the sum stored in the private data member `m_sum`.

```
#include <iostream>

class Data{
   public:
      Data(void);
      void addNum(int i);
      int getSum();
   private:
      int m_sum;
};
```

```
Data::Data (){
    m_sum = 0; // initialize to 0 */
}

/* add member functions here */

int main() {
    Data d;
    int i, sum1=0, sum2;
    for(i = 0; i<10; i++) {
        d.addNum(i);
        sum1 += i;
    }
    sum2 = d.getSum();
    printf("sum1 = %d\n", sum1);
    printf("sum2 = %d\n", sum2);
}
```

2. Complete the following program with the constructor `Data()`, and the member functions `print()` and `length()`. The function `print()` prints out the string passed in the argument and adds the length of the string in the private member `m_len`. The function `length()` obtains the total length of strings printed out by the member function `print()` stored in the private data member `m_len`.

```
#include <iostream>
#include <string.h>

class Data{
    public:
        Data();
        void print(char *);
        int length();
    private:
        int m_len;
};

int main() {
    Data d;
    int len;
    d.print("1234");
    d.print("abcd");
    len = d.length();
    printf("len= %d\n", len); /* this should give 'len=8' */
}

/* add constructor and member functions here */
```

3. State whether the following are true or false. If false, briefly explain why.

   a. Both class and structure in C++ allow member functions to perform operations on their members.

b.
```
class Rectangle_Area {
    int length;
    int width;
};
```

Just like members in structs, the members in the class Rectangle_Area, `length` and `width`, are private by default.

c. The following code fragment is legal:

```
class Student {
    int id;
    int grade;
public:
    char *name;
};

int main() {
    ...
    id = 2;         // set member id to 2;
}
```

d. No return value needs to be specified for a constructor.

e. Assume that class `Student` has the following declaration:

```
class Student {
  private:
    int id;
  public:
    void setId(int sid);
};
```

The code

```
void Student::setId(int sid) {
    id = sid;
}
```

is the same as

```
void Student::setId(int sid) {
    this->id = sid;
}
```

f. A class inside a member function is visible to other member functions if the member function in which it is defined in is declared public.

4. Fill in the blanks in the following statements.

a. Class members are accessed with the _____ operator if it is an object of the class. But they are accessed with the _____ operator if it is a pointer to an object of the class.

b. A _____ is a member function that by convention is used for data members' initializations.

c. The _____ pointer points to its own object address.

d. The _____ and _____ operators in C++ have the same uses as the functions **malloc()** and **free()** in C, respectively.
e. The keyword _____ specifies that the variable is shared among different objects of a class.
f. Members of a class specified as _____ are accessible anywhere an object of the class is in scope.

5. Find the error(s) in each of the following code fragments and explain how to correct it (them).

a. The following prototypes are declared in the class `Student`:

```
char * Student(const char *, const char *);
   ...
void ~Student(int);
```

b.

```
class Student {
     public:
       ...
     private:
       int id = -1;
       int phone_num = -1;
       ...
};
```

c.

```
class Student {
     public:
       int getId(char *name);
       ...
     private:
       ...
};

int main() {
     Student s;
     int id;
     ...
     id = s->getId("Aaron");
     ...
}
```

d.

```
#include "Student.h"

int main() {
     class Student *s = new Student[10];
     ...
     delete s;
}
```

e.

```
class Circle: {
     private
       float X;
       float Y;
       float R;
```

```
        public
          setC(float, float);
          setR(float);
    }
```

6. Assume that the class `Student` has two private data members: `id`, set to 101, and `phone_number`, set to 4158349039. The values of `id` and `phone_number` can be retrieved only using `getId()` and `getPN()`. Write a function **main()** that prints the values of `id` and `phone_number` without instantiating any `Student` object.
7. Create a class called `Rectangle`. The class has the data members `width` and `length`. It has five member functions: `perimeter()`, `area()`, `set()`, `getLength()`, and `getWidth()`. The `set` function is used to set the length and width of a rectangle. The functions `getLength()`, `getWidth()`, `perimeter()`, and `area()` return the length, width, perimeter, and area of the rectangle, respectively. The `set()` function should make sure that the values of `width` and `length` are both floating point numbers between 0.0 and 20.0. If the input value is outside this range, the default value of 1.0 will be assigned. Test the class with a rectangle of the length of 2 and width of 3.
8. Modify Programs 19.5 and 19.6 by adding a member function `CStudent::file(char * filename)`, which will save the ID and name of the student in the file `filename` passed in the argument of the member function, as illustrated in the program `file.cpp` below.

```
/* File: file.cpp */
#include "student.h"

int main() {
    class CStudent s1 = CStudent(101,"John");
    class CStudent s2 = CStudent(102,"Doe");

    s1.print();
    s2.print();
    s1.file("John");
    s2.file("Doe");
    return 0;
}
```

CHAPTER 20

Two- and Three-Dimensional Plotting in C++

As the saying goes, "a picture is worth a thousand words." Graphical plotting is important for the visualization, efficient representation, and interpretation of numerical results. But the C and C++ standard do not support graphical plotting by default. Developers typically generate data in a file and then use other software packages, such as Microsoft Excel, to plot the data in the file. However, this is an inconvenient process for the development of algorithms. In this chapter, a plotting class in the C++ graphical library called SoftIntegration Graphical Library (SIGL) is introduced. This library might be the simplest possible solution for two- and three-dimensional graphical plottings within the framework of C/C++. Two- and three-dimensional graphical plots can be easily generated by plotting functions or member functions in the library. Plots can be created from data arrays or files, and they can be displayed on the screen, saved as an image file in different file formats, or output to the **stdout** stream in a proper image format for display in a Web browser through a Web server.

We have already used some plotting functions of this plotting library, such as **plotxy(), plotxyz(), fplotxy()**, and **fplotxyz()**, in previous chapters. To use the SIGL library, a program needs to include the header file **chplot.h**, which contains the definition of the plotting class and its member functions, function prototypes, and macros. At the end of this chapter, we will describe how to compile and link a C++ program using functions or member functions in the SIGL library. However, the SIGL graphical library is Ch-compatible. A program using the plotting class and functions in SIGL can readily run in Ch interpretively without compilation.

20.1 Using a Plotting Class to Plot Multiple Sets of Data

In section 10.6 in Chapter 10, the function **plotxy()** is used to plot data in arrays. Program 20.1 provides a simple example of using the **plotxy()** function for generating the plot of a sine wave for x from 0 to 2π radians. The variables `x0` and `xf` represent the initial and final values of x, respectively. The macro N is defined as the number of 37 points. A **for** loop is used to generate 37 data points for the plot, which is shown in Figure 20.1. The statement

```
x[i] = x0+i*(xf - x0)/(N-1);
```

generates the x-coordinates of the plot with the number of points specified in the macro N for x ranging from `t0` to `tf`. The title of the plot and axes are specified as the strings `"function sin(x)"`, `"x"`, and `"sin(x)"`, respectively.

```
/* File: plotxy.cpp
   Plot sin(x) from 0 to 2PI using plotxy() */
#include <math.h>    // for sin() and M_PI
#include <chplot.h> // for plotxy()

#define N 37          // number of points for plotting

int main() {
    double x[N], y[N], x0, xf;
    int i;

    x0 = 0;
    xf = 2*M_PI;
    for(i=0; i<N; i++)  {
        x[i] = x0 + i*(xf - x0)/(N-1);
        y[i] = sin(x[i]);
    }
    plotxy(x, y, N, "function sin(x)", "x", "sin(x)");
    return 0;
}
```

Program 20.1: Plotting data using the function **plotxy()**.

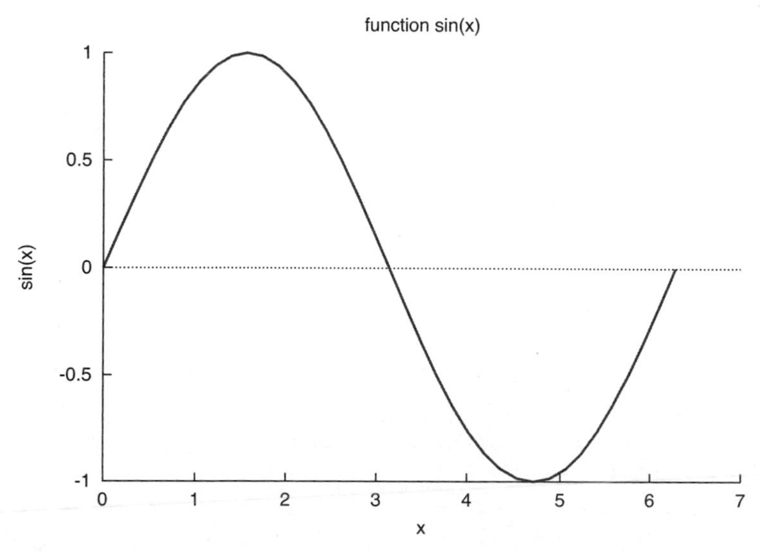

Figure 20.1: The plot generated by Program 20.1.

The function **plotxy**() has limited capabilities to construct a plot. For example, it cannot add legends for multiple curves in the same plot. The plotting class **CPlot** enables high-level creation and manipulation of plots for applications. Many member functions of the class **CPlot** can be used to fine-tune a plot. Detailed descriptions of each function can be found in the Users Guide for SIGL.

The plotting class **CPlot** can be used to implement other simple plotting functions. For example, the function call

```
plotxy(x, y, n, title, xlabel, ylabel);
```

is equivalent to

```
CPlot plot;
plot.title(title);
plot.label(PLOT_AXIS_X, xlabel);
plot.label(PLOT_AXIS_Y, ylabel);
plot.data2DCurve(x, y, n);
plot.plotting();
```

as shown in Program 20.2, which generates the same plot displayed in Figure 20.1.

```
/* File: plotclass.cpp
   Plot sin(x) from 0 to 2PI using class CPlot */
#include <math.h>    // for sin() and M_PI
#include <chplot.h> // for CPlot

#define N 37         // number of points for plotting

int main() {
    double x[N], y[N], x0, xf;
    char title[] = "function sin(x)",
         xlabel[] = "x",
         ylabel[] = "sin(x)";
    int i;
    CPlot plot;

    x0 = 0;
    xf = 2*M_PI;
    for(i=0; i<N; i++)  {
        x[i] = x0 + i*(xf - x0)/(N-1);
        y[i] = sin(x[i]);
    }
    /* use member functions of class CPlot */
    plot.title(title);
    plot.label(PLOT_AXIS_X, xlabel);
    plot.label(PLOT_AXIS_Y, ylabel);
    plot.data2DCurve(x, y, N);
    plot.plotting();
    return 0;
}
```

Program 20.2: Plotting data using the plotting class **CPlot**.

Table 20.1 The macros for axes.

PLOT_AXIS_X	Selects the x axis only.
PLOT_AXIS_X2	Selects the x2 axis only.
PLOT_AXIS_Y	Selects the y axis only.
PLOT_AXIS_Y2	Selects the y2 axis only.
PLOT_AXIS_Z	Selects the z axis only.
PLOT_AXIS_XY	Selects the x and y axes.
PLOT_AXIS_XYZ	Selects the x, y, and z axes.

The data for the plotting of a two-dimensional curve are added to an instance of **CPlot** class by the member function **CPlot::data2DCurve**()

```
int CPlot::data2DCurve(double x[], double y[], int n);
```

Both one-dimensional arrays `x` and `y` have the same number of elements of size `n`.

The title and labels on axes are annotated using the corresponding member functions **CPlot::title()**

```
void CPlot::title(char *title);
```

and **CPlot::label**()

```
void CPlot::label(int axis, char *label);
```

respectively. The argument *axis* of the member function **CPlot**::**label**() is the axis to be set. The valid macros for *axis*, defined in the header file **chplot.h**, are listed in Table 20.1. The axis x refers to the x axis on the bottom, the axis y refers to the y axis on the left, the axis $x2$ refers to the $x2$ axis on the top, and the axis $y2$ refers to the $y2$ axis on the right. At the point where the member function **CPlot**::**plotting**() is called, a plot is generated.

Similarly, the function call

```
fplotxy(func, x0, xf, num, title. xlabel, ylabel);
```

is equivalent to

```
CPlot plot;
plot.title(title);
plot.label(PLOT_AXIS_X, xlabel);
plot.label(PLOT_AXIS_Y, ylabel);
plot.func2D(x0, xf, num, func);
plot.plotting();
```

The member function **CPlot::fun2D**()

```
void CPlot::func2D(double x0, double xf, int num,
                   double (*func)(double x));
```

adds a set of data using a function pointed by `func` in the range from `x0` to `xf` with `num` points to a previously declared instance of the **CPlot** class. The function to be plotted shall have the function prototype of

```
double func(double x);
```

The member function **CPlot::funcp2D**()

```
void CPlot::funcp2D(double x0, double xf, double num,
            double (*func)(double x, void *param), void *param);
```

can be used to plot a function with parameters. The function to be plotted has the function prototype of

```
double func(double x, void *param);
```

The parameter from the calling function is passed to the plotting function in the second argument. Using a generic pointer for parameters, different numbers of arguments and data types can be handled. For multiple parameters of the same data type, one can pass the parameters using an array. For multiple parameters of different data types, a structure can be used to hold the parameters and a pointer to structure can be passed to the function. Inside the plotting function, the argument `param` of generic type is cast into the proper data type. If there is no parameter, NULL can be passed as the last argument of the member function **funcp2D**(). Using a generic pointer to pass information from a calling function to the callback function is commonly used in C.

As an example, Program 8.3 in section 8.1.1 in Chapter 8 plots the trajectory for a projectile. The variables `v0` and `theta0` for initial speed and initial projection angle, respectively, are declared as global variables. They can be shared in different functions so that they need to be calculated once. However, to avoid the name space conflict, the use of global variables should be minimized. Using a generic pointer as described in section 11.12 in Chapter 11 and section 13.1.9 in Chapter 13, the member function **funcp2D**() can be employed to avoid using global variables, as shown in Program 20.3. The variable `initc` of the structure `InitCond` is used to hold the initial projection angle θ_0 and the initial speed v_0, which are calculated only once in the function **main**(). The address of the structure is passed to the second argument of the function `traj()` through

```
/* File: projectilestruct.cpp
   Plot a projectile without using global variable */
#include <math.h>          // for sin(), cos(), tan()
#include <chplot.h>        // for CPlot

#define M_G 9.81           // gravitational constant g
#define N 100              // number of points for plotting

struct InitCond {          // define struct InitCond
   double theta0;          // member for projection angle
   double v0;              // member for initial velocity
};

double traj(double x, void *param) {
   double theta0,          // variable for projection angle
          v0,              // variable for initial velocity
          y;               // y coordinate
   struct InitCond *initptr;
```

Program 20.3: A program to plot the trajectory for a projectile without global variables. (*Continued*)

```
    initcptr = (struct InitCond *)param;  // cast to proper pointer type
    theta0 = initcptr->theta0;            // access value from the pointer
    v0 = initcptr->v0;
    y = tan(theta0)*x - M_G*x*x/(2*v0*v0*cos(theta0)*cos(theta0));
    return y;
}

int main() {
    struct InitCond initc; // variables for projection angle and initial velocity
    double x0=0, xf;
    CPlot plot;


    initc.theta0 = 15*M_PI/180;    // projection angle in rad
    initc.v0 = 35.0;               // initial velocity
    xf = initc.v0*initc.v0*sin(2*initc.theta0)/M_G;    // the distance
    plot.title("A projectile with the initial projection angle 15 degrees");
    plot.label(PLOT_AXIS_X, "x (m)");
    plot.label(PLOT_AXIS_Y, "y (m)");
    plot.funcp2D(x0, xf, N, traj, &initc); // address of initc is passed
    plot.plotting();
}
```

Program 20.3: *(Continued)*

the last argument of the member function **funcp2D**() using generic pointers for different parameters. The initial projection angle θ_0 and initial speed v_0 are retrieved from the second argument of the function `traj()` by the variable `initcptr` of pointer to structure `InitCond`. In this example, we could also use an array of two elements to hold the initial projection angle and speed inside the main() function and pass the array to the plotting function `traj()`. The output from Program 20.3 is the same as the one shown in Figure 6.2 in section 6.7 in Chapter 6.

The data for plotting a three-dimensional curve can also be added to an instance of **CPlot** class by the member function **CPlot::data3DCurve**()

```
int CPlot::data3DCurve(double  x[], double y[], double z[], int n);
```

One-dimensional arrays `x`, `y`, and `z` shall have the same number of elements of size `n`.

A set of data for three-dimensional surface plotting can be added to an instance of the **CPlot** class by the member function **CPlot::data3DSurface**()

```
int CPlot::data3DSurface(double  x[], double y[], double z[],
                          int nx, int ny);
```

If the one-dimensional array `x` has the number of elements of *nx* and the one-dimensional array *y* has *ny*, the number of elements of one-dimensional array *z* shall be the product of `nx` and `ny`. In a Cartesian coordinate system, the arrays *x*, *y*, and *z* represent values in X, Y, and Z coordinates, respectively.

A set of data based on a function with two variables can also be added to an instance of a plotting class by the member function **CPlot::func3D**()

```
void CPlot::func3D(double x0, double xf, double y0, double yf,
                   int num, int numy, double (*func)(double x, y));
```

It adds a set of data using a function pointed by `func` in the range from `x0` to `xf` with `num` points to a previously declared instance of the **CPlot** class. It plots the function with the two variables x and y in the range $x0 \leq x \leq xf$ with `numx` points and $y0 \leq y \leq$ with `numy` points, respectively. The function to be plotted, `func`, is specified as a pointer to a function that takes two arguments and returns a value of double type with the function prototype of

```
double func(double x, double y);
```

Many other member functions of the plotting class can be used to specify the desired features for the generated plot and to create different output.

As an example for plotting with multiple data sets, a plot with two sets of data for sine and cosine functions from 0 to 360 degrees with legends, shown in Figure 20.2, is generated by Program 20.4. In Program 20.4, the array `x` contains the data for the x-coordinates, and the arrays `y1` and `y2` each contain a data set for the y-coordinates. The member function **CPlot::data2DCurve**() is called twice to add two sets of data to the plot. A legend can be added to the plot by the member function **CPlot::legend**()

```
void CPlot::legend(char *legend, int num);
```

The argument `legend` is a string of characters. The number of data sets, with which the legend is associated, is indicated by the second argument `num` of int type. The numbering of the data sets starts with zero. New legends will replace previously specified legends. This member function shall be called after plotting data have been added by the member function **CPlot::data2DCurve**().

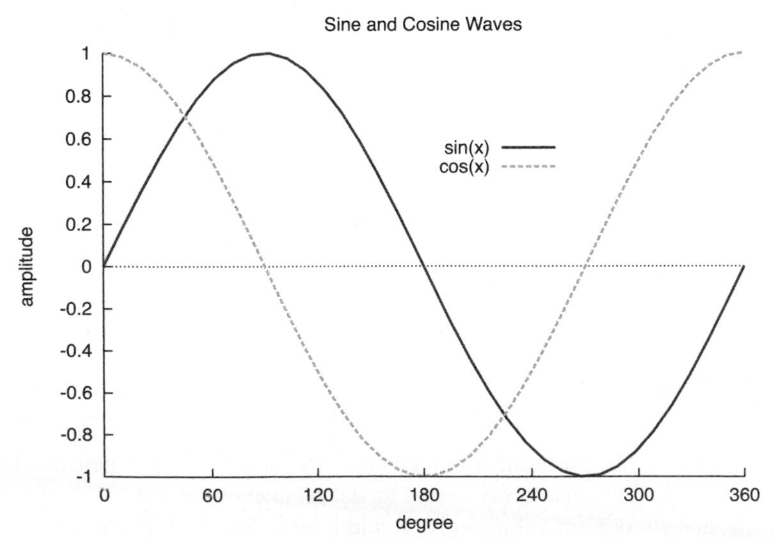

Figure 20.2: A plot generated by Program 20.4 with two sets of data and legends.

```
/* File: legend.cpp
   Use legend for a plot with multiple curves */
#include <math.h>     // for sin(), cos(), M_PI
#include <chplot.h>  // for CPlot

#define N 36

int main() {
    int i;
    double x0, xf, x[N], y1[N], y2[N];
    char *title="Sine and Cosine Waves",
         *xlabel="degree", *ylabel="amplitude";
    CPlot plot;

    x0 = 0;
    xf = 360;
    for(i = 0; i < N; i++) {
        x[i]  = x0 + i*(xf - x0)/(N-1);
        y1[i] = sin(x[i]*M_PI/180);
        y2[i] = cos(x[i]*M_PI/180);
    }
    plot.title(title);
    plot.label(PLOT_AXIS_X, xlabel);
    plot.label(PLOT_AXIS_Y, ylabel);
    plot.data2DCurve(x, y1, N);
    plot.data2DCurve(x, y2, N);
    plot.legend("sin(x)", 0);          // add legend for 1st curve
    plot.legend("cos(x)", 1);          // add legend for 2nd curve
    plot.legendLocation(260, 0.6);     // set the location for legends
    plot.axisRange(PLOT_AXIS_X, 0.0, 360.0);       // set axis range
    plot.ticsRange(PLOT_AXIS_X, 60.0, 0.0, 360.0); // set tics marks
    plot.plotting();
    return 0;
}
```

Program 20.4: A program for plotting two sets of data with legends.

The member function **CPlot::legendLocation**()

```
void CPlot::legendLocation(double x, double y, ... /* [double z] */);
```

specifies the position of the plot legend using plot coordinates (x, y, z) of double type. For a two-dimensional plot, only the coordinates (x, y) are needed. The position specified is the location of the top part of the space separating the markers and labels of the legend, as shown in Figure 20.3. By default, the location of the legend is near the upper-right corner of the plot.

The range of an axis can be set by the member function **CPlot::axisRange**(),

```
void CPlot::axisRange(int axis, double minimum, double maximum);
```

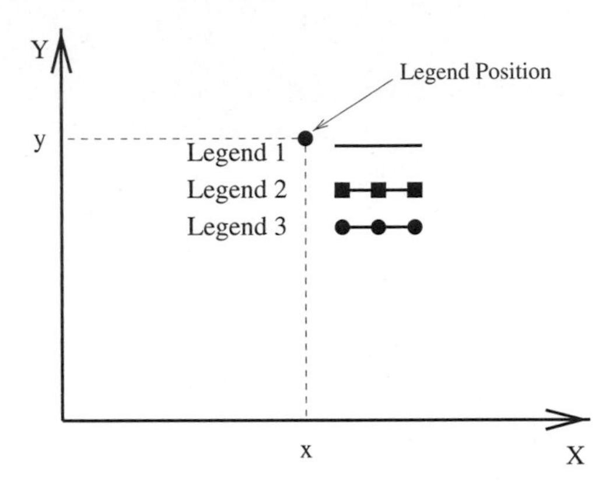

Figure 20.3: The position of a legend.

The valid macros for *axis* are listed in Table 20.1. Each of the four borders x (bottom), $x2$ (top), y (left), and $y2$ (right) can be used as an independent axis. The minimum and maximum values for an axis are given in the second and third arguments, respectively. The tick marks on an axis can be set by the function **CPlot**::**ticsRange**()

```
void CPlot::ticsRange(int axis, double incr, ...
                      /* [double start], [double end] */);
```

The increment between tick marks is given in the variable *incr*. By default, this value is calculated internally. The start and end positions for tick marks are optional arguments. For example, the following function calls in Program 20.4

```
plot.axisRange(PLOT_AXIS_X, 0.0, 360.0);
plot.ticsRange(PLOT_AXIS_X, 60.0, 0.0, 360.0);
```

set the range of the x-axis from 0 to 360 degrees with tick marks at every 60 degrees.

By default, points in a plot are connected as a line. The member function **CPlot**::**plotType**()

```
void CPlot::plotType(int plottype, int num, ...);
```

can be used to change this default plot type. The first argument `plottype` specifies the plot type. The second argument `num` is the number of data set to which the plot type applies. For example, Program 10.19 uses this member function to create a plot with scattered points for the distance of a moving body versus time, as shown in Figure 10.8 in Chapter 10. Using the same experimental data in Program 10.19, Program 20.5, with the output shown in Figure 20.4, calls the member function

```
plot.plotType(PLOT_PLOTTYPE_FILLEDCURVES, num, "y1=0");
```

to plot a filled curve with respect to the x1-axis as specified by `y1 = 0` in the third argument for the option of the filled curve. The filled color is specified by the fourth argument of the function call

```
plot.lineType(num, linetype, linewidth, "green");
```

The member function **CPlot**::**lincType**()

```
void CPlot::lineType(int num, int type, int width, ... /* char *color */);
```

```
/* File: filledcurve.cpp
   Plot data in a filled curve */
#include <chplot.h> // for CPlot

int main() {
    /* declare and initialize the original data */
    double t[] = {0.0, 3.0, 5.0, 8.0,  10.0, 12.0, 15.0, 18.0};
    double y[] = {2.0, 5.2, 6.0, 10.0, 10.4, 13.4, 14.8, 18.0};
    int n, num=0;  // number of data points and data set number
    CPlot plot;    // instantiate a plotting class
    int linetype, linewidth;

    n = sizeof(t)/sizeof(double); // calculate the number of data points

    /* Setup for the entire plot */
    plot.label(PLOT_AXIS_X, "t (second)");
    plot.label(PLOT_AXIS_Y, "y (meter)");
    plot.border(PLOT_BORDER_ALL, PLOT_ON); // display all four boards
    /* add grid, always on the front with line width 2 */
    plot.grid(PLOT_ON, "front linewidth 2");

    /* add data t[] and y[] as the 1st set of data for plotting
       in filled curve with axis y1=0 and color specified by line type 2 */
    plot.data2DCurve(t, y, n);
    plot.plotType(PLOT_PLOTTYPE_FILLEDCURVES, num, "y1=0");
    linetype = 1;   // line type
    linewidth = 1;  // line width
    plot.lineType(num, linetype, linewidth, "green");

    /* add data t[] and y[] as the 2nd set of data for plotting in lines */
    plot.data2DCurve(t, y, n);
    linetype = 1;   // line type
    linewidth = 4;  // line width,
    plot.lineType(++num, linetype, linewidth, "red");

    plot.plotting();
    return 0;
}
```

Program 20.5: A program for plotting two sets of data, one of which is a filled curve.

can be used to change the attributes of a line. The first argument `num` is the number of data set to which the line type applies. The second argument `type` specifies a line type. The third argument `width` specifies the width of a line. An optional fourth argument can specify the color of a line by a color name or RGB value, such as `"blue"` or `"#0000ff"` for color blue. The default line type, width, and color for the second set of data in Program 20.5 are changed by the function call

```
plot.lineType(++num, linetype, linewidth, "red");
```

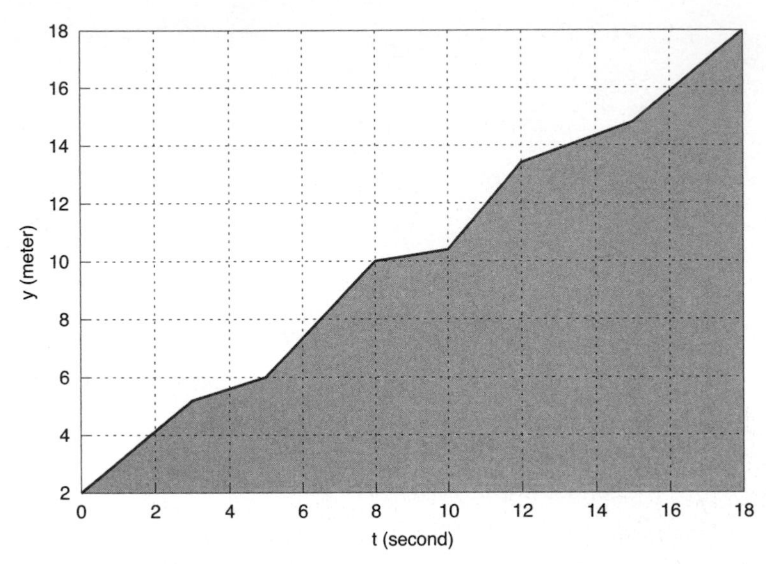

Figure 20.4: A plot generated by Program 20.5 with two sets of data, one of which is a filled curve.

The member function **CPlot::border()**

```
void CPlot::border(int location, int flag);
```

turns on or off a border display around the plot. By default, the border is drawn on the left and bottom sides for two-dimensional plots, and on all sides on the x-y plane for three-dimensional plots. The valid `location` for the function **CPlot::border()** is given in Table 20.2. The `flag` can be set to **PLOT_ON** to enable the drawing of the border, or **PLOT_OFF** to disable the drawing of the border. The function call in Program 20.5

```
plot.border(PLOT_BORDER_ALL, PLOT_ON);
```

displays all four borders.

The member function **CPlot::grid()**

```
void CPlot::grid(int flag, ... /* char *option */);
```

turns the display of a grid on the x-y plane on or off. The function call in Program 20.5

```
plot.grid(PLOT_ON, "front linewidth 2");
```

makes the grid displayed on the entire plot with the grid line width of 2. Without the option `front`, the filled part on the plot would have no grid.

Table 20.2 The macros for border locations.

PLOT_BORDER_BOTTOM	The bottom of the plot
PLOT_BORDER_LEFT	The left side of the plot
PLOT_BORDER_TOP	The top of the plot
PLOT_BORDER_RIGHT	The right side of the plot
PLOT_BORDER_ALL	All sides of the plot

The member function **CPlot::enhanceText**()

```
void CPlot::enhanceText(void);
```

turns on the enhanced text mode for terminal and output files in PostScript, PNG, JPEG, GIF formats that support additional text formatting information embedded in the text string. With this member function call, special symbols can be used in text such as those passed as arguments of member functions **CPlot::label**(), **CPlot::legend**(), **CPlot::text**(), and **CPlot::title**(). The detailed syntax and character codes for the enhanced text are presented in *Ch Reference Guide* available in `CHHOME/docs/chref.pdf`. For example, Program 17.8 in Chapter 17 uses the enhanced text to display the Greek symbols ω_n and ζ in Figure 17.8. Program 20.6 displays the mathematical symbol m/s^2 in Figure 20.5.

20.2 Multiple Plots in the Same Figure

In some applications, more than two sets of data with different units need to be plotted in the same figure. For example, one may plot the position, velocity, and acceleration of a moving particle versus time. Because these three quantities have different units, we cannot draw these three curves in the same plot. But the x-coordinates for the time are the same for three curves. It will be desirable to draw them in the same figure for comparison. If more than two sets of data with different units are to be plotted in the same figure, subplots in Ch can be used.

Multiple plots can be created in the same figure using the member function **CPlot::subplot**()

```
int CPlot::subplot(int row, int col);
```

The function **CPlot::subplot**() breaks the figure into an `m`-by-`n` matrix of small subplots. The subplots are numbered as if there were a two-dimensional matrix with the numbers of rows and columns specified in its arguments. Each index starts with 0. A pointer to the **CPlot** class as a handle for a subplot at the location `(i,j)` can be obtained by the member function **CPlot::getSubplot**()

```
CPlot *CPlot::getSubplot(int row, int col);
```

where `row` and `col` are the row and column numbers of the desired subplot element, respectively. Numbering starts with zero. Each subplot can be annotated with title, label, etc., as if it were a separate plot.

An Application Example

Position, Velocity, and Acceleration of a Moving Particle

Problem Statement:

The position coordinate of a particle that is confined to move along a straight line is given by

$$x = 2t^3 - 24t + 6$$

where x is measured in meters from a convenient origin and t is the time in seconds. The velocity and acceleration of the particle can be obtained by successive differentiation of x with respect to time as follows:

$$v = 6t^2 - 24$$

$$a = 12t$$

where v is the velocity in m/s and a is the acceleration in m/s^2. Plot the position, velocity, and acceleration of the particle versus time in the range of $0 \le t \le 4$ in a figure.

Because the position, velocity, and acceleration have different units, we can plot them using subplots in a figure. Program 20.6 breaks a plot with three subplots in a 3-by-1 matrix. The element (0, 0) is for position, (1, 0) for velocity, and (2, 0) for acceleration. Figure 20.5 displays the plot produced by Program 20.6. In Program 20.6, the plotting data for position, velocity, and acceleration are generated by functions and added to the plotting object by the member function **func2D**(). Each subplot has its own labels for its coordinates. The tick marks for each subplot are specified by the member function **ticsRange**(). The incremental value for tick marks may need to be adjusted after an initial plot is displayed. The member function **enhanceText()** allows the text `accel (m/s^2)` to be displayed in the enhanced text in the proper mathematical symbol m/s^2 for the unit of the acceleration for the label in the y-axis in the last subplot.

```
/* File: posvelaccel.cpp
   Plot position, velocity, and acceleration in subplots in the same figure */
#include <math.h>
#include <chplot.h>

double position(double t) {       // function for position
    return 2*t*t*t - 24*t + 6;
}

double velocity(double t) {       // function for velocity
    return 6*t*t - 24;
}

double accel(double t) {          // function for acceleration
    return 12*t;
}

int main() {
    double t0 = 0, tf = 4;
    int num = 100;
    CPlot subplot, *plot;

    subplot.subplot(3, 1);        // create 3x1 subplots
    subplot.enhanceText();        // using enhanced text
    /* subplot for position */
    plot = subplot.getSubplot(0, 0);
    plot->label(PLOT_AXIS_X, "time (s)");
    plot->label(PLOT_AXIS_Y, "position (m)");
    plot->func2D(t0, tf, num, position);
    plot->ticsRange(PLOT_AXIS_Y, 10);

    /* subplot for velocity */
    plot = subplot.getSubplot(1, 0);
    plot->label(PLOT_AXIS_X, "time (s)");
    plot->label(PLOT_AXIS_Y, "velocity (m/s)");
```

Program 20.6: A program to plot the position, velocity, and acceleration using subplots. (*Continued*)

```
    plot->func2D(t0, tf, num, velocity);
    plot->ticsRange(PLOT_AXIS_Y, 20);

    /* subplot for acceleration */
    plot = subplot.getSubplot(2, 0);
    plot->label(PLOT_AXIS_X, "time (s)");
    plot->label(PLOT_AXIS_Y, "accel (m/s^2)"); // enhanced text for m/s^2
    plot->func2D(t0, tf, num, accel);
    plot->ticsRange(PLOT_AXIS_Y, 10);

    subplot.plotting();          // plot all subplots
}
```

Program 20.6: (*Continued*)

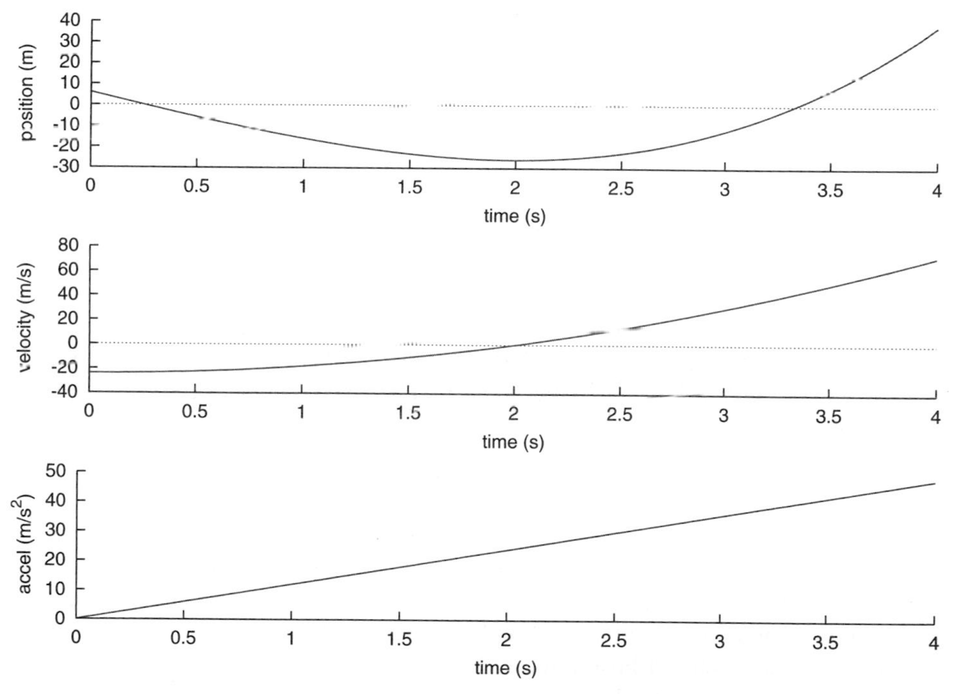

Figure 20.5 The position, velocity, and acceleration in subplots generated by Program 20.6.

20.3 Copying, Printing, and Saving a Plot

In Windows, the plots such as the one displayed in Figure 20.1 can be copied to the clipboard first, then pasted into other documents, such as Word documents and PowerPoint presentation slides. Clicking the plot icon on the upper left corner of the plot will bring up several menus. Click `Copy to Clipboard` under the `Options` menu, as shown in Figure 20.6. Doing this will save the plot in the clipboard first. Then the plot can be printed out by clicking `Print` under the `Options` menu.

```
int main() {
    double a[N], p[N], t[N], t0, tf;
    double mu, m;
    int i;
    CPlot plot;

    mu = 0.2;
    m = 5.0;
    t0 = 0.0;
    tf = 10.0;
    for(i=0; i<N; i++) {
        t[i] = t0+i*(tf - t0)/(N-1);
        p[i] = 4*sin(t[i]-3)+20;
        a[i] = (p[i]-mu*m*M_G)/m;
    }
    /* Setup for the entire plot */
    plot.title("force and acceleration");
    plot.label(PLOT_AXIS_X, "time (s)");
    plot.border(PLOT_BORDER_ALL, PLOT_ON); // display all four borders

    /* Setup for the acceleration using axes x1 and y1 */
    plot.label(PLOT_AXIS_Y, "accel (m/s^2)");
    plot.data2DCurve(t, a, N);
    plot.legend("acceleration", 0);  // set legend for 1st curve

    /* Setup for the force using axes x1 and y2 */
    plot.label(PLOT_AXIS_Y2, "force (N)");
    plot.data2DCurve(t, p, N);
    plot.axisRange(PLOT_AXIS_Y2, 15, 25);
    plot.ticsRange(PLOT_AXIS_Y2, 5);
    plot.legend("force", 1);   // set legend for 2nd curve
    plot.axes(1, "x1y2");      // use axes x1 and y2 for 2nd curve
    plot.tics(PLOT_AXIS_Y2, PLOT_ON);

    plot.plotting();
    return 0;
}
```

Program 20.7: (*Continued*)

Because the $y2$ axis is used, the border for all sides and ticks on the $y2$ axis are turned on. The $y2$ axis ranges from 15 to 25 with the incremental tick marks of 5. Because the acceleration is a linear function of the external force in this application, the shapes of both acceleration and force are similar.

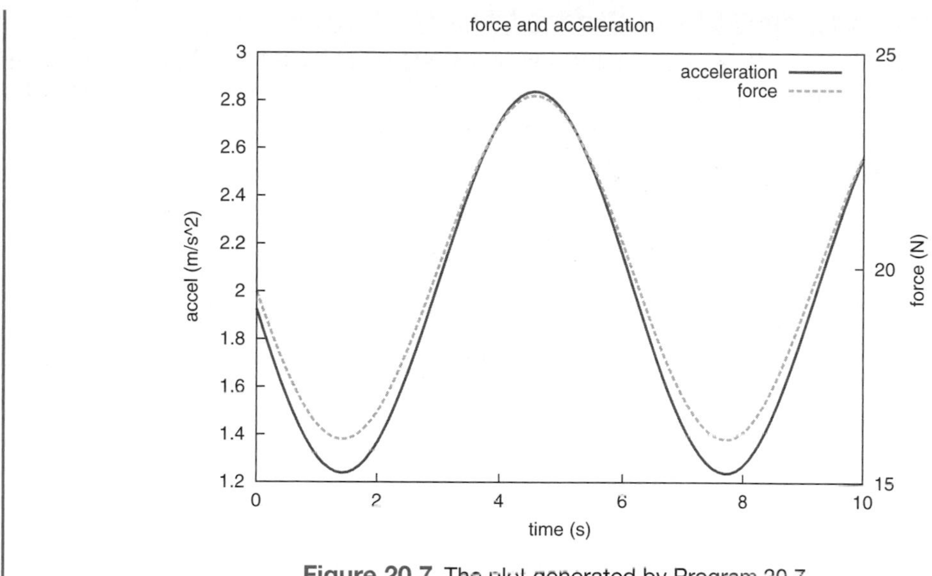

Figure 20.7 The plot generated by Program 20.7.

20.5 Making It Work

20.5.1 Compiling Programs Using the SIGL C++ Plotting Library

Plotting features described in this chapter are readily available in Ch. However, a program using SIGL C++ plotting library can also be compiled using a C++ compiler.

In this section, we will describe how to compile and link a C++ program using the SIGL library. The process of compiling a C++ program in Unix is slightly different from that in Windows.

Compiling Programs Using the SIGL C++ Plotting Library in Unix

In Unix, assume that the environment variable **SILIB_HOME** for the home directory of SoftIntegration Graphical Library is /usr/silib. Otherwise, change /usr/ch below to the directory for **SILIB_HOME**. With the C++ compiler command **g++, CC, c++** in Unix, use one of the following commands to compile and link the C++ program `plot.cpp`:

```
> g++ plotxy.cpp -I/usr/silib/include -L/usr/silib/lib -lchplot -lm
> CC  plotxy.cpp -I/usr/silib/include -L/usr/silib/lib -lchplot -lm
> c++ plotxy.cpp -I/usr/silib/include -L/usr/silib/lib -lchplot -lm
```

where option `-I` specifies the included path for header files, option `-L` specifies the search path for libraries, and option `-l` specifies a library to be linked. For example, options `-lchplot` and `-lm` will link the program with graphical and mathematical libraries, respectively. The above command will create executable program `a.out`.

Compiling Programs Using the SIGL C++ Plotting Library in Windows

For Visual C++ in Windows, assume that the environment variable **SILIB_HOME** for the home directory of the graphical library is `C:/silib`. Otherwise, change `C:/silib` below to the directory for **SILIB_HOME**. Use the command below to compile and link the program `plotxy.cpp` in a Ch command shell:

```
> cl plotxy.cpp -IC:/silib/include C:/silib/lib/libchplot.lib
```

It compiles the source code `plotxy.cpp` and links the graphical library `libchplot.lib` to create an executable program `accelplot.exe`. If the program `plotxy.cpp` uses the macro **M_PI** in the header file `math.h`, the macro `_USE_MATH_DEFINES` can be defined before **math.h** is included, as shown below.

```
> cl plotxy.cpp -IC:/silib/include C:/silib/lib/libchplot.lib -D_USE_MATH_DEFINES
```

Compiling Programs Using the SIGL C++ Plotting Library in ChIDE

The most simple way to compile a C++ program using SIGL in Windows is to use ChIDE, as described in section 2.2.5 in Chapter 2. You can readily edit, compile, and link the program using the same graphical user interface (GUI) windows.

Exercises

1. Write a program to plot the function $f(x) = 2x^2 \sin(x)$ versus x when x varies within the range of -8.5 radians $\leq x \leq 8.5$ radians.
   a. Use the plotting function **plotxy**().
   b. The X axis shall range from `xmin` of -10 to `xmax` of 10 with a tick mark at the incremental of 1.
2. Write a program to plot the functions $y1 = e^x + \sqrt{x}$ and $y2 = 10\sin(x)$ from $x = 0$ to π without labels in both, the x and y axes. The plot shall have legends of `y1` and `y2` for the curves of these two functions, with 50 points for each curve.
3. Using the temperature conversion formula shown below,

$$F = \frac{9}{5}C + 32$$

   write a program to plot the temperature in Fahrenheit with respect to the temperature in Celsius from 0°C to 100°C using a filled curve as shown in Figure 20.4.
4. A projectile is fired into the air with an initial speed v_0 of 35 m/s and an initial projection angle of $\theta_0 = 15°$. The trajectory can be expressed in x- and y-coordinates using equations (6.3) and (6.4) in section 6.7. The initial speed and and projection angle are passed to the function for the y-coordinate using a structure in Program 20.3. Modify Program 20.3 to plot the trajectory. Store the initial speed and and projection angle in an array with two elements in the function **main**(). Pass this array to the function for the y-coordinate.
5. A projectile is fired into the air with an initial speed v_0 of 35.0 m/s. Plot the trajectories for initial projection angles of $\theta_0 = 15°, 30°, 45°, 60°, 75°$, and $90°$, with 100 points for each trajectory in a single plot. The trajectory can be expressed in x- and y-coordinates using equations (6.3) and (6.4) in section 6.7 in Chapter 6. You may use the following member function call:

   plot.border(PLOT_BORDER_LEFT, PLOT_OFF);

to remove the border on the left of the plot. Perform the following actions:

a. Use arrays to store the x and y coordinates of a trajectory.
b. Use arrays to store the x and y coordinates of a trajectory. Use a loop for the initial projection angles.
c. Use global variables for v_0 and θ_0, and the member function **func2D**() to plot trajectories. Use a loop for the initial projection angles.
d. Use the member function **funcp2D**() without global variables to plot trajectories. Use a loop for the initial projection angles.

6. The value of $\sigma > 0$ in equation (6.10) in Exercise 33 in Chapter 6 determines the shape of the probability density functions shown in Figure 6.12. (a) Given $\mu = -2$, plot the probability density functions for σ equal to 0.5, 1, 2, and 3 in a single plot, with x in the range $-10 \leq x \leq 10$. Define the probability density function and σ in the function **main**(). Pass them to the member function **funcp2D**() of the plotting class **CPlot**. (b) Fill the probability density function curves with respect to the $x1$ axis with colors.

7. A *dot diagram* as shown in the illustration is very useful for displaying a small set of data. The diagram allows us to quickly and easily see the *location* or *central tendency* in the data and the *spread* or *variability*. For example, the middle of the data shown in the diagram is very close to 75.003. Plot the dot diagram shown in the illustration using the data for the measured piston rings in Exercise 15 in Chapter 10. You may use the following member function calls of the plotting class **CPlot**. The details for these functions can be found in *Ch Reference Guide* available in the PDF file `CHHOME/docs/chref.pdf`.

```
plot.plotType(PLOT_PLOTTYPE_POINTS, 0);  // use plot type of points
plot.axis(PLOT_AXIS_Y, PLOT_OFF);        // do not display y axis
plot.border(PLOT_BORDER_LEFT, PLOT_OFF); // remove board on the left
// Assume that the Y coordinate for each point is 1
plot.axisRange(PLOT_AXIS_Y, 0.9, 1.1);
plot.size(1, 0.5);                     // reduce the size of y in half
plot.tics(PLOT_AXIS_Y, PLOT_OFF);      // no tics on y axis
```

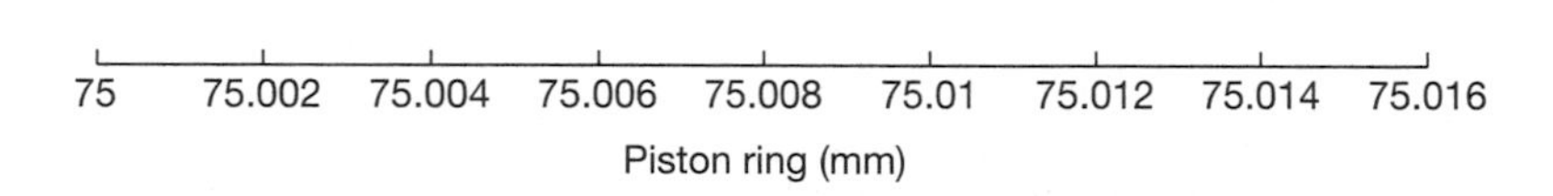

8. Let $f(x) = x^2 - 3$ for $x \geq 0$ and the inverse function $f^{-1}(x) = g(x)$ is $\sqrt{x+3}$ with $x \geq -3$, as shown in Figure 4.7 in Chapter 4. Write a program to plot the functions $f(x)$ and $g(x)$

9. The left end of the beam shown in the illustration is fixed and the right end is simply supported. When the beam is under a uniform load w, the displacement, shear, and moment of the beam along the axis can be expressed as follows:

$$y = \frac{wx^2}{48EI}(l - x)(2x - 3l)$$

$$V = \frac{5wl}{8} - wx$$

$$M = \frac{w}{8}\left(4x^2 + 5lx - l^2\right)$$

where x is the distance from the fixed end, l the length of the beam, E Youngs modulus, and I the second moment of area. Given $l = 1.6$ m, $w = 15$ Newton/m, E = 300000 MPa, and I = 8.310^{-6}m^4, plot the displacement, shear, and moment diagrams versus the distance x in the same diagram using subplots.

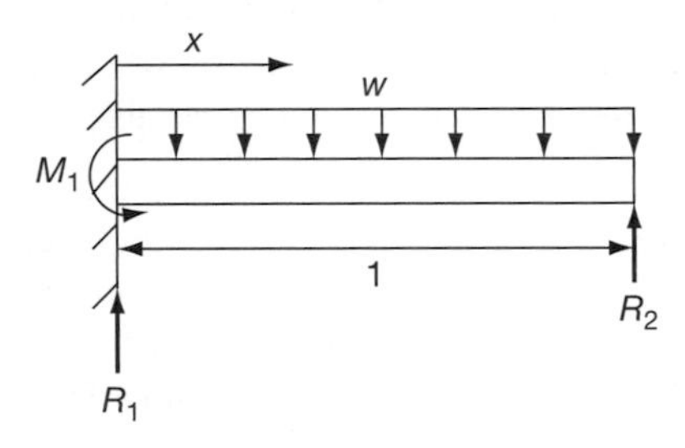

10. The position, velocity, and acceleration for the mass of the critically damped free vibration system described in Exercise 35 in Chapter 6 are

$$x(t) = 4(1 - 3t)e^{-3t}$$
$$v(t) = -24e^{-3t} + 36te^{-3t}$$
$$a(t) = 108(1 - t)e^{-3t}$$

Plot the position, velocity, and acceleration versus time for $0 \leq t \leq 4$ in the same illustration using subplots.

11. The following two functions describe the oscillations in two electrical circuits, or vibration in x and y directions of a mechanical system.

$$x(t) = 10e^{-0.5t}\sin(3t + 2)$$
$$y(t) = 0.5e^{-0.4t}\cos(5t - 4)$$

   a. Plot these two functions on the same illustration using the same coordinates.
   b. Because the magnitude of y is smaller than x, plot these two functions on the same figure using Y and $Y2$ coordinates for $x(t)$ and $y(t)$, respectively, with different scales.

12. Write a program to plot functions

$$f_1(x) = \sin(x^2) + 1/x^2$$
$$f_2(x) = \cos(x^2) + 1/x^3$$

with 50 points from $1 \leq x \leq 2$ with x label of `x`, y label of `function`, and legends for `f1` and `f2`.

13. Write a program to plot the functions $f_1(x) = 2x^2\sin(x)$ and $f_2(x) = 10\cos(x)$ versus x when x varies within the range of 0 to 2π using 360 points. The plot shall have legends $f_1(x)$ and $f_2(x)$ for curves of these two functions. The label on the x-axis shall display `x`, whereas the label on the y-axis shall display `f1 and f2`. The plot will be exported to an external file called `plot.eps` in a color-encapsulated Postscript file format.

14. Plot the functions $f_1(x) = x^2 + 3x + 1$ and $f_2(x) = 1/x^2 - 5x$ in the range $[-10, 10]$ for x with incremental tick marks every 2 units.

   a. Display two curves with a legend for each curve in the same plot.
   b. Display two plots, one for each function, in the same illustration using the member function **CPlot::subplot()** of the plotting class **CPlot**.

15. Plot the function $y = e^{x\sin(x)}$ with a logarithmic scale y-axis.

16. Plot the function $y = \sin(x)x$ from $x = 0$ to 2π with a label in the x-axis as *variable x* and a label in the y-axis as $y = \sin(x)x$. The plot shall have the text `This is the text` at the location $(x, y) = (3, 1.2)$.

a. Turn off autoscaling of the axis y.
b. Add an arrow to point from the text to the curve.
c. Add four borders of the plot and grids.

17. Plot the three-dimensional function $z = \sin(x)\sin(y)$ for x and y in the ranges of $0 \le x \le 3\pi$ and $0 \le y \le 3\pi$ in the following ways:

a. Using the class **CPlot** to plot the surface $z(x, y)$.
b. Using the function **plotxyz**() to plot it.
c. Using the function **fplotxyz**() to plot it.
d. Using the function **plotxyzf**() to plot it.
e. Plotting it with contours at the base with 10 levels.

18. Create a polar plot of the function $f(x) = 3\sin(\theta)\cos(2\theta)$ for $0 \le \theta \le 360°$ with $1°$ increments. Provide a title and labels for the x and y axes.

19. Create a three-dimensional plot of the function $g(x, y) = 3xy^2 + \sin(x)\tan(y)$, where $0 \le x \le 10$ and $0 \le y \le 10$ with 50 sets of data points. Output this plot into a file called plot.png in *PNG* file format.

20. Create a contour plot of the function $f(x) = \sin(r)\cos(r)/r$, where $r = \sqrt{x^2 + y^2}$. Let $-10 \le x \le 10$ and $-10 \le y \le 10$ with 30 sets of data points. The three-dimensional plot shall have five contour levels with a legend for function.

21. The xyz coordinates of a particle are given by

$$x = (0.5 + 5t)\sin\left(\frac{2\pi}{3}t\right)\cos(4\pi t)$$

$$y = (0.5 + 5t)\sin\left(\frac{2\pi}{3}t\right)\sin(4\pi t)$$

$$z = (0.5 + 5t)\cos\left(\frac{2\pi}{3}t\right)$$

where t is time in minutes. Obtain the three-dimensional plot of the particle for $0 \le t \le 0.2$ minutes.

22. Obtain the surface plot with contour at the base for the function $z = x(x + 3) - 2xy + 4y^2$.

PART III

Numerical Computing in Ch

CHAPTER 21

Computational Arrays and Matrix Computations in Ch

Matrix notations are commonly used in solving problems in engineering and science. For example, as we explained in section 10.6.1 in Chapter 10, the regression coefficients b and v of the linear equation

$$y = b + vt \tag{21.1}$$

can be determined by the least squares method. The formulas for b and v are given in equations (10.9) and (10.8), respectively. Alternatively, the least squares method for linear regression can be formulated using matrix notation. The relation between y_i and t_i can be written

$$\boldsymbol{y} = \boldsymbol{A}\boldsymbol{x} \tag{21.2}$$

where

$$\boldsymbol{y} = \begin{bmatrix} y_1 \\ y_2 \\ \vdots \\ y_n \end{bmatrix}, \quad \boldsymbol{A} = \begin{bmatrix} 1 & t_1 \\ 1 & t_2 \\ \vdots & \vdots \\ 1 & t_n \end{bmatrix}, \quad \boldsymbol{x} = \begin{bmatrix} b \\ v \end{bmatrix} \tag{21.3}$$

The vector $\boldsymbol{y}$ and matrix $\boldsymbol{A}$ contain the values for each sample point. The vector $\boldsymbol{x}$ for the two regression coefficients is to be calculated. It can be shown that the least squares solution for this linear regression is given by solving

$$\boldsymbol{A}^T\boldsymbol{A}\boldsymbol{x} = \boldsymbol{A}^T\boldsymbol{y} \tag{21.4}$$

which is a set of two equations in two unknowns b and v in the vector $\boldsymbol{x}$. Formally, equation (21.4) is obtained by premultiplying equation (21.2) by $\boldsymbol{A}^T$, the transpose of matrix $\boldsymbol{A}$. In this chapter, computational arrays in Ch are introduced. Using computational arrays, equation (21.4) can be conveniently solved by Program 21.9, which will be described later in this chapter.

Arrays in C are intimately tied with pointers. For comparison purposes with computational arrays, these arrays are called *C arrays*. For numerical computing and data analysis, *computational arrays* in Ch are first-class objects with more information than regular C arrays. They are not part of the C standard. Many operators, including arithmetic operators, are overloaded to handle computational arrays.

The notations used in this chapter are listed in Table 21.1. A digital number may follow a symbol for multiple variables. For example, symbols **V**, **V1**, and **V2** are used for vectors; symbols **A**, **A1**, and **A2** stand for vectors, matrices, or high-dimensional arrays.

Table 21.1 Shape and data type notations.

Symbol	Meaning
	Shape
A	Vector, matrix, or high-dimension arrays of char, int, float, double, long double,
	float complex, double complex, and long double complex
B	Vector, matrix, or high-dimension arrays of char, int, float, and double
I	Vector, matrix, or high-dimension arrays with integral data types of char, int
M	Two-dimensional matrix of char, int, float, double, float complex, or double complex
V	One-dimensional vector of char, int, float, double, long double, float complex, double complex, and long double complex
a	Scalar of char, int, float, double, long double, float complex, double complex, and long double complex
s	Scalar of char, int, float, double, long double, float complex, double complex, and long double complex
	Data type
b	bool
c	char
h	short
i	int
f	float
d	double
z	complex
p	Higher-order data type of operands in operations or arguments in functions
k	The same data type of the original operand or argument
m	The same data type of the original operand or argument, double if the data type of the original operand or argument is char or int
	Data type modifier
u	Unsigned
l	Long

21.1 Declaration and Initialization of Computational Arrays

Similar to C arrays, a one-dimensional computational array is declared with the following format:

```
array type name[expr] = {optional initializers};
```

where the type qualifier **array**, defined as a macro in the header file **array.h**, specifies that the declaration is for a computational array. A program using computational arrays should include the header file **array.h**.

In command mode, the type qualifier **array** is defined as an alias by default. The symbol `type` contains the declaration specifiers that specify a data type of the array, such as int. The symbol `name` is a declarator that contains an identifier. The delimiters `[` and `]` delimit an optional integral expression `expr`, which specifies the number of elements of the array. If `expr` is a constant integral expression, it shall have a value greater than zero. If it is not a constant expression, it is evaluated at program execution time and shall evaluate to a value greater than zero. A computational array whose size is determined at program execution time is called a *variable-length computational array*. Like in a C array, if the size expression `expr` is not present, the array type is an incomplete type. An incomplete array occurs in array declarations, function arguments, and extern declarations. They are completed by array initializations, function calls, and declarations, which will be described later. For a fully specified computational array, the expression `expr` can take the form `lower:upper` to specify the subscript range from `lower` to `upper`. The initialization of a computational array with initializers at the declaration is the same as that for C arrays. The declaration of multidimensional computational arrays is also similar to that for C arrays. For example, two pairs of the delimiters `[` and `]` are used to specify the row and column of a two-dimensional array.

The declaraion statement

```
array int a[5];
```

declares a computational array `a` with five elements.

Like C arrays, computational arrays are also row-wise. For example, for the computational array `b` declared below:

```
array int b[2][3];
```

assume that the address of the computational array `b` of dimension 2x3 is 0x2000. The internal memory layout of the array `b`, is shown in Figure 10.2 in Chapter 10. The layout of the data for a computational array inside the memory is the same as that for a C array.

The extent and range of subscripts for each dimension are fully specified for a *fully-specified-shape array*. The computational arrays below are fully specified:

```
array int c1[10];              // c1[0],  ...,  c1[9]
array int c2[0:9];             // c2[0],  ...,  c2[9]
array int c3[1:10];            // c3[1],  ...,  c3[10]
array double  c4[10][10];      // c4[0:9][0:9]
array complex c5[1:10][1:10];  // c5[1:10][1:10]
```

where the symbol '`:`' is used to specify the range of the subscripts of the arrays. By default, it is from 0 to `n-1`, where `n` is the number in the operator [] to specify the size of the array.

Computational arrays can be initialized when they are declared in the same manner as C arrays. By default, computational arrays are initialized to zero. If not enough initializers are specified, the unspecified elements are initialized to zero by default. For example,

```
array int d1[3]  = {1, 2, 3};
array int d2[3]= {2.3e1, 4.2F, 4.6};           // d2={23,2,3}
array double d3[] = {0.0, -0.0};               // d3={0.0, -0.0, 0.0}
array double d4[][3] = {{1, 2}, {1, 2, 3}}; // d4={{1,2,0},{1,2,3}}
array double d5[2][3] = {1, 2, 3, 1};          // d5={{1,2,3},{1,0,0}}
```

21.2 Array References

21.2.1 Whole Arrays

For a C array, the name of the array contains the address of the array. The name of a computational array refers to the whole array. If two computational arrays have the same number of elements in each dimension, even with different subscript ranges, the assignment operator '=' can be used to assign arrays element-wise. For example, in the execution of the commands

```
> array double a[0:3], b[1:4];
> array int c[4] = { 1, 2, 3, 4}
> b = c
1.0000 2.0000 3.0000 4.0000
> a = b+c
2.0000 4.0000 6.0000 8.0000
```

The subscript range for the array `b` is from 1 to 4, whereas for the arrays `a` and `c`, it is from 0 to 3. We can assign array `c` to array `b`. Later, the arrays `b` and `c` are added element-wise and assigned to the array `a`.

One-dimensional arrays, such as `a` and `b`, are treated as vectors, just as in linear algebra. This feature makes programs much simpler compared to programs using regular C arrays. As an example, the vector $\boldsymbol{x}$ and the matrix $\boldsymbol{Y}$ are defined by the formulas below.

$$\boldsymbol{x} = (\boldsymbol{A} + \boldsymbol{B})\boldsymbol{v}$$
$$\boldsymbol{Y} = 3\boldsymbol{A}\boldsymbol{C}$$

In section 10.8.2 in Chapter 10, the vector $\boldsymbol{x}$ and matrix $\boldsymbol{Y}$ are calculated by Program 10.29, with the matricies $\boldsymbol{A}$, $\boldsymbol{B}$, and $\boldsymbol{C}$ and the vector $\boldsymbol{v}$ specified in equation (10.42). Program 10.29 uses regular C arrays to handle matrices and vectors with multiple nested loops. Program 21.1 uses computational arrays to represent vectors and matrices. Both Programs 21.1 and 10.29 calculate the vector $\boldsymbol{x}$ and the matrix $\boldsymbol{Y}$ for the same matricies $\boldsymbol{A}$, $\boldsymbol{B}$, and $\boldsymbol{C}$ and the vector $\boldsymbol{v}$. The output from these two programs is the same and is shown in Figure 10.13. Clearly, Program 21.1 contains fewer lines of code and is more readable and easier to maintain. Details about addition and multiplication operations for computational arrays are described later in this chapter. Note that the **array** qualifier is defined as a macro in the header file **array.h**. To use the computational array, the program should include this header file.

```
/* File: matrixexpr.ch
   Calculate matrix formulas x = (A+B)v and y = 3A*C */
#include <stdio.h>
#include <array.h>  /* for 'array' type qualifier */

/* for multiplication A[M1][N1]*C[M2][N2], N1 must equal to M2 */
#define M1 2 /* number of rows for A, B, v */
#define N1 3 /* number of columns for A, B */
```

Program 21.1: Declaring and using computational arrays. (*Continued*)

```
#define M2 3 /* number of rows for C */
#define N2 2 /* number of columns for C */

int main() {
  /* declare and initialize matrices A, B, C and vector v */
  array double a[M1][N1] = {{1,2,3},{4,5,6}};
  array double b[M1][N1] = {{4,5,6},{7,8,9}};
  array double c[M2][N2] = {{1,2},{3,4},{5,6}};
  array double v[N1] = {1,2,3};
  /* declare x and y */
  array double x[M1], y[M1][N2];

  x = (a+b)*v;                 /* calculate x=(A+B)v */
  printf("x = \n%g", x);       /* display vector x */
  y = 3*a*c;                   /* calculate y=3A*C */
  printf("y = \n%g", y);       /* display matrix y */
  return 0;
}
```

Program 21.1: *(Continued)*

21.2.2 Array Elements

Similar to C arrays, the operator `[n]` can be used to access elements of computational arrays, where `n` is a valid subscript. For example, the following code fragment

```
array int a[20], b[20];
b[1] = a[2]+b[2];
```

adds the third element of `a` to the third element of `b` and saves the result to the second element of `b`.

21.3 Formatted Input and Output for Computational Arrays

Like C arrays, the input of computational arrays shall be handled element by element. For example,

```
> array int  a[2]
> scanf("%d", &a[0])
10
> a
10 0
```

The address of an element of the array `a` is obtained by applying the address operator `&` to the element. The address of the first element `a[0]` can be obtained by the expression `&a[0]`. In the above example, the address of the first element `a[0]` of the array `a` is passed to the function **scanf**() to obtain its value.

The family of the output functions **fprintf()**, **sprintf()**, **printf()**, and so forth, can be used to print out all elements of a computational array once. The output format specifier of these functions is applied to each element of the array. For example,

```
> array int a[3] = {1,2,3}
> array int b[2][3] = {1,2,3,4,5,6}
> printf("a = %d", a);
a = 1 2 3
> printf("b = \n%d", b);
b =
1 2 3
4 5 6
```

For computational arrays with large extents, 74 characters, including elements of arrays and delimiting spaces at each line, will be printed out. For example, each element of the array a below has the same value of 90. The output is wrapped in the subsequent line beyond 74 characters.

```
> array int a[2][50] = 90
> a
90 90 90 90 90 90 90 90 90 90 90 90 90 90 90 90 90 90 90 90 90 90 90 90 90
90 90 90 90 90 90 90 90 90 90 90 90 90 90 90 90 90 90 90 90 90 90 90 90 90
90 90 90 90 90 90 90 90 90 90 90 90 90 90 90 90 90 90 90 90 90 90 90 90 90
90 90 90 90 90 90 90 90 90 90 90 90 90 90 90 90 90 90 90 90 90 90 90 90 90
>
```

A multidimensional array will be printed out in multiple two-dimensional arrays with the rows and columns of the last two extents of the array, as shown below.

```
> array int a[2][2][3] = {1, 2, 3, 4, 5, 6, 7, 8, 9, 10, 11, 12}
> a
1 2 3
4 5 6

7 8 9
10 11 12
```

By default, a one-dimensional array is a column vector in Ch. For a one-dimensional array of a column or row vector, the output is printed out as a row vector even if it is a column vector. For example,

```
> array int a[3] = {1,2,3}
> a                       // column vector
1 2 3
> transpose(a)            // row vector
1 2 3
```

The vector `a` is a column vector, the transpose of `a`, `transpose(a)`, is a row vector. When they are printed out, both are displayed as row vectors. More information about the generic function **transpose**() will be described in section 21.10.

21.4 Implicit Data Type Conversion for Computational Arrays

In computational array operations, the data types of operands will be checked for compatibility. If data types do not match, Ch will signal an error and print out some informative messages for the convenience of program debugging. However, some data type conversion rules have been built into Ch so that they can be invoked whenever necessary. This will save many explicit type conversion commands for a program. The data type hierarchy for computational arrays is the same as that for the scalar data types shown in Figure 4.1 in Chapter 4. The char is the lowest data type, and double complex is the highest data type. The default conversion rules are summarized as follows:

1. Arrays of char, int, float, and double can be converted according to data conversion rules of the corresponding scalar types.
2. Arrays of char, int, float, and double can be converted to arrays of complex, with the imaginary part of each element being zero. When casting an array of real numbers to an array of complex numbers, the values of the elements Inf and −Inf become ComplexInf, and the value of the element NaN becomes ComplexNaN. Conversion from array of double to array of complex may cause information to be lost.
3. In binary operations, such as addition, subtraction, multiplication, and division with arrays of mixed data types, the result of the operation will carry the higher data type of two operands. For example, the result of adding an array of int and an array of double will result in an array of double.

The following code segment will illustrate how arrays with different data types are automatically converted.

```
> array int i[2] = {1, 2}
> array float f[2]
> array double d [2]
> f = i              // float = int
1.00 2.00
> d = f + i          // double = float + int
2.0000 4.0000
>
```

For the operation `d = f + i`, elements of the arrays `f` and `i` of float and int types, respectively, are added with the result of a computational array of float type. The resultant computational array of float type is then cast to a computational array of double type and assigned to the variable `d` of computational array of double type. Data type conversion for various array operations are discussed in detail in the next section.

21.5 Array Operations

21.5.1 Arithmetic Operations

The arithmetic operations for computational arrays are listed in Table 21.2. The symbol **A**/k indicates that the results are arrays with the same shape and data type of the operand. For the symbol **A**/p, the result is

Table 21.2 Array arithmetic operations.

Definition	Operation	Result
Unary plus	+**A**	A/k
Unary minus	−**A**	A/k
Addition	**A1** + **A2**	A/p
Addition	**A** + [s]	A/p
Addition	[s] + **A**	A/p
Subtraction	**A1** − **A2**	A/p
Subtraction	**A** − [s]	A/p
Subtraction	[s] − **A**	A/p
Multiplication	**A1** ∗ **A2**	A/p or a/p
Multiplication	**A** ∗ s	A/p
Multiplication	s ∗ **A**	A/p
Division	**A**/s	A/p
Array multiplication	**A1**. ∗ **A2**	A/p
Array division	**A1**./**A2**	A/p
Array division	[s]./**A2**	A/p

the same shape and a higher-order of data type of two operands. These symbols are described in Table 21.1. The arithmetic operations include the unary plus operator '+', the unary minus operator '-', the addition operator '+', the subtraction operator '-', the multiplication operator '*', the division operator '/', the array multiplication operator '.*', and the array division operator './'. The operator '*' is for the multiplication of two arrays of one-dimensional vectors or two-dimensional matrices. The multiplication of two arrays follows the rule of linear algebra. For the element-wise array multiplication operator '.*' and the element-wise array division operator './', the operation is performed on each corresponding element of two array operands, which shall be of the same shape (dimension and extent). For the element-wise array multiplication `A.*B` of two-dimensional arrays **A**, with elements a_{ij}, and **B**, with elements b_{ij} of the same shape, the result is an array with the same shape with elements defined by

$$c_{ij} = a_{ij} * b_{ij}$$

For one-dimensional arrays, the result is

$$c_i = a_i * b_i$$

For the element-wise array division `A./B` of two-dimensional arrays, the result is defined as $c_{ij} = a_{ij}/b_{ij}$. For one-dimensional arrays, the result is $c_i = a_i/b_i$.

The data type of the result of the operation of the unary plus operator or the unary minus operator is the same as that of the operand. The resulting data types of the other operations in Table 21.2 will have the higher order data type of the operands in operations. If one of the operands of the addition or subtraction operator is a scalar and the other is a computational array, the scalar will be promoted to a computational array for the corresponding array operation. If the numerator of the array division operator '`./`' is a scalar, it will be promoted to a computational array.

Applications of these operations are illustrated in the commands below. For example,

```
> array int a1[2][2] = {1, 0, 2, 3}
> array int a2[2][2] = {0, 5, 2, 2}
> double s = 2.0
> a1 * a2
0 5
6 16
> a1 .* a2
0 0
4 6
> a1/s
0.50 0.00
1.00 1.50
> a1 +2
3 2
4 5
```

For the multiplication of two arrays, the dimensions of the arrays have to follow the rule of linear algebra, as shown below.

```
> array int a1[2][3] = {1, 2, 3, 4, 5, 6}
> array int a2[3][2] = {1, 2, 3, 4, 5, 6}
> array int b[3] = {1, 2, 3}
> a1*a2
22 28
49 64
> a1*b
14 32
> a1*a1
ERROR: array dimensions do not match for matrix operations
```

In a special case, the result of the multiplication of two arrays is a scalar instead of an array, if the shapes of arrays **A1** and **A2** are $(1 \times n)$ and $(n \times 1)$, where n is 1, 2, 3, ... For example,

```
> int i
> array int a[1] = {10}
> array int b[1] = {20}
> array int c[2] = {1, 2}
> i = a * b  // (1x1) * (1x1), the result is a scalar
200
> b = a + b  // it's an array
30
```

```
> transpose(c) * c // (1x2) * (2x1), the result is a scalar
5
> c * transpose(c) // (2x1) * (1x2), the result is an array
1 2
2 4
```

The result of `a * b` is an integer, and so is `transpose(c) * c`. The one-dimensional array by default is a column vector with the shape of $(n \times 1)$ at declaration and calculation. For example, `c` has the shape of (2×1) instead of (1×2).

The element-wide array multiplication operator '`.*`' and element-wise array division operator '`./`' are useful to handle mathematical formulas without loops such as **for** loops and **while** loops. For example, the plot of the function $y(x) = 2/x + \sin(x^2)$ in the range of $0.1 \le x \le 6.2$ with 100 points can be created as follows:

```
> array double x[100], y[100]
> lindata(0.1, 6.2, x)
> y =  2.0./x +sin(x.*x)
> plotxy(x, y)
```

The output of a plot is displayed in Figure 21.1. Details about the generic mathematical function **sin()** for handling arguments of array type will be described later in this chapter. Note that for the computational array `x`, the expression `2./x` is interpreted as `2.0/x`, not the array operation `2 ./ x`. Therefore, `2./x` is invalid because of unmatched array dimensions. The function call of `lindata(0.1, 6.2, x)` assigns linearly spaced values starting with 0.1 and ending with 6.2 for elements of the array x. The function **lindata()** is

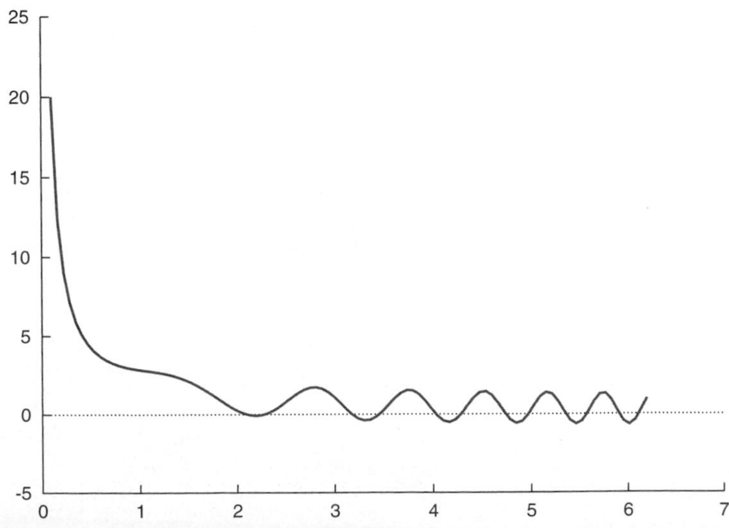

Figure 21.1: An interactively generated plot for the function $y(x) = 2/x + \sin(x^2)$.

prototyped in the header file **numeric.h** as follows:

```
int lindata(double first, double last, ...
            /* type a[:]...[:] | type *a, int n */);
```

The **lindata()** function generates linearly spaced data with the initial and final values specified by the input arguments `first` and `last`, respectively. The result is passed back to the third passed argument of array type. When the third argument is of pointer type, the fourth argument is used to specify the number of elements. The total number of data points generated is passed as the return value. For example,

```
> array double a[5]
> lindata(0, 2, a)
> a
0.0000 0.5000 1.0000 1.5000 2.0000
```

21.5.2 Assignment Operations

The assignment operations for computational arrays are listed in Table 21.3. They include simple assignment '=' and compound assignments, which include the assign sum operator '+=', the assign difference operator '-=', the assign product operator '*=', and the assign quotient operator '/='. The data types of the results of operations of these operators are the same as those of the left operands.

Applications of these operations are illustrated in the commands below.

```
> array int a1[4] = {1, 0, 2, 3}
> array int a2[4] = {0, 5, 2, 2}
> a1 += a2
1 5 4 5
```

21.5.3 Increment and Decrement Operations

The increment and decrement operations for computational arrays are listed in Table 21.4. They include the increment operator '++' and the decrement operator '--', which add 1 to and subtract 1 from each element of the array, respectively. The resulting data type of these operations are the same as those of the original operands.

Table 21.3 Array assignment operations.

Definition	Operation	Result
Assignment	**A1** = **A2**	**A**/k
Assignment	**A** = [*s*]	**A**/k
Assign sum	**A1**+= **A2**	**A**/k
Assign difference	**A1**-= **A2**	**A**/k
Assign product	**A1***= **A2**	**A**/k
Assign product	**A1***= *s*	**A**/k
Assign quotient	**A1**/= *s*	**A**/k

Table 21.4 Array increment and decrement operations.

Definition	Operation	Result
Plus	**A**++	**A**/k
Plus	++**A**	**A**/k
Minus	**A**--	**A**/k
Minus	--**A**	**A**/k

Applications of these operations are illustrated in the commands below.

```
> array int a1[4] = {1, 0, 2, 3}
> array int a2[4] = {0, 5, 2, 2}
> a1++
1 0 2 3
> a1
2 1 3 4
> --a2
-1 4 1 1
```

21.5.4 Relational Operations

The relational operations for computational arrays are listed in Table 21.5. They include the less than operator '<', the less than equal operator '<=', the equal operator '==', the greater than equal operator '>=', the greater than operator '>', and the not equal operator '!='. Using these operators results in an array of int type, with values of either 0 or 1, depending on how each element of the array compares. For these binary operators, if one of the operands is a computational array and the other is a scalar, the scalar will be promoted to a computational array with the shape of the array operand. Applications of these operations are illustrated in the commands below.

```
> array int a1[4] = {1, 0, 2, 3}
> array int a2[4] = {0, 5, 2, 2}
> a1 < a2
0 1 0 0
> a1 >=  a2
1 0 1 1
```

21.5.5 Logic Operations

The logic operations for computational arrays are listed in Table 21.6. They include the AND operator '&&', the XOR operator '^^', the OR operator '||', and the NOT operator '!'. The results of evaluating with these operators are arrays of int type, with values of either 0 or 1. For these binary operators, if one of the operands is a computational array and the other is a scalar, the scalar will be promoted to a computational array with the shape of the array operand.

Table 21.5 Array relational operations.

Definition	Operation	Result
Less than	**B1** < **B2**	I/i
Less than	**B1** < [*s*]	I/i
Less than	[*s*] < **B2**	I/i
Less equal	**B1** <= **B2**	I/i
Less equal	**B1** <= [*s*]	I/i
Less equal	[*s*] <= **B2**	I/i
Equal	**A1** == **A2**	I/i
Equal	**A1** == [*s*]	I/i
Equal	[*s*] == **A2**	I/i
Equal	*NULL* == **A1**	b
Equal	**A1** == *NULL*	b
Greater equal	**B1** >= **B2**	I/i
Greater equal	**B1** >= [*s*]	I/i
Greater equal	[*s*] >= **B2**	I/i
Greater than	**B1** > **B2**	I/i
Greater than	**B1** > [*s*]	I/i
Greater than	[*s*] > **B2**	I/i
Not equal	**A1** ! = **A2**	I/i
Not equal	**A1** ! = [*s*]	I/i
Not equal	[*s*]! = **A2**	I/i
Not equal	**A1** ! = *NULL*	b
Not equal	*NULL* ! = **A1**	b

Applications of these operations are illustrated in the commands below.

```
> array int a1[4] = {1, 0, 2, 3}
> array int a2[4] = {0, 5, 2, 2}
> a1 && a2
0 0 1 1
> a1 ||  a2
1 1 1 1
```

21.5.6 Conditional Operation

The conditional operator '`?:`' can be applied to computational arrays in Ch. If this is the case, the first operand of a conditional expression shall have scalar type, and the other two operands are computational arrays of the same shape. The result is a computational array with the higher-order type of these two operands.

Table 21.6 Array logic operations.

Definition	Operation	Result
AND	**A1** && **A2**	**I**/i
AND	**A1** && [*s*]	**I**/i
AND	[*s*]&& **A2**	**I**/i
XOR	**A1** ^^ **A2**	**I**/i
XOR	**A1** ^^ [*s*]	**I**/i
XOR	[*s*] ^^ **A2**	**I**/i
OR	**A1** || **A2**	**I**/i
OR	**A1** || [*s*]	**I**/i
OR	[*s*]|| **A2**	**I**/i
NOT	!**A**	**I**/i

Applications of the conditional operation are illustrated in the commands below.

```
> array int a[2][3] = 1, b[2][3]=2
> array float f[2][3] = 3.0
> 1 ? a:b // operands of array
1 1 1
1 1 1
> 0 ? f:b  // operands of array
3.00 3.00 3.00
3.00 3.00 3.00
```

In these two examples, both the second and third operands have the same shape, which are (2×3) and (2×2), respectively. The result of the latter example is a computational array of type float, because the type of the second operand is float, which has a higher order than int type of the third operand.

21.5.7 Address Operations

The address operator '`&`' can also be used to get the address of a computational array or the address of an element of a computational array. The commands below illustrate how the address operator works.

```
array int a[0:9], b[2][3];
int *ptr;
ptr = &a;          // the address of a
ptr = &a[2]        // the address of third element of a
ptr = &b;          // the address of b
ptr = &b[1][2];    // the address of an element of b
```

The address operator '`&`' applied to a computational array gives the address of the first element of the array. For the sample commands below, `&a` gives the address of `a[0][0]` and `&b` gives the address of `b[0][0]`.

The address operator '&' before an element of a computational array gives the address of this element. For example, &b[1][0][0] gives the address of b[1][0][0], as shown below.

```
> array int a[2][2] = {1, 2, 3, 4}
> array int b[2][2][2] = {1, 2, 3, 4, 5, 6, 7, 8}
> &a
4005e3e0
> &a[0][0]                  // same as &a
4005e3e0
> &b
4005e4e0
> &b[0][0][0]               // same as &b
4005e4e0
> &b[1][0][0]
4005e4f0
```

21.5.8 Cast Operations

Because Ch allows array operations of computational arrays with different types, or even operations with computational arrays and C arrays, the cast operation is sometimes important to prevent confusion.

Below are some examples of cast operations for computational arrays.

```
array double a[3][1], b[3], c[4][3];
array int d[3][1];
a = (array double [3][1])b;        // cast [3] to [3][1]
b = (array double [3])a;           // cast [3][1] to [3]
b = (array double [3])&c[1][0];    // cast 2nd row of c to vector b
b = (array double [3])&c[2][0];    // cast 3rd row of c to vector b
c = (array double [4][3])4;        // cast scalar to array
d = (array int [3][1])a;           // cast double to int
```

Through cast operations, the assignment operations can be performed for two computational arrays. For example, the extent of the last dimension of the array c is the same as that of the array b. Although a has the different extent in the last dimension, it also has the same amount of memory of the array b. Note that scalars may be cast as computational arrays. The statement c = (array double [4][3])4 above will set all the elements of the array c to 4. It is also possible to cast computational arrays of one data type to another, such as in the last operation above.

If the number of array elements in the cast operation is smaller than the number of array elements in the operand, the extra elements of the operand are ignored. If the number of array elements in the cast operation is larger than the number of array elements in the operand, the remaining elements of the resulting array are filled with 0s. For example,

```
> array double a[3] = {1,2,3}
> (array int [2])a
1 2
> (array int [4])a
1 2 3 0
```

The casting operator preceding an array can give the address or value of the first element of the array. If the type is a pointer, it gives the address of the first element of the array. Otherwise, it gives the value of the first element. For example,

```
> array int a[2][2] = {1, 2, 3, 4}
> (int *)a
4005ef10
> &a
4005ef10
> (int)a
1
```

21.6 Promotion of Scalars to Computational Arrays in Operations

A scalar value can be cast to a computational array explicitly. But the scalar operand will be promoted to a computational array implicitly for addition, subtraction, array division, assignment, logic, and relational operations if the other operand is a computational array. An array promotion is used for operations with two-array operands, that is, the operand of a scalar in the operation internally is treated as an array in which the value of each element equals this scalar value. In some cases, array promotions make programming easier. Consider the following statements, where 2 is added to each element of the computational array a with a single statement. If a were a regular C array, the process would require some sort of loop.

```
> array int a[2][2] = {1, 0, 2, 3}
> a1 + 2                      // 2 is promoted to array
3 2
4 5
```

Table 21.7 provides a list of operations with implicit array promotion.

21.7 Passing Computational Arrays to Functions

Computational arrays can also be passed to a function in the same manner as regular C arrays.

21.7.1 Fully-Specified-Shape Arrays

Program 21.2 demonstrates how fully-specified-shape arrays are used as arguments of a function. In Program 21.2, the function sum1() with arguments of fully-specified-shape arrays is called to calculate the matrix expression of the dimension 2x3:

$$\mathbf{b} = \mathbf{a} + \mathbf{2} * \mathbf{a}, \tag{21.5}$$

and returns the sum of values for each element of the array a. If the argument of a function is defined as a fully-specified-shape array, addresses of arrays are passed to this function. The output of Program 21.2 is displayed in Figure 21.2.

Table 21.7 Operations with array promotions.

Definition	Operation	Promotion	Result
Assignment	$\mathbf{A} = s$	$\mathbf{A} = [s]$	A/k
Addition	$\mathbf{A} + s$	$\mathbf{A} + [s]$	A/p
Addition	$s + \mathbf{A}$	$[s] + \mathbf{A}$	A/p
Subtraction	$\mathbf{A} - s$	$\mathbf{A} - [s]$	A/p
Subtraction	$s - \mathbf{A}$	$[s] - \mathbf{A}$	A/p
Division	$s \,./\, \mathbf{A}$	$[s] \,./\, \mathbf{A}$	A/p
Less than	$\mathbf{B} < s$	$\mathbf{B} < [s]$	I/i
Less than	$s < \mathbf{B}$	$[s] < \mathbf{B}$	I/i
Less equal	$\mathbf{B} <= s$	$\mathbf{B} <= [s]$	I/i
Less equal	$s <= \mathbf{B}$	$[s] <= \mathbf{B}$	I/i
Equal	$\mathbf{A} == s$	$\mathbf{A} == [s]$	I/i
Equal	$s == \mathbf{A}$	$[s] == \mathbf{A}$	I/i
Greater equal	$\mathbf{B} >= s$	$\mathbf{B} >= [s]$	I/i
Greater equal	$s >= \mathbf{B}$	$[s] >= \mathbf{B}$	I/i
Greater than	$\mathbf{B} > s$	$\mathbf{B} > [s]$	I/i
Greater than	$s > \mathbf{B}$	$[s] > \mathbf{B}$	I/i
Not equal	$\mathbf{A} \,!= s$	$\mathbf{A} \,!= [s]$	I/i
Not equal	$s \,!= \mathbf{A}$	$[s] \,!= \mathbf{A}$	I/i
XOR	$\mathbf{B} \wedge\wedge s$	$\mathbf{B} \wedge\wedge [s]$	I/i
XOR	$s \wedge\wedge \mathbf{B}$	$[s] \wedge\wedge \mathbf{B}$	I/i
OR	$\mathbf{B} \Vert s$	$\mathbf{B} \Vert [s]$	I/i
OR	$s \Vert \mathbf{B}$	$[s] \Vert \mathbf{B}$	I/i
AND	$\mathbf{B} \&\& s$	$\mathbf{B} \&\& [s]$	I/i
AND	$s \&\& \mathbf{B}$	$[s] \&\& \mathbf{B}$	I/i

```
/* File: passfullarray.ch
   Pass fully-specified-shape arrays to a function   */
#include <stdio.h>
#include <array.h>    // for 'array' type qualifier
#define N 2           // number of rows of arrays a and b
#define M 3           // number of columns of arrays a and b

/* function passes fully-specified-shape arrays a and b */
double sum1(array double a[N][M], array double b[N][M]) {
```

Program 21.2: Passing computational arrays of fixed shape. (*Continued*)

```
    double sum = 0;
    int i, j;

    b = a + 2 * a;          // matrix computation for b = 3*a
    for(i=0; i<N; i++)      // sum all elements of array a
        for(j=0; j<M; j++)
            sum += a[i][j];
    return sum;             // return the sum of all elements of array a
}

int main() {
    double sum;
    array double b[N][M], a[N][M] = {1, 2, 3,
                                     4, 5, 6};

    sum = sum1(a, b);
    printf("b = \n%g", b);    // print b passed back from sum1()
    printf("sum = %g\n", sum);
    return 0;
}
```

Program 21.2: *(Continued)*

```
b =
3 6 9
12 15 18
sum = 21
```

Figure 21.2: The output from Program 21.2 and Program 21.5.

21.7.2 Variable Length Arrays

The arguments `a` and `b` of the function `sum1()` in the previous example are declared as fully-specified-shape arrays. This is not a flexible way to handle arrays with different extents in each dimension. Like variable length arrays (VLAs) in C99, a *variable length computational array* can be declared in a function parameter as a formal argument that takes the shape of the actual argument passed to it. That is, the arrays for actual and formal arguments have the same rank and extent in each dimension. The bounds of the array shall be an integral variable declared in the same function prototype prior to the array argument, as shown in Program 21.3 with the function prototype

```
double sum2(int n, int m, array double a[n][m], array double b[n][m]);
```

The array bounds for a VLA, such as `m` and `n`, have to be declared before an array definition. In a function prototype, the size of an array can be replaced by the symbol '`*`' and without the variable name as shown below.

```
double sum2(int n, int m, array double a[*][*], array double [*][*]);
```

```
/* File: passvla.ch
   Pass variable length arrays to a function  */
#include <stdio.h>
#include <array.h>   // for 'array' type qualifier

/* Function prototypes */
double sum2(int n, int m, array double a[n][m], array double b[n][m]);
double sum2(int n, int m, array double a[*][*], array double [*][*]);

/* function passes variable length arrays a and b */
double sum2(int n, int m, array double a[n][m], array double b[n][m]){
    double sum = 0;
    int i, j;

    printf("n = %d, m = %d\n", n, m); // print passed n and m
    b = a + 2 * a;            // matrix computation for b = 3*a
    for(i=0; i<n; i++)        // sum all elements of array a
       for(j=0; j<m; j++)
          sum += a[i][j];
    return sum;
}

int main() {
    double sum;
    array double b1[2][3], a1[2][3] = {1, 2, 3,
                                       4, 5, 6};
    array double b2[3][4], a2[3][4] = {1, 2, 3, 4,
                                       5, 6, 7, 8,
                                       9, 10, 11, 12};

    sum = sum2(2, 3, a1, b1);        // pass 2x3 matrices a1 and b1
    printf("b1 = \n%g", b1);         // print b1 passed back from sum2()
    printf("sum = %g\n\n",  sum);
    sum = sum2(3, 4, a2, b2);        // pass 3x4 matrices a2 and b2
    printf("b2 = \n%g", b2);         // print b2 passed back from sum2()
    printf("sum = %g\n",  sum);
    return 0;
}
```

Program 21.3: Passing computational arrays of different shapes using variable length arrays.

In Program 21.3, the function `sum2()`, which takes four arguments. The first two arguments, `n` and `m`, are the number of rows and columns for the remaining two arguments of variable length arrays `a` and `b`. Like the function `sum1()` in Program 21.2, the function `sum2()` in Program 21.3 calculates the same matrix expression

$$\mathbf{b} = \mathbf{a} + \mathbf{2} * \mathbf{a}, \tag{21.6}$$

```
n = 2, m = 3
b1 =
3 6 9
12 15 18
sum = 21

n = 3, m = 4
b2 =
3 6 9 12
15 18 21 24
27 30 33 36
sum = 78
```

Figure 21.3: The output from Programs 21.3 and 21.4.

and also returns the sum of the values for each element of the array a. The number of rows and columns for the array a are passed from the arguments of the function, instead of constants. The output of Program 21.3 is displayed in Figure 21.3.

21.7.3 Assumed-Shape Arrays

The function `sum1()` in Program 21.2 takes two arguments of fully-specified-shape arrays. The function `sum2()` in Program 21.3 takes four arguments, two integers for array bounds of the remaining two variable length arrays a and b. It is assumed that the array bounds for the arrays a and b are the same. If they are different, then four arguments of integer type need to be passed, two for each two-dimensional array.

Ch provides assumed-shape arrays to deal with arrays of variable length. If arguments are declared as *assumed-shape arrays* using a colon as an array subscript, they can take arrays that have the same dimension but a different number of elements in each dimension. The dimension information for an assumed-shape array can be obtained at runtime inside the function.

Assumed-shape arrays declared with a colon as array subscripts are shown below.

```
int funct1(array int a[:][:], b[:]);
int func2(array double c[:]);
```

We can rewrite Programs 21.2 and 21.3 to use a function with arguments of assumed-shape arrays. In Program 21.4, the function `sum3()`, which takes two arguments of assumed-shape array, is called to calculate the same matrix expression:

$$\mathbf{b} = \mathbf{a} + 2 * \mathbf{a} \tag{21.7}$$

```
/* File: passassumeshape.ch
   Pass variable length arrays to a function using assumed-shape arrays */
#include <stdio.h>
#include <array.h>   // for 'array' type qualifier
```

Program 21.4: Passing computational arrays of different shapes using assumed-shape arrays. (*Continued*)

```
/* function passes variable length arrays using assumed-shape arrays a and b */
double sum3(array double a[:][:], array double b[:][:]){
    /* obtain n and m, the number of rows and columns */
    int n = shape(a, 0), m = shape(a, 1);
    /* or array int dim[2] = shape(a);
          int n = dim[0], m = dim[1]; */
    double sum = 0;
    int i, j;

    printf("n = %d, m = %d\n", n, m); // print passed n and m
    b = a + 2 * a;           // matrix computation for b = 3*a
    for(i=0; i<n; i++)       // sum all elements of array a
       for(j=0; j<m; j++)
          sum += a[i][j];
    return sum;
}

int main() {
    double sum;
    array double b1[2][3], a1[2][3] = {1, 2, 3,
                                        4, 5, 6};
    array double b2[3][4], a2[3][4] = {1, 2, 3, 4,
                                        5, 6, 7, 8,
                                        9, 10, 11, 12};

    sum = sum3(a1, b1);              // pass 2x3 matrices a1 and b1
    printf("b1 = \n%g", b1);         // print b1 passed back from sum2()
    printf("sum = %g\n\n", sum);
    sum = sum3(a2, b2);              // pass 3x4 matrices a2 and b2
    printf("b2 = \n%g", b2);         // print b2 passed back from sum2()
    printf("sum = %g\n", sum);
    return 0;
}
```

Program 21.4: *(Continued)*

and also returns the sum of the values for each element of the array `a`. The output of Program 21.4 is the same as the one from Program 21.3, as shown in Figure 21.3.

If the argument of a function is defined as an assumed-shape array, not only addresses but also boundaries of arrays are passed to this function. So arrays with different numbers of elements in each dimension can be passed to the same function. For example, in Program 21.4, the arrays `a1` and `a2` have the same dimension, but the extents are different. They can be passed to the same argument of the function `sum3()`. Similarly, the arrays `b1` and `b2` of different extents are also passed to the same argument. The generic function **shape()** can be used to obtain the extent of each dimension of the assumed-shape array. If a single argument of the function **shape()** is of array type, it returns its shape as a computational array of int type as if the function were prototyped as

```
array int shape(array type [:]...[:])[:];
```

where `type` can be any valid type for computational arrays. If the argument of the function **shape()** is a one-dimensional array, the return value is a computational array of size 1x1. Thus, the return value may be cast to a scalar. The function **shape()** can also be used to obtain the extent of a specified dimension for an array. In this case, it acts as if the function were prototyped as

```
int shape(array type [:]...[:], int index);
```

For example,

```
> array int a[3][4], b[5]
> shape(a)
3 4
> shape(a, 0)
3
> shape(a, 1)
4
> shape(b)
5
> (int)shape(b)     // cast 1x1 array to scalar
5
> (int)shape(shape(a))
2
```

The function call `shape(b)` in the above function returns a computational array of size 1x1. It can be cast to a scalar by the expression `(int)shape(b)`. Similarly, a scalar value can be obtained from the expression `(int) shape(shape(a))`.

21.8 Deferred-Shape Arrays

Ch supports *deferred-shape computational arrays*, which is another way to handle arrays with different numbers of elements in each dimension at runtime. A one-dimensional deferred-shape computational array is declared with the following format:

```
array type name[expr];
```

where `expr` is a nonconstant expression, which is evaluated at runtime. It declares `name` as a deferred-shape computational array with the data type specified by `type`. Examples of the declaration of deferred-shape arrays `A` and `C` are shown below:

```
array int A[n][m], B[m];
array double C[m];
```

where `n` and `m` are variables of int type.

```
/* File: defshape.ch
   Use deferred shape arrays */
#include <array.h>    // for 'array' type qualifier
#define N 2
#define M 3

/* pass arrays of variable length using assumed-shape */
double defshape(array double a[:][:], int n, int m) {
    array double b[n][m];    // b is a deferred-shape array
    double sum = 0;
    int i, j;

    b = a + 2 * a;            // matrix computation for b = 3*a
    for(i=0; i<n; i++)        // sum all elements of array a
      for(j=0; j<m; j++)
        sum += a[i][j];
    printf("b = \n%g", b);
    return sum;
}

int main() {
    double sum;
    array double a1[N][M] = {1, 2, 3,
                             4, 5, 6};

    sum = defshape(a1, N, M);
    printf("sum = %g\n", sum);
    return 0;
}
```

Program 21.5: Using computational arrays of deferred shape.

Program 21.5 demonstrates how to use a deferred-shape array within a function. The array `b` in the function `defshape()` is deferred. The shape of the array `b` is derived from the shape of the array `a`. The output of Program 21.5 is the same as that of Program 21.2, shown in Figure 21.2.

21.9 Functions Returning Computational Arrays

A function can return computational arrays as first-class objects. For a function that returns a computational array, the rank of the returned array in the function definition and that of an array expression following a return statement inside the function must be the same.

21.9.1 Functions Returning Computational Arrays of Fixed Length

The prototype of functions returning computational arrays of fixed length is as follows:

```
array datatype funcname(argument_list) [n1]...[nm];
```

where `n1` and `nm` are constant integers, such as 2 and 3, for the lengths of the corresponding dimensions. The number of the symbol `[]` following the closing parenthesis of the function argument list indicates the rank of the returned computational array.

Program 21.6 is an example to demonstrate how a function returns a computational array to the calling function. The function `funct()` of this program returns the following result of the matrix expression of the dimension 2x3:

$$\mathbf{b} = \mathbf{2} * \mathbf{a} \tag{21.8}$$

The output of Program 21.6 is shown in Figure 21.4.

```
/* File: retfix.ch
   Function returns arrays of fixed length */
#include <array.h>  // for 'array' type qualifier

/* function prototype, returning 2x3 computational arrays */
array int funct(array int a[2][3])[2][3];

int main() {
    array int a[2][3] = {1, 2, 3, 4, 5, 6}, b[2][3];

    b = funct(a);   // call function returning array
    printf("a[1][2] = %d\n", a[1][2]);
    printf("b[1][2] = %d\n", b[1][2]);
    printf("b = \n%d", b);
    return 0;
}


/* function returning 2x3 computational arrays */
array int funct(array int a[2][3])[2][3] {
    array int b[2][3];

    b = 2*a;
    return b;
}
```

Program 21.6: A function returning a computational array of fixed length.

```
a[1][2] = 6
b[1][2] = 12
b =
2 4 6
8 10 12
```

Figure 21.4: The output from Program 21.6.

21.9.2 Functions Returning Computational Arrays of Variable Length

The prototype of functions returning computational arrays of variable length is as follows:

```
array datatype funcname(argument_list) [:]...[:]
```

The number of the symbol `[:]` following the closing parenthesis of the function argument list indicates the rank of the returned computational array.

Program 21.7 provides an example of a function that returns a computational array of variable length. The dimensions of the returned arrays in the function calls of `func2(a)` and `func2(b)` are different. The output of Program 21.7 is shown in Figure 21.5.

```
/* File: retvla.ch
   Function returns arrays of variable length arrays */
#include <array.h>  // for 'array' type qualifier

/* function returning variable length arrays */
array int func2(array int a[:])[:] {
    int n = (int)shape(a);   // get the size of the passed array
    array int x[n];

    printf("n = %d\n", n);
    x = 2*a;                 // multiply each element by 2 for array a
    return x;
}

int main() {
    array int a[2] = {1, 2};
    array int b[5] = {10, 20, 30, 40, 50};

    a = func2(a);  // call function returning array
    printf("a = %d\n", a);
    b = func2(b);  // call function returning array
    printf("b = %d", b);
    return 0;
}
```

Program 21.7: A function returning a computational array of variable length.

```
n = 2
a = 2 4

n = 5
b = 20 40 60 80 100
```

Figure 21.5: The output from Program 21.7.

21.10 Type Generic Array Functions

The function **shape()**, presented in section 21.7.3, is a generic function. In addition, commonly used generic mathematical functions are overloaded to handle computational arrays. They are overloaded to handle arguments of different dimensions, lengths, and data types.

For an argument of computational array type, the function **abs()** returns an array with the absolute value of each element. For an argument of complex type, each element contains the magnitude of the corresponding complex number. The function is handled as if it were prototyped as

```
array int abs(array int a[:]...[:])[:]...[:]
array float abs(array float a[:]...[:])[:]...[:]
array float abs(array float complex a[:]...[:])[:]...[:]
array double abs(array double a[:]...[:])[:]...[:]
array double abs(array double complex a[:]...[:])[:]...[:]
```

For example,

```
> array int a[2][3] = {-1, 2, 3, -4, -5, 6}
> abs(a)
1 2 3
4 5 6
> array complex b[3] = {complex(3, 4), 4, -5}
> abs(b)
5.0000 4.0000 5.0000
```

The mathematical functions **acos()**, **acosh()**, **asin()**, **asinh()**, **atan()**, **atanh()**, **ceil()**, **cos()**, **cosh()**, **exp()**, **floor()**, **log()**, **log10()**, **sin()**, **sinh()**, **sqrt()**, **tan()**, and **tanh()** have only one argument. They are overloaded to handle arguments of different dimensions, lengths, and data types. If the data type of the input argument is an integral type, it will be promoted to float for computation. For array arguments, they behave as if they were prototyped as

```
array float func(array float a[:]...[:])[:]...[:]
array double func(array double a[:]...[:])[:]...[:]
array float complex func(array float complex a[:]...[:])[:]...[:]
array double complex func(array double complex a[:]...[:])[:]...[:]
```

where `func` is one of the above mathematical functions. If the data type of the input argument is integral type, it will be promoted to float for computation. For example,

```
> array int a[2][3] = {-1, 2, 3, -4, -5, 6}
> sin(a)
-0.84 0.91 0.14
0.76 0.96 -0.28
> array complex b[3] = {complex(3, 4), 4, -5}
> sin(b)
complex(3.8537,-27.0168) complex(-0.7568,-0.0000) complex(0.9589,0.0000)
```

For array arguments, the function **atan2()** acts as if it were prototyped as

```
array float           atan2(array float y[:]...[:],
                            array float x[:]...[:])[:]...[:]
array double          atan2(array double y[:]...[:],
                            array double x[:]...[:])[:]...[:]
array float complex   atan2(array float complex y[:]...[:],
                            array float complex x[:]...[:])[:]...[:]
array double complex  atan2(array double complex y[:]...[:],
                            array double complex x[:]...[:])[:]...[:]
```

The function **atan2()** has two arguments. The data type of both computational arrays shall be the same. If data types of both arguments are integral type, they will be promoted to float for computation. For example,

```
> array int   y[4]={1,-2, 3,  -4}
> array float x[4]={5, 6, -7, -8}
> atan2(y, x)
0.20 -0.32 2.74 -2.68
```

If the first argument of the function **pow(a, x)** is a computational array with shape of NxN and the second is an integral type, it will return a computational array of the same type and dimension as the first argument as if the function were prototyped as

```
array int pow(array int a[:][:], int x)[:][:]
array float pow(array float a[:][:], int x)[:][:]
array double pow(array double a[:][:], int x)[:][:]
array float complex pow(array float complex a[:][:], int x)[:][:]
array double complex pow(array double complex a[:][:], int x)[:][:]
```

In this case, the array function **pow(a, x)** behaves like matrix multiplication. For example,

```
> array int a[2][2] = {-1, 2, 3, -4}
> pow(a, 2)
7 -10
-15 22
> a*a
7 -10
-15 22
```

If both arguments of the array function **pow()** are computational array type, it will return an array with the value of each element calculated by the scalar function **pow()** with the corresponding elements of the two input arrays. In this case, the data types of the two input arrays shall be the same as if the function were prototyped as

```
array int           pow(array int y[:]...[:],
                        array int x[:]...[:])[:]...[:]
```

```
array float          pow(array float y[:]...[:],
                         array float x[:]...[:])[:]...[:]
array double         pow(array double y[:]...[:],
                         array double x[:]...[:])[:]...[:]
array float complex  pow(array float complex y[:]...[:],
                         array float complex x[:]...[:])[:]...[:]
array double complex pow(array double complex y[:]...[:],
                         array double complex x[:]...[:])[:]...[:]
```

For example,

```
> array int a[3] = {-1, 2, 3}
> pow(a, a)
-1 4 27
```

The functions **real()** and **imag()** will give the real and imaginary parts of the input argument. For array arguments, they behave as if they were prototyped as

```
array float func(array float a[:]...[:])[:]...[:]
array double func(array double a[:]...[:])[:]...[:]
array float func(array float complex a[:]...[:])[:]...[:]
array double func(array double complex a[:]...[:])[:]...[:]
```

where `func` is either **real** or **imag**. If the data type of the input argument is integral type, it will be promoted to float for computation. For example,

```
> array int a[3] = {-1, 2, 3}
> real(a)
-1.00 2.00 3.00
> array complex z[3] = {complex(1,2), complex(-3, -4), complex(0, -6)}
> real(z)
1.0000 -3.0000 0.0000
> imag(z)
2.0000 -4.0000 -6.0000
```

The array function **transpose()** returns a transpose of the input array of one or two dimensions. If the input array is of size NxM, the size of the returned array is MxN. By default, a one-dimensional array is a column vector. If the input array is a column vector of size Nx1, the return array is a row vector of 1xN and vice versa. The data type of the returned array is the same as the input array as if the function were prototyped as

```
array type transpose(array type a[:])[:]
array type transpose(array type a[:][:])[:][:]
```

where `type` can be any valid type for a computational array. For example,

```
> array float a[2][3]={1,2,3,4,5,6}
1.00 2.00 3.00
4.00 5.00 6.00
> transpose(a)
1.00 4.00
2.00 5.00
3.00 6.00
> array int b[3] = {1, 2, 3}
> a*b
14.00 32.00
> transpose(b)*b
14
> b*transpose(b)
1 2 3
2 4 6
3 6 9
```

As an example, in section 10.6.3, regular C arrays are used in Program 10.22 to plot a three-dimensional helix curve shown in Figure 10.10 in Chapter 10. The curve is modeled by the parametric equations (10.10) and (10.11) in terms of the parameter t. The same plot can be generated by Program 21.8 using computational arrays. In Program 21.8, the function **lindata()** is used to fill the computational array `t` of 300 elements with values from 0 to 10π linearly. The arrays of values from the type generic functions **sin()** and **cos()** are then assigned to the arrays `x` and `y`, respectively. Arguments of either regular C arrays or computational arrays for plotting data can be passed to the function **plotxyz()** for plotting.

```
/* File: helix.ch
   Plot 3D curve using plotxyz() with computational array */
#include <math.h>     // for sin() and cos()
#include <chplot.h>   // for plotxyz() and 'array' type qualifier

#define N 300         // number of data points for the 3D curve

int main() {
    /* declare arrays for plotting, t is coordinates in z-axis  */
    array double x[N], y[N], t[N];

    lindata(0, 10*M_PI, t); // fill array t from 0 to 10PI linearly
    x = sin(t);             // calculate array x with sin(t)
    y = cos(t);             // calculate array y with cos(t)
    /* plot 3D curve using plotxyz() */
    plotxyz(x, y, t, N, "Helix", "sin(t)", "cos(t)", "t");
    return 0;
}
```

Program 21.8: Plotting a three-dimensional curve using computational arrays.

21.11 Relationship Between Computational Arrays and C Arrays

A C array is only an address or a pointer, whereas a computational array in Ch is a first-class object that contains more information. As mentioned earlier in this chapter, a computational array is declared with the type qualifier **array**. Computational arrays can support many operators, while C arrays cannot. Given the same extents, the value of each element of a C array can be assigned to a computational array. For example,

```
int a[3][4];         // C array, 'a' represents an address or a pointer
array int A[3][4]; // Ch computational array
A = a;               // OK
```

In the above example, the values for each element of the array a is copied to the corresponding element of the computational array A.

C arrays can be passed to functions that take computational arrays as arguments, and vice versa. For example,

```
int f1(array int A[3][4]); // argument is computational array
int f2(int a[3][4]);       // argument is C array
f1(a); // OK
f1(A); // OK
f2(a); // OK
f2(A); // OK
```

If the variable of a C array is used as an address of the memory for the array, the address of the computational array shall be used for the equivalent code. For example,

```
int f3(int *a);               // argument is a pointer
f3(a);          // OK
f3(&A[0][0]); // OK
```

Application Examples

Linear Regression

Problem Statement:
For measured positions of a moving body at various times in Table 4.3 in Chapter 4, Program 10.19 in Chapter 10 uses the statistical library to calculate the linear regression coefficients v and b using equations (10.9) and (10.8), respectively, and plot the original data and fitted straight line. Calculate the linear regression coefficients v and b based on the matrix equation (21.4).

Program 21.9 uses the function **linsolve()** to calculate the linear regression coefficients v and b based on equation (21.4). Details about the function **linsolve()** will be presented in section 22.5 in Chapter 22. The transpose of a matrix is obtained by the function **transpose()**. Thc output from Program 21.9 is the same as that from Program 10.19, shown in Figures 10.8 and 10.9.

```
/* File: linreg.ch
   Perform linear regression analysis for a set of data in computational arrays.
   Plot the fitted line in comparison with the original scattered data points */
#include <stdio.h>
#include <numeric.h> /* for 'array' and linsolve() */
#include <chplot.h>  /* for class CPlot for plotting */
#define N      8     /* number of points for sample data */
#define NUM    100   /* number of points for plotting */
double b, v;         /* linear regression coefficients */

/* linear function y = b + v*t */
double func(double t) {
    double y;
    y = b + v*t;
    return y;
}

int main() {
    /* declare and initialize the original data */
    array double t[N] = {0, 3,   5, 8,  10,   12,   15,   18};
    array double y[N] = {2, 5.2, 6, 10, 10.4, 13.4, 14.8, 18}, x[2];
    array double a[N][2]; /* declare array a */
    CPlot plot;           /* instantiate a plotting class */
    int i;                /* index variable for a for-loop */

    /* initialize array a based on the matrix formula for linear regression */
    for(i=0; i<N; i++) {
       a[i][0] = 1;
       a[i][1] = t[i];
    }
    /* calculate the linear regression coefficients based on the formulas */
    linsolve(x, transpose(a)*a, transpose(a)*y);
    /* or  x = inverse(transpose(a)*a)*transpose(a)*y; */
    b = x[0];
    v = x[1];
    /* display the linear regresson coefficients v and b, and find y(11.0) */
    printf("v = %.2f\n", v);
    printf("b = %.2f\n", b);
    printf("y is = %.2f (m) at time t = 11 (s)\n", func(11.0));

   /* set the label on the x-axis */
    plot.label(PLOT_AXIS_X, "t (second)");
    /* set the label on the y-axis */
    plot.label(PLOT_AXIS_Y, "y (meter)");
```

Program 21.9: A program for straight-line fitting of data using computational arrays. (*Continued*)

```
    /* set the range for x-axis from 0 to 18 */
    plot.axisRange(PLOT_AXIS_Y, 0.0, 18.0);
    /* add data y[] and t[] as the 1st set of data for plotting */
    plot.data2DCurve(t, y, N);
    /* set the scattered point plot type for the 1st set of data */
    plot.plotType(PLOT_PLOTTYPE_POINTS, 0);
    /* set function func() to be plotted from t[0] to t[n-1] with NUM points */
    plot.func2D(t[0], t[N-1], NUM, func);
    /* after the above setup, ready and go, plot and display it! */
    plot.plotting();
    return 0;
}
```

Program 21.9: *(Continued)*

Force and Acceleration of a Moving Body

Problem Statement:
For the mechanical system shown in Figure 2.12, given mass $m = 5$ kilograms (kg), gravitational acceleration constant $g = 9.81 m/s^2$, coefficient of kinetic friction $\mu = 0.2$, and applied force p expressed as a function of time t in the formula

$$p(t) = 4\sin(t - 3) + 20 \tag{21.9}$$

write a program to plot the acceleration from $t = 0$ to $t = 10$ seconds. Solve the problem using the following different methods.

1. Using computational arrays to store the values for time, force, and acceleration, plot the acceleration curve for the external force equation (21.9) with the number of points equal to 100.
2. Using variable-length computational arrays, generate acceleration plots using the formula (21.9) for the external force $p(t)$ using both 11 and 100 data points.
3. Repeat the above process using assumed-shape computational arrays.
4. Repeat the above process using a function that returns computational arrays for accelerations.

The steps performed to solve these problems are similar to the ones used before. However, applications of computational arrays are illustrated in the programs. Program 21.10 is the solution for the first part of the problem. It uses the computational arrays `a`, `t`, and `p` to store the values for acceleration, time, and force, respectively. There is no loop such as a **for** loop used in the application program so that the code is more readable. Also, acceleration plots are generated for the two different external forces specified above. The plot for $p = 4\sin(t - 3) + 20$ is the same as the one shown in Figure 6.4 in Chapter 6. Program 21.10 also generates the plot for acceleration with the external force $p = 4(t^2 - 3) + 20$.

For the second part of the problem, the function `accelvla()` in Program 21.11 uses variable-length computational arrays to plot the acceleration of the system with respect to time. The size of the array is passed as an argument to the function.

Similarly, for the third part of the problem, the function `accelassumeshape()` of Program 21.12 also generates acceleration plots of the system, but it uses assumed-shape arrays instead of variable-length arrays. The **shape()** function is used on the array argument `a` to determine the number of data points to plot.

For the fourth part of the problem, the function `accelreturnarray()` in Program 21.13 first uses the computational array `t` to determine the size of the arrays `a` and `p` for the acceleration and the external force, respectively. Once the acceleration values are calculated with the computational arrays, the function `accelreturnarray()` then returns the array `a` to the function **main()** to plot the acceleration curves.

Note that in Programs 21.11 to 21.13, the function **lindata()** is used to generate data points for time `t` from 0 to 10 seconds. The plot generated by Programs 21.11 to 21.13 with 11 data points is the same as one shown in Figure 6.3. The plot generated by Programs 21.11 to 21.13 with 100 data points is displayed in Figure 6.4.

```
/* File: accelcharray.ch
   Calculate and plot accelerations using computational arrays */
#include <numeric.h> // for lindata(), sin(), and 'array' type qualifier
#include <chplot.h>  // for plotxy()

#define M_G 9.81        // gravitational acceleration constant g
#define N 100           // number of points for plotting

int main() {
    array double a[N], t[N], p[N]; // declare computational arrays
    double mu, m, t0, tf;          // declare variables

    mu = 0.2;               // mu
    m = 5.0;                // mass
    t0 = 0.0;               // initial time 0 second
    tf = 10.0;              // final time 10 seconds
    lindata(t0, tf, t);     // fill array t from t0 to tf linearly

    p = 4*(sin(t-3))+20; // p = 4sin(t-3)+20
    a = (p-mu*m*M_G)/m;  // a = (p-mu*m*M_G)/m
    plotxy(t, a, N, "Acceleration Plot", "time (s)", "accel (m/s^2)");

    p = 4*(t.*t-3)+20;   // p = 4(t*t-3)+20
    a = (p-mu*m*M_G)/m;  // a = (p-mu*m*M_G)/m
    plotxy(t, a, N, "Acceleration Plot", "time (s)", "accel (m/s^2)");
    return 0;
}
```

Program 21.10: Calculating accelerations using computational arrays.

```
/* File: accelcharrayvla.ch
   Calculate and plot accels using variable length computational arrays */
#include <numeric.h> // for lindata(), sin(), and 'array' type qualifier
#include <chplot.h>  // for plotxy()
```

Program 21.11: Calculating accelerations with variable length of computational arrays. (*Continued*)

```
#define M_G 9.81      // gravitational acceleration constant g
#define N1 11         // number of points for plotting
#define N2 100        // number of points for plotting

/* function passes variable length arrays */
void accelvla(int n, array double a[n]) {
    array double t[n], p[n]; // declare deferred-shape arrays t and p
    double mu, m, t0, tf;    // declare variables
    mu = 0.2;                // mu
    m = 5.0;                 // mass
    t0 = 0.0;                // initial time 0 second
    tf = 10.0;               // final time 10 seconds
    lindata(t0, tf, t);      // fill array t from t0 to tf linearly
    p = 4*(sin(t-3))+20;     // p = 4sin(t-3)+20
    a = (p-mu*m*M_G)/m;      // a = (p-mu*m*M_G)/m
    plotxy(t, a, n, "Acceleration Plot", "time (s)", "accel (m/s^2)");
}

int main() {
    array double a1[N1], a2[N2];  // declare arrays with different size

    accelvla(N1, a1);             // pass array a1 with N1 elements
    accelvla(N2, a2);             // pass array a2 with N2 elements
    return 0;
}
```

Program 21.11: *(Continued)*

```
/* File: accelcharrayassumeshape.ch
   Calculate and plot accelerations using assumed-shape array */
#include <numeric.h> // for lindata(), sin(), and 'array' type qualifier
#include <chplot.h>  // for plotxy()

#define M_G 9.81      // gravitational acceleration constant g
#define N1 11         // number of points for plotting
#define N2 100        // number of points for plotting

/* function passes variable length arrays through assumed-shape array */
void accelassumeshape(array double a[:]) {
    int n = (int)shape(a);   // obtain the size of the array a
    array double t[n], p[n]; // declare deferred-shape ararys t and p
    double mu, m, t0, tf;    // declare variables
```

Program 21.12: Calculating accelerations using computational arrays of assumed shape. *(Continued)*

```
    mu = 0.2;                    // mu
    m = 5.0;                     // mass
    t0 = 0.0;                    // initial time 0 second
    tf = 10.0;                   // final time 10 seconds
    lindata(t0, tf, t);          // fill array t from t0 to tf linearly
    p = 4*(sin(t-3))+20;         // p = 4sin(t-3)+20
    a = (p-mu*m*M_G)/m;          // a = (p-mu*m*M_G)/m
    plotxy(t, a, n, "Acceleration Plot", "time (s)", "accel (m/s^2)");
}

int main() {
    array double a1[N1], a2[N2];  // declare arrays with different size

    accelassumeshape(a1);           // pass array a1 with N1 elements
    accelassumeshape(a2);           // pass array a2 with N2 elements
    return 0;
}
```

Program 21.12: *(Continued)*

```
/* File: accelcharrayreturn.ch
   Calculate and plot accelerations using a function returning arrays */
#include <numeric.h> // for lindata(), sin(), and 'array' type qualifier
#include <chplot.h>  // for plotxy()

#define M_G 9.81      // gravitational acceleration constant g
#define N1 11         // number of points for plotting
#define N2 100        // number of points for plotting

/* function passes variable length arrays using assumed-shape array
   and returns array of variable length */
array double accelreturnarray(array double t[:])[:] {
    int n = (int)shape(t);   // obtain the array size
    array double a[n], p[n]; // declare deferred-shape arrays a and p
    double mu, m;            // declare mu and mass m

    mu = 0.2;                // mu
    m = 5.0;                 // mass
    p = 4*(sin(t-3))+20;     // p = 4sin(t-3)+20
    a = (p-mu*m*M_G)/m;      // a = (p-mu*m*M_G)/m
    return a;                // return array a
}
```

Program 21.13: Calculating accelerations with functions returning a computational array. *(Continued)*

```
int main() {
    /* declare arrays of different sizes */
    array double t1[N1], t2[N2];
    array double a1[N1], a2[N2];
    double t0, tf;

    t0 = 0.0;                    // initial time 0 second
    tf = 10.0;                   // final time 10 seconds
    lindata(t0, tf, t1);         // fill array t1 from t0 to tf linearly
    /* pass array t1 to function which returns acclerations in an array */
    a1 = accelreturnarray(t1);
    plotxy(t1, a1, "Acceleration Plot", "time (s)", "accel (m/s^2)");

    lindata(t0, tf, t2);         // fill array t2 from t0 to tf linearly
    /* pass array t2 to function which returns acclerations in an array */
    a2 = accelreturnarray(t2);
    plotxy(t2, a2, "Acceleration Plot", "time (s)", "accel (m/s^2)");
    return 0;
}
```

Program 21.13: *(Continued)*

Exercises

1. Is **array** a keyword in Ch? If not, when will it become a type qualifier?
2. Point out the errors in the following code fragments.

a.
```
array int a[3] = {1,2,3}, b[2];
b = 10 + a;
```
b.
```
array int a[3] = {1,2,3}, b[3];
b = (array int [3])10./a;
```
c.
```
array int A[3][4], B[3][4];
A = B+10;
A = A*A + A;
```

3. The variable `m` is declared as a 2x3 matrix of int type. Write an initializer for *m* that places 1s in the first column, 2s in the second column, and 3s in the third column.
4. Use computational arrays to solve the problems in Exercise 38 in Chapter 10.
5. Use computational arrays to solve the problems in Exercise 39 in Chapter 10.
6. Use computational arrays to solve the problems in Exercise 40 in Chapter 10.
7. For matrix A in Exercise 40 in Chapter 10, calculate the following expressions:

   (a) $\boldsymbol{A} + \boldsymbol{A}$, (b) $5\boldsymbol{A}$

   (i) using C arrays and (ii) using computational arrays.

8. Given

a.

$$A = \begin{bmatrix} 5 & 2 & 2 \\ 4 & 5 & 6 \\ 7 & 8 & 9 \end{bmatrix}, \boldsymbol{B} = \begin{bmatrix} 7 & 8 & 9 \\ 1 & 2 & 3 \\ 4 & 5 & 6 \end{bmatrix}, \text{ and } \boldsymbol{b} = \begin{bmatrix} 1 \\ 4 \\ 7 \end{bmatrix}$$

b.

$$A = \begin{bmatrix} 1 & 2 \\ 4 & 5 \end{bmatrix}, \boldsymbol{B} = \begin{bmatrix} 7 & 8 \\ 1 & 2 \end{bmatrix}, \text{ and } \boldsymbol{b} = \begin{bmatrix} 1 \\ 4 \end{bmatrix}$$

write a program to compute **x, Y**, and **Z** in the following equations:

$$\mathbf{Y} = \sin(\mathbf{5AB} + \mathbf{B}^{\mathrm{T}}\mathbf{A} + \mathbf{A}^2)$$
$$\mathbf{Z} = (\mathbf{5AB} + \mathbf{B}^{\mathrm{T}}\mathbf{A} + \mathbf{A}^2)^{50}$$

(1) Calculate **Y** and **Z** inside the function main().
(2) The values for **Y** and **Z** shall be calculated and printed out inside the function `f()`, which is called by `f(3, A1, B1, b1)` and `f(2, A2, B2, b2)` for problems (a) and (b), respectively.
(3) The values for **Y** and **Z** shall be calculated and printed out inside the function `f()`, which is called by `f(A1, B1, b1)` and `f(A2, B2, b2)` for problems (a) and (b), respectively.

9. Write a function called `summary()`, which will add each element of the array arguments passed in.

```
#include <stdio.h>
double summary(array int a[2], array int b[:],
               array double c[:][:]);

int main(){
   int a[2]={1, 2}, b[3] = {1, 2, 3};
   double c1[2][3] = {1, 2, 3, 4, 5, 6};
   double c2[3][4] = {1, 2, 3, 4, 5, 6, 7, 8, 9, 10, 11, 12};
   double s;
   s =  summary(a, a, c1);
   printf("s = %f\n", s);
   s =  summary(a, b, c2);
   printf("s = %f\n", s);
}
double summary(array int a[2], array int b[:],
               array double c[:][:]) {
```

10. Write a function to compute and return the following matrix equation:

$$f(\mathbf{A}, \mathbf{B}, c) = \mathbf{A}. * \mathbf{B} + c\mathbf{B}$$

where 2-by-4 matrices **A** and **B** and constant c are arguments of the function. Calculate $f(\mathbf{A}, \mathbf{B}, c)$ with $A = \begin{bmatrix} 1 & 2 & 2 & 5 \\ 5 & 7 & 3 & 2 \end{bmatrix}, B = \begin{bmatrix} 5 & 7 & 3 & 2 \\ 1 & 2 & 2 & 5 \end{bmatrix}$, and $c = 3$.

11. Modify the programs `linearsys1.c` and `linear1()` in Exercise 36 in Chapter 11 as `linearsys2.c` and `linear2()`. The function `linear2()` should be implemented as a Ch function file `linear2.chf` using an array of assumed shape with the following function prototypes:

```
void linear2(array double B[:][:], array double A[:][:]);
int main() {
```

```
    array double B1[3][4], A1[3][4] = {....};
    array double B2[2][3], A2[2][3] = {...};
    /* add code here */
    linear2(B1, A1);
    linear2(B2, A2);
    /* print out result of B1 and B2 here */
}
```

12. Plot the following functions using the function **plotxy()** with x from -5 to 5 without using a loop structure.

  a. $f(x) = x \sin x$
  b. $g(x) = 3x^2 + x$
  c. $h(x) = x^2 \sin x^2 + 5$

13. Compute values of the function

$$f_{10}(x) = x^2 + 5\sin(10x),$$

and plot it based on the instructions in Exercise 11 in Chapter 6. Use computational arrays without a loop for computation. You may display the output in the format shown in Figure 5.16 in Chapter 5 using a loop.

14. Program 10.8 in Chapter 10 rolls a six-sided die 6000 times randomly. Calculate the frequencies for each face (the number of times each side will come up). A C array is used to keep frequencies for each face. Modify the program to use a Ch array with an index ranging from 1 to 6. Roll the die 60,000 times.

15. A projectile is fired into the air with an initial speed v_0 of 35 m/s and an initial projection angle of $\theta_0 = 15°$. Plot its trajectory of y versus x without a loop using computational arrays for x and y with 100 points. The trajectory can be expressed in x-y coordinates using equations (6.3) and (6.4) in section 6.7 in Chapter 6.

16. Plot the humps function shown in Figure 6.11 in Chapter 6 for x in the range $-1 \le x \le 2$. Without a loop, use a computational array for x with 100 points.

17. Plot the probability density function shown in Figure 6.12 in Chapter 6 for x in the range $-4 \le x \le 8$ with $\mu = 2$ and $\sigma = 3$. Without a loop, use computational arrays for x and f with 100 points.

18. Plot the first four terms and partial sums $f_1(x)$, $f_2(x)$, $f_3(x)$, and $f_4(x)$ of the Fourier series for the periodic function defined in Exercise 34 in Chapter 6 for x in the range of $-\pi$ to π in the same figure without a loop. Use the computational arrays for x and the first four terms s_i and partial sums f_i with 100 points.

19. Plot the responses of distance versus time for the overdamped, critically damped, and underdamped mechanical systems defined in Exercise 35 in Chapter 6 without a loop using computational arrays for distance x and time t with 100 points.

20. Plot sinusoids $s_1(t)$ and $s_2(t)$ and signal $s = s_1(t) + s_2(t)$, defined in Exercise 36 in Chapter 6, without a loop using the computational arrays for signals s_1, s_2, and s, and time t with 200 points.

21. For the curvelinear motion of a particle defined in Exercise 55 in Chapter 10, plot the path of the particle for $0 \le t \le 5$ without using loops.

22. For the harmonic motion of a particle defined in Exercise 56 in Chapter 10, plot the path of the particle for $0 \le t \le 7$ without using loops.

23. For thc three-dimensional spiral motion of a particle defined in Exercise 57 in Chapter 10, plot the path of the particle for $0 \le t \le 10\pi$ without using loops.

24. Plot the temperature conversion function specified in Exercise 3 in Chapter 20 using computational arrays.

25. Let $f(x) = x^2 - 3$ for $x \geq 0$, the inverse function $f^{-1}(x) = g(x)$ is $\sqrt{x+3}$ with $x \geq -3$ as shown in Figure 4.7 in Chapter 4. Write a program using computational arrays to plot the functions $f(x)$ and $g(x)$.
26. Solve the linear regression problem in Exercise 59 in Chapter 10 in matrix notation using computational arrays.
27. Solve the linear regression problem in Exercise 60 in Chapter 10 in matrix notation using computational arrays.
28. Solve the linear regression problem in Exercise 61 in Chapter 10 in matrix notation using computational arrays.
29. Solve the linear regression problem in Exercise 62 in Chapter 10 in matrix notation using computational arrays.

CHAPTER 22

‡Advanced Numerical Analysis in Ch

Numerical analysis in Ch is the simplist possible extension in the spirit of C. Complicated problems in numerical analysis can often be solved with just one function call in Ch. The advanced features for numerical analysis in Ch are very useful for applications in engineering and science. The category of numerical analysis functions in Ch is listed in Table 22.1. The function prototypes for numerical analysis are included in the header file **numeric.h**. In this chapter, some commonly used numerical analysis functions are presented. The detailed description of each function can be found in *The Ch Language Environment—Reference Guide*.

Table 22.1 Category of numerical analysis functions in Ch.

Data analysis and statistics
Data interpolation and curve fitting
Minimization or maximization of functions
Polynomials
Nonlinear equations
Ordinary differential equations
Derivatives
Integration
Matrix analysis functions
Matrix decomposition
Special matrices
Linear equations
Eigenvalues and eigenvectors
Fast Fourier transforms
Convolution and filtering
Cross-correlation
Special mathematical functions

22.1 Solving Nonlinear Equations

The function **fzero**() with the prototype of

```
int fzero(double *x, double (*func)(double), ...
        /* [double x0] | [double x02[2]*/);
```

finds a zero position of a nonlinear function with one variable. The argument `func` is a pointer to the function given by the user. The position where the function is zero is passed by the argument `x`. The argument `x0` contains the initial guess for the zero position. The argument `x02` is a vector with two elements and double type. The function shall be bracketed in the interval of [`x02[0]`, `x02[1]`] so that the sign of `func(x02[0])` differs from the sign of `func(x02[1])`. Otherwise, an error occurs. The function **fzero**() returns 0 on success and -1 on failure.

For example, the zero position 1.414213 of function

$$f(x) = x^2 - 2$$

can be obtained with an initial guess of $x_0 = 2.0$ by the following commands:

```
> double x, func1(double x) { return x*x-2.0;}
> fzero(&x, func1, 2.0);
> x
1.4142
> double x02[2]={-2, 0}
> fzero(&x, func1, x02);
> x
-1.4142
```

22.2 Solving Systems of Nonlinear Equations

A system of nonlinear equations can be found by using the function **fsolve**(). The function **fsolve**() has the prototype of

```
int fsolve(double x[:], void (*func)(double[], double []), double x0[:]);
```

The array arguments `x` and `x0` contain the calculated zero position and its initial guess, respectively. The user function `func` has two arguments, one for input and another one for the values of the functions. The input argument is an n-dimensional array, and the function values calculated will be delivered by the second array argument of the same dimension. The number of dimensions is taken from the function given by the user internally. The function **fsolve**() returns 0 on success and -1 on failure.

For example, the nonlinear system of the two equations

$$f_0 = -(x_0^2 + x_1^2 - 2.0) = 0$$
$$f_1 = e^{x_0 - 1.0} + x_1^3 - 2.0 = 0$$

has a zero point at (1, 1). It can be solved by using the function **fsolve**() with the initial guesses of zero point at $x_0 = 2.0$, and $x_1 = 0.5$ using the following commands:

```
> void func2(double x[], double f[]){f[0]=-(x[0]*x[0]+x[1]*x[1]-2.0);\
  f[1]=exp(x[0]-1.0)+x[1]*x[1]*x[1]-2.0;}
> array double x[2], x0[2] = {2.0, 0.5};
> fsolve(x, func2, x0);
> x
1.0000 1.0000
```

22.3 Finding Roots of Polynomials

The function **roots**(), with the prototype of

```
int roots(... /* double [complex] x[:], double [complex] p[:] */);
```

finds the roots of the polynomial

$$p = p_0 x^n + p_1 x^{n-1} + \cdots + p_{n-1} x + p_n$$

The function can handle polynomials with coefficients of double or double complex type. The arguments p and x contain the coefficients and roots of a polynomial, respectively. The function returns 0 on success and −1 on failure.

For example, the roots of the polynomial

$$p = x^2 - 2x + 1$$

can be determined by the following command-line executions:

```
> array double x[2]
> array double p[3] = {1, -2, 1}          /* p = x^2-2x+1 */
> roots(x, p)
> x
1.0000  1.0000
>
```

The **roots**() function can also calculate the complex roots of a polynomial. For example, the polynomial

$$p = x^4 - 12x^3 + 25x + 116$$

has two roots of complex numbers and two roots of real numbers, which can be obtained by the following commands:

```
> array double x[4], p[5]  = {1, -12, 0, 25, 116}
> array double complex z[4]
> roots(x, p)
> x
11.7473 2.7028 NaN NaN
> roots(z, p)
```

```
> z
complex(11.7473,0.0000) complex(2.7028,0.0000) \
complex(-1.2251,1.4672) complex(-1.2251,-1.4672)
```

22.4 Multiplication of Polynomials

The function **conv()**, with the prototype of

```
int conv(... /* double [complex] c[:], double [complex] x[:],
                double [complex] y[:] */);
```

multiplies two polynomials represented by arrays x and y. If the array size for x is n and the size for y is m, the product of the multiplication of two polynomials is a one-dimensional array c of size $n+m-1$. The function returns 0 on success and -1 on failure. As an example, for the polynomials

$$x(s) = 2s^2 - 7s + 3$$
$$y(s) = s^2 + 2s + 101$$

the product $c(s) = x(s)y(s) = 2s^4 - 3^3 + 191s^2 - 701s + 303$ can be obtained as follows:

```
> array double x[3] ={2, -7, 3}
> array double y[3] ={1, 2, 101}
> array double c[5]
> conv(c, x, y)
> c
2.0000 -3.0000 191.0000 -701.0000 303.0000
```

The division of two polynomials can be performed by the function **decon()**. The details about **decon()** can be found in the *Ch Reference Guide*.

An Application Example

Finding Poles of a Transfer Function

In control theory, there are two main methods for analyzing feedback systems: the *transfer function* method for frequency domain, and the state space method. In the transfer function method, the focus is on the locations in the complex *s-plane* where the transfer function becomes infinite (the *poles*) or zero (the *zeros*). As an example, a control system is represented in its transfer function as follows:

$$G(s) = \frac{s+1}{(2s^2 - 7s + 3)(s^2 + 2s + 101)} \tag{22.1}$$

the zero of this transfer function is -1. The roots of polynomials $(2s^2 - 7s + 3)$ and $(s^2 + 2s + 101)$ are the poles of the transfer function $G(s)$. We can write a program to find its poles. For illustrative purposes, we multiply these two polynomials in the denominator first using the function **conv()**, then using the function **roots**() to find the roots of the resultant polynomial, as shown in Program 22.1. The output from Program 22.1 is shown below.

```
denominator =    2.00   -3.00  191.00 -701.00  303.00
poles = complex(-1,10) complex(-1,-10) complex(0.5,0) complex(3,0)
```

There are four poles $-1 + i10, -1 - i10, 0.5$, and 3 for the transfer function $G(s)$. Two of them are complex numbers.

```
/* File: poles.ch
   Multiply polynomials and find poles of a transfer function */
#include <stdio.h>
#include <numeric.h> /* for conv() and roots() */

/* define dimensions for arrays */
#define N1 3          /* p1 = 2s^2 - 7s + 3 */
#define N2 3          /* p2 = s^2 + 2s + 101 */
#define N (N1+N2-1) /* den = (s^2 + 2s + 82)(s^2 + 2s + 101) */
#define NN (N-1)      /* roots for den = p1*p2 */

int main() {
   double p1[N1] = {2, -7, 3};   /* p1 = 2s^2 - 7s + 3 */
   double p2[N2] = {1, 2, 101}; /* p2 = s^2 + 2s + 101 */
   double den[N];                 /* den = p1*p2 */
   complex poles[NN];             /* poles for denominator for den */
   int i;

   conv(den,p1,p2);   /* den = (2s^2 - 7s + 3)(s^2 + 2s + 101)
                            = 2s^4 - 3s^3 + 191s^2 - 701s + 303 */
   printf("denominator =");
   for(i=0; i<N; i++) {
     printf("%8.2f", den[i]);
   }

   roots(poles, den);   /* find roots for den = p1*p2 */
   printf("\npoles = ");
   for(i=0; i<NN; i++) {
      printf("%g ", poles[i]);
   }
   printf("\n");
   return 0;
}
```

Program 22.1: Finding poles of a transfer function.

22.5 Solving Systems of Linear Equations and Inverse of Matrices

A system of linear equations

$$\mathbf{Ax} = \mathbf{b}$$

can be solved by various functions in Ch. If matrix **A** is an n-by-n square matrix of real or complex type, it can be solved by the function **linsolve**(). The function **linsolve**() uses LU decomposition with partial pivoting and row interchanges to factor the matrix **A** as **A** = **PLU**, where **P** is a permulation matrix, **L** is a unit lower triangular, and **U** is an upper triangular. The factored form of **A** is then used to solve the system of equations for **x**. The function **linsolve**(), with the prototype of

```
int linsolve(double x[:], double a[:][:], double b[:])
```

takes the arguments x, a, and b, corresponding to **x, A**, and **b** in a system of linear equations **Ax** = **b**, respectively. They can be arrays of double type. The function **linsolve**() returns 0 if the equation can be solved successfully; otherwise it returns −1.

For example, Equation (10.49) presented in section 10.8.3 in Chapter 10 can be solved by Program 10.30 in Chapter 10 which is equivalent to Program 10.31 in Chapter 10. Both use the same function in CLAPACK to solve a system of linear equations and have the same output. Equation (10.49) can also be solved interactively as follows:

```
> array double a[3][3] = {3, 5, 6, 4, 2, 1, 0, 7, 1}
> array double x[3], b[3] = {-1, 8, 5}
> linsolve(x, a, b)
> x
2.0000 1.0000 -2.0000
> a*x
-1.0000 8.0000 5.0000
```

The inverse $\mathbf{A}^{-1}$ of a square matrix **A** is defined as

$$\mathbf{A}^{-1}\mathbf{A} = \mathbf{A}\mathbf{A}^{-1} = \mathbf{I}.$$

To obtain its inverse, the matrix **A** shall not be singular. The inverse matrix $\mathbf{A}^{-1}$ of the matrix **A** of real type can be calculated by the function **inverse**(), with the prototype of

```
array double inverse(double a[:][:], ... /* [int *status] */)[:][:];
```

The function returns the inverse of the matrix a. The optional argument status gives the status of the calculation. If the calculation is successful, status is 0; otherwise status is negative.

In the example below, the inverse of matrix **A** presented in equation (10.46) in Chapter 10 is obtained by the function **inverse**(). The system of linear equations then can be solved by the equation $\mathbf{x} = \mathbf{A}^{-1}\mathbf{b}$.

```
> array double a[3][3] = {3, 5, 6, 4, 2, 1, 0, 7, 1}
> array double ai[3][3], b[3] = {-1, 8, 5}
> ai=inverse(a)
-0.0376 0.2782 -0.0526
-0.0301 0.0226 0.1579
0.2105 -0.1579 -0.1053
> ai*b
2.0000 1.0000 -2.0000
```

22.6 Finding Eigenvalues and Eigenvectors

The eigenvalue λ and eigenvector **V** of the square matrix **A** are defined as

$$\mathbf{AV} = \lambda \mathbf{V}$$

If the matrix **A** is not symmetrical or not all elements are of real type, its eigenvalue λ and eigenvector **V** could be complex numbers.

The function **eigen**(), with the prototype of

```
int eigen(... /* double [complex] a[:][:],
                 double [complex] evalues[:],
                 double [complex] evectors[:][:],
                 [char *mode] */);
```

calculates the eigenvalue `evalues` and eigenvector `evectors` of the matrix `a` with dimension n-by-n. The syntaxes for calling this function are as follows:

```
eigen(a, evalues);
eigen(a, evalues, evectors);
eigen(a, evalues, evectors, mode);
```

The computed eigenvalues and eigenvectors are passed as arguments of `evectors` and `evectors` of the function, respectively. The arrays `a`, `evalues`, and `evectors` shall be double or double complex type. The computed eigenvectors are normalized so that the norm of each eigenvector equals 1. The argument `mode` is used to indicate if a preliminary balancing step before the calculation is performed or not. Generally, balancing improves the condition of the input matrix, enabling more accurate computation of the eigenvalues and eigenvectors. But it also may lead to incorrect eigenvectors in some special cases. By default, a preliminary balancing step is taken.

For example, for the matrices below

$$\mathbf{A} = \begin{bmatrix} 0.8 & 0.2 & 0.1 \\ 0.2 & 0.7 & 0.3 \\ 0.1 & 0.3 & 0.6 \end{bmatrix}, \mathbf{B} = \begin{bmatrix} 0.8 & 0.2 & 0.1 \\ 0.1 & 0.7 & 0.3 \\ 0.1 & 0.1 & 0.6 \end{bmatrix}, \mathbf{C} = \begin{bmatrix} 3 & 9 & 23 \\ 2 & 2 & 1 \\ -7 & 1 & -9 \end{bmatrix},$$

the matrix **A** is symmetrical with real eigenvalues, **B** is nonsymmetrical with real eigenvalues, and **C** is nonsymmetrical with complex eigenvalues. The eigenvalues and eigenvectors of these three matrices can be calculated by the following commands:

```
> array double a[3][3] = {0.8,0.2,0.1, 0.2,0.7,0.3, 0.1,0.3,0.6}
> array double b[3][3] = {0.8,0.2,0.1, 0.1,0.7,0.3, 0.1,0.1,0.6}
> array double c[3][3] = {3, 9, 23, 2, 2, 1, -7, 1, -9}
> array double evalues[3], evectors[3][3]
> array double complex zvalues[3], zvectors[3][3]
> eigen(b, evalues, evectors)
> evalues
1.1088 0.6526 0.3386
> evectors
0.5795 0.8035 0.1362
0.6471 -0.3520 -0.6763
0.4954 -0.4801 0.7239
> eigen(b, evalues)
> evalues
1.0000 0.6000 0.5000
> eigen(c, evalues)
> evalues
NaN NaN 3.2417
> eigen(c, zvalues, zvectors)
> printf("%.3f", zvalues)
complex(-3.621,10.647) complex(-3.621,-10.647) complex(3.242,0.000)
> printf("%.3f", zvectors)
complex(0.854,0.000) complex(0.854,0.000) complex(0.604,0.000)
complex(-0.024,-0.125) complex(-0.024,0.125) complex(0.744,0.000)
complex(-0.236,0.445) complex(-0.236,-0.445) complex(-0.285,0.000)
```

22.7 Solving Ordinary Differential Equations

The function **oderk**(), with the prototype of

```
int oderk( void (*func)(double x, double y[], double dydx[], void *param),
        double t0, double tf, double y0[:], void *param,
        double t[:], double *y, ... /* double tol */);
```

numerically solves an ordinary differential equation (ODE):

$$\frac{dy}{dt} = \text{func}(t, y, p)$$

or a system of ODEs:

$$\frac{d\mathbf{y}}{dt} = \mathbf{func}(t, \mathbf{y}, p)$$

using a Runge-Kutta method. The function can be called using one of the following forms. The argument `param` is used to pass information from the calling function to the ODE function. The argument `func` is specified as a pointer to function for a first-order differential equation. The initial and final values for `t` are specified as the arguments `t0` and `tf`. The argument `y0` of array type contains the initial values of differential equations. Its dimension equals the number of dependent variables. If successful, this function returns the number of points calculated in the interval between `t0` and `tf`. Otherwise, it returns −1. The vector `t` contains the values between `t0` and `tf` in which the ODE function is solved and the results are stored in the memory pointed to by the variable `y`. The user shall pass the address of a one-dimensional array for an ODE or the address of a two-dimensional array for a system of ODEs to the argument `y` of the function **oderk**(). If the optional argument `tol` is passed, the algorithm uses the user-specified tolerance to decide the iteration stop. Otherwise, the value of 10^{-8} is used by default. In general, the user should guess how many points it would produce and define the size of the arrays *t* and *y* accordingly. The function **oderk**() will automatically pad the leftover space in `t` and `y` with results at `tf`.

For example, the ODE

$$\frac{dy}{dt} = \sin(t)$$

with the initial condition $t_0 = -\pi$ and $y_0 = 1.0$ can be solved with more than 50 points in the interval $t_0 = -\pi$ to $t_f = \pi$ by the following commands:

```
> double t[50], y[50], y00[1]={1.0}
> void func(double t, double y[], double dydt[], void *param){dydt[0]=sin(t);}
> oderk(func, -3.14, 3.14, y00, NULL, t, y)
34
> plotxy(t, y)
```

As displayed in the above code, although 50 elements have been allocated for the arrays `t` and `y`, only the first 34 elements have the values from the ODE solution. The remaining elements are filled with the values at the end point `tf`. The output from the above code is displayed in Figure 22.1.

The function **oderk**() can be used to solve the Van der Pol equation

$$\frac{d^2u}{dt^2} - \mu(1-u^2)\frac{du}{dt} + u = 0$$

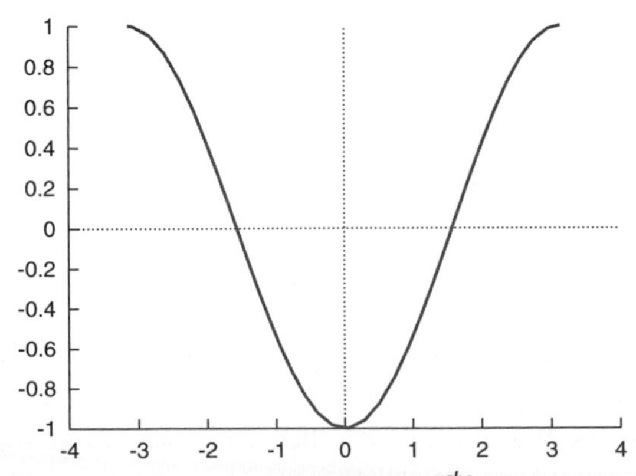

Figure 22.1: The plot as a solution for the ODE equation $\frac{dy}{dt} = \sin(t)$ in the range of $-\pi \leq t \leq \pi$.

in the range of $1 \leq t \leq 30$ with $\mu = 2$, and the initial condition $t_0 = 1$, $u(t_0) = 1$ and $u'(t_0) = 0$. The Van der Pol equation can be reformulated as a set of first-order differential equations with two dependent variables first. Let

$$y_0 = u$$
$$y_1 = \frac{du}{dt}$$

then

$$\frac{dy_0}{dt} = \frac{du}{dt} = y_1$$
$$\frac{dy_1}{dt} = \frac{d^2u}{dt^2} = \mu(1 - u^2)\frac{du}{dt} - u = \mu(1 - y_0^2)y_1 - y_0$$

with the initial condition $t_0 = 1$, $y_0(t_0) = 1$ and $y_1(t_0) = 0$. Program 22.2 solves the Van der Pol equation with the above initial condition in the range of $1 \leq t \leq 30$. The parameter μ is passed from the function **main**() to the ODE function through the argument `param`. The output from Program 22.2 is displayed in Figure 22.2.

```
/* File: oderk.ch
   Solve an ordinary different equation, the van der Pol equation,
   using function oderk() in Runge Kutta method */
#include <chplot.h>     // plotxy()
#include <numeric.h>    // header file numerical functions, for oderk()

#define NVAR 2          // number of dependent variables y1 and y2,
                        // or order of the equation
#define POINTS 256      // maximum number of points for ODE

/* function for differential equation */
void func(double t, double y[], double dydt[], void *param) {
    double mu;               // mu in the van der Pol equation

    /* obtain mu passed from call oderk(func, t0, tf, y0, &mu, t, y); */
    mu = *(double*)param;
    dydt[0] = y[1];                          // 1st equation in the ODE
    dydt[1]=mu*(1-y[0]*y[0])*y[1] - y[0]; // 2nd equation in the ODE
}

int main() {
    double t0=1, tf=30, y0[NVAR] = {1, 0}; // initial condition
    /* arrays to keep the results from the ODE solver oderk() */
    double t[POINTS], y[NVAR][POINTS];
    double mu = 2;                         //  declare and initialize mu
```

Program 22.2: Solving the Van der Pol equation. (*Continued*)

```
    /* call oderk() to solve the van der Pol equation with t and y */
    oderk(func, t0, tf, y0, &mu, t, y);
    /* plot y1 and y2 versus t, 2D array y contains y[0] and y[1] */
    plotxy(t, y, "The solution for the van der Pol equation", "t (seconds)",
           "y1 and y2");
    return 0;
}
```

Program 22.2: (*Continued*)

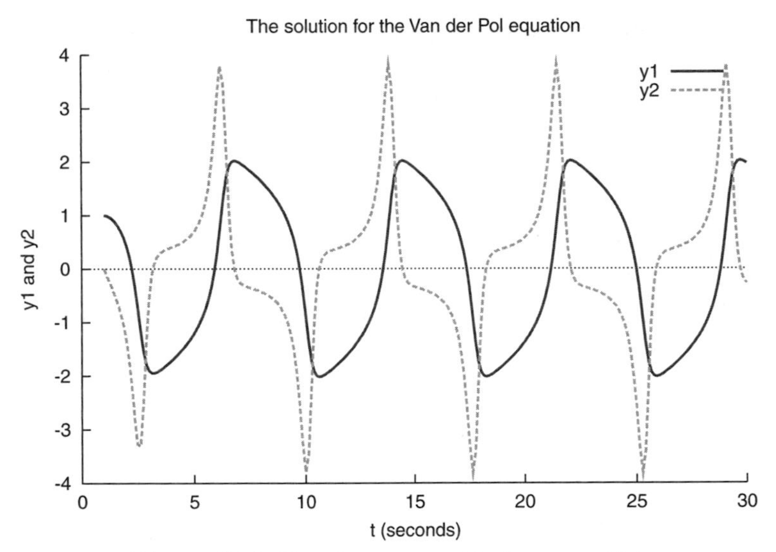

Figure 22.2: The plot generated by Program 22.2.

Exercises

1. Note the following polynomial equations.

(a) $p_1(x) = x^3 + 7x^2 - 20x - 96.$
(b) $p_2(x) = x^4 - 12x^3 - 25x + 116.$
(c) $p_3(x) = x^4 - x - 10.$
(d) $p_4(x) = x^3 - 8x^2 + 17x - 10.$
(e) $p_5(x) = x^4 - 5x^3 - 12x^2 + 76x - 79.$

a. For each, calculate the roots.
b. For each, evaluate the value of the polynomial at $x = 3.5$.

2. For polynomials in Exercise 1, obtain products from the multiplication of polynomials as follows:
(a) $p_1(x)p_2(x)$, (b) $p_2(x)p_3(x)$, (c) $p_2(x)p_3(x)p_4(x)$, (d) $p_1(x)p_2(x)p_4(x)p_5(x)$,
(e) $p_2(x)p_3(x)p_4(x)p_5(x)$.

3. Solve for two roots of the nonlinear equation for the humps function shown in Figure 6.11 in Chapter 6.
4. The formula for the volume of a sphere is $\frac{4}{3}\pi r^3$, where r is the radius of the sphere. If the volume of a sphere is 90 m^3, write a program to calculate the radius of the sphere. Plot the function $f(r) = \frac{4}{3}\pi r^3 - 90$ in the range $-5 \leq r \leq 5$.
5. Solve for three roots of the third-order polynomial function shown in Figure 6.13 in Chapter 6.
6. Solve the following nonlinear equations with initial guesses.

   a. $e^{-x} = \sin(x)$ with $x_0 = 0$. This nonlinear equation has infinite solutions.

   b. $\log(x) = \cos(x)$ with the solution located within the range $1 \leq x \leq 2$.

   c. $f_1(x, y) = x^2 + y^2 - 2 = 0$
   $f_2(x, y) = e^{y-1} + x^5 - 1 = 0$
   $x_0 = 0$, $y_0 = 0$

7. For the matrices below,

$$\mathbf{A} = \begin{bmatrix} 1 & 2 & 2 & 5 \\ 2 & 4 & 6 & 4 \\ 2 & 6 & 9 & 3 \\ 5 & 4 & 3 & 2 \end{bmatrix}, \mathbf{B} = \begin{bmatrix} 1 & 2 & 2 \\ 2 & 4 & 6 \\ 2 & 6 & 9 \end{bmatrix}, \mathbf{C} = \begin{bmatrix} 1 & 2 & 2 \\ 3 & 4 & 6 \\ 4 & 6 & 9 \end{bmatrix}$$

   a. Calculate the eigenvalues and eigenvectors.

   b. Calculate the inverse matrices.

8. A stress tensor for a stress element shown in the illustration can be represented by the matrix

$$\begin{bmatrix} \sigma_x & \tau_{xy} & \tau_{xz} \\ \tau_{yx} & \sigma_y & \tau_{yz} \\ \tau_{zx} & \tau_{zy} & \sigma_z \end{bmatrix}$$

The eigenvalues and eigenvectors of the matrix are the principal stresses $\sigma_1, \sigma_2, \sigma_3$ and their corresponding direction cosines, respectively. Given a stress element with $\sigma_x = 100$ MPa, $\sigma_y = 20$ MPa, $\sigma_z = -30$ MPa, $\tau_{xy} = -40$ MPa, $\tau_{yz} = 0$ MPa, and $\tau_{zx} = 20$ MPa, find the principal stresses and their corresponding direction cosines.

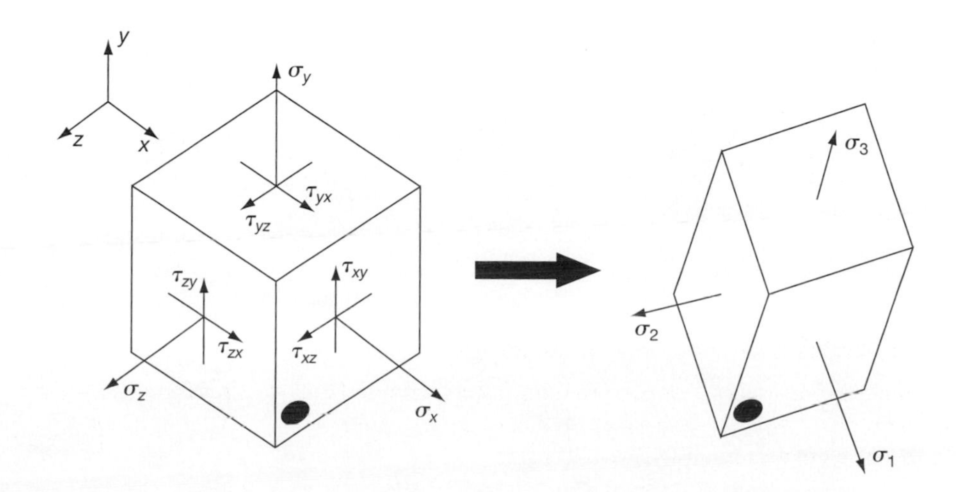

9. Solve for the linear system of equation

$$\mathbf{Ax} = \mathbf{b}$$

with

$$\mathbf{A} = \begin{bmatrix} 1 & 2 & 2 & 5 \\ 2 & 4 & 6 & 4 \\ 2 & 6 & 9 & 3 \\ 5 & 4 & 3 & 2 \end{bmatrix}, \quad \mathbf{b} = \begin{bmatrix} 1 \\ 2 \\ 2 \\ 3 \end{bmatrix}$$

10. Solve the problems in Exercise 43 in Chapter 10 using the function **linsolve()**.

11. Solve Exercise 44 in Chapter 10 using the function **linsolve()**.

12. Solve Exercise 45 in Chapter 10 using the function **linsolve()**.

13. Solve the initial value problem with the following ordinary differential equations numerically. Plot the solutions for both y and y' from $t = 0$ to $t = 3$ with 50 points.

a. $y''(t) - 2y'(t) + 10y(t) = 0$, $y(0) = 4$, $y'(0) = 1$.

b. $\dfrac{d^2y}{dt^2} + 9\sin(y) = 0$, $y(0) = 1, \dot{y}(0) = 0$

14. For matrices $\boldsymbol{A}$ and $\boldsymbol{B}$, and vector $\boldsymbol{b}$ given in Exercise 8 in Chapter 21, calculate the vector $\mathbf{x}$ in the following equation:

$$(\mathbf{5AB} + \mathbf{B^TA} + \mathbf{A^2})\mathbf{x} = \mathbf{b}$$

15. Solve Exercise 35(c) in Chapter 6 using the function **fsolve()**.

PART IV

Numerical Computing in MATLAB

CHAPTER 23

Introduction to MATLAB and Comparison Study with C/Ch

MATLAB is a proprietary programming software package developed by the MathWorks, Inc. Its name is derived from the term MATrix LABoratory. It is a software tool used primarily for scientific and engineering analysis. The MATLAB software is capable of solving many numerical-oriented problems. Like Ch, MATLAB is interpretive. It can execute either single line statements or a script file, which is composed of several statements. Almost all features in MATLAB are available in Ch. In this chapter, MATLAB will be introduced briefly in comparison with C99 and Ch.

23.1 Variables

MATLAB is a typeless software package. It is case-sensitive. Variable names should begin with a letter and can have a maximum length of 31 characters. The names are limited to combinations of letters, numbers, and underscores. All variables are treated as arrays of double precision floating-point complex data types in MATLAB. Thus, a variable can be used without declaration. Scalar quantities are automatically considered as 1×1 dimensional arrays. When an integer is used in MATLAB, it can be viewed as a variable of **int** type in C. Similarly, a double precision floating-point number in MATLAB is like a C variable of **double** data type. A matrix or vector in MATLAB is equivalent to a computational array of **double** data type in Ch. For a matrix of complex numbers in MATLAB, the Ch equivalent data type is a computational array of **double complex** type. For example, variables in MATLAB can be initialized as follows:

```
x = 3;
y = 4.5;
a = [1 2 3];
b = [1 2 3; 4 5 6];
```

Note that x and y are variables of scalar types, and a and b are arrays of size 1×3 and 2×3, respectively. More details about arrays and matrices are given in the next section. Similar to Ch, variables can be used interactively in command mode, as shown below.

```
>> x = 3
x =
     3
```

```
>> x+4
ans =
      7
>> y = x*x + 4
y =
     13
>> z = cos(0)
z =
     1
>> sqrt(x+1)
ans =
      2
```

The above example shows that variables may be used in assignment and arithmetic operations in the interactive command mode. Furthermore, variables may also be used as arguments of functions, as shown by the interactive execution of `sqrt(x+1)`. Notice the similarities between the interactive command modes in MATLAB and Ch. Both have the same functionalities of a high-end scientific calculator. Mathematical operations can be performed interactively.

An Application Example

Recall the sample application problem in Chapter 3, which is repeated below.

Problem Statement:

For the mechanical system shown in Figure 2.12, given mass $m = 5$ kilograms (kg) and coefficient of kinetic friction $\mu = 0.2$, the applied force p is constant at 20 Newtons (N). Write a program to calculate the acceleration of the system.

The solution to the above problem statement was provided as Program 3.2, which was written in C code. A similar Ch program is listed in Program 23.1. The preprocessing directive **#include** and the **main()** function are not required for the Ch program. The equivalent MATLAB program to the C and Ch programs is listed as Program 23.2. Program 23.2 is almost identical to Program 23.1 except that the Ch program requires the declaration of its variables. Note that all MATLAB programs must have the file extension **.m**.

```
/* File: accelvar.ch */
double g, mu, m, p, a;

g = 9.81;
mu = 0.2;
m = 5.0;
p = 20.0;
a = (p-mu*m*g)/m;
printf("Acceleration a = %f (m/s^2)\n", a);
```

Program 23.1: Calculating the acceleration using variables in Ch.

```
% File: accelvar.m
g = 9.81;
mu = 0.2;
m = 5.0;
p = 20.0;

a = (p-mu*m*g)/m;
fprintf('Acceleration a = %.2f (m/s^2)\n', a);
```

Program 23.2: The equivalent MATLAB program for `accelvar.ch` in Ch listed in Program 23.1.

Equivalent to `'//'` in C, the symbol `'%'` can be used to comment out a line of MATLAB code. The function **fprintf()** in MATLAB is equivalent to **printf()** and **fprintf()** in C. More details about the function **fprintf()** will be presented in section 23.6. Note that strings in MATLAB are enclosed in single quotes rather than double quotes in C. There is no distinction between a character and string in MATLAB. A character is considered a single-character string.

23.2 Arrays and Matrices

As pointed out in the previous section, all variables in MATLAB are considered as arrays of double precision floating-point complex numbers. Arrays in C are stored in row-wise, whereas arrays in MATLAB are stored in column-wise. However, an array is assigned row-wise. For example, the array `a` with dimensions of 3×4 is composed of 3 rows and 4 columns. It can be initialized as follows:

```
a = [1 2 3 4; 5 6 7 8; 9 10 11 12];
```

where the elements of the array `a` are specified row-by-row. Note that a semicolon `';'` separates each row. A column vector can be specified as

```
b = [1; 2; 3];
```

or

```
b = [1 2 3]';
```

where the prime symbol `'` denotes the transpose of that matrix, which is equivalent to using the function **transpose()** in Ch.

MATLAB also provides simplified methods for initializing special arrays and matrices. For example, the statement

```
c = 0:9
```

specifies a row vector of 10 elements, such as

```
c = [0 1 2 3 4 5 6 7 8 9];
```

A row vector in which the values of its elements range from *minval* to *maxval* with an increment of *inc* can be specified as `d = minval:inc:maxval`. For example, the compact statement

```
d = 1:0.5:4
```

is the same as the statement

```
d = [1.5 2.0 2.5 3.0 3.5 4.0];
```

An identity matrix can be declared with the function **eye(n)** in MATLAB, where n corresponds to the order of the matrix. For example, the 3×3 identity matrix

$$\mathbf{A} = \begin{bmatrix} 1 & 0 & 0 \\ 0 & 1 & 0 \\ 0 & 0 & 1 \end{bmatrix}$$

is specified as

```
>> A = eye(3)
A =
     1     0     0
     0     1     0
     0     0     1
```

which is equivalent to

```
array double A[3][3] = identitymatrix(3);
```

in Ch. To specify an $n \times n$ matrix with all its elements equal to 1, the function **ones(n)** can be used. Thus, the statement

```
>> B = ones(3)
B =
     1     1     1
     1     1     1
     1     1     1
```

is equivalent to

```
array double B[3][3] = 1;
```

in Ch. To create an $m \times n$ matrix filled with zeros, the **zeros(m, n)** function can be used. For example,

```
>> D = zeros(2, 4)
D =
     0     0     0     0
     0     0     0     0
```

is equivalent to

```
array double D[2][4];
```

in Ch. Note that the elements of arrays in Ch are automatically initialized to 0.

MATLAB uses a pair of parentheses `()` to reference an array element, while C uses square brackets `[]`. The array index starts with 1 in MATLAB, whereas the array index starts with 0 by default in C. Thus, the ith element of the array a can be referenced by `a(i)` in MATLAB and `a[i-1]` in C. The element `b(i,j)` in MATLAB is equivalent to the element `b[i-i][j-1]` in C.

The **size()** function can be used to determine the size of a matrix in MATLAB. Its syntaxes are as follows:

```
d = size(A)
[m, n] = size(A)
i = size(A, dim)
```

As an example, consider `A` to be a 2×3 matrix. The statement `d = size(A)` would have the row vector `d = [2 3]`, where the two numbers correspond to the number of rows and columns of the matrix, respectively. The second calling syntax `[m, n] = size(A)` returns the numbers of rows and columns to `m` and `n`, respectively. If a scalar is specified as a second input argument for the function **size()**, then it will return the length of the dimension specified by the scalar `dim`. For example,

```
>> A = [1 2 3; 4 5 6];
>> m = size(A, 1)               % determine the number of rows
m =
     2
```

Note that the **size()** function is similar to the **shape()** function in Ch. Table 23.6 in section 23.12 contains comparison of the function **size()** in the MATLAB **shape()** function in Ch.

An Application Example

Problem Statement:
For the mechanical system shown in Figure 2.12, given mass $m = 5$ kilograms (kg) and coefficient of kinetic friction $\mu = 0.2$, the applied force p is expressed as a function of time t in

$$p(t) = 4\sin(t - 3) + 20$$

Write a program to calculate and print the acceleration **a** when $t = 0$ to $t = 10$ seconds with a step size of 1 second.

As in section 23.1, the solution for the above problem statement was provided in Chapter 10 as Program 10.6 in C. The solution for the problem in MATLAB is listed as Program 23.3. The arrays `t` and `a` are used without initialization. Note that the structure for the **for** loop in MATLAB is slightly different from the structure in C. The line

```
for i=1:n
```

initializes the variable `i` to 1 and executes the statements within the loop while incrementing `i` by 1 until `i` is `n`. The end of the **for** loop is indicated by the keyword **end**. More information about the control flow in MATLAB will be described in section 23.5.

```
% File: accelarray.m
g = 9.81;
mu = 0.2;
m = 5.0;
t0 = 0.0;
```

Program 23.3: The equivalent MATLAB program for `accelarray.c` in C listed in Program 10.6. *(Continued)*

```
tf = 10.0;
n = 11;

for i=1:n
   t(i) = t0+(i-1)*(tf - t0)/(n-1);
   p = 4*(t(i)-3)+20;
   a(i) = (p-mu*m*g)/m;
end

fprintf('\ntime (s)  accel (m/s^2)\n');
fprintf('-----------------------\n');
for i=1:n
   fprintf('%8.4f    %8.4f\n', t(i), a(i));
end
```

Program 23.3: (*Continued*)

23.3 Complex Numbers

Complex numbers are handled automatically in MATLAB. Either `i` or `j` can be used to specify the imaginary part of a complex number. For example, `z = 3 - 4i` initializes the variable `z` to equal the complex number $3-i4$. Notice that unlike `2 - 3*I` in C, MATLAB does not require the multiplication symbol `'*'` between i and the imaginary scalar number 4. However, the use of the multiplication symbol is also allowed in MATLAB, provided that `i` has not been associated as a variable. For example,

```
>> z = 3 - 4*i
z =
   3.0000 - 4.0000i           % complex number
>> i = 4;
>> z = 3 - 4*i
z =
  -11.0000                    % real number
```

The magnitude and phase angle of a complex number can be determined by the functions **abs()** and **angle()** in MATLAB, respectively. Real and imaginary parts of a complex number or an array of complex numbers can be obtained by the functions **real()** and **imag()**, respectively. The functions **abs()**, **real()**, and **imag()** are the same in both Ch and MATLAB. The function **angle()** is equivalent to the function **carg()** in C or **arg()** in Ch. For example,

```
>> z = 3 - 4i
z =
   3.0000 - 4.0000i
>> z + z
ans =
   6.0000 - 8.0000i
```

```
>> abs(z)
ans =
     5
>> angle(z)
ans =
   -0.9273
>> real(z)
ans =
     3
>> imag(z)
ans =
    -4
```

23.4 Operators

Operators used in MATLAB and Ch are compared in this section. Table 23.1 lists the symbols along with their meanings used in the comparison for operators in Table 23.2. For example, according to Table 23.1, the symbol `'A'` in Table 23.2 stands for an array of real or complex type. Some of the operators listed in

Table 23.1 Symbols used for comparison of MATLAB and Ch.

Symbol	Data type
x	Scalar or computational array of real or complex type
A, Ai, B, Bi	Computational arrays of real or complex type
Av, Avi, Bv, Bvi	One-dimensional computational arrays of real or complex type
R, Ri	Computational arrays of real type
Rv, Rvi	One-dimensional computational arrays of real type
I, Ii	Computational arrays of integral type
Iv, Ivi	One-dimensional computational arrays of integral type
C, Ci	Arrays of char type
Z, Zi	Computational arrays of complex type
Zv, Zvi	One-dimensional computational arrays of complex type
s	Scalar of real or complex type
z	Scalar complex type
r	Scalar real type
f	Scalar floating-point type
i	Scalar integral type
p	Pointer type
str	A string

Table 23.2 Comparison of operators in MATLAB and Ch.

<table>
<tr><th>Operator</th><th>MATLAB</th><th>Ch</th></tr>
<tr><td>~</td><td>~A
~s</td><td>!A
!s</td></tr>
<tr><td>+</td><td>+A
+s</td><td>+A
+s</td></tr>
<tr><td>−</td><td>−A
−s</td><td>−A
−s</td></tr>
<tr><td><</td><td>A<B
A<s
s<A</td><td>A<B
A<r
r<A</td></tr>
<tr><td>~=</td><td>A~=B
A~=s
s~=A</td><td>A! =B
A! =s
s! =A</td></tr>
<tr><td>|</td><td>A|B
A|s
s|A</td><td>A||B
A||r
r||A</td></tr>
<tr><td>&</td><td>A& B
A& s
s& A</td><td>A&& B
A&& s
s&& A</td></tr>
<tr><td>+</td><td>A+B
A+s
s+A
A= A+B
A= A+B</td><td>A+B
A+s
s+A
A= A+B
A+= B</td></tr>
<tr><td>−</td><td>A−B
A−s
s−A
A= A−B</td><td>A−B
A−s
s−A
A−= B</td></tr>
<tr><td>*</td><td>A*B
A*s
s*A
A= A*B
A= A*B</td><td>A*B
A*s
s*A
A= A*B
A*= B</td></tr>
<tr><td>/</td><td>A= A1/B1
A/s
A= A/s
A= A/s</td><td>A=A1*inverse(B1)
A/s
A= A/s
A/= s</td></tr>
<tr><td>^</td><td>i1^i2
s1^s2
I^i
A^i</td><td>pow(i1,i2)
pow(s1,s2)
pow(I,i)
pow(A,i)</td></tr>
</table>

(Continued)

Table 23.2 (*Continued*)

Operator	MATLAB	Ch
\	*A=A1\B1*	*A=***inverse**(*A1*)∗*B1*
\	*Av=A\Bv'*	**linsolve**(*Av,A,Bv*) *Av=***inverse**(*A*)∗*Bv* **llsqsolve**(*Bv, A,Av*)
'	*A'*	**transpose**(*A*)
'	*Z'*	**transpose**(**conj**(*Z*))
.*	*A.*B*	*A.*B*
./	*A./B*	*A./B*
./	*s./B*	*s./A*
.^	*A.^B*	**pow**(*A, B*)
.^	*A.^s*	**pow**(*A,* (**array double** [n])*s*)
.^	*s.^A*	**pow**((**array double** [n])*s, A*)
.\	*A.\B*	(not valid)

Table 23.2 correspond to relational, logical and arithmetic operators. There are also differences in the syntaxes of some of the operators. For example, the NOT operator is indicated by `'~'` in MATLAB and `'!'` in C. Also, the OR and AND operators are specified by `'|'` and `'&'`, instead of `'||'` and `'&&'` in C, respectively. MATLAB has an exponential operator `'^'`, such as `x^2` for x^2.

Matrix operations in MATLAB and Ch differ slightly as well. For example, the matrix expression $A = A_1 B_1^{-1}$ is specified in MATLAB as `A = A1/B1` and `A = A1*inverse(B1)` in Ch. At this point, it should be noted that MATLAB has two operators to specify the inverse of a matrix: `'/'`, as previously mentioned, and `'\'`. The `'\'` operator, as in `A = A1\B1`, indicates the matrix operation $A = A_1^{-1} B_1$. In this case, the matrix A_1 is inverted. In Ch, the matrix operation $A = A_1^{-1} B_1$ is simply `A1 = inverse(A1)*B1`, which better matches the mathematical representation. To obtain the transpose of a matrix, the MATLAB operator `'` can be used. For example, `A'` is mathematically equivalent to A^T. The function **transpose()** in Ch has the same functionality as `'` in MATLAB. To perform element-wise multiplication and division, the operators `'.*'` and `'./'` can be used in both MATLAB and Ch, respectively. The operation `A = A1./B1` is equivalent to `A = B1.\A1`. The `'.^'` operator performs element-wise exponentiation and is similar to the regular exponential operator `'^'`. However, the `'^'` operator is defined only for matrix exponentiation of square matrices, whereas the element-wise matrix exponentiation operator `'.^'` is valid for variable dimensional matrices.

23.5 Control Flow

Table 23.3 lists the syntaxes for the various control flows in both MATLAB and C. The most noticeable difference between the types of syntax is the use of brackets `{}` in C to indicate the beginning and end of a control flow rather than the keyword **end** to specify the end of a control flow in MATLAB. For the beginning

Table 23.3 Control-flow comparisons between MATLAB and C.

Description	MATLAB	C

for loop	`for i=n1:n2:n3`
	`statements`
	`end`
	
	`for i=n1:n3`
	`statements`
	`end`
		`for (i=n1; i<=n3; i+=n2) {`
		`statements`
		`}`
		
		`for(i=n1; i<=n3; i++) {`
		`statements`
		`}`

while loop	`while expr`
	`statements`
	`end`
		`while(expr) {`
		`statements`
		`}`

if	`if expr`
	`statements`
	`end`
		`if (expr) {`
		`statements`
		`}`

if-else	`if expr1`
	`statements1`
	
	`else`
	`statements2`
	`end`
		`if (expr1) {`
		`statements1`
		`}`
		`else {`
		`statements2`
		`}`

if-else if-else	`if expr1`
	`statements1`
	
	`elseif expr2`
	`statements2`
	
	`else`
	`statements3`
	`end`
		`if (expr1) {`
		`statements1`
		`}`
		`else if(expr2) {`
		`statements2`
		`}`
		`else {`
		`statements3`
		`}`

of the **for** loop in MATLAB,

```
for i=n1:n2:n3
```

the variable `i` is initialized to the value of `n1`, whereas `n2` and `n3` correspond to the step size and terminating condition, respectively. Thus for every pass through the loop, `i` is incremented by `n2` and then checked to see whether it is equal to or greater than `n3`; if this is so, the **for** loop terminates. For the notion of

```
for i = n1:n3
```

the default increment step size of 1 is used. A **break** statement inside a **for** loop or **while** loop will exit the innermost loop. It behaves the same in both MATLAB and C. Porting a **for** loop in MATLAB to a **for** loop in C is very simple. Porting a **for** loop in C to a **for** loop in MATLAB might not be as straightforward, however.

For example, the **for** loop below in C

```
for(i=n1; i<n3 && i<j; i++) {
   statements
}
```

might be translated into MATLAB code as follows:

```
for i=n1:n3-1
    if(i<j)
       statements
    end
end
```

The other control flow sequences for MATLAB in Table 23.3 are relatively identical to those in C and are self-explanatory.

An Application Example

Recall the C program `accelmpts.c` listed as Program 5.15 in Chapter 5, which uses a **for** loop and a conditional **if-else** statement to solve the problem statement below.

Problem Statement:
For the mechanical system shown in Figure 2.12, given mass $m = 5$ kilograms (kg) and coefficient of kinetic friction $\mu = 0.2$, the applied force p is expressed as a function of time t in

$$p(t) = \begin{cases} 4(t+2) & \text{if} \quad t \geq 3 \\ 20 & \text{if} \quad t < 3 \end{cases}$$

Write a program to calculate and print the resulting accelerations of the rigid body from $t = 0$ to 10 seconds with a step size of 1 second.

The equivalent MATLAB program is listed in Program 23.4. Notice that the **for** loop in this program specifies only two conditions: the initialization condition `i=0` and the terminating condition (when `i=10`). The variable `i` is automatically incremented by 1 for each repetition of the loop.

```
% File: accelmpts.m
g = 9.81;
mu = 0.2;
m = 5.0;
step = 1;
t0 = 0.0;
tf = 10.0;
n = (tf - t0)/step + 1;
```

Program 23.4: The equivalent MATLAB program for `accelmpts.c` in C listed in Program 5.15. *(Continued)*

```
fprintf('\ntime (s)   accel (m/s^2)\n');
fprintf('\n-----------------------\n');
for i=0:n-1   % for i = 0:1:n-1
   t = t0 + i*step;
   if t<=3
      p = 20;
   else
      p = 4*(t+2);
   end

   a = (p-mu*m*g)/m;
   fprintf('%3.0f        %8.4f\n', t, a);
end
```

Program 23.4: (*Continued*)

23.6 Formatted Input and Output

23.6.1 The function input()

The function **input()** can be used to prompt the user for an input and then record that input. For example,

```
>> age = input('Enter your age: ')
Enter your age: 15
>> age
age =
     15
```

In this example, the user is prompted to enter his or her age, which is then recorded into the variable `age`. The statement

```
age = input('Enter your age: ')
```

is equivalent to

```
age = getnum("Enter your age: ");
```

in Ch. However, the function **input()** can also accept a string. It has capabilities of the function **scanf()** in C.

23.6.2 Format Specifiers

Similar to Ch, by default, MATLAB will display an integer if the output value is an integer. If the output is a real number, then the output is displayed with four digits following the decimal point. If the significant digits in the result of some calculation is outside the default range, then MATLAB will display the result in scientific notation.

Furthermore, MATLAB also have functions such as **sprintf()** and **fprintf()** for printing formatted output. These functions are similar to their C equivalents. The function **sprintf()** prints formatted data to a string `s` with the following syntax:

```
s = sprintf('format', A)
```

The function **fprintf()**, with the syntaxes shown below

```
fprintf(fid, 'format', A)
fprintf('format', A)
```

prints formatted data to a file specified by `fid` described in section 23.7 or to the terminal screen, respectively. Like their C-equivalent functions, the output can be formatted with the conversion specifiers `'%d'`, `'%i'`, `'%o'`, `'%u'`, `'%x'`, `'%X'`, `'%f'`, `'%e'`, `'%E'`, `'%g'`, `'%G'`, `'%c'`, and `'%s'`. The field width, precision, etc. for the format control string `'format'` of the function **fprintf()** in MATLAB is similar to those in C. Refer to Chapter 9 for more information concerning formatted output with the functions **sprintf()** and **fprintf()**.

The values of all elements of an array can be displayed by function **display()**. The function displays both the variable name or expression and its contents. A text string can also be displayed by this function. The function **disp()** is the same as the function **display()**, except that **disp()** displays only the values of its argument. For example,

```
>> A = [1 2; 3 4];
>> display(A)
A =
     1     2
     3     4
>> disp(A)
     1     2
     3     4
```

The function **disp()** in MATLAB is equivalent to the function **printf()** in Ch. It can be used to print out the values of its arguments of different data types using the default format specifiers in the standard output presented in Table 3.5 in Chapter 3.

A semicolon `';'` terminates a statement in C. In MATLAB, the result of the operation of a statement without a semicolon at the end is printed out using the function **display()**. The presence of a semicolon suppresses the display of the result of the statement. This feature can be useful for debugging. You may just simply remove a semicolon at the end of a statement to print out the value of a variable or expression. For example,

```
>> i = 4+5;                % semicolon present
>> i
i =
     9
```

whereas

```
>> i = 4+5                 % semicolon missing
i =
     9
```

An Application Example

Consider the following problem statement, which was solved by Program 3.7 in Chapter 3.

Problem Statement:
For the mechanical system shown in Figure 2.12 given mass $m = 5$ kilograms (kg) and coefficient of kinetic friction $\mu = 0.2$, the applied force p is expressed as a function of time t in

$$p(t) = 4\sin(t - 3) + 20$$

Write a program to calculate the acceleration **a** according to the input values of `m`, μ, and `t`.

Program 3.7 used inputs for `m`, `mu`, and `t` to calculate the acceleration of the described system. The MATLAB equivalent of Program 3.7 is listed in Program 23.5. It uses the function **input()** to prompt the user to input values for the mass, coefficient of friction, and time, which are stored in the appropriate variables. The function **fprintf()** is used to display the mass, μ, and time values that the user typed in, as well as to print out the calculated acceleration value. Creating the function `force()` will be described in section 23.9.

```
% File: accelio.m
g = 9.81;

fprintf('***** Acceleration Calculator *****\n\n');
m = input('Please enter value for mass in kilogram: ');
fprintf('mass is %f (kg)\n\n', m);
mu = input('Please enter value for friction coefficient: ');
fprintf('friction coefficient is %f\n\n', mu);
t = input('Please enter value for time in second: ');
fprintf('time is %f (s)\n\n', t);
p = 4*(t-3)+20;
a = (p-mu*m*g)/m;
fprintf('Acceleration a = %f (m/s^2)\n', a);
```

Program 23.5: The equivalent MATLAB program for `accelio.c` in C listed in Program 3.7.

23.7 File Processing

The set of functions for file processing in MATLAB is similar to that for C. Table 23.4 lists some of the file input/output functions available in MATLAB along with a brief description and a syntax example. For the function **fopen()**, `permission` corresponds to either `'r'`, `'r+'`, `'w'`, `'w+'`, `'a'`, and `a+'`, where these mode specifiers are similar to the ones in C. The specifier `'r'` is for reading, `'r+'` is for reading and writing, etc. The `format` argument for the functions **fscanf()** and **fprintf()** specifies the format of the data to be read from or written to the file, respectively.

Table 23.4 File-processing functions in MATLAB.

Function	Description	Syntax
fopen()	Opens a file.	`fid = fopen('filename', 'permission')`
fclose()	Closes a file.	`status = fclose(fid)`
fread()	Reads binary data from a file.	`A = fread(fid)`
fwrite()	Writes binary data from a MATLAB matrix to a file.	`count = fwrite(fid, A, 'precision')`
fscanf()	Reads formatted data from a file.	`A = fscanf(fid, 'format', num)`
fprintf()	Writes formatted data to a file.	`count = fprintf(fid, 'format', A)`

An Application Example

The problem statement below, originally from Chapter 14, was about file processing in C. The C solution to this problem is listed in Programs 14.3 and 14.5. This problem can also be solved in MATLAB, and Programs 23.6 and 23.7 list the MATLAB equivalent of Programs 14.3 and 14.5, respectively.

```
% File: accelo.m
g = 9.81;
N = 11;
mu = 0.2;
m = 5.0;
step = 1;
t0 = 0.0;
tf = 10.0;
n = (tf - t0)/step + 1;

fid = fopen('accel.txt', 'w');
if fid == -1
   fprintf('Error: cannot open accel.txt for writing\n');
end

for i=0:n-1  % for i = 0:1:n-1
   t = t0 + i*step;
   p = 4*(t-3)+20;
   a = (p-mu*m*g)/m;
   fprintf(fid, '%f\n', a);
end
fclose(fid);
fprintf('Done!  Finished writing data to file accel.txt.\n');
```

Program 23.6: The equivalent MATLAB program for `accelo.c` in C listed in Program 14.3.

```
% File: acceli.m
fid = fopen('accel.txt', 'r');
if fid == -1
  fprintf('Error: cannot open accel.txt for reading\n');
end

a = fscanf(fid, '%f', 1);
while(~feof(fid))
    fprintf('%f\n', a);
    a = fscanf(fid, '%f', 1);
end
fclose(fid);
```

Program 23.7: The equivalent MATLAB program for `acceli.c` in C listed in Program 14.5.

Problem Statement:
For the mechanical system shown in Figure 2.12, given mass $m = 5$ kilograms (kg) and coefficient of kinetic friction $\mu = 0.2$, the applied force p is expressed as a function of time t in

$$p(t) = 4\sin(t - 3) + 20$$

Write a program to calculate the accelerations a during $t = 0$ to $t = 10$ with time step 1 and save the accelerations into a text file, named `accel.txt`. Then write another program to read the accelerations from the file `accel.txt` and print them out.

In Program 23.6, the statements

```
fid = fopen('accel.txt', 'w');
if fid == -1
  fprintf('Error: cannot open accel.txt for writing\n');
end
```

create and open the file `accel.txt` for writing. However, if there is a problem in the creation or opening of the file (i.e., `fid == -1`), an error message will be displayed. This is equivalent to the C code below.

```
fp = fopen("accel.txt", "w");
if(fp == NULL) {
  printf("Error: cannot open accel.txt for writing\n");
}
```

The file `accel.txt` is closed after the calculated acceleration values for $t = 1$ to $t = 10$ seconds have been written into the file.

Program 23.7 uses the **fopen()** function with the permission `'r'` to read the contents of file `accel.txt`. Again, if there is a problem with opening the file, an error message stored in the string `message` will be displayed. Like the corresponding C program, the data in the file is read into the variable a by the **fscanf()** function, one at a time inside a **while** loop, and then printed out by the function **fprintf()**. The function **feof()** returns a nonzero value when the end of file (EOF) is reached. The format `'%f'` for the functions **fscanf()** and **fprintf()** indicates that the data to be read is in a floating-point value. The third argument of the function **fscanf()** indicates that only one floating-point number is read.

23.7.1 Reading and Writing Whole Arrays in a File

The uniform data in a file can also be read from a file and saved into an array, as shown in Program 23.8. The variable a in this program is a column vector, and its size is determined by the number of values in the file accel.txt. Because there are 11 acceleration values in 11 lines in the file, the dimension of the array a is 11 × 1. Function **fscanf()** and **fprintf()** can be used to read and print as entire array, respectively. The output of Program 23.8 is shown as follows:

```
a = -0.36 0.43 1.24 2.04 2.84 3.64 4.44 5.24 6.04 6.84 7.64
```

```
% File: acceli2.m
% read and print all data once
fid = fopen('accel.txt', 'r');

if fid == -1
    fprintf('Error: cannot open accel.txt for reading\n');
end

a = fscanf(fid, '%f');
fprintf('a = %.2f ', a);
fclose(fid);
```

Program 23.8: Reading data from a file and storing them into an array.

23.8 Two- and Three-Dimensional Plotting

Two- and three-dimensional plotting can be accomplished by the functions **plot()** and **plot3()** in MATLAB, equivalent to the functions **plotxy()** and **plotxyz()** in Ch, respectively. The function **plot()** can be invoked in one of the following syntaxes.

```
plot(y);
plot(x, y);
plot(x, y, 'linetype');
plot(x1, y1, 'linetype1', x2, y2, linetype2', ...);
```

The first syntax will plot the contents of array y with respect to their indices. The second syntax will plot the vector x versus the vector y. The argument linetype, in the third syntax of **plot()**, allows the user to specify the line type of the curve. The fourth syntax is an example to show how multiple curves can be placed into one plot. The various line types, plot symbols, and colors available in MATLAB are shown in Table 23.5. For example, plot(x, y, 'r*') plots a red star at each data point of x and y.

Note that as in Ch, the title, x-label, and y-label are specified with functions **title()**, **xlabel()**, and **ylabel()**, respectively.

To generate multiple plots in a single program, the command **pause** can be used to separate each plot. However, to have multiple curves in a single plot, the command **hold** can be used to hold the previously plotted curve in the plotting window. The function **legend()** can be used to add legends for each curve.

For three-dimensional plotting, the function **plot3()** is analogous to the function **plot()**. Three values are now required in order to make a point of a curve in three dimensions. The line types, symbols, and colors available for the **plot()** function are also available for the **plot3()** function.

Table 23.5 Line types, symbols, and colors for plotting.

Symbol	Line types	Symbol	Colors
.	Point	y	Yellow
o	Circle	m	Magenta
x	X-mark	c	Cyan
+	Plus	r	Red
*	Star	g	Green
-	Solid line	b	Blue
:	Dotted line	w	White
-.	Dash-dot line	k	Black
--	Dashed line		

An Application Example

For a plotting example, consider the problem statement below.

Problem Statement:
For the mechanical system shown in Figure 2.12, given mass $m = 5$ kilograms (kg) and coefficient of kinetic friction $\mu = 0.2$, the applied force p is expressed as a function of time t in

$$p(t) = 4\sin(t - 3) + 20$$

Write a program to calculate the accelerations **a** for $t = 0$ to $t = 10$ seconds with 11 and 100 data points. Plot the results.

Although this problem is solved in Chapter 10 with Program 10.18, with the output plot shown in Figure 6.4 in Chapter 6, Program 23.9 provides the solution in a MATLAB script file. The plot is displayed

```
% File: acceldata2DCurve.m
g = 9.81;
N1 = 11;
N2 = 100;
mu = 0.2;
m = 5.0;
t0 = 0.0;
tf = 10.0;

for i=1:N1
    t1(i) = t0+(i-1)*(tf - t0)/(N1-1);
    p1 = 4*sin(t1(i)-3)+20;
    a1(i) = (p1-mu*m*g)/m;
end

for i=1:N2
    t2(i) = t0+(i-1)*(tf - t0)/(N2-1);
```

Program 23.9: The equivalent MATLAB program for `acceldata2DCurve.cpp` in C listed in Program 10.18. *(Continued)*

```
    p2 = 4*sin(t2(i)-3)+20;
    a2(i) = (p2-mu*m*g)/m;
end

plot(t1, a1);
xlabel('time (s)');
ylabel('accel (m/s^2)');
title('Acceleration Plot');
hold;                               % one plot with two curves
plot(t2, a2, '.');                  % using points for the 2nd curve
legend('11 points', '100 points'); % add legends
```

Program 23.9: (*Continued*)

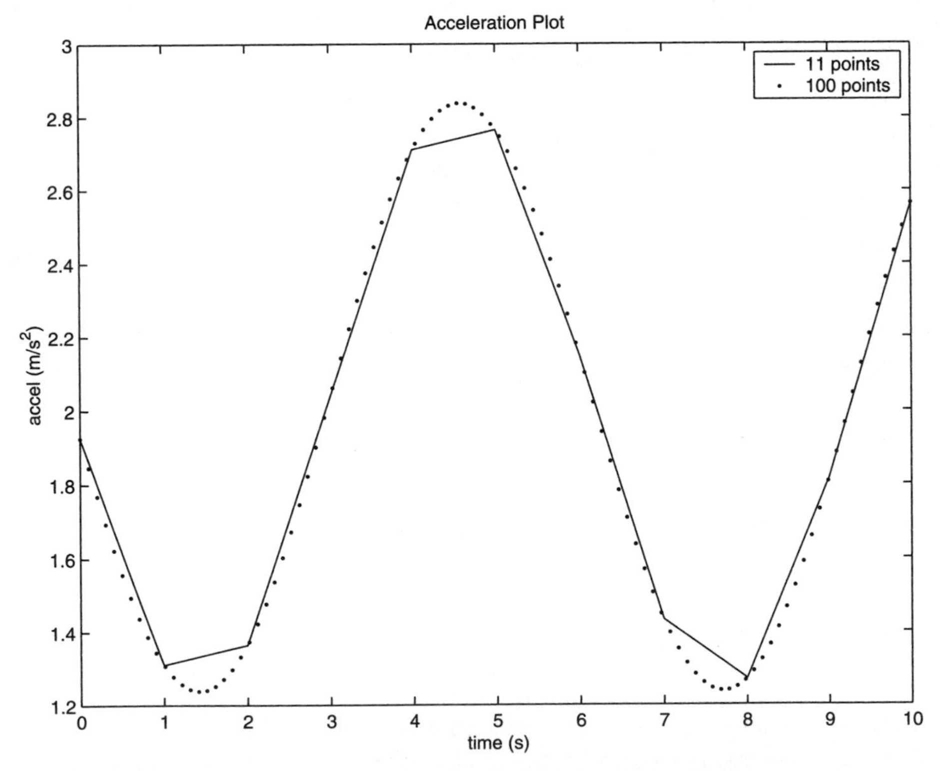

Figure 23.1 The plot generated by Program 23.9.

in Figure 23.1. By default, each curve is plotted in a solid line. The line type for the second curve is changed to the point. The program uses the command **hold** to place multiple curves in a single plot. Alternatively, the code for plotting at the end of Program 10.18 can be replaced by calling the function **plot()** with multiple data sets as follows:

```
% plot two curves, using points for the 2nd curve
plot(t1, a1, t2, a2, '.');
```

```
xlabel('time (s)');
ylabel('accel (m/s^2)');
title('Acceleration Plot');
legend('11 points', '100 points'); % add legends
```

23.9 Functions and M-Files

MATLAB script files, or *M-files*, are similar to program files in C. All the previous example programs presented in this chapter are M-files for analyzing the acceleration of a dynamic system.

Like C, MATLAB allows users to create user-defined functions. However, functions cannot be defined within a script file. Instead, MATLAB functions are defined in their own separate files with the file extension `.m`, just like a script file. The first line of a function M-file, also known as the *function-declaration line*, begins with the keyword **function** followed by the calling syntax for the function. For example, the function `func1()` with a return value and one argument, defined in the function file `func.m`, can be declared as follows:

```
function out = func1(in)
```

The input and output variables identified in the function-declaration line are local variables of the function. Note that the function name should be identical to the function file name. The function `func1()` can be called by

```
retval = func1(arg);
```

A function without a return value can be declared by

```
function func2(in)
```

and called by

```
func2(arg);
```

The syntax for a function with multiple return values is shown as follows:

```
function [out1, out2] = func3(in1, in2)
```

The function `func3()` can be called by

```
[retval1, retval2] = func3(arg1, arg2);
```

Typically, comment lines are added after the function-declaration line to explain the purpose of the function as well as some of the possible calling syntaxes. Following the comment lines are the MATLAB statements that compose the body. A function M-file terminates after the last statement in the file is executed or whenever a **return** statement is encountered.

Function M-files can contain calls to script files and other function M-files. Functions in addition to the primary function may be included within a function M-file. These *subfunctions* may be called by the primary function or another subfunction. Subfunction definitions shall be appended to the end of the primary function definition.

In Ch, function files are searched based on the directories specified in the system variable **_fpath**. Commands or programs are based on the system variable **_path**. In MATLAB, the default search path for script and function M-files are set by the script file `pathdef.m`. Additional search paths may be included in a variety of ways. For example, the `Path Browser` can be used to include another directory into the MATLAB search path. This tool can be found under the `File->Set Path` menu.

Additionally, the search path can be edited by the functions **path()**, **addpath()**, and **rmpath()** in the MATLAB command window. Typing **path** alone prints out the current setting of the MATLAB search path. This is similar to entering the keyword **matlabpath** at the command prompt. If one or two strings are used as arguments in the function **path()**, such as

```
path(p);                % p is a string
path(p1, p2);           % p1 and p2 are strings
```

the search path is changed into either the string `p` or the concatenation of the two path strings `p1` and `p2`, respectively. To add a new directory path to the MATLAB search path, the function **addpath()** can be used. For example,

```
addpath('path');
```

prepends the directory specified by the string `path` to the search path. In contrast, the statement

```
rmpath('path');
```

removes the `path` directory from the MATLAB search path.

Application Examples

Calculating the Acceleration of a Moving Body

Problem Statement:
For the mechanical system shown in Figure 2.12, given mass $m = 5$ kilograms (kg) and coefficient of kinetic friction $\mu = 0.2$, the applied force p is expressed as a function of time t in

$$p(t) = 4(t - 3) + 20$$

Write a program to calculate the acceleration **a** when $t = 2$ seconds.

1. Use a function to calculate the applied force.
2. Use a function to calculate the acceleration with a subfunction for force.

The first part in the above problem statement was previously solved by Program 6.3 in Chapter 6. The program defines a `force()` function to calculate the external force acting on the system and then uses this value to determine the acceleration of the dynamic system. An equivalent set of files for solving the above problem are Programs 6.21 and 6.20, which are a Ch application program and a function file, respectively. Program 6.20 is the function file that contains the definition of the function `force()`, which Program 6.21 uses to calculate the external force prior to determining the acceleration of the system described in the problem statement. The MATLAB equivalent of Programs 6.21 and 6.20 are listed as Programs 23.10 and 23.11, respectively. Program 23.10 is the MATLAB script file that calls the `force()` function defined in the function M-file `force.m`.

```
% File: accelfun.m
mu = 0.2;
m = 5.0;
g = 9.81;
t = 2.0;

p = force(t);
a = (p-mu*m*g)/m;
fprintf('Acceleration = %f (m/s^2)\n', a);
```

Program 23.10: The equivalent MATLAB program for `accelfun.c` in C listed in Program 6.3.

```
% File: force.m
function p = force(t)
p = 4*(t-3)+20;
```

Program 23.11: The function file for the function `force()` used by the program `accelfun.m`.

```
% File: accel.m
function a = accel(t, mu, m)

g = 9.81;
p = local_force(t);
a = (p - mu*m*g)/m;

function p = local_force(t)

p = 4*(t-3) + 20;
```

Program 23.12: The function file for the function `accel()` with a subfunction.

```
% File: accel_subfunc.m
mu = 0.2;
m = 5.0;
t = 2.0;

a = accel(t, mu, m)
```

Program 23.13: Using the function `accel()` with the subfunction `local_force()`.

Programs 23.12 and 23.13 are the solutions to the second part of the problem statement above. Program 23.13 contains the primary function `accel()` to calculate the acceleration of the dynamic system and the subfunction `force()`, which is used by the function `accel()` to calculate the external force exerted on the system. Programs 23.12 and 23.13 are equivalent to Program 6.4.

Calculating the Area and Circumference of a Metal Disc

Program 11.5 in Chapter 11 calculates the area and circumference of a metal disc with the radius of 3.5 meters. The results are passed back to the calling function using pointers. The same problem is solved in Ch and C++. The function `discref()` in Program 18.6 in Chapter 18 passes the calculated area and circumference of a metal disc to the calling function by reference.

For the comparison, the same problem is solved in MATLAB here using a function to calculate both area and circumference. Program 23.14 defines the function `disc()` with two return variables `area` and `circum`. The mathematical constant π can be represented using the variable **pi** in MATLAB as shown in Program 23.14. Program 23.15 calls the function `disc()` defined in Program 23.14 to calculate the area and circumference of a metal disc with the radius of 3.5 meters. The output from Program 23.15 is shown in Figure 11.11 in Chapter 11. It is the same as those from Program 11.5 in Chapter 11 and Program 18.6 in Chapter 18.

```
% File: disc.m
function [area, circum] = disc(radius)

area = pi*radius*radius;
circum = 2*pi*radius;
```

Program 23.14 The function file for the function `disc()` with two return values.

```
% File: discfun.m

radius = 3.5;
[area, circum] = disc(radius);
fprintf('\narea = %f (m^2)\n', area);
fprintf('circumference = %f (m)\n', circum);
```

Program 23.15 Using the function `disc()` with two return values.

23.10 Comparison Between MATLAB Arrays and Ch Computational Arrays

MATLAB arrays and computational arrays in Ch have very similar objects. As previously illustrated, both arrays are first-class objects and can be used to perform matrix operations. MATLAB arrays and Ch computational arrays can use the **linspace()** and **lindata()** functions, respectively, to quickly set values to the elements. The statements

```
array double a[100];
lindata(0, 10, a); // or lindata(0, 10, a, 100);
```

in Ch, or

```
a = linspace(0, 10, 100);
```

in MATLAB, sets the element values of the array a from 0 to 10 with an increment step size of 0.1. Like computational arrays in Ch, arrays in MATLAB can be passed as arguments to functions. In addition, MATLAB functions can return arrays, as illustrated in an application example presented later in this section.

If $\mathbf{A}_1$ and $\mathbf{A}_2$ are two arrays, in general, the matrix expression $\mathbf{A}_1/\mathbf{A}_2$ is undefined mathematically in linear algebra. However, $\mathbf{A}_1/\mathbf{A}_2$ in MATLAB is defined as the product of $\mathbf{A}_1$ and the inverse matrix of $\mathbf{A}_2$; that is, $\mathbf{A}_1/\mathbf{A}_2$ is the same as $\mathbf{A}_1\mathbf{A}_2^{-1}$. This kind of operator overloading for division is quite confusing for students of linear algebra. This may lead students to use the expression $\mathbf{x} = \mathbf{b}/\mathbf{A}$ as a solution to the system of linear equations $\mathbf{Ax} = \mathbf{b}$. To avoid such a mistake, one of the guiding principles in designing Ch is to follow the mathematical conventions. For example, the element-wise division of two matrices $\mathbf{A}_1$ and $\mathbf{A}_2$ with the same rank is programmed in Ch as `A1./A2`; and the product of $\mathbf{A}_1$ and the inverse of matrix $\mathbf{A}_2$ are written as `A1*inverse(A2)`. The expression $s = \mathbf{v}^T\mathbf{Av}$ is translated into `transpose(v)*A*v` in Ch.

An Application Example

Force and Acceleration of a Moving Body

The four problems for analysis of the force and acceleration of a moving body described in section 21.11 are solved by Programs 21.10 to 21.13 in Chapter 21. These problems are solved here using MATLAB. The MATLAB equivalent of Program 21.10 is Program 23.16. It uses arrays to store values for time, force, and acceleration. The command **pause** is used to create two separate plots. The user needs to hit the return key on the keyboard to display the second plot.

```
% File: accelcharray.m
g = 9.81;
N = 100;
mu = 0.2;
m = 5.0;
t0 = 0.0;
tf = 10.0;

t = linspace(t0, tf, N);
p = 4*(sin(t)-3)+20;
a = (p-mu*m*g)/m;
plot(t, a);
xlabel('time (s)');
ylabel('accel (m/s^2)');
title('Acceleration Plot');
pause;  % pause for two separate plots, hold for one plot with two curves

p = 4*(t.*t-3)+20;
a = (p-mu*m*g)/m;
plot(t, a);
```

Program 23.16: The equivalent MATLAB program for `accelcharray.ch` in Ch listed in Program 21.10.

Program 23.17, with the function M-file listed in Program 23.18, is the MATLAB equivalent of Program 21.11 using variable-length computational arrays in Ch. The use of assumed-shape computational arrays in Ch allows the user to pass arrays to functions without explicitly specifying the array size. The function `accelvla()` has no return value. The grids on the plot are created by the command **grid**.

In MATLAB, Programs 23.19 and 23.20 have the same functionality as Program 21.12 in Ch. Programs 23.21 and 23.22 can be used to fulfill the last requirement of the problem statement above in MATLAB. Program 23.22 is a function M-file used to calculate the acceleration values from time $t = 0$ to $t = 10$ seconds and to return them as a one-dimensional array.

Programs 23.21 and 23.22 are equivalent to Program 21.13. The function `accelreturnarray()` returns an array.

```
% File: accelcharrayvla.m
N1 = 11;
N2 = 100;

a1 = linspace(0, 0, N1);
a2 = linspace(0, 0, N2);

accelvla(N1, a1);
pause;
accelvla(N2, a2);
```

Program 23.17: The equivalent MATLAB program for `accelcharrayvla.ch` in Ch listed in Program 21.11.

```
% File: accelvla.m
function accelvla(n, a)

g = 9.81;
mu = 0.2;
m = 5.0;
t0 = 0.0;
tf = 10.0;

t = linspace(t0, tf, N);
p = 4*(sin(t-3))+20;
a = (p-mu*m*g)/m;

plot(t, a);
title('Acceleration Plot');
xlabel('time (s)');
ylabel('accel (m/s^2)');
grid;
```

Program 23.18: The function file used by the program `accelcharrayvla.m`.

```
% File: accelcharrayassumeshape.m
N1 = 11;
N2 = 100;

a1 = linspace(0, 0, N1); % a1 is 1xN1 matrix
a2 = linspace(0, 0, N2); % a2 is 1xN2 matrix

accelassumeshape(a1);
pause;
accelassumeshape(a2);
```

Program 23.19: The equivalent MATLAB program for `accelcharrayassumeshape.ch` in Ch listed in Program 21.12.

```
% File: accelassumeshape.m
function accelassumeshape(a)

g = 9.81;
mu = 0.2;
m = 5.0;
t0 = 0.0;
tf = 10.0;
n = size(a, 2);  % obtain the number of columns for a

t = linspace(t0, tf, n);
p = 4*(sin(t-3))+20;
a = (p-mu*m*g)/m;

plot(t, a);
title('Acceleration Plot');
xlabel('time (s)');
ylabel('accel (m/s^2)');
grid;
```

Program 23.20: The function file used by the program `accelcharrayassumeshape.m`.

```
% File: accelcharrayreturn.m
N1 = 11;
N2 = 100;
t0 = 0.0;
tf = 10.0;

t1 = linspace(t0, tf, N1);
a1 = accelreturnarray(t1);
```

Program 23.21: The equivalent MATLAB program for `accelcharrayreturn.ch` in Ch listed in Program 21.13. (*Continued*)

```
plot(t1, a1);
title('Acceleration Plot');
xlabel('time (s)');
ylabel('accel (m/s^2)');
grid;

pause;

t2 = linspace(t0, tf, N2);
a2 = accelreturnarray(t2);
plot(t2, a2);
title('Acceleration Plot');
xlabel('time (s)');
ylabel('accel (m/s^2)');
grid;
```

Program 23.21: (*Continued*)

```
% File: accelreturnarray.m
function a = accelreturnarray(t)

g = 9.81;
mu = 0.2;
m = 5.0;

p = 4*(sin(t-3))+20;
a = (p-mu*m*g)/m;
```

Program 23.22: The function file used by the program `accelcharrayreturn.m`.

23.11 ‡Advanced Numerical Analysis Functions

Aside from the typical mathematical functions such as the **sqrt()** function for calculating the square root of a number, many advanced numerical analysis functions are available. These advanced numerical functions in MATLAB are similar to those in Ch. In this section, functions for solving linear equations, nonlinear systems of equations, roots of polynomials, the multiplication of polynomials, differential equations, and eigenvalues and eigenvectors will be described. The functions **fzero()**, **fsolve()**, **roots()**, **conv()**, **inverse()**, **eigen()**, and **oderk()** in Ch, described in Chapter 22, are similar to the functions **fzero()**, **fsolve()**, **roots()**, **conv()**, **inv()**, **eig()**, and **ode23()** or **ode45()**, in MATLAB, respectively. For comparison, the same problems solved by these Ch functions in Chapter 22 will be solved in MATLAB correspondingly.

23.11.1 Solving Nonlinear Equations

The function **fzero()**, with the typical calling syntax of

```
z = fzero('func', x0)
```

```
% File: func1.m
function y = func1(x)

y = x^2 - 2;
```

Program 23.23: A nonlinear function solved by the function **fzero**().

finds a zero of the function corresponding to the name `'func'` that is closest to the initial guess of `x0`. For example, the zero of the function $f(x) = x^2 - 2$ can be found by first writing a M-file, say `func1.m` as shown in Program 23.23, which defines the function $f(x)$. Then the following statement determines the zero near 2:

```
>> x = fzero('func1', 2)
x =
    1.4142
```

23.11.2 Solving Systems of Nonlinear Equations

The **fsolve()** function in MATLAB is used to solve a system of nonlinear equations by a least-squares method. Its calling syntax is as follows:

```
x = fsolve(func, x0)
```

The argument `x0` contains values for the initial guess to the solutions, whereas `func` refers to a function M-file that includes the nonlinear equations to be solved. The function specified by `func` should have one input argument and a vector output value. The output of the function **fsolve()** is stored into the array `x`. Given the following nonlinear system of two equations,

$$f_0 = -(x_0^2 + x_1^2 - 2.0) = 0$$
$$f_1 = e^{x_0 - 1.0} + x_1^3 - 2.0 = 0$$

the MATLAB commands below can be used to solve the two equations.

```
>> x = fsolve('func2', [2.0 0.5])
x =
   -0.0902    1.2417
```

The function `func2()` with the function file `func2.m` is shown in Program 23.24.

```
% File: func2.m
function f = func2(x)

f = zeros(2)';
f(1)  = -x(1)^2 + x(2)^2 - 2.0;
f(2)  = exp(x(1)-1.0) + x(2)^3 - 2.0;
```

Program 23.24: A system of nonlinear equations solved by the function **fsolve**().

23.11.3 Finding Roots of Polynomials

To obtain the roots of a polynomial, the function **roots()** can be used. Its syntax is as follows:

```
r = roots(p)
```

where the variable p is the polynomial in the form of $c_1 s^n + c_2 s^{n-1} + \cdots + c_n s + c_{n+1}$. For example, the polynomial $p = x^2 - 2x + 1$ is represented in MATLAB as `p = [1 -2 1]`, where each element of the vector is the coefficients of the polynomial. The roots of the polynomial $p = x^2 - 2x + 1$ are 1, which are determined by the MATLAB statements below.

```
>> p = [1 -2 1];
>> r = roots(p)
r =
     1
     1
```

As another example, the roots of the polynomial $p = x^4 - 12x^3 + 25x + 116$ can be calculated as follows:

```
>> p = [1 -12 0 25 116];
>> r = roots(p)
r =
   11.7473
    2.7028
   -1.2251 + 1.4672i
   -1.2251 - 1.4672i
```

23.11.4 Multiplication of Polynomials

The **conv()** function, with the syntax

```
c = conv(x, y)
```

can be used to multiply two polynomials represented by the arrays x and y. For example, for the polynomials

$$x(s) = 2s^2 - 7s + 3$$

$$y(s) = s^2 + 2s + 101$$

the product $c(s) = x(s)y(s) = 2s^4 - 3^3 + 191s^2 - 701s + 303$ can be obtained as follows:

```
>> x =[2  -7  3];
>> y =[1 2 101];
>> c = conv(x, y)
c =
     2  -3  191 -701 303
```

23.11.5 Solving Systems of Linear Equations and Inverse of Matrices

The **inv()** function, with syntax

```
y = inv(x)
```

performs the inverse operation on the square matrix x. This function can be used to solve a system of linear equations, such as $\mathbf{Ax} = \mathbf{b}$. The solution $\mathbf{x} = \mathbf{A}^{-1}\mathbf{b}$ can be written in MATLAB as `x = inv(A)*b` or `x = A\b`. For example, given the matrix equation

$$\begin{bmatrix} 3 & 0 & 6 \\ 0 & 2 & 1 \\ 1 & 0 & 1 \end{bmatrix} \begin{bmatrix} x_1 \\ x_2 \\ x_3 \end{bmatrix} = \begin{bmatrix} 2 \\ 12 \\ 25 \end{bmatrix}$$

the solutions for x_1, x_2, and x_3 can be determined by the following MATLAB command-line statements:

```
>> A = [3 0 6; 0 2 1; 1 0 1];
>> b = [2 3 25]';
>> x = inv(A)*b                    % or x = A\b
x =
   49.3333
   13.6667
  -24.3333
```

23.11.6 Finding Eigenvalues and Eigenvectors

Recall the *eigenvalue problem* from mathematics used to determine the nontrivial solutions of the equation

$$\mathbf{Ax} = \lambda \mathbf{x} \tag{23.1}$$

where $\mathbf{A}$ is an $n \times n$ matrix, $\mathbf{x}$ is a column vector of length n, and λ is a scalar. The eigenvalue problem states that there are n values for λ that will satisfy equation (23.1). These values of λ are referred to as *eigenvalues*, and the corresponding values for $\mathbf{x}$ are called *eigenvectors*.

The function **eig()** in MATLAB can be used to solve for the eigenvalues and eigenvectors. The calling syntaxes for this function are as follows:

```
D = eig(A)
[V, D] = eig(A)
```

The first calling syntax will solve for the eigenvalues of the matrix $\mathbf{A}$, whereas the second calling syntax will solve for both eigenvalues and their corresponding eigenvectors. The eigenvalues and eigenvectors are stored in the matrix variables $\mathbf{D}$ and $\mathbf{V}$, respectively. The matrix $\mathbf{D}$ is a diagonal matrix where each value of the diagonal represents an eigenvalue. The matrix $\mathbf{V}$ is a full matrix whose columns are the corresponding eigenvectors, such as the following for a 3×3 matrix:

$$\mathbf{D} = \begin{bmatrix} \lambda_1 & 0 & 0 \\ 0 & \lambda_2 & 0 \\ 0 & 0 & \lambda_3 \end{bmatrix}$$

$$\mathbf{V} = \begin{bmatrix} \mathbf{v_1} & \mathbf{v_2} & \mathbf{v_3} \end{bmatrix}$$

As an example, consider the 3×3 matrix

$$\mathbf{A} = \begin{bmatrix} 0.8 & 0.2 & 0.1 \\ 0.2 & 0.7 & 0.3 \\ 0.1 & 0.3 & 0.6 \end{bmatrix}$$

whose eigenvalues and eigenvectors can be determined by the following command-line statements in MATLAB:

```
>> A = [0.8 0.2 0.1; 0.2 0.7 0.3; 0.1 0.3 0.6];
>> [V, D] = eig(A);
>> V
V =
   -0.1362    0.8035   -0.5795
    0.6763   -0.3520   -0.6471
   -0.7239   -0.4801   -0.4954
>> D
D =
    0.3386         0         0
         0    0.6526         0
         0         0    1.1088
```

Thus, the eigenvalues are $\lambda_1 = 0.3386$, $\lambda_2 = 0.6526$, and $\lambda_3 = 1.1088$, and the corresponding eigenvectors are

$$\mathbf{v}_1 = \begin{bmatrix} -0.1362 \\ 0.6763 \\ -0.7239 \end{bmatrix}, \mathbf{v}_2 = \begin{bmatrix} 0.8035 \\ -0.3520 \\ -0.4801 \end{bmatrix}, \mathbf{v}_2 = \begin{bmatrix} -0.5795 \\ -0.6471 \\ -0.4954 \end{bmatrix}$$

23.11.7 Solving Ordinary Differential Equations

The functions **ode23()** or **ode45()** can be used to solve ordinary differential equations. Their simplest calling syntaxes are as follows:

```
[y, t] = ode23('yprime', t0, tf, y0)
[y, t] = ode45('yprime', t0, tf, y0)
```

The function **ode23()** integrates a system of ordinary differential equations using second- and third-order Runge-Kutta formulas, whereas the function **ode45()** uses fourth- and fifth-order formulas. The argument `yprime` corresponds to a function M-file that defines the differential equations to be integrated. The arguments `t0` and `tf` are the initial and final integration times, respectively, and `y0` is a column vector containing the initial conditions of the equations. Either function will produce two column vectors as outputs, `t` for time and `y` for the state corresponding to time.

For example, the Van der Pol equation given as

$$\ddot{u} - \mu(1 - u^2)\dot{u} + u = 0 \tag{23.2}$$

can be represented in MATLAB with the function M-file in Program 23.25 with $\mu = 2$ and the file name `func.m`.

Note that the output variable `dydt` must be a column vector. This was accomplished by the statement `dydt = zeros(2)'`, which made `dydt` as a 2×1 vector with elements initialized to 0. Otherwise, the `dydt` vector could have been entered as

```
dydt = [y(2); mu*(1-y(2)^2)*y(2) - y(1)];
```

With the Van der Pol equation defined in the file `func.m` and given $t_1 = 0$, $t_f = 30$, and $y_0 = [1, 0]^T$, the following commands can be used to solve the ordinary differential equation:

```
% File: func.m
% Van der Pol equation
function dydt = func(t, y)

mu = 2;
dydt = zeros(2)';
dydt(1) = y(2);
dydt(2) = mu*(1-y(1)^2)*y(2) - y(1);
```

Program 23.25 A function for the Van der Pol equation.

```
>> t0 = 1;   tf = 30;
>> y0 = [1; 0];
>> [t, y] = ode23('func', t0, tf, y0);
```

To obtain a visualization of the output, the function **plot()** can be used to plot the solutions of the Van der Pol equation.

23.12 Comparison of Functions in MATLAB and C/Ch

Table 23.6 lists the functions and constants available in MATLAB in alphabetical order along with their equivalents in C/Ch. As one can see, porting MATLAB code to Ch code is quite easy. Most of the syntax for the functions in Ch is similar to that in MATLAB. Because C/Ch is a typed language, whereas MATLAB is a typeless mathematical software package, a few functions, such as **isempty**(), are available in MATLAB but not in C/Ch. However, the important functions for scientific computing and engineering analysis, such as those described in the previous sections, are readily available and can be used according to the syntaxes shown in Table 23.6. The definitions of the symbols in the arguments and lvalues of the functions in Table 23.6 can be found in Table 23.1.

Table 23.6 Comparison of functions in MATLAB and Ch.

Function	MATLAB	Ch
abs	*r*=**abs**(*s*) *A*=**abs**(*A*) *Iv*=**abs**('*str*')	*r*=**abs**(*s*) *A*=**abs**(*A*) **array int** *Iv*[**strlen**("*str*")]= {'*s*', '*t*', '*r*'}
acos	*x*=**acos**(*x*)	*x*=**acos**(*x*)
acosh	*x*=**acosh**(*x*)	*x*=**acosh**(*x*)
addpath	**addpath**('/new/dir', /new/dir2')	_path=**stradd**("/new/dir1;/new/dir2;", _path)
all	*i*=**all**(*A*)	*i*=**sum**(!*A*=0)==0
angle	*r*=**angle**(*z*)	*r*=**carg**(*z*)
any	*i*=**any**(*A*)	*i*=**sum**(*A*! =0)! =0
asin	*x*=**asin**(*x*)	*x*=**asin**(*x*)

(Continued)

Table 23.6 *(Continued)*

Function	MATLAB	Ch
asinh	*x*=**asinh**(*x*)	*x*=**asinh**(*x*)
atan	*x*=**atan**(*x*)	*x*=**atan**(*x*)
atan2	*r*=**atan2**(*r1*, *r2*)	*r*=**atan2**(*r1*, *r2*)
atanh	*x*=**atanh**(*x*)	*x*=**atanh**(*x*)
balance	[*A*, *B*] = **balance**(*A1*)	**balance**(*A1*, *A*, *B*)
base2dec	*i*=**base2dec**('*str*', *i2*)	*i*=**strtol**("*str*", **NULL**, *i2*)
bin2dec	**bin2dec**('*01010*')	
blanks	*str*=**blank**(*n*)	" "
ceil	*x*=**ceil**(*x*)	*s*=**ceil**(*s*)
choly	*A*= **chol**(*A1*)	**choldecomp**(*A1*, *A*)
clear	**clear** `name` **clear** `name`	**remvar** `name` **#pragma** remvar(`name`)
compan	*A*=**compan**(*Av*)	*R*=**companionmatrix**(*Rv*) *Z*=**ccompanionmatrix**(*Zv*)
cond	*r*=**cond**(*A*)	*r*=**condnum**(*A*)
condest	*r*=**condest**(*A*)	*r*=**condnum**(*A*)
conj	*x*=**conj**(*x*)	*x*=**conj**(*x*)
conv	*Av*= **conv**(*Av1*, *Av2*)	**conv**(*Av*, *Av1*, *Av1*)
conv2	*A*= **conv2**(*A1*, *A2*)	**conv2**(*A*, *A1*, *A2*)
corrcoef	*R*= **corrcoef**(*R1*)	**corrcoef**(*R*, *R1*)
corr2	*r*= **corr2**(*R1*, *R2*)	*r*= **correlation2**(*R1*, *R2*)
cos	*x*=**cos**(*x*)	*x*=**cos**(*x*)
cosh	*x*=**cosh**(*x*)	*x*=**cosh**(*x*)
cov	*R*= **cov**(*R1*)	**covariance**(*R*, *R1*)
cross	*Rv*=**cross**(*Rv1*, *Rv2*)	*Rv*=**cross**(*Rv1*, *Rv2*)
cumprod	*A*= **cumprod**(*A1*') *A*= **cumprod**(*A1*) *Av*=**cumprod**(*Av1*)	**cumprod**(*A*, *A1*) **cumprod**(*A*, **transpose**(*A1*)) **cumprod**(*Av*, *Av1*)
cumsum	*A*= **cumsum**(*A1*') *A*= **cumsum**(*A1*) *Av*= **cumsum**(*Av1*)	**cumsum**(*A*, *A1*) **cumsum**(*A*, **transpose**(*A1*)) **cumsum**(*Av*, *Av1*)
dec2base	*str*= **dec2base**(*i1*, *i2*)	
dec2bin	*i*=**dec2bin**(*i2*)	**printf**("*%b*", *i2*) **printf**("*%10b*", *i2*)
dec2hex	*str*=**dec2hex**(*x*)	**sprintf**(*str*,"*%x*", *r*)

Table 23.6 (*Continued*)

Function	MATLAB	Ch
deconv	*A*=**deconv**(*A1*, *B1*) [*A*, *B*]=**deconv**(*A1*, *B1*)	**deconv**(*A*, *A1*, *B1*) **deconv**(*A*, *A1*, *B1*, *B*)
deblank()	**deblank**('*str*')	(not valid)
det	*s*=**det**(*A*)	*r*=**determinant**(*A*) *z*=**cdeterminant**(Z)
diag	*Av*=**diag**(*A*) *A*=**diag**(*Av*)	*Rv*=**diagonal**(*R*) *Zv*=**diagonal**(*Z*) *R*=**diagonalmatrix**(*Rv*) *Z*=**cdiagonalmatrix**(*Zv*)
diff	*A*=**diff**(*A*)	*Rv*=**difference**(*Rv*) *r*=**derivative**(*func*, *r*) *R*=**derivatives**(*func*, *R*)
disp	**disp**(*i*) **disp**(*f*) **disp**(*str*) **disp**(*A*)	**printf**("%d", *i*) or **printf**(i) **printf**("%f", *f*) or **printf**(f) **printf**("%s", *str*) or **printf**(str) **printf**("%d", *A*) or **printf**(A)
display	**display**(*i*) **display**(*f*) **display**(*str*) **display**(*A*)	**printf**("%d", *i*) or **printf**(i) **printf**("%f", *f*) or **printf**(f) **printf**("%s", *str*) or **printf**(str) **printf**("%d", *A*) or **printf**(A)
dot	*x*=**dot**(*Av1*, *Av2*)	*r*=**dot**(*Rv1*, *Rv2*)
dot	*x*=**dot**(*Av1*, *Av2*)	*r*=**dot**(*Rv1*, *Rv2*)
eig	*Av*=**eig**(*A1*) [*Av*, *B*]=**eig**(*A1*) [*Av*, *B*]=**eig**(*A1*, 'nobalance')	**eigen**(*Av*, *NULL*, *A1*) **eigen**(*Av*, *B*, *A1*) **eigen**(*Av*, *B*, *A1*, "nobalance")
eps	**eps**	**#include<float.h>** FLT_EPSILON, DBL_EPSILON
eval	**eval**('cmd') **eval**('expr') **eval**(*try*, *catch*)	**system**("cmd") **streval**("expr")
eye	*R*=**eye**(*i*)	*R*=**identitymatrix**(*i*)
exp	*x*=**exp**(*x*)	*x*=**exp**(*x*)
expm	*A*= **expm**(*A1*)	**expm**(*A*, *A1*)
fclose	**fclose**	*See* **fclose**()
feval	**feval**('*fun*')	**streval**("*fun*")
feof	**feof**	*See* **feof**()
ferror	**ferror**	*See* **perror**() and other I/O functions
fft	*Av*= **fft**(*Av1*) *Av*= **fft**(*Av1*, *i*)	**fft**(*Av*, *Av1*) *A*= **fft**(*A1*, *i*)

(*Continued*)

Table 23.6 ***(Continued)***

Function	MATLAB	Ch
fft2	*A*=**fft2**(*A1*) *A*= **fft**(*A1*, *i1*, *i2*)	**fft**(*A*, *A1*) *Iv*[0]=*i1*, *Iv*[*1*] =*i2*, *A*= **fft**(*A1*, *Iv*)
fftn	*A*=**fftn**(*A1*) *A*= **fftn**(*A1*, *i*)	**fft**(*A*, *A1*) /* 3D only */ *Iv*[0]=*Iv*[*1*]=*Iv*[2]=*i*, **fft**(*A*, *A1*, *Iv*) /* 3D only */
fftshift	*A*= **fftshift**(*A1*)	
fgetl	*str*= **fgetl**(*fid*)	*i*=**strlen**(*str*) **getline**(*fid*, *str*, *i*)
fgets	**fgets**	*See* **fgets**()
fix	*i*=**fix**(*r*)	*i*=*r*
filter	*Av*= **filter**(*Bv1*, *Bv2*, *Av1*)	**filter**(*Bv1*, *Bv2*, *Av1*, *Av*)
filter2	*A*= **filter2**(*A1*, *B1*)	**filter2**(*A*, *A1*, *B1*)
finite	*i*=**finite**(*s*) *I*=**finite**(*A*)	*i*=**isfinite**(*s*) **fevalarray**(*I*, **isfinite**, *R*);
find()	*i*=**find**(*x*) [*r*, *c*]=**find**(*x*) *I*= **find**(*A*)	 *i*=**findvalue**(*I*, *A*) /* i is # of values found */
findstr()	*i*=**findstr**('*str1*', '*str2*')	*p*=**strstr**(*str1*, *str2*)
fliplr	*A*= **fliplr**(*A1*)	**fliplr**(*A*, *A1*)
flipud	*A*= **flipud**(*A1*)	**flipud**(*A*, *A1*)
floor	**floor**(*x*)	**floor**(*x*)
flops	**flops**	(Not valid)
fmin	*r*= **fmin**('*fun*', *r1*, *r2*)	**fminimum**(*r*3, *r*, *fun*, *r1*, *r2*)
fmins	*Rv*= **fmins**('*fun*', *Rv1*)	**fminimums**(*r*3, *Rv*, *fun*, *Rv1*)
fplot	**fplot**('*fun*', [*r1r2*])	**fplotxy**(*fun*, *r1*, *r2*) **fplotxyz**() **CPlot**:MemberFunctions()
fprintf	**fprintf**()	see **fprintf**()
fread	**fread**()	see **fread**()
frewind	**frewind**()	see **frewind**()
fscanf	**fscanf**()	see **fscanf**()
fseek	**fseek**()	see **fseek**()
ftell	**ftell**()	see **ftell**()
funm	*R*= **funm**(*R1*, '*fun*') *Z*= **funm**(*Z*, '*fun*')	**funm**(*R*, *fun*, *R1*) **cfunm**(*Z*, /* complex */ cfun, *Z1*)
fwrite	**fwrite**()	see **fwrite**()
fsolve	*R*= **fsolve**('*fun*', *Ri*)	**fsolve**(*R*, *fun*, *Ri*)

Table 23.6 ***(Continued)***

Function	MATLAB	Ch
fzero	*r*= **fzero**('*fun*', *r1*)	**fzero**(*r*, *fun*, *r1*)
gallery	*A*=**gallery**(*name*, *arg1*) *A*=**gallery**(*name*, *arg1*, *arg2*) *A*=**gallery**(*name*, *arg1*, *arg2*, *arg3*) *A*=**gallery**('*caychy*', *Av1*) *A*=**gallery**('*caychy*', *Av1*, *Av2*) *A*=**gallery**('*chebvand*', *Av1*) *A*=**gallery**('*chebvand*', *i*, *Av1*) *A*=**gallery**('*chow*', *i*) *A*=**gallery**('*chow*', *i*, *r1*) *A*=**gallery**('*chow*', *i*, *r1*, *r2*) *A*=**gallery**('*circul*', *Av1*) *A*=**gallery**('*clement*', *i1*, *i2*) *A*=**gallery**('*dramadah*', *i1*) *A*=**gallery**('*dramadah*', *i1*, *i2*) *A*=**gallery**('*fiedler*', *Av1*) *A*=**gallery**('*frank*', *i1*) *A*=**gallery**('*frank*', *i1*, *i2*) *A*=**gallery**('*gearmat*', *i1*) *A*=**gallery**('*wilk*', *i1*) *AV*=**gallery**('*house*', *Av1*) [*AV*, *r*]=**gallery**('*house*', *Av1*)	*A*=**specialmatrix**(Name, *arg1*) *A*=**specialmatrix**(*Name*, *arg1*, *arg2*) *A*=**specialmatrix**(*Name*, *arg1*, *arg2*, *arg3*) **specialmatrix**("*Cauchy*", *Av1*) **specialmatrix**("*Cauchy*", *Av1*, *Av2*) **specialmatrix**("*ChebyshevVandemonde*", *Av1*) **specialmatrix**("*ChebyshevVandemonde*", *Av1*, *i*) **specialmatrix**("*Chow*", *i*) **specialmatrix**("*Chow*", *i*, *r1*) **specialmatrix**("*Chow*", *i*, *r1*, *r2*) **specialmatrix**("*Circul*", *Av1*) **specialmatrix**("*Clement*", *i1*, *i2*) **specialmatrix**("*DenavitHartenberg*", *r1*, *r2*, *r3*, *r4*) **specialmatrix**("*DenavitHartenberg2*", *r1*, *r2*, *r3*, *r4*) **specialmatrix**("*Dramadah*", *i1*) **specialmatrix**("*Dramadah*", *i1*, *i2*) **specialmatrix**("*Fiedler*", *Av1*) **specialmatrix**("Frank", *i1*) **specialmatrix**("*Frank*", *i1*, *i2*) **specialmatrix**("Gear", *i1*) **specialmatrix**("*Wilkinson*", *i1*) **householdermatrix**(*Av1*, *Av*) **householdermatrix**(*Av1*, *Av*, *r*)
gcd()	*I*= **gcd**(*I1*, *I2*) [*I*, *I3*, *I4*]=**gcd**(*I1*, *I2*)	**gcd**(*I1*, *I2*, *I*) **gcd**(*I1*, *I2*, *I*, *I3*, *I4*)
hadamard	*A*=**hadamard**(*i1*)	**specialmatrix**("*Hadamard*", *i1*)
hankel	*A*=**hankel**(*Av1*) *A*=**hankel**(*Av1*, *Av1*)	**specialmatrix**("*Hankel*", *Av1*) **specialmatrix**("*Hankel*", *Av1*, *Av2*)
hex2dec	*i*=**hex2dec**('*str*')	*i*=**strtol**("*str*", *NULL*, *16*)
hex2num()	*r*=**hex2num**('*str*')	
hess	[*B*, *A*] = **hess**(*A1*)	**hessdecomp**(*A1*, *A*, *B*)
hilb	*A*=**hilb**(*i1*)	**specialmatrix**("*Hilbert*", *i1*)
hist	**hist**()	**histogram**()
i	**i**	**#include<complex.h>** **I**
ifft	*Av*=**ifft**(*Av1*) *Av*=**ifft**(*Av1*, *i*)	**ifft**(*Av*, *Av1*) **ifft**(*A*, *A1*, *i*)
ifft2	*A*=**ifft2**(*A1*) *A*= **ifft**(*A1*, *i1*, *i2*)	**ifft**(*A*, *A1*) *Iv*[0]=*i1*, *Iv*[two] =*i2*, **ifft2**(*A*, *A1*, *Iv*)
ifftn	*A*=**ifftn**(*A1*) *A*= **iftn**(*A1*, *i*)	**ifft**(*A*, *A1*) /* 3D only */ *Iv*[0]=*Iv*[*1*]=*Iv*[2]=*i*, **ifft**(*A*, *A1*, *Iv*)

(Continued)

Table 23.6 (*Continued*)

Function	MATLAB	Ch
imag	*r*=**imag**(*s*) *R*=**imag**(*A*)	*r*=**imag**(*s*) *R*=**imag**(*A*)
inf	**inf**	Inf
input	*s*=**input**(*str*)	*r*=**getnum**(*str*, *r*)
int2str	*str*=**int2str**(*i*)	**sprintf**(*str*, ''%d"", *i*)
interp1	*Ri*=**interp1**(*R1*, *R2*, *Ri1*) *Ri*=**interp1**(*R1*, *R2*, *Ri1*,'*linear*') *Ri*=**interp1**(*R1*, *R2*, *Ri1*,'*spline*')	**interp1**(*Ri*, *Ri1*, *R1*, *R2*, "*linear*") **interp1**(*Ri*, *Ri1*, *R1*, *R2*, "*linear*") **interp1**(*Ri*, *Ri1*, *R1*, *R2*, "*spline*")
interp2	*Ri*=**interp2**(*R1*, *R2*, *R3*, *Ri1*, *Ri2*) *Ri*=**interp2**(*R1*, *R2*, *R3*, *Ri1*, *Ri2*, '*linear*') *Ri*= **interp2**(*R1*, *R2*, *R3*, *Ri1*, *Ri2*, '*spline*')	**interp2**(*Ri*, *Ri1*, *Ri2*, *R1*, *R2*, *R3*, "*linear*") **interp2**(*Ri*, *Ri1*, *Ri2*, *R1*, *R2*, *R3*, "*linear*") **interp2**(*Ri*, *Ri1*, *Ri2*, *R1*, *R2*, *R3*, "*spline*")
inv	*A*=**inv**(*A*)	*R*=**inverse**(*R*) *Z*=**cinverse**(*Z*)
invhilb	*A*=**invhilb**(*i1*)	**specialmatrix**("*InverseHilbert*", *i1*)
isempty	*i*=**isempty**(*A*)	(not valid)
isglobal	*i*=**isglobal**(*x*)	**#include**<chshell.h > **isvar**("*x*")**==CH_SYSTEMVAR**
ishold	*i*=**ishold**	(not valid)
isieee	*i*=**isieee**	(not valid)
isinf	*i*=**isinf**(*s*) *I*=**isinf**(*A*)	*i*=**isinf**(*s*) **fevalarray**(*I*, **isinf**, *R*);
isletter	*i*=**isletter**(*s*) *I*=**isletter**(*A*)	*i*=**isalpha**(*s*) **fevalarray**(*I*, **isalpha**, *R*);
isnan	*i*=**isnan**(*s*) *I*=**isnan**(*A*)	*i*=**isnan**(*s*) **fevalarray**(*I*, **isnan**, *R*);
isreal	*i*=**isreal**(*s*)	*i*=**elementtype**(*x*) != **elementtype**(**complex**) && **elementtype**(*x*) != **elementtype**(**double complex**)
isspace	*i*=**isspace**(*s*) *I*=**isspace**(*A*)	*i*=**isspace**(*s*) **fevalarray**(*I*, **isspace**, *R*);
issparse	*i*=**issparse**(*x*)	
isstr	*i*=**isstr**(*x*)	*i*=**elementtype**(*x*) == **elementtype**(*string_t*)
isstudent	*i*=**isstudent**	*i*=**isstudent**()
isunix	*i*=**isunix**	**#ifndef _WIN32_**
isvms	*i*=**isvms**	(not valid)
invhilb()	*A*= **invhilb**(*i*)	
j	**j**	**#include**<**complex.h**> I

Table 23.6 ***(Continued)***

Function	MATLAB	Ch
lasterr	**lasterr**('')	see **perror**(), **strerror**()
lcm()	*I*= **lcm**(*I1*, *I2*)	**lcm**(*I*, *I1*, *I2*)
length	*i*=**length**(*A*)	*i*=**max**(**shape**(*A*))
linspace	*x*=**linspace**(*first*, *last*, *n*) *x*=**linspace**(*first*, *last*, *n*)	**lindata**(*first*, *last*, *x*) **lindata**(*first*, *last*, *x*, *n*)
loglog	*x*=**loglog**(*x*, *y*)	plot.loglog(*x*, *y*)
loglog	*x*=**loglog**(*x*, *y*)	plot.data2D(*x*, *y*) plot.scaleType(PLOT_AXIS_X, PLOT_SCALETYPE_LOG) plot.scaleType(PLOT_AXIS_Y, PLOT_SCALETYPE_LOG)
logspace	*x*=**logspace**(*first*, *last*, *n*)	**logspace**(*x*, *first*, *last*)
log	*x*=**log**(*x*)	*x*=**log**(*x*)
log10	*x*=**log10**(*x*)	*x*=**log10**(*x*)
log2	*x*=**log2**(*x*) *r*=**log2**(*r*)	*x*=**log**(*x*)/**log**(*2*) *r*=**log2**(*r*)
logm	*A*=**logm**(*A1*)	**logm**(*A*, *A1*)
lower	*str*=**lower**('*str*')	see **tolower**()
lscov	*R*= **lscov**(*A1*, *R1*, *A2*) [*R*, *R2*]=**lscov**(*A1*, *R1*, *A2*)	**llsqcovsolve**(*R*, *A1*, *R1*, *A2*) **llsqcovsolve**(*R*, *A1*, *R1*, *A2*, *R2*)
lu	[*R1*, *R2*]=**lu**(*A*) [*R1*, *R2*, *I*]=**lu**(*A*)	**ludecomp**(*A*, *R1*, *R2*) **ludecomp**(*A*, *R1*, *R2*, *I*)
magic()	*A*=**magic**(*i1*) *Zv*= **mean**(*Z*)	**specialmatrix**("*Magic*", *i1*) **cmean**(*Z*, *Zv*)
max	*r*=**max**(*s1*, *s2*) *r*=**max**(*Av*) *Rv*=**max**(*A*)	*r*=**max**(*r1*, *r2*) *r*=**max**(*R*) *Rv*=**maxv**(*R*) *Rv*=**transpose**(**maxv**(**transpose**(*R*)))
min	*r*=**min**(*s1*, *s2*) *r*=**min**(*Av*) *Rv*=**min**(*A*)	*r*=**min**(*r1*, *r2*) *r*=**min**(*R*) *Rv*=**minv**(*R*) *Rv*=**transpose**(**minv**(**transpose**(*R*))
mean	*r*=**mean**(*R*) *Rv*=**mean**(*R*) *z*= **mean**(*Z*)	*r*=**mean**(*R*) *r*=**mean**(*R*, *Rv*) **mean**(**transpose**(*R*), *Rv*) *z*=**cmean**(*Z*)
median	*r*=**median**(*R*) *Rv*=**median**(*R*)	*r*=**median**(*R*) *r*=**median**(*R*, *Rv*) **median**(**transpose**(*R*), *Rv*)
mod	*i*=**mod**(*i1*, *i2*) *r*=**mod**(*r1*, *r2*)	*i*=*i1*%*i2* *r*=**fmod**(*r1*, *r2*)

(Continued)

Table 23.6 *(Continued)*

Function	MATLAB	Ch
NaN	**NaN**	**NaN**
nargin	**nargin**	(not valid)
nargout	**nargout**	(not valid)
nextpow2	i=**nextpow2**(r) i=**nextpow2**(z) i=**nextpow2**(Av)	i=**ceil**(**log2**(r)) i=**ceil**(**log2**(**abs**(z))) i=**ceil**(**log2**((**int**)**shape**(Av)))
nnls()	R=**nnls**(A1, R1) R=**nnls**(A1, R1, r) [R, R2]=**nnls**(A1, R1) [R, R2]=**nnls**(A1, R1, r)	**llsqnonnegsolve**(R, A1, R1) **llsqnonnegsolve**(R, A1, R1, R) **llsqnonnegsolve**(R, A1, R1,0.0, R2) **llsqnonnegsolve**(R, A1, R1, r, R2)
norm	**norm**(A) **norm**(A, 1) **norm**(A, 2) **norm**(A, inf) **norm**(A,'fro') **norm**(Av) **norm**(Av, inf) **norm**(Av,-inf) **norm**(Av,p)	**norm**(A, "2") **norm**(A, "1") **norm**(A, "2") **norm**(A, "i") **norm**(A, "f") **norm**(Av, "2") **norm**(Av, "i") **norm**(Av, "-i") **norm**(Av, "p")
numtwostr	str=**numtwostr**(s)	**sprintf**(str, "%", s)
null	A=**null**(Ai)	**nullspace**(A, Ai)
ones	**ones**(i1) **ones**(i1, i2) **ones**(**size**(A))	(**array int a**[i1][i1])1 (**array int a**[ii1][i2])1 **array int** dim[2]=**shape**(A); (**array int a**[dim[0]][dim[1]])1
ode23	[Rv1, Rv2]= **ode23**('fun', r1, r2, Rv)	**oderk**(fun, r1, r2, Rv, NULL, Rv1, Rv2)
ode45	[Rv1, Rv2]= **ode45**('fun', r1, r2, Rv)	**oderk**(fun, r1, r2, Rv, NULL, Rv1, Rv2)
orth	A= **orth**(Ai)	**orthonormalbase**(A, Ai)
pascal()	A=**pascal**(i1) A=**pascal**(i1, i2)	**specialmatrix**("Pascal", i1) **specialmatrix**("Pascal", i1, i2)
pi	**pi**	**#include<math.h>** **M_PI**
pinv	A1=**pinv**(A)	R1=**pinverse**(R)
poly	Av=**poly**(A) Bv=**poly**(Av)	**charpolycoef**(Av, A) **polycoef**(Bv, Av)
polyder	Av= **polyder**(Bv)	**polyder**(Av, Bv)
polyder2	Av= **polyder**(Av1, Bv1) [Av, Bv] = **polyder**(Av1, Bv1)	**polyder2**(Av, NULL, Av1, Bv1) **polyder2**(Av, Bv, Av1, Bv1)
polyfit	Rv=**polyfit**(Rv1, Rv2, i)	**polyfit**(Rv, Rv1, Rv2)

Table 23.6 ***(Continued)***

Function	MATLAB	Ch
polyval	*r*= **polyval**(*Rv1*, *r1*) *r*= **polyval**(*Rv1*, *r1*, *Rv*) *z*= **polyval**(*Av1*, *s*) *z*= **polyval**(*Av1*, *s*, *Av*) *Av*= **polyval**(*Bv*, *Av1*) *A*=**polyval**(*Av*, *A1*)	*r*= **polyeval**(*Rv1*, *r1*) *r*= **polyeval**(*Rv1*, *r1*, *Rv*) *z*= **cpolyeval**(*Av1*, *s*) z = **cpolyeval**(*Av1*, *s*, *Av*) **polyevalarray**(*Av*, *Bv*, *Av1*) **polyevalm**(*A*, *Av*, *A1*)
polyvalm()	*A*=**polyvalm**(*Av*, *A1*)	**polyevalm**(*A*, *Av*, *A1*)
plot	**plot**(Rva,Rvb)	**plotxy**(*Rv1*, *Rv2*) **plotxyf**(*file*) **CPlot**:MemberFunctions()
plot3	**plot3**(*Rv1*, *Rv2*, *Rv3*)	**plotxyz**(*Rv1*, *Rv2*, *Rv3*) **plotxyzf**(*file*) **CPlot**:MemberFunctions()
prod	*s*=**prod**(*A*) *Av*=**prod**(*A*) *Av*=**prod**(*A*, 1) *Av*=**prod**(*A*, 2)	*r*=**product**(*R*) z=**cproduct**(Z) *r*=**product**(*R*, *Rv*) *r*=**product**(*R*, *Rv*) *r*=**product**(**transpose**(*R*), *Rv*) *z*=**cproduct**(*Z*, *Zv*) **product**(**transpose**(*R*), *Rv*) **cproduct**(**transpose**(*Z*), *Zv*)
quad	*r*=**quad**('*fun*', *r1*, *r2*)	*r*=**integral1**(*fun*, *r1*, *r2*)
quadeight	*r*=**quadeight**('*fun*', *r1*, *r2*)	*r*=**integral1**(*fun*, *r1*, *r2*)
qr	[*A1*, *A2*] = **qr**(*A*) [*A1*, *A2*, *A3*] = **qr**(*A*) [*A1*, *A2*]=**qr**(*A*) [*A1*, *A2*]=**qr**(*A*, **zero**)	**qrdecomp**(*A*, *A1*, *A2*) **qrdecomp**(*A*, *A1*, *A2*) **qrdecomp**(*A*, *A1*, *A2*)
qrdelete	[*A1*, **itBa**] = **qrdelete**(*A*, *B*, *i2*)	**qrdelete**(*A1*, **itBa**, *A*, *B*, *i2*)
qrinsert	[*A1*, **itBa**] = **qrdelete**(*A*, *B*, *i2*, *Av*)	**qrdelete**(*A1*, **itBa**, *A*, *B*, *i2*, *Av*)
rank	*i*= **rank**(*A*) *i*= **rank**(*A*, *r*)	*i*= **rank**(*A*) *i*= **rank**(*A*)
real	*r*=**real**(*s*) *R*=**real**(*A*)	*r*=**real**(*s*) *R*=**real**(*A*)
realmax	**realmax**	**#include<float.h>** FLT_MAX, DBL_MAX
realmin	**realmin**	**#include<float.h>** FLT_MIN, DBL_MIN
rem	*r*=**rem**(*r1*, *r2*)	*r*=**fmod**(*r1*, *r2*) *r*=**remainder**(*r1*, *r2*)+*r2*
residue	[*Av*, *Bv*,Rv]=**residue**(*Rv1*, *Rv2*)	**residue**(*Rv1*, *Rv2*, *Av*, *Bv*, *Rv*)

(Continued)

Table 23.6 (*Continued*)

Function	MATLAB	Ch
round	*i*=**round**(*r*)	*i*=(**int**)(*r*>0?*r*+0.5:*r*-0.5)
roots	*Av*=**roots**(*Bv*)	**roots**(*Av*, *Bv*)
rosser	*A*=**rosser**()	**specialmatrix**("*Rosser*")
rot90(*A*)	*A*= **rot90**(*A1*) *A*= **rot90**(*A1*, *i*)	**rot90**(*A*, *A1*) **rot90**(*A*, *A1*, *i*)
rand	*r*=**rand**()	*r*=**urand**()
randn	*R*=**rand**(*i1*, *i2*)	**urand**(*R*)
rcond	*r*= **rcond**(*A*)	*r*= **rcondnum**(*A*)
reshape	**reshape**(*A*, *m*, *n*)	(**array** type [m][n])*A*
rsf2csf	[*A1*, **itBa**] = **rsf2csf**(*A*, *B*)	**rsf2csf**(*A1*, **itBa**, *A*, *B*)
schur	*A1*= **schur**(*A*) [*A1*, *A2*] = **schur**(*A*)	**schurdecomp**(*A*, *A1*, *NULL*) **schurdecomp**(*A*, *A1*, *A2*)
semilogx	*x*=**semilogx**(*x*, *y*)	plot.semilogx(*x*, *y*)
semilogx	*x*=**semilogx**(*x*, *y*)	plot.data2D(*x*, *y*) plot.scaleType(PLOT_AXIS_X, PLOT_SCALETYPE_LOG)
semilogy	*x*=**semilogy**(*x*, *y*)	plot.semilogy(*x*, *y*)
semilogy	*x*=**semilogy**(*x*, *y*)	plot.data2D(*x*, *y*) plot.scaleType(PLOT_AXIS_Y, PLOT_SCALETYPE_LOG)
sign	*i*=**sign**(*r*) *z*=**sign**(*z*)	*i*=**sign**(*r*) *z*=*z*/**abs**(*z*)
sqrt	*x*=**sqrt**(*x*)	*x*=**sqrt**(*x*)
sqrtm	*A*= **sqrtm**(*A1*)	**sqrtm**(*A*, *A1*)
size	*Iv*=**size**(*A*) [*i1*, *i2*]=**size**(*A*) *i*=**size**(*A*, *1*) *i*=**size**(*A*, *2*)	*Iv*=**shape**(*A*) *Iv*=**shape**(*A*); *i1*=*Iv*[0]; *i2*=*Iv*[*1*] *i*= (**int**)**shape**(*A*) *Iv*=**shape**(*A*); *i*=*Iv*[*1*]
sort	*Av*=**sort**(*Av1*) *A*=**sort**(*A1*) *A*=**sortrows**(*A1*) [*Av*, I]=**sort**(*Av1*) [*A*, *I*]=**sort**(*A1*) [*A*, *I*]=**sortrows**(*A1*)	**sort**(*Av*, *Av1*) **sort**(*Av*, *Av1*, "array") **sort**(*A*, *A1*, "column") **sort**(*A*, *A1*, "row") **sort**(*Av*, *Av1*, "array", I) **sort**(*Av*, *Av1*, NULL, I) **sort**(*A*, *A1*, "column", I) **sort**(*A*, *A1*, "rows", I)
spline	*Ri*= **spline**(*R1*, *R2*, *Ri1*) *ri*= **spline**(*R1*, *R2*, *r*) *Ri*= **spline**(*R1*, *R2*, *Ri1*)	**interp1**(*Ri*, *R1i*, *R2i*, "*spline*") **CSpline**::**Interp**(r) **CSpline**::**Interpm**(*Ri1*, *Ri*)
sprintf	**sprintf**()	*See* **sprintf**()

Table 23.6 ***(Continued)***

Function	MATLAB	Ch
sscanf	**sscanf**()	*See* **sscanf**()
std	*r*=**std**(*R*) *Rv*=**std**(*R*)	*r*=**std**(*R*) *r*=**std**(R, Rv) **std**(**transpose**(*R*), *Rv*)
str2mat	C=**str2mat**('*str1*', '*str2*', ...)	**str2mat**(*C*, *str1*, *str2*)
str2num	*i*=**str2num**('*str*')	*i*=**atol**(*str*), see **strtod**()
strcmp	**strcmp**('*str1*', '*str2*')	!**strcmp**("*str1*", "*str2*")
strrep	*str*= **strrep**('*str1*', '*str2*', '*str3*')	*str*=**strrep**(*str1*, *str2*, *str3*)
strtok	**strtok**	*See* **strtok**(), **strtok_r**()
subplot	**subplot**()	**CPlot**::**subplot**() **CPlot**::**getSubplot**()
sum	*r*=**sum**(*A*) *Av*=**sum**(*A*)	*r*=**sum**(*R*) *z*=**csum**(*Z*) *r*=**sum**(*R*, *Rv*) *z*=**csum**(Z, *Zv*) **sum**(**transpose**(*R*), *Rv*) **csum**(**transpose**(*Z*), *Zv*)
svd	*R*= **svd**(*A*) [*A1*, *R*, *A2*] = **svd**(*A*))	**svd**(*A*, *R*, *NULL*, *NULL*) **svd**(*A*, *R*, *A1*, *A2*)
tan	*x*=**tan**(*x*)	*x*=**tan**(*x*)
tanh	*x*=**tanh**(*x*)	*x*=**tanh**(*x*)
toeplititz	*A*=**toeplititz**(*Av1*) *A*=**toeplititz**(*Av1*, *Av2*)	**specialmatrix**("*Toeplititz*", *Av1*) **specialmatrix**("*Toeplititz*", *Av1*, *Av2*)
trace	*s*=**trace**(*A*)	*r*=**trace**(*R*) *z*=**ctrace**(Z)
trapz	*r*=**trapz**(Rva, Rvb)	*See* **integral1**()
tril	*A1*=**tril**(*A*) *Z1*=**tril**(Z) *A1*=**tril**(*A*, i) *Z1*=**tril**(Z, i)	*A1*=**triangularmatrix**("*lower*", *A*) *Z1*=**ctriangularmatrix**("*lower*", *Z*) *A1*=**triangularmatrix**("*lower*", *A*, *i*) *Z1*=**ctriangularmatrix**("*lower*", *Z*, *i*)
triu	*A1*=**triu**(*A*) *Z1*=**triu**(Z) *A1*=**triu**(*A*, i) *Z1*=**triu**(*Z*, *i*)	*A1*=**triangularmatrix**("*upper*", *A*) *Z1*=**ctriangularmatrix**("*upper*", *Z*) *A1*=**triangularmatrix**("*upper*", *A*, *i*) *Z1*=**ctriangularmatrix**("*upper*", *Z*, *i*)
vander	*R*=**vander**(*Rv*) *A*=**vander**(*Av*)	*R*=**vandermatrix**(*Rv*) **specialmatrix**("*Vandermonde*", *Av*)
unwrap()	*A*=**unwrap**(*A1*) *A*=**unwrap**(*A1*, r)	**unwrap**(*A*, *A1*) **unwrap**(*A*, *A1*, *r*)

(Continued)

Table 23.6 (*Continued*)

Function	MATLAB	Ch
upper	*str*=**upper**('str')	*See* **toupper**()
who	**who**	**stackvar**
xcorr	*Av*= **xcorr**(*Av1*, *Av2*)	**xcorr**(*Av*, *Av1*, *Av2*)
xor	**xor**(*A*, *B*) **xor**(*A*, *s*) **xor**(s, *A*)	*A*^^ *B* *A*^^ *r* *r*^^ *A*
zeros	**zeros**(*i1*) **zeros**(*i1*, *i2*) **zeros**(**size**(*A*))	(**array int**[*i1*][*i1*]) *0* (**array int**[*i1*][*i2*]) *0* **array int** dim[2]=**shape**(*A*); (**array int** [dim[*0*]][dim[*1*]]) *0*
2D/3D plotting functions	*See* class **CPlot**	

Exercises

1. Write a MATLAB program to solve Exercise 6 in Chapter 5.
2. Write a MATLAB program to solve Exercise 8 in Chapter 5.
3. Write a MATLAB program to solve Exercise 8 in Chapter 6.
4. Write a MATLAB program to solve Exercise 9 in Chapter 6.
5. Write a MATLAB program to solve Exercise 2 in Chapter 14.
6. Write a MATLAB program to solve Exercise 3 in Chapter 14.
7. Write a MATLAB program to solve Exercise 4 in Chapter 14.
8. Write a MATLAB program to solve Exercise 6 in Chapter 21.
9. Write a MATLAB program to solve Exercise 8 in Chapter 21.
10. Write a MATLAB program to solve Exercise 9 in Chapter 21.
11. Write a MATLAB program to solve Exercise 10 in Chapter 21.
12. Write a MATLAB program to solve Exercise 12(a) in Chapter 21.
13. Write a MATLAB program to solve Exercise 12(b) in Chapter 21.
14. Write a MATLAB program to solve Exercise 12(c) in Chapter 21.
15. Write a MATLAB program to solve Exercise 14 in Chapter 22.

APPENDIX A

Keywords

A.1 Keywords in C

A.1.1 Preprocessing Directives

The preprocessing directives operators available in C are as follows:

#include #define #undef #if #ifdef #ifndef #elif #else #endif #error #line #pragma
 # ## defined()

A.1.2 Control Keywords

Control keywords control the order of execution of program blocks. For functions, these keywords are **main** and **return**. The conditional keywords are **if**, **else**, **switch**, **case**, and **default**. For loops, they are **while**, **do**, and **for**. To transfer control to another block, the keywords **break**, **continue**, and **goto** are available.

A.1.3 Types and Declarations

The following types and declarations are available in C:

Integer types: **char**, **short**, **int**, **long**, **signed**, **unsigned**

Real types: **double**, **float**, **long double**

Complex types: **complex**, **float complex**, **double complex**

Unknown or generic type: **void**

Type qualifiers: **const**, **volatile**, **restrict**

Storage class: **auto**, **static**, **extern**, **register**

Type operator: **sizeof**

Create new type names: **typedef**

Define new data type descriptions: **struct**, **enum**, **union**

A.2 Keywords in C++ Supported in Ch

class delete new private public this using

A.3 List of Keywords

An alphabetical list of C and C++ reserved keywords used in Ch are as follows:

auto break const complex char case continue class double default delete do else enum extern float for goto if inline int long new operator private public register restrict return scanf static struct short signed sizeof switch this union unsigned volatile void while

A.4 Keywords in Ch Only

The following additional keywords have been added in Ch:

ComplexInf ComplexNaN Inf NaN NULL array foreach fprintf printf scanf string_t

A.5 Punctuators

A punctuator is a symbol that has independent syntactic and semantic significance. Depending on context, it may specify an operation to be performed in which case it is known as an *operator*. An *operand* is an entity on which an operator acts. The following punctuators are valid in C:

```
! != # ## % %= & && &= * *= + ++ += - -- -=
-> . .* ./ / /= < << <<= <= = == > >= >> >>= ?
^ ^= ^^ " ' { | |= || } ~
```

APPENDIX B

C99 Features Supported in Ch

Ch supports all features in the C89 Standard. Ch also supports the following major new features added in the ISO C99 Standard:

1. The features of IEEE 754 standard for floating-point arithmetic are transparent to users. Real numbers are represented in the entire real line with metanumbers ±0.0, ±Inf, and Not-a-Number (NaN). Mathematical functions with real numbers are defined in the entire real domain.
2. Data types of float complex, double complex, and long double complex.
3. Data types of long long and unsigned long long.
4. Variable-length arrays (VLAs).
5. Type-generic math functions in the header file **tgmath.h** for polymorphism.
6. Mixed executable code and declaration, as shown below:

```
x = 4;
int n = 2*x;
int a[n];
```

7. The C++ style comment symbol `//`.
8. The identifier **__func__** inside a function or member function of a class contains the name of the function.
9. Support the header file **stdbool.h** with type **bool**, and the macros **true** and **false**.
10. Support the header files **complex.h**, **fenv.h**, **inttypes.h**, **iso646.h**, **stdbool.h**, **tgmath.h**, **wchar.h**, and **wctype.h**.
11. The implicit int declaration is removed:

```
fun(int i) { // ERROR: implicit int type for fun
    ...
}
int fun2(i) { // ERROR: implicit int type for i
    ...
}
```

12. Add **va_copy()** in the header file **stdarg.h**.
13. The keywords **restrict** and **inline** are recognized.
14. The hexadecimal floating-point constants.

APPENDIX C

C++ Features Supported in Ch

1. Member function.
2. Mixed executable code and declaration.
3. The **this** pointer.
4. Reference type and pass-by-reference.
5. Function-style type conversion.
6. Classes declared by the type specifier **class**.
7. Private/public data and functions declared by the type modifiers **private** and **public**. Members of a class definition are assumed to be private until a **public** declaration is given.
8. Static member of class/struct/union.
9. Const member functions.
10. The **new** and **delete** operators.
11. The constructor and destructor.
12. Polymorphic functions.
13. The scope resolution operator `::` for member function definitions, static members, and global variables, such as `::g` for the global variable *g* in a local scope.
14. The I/O **cout**, **cerr**, and **cin** with **endl** and **ends**.
15. The following **using** directive for **cout**, **cerr**, **cin**, **endl**, and **ends**:

```
using std::cout;
using std::cin;
using std::cerr;
using std::endl;
using std::ends;
```

    or

```
using namespace std;
```

16. Arguments for variadic functions are optional.

```
int func(...); // ok in C++/Ch, not valid in C.
```

APPENDIX D

The ASCII Character Set

Table D.1 The ASCII character set.

Dec	Hex	Octal	ASCII	HTML	Name	Dec	Hex	Octal	ASCII	HTML
0	0	0	Ctrl@	%00	NUL	32	20	40	SPACE	%20
1	1	1	Ctrl/A	%01	SOH	33	21	41	!	%21
2	2	2	Ctrl/B	%02	STX	34	22	42	”	%22
3	3	3	Ctrl/C	%03	ETX	35	23	43	#	%23
4	4	4	Ctrl/D	%04	EQT	36	24	44	$	%24
5	5	5	Ctrl/E	%05	ENQ	37	25	45	%	%25
6	6	6	Ctrl/F	%06	ACK	38	26	46	&	%26
7	7	7	Ctrl/G	%07	BEL \a	39	27	47	`	%27
8	8	10	Ctrl/H	%08	BS \b	40	28	50	(	%28
9	9	11	Ctrl/I	%09	TAB \t	41	29	51	)	%29
10	A	12	Ctrl/J	%0A	LF \n	42	2A	52	*	%2A
11	B	13	Ctrl/K	%0B	VT \v	43	2B	53	+	%2B
12	C	14	Ctrl/L	%0C	FF \f	44	2C	54	,	%2C
13	D	15	Ctrl/M	%0D	VR \r	45	2D	55	-	%2D
14	E	16	Ctrl/N	%0E	SO	46	2E	56	.	%2E
15	F	17	Ctrl/O	%0F	SI	47	2F	57	/	%2F
16	10	20	Ctrl/P	%10	DLE	48	30	60	0	0
17	11	21	Ctrl/Q	%11	DC1	49	31	61	1	1
18	12	22	Ctrl/R	%12	DC2	50	32	62	2	2
19	13	23	Ctrl/S	%13	DC3	51	33	63	3	3
20	14	24	Ctrl/T	%14	DC4	52	34	64	4	4
21	15	25	Ctrl/U	%15	NAK	53	35	65	5	5
22	16	26	Ctrl/V	%16	SYN	54	36	66	6	6
23	17	27	Ctrl/W	%17	ETB	55	37	67	7	7
24	18	30	Ctrl/X	%18	CAN	56	38	70	8	8
25	19	31	Ctrl/Y	%19	EM	57	39	71	9	9
26	1A	32	Ctrl/Z	%1A	SUB	58	3A	72	:	%3A
27	1B	33	Ctrl [	%1B	ESC	59	3B	73	;	%3B
28	1C	34	Ctrl\	%1C	FS	60	3C	74	<	%3C
29	1D	35	Ctrl]	%1D	GS	61	3D	75	=	%3D
30	1E	36	Ctrl^	%1E	RS	62	3E	76	>	%3E
31	1F	37	Ctrl_	%1F	US	63	3F	77	?	%3F

(Continued)

Table D.1 (*Continued*)

Dec	Hex	Octal	ASCII	HTML	Dec	Hex	Octal	ASCII	HTML
64	40	100	@	%40	96	60	140	'	%60
65	41	101	A	A	97	61	141	a	a
66	42	102	B	B	98	62	142	b	b
67	43	103	C	C	99	63	143	c	c
68	44	104	D	D	100	64	144	d	d
69	45	105	E	E	101	65	145	e	e
70	46	106	F	F	102	66	146	f	f
71	47	107	G	G	103	67	147	g	g
72	48	110	H	H	104	68	150	h	h
73	49	111	I	I	105	69	151	i	i
74	4A	112	J	J	106	6A	152	j	j
75	4B	113	K	K	107	6B	153	k	k
76	4C	114	L	L	108	6C	154	l	l
77	4D	115	M	M	109	6D	155	m	m
78	4E	116	N	N	110	6E	156	n	n
79	4F	117	O	O	111	6F	157	o	o
80	50	120	P	P	112	70	160	p	p
81	51	121	Q	Q	113	71	161	q	q
82	52	122	R	R	114	72	162	r	r
83	53	123	S	S	115	73	163	s	s
84	54	124	T	T	116	74	164	t	t
85	55	125	U	U	117	75	165	u	u
86	56	126	V	V	118	76	166	v	v
87	57	127	W	W	119	77	167	w	w
88	58	130	X	X	120	78	170	x	x
89	59	131	Y	Y	121	79	171	y	y
90	5A	132	Z	Z	122	7A	172	z	z
91	5B	133	[	%5B	123	7B	173	{	%7B
92	5C	134	\	%5C	124	7C	174	|	%7C
93	5D	135	]	%5D	125	7D	175	}	%7D
94	5E	136	^	%5E	126	7E	176	~	%7E
95	5F	137	_	%5F	127	7F	177	del	%7F

Index

A

D

E

F

G

M

P

V

W

X

Z

License Agreement and Limited Warranty

The software in the CD is distributed "AS IS" without any warranty. Neither the author, SoftIntegration, Inc., nor The McGraw-Hill Companies, Inc. makes any representation, or warranty, either express or implied, with respect to the software programs, their quality, accuracy, or fitness for a specific purpose. Therefore, neither the author, SoftIntegration, Inc., nor The McGraw-Hill Companies, Inc. shall have any liability to you or any other person or entity with respect to any liability, loss, or damage caused or alleged to have caused directly or indirectly by the programs contained on the media. This includes, but not limited to, interruption of service, loss of data, loss of classroom time, loss of consulting or anticipatory profits, or consequential damages from the use of these programs, even if the author, SoftInt ... dvised of the possibilities of such damages. If the n ...

Ch® Student Edition vers ... d by a registered student of an educational institut ... t to the SoftIntegration Ch Student Edition End- ... the CD or the Web site http://www.softintegratic ... ition End-User License Agreement. By opening ... litions of these licenses. If you do not agree, do n ...

Ch® Student Editi...

Ch is an embeddable C/C ... - and three-dimensional plotting, numerical comp ... ell and integrated development environment (Ch ... expressions, statements, functions, and programs ... conventional command shell to run other executa ... cute C/C++ programs in a user-friendly integrated ... oftIntegration Graphical Library (SIGL) for comp ... plotting functions using a C++ compiler.

Contents of the C...

- Ch® Student Editio ... mentation of Ch Installation and System Ad ... eference Guide, Ch SDK User's Guide, and ...

System Requiren...

- PC with Pentium-...
- Microsoft Window...
- 88 MB disk space ...

Installation of the...

The contents of the CD ... p screen does not pop up automatically when yo ... e file **setup.exe** to install the software.

Ch® Student Edi...

Ch® Student Edition ... he Web site http://www.softintegration.com, su ... dows.

Ch, ChIDE, and SoftIntegration are registered trademarks of SoftIntegration, Inc.